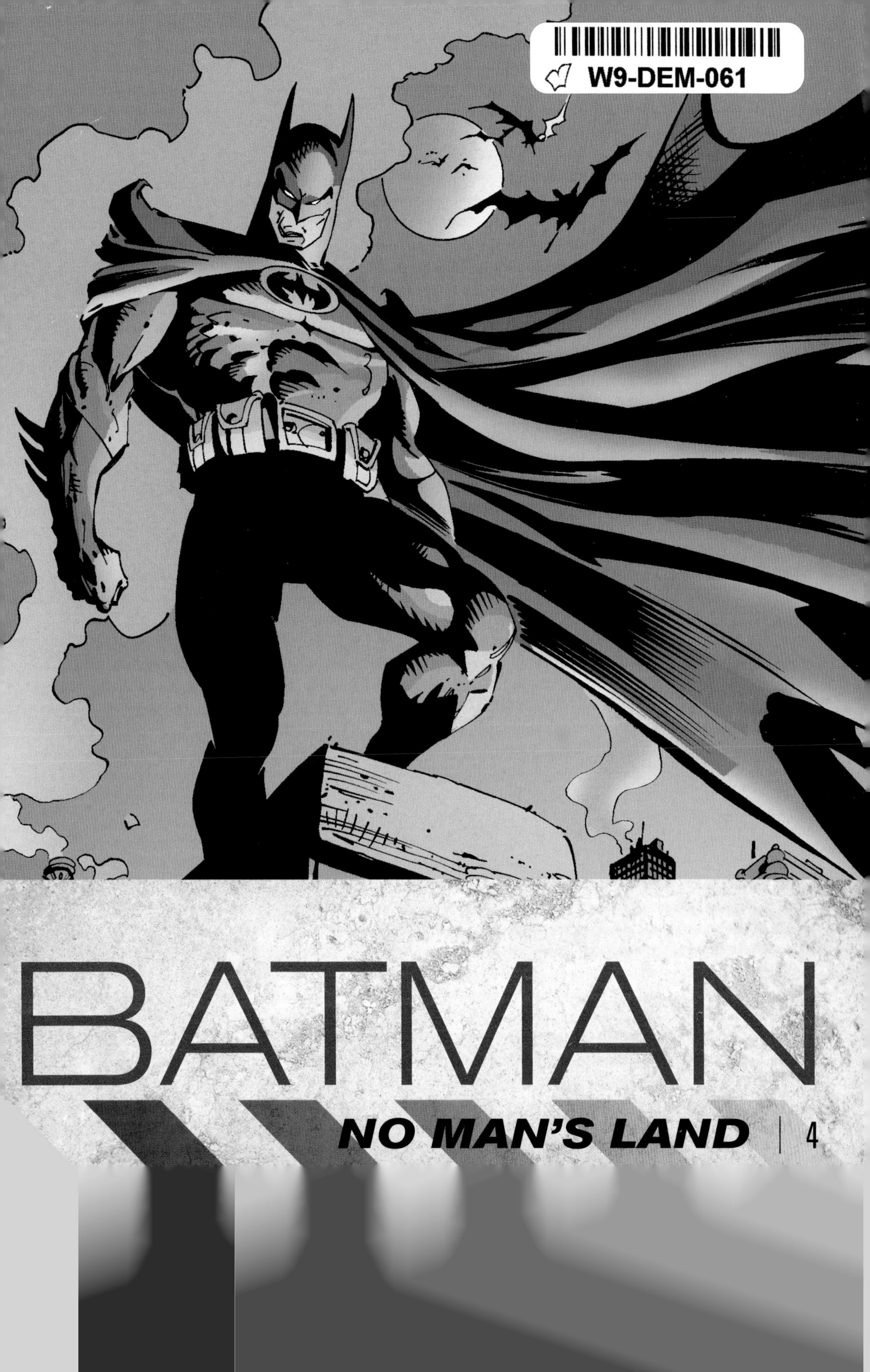

BATMAN

NO MAN'S LAND | 4

Jordan B. Gorfinkel Darren Vincenzo
Dennis O'Neil Matt Idelson Mike Carlin
Editors – Original Series

Joseph Illidge
Associate Editor – Original Series

Frank Berrios
Assistant Editor – Original Series

Rowena Yow
Editor

Robbin Brosterman
Design Director – Books

Brainchild Studios/NYC
Publication Design

Bob Harras
VP – Editor-in-Chief

Diane Nelson
President

Dan DiDio and Jim Lee
Co-Publishers

Geoff Johns
Chief Creative Officer

John Rood
Executive VP – Sales, Marketing and
Business Development

Amy Genkins
Senior VP – Business and Legal Affairs

Nairi Gardiner
Senior VP – Finance

Jeff Boison
VP – Publishing Operations

Mark Chiarello
VP – Art Direction and Design

John Cunningham
VP – Marketing

Terri Cunningham
VP – Talent Relations and Services

Alison Gill
Senior VP – Manufacturing and Operations

Hank Kanalz
Senior VP – Digital

Jay Kogan
VP – Business and Legal Affairs,
Publishing

Jack Mahan
VP – Business Affairs, Talent

Nick Napolitano
VP – Manufacturing Administration

Sue Pohja
VP – Book Sales

Courtney Simmons
Senior VP – Publicity

Bob Wayne
Senior VP – Sales

BATMAN: NO MAN'S LAND VOLUME 4

DC Comics, 1700 Broadway, New York, NY 10019
A Warner Bros. Entertainment Company.
Printed by RR Donnelley, Salem, VA, USA. 11/2/12. First Printing.
ISBN: 978-1-4012-3564-2

SUSTAINABLE
FORESTRY
INITIATIVE

Certified Chain of Custody
At Least 20% Certified Forest Content

TABLE OF CONTENTS

BATMAN CREATED BY BOB KANE

**COLLECTION COVER BY
BILL SIENKIEWICZ**

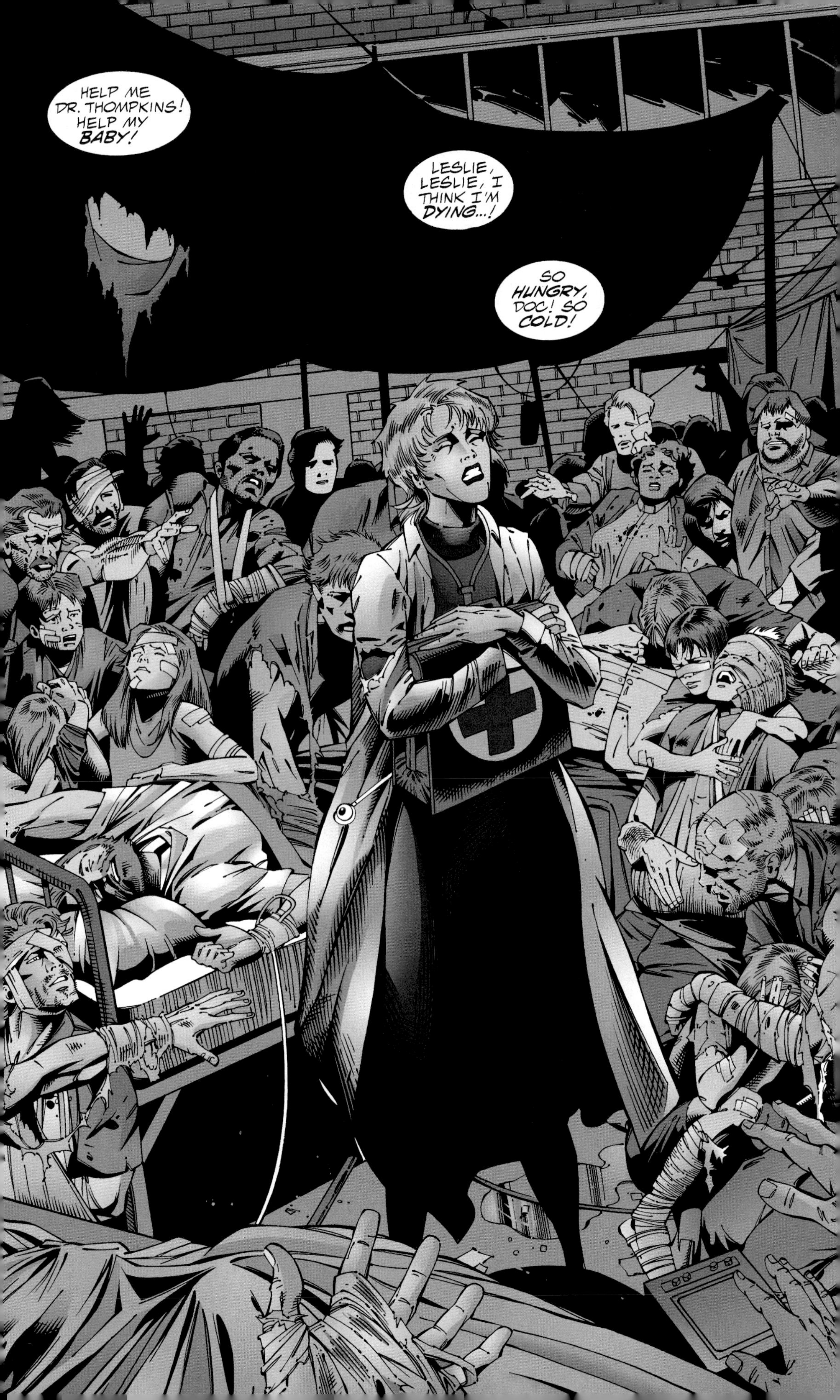

HELP ME DR. THOMPKINS! HELP MY BABY!
LESLIE, LESLIE, I THINK I'M DYING...!
SO HUNGRY, DOC! SO COLD!

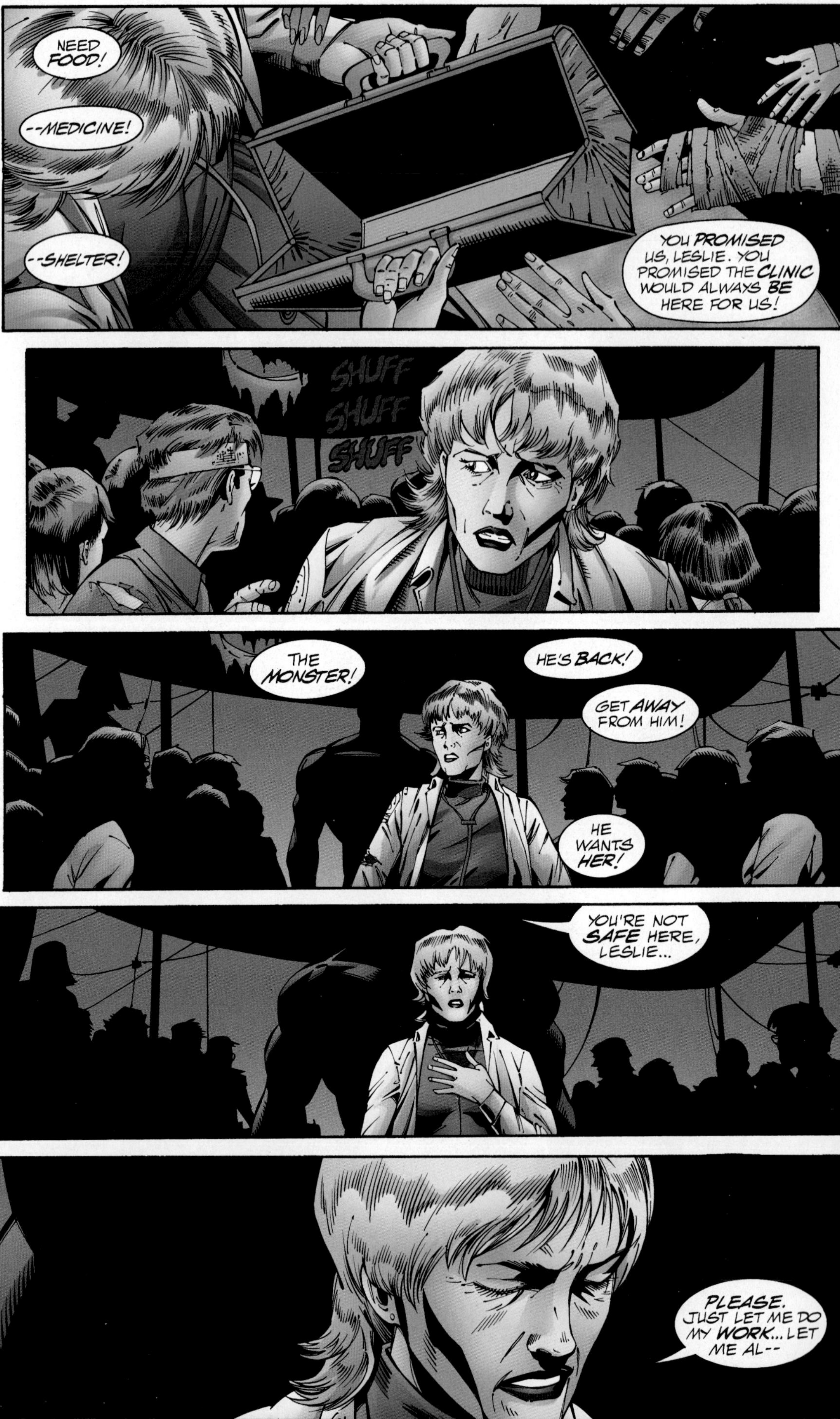
NEED FOOD!
--MEDICINE!
--SHELTER!
YOU PROMISED US, LESLIE. YOU PROMISED THE CLINIC WOULD ALWAYS BE HERE FOR US!
SHUFF SHUFF SHUFF
THE MONSTER!
HE'S BACK!
GET AWAY FROM HIM!
HE WANTS HER!
YOU'RE NOT SAFE HERE, LESLIE...
PLEASE. JUST LET ME DO MY WORK... LET ME AL--

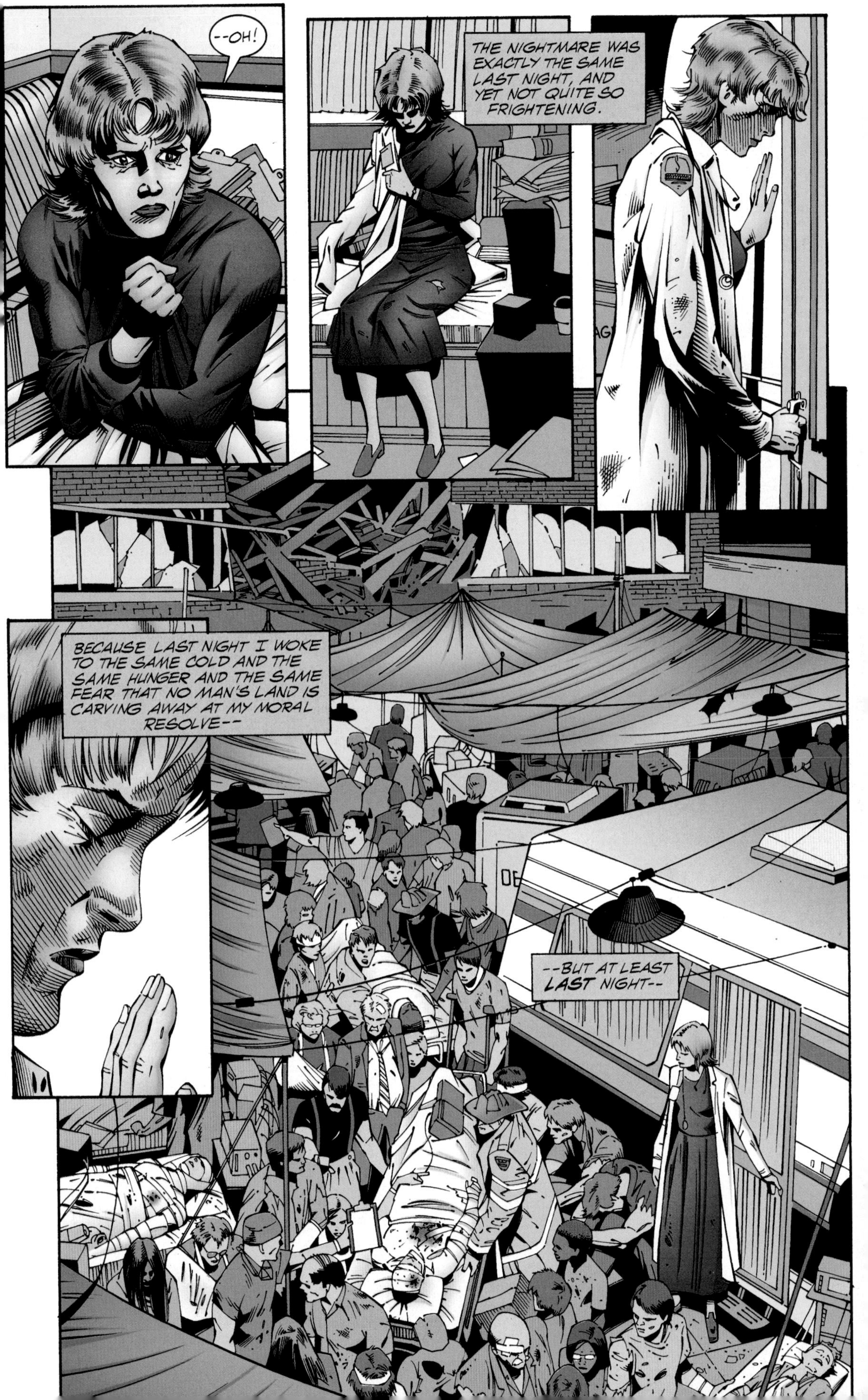
--OH!
THE NIGHTMARE WAS EXACTLY THE SAME LAST NIGHT, AND YET NOT QUITE SO FRIGHTENING.
BECAUSE LAST NIGHT I WOKE TO THE SAME COLD AND THE SAME HUNGER AND THE SAME FEAR THAT NO MAN'S LAND IS CARVING AWAY AT MY MORAL RESOLVE--
--BUT AT LEAST LAST NIGHT--

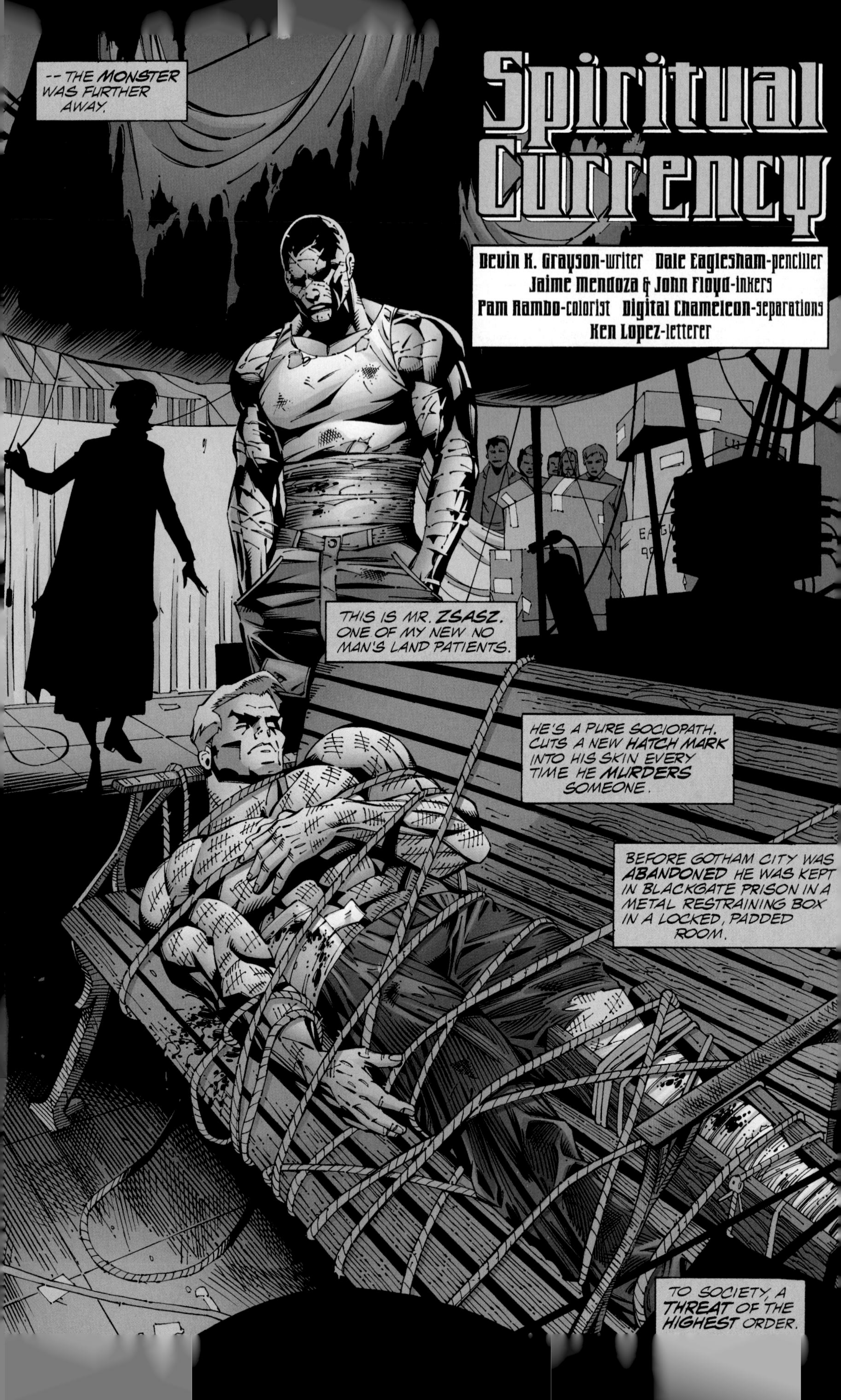

-- THE MONSTER WAS FURTHER AWAY.
Spiritual Currency
Devin K. Grayson-writer Dale Eaglesham-penciller
Jaime Mendoza & John Floyd-inkers
Pam Rambo-colorist Digital Chameleon-separations
Ken Lopez-letterer
THIS IS MR. ZSASZ. ONE OF MY NEW NO MAN'S LAND PATIENTS.
HE'S A PURE SOCIOPATH. CUTS A NEW HATCH MARK INTO HIS SKIN EVERY TIME HE MURDERS SOMEONE.
BEFORE GOTHAM CITY WAS ABANDONED HE WAS KEPT IN BLACKGATE PRISON IN A METAL RESTRAINING BOX IN A LOCKED, PADDED ROOM.
TO SOCIETY, A THREAT OF THE HIGHEST ORDER.

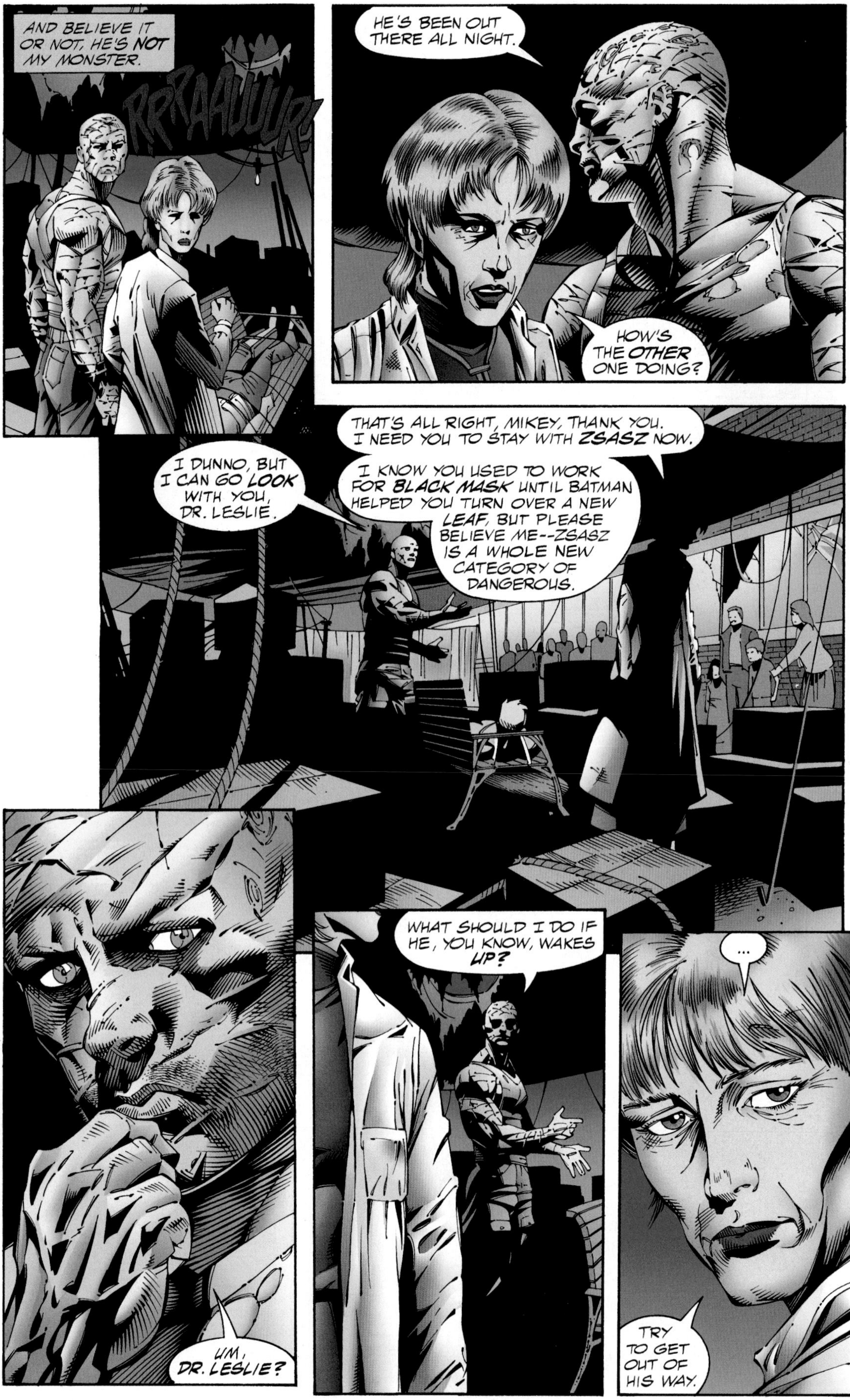
AND BELIEVE IT OR NOT, HE'S NOT MY MONSTER.
RRRAAUUUR!
HE'S BEEN OUT THERE ALL NIGHT.
HOW'S THE OTHER ONE DOING?
I DUNNO, BUT I CAN GO LOOK WITH YOU, DR. LESLIE.
THAT'S ALL RIGHT, MIKEY, THANK YOU. I NEED YOU TO STAY WITH ZSASZ NOW.
I KNOW YOU USED TO WORK FOR BLACK MASK UNTIL BATMAN HELPED YOU TURN OVER A NEW LEAF, BUT PLEASE BELIEVE ME--ZSASZ IS A WHOLE NEW CATEGORY OF DANGEROUS.
UM, DR. LESLIE?
WHAT SHOULD I DO IF HE, YOU KNOW, WAKES UP?
...
TRY TO GET OUT OF HIS WAY.

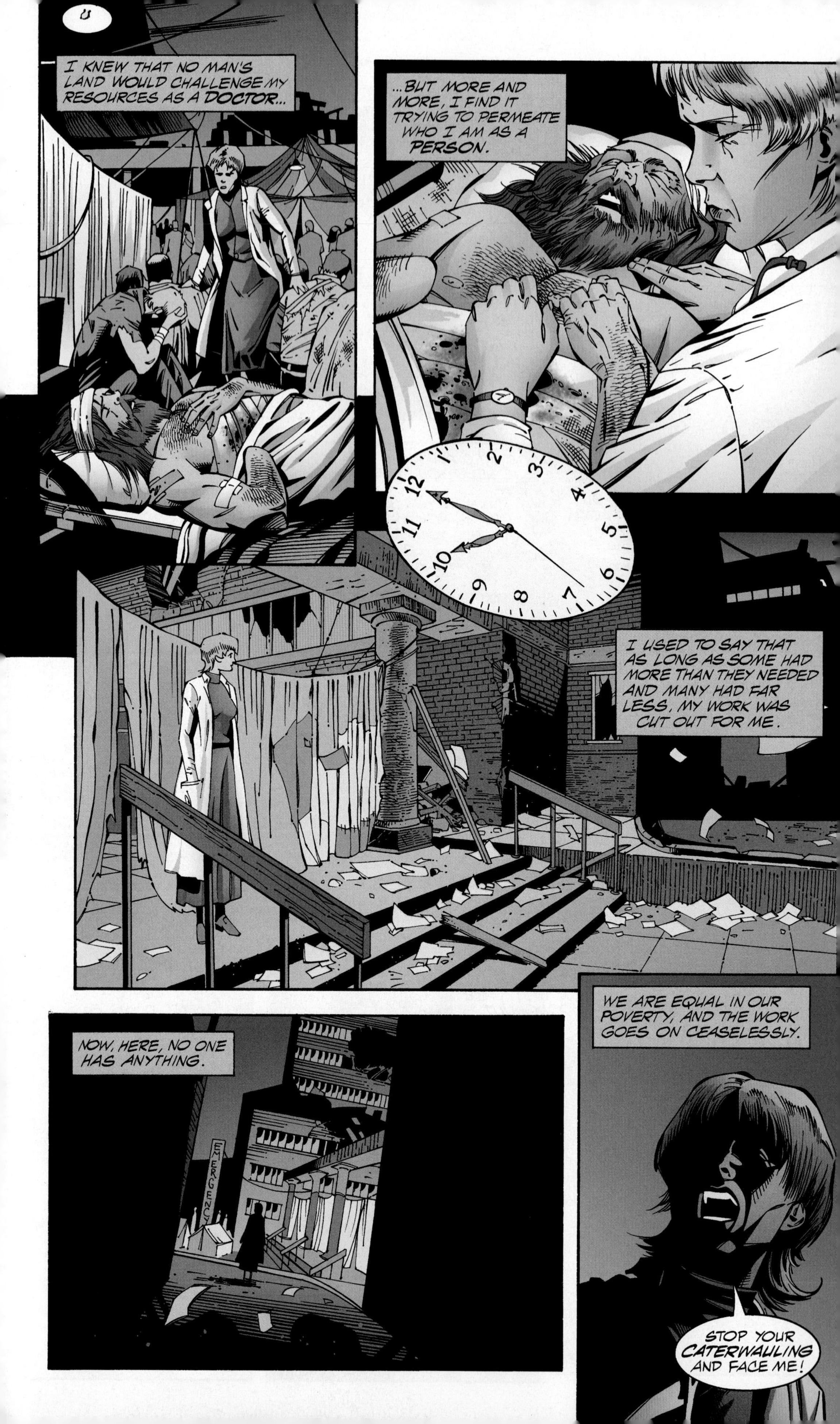
I KNEW THAT NO MAN'S LAND WOULD CHALLENGE MY RESOURCES AS A DOCTOR...
...BUT MORE AND MORE, I FIND IT TRYING TO PERMEATE WHO I AM AS A PERSON.
I USED TO SAY THAT AS LONG AS SOME HAD MORE THAN THEY NEEDED AND MANY HAD FAR LESS, MY WORK WAS CUT OUT FOR ME.
NOW, HERE, NO ONE HAS ANYTHING.
EMERGENCY
WE ARE EQUAL IN OUR POVERTY, AND THE WORK GOES ON CEASELESSLY.
STOP YOUR CATERWAULING AND FACE ME!

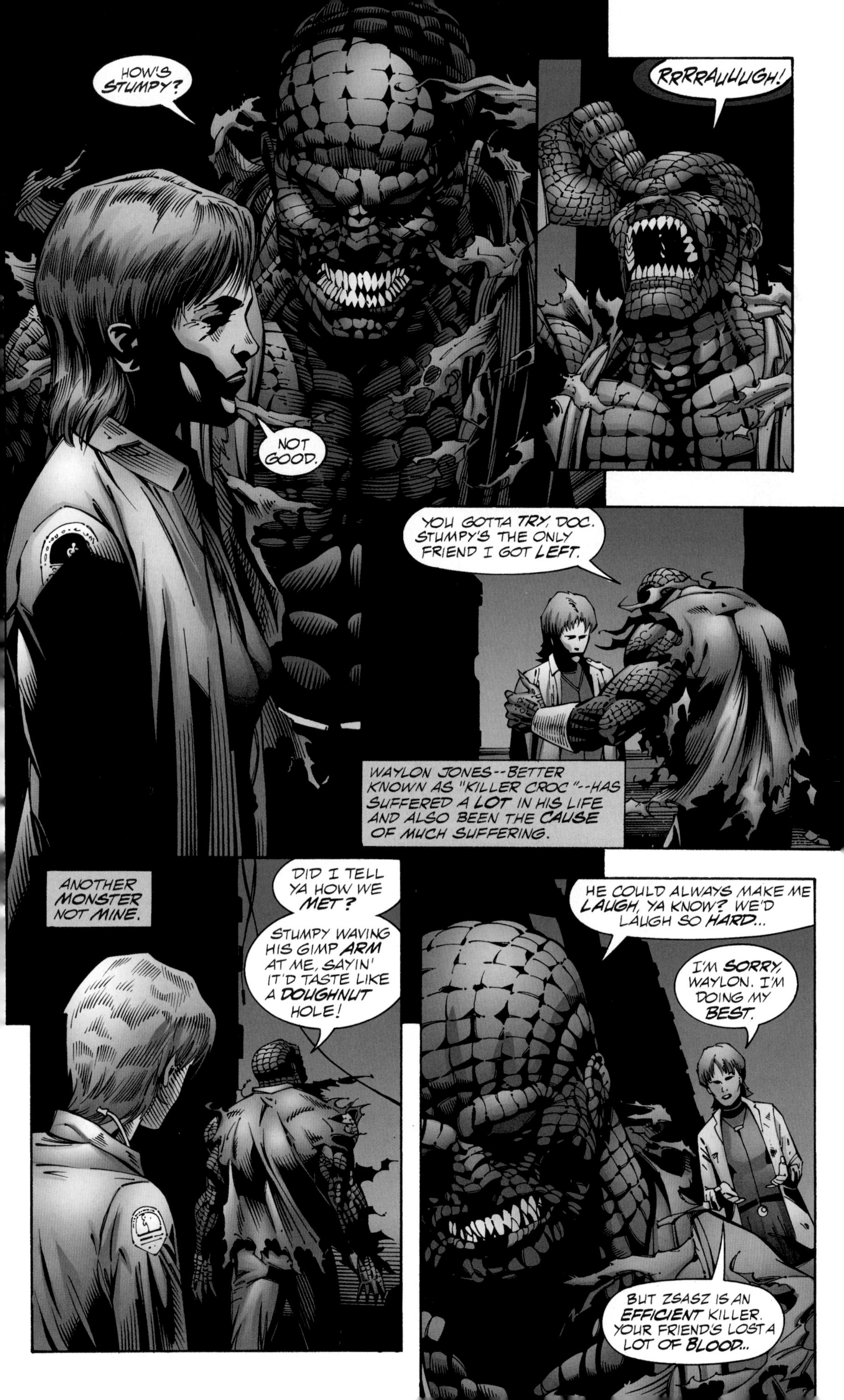
HOW'S STUMPY?
NOT GOOD.
RRRRAUUUGH!
YOU GOTTA TRY, DOC. STUMPY'S THE ONLY FRIEND I GOT LEFT.
WAYLON JONES--BETTER KNOWN AS "KILLER CROC"--HAS SUFFERED A LOT IN HIS LIFE AND ALSO BEEN THE CAUSE OF MUCH SUFFERING.
ANOTHER MONSTER NOT MINE.
DID I TELL YA HOW WE MET?
STUMPY WAVING HIS GIMP ARM AT ME, SAYIN' IT'D TASTE LIKE A DOUGHNUT HOLE!
HE COULD ALWAYS MAKE ME LAUGH, YA KNOW? WE'D LAUGH SO HARD...
I'M SORRY, WAYLON. I'M DOING MY BEST.
BUT ZSASZ IS AN EFFICIENT KILLER. YOUR FRIEND'S LOST A LOT OF BLOOD...

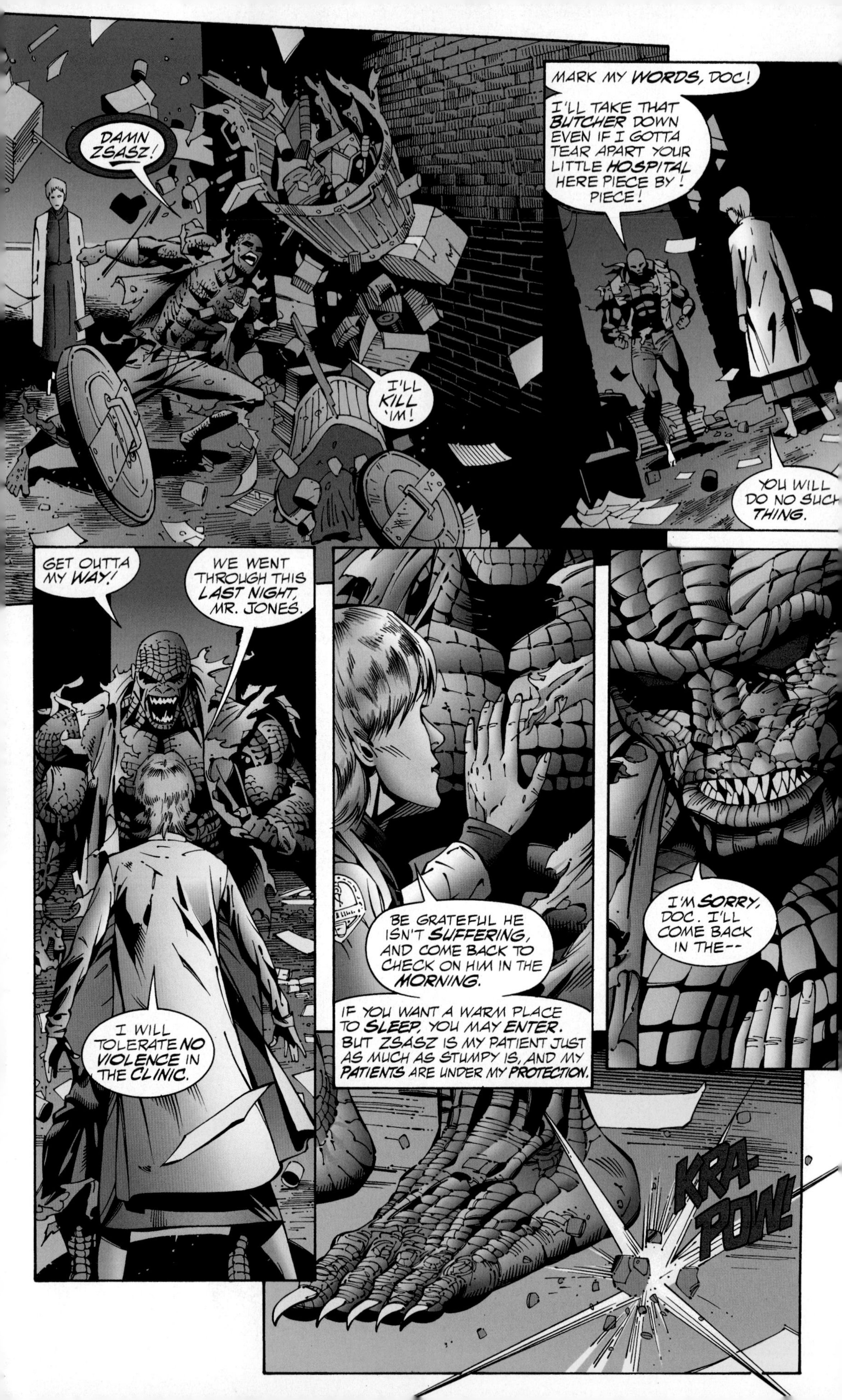
DAMN ZSASZ!
I'LL KILL 'IM!
MARK MY WORDS, DOC!
I'LL TAKE THAT BUTCHER DOWN EVEN IF I GOTTA TEAR APART YOUR LITTLE HOSPITAL HERE PIECE BY ! PIECE!
YOU WILL DO NO SUCH THING.
GET OUTTA MY WAY!
WE WENT THROUGH THIS LAST NIGHT, MR. JONES.
I WILL TOLERATE NO VIOLENCE IN THE CLINIC.
BE GRATEFUL HE ISN'T SUFFERING, AND COME BACK TO CHECK ON HIM IN THE MORNING.
IF YOU WANT A WARM PLACE TO SLEEP, YOU MAY ENTER. BUT ZSASZ IS MY PATIENT JUST AS MUCH AS STUMPY IS, AND MY PATIENTS ARE UNDER MY PROTECTION.
I'M SORRY, DOC. I'LL COME BACK IN THE--
KRA-POW!

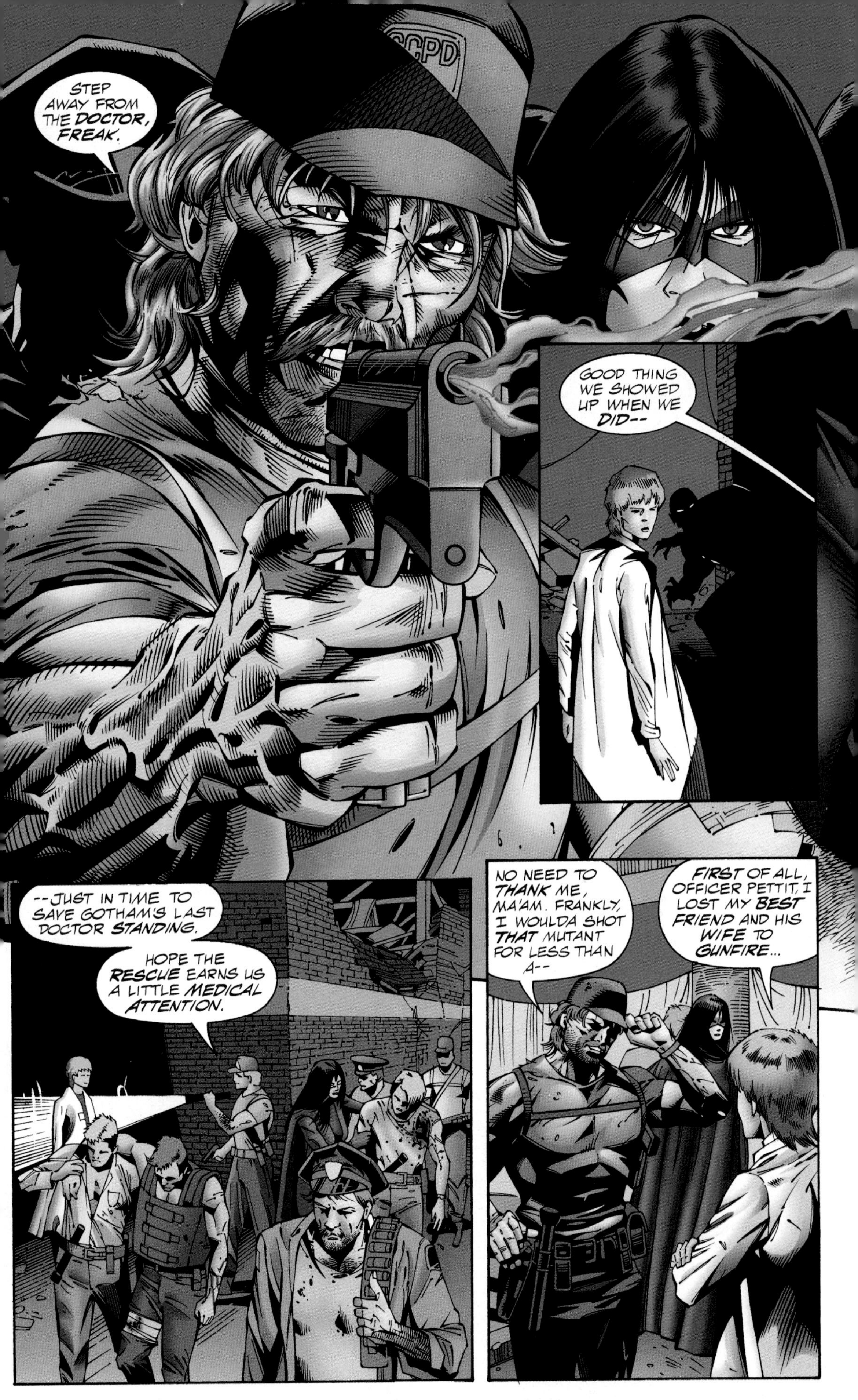
STEP AWAY FROM THE DOCTOR, FREAK.
GCPD
GOOD THING WE SHOWED UP WHEN WE DID--
--JUST IN TIME TO SAVE GOTHAM'S LAST DOCTOR STANDING.
HOPE THE RESCUE EARNS US A LITTLE MEDICAL ATTENTION.
NO NEED TO THANK ME, MA'AM. FRANKLY, I WOULDA SHOT THAT MUTANT FOR LESS THAN A--
FIRST OF ALL, OFFICER PETTIT, I LOST MY BEST FRIEND AND HIS WIFE TO GUNFIRE...

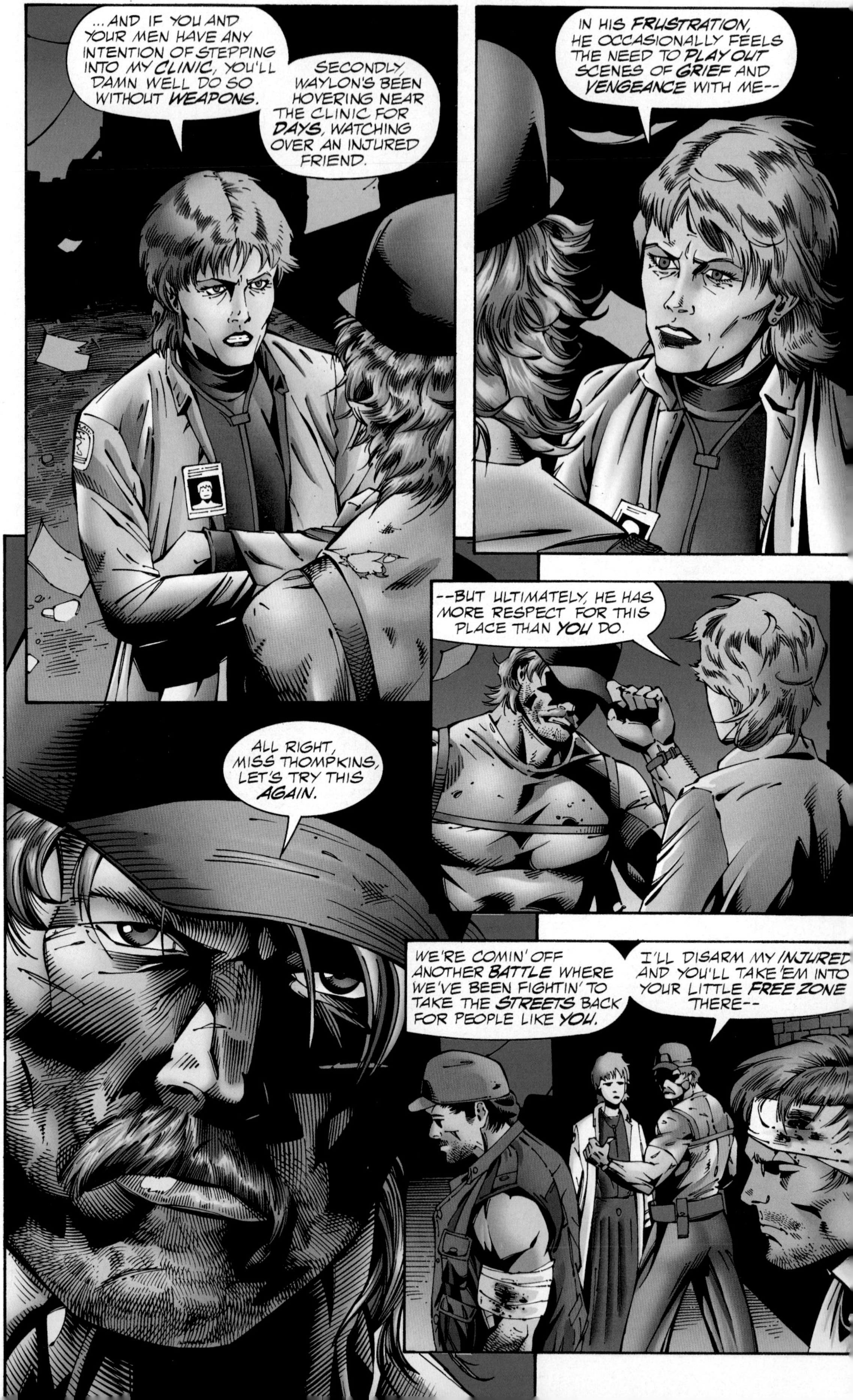

...AND IF YOU AND YOUR MEN HAVE ANY INTENTION OF STEPPING INTO MY CLINIC, YOU'LL DAMN WELL DO SO WITHOUT WEAPONS.
SECONDLY, WAYLON'S BEEN HOVERING NEAR THE CLINIC FOR DAYS, WATCHING OVER AN INJURED FRIEND.
IN HIS FRUSTRATION, HE OCCASIONALLY FEELS THE NEED TO PLAY OUT SCENES OF GRIEF AND VENGEANCE WITH ME--
--BUT ULTIMATELY, HE HAS MORE RESPECT FOR THIS PLACE THAN YOU DO.
ALL RIGHT, MISS THOMPKINS, LET'S TRY THIS AGAIN.
WE'RE COMIN' OFF ANOTHER BATTLE WHERE WE'VE BEEN FIGHTIN' TO TAKE THE STREETS BACK FOR PEOPLE LIKE YOU.
I'LL DISARM MY INJURED AND YOU'LL TAKE 'EM INTO YOUR LITTLE FREE ZONE THERE--

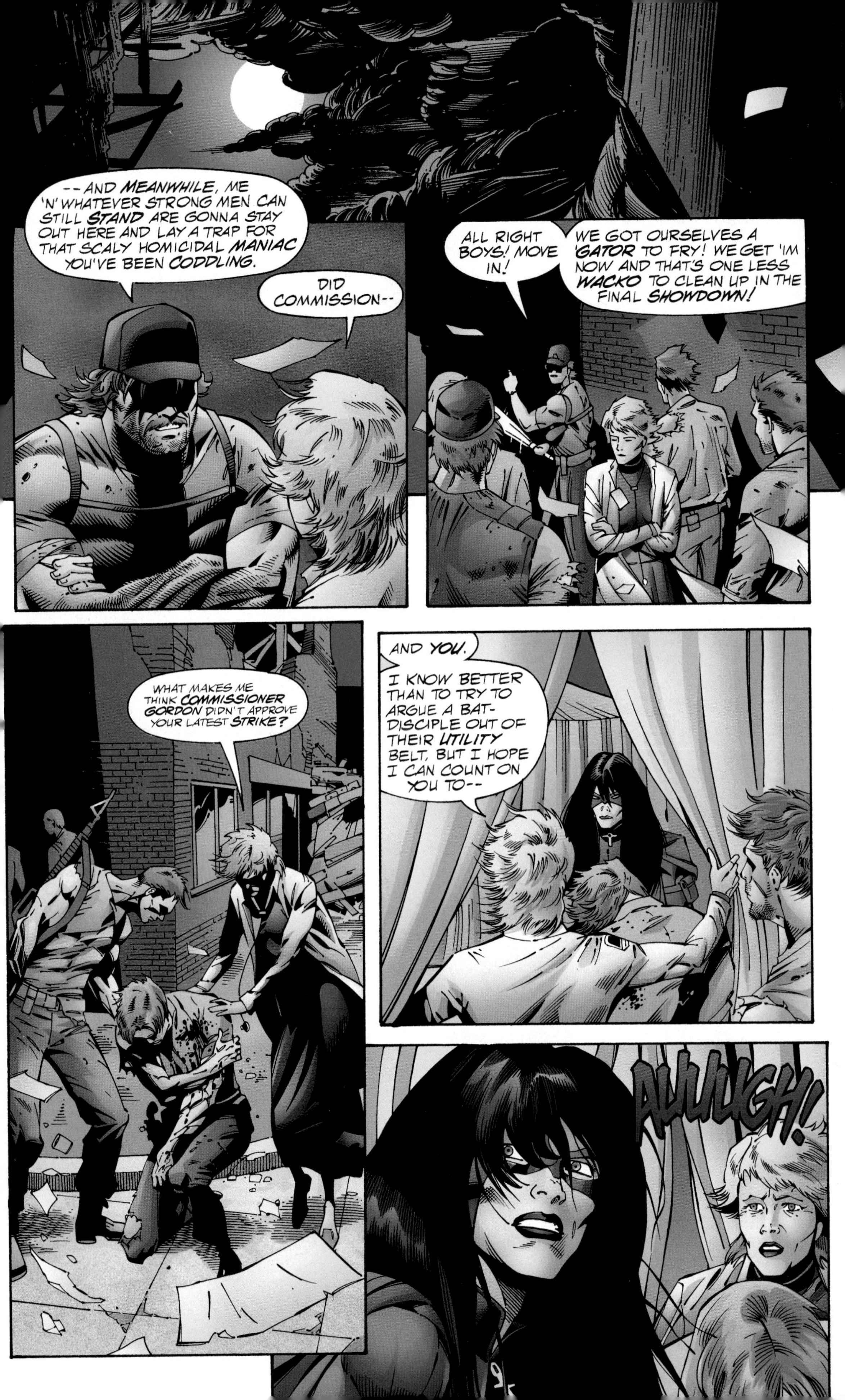
--AND MEANWHILE, ME 'N' WHATEVER STRONG MEN CAN STILL STAND ARE GONNA STAY OUT HERE AND LAY A TRAP FOR THAT SCALY HOMICIDAL MANIAC YOU'VE BEEN CODDLING.
DID COMMISSION--
ALL RIGHT BOYS! MOVE IN!
WE GOT OURSELVES A 'GATOR TO FRY! WE GET 'IM NOW AND THAT'S ONE LESS WACKO TO CLEAN UP IN THE FINAL SHOWDOWN!
WHAT MAKES ME THINK COMMISSIONER GORDON DIDN'T APPROVE YOUR LATEST STRIKE?
AND YOU.
I KNOW BETTER THAN TO TRY TO ARGUE A BAT-DISCIPLE OUT OF THEIR UTILITY BELT, BUT I HOPE I CAN COUNT ON YOU TO--
AUUUGH!

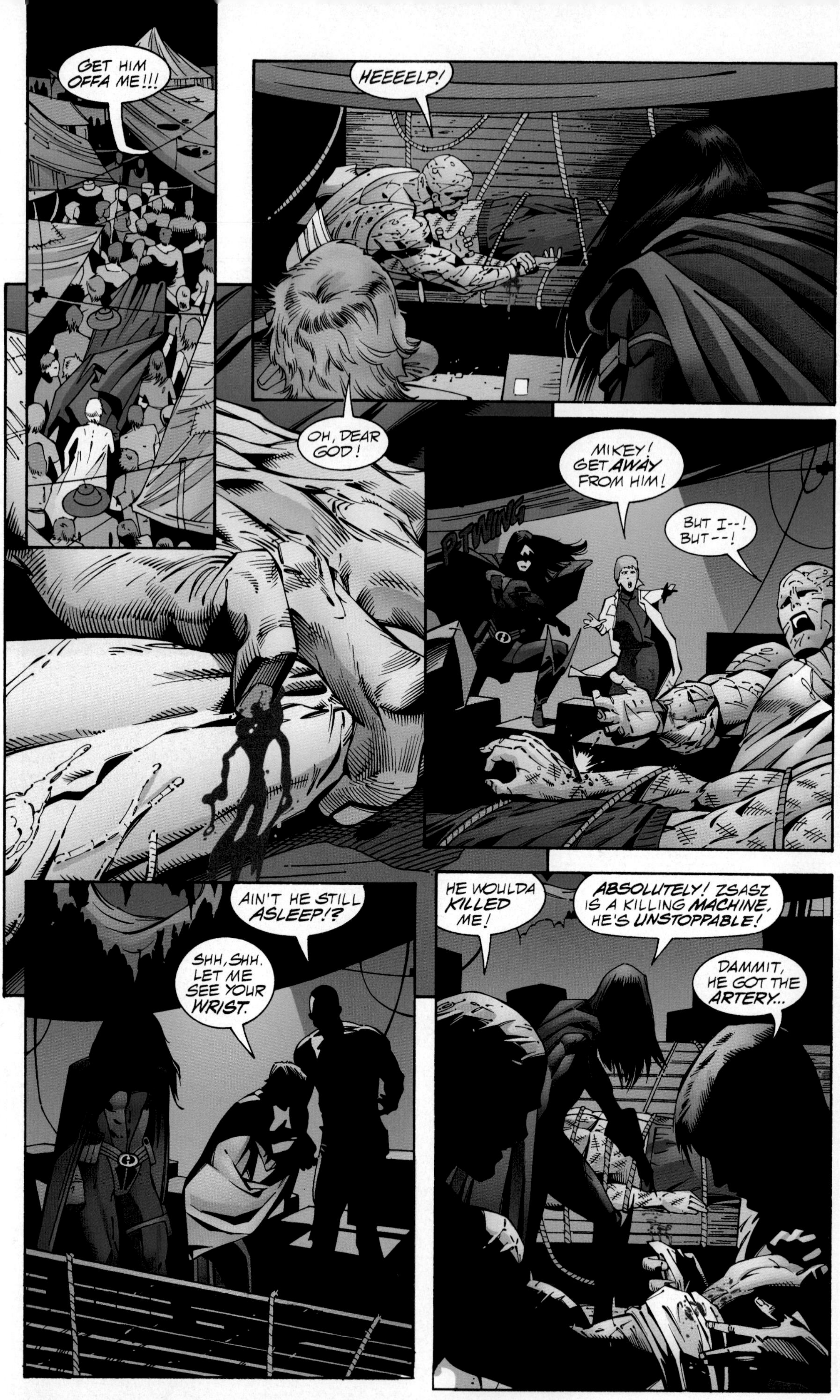
GET HIM OFFA ME!!!
HEEEELP!
OH, DEAR GOD!
MIKEY! GET AWAY FROM HIM!
P-TWING
BUT I--! BUT--!
AIN'T HE STILL ASLEEP!?
SHH, SHH. LET ME SEE YOUR WRIST.
HE WOULDA KILLED ME!
ABSOLUTELY! ZSASZ IS A KILLING MACHINE, HE'S UNSTOPPABLE!
DAMMIT, HE GOT THE ARTERY...

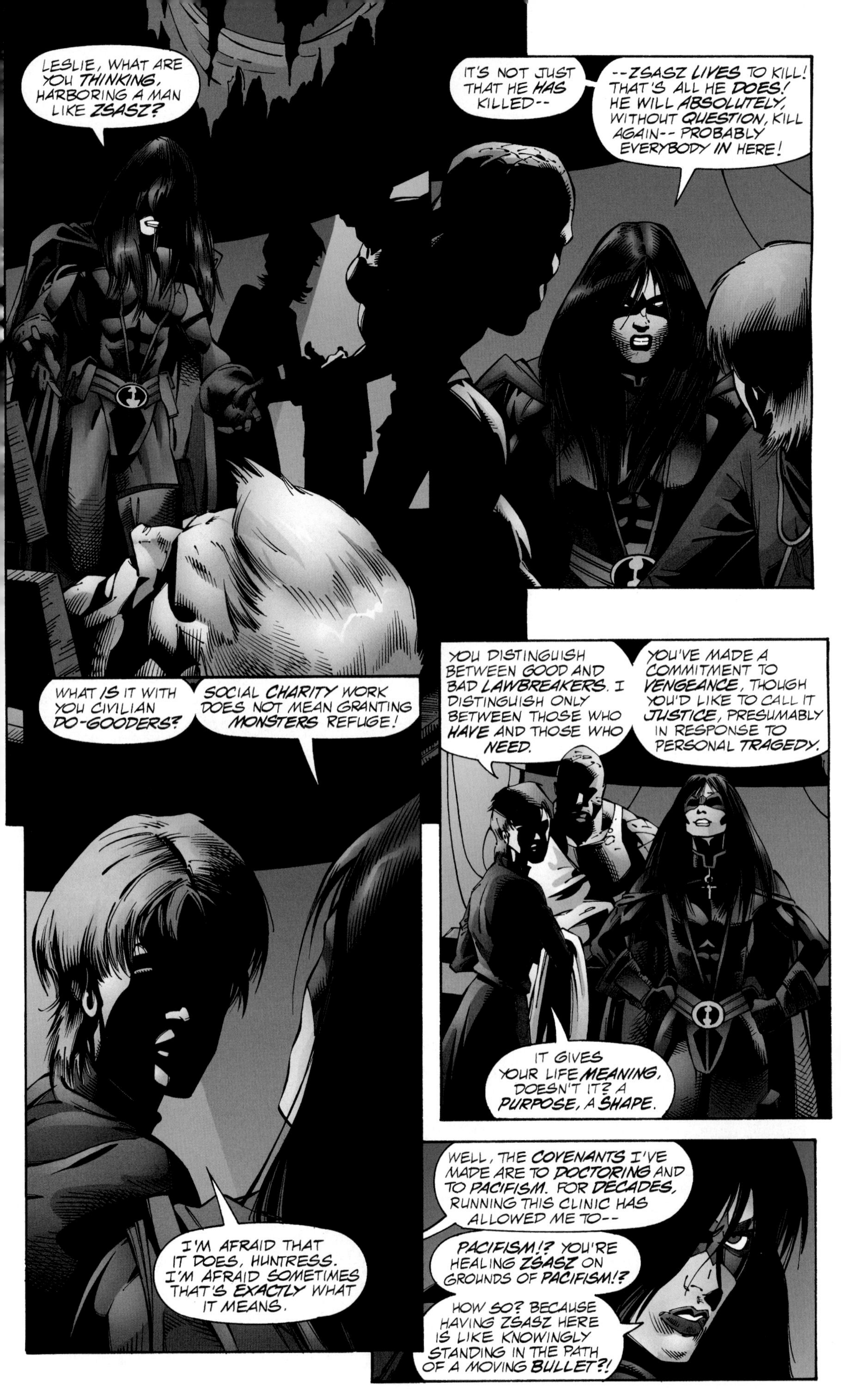

LESLIE, WHAT ARE YOU THINKING, HARBORING A MAN LIKE ZSASZ?
IT'S NOT JUST THAT HE HAS KILLED--
--ZSASZ LIVES TO KILL! THAT'S ALL HE DOES! HE WILL ABSOLUTELY, WITHOUT QUESTION, KILL AGAIN-- PROBABLY EVERYBODY IN HERE!
WHAT IS IT WITH YOU CIVILIAN DO-GOODERS?
SOCIAL CHARITY WORK DOES NOT MEAN GRANTING MONSTERS REFUGE!
YOU DISTINGUISH BETWEEN GOOD AND BAD LAWBREAKERS. I DISTINGUISH ONLY BETWEEN THOSE WHO HAVE AND THOSE WHO NEED.
YOU'VE MADE A COMMITMENT TO VENGEANCE, THOUGH YOU'D LIKE TO CALL IT JUSTICE, PRESUMABLY IN RESPONSE TO PERSONAL TRAGEDY.
IT GIVES YOUR LIFE MEANING, DOESN'T IT? A PURPOSE, A SHAPE.
I'M AFRAID THAT IT DOES, HUNTRESS. I'M AFRAID SOMETIMES THAT'S EXACTLY WHAT IT MEANS.
WELL, THE COVENANTS I'VE MADE ARE TO DOCTORING AND TO PACIFISM. FOR DECADES, RUNNING THIS CLINIC HAS ALLOWED ME TO--
PACIFISM!? YOU'RE HEALING ZSASZ ON GROUNDS OF PACIFISM!?
HOW SO? BECAUSE HAVING ZSASZ HERE IS LIKE KNOWINGLY STANDING IN THE PATH OF A MOVING BULLET?!

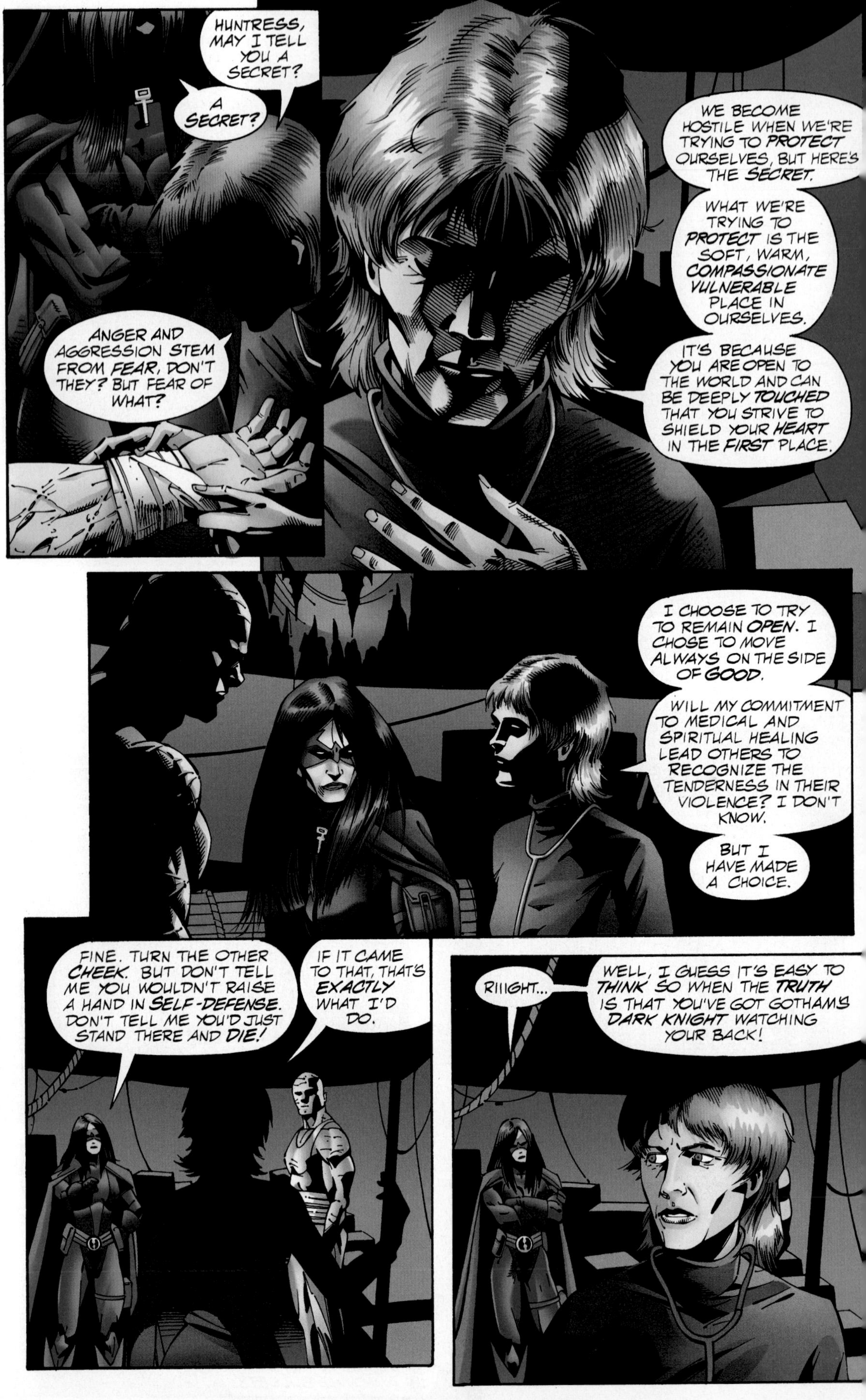
HUNTRESS, MAY I TELL YOU A SECRET?
A SECRET?
ANGER AND AGGRESSION STEM FROM FEAR, DON'T THEY? BUT FEAR OF WHAT?
WE BECOME HOSTILE WHEN WE'RE TRYING TO PROTECT OURSELVES, BUT HERE'S THE SECRET.
WHAT WE'RE TRYING TO PROTECT IS THE SOFT, WARM, COMPASSIONATE VULNERABLE PLACE IN OURSELVES.
IT'S BECAUSE YOU ARE OPEN TO THE WORLD AND CAN BE DEEPLY TOUCHED THAT YOU STRIVE TO SHIELD YOUR HEART IN THE FIRST PLACE.
I CHOOSE TO TRY TO REMAIN OPEN. I CHOSE TO MOVE ALWAYS ON THE SIDE OF GOOD.
WILL MY COMMITMENT TO MEDICAL AND SPIRITUAL HEALING LEAD OTHERS TO RECOGNIZE THE TENDERNESS IN THEIR VIOLENCE? I DON'T KNOW.
BUT I HAVE MADE A CHOICE.
FINE. TURN THE OTHER CHEEK. BUT DON'T TELL ME YOU WOULDN'T RAISE A HAND IN SELF-DEFENSE. DON'T TELL ME YOU'D JUST STAND THERE AND DIE!
IF IT CAME TO THAT, THAT'S EXACTLY WHAT I'D DO.
RIIIGHT...
WELL, I GUESS IT'S EASY TO THINK SO WHEN THE TRUTH IS THAT YOU'VE GOT GOTHAM'S DARK KNIGHT WATCHING YOUR BACK!

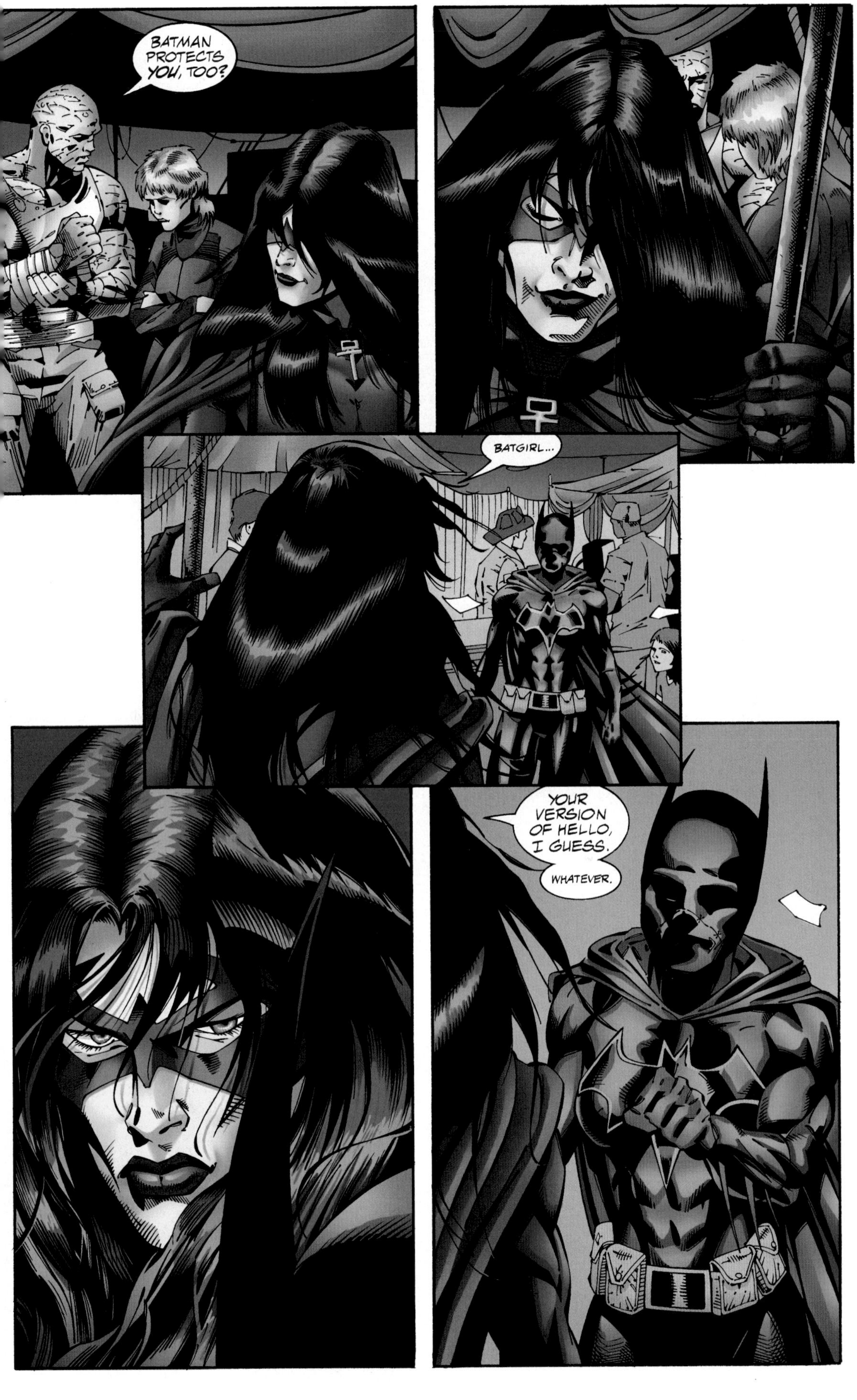
BATMAN PROTECTS YOU, TOO?
BATGIRL...
YOUR VERSION OF HELLO, I GUESS.
WHATEVER.

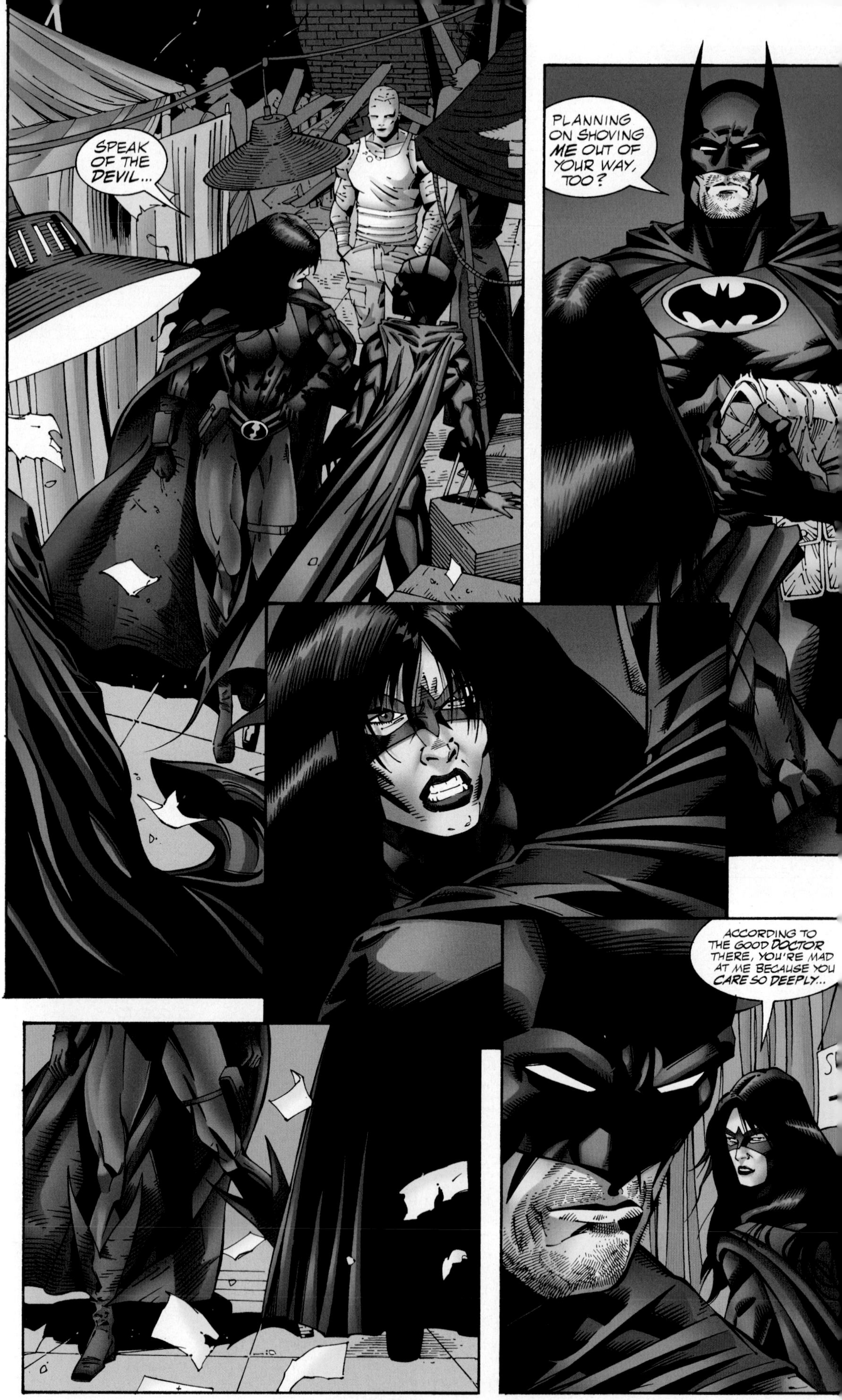
SPEAK OF THE DEVIL...
PLANNING ON SHOVING ME OUT OF YOUR WAY, TOO?
ACCORDING TO THE GOOD DOCTOR THERE, YOU'RE MAD AT ME BECAUSE YOU CARE SO DEEPLY...

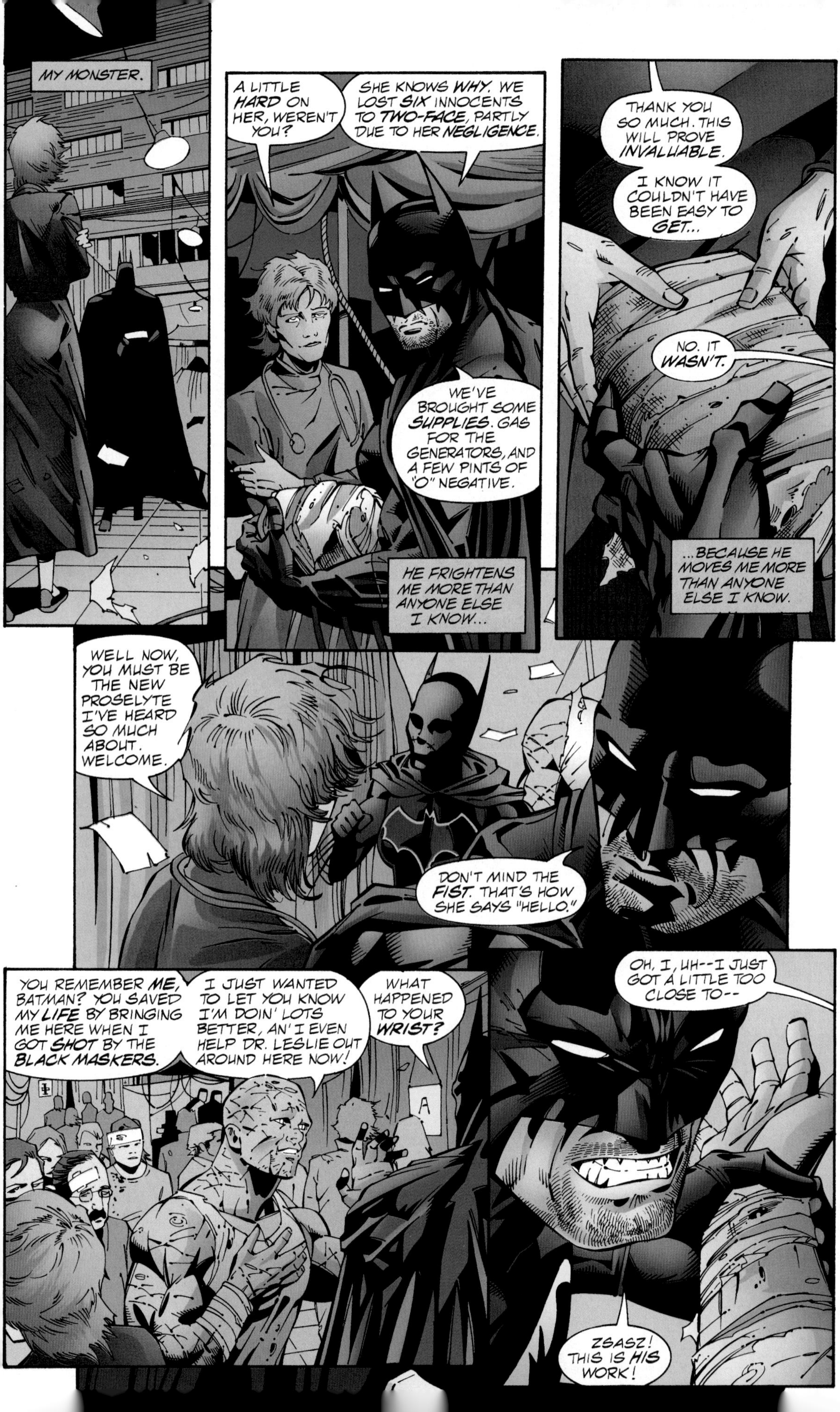

MY MONSTER.
A LITTLE HARD ON HER, WEREN'T YOU?
SHE KNOWS WHY. WE LOST SIX INNOCENTS TO TWO-FACE, PARTLY DUE TO HER NEGLIGENCE.
WE'VE BROUGHT SOME SUPPLIES. GAS FOR THE GENERATORS, AND A FEW PINTS OF "O" NEGATIVE.
HE FRIGHTENS ME MORE THAN ANYONE ELSE I KNOW...
THANK YOU SO MUCH. THIS WILL PROVE INVALUABLE.
I KNOW IT COULDN'T HAVE BEEN EASY TO GET...
NO. IT WASN'T.
...BECAUSE HE MOVES ME MORE THAN ANYONE ELSE I KNOW.
WELL NOW, YOU MUST BE THE NEW PROSELYTE I'VE HEARD SO MUCH ABOUT. WELCOME.
DON'T MIND THE FIST. THAT'S HOW SHE SAYS "HELLO."
YOU REMEMBER ME, BATMAN? YOU SAVED MY LIFE BY BRINGING ME HERE WHEN I GOT SHOT BY THE BLACK MASKERS.
I JUST WANTED TO LET YOU KNOW I'M DOIN' LOTS BETTER, AN' I EVEN HELP DR. LESLIE OUT AROUND HERE NOW!
WHAT HAPPENED TO YOUR WRIST?
OH, I, UH--I JUST GOT A LITTLE TOO CLOSE TO--
ZSASZ! THIS IS HIS WORK!

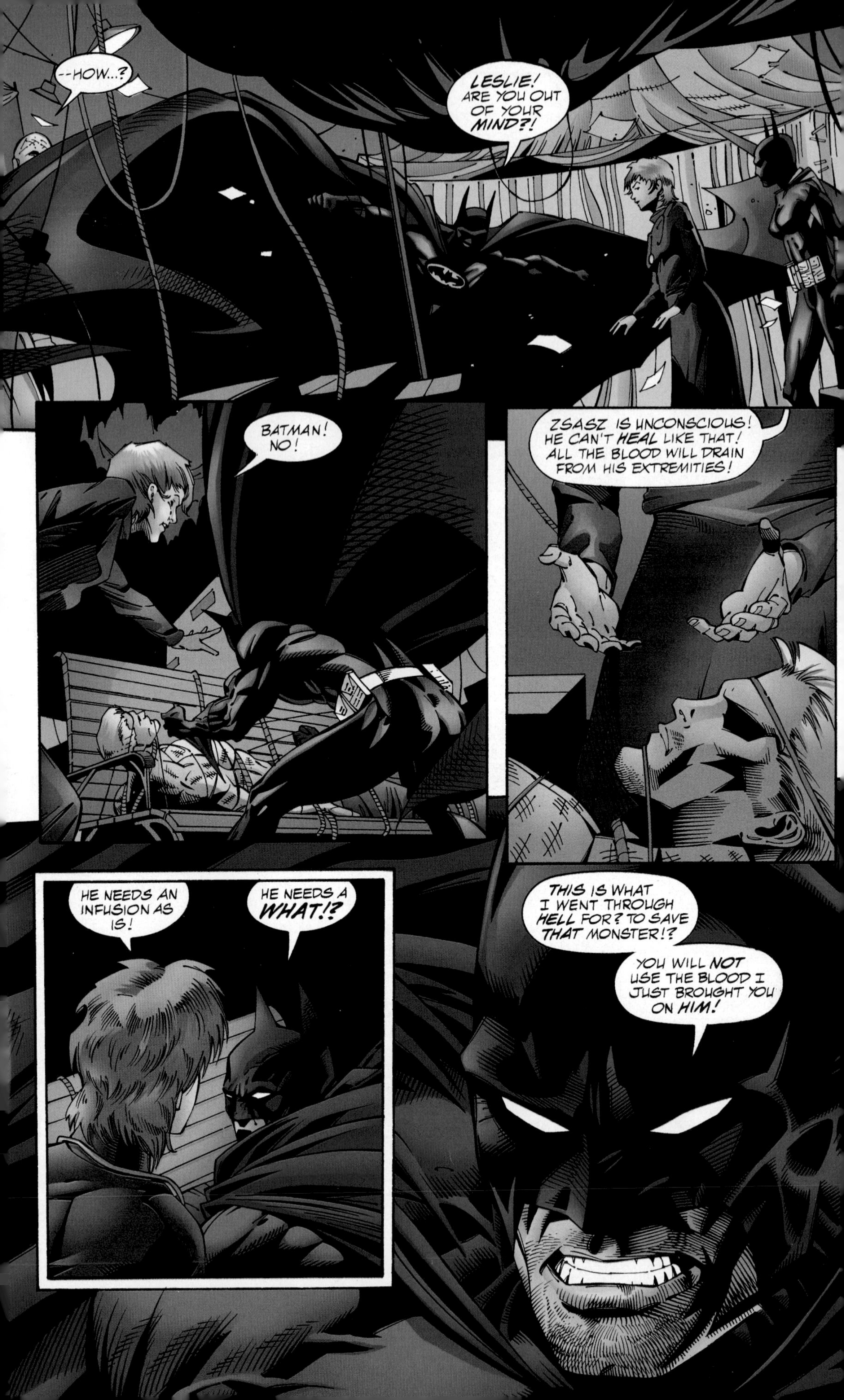
--HOW...?
LESLIE! ARE YOU OUT OF YOUR MIND?!
BATMAN! NO!
ZSASZ IS UNCONSCIOUS! HE CAN'T HEAL LIKE THAT! ALL THE BLOOD WILL DRAIN FROM HIS EXTREMITIES!
HE NEEDS AN INFUSION AS IS!
HE NEEDS A WHAT!?
THIS IS WHAT I WENT THROUGH HELL FOR? TO SAVE THAT MONSTER!?
YOU WILL NOT USE THE BLOOD I JUST BROUGHT YOU ON HIM!

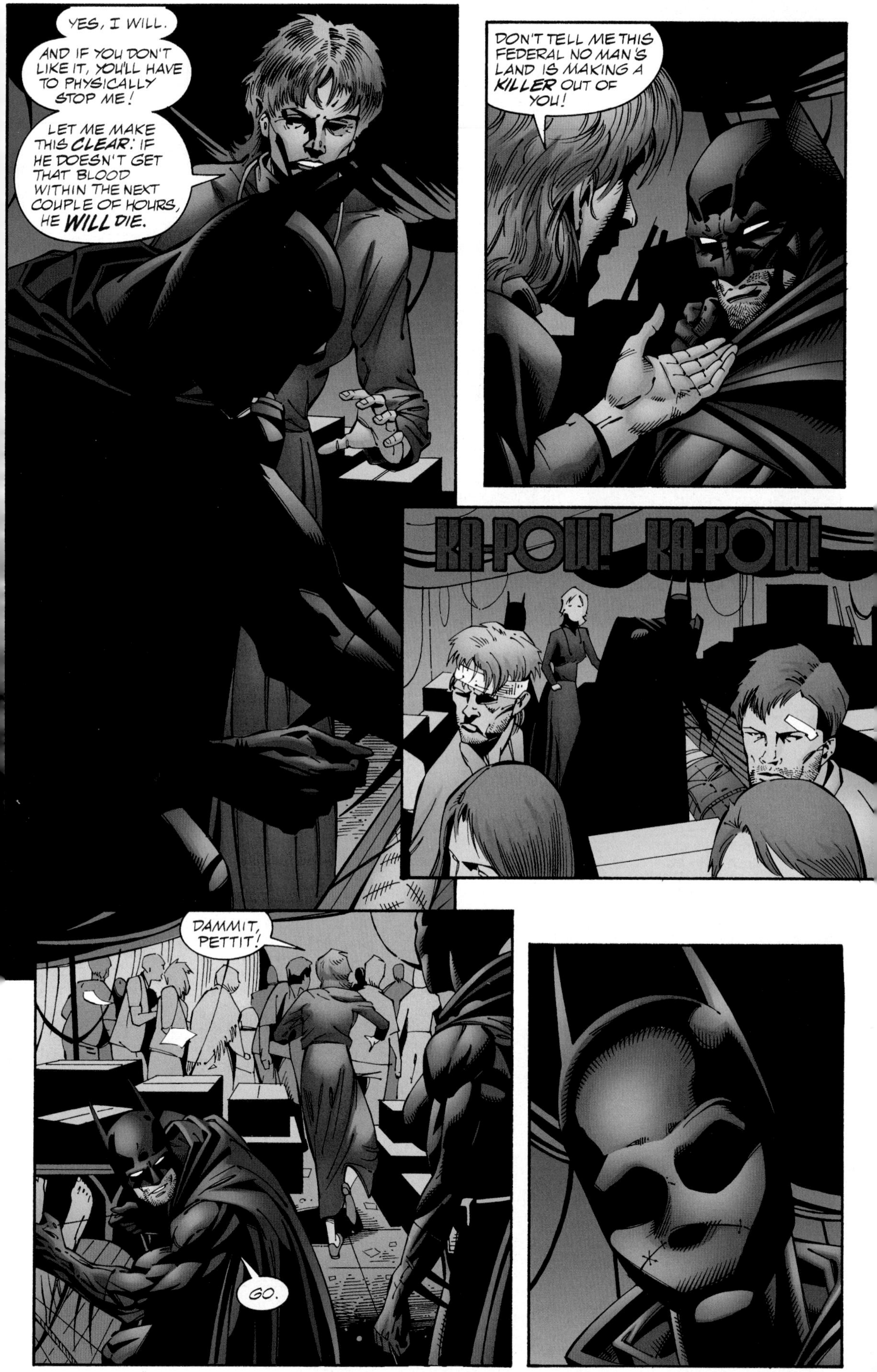
YES, I WILL.
AND IF YOU DON'T LIKE IT, YOU'LL HAVE TO PHYSICALLY STOP ME!
LET ME MAKE THIS CLEAR: IF HE DOESN'T GET THAT BLOOD WITHIN THE NEXT COUPLE OF HOURS, HE WILL DIE.
DON'T TELL ME THIS FEDERAL NO MAN'S LAND IS MAKING A KILLER OUT OF YOU!
KA-POW! KA-POW!
DAMMIT, PETTIT!
GO.

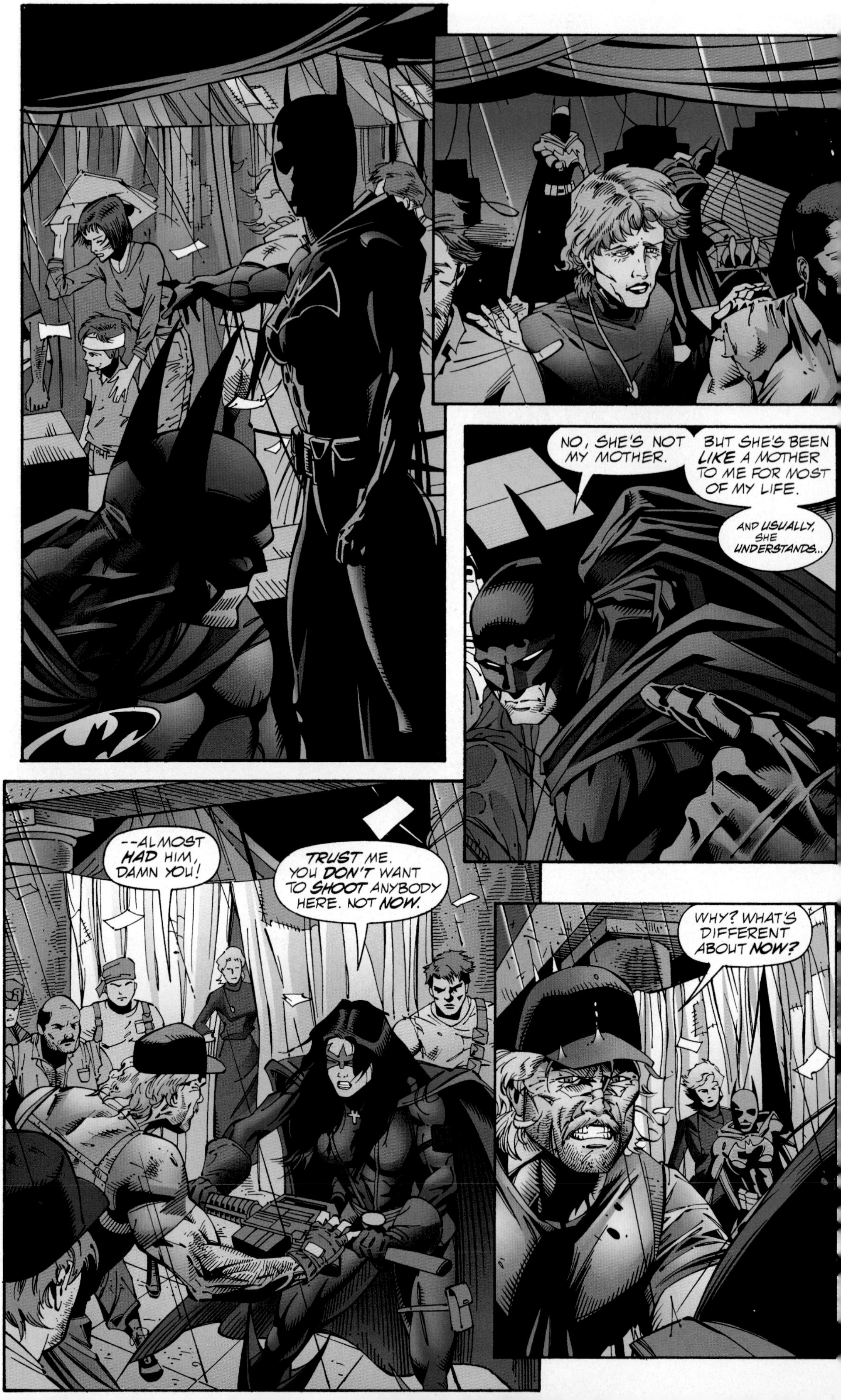
NO, SHE'S NOT MY MOTHER.
BUT SHE'S BEEN LIKE A MOTHER TO ME FOR MOST OF MY LIFE.
AND USUALLY, SHE UNDERSTANDS...
--ALMOST HAD HIM, DAMN YOU!
TRUST ME. YOU DON'T WANT TO SHOOT ANYBODY HERE. NOT NOW.
WHY? WHAT'S DIFFERENT ABOUT NOW?

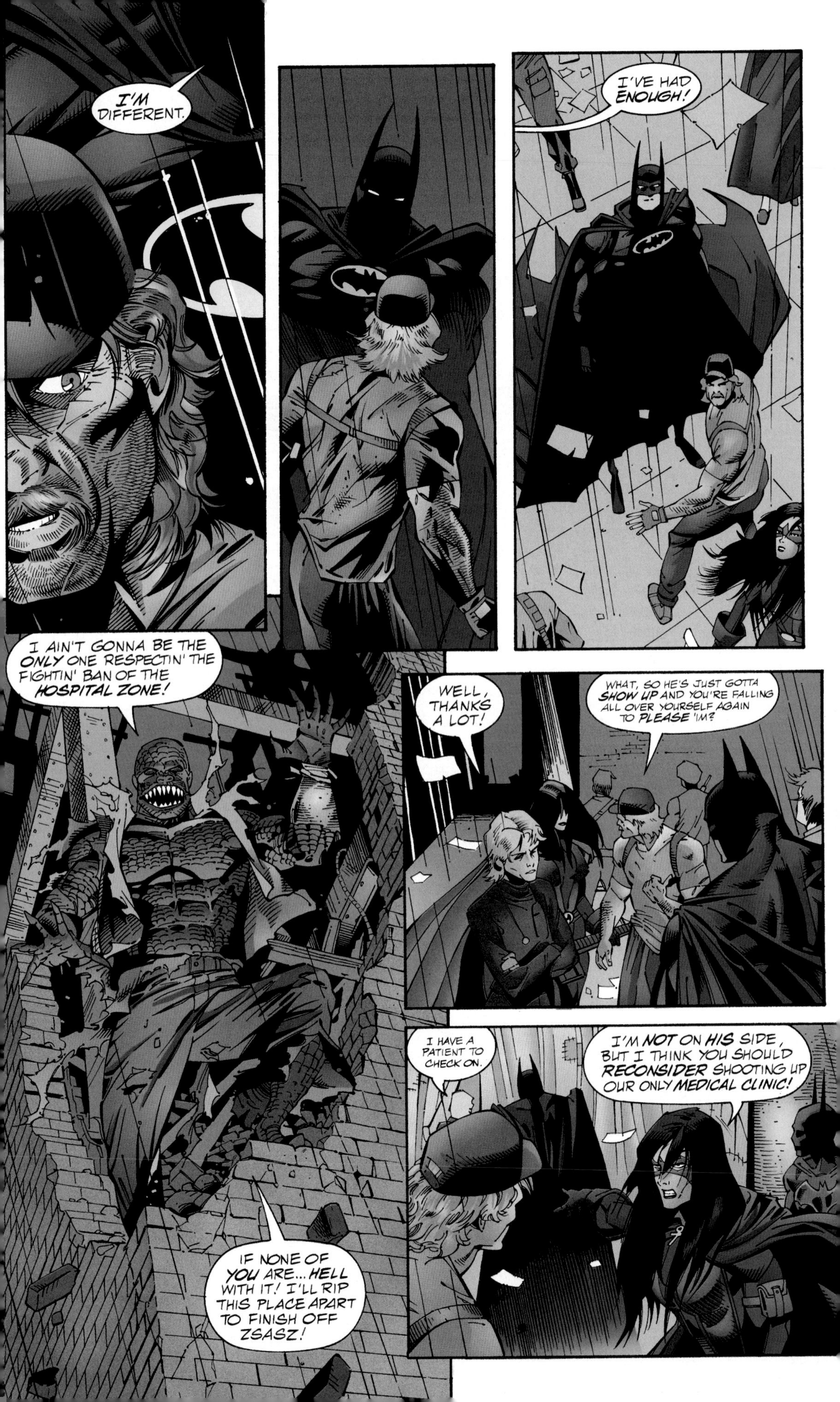
I'M DIFFERENT.
I'VE HAD ENOUGH!
I AIN'T GONNA BE THE ONLY ONE RESPECTIN' THE FIGHTIN' BAN OF THE HOSPITAL ZONE!
IF NONE OF YOU ARE... HELL WITH IT! I'LL RIP THIS PLACE APART TO FINISH OFF ZSASZ!
WELL, THANKS A LOT!
WHAT, SO HE'S JUST GOTTA SHOW UP AND YOU'RE FALLING ALL OVER YOURSELF AGAIN TO PLEASE 'IM?
I HAVE A PATIENT TO CHECK ON.
I'M NOT ON HIS SIDE, BUT I THINK YOU SHOULD RECONSIDER SHOOTING UP OUR ONLY MEDICAL CLINIC!

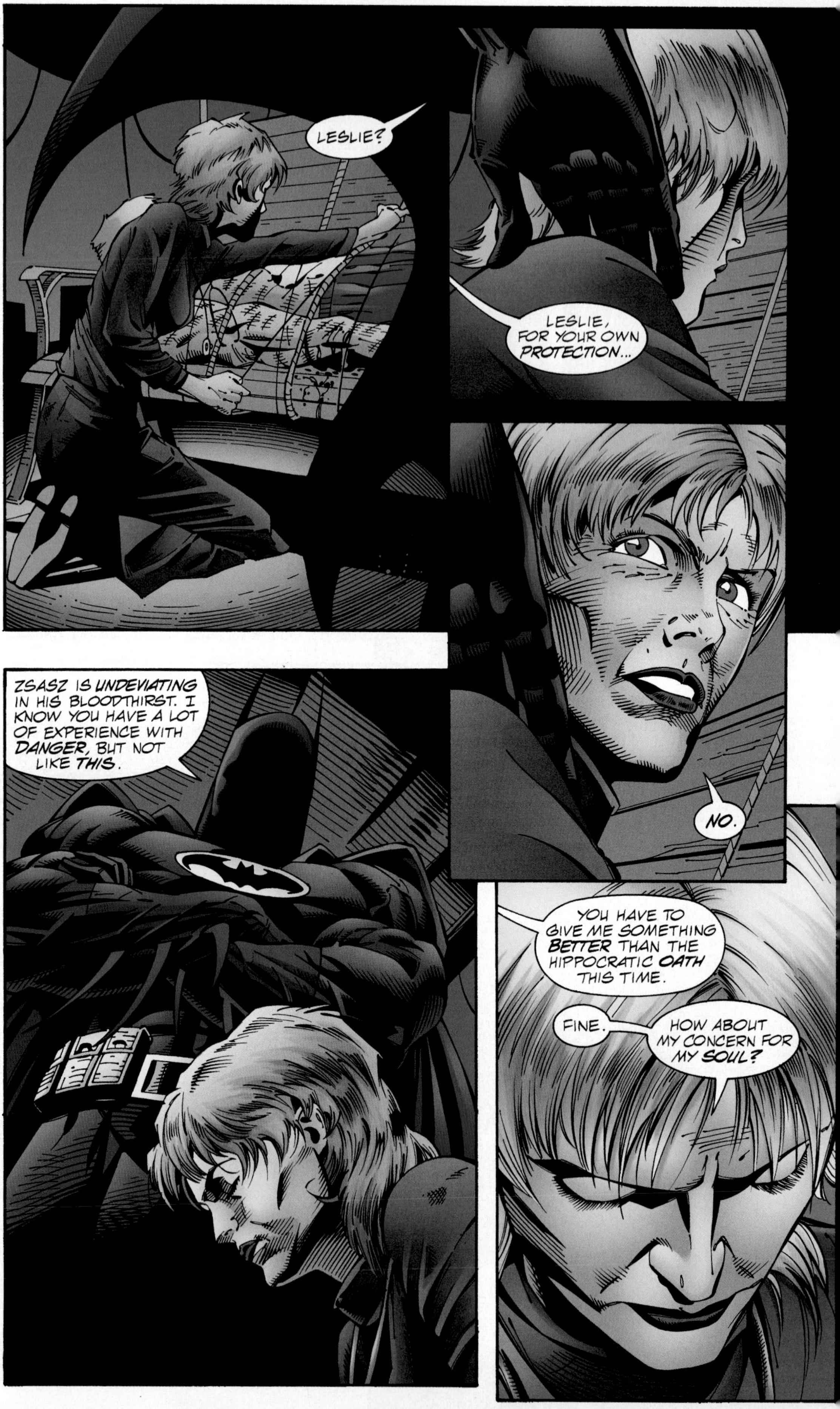
LESLIE?
LESLIE, FOR YOUR OWN PROTECTION...
NO.
ZSASZ IS UNDEVIATING IN HIS BLOODTHIRST. I KNOW YOU HAVE A LOT OF EXPERIENCE WITH DANGER, BUT NOT LIKE THIS.
YOU HAVE TO GIVE ME SOMETHING BETTER THAN THE HIPPOCRATIC OATH THIS TIME.
FINE.
HOW ABOUT MY CONCERN FOR MY SOUL?

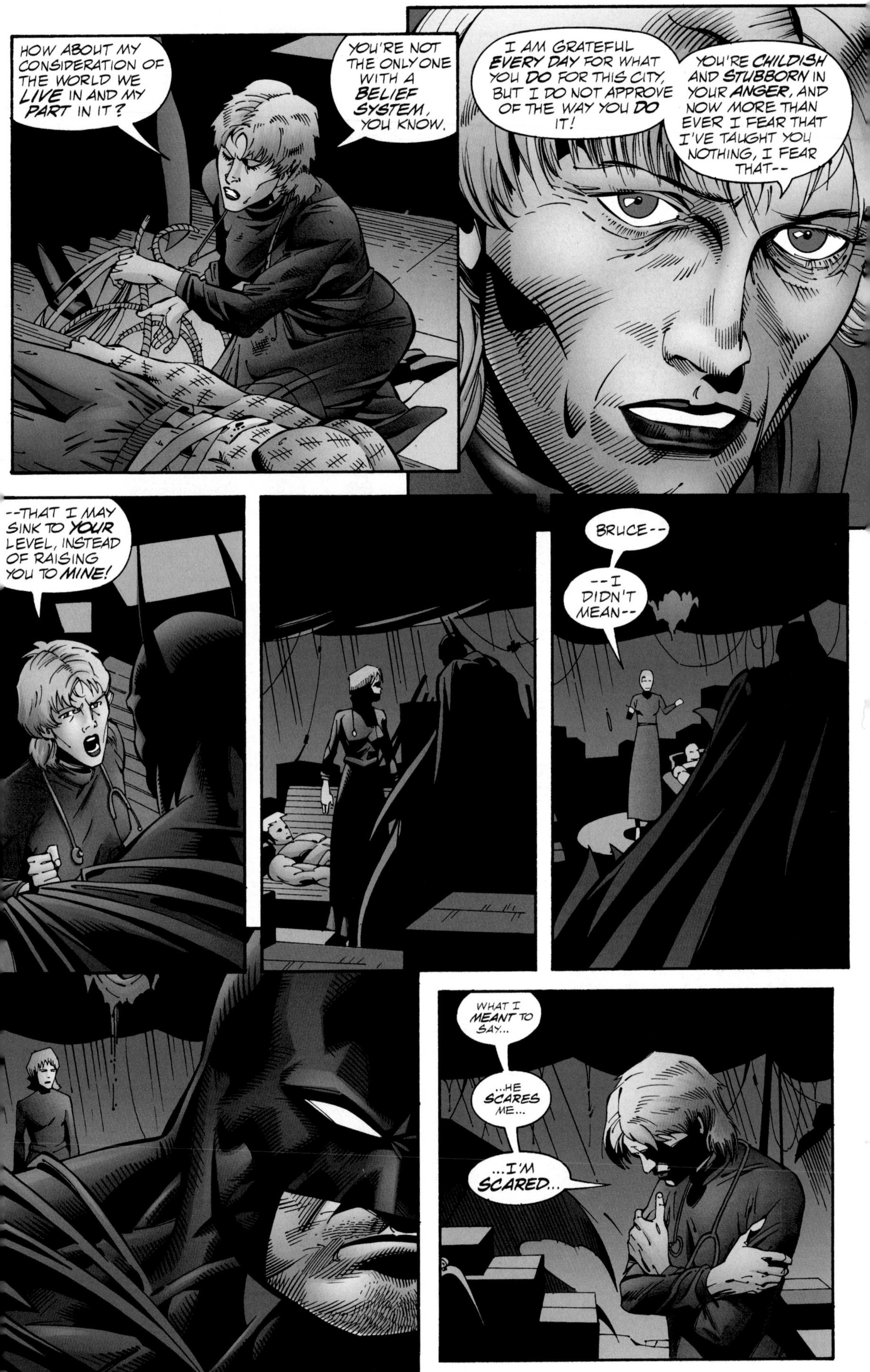
HOW ABOUT MY CONSIDERATION OF THE WORLD WE LIVE IN AND MY PART IN IT?
YOU'RE NOT THE ONLY ONE WITH A BELIEF SYSTEM, YOU KNOW.
I AM GRATEFUL EVERY DAY FOR WHAT YOU DO FOR THIS CITY, BUT I DO NOT APPROVE OF THE WAY YOU DO IT!
YOU'RE CHILDISH AND STUBBORN IN YOUR ANGER, AND NOW MORE THAN EVER I FEAR THAT I'VE TAUGHT YOU NOTHING, I FEAR THAT--
--THAT I MAY SINK TO YOUR LEVEL, INSTEAD OF RAISING YOU TO MINE!
BRUCE--
--I DIDN'T MEAN--
WHAT I MEANT TO SAY...
...HE SCARES ME...
...I'M SCARED...

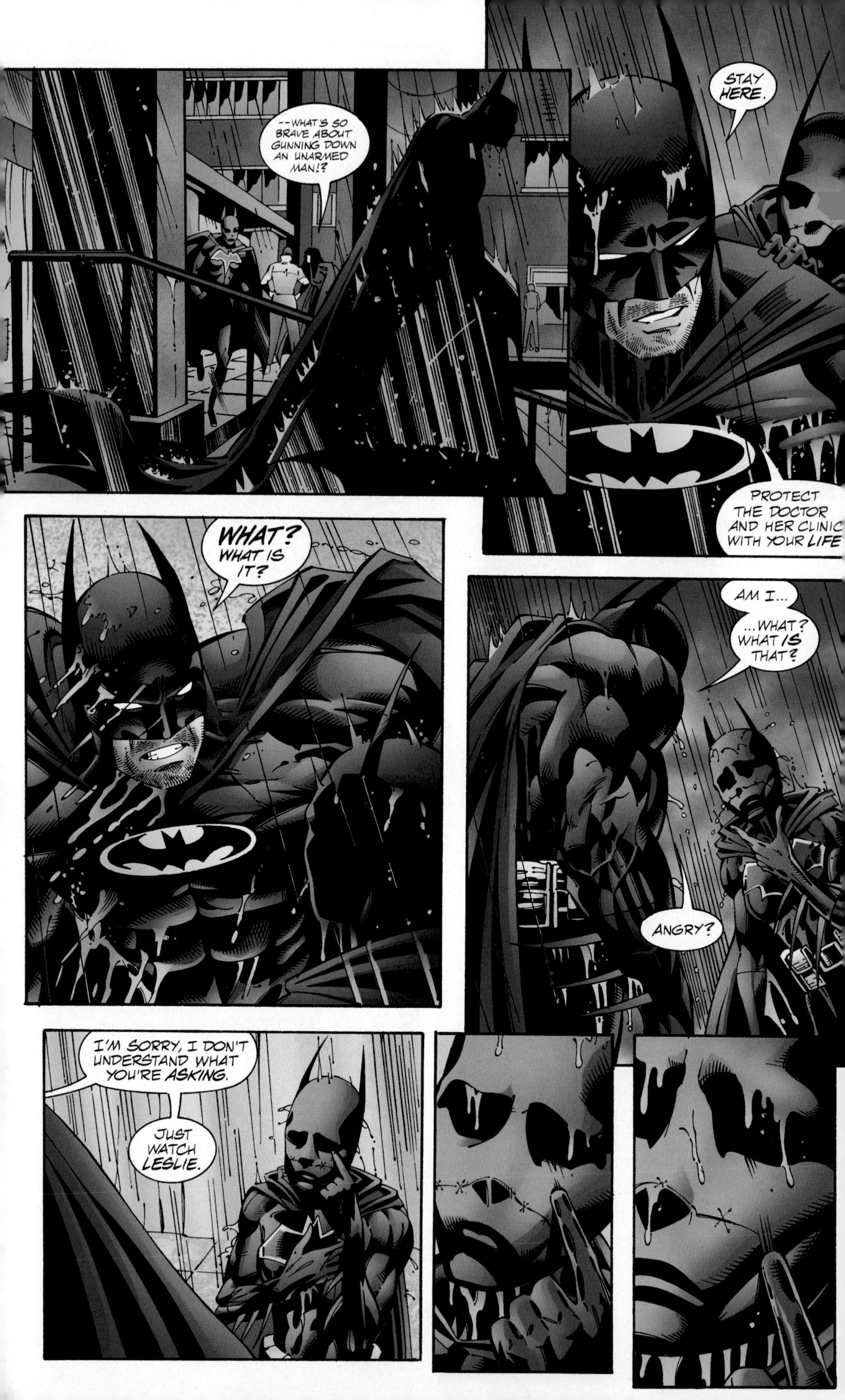
--WHAT'S SO BRAVE ABOUT GUNNING DOWN AN UNARMED MAN!?
STAY HERE.
PROTECT THE DOCTOR AND HER CLINIC WITH YOUR LIFE
WHAT? WHAT IS IT?
AM I...
...WHAT? WHAT IS THAT?
ANGRY?
I'M SORRY, I DON'T UNDERSTAND WHAT YOU'RE ASKING.
JUST WATCH LESLIE.

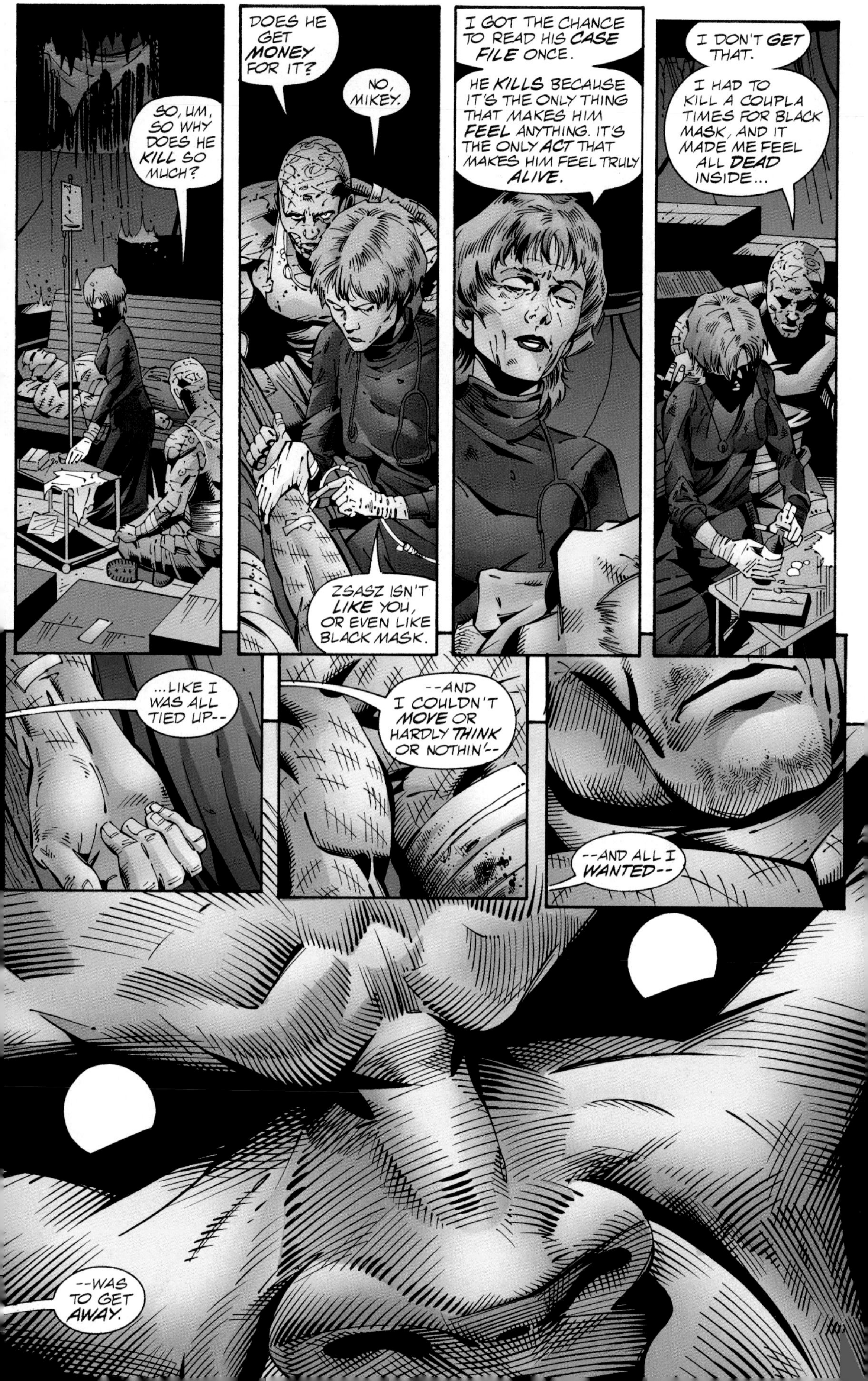

SO, UM, SO WHY DOES HE KILL SO MUCH?
DOES HE GET MONEY FOR IT?
NO, MIKEY.
ZSASZ ISN'T LIKE YOU, OR EVEN LIKE BLACK MASK.
I GOT THE CHANCE TO READ HIS CASE FILE ONCE.
HE KILLS BECAUSE IT'S THE ONLY THING THAT MAKES HIM FEEL ANYTHING. IT'S THE ONLY ACT THAT MAKES HIM FEEL TRULY ALIVE.
I DON'T GET THAT.
I HAD TO KILL A COUPLA TIMES FOR BLACK MASK, AND IT MADE ME FEEL ALL DEAD INSIDE...
...LIKE I WAS ALL TIED UP--
--AND I COULDN'T MOVE OR HARDLY THINK OR NOTHIN'--
--AND ALL I WANTED--
--WAS TO GET AWAY.

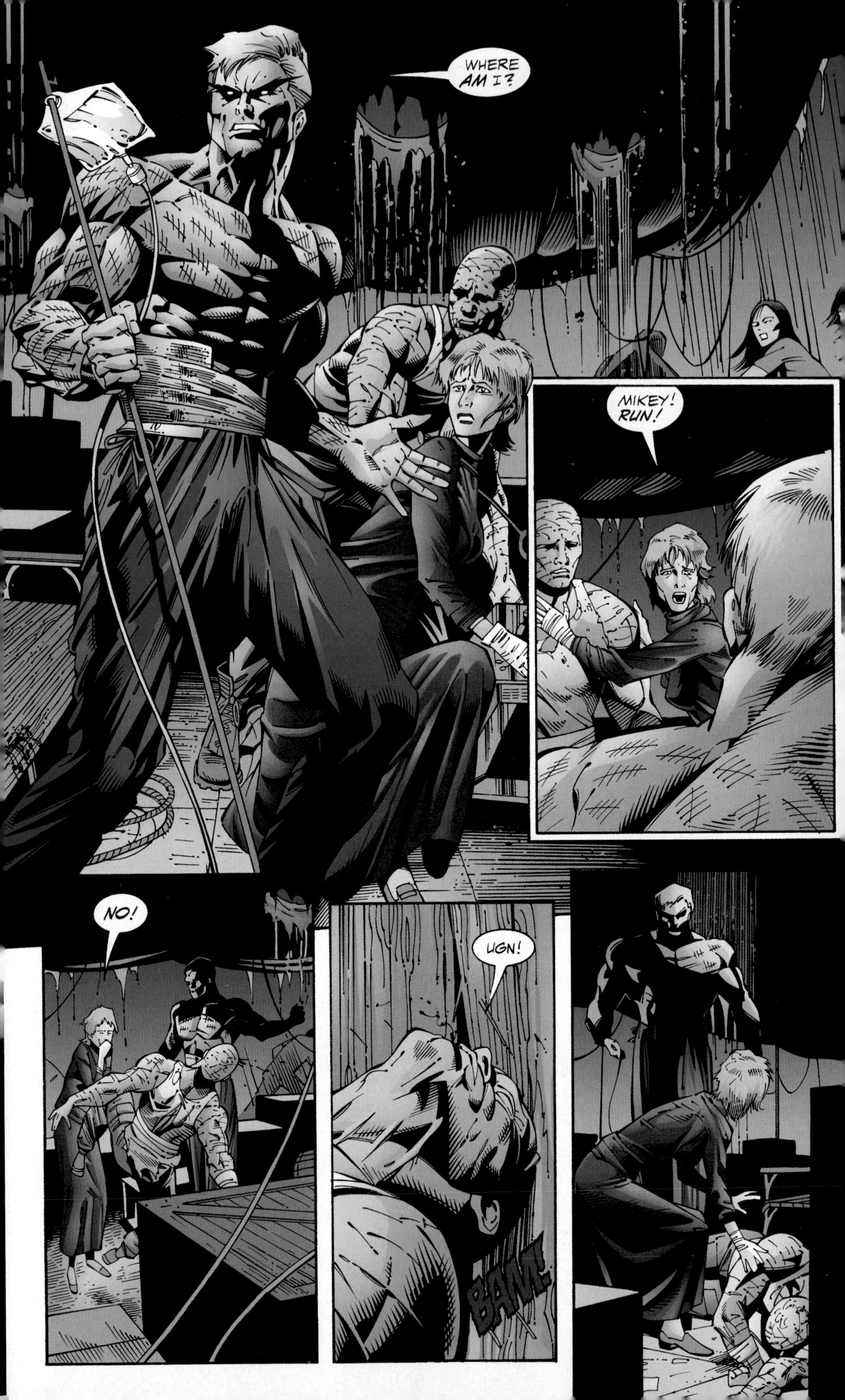
WHERE AM I?
MIKEY! RUN!
NO!
UGN!
BAM!

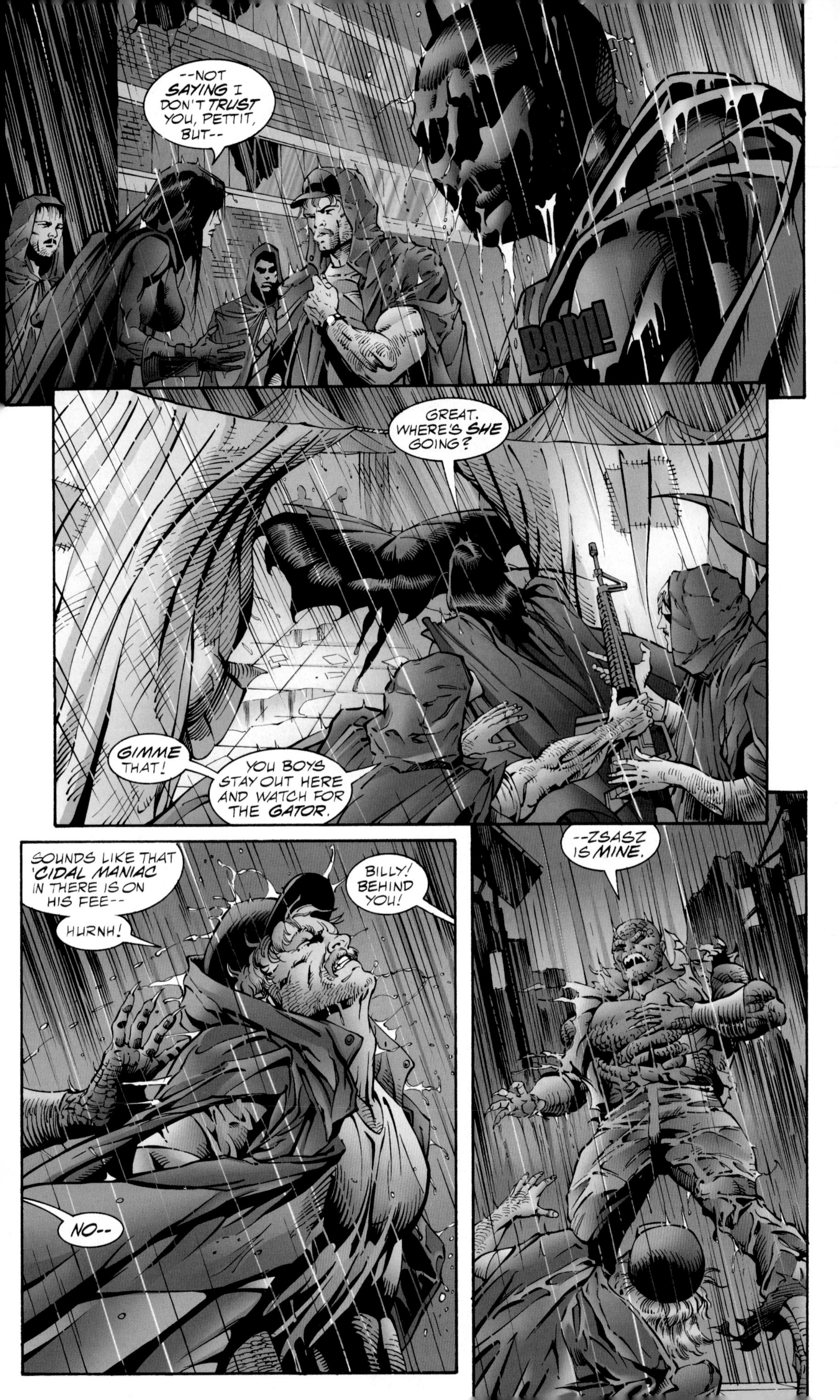
--NOT SAYING I DON'T TRUST YOU, PETTIT, BUT--
BAM!
GREAT. WHERE'S SHE GOING?
GIMME THAT!
YOU BOYS STAY OUT HERE AND WATCH FOR THE GATOR.
SOUNDS LIKE THAT 'CIDAL MANIAC IN THERE IS ON HIS FEE--
HURNH!
BILLY! BEHIND YOU!
NO--
--ZSASZ IS MINE.

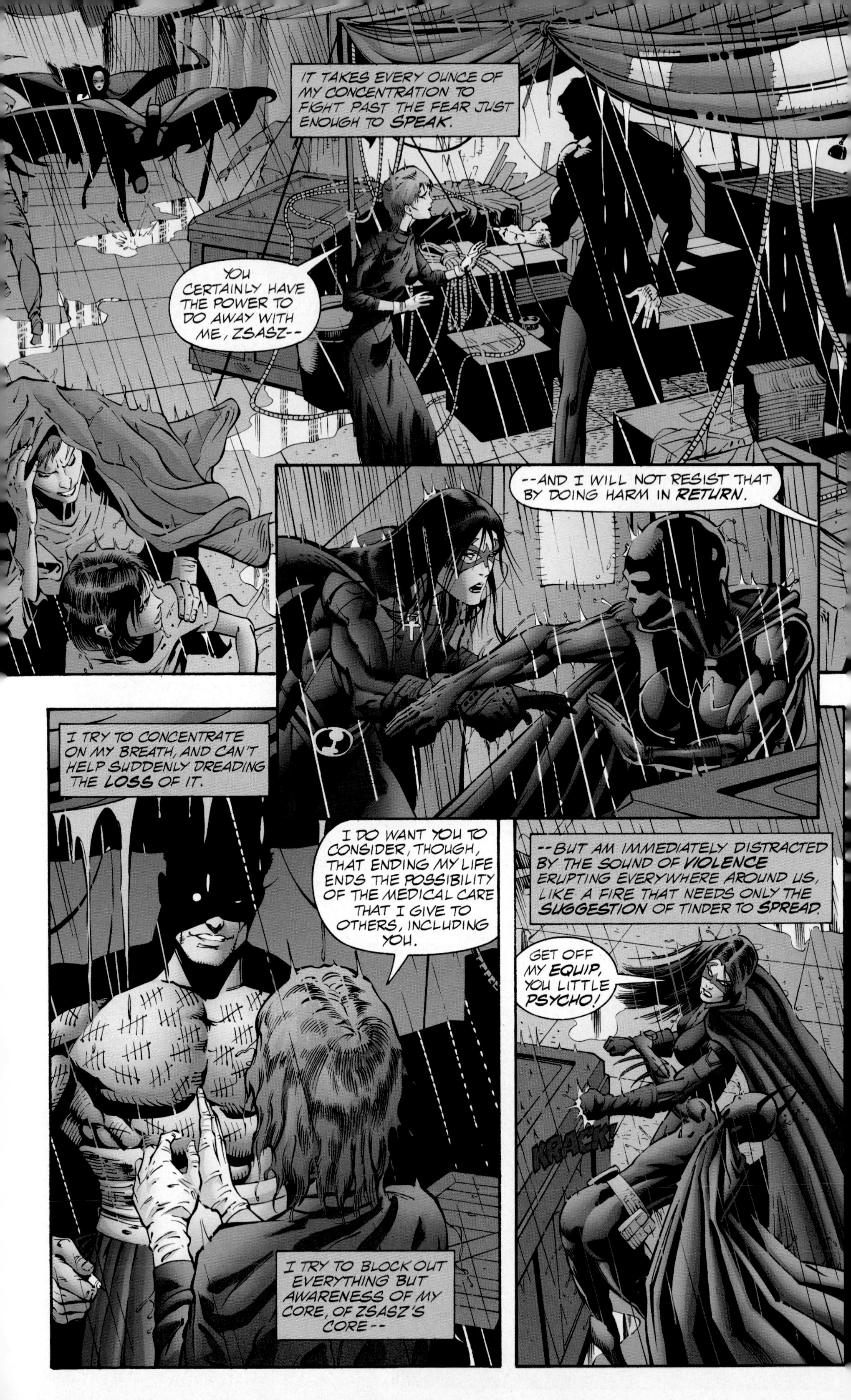
IT TAKES EVERY OUNCE OF MY CONCENTRATION TO FIGHT PAST THE FEAR JUST ENOUGH TO SPEAK.
YOU CERTAINLY HAVE THE POWER TO DO AWAY WITH ME, ZSASZ--
--AND I WILL NOT RESIST THAT BY DOING HARM IN RETURN.
I TRY TO CONCENTRATE ON MY BREATH, AND CAN'T HELP SUDDENLY DREADING THE LOSS OF IT.
I DO WANT YOU TO CONSIDER, THOUGH, THAT ENDING MY LIFE ENDS THE POSSIBILITY OF THE MEDICAL CARE THAT I GIVE TO OTHERS, INCLUDING YOU.
I TRY TO BLOCK OUT EVERYTHING BUT AWARENESS OF MY CORE, OF ZSASZ'S CORE--
--BUT AM IMMEDIATELY DISTRACTED BY THE SOUND OF VIOLENCE ERUPTING EVERYWHERE AROUND US, LIKE A FIRE THAT NEEDS ONLY THE SUGGESTION OF TINDER TO SPREAD.
GET OFF MY EQUIP, YOU LITTLE PSYCHO!
KRACK!

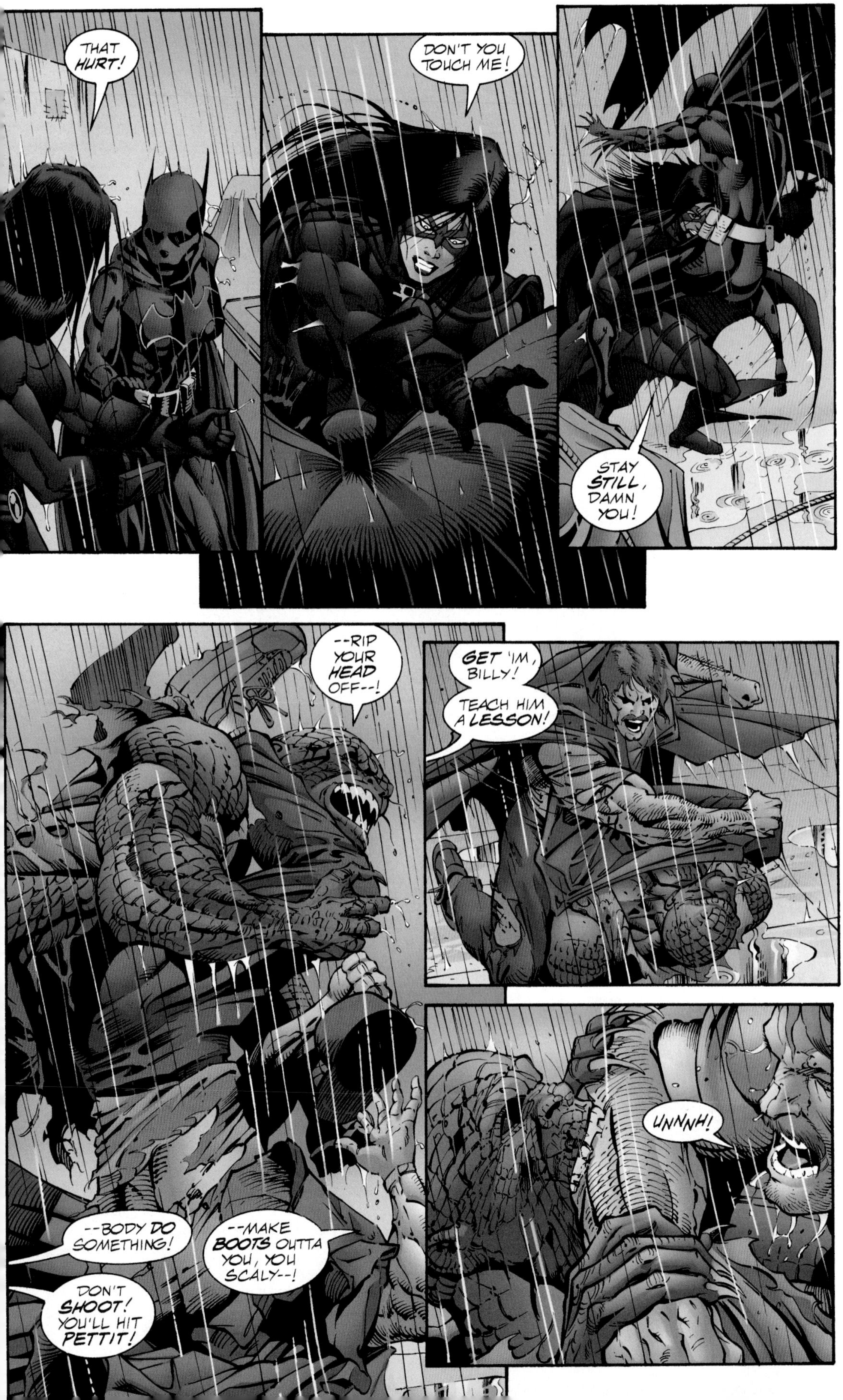
THAT HURT!
DON'T YOU TOUCH ME!
STAY STILL, DAMN YOU!
--RIP YOUR HEAD OFF--!
GET 'IM, BILLY!
TEACH HIM A LESSON!
--BODY DO SOMETHING!
DON'T SHOOT! YOU'LL HIT PETTIT!
--MAKE BOOTS OUTTA YOU, YOU SCALY--!
UNNNH!

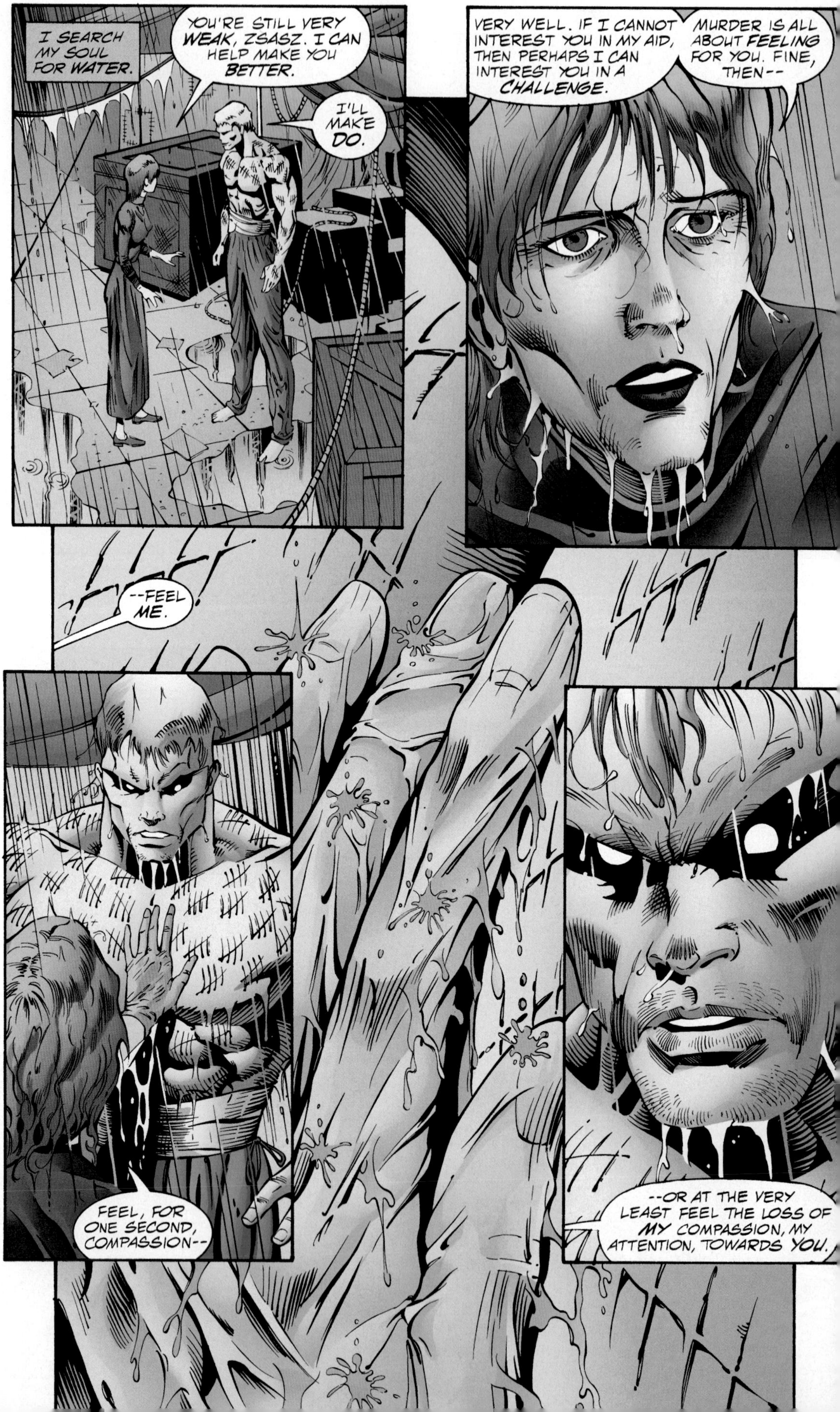
I SEARCH MY SOUL FOR WATER.
YOU'RE STILL VERY WEAK, ZSASZ. I CAN HELP MAKE YOU BETTER.
I'LL MAKE DO.
VERY WELL. IF I CANNOT INTEREST YOU IN MY AID, THEN PERHAPS I CAN INTEREST YOU IN A CHALLENGE.
MURDER IS ALL ABOUT FEELING FOR YOU. FINE, THEN--
--FEEL ME.
FEEL, FOR ONE SECOND, COMPASSION--
--OR AT THE VERY LEAST FEEL THE LOSS OF MY COMPASSION, MY ATTENTION, TOWARDS YOU.

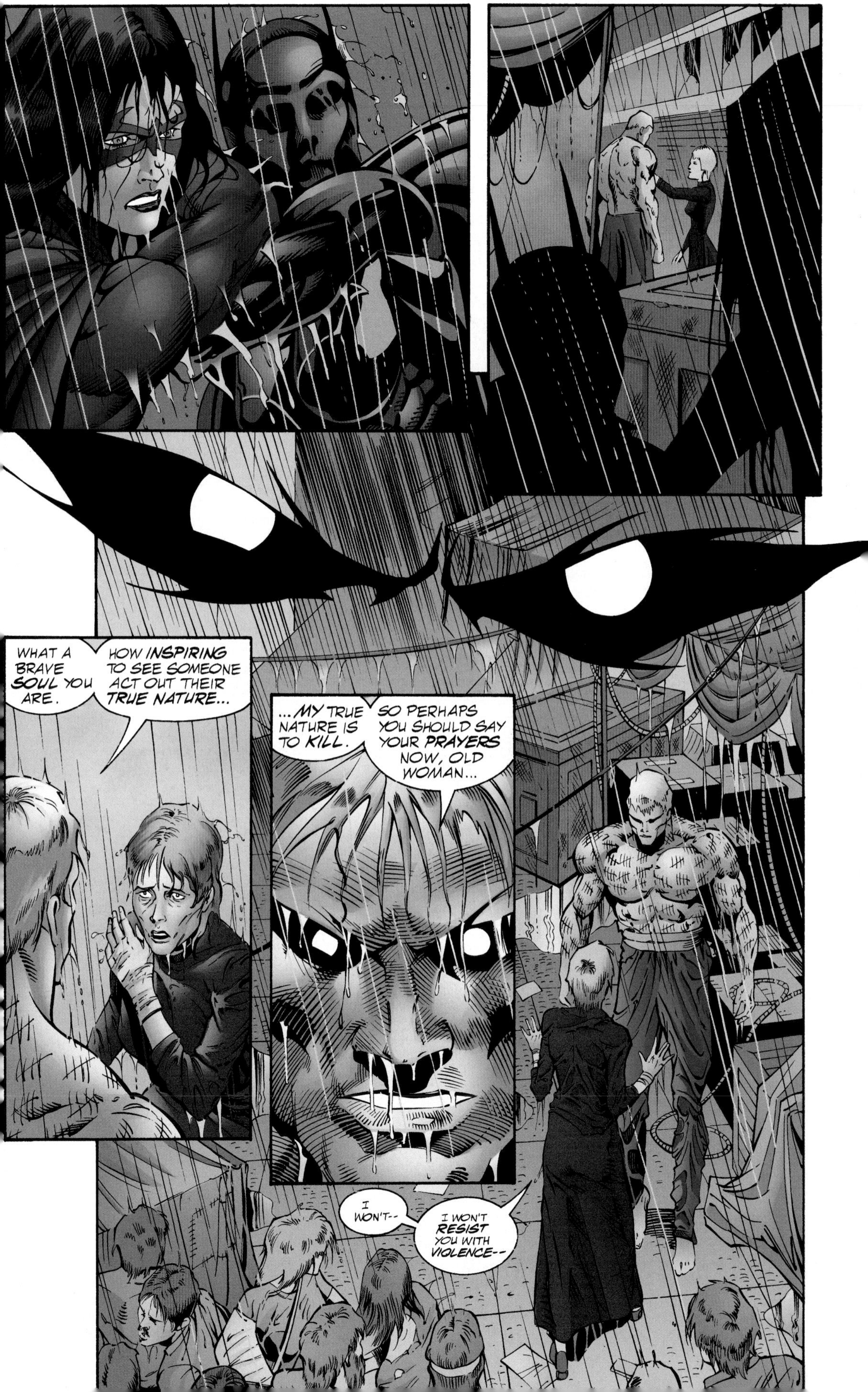
WHAT A BRAVE SOUL YOU ARE.
HOW INSPIRING TO SEE SOMEONE ACT OUT THEIR TRUE NATURE...
...MY TRUE NATURE IS TO KILL.
SO PERHAPS YOU SHOULD SAY YOUR PRAYERS NOW, OLD WOMAN...
I WON'T--
I WON'T RESIST YOU WITH VIOLENCE--

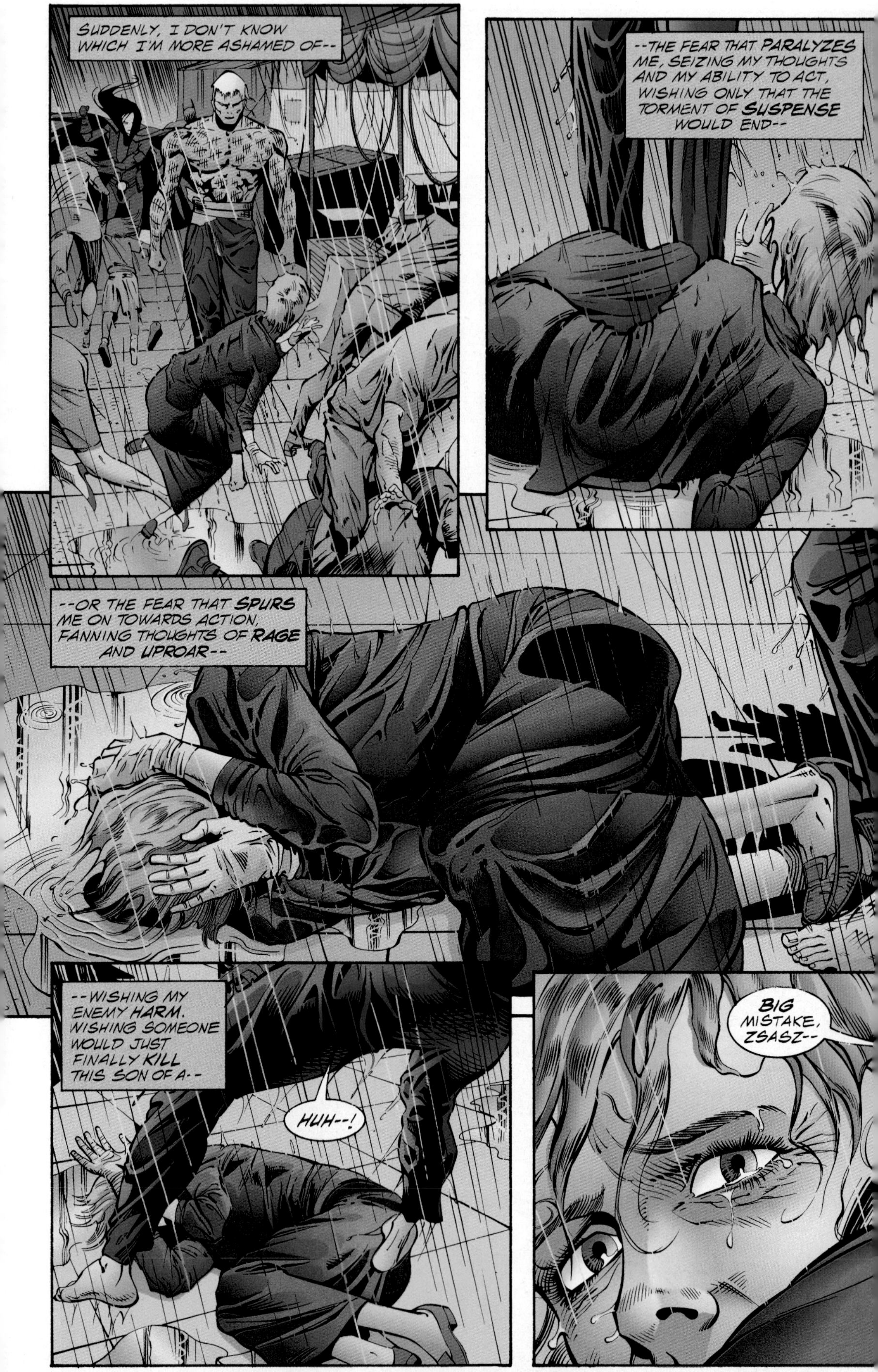
SUDDENLY, I DON'T KNOW WHICH I'M MORE ASHAMED OF--
--THE FEAR THAT PARALYZES ME, SEIZING MY THOUGHTS AND MY ABILITY TO ACT, WISHING ONLY THAT THE TORMENT OF SUSPENSE WOULD END--
--OR THE FEAR THAT SPURS ME ON TOWARDS ACTION, FANNING THOUGHTS OF RAGE AND UPROAR--
--WISHING MY ENEMY HARM. WISHING SOMEONE WOULD JUST FINALLY KILL THIS SON OF A--
HUH--!
BIG MISTAKE, ZSASZ--

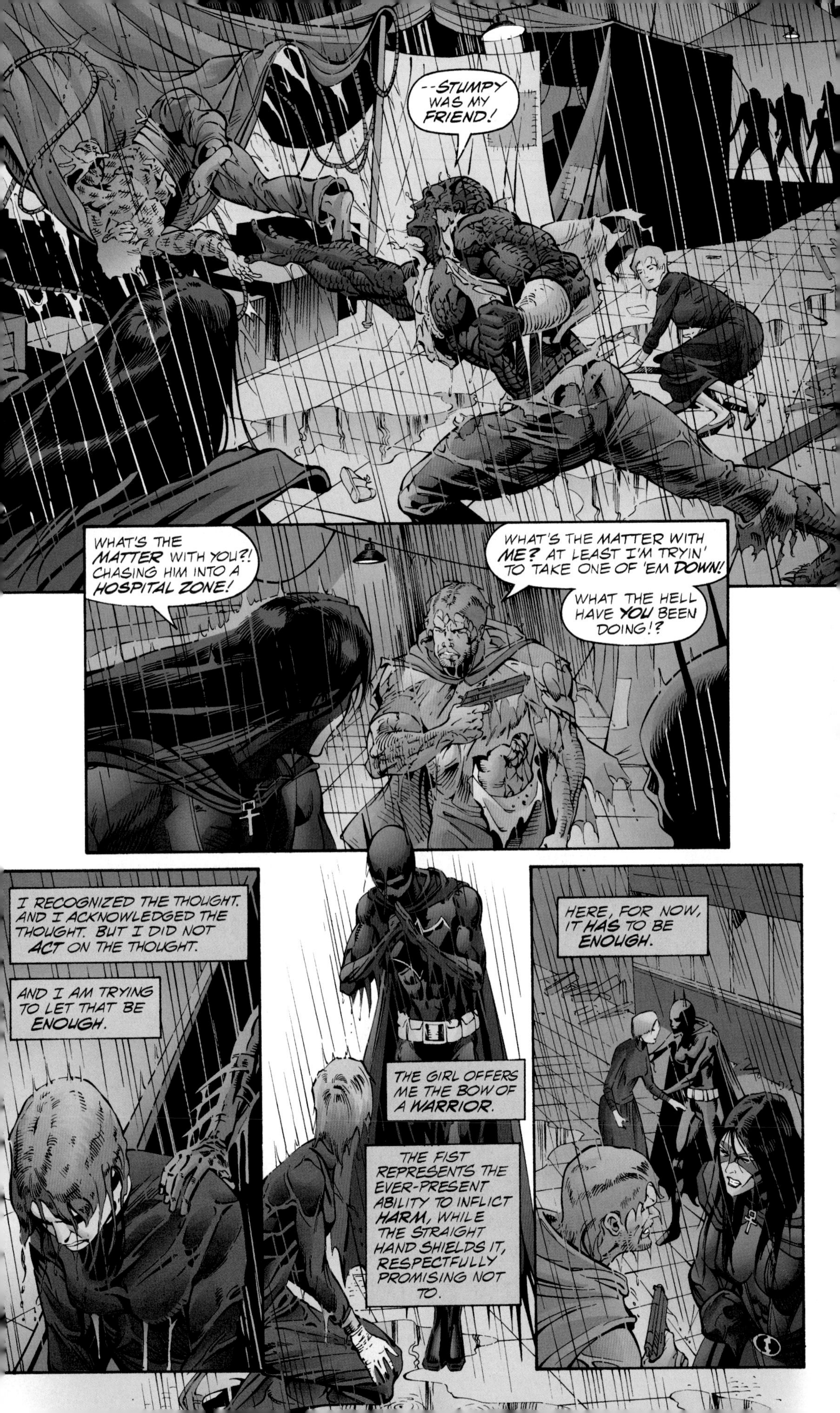
--STUMPY WAS MY FRIEND!
WHAT'S THE MATTER WITH YOU?! CHASING HIM INTO A HOSPITAL ZONE!
WHAT'S THE MATTER WITH ME? AT LEAST I'M TRYIN' TO TAKE ONE OF 'EM DOWN!
WHAT THE HELL HAVE YOU BEEN DOING!?
I RECOGNIZED THE THOUGHT. AND I ACKNOWLEDGED THE THOUGHT. BUT I DID NOT ACT ON THE THOUGHT.
AND I AM TRYING TO LET THAT BE ENOUGH.
THE GIRL OFFERS ME THE BOW OF A WARRIOR.
THE FIST REPRESENTS THE EVER-PRESENT ABILITY TO INFLICT HARM, WHILE THE STRAIGHT HAND SHIELDS IT, RESPECTFULLY PROMISING NOT TO.
HERE, FOR NOW, IT HAS TO BE ENOUGH.

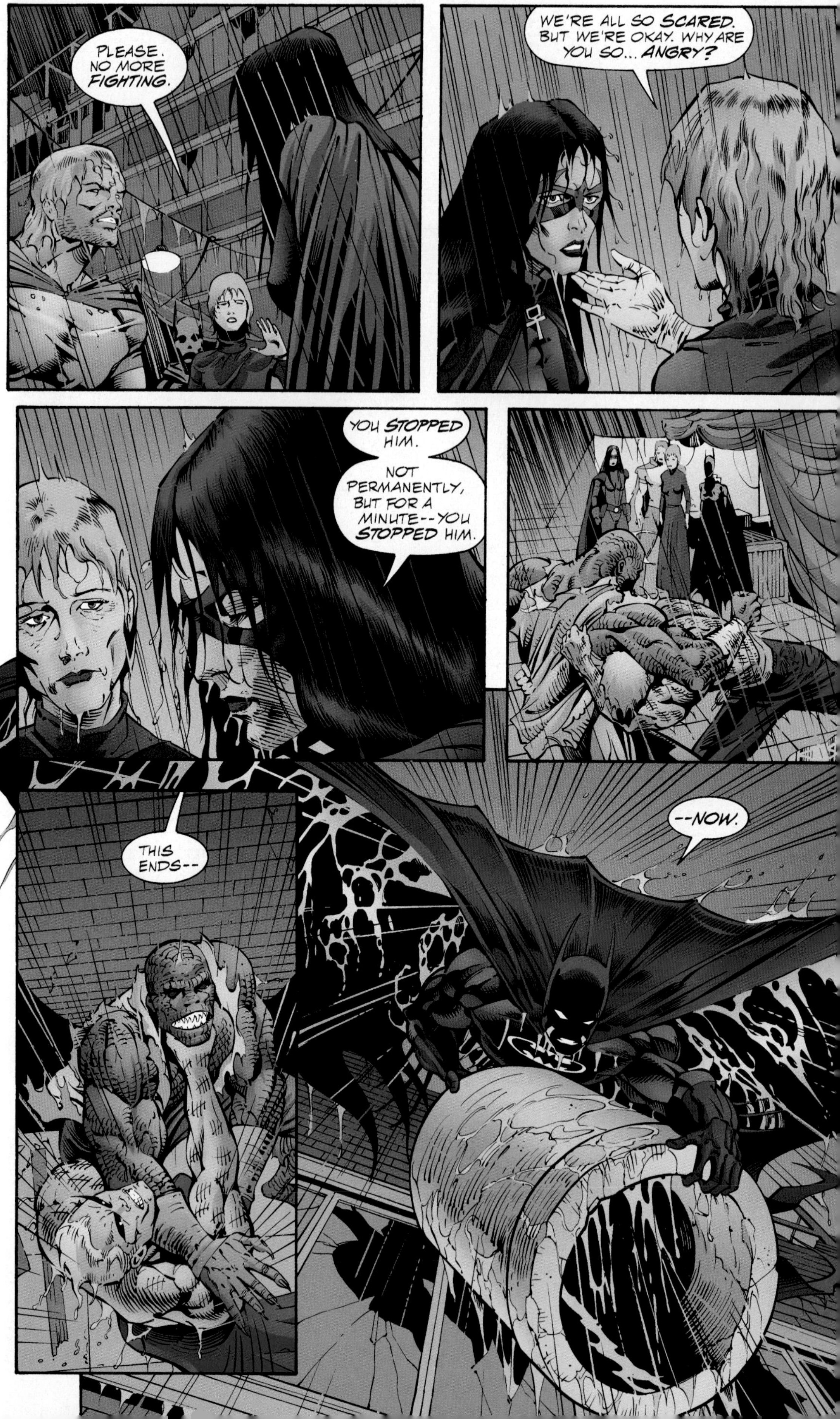
PLEASE. NO MORE FIGHTING.
WE'RE ALL SO SCARED. BUT WE'RE OKAY. WHY ARE YOU SO... ANGRY?
YOU STOPPED HIM.
NOT PERMANENTLY, BUT FOR A MINUTE--YOU STOPPED HIM.
THIS ENDS--
--NOW.

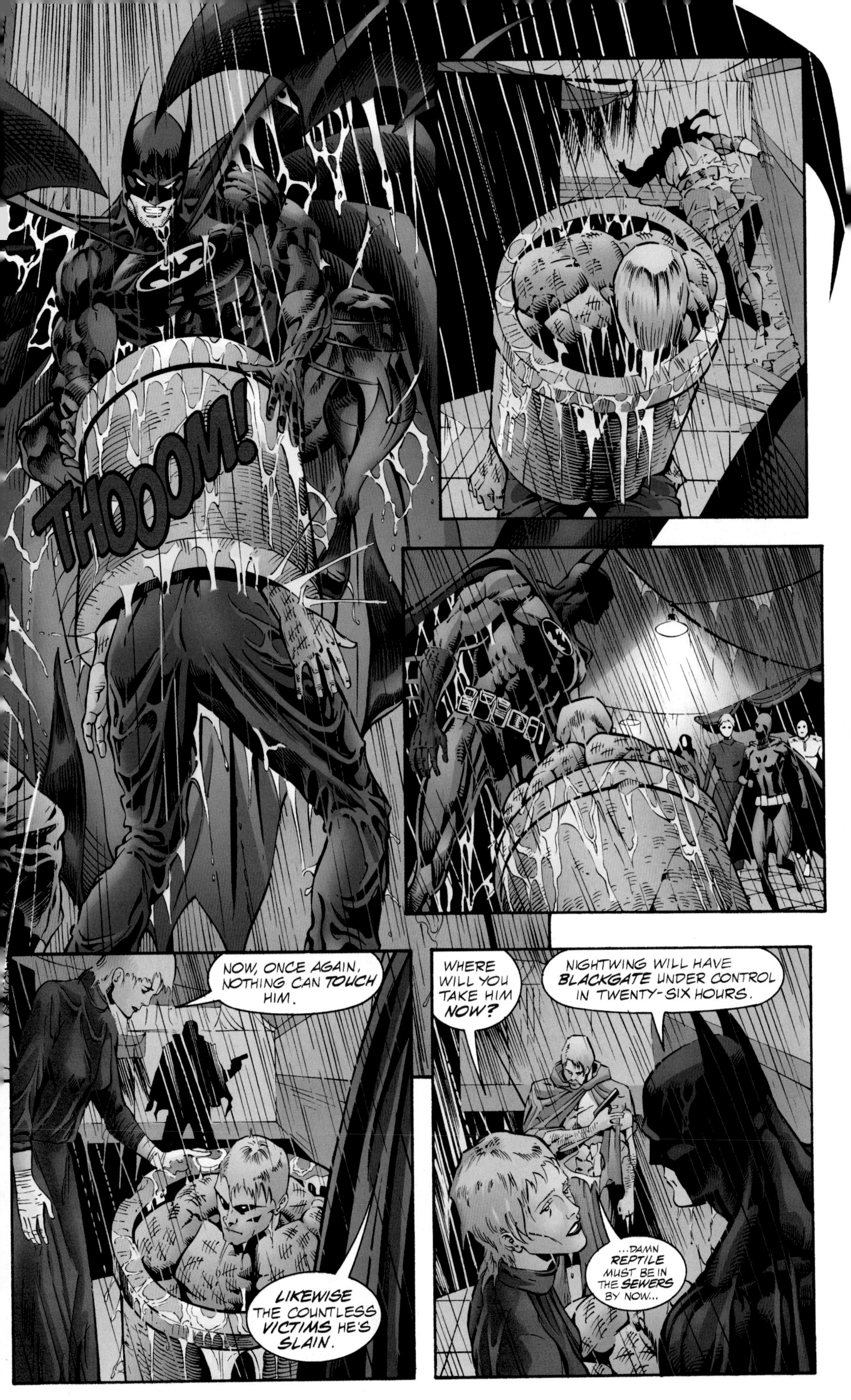
THOOOM!
NOW, ONCE AGAIN, NOTHING CAN TOUCH HIM.
LIKEWISE THE COUNTLESS VICTIMS HE'S SLAIN.
WHERE WILL YOU TAKE HIM NOW?
NIGHTWING WILL HAVE BLACKGATE UNDER CONTROL IN TWENTY-SIX HOURS.
...DAMN REPTILE MUST BE IN THE SEWERS BY NOW...

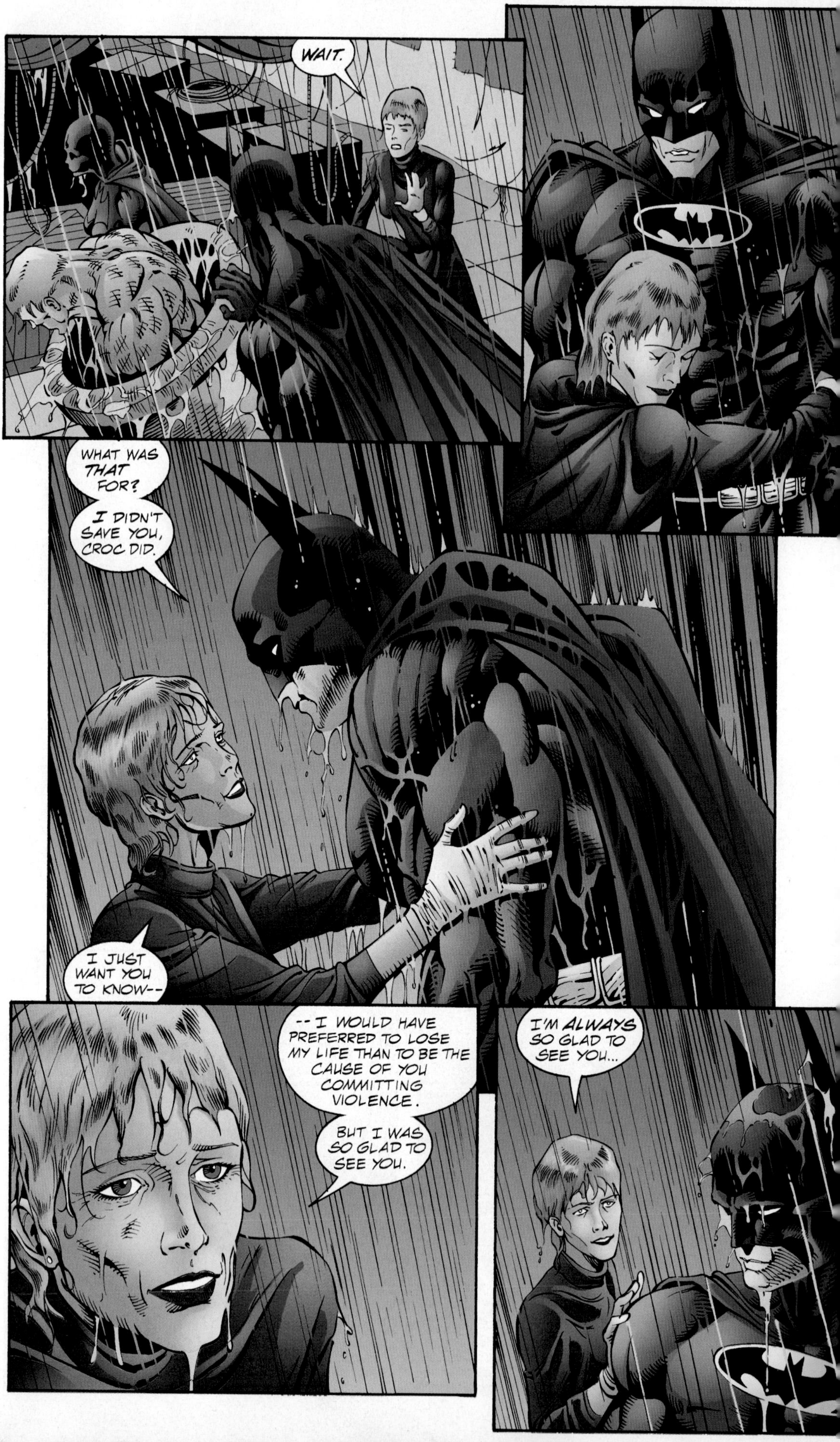
WAIT.
WHAT WAS THAT FOR?
I DIDN'T SAVE YOU, CROC DID.
I JUST WANT YOU TO KNOW--
-- I WOULD HAVE PREFERRED TO LOSE MY LIFE THAN TO BE THE CAUSE OF YOU COMMITTING VIOLENCE.
BUT I WAS SO GLAD TO SEE YOU.
I'M ALWAYS SO GLAD TO SEE YOU...

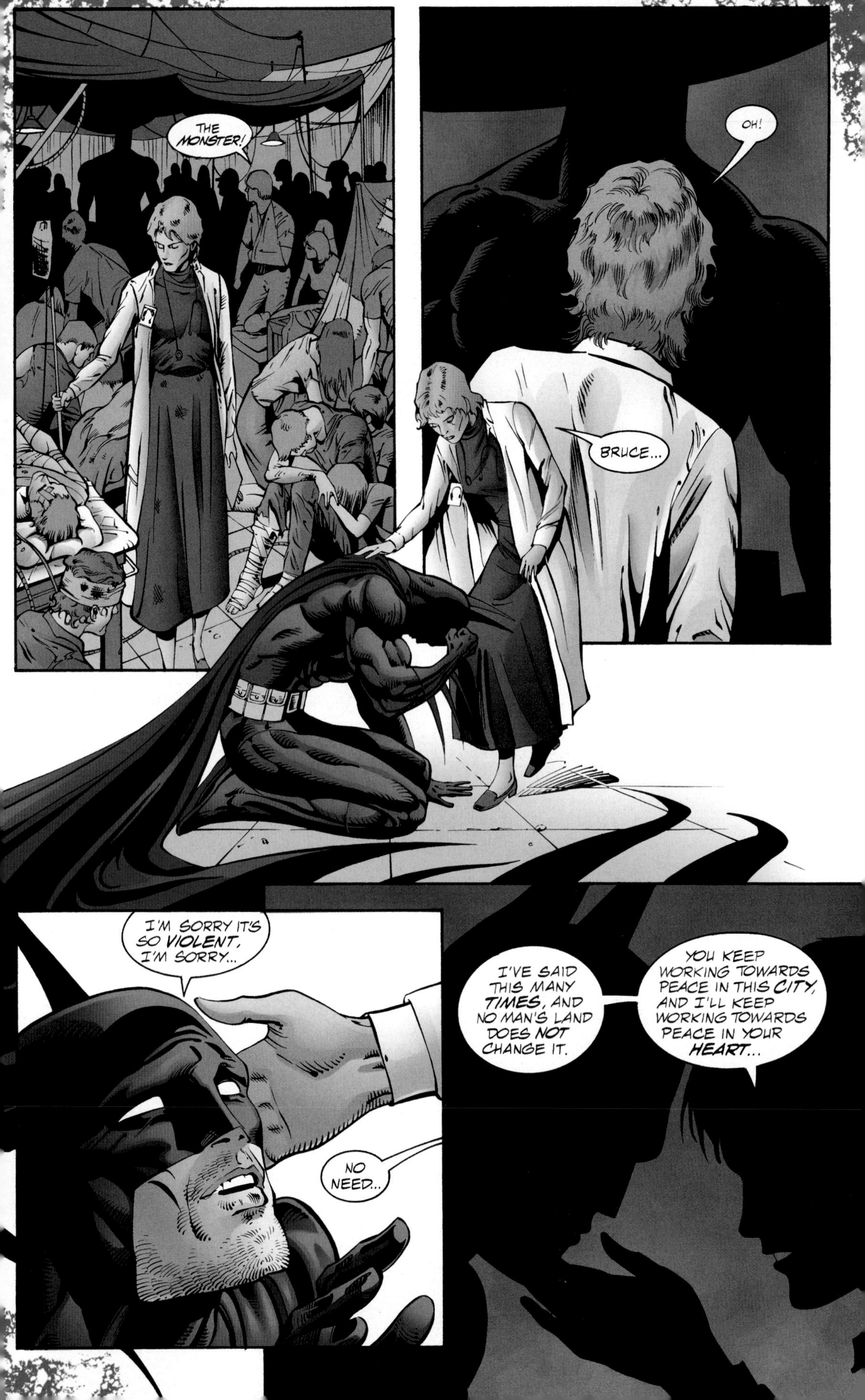
THE MONSTER!
OH!
BRUCE...
I'M SORRY IT'S SO VIOLENT, I'M SORRY...
NO NEED...
I'VE SAID THIS MANY TIMES, AND NO MAN'S LAND DOES NOT CHANGE IT.
YOU KEEP WORKING TOWARDS PEACE IN THIS CITY, AND I'LL KEEP WORKING TOWARDS PEACE IN YOUR HEART...

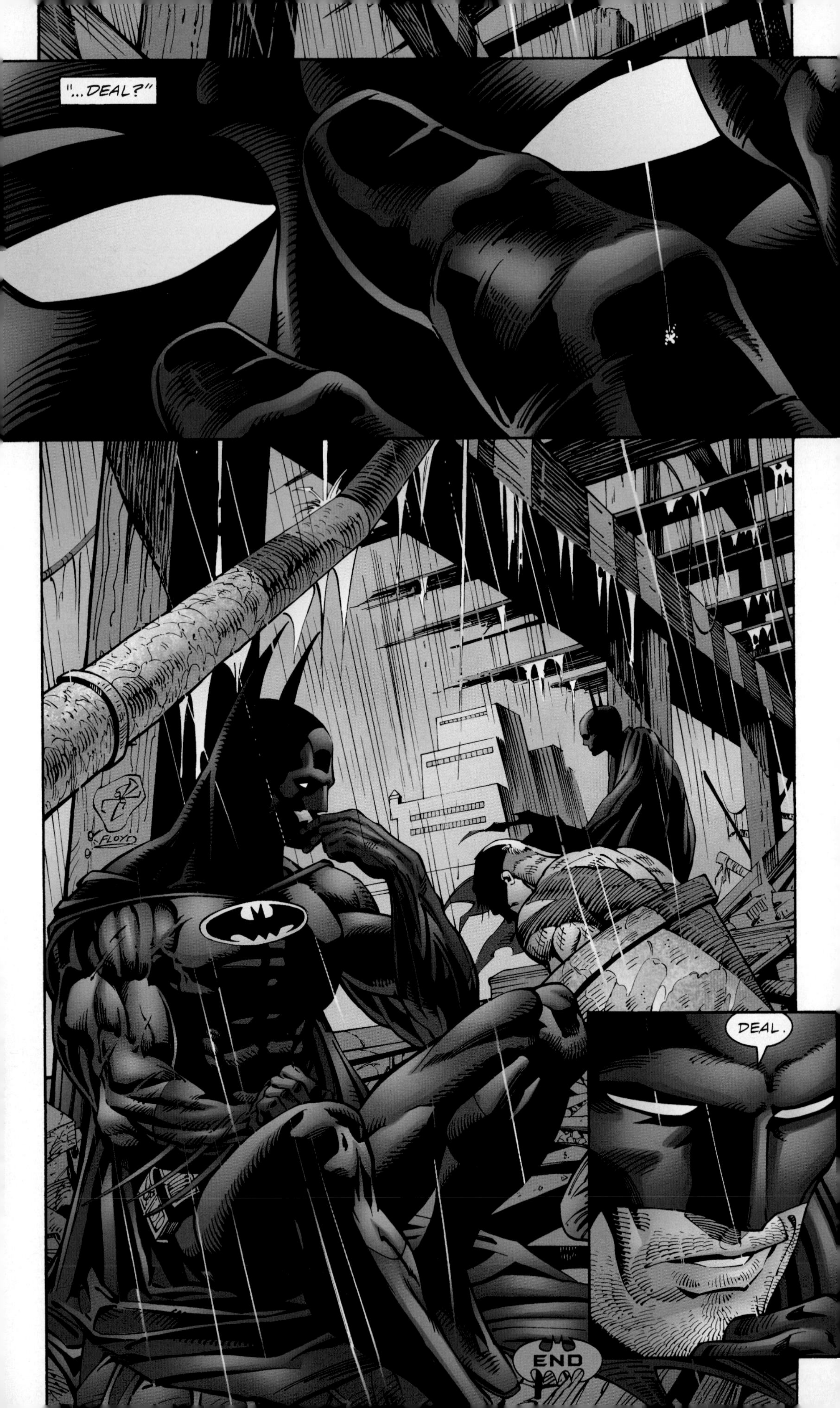
"...DEAL?"
DEAL.
END

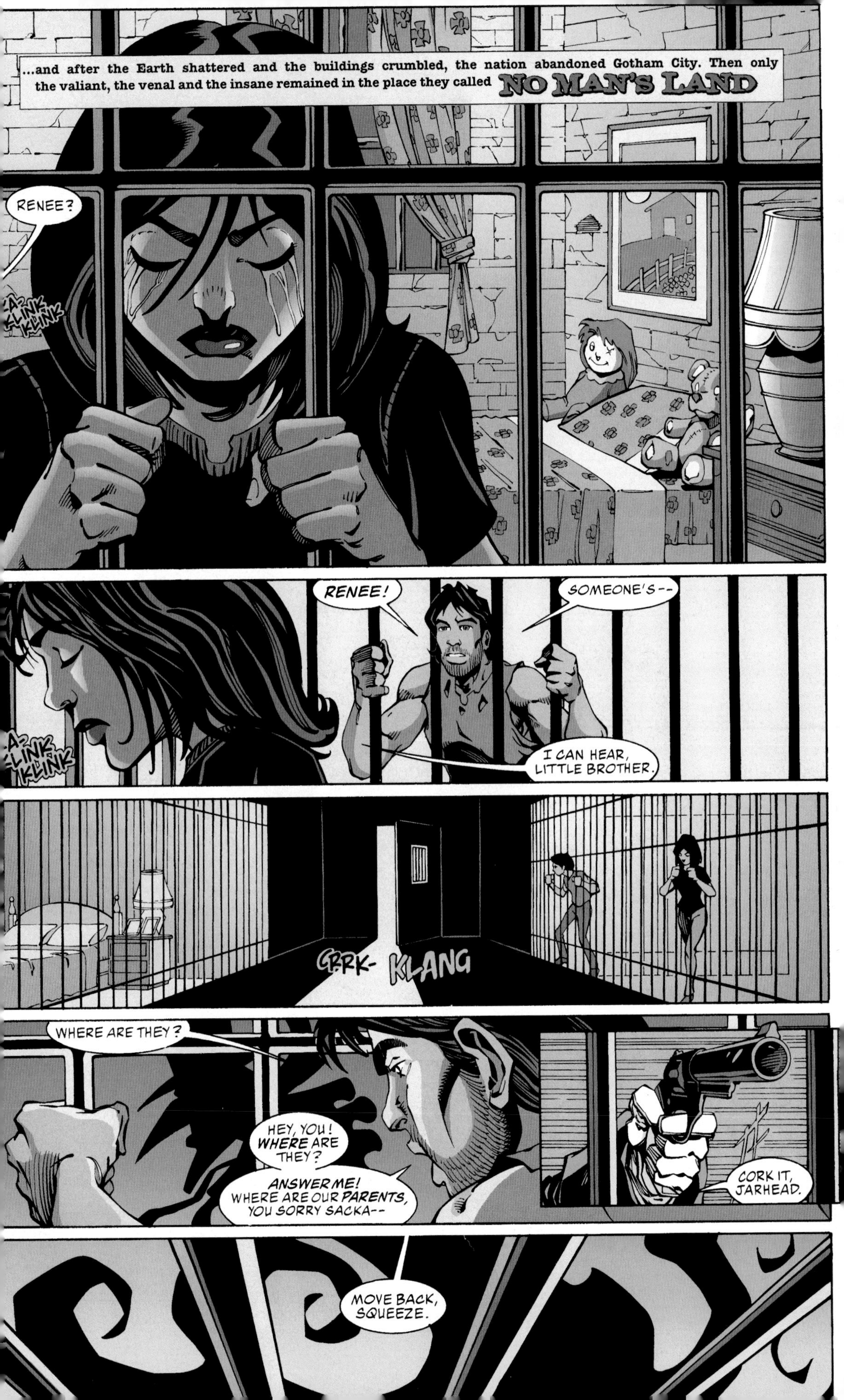
...and after the Earth shattered and the buildings crumbled, the nation abandoned Gotham City. Then only the valiant, the venal and the insane remained in the place they called NO MAN'S LAND
RENEE?
A-KLINK KLINK
RENEE!
SOMEONE'S--
I CAN HEAR, LITTLE BROTHER.
A-KLINK KLINK
CRRK- KLANG
WHERE ARE THEY?
HEY, YOU! WHERE ARE THEY?
ANSWER ME! WHERE ARE OUR PARENTS, YOU SORRY SACKA--
CORK IT, JARHEAD.
MOVE BACK, SQUEEZE.

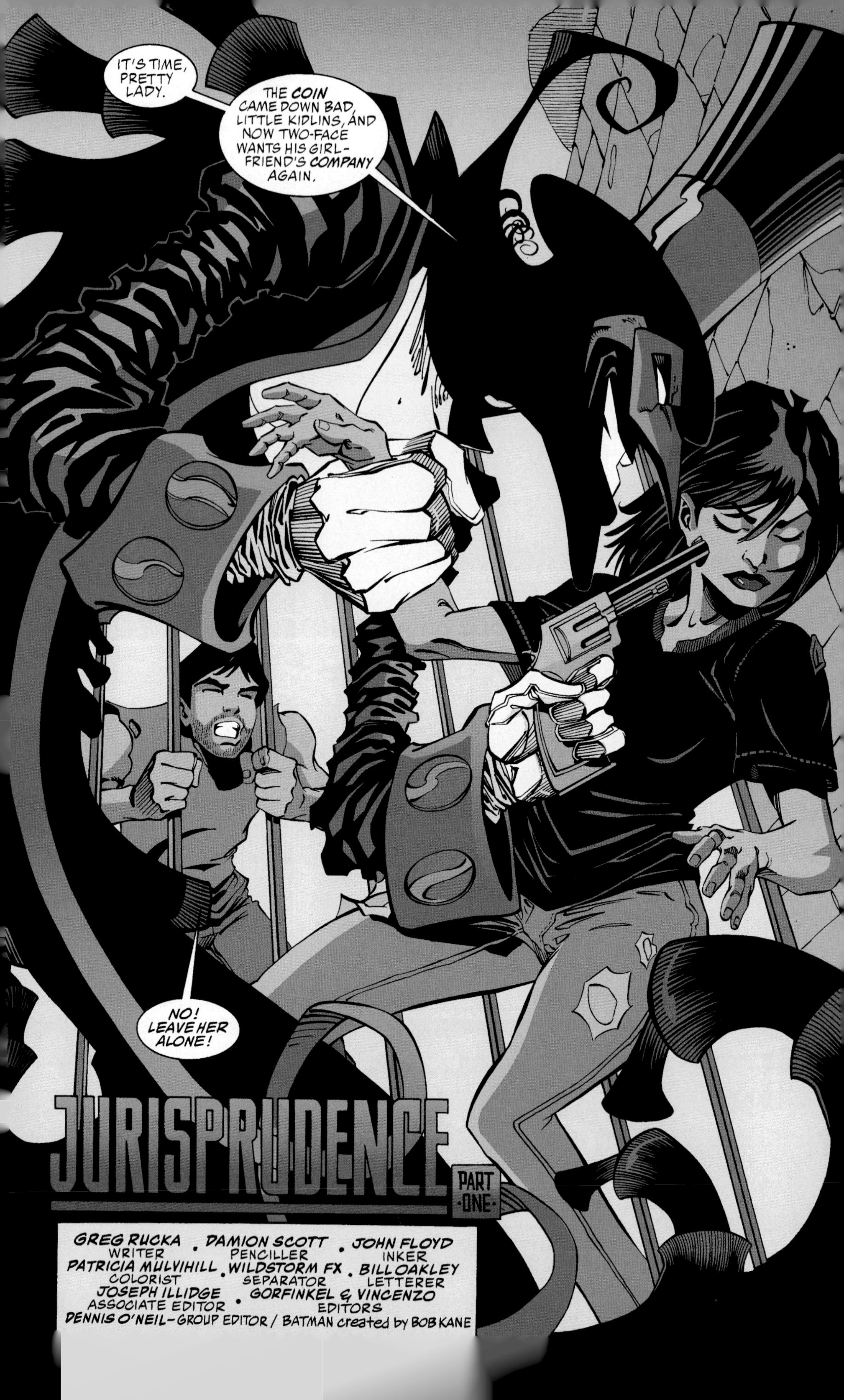
IT'S TIME, PRETTY LADY.
THE COIN CAME DOWN BAD, LITTLE KIDLINS, AND NOW TWO-FACE WANTS HIS GIRL-FRIEND'S COMPANY AGAIN.
NO! LEAVE HER ALONE!
JURISPRUDENCE PART ONE
GREG RUCKA WRITER . DAMION SCOTT PENCILLER . JOHN FLOYD INKER
PATRICIA MULVIHILL COLORIST . WILDSTORM FX SEPARATOR . BILL OAKLEY LETTERER
JOSEPH ILLIDGE ASSOCIATE EDITOR . GORFINKEL & VINCENZO EDITORS
DENNIS O'NEIL-GROUP EDITOR / BATMAN created by BOB KANE

YOU HURT MY **SISTER** I'LL KILL YOU, UNDERSTAND I'LL **KILL** YOU--

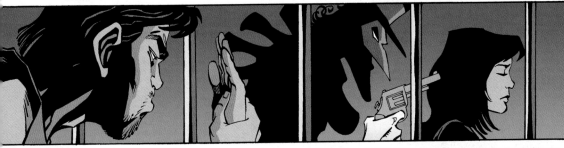

--TALK TOO MUCH, LITTLE BOY!

AH!

KA-KLANK

SHAK

NO... NOT RENEE... NOT MY SISTER...

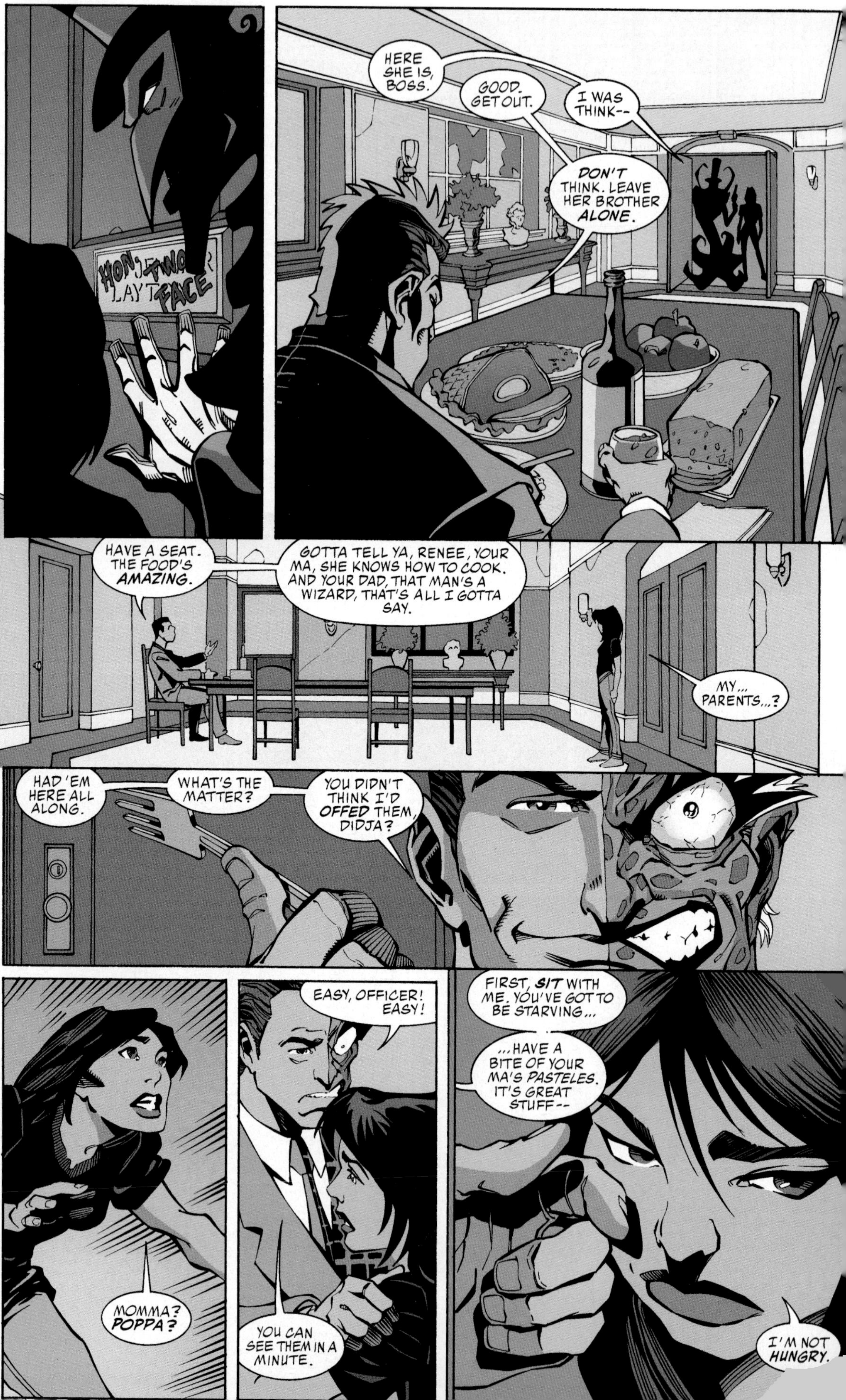
HON. JEN... TWO FACE LAYT...
HERE SHE IS, BOSS.
GOOD. GET OUT.
I WAS THINK--
DON'T THINK. LEAVE HER BROTHER ALONE.
HAVE A SEAT. THE FOOD'S AMAZING.
GOTTA TELL YA, RENEE, YOUR MA, SHE KNOWS HOW TO COOK. AND YOUR DAD, THAT MAN'S A WIZARD, THAT'S ALL I GOTTA SAY.
MY... PARENTS...?
HAD 'EM HERE ALL ALONG.
WHAT'S THE MATTER?
YOU DIDN'T THINK I'D OFFED THEM, DIDJA?
MOMMA? POPPA?
EASY, OFFICER! EASY!
YOU CAN SEE THEM IN A MINUTE.
FIRST, SIT WITH ME. YOU'VE GOT TO BE STARVING...
...HAVE A BITE OF YOUR MA'S PASTELES. IT'S GREAT STUFF--
I'M NOT HUNGRY.

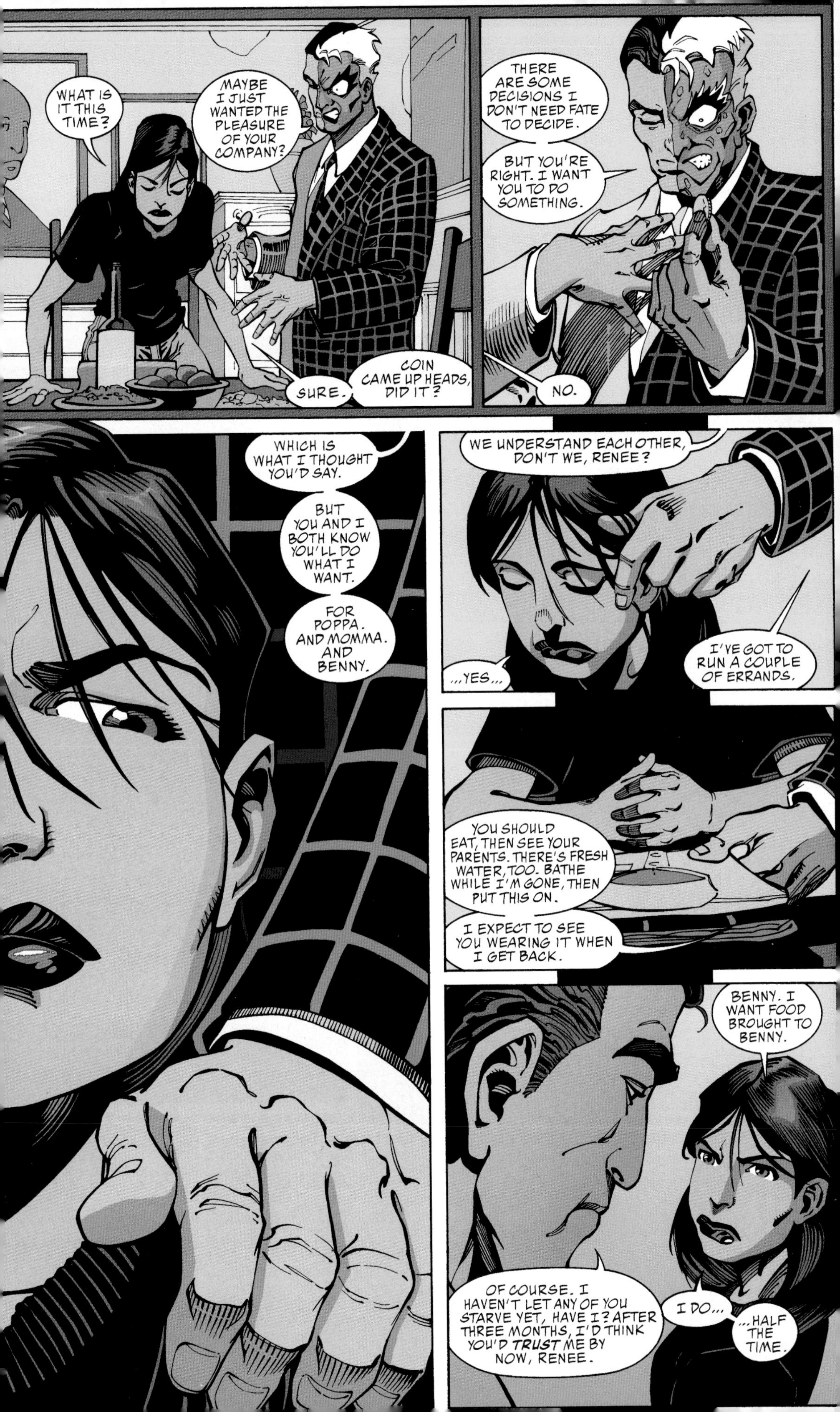
WHAT IS IT THIS TIME?
MAYBE I JUST WANTED THE PLEASURE OF YOUR COMPANY?
SURE.
COIN CAME UP HEADS, DID IT?
THERE ARE SOME DECISIONS I DON'T NEED FATE TO DECIDE.
BUT YOU'RE RIGHT. I WANT YOU TO DO SOMETHING.
NO.
WHICH IS WHAT I THOUGHT YOU'D SAY.
BUT YOU AND I BOTH KNOW YOU'LL DO WHAT I WANT.
FOR POPPA. AND MOMMA. AND BENNY.
WE UNDERSTAND EACH OTHER, DON'T WE, RENEE?
...YES...
I'VE GOT TO RUN A COUPLE OF ERRANDS.
YOU SHOULD EAT, THEN SEE YOUR PARENTS. THERE'S FRESH WATER, TOO. BATHE WHILE I'M GONE, THEN PUT THIS ON.
I EXPECT TO SEE YOU WEARING IT WHEN I GET BACK.
BENNY. I WANT FOOD BROUGHT TO BENNY.
OF COURSE. I HAVEN'T LET ANY OF YOU STARVE YET, HAVE I? AFTER THREE MONTHS, I'D THINK YOU'D *TRUST* ME BY NOW, RENEE.
I DO...
...HALF THE TIME.

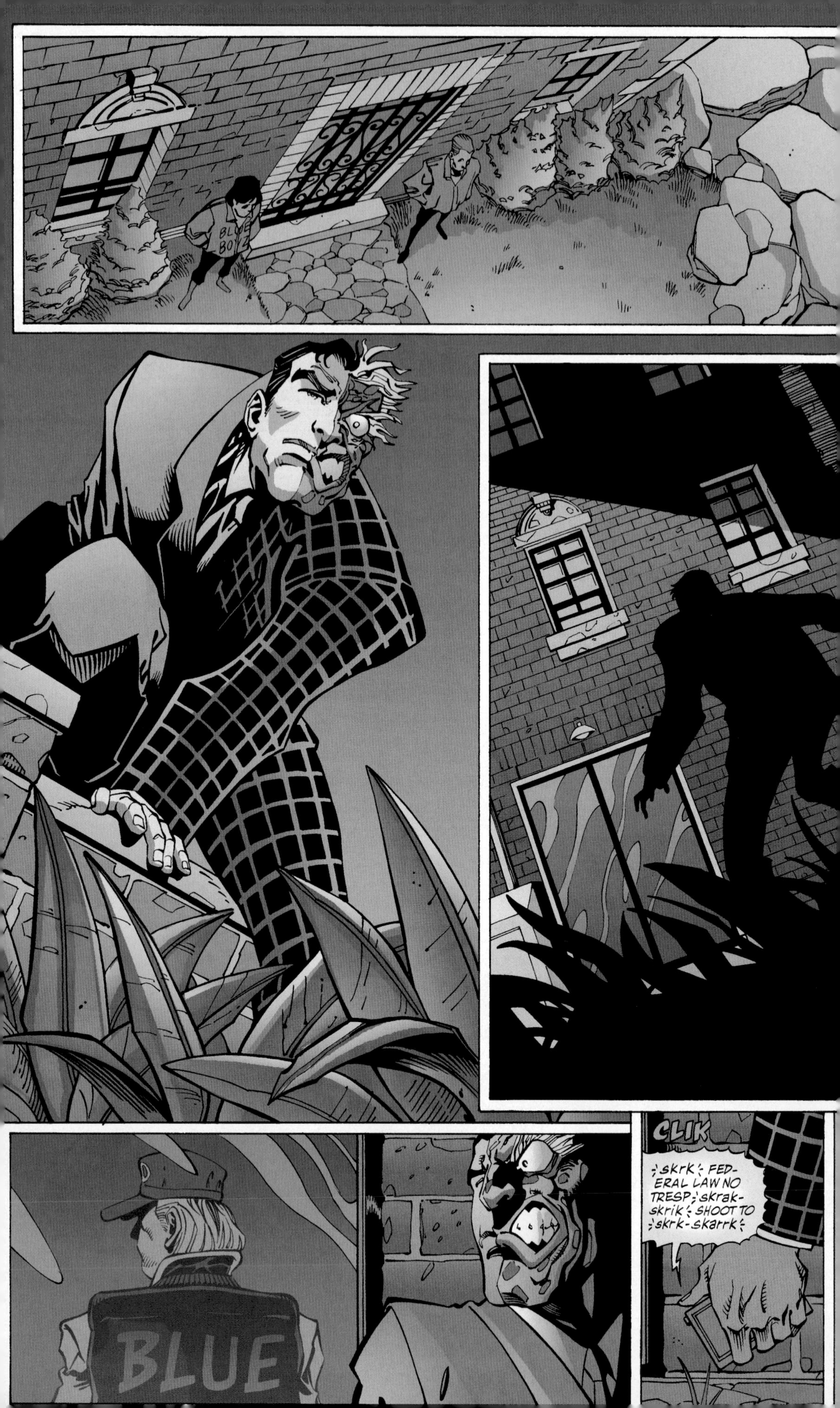
BLUE BOYZ
CLIK
skrk FEDERAL LAW NO TRESP skrak-skrik SHOOT TO skrk-skarrk
BLUE

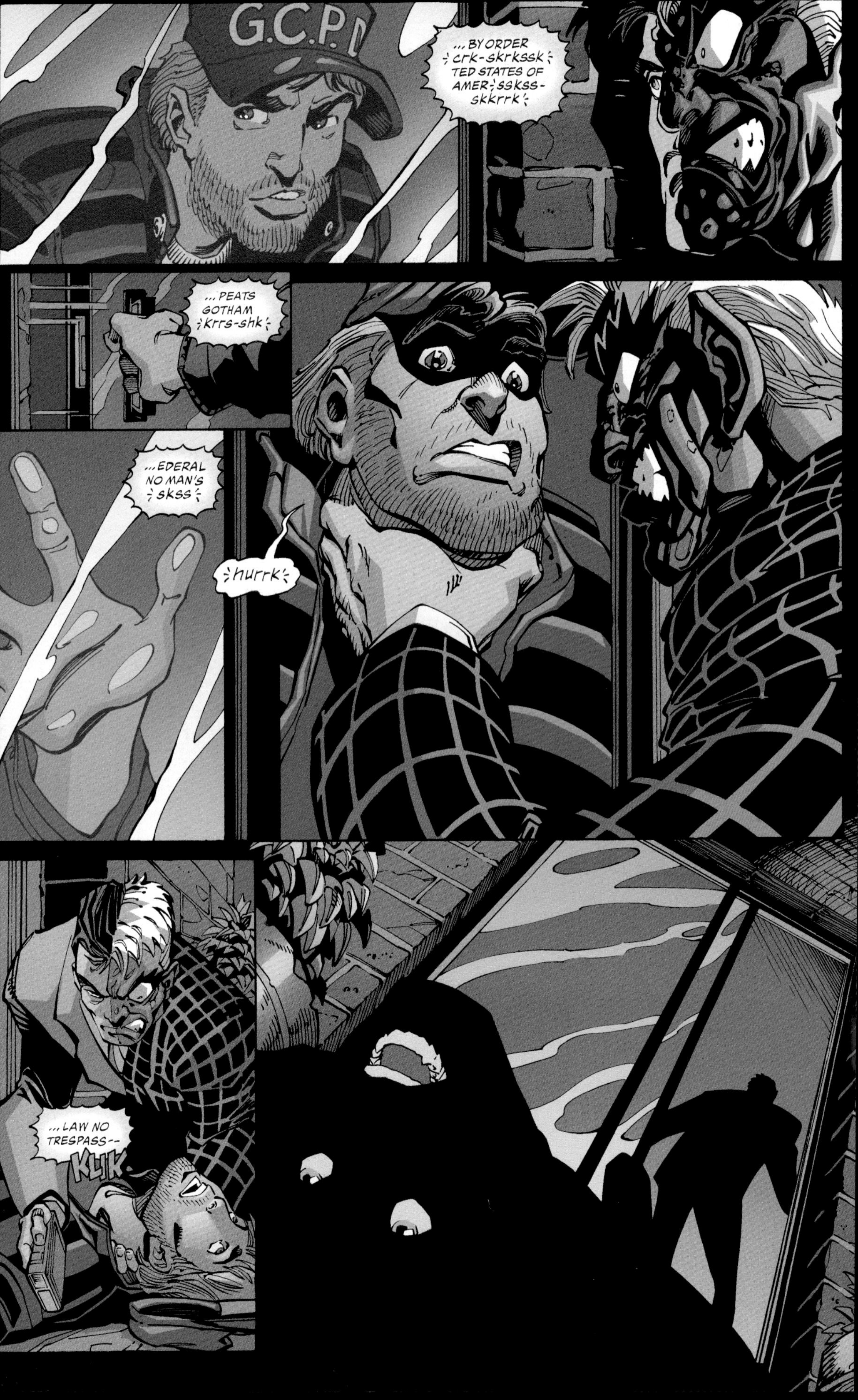

...BY ORDER crk-skrkssk TED STATES OF AMER ssksss-skkrrk
...PEATS GOTHAM krrs-shk
...EDERAL NO MAN'S sksss
hurrk
...LAW NO TRESPASS--
KLIK

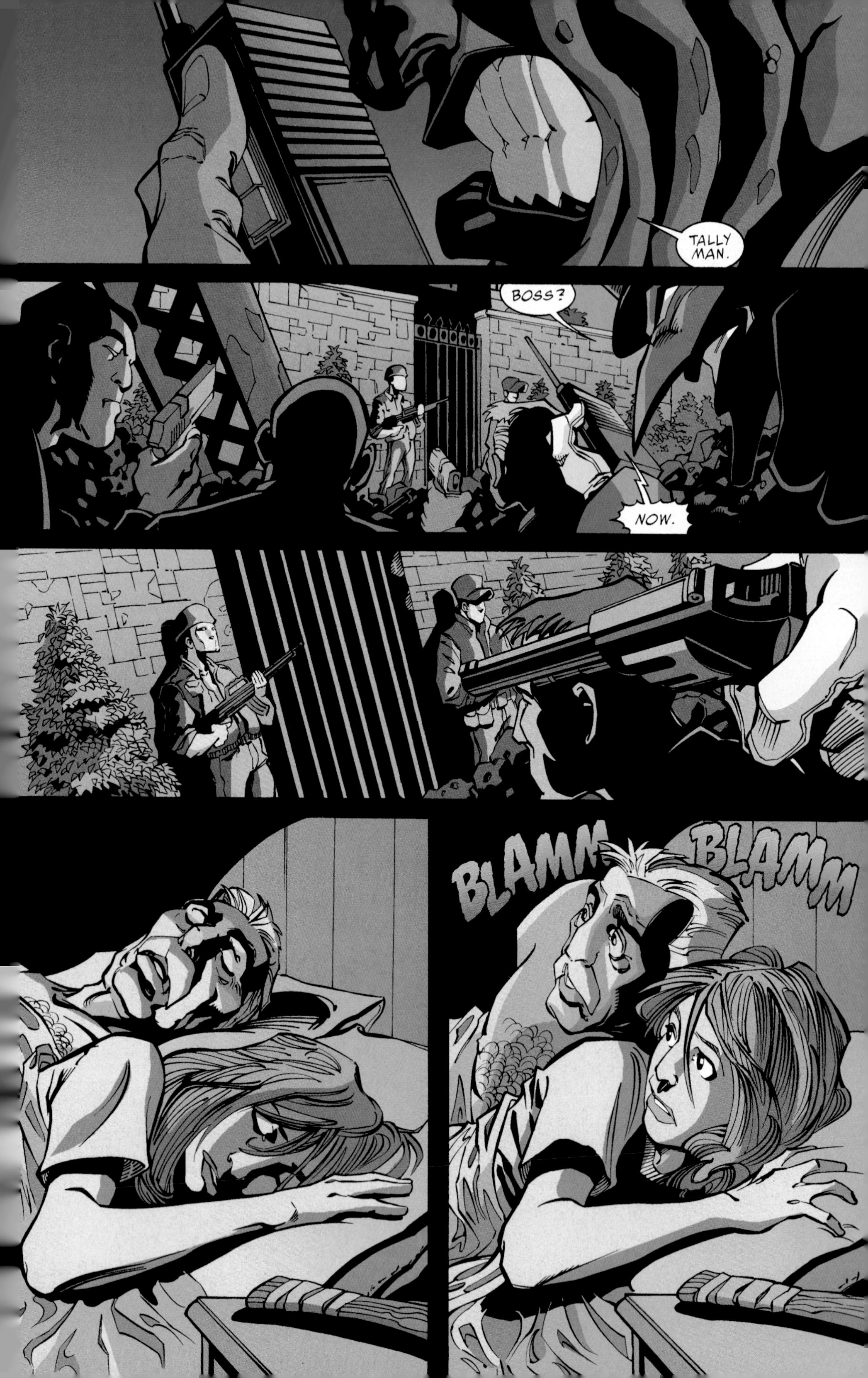
TALLY MAN.
BOSS?
NOW.
BLAMM
BLAMM

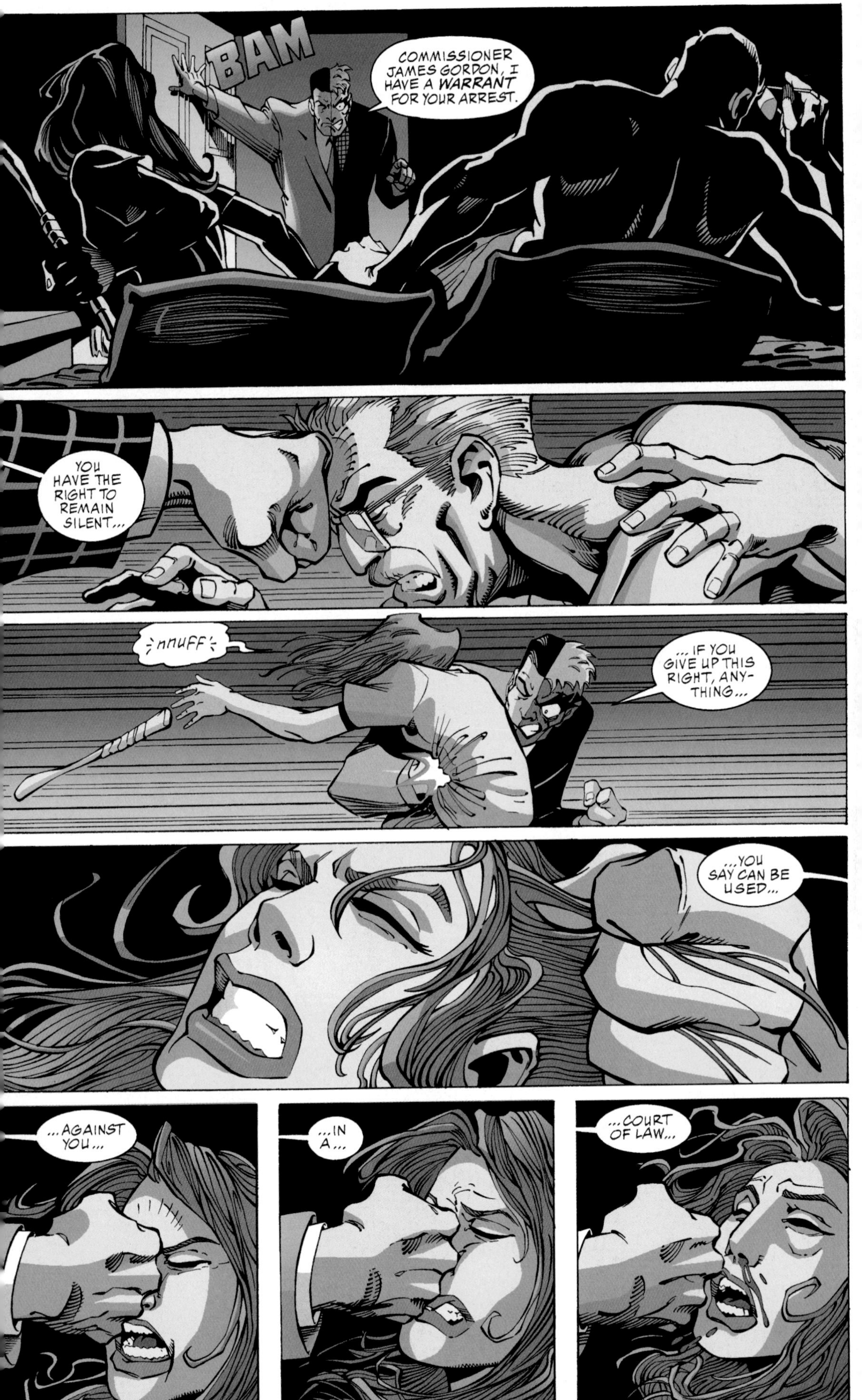
BAM
COMMISSIONER JAMES GORDON, I HAVE A WARRANT FOR YOUR ARREST.
YOU HAVE THE RIGHT TO REMAIN SILENT...
nnUFF
...IF YOU GIVE UP THIS RIGHT, ANY-THING...
...YOU SAY CAN BE USED...
...AGAINST YOU...
...IN A...
...COURT OF LAW...

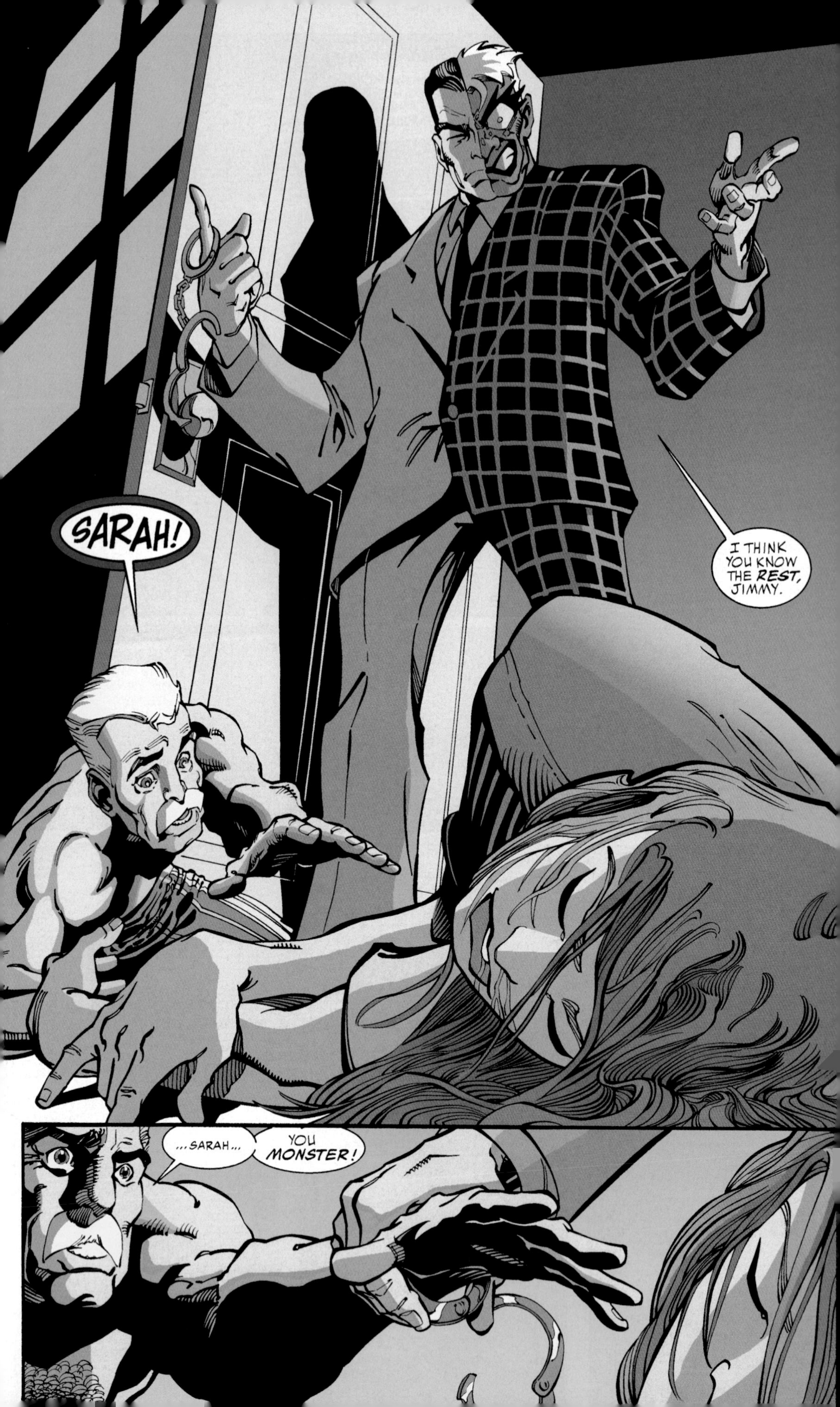

SARAH!
I THINK YOU KNOW THE *REST*, JIMMY.
...SARAH...
YOU *MONSTER*!

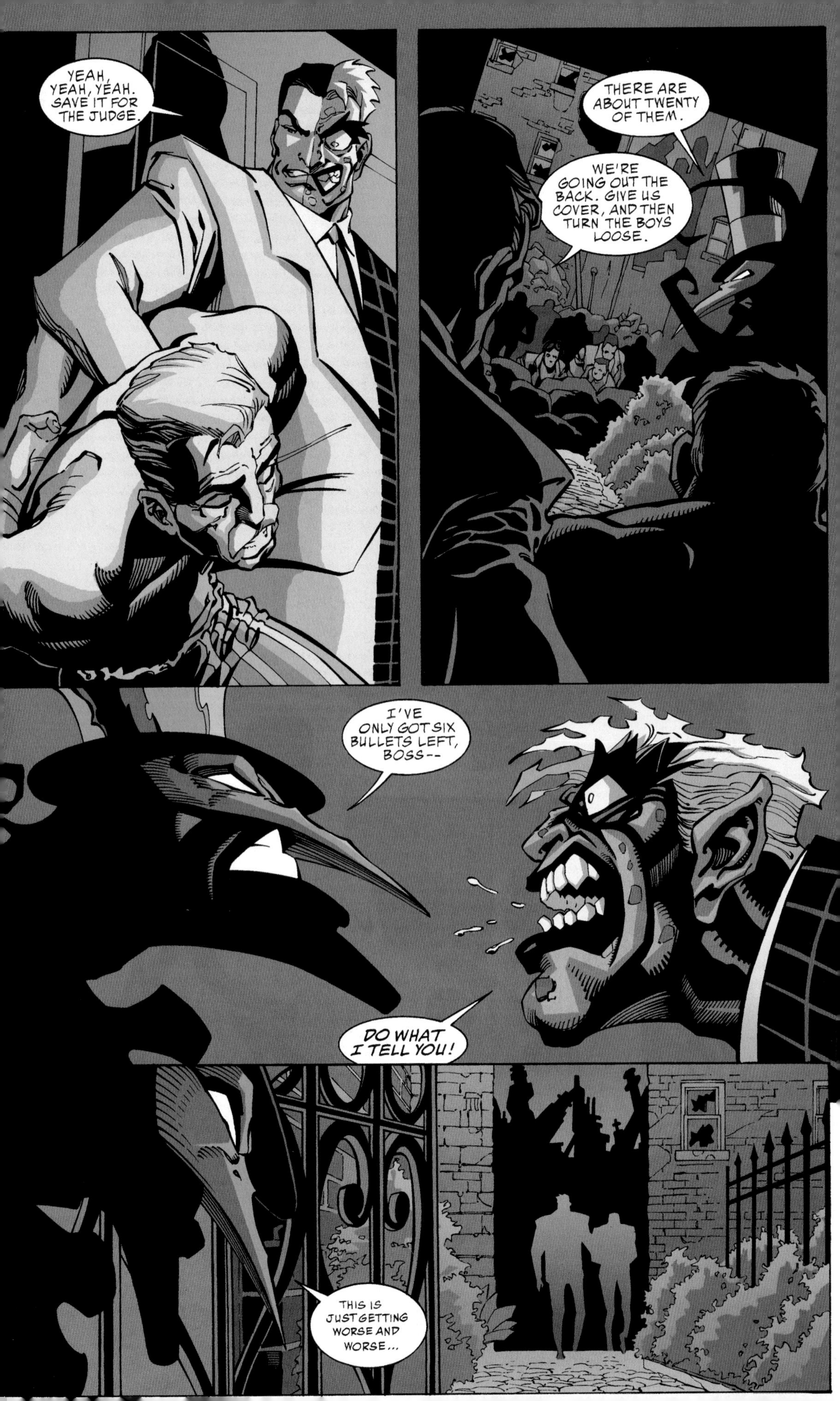

YEAH, YEAH, YEAH. SAVE IT FOR THE JUDGE.
THERE ARE ABOUT TWENTY OF THEM.
WE'RE GOING OUT THE BACK. GIVE US COVER, AND THEN TURN THE BOYS LOOSE.
I'VE ONLY GOT SIX BULLETS LEFT, BOSS--
DO WHAT I TELL YOU!
THIS IS JUST GETTING WORSE AND WORSE...

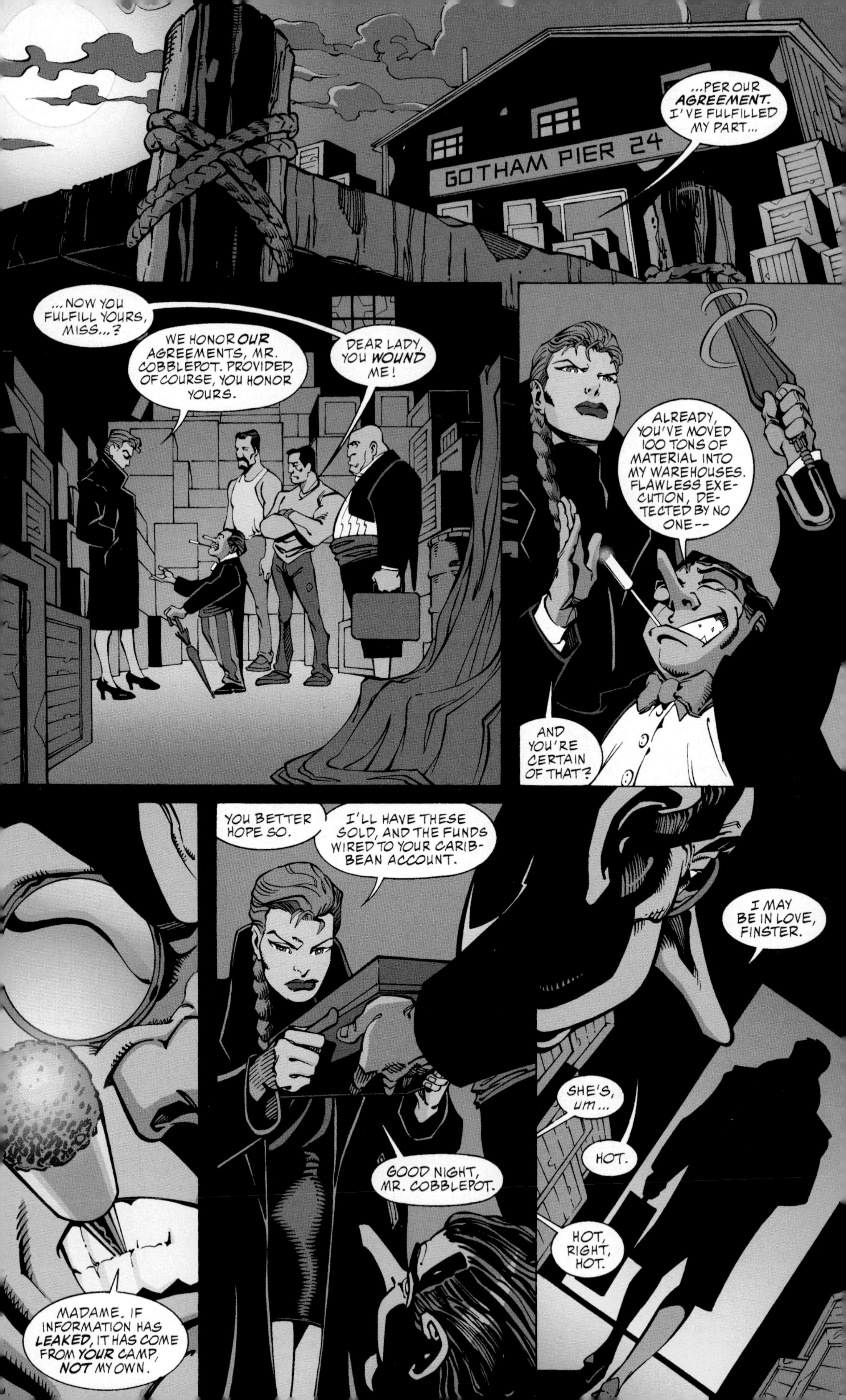
GOTHAM PIER 24
...PER OUR AGREEMENT. I'VE FULFILLED MY PART...
...NOW YOU FULFILL YOURS, MISS...?
WE HONOR OUR AGREEMENTS, MR. COBBLEPOT. PROVIDED, OF COURSE, YOU HONOR YOURS.
DEAR LADY, YOU WOUND ME!
ALREADY, YOU'VE MOVED 100 TONS OF MATERIAL INTO MY WAREHOUSES. FLAWLESS EXE-CUTION, DE-TECTED BY NO ONE--
AND YOU'RE CERTAIN OF THAT?
MADAME. IF INFORMATION HAS LEAKED, IT HAS COME FROM YOUR CAMP, NOT MY OWN.
YOU BETTER HOPE SO.
I'LL HAVE THESE SOLD, AND THE FUNDS WIRED TO YOUR CARIB-BEAN ACCOUNT.
GOOD NIGHT, MR. COBBLEPOT.
I MAY BE IN LOVE, FINSTER.
SHE'S, UM...
HOT.
HOT, RIGHT, HOT.

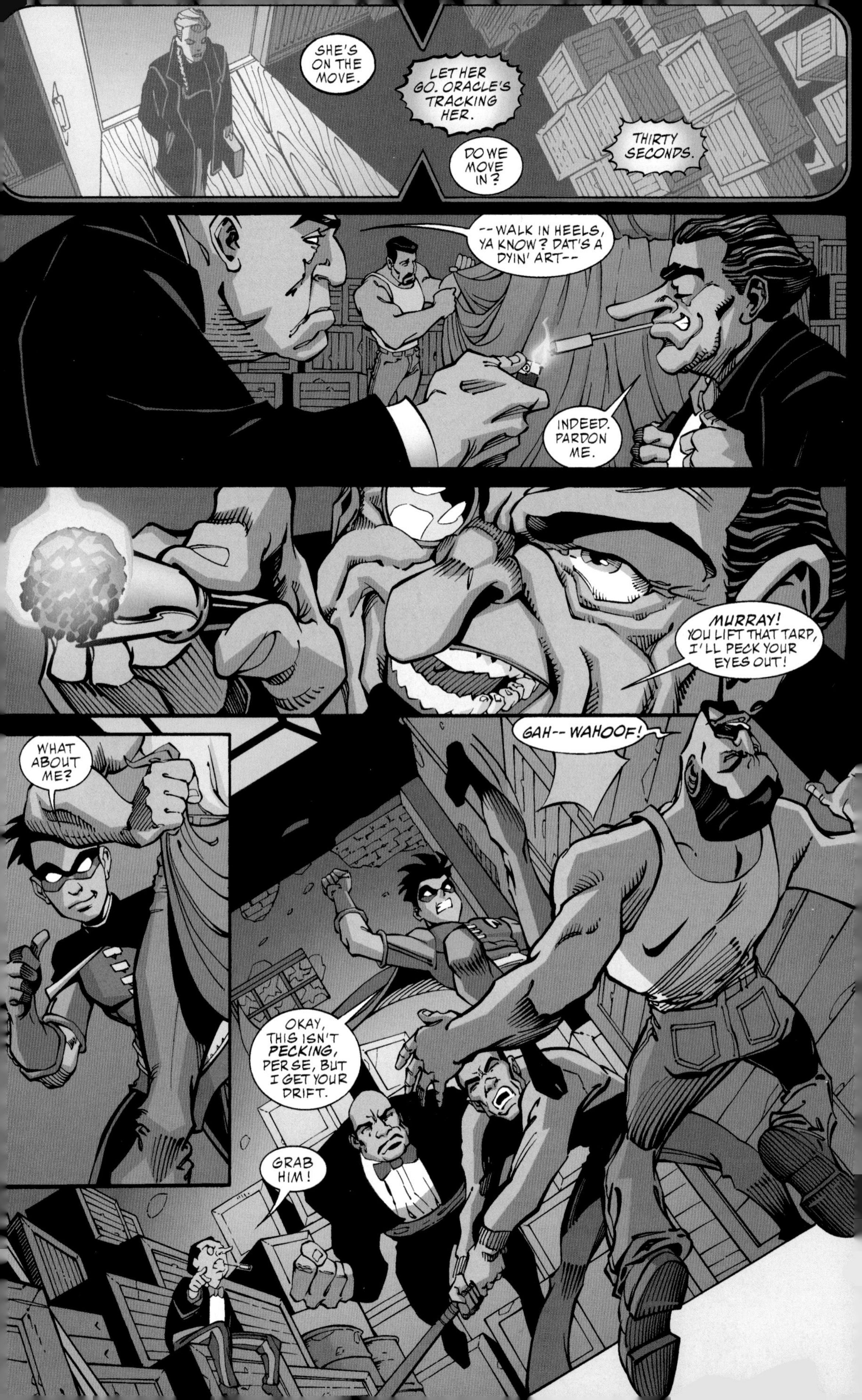
SHE'S ON THE MOVE.
LET HER GO. ORACLE'S TRACKING HER.
DO WE MOVE IN?
THIRTY SECONDS.
--WALK IN HEELS, YA KNOW? DAT'S A DYIN' ART--
INDEED. PARDON ME.
MURRAY! YOU LIFT THAT TARP, I'LL PECK YOUR EYES OUT!
WHAT ABOUT ME?
GAH-- WAHOOF!
OKAY, THIS ISN'T PECKING, PER SE, BUT I GET YOUR DRIFT.
GRAB HIM!

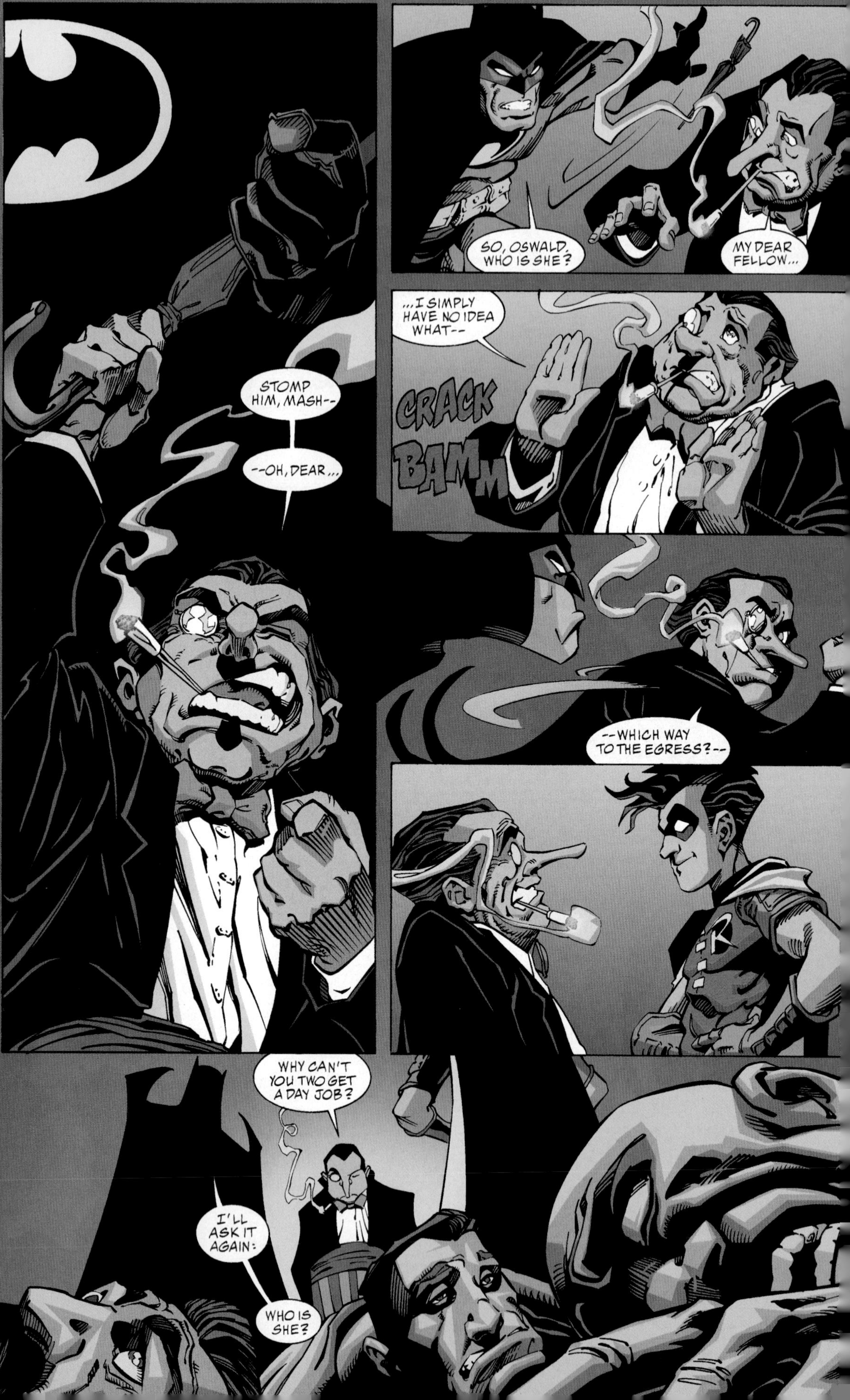
SO, OSWALD, WHO IS SHE?
MY DEAR FELLOW...
...I SIMPLY HAVE NO IDEA WHAT--
CRACK
BAMM
STOMP HIM, MASH--
--OH, DEAR...
--WHICH WAY TO THE EGRESS?--
WHY CAN'T YOU TWO GET A DAY JOB?
I'LL ASK IT AGAIN:
WHO IS SHE?

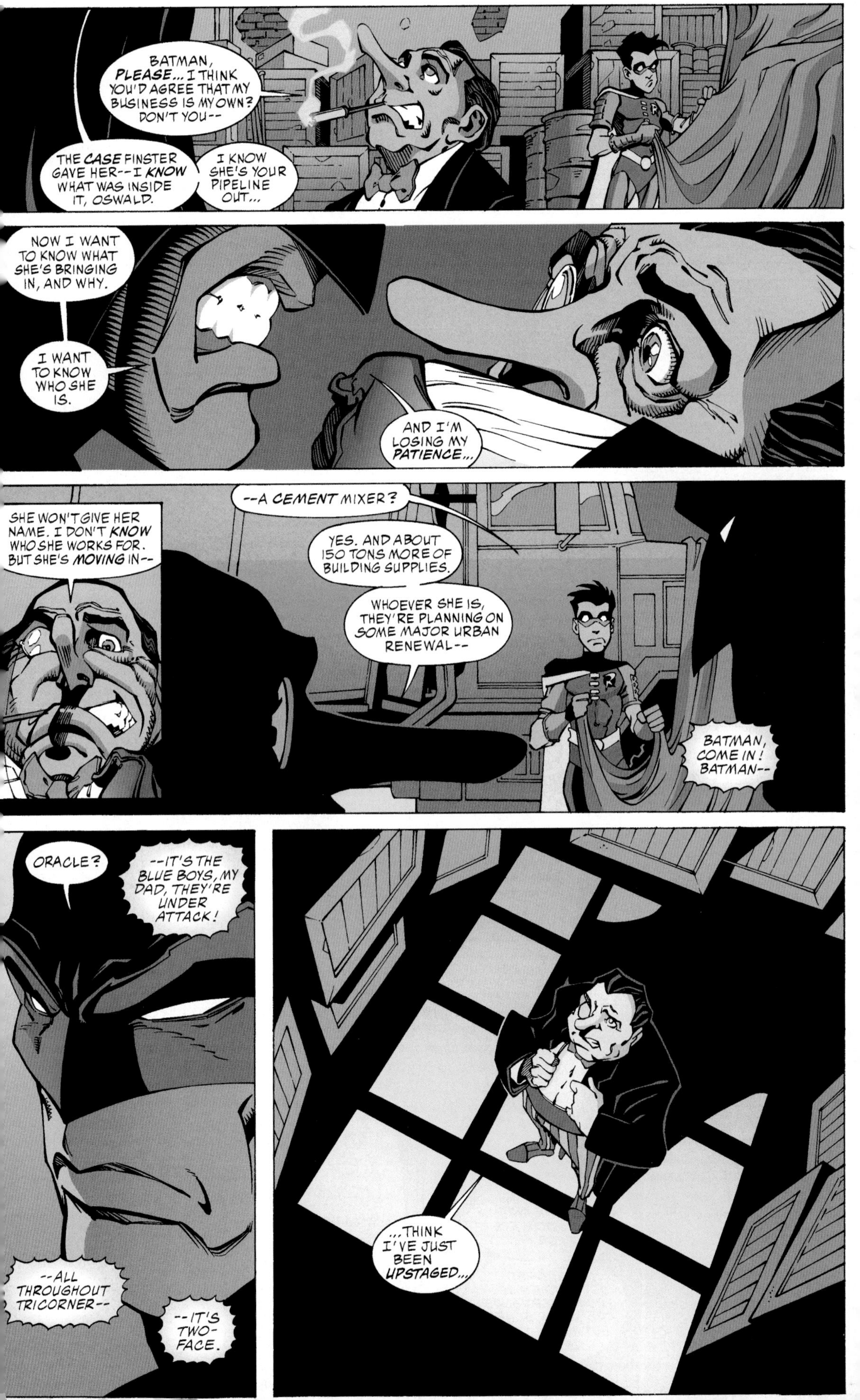
BATMAN, PLEASE... I THINK YOU'D AGREE THAT MY BUSINESS IS MY OWN? DON'T YOU--
THE CASE FINSTER GAVE HER--I KNOW WHAT WAS INSIDE IT, OSWALD.
I KNOW SHE'S YOUR PIPELINE OUT...
NOW I WANT TO KNOW WHAT SHE'S BRINGING IN, AND WHY.
I WANT TO KNOW WHO SHE IS.
AND I'M LOSING MY PATIENCE...
SHE WON'T GIVE HER NAME. I DON'T KNOW WHO SHE WORKS FOR. BUT SHE'S MOVING IN--
--A CEMENT MIXER?
YES. AND ABOUT 150 TONS MORE OF BUILDING SUPPLIES.
WHOEVER SHE IS, THEY'RE PLANNING ON SOME MAJOR URBAN RENEWAL--
BATMAN, COME IN! BATMAN--
ORACLE?
--IT'S THE BLUE BOYS, MY DAD, THEY'RE UNDER ATTACK!
--ALL THROUGHOUT TRICORNER--
--IT'S TWO-FACE.
...THINK I'VE JUST BEEN UPSTAGED...

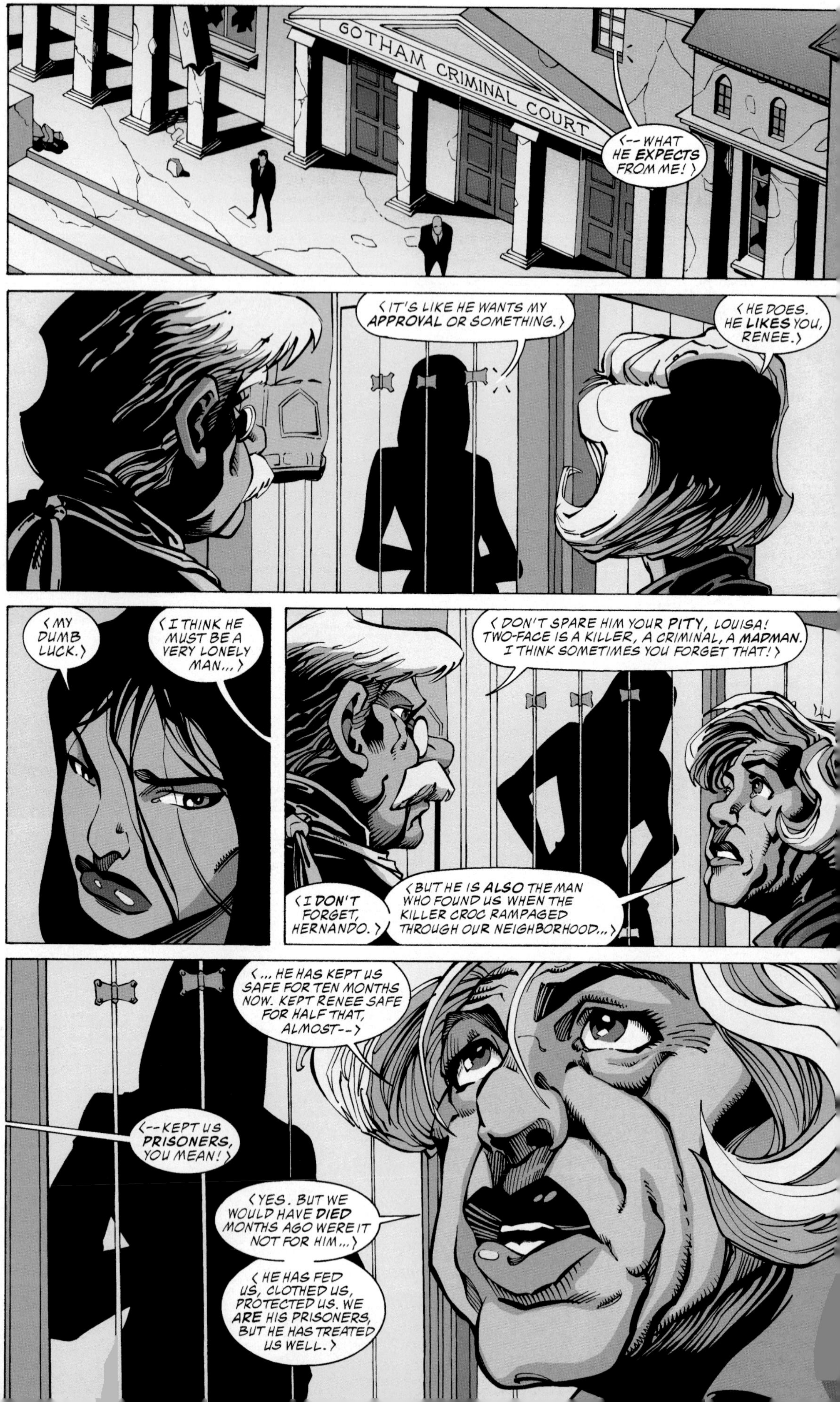

GOTHAM CRIMINAL COURT
<-- WHAT HE EXPECTS FROM ME! >
< IT'S LIKE HE WANTS MY APPROVAL OR SOMETHING. >
< HE DOES. HE LIKES YOU, RENEE. >
< MY DUMB LUCK. >
< I THINK HE MUST BE A VERY LONELY MAN... >
< DON'T SPARE HIM YOUR PITY, LOUISA! TWO-FACE IS A KILLER, A CRIMINAL, A MADMAN. I THINK SOMETIMES YOU FORGET THAT! >
< I DON'T FORGET, HERNANDO. >
< BUT HE IS ALSO THE MAN WHO FOUND US WHEN THE KILLER CROC RAMPAGED THROUGH OUR NEIGHBORHOOD... >
< ... HE HAS KEPT US SAFE FOR TEN MONTHS NOW. KEPT RENEE SAFE FOR HALF THAT, ALMOST-- >
<-- KEPT US PRISONERS, YOU MEAN! >
< YES. BUT WE WOULD HAVE DIED MONTHS AGO WERE IT NOT FOR HIM... >
< HE HAS FED US, CLOTHED US, PROTECTED US. WE ARE HIS PRISONERS, BUT HE HAS TREATED US WELL. >

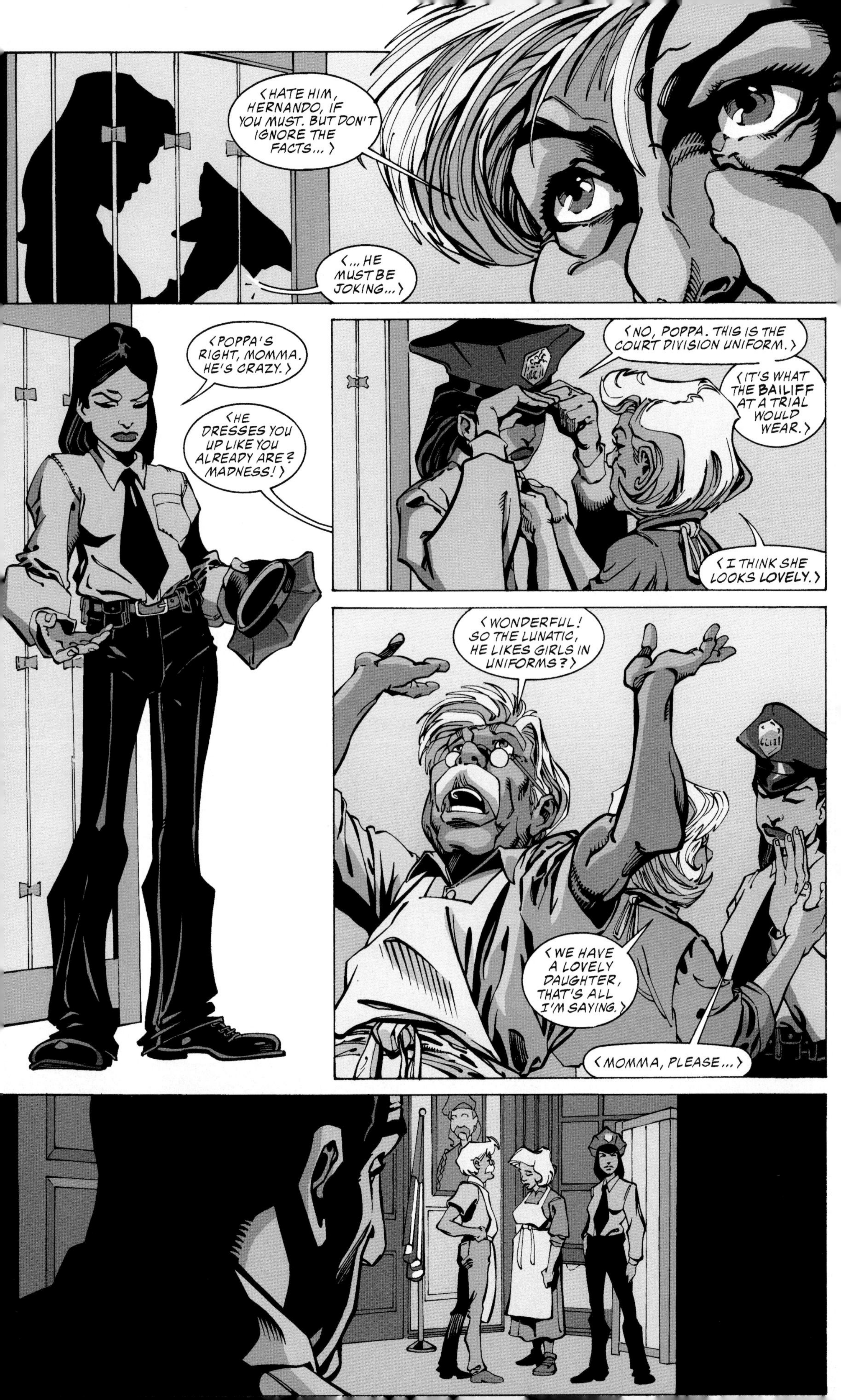

<HATE HIM, HERNANDO, IF YOU MUST. BUT DON'T IGNORE THE FACTS...>
<...HE MUST BE JOKING...>
<POPPA'S RIGHT, MOMMA. HE'S CRAZY.>
<HE DRESSES YOU UP LIKE YOU ALREADY ARE? MADNESS!>
<NO, POPPA. THIS IS THE COURT DIVISION UNIFORM.>
<IT'S WHAT THE BAILIFF AT A TRIAL WOULD WEAR.>
<I THINK SHE LOOKS LOVELY.>
<WONDERFUL! SO THE LUNATIC, HE LIKES GIRLS IN UNIFORMS?>
<WE HAVE A LOVELY DAUGHTER, THAT'S ALL I'M SAYING.>
<MOMMA, PLEASE...>

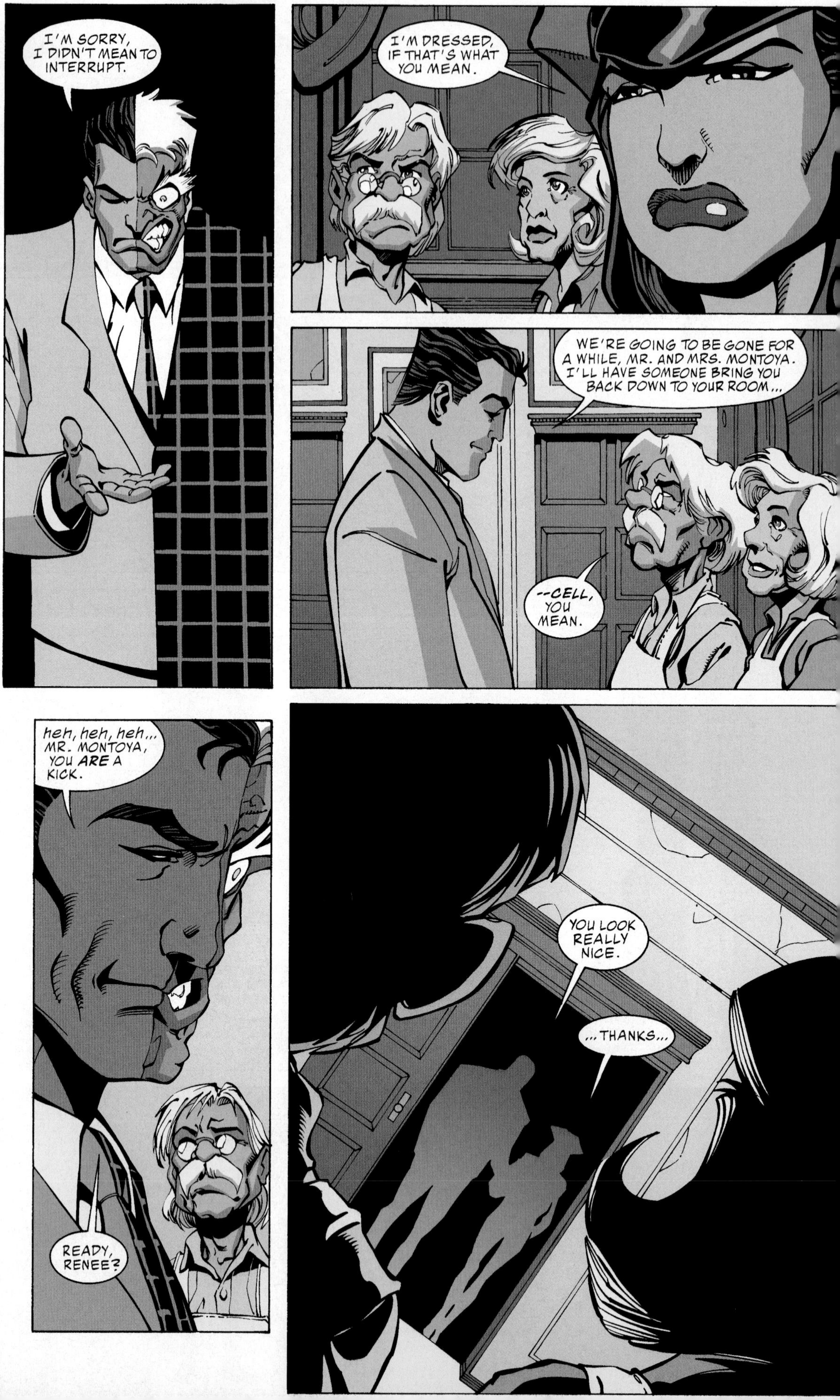
I'M SORRY, I DIDN'T MEAN TO INTERRUPT.
I'M DRESSED, IF THAT'S WHAT YOU MEAN.
WE'RE GOING TO BE GONE FOR A WHILE, MR. AND MRS. MONTOYA. I'LL HAVE SOMEONE BRING YOU BACK DOWN TO YOUR ROOM...
--CELL, YOU MEAN.
heh, heh, heh... MR. MONTOYA, YOU ARE A KICK.
READY, RENEE?
YOU LOOK REALLY NICE.
...THANKS...

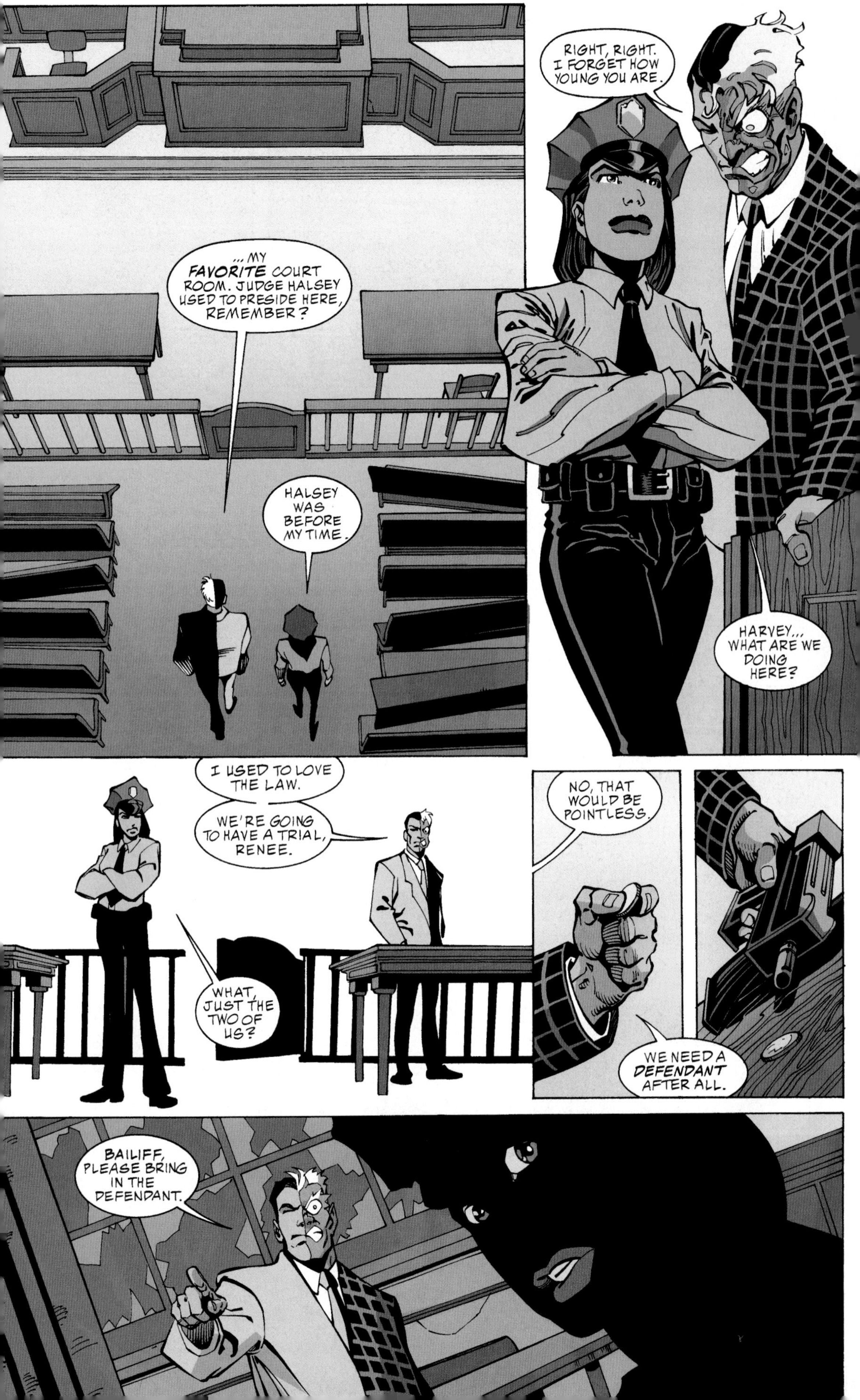
...MY FAVORITE COURT ROOM. JUDGE HALSEY USED TO PRESIDE HERE, REMEMBER?
HALSEY WAS BEFORE MY TIME.
RIGHT, RIGHT. I FORGET HOW YOUNG YOU ARE.
HARVEY... WHAT ARE WE DOING HERE?
I USED TO LOVE THE LAW.
WE'RE GOING TO HAVE A TRIAL, RENEE.
WHAT, JUST THE TWO OF US?
NO, THAT WOULD BE POINTLESS.
WE NEED A DEFENDANT AFTER ALL.
BAILIFF, PLEASE BRING IN THE DEFENDANT.

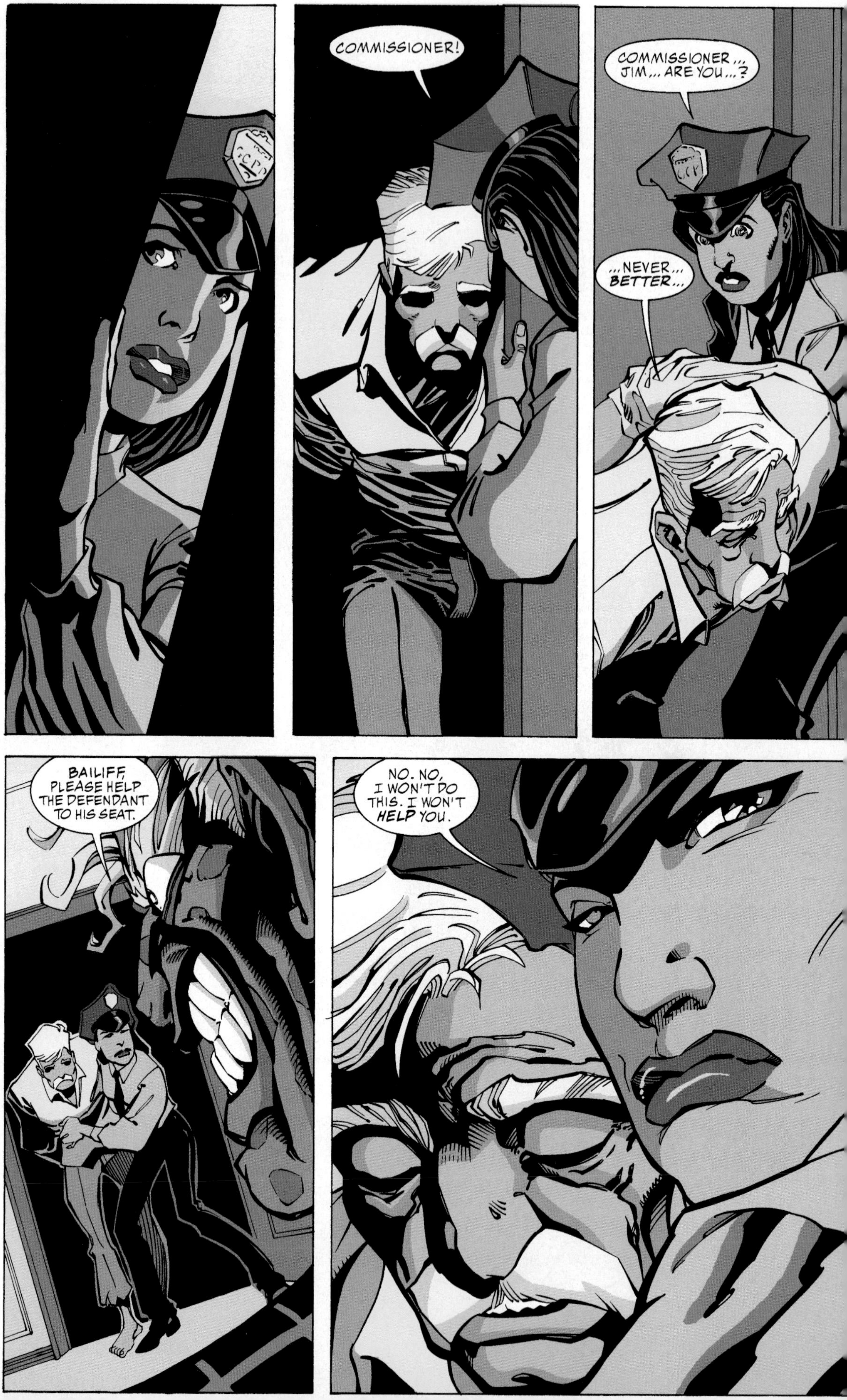
COMMISSIONER!
COMMISSIONER... JIM... ARE YOU...?
...NEVER... BETTER...
BAILIFF, PLEASE HELP THE DEFENDANT TO HIS SEAT.
NO. NO, I WON'T DO THIS. I WON'T HELP YOU.

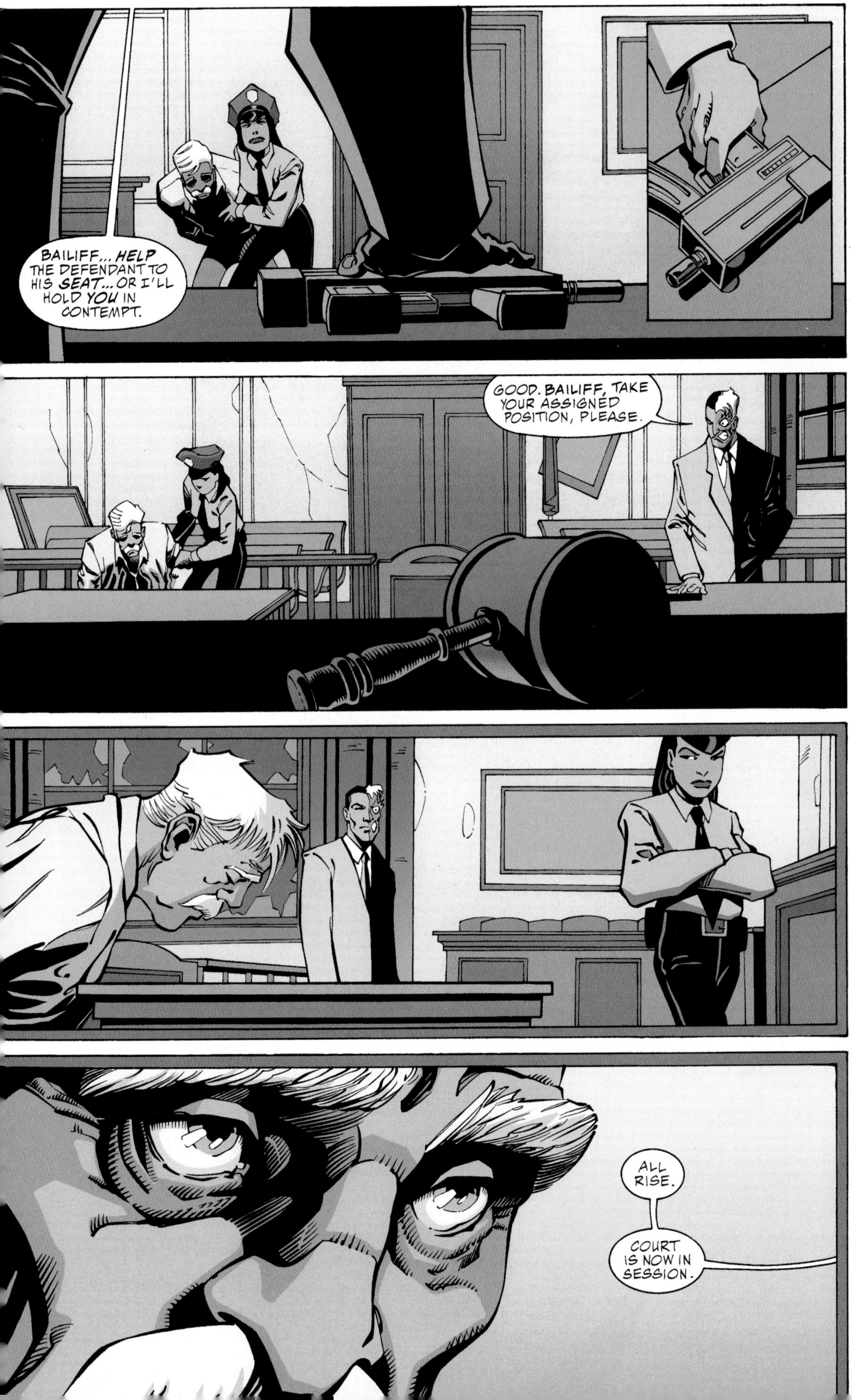
BAILIFF... HELP THE DEFENDANT TO HIS SEAT... OR I'LL HOLD YOU IN CONTEMPT.
GOOD. BAILIFF, TAKE YOUR ASSIGNED POSITION, PLEASE.
ALL RISE.
COURT IS NOW IN SESSION.

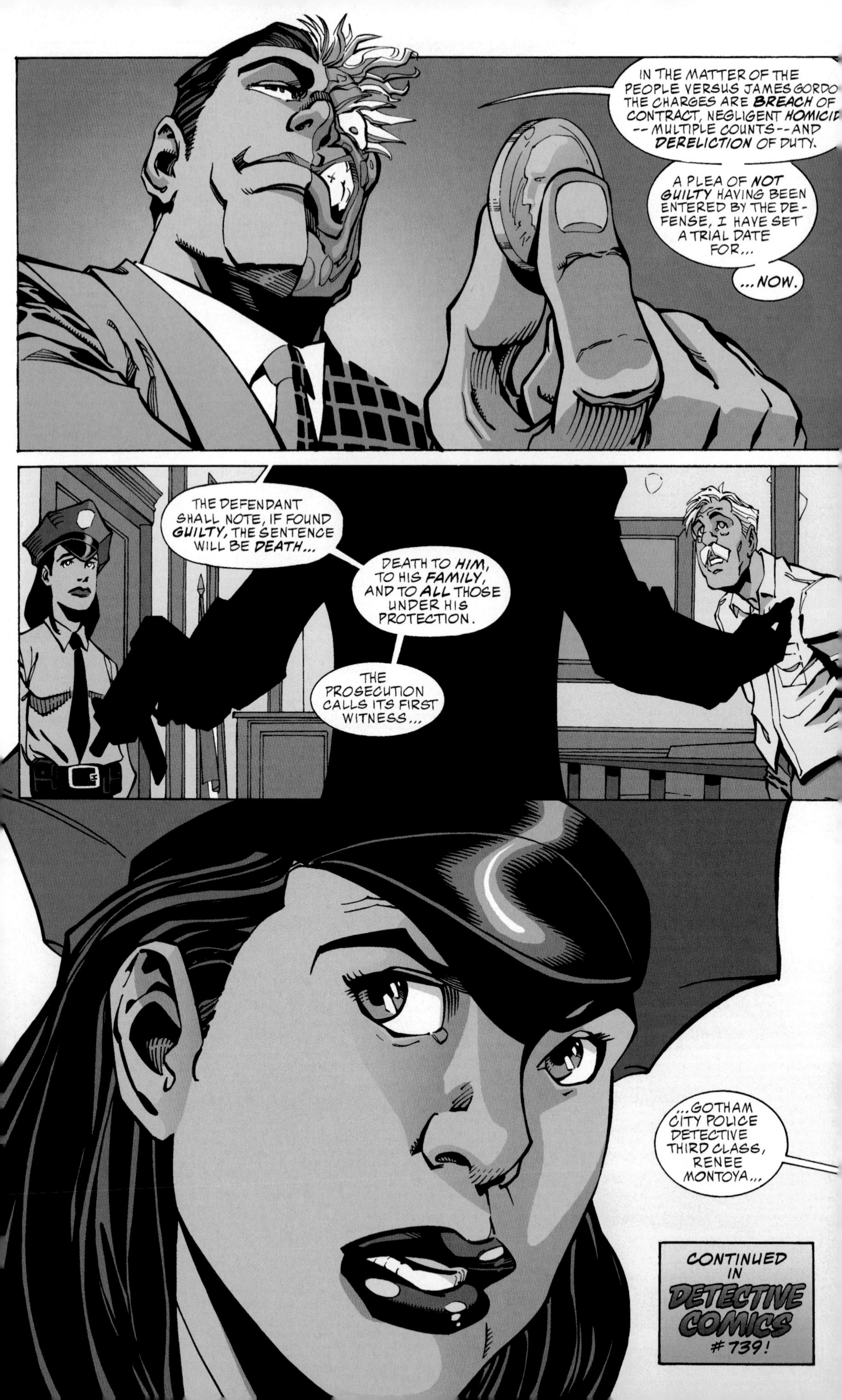

IN THE MATTER OF THE PEOPLE VERSUS JAMES GORDO THE CHARGES ARE BREACH OF CONTRACT, NEGLIGENT HOMICID -- MULTIPLE COUNTS--AND DERELICTION OF DUTY.
A PLEA OF NOT GUILTY HAVING BEEN ENTERED BY THE DE-FENSE, I HAVE SET A TRIAL DATE FOR...
...NOW.
THE DEFENDANT SHALL NOTE, IF FOUND GUILTY, THE SENTENCE WILL BE DEATH...
DEATH TO HIM, TO HIS FAMILY, AND TO ALL THOSE UNDER HIS PROTECTION.
THE PROSECUTION CALLS ITS FIRST WITNESS...
...GOTHAM CITY POLICE DETECTIVE THIRD CLASS, RENEE MONTOYA...
CONTINUED IN DETECTIVE COMICS #739!

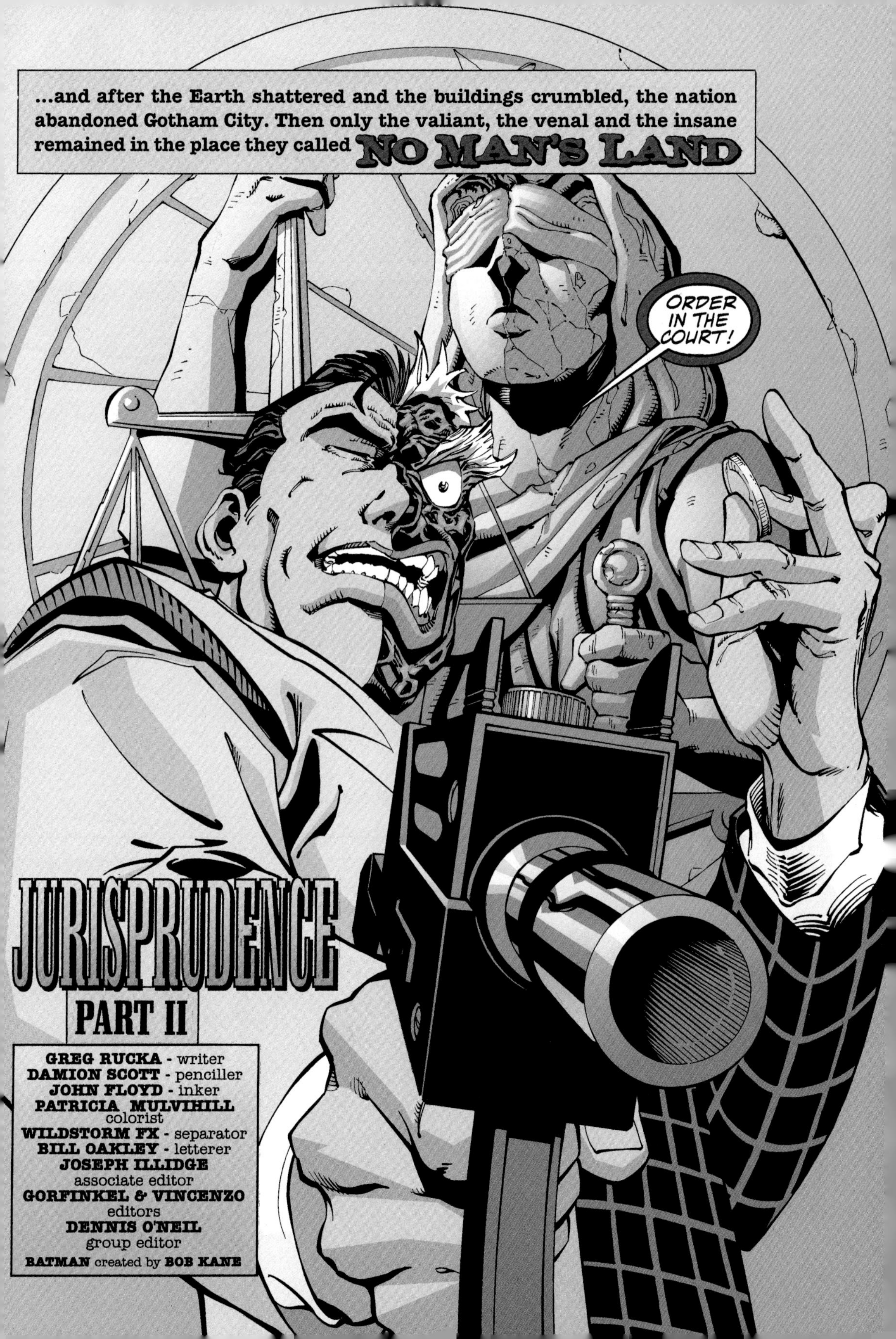
...and after the Earth shattered and the buildings crumbled, the nation abandoned Gotham City. Then only the valiant, the venal and the insane remained in the place they called NO MAN'S LAND
ORDER IN THE COURT!
JURISPRUDENCE
PART II
GREG RUCKA - writer
DAMION SCOTT - penciller
JOHN FLOYD - inker
PATRICIA MULVIHILL colorist
WILDSTORM FX - separator
BILL OAKLEY - letterer
JOSEPH ILLIDGE associate editor
GORFINKEL & VINCENZO editors
DENNIS O'NEIL group editor
BATMAN created by BOB KANE

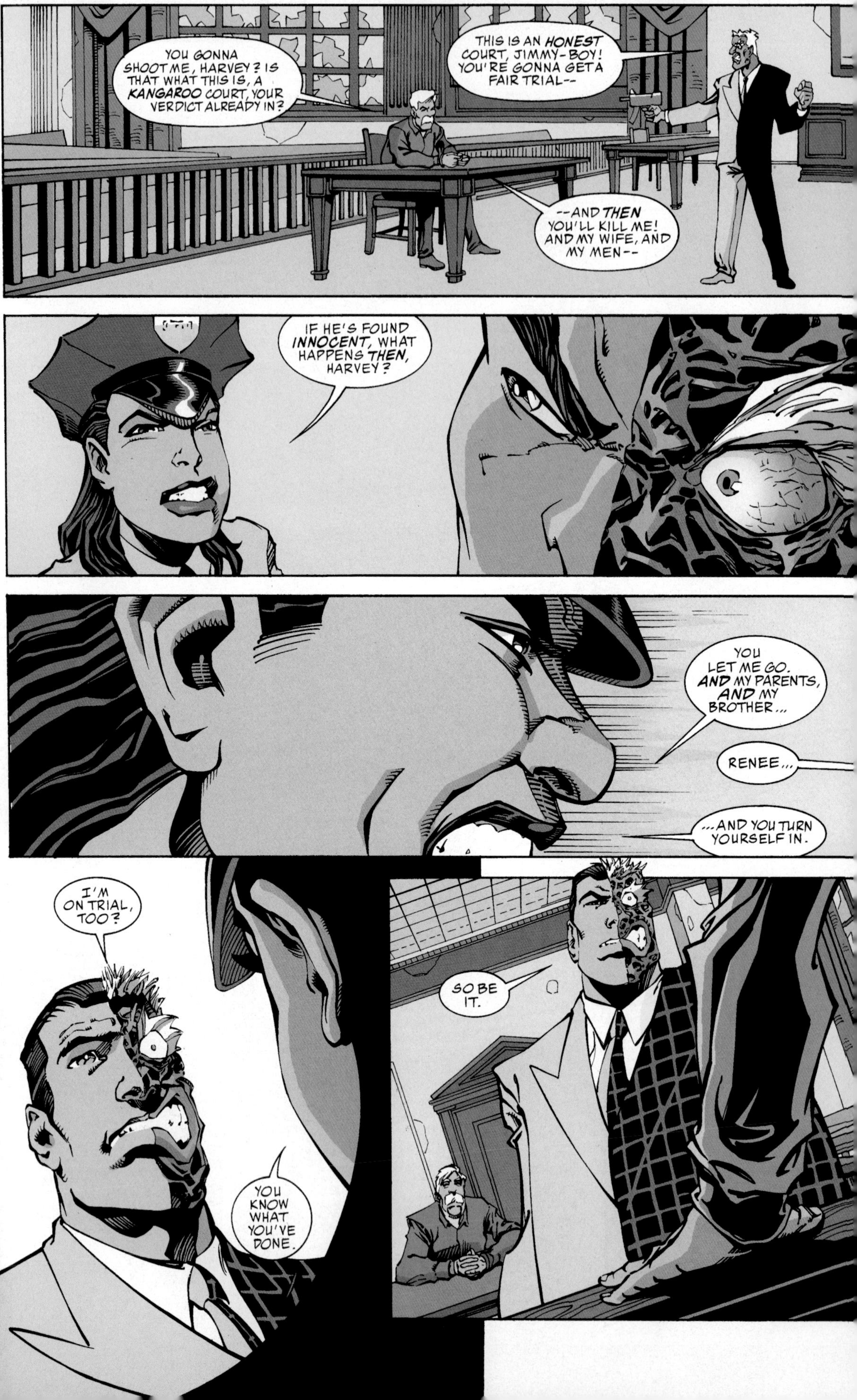
YOU GONNA SHOOT ME, HARVEY? IS THAT WHAT THIS IS, A KANGAROO COURT, YOUR VERDICT ALREADY IN?
THIS IS AN HONEST COURT, JIMMY-BOY! YOU'RE GONNA GET A FAIR TRIAL--
--AND THEN YOU'LL KILL ME! AND MY WIFE, AND MY MEN--
IF HE'S FOUND INNOCENT, WHAT HAPPENS THEN, HARVEY?
YOU LET ME GO. AND MY PARENTS, AND MY BROTHER...
RENEE...
...AND YOU TURN YOURSELF IN.
I'M ON TRIAL, TOO?
YOU KNOW WHAT YOU'VE DONE.
SO BE IT.

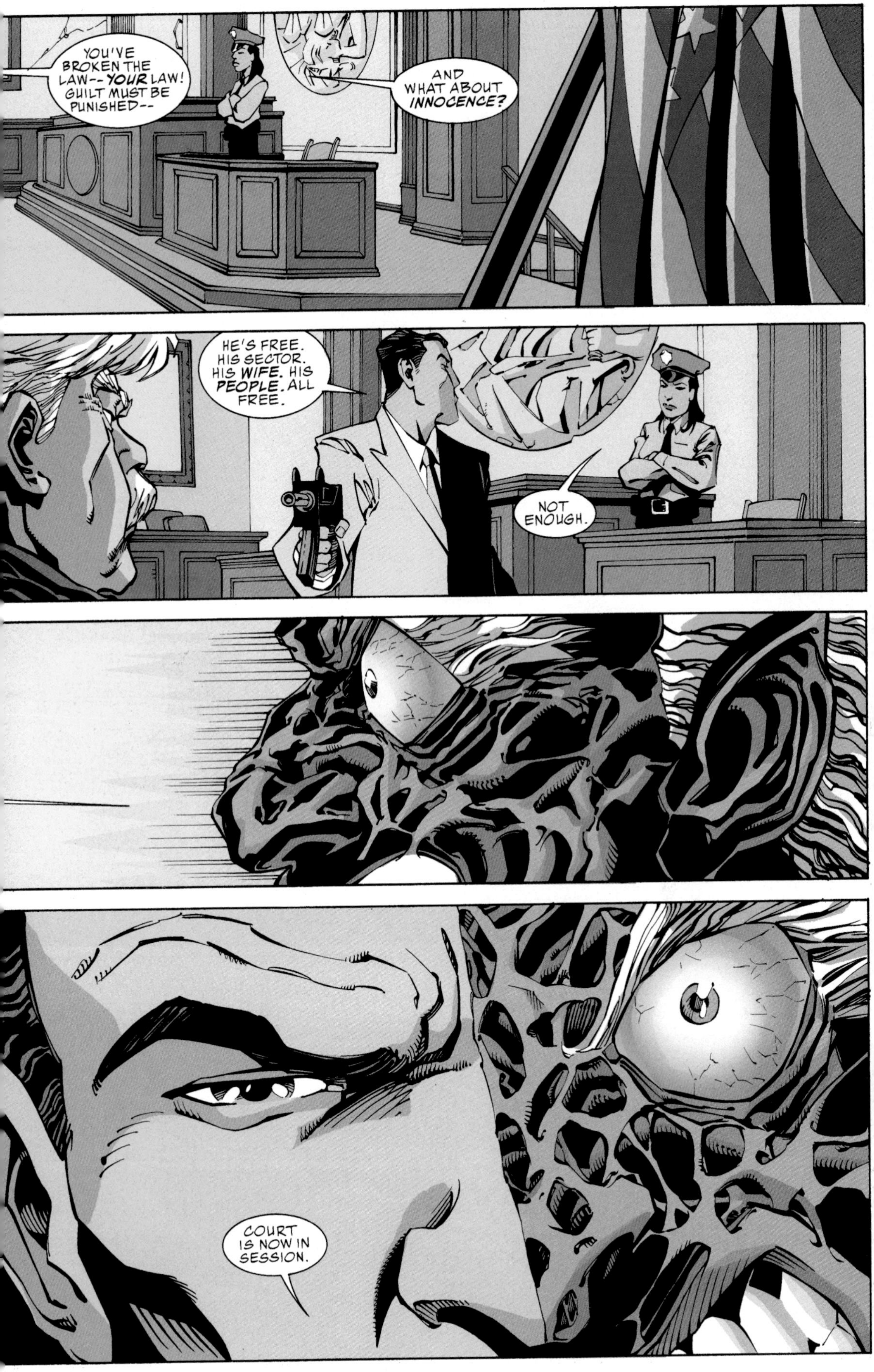
YOU'VE BROKEN THE LAW-- YOUR LAW! GUILT MUST BE PUNISHED--
AND WHAT ABOUT INNOCENCE?
HE'S FREE. HIS SECTOR. HIS WIFE. HIS PEOPLE. ALL FREE.
NOT ENOUGH.
COURT IS NOW IN SESSION.

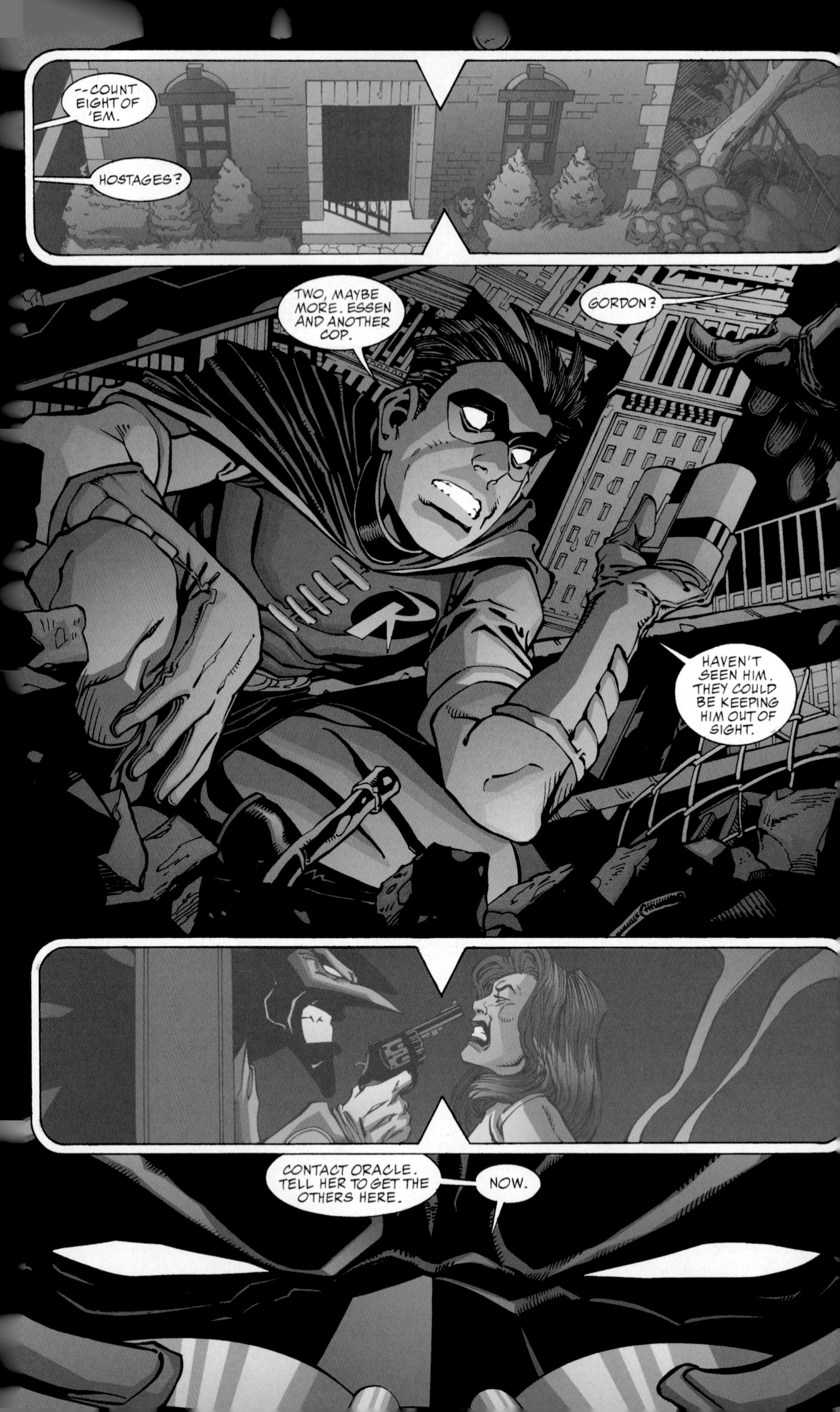
--COUNT EIGHT OF 'EM.
HOSTAGES?
TWO, MAYBE MORE. ESSEN AND ANOTHER COP.
GORDON?
HAVEN'T SEEN HIM. THEY COULD BE KEEPING HIM OUT OF SIGHT.
CONTACT ORACLE. TELL HER TO GET THE OTHERS HERE.
NOW.

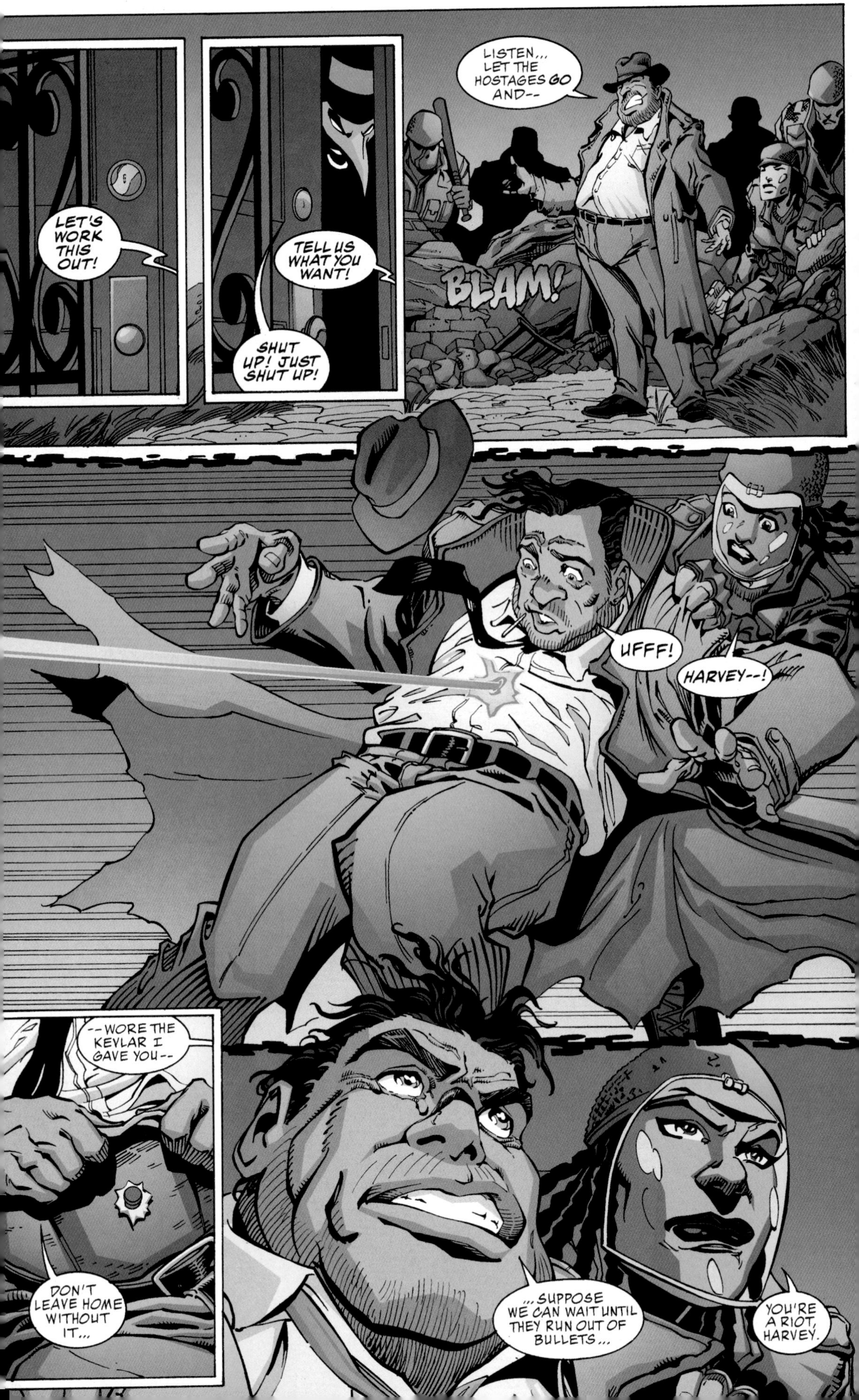
LET'S WORK THIS OUT!
TELL US WHAT YOU WANT!
SHUT UP! JUST SHUT UP!
LISTEN... LET THE HOSTAGES GO AND--
BLAM!
UFFF!
HARVEY--!
--WORE THE KEVLAR I GAVE YOU--
DON'T LEAVE HOME WITHOUT IT...
...SUPPOSE WE CAN WAIT UNTIL THEY RUN OUT OF BULLETS...
YOU'RE A RIOT, HARVEY.

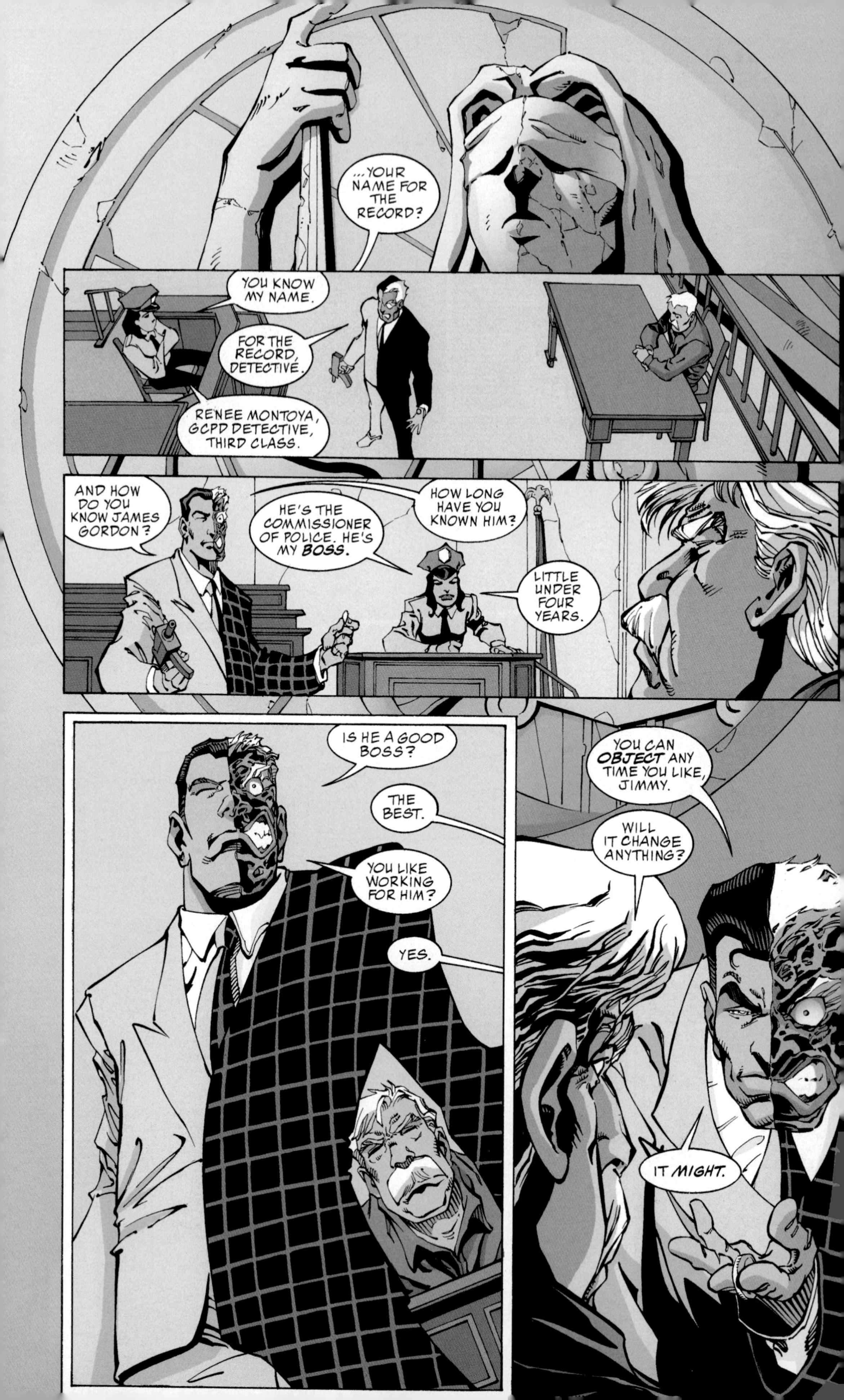
...YOUR NAME FOR THE RECORD?
YOU KNOW MY NAME.
FOR THE RECORD, DETECTIVE.
RENEE MONTOYA, GCPD DETECTIVE, THIRD CLASS.
AND HOW DO YOU KNOW JAMES GORDON?
HE'S THE COMMISSIONER OF POLICE. HE'S MY BOSS.
HOW LONG HAVE YOU KNOWN HIM?
LITTLE UNDER FOUR YEARS.
IS HE A GOOD BOSS?
THE BEST.
YOU LIKE WORKING FOR HIM?
YES.
YOU CAN OBJECT ANY TIME YOU LIKE, JIMMY.
WILL IT CHANGE ANYTHING?
IT MIGHT.

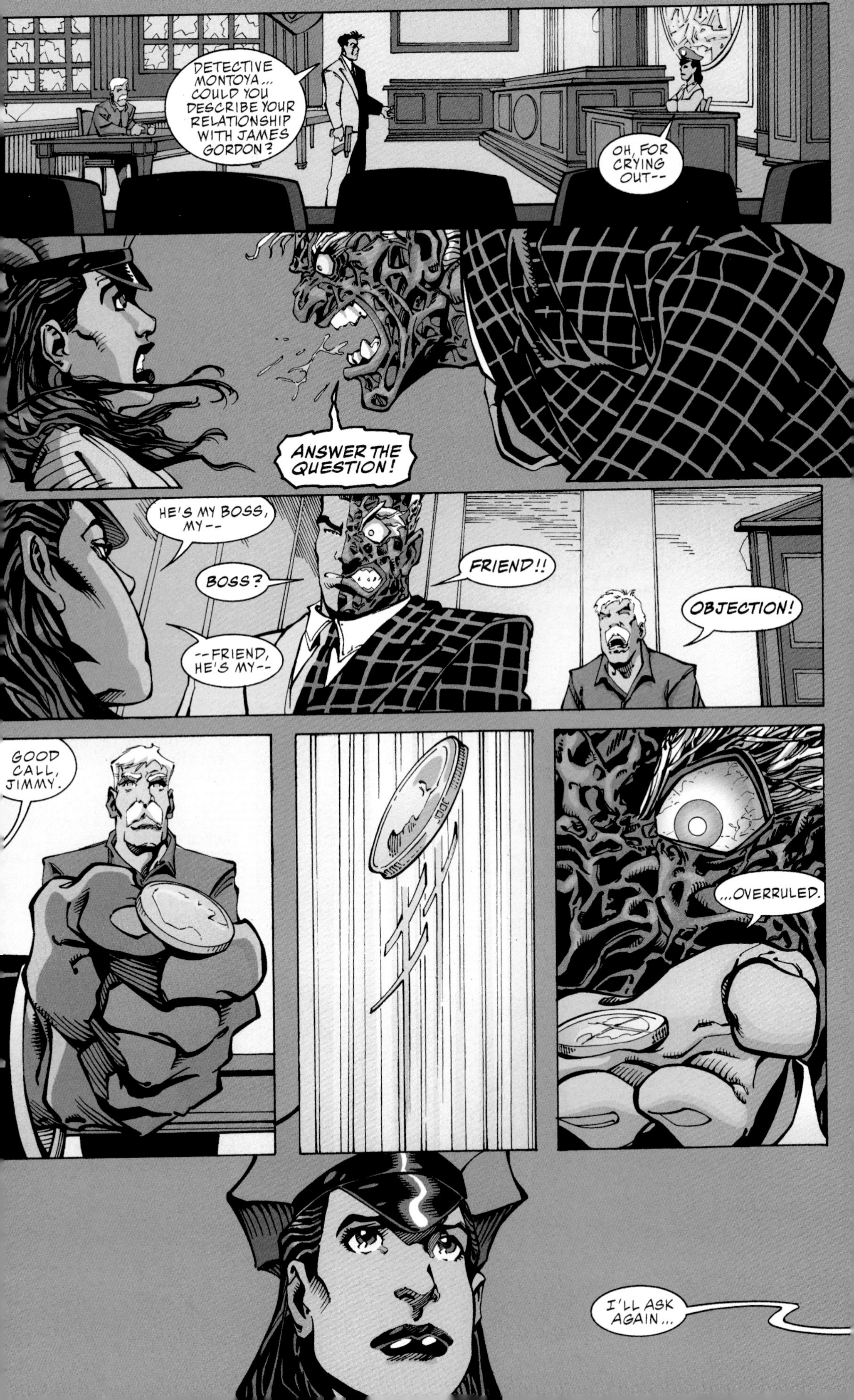
DETECTIVE MONTOYA... COULD YOU DESCRIBE YOUR RELATIONSHIP WITH JAMES GORDON?
OH, FOR CRYING OUT--
ANSWER THE QUESTION!
HE'S MY BOSS, MY--
BOSS?
--FRIEND, HE'S MY--
FRIEND!!
OBJECTION!
GOOD CALL, JIMMY.
...OVERRULED.
I'LL ASK AGAIN...

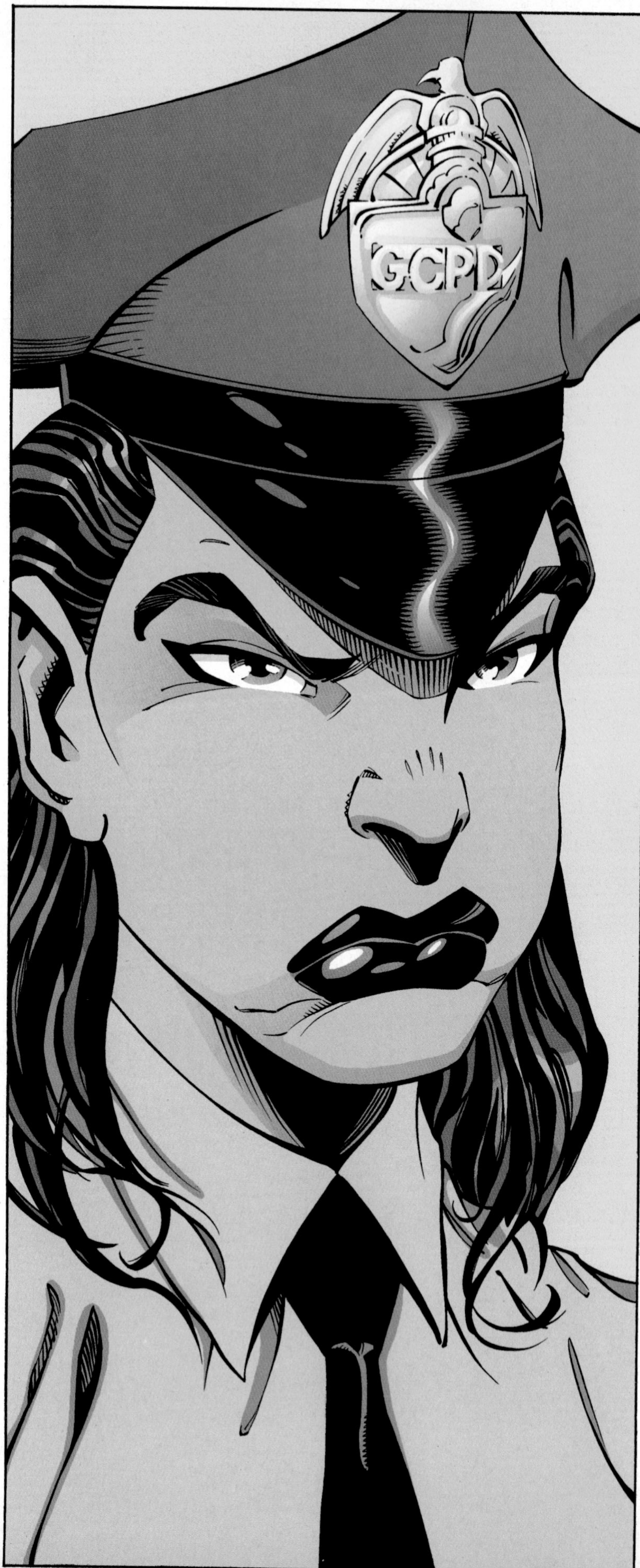
GCPD

Q [Mr.H.Dent]: Please tell the court what the defendant asked you to do on day 190 of NML.

A [Det. 3rd R. Montoya]:

Dammit, Harvey, you know---

Q: Answer the question, Detective Montoya!

A: ...he told me to talk to you.

Q: Why?

A: He wanted your help.

Q: You disapproved of this?

A: Yes.

Q: Why?

A: Because you're a murderer and you're crazy, that's why.

Q: Answer without editorializing, if you please, Detective.

A: ...because we're cops. You're a criminal. Working with you is morally and ethically wrong.

Q: It is in fact illegal.

A: Yes.

Q: Why did he send you to talk to me, and no other cop?

A: ...he knew...he knew that you and I had met before NML was declared...that you'd let me keep that coin...

Q: Was that the only reason?

A: ...no. He didn't want...he didn't want anyone else to know that he was dealing with you.

Q: Did you want to talk to me? Detective? Answer the question, please.

A: ...no.

Q: Why not?

A: You scare me.

Q: But you brought his message anyway, correct?

A: Yes.

Q: Why?

A: I couldn't say no.

[Comm.J.Gordon]:

Objection!

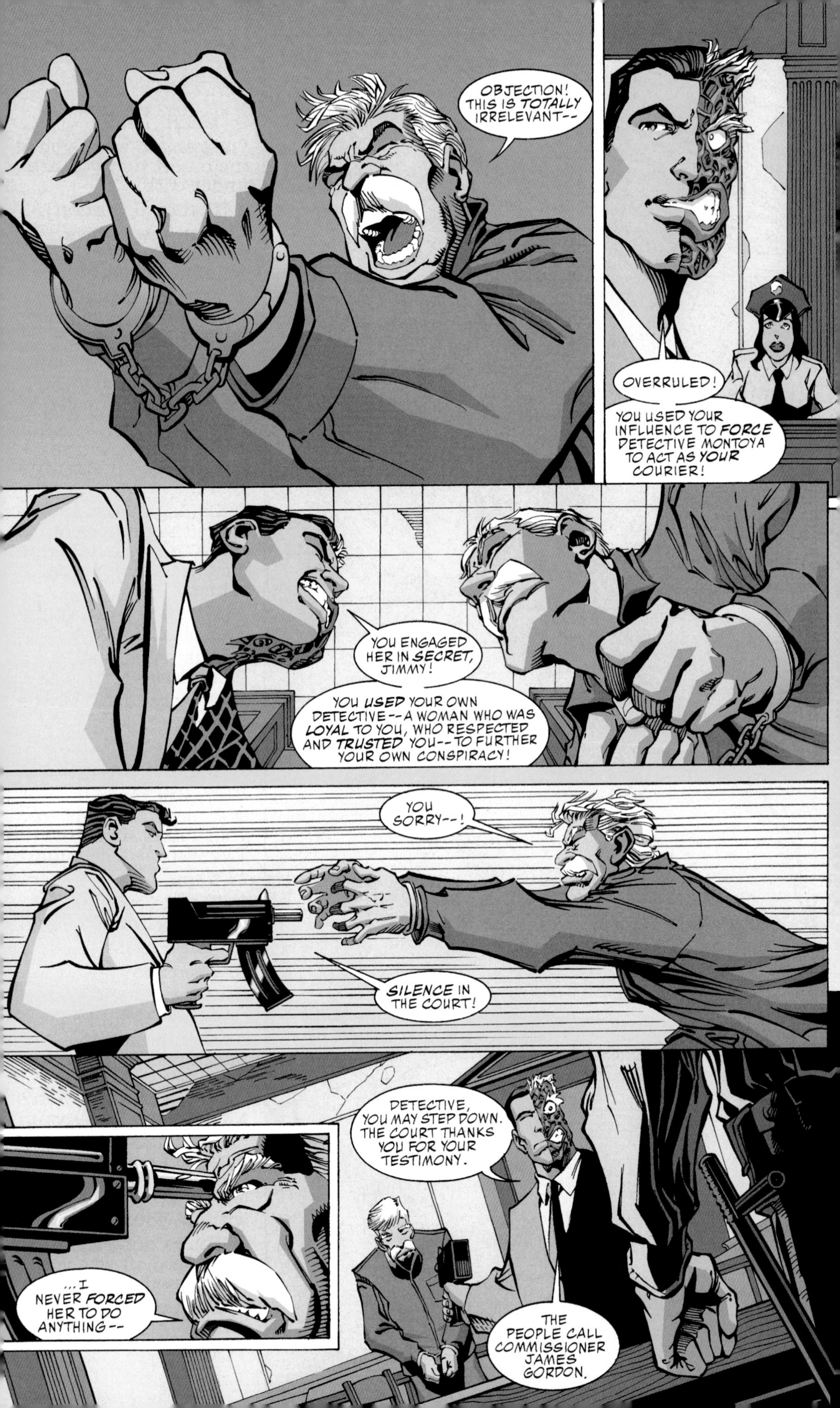
OBJECTION! THIS IS TOTALLY IRRELEVANT--
OVERRULED!
YOU USED YOUR INFLUENCE TO FORCE DETECTIVE MONTOYA TO ACT AS YOUR COURIER!
YOU ENGAGED HER IN SECRET, JIMMY!
YOU USED YOUR OWN DETECTIVE--A WOMAN WHO WAS LOYAL TO YOU, WHO RESPECTED AND TRUSTED YOU--TO FURTHER YOUR OWN CONSPIRACY!
YOU SORRY--!
SILENCE IN THE COURT!
...I NEVER FORCED HER TO DO ANYTHING--
DETECTIVE, YOU MAY STEP DOWN. THE COURT THANKS YOU FOR YOUR TESTIMONY.
THE PEOPLE CALL COMMISSIONER JAMES GORDON.

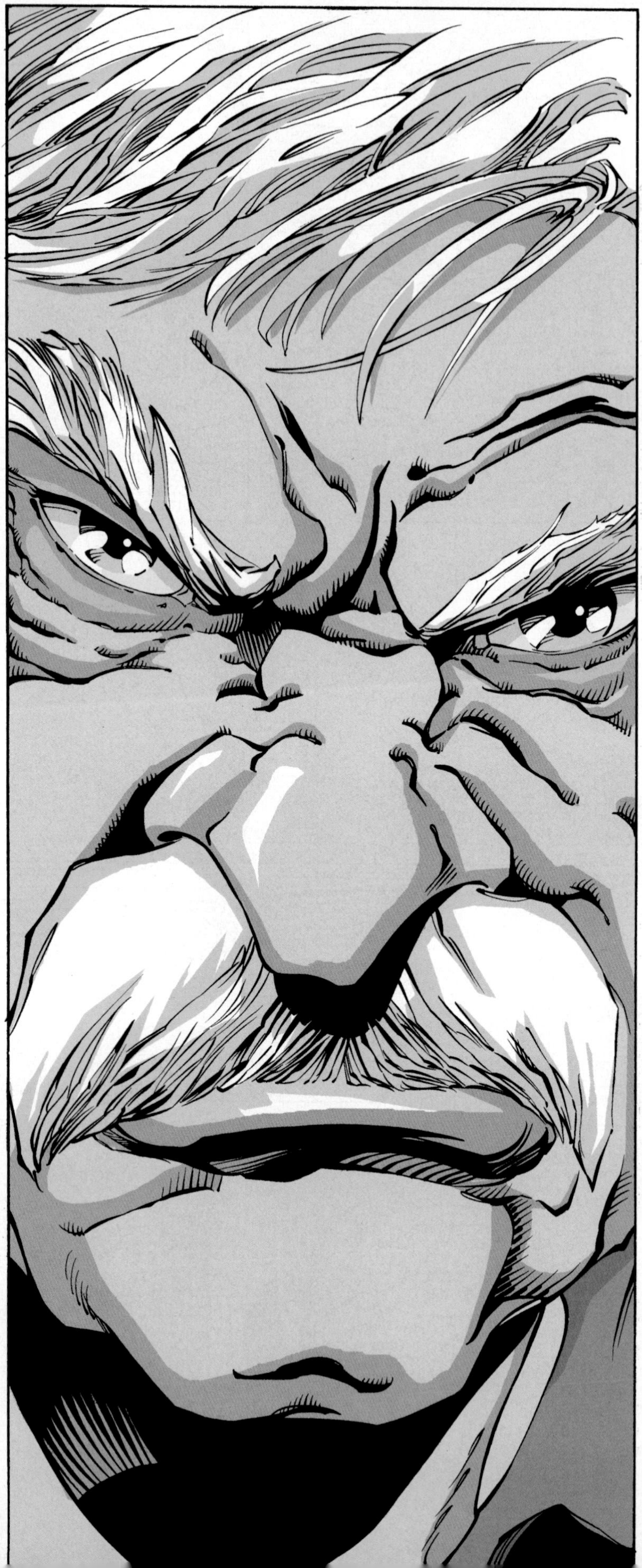

Q [Mr. H. Dent]:
I'm going to warn you at the outset that you are under oath.

A [Comm. J.Gordon]:
I know how to give testimony, you sanctimonious--

Q: Are you acquainted with the criminal known as Two-Face?

A: Looking right at him.

Q: How long have you known him? Answer, please.

A: As Two-Face? I've known you almost nine years.

Q: Could you list for the court the number of times he's been taken into custody, and for what crimes?

A: Where are you going with this, Harvey?

Q: Answer, please, Commissioner.

A: Twenty times. Maybe more.

Q: For?

A: Name it. Everything from murder to larceny.

Q: There's no doubt in your mind, then, that Two-Face is a criminal?

A: None.

Q: Would you consider him dangerous?

A: Wait a min---

Q: Yes or no?

A: ...yes.

Q: So why would you have entered into a mutual defense agreement with him? Commissioner Gordon?

A: You know why! You had the men and the muscle. I couldn't protect my people or what's left of this city without your help!

Q: You've done it in the past. Batman was your sanctioned---

A: Don't talk to me about him!

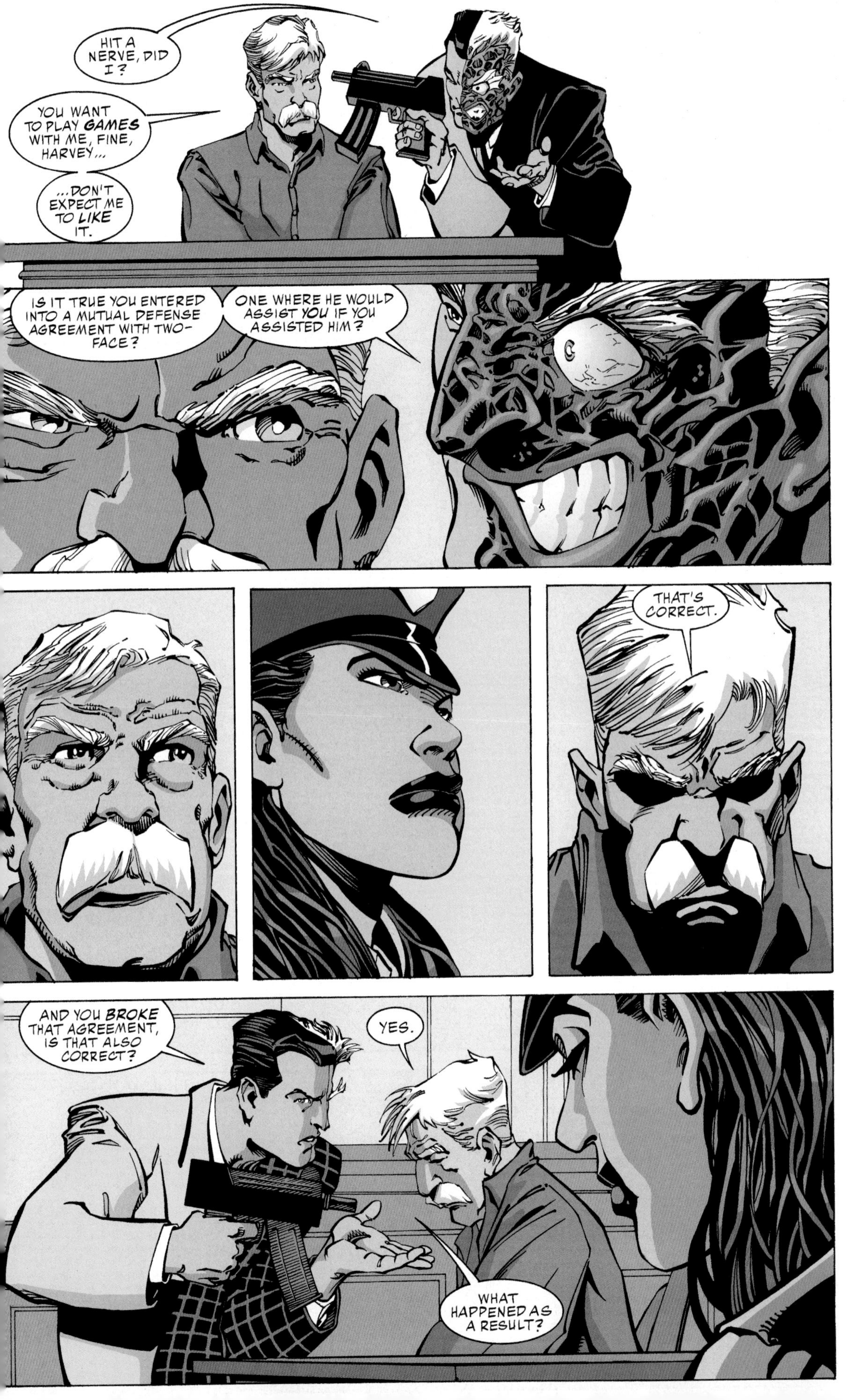

HIT A NERVE, DID I?
YOU WANT TO PLAY **GAMES** WITH ME, FINE, HARVEY...
...DON'T EXPECT ME TO **LIKE** IT.
IS IT TRUE YOU ENTERED INTO A MUTUAL DEFENSE AGREEMENT WITH TWO-FACE?
ONE WHERE HE WOULD ASSIST **YOU** IF YOU ASSISTED HIM?
THAT'S CORRECT.
AND YOU **BROKE** THAT AGREEMENT, IS THAT ALSO CORRECT?
YES.
WHAT HAPPENED AS A RESULT?

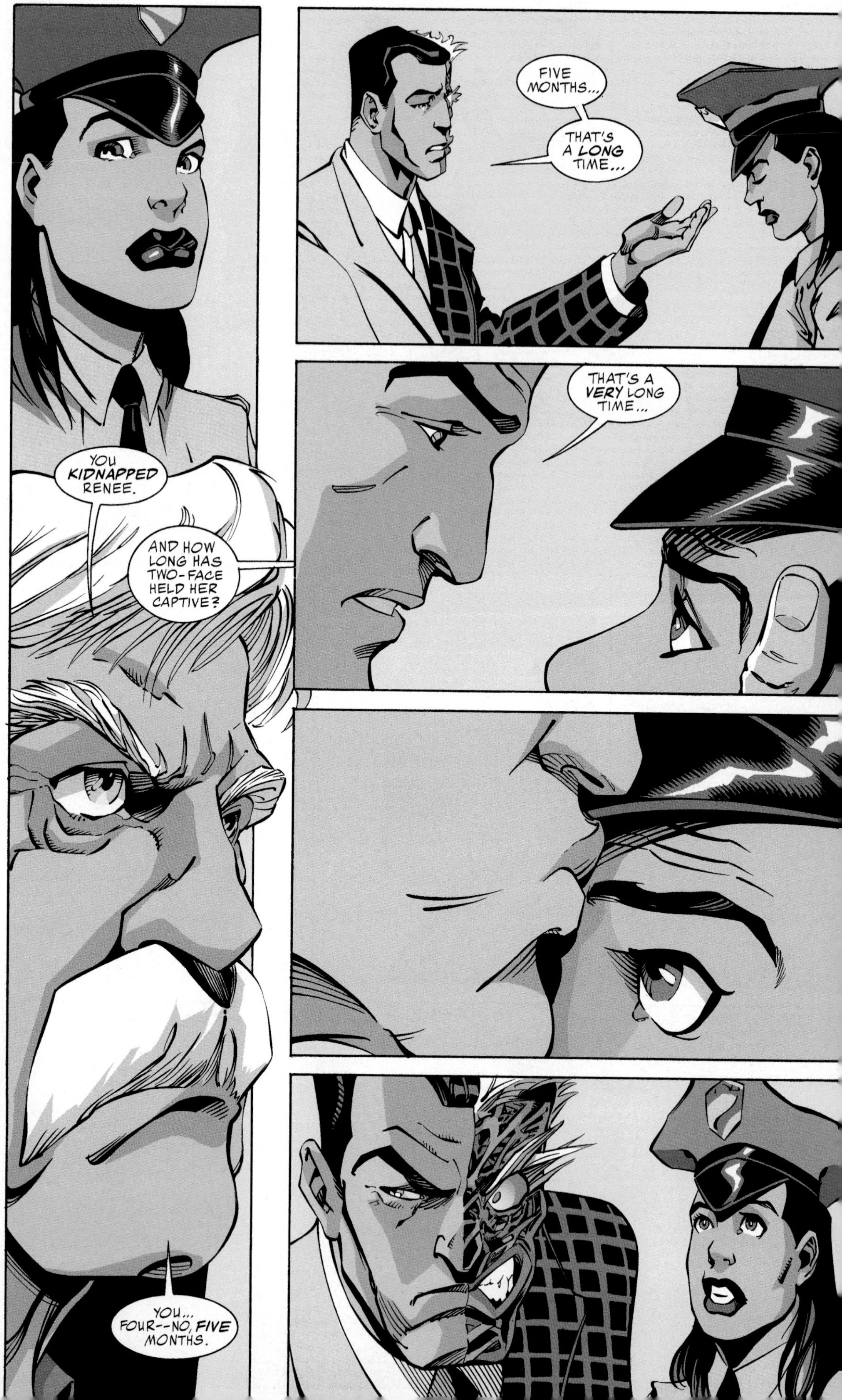

FIVE MONTHS...
THAT'S A LONG TIME...
YOU KIDNAPPED RENEE.
AND HOW LONG HAS TWO-FACE HELD HER CAPTIVE?
THAT'S A VERY LONG TIME...
YOU... FOUR--NO, FIVE MONTHS.

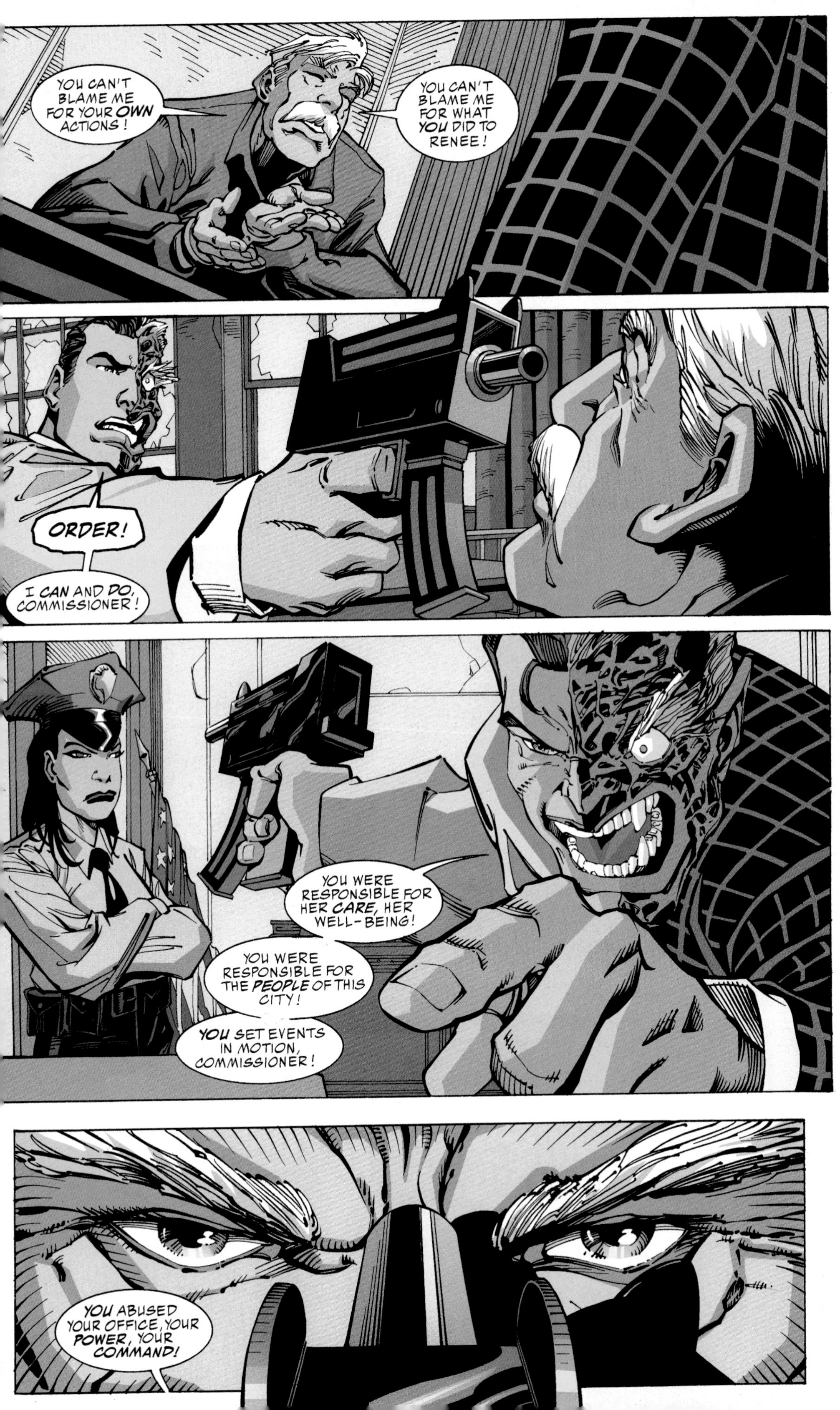
YOU CAN'T BLAME ME FOR YOUR OWN ACTIONS!
YOU CAN'T BLAME ME FOR WHAT YOU DID TO RENEE!
ORDER!
I CAN AND DO, COMMISSIONER!
YOU WERE RESPONSIBLE FOR HER CARE, HER WELL-BEING!
YOU WERE RESPONSIBLE FOR THE PEOPLE OF THIS CITY!
YOU SET EVENTS IN MOTION, COMMISSIONER!
YOU ABUSED YOUR OFFICE, YOUR POWER, YOUR COMMAND!

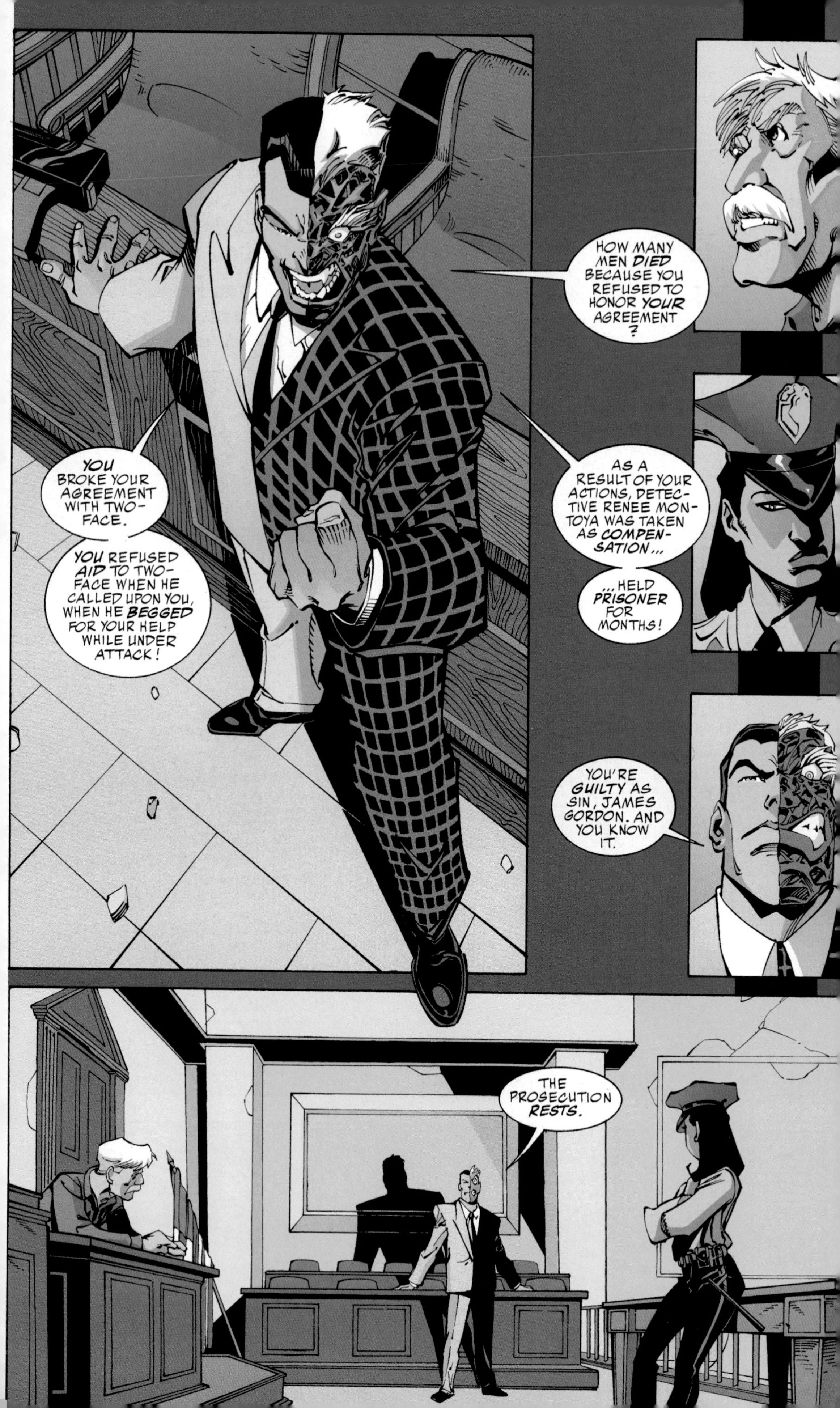
YOU BROKE YOUR AGREEMENT WITH TWO-FACE.
YOU REFUSED AID TO TWO-FACE WHEN HE CALLED UPON YOU, WHEN HE BEGGED FOR YOUR HELP WHILE UNDER ATTACK!
HOW MANY MEN DIED BECAUSE YOU REFUSED TO HONOR YOUR AGREEMENT?
AS A RESULT OF YOUR ACTIONS, DETECTIVE RENEE MONTOYA WAS TAKEN AS COMPENSATION...
...HELD PRISONER FOR MONTHS!
YOU'RE GUILTY AS SIN, JAMES GORDON. AND YOU KNOW IT.
THE PROSECUTION RESTS.

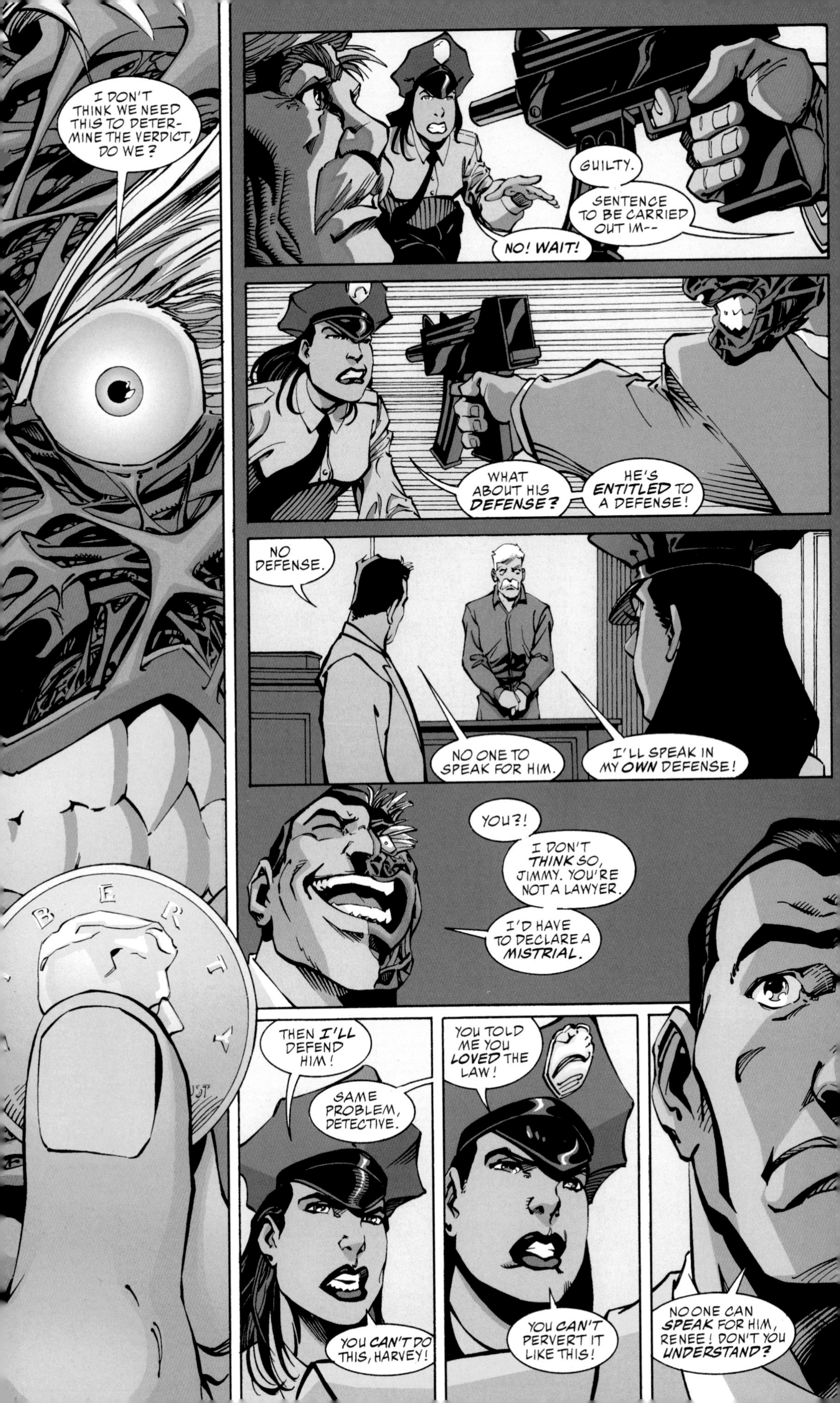

I DON'T THINK WE NEED THIS TO DETERMINE THE VERDICT, DO WE?
GUILTY.
SENTENCE TO BE CARRIED OUT IM--
NO! WAIT!
WHAT ABOUT HIS DEFENSE?
HE'S ENTITLED TO A DEFENSE!
NO DEFENSE.
NO ONE TO SPEAK FOR HIM.
I'LL SPEAK IN MY OWN DEFENSE!
YOU?!
I DON'T THINK SO, JIMMY. YOU'RE NOT A LAWYER.
I'D HAVE TO DECLARE A MISTRIAL.
THEN I'LL DEFEND HIM!
SAME PROBLEM, DETECTIVE.
YOU CAN'T DO THIS, HARVEY!
YOU TOLD ME YOU LOVED THE LAW!
YOU CAN'T PERVERT IT LIKE THIS!
NO ONE CAN SPEAK FOR HIM, RENEE! DON'T YOU UNDERSTAND?
LIBERTY

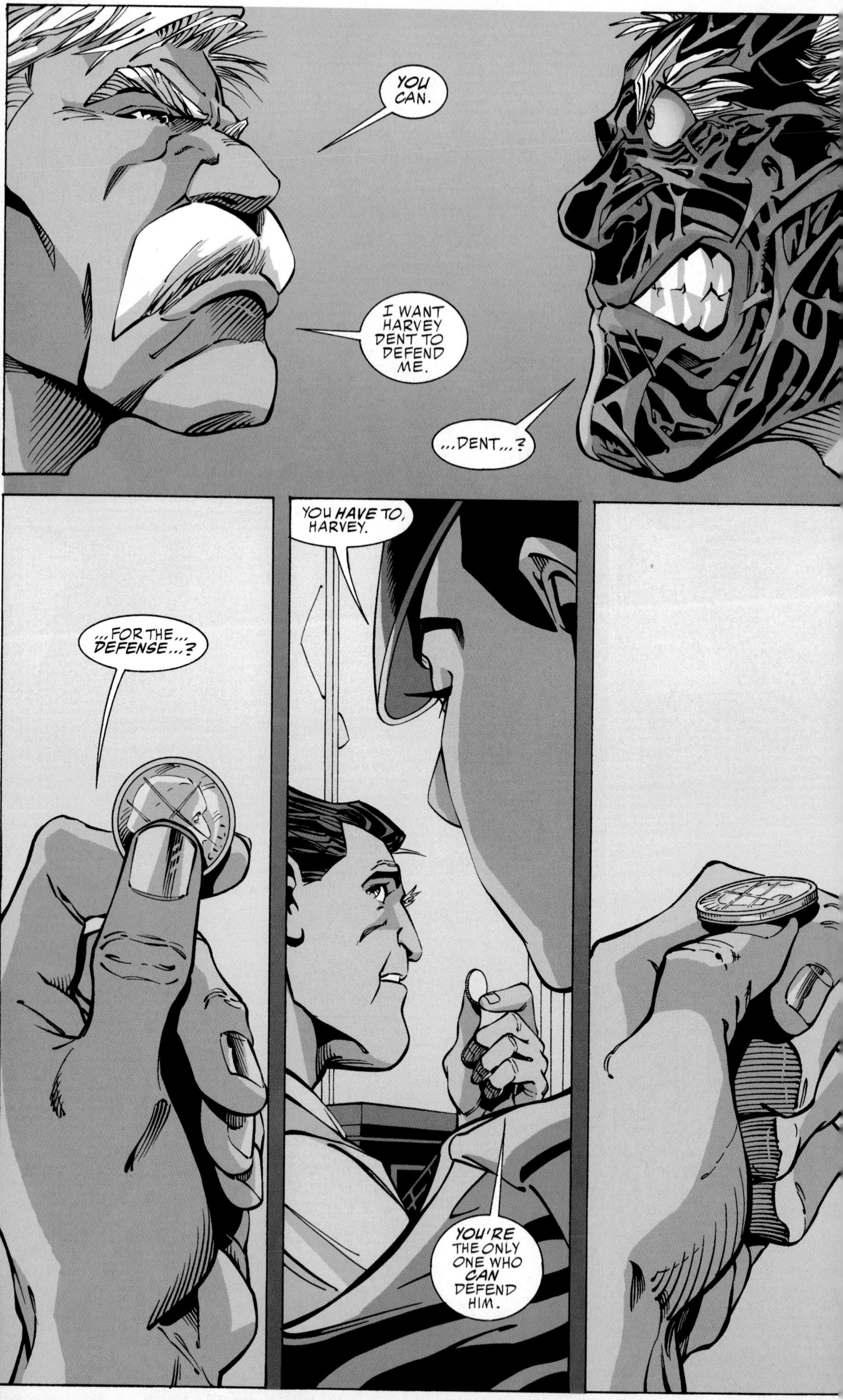
YOU CAN.
I WANT HARVEY DENT TO DEFEND ME.
...DENT...?
...FOR THE... DEFENSE...?
YOU HAVE TO, HARVEY.
YOU'RE THE ONLY ONE WHO CAN DEFEND HIM.

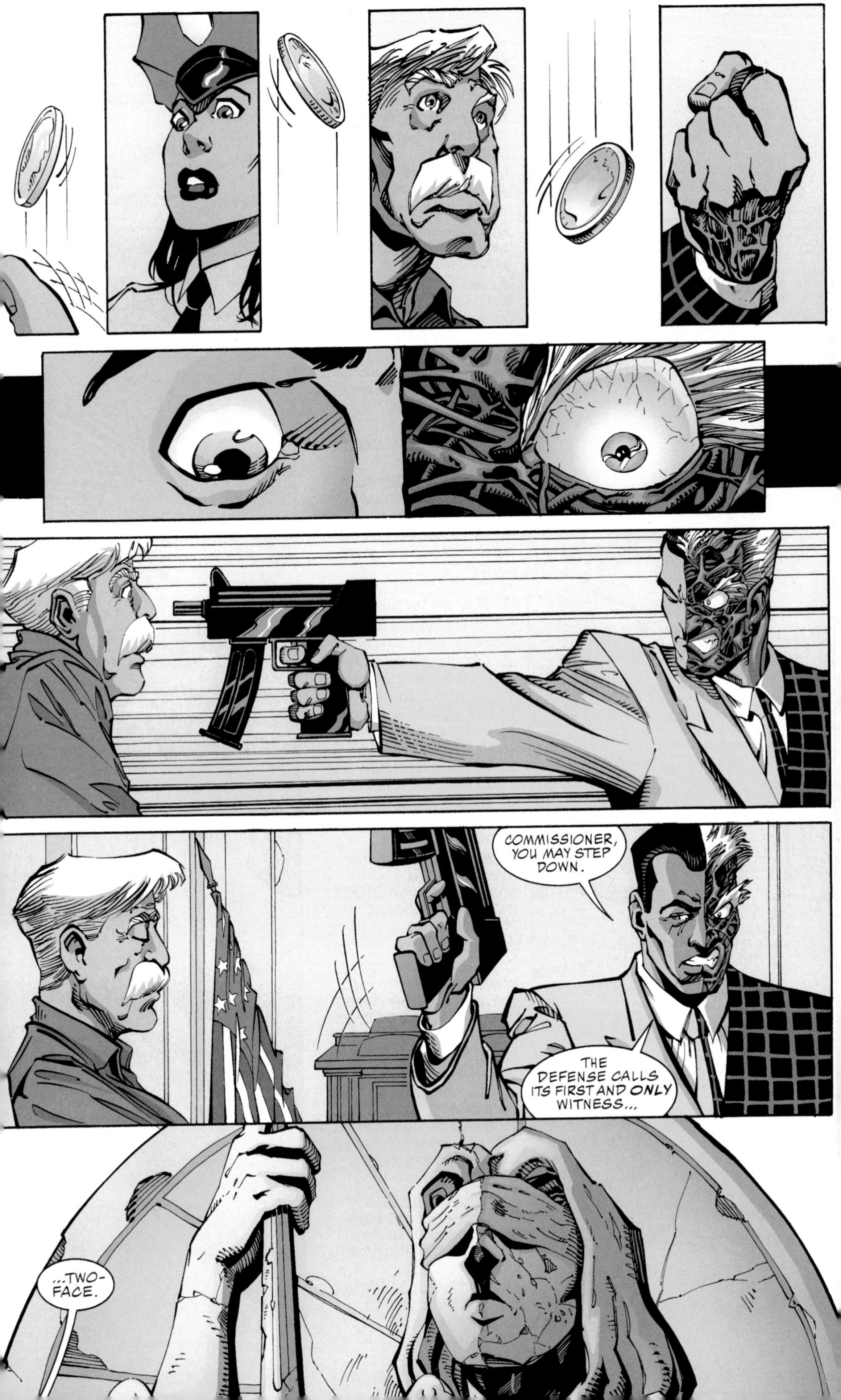
COMMISSIONER, YOU MAY STEP DOWN.
THE DEFENSE CALLS ITS FIRST AND ONLY WITNESS...
...TWO-FACE.

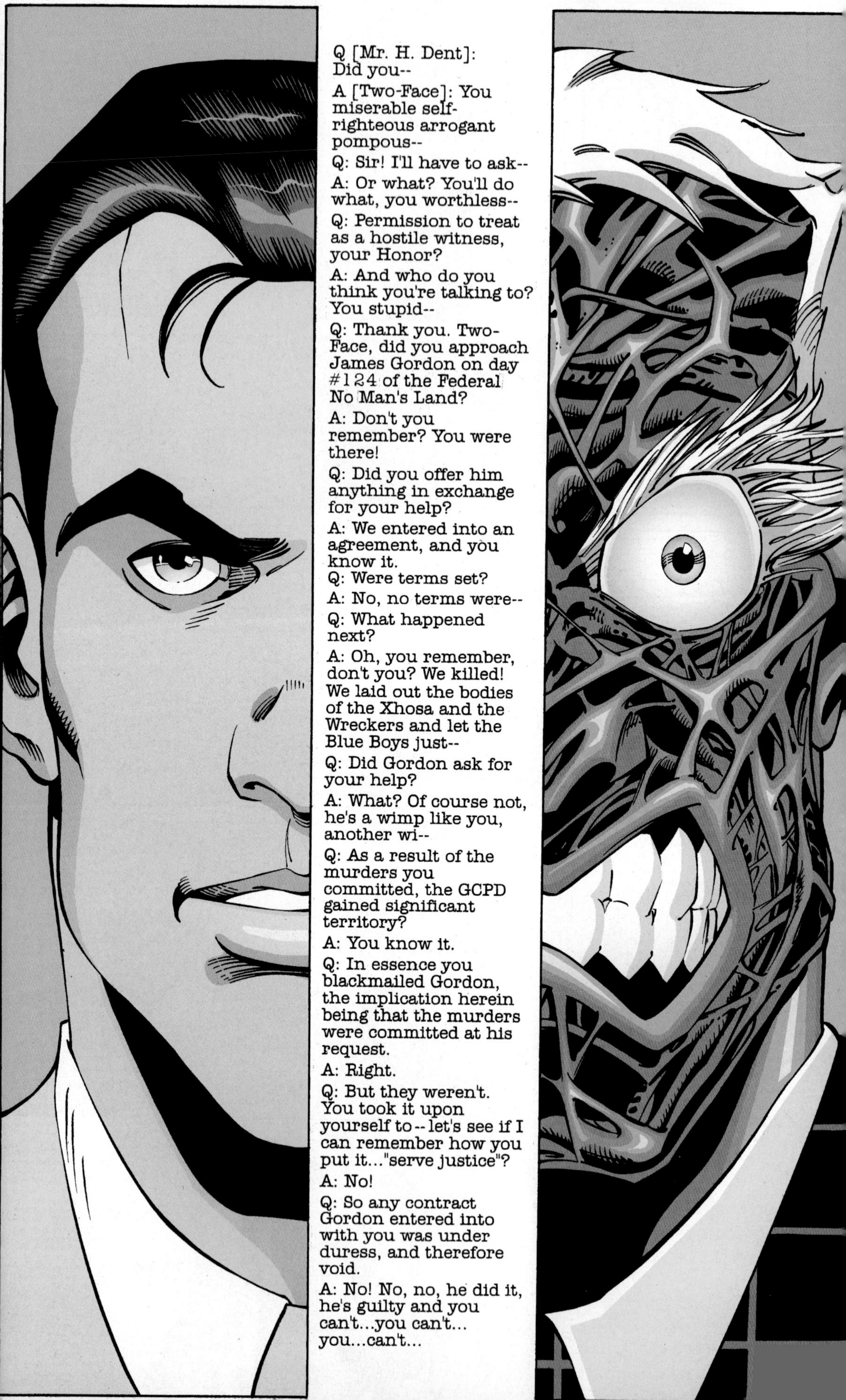
Q [Mr. H. Dent]: Did you--
A [Two-Face]: You miserable self-righteous arrogant pompous--
Q: Sir! I'll have to ask--
A: Or what? You'll do what, you worthless--
Q: Permission to treat as a hostile witness, your Honor?
A: And who do you think you're talking to? You stupid--
Q: Thank you. Two-Face, did you approach James Gordon on day #124 of the Federal No Man's Land?
A: Don't you remember? You were there!
Q: Did you offer him anything in exchange for your help?
A: We entered into an agreement, and you know it.
Q: Were terms set?
A: No, no terms were--
Q: What happened next?
A: Oh, you remember, don't you? We killed! We laid out the bodies of the Xhosa and the Wreckers and let the Blue Boys just--
Q: Did Gordon ask for your help?
A: What? Of course not, he's a wimp like you, another wi--
Q: As a result of the murders you committed, the GCPD gained significant territory?
A: You know it.
Q: In essence you blackmailed Gordon, the implication herein being that the murders were committed at his request.
A: Right.
Q: But they weren't. You took it upon yourself to -- let's see if I can remember how you put it..."serve justice"?
A: No!
Q: So any contract Gordon entered into with you was under duress, and therefore void.
A: No! No, no, he did it, he's guilty and you can't...you can't... you...can't...

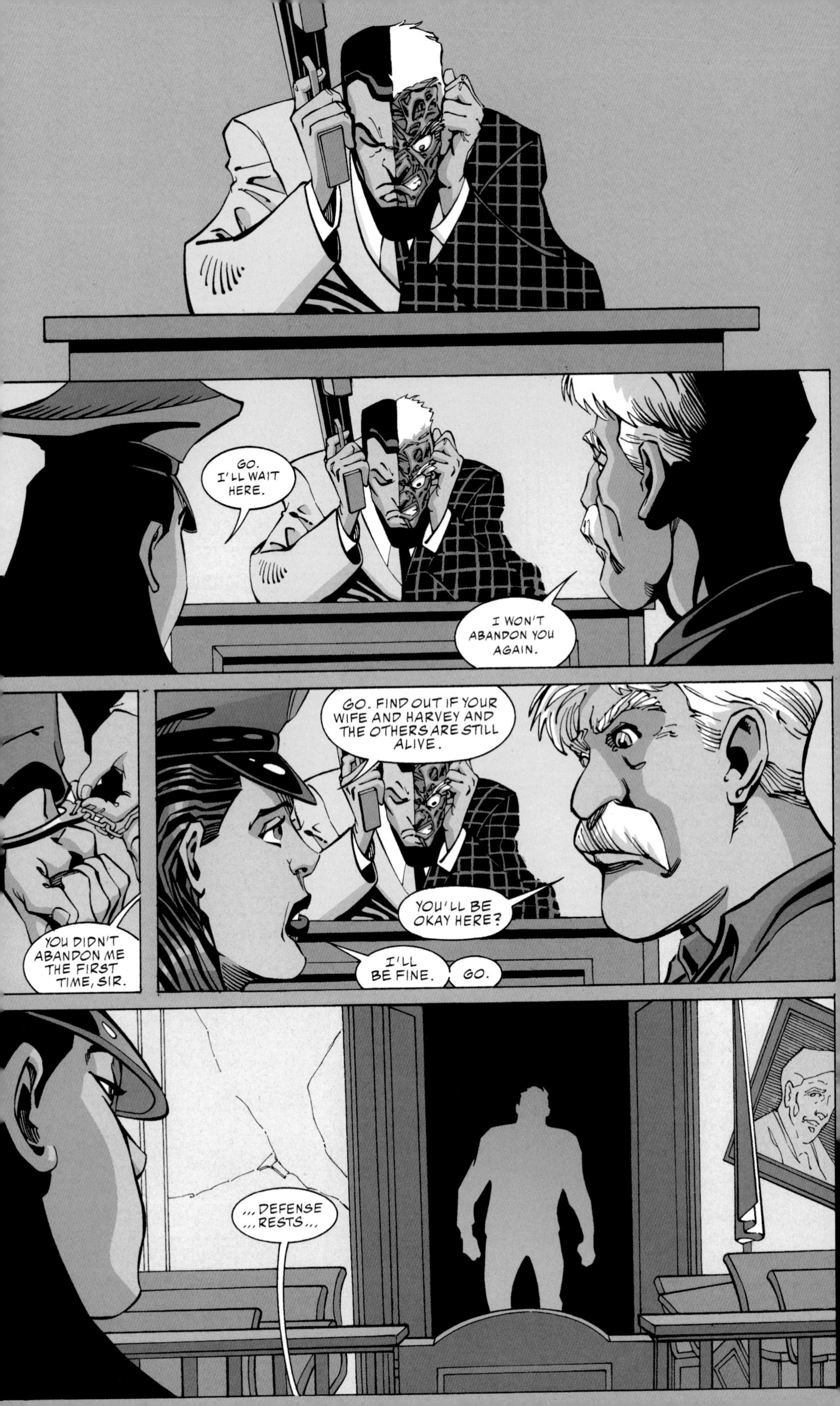

GO. I'LL WAIT HERE.
I WON'T ABANDON YOU AGAIN.
YOU DIDN'T ABANDON ME THE FIRST TIME, SIR.
GO. FIND OUT IF YOUR WIFE AND HARVEY AND THE OTHERS ARE STILL ALIVE.
YOU'LL BE OKAY HERE?
I'LL BE FINE.
GO.
...DEFENSE ...RESTS...

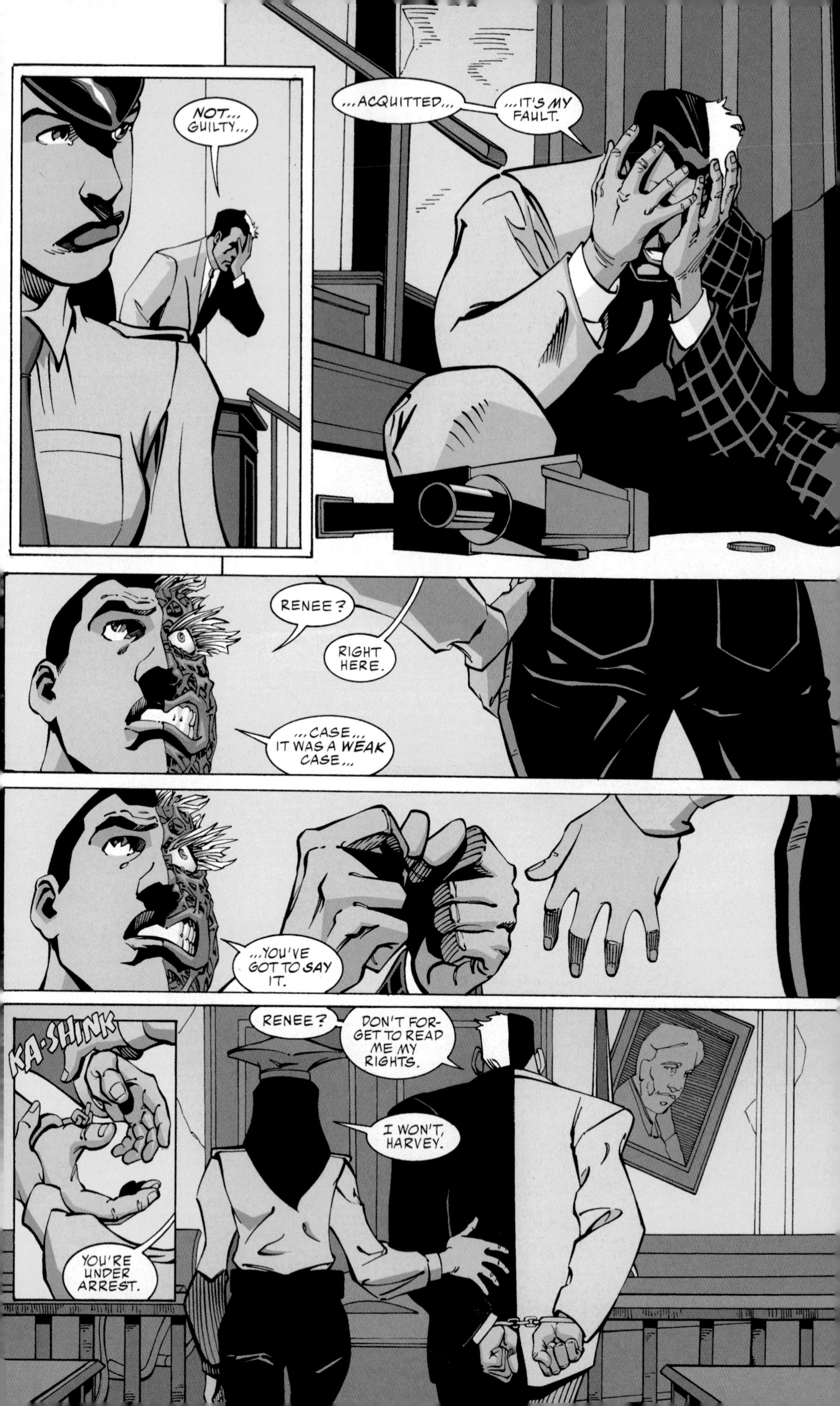
NOT... GUILTY...
...ACQUITTED...
...IT'S MY FAULT.
RENEE?
RIGHT HERE.
...CASE... IT WAS A WEAK CASE...
...YOU'VE GOT TO SAY IT.
KA-SHINK
YOU'RE UNDER ARREST.
RENEE?
DON'T FOR-GET TO READ ME MY RIGHTS.
I WON'T, HARVEY.

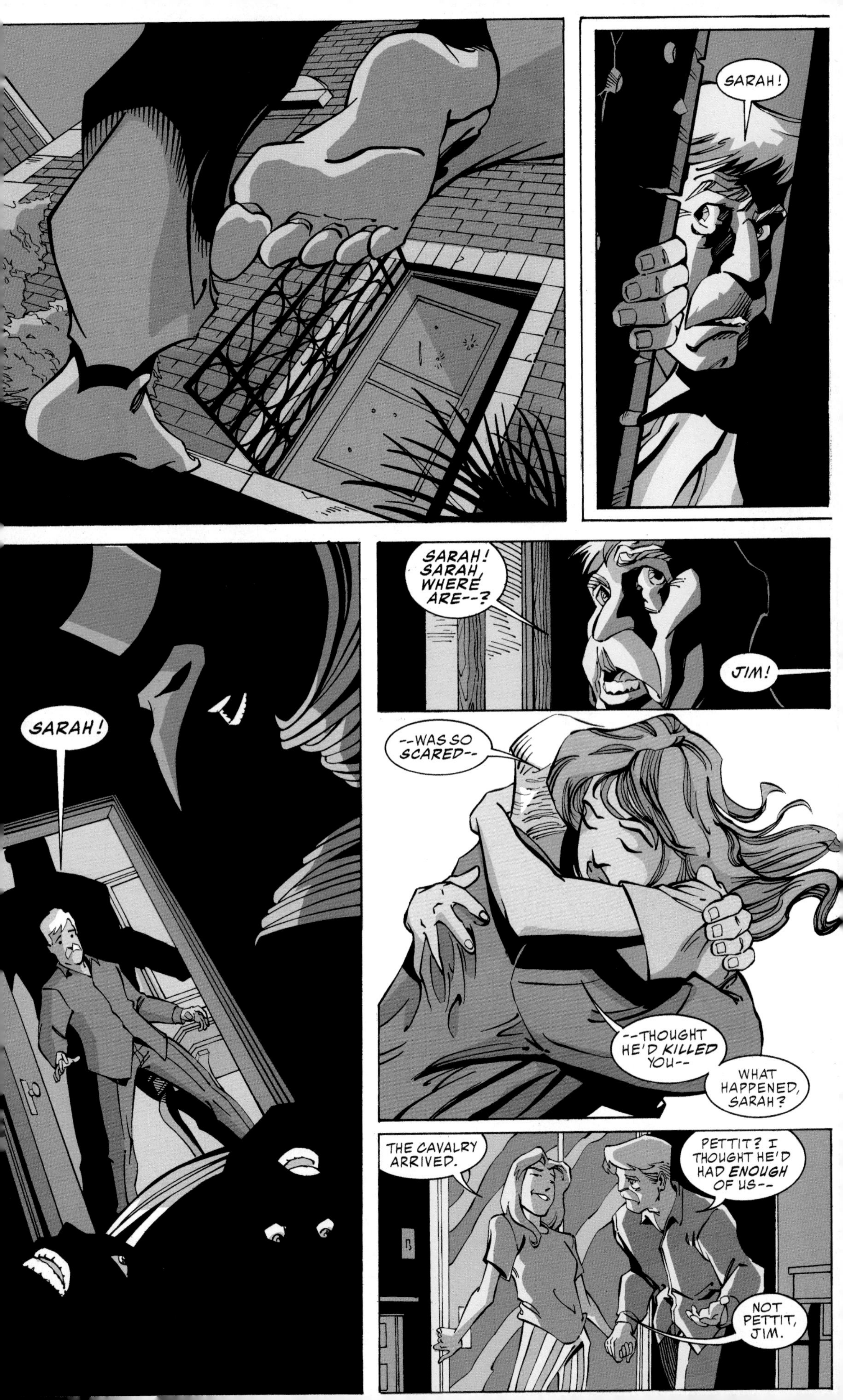
SARAH!
SARAH!
SARAH! SARAH, WHERE ARE--?
JIM!
--WAS SO SCARED--
--THOUGHT HE'D KILLED YOU--
WHAT HAPPENED, SARAH?
THE CAVALRY ARRIVED.
PETTIT? I THOUGHT HE'D HAD ENOUGH OF US--
NOT PETTIT, JIM.

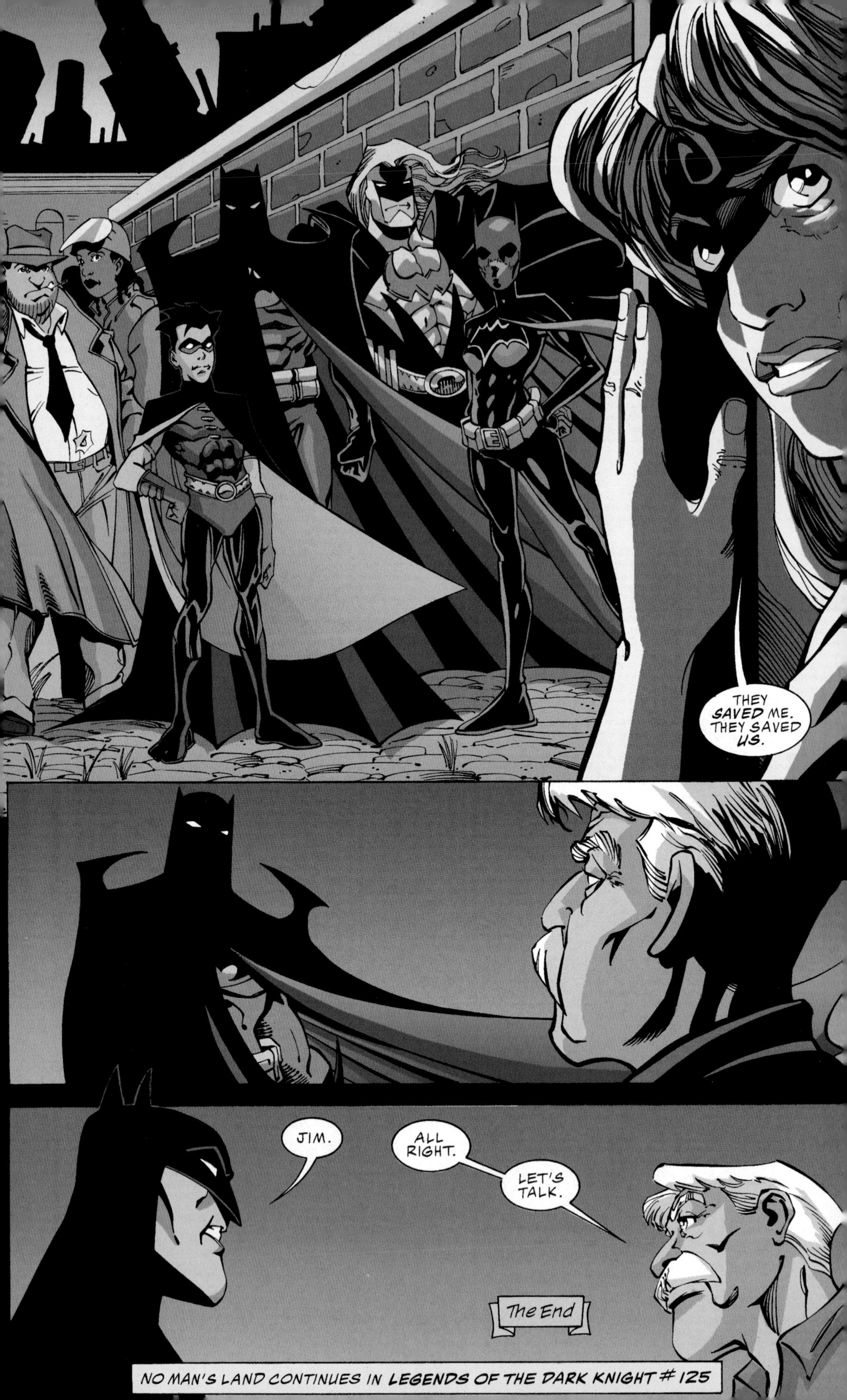
THEY SAVED ME. THEY SAVED US.
JIM.
ALL RIGHT.
LET'S TALK.
The End
NO MAN'S LAND CONTINUES IN LEGENDS OF THE DARK KNIGHT #125

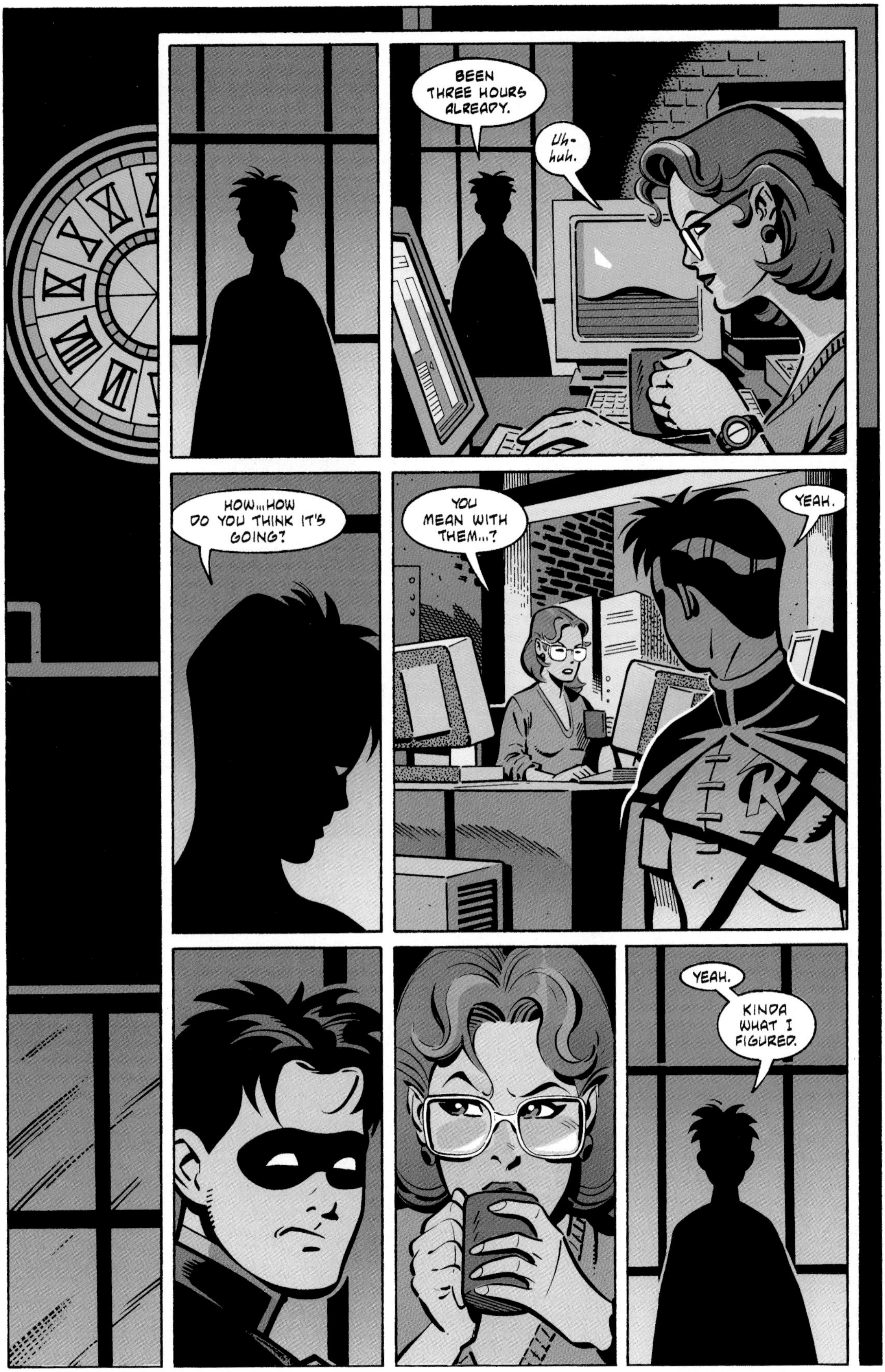

BEEN THREE HOURS ALREADY.
Uh-huh.
HOW...HOW DO YOU THINK IT'S GOING?
YOU MEAN WITH THEM...?
YEAH.
YEAH.
KINDA WHAT I FIGURED.

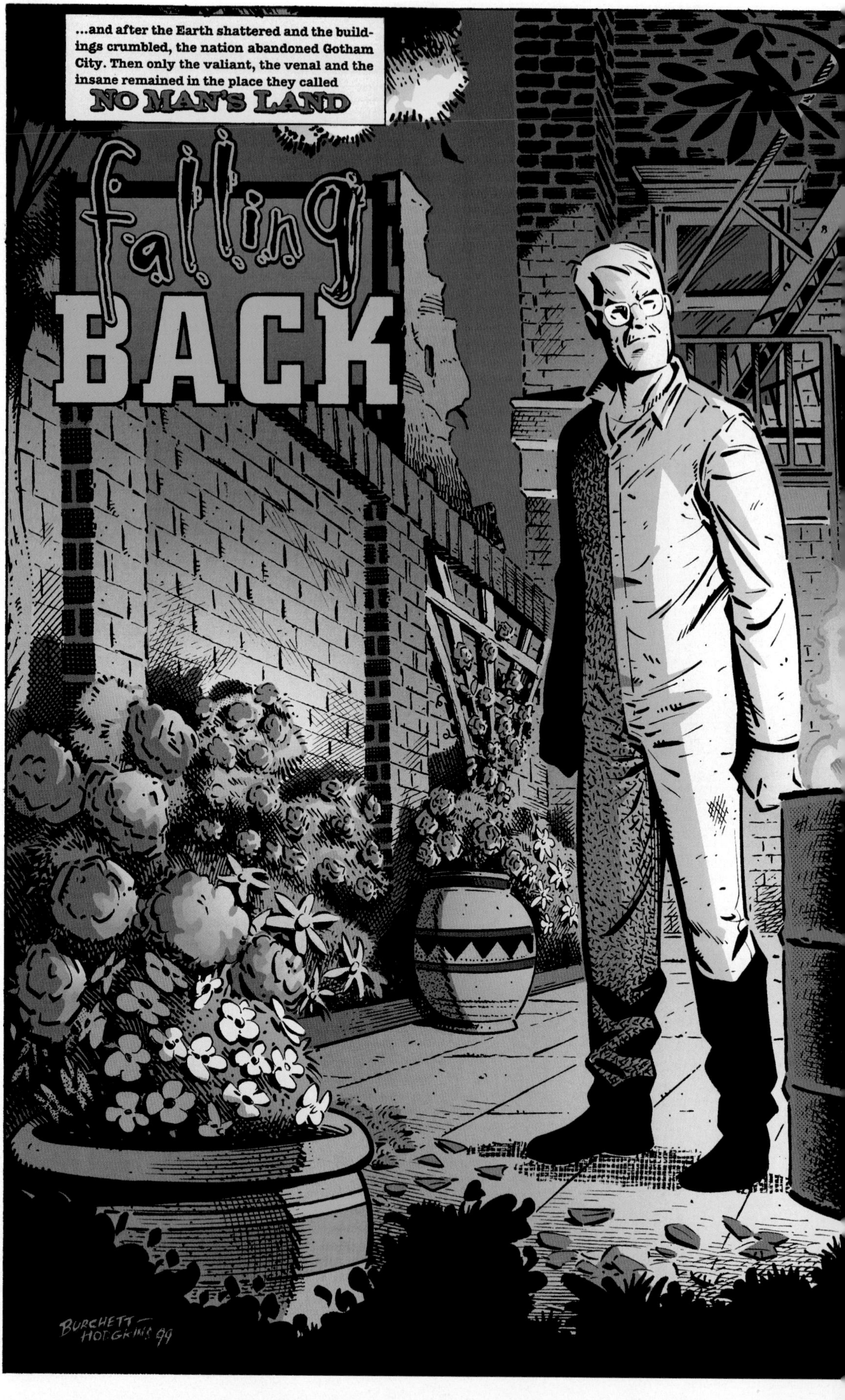
...and after the Earth shattered and the buildings crumbled, the nation abandoned Gotham City. Then only the valiant, the venal and the insane remained in the place they called
NO MAN'S LAND
falling
BACK
BURCHETT — HODGKINS '99

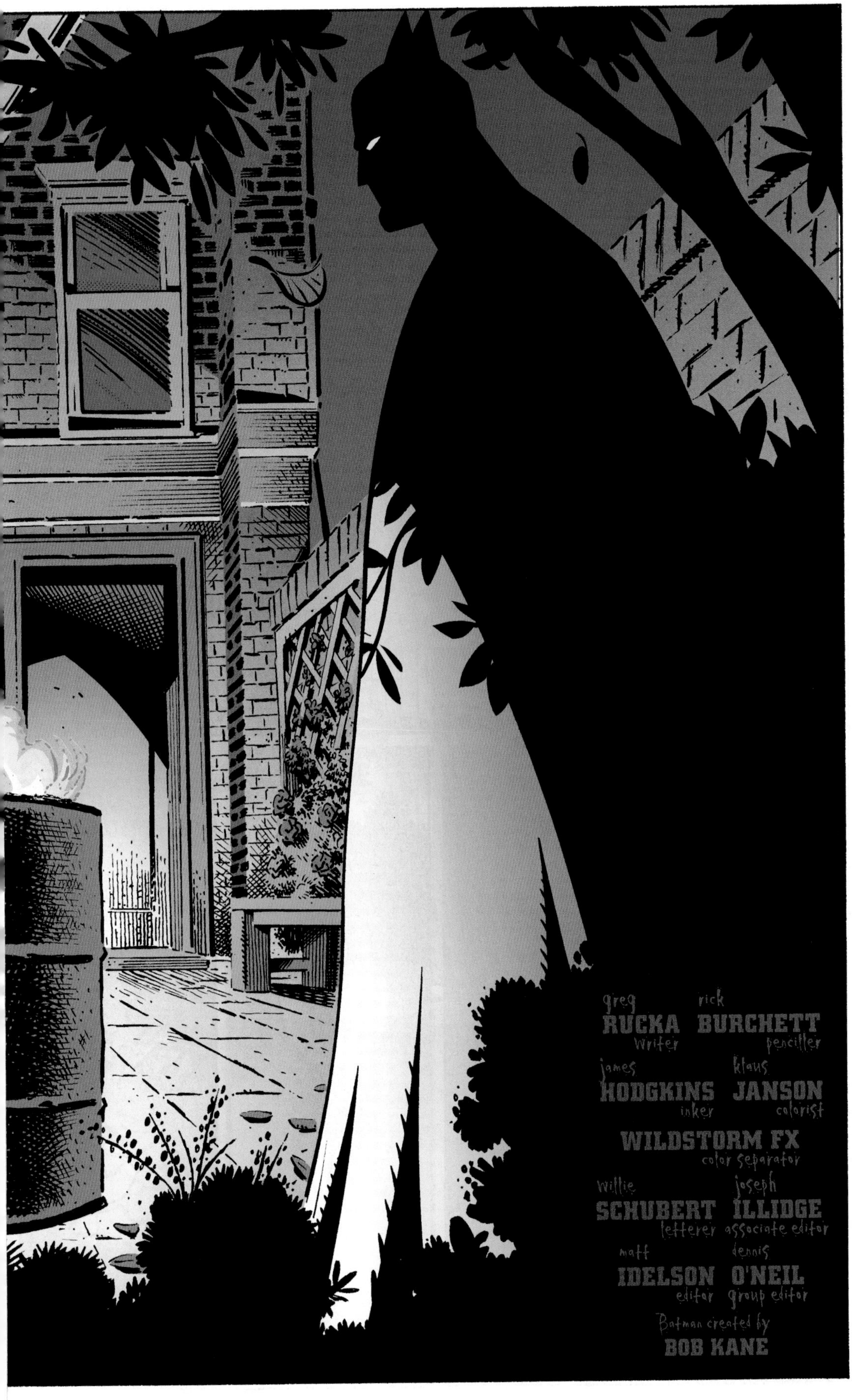
greg RUCKA writer
rick BURCHETT penciller
james HODGKINS inker
klaus JANSON colorist
WILDSTORM FX color separator
willie SCHUBERT letterer
joseph ILLIDGE associate editor
matt IDELSON editor
dennis O'NEIL group editor
Batman created by BOB KANE

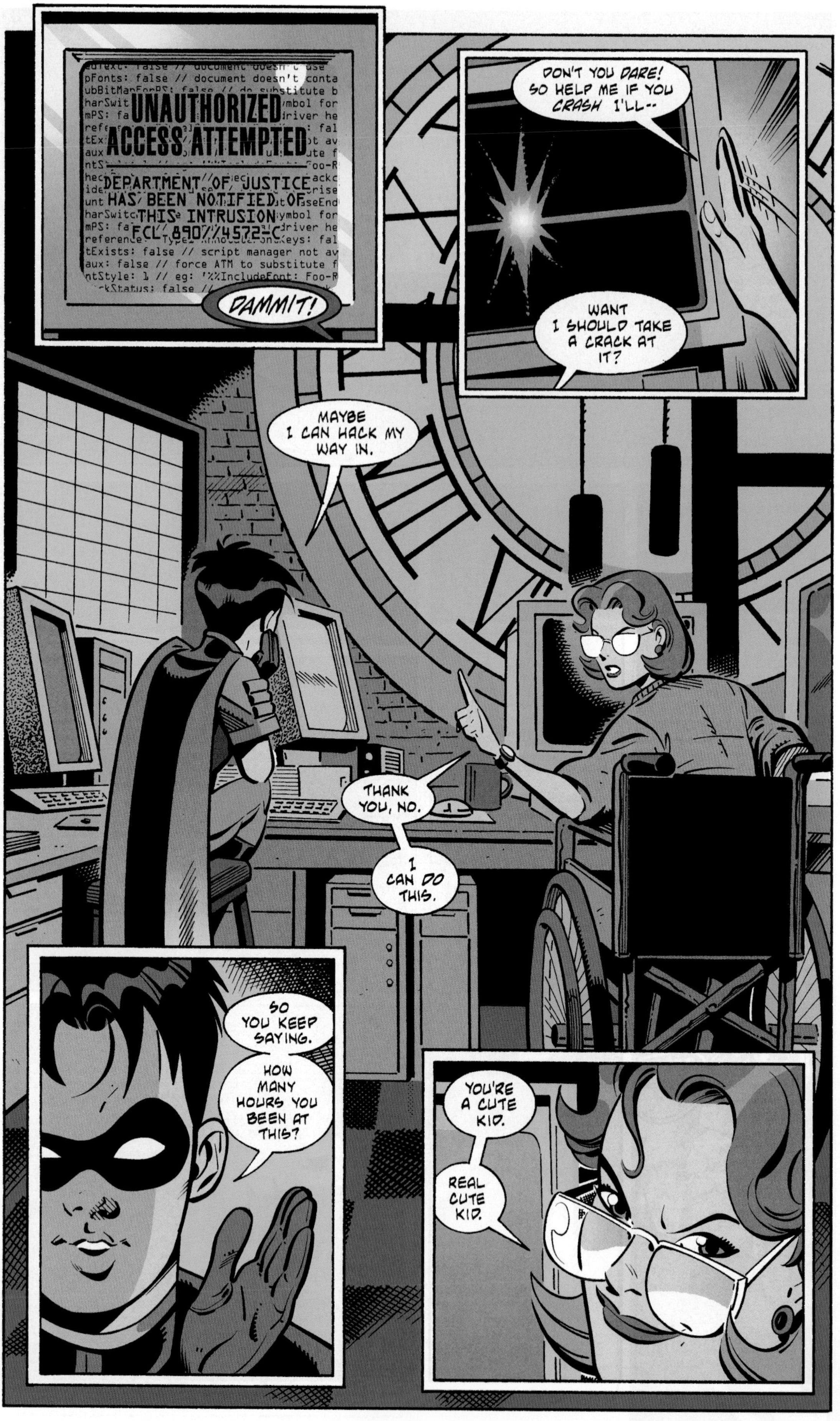
UNAUTHORIZED ACCESS ATTEMPTED
DEPARTMENT OF JUSTICE HAS BEEN NOTIFIED OF THIS INTRUSION
FCL 890%4572-C
DAMMIT!
DON'T YOU DARE! SO HELP ME IF YOU CRASH I'LL--
WANT I SHOULD TAKE A CRACK AT IT?
MAYBE I CAN HACK MY WAY IN.
THANK YOU, NO.
I CAN DO THIS.
SO YOU KEEP SAYING.
HOW MANY HOURS YOU BEEN AT THIS?
YOU'RE A CUTE KID.
REAL CUTE KID.

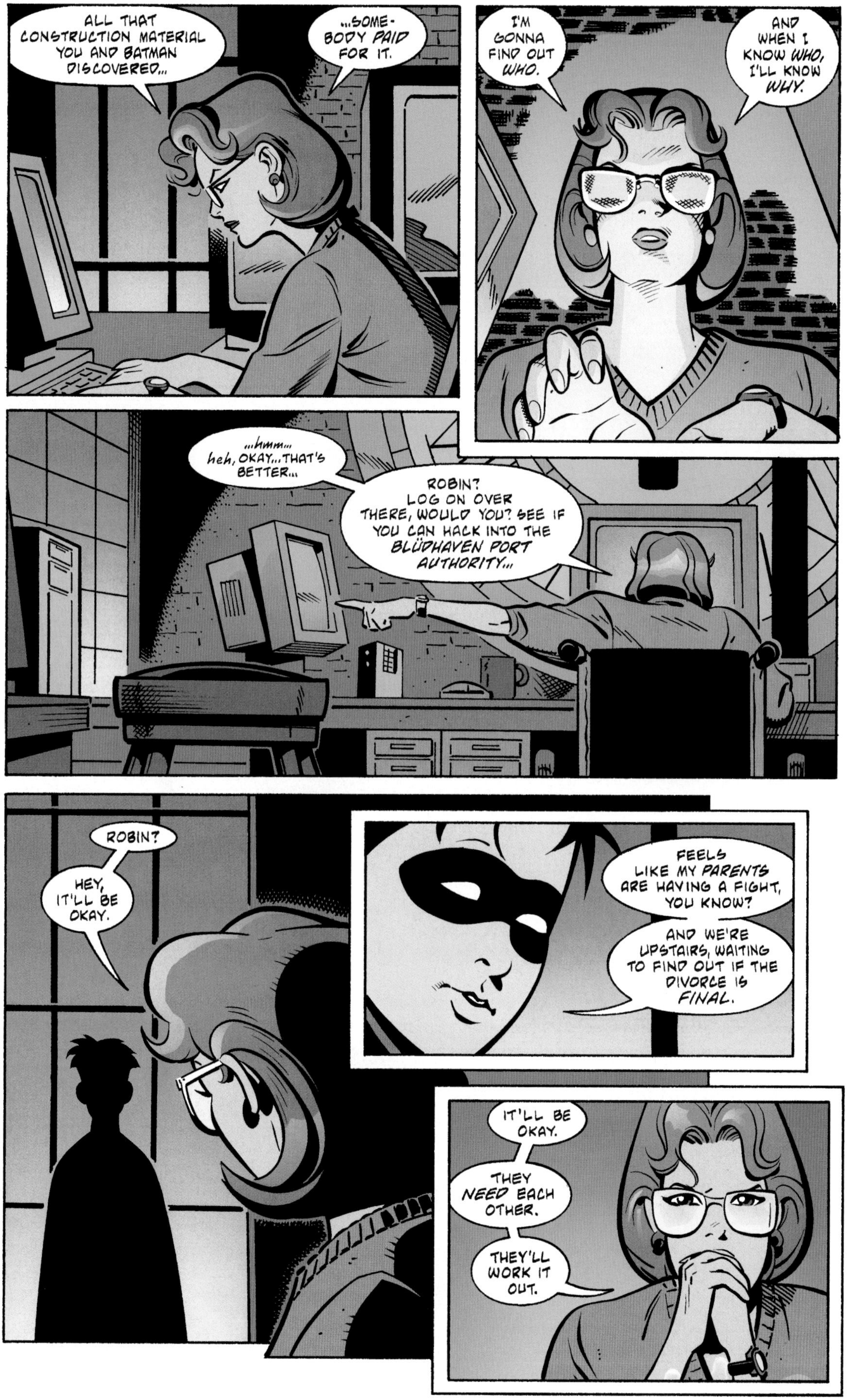
ALL THAT CONSTRUCTION MATERIAL YOU AND BATMAN DISCOVERED...
...SOME-BODY PAID FOR IT.
I'M GONNA FIND OUT WHO.
AND WHEN I KNOW WHO, I'LL KNOW WHY.
...hmm... heh, OKAY...THAT'S BETTER...
ROBIN? LOG ON OVER THERE, WOULD YOU? SEE IF YOU CAN HACK INTO THE BLÜDHAVEN PORT AUTHORITY...
ROBIN?
HEY, IT'LL BE OKAY.
FEELS LIKE MY PARENTS ARE HAVING A FIGHT, YOU KNOW?
AND WE'RE UPSTAIRS, WAITING TO FIND OUT IF THE DIVORCE IS FINAL.
IT'LL BE OKAY.
THEY NEED EACH OTHER.
THEY'LL WORK IT OUT.

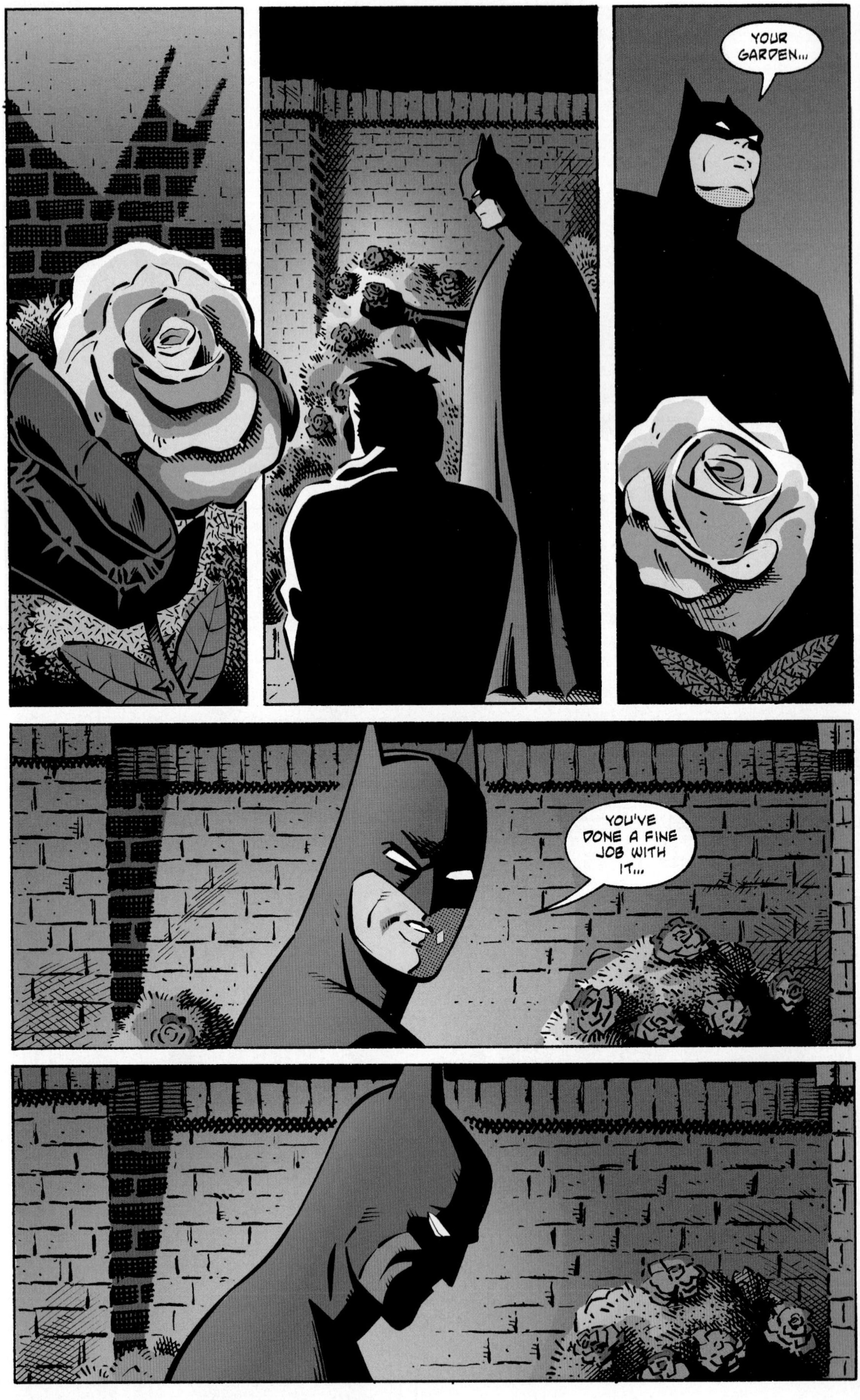
YOUR GARDEN...
YOU'VE DONE A FINE JOB WITH IT...

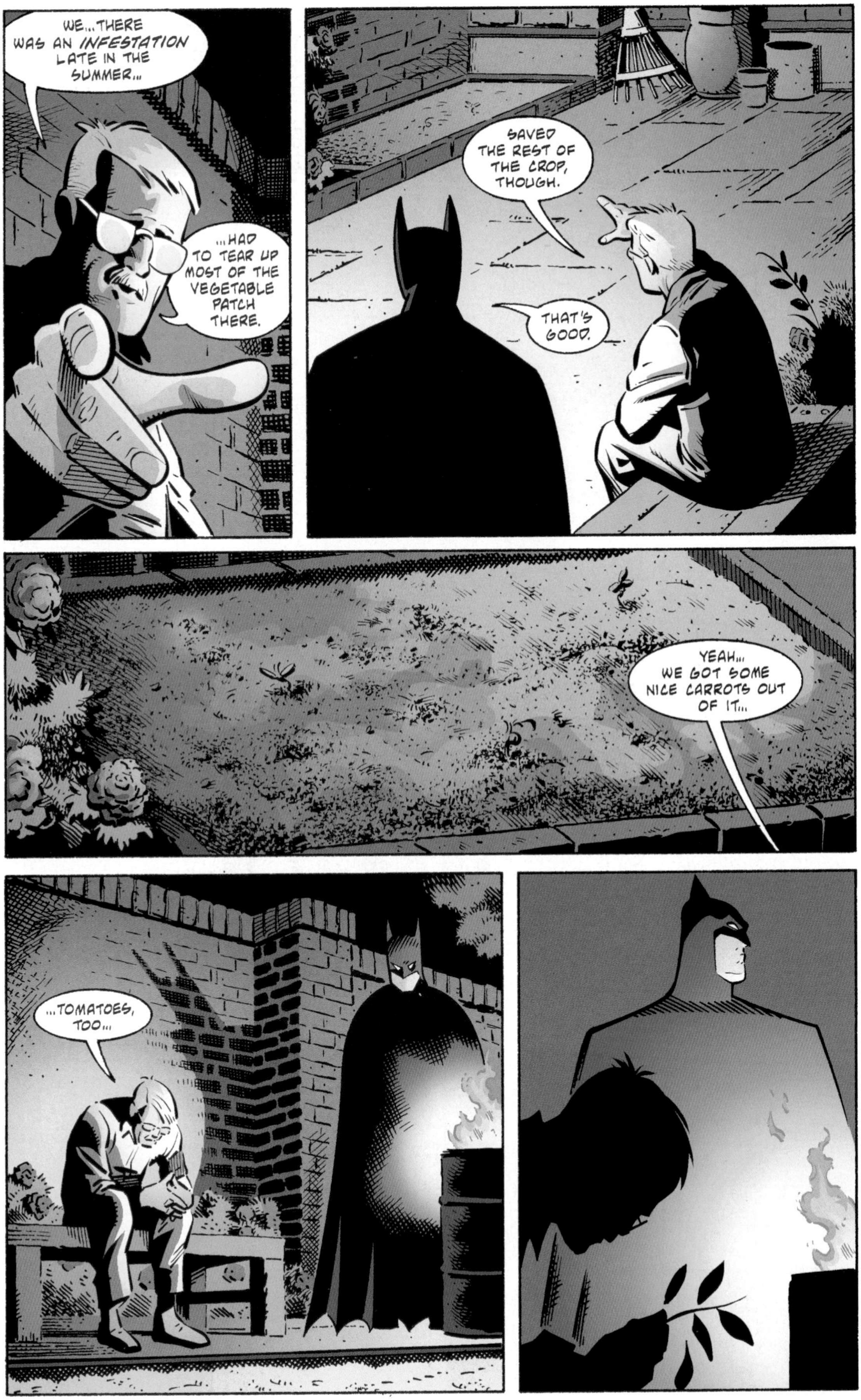
WE... THERE WAS AN *INFESTATION* LATE IN THE SUMMER...
...HAD TO TEAR UP MOST OF THE VEGETABLE PATCH THERE.
SAVED THE REST OF THE CROP, THOUGH.
THAT'S GOOD.
YEAH... WE GOT SOME NICE CARROTS OUT OF IT...
...TOMATOES, TOO...

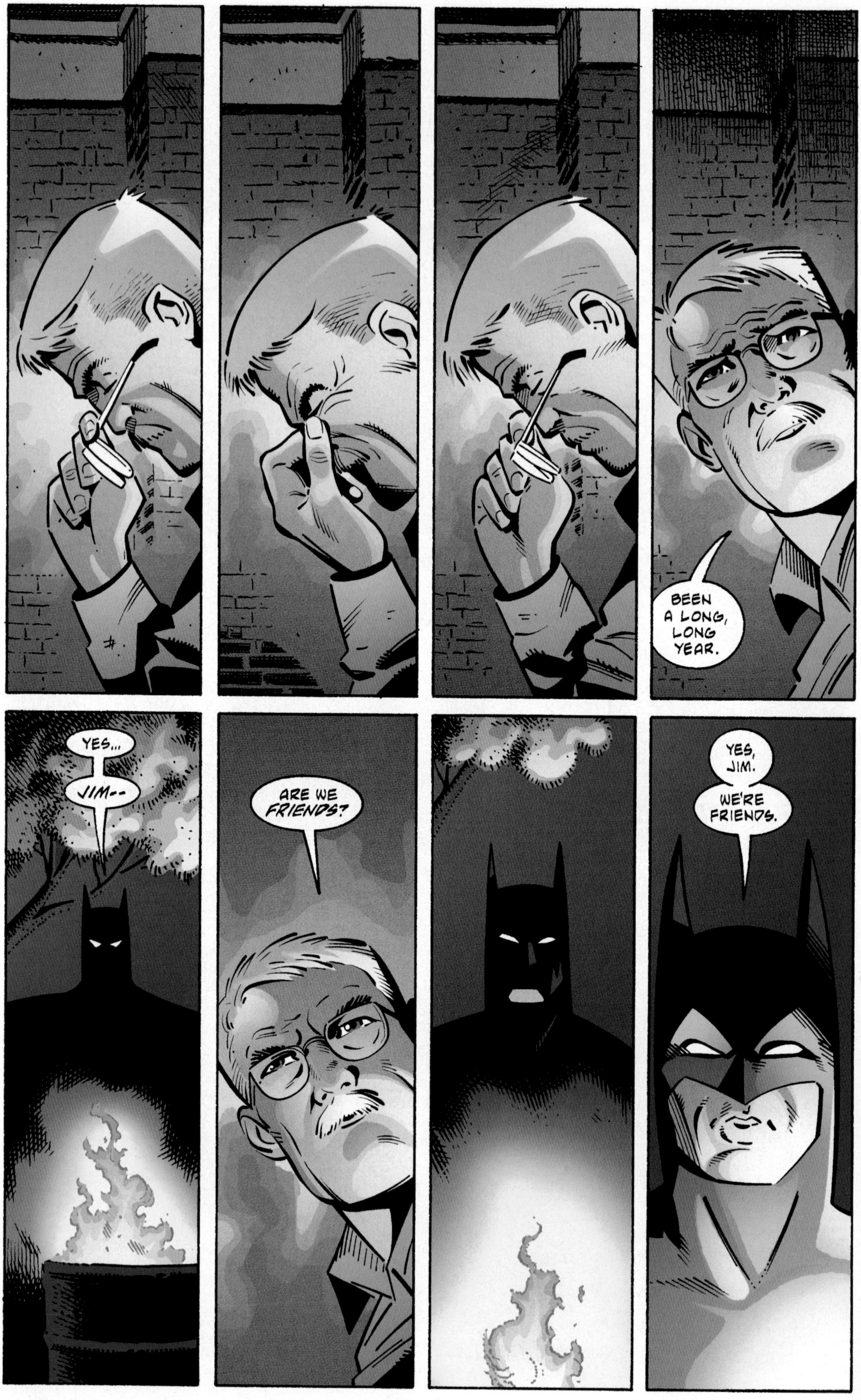
BEEN A LONG, LONG YEAR.
YES...
JIM--
ARE WE FRIENDS?
YES, JIM.
WE'RE FRIENDS.

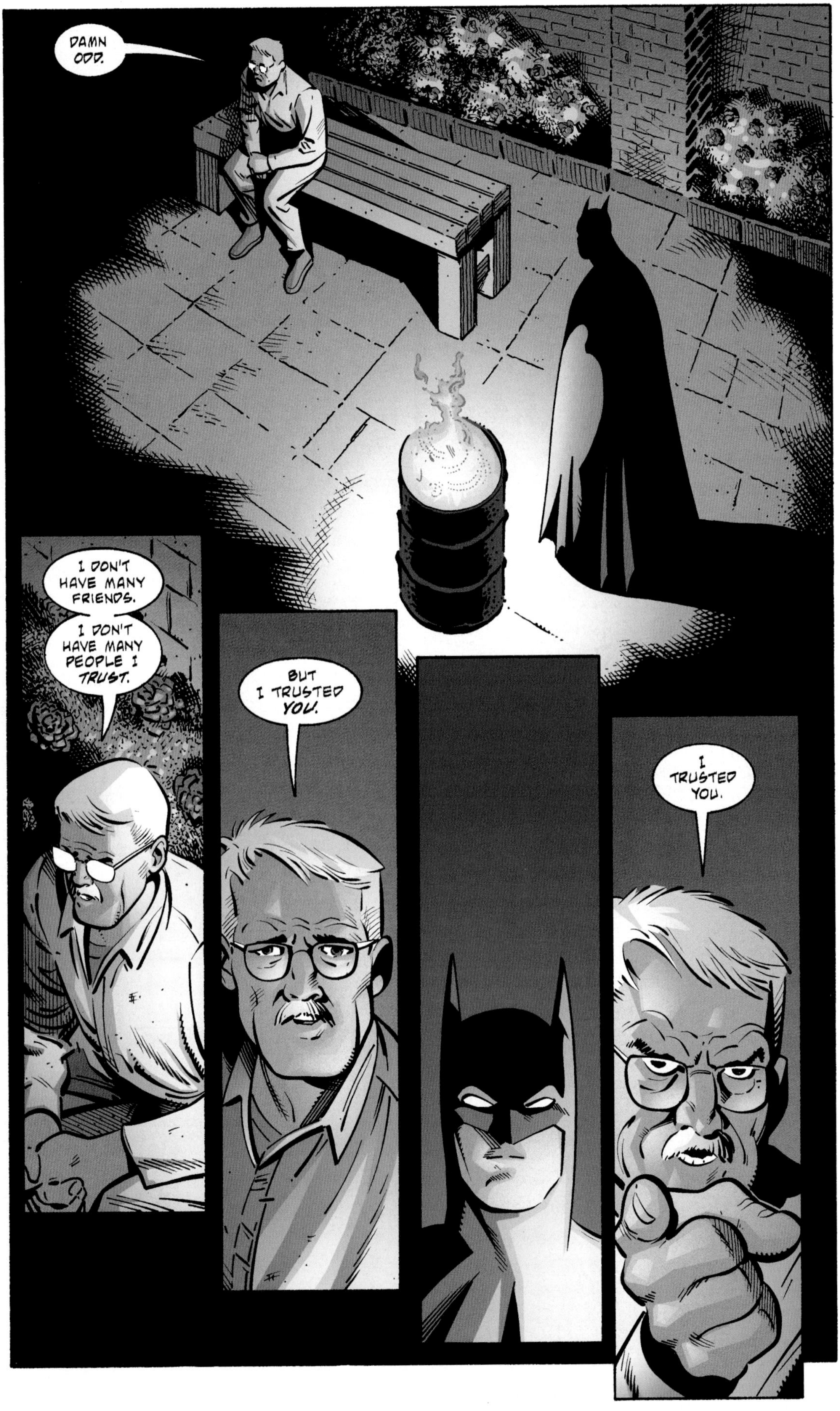
DAMN ODD.
I DON'T HAVE MANY FRIENDS.
I DON'T HAVE MANY PEOPLE I *TRUST*.
BUT I TRUSTED *YOU*.
I TRUSTED YOU.

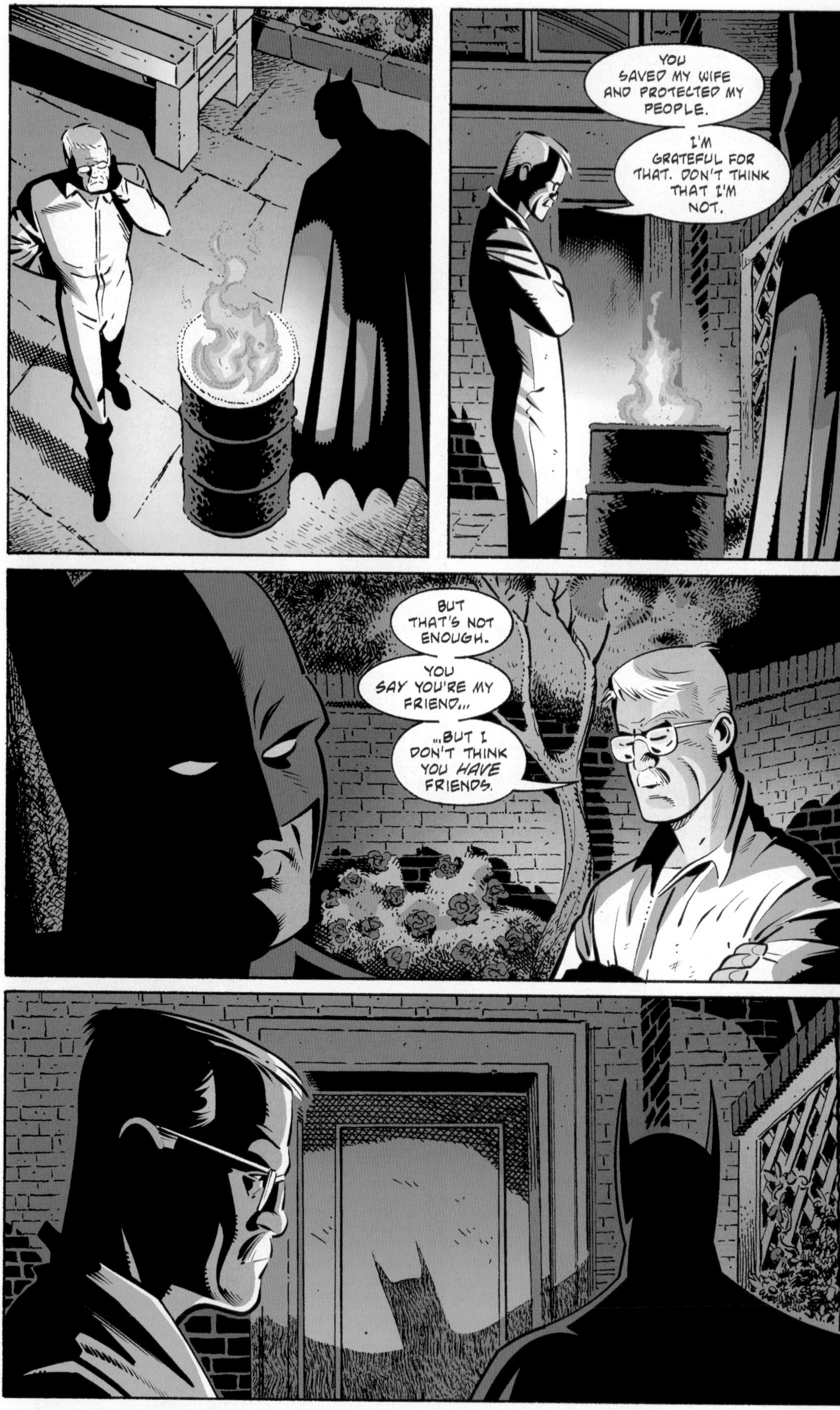

YOU SAVED MY WIFE AND PROTECTED MY PEOPLE.
I'M GRATEFUL FOR THAT. DON'T THINK THAT I'M NOT.
BUT THAT'S NOT ENOUGH.
YOU SAY YOU'RE MY FRIEND...
...BUT I DON'T THINK YOU *HAVE* FRIENDS.

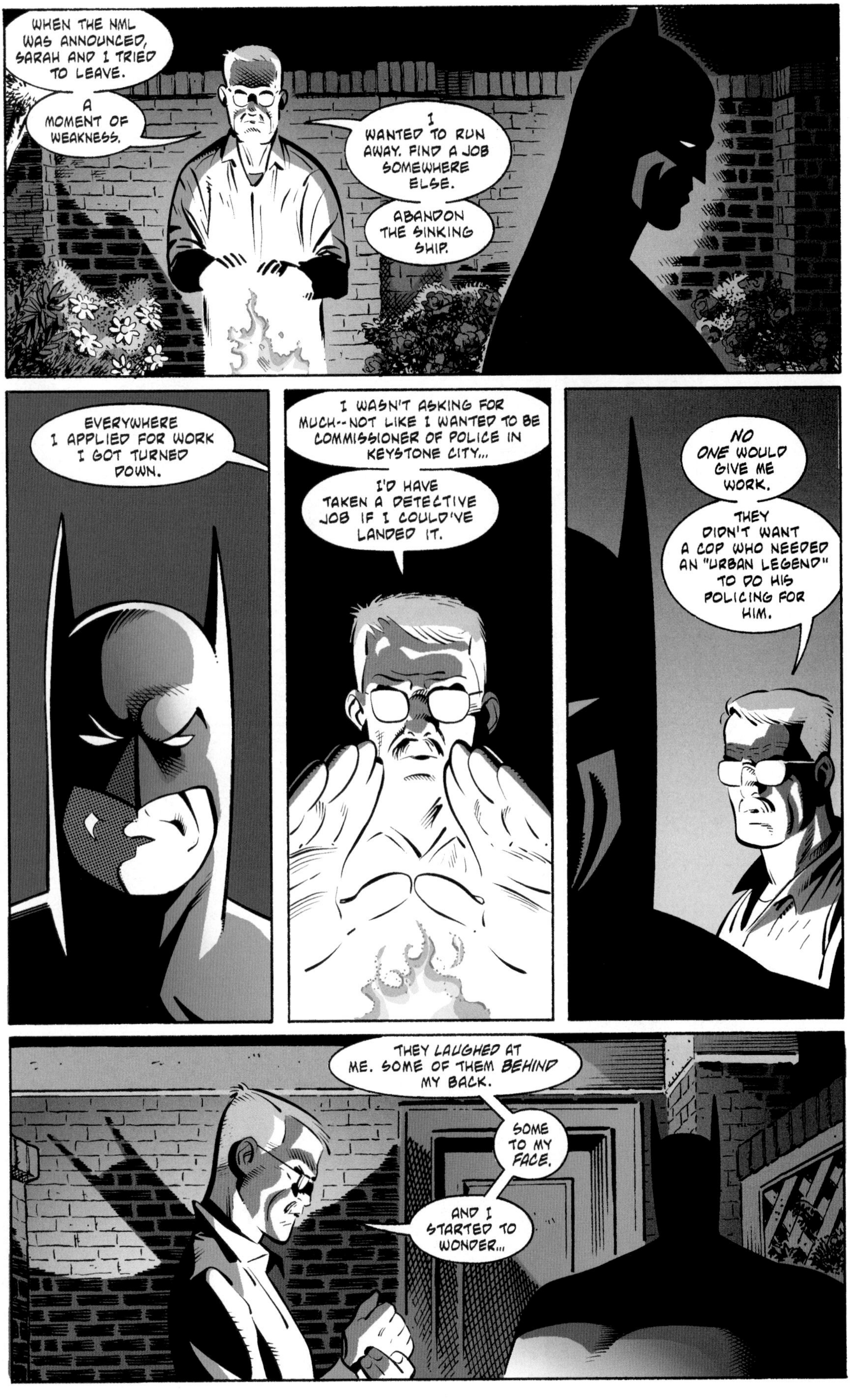
WHEN THE NML WAS ANNOUNCED, SARAH AND I TRIED TO LEAVE.
A MOMENT OF WEAKNESS.
I WANTED TO RUN AWAY. FIND A JOB SOMEWHERE ELSE.
ABANDON THE SINKING SHIP.
EVERYWHERE I APPLIED FOR WORK I GOT TURNED DOWN.
I WASN'T ASKING FOR MUCH--NOT LIKE I WANTED TO BE COMMISSIONER OF POLICE IN KEYSTONE CITY...
I'D HAVE TAKEN A DETECTIVE JOB IF I COULD'VE LANDED IT.
NO ONE WOULD GIVE ME WORK.
THEY DIDN'T WANT A COP WHO NEEDED AN "URBAN LEGEND" TO DO HIS POLICING FOR HIM.
THEY LAUGHED AT ME. SOME OF THEM BEHIND MY BACK.
SOME TO MY FACE.
AND I STARTED TO WONDER...

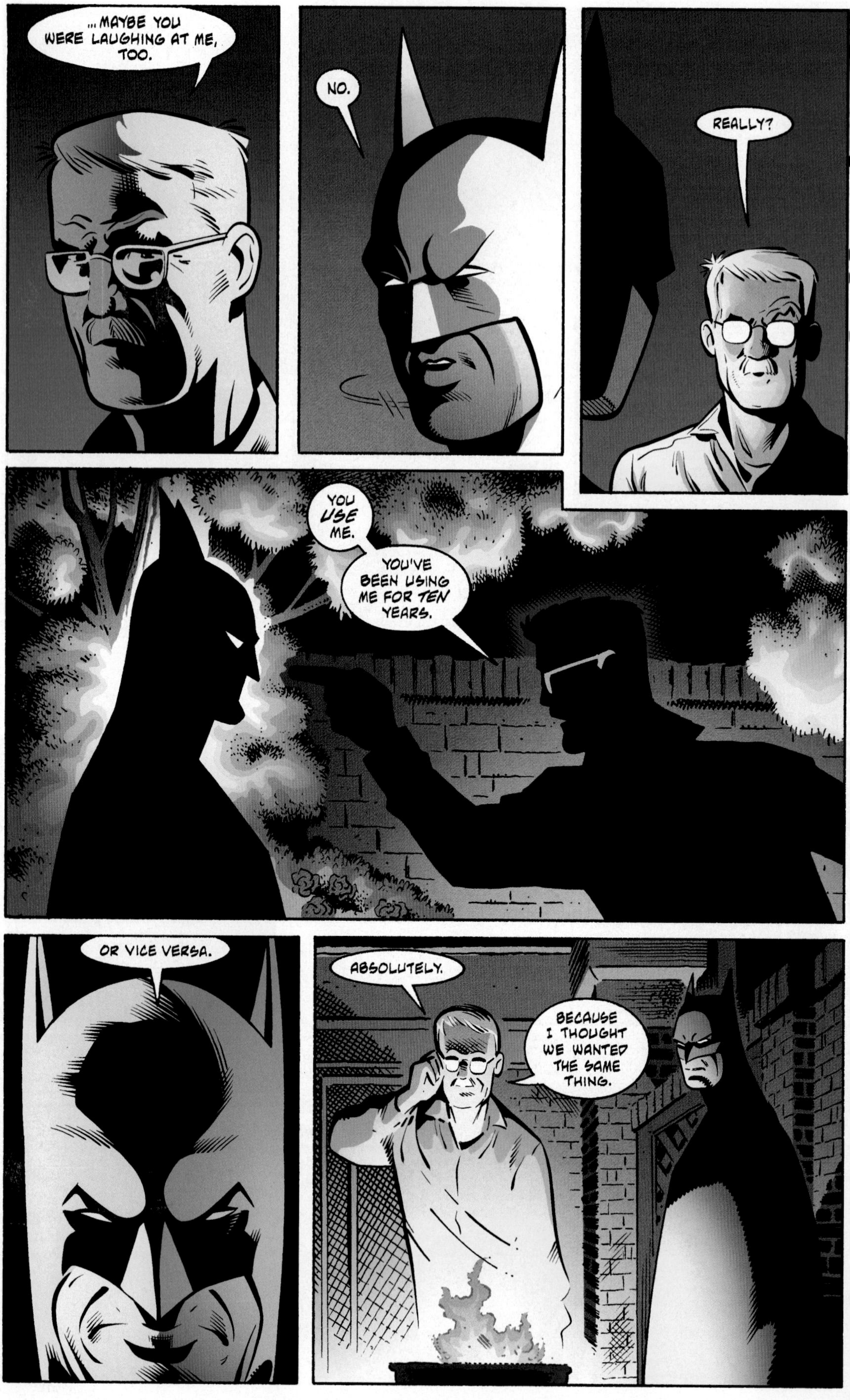
...MAYBE YOU WERE LAUGHING AT ME, TOO.
NO.
REALLY?
YOU *USE* ME.
YOU'VE BEEN USING ME FOR *TEN* YEARS.
OR VICE VERSA.
ABSOLUTELY.
BECAUSE I THOUGHT WE WANTED THE SAME THING.

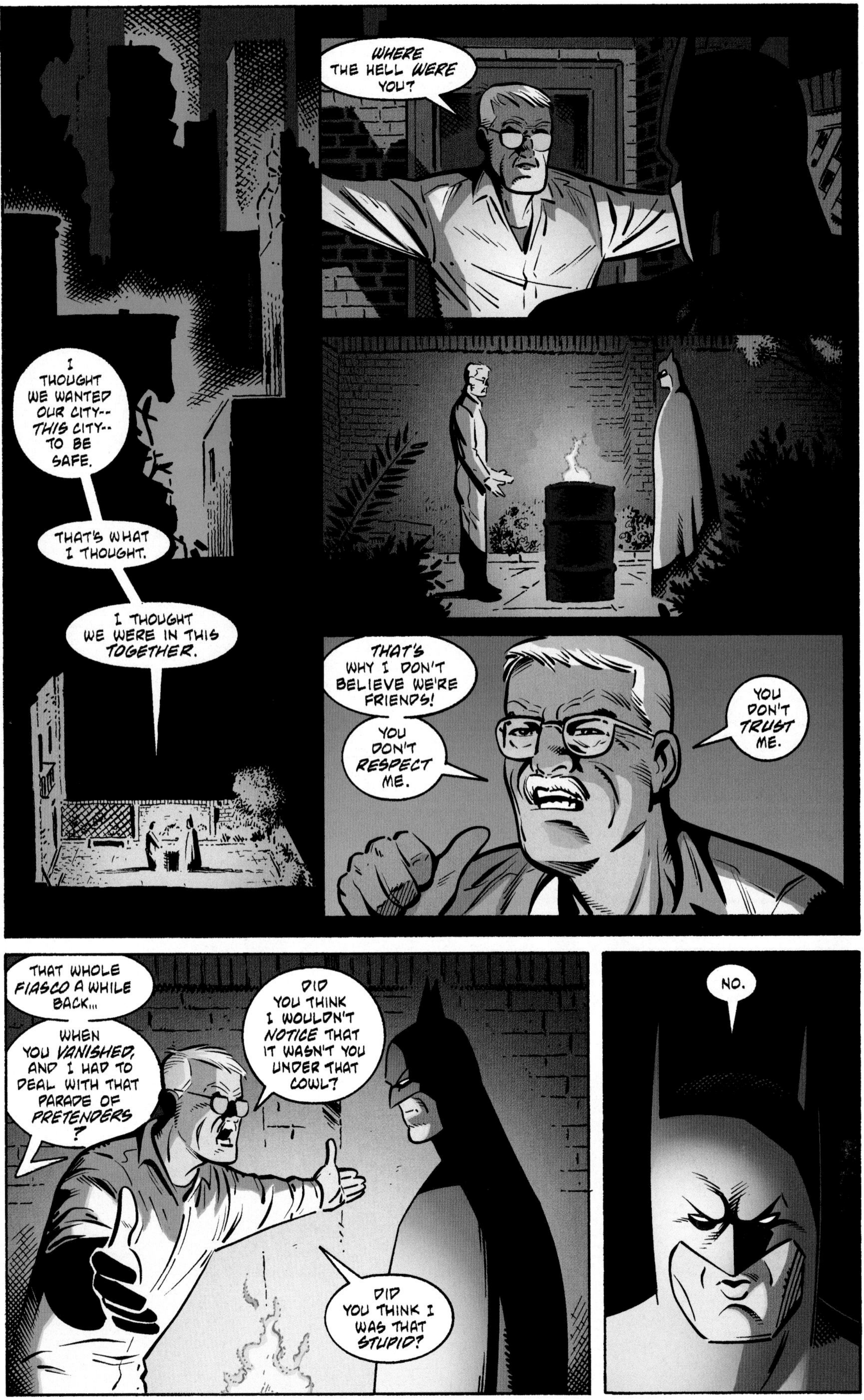
WHERE THE HELL WERE YOU?
I THOUGHT WE WANTED OUR CITY-- THIS CITY-- TO BE SAFE.
THAT'S WHAT I THOUGHT.
I THOUGHT WE WERE IN THIS TOGETHER.
THAT'S WHY I DON'T BELIEVE WE'RE FRIENDS!
YOU DON'T RESPECT ME.
YOU DON'T TRUST ME.
THAT WHOLE FIASCO A WHILE BACK...
WHEN YOU VANISHED, AND I HAD TO DEAL WITH THAT PARADE OF PRETENDERS?
DID YOU THINK I WOULDN'T NOTICE THAT IT WASN'T YOU UNDER THAT COWL?
DID YOU THINK I WAS THAT STUPID?
NO.

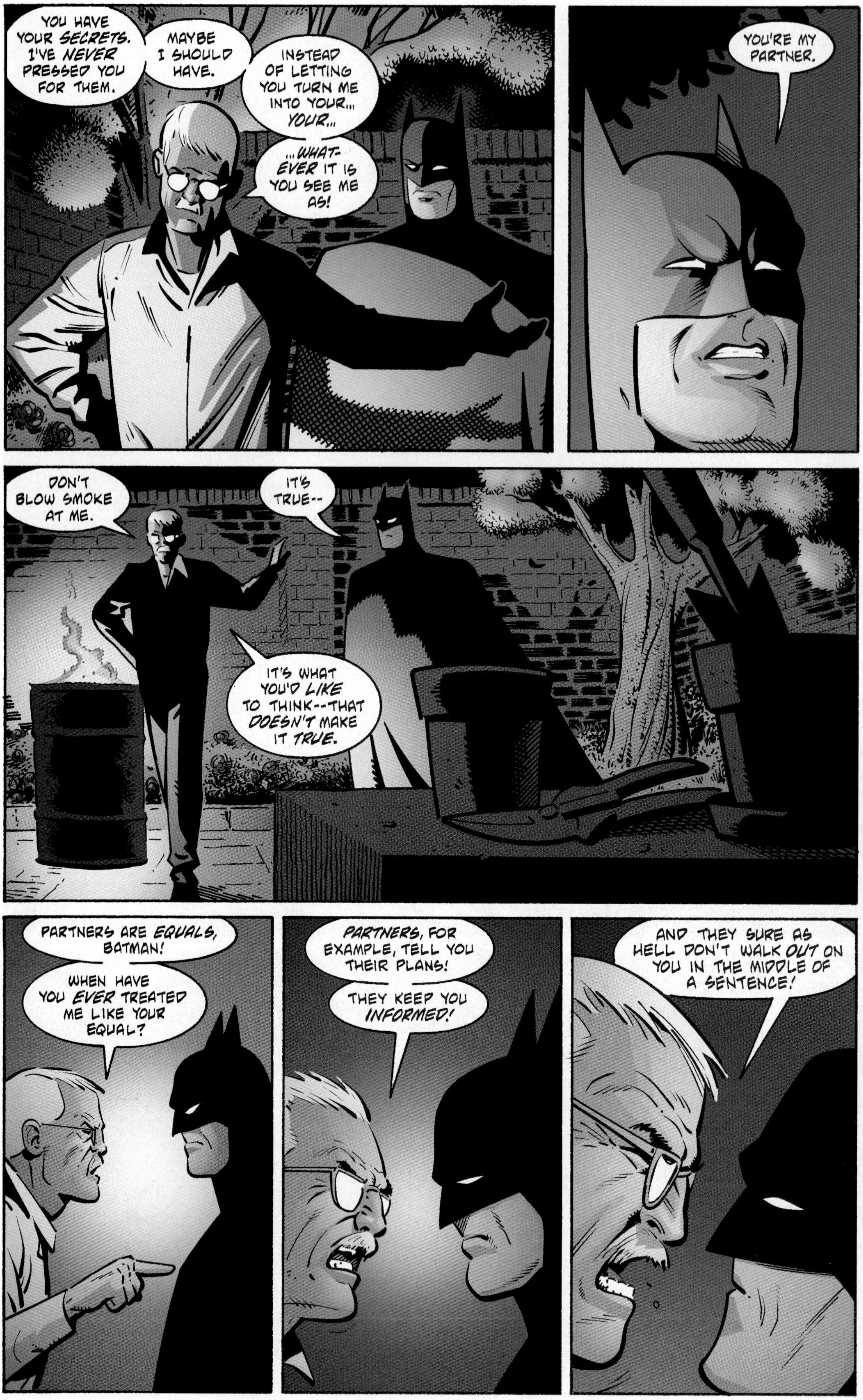
YOU HAVE YOUR SECRETS. I'VE NEVER PRESSED YOU FOR THEM.
MAYBE I SHOULD HAVE.
INSTEAD OF LETTING YOU TURN ME INTO YOUR... YOUR...
...WHAT-EVER IT IS YOU SEE ME AS!
YOU'RE MY PARTNER.
DON'T BLOW SMOKE AT ME.
IT'S TRUE--
IT'S WHAT YOU'D LIKE TO THINK--THAT DOESN'T MAKE IT TRUE.
PARTNERS ARE EQUALS, BATMAN!
WHEN HAVE YOU EVER TREATED ME LIKE YOUR EQUAL?
PARTNERS, FOR EXAMPLE, TELL YOU THEIR PLANS!
THEY KEEP YOU INFORMED!
AND THEY SURE AS HELL DON'T WALK OUT ON YOU IN THE MIDDLE OF A SENTENCE!

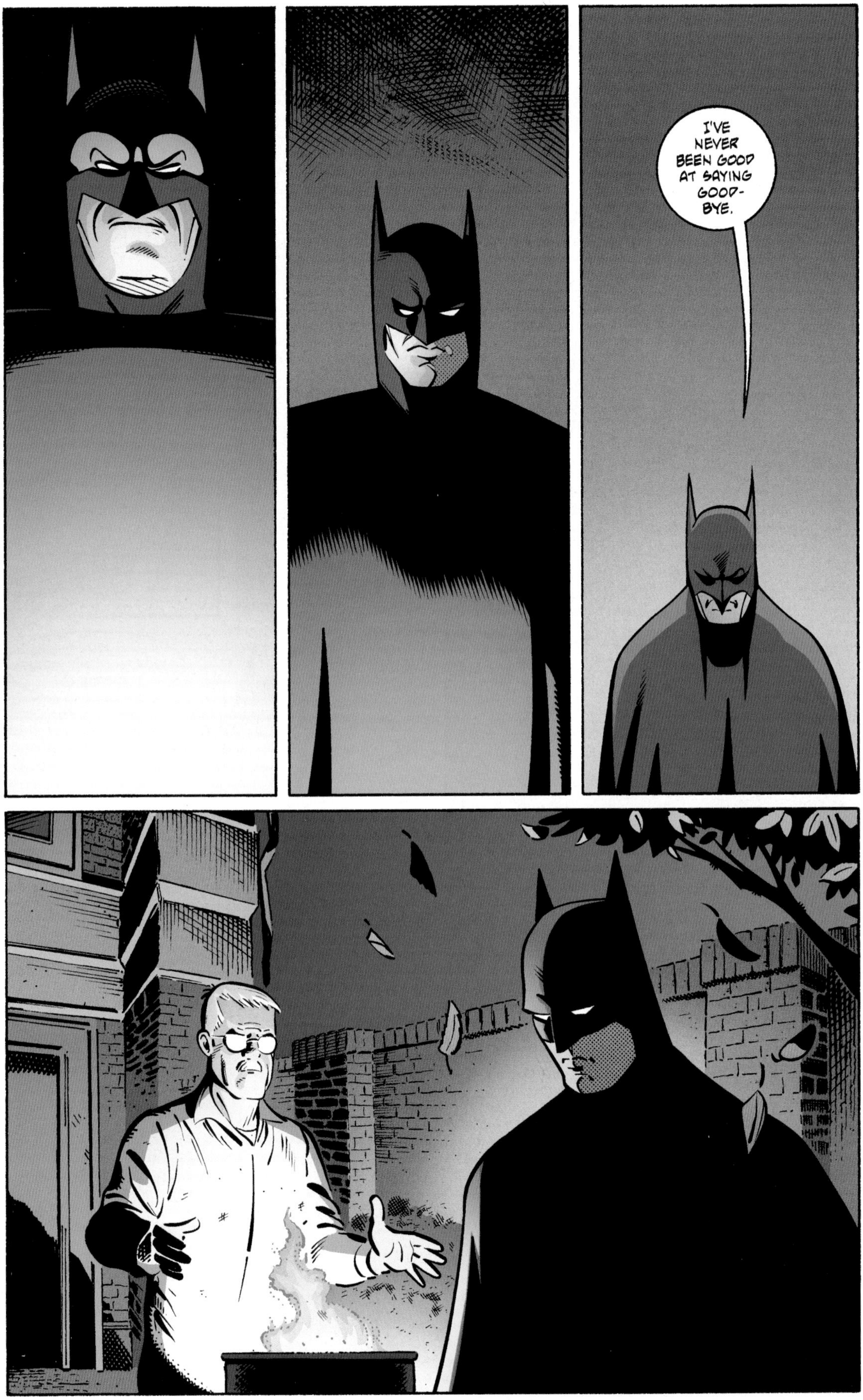
I'VE NEVER BEEN GOOD AT SAYING GOOD-BYE.

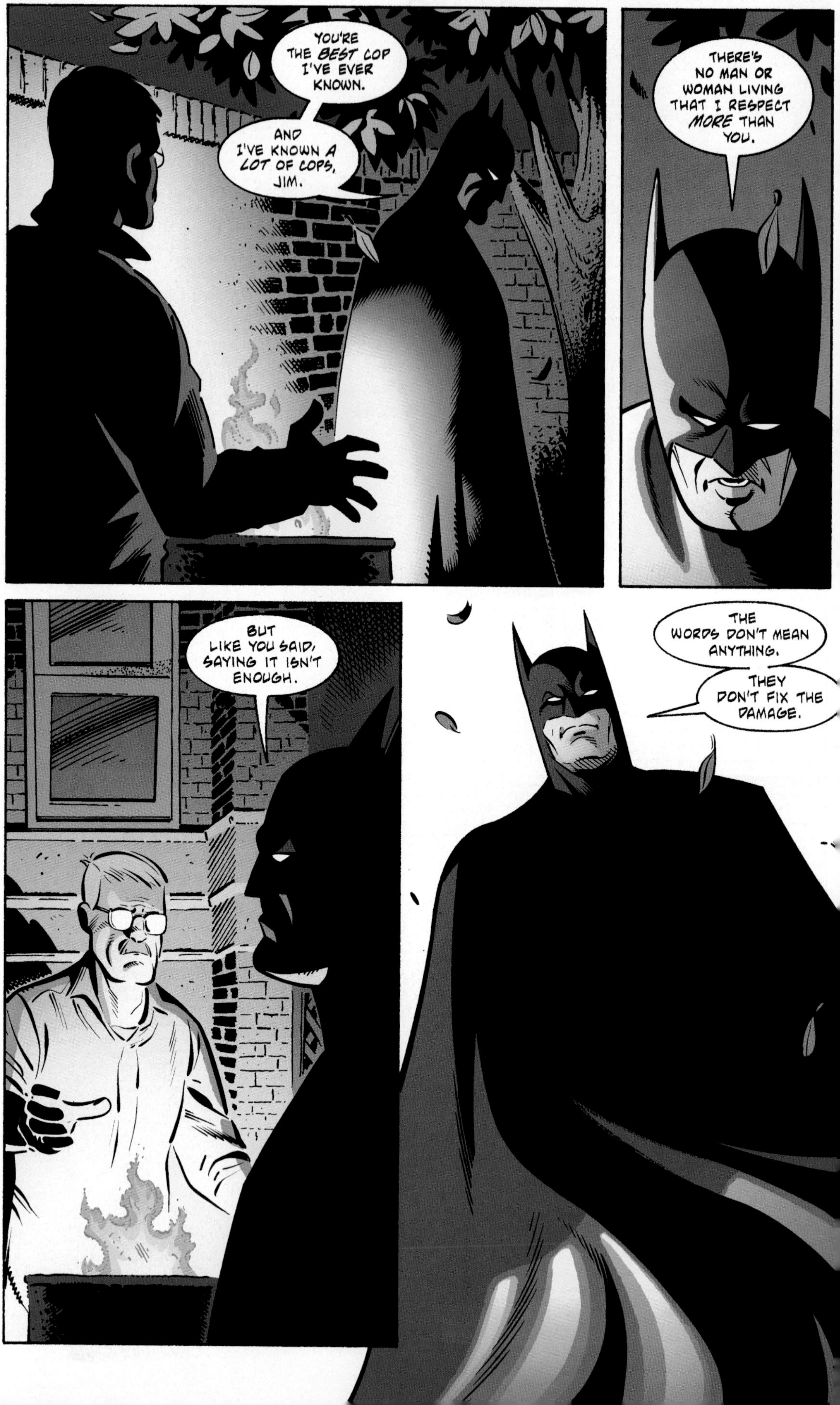
YOU'RE THE BEST COP I'VE EVER KNOWN.
AND I'VE KNOWN A LOT OF COPS, JIM.
THERE'S NO MAN OR WOMAN LIVING THAT I RESPECT MORE THAN YOU.
BUT LIKE YOU SAID, SAYING IT ISN'T ENOUGH.
THE WORDS DON'T MEAN ANYTHING.
THEY DON'T FIX THE DAMAGE.

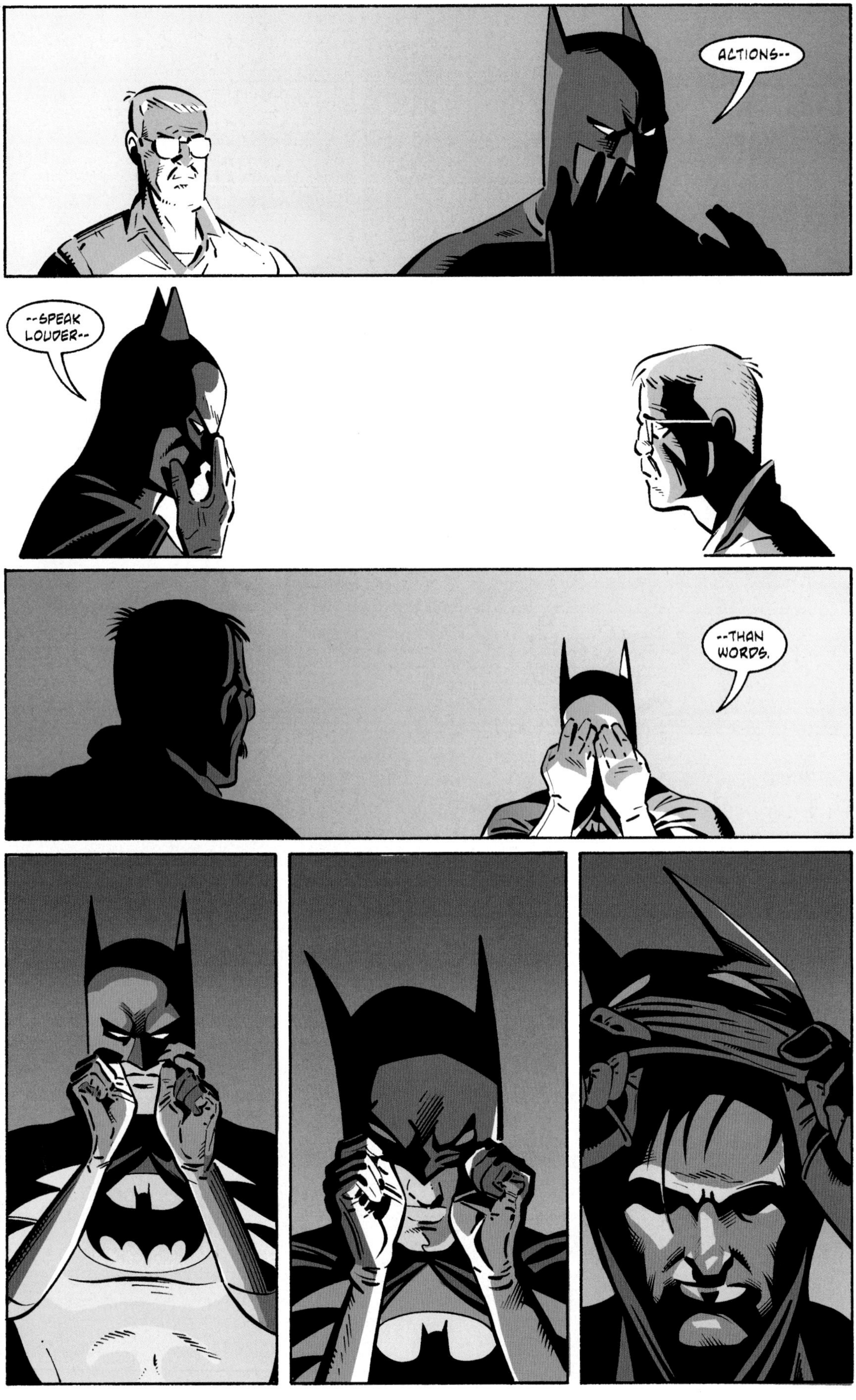
ACTIONS--
--SPEAK LOUDER--
--THAN WORDS.

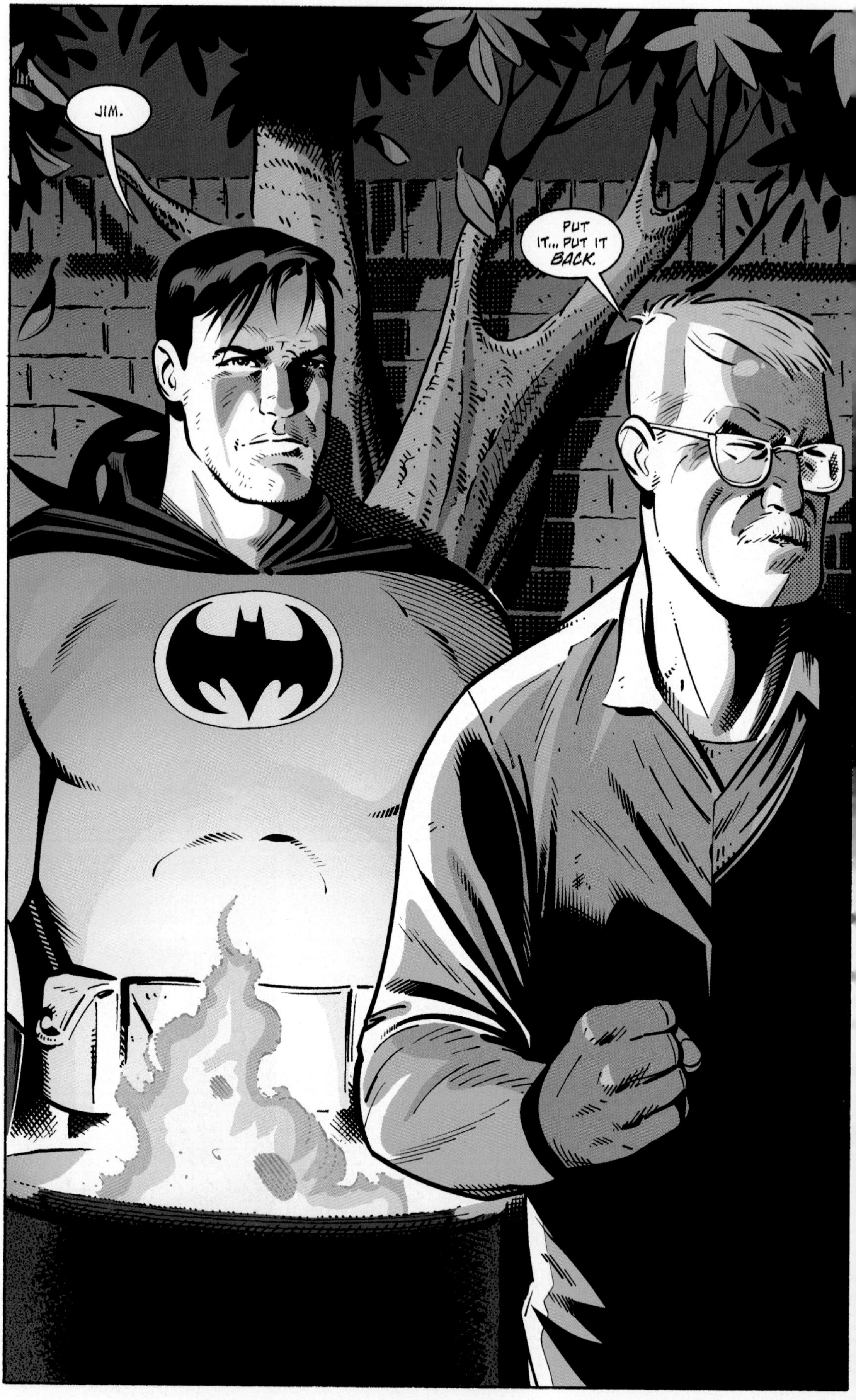
JIM.
PUT IT... PUT IT BACK.

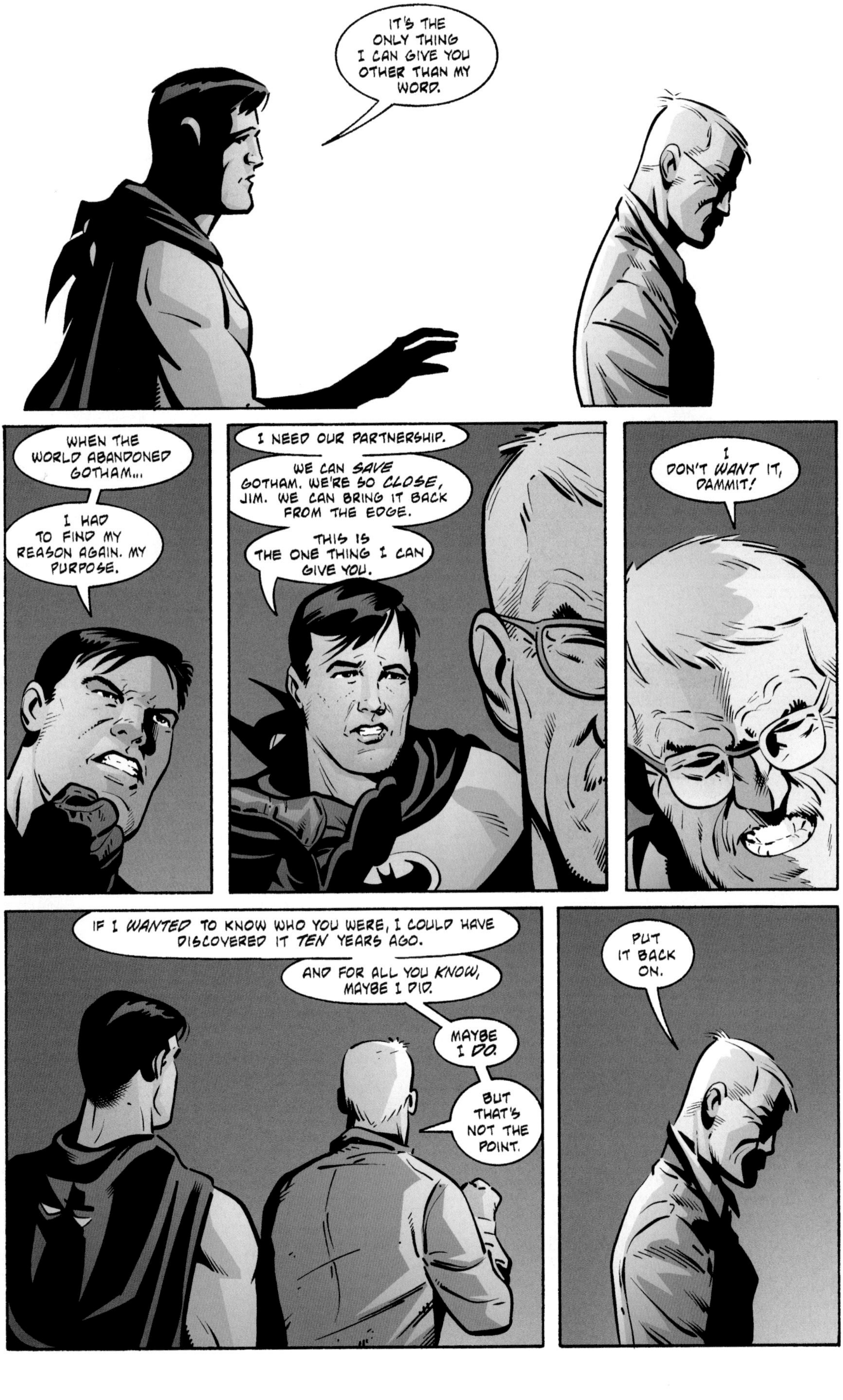
IT'S THE ONLY THING I CAN GIVE YOU OTHER THAN MY WORD.
WHEN THE WORLD ABANDONED GOTHAM...
I HAD TO FIND MY REASON AGAIN. MY PURPOSE.
I NEED OUR PARTNERSHIP.
WE CAN SAVE GOTHAM. WE'RE SO CLOSE, JIM. WE CAN BRING IT BACK FROM THE EDGE.
THIS IS THE ONE THING I CAN GIVE YOU.
I DON'T WANT IT, DAMMIT!
IF I WANTED TO KNOW WHO YOU WERE, I COULD HAVE DISCOVERED IT TEN YEARS AGO.
AND FOR ALL YOU KNOW, MAYBE I DID.
MAYBE I DO.
BUT THAT'S NOT THE POINT.
PUT IT BACK ON.

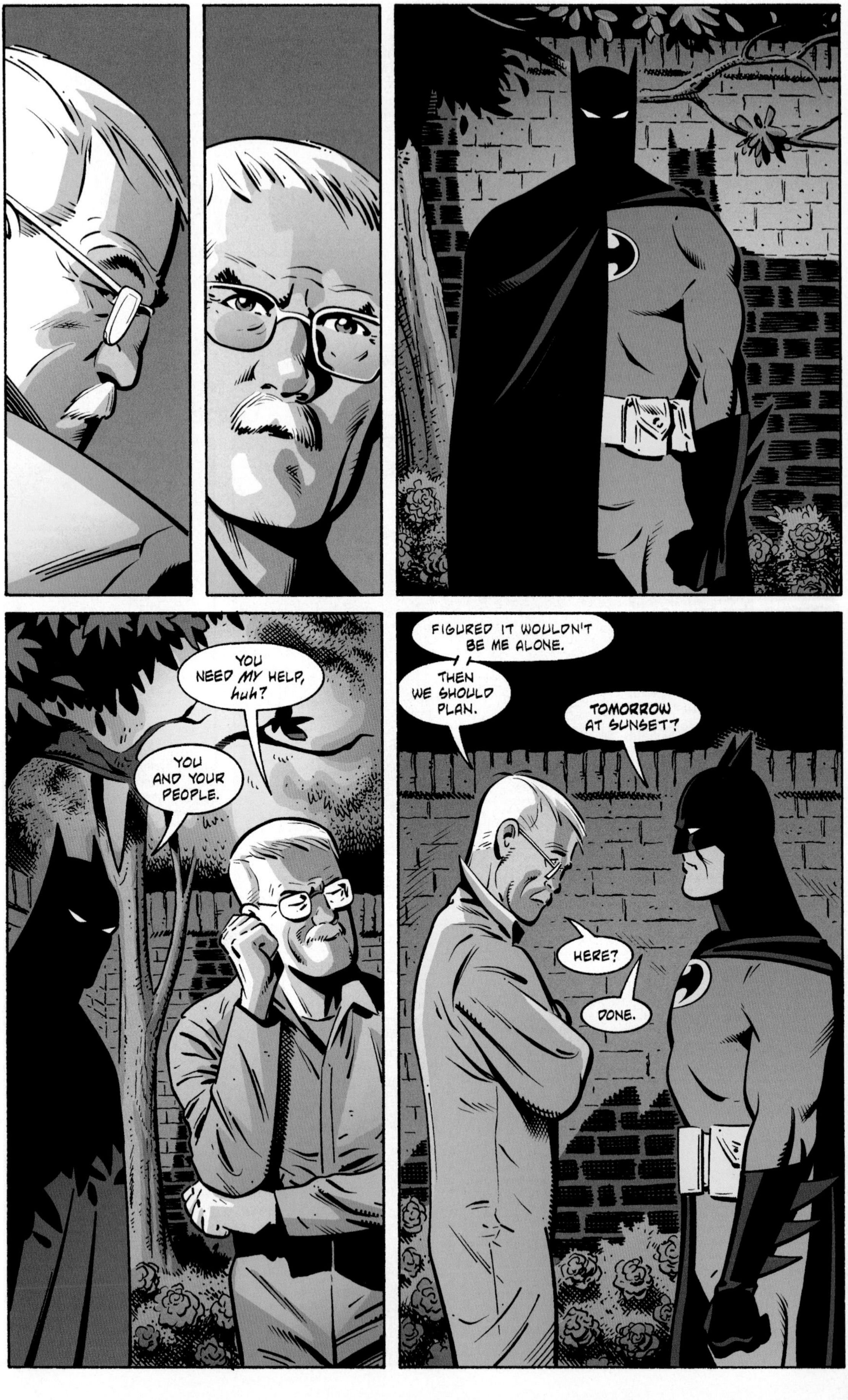
YOU NEED MY HELP, huh?
YOU AND YOUR PEOPLE.
FIGURED IT WOULDN'T BE ME ALONE.
THEN WE SHOULD PLAN.
TOMORROW AT SUNSET?
HERE?
DONE.

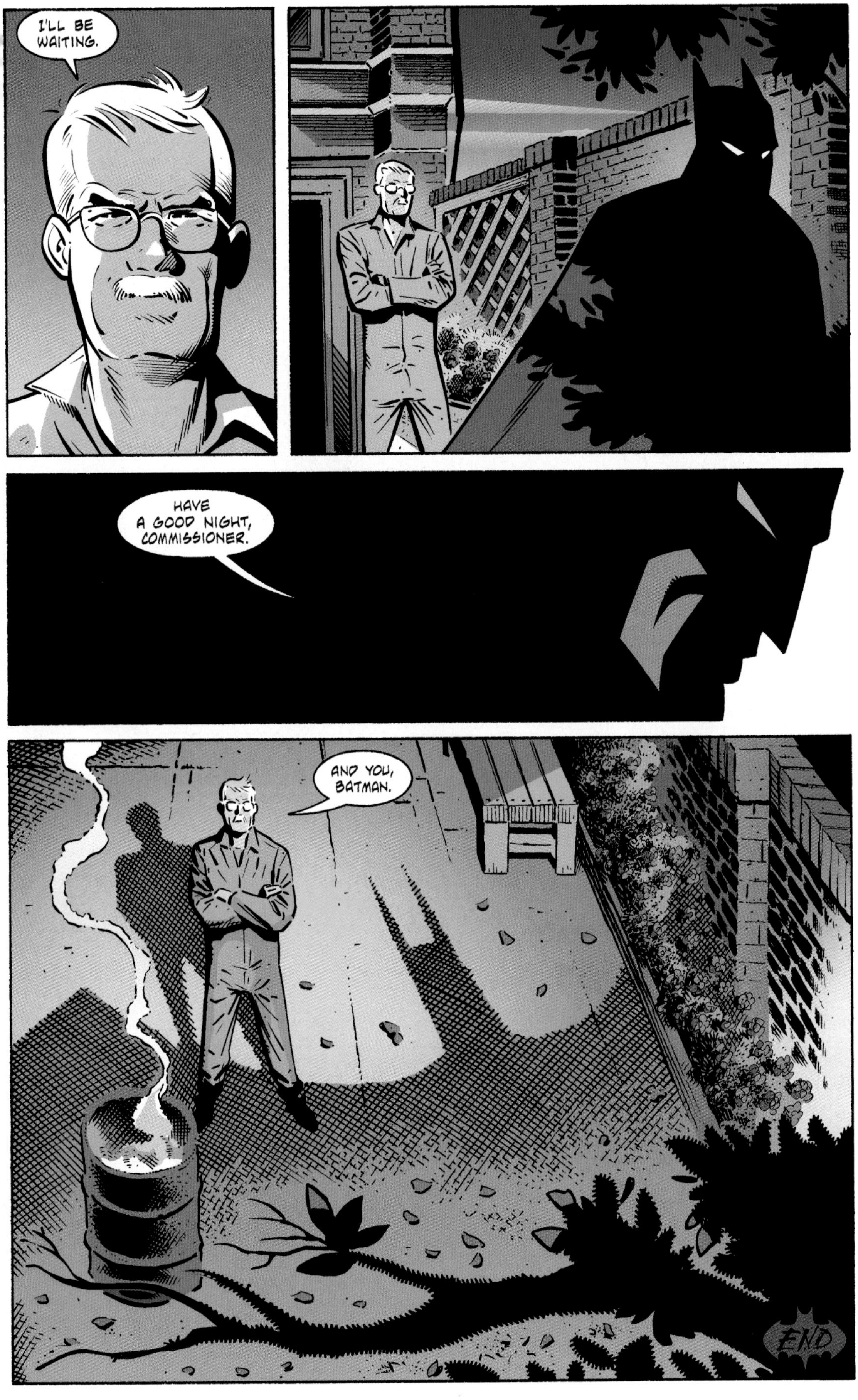
I'LL BE WAITING.
HAVE A GOOD NIGHT, COMMISSIONER.
AND YOU, BATMAN.
END

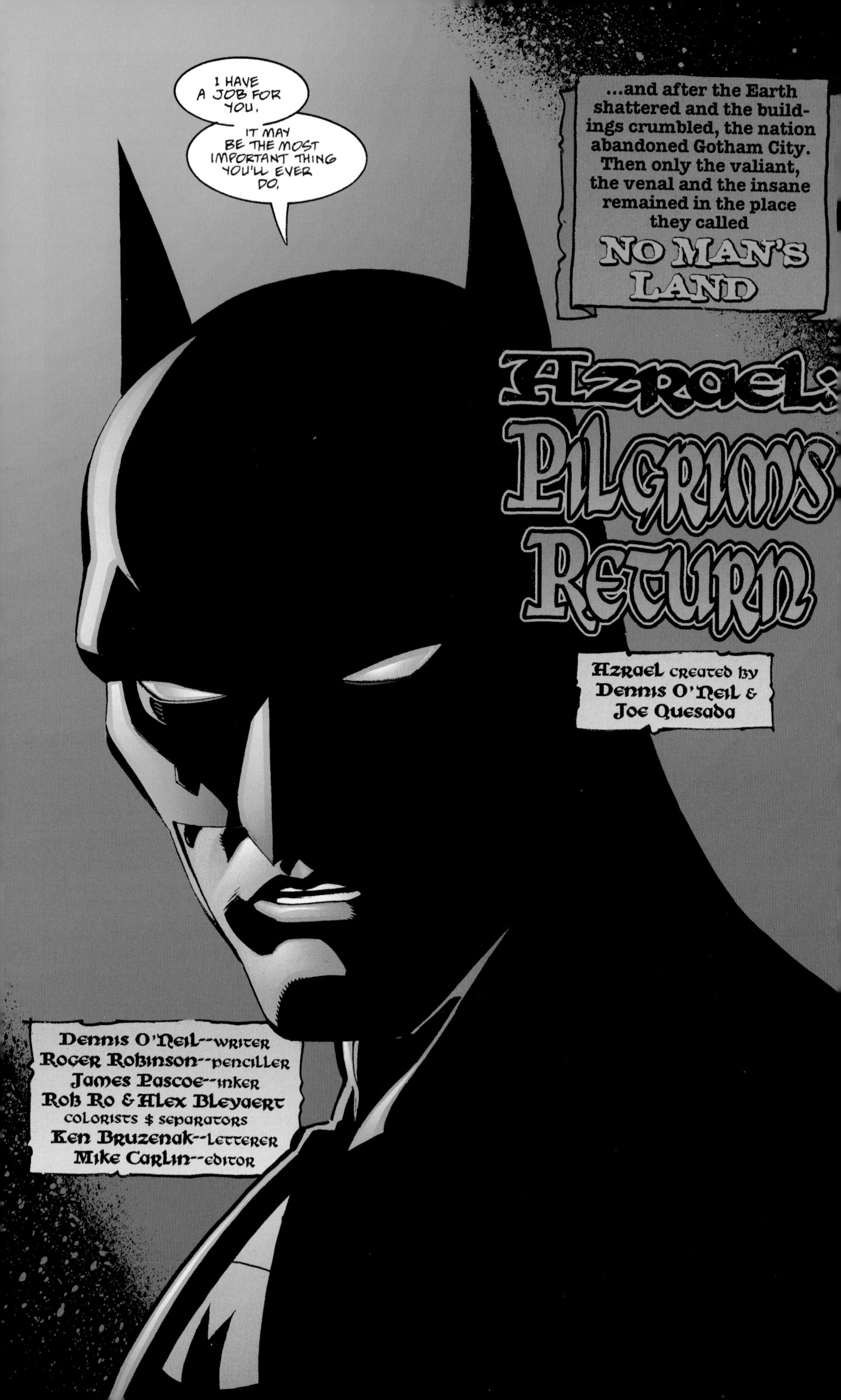

I HAVE A JOB FOR YOU.
IT MAY BE THE MOST IMPORTANT THING YOU'LL EVER DO.
...and after the Earth shattered and the buildings crumbled, the nation abandoned Gotham City. Then only the valiant, the venal and the insane remained in the place they called
NO MAN'S LAND
Azrael: Pilgrim's Return
Azrael created by Dennis O'Neil & Joe Quesada
Dennis O'Neil--writer
Roger Robinson--penciller
James Pascoe--inker
Rob Ro & Alex Bleyaert
colorists $ separators
Ken Bruzenak--letterer
Mike Carlin--editor

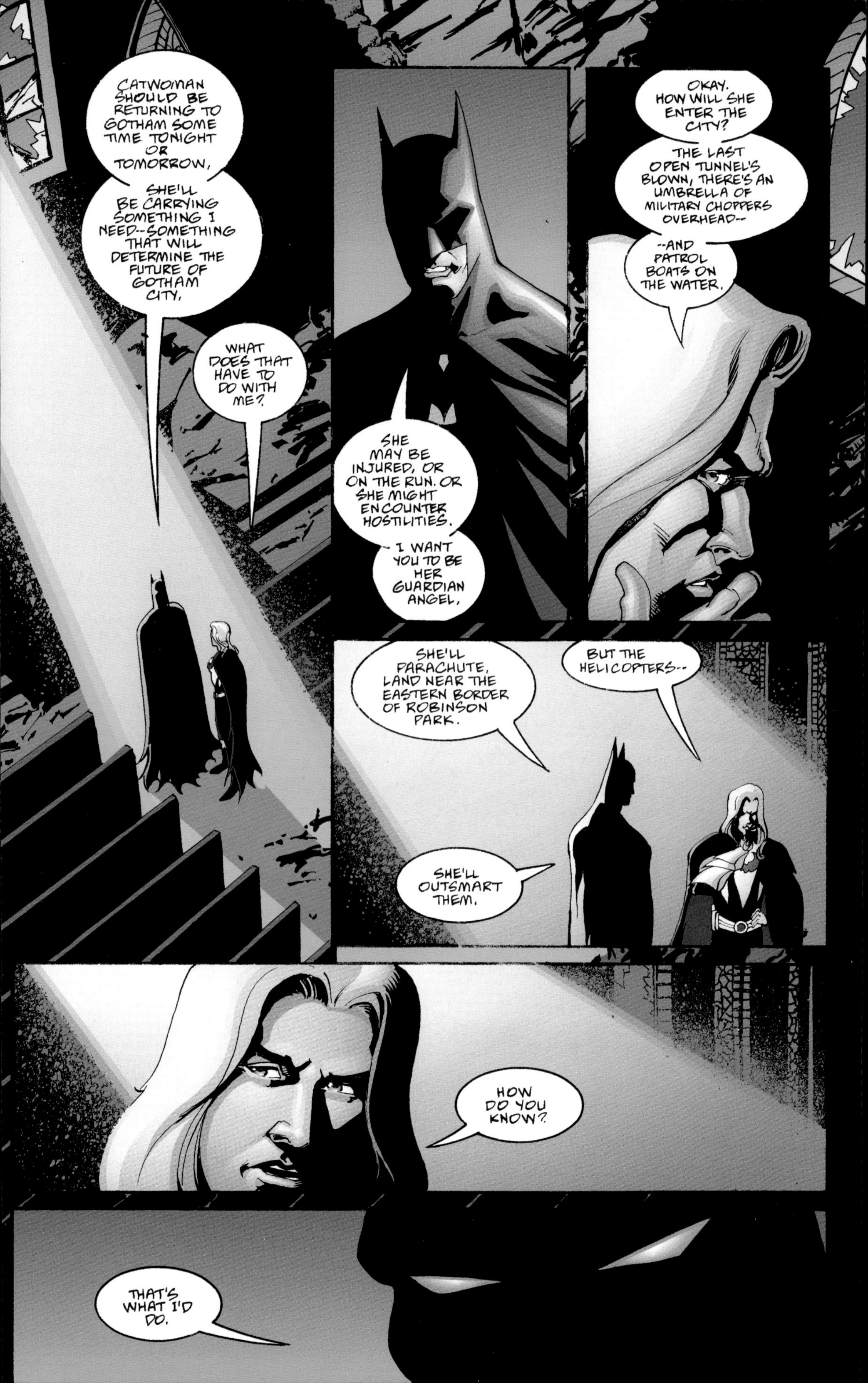
CATWOMAN SHOULD BE RETURNING TO GOTHAM SOME TIME TONIGHT OR TOMORROW.
SHE'LL BE CARRYING SOMETHING I NEED--SOMETHING THAT WILL DETERMINE THE FUTURE OF GOTHAM CITY.
WHAT DOES THAT HAVE TO DO WITH ME?
SHE MAY BE INJURED, OR ON THE RUN. OR SHE MIGHT ENCOUNTER HOSTILITIES.
I WANT YOU TO BE HER GUARDIAN ANGEL.
OKAY. HOW WILL SHE ENTER THE CITY?
THE LAST OPEN TUNNEL'S BLOWN, THERE'S AN UMBRELLA OF MILITARY CHOPPERS OVERHEAD--
--AND PATROL BOATS ON THE WATER.
SHE'LL PARACHUTE, LAND NEAR THE EASTERN BORDER OF ROBINSON PARK.
BUT THE HELICOPTERS--
SHE'LL OUTSMART THEM.
HOW DO YOU KNOW?
THAT'S WHAT I'D DO.

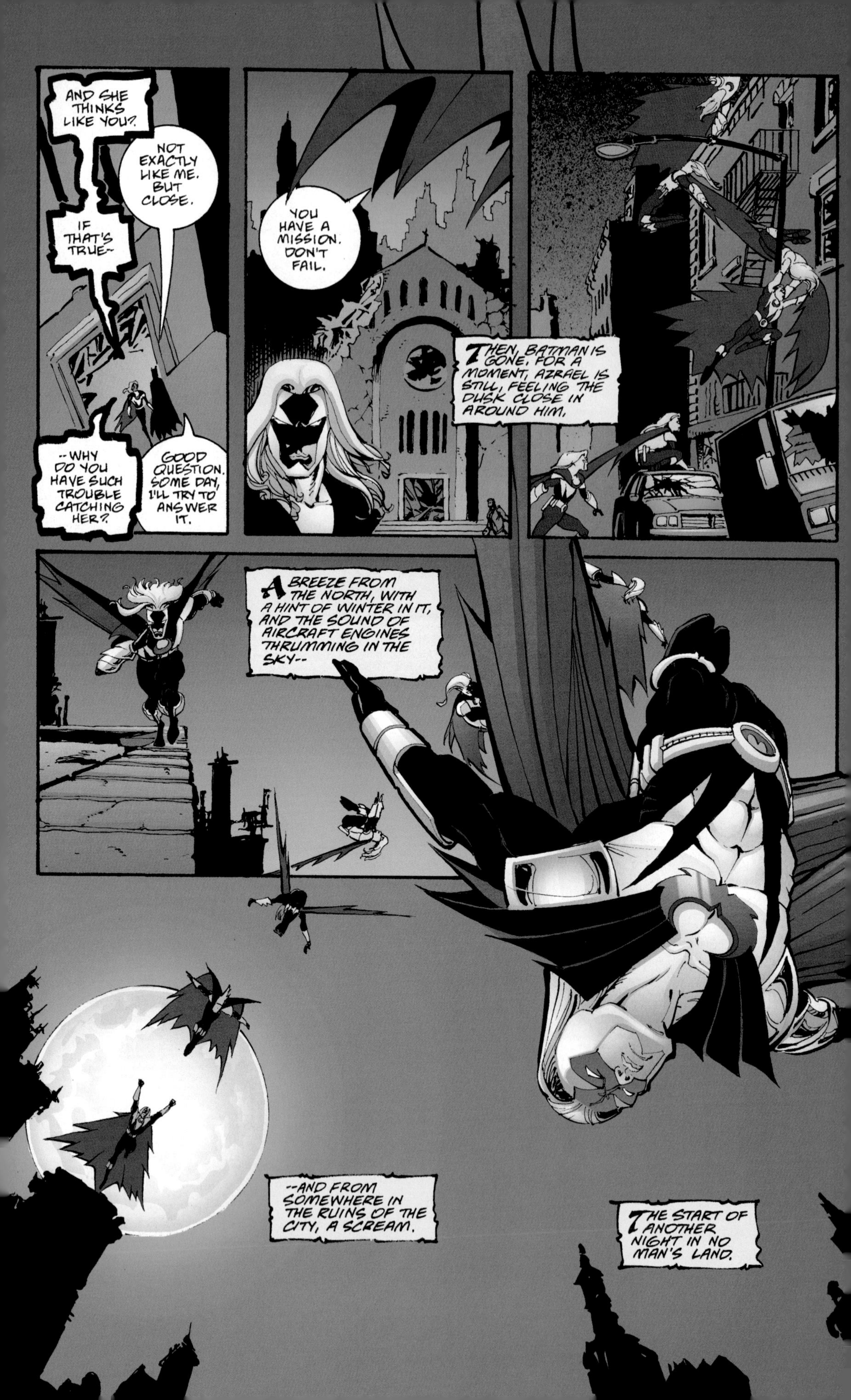
AND SHE THINKS LIKE YOU?
NOT EXACTLY LIKE ME. BUT CLOSE.
IF THAT'S TRUE--
--WHY DO YOU HAVE SUCH TROUBLE CATCHING HER?
GOOD QUESTION. SOME DAY, I'LL TRY TO ANSWER IT.
YOU HAVE A MISSION. DON'T FAIL.
THEN, BATMAN IS GONE. FOR A MOMENT, AZRAEL IS STILL, FEELING THE DUSK CLOSE IN AROUND HIM.
A BREEZE FROM THE NORTH, WITH A HINT OF WINTER IN IT, AND THE SOUND OF AIRCRAFT ENGINES THRUMMING IN THE SKY--
--AND FROM SOMEWHERE IN THE RUINS OF THE CITY, A SCREAM.
THE START OF ANOTHER NIGHT IN NO MAN'S LAND.

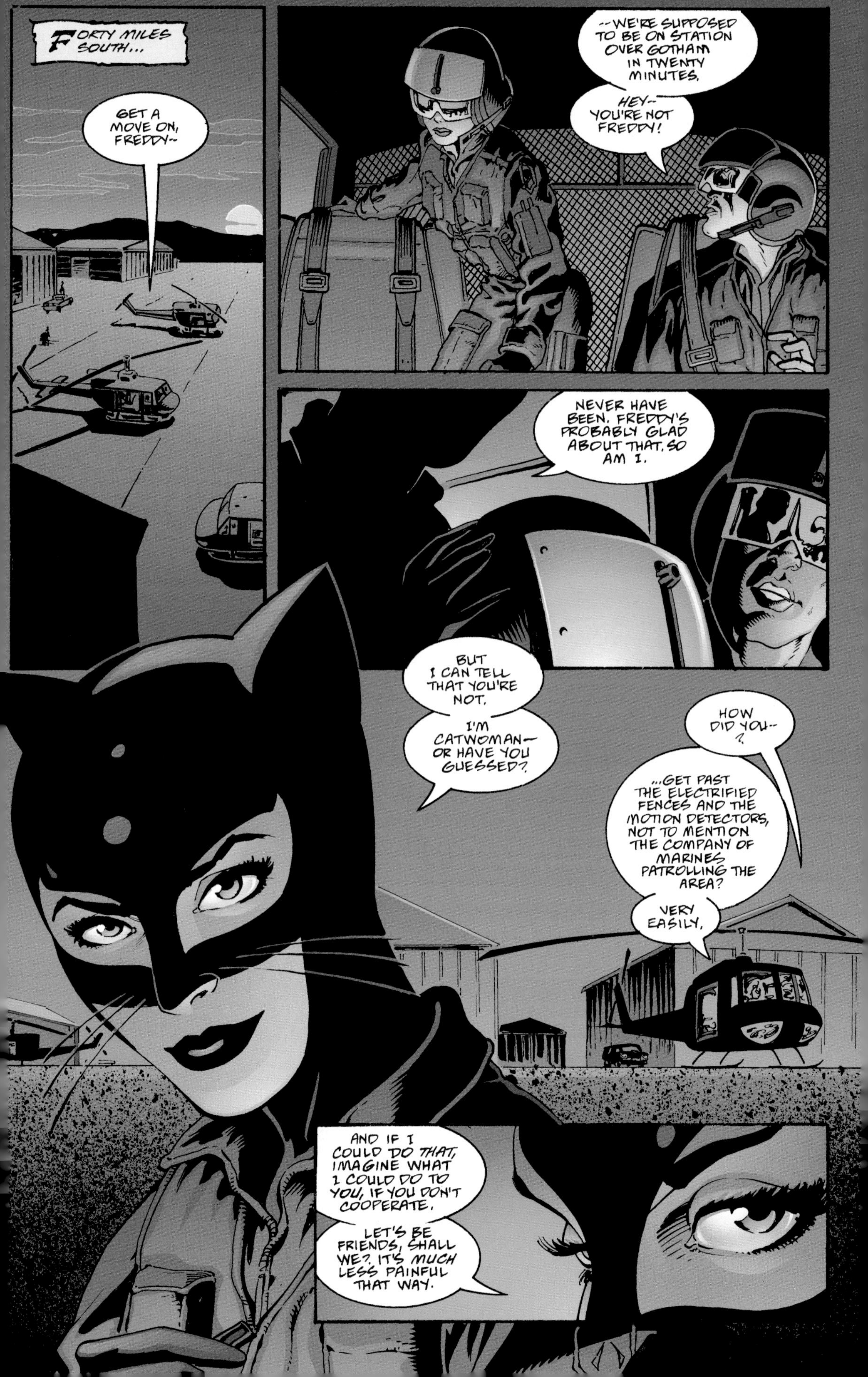
FORTY MILES SOUTH...
GET A MOVE ON, FREDDY--
--WE'RE SUPPOSED TO BE ON STATION OVER GOTHAM IN TWENTY MINUTES.
HEY-- YOU'RE NOT FREDDY!
NEVER HAVE BEEN. FREDDY'S PROBABLY GLAD ABOUT THAT. SO AM I.
BUT I CAN TELL THAT YOU'RE NOT.
I'M CATWOMAN-- OR HAVE YOU GUESSED?
HOW DID YOU-- ?
...GET PAST THE ELECTRIFIED FENCES AND THE MOTION DETECTORS, NOT TO MENTION THE COMPANY OF MARINES PATROLLING THE AREA?
VERY EASILY.
AND IF I COULD DO THAT, IMAGINE WHAT I COULD DO TO YOU, IF YOU DON'T COOPERATE.
LET'S BE FRIENDS, SHALL WE? IT'S MUCH LESS PAINFUL THAT WAY.

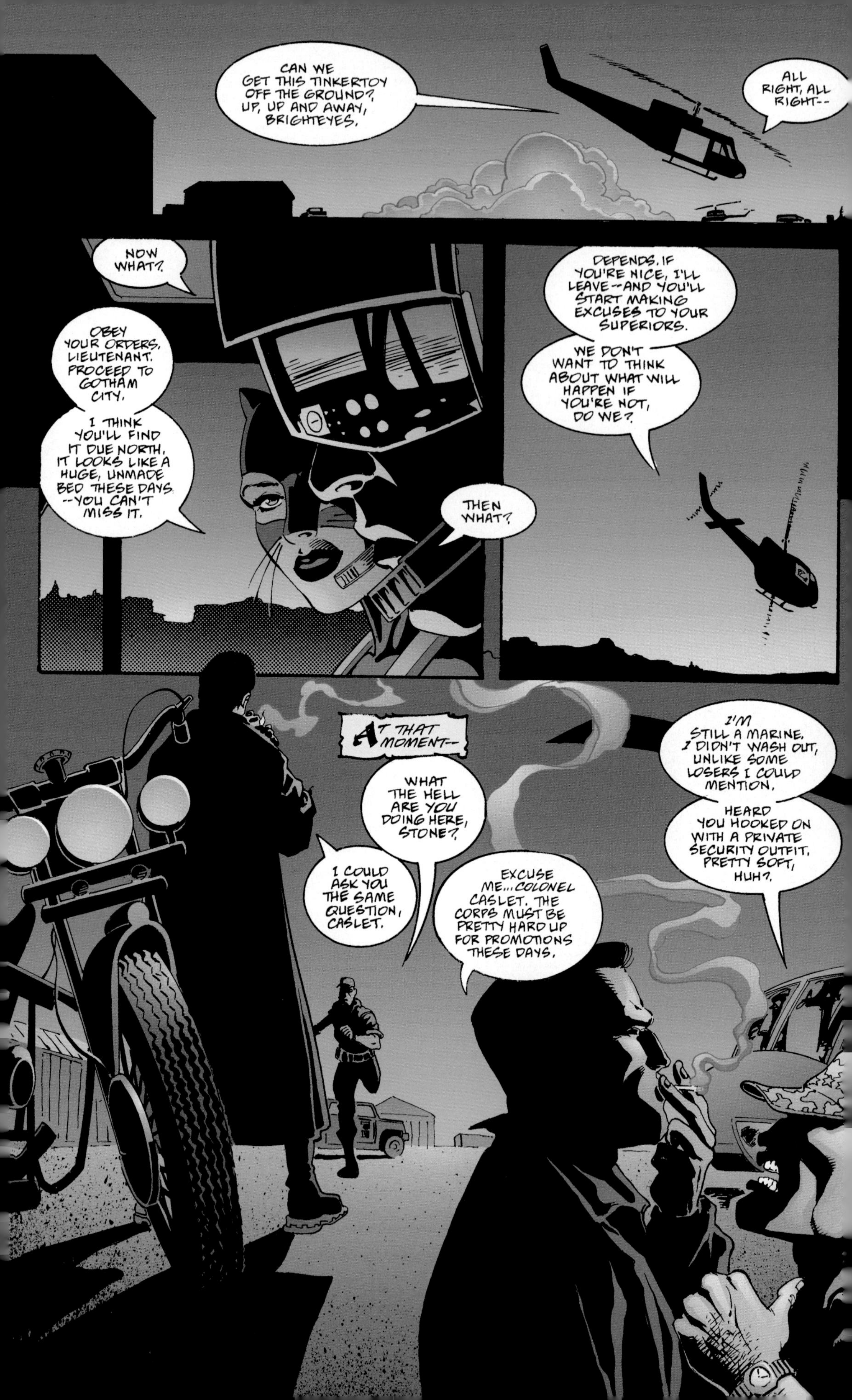
CAN WE GET THIS TINKERTOY OFF THE GROUND? UP, UP AND AWAY, BRIGHTEYES.
ALL RIGHT, ALL RIGHT--
NOW WHAT?
OBEY YOUR ORDERS, LIEUTENANT. PROCEED TO GOTHAM CITY.
I THINK YOU'LL FIND IT DUE NORTH. IT LOOKS LIKE A HUGE, UNMADE BED THESE DAYS. --YOU CAN'T MISS IT.
THEN WHAT?
DEPENDS. IF YOU'RE NICE, I'LL LEAVE--AND YOU'LL START MAKING EXCUSES TO YOUR SUPERIORS.
WE DON'T WANT TO THINK ABOUT WHAT WILL HAPPEN IF YOU'RE NOT, DO WE?
AT THAT MOMENT--
WHAT THE HELL ARE YOU DOING HERE, STONE?
I COULD ASK YOU THE SAME QUESTION, CASLET.
EXCUSE ME...COLONEL CASLET. THE CORPS MUST BE PRETTY HARD UP FOR PROMOTIONS THESE DAYS.
I'M STILL A MARINE. I DIDN'T WASH OUT, UNLIKE SOME LOSERS I COULD MENTION.
HEARD YOU HOOKED ON WITH A PRIVATE SECURITY OUTFIT. PRETTY SOFT, HUH?

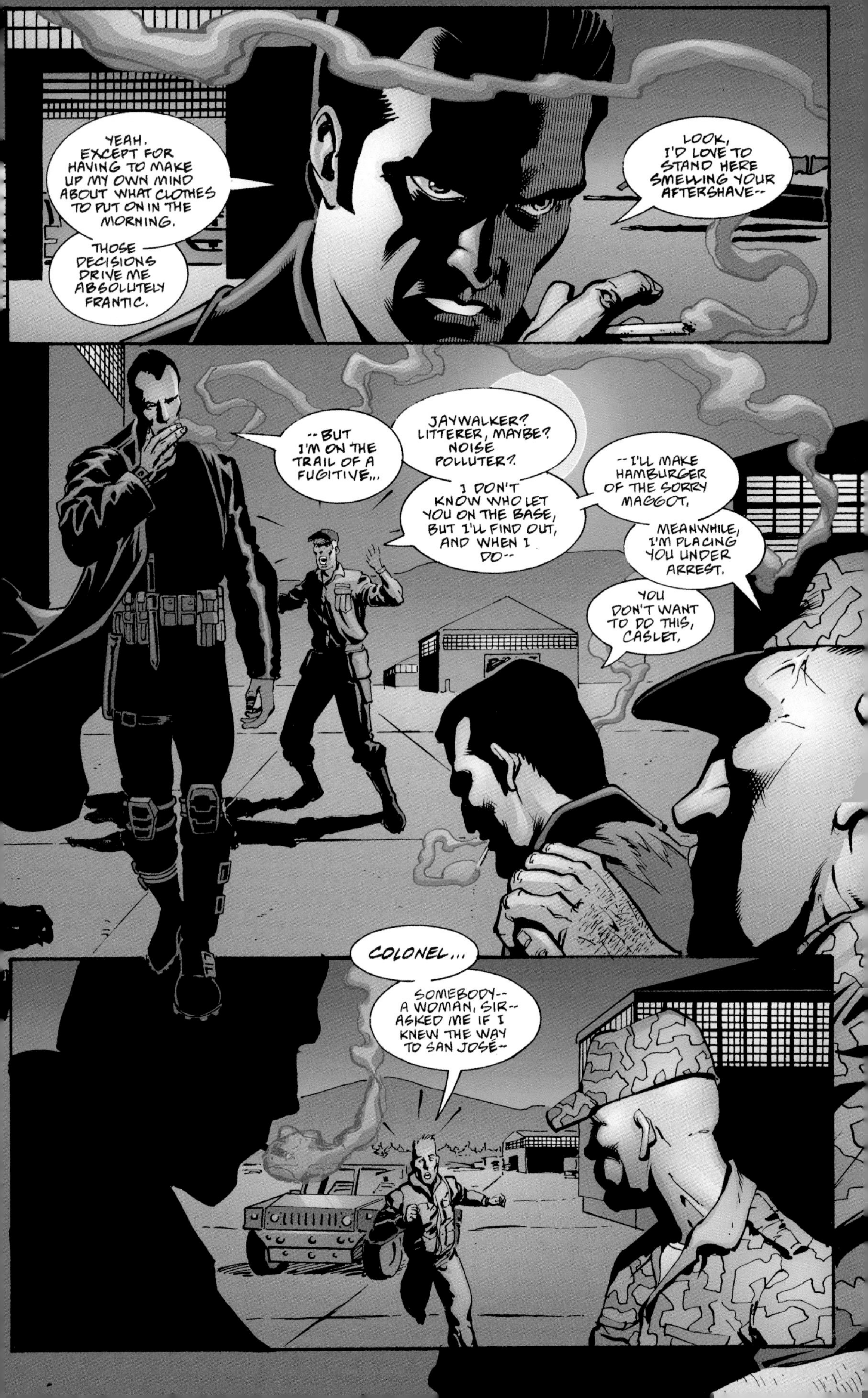
YEAH. EXCEPT FOR HAVING TO MAKE UP MY OWN MIND ABOUT WHAT CLOTHES TO PUT ON IN THE MORNING.
THOSE DECISIONS DRIVE ME ABSOLUTELY FRANTIC.
LOOK, I'D LOVE TO STAND HERE SMELLING YOUR AFTERSHAVE--
--BUT I'M ON THE TRAIL OF A FUGITIVE...
JAYWALKER? LITTERER, MAYBE? NOISE POLLUTER?
I DON'T KNOW WHO LET YOU ON THE BASE, BUT I'LL FIND OUT, AND WHEN I DO--
--I'LL MAKE HAMBURGER OF THE SORRY MAGGOT.
MEANWHILE, I'M PLACING YOU UNDER ARREST.
YOU DON'T WANT TO DO THIS, CASLET.
COLONEL...
SOMEBODY-- A WOMAN, SIR-- ASKED ME IF I KNEW THE WAY TO SAN JOSÉ--

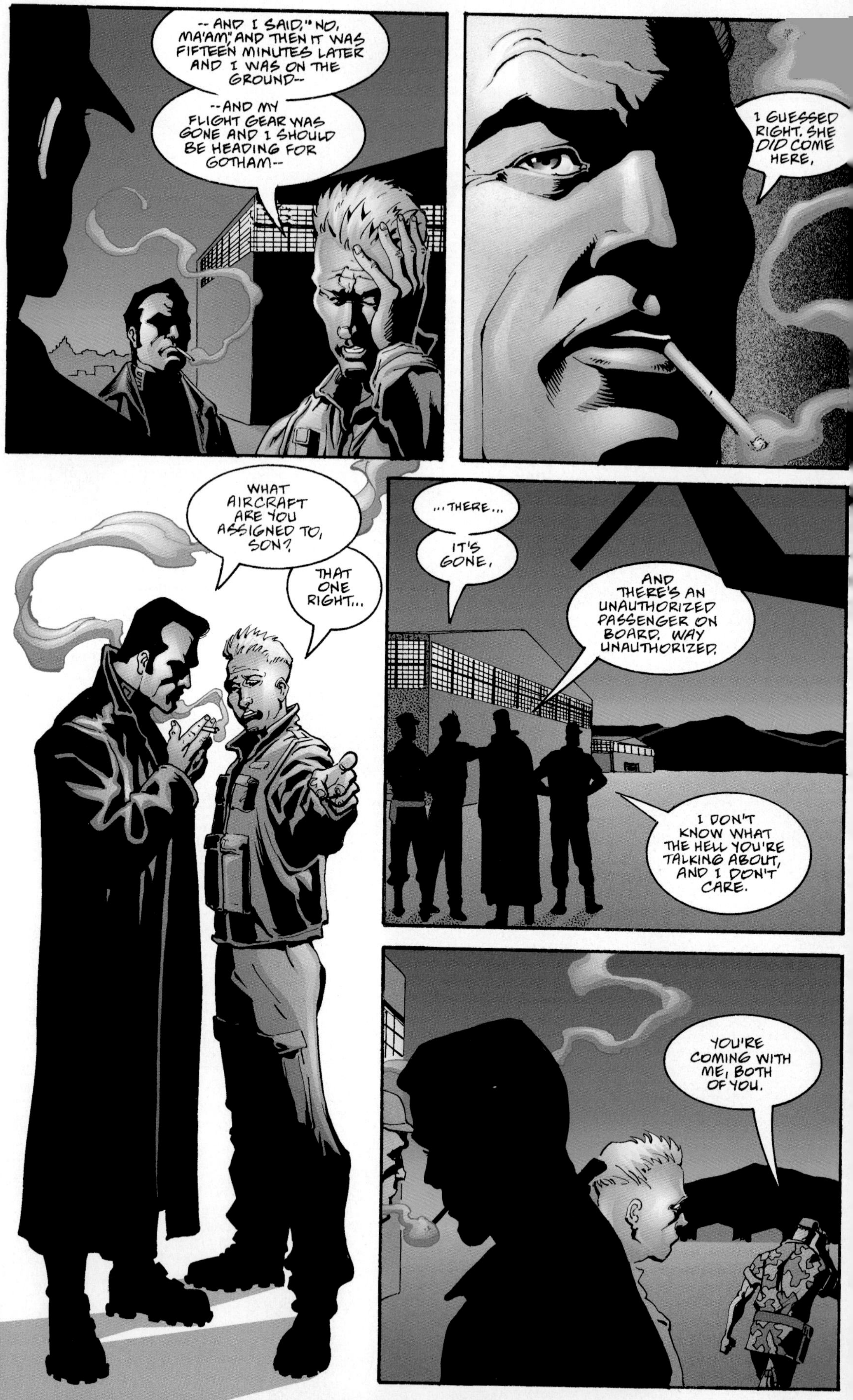
-- AND I SAID, "NO, MA'AM," AND THEN IT WAS FIFTEEN MINUTES LATER AND I WAS ON THE GROUND--
--AND MY FLIGHT GEAR WAS GONE AND I SHOULD BE HEADING FOR GOTHAM--
I GUESSED RIGHT. SHE *DID* COME HERE.
WHAT AIRCRAFT ARE YOU ASSIGNED TO, SON?
THAT ONE RIGHT...
...THERE...
IT'S GONE.
AND THERE'S AN UNAUTHORIZED PASSENGER ON BOARD. WAY UNAUTHORIZED.
I DON'T KNOW WHAT THE HELL YOU'RE TALKING ABOUT, AND I DON'T CARE.
YOU'RE COMING WITH ME, BOTH OF YOU.

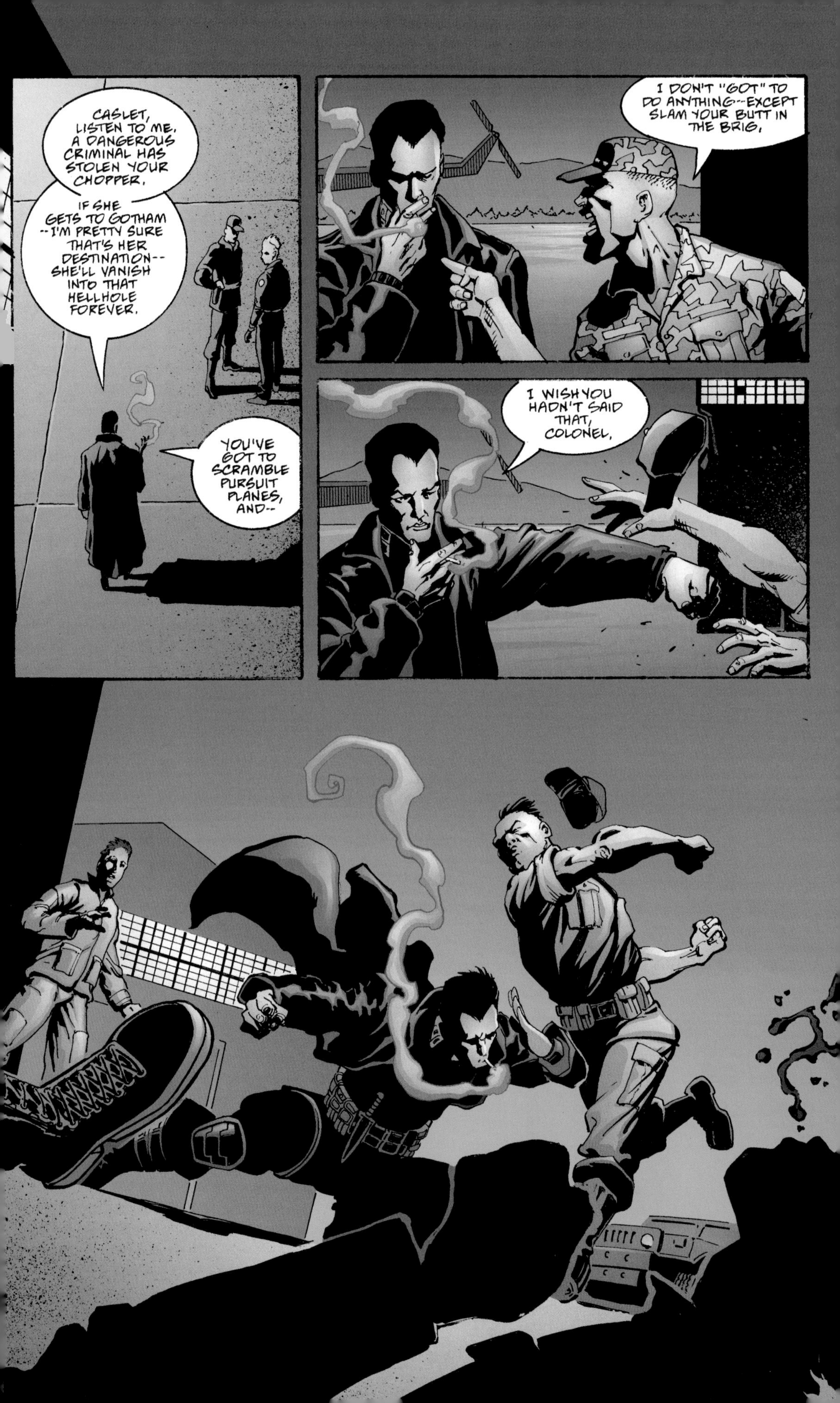
CASLET, LISTEN TO ME. A DANGEROUS CRIMINAL HAS STOLEN YOUR CHOPPER.
IF SHE GETS TO GOTHAM --I'M PRETTY SURE THAT'S HER DESTINATION-- SHE'LL VANISH INTO THAT HELLHOLE FOREVER.
YOU'VE GOT TO SCRAMBLE PURSUIT PLANES, AND--
I DON'T "GOT" TO DO ANYTHING--EXCEPT SLAM YOUR BUTT IN THE BRIG.
I WISH YOU HADN'T SAID THAT, COLONEL.

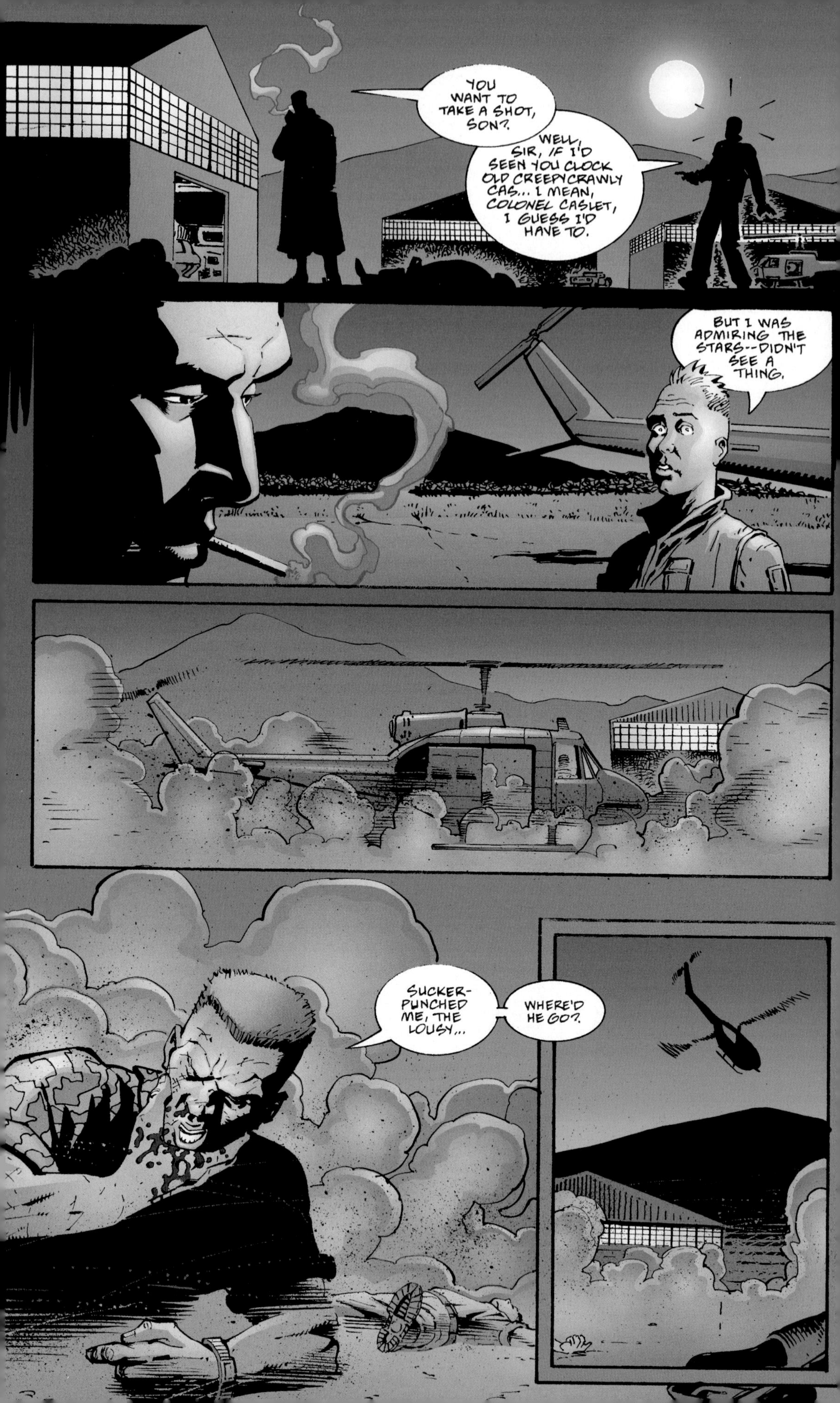
YOU WANT TO TAKE A SHOT, SON?
WELL, SIR, IF I'D SEEN YOU CLOCK OLD CREEPYCRAWLY CAS... I MEAN, COLONEL CASLET, I GUESS I'D HAVE TO.
BUT I WAS ADMIRING THE STARS--DIDN'T SEE A THING.
SUCKER-PUNCHED ME, THE LOUSY...
WHERE'D HE GO?

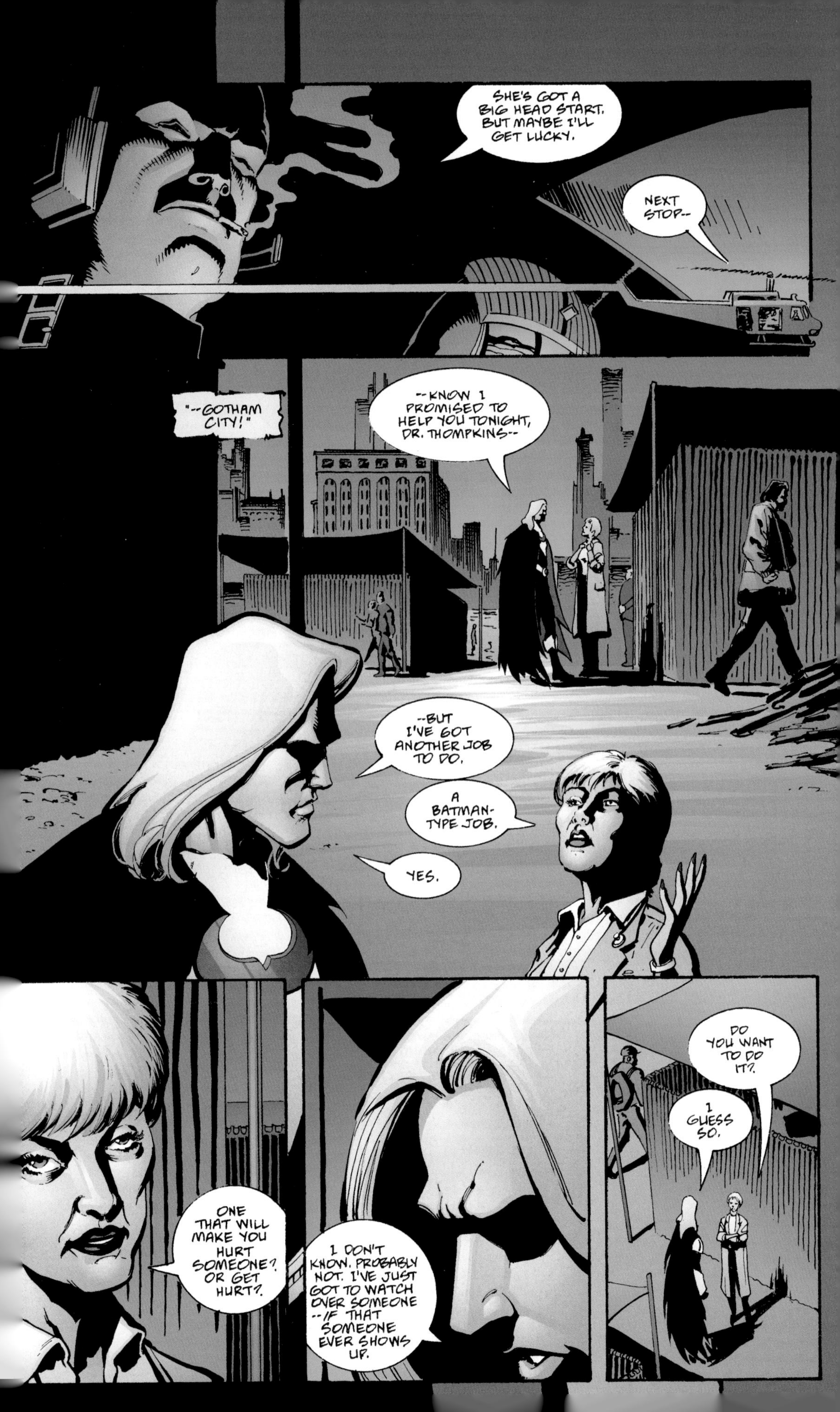
SHE'S GOT A BIG HEAD START. BUT MAYBE I'LL GET LUCKY.
NEXT STOP--
"--GOTHAM CITY!"
--KNOW I PROMISED TO HELP YOU TONIGHT, DR. THOMPKINS--
--BUT I'VE GOT ANOTHER JOB TO DO.
A BATMAN-TYPE JOB.
YES.
ONE THAT WILL MAKE YOU HURT SOMEONE? OR GET HURT?
I DON'T KNOW. PROBABLY NOT. I'VE JUST GOT TO WATCH OVER SOMEONE --IF THAT SOMEONE EVER SHOWS UP.
DO YOU WANT TO DO IT?
I GUESS SO.

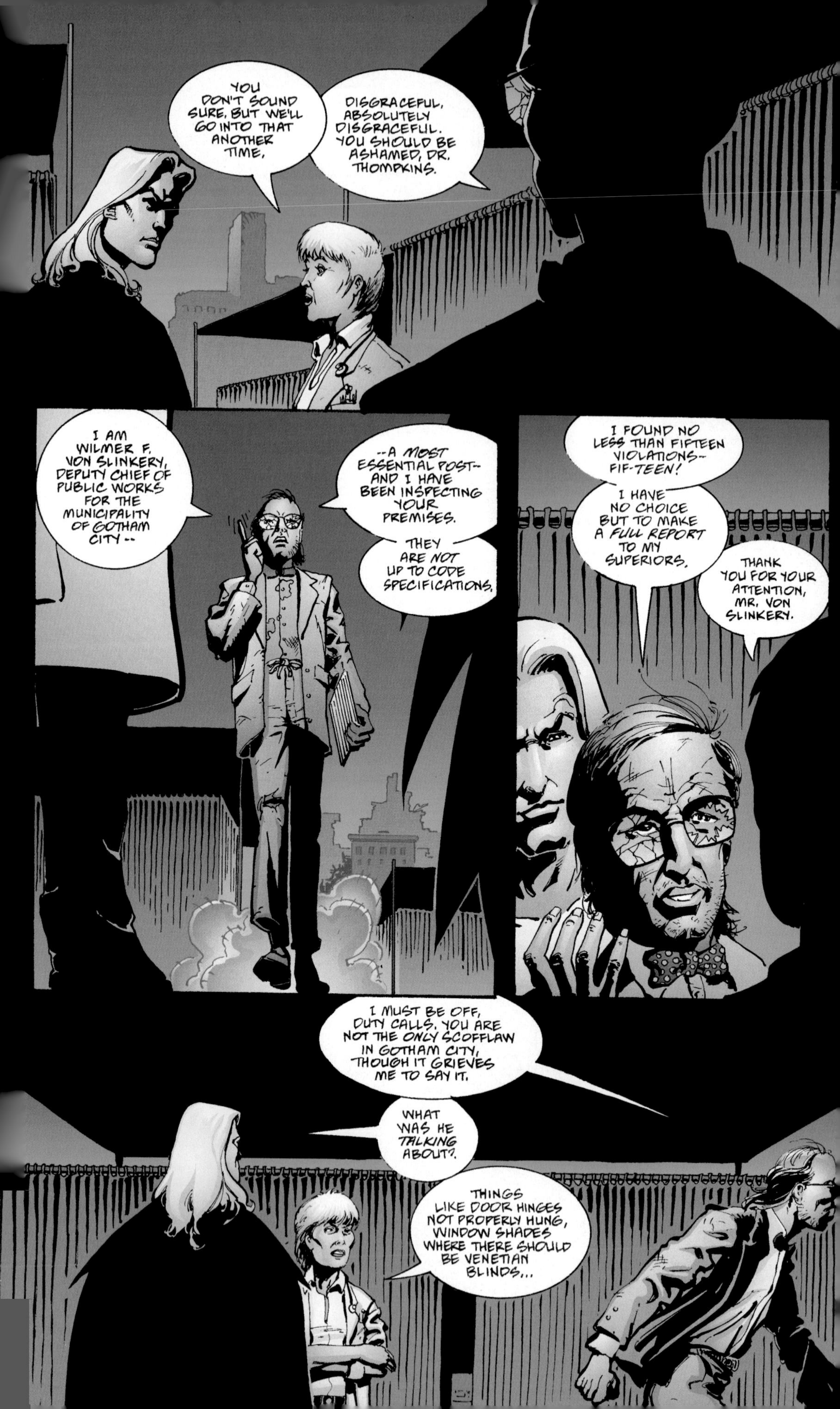

YOU DON'T SOUND SURE, BUT WE'LL GO INTO THAT ANOTHER TIME.
DISGRACEFUL, ABSOLUTELY DISGRACEFUL. YOU SHOULD BE ASHAMED, DR. THOMPKINS.
I AM WILMER F. VON SLINKERY, DEPUTY CHIEF OF PUBLIC WORKS FOR THE MUNICIPALITY OF GOTHAM CITY --
--A MOST ESSENTIAL POST-- AND I HAVE BEEN INSPECTING YOUR PREMISES.
THEY ARE NOT UP TO CODE SPECIFICATIONS.
I FOUND NO LESS THAN FIFTEEN VIOLATIONS-- FIF-TEEN!
I HAVE NO CHOICE BUT TO MAKE A FULL REPORT TO MY SUPERIORS.
THANK YOU FOR YOUR ATTENTION, MR. VON SLINKERY.
I MUST BE OFF, DUTY CALLS. YOU ARE NOT THE ONLY SCOFFLAW IN GOTHAM CITY, THOUGH IT GRIEVES ME TO SAY IT.
WHAT WAS HE TALKING ABOUT?
THINGS LIKE DOOR HINGES NOT PROPERLY HUNG, WINDOW SHADES WHERE THERE SHOULD BE VENETIAN BLINDS...

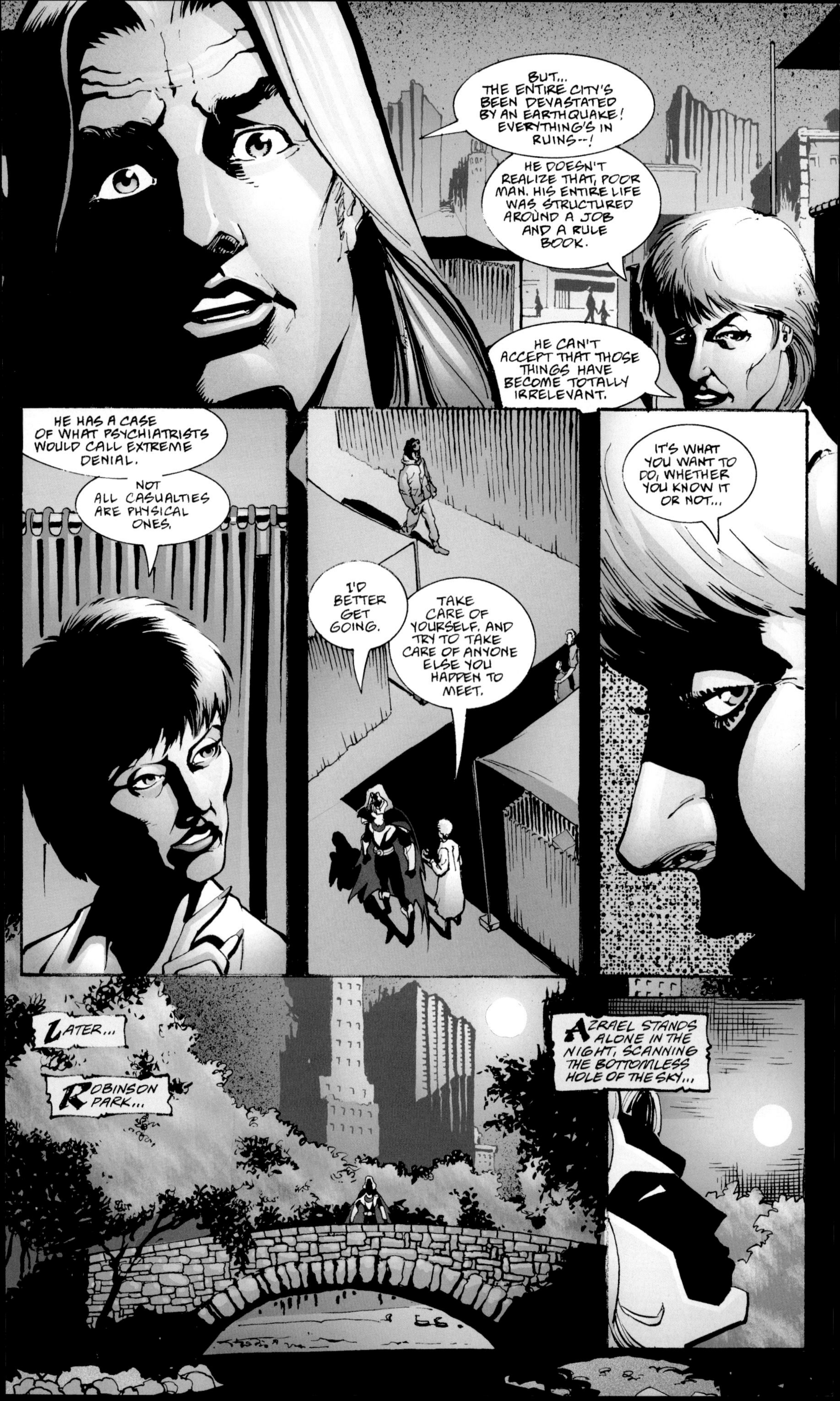
BUT... THE ENTIRE CITY'S BEEN DEVASTATED BY AN EARTHQUAKE! EVERYTHING'S IN RUINS--!
HE DOESN'T REALIZE THAT, POOR MAN. HIS ENTIRE LIFE WAS STRUCTURED AROUND A JOB AND A RULE BOOK.
HE CAN'T ACCEPT THAT THOSE THINGS HAVE BECOME TOTALLY IRRELEVANT.
HE HAS A CASE OF WHAT PSYCHIATRISTS WOULD CALL EXTREME DENIAL.
NOT ALL CASUALTIES ARE PHYSICAL ONES.
I'D BETTER GET GOING.
TAKE CARE OF YOURSELF, AND TRY TO TAKE CARE OF ANYONE ELSE YOU HAPPEN TO MEET.
IT'S WHAT YOU WANT TO DO, WHETHER YOU KNOW IT OR NOT...
LATER...
ROBINSON PARK...
AZRAEL STANDS ALONE IN THE NIGHT, SCANNING THE BOTTOMLESS HOLE OF THE SKY...

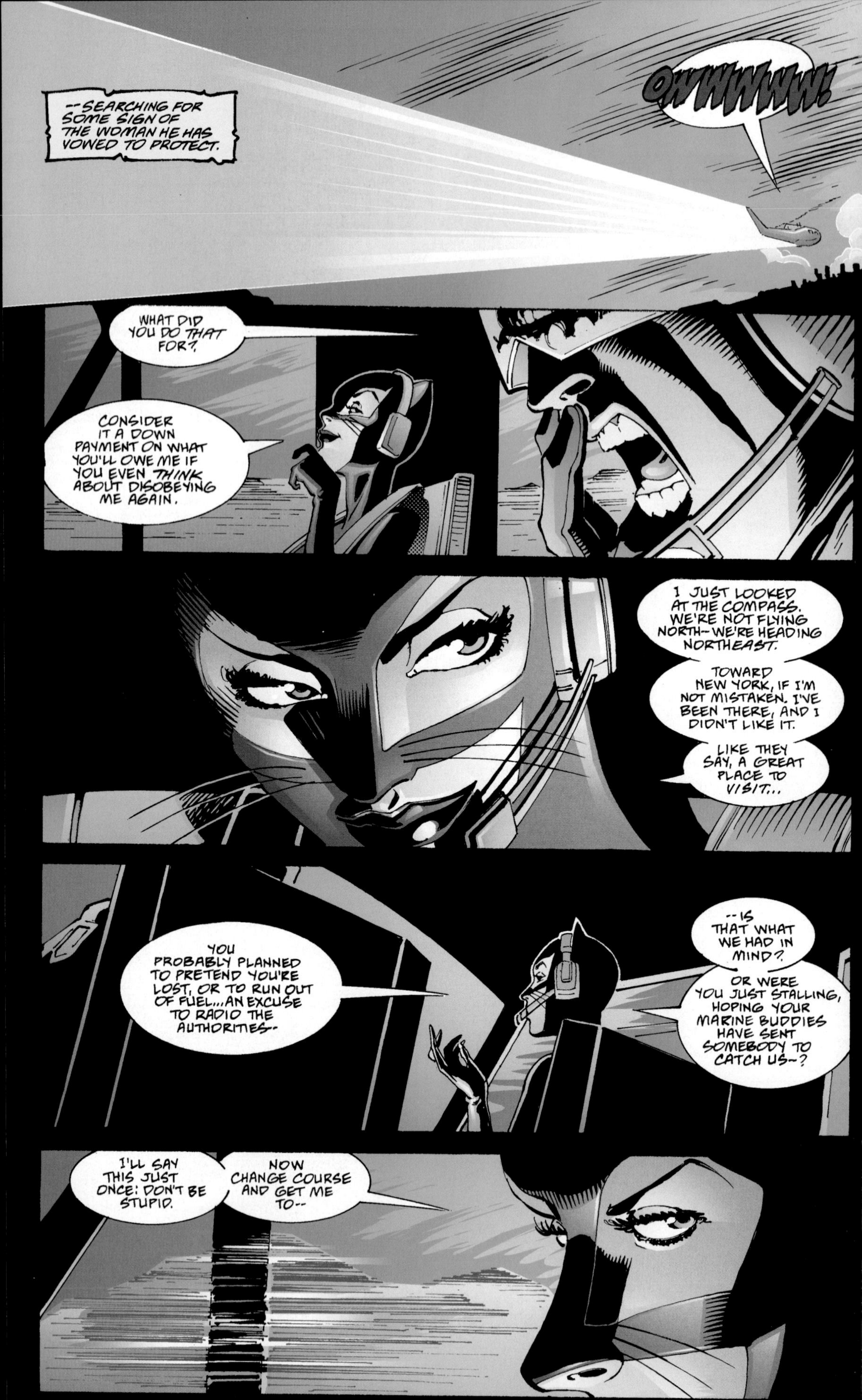
--SEARCHING FOR SOME SIGN OF THE WOMAN HE HAS VOWED TO PROTECT.
OWWWWW!
WHAT DID YOU DO THAT FOR?
CONSIDER IT A DOWN PAYMENT ON WHAT YOU'LL OWE ME IF YOU EVEN THINK ABOUT DISOBEYING ME AGAIN.
I JUST LOOKED AT THE COMPASS. WE'RE NOT FLYING NORTH-- WE'RE HEADING NORTHEAST.
TOWARD NEW YORK, IF I'M NOT MISTAKEN. I'VE BEEN THERE, AND I DIDN'T LIKE IT.
LIKE THEY SAY, A GREAT PLACE TO VISIT...
YOU PROBABLY PLANNED TO PRETEND YOU'RE LOST, OR TO RUN OUT OF FUEL...AN EXCUSE TO RADIO THE AUTHORITIES-
--IS THAT WHAT WE HAD IN MIND?
OR WERE YOU JUST STALLING, HOPING YOUR MARINE BUDDIES HAVE SENT SOMEBODY TO CATCH US--?
I'LL SAY THIS JUST ONCE: DON'T BE STUPID.
NOW CHANGE COURSE AND GET ME TO--

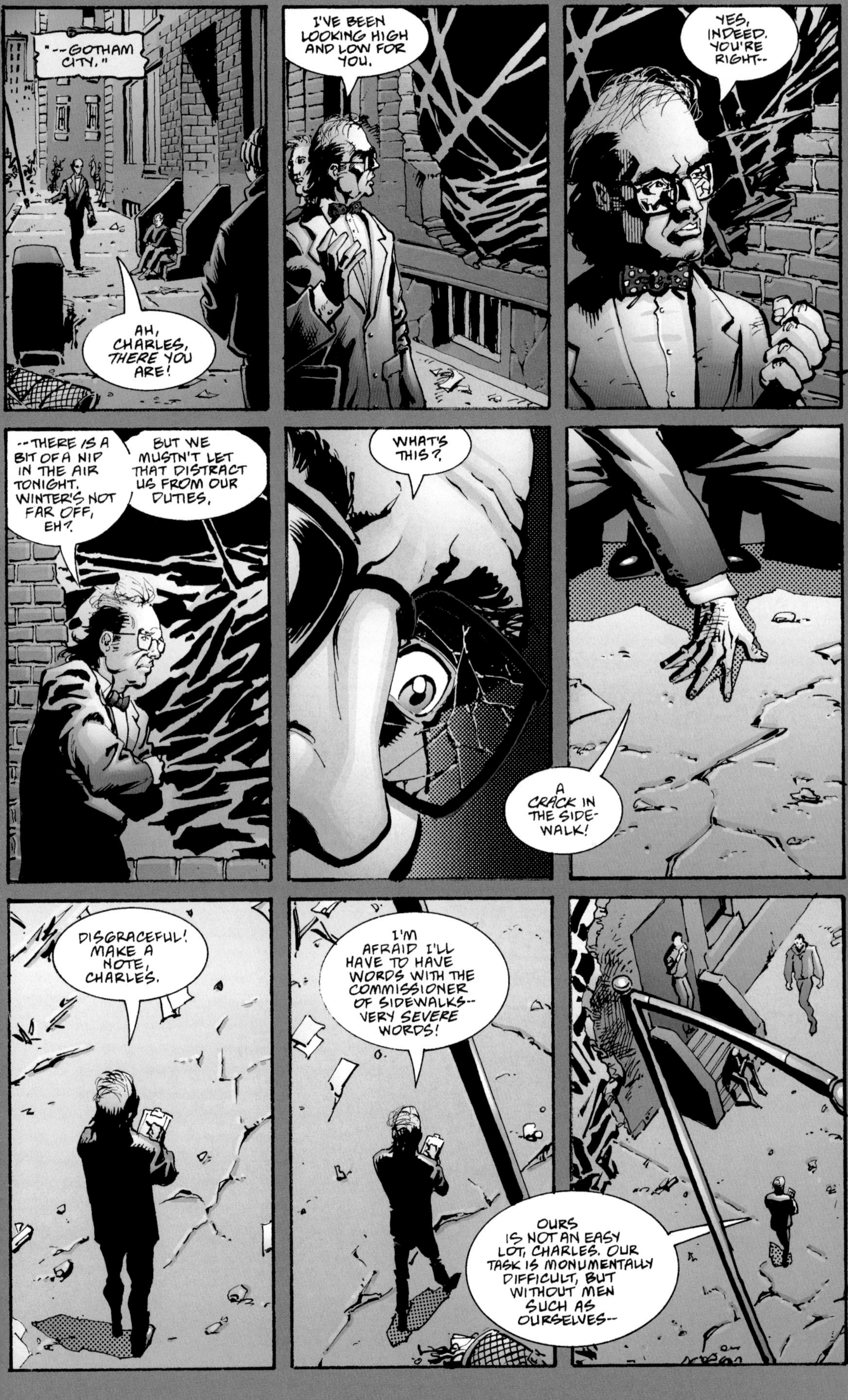
"--GOTHAM CITY."
AH, CHARLES, THERE YOU ARE!
I'VE BEEN LOOKING HIGH AND LOW FOR YOU.
YES, INDEED. YOU'RE RIGHT--
--THERE IS A BIT OF A NIP IN THE AIR TONIGHT. WINTER'S NOT FAR OFF, EH?
BUT WE MUSTN'T LET THAT DISTRACT US FROM OUR DUTIES.
WHAT'S THIS?
A CRACK IN THE SIDE-WALK!
DISGRACEFUL! MAKE A NOTE, CHARLES.
I'M AFRAID I'LL HAVE TO HAVE WORDS WITH THE COMMISSIONER OF SIDEWALKS-- VERY SEVERE WORDS!
OURS IS NOT AN EASY LOT, CHARLES. OUR TASK IS MONUMENTALLY DIFFICULT, BUT WITHOUT MEN SUCH AS OURSELVES--

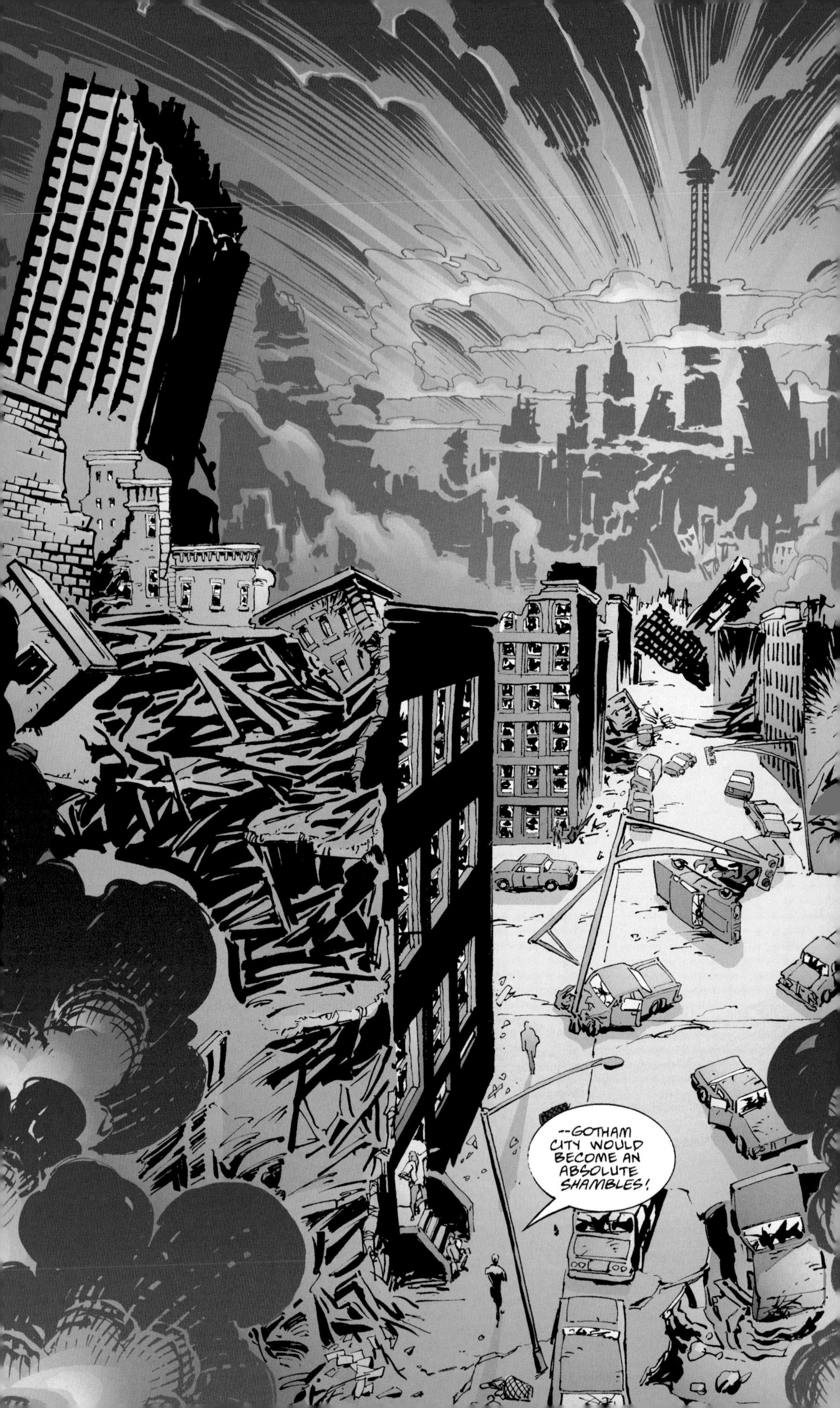
--GOTHAM CITY WOULD BECOME AN ABSOLUTE SHAMBLES!

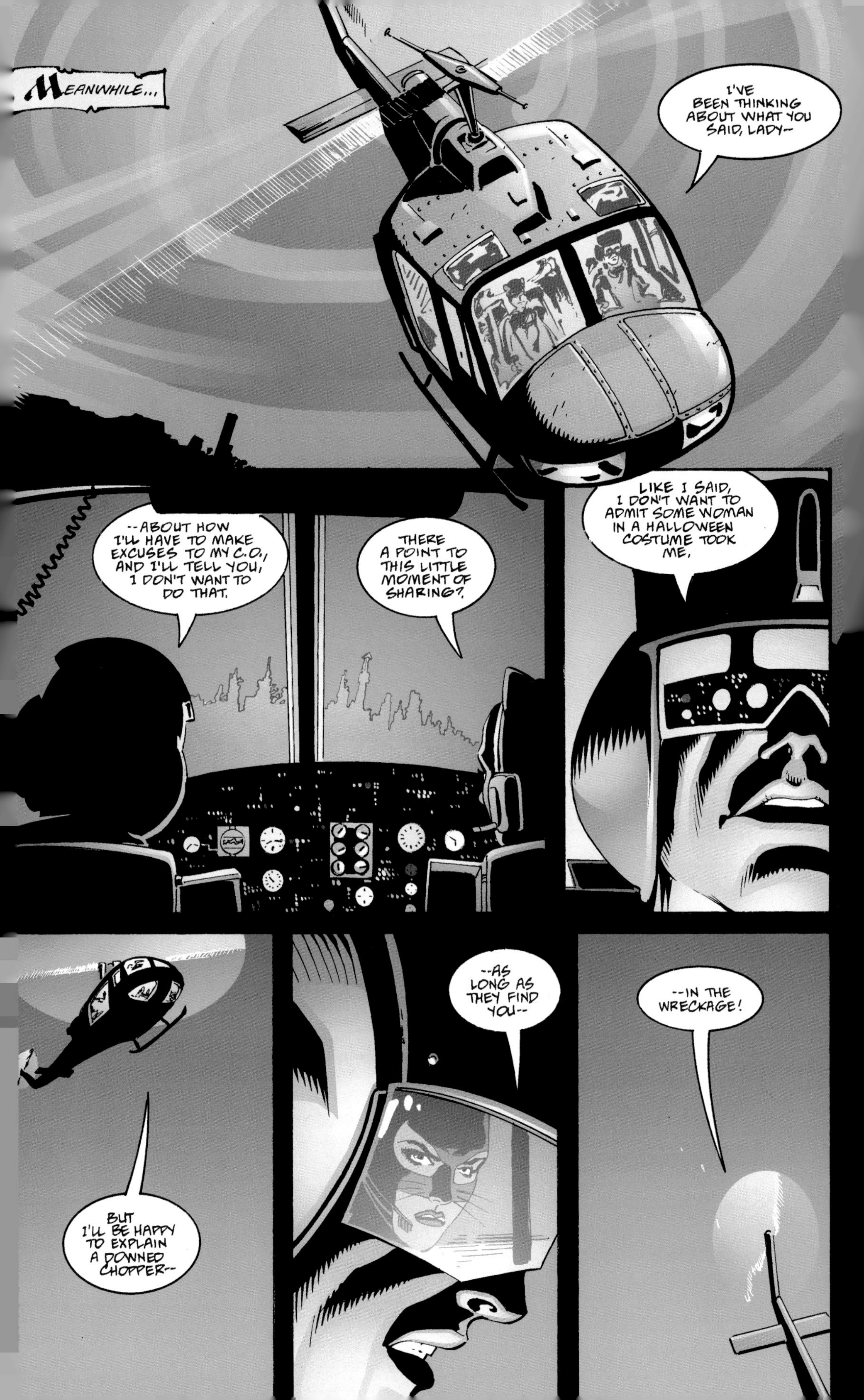
MEANWHILE...
I'VE BEEN THINKING ABOUT WHAT YOU SAID, LADY--
--ABOUT HOW I'LL HAVE TO MAKE EXCUSES TO MY C.O., AND I'LL TELL YOU, I DON'T WANT TO DO THAT.
THERE A POINT TO THIS LITTLE MOMENT OF SHARING?
LIKE I SAID, I DON'T WANT TO ADMIT SOME WOMAN IN A HALLOWEEN COSTUME TOOK ME.
BUT I'LL BE HAPPY TO EXPLAIN A DOWNED CHOPPER--
--AS LONG AS THEY FIND YOU--
--IN THE WRECKAGE!

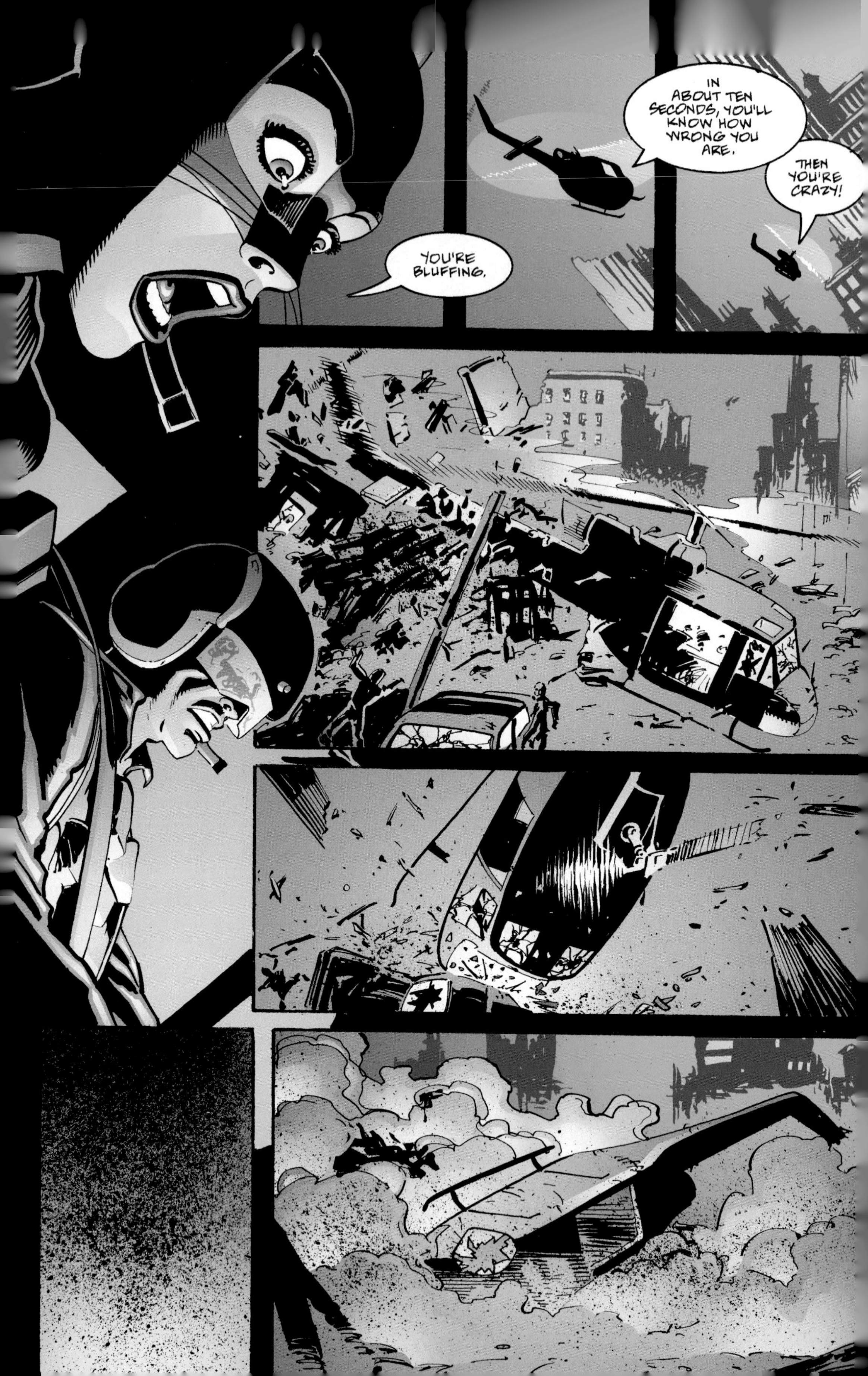
YOU'RE BLUFFING.
IN ABOUT TEN SECONDS, YOU'LL KNOW HOW WRONG YOU ARE.
THEN YOU'RE CRAZY!

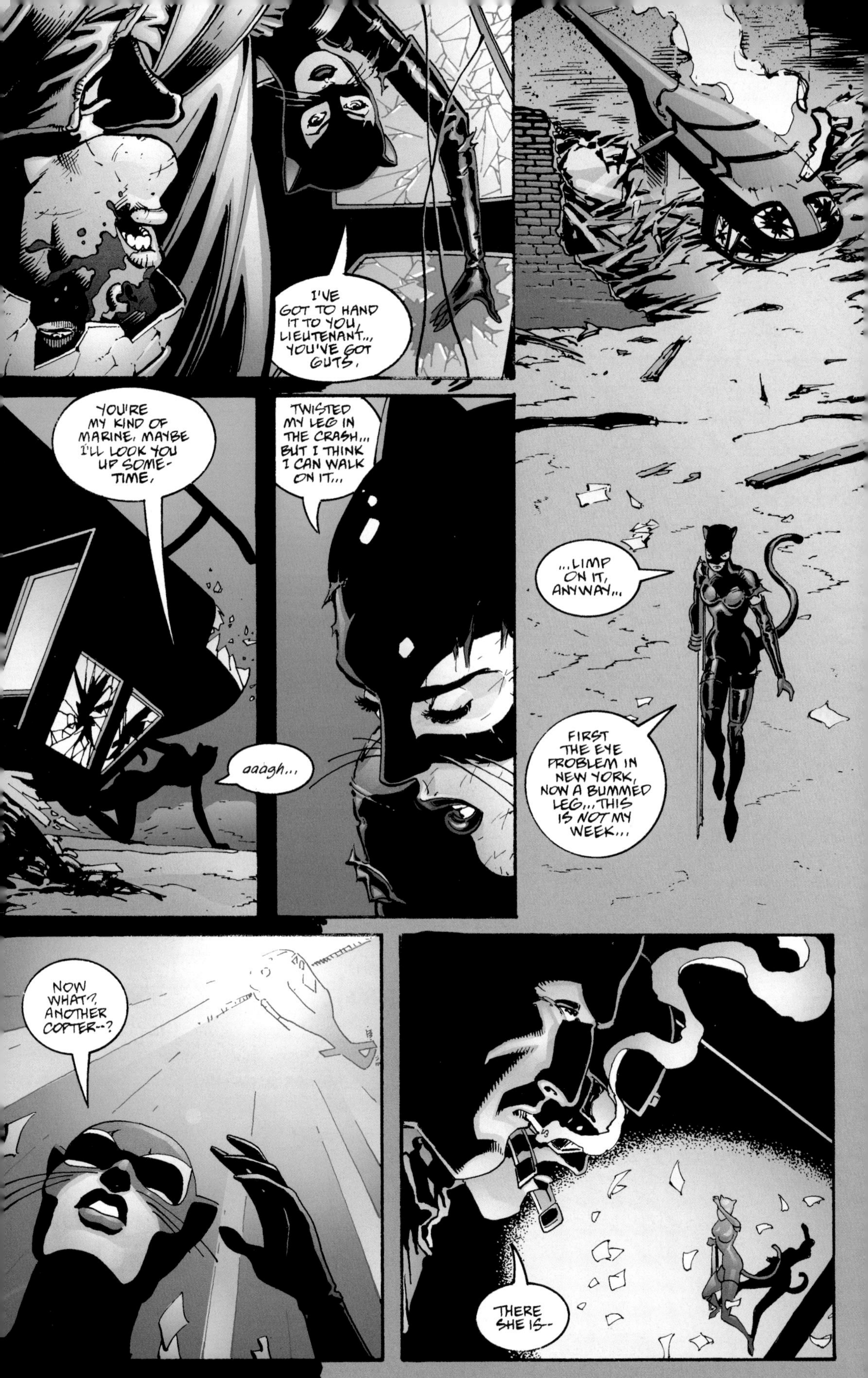
I'VE GOT TO HAND IT TO YOU, LIEUTENANT... YOU'VE GOT GUTS.
YOU'RE MY KIND OF MARINE. MAYBE I'LL LOOK YOU UP SOMETIME.
TWISTED MY LEG IN THE CRASH... BUT I THINK I CAN WALK ON IT...
aaagh...
...LIMP ON IT, ANYWAY...
FIRST THE EYE PROBLEM IN NEW YORK, NOW A BUMMED LEG... THIS IS NOT MY WEEK...
NOW WHAT?, ANOTHER COPTER--?
THERE SHE IS--

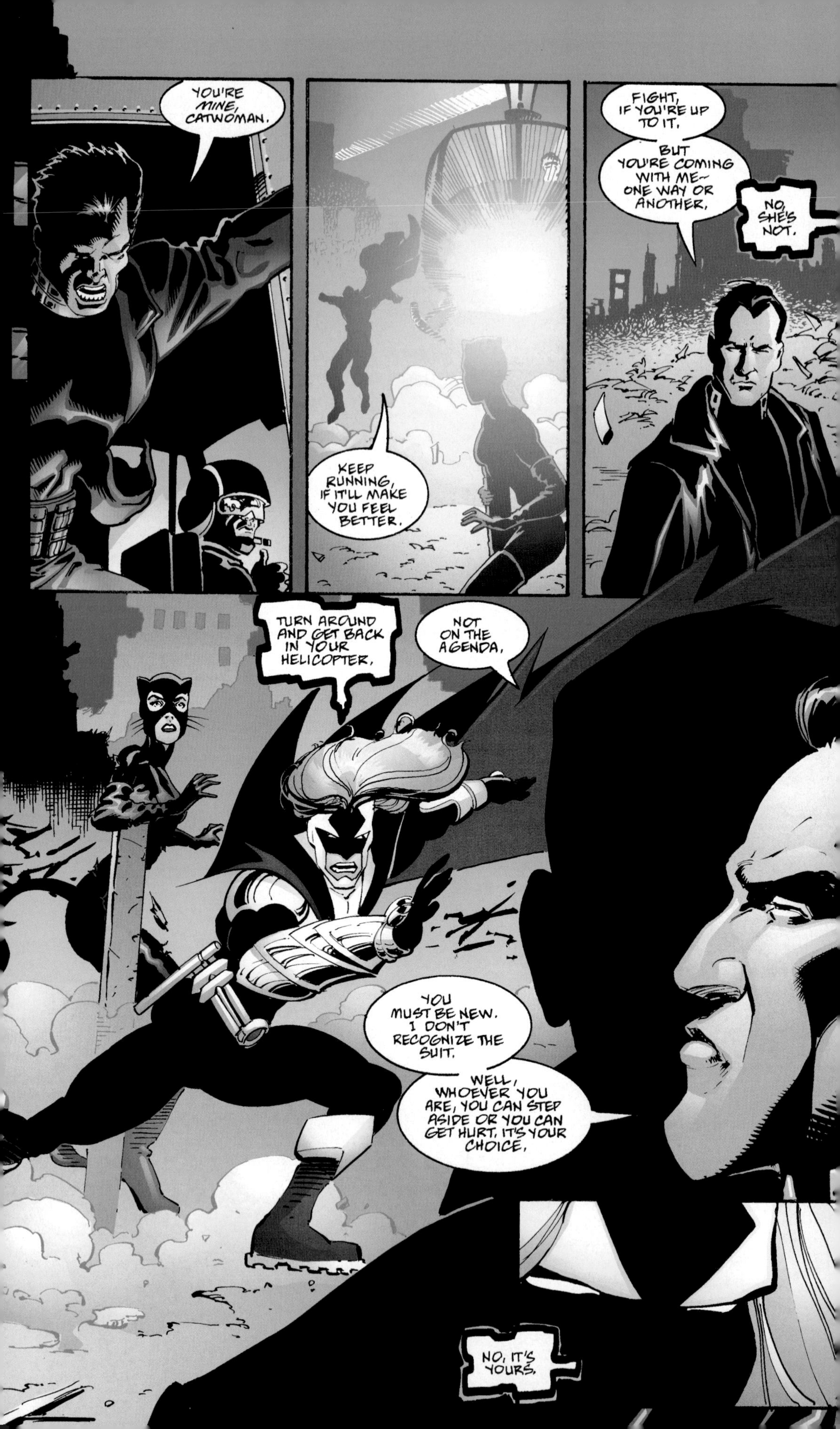
YOU'RE MINE, CATWOMAN.
KEEP RUNNING, IF IT'LL MAKE YOU FEEL BETTER.
FIGHT, IF YOU'RE UP TO IT.
BUT YOU'RE COMING WITH ME-- ONE WAY OR ANOTHER.
NO, SHE'S NOT.
TURN AROUND AND GET BACK IN YOUR HELICOPTER.
NOT ON THE AGENDA.
YOU MUST BE NEW. I DON'T RECOGNIZE THE SUIT.
WELL, WHOEVER YOU ARE, YOU CAN STEP ASIDE OR YOU CAN GET HURT. IT'S YOUR CHOICE.
NO, IT'S YOURS.

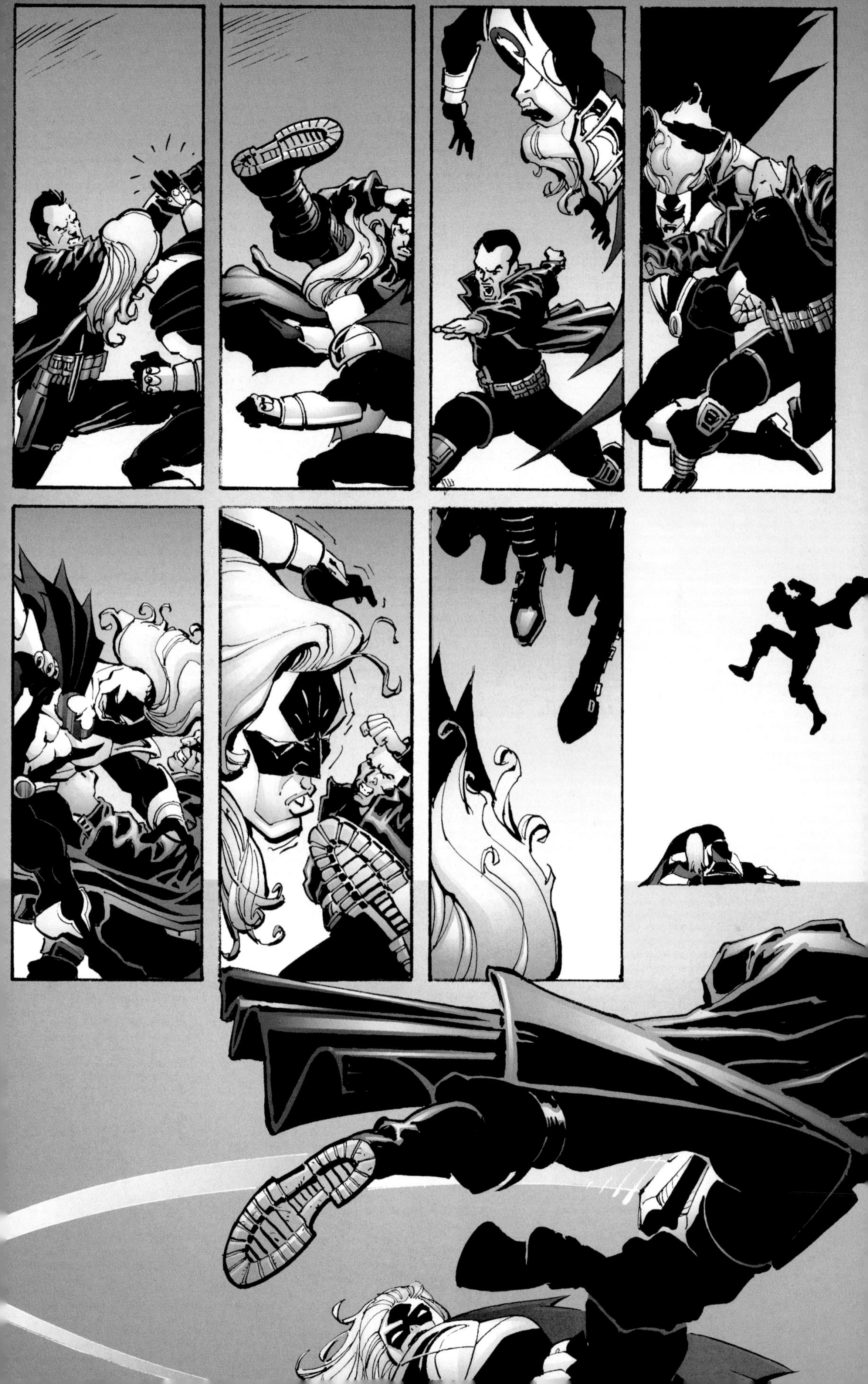

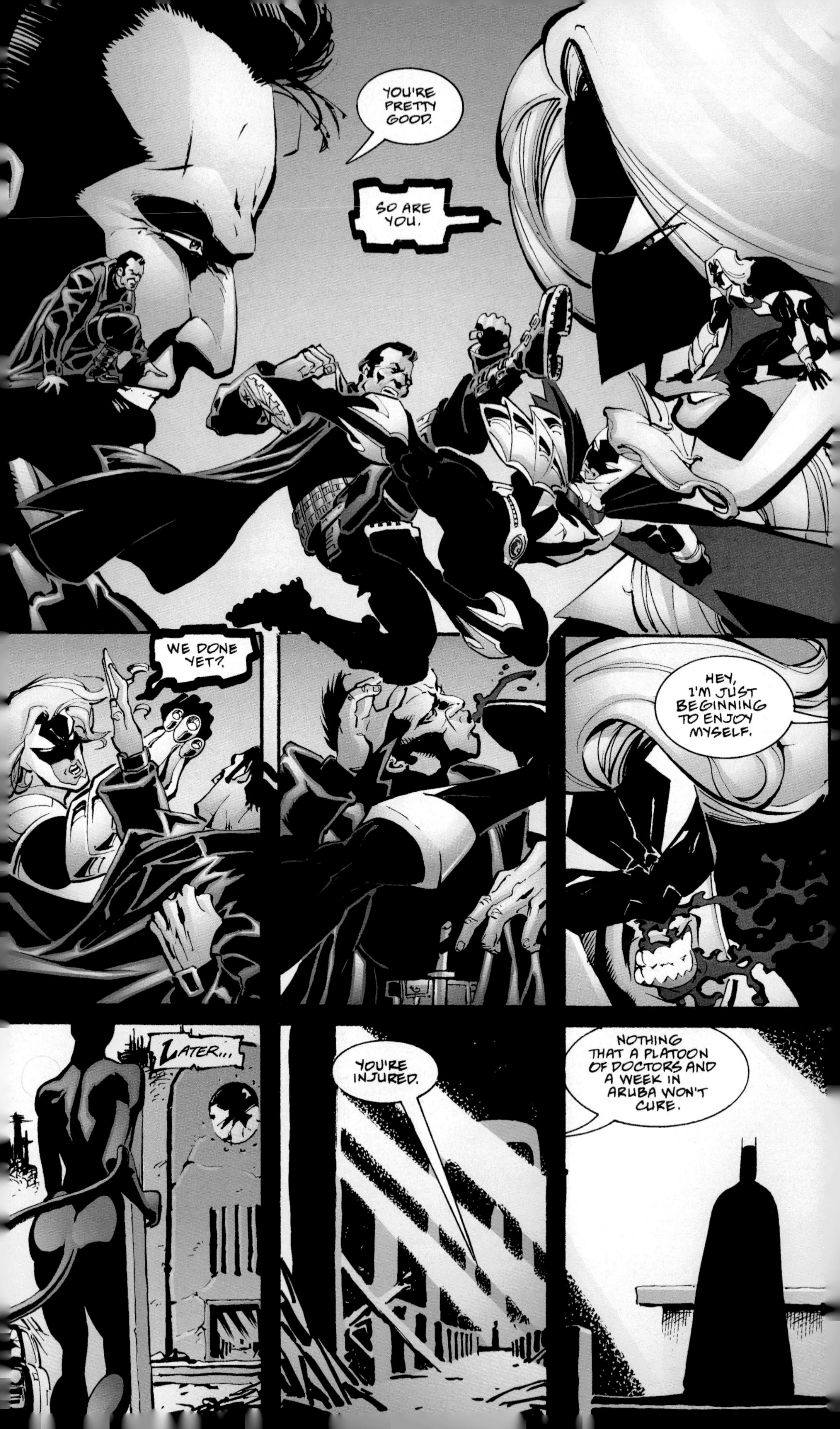
YOU'RE PRETTY GOOD.
SO ARE YOU.
WE DONE YET?
HEY, I'M JUST BEGINNING TO ENJOY MYSELF.
LATER...
YOU'RE INJURED.
NOTHING THAT A PLATOON OF DOCTORS AND A WEEK IN ARUBA WON'T CURE.

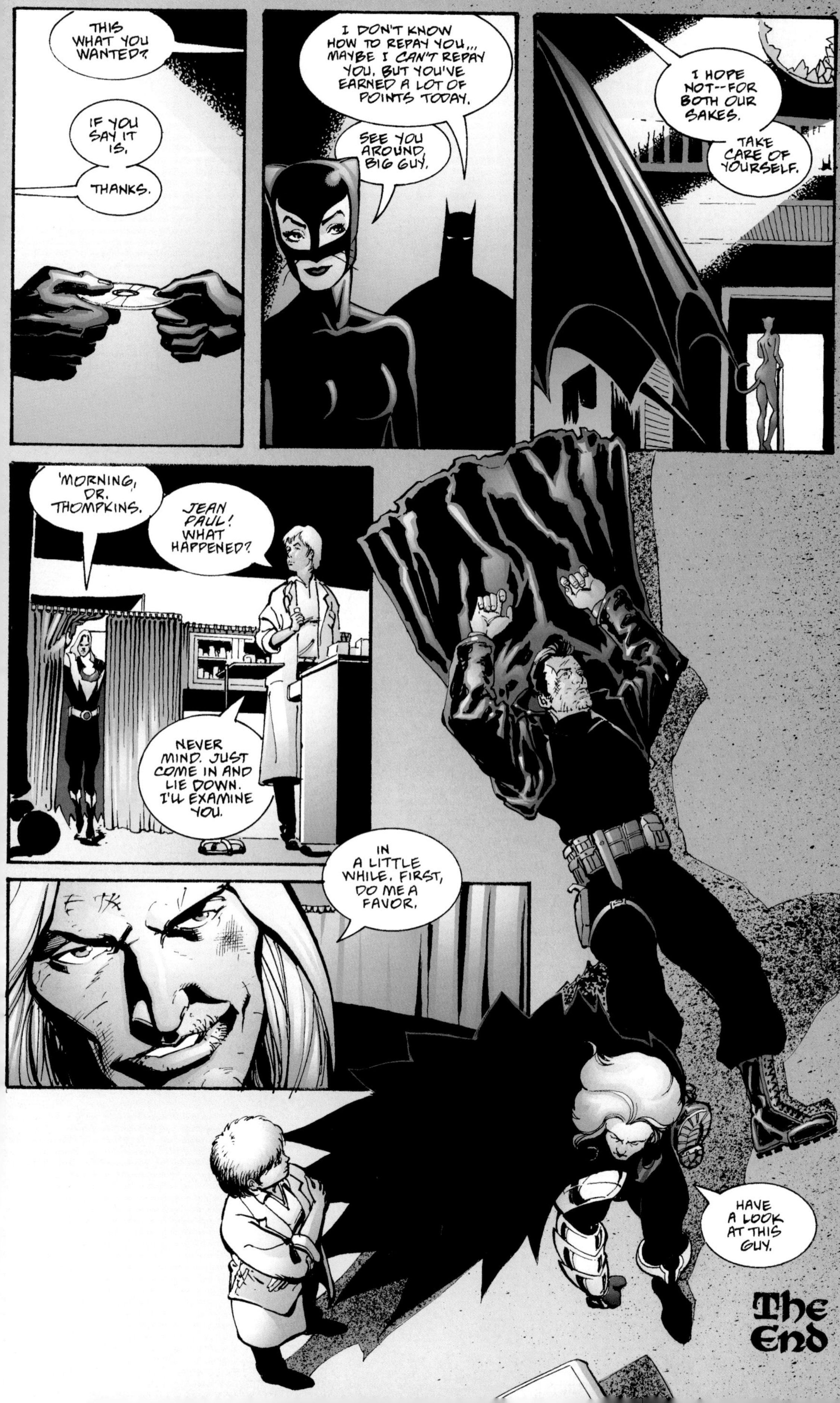
THIS WHAT YOU WANTED?
IF YOU SAY IT IS.
THANKS.
I DON'T KNOW HOW TO REPAY YOU... MAYBE I CAN'T REPAY YOU. BUT YOU'VE EARNED A LOT OF POINTS TODAY.
SEE YOU AROUND, BIG GUY.
I HOPE NOT--FOR BOTH OUR SAKES.
TAKE CARE OF YOURSELF.
'MORNING, DR. THOMPKINS.
JEAN PAUL! WHAT HAPPENED?
NEVER MIND. JUST COME IN AND LIE DOWN. I'LL EXAMINE YOU.
IN A LITTLE WHILE. FIRST, DO ME A FAVOR.
HAVE A LOOK AT THIS GUY.
The End

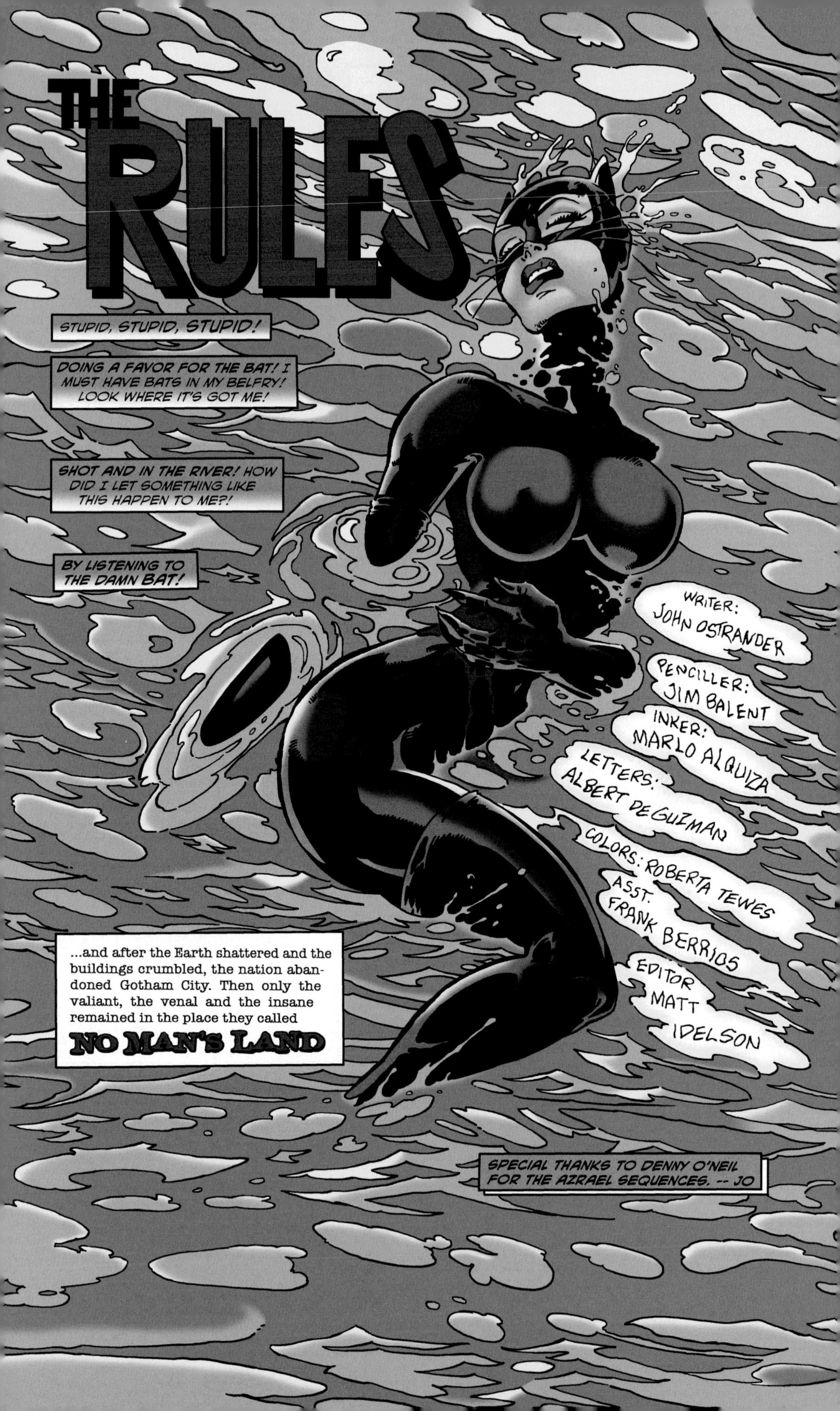

THE RULES
STUPID, STUPID, STUPID!
DOING A FAVOR FOR THE BAT! I MUST HAVE BATS IN MY BELFRY! LOOK WHERE IT'S GOT ME!
SHOT AND IN THE RIVER! HOW DID I LET SOMETHING LIKE THIS HAPPEN TO ME?!
BY LISTENING TO THE DAMN BAT!
WRITER: JOHN OSTRANDER
PENCILLER: JIM BALENT
INKER: MARLO ALQUIZA
LETTERS: ALBERT DEGUZMAN
COLORS: ROBERTA TEWES
ASST. FRANK BERRIOS
EDITOR MATT IDELSON
...and after the Earth shattered and the buildings crumbled, the nation abandoned Gotham City. Then only the valiant, the venal and the insane remained in the place they called
NO MAN'S LAND
SPECIAL THANKS TO DENNY O'NEIL FOR THE AZRAEL SEQUENCES. -- JO

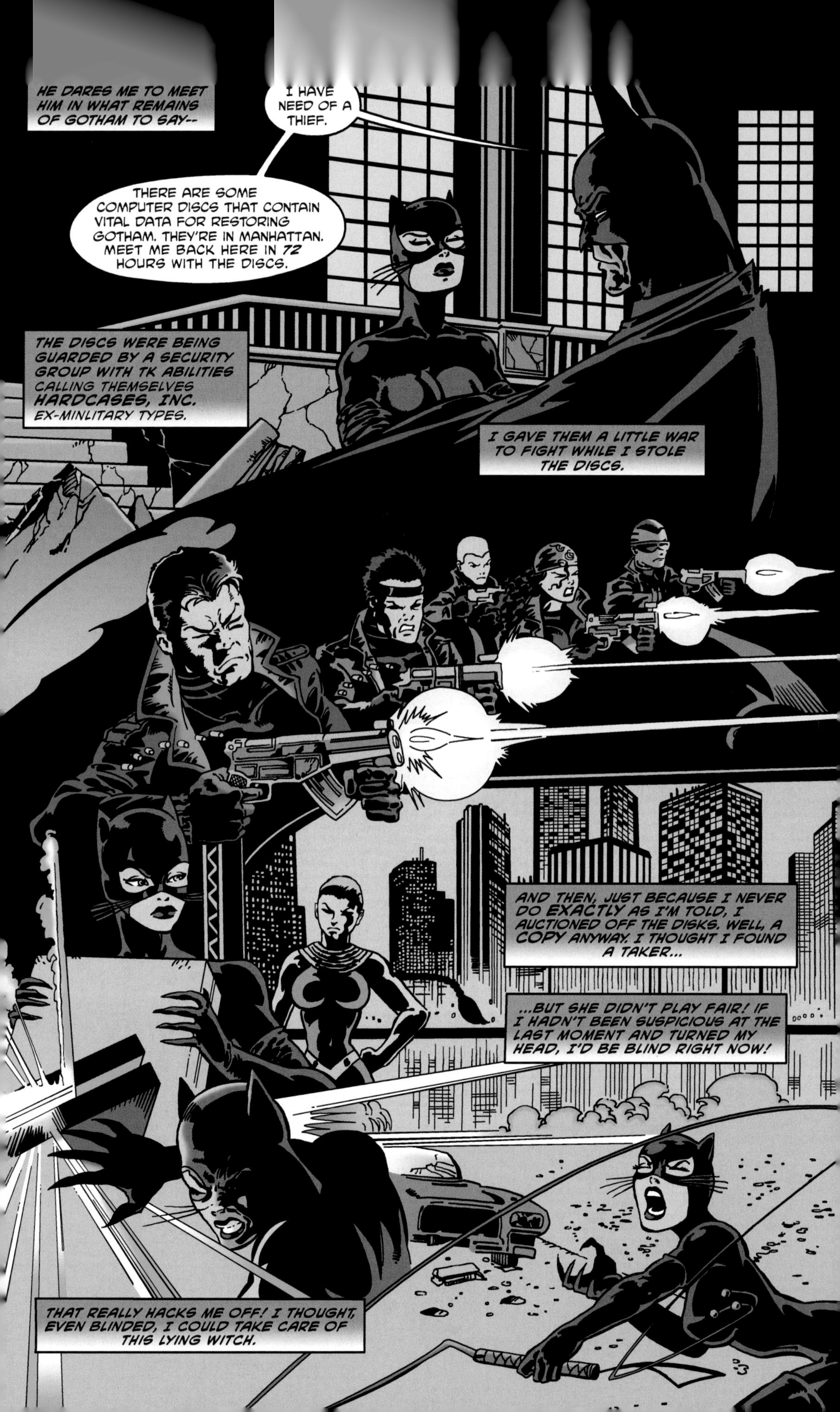

HE DARES ME TO MEET HIM IN WHAT REMAINS OF GOTHAM TO SAY--
I HAVE NEED OF A THIEF.
THERE ARE SOME COMPUTER DISCS THAT CONTAIN VITAL DATA FOR RESTORING GOTHAM. THEY'RE IN MANHATTAN. MEET ME BACK HERE IN 72 HOURS WITH THE DISCS.
THE DISCS WERE BEING GUARDED BY A SECURITY GROUP WITH TK ABILITIES CALLING THEMSELVES HARDCASES, INC. EX-MINLITARY TYPES.
I GAVE THEM A LITTLE WAR TO FIGHT WHILE I STOLE THE DISCS.
AND THEN, JUST BECAUSE I NEVER DO EXACTLY AS I'M TOLD, I AUCTIONED OFF THE DISKS. WELL, A COPY ANYWAY. I THOUGHT I FOUND A TAKER...
...BUT SHE DIDN'T PLAY FAIR! IF I HADN'T BEEN SUSPICIOUS AT THE LAST MOMENT AND TURNED MY HEAD, I'D BE BLIND RIGHT NOW!
THAT REALLY HACKS ME OFF! I THOUGHT, EVEN BLINDED, I COULD TAKE CARE OF THIS LYING WITCH.

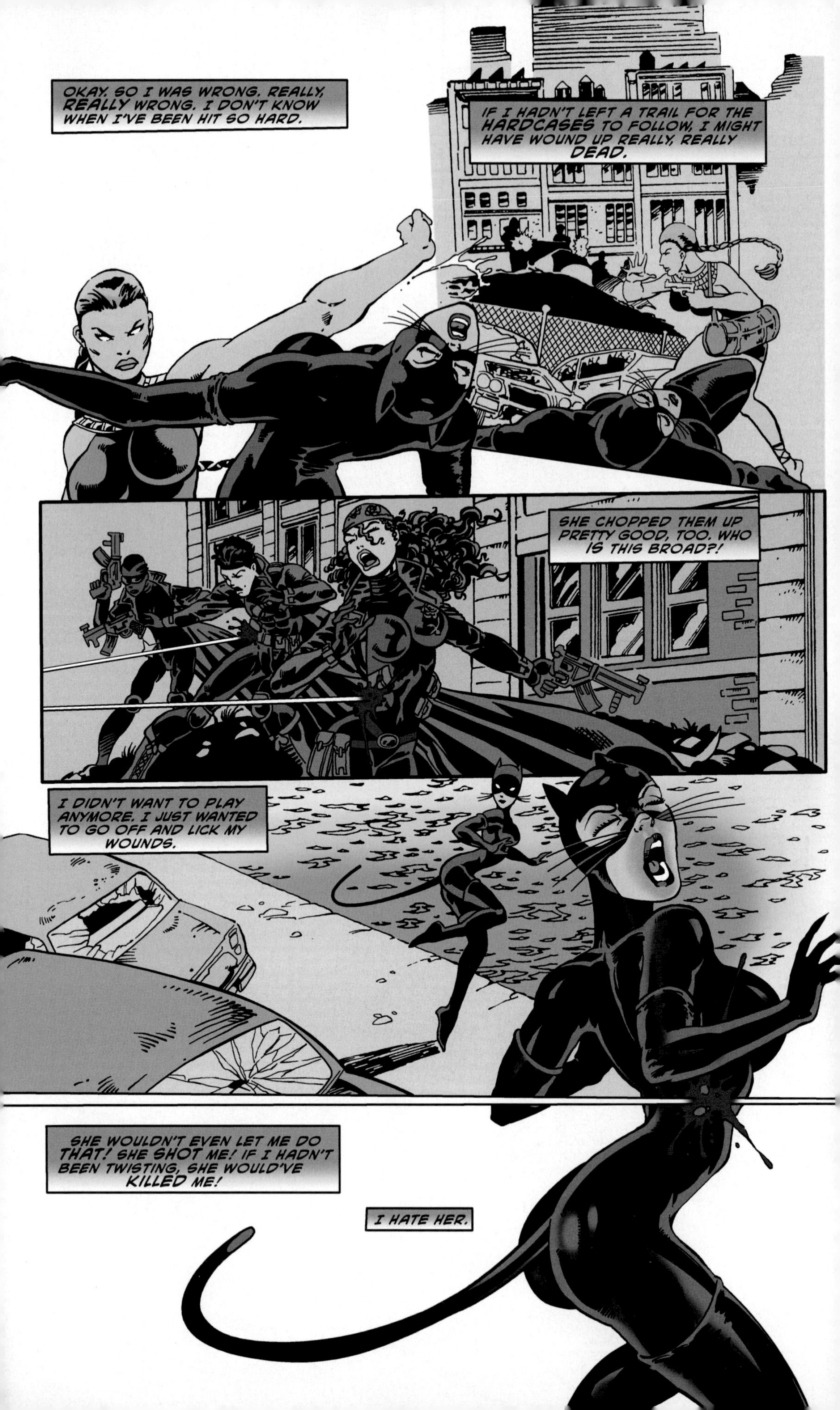
OKAY, SO I WAS WRONG. REALLY, REALLY WRONG. I DON'T KNOW WHEN I'VE BEEN HIT SO HARD.
IF I HADN'T LEFT A TRAIL FOR THE HARDCASES TO FOLLOW, I MIGHT HAVE WOUND UP REALLY, REALLY DEAD.
SHE CHOPPED THEM UP PRETTY GOOD, TOO. WHO IS THIS BROAD?!
I DIDN'T WANT TO PLAY ANYMORE. I JUST WANTED TO GO OFF AND LICK MY WOUNDS.
SHE WOULDN'T EVEN LET ME DO THAT! SHE SHOT ME! IF I HADN'T BEEN TWISTING, SHE WOULD'VE KILLED ME!
I HATE HER.

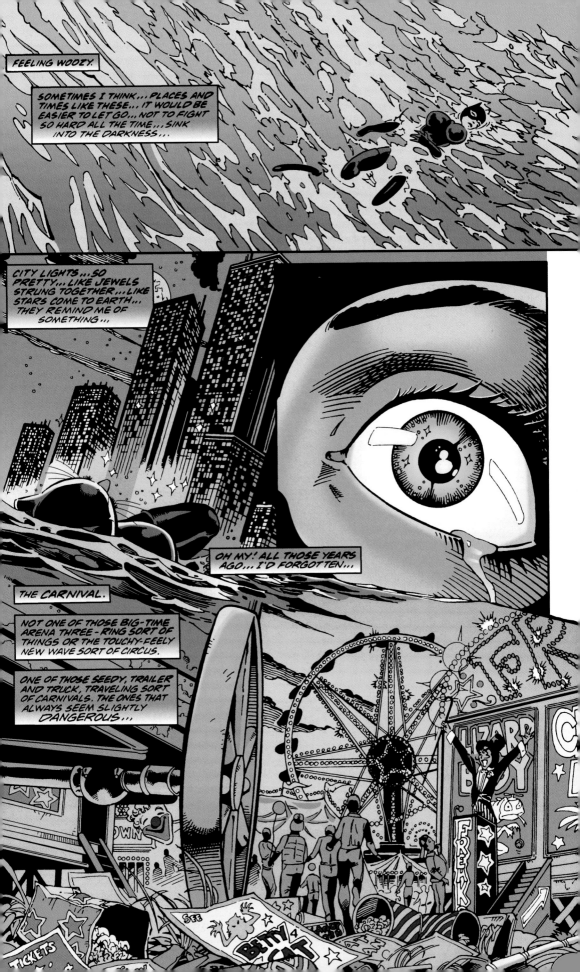

FEELING WOOZY.

SOMETIMES I THINK...PLACES AND TIMES LIKE THESE...IT WOULD BE EASIER TO LET GO...NOT TO FIGHT SO HARD ALL THE TIME...SINK INTO THE DARKNESS...

CITY LIGHTS...SO PRETTY...LIKE JEWELS STRUNG TOGETHER...LIKE STARS COME TO EARTH... THEY REMIND ME OF SOMETHING...

OH MY! ALL THOSE YEARS AGO...I'D FORGOTTEN...

THE CARNIVAL.

NOT ONE OF THOSE BIG-TIME ARENA THREE-RING SORT OF THINGS OR THE TOUCHY-FEELY NEW WAVE SORT OF CIRCUS.

ONE OF THOSE SEEDY, TRAILER AND TRUCK, TRAVELING SORT OF CARNIVALS. THE ONES THAT ALWAYS SEEM SLIGHTLY DANGEROUS...

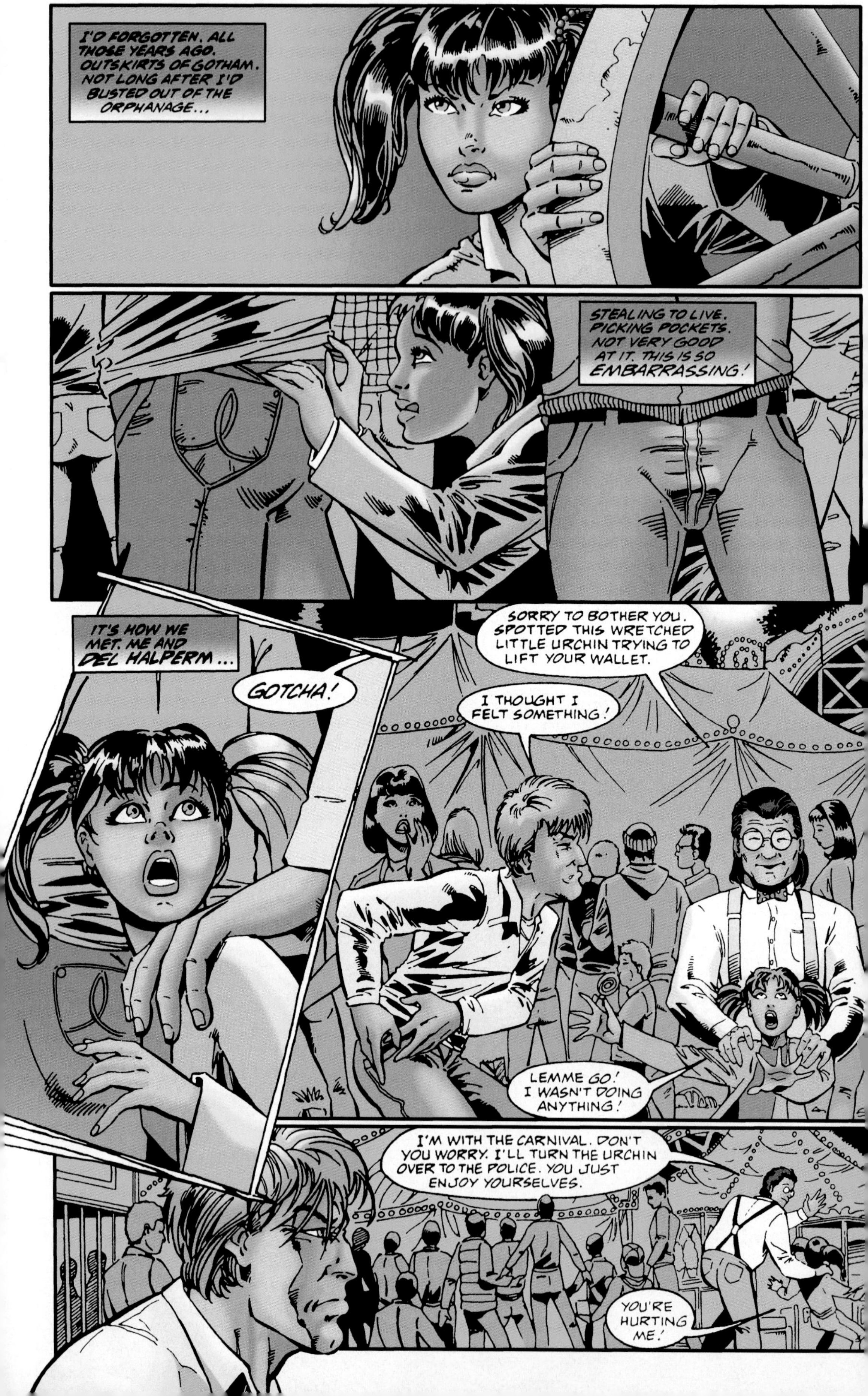

I'D FORGOTTEN. ALL THOSE YEARS AGO. OUTSKIRTS OF GOTHAM. NOT LONG AFTER I'D BUSTED OUT OF THE ORPHANAGE...
STEALING TO LIVE. PICKING POCKETS. NOT VERY GOOD AT IT. THIS IS SO EMBARRASSING!
IT'S HOW WE MET. ME AND DEL HALPERM...
GOTCHA!
SORRY TO BOTHER YOU. SPOTTED THIS WRETCHED LITTLE URCHIN TRYING TO LIFT YOUR WALLET.
I THOUGHT I FELT SOMETHING!
LEMME GO! I WASN'T DOING ANYTHING!
I'M WITH THE CARNIVAL. DON'T YOU WORRY. I'LL TURN THE URCHIN OVER TO THE POLICE. YOU JUST ENJOY YOURSELVES.
YOU'RE HURTING ME!

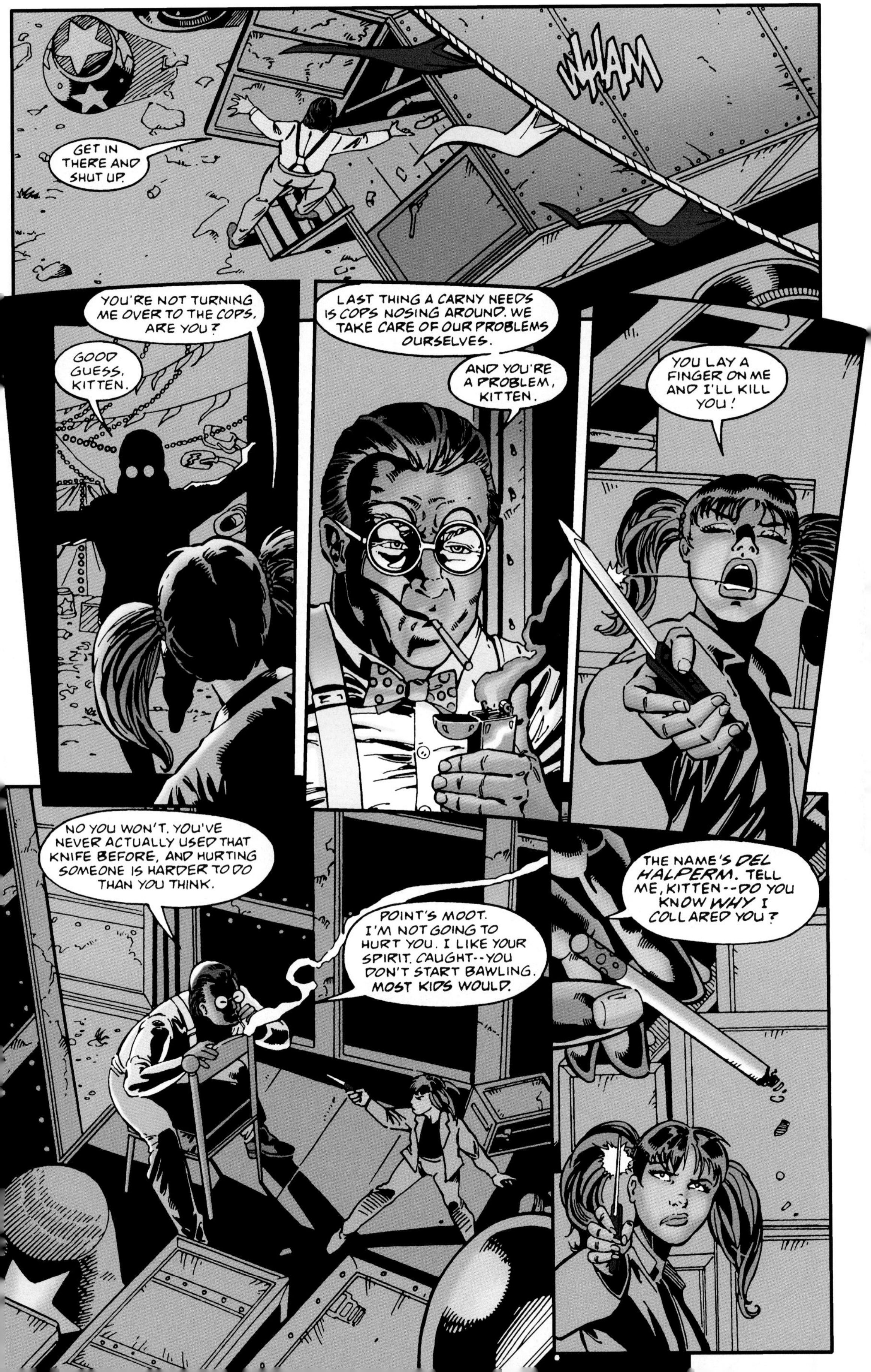
WHAM
GET IN THERE AND SHUT UP.
YOU'RE NOT TURNING ME OVER TO THE COPS, ARE YOU?
GOOD GUESS, KITTEN.
LAST THING A CARNY NEEDS IS COPS NOSING AROUND. WE TAKE CARE OF OUR PROBLEMS OURSELVES.
AND YOU'RE A PROBLEM, KITTEN.
YOU LAY A FINGER ON ME AND I'LL KILL YOU!
NO YOU WON'T. YOU'VE NEVER ACTUALLY USED THAT KNIFE BEFORE, AND HURTING SOMEONE IS HARDER TO DO THAN YOU THINK.
POINT'S MOOT. I'M NOT GOING TO HURT YOU. I LIKE YOUR SPIRIT. CAUGHT--YOU DON'T START BAWLING. MOST KIDS WOULD.
THE NAME'S DEL HALPERM. TELL ME, KITTEN--DO YOU KNOW WHY I COLLARED YOU?

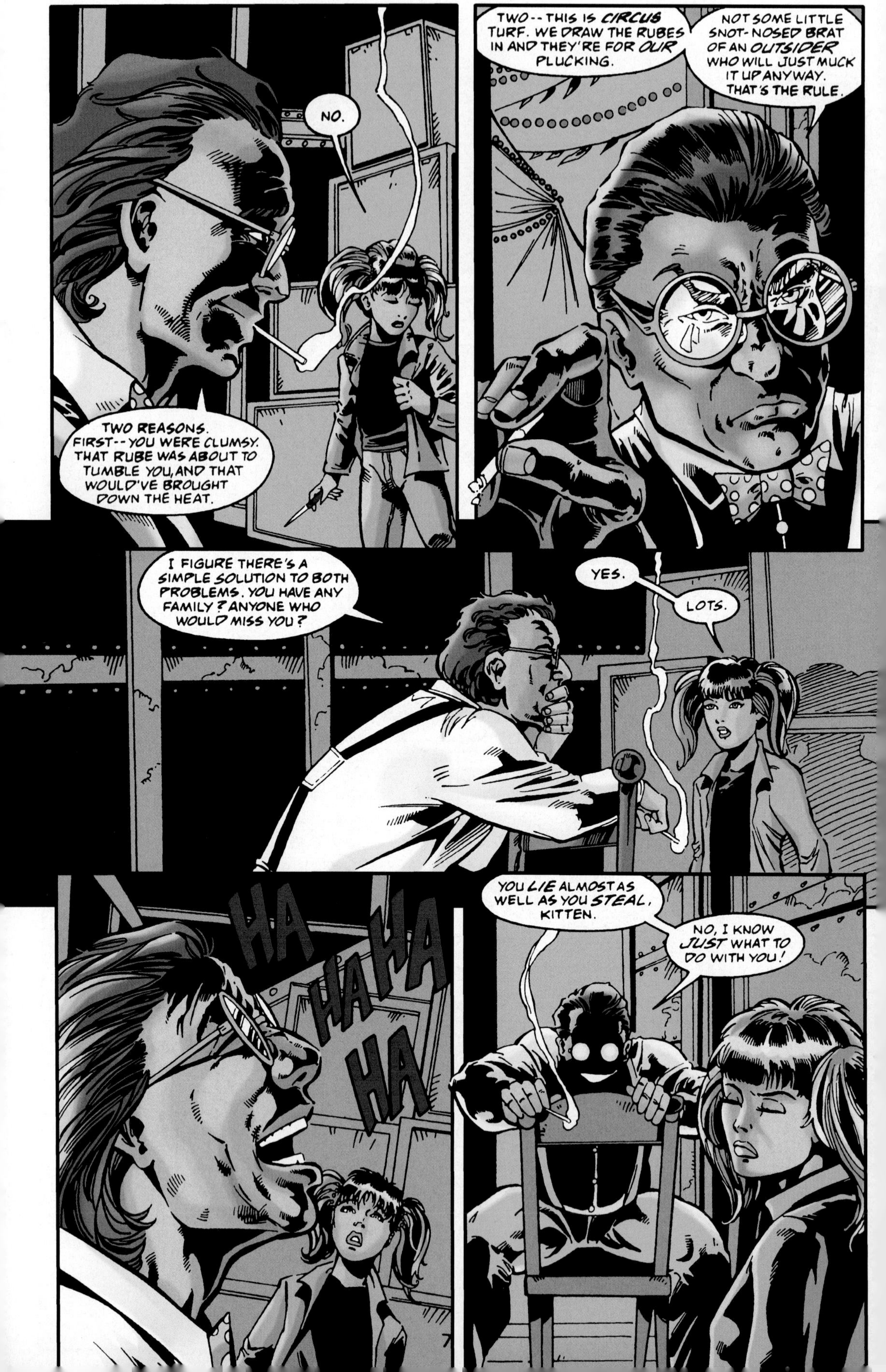
NO.
TWO REASONS. FIRST-- YOU WERE CLUMSY. THAT RUBE WAS ABOUT TO TUMBLE YOU, AND THAT WOULD'VE BROUGHT DOWN THE HEAT.
TWO-- THIS IS CIRCUS TURF. WE DRAW THE RUBES IN AND THEY'RE FOR OUR PLUCKING.
NOT SOME LITTLE SNOT-NOSED BRAT OF AN OUTSIDER WHO WILL JUST MUCK IT UP ANYWAY. THAT'S THE RULE.
I FIGURE THERE'S A SIMPLE SOLUTION TO BOTH PROBLEMS. YOU HAVE ANY FAMILY? ANYONE WHO WOULD MISS YOU?
YES.
LOTS.
HA HA HA HA HA
YOU LIE ALMOST AS WELL AS YOU STEAL, KITTEN.
NO, I KNOW JUST WHAT TO DO WITH YOU!

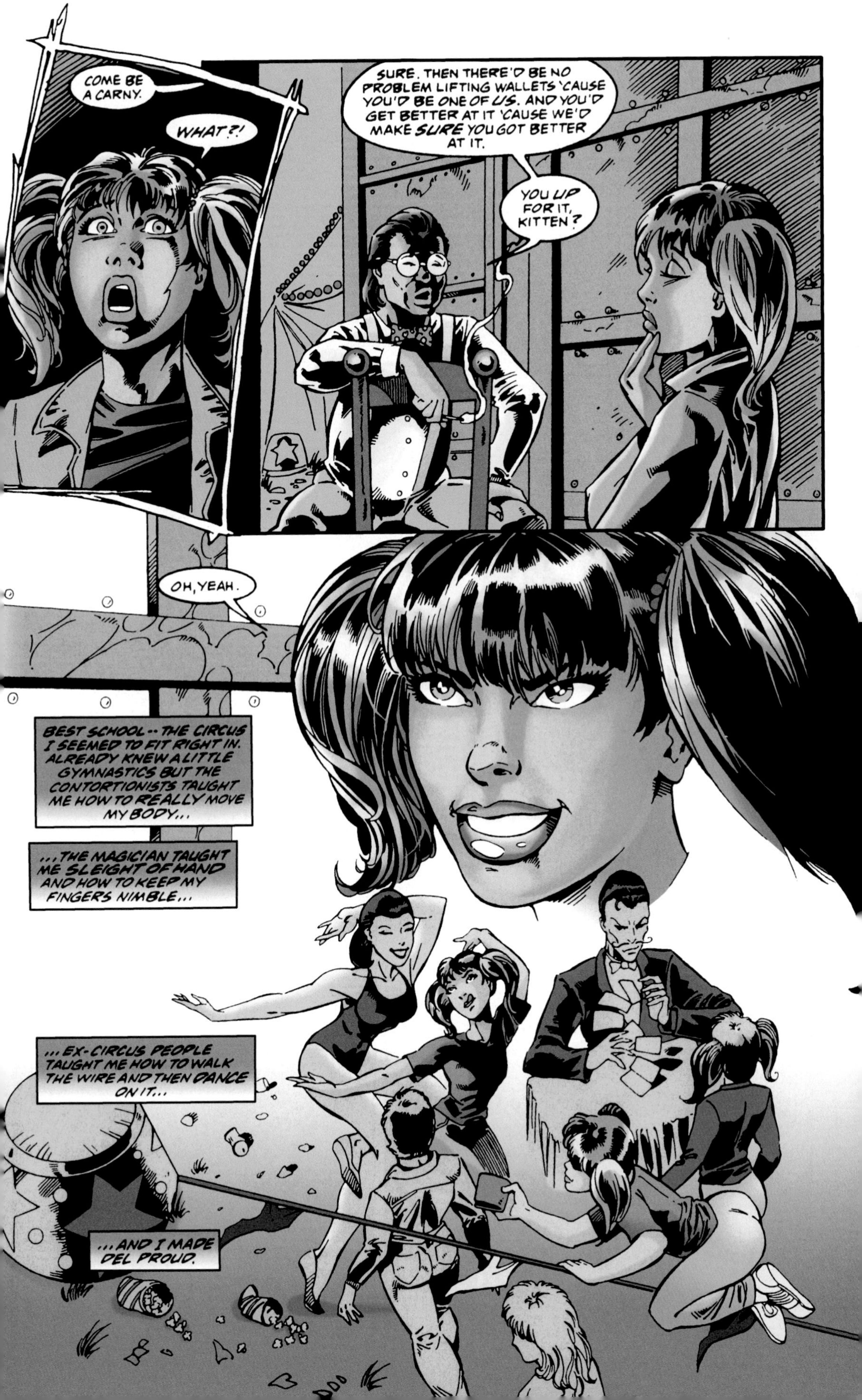
COME BE A CARNY.
WHAT?!
SURE. THEN THERE'D BE NO PROBLEM LIFTING WALLETS 'CAUSE YOU'D BE ONE OF US. AND YOU'D GET BETTER AT IT 'CAUSE WE'D MAKE SURE YOU GOT BETTER AT IT.
YOU UP FOR IT, KITTEN?
OH, YEAH.
BEST SCHOOL -- THE CIRCUS I SEEMED TO FIT RIGHT IN. ALREADY KNEW A LITTLE GYMNASTICS BUT THE CONTORTIONISTS TAUGHT ME HOW TO REALLY MOVE MY BODY...
...THE MAGICIAN TAUGHT ME SLEIGHT OF HAND AND HOW TO KEEP MY FINGERS NIMBLE...
...EX-CIRCUS PEOPLE TAUGHT ME HOW TO WALK THE WIRE AND THEN DANCE ON IT...
...AND I MADE DEL PROUD.

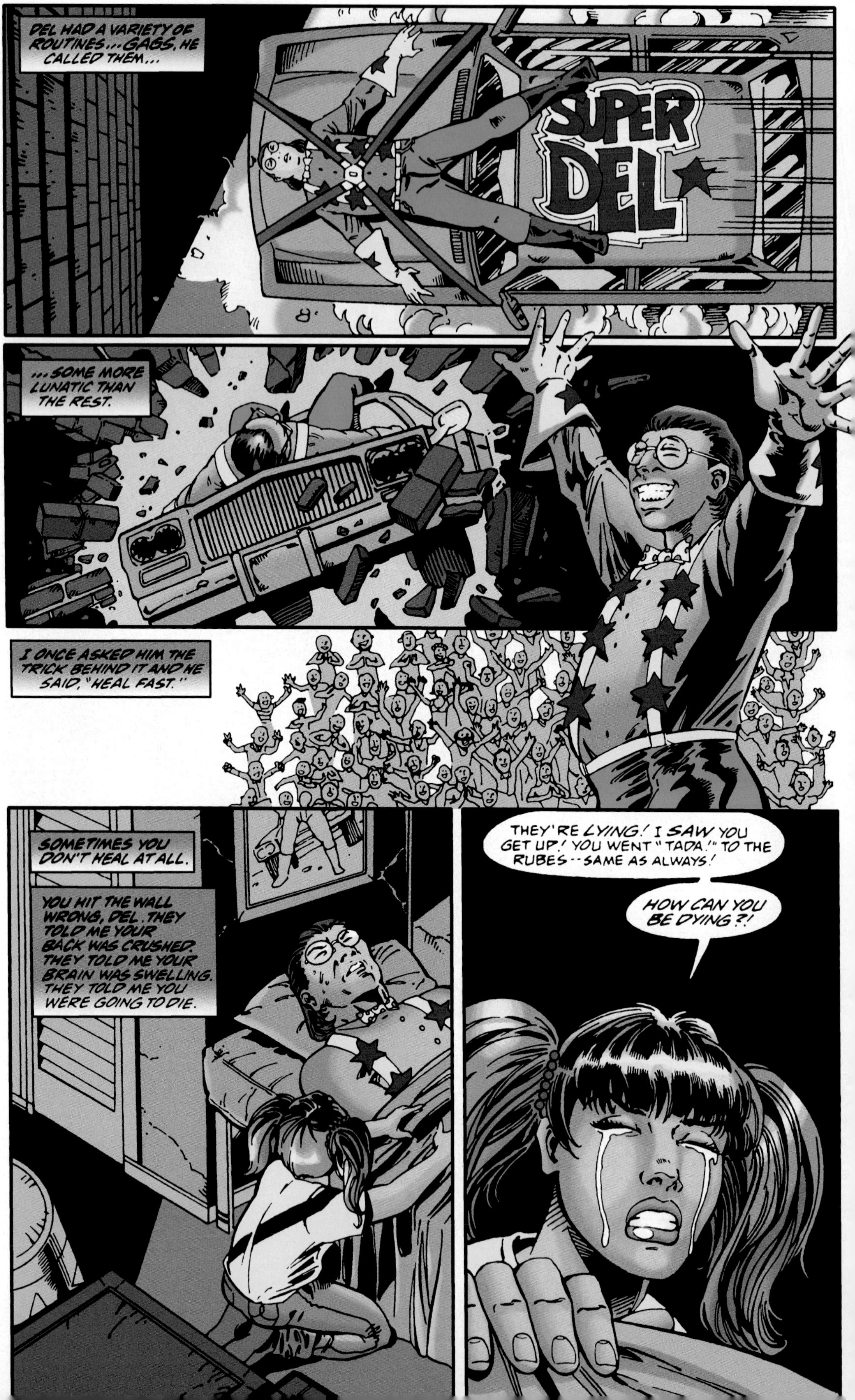

DEL HAD A VARIETY OF ROUTINES... GAGS, HE CALLED THEM...
SUPER DEL
...SOME MORE LUNATIC THAN THE REST.
I ONCE ASKED HIM THE TRICK BEHIND IT AND HE SAID, "HEAL FAST."
SOMETIMES YOU DON'T HEAL AT ALL.
YOU HIT THE WALL WRONG, DEL. THEY TOLD ME YOUR BACK WAS CRUSHED. THEY TOLD ME YOUR BRAIN WAS SWELLING. THEY TOLD ME YOU WERE GOING TO DIE.
THEY'RE LYING! I SAW YOU GET UP! YOU WENT "TADA!" TO THE RUBES--SAME AS ALWAYS!
HOW CAN YOU BE DYING?!

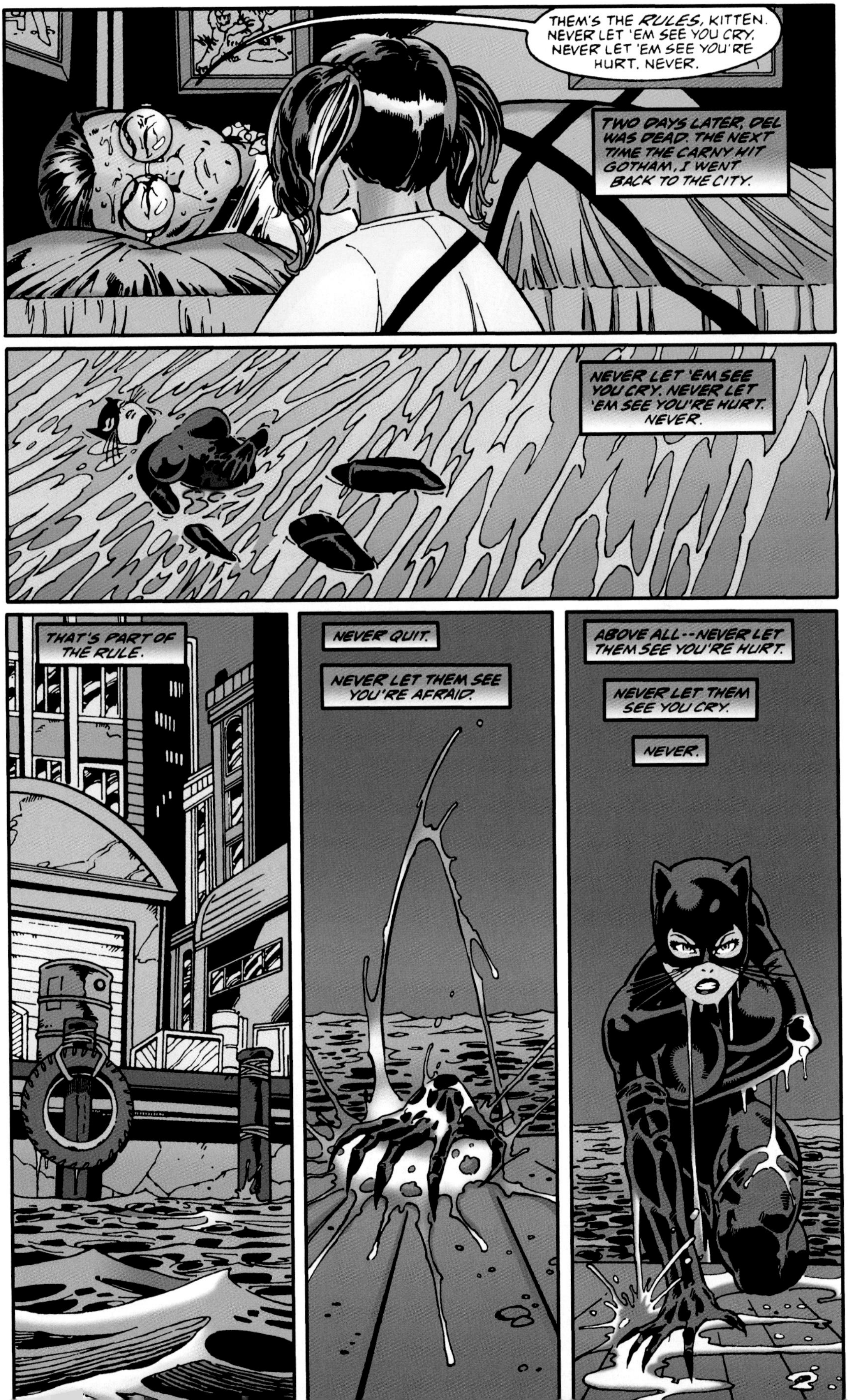
THEM'S THE RULES, KITTEN. NEVER LET 'EM SEE YOU CRY. NEVER LET 'EM SEE YOU'RE HURT. NEVER.
TWO DAYS LATER, DEL WAS DEAD. THE NEXT TIME THE CARNY HIT GOTHAM, I WENT BACK TO THE CITY.
NEVER LET 'EM SEE YOU CRY. NEVER LET 'EM SEE YOU'RE HURT. NEVER.
THAT'S PART OF THE RULE.
NEVER QUIT.
NEVER LET THEM SEE YOU'RE AFRAID.
ABOVE ALL--NEVER LET THEM SEE YOU'RE HURT.
NEVER LET THEM SEE YOU CRY.
NEVER.

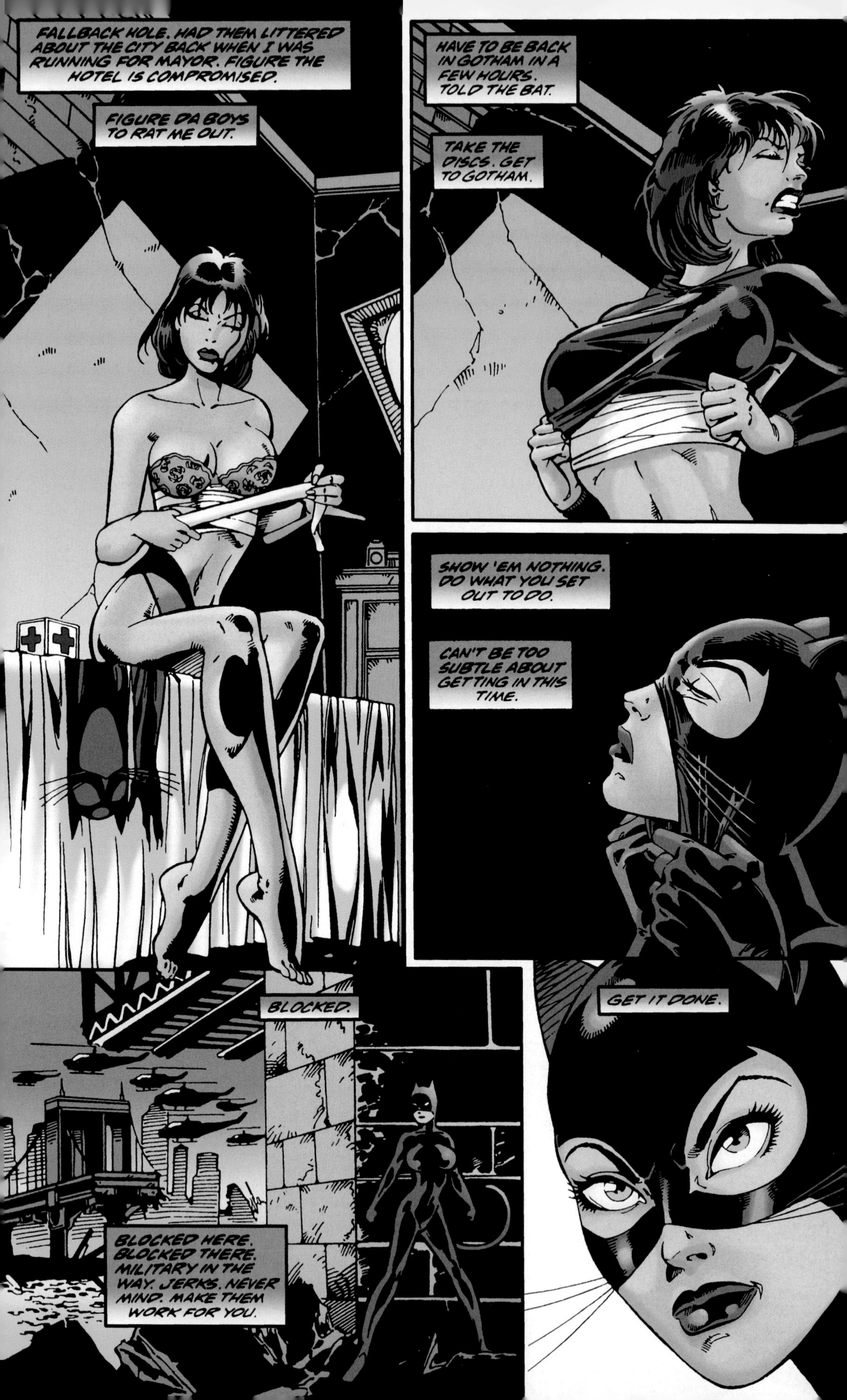
FALLBACK HOLE. HAD THEM LITTERED ABOUT THE CITY BACK WHEN I WAS RUNNING FOR MAYOR. FIGURE THE HOTEL IS COMPROMISED.
FIGURE DA BOYS TO RAT ME OUT.
HAVE TO BE BACK IN GOTHAM IN A FEW HOURS. TOLD THE BAT.
TAKE THE DISCS. GET TO GOTHAM.
SHOW 'EM NOTHING. DO WHAT YOU SET OUT TO DO.
CAN'T BE TOO SUBTLE ABOUT GETTING IN THIS TIME.
BLOCKED.
BLOCKED HERE. BLOCKED THERE. MILITARY IN THE WAY. JERKS. NEVER MIND. MAKE THEM WORK FOR YOU.
GET IT DONE.

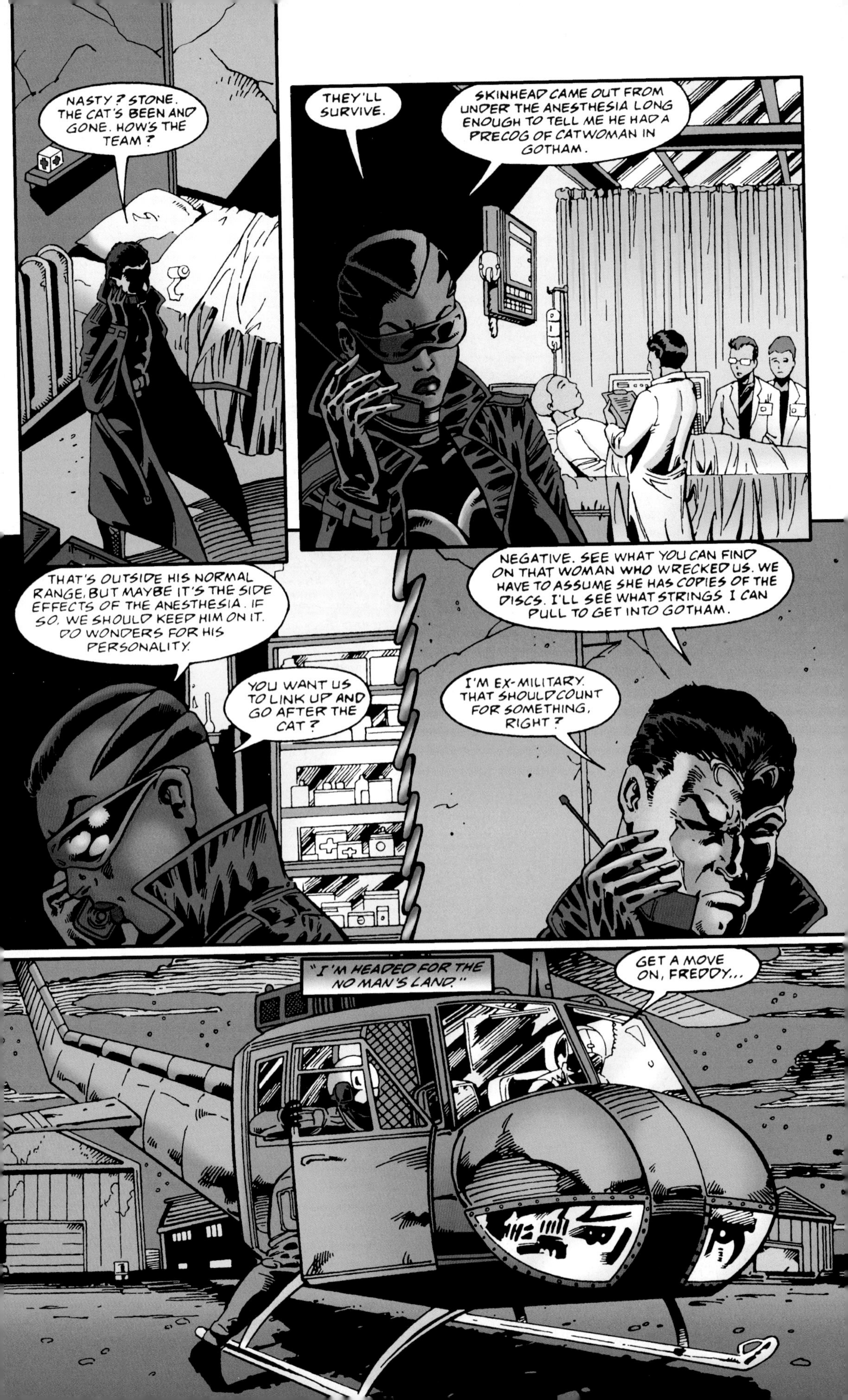

NASTY? STONE. THE CAT'S BEEN AND GONE. HOW'S THE TEAM?
THEY'LL SURVIVE.
SKINHEAD CAME OUT FROM UNDER THE ANESTHESIA LONG ENOUGH TO TELL ME HE HAD A PRECOG OF CATWOMAN IN GOTHAM.
THAT'S OUTSIDE HIS NORMAL RANGE, BUT MAYBE IT'S THE SIDE EFFECTS OF THE ANESTHESIA. IF SO, WE SHOULD KEEP HIM ON IT. DO WONDERS FOR HIS PERSONALITY.
YOU WANT US TO LINK UP AND GO AFTER THE CAT?
NEGATIVE. SEE WHAT YOU CAN FIND ON THAT WOMAN WHO WRECKED US. WE HAVE TO ASSUME SHE HAS COPIES OF THE DISCS. I'LL SEE WHAT STRINGS I CAN PULL TO GET INTO GOTHAM.
I'M EX-MILITARY. THAT SHOULD COUNT FOR SOMETHING, RIGHT?
"I'M HEADED FOR THE NO MAN'S LAND."
GET A MOVE ON, FREDDY...

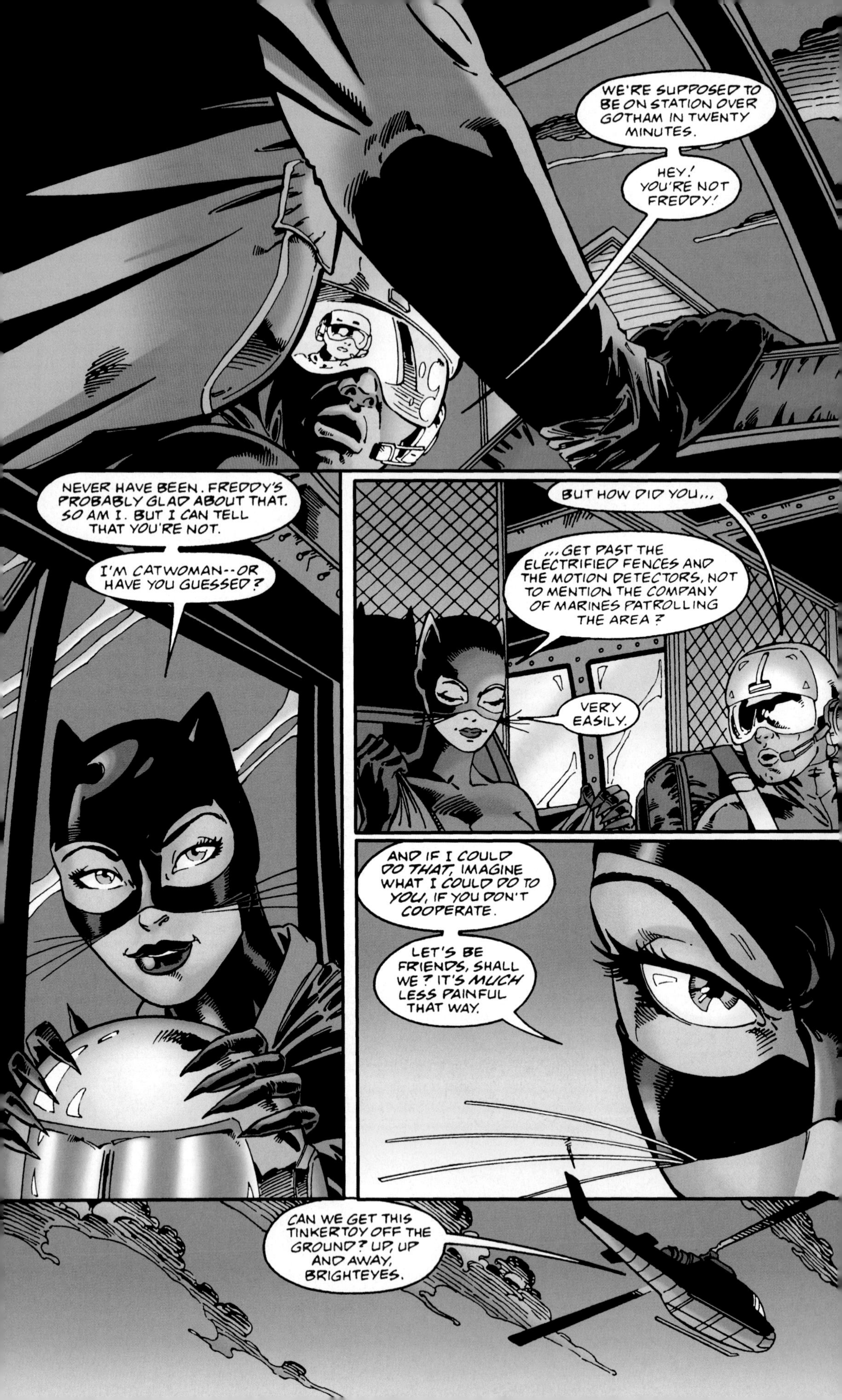

WE'RE SUPPOSED TO BE ON STATION OVER GOTHAM IN TWENTY MINUTES.
HEY! YOU'RE NOT FREDDY!
NEVER HAVE BEEN. FREDDY'S PROBABLY GLAD ABOUT THAT. SO AM I. BUT I CAN TELL THAT YOU'RE NOT.
I'M CATWOMAN--OR HAVE YOU GUESSED?
BUT HOW DID YOU...
...GET PAST THE ELECTRIFIED FENCES AND THE MOTION DETECTORS, NOT TO MENTION THE COMPANY OF MARINES PATROLLING THE AREA?
VERY EASILY.
AND IF I COULD DO THAT, IMAGINE WHAT I COULD DO TO YOU, IF YOU DON'T COOPERATE.
LET'S BE FRIENDS, SHALL WE? IT'S MUCH LESS PAINFUL THAT WAY.
CAN WE GET THIS TINKERTOY OFF THE GROUND? UP, UP AND AWAY, BRIGHTEYES.

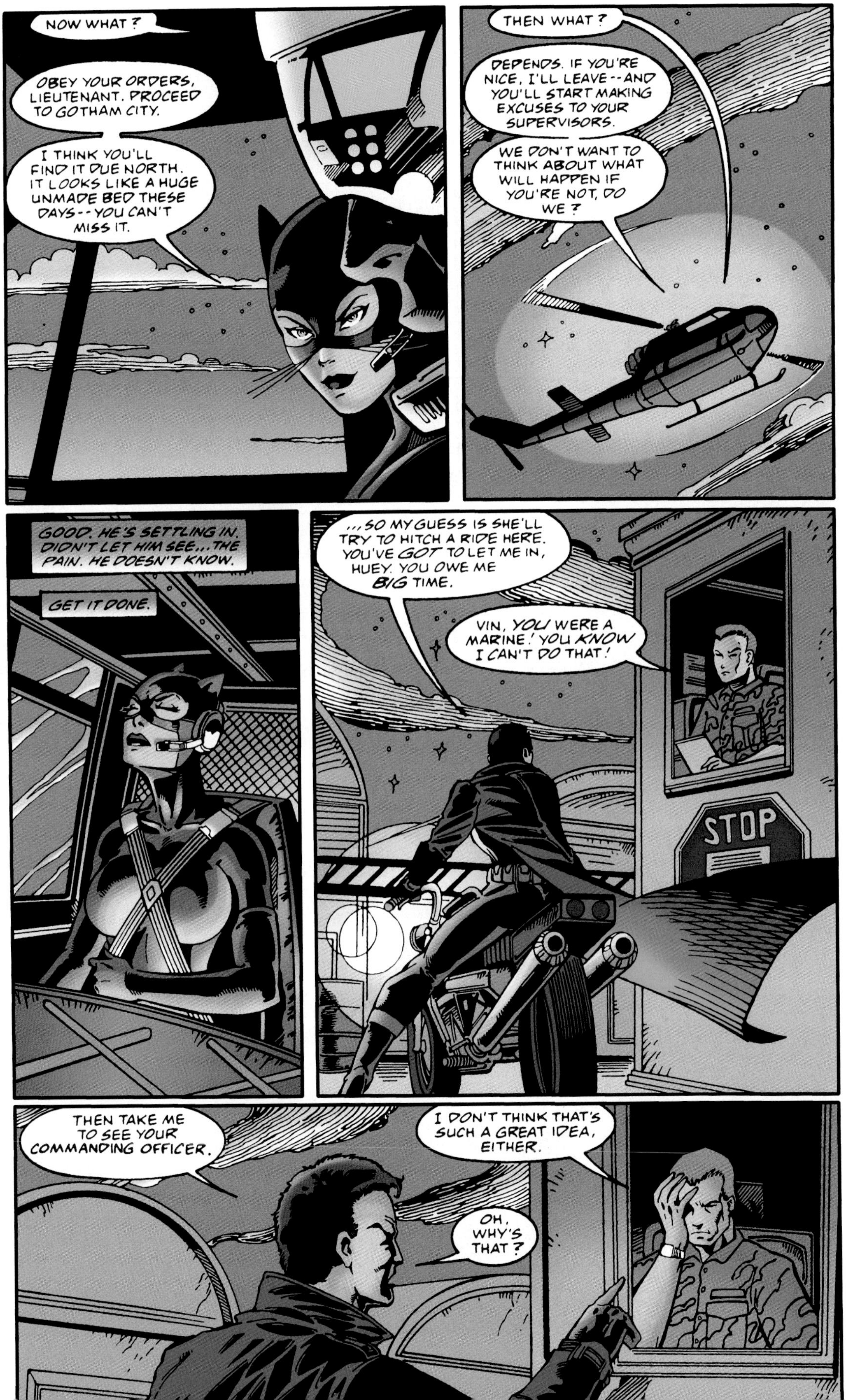
NOW WHAT?
OBEY YOUR ORDERS, LIEUTENANT. PROCEED TO GOTHAM CITY.
I THINK YOU'LL FIND IT DUE NORTH. IT LOOKS LIKE A HUGE UNMADE BED THESE DAYS--YOU CAN'T MISS IT.
THEN WHAT?
DEPENDS. IF YOU'RE NICE, I'LL LEAVE--AND YOU'LL START MAKING EXCUSES TO YOUR SUPERVISORS.
WE DON'T WANT TO THINK ABOUT WHAT WILL HAPPEN IF YOU'RE NOT, DO WE?
GOOD. HE'S SETTLING IN. DIDN'T LET HIM SEE... THE PAIN. HE DOESN'T KNOW.
GET IT DONE.
...SO MY GUESS IS SHE'LL TRY TO HITCH A RIDE HERE. YOU'VE GOT TO LET ME IN, HUEY. YOU OWE ME BIG TIME.
VIN, YOU WERE A MARINE! YOU KNOW I CAN'T DO THAT!
STOP
THEN TAKE ME TO SEE YOUR COMMANDING OFFICER.
I DON'T THINK THAT'S SUCH A GREAT IDEA, EITHER.
OH, WHY'S THAT?

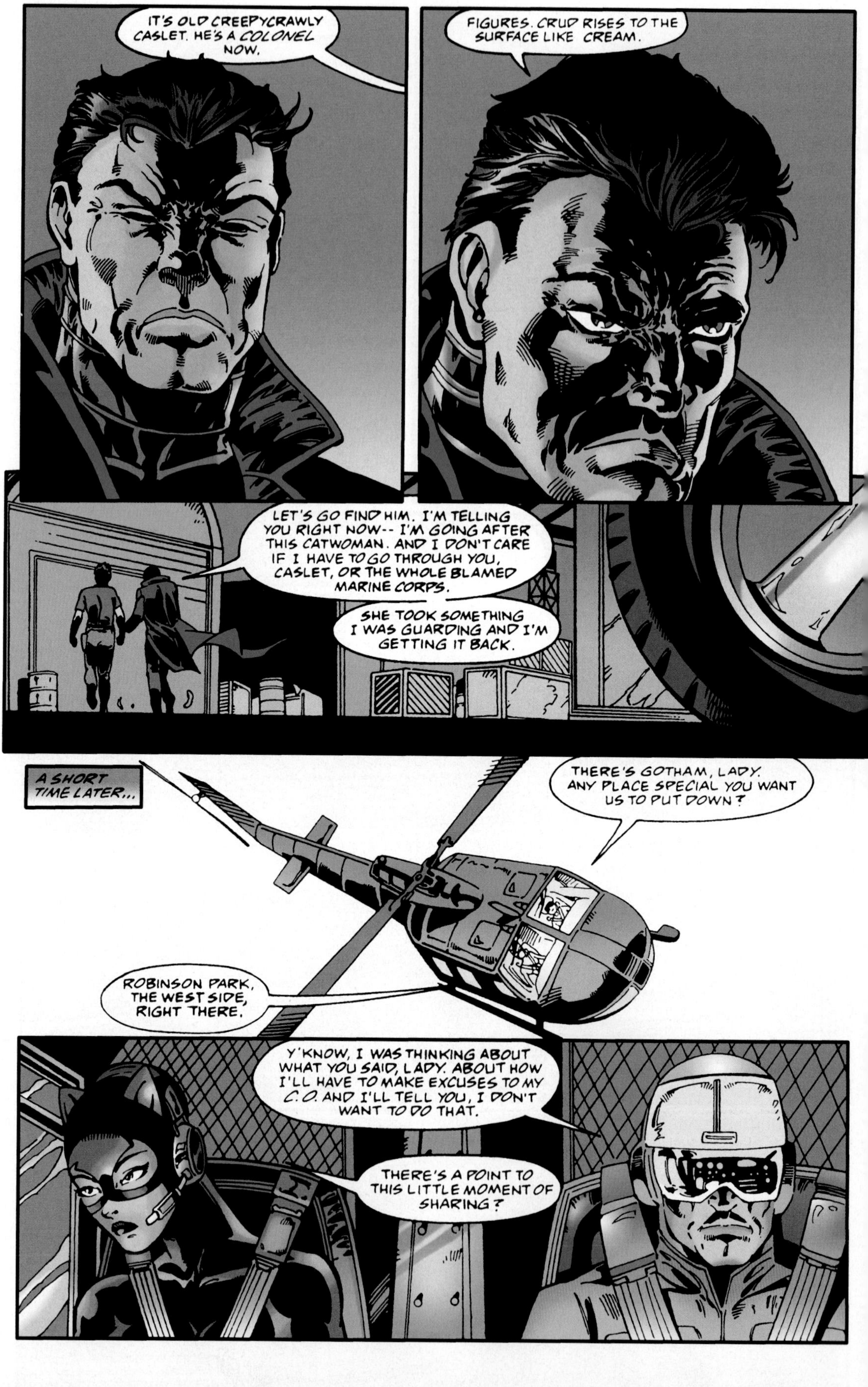
IT'S OLD CREEPYCRAWLY CASLET. HE'S A COLONEL NOW.
FIGURES. CRUD RISES TO THE SURFACE LIKE CREAM.
LET'S GO FIND HIM. I'M TELLING YOU RIGHT NOW-- I'M GOING AFTER THIS CATWOMAN. AND I DON'T CARE IF I HAVE TO GO THROUGH YOU, CASLET, OR THE WHOLE BLAMED MARINE CORPS.
SHE TOOK SOMETHING I WAS GUARDING AND I'M GETTING IT BACK.
A SHORT TIME LATER...
THERE'S GOTHAM, LADY. ANY PLACE SPECIAL YOU WANT US TO PUT DOWN?
ROBINSON PARK, THE WEST SIDE, RIGHT THERE.
Y'KNOW, I WAS THINKING ABOUT WHAT YOU SAID, LADY. ABOUT HOW I'LL HAVE TO MAKE EXCUSES TO MY C.O. AND I'LL TELL YOU, I DON'T WANT TO DO THAT.
THERE'S A POINT TO THIS LITTLE MOMENT OF SHARING?

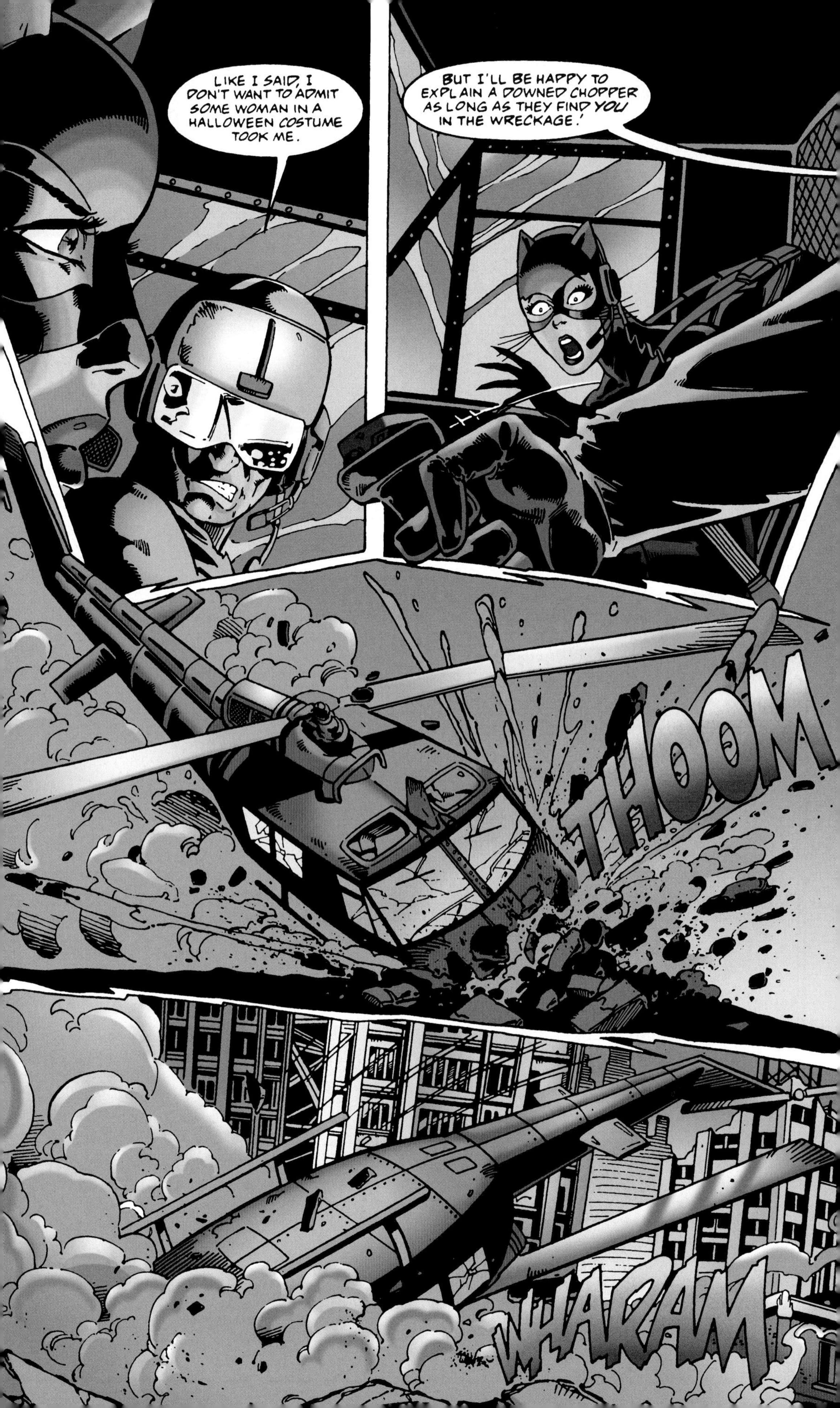

LIKE I SAID, I DON'T WANT TO ADMIT SOME WOMAN IN A HALLOWEEN COSTUME TOOK ME.
BUT I'LL BE HAPPY TO EXPLAIN A DOWNED CHOPPER AS LONG AS THEY FIND YOU IN THE WRECKAGE!
THOOM
WHAAM

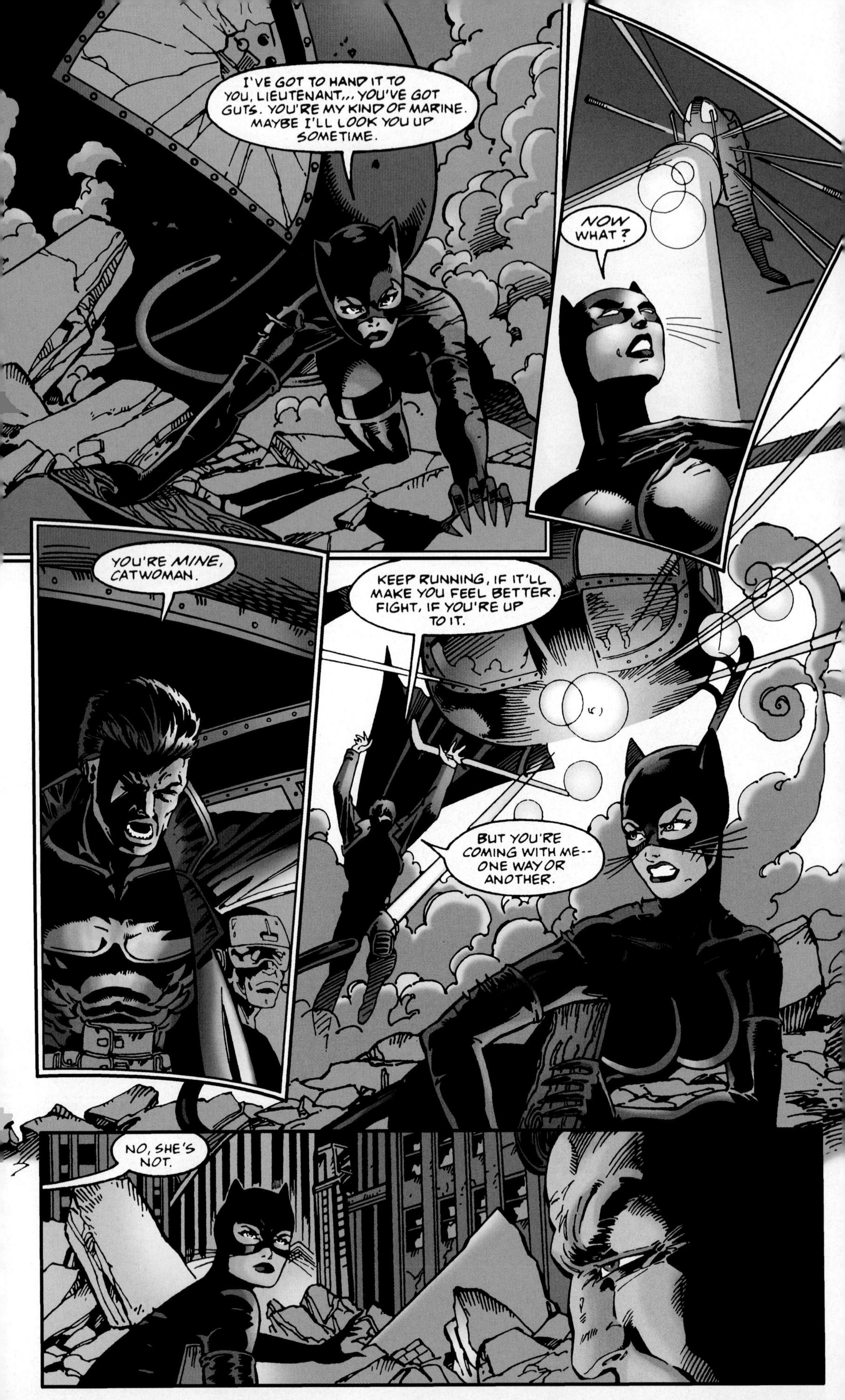
I'VE GOT TO HAND IT TO YOU, LIEUTENANT... YOU'VE GOT GUTS. YOU'RE MY KIND OF MARINE. MAYBE I'LL LOOK YOU UP SOMETIME.
NOW WHAT?
YOU'RE MINE, CATWOMAN.
KEEP RUNNING, IF IT'LL MAKE YOU FEEL BETTER. FIGHT, IF YOU'RE UP TO IT.
BUT YOU'RE COMING WITH ME-- ONE WAY OR ANOTHER.
NO, SHE'S NOT.

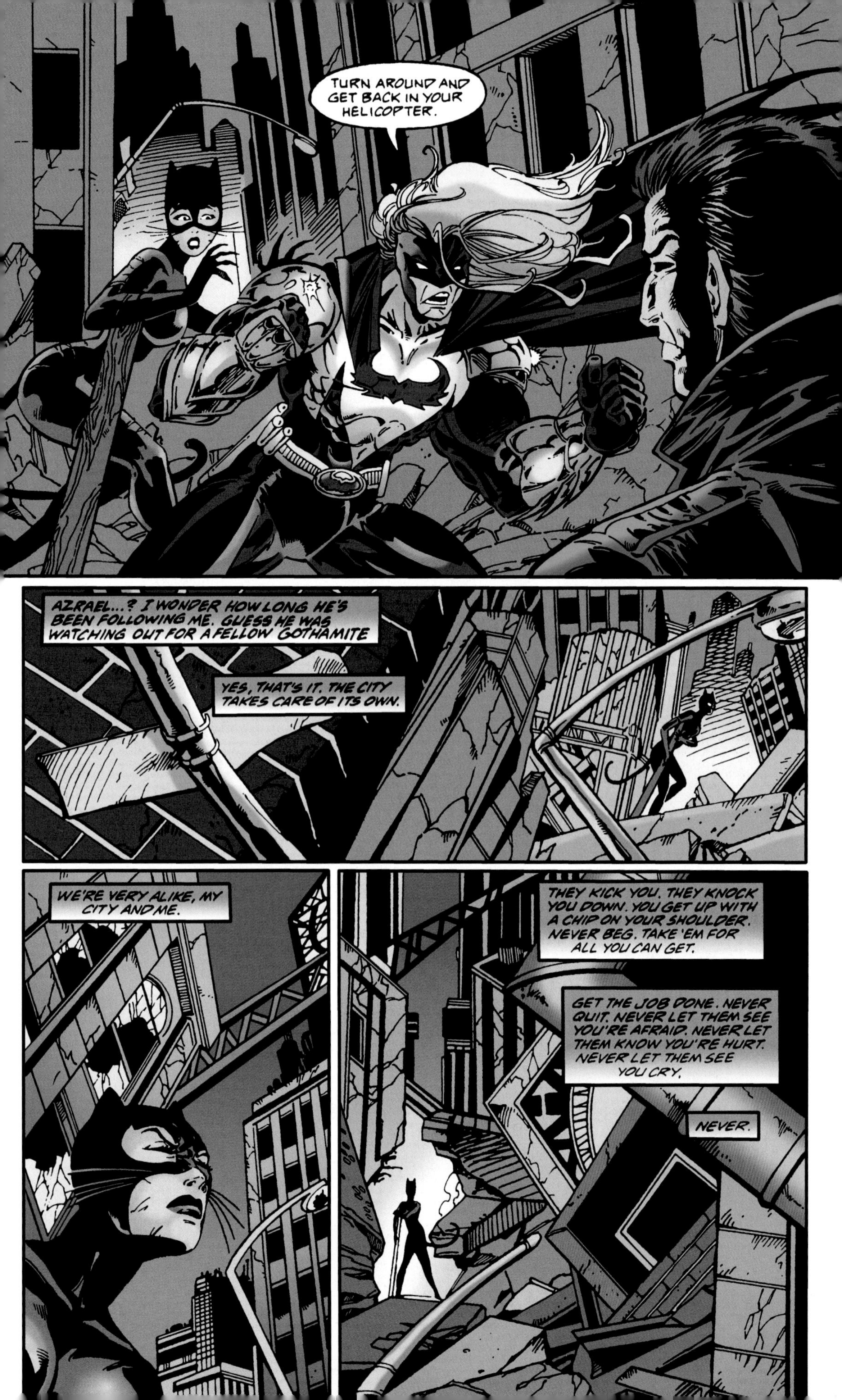
TURN AROUND AND GET BACK IN YOUR HELICOPTER.
AZRAEL...? I WONDER HOW LONG HE'S BEEN FOLLOWING ME. GUESS HE WAS WATCHING OUT FOR A FELLOW GOTHAMITE
YES, THAT'S IT. THE CITY TAKES CARE OF ITS OWN.
WE'RE VERY ALIKE, MY CITY AND ME.
THEY KICK YOU. THEY KNOCK YOU DOWN. YOU GET UP WITH A CHIP ON YOUR SHOULDER. NEVER BEG. TAKE 'EM FOR ALL YOU CAN GET.
GET THE JOB DONE. NEVER QUIT. NEVER LET THEM SEE YOU'RE AFRAID. NEVER LET THEM KNOW YOU'RE HURT. NEVER LET THEM SEE YOU CRY.
NEVER.

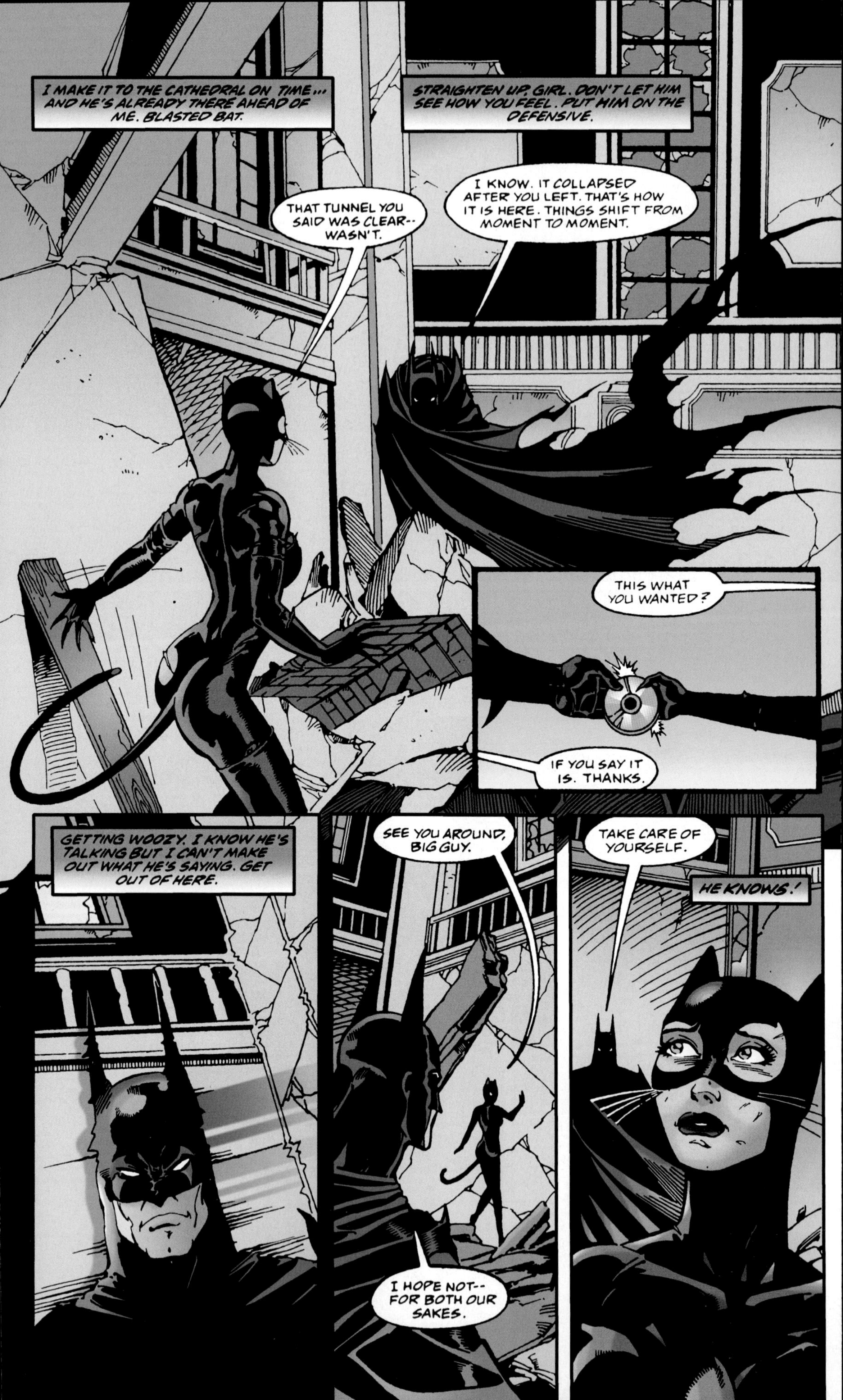

I MAKE IT TO THE CATHEDRAL ON TIME... AND HE'S ALREADY THERE AHEAD OF ME. BLASTED BAT.
STRAIGHTEN UP, GIRL. DON'T LET HIM SEE HOW YOU FEEL. PUT HIM ON THE DEFENSIVE.
THAT TUNNEL YOU SAID WAS CLEAR-- WASN'T.
I KNOW. IT COLLAPSED AFTER YOU LEFT. THAT'S HOW IT IS HERE. THINGS SHIFT FROM MOMENT TO MOMENT.
THIS WHAT YOU WANTED?
IF YOU SAY IT IS. THANKS.
GETTING WOOZY. I KNOW HE'S TALKING BUT I CAN'T MAKE OUT WHAT HE'S SAYING. GET OUT OF HERE.
SEE YOU AROUND, BIG GUY.
I HOPE NOT-- FOR BOTH OUR SAKES.
TAKE CARE OF YOURSELF.
HE KNOWS!

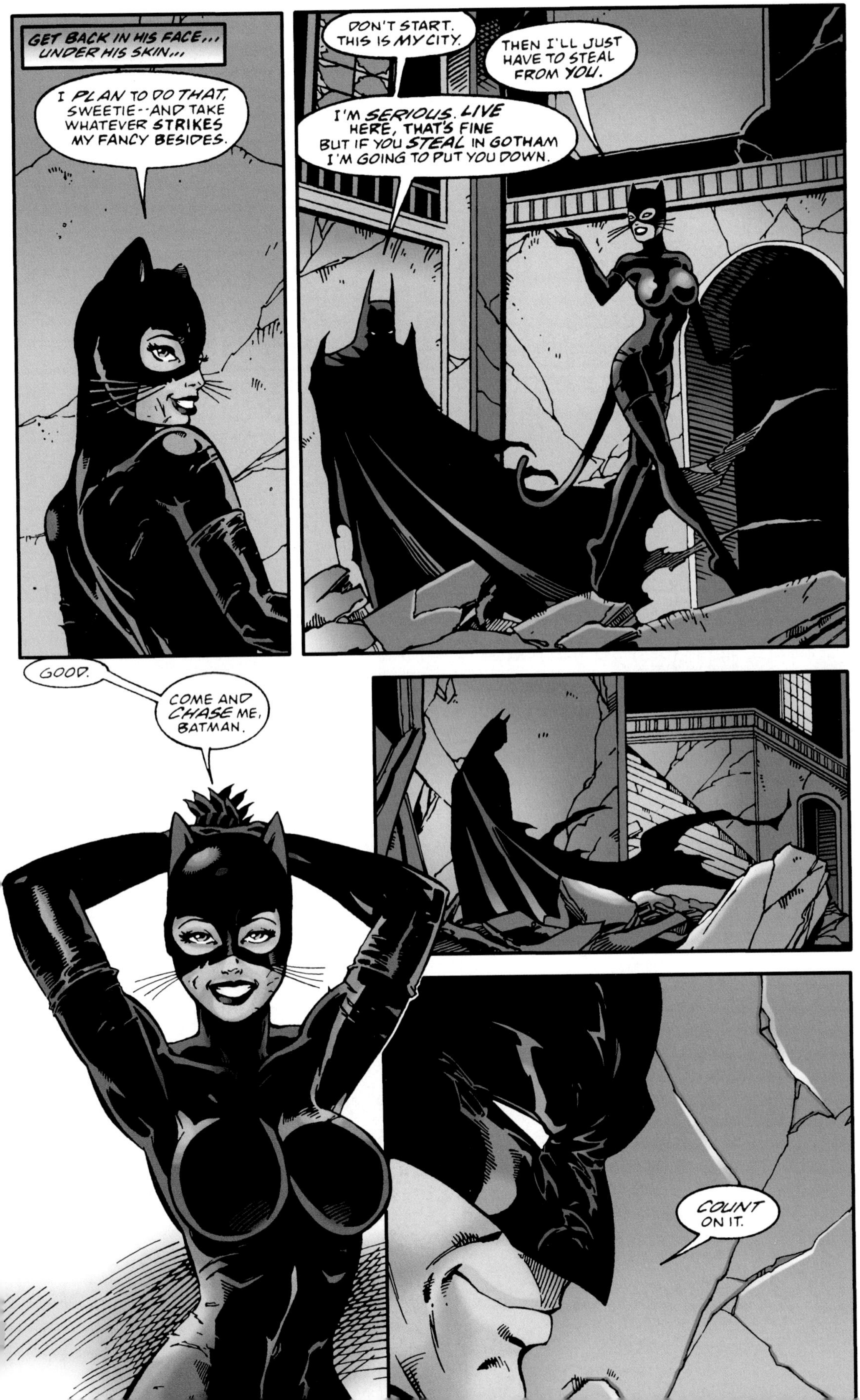
GET BACK IN HIS FACE... UNDER HIS SKIN...
I PLAN TO DO THAT, SWEETIE--AND TAKE WHATEVER STRIKES MY FANCY BESIDES.
DON'T START. THIS IS MY CITY.
THEN I'LL JUST HAVE TO STEAL FROM YOU.
I'M SERIOUS. LIVE HERE, THAT'S FINE BUT IF YOU STEAL IN GOTHAM I'M GOING TO PUT YOU DOWN.
GOOD.
COME AND CHASE ME, BATMAN.
COUNT ON IT.

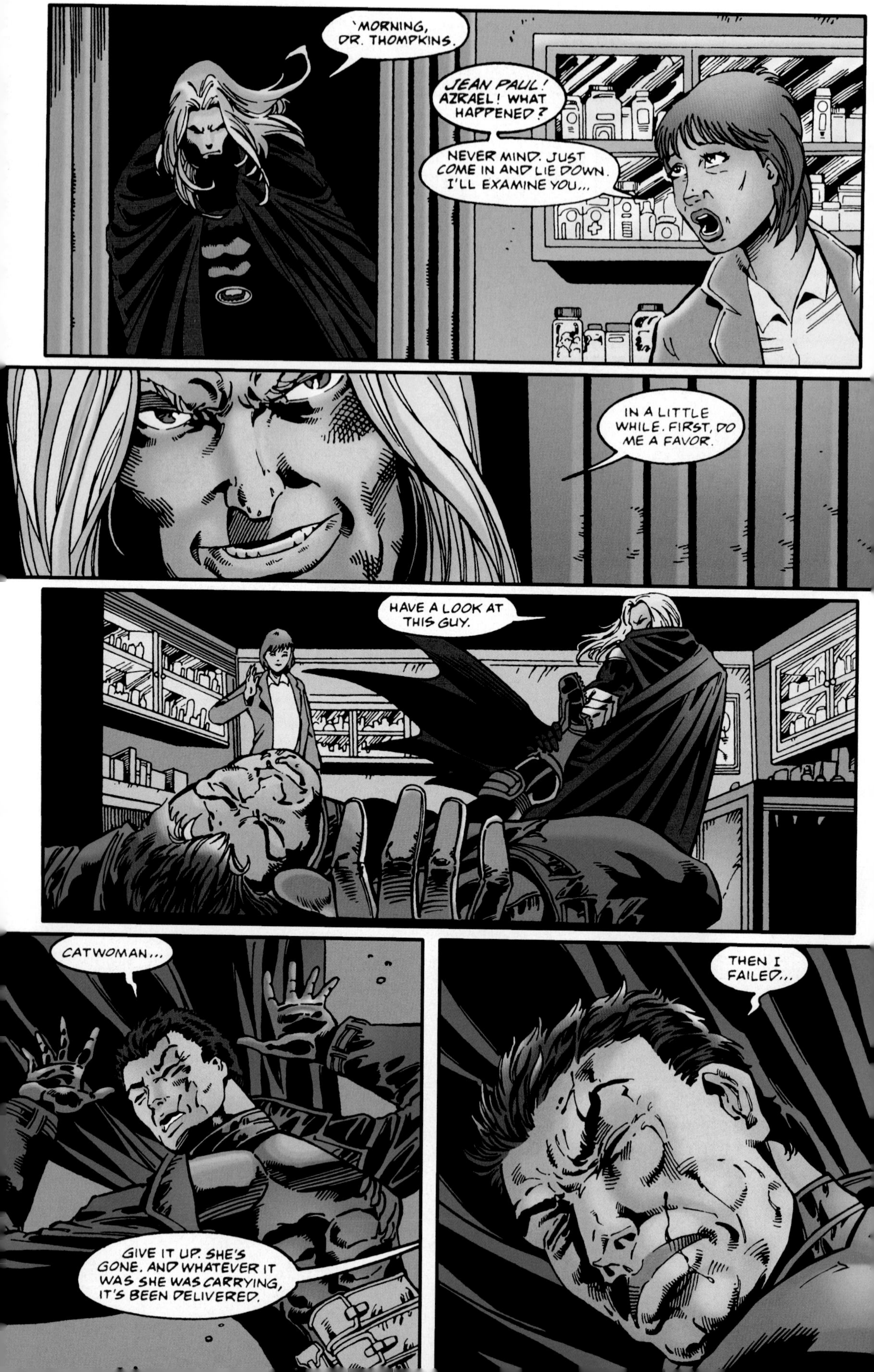
'MORNING, DR. THOMPKINS.
JEAN PAUL! AZRAEL! WHAT HAPPENED?
NEVER MIND. JUST COME IN AND LIE DOWN. I'LL EXAMINE YOU...
IN A LITTLE WHILE. FIRST, DO ME A FAVOR.
HAVE A LOOK AT THIS GUY.
CATWOMAN...
GIVE IT UP. SHE'S GONE. AND WHATEVER IT WAS SHE WAS CARRYING, IT'S BEEN DELIVERED.
THEN I FAILED...

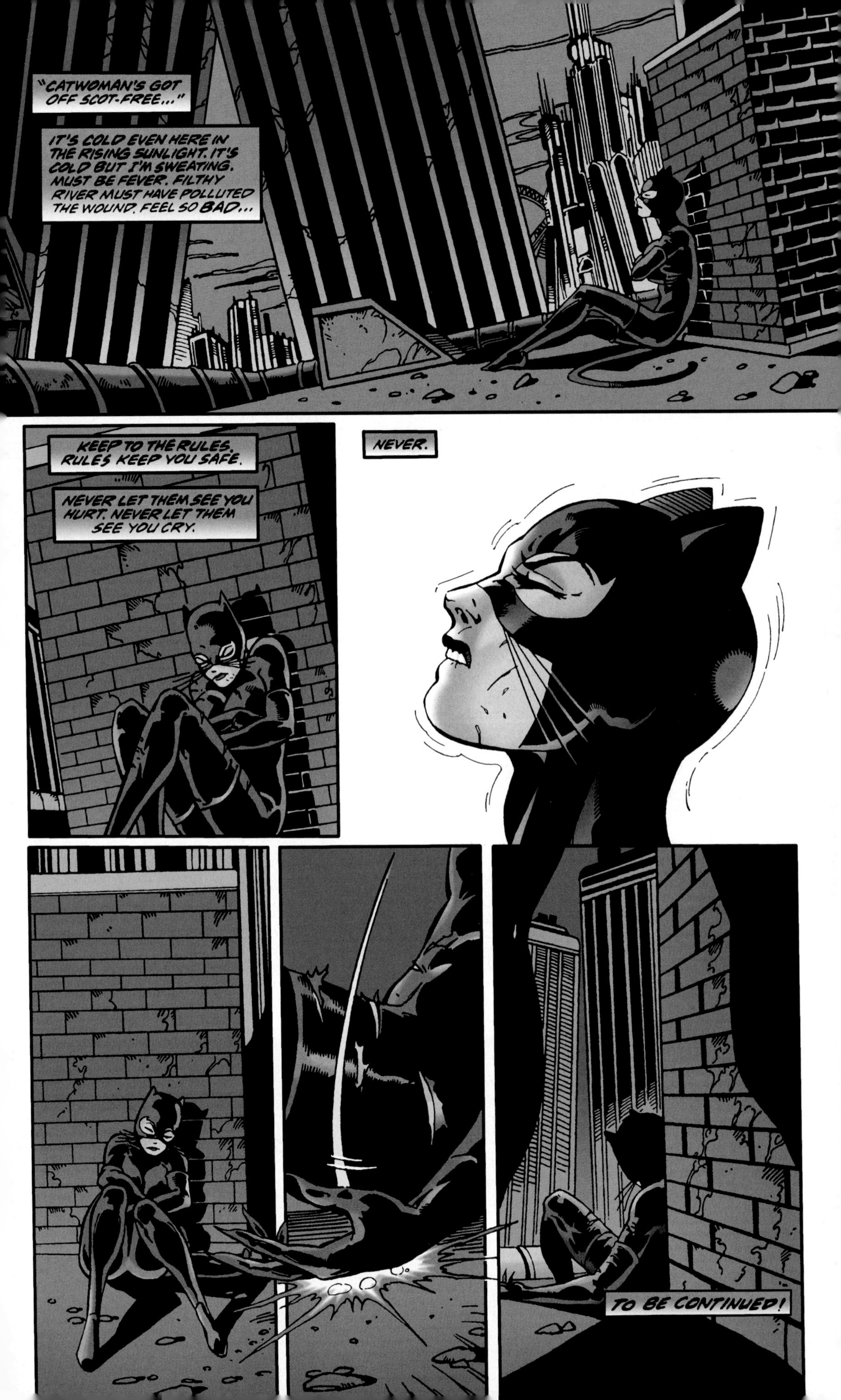
"CATWOMAN'S GOT OFF SCOT-FREE..."
IT'S COLD EVEN HERE IN THE RISING SUNLIGHT. IT'S COLD BUT I'M SWEATING. MUST BE FEVER. FILTHY RIVER MUST HAVE POLLUTED THE WOUND. FEEL SO BAD...
KEEP TO THE RULES. RULES KEEP YOU SAFE.
NEVER LET THEM SEE YOU HURT. NEVER LET THEM SEE YOU CRY.
NEVER.
TO BE CONTINUED!

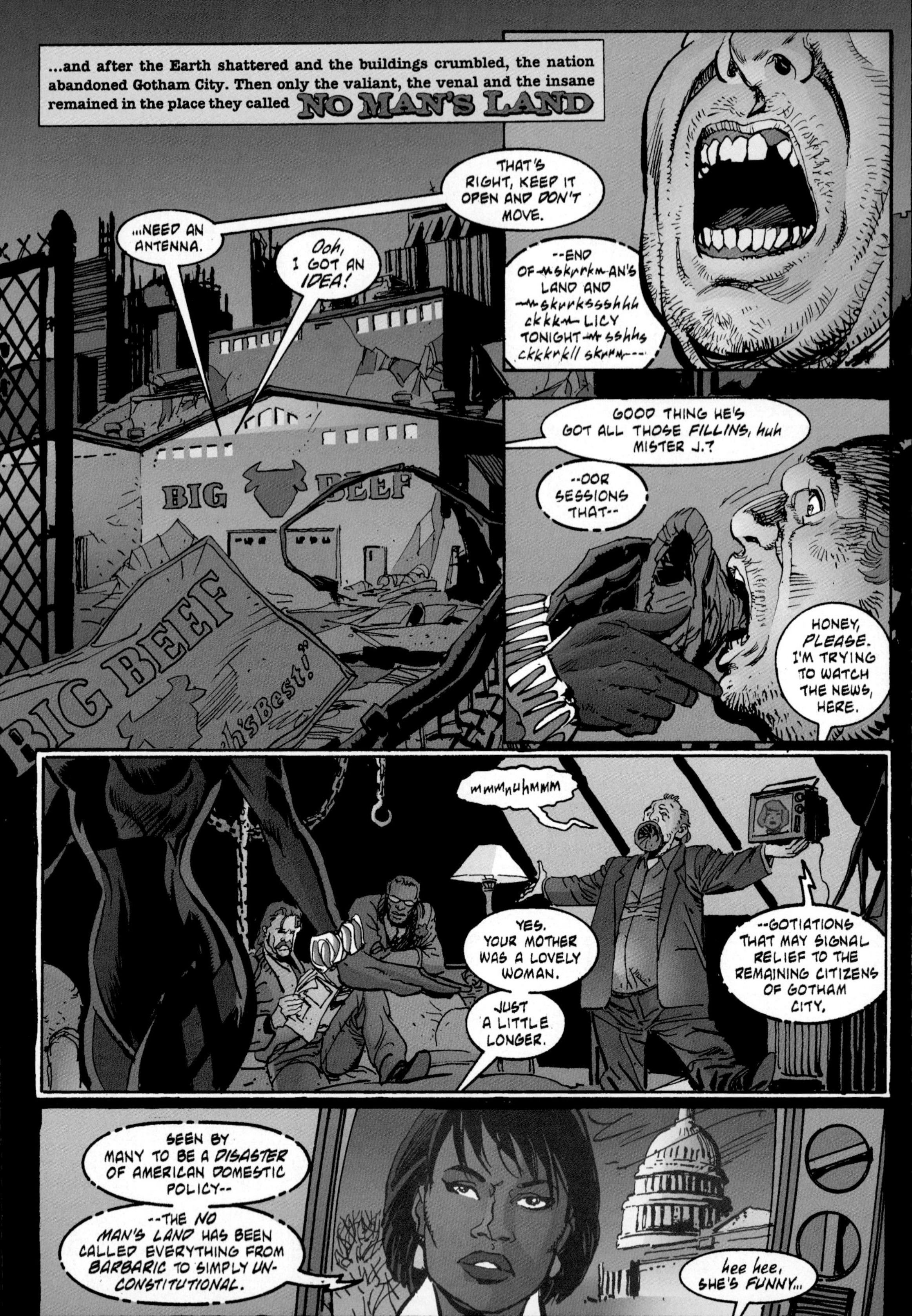
...and after the Earth shattered and the buildings crumbled, the nation abandoned Gotham City. Then only the valiant, the venal and the insane remained in the place they called NO MAN'S LAND
...NEED AN ANTENNA.
THAT'S RIGHT, KEEP IT OPEN AND DON'T MOVE.
Ooh, I GOT AN IDEA!
--END OF ~skrrkm~AN'S LAND AND ~mskrrksssshhh ckkkm~ LICY TONIGHT ~m sshhs ckkkrkll skrmm---
BIG BEEF
BIG BEEF
GOOD THING HE'S GOT ALL THOSE FILLINS, huh MISTER J.?
--OOR SESSIONS THAT--
HONEY, PLEASE. I'M TRYING TO WATCH THE NEWS, HERE.
mmmnuhmmm
YES. YOUR MOTHER WAS A LOVELY WOMAN.
JUST A LITTLE LONGER.
--GOTIATIONS THAT MAY SIGNAL RELIEF TO THE REMAINING CITIZENS OF GOTHAM CITY.
SEEN BY MANY TO BE A DISASTER OF AMERICAN DOMESTIC POLICY--
--THE NO MAN'S LAND HAS BEEN CALLED EVERYTHING FROM BARBARIC TO SIMPLY UN-CONSTITUTIONAL.
hee hee, SHE'S FUNNY...

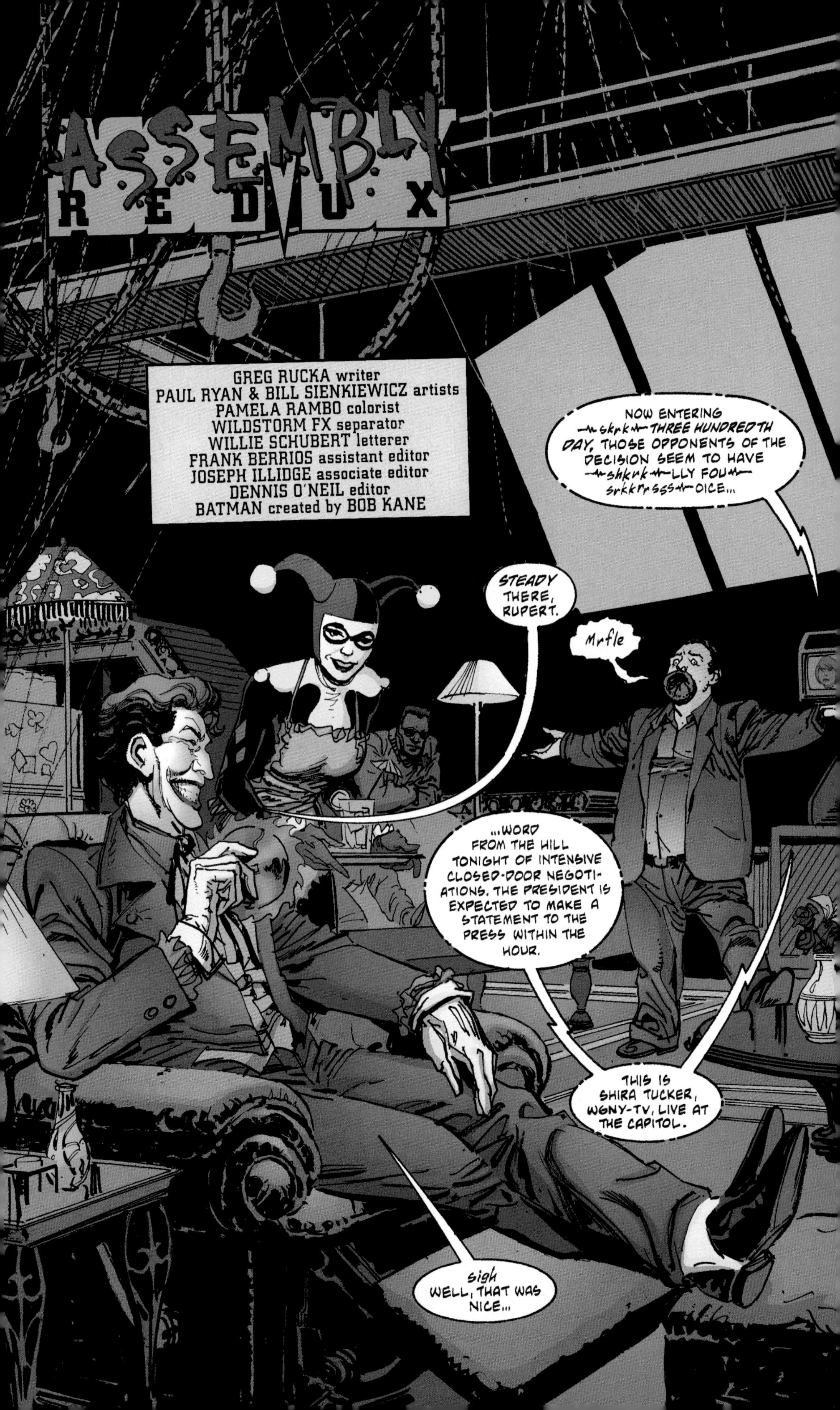
ASSEMBLY
REDUX
GREG RUCKA writer
PAUL RYAN & BILL SIENKIEWICZ artists
PAMELA RAMBO colorist
WILDSTORM FX separator
WILLIE SCHUBERT letterer
FRANK BERRIOS assistant editor
JOSEPH ILLIDGE associate editor
DENNIS O'NEIL editor
BATMAN created by BOB KANE
NOW ENTERING —skrk— THREE HUNDREDTH DAY, THOSE OPPONENTS OF THE DECISION SEEM TO HAVE —shkrk—LLY FOU— srkkrrsss—OICE...
STEADY THERE, RUPERT.
Mrfle
...WORD FROM THE HILL TONIGHT OF INTENSIVE CLOSED-DOOR NEGOTIATIONS. THE PRESIDENT IS EXPECTED TO MAKE A STATEMENT TO THE PRESS WITHIN THE HOUR.
THIS IS SHIRA TUCKER, WGNY-TV, LIVE AT THE CAPITOL.
sigh WELL, THAT WAS NICE...

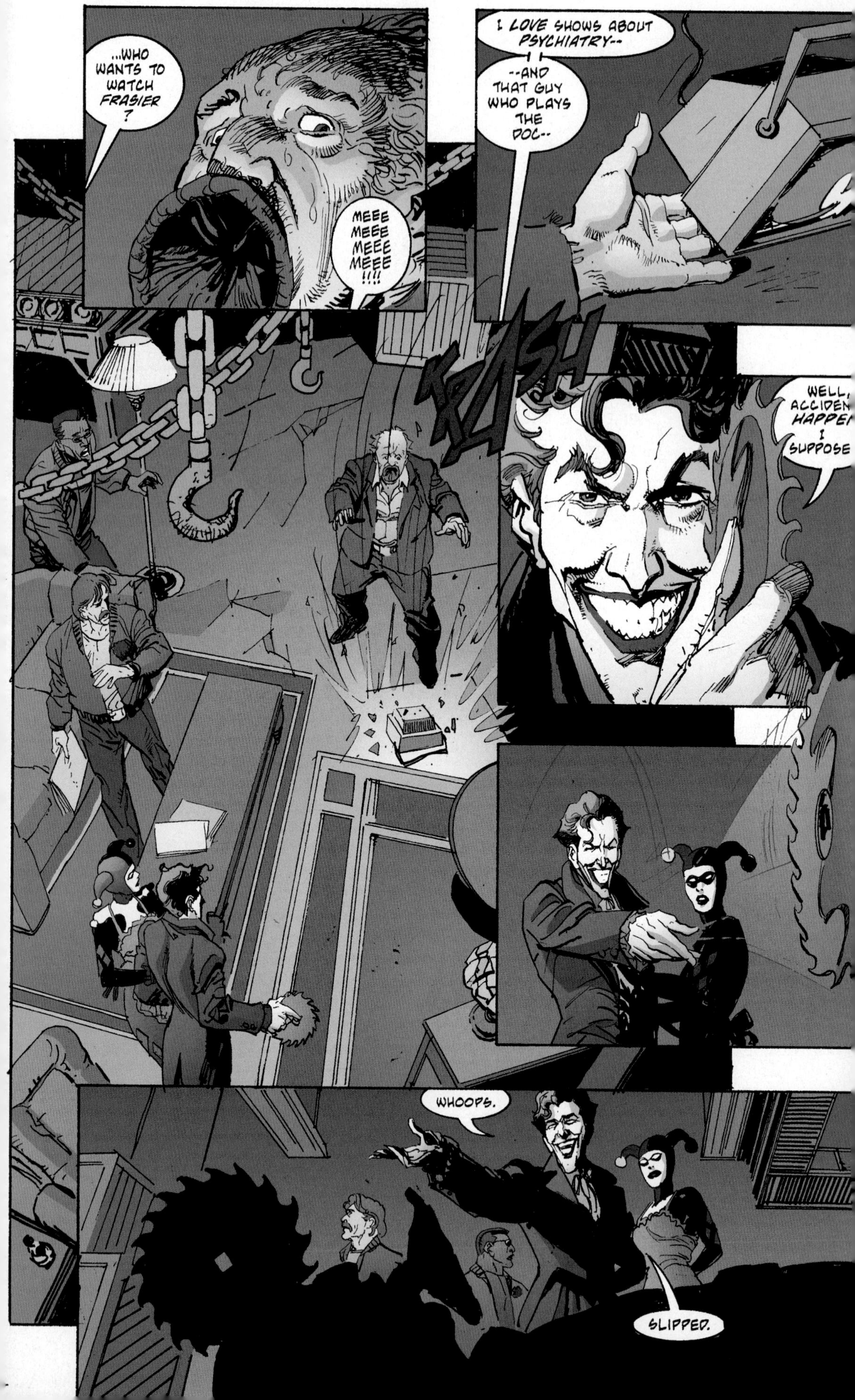

...WHO WANTS TO WATCH FRASIER ?
MEEE MEEE MEEE MEEE !!!!
I LOVE SHOWS ABOUT PSYCHIATRY--
--AND THAT GUY WHO PLAYS THE DOC--
KRASH
WHOOPS.
SLIPPED.

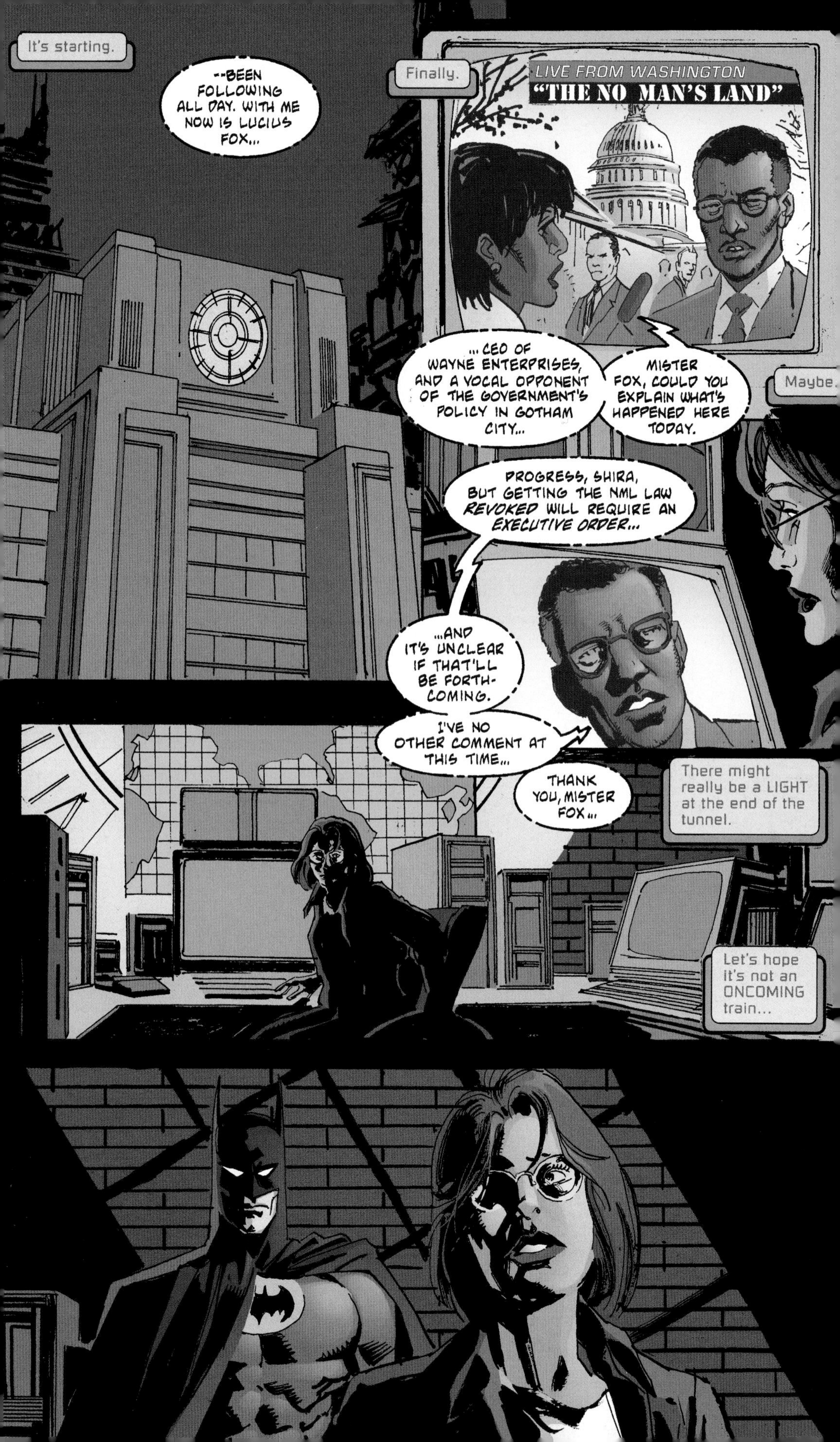

It's starting.
--BEEN FOLLOWING ALL DAY. WITH ME NOW IS LUCIUS FOX...
Finally.
LIVE FROM WASHINGTON
"THE NO MAN'S LAND"
...CEO OF WAYNE ENTERPRISES, AND A VOCAL OPPONENT OF THE GOVERNMENT'S POLICY IN GOTHAM CITY...
MISTER FOX, COULD YOU EXPLAIN WHAT'S HAPPENED HERE TODAY.
Maybe.
PROGRESS, SHIRA, BUT GETTING THE NML LAW REVOKED WILL REQUIRE AN EXECUTIVE ORDER...
...AND IT'S UNCLEAR IF THAT'LL BE FORTH-COMING.
I'VE NO OTHER COMMENT AT THIS TIME...
THANK YOU, MISTER FOX...
There might really be a LIGHT at the end of the tunnel.
Let's hope it's not an ONCOMING train...

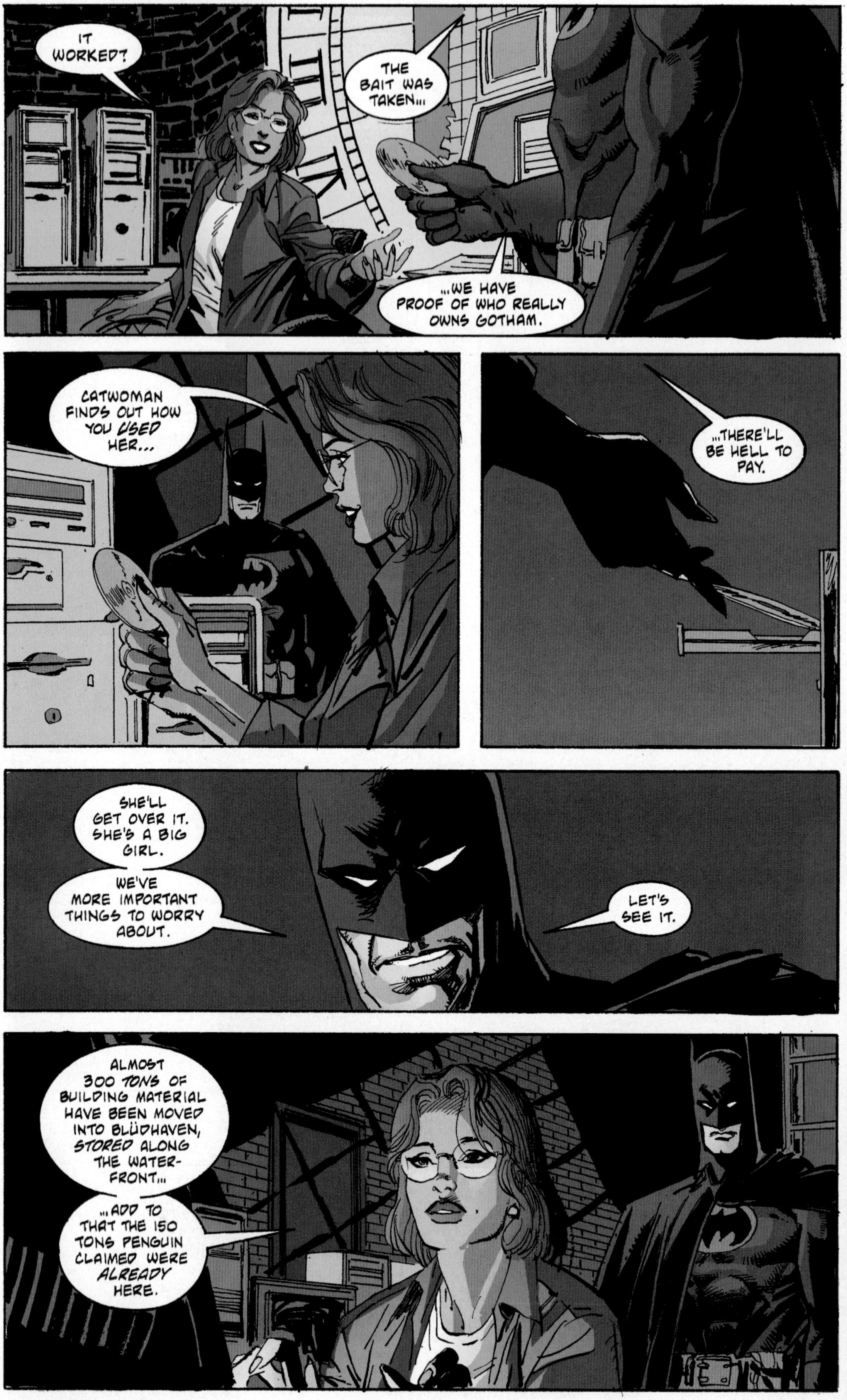
IT WORKED?
THE BAIT WAS TAKEN...
...WE HAVE PROOF OF WHO REALLY OWNS GOTHAM.
CATWOMAN FINDS OUT HOW YOU *USED* HER...
...THERE'LL BE HELL TO PAY.
SHE'LL GET OVER IT. SHE'S A BIG GIRL.
WE'VE MORE IMPORTANT THINGS TO WORRY ABOUT.
LET'S SEE IT.
ALMOST 300 *TONS* OF BUILDING MATERIAL HAVE BEEN MOVED INTO BLÜDHAVEN, *STORED* ALONG THE WATER-FRONT...
...ADD TO THAT THE 150 TONS PENGUIN CLAIMED WERE *ALREADY* HERE.

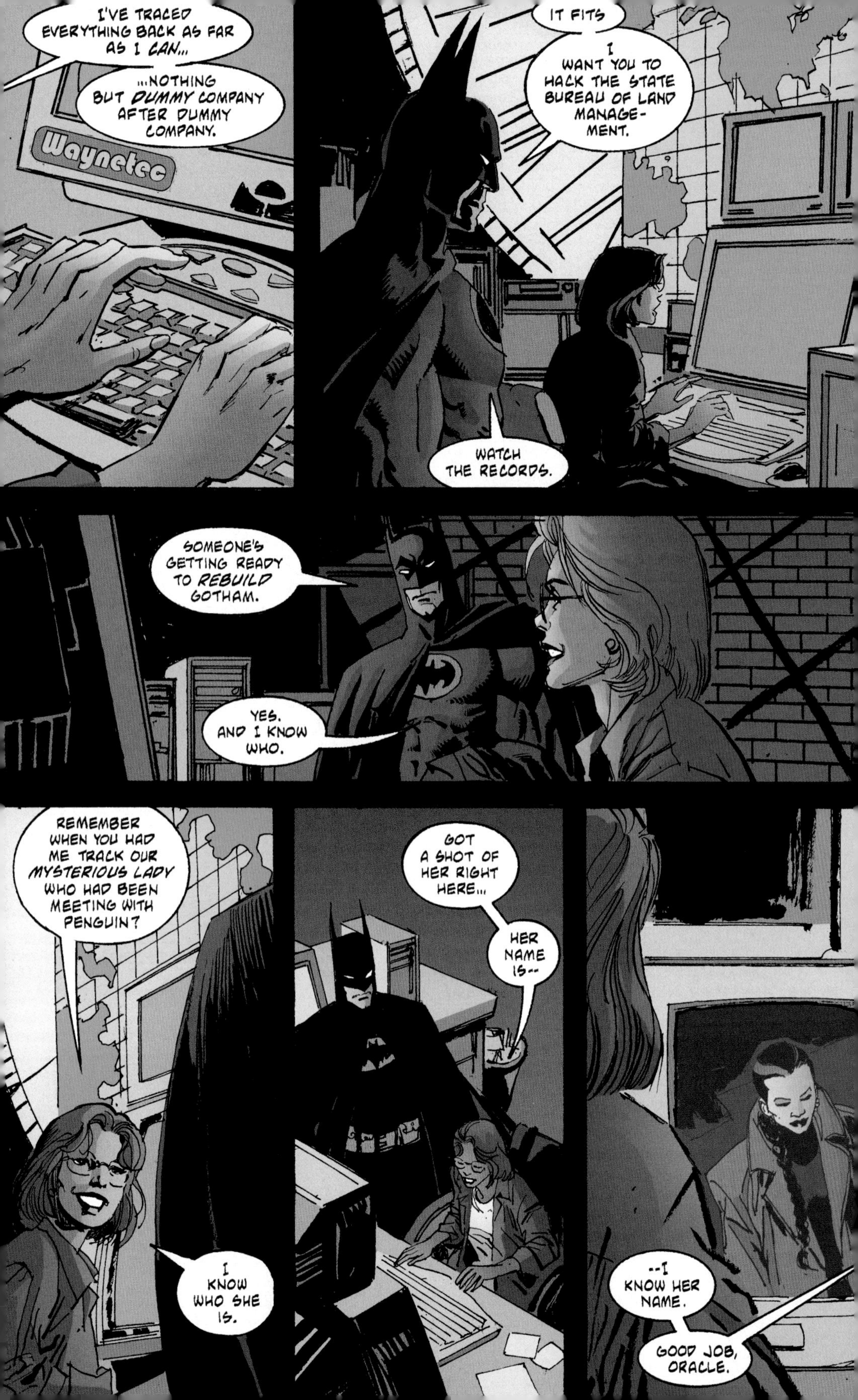
I'VE TRACED EVERYTHING BACK AS FAR AS I CAN...
...NOTHING BUT DUMMY COMPANY AFTER DUMMY COMPANY.
Waynetec
IT FITS
I WANT YOU TO HACK THE STATE BUREAU OF LAND MANAGE-MENT.
WATCH THE RECORDS.
SOMEONE'S GETTING READY TO REBUILD GOTHAM.
YES. AND I KNOW WHO.
REMEMBER WHEN YOU HAD ME TRACK OUR MYSTERIOUS LADY WHO HAD BEEN MEETING WITH PENGUIN?
I KNOW WHO SHE IS.
GOT A SHOT OF HER RIGHT HERE...
HER NAME IS--
--I KNOW HER NAME.
GOOD JOB, ORACLE.

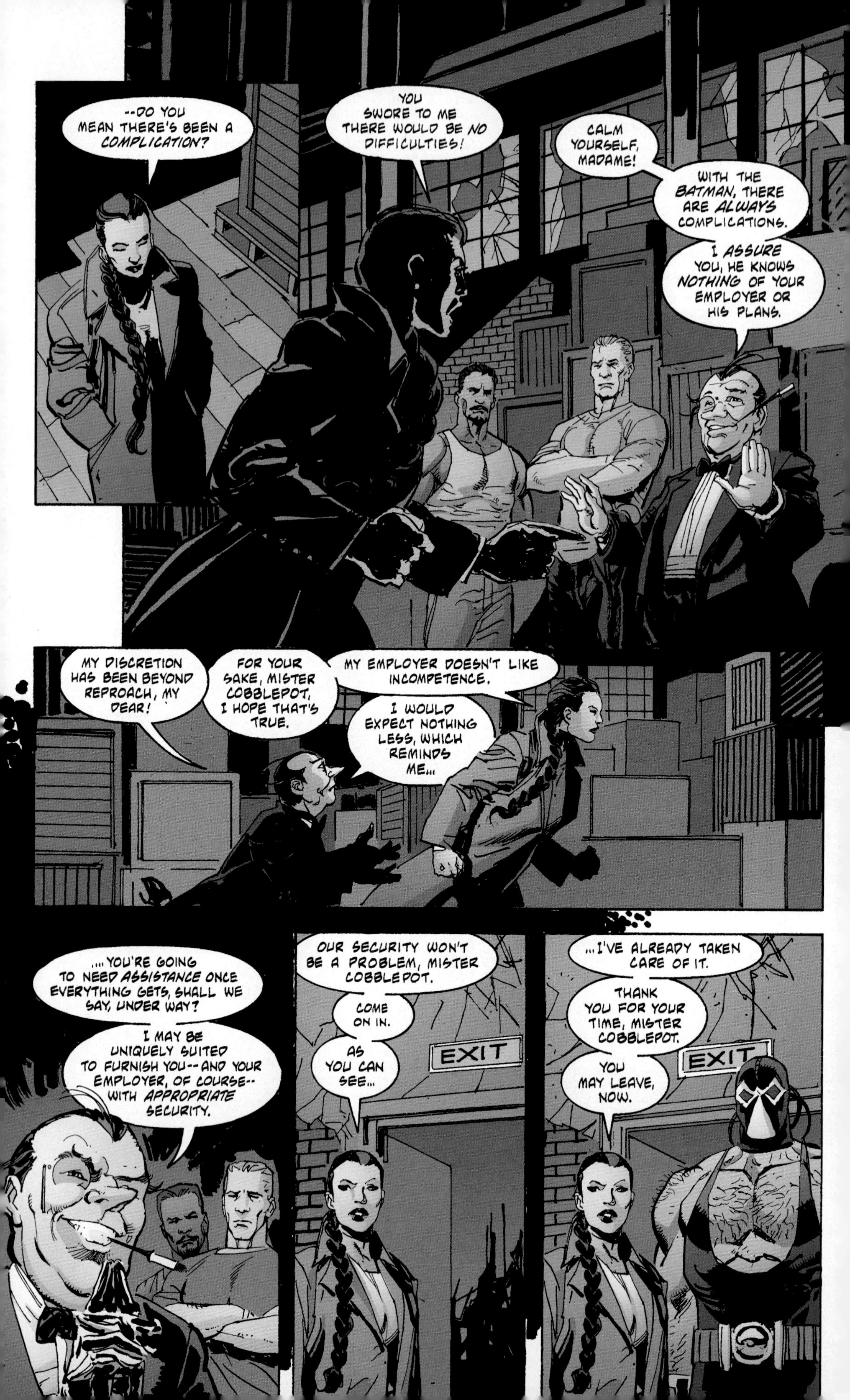
--DO YOU MEAN THERE'S BEEN A *COMPLICATION?*
YOU SWORE TO ME THERE WOULD BE *NO* DIFFICULTIES!
CALM YOURSELF, MADAME!
WITH THE *BATMAN,* THERE ARE *ALWAYS* COMPLICATIONS.
I *ASSURE* YOU, HE KNOWS *NOTHING* OF YOUR EMPLOYER OR HIS PLANS.
MY DISCRETION HAS BEEN BEYOND REPROACH, MY DEAR!
FOR YOUR SAKE, MISTER COBBLEPOT, I HOPE THAT'S TRUE.
MY EMPLOYER DOESN'T LIKE INCOMPETENCE.
I WOULD EXPECT NOTHING LESS, WHICH REMINDS ME...
....YOU'RE GOING TO NEED *ASSISTANCE* ONCE EVERYTHING GETS, SHALL WE SAY, UNDER WAY?
I MAY BE UNIQUELY SUITED TO FURNISH YOU--AND YOUR EMPLOYER, OF COURSE--WITH *APPROPRIATE* SECURITY.
OUR SECURITY WON'T BE A PROBLEM, MISTER COBBLEPOT.
COME ON IN.
AS YOU CAN SEE...
EXIT
...I'VE ALREADY TAKEN CARE OF IT.
THANK YOU FOR YOUR TIME, MISTER COBBLEPOT.
YOU MAY LEAVE, NOW.
EXIT

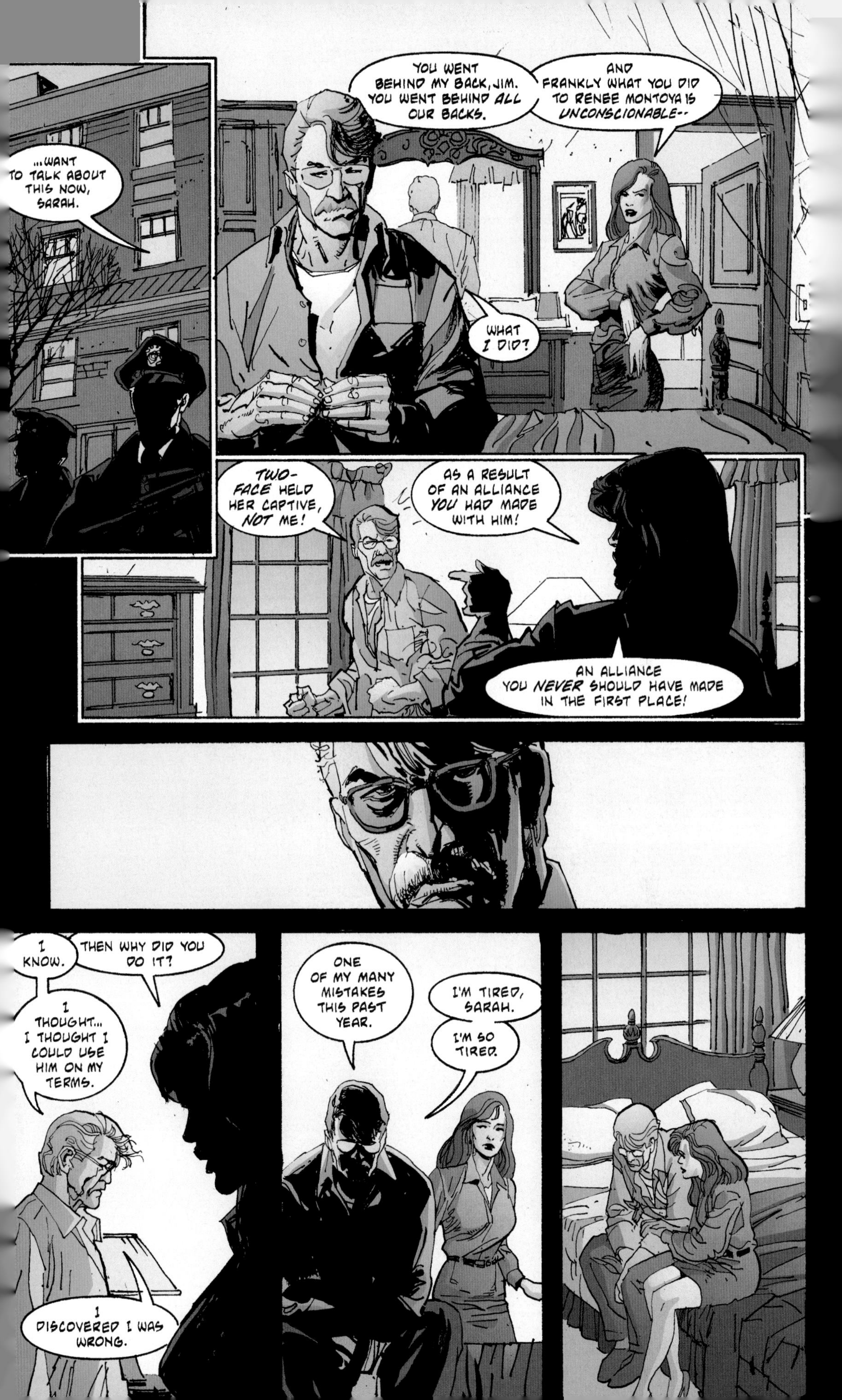
...WANT TO TALK ABOUT THIS NOW, SARAH.
YOU WENT BEHIND MY BACK, JIM. YOU WENT BEHIND ALL OUR BACKS.
AND FRANKLY WHAT YOU DID TO RENEE MONTOYA IS UNCONSCIONABLE--
WHAT I DID?
TWO-FACE HELD HER CAPTIVE, NOT ME!
AS A RESULT OF AN ALLIANCE YOU HAD MADE WITH HIM!
AN ALLIANCE YOU NEVER SHOULD HAVE MADE IN THE FIRST PLACE!
I KNOW.
THEN WHY DID YOU DO IT?
I THOUGHT... I THOUGHT I COULD USE HIM ON MY TERMS.
I DISCOVERED I WAS WRONG.
ONE OF MY MANY MISTAKES THIS PAST YEAR.
I'M TIRED, SARAH.
I'M SO TIRED.

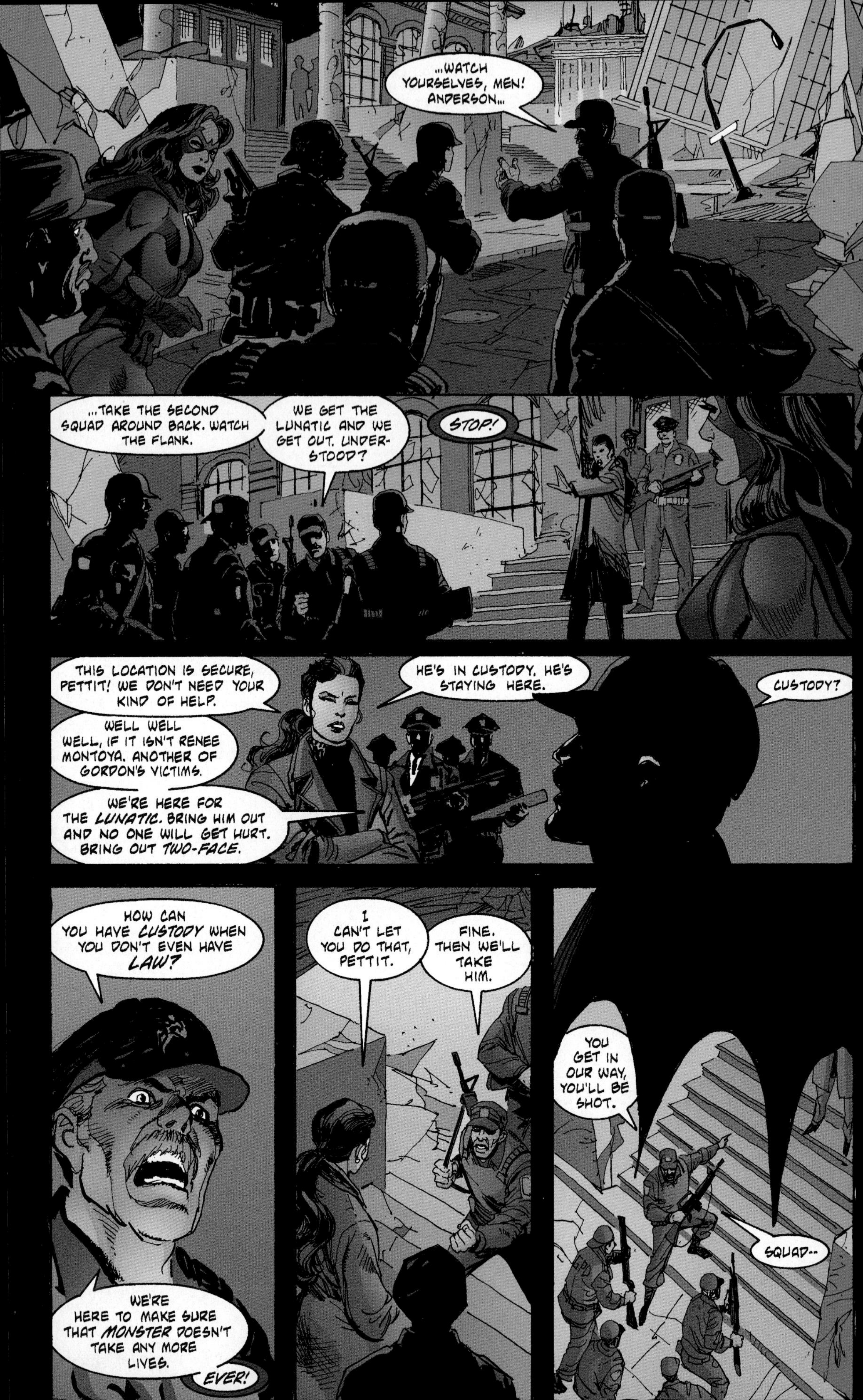
...WATCH YOURSELVES, MEN! ANDERSON...
...TAKE THE SECOND SQUAD AROUND BACK. WATCH THE FLANK.
WE GET THE LUNATIC AND WE GET OUT. UNDER-STOOD?
STOP!
THIS LOCATION IS SECURE, PETTIT! WE DON'T NEED YOUR KIND OF HELP.
WELL WELL WELL, IF IT ISN'T RENEE MONTOYA. ANOTHER OF GORDON'S VICTIMS.
WE'RE HERE FOR THE LUNATIC. BRING HIM OUT AND NO ONE WILL GET HURT. BRING OUT TWO-FACE.
HE'S IN CUSTODY. HE'S STAYING HERE.
CUSTODY?
HOW CAN YOU HAVE CUSTODY WHEN YOU DON'T EVEN HAVE LAW?
WE'RE HERE TO MAKE SURE THAT MONSTER DOESN'T TAKE ANY MORE LIVES.
EVER!
I CAN'T LET YOU DO THAT, PETTIT.
FINE. THEN WE'LL TAKE HIM.
YOU GET IN OUR WAY, YOU'LL BE SHOT.
SQUAD--

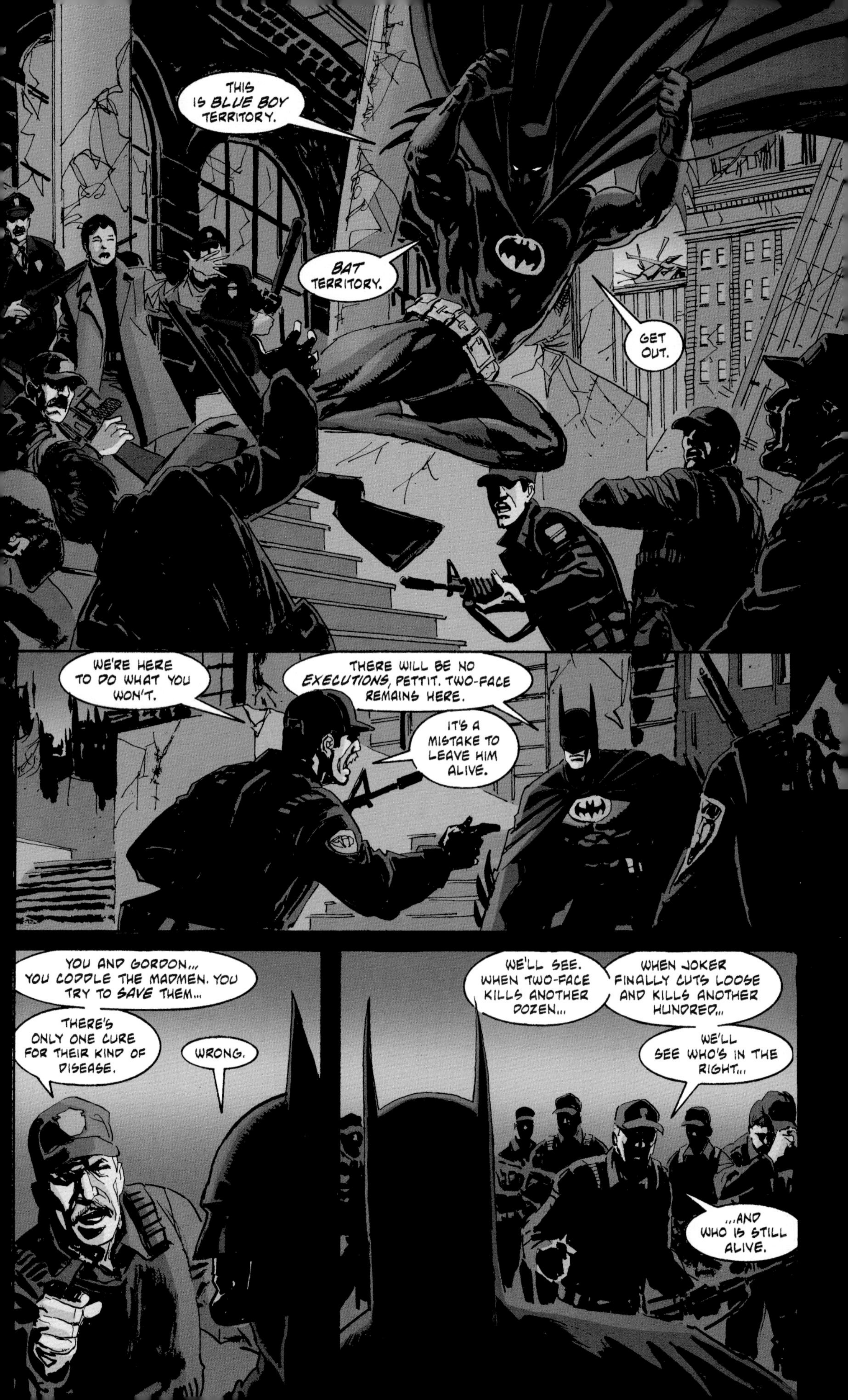
THIS IS *BLUE BOY* TERRITORY.
BAT TERRITORY.
GET OUT.
WE'RE HERE TO DO WHAT YOU WON'T.
THERE WILL BE NO *EXECUTIONS*, PETTIT. TWO-FACE REMAINS HERE.
IT'S A MISTAKE TO LEAVE HIM ALIVE.
YOU AND GORDON... YOU CODDLE THE MADMEN. YOU TRY TO *SAVE* THEM...
THERE'S ONLY ONE CURE FOR THEIR KIND OF DISEASE.
WRONG.
WE'LL SEE. WHEN TWO-FACE KILLS ANOTHER DOZEN...
WHEN JOKER FINALLY CUTS LOOSE AND KILLS ANOTHER HUNDRED...
WE'LL SEE WHO'S IN THE RIGHT...
...AND WHO IS STILL ALIVE.

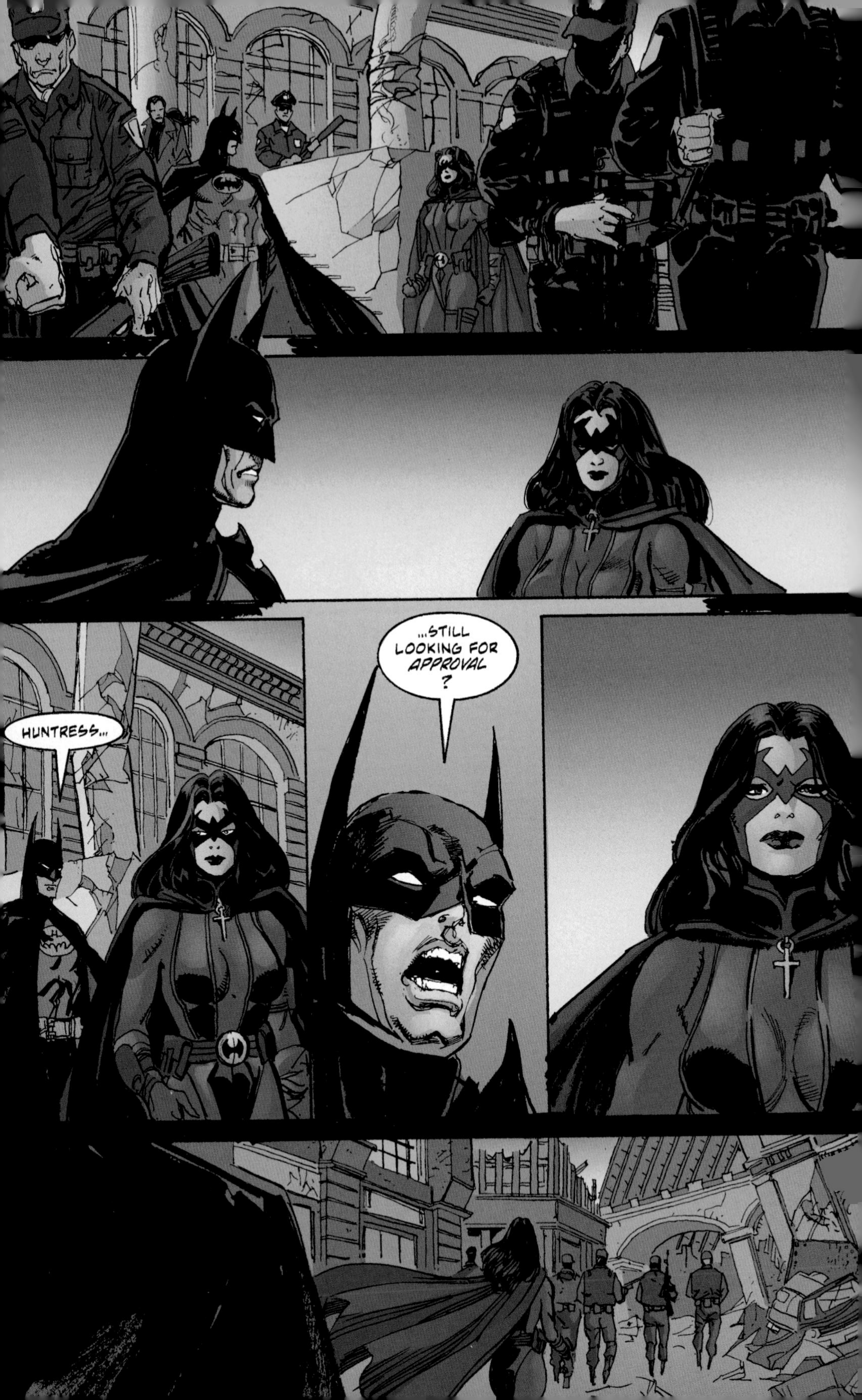
HUNTRESS...
...STILL LOOKING FOR APPROVAL ?

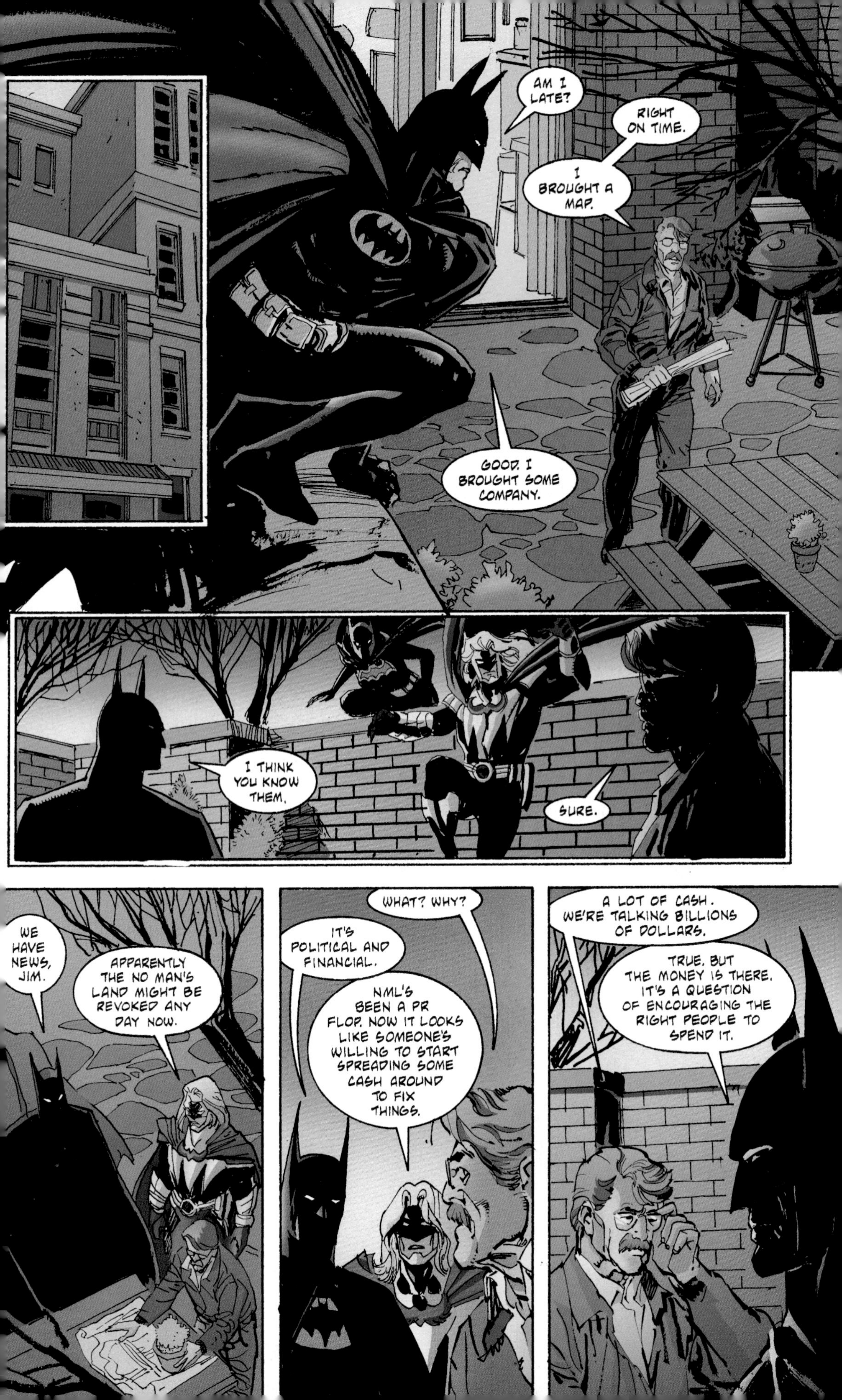
AM I LATE?
RIGHT ON TIME.
I BROUGHT A MAP.
GOOD. I BROUGHT SOME COMPANY.
I THINK YOU KNOW THEM.
SURE.
WE HAVE NEWS, JIM.
APPARENTLY THE NO MAN'S LAND MIGHT BE REVOKED ANY DAY NOW.
WHAT? WHY?
IT'S POLITICAL AND FINANCIAL.
NML'S BEEN A PR FLOP. NOW IT LOOKS LIKE SOMEONE'S WILLING TO START SPREADING SOME CASH AROUND TO FIX THINGS.
A LOT OF CASH. WE'RE TALKING BILLIONS OF DOLLARS.
TRUE, BUT THE MONEY IS THERE. IT'S A QUESTION OF ENCOURAGING THE RIGHT PEOPLE TO SPEND IT.

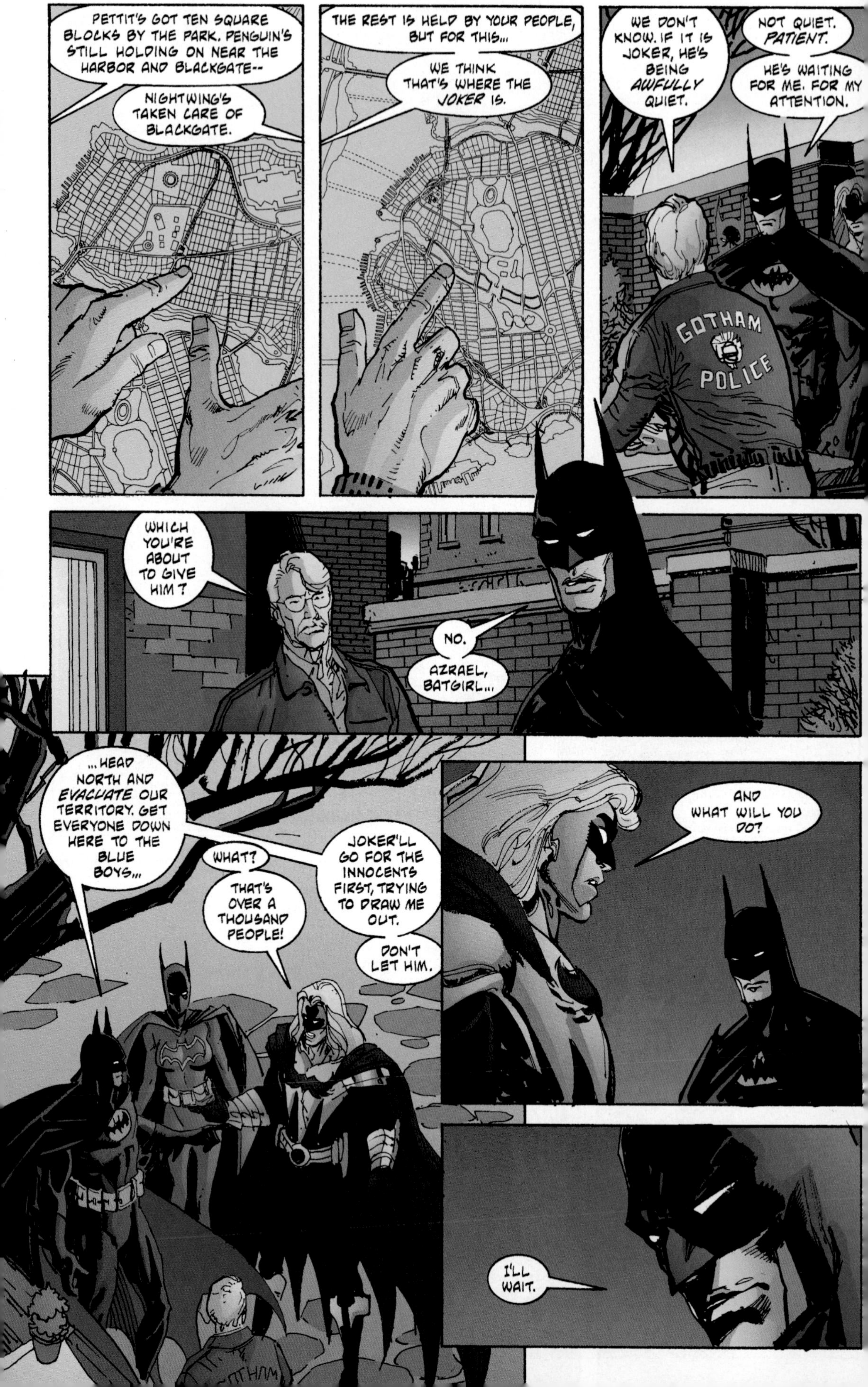

PETTIT'S GOT TEN SQUARE BLOCKS BY THE PARK. PENGUIN'S STILL HOLDING ON NEAR THE HARBOR AND BLACKGATE--
NIGHTWING'S TAKEN CARE OF BLACKGATE.
THE REST IS HELD BY YOUR PEOPLE, BUT FOR THIS...
WE THINK THAT'S WHERE THE JOKER IS.
WE DON'T KNOW. IF IT IS JOKER, HE'S BEING AWFULLY QUIET.
NOT QUIET. PATIENT.
HE'S WAITING FOR ME. FOR MY ATTENTION.
GOTHAM POLICE
WHICH YOU'RE ABOUT TO GIVE HIM?
NO.
AZRAEL, BATGIRL...
...HEAD NORTH AND EVACUATE OUR TERRITORY. GET EVERYONE DOWN HERE TO THE BLUE BOYS...
WHAT?
THAT'S OVER A THOUSAND PEOPLE!
JOKER'LL GO FOR THE INNOCENTS FIRST, TRYING TO DRAW ME OUT.
DON'T LET HIM.
AND WHAT WILL YOU DO?
I'LL WAIT.

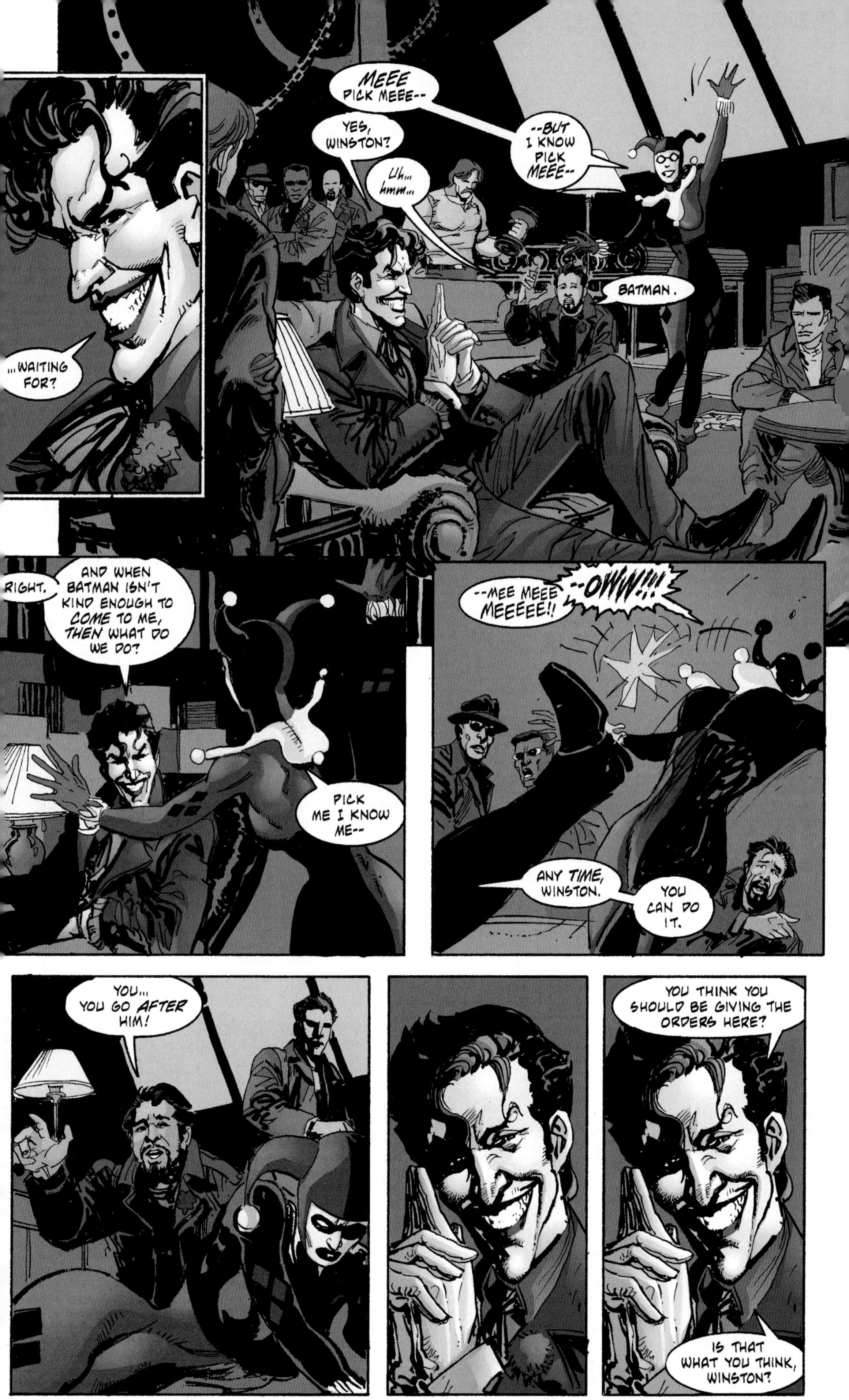
...WAITING FOR?
MEEE PICK MEEE--
YES, WINSTON?
--BUT I KNOW PICK MEEE--
Uh... hmm...
BATMAN.
RIGHT.
AND WHEN BATMAN ISN'T KIND ENOUGH TO COME TO ME, THEN WHAT DO WE DO?
PICK ME I KNOW ME--
--MEE MEEE MEEEEE!!
--OWW!!!
ANY TIME, WINSTON.
YOU CAN DO IT.
YOU... YOU GO AFTER HIM!
YOU THINK YOU SHOULD BE GIVING THE ORDERS HERE?
IS THAT WHAT YOU THINK, WINSTON?

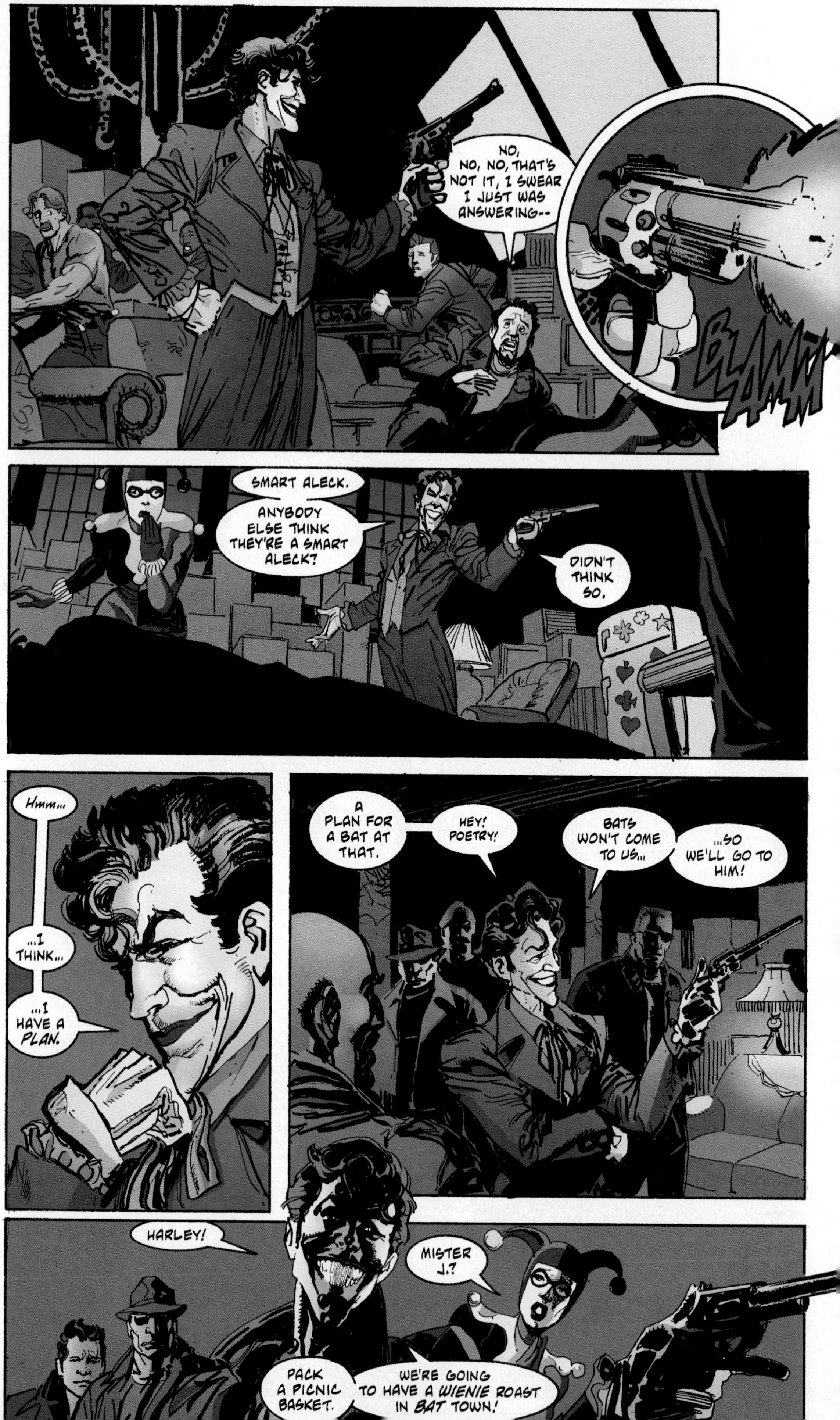
NO, NO, NO, THAT'S NOT IT, I SWEAR I JUST WAS ANSWERING--
BLAMM
SMART ALECK.
ANYBODY ELSE THINK THEY'RE A SMART ALECK?
DIDN'T THINK SO.
Hmm...
...I THINK...
...I HAVE A PLAN.
A PLAN FOR A BAT AT THAT.
HEY! POETRY!
BATS WON'T COME TO US...
...SO WE'LL GO TO HIM!
HARLEY!
MISTER J.?
PACK A PICNIC BASKET.
WE'RE GOING TO HAVE A WIENIE ROAST IN BAT TOWN!

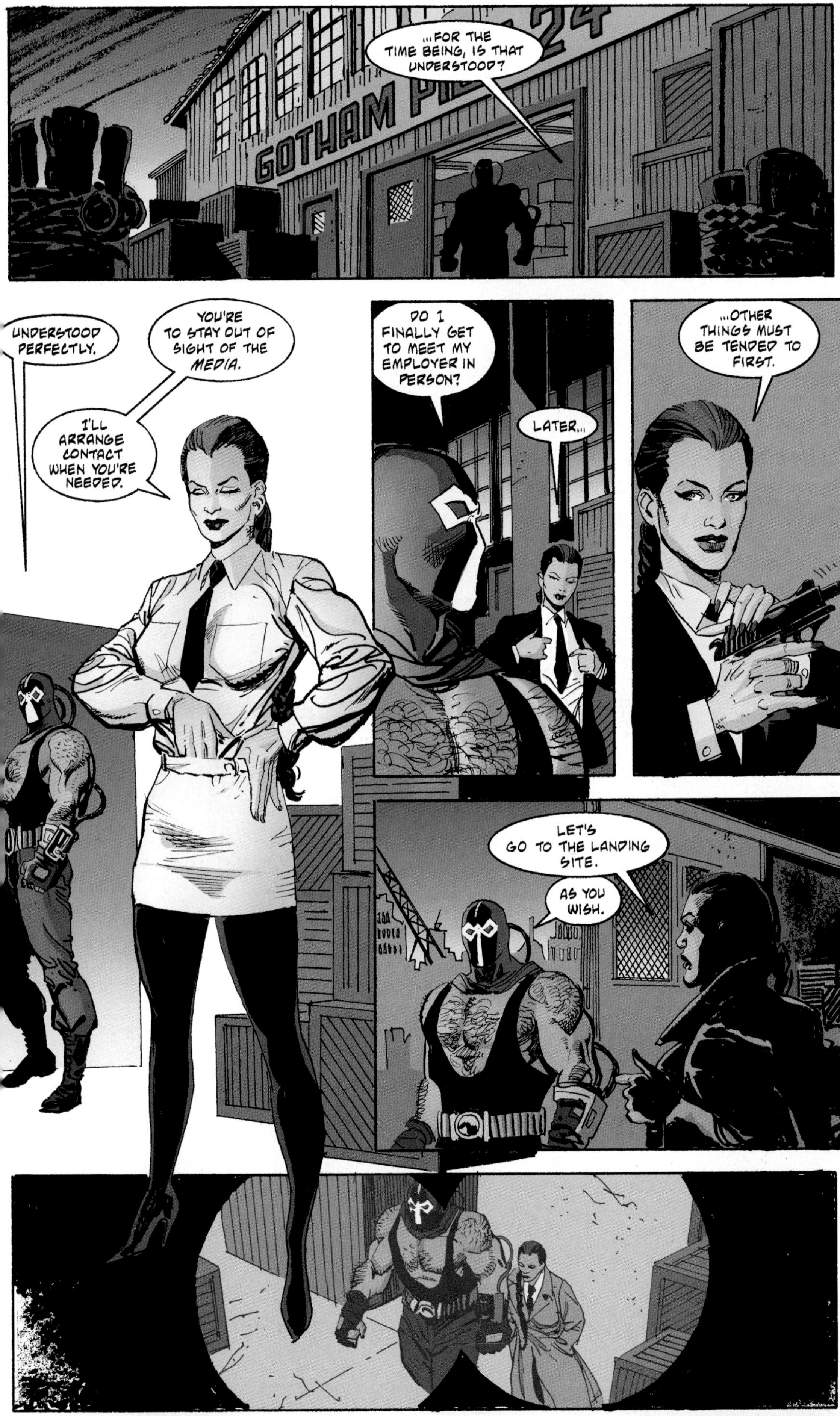
GOTHAM PIER 24
...FOR THE TIME BEING, IS THAT UNDERSTOOD?
UNDERSTOOD PERFECTLY.
YOU'RE TO STAY OUT OF SIGHT OF THE MEDIA.
I'LL ARRANGE CONTACT WHEN YOU'RE NEEDED.
DO I FINALLY GET TO MEET MY EMPLOYER IN PERSON?
LATER...
...OTHER THINGS MUST BE TENDED TO FIRST.
LET'S GO TO THE LANDING SITE.
AS YOU WISH.

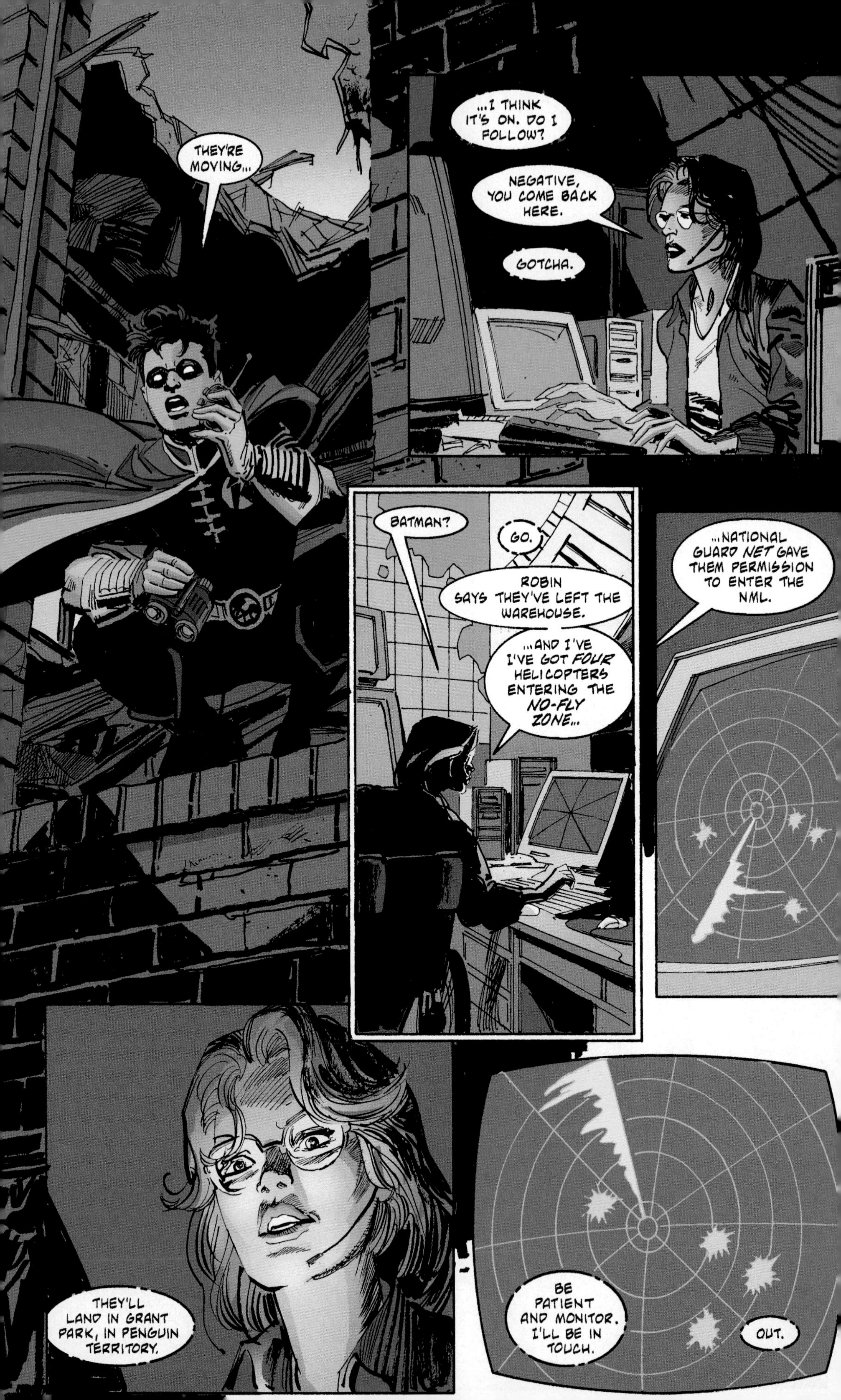

THEY'RE MOVING...
...I THINK IT'S ON. DO I FOLLOW?
NEGATIVE, YOU COME BACK HERE.
GOTCHA.
BATMAN?
GO.
ROBIN SAYS THEY'VE LEFT THE WAREHOUSE.
...AND I'VE I'VE GOT FOUR HELICOPTERS ENTERING THE NO-FLY ZONE...
...NATIONAL GUARD NET GAVE THEM PERMISSION TO ENTER THE NML.
THEY'LL LAND IN GRANT PARK, IN PENGUIN TERRITORY.
BE PATIENT AND MONITOR. I'LL BE IN TOUCH.
OUT.

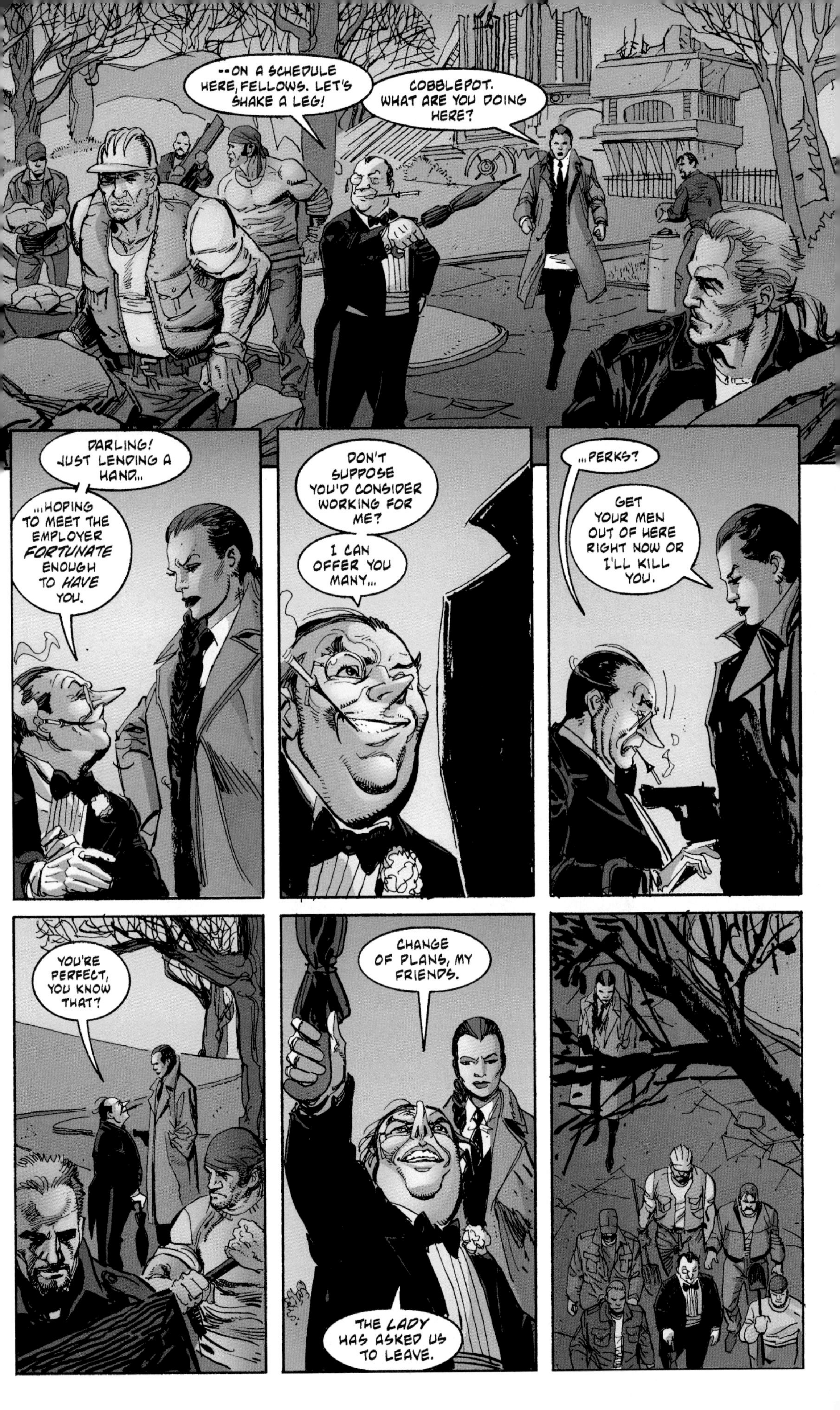
--ON A SCHEDULE HERE, FELLOWS. LET'S SHAKE A LEG!
COBBLEPOT. WHAT ARE YOU DOING HERE?
DARLING! JUST LENDING A HAND...
...HOPING TO MEET THE EMPLOYER *FORTUNATE* ENOUGH TO *HAVE* YOU.
DON'T SUPPOSE YOU'D CONSIDER WORKING FOR ME?
I CAN OFFER YOU MANY...
...PERKS?
GET YOUR MEN OUT OF HERE RIGHT NOW OR I'LL KILL YOU.
YOU'RE PERFECT, YOU KNOW THAT?
CHANGE OF PLANS, MY FRIENDS.
THE *LADY* HAS ASKED US TO LEAVE.

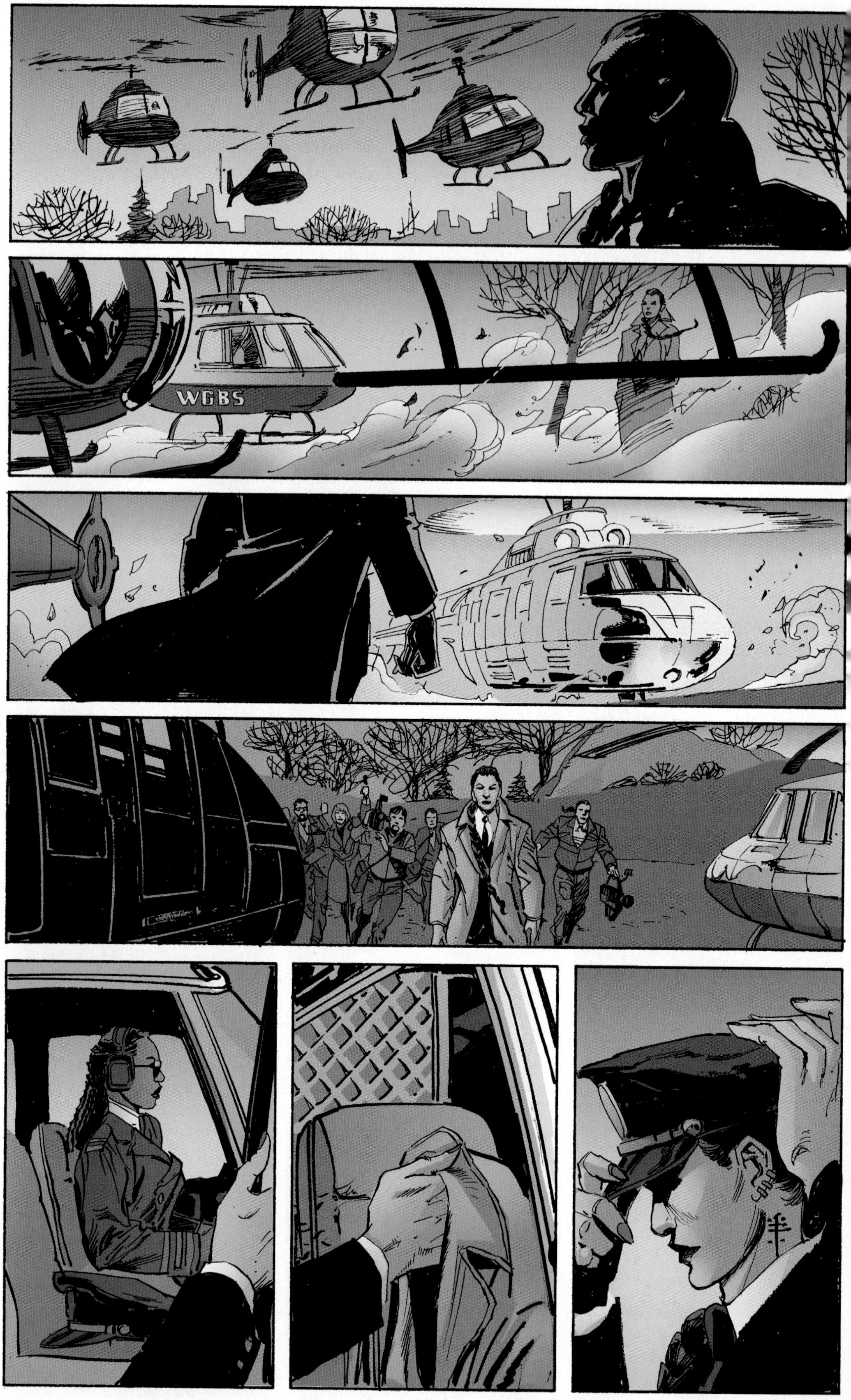
WGBS

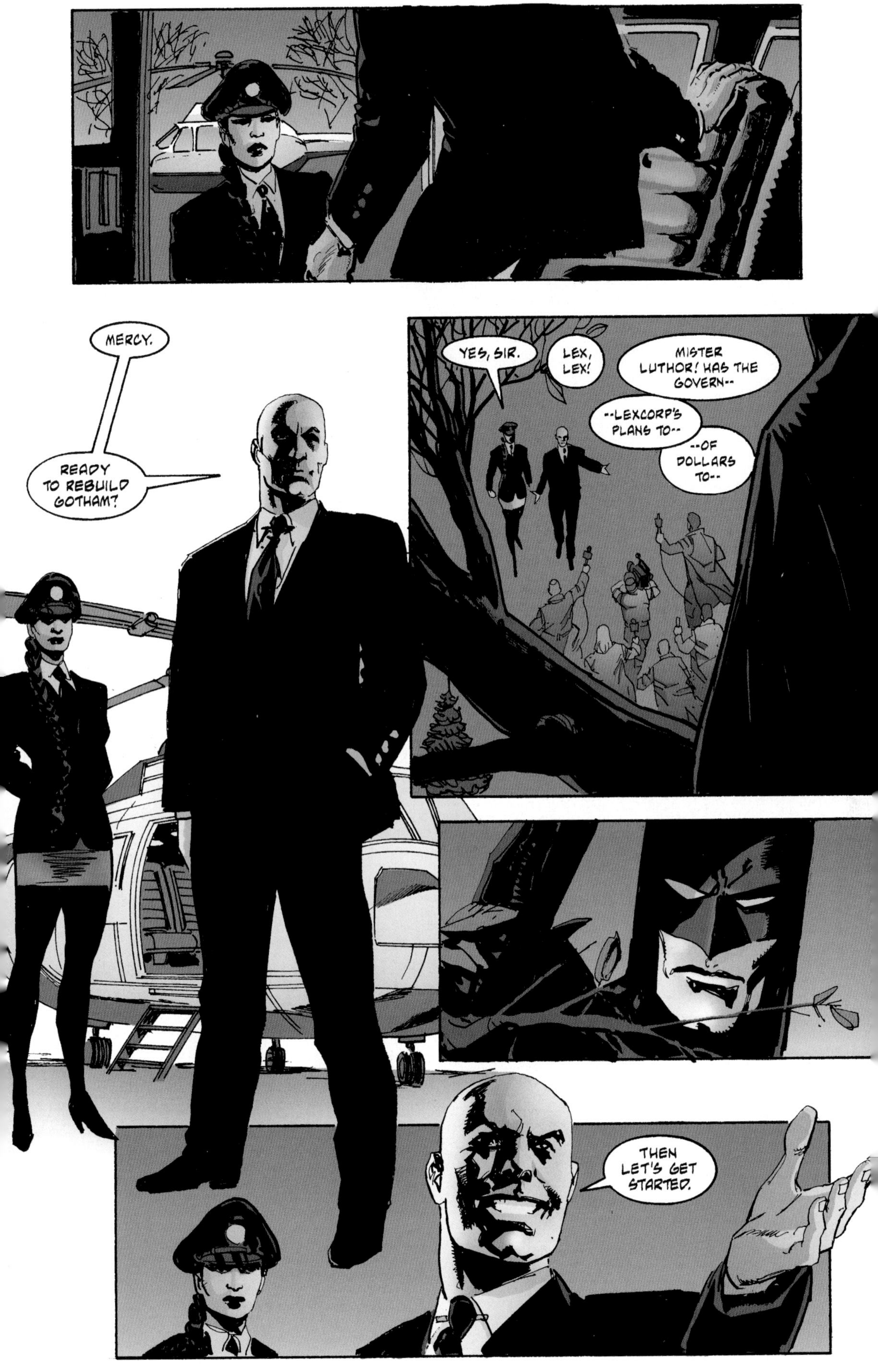
MERCY.
READY TO REBUILD GOTHAM?
YES, SIR.
LEX, LEX!
MISTER LUTHOR! HAS THE GOVERN--
--LEXCORP'S PLANS TO--
--OF DOLLARS TO--
THEN LET'S GET STARTED.

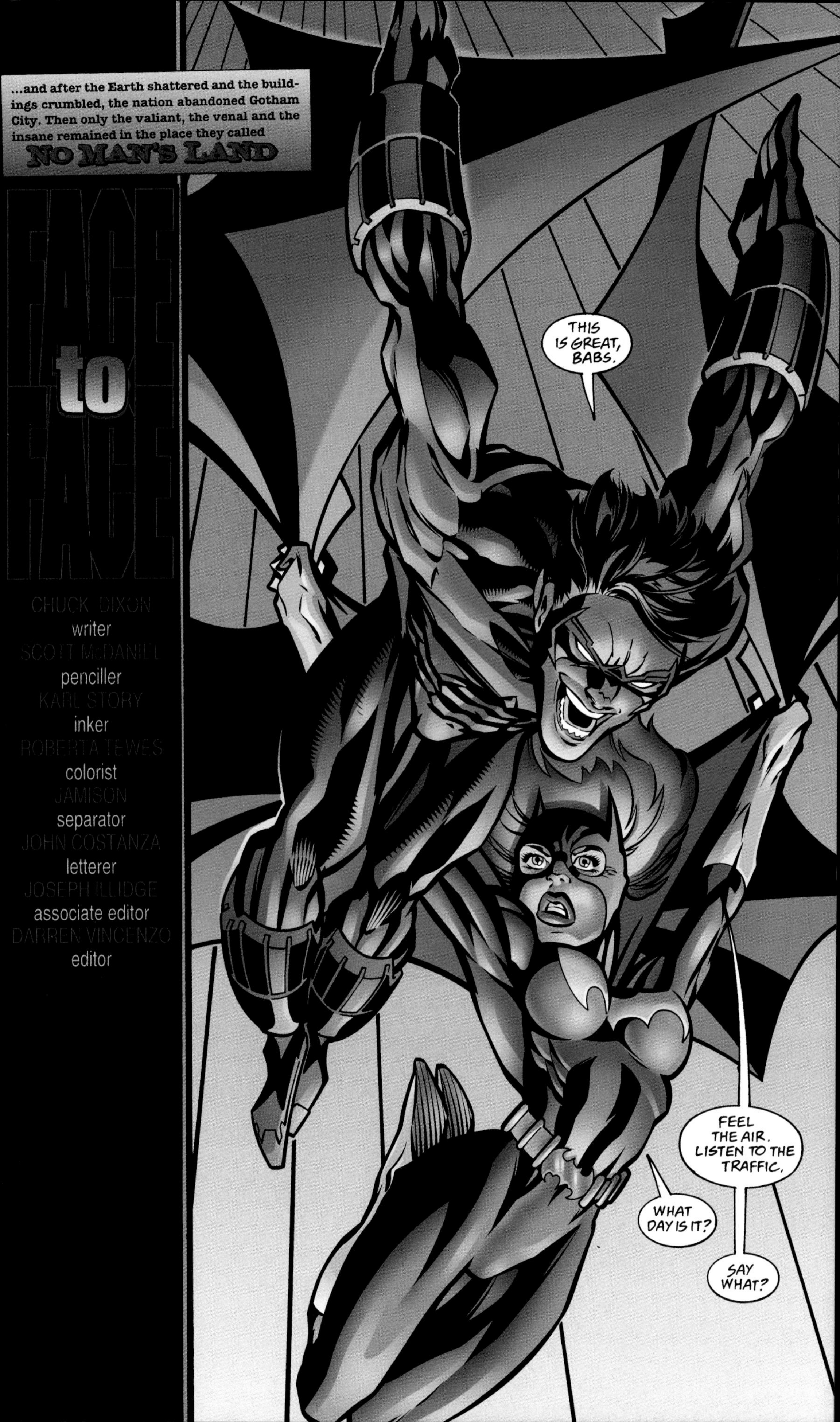

...and after the Earth shattered and the buildings crumbled, the nation abandoned Gotham City. Then only the valiant, the venal and the insane remained in the place they called
NO MAN'S LAND
FACE to FACE
CHUCK DIXON
writer
SCOTT McDANIEL
penciller
KARL STORY
inker
ROBERTA TEWES
colorist
JAMISON
separator
JOHN COSTANZA
letterer
JOSEPH ILLIDGE
associate editor
DARREN VINCENZO
editor
THIS IS GREAT, BABS.
FEEL THE AIR. LISTEN TO THE TRAFFIC.
WHAT DAY IS IT?
SAY WHAT?

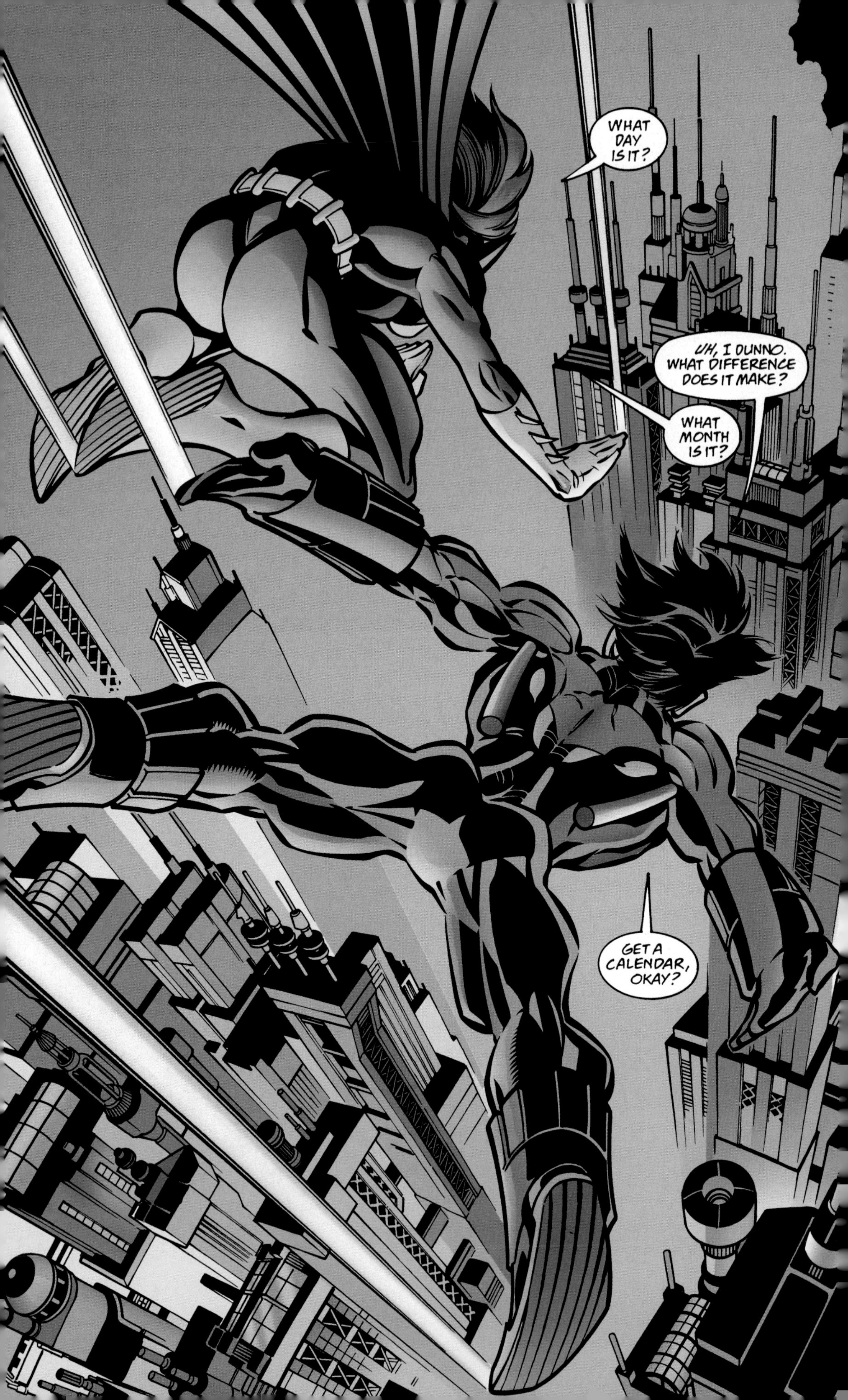
WHAT DAY IS IT?
UH, I DUNNO. WHAT DIFFERENCE DOES IT MAKE?
WHAT MONTH IS IT?
GET A CALENDAR, OKAY?

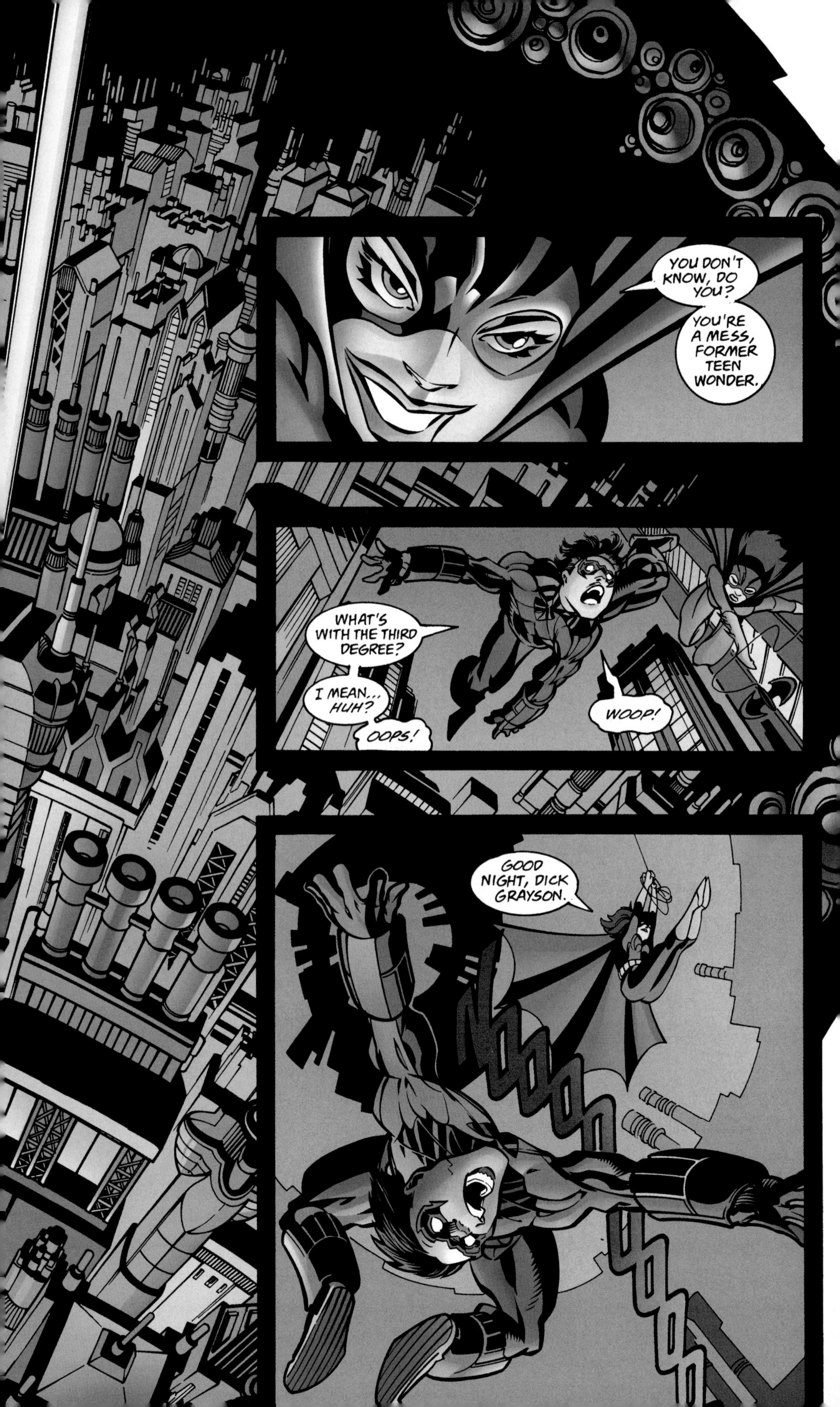
YOU DON'T KNOW, DO YOU?
YOU'RE A MESS, FORMER TEEN WONDER.
WHAT'S WITH THE THIRD DEGREE?
I MEAN... HUH?
OOPS!
WOOP!
GOOD NIGHT, DICK GRAYSON.

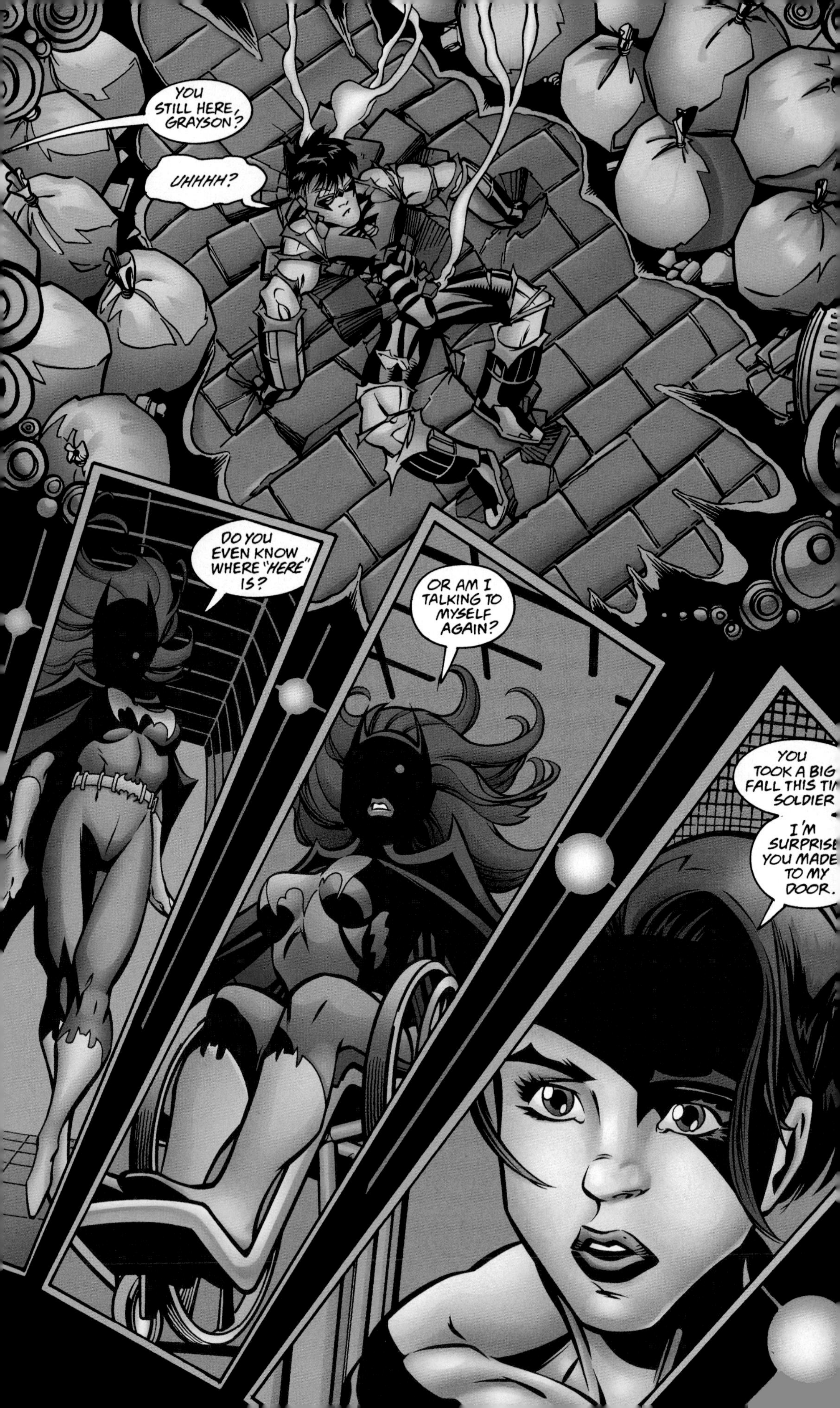
YOU STILL HERE, GRAYSON?
UHHHH?
DO YOU EVEN KNOW WHERE "HERE" IS?
OR AM I TALKING TO MYSELF AGAIN?
YOU TOOK A BIG FALL THIS TI
SOLDIER
I'M SURPRIS
YOU MADE
TO MY DOOR.

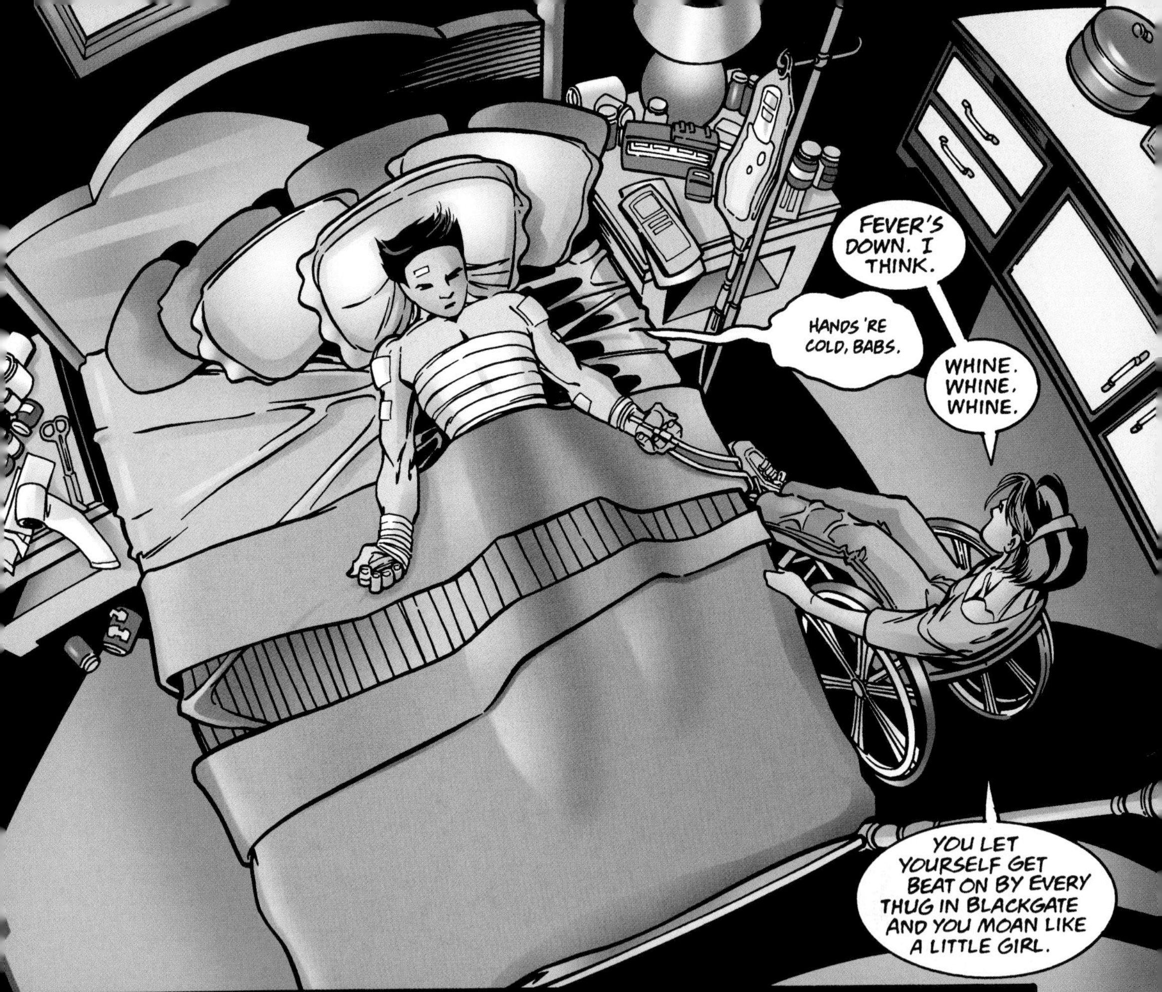
FEVER'S DOWN. I THINK.
HANDS 'RE COLD, BABS.
WHINE. WHINE. WHINE.
YOU LET YOURSELF GET BEAT ON BY EVERY THUG IN BLACKGATE AND YOU MOAN LIKE A LITTLE GIRL.

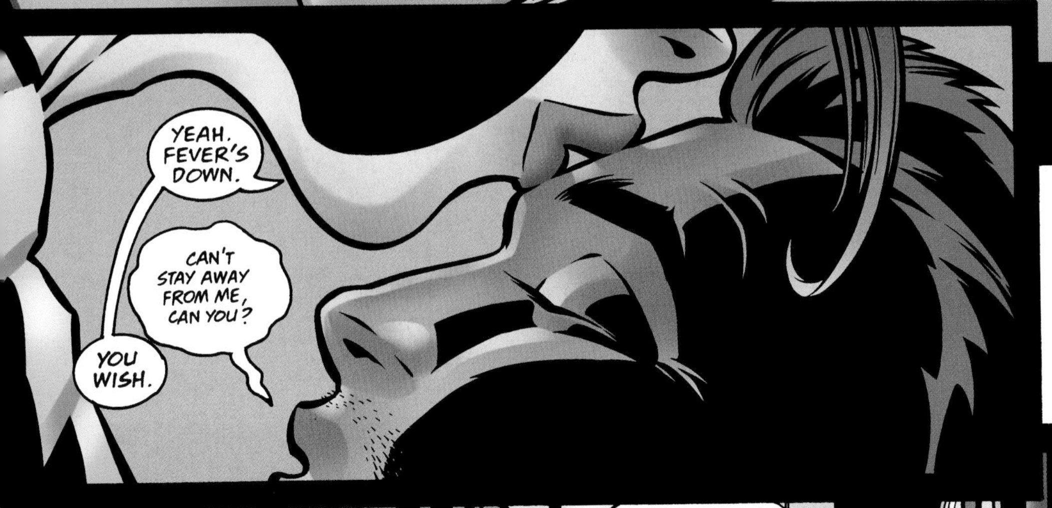
YEAH. FEVER'S DOWN.
CAN'T STAY AWAY FROM ME, CAN YOU?
YOU WISH.

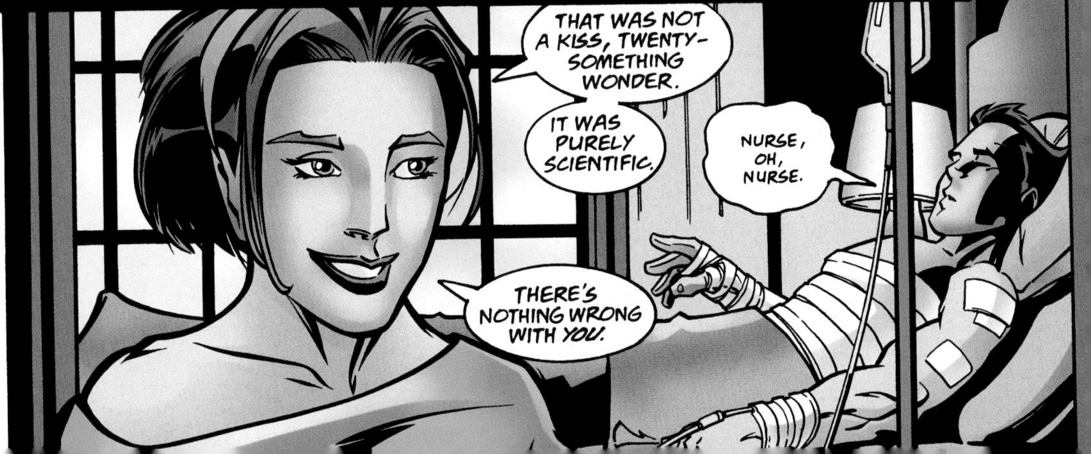
THAT WAS NOT A KISS, TWENTY-SOMETHING WONDER.
IT WAS PURELY SCIENTIFIC.
NURSE, OH, NURSE.
THERE'S NOTHING WRONG WITH YOU.

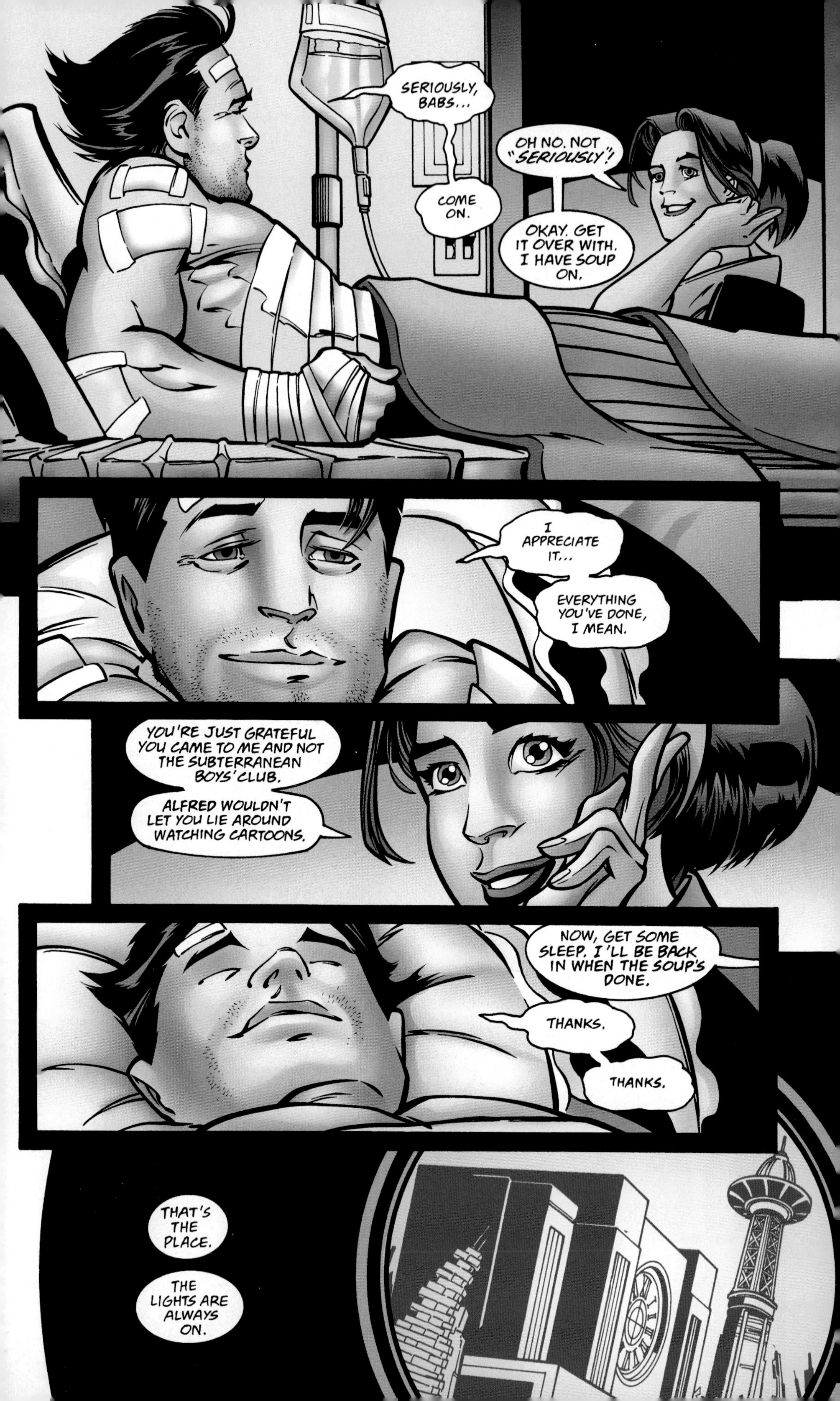
SERIOUSLY, BABS...
COME ON.
OH NO. NOT "SERIOUSLY"!
OKAY. GET IT OVER WITH. I HAVE SOUP ON.
I APPRECIATE IT...
EVERYTHING YOU'VE DONE, I MEAN.
YOU'RE JUST GRATEFUL YOU CAME TO ME AND NOT THE SUBTERRANEAN BOYS' CLUB.
ALFRED WOULDN'T LET YOU LIE AROUND WATCHING CARTOONS.
NOW, GET SOME SLEEP. I'LL BE BACK IN WHEN THE SOUP'S DONE.
THANKS.
THANKS.
THAT'S THE PLACE.
THE LIGHTS ARE ALWAYS ON.

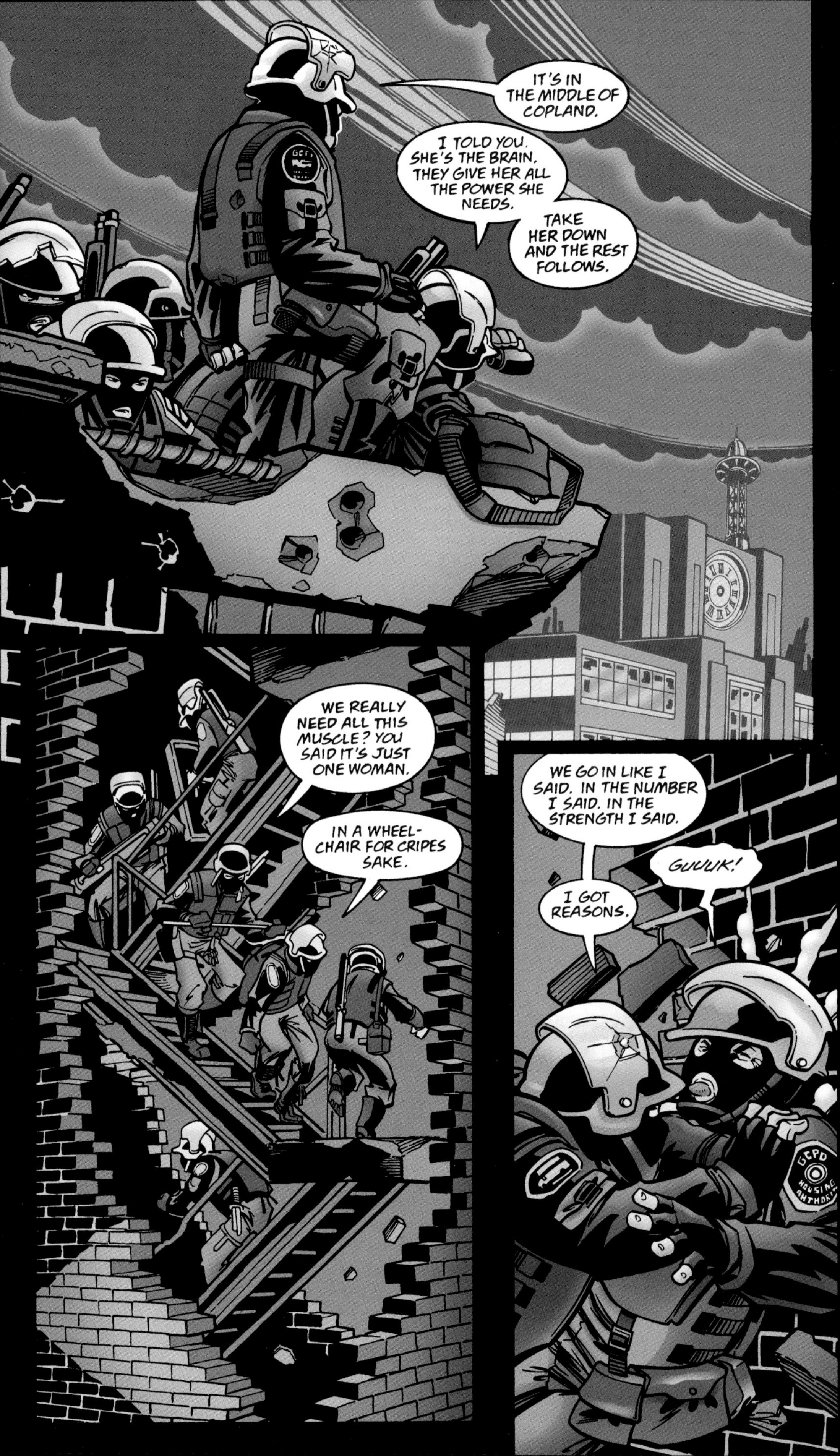
IT'S IN THE MIDDLE OF COPLAND.
I TOLD YOU. SHE'S THE BRAIN. THEY GIVE HER ALL THE POWER SHE NEEDS.
TAKE HER DOWN AND THE REST FOLLOWS.
WE REALLY NEED ALL THIS MUSCLE? YOU SAID IT'S JUST ONE WOMAN.
IN A WHEEL-CHAIR FOR CRIPES SAKE.
WE GO IN LIKE I SAID. IN THE NUMBER I SAID. IN THE STRENGTH I SAID.
I GOT REASONS.
GUUUK!

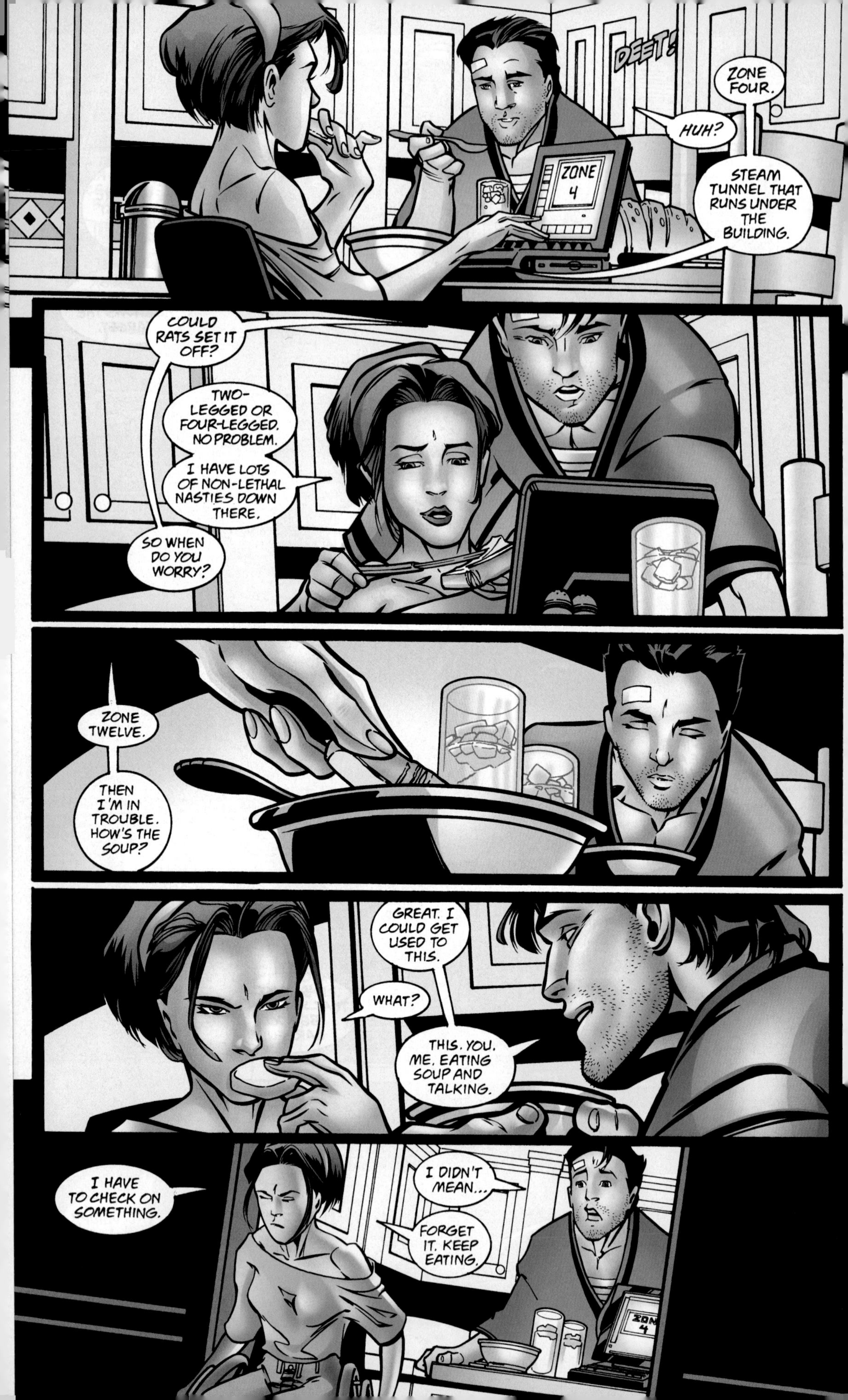
DEET!
ZONE FOUR.
HUH?
STEAM TUNNEL THAT RUNS UNDER THE BUILDING.
ZONE 4
COULD RATS SET IT OFF?
TWO-LEGGED OR FOUR-LEGGED. NO PROBLEM.
I HAVE LOTS OF NON-LETHAL NASTIES DOWN THERE.
SO WHEN DO YOU WORRY?
ZONE TWELVE.
THEN I'M IN TROUBLE. HOW'S THE SOUP?
GREAT. I COULD GET USED TO THIS.
WHAT?
THIS. YOU. ME. EATING SOUP AND TALKING.
I HAVE TO CHECK ON SOMETHING.
I DIDN'T MEAN...
FORGET IT. KEEP EATING.

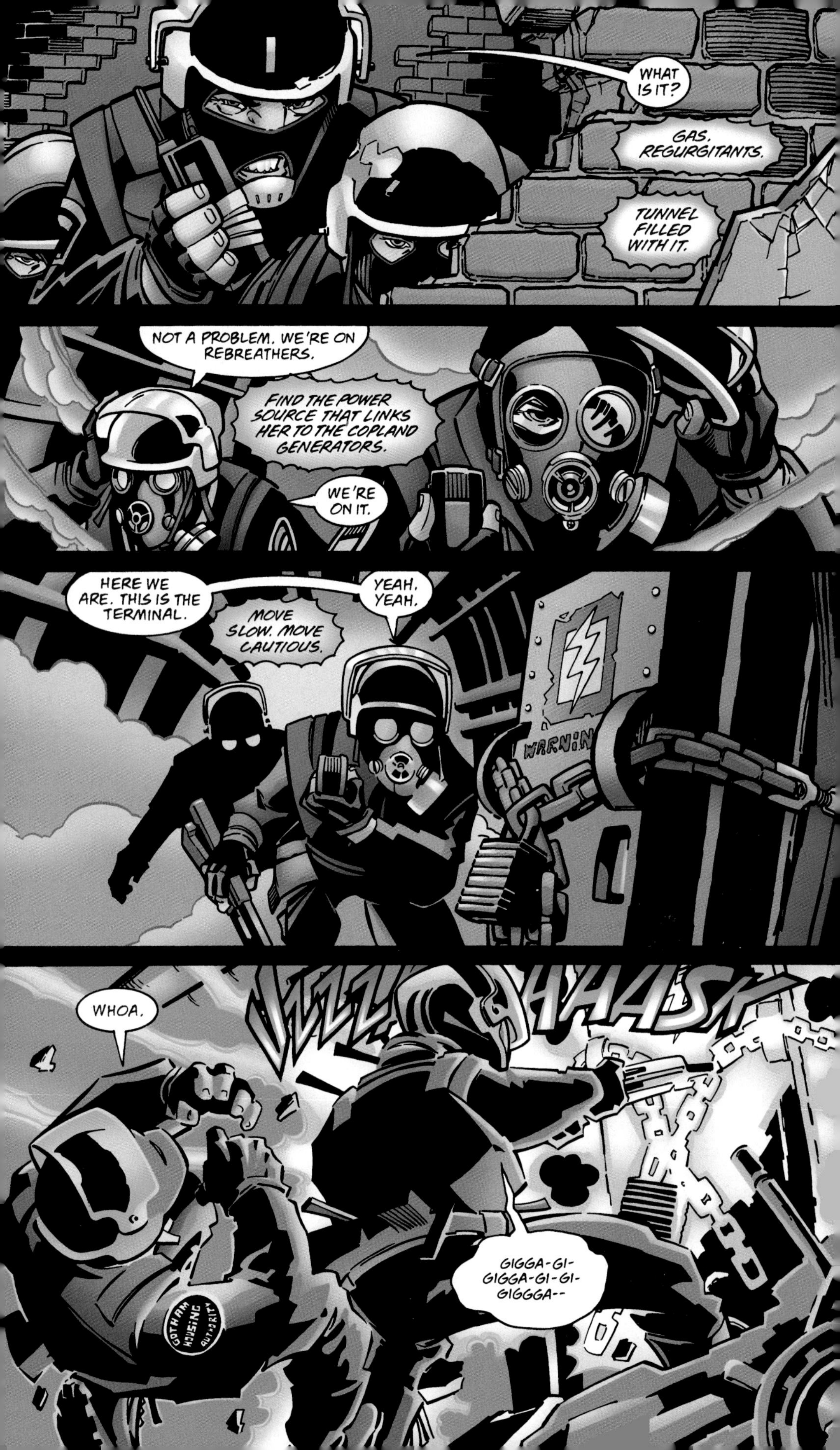
WHAT IS IT?
GAS. REGURGITANTS.
TUNNEL FILLED WITH IT.
NOT A PROBLEM. WE'RE ON REBREATHERS.
FIND THE POWER SOURCE THAT LINKS HER TO THE COPLAND GENERATORS.
WE'RE ON IT.
HERE WE ARE. THIS IS THE TERMINAL.
YEAH. YEAH.
MOVE SLOW. MOVE CAUTIOUS.
WHOA.
GIGGA-GI-GIGGA-GI-GI-GIGGGA--

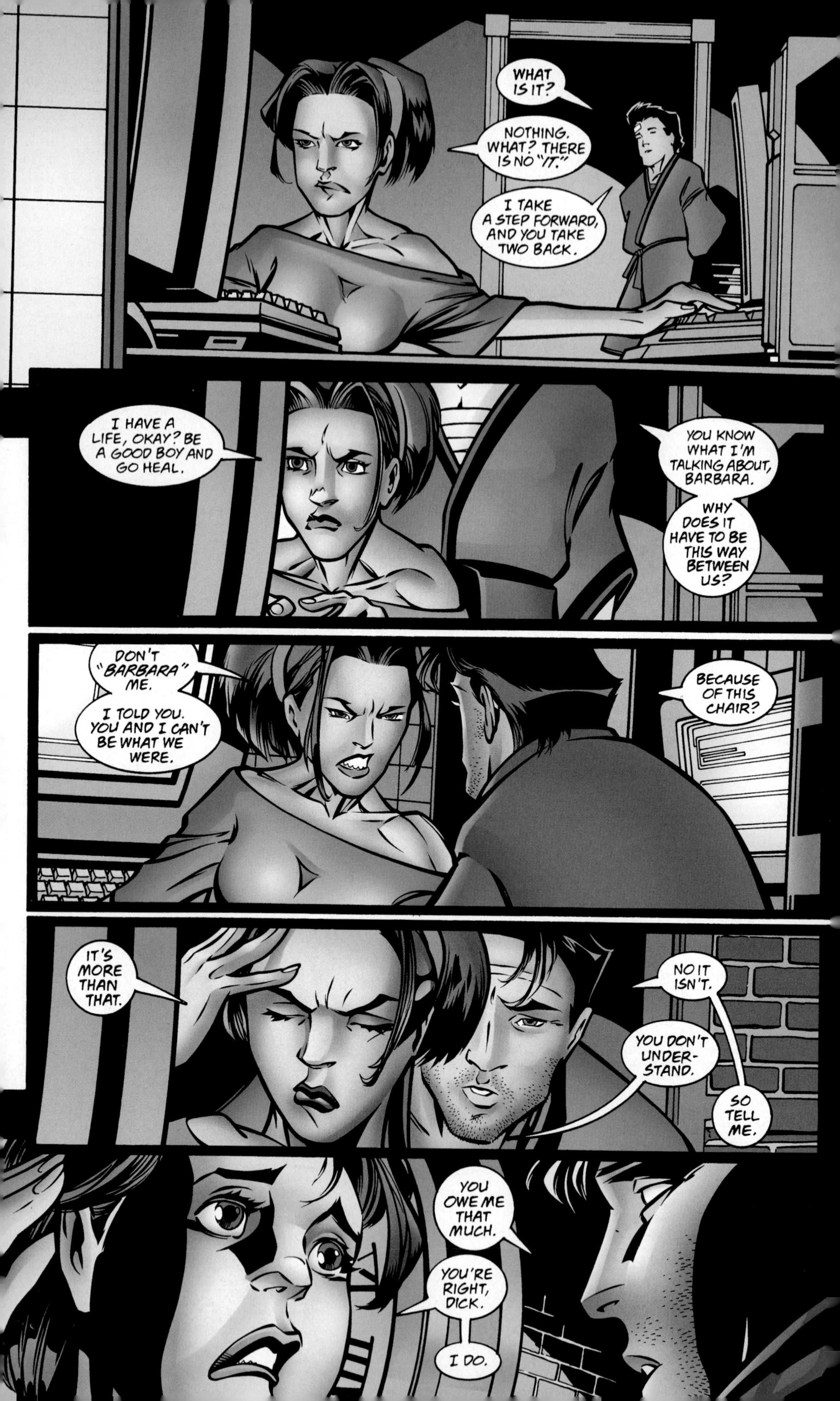
WHAT IS IT?
NOTHING. WHAT? THERE IS NO "IT."
I TAKE A STEP FORWARD, AND YOU TAKE TWO BACK.
I HAVE A LIFE, OKAY? BE A GOOD BOY AND GO HEAL.
YOU KNOW WHAT I'M TALKING ABOUT, BARBARA.
WHY DOES IT HAVE TO BE THIS WAY BETWEEN US?
DON'T "BARBARA" ME.
I TOLD YOU. YOU AND I CAN'T BE WHAT WE WERE.
BECAUSE OF THIS CHAIR?
IT'S MORE THAN THAT.
NO IT ISN'T.
YOU DON'T UNDER-STAND.
SO TELL ME.
YOU OWE ME THAT MUCH.
YOU'RE RIGHT, DICK.
I DO.

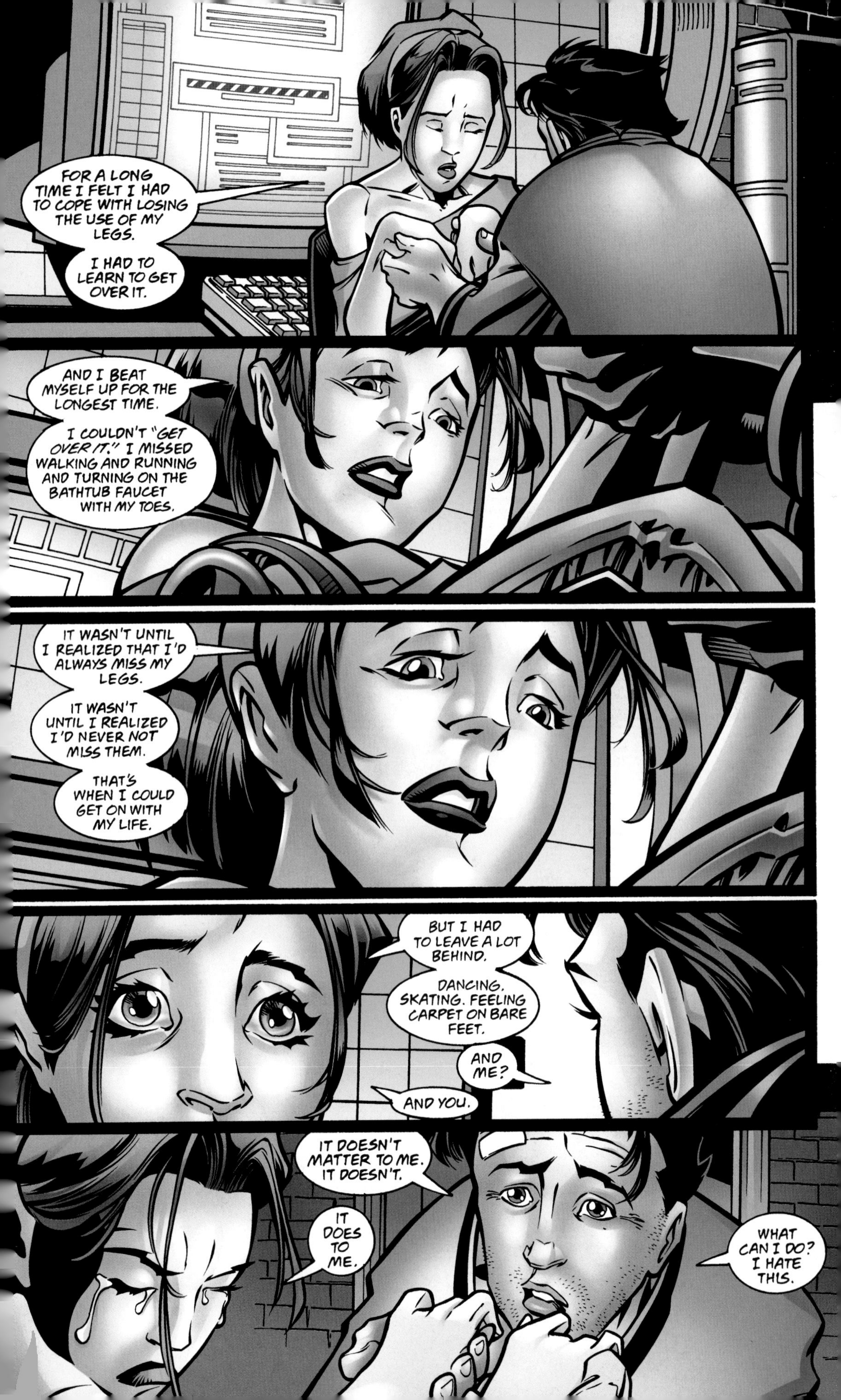

FOR A LONG TIME I FELT I HAD TO COPE WITH LOSING THE USE OF MY LEGS.
I HAD TO LEARN TO GET OVER IT.
AND I BEAT MYSELF UP FOR THE LONGEST TIME.
I COULDN'T "GET OVER IT." I MISSED WALKING AND RUNNING AND TURNING ON THE BATHTUB FAUCET WITH MY TOES.
IT WASN'T UNTIL I REALIZED THAT I'D ALWAYS MISS MY LEGS.
IT WASN'T UNTIL I REALIZED I'D NEVER NOT MISS THEM.
THAT'S WHEN I COULD GET ON WITH MY LIFE.
BUT I HAD TO LEAVE A LOT BEHIND.
DANCING. SKATING. FEELING CARPET ON BARE FEET.
AND ME?
AND YOU.
IT DOESN'T MATTER TO ME. IT DOESN'T.
IT DOES TO ME.
WHAT CAN I DO? I HATE THIS.

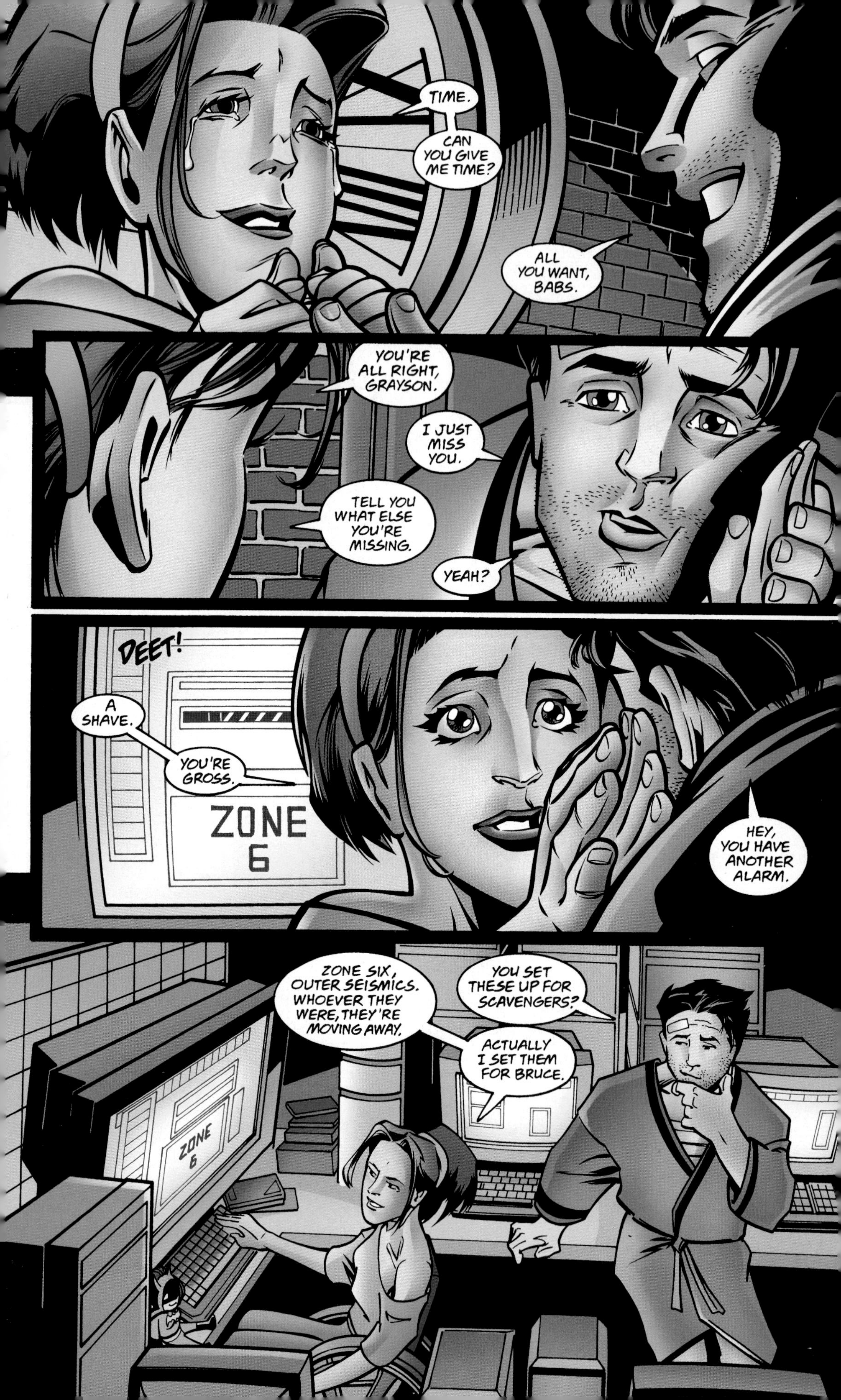
TIME.
CAN YOU GIVE ME TIME?
ALL YOU WANT, BABS.
YOU'RE ALL RIGHT, GRAYSON.
I JUST MISS YOU.
TELL YOU WHAT ELSE YOU'RE MISSING.
YEAH?
DEET!
A SHAVE.
YOU'RE GROSS.
ZONE 6
HEY, YOU HAVE ANOTHER ALARM.
ZONE SIX, OUTER SEISMICS. WHOEVER THEY WERE, THEY'RE MOVING AWAY.
YOU SET THESE UP FOR SCAVENGERS?
ACTUALLY I SET THEM FOR BRUCE.
ZONE 6

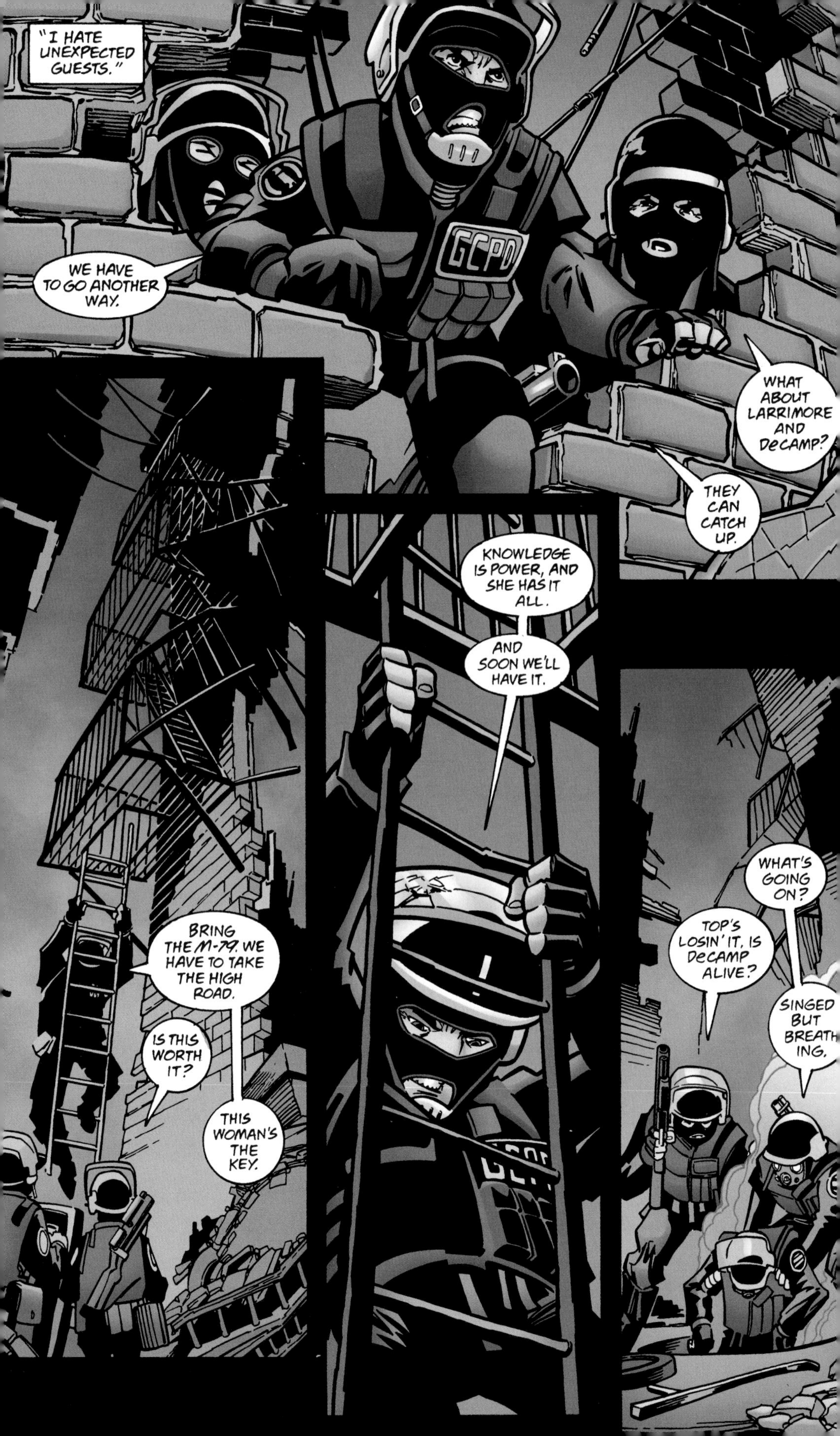
"I HATE UNEXPECTED GUESTS."
GCPD
WE HAVE TO GO ANOTHER WAY.
WHAT ABOUT LARRIMORE AND DeCAMP?
THEY CAN CATCH UP.
KNOWLEDGE IS POWER, AND SHE HAS IT ALL.
AND SOON WE'LL HAVE IT.
BRING THE M-79. WE HAVE TO TAKE THE HIGH ROAD.
IS THIS WORTH IT?
THIS WOMAN'S THE KEY.
WHAT'S GOING ON?
TOP'S LOSIN' IT. IS DeCAMP ALIVE?
SINGED BUT BREATH ING.

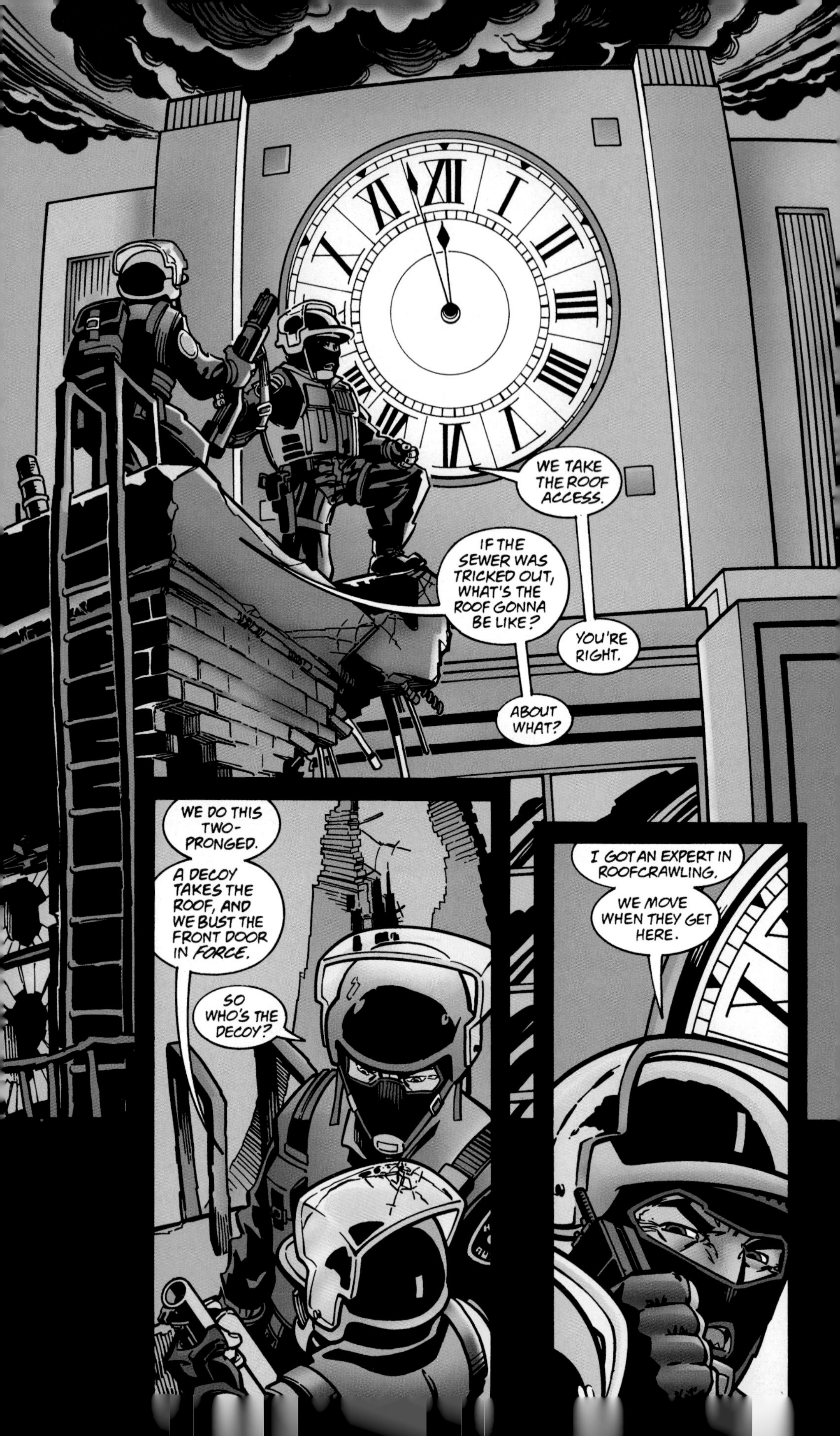
WE TAKE THE ROOF ACCESS.
IF THE SEWER WAS TRICKED OUT, WHAT'S THE ROOF GONNA BE LIKE?
YOU'RE RIGHT.
ABOUT WHAT?
WE DO THIS TWO-PRONGED.
A DECOY TAKES THE ROOF, AND WE BUST THE FRONT DOOR IN FORCE.
SO WHO'S THE DECOY?
I GOT AN EXPERT IN ROOFCRAWLING.
WE MOVE WHEN THEY GET HERE.

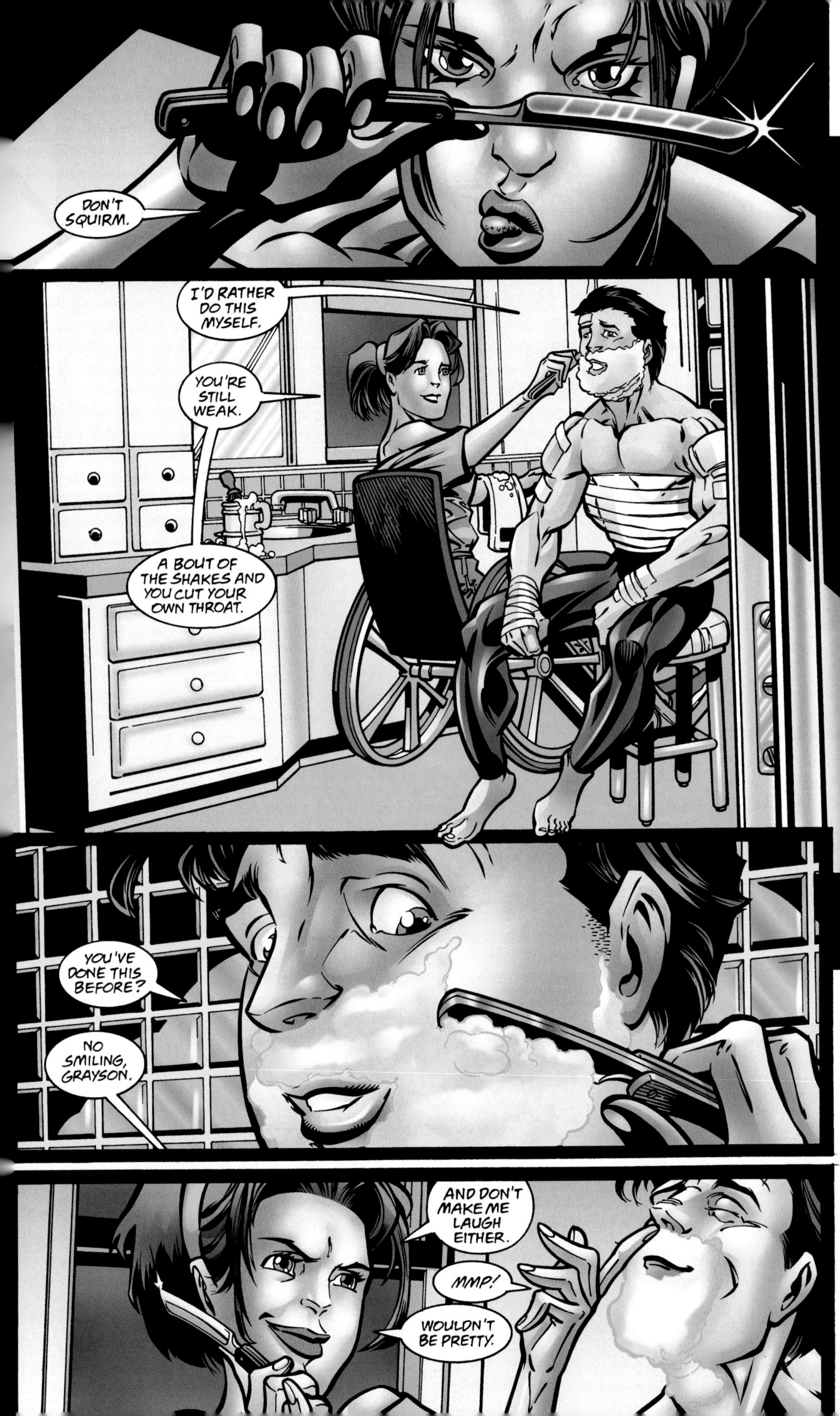
DON'T SQUIRM.
I'D RATHER DO THIS MYSELF.
YOU'RE STILL WEAK.
A BOUT OF THE SHAKES AND YOU CUT YOUR OWN THROAT.
YOU'VE DONE THIS BEFORE?
NO SMILING, GRAYSON.
AND DON'T MAKE ME LAUGH EITHER.
MMP!
WOULDN'T BE PRETTY.

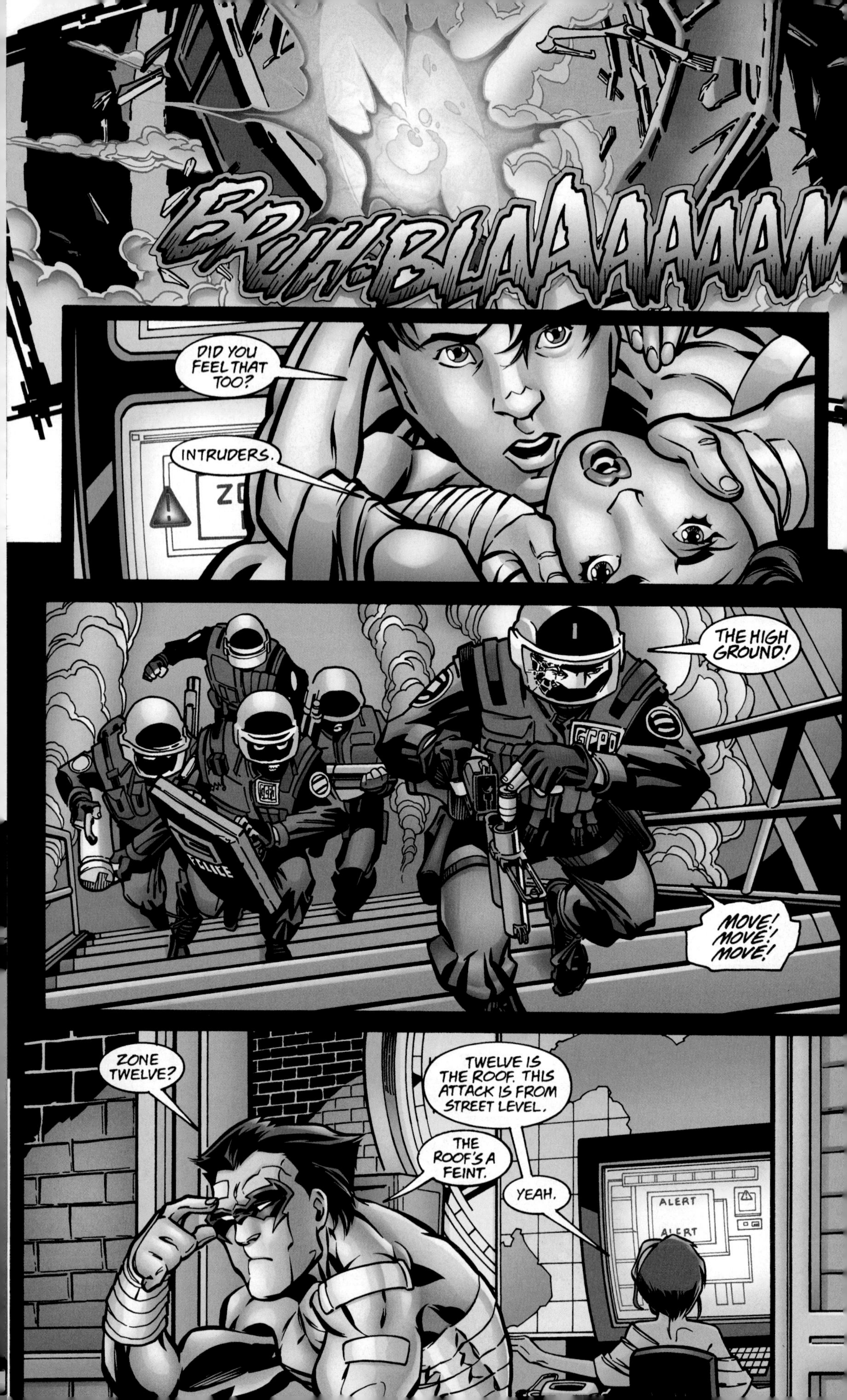
BRUHBLAAAAAAM
DID YOU FEEL THAT TOO?
INTRUDERS.
THE HIGH GROUND!
MOVE! MOVE! MOVE!
POLICE
ZONE TWELVE?
TWELVE IS THE ROOF. THIS ATTACK IS FROM STREET LEVEL.
THE ROOF'S A FEINT.
YEAH.
ALERT
ALERT

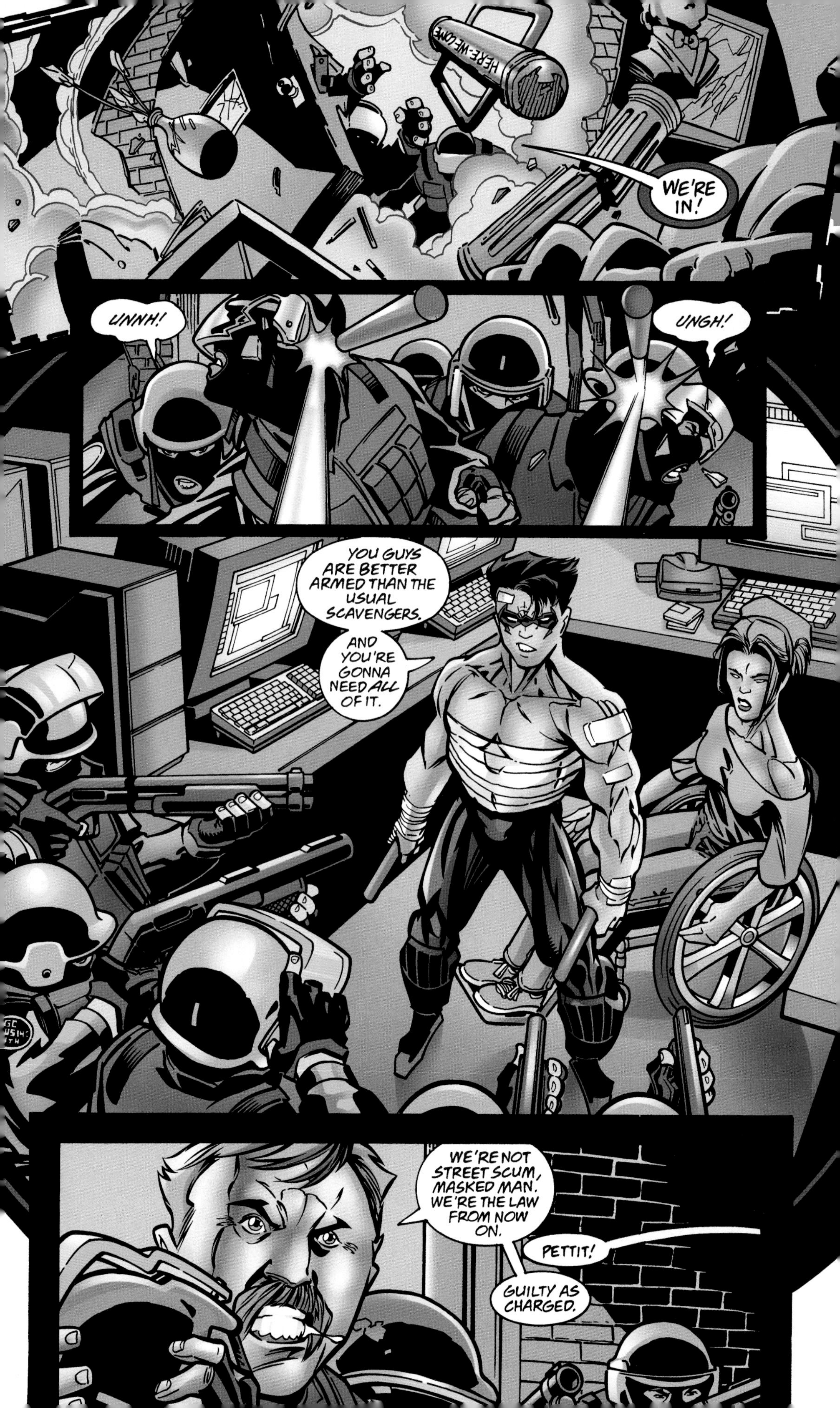
HERE-WE COME
WE'RE IN!
UNNH!
UNGH!
YOU GUYS ARE BETTER ARMED THAN THE USUAL SCAVENGERS.
AND YOU'RE GONNA NEED ALL OF IT.
WE'RE NOT STREET SCUM, MASKED MAN. WE'RE THE LAW FROM NOW ON.
PETTIT!
GUILTY AS CHARGED.

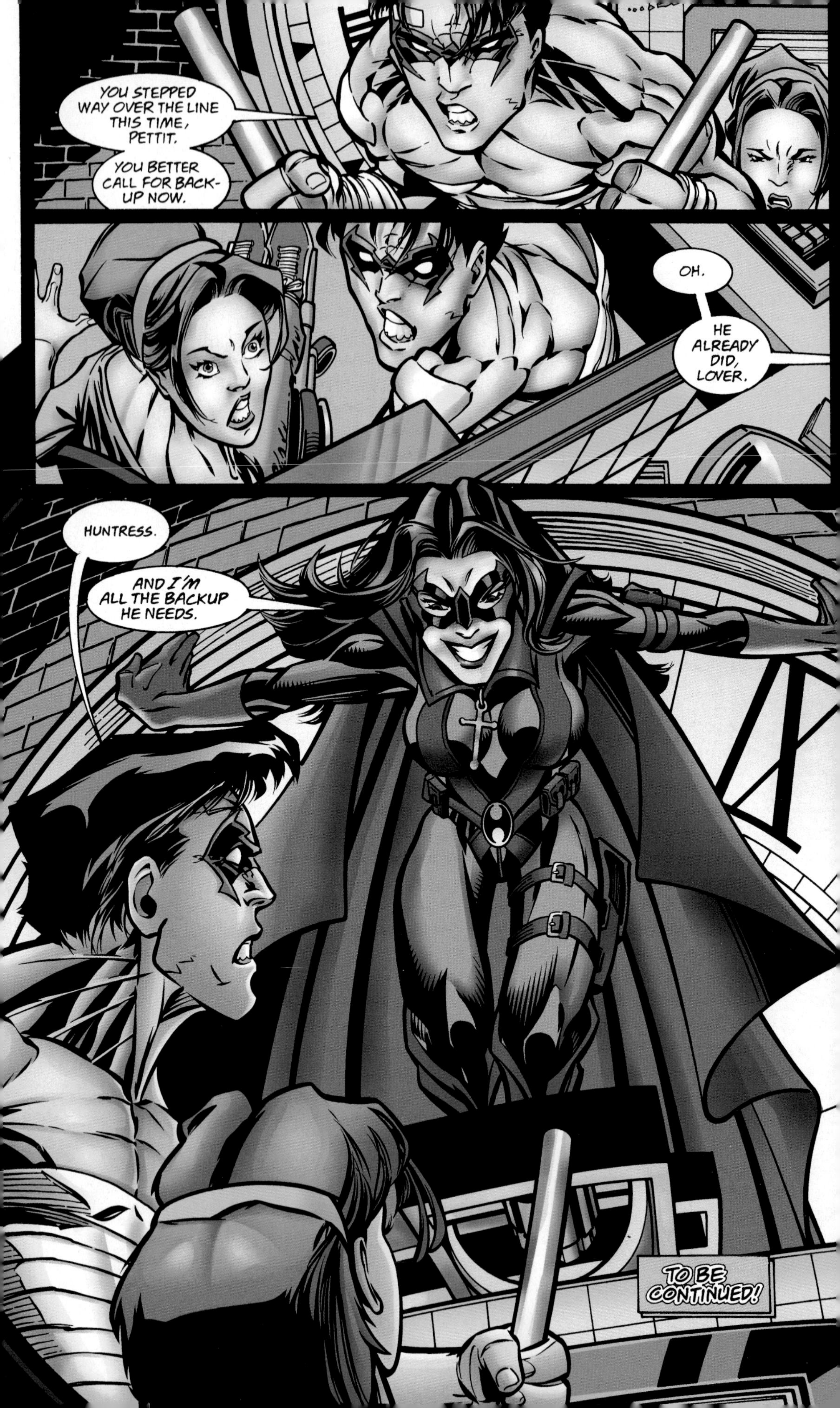
YOU STEPPED WAY OVER THE LINE THIS TIME, PETTIT.
YOU BETTER CALL FOR BACK-UP NOW.
OH.
HE ALREADY DID, LOVER.
HUNTRESS.
AND I'M ALL THE BACKUP HE NEEDS.
TO BE CONTINUED!

BY FORCE OF ARMS

Chuck Dixon
writer
Scott McDaniel
penciller
Karl Story
inker
Roberta Tewes
colorist
ohn Costanza
letterer
Jamison
separator
Joseph Illidge
assoc. editor
arren Vincenzo
general

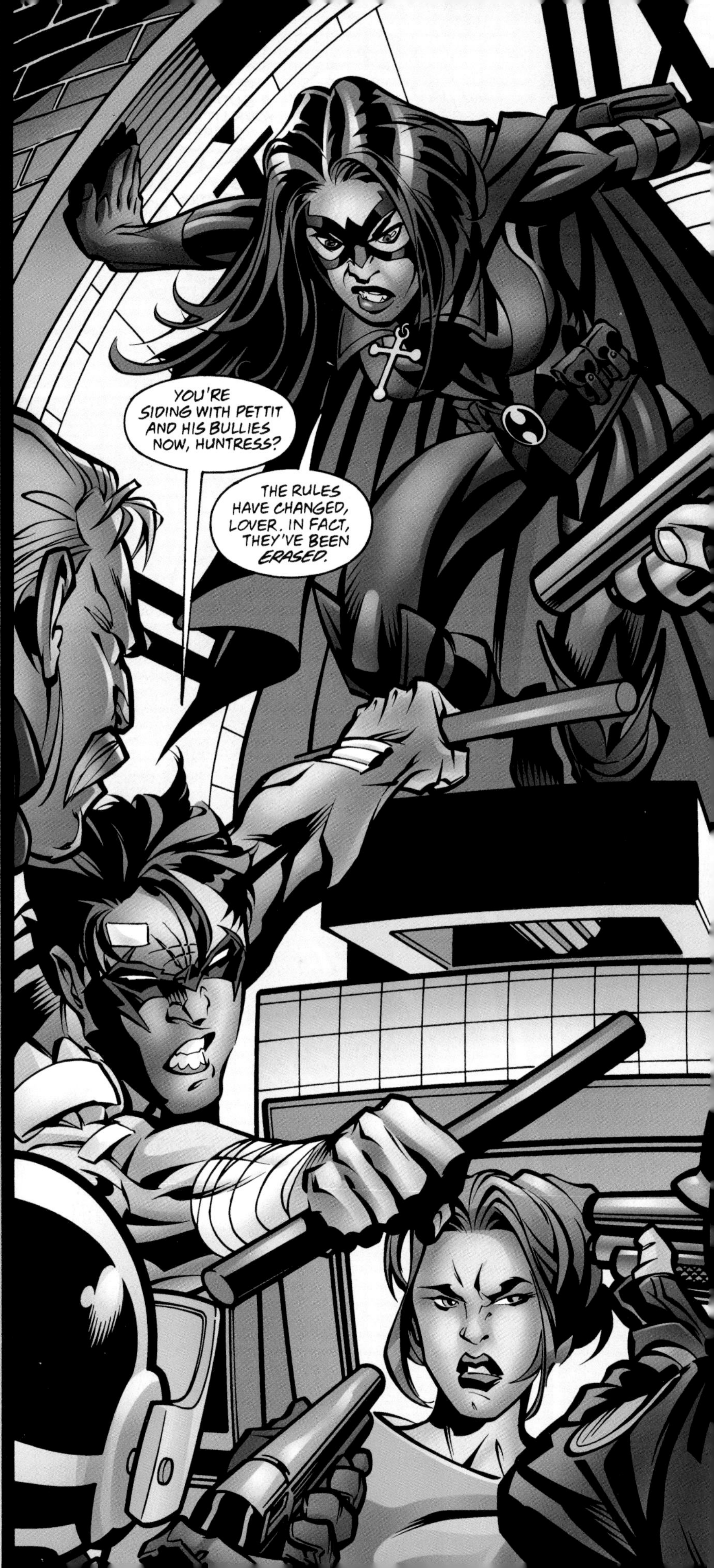
YOU'RE SIDING WITH PETTIT AND HIS BULLIES NOW, HUNTRESS?
THE RULES HAVE CHANGED, LOVER. IN FACT, THEY'VE BEEN *ERASED*.

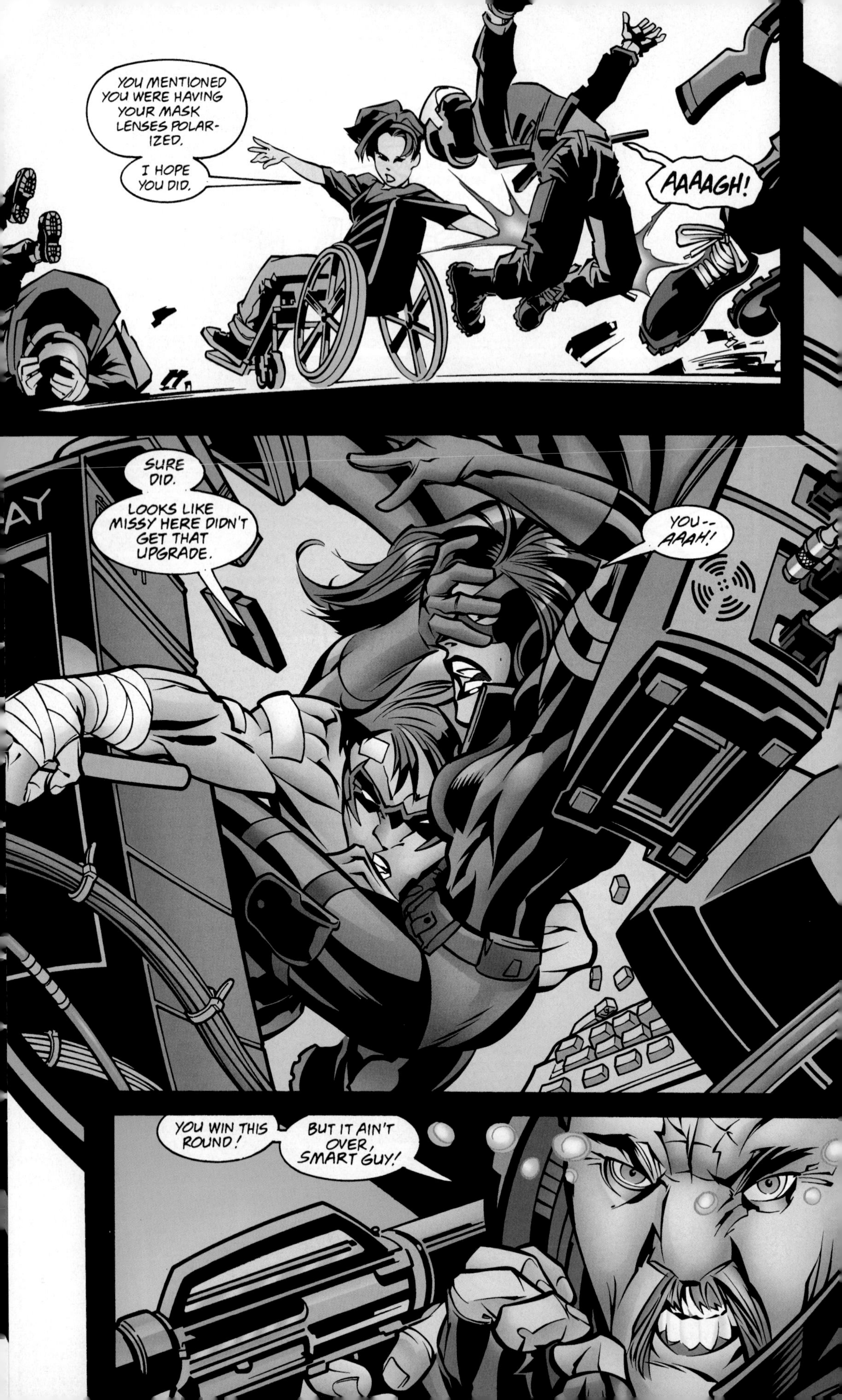
YOU MENTIONED YOU WERE HAVING YOUR MASK LENSES POLAR-IZED.
I HOPE YOU DID.
AAAAGH!
SURE DID.
LOOKS LIKE MISSY HERE DIDN'T GET THAT UPGRADE.
YOU-- AAAH!
YOU WIN THIS ROUND!
BUT IT AIN'T OVER, SMART GUY!

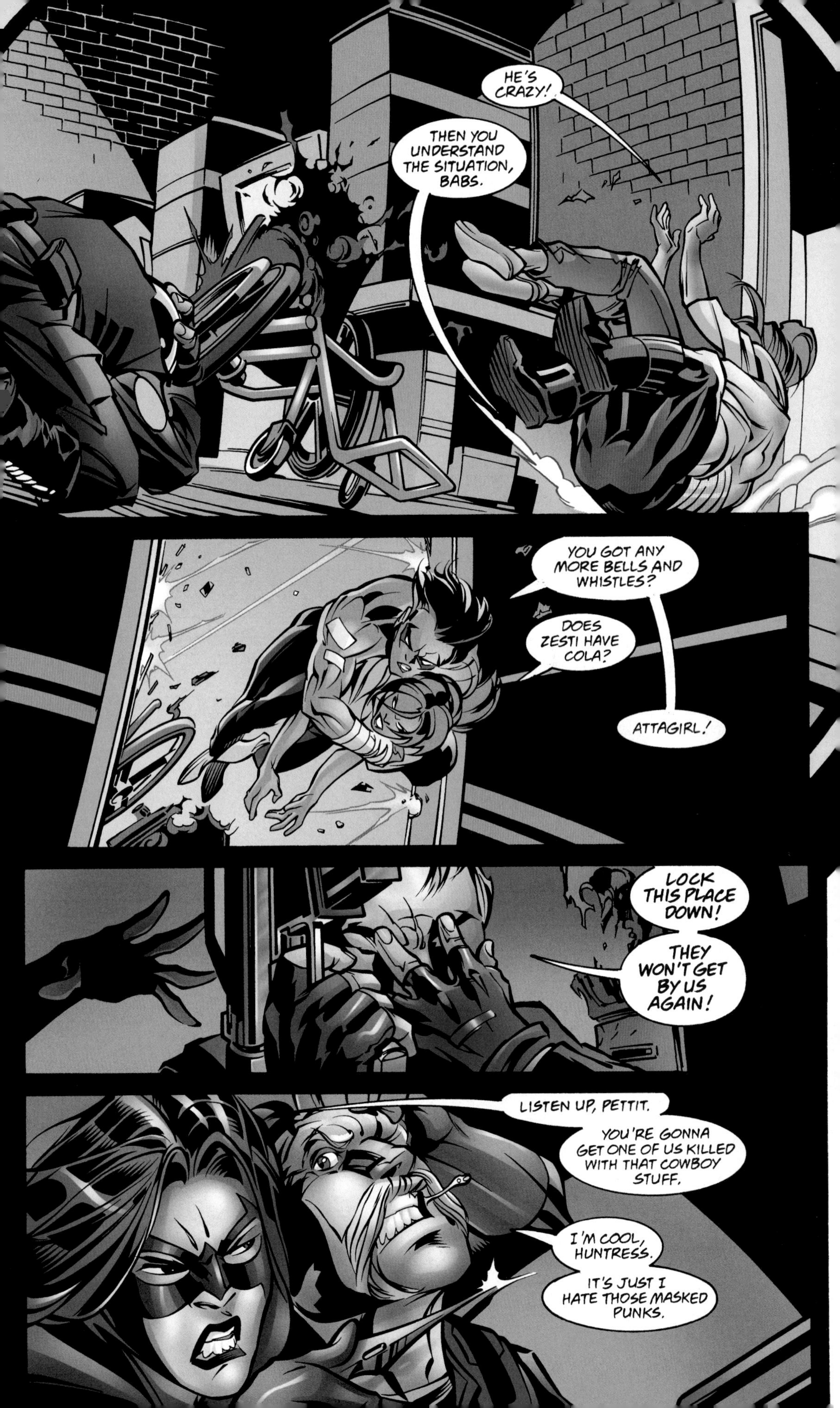
HE'S CRAZY!
THEN YOU UNDERSTAND THE SITUATION, BABS.
YOU GOT ANY MORE BELLS AND WHISTLES?
DOES ZESTI HAVE COLA?
ATTAGIRL!
LOCK THIS PLACE DOWN!
THEY WON'T GET BY US AGAIN!
LISTEN UP, PETTIT.
YOU'RE GONNA GET ONE OF US KILLED WITH THAT COWBOY STUFF.
I'M COOL, HUNTRESS.
IT'S JUST I HATE THOSE MASKED PUNKS.

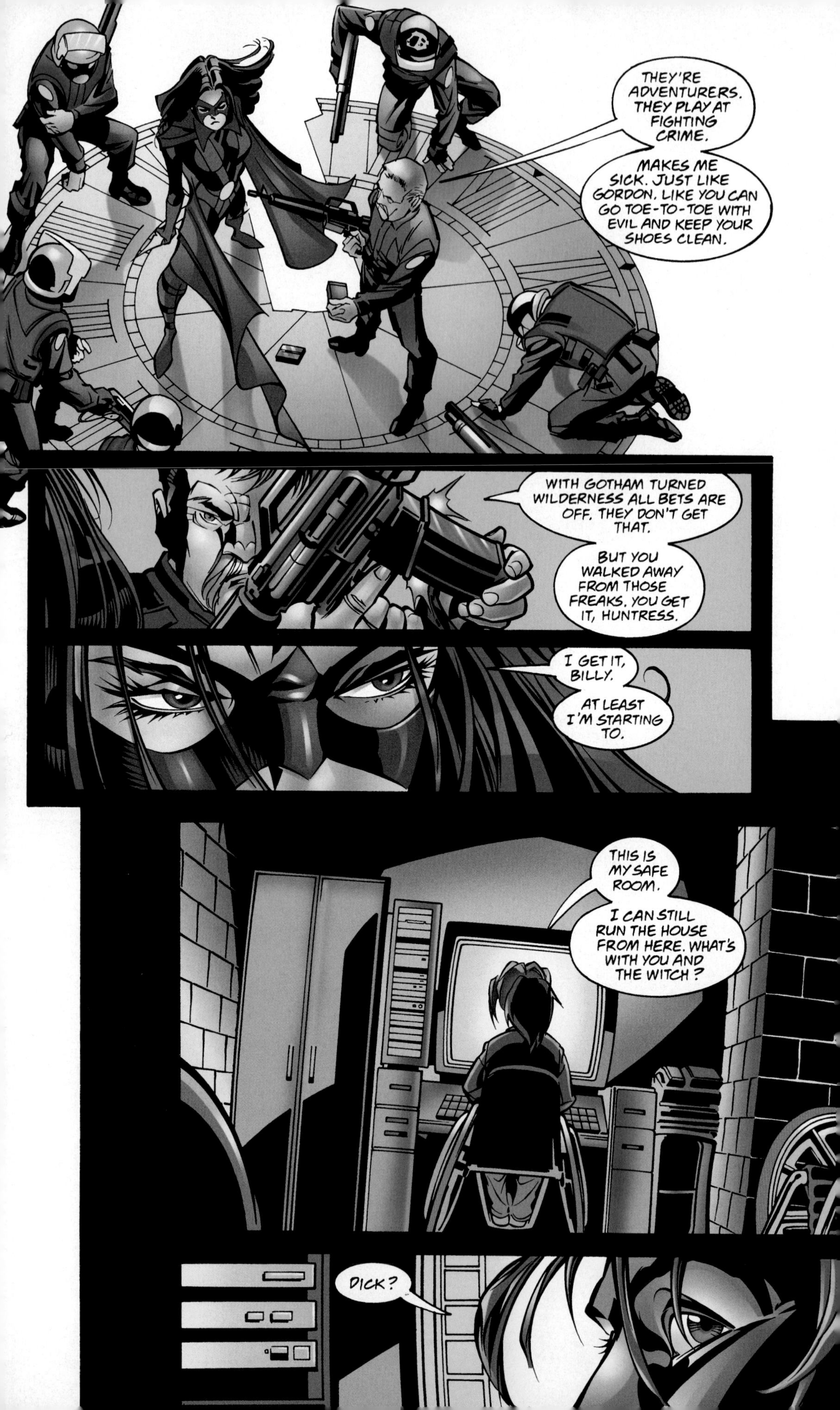
THEY'RE ADVENTURERS. THEY PLAY AT FIGHTING CRIME.
MAKES ME SICK. JUST LIKE GORDON. LIKE YOU CAN GO TOE-TO-TOE WITH EVIL AND KEEP YOUR SHOES CLEAN.
WITH GOTHAM TURNED WILDERNESS ALL BETS ARE OFF. THEY DON'T GET THAT.
BUT YOU WALKED AWAY FROM THOSE FREAKS. YOU GET IT, HUNTRESS.
I GET IT, BILLY.
AT LEAST I'M STARTING TO.
THIS IS MY SAFE ROOM.
I CAN STILL RUN THE HOUSE FROM HERE. WHAT'S WITH YOU AND THE WITCH?
DICK?

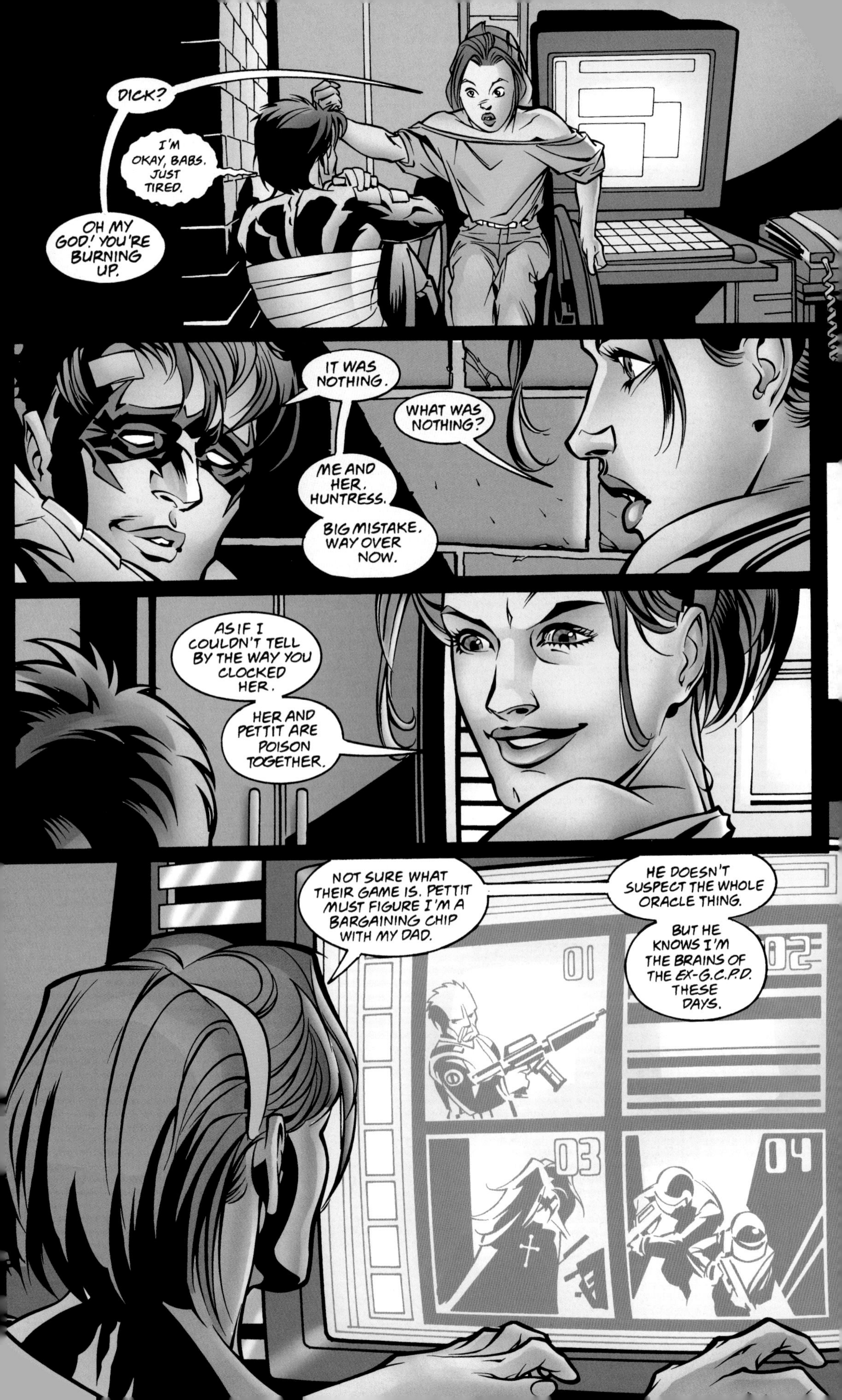
DICK?
I'M OKAY, BABS. JUST TIRED.
OH MY GOD! YOU'RE BURNING UP.
IT WAS NOTHING.
WHAT WAS NOTHING?
ME AND HER. HUNTRESS.
BIG MISTAKE. WAY OVER NOW.
AS IF I COULDN'T TELL BY THE WAY YOU CLOCKED HER.
HER AND PETTIT ARE POISON TOGETHER.
NOT SURE WHAT THEIR GAME IS. PETTIT MUST FIGURE I'M A BARGAINING CHIP WITH MY DAD.
HE DOESN'T SUSPECT THE WHOLE ORACLE THING.
BUT HE KNOWS I'M THE BRAINS OF THE EX-G.C.P.D. THESE DAYS.
01
02
03
04

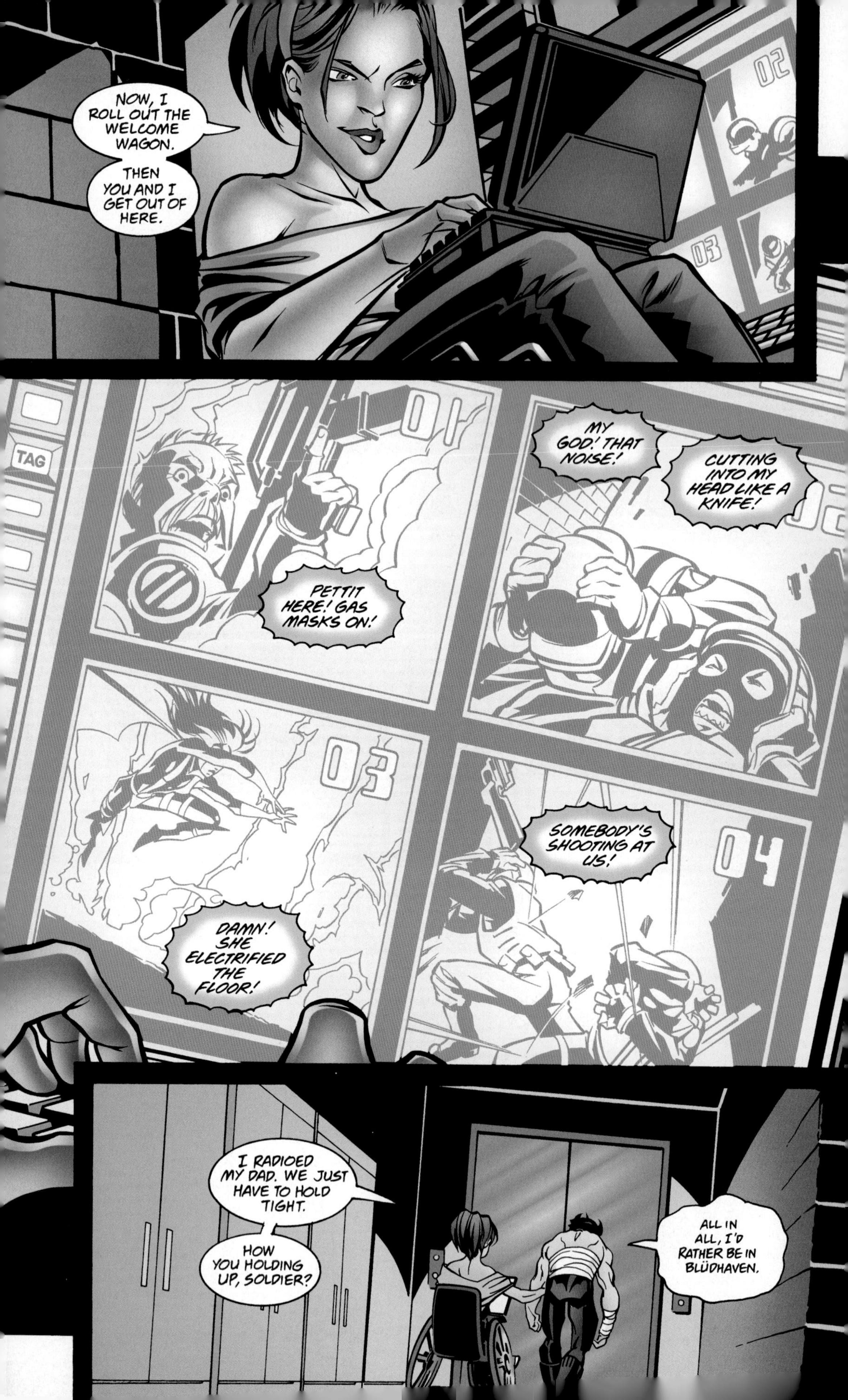
NOW, I ROLL OUT THE WELCOME WAGON.
THEN YOU AND I GET OUT OF HERE.
TAG
PETTIT HERE! GAS MASKS ON!
MY GOD! THAT NOISE!
CUTTING INTO MY HEAD LIKE A KNIFE!
DAMN! SHE ELECTRIFIED THE FLOOR!
SOMEBODY'S SHOOTING AT US!
I RADIOED MY DAD. WE JUST HAVE TO HOLD TIGHT.
HOW YOU HOLDING UP, SOLDIER?
ALL IN ALL, I'D RATHER BE IN BLÜDHAVEN.

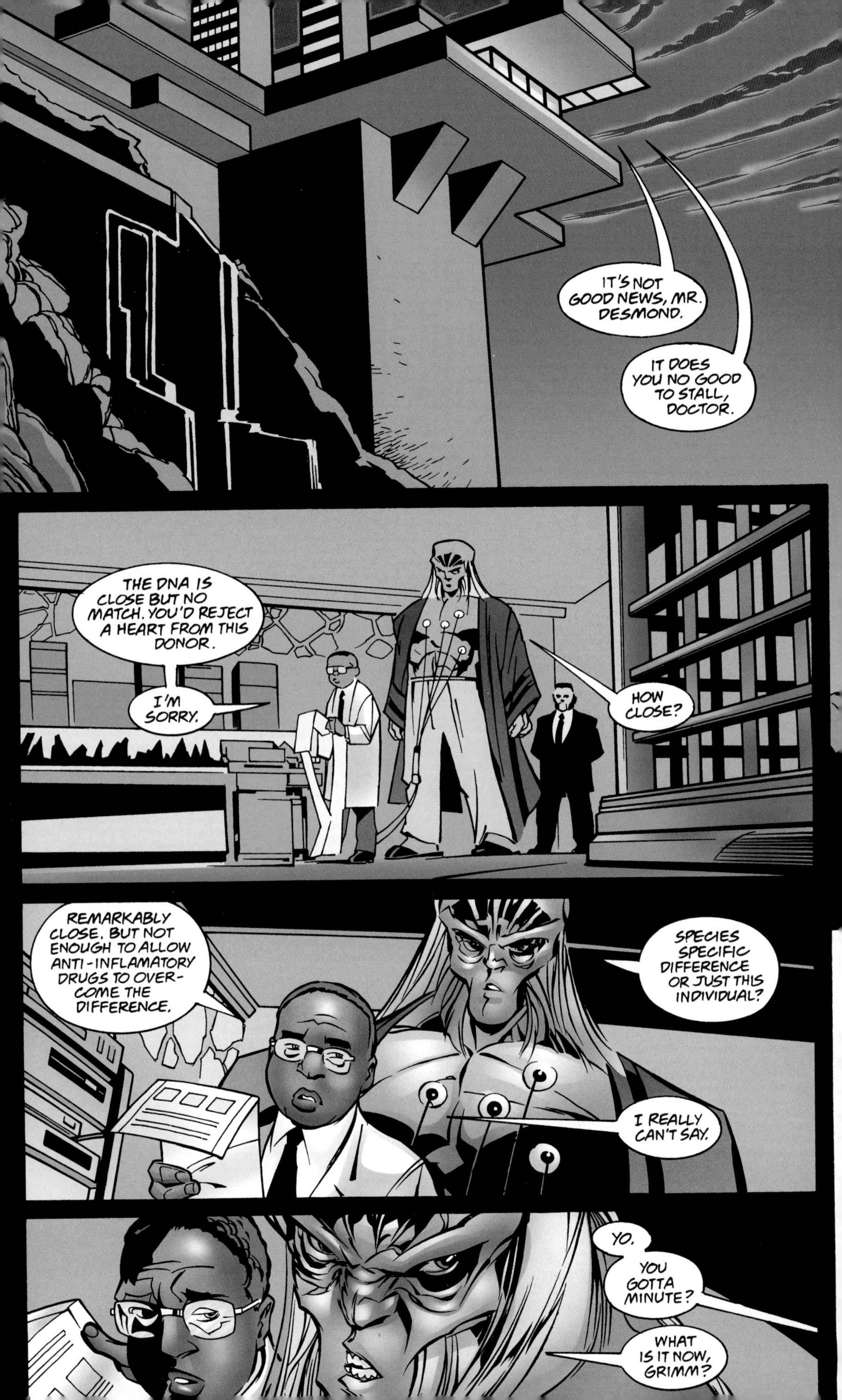
IT'S NOT GOOD NEWS, MR. DESMOND.
IT DOES YOU NO GOOD TO STALL, DOCTOR.
THE DNA IS CLOSE BUT NO MATCH. YOU'D REJECT A HEART FROM THIS DONOR.
I'M SORRY.
HOW CLOSE?
REMARKABLY CLOSE. BUT NOT ENOUGH TO ALLOW ANTI-INFLAMATORY DRUGS TO OVER-COME THE DIFFERENCE.
SPECIES SPECIFIC DIFFERENCE OR JUST THIS INDIVIDUAL?
I REALLY CAN'T SAY.
YO.
YOU GOTTA MINUTE?
WHAT IS IT NOW, GRIMM?

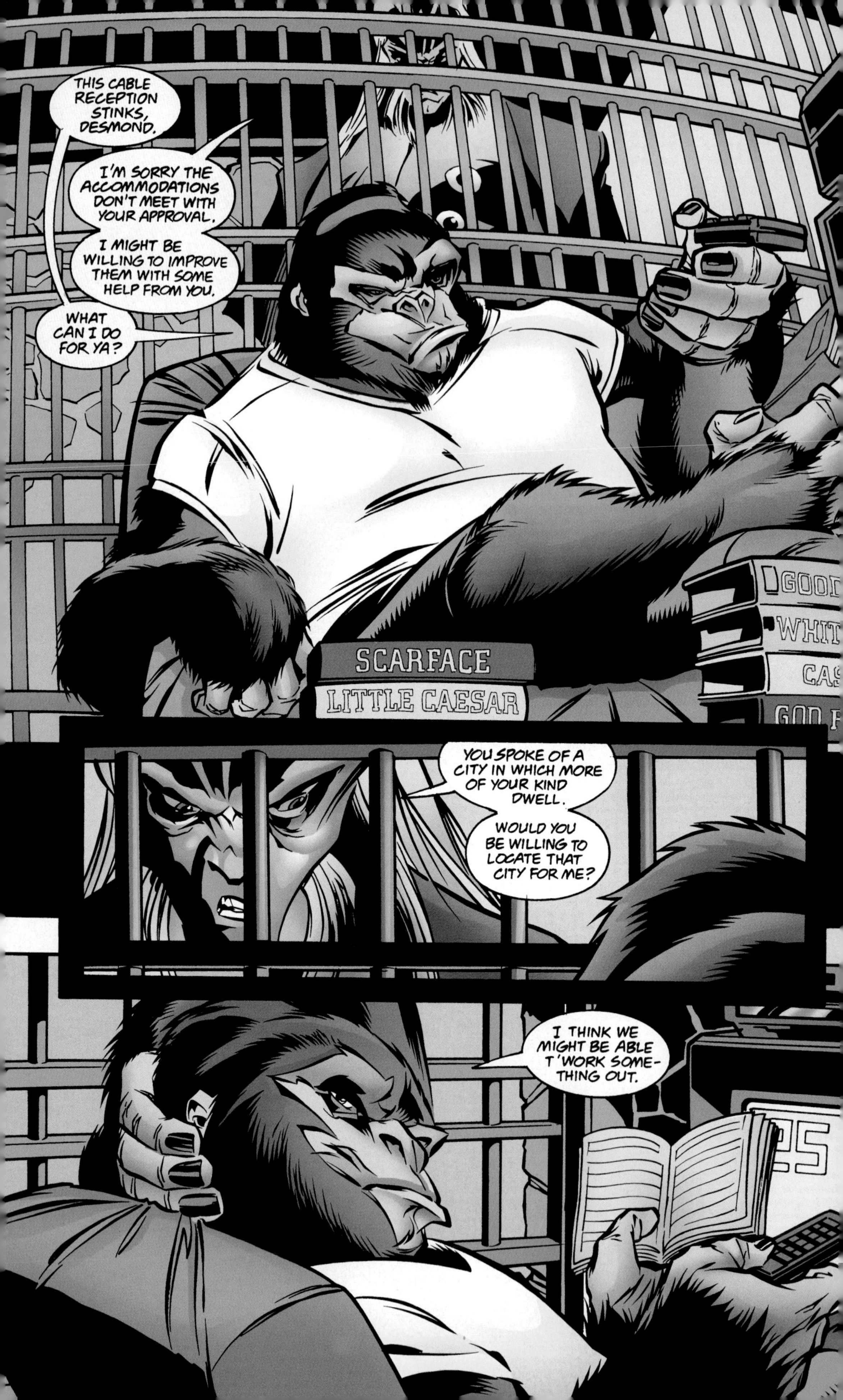

THIS CABLE RECEPTION STINKS, DESMOND.
I'M SORRY THE ACCOMMODATIONS DON'T MEET WITH YOUR APPROVAL.
I MIGHT BE WILLING TO IMPROVE THEM WITH SOME HELP FROM YOU.
WHAT CAN I DO FOR YA?
SCARFACE
LITTLE CAESAR
YOU SPOKE OF A CITY IN WHICH MORE OF YOUR KIND DWELL.
WOULD YOU BE WILLING TO LOCATE THAT CITY FOR ME?
I THINK WE MIGHT BE ABLE T'WORK SOMETHING OUT.

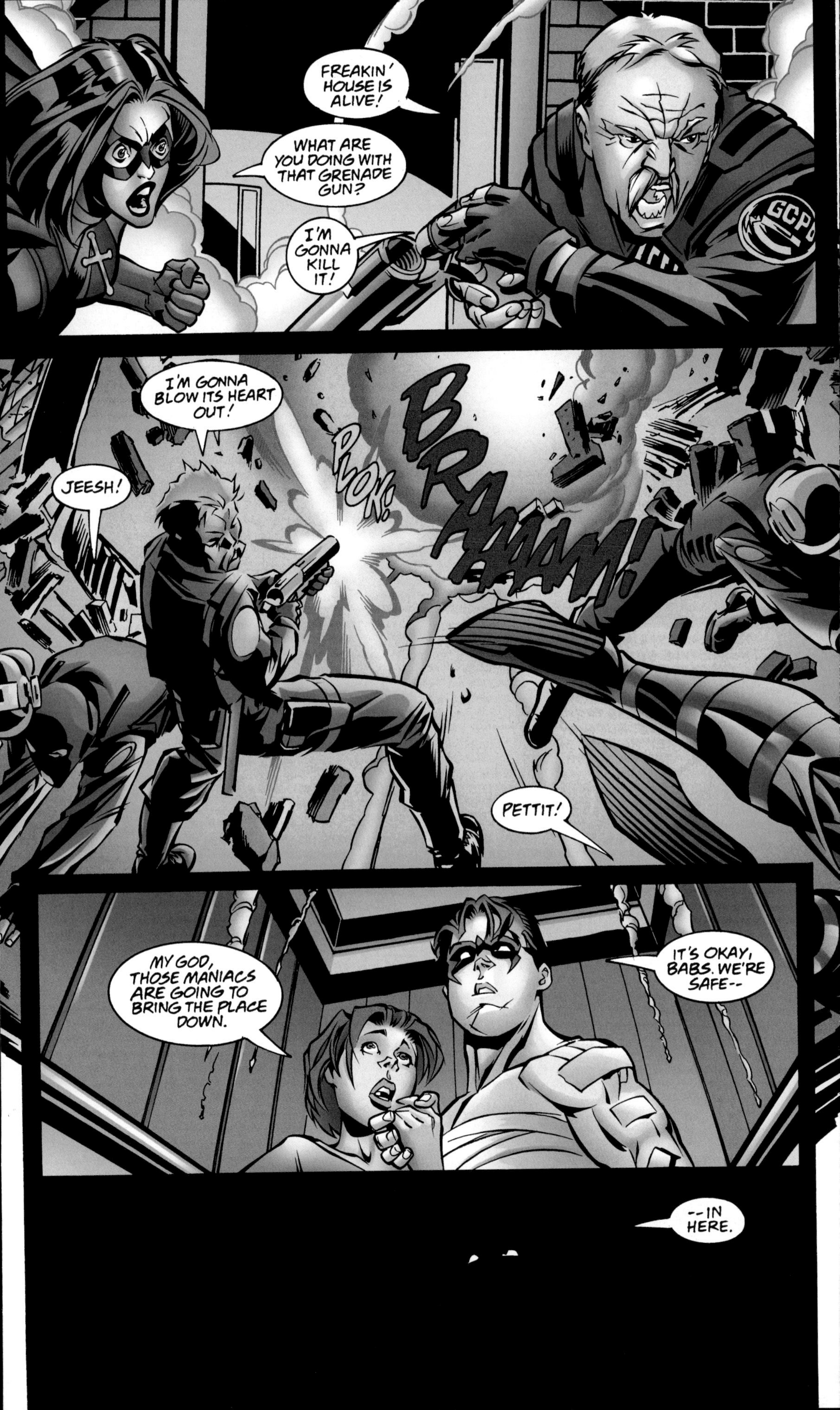
FREAKIN' HOUSE IS ALIVE!
WHAT ARE YOU DOING WITH THAT GRENADE GUN?
I'M GONNA KILL IT!
GCPD
I'M GONNA BLOW ITS HEART OUT!
PLOK!
BRAAAAAM!
JEESH!
PETTIT!
MY GOD, THOSE MANIACS ARE GOING TO BRING THE PLACE DOWN.
IT'S OKAY, BABS. WE'RE SAFE--
--IN HERE.

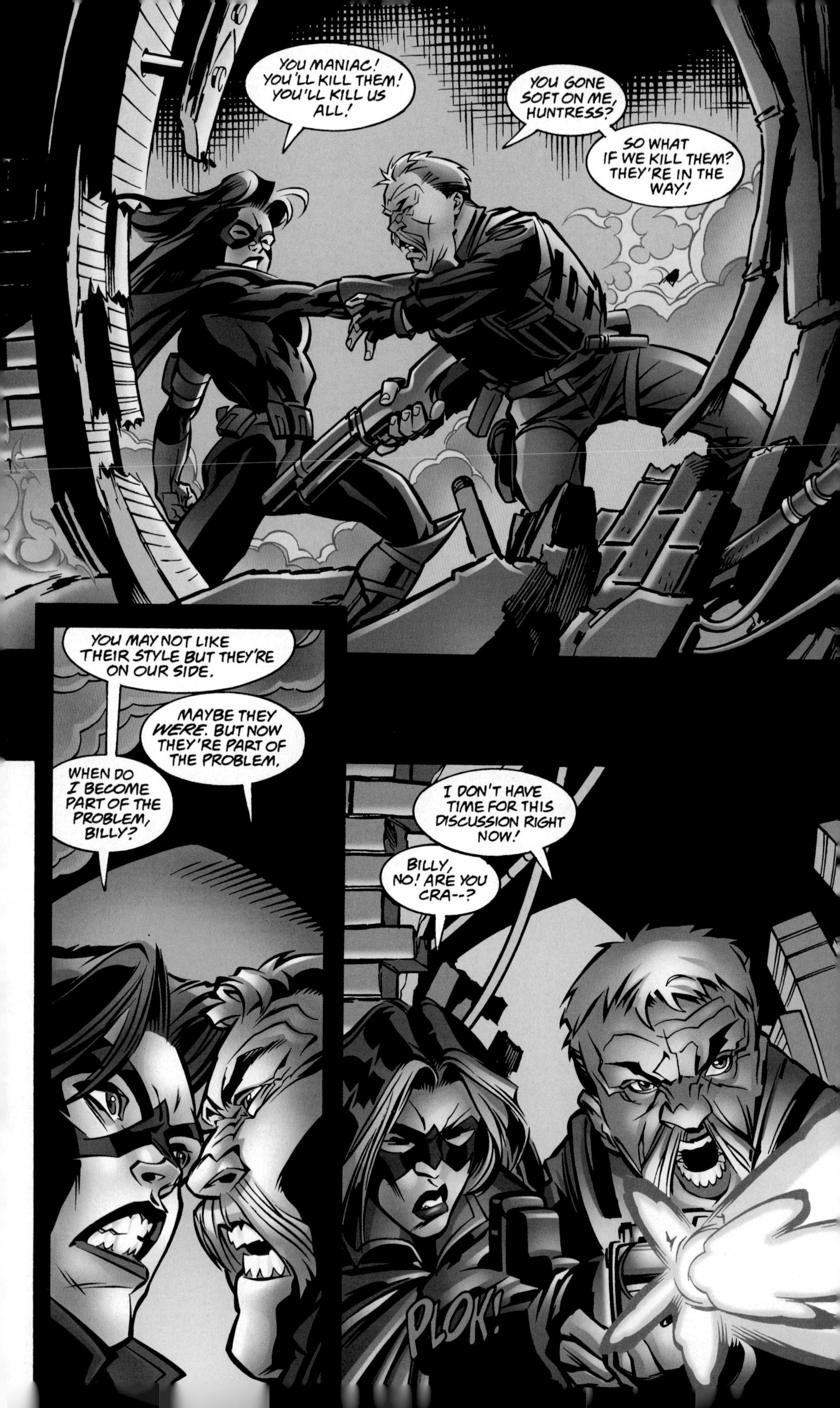
YOU MANIAC! YOU'LL KILL THEM! YOU'LL KILL US ALL!
YOU GONE SOFT ON ME, HUNTRESS?
SO WHAT IF WE KILL THEM? THEY'RE IN THE WAY!
YOU MAY NOT LIKE THEIR STYLE BUT THEY'RE ON OUR SIDE.
MAYBE THEY WERE. BUT NOW THEY'RE PART OF THE PROBLEM.
WHEN DO I BECOME PART OF THE PROBLEM, BILLY?
I DON'T HAVE TIME FOR THIS DISCUSSION RIGHT NOW!
BILLY, NO! ARE YOU CRA--?
PLOK!

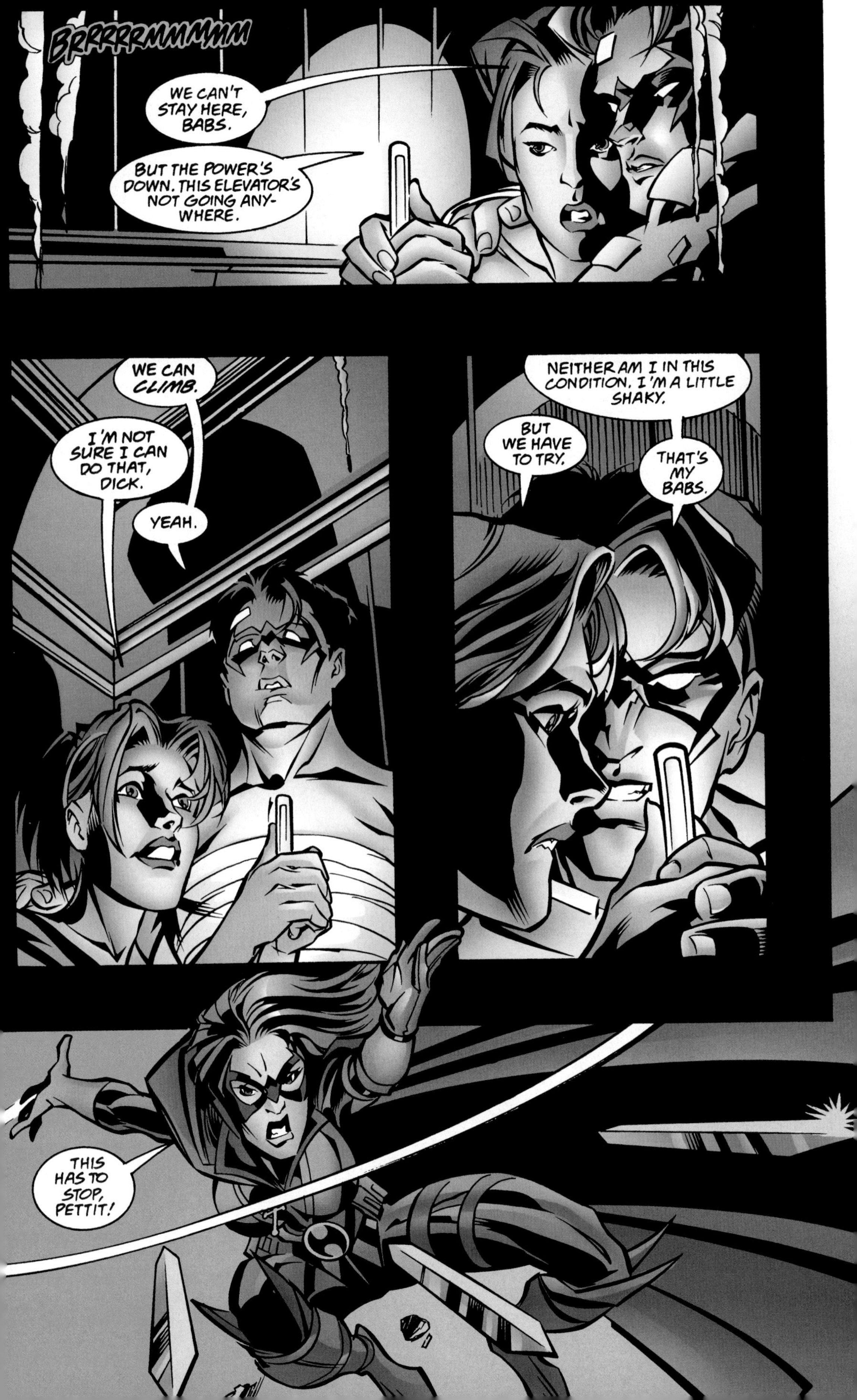
BRRRRRMMMMMM
WE CAN'T STAY HERE, BABS.
BUT THE POWER'S DOWN. THIS ELEVATOR'S NOT GOING ANY-WHERE.
WE CAN CLIMB.
I'M NOT SURE I CAN DO THAT, DICK.
YEAH.
NEITHER AM I IN THIS CONDITION. I'M A LITTLE SHAKY.
BUT WE HAVE TO TRY.
THAT'S MY BABS.
THIS HAS TO STOP, PETTIT!

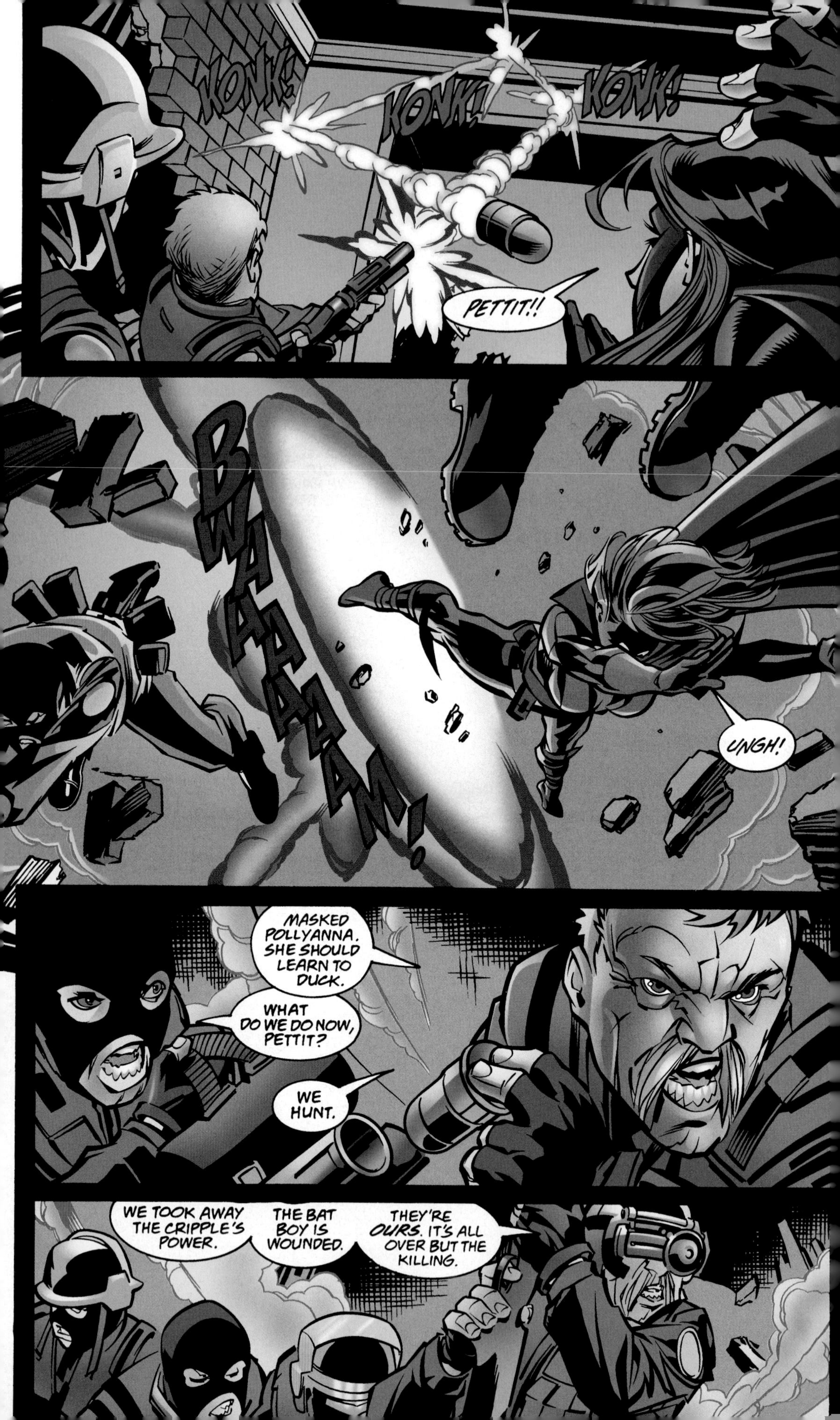
KONK!
KONK!
KONK!
PETTIT!!
BWAAAAAAAM!
UNGH!
MASKED POLLYANNA. SHE SHOULD LEARN TO DUCK.
WHAT DO WE DO NOW, PETTIT?
WE HUNT.
WE TOOK AWAY THE CRIPPLE'S POWER.
THE BAT BOY IS WOUNDED.
THEY'RE OURS. IT'S ALL OVER BUT THE KILLING.

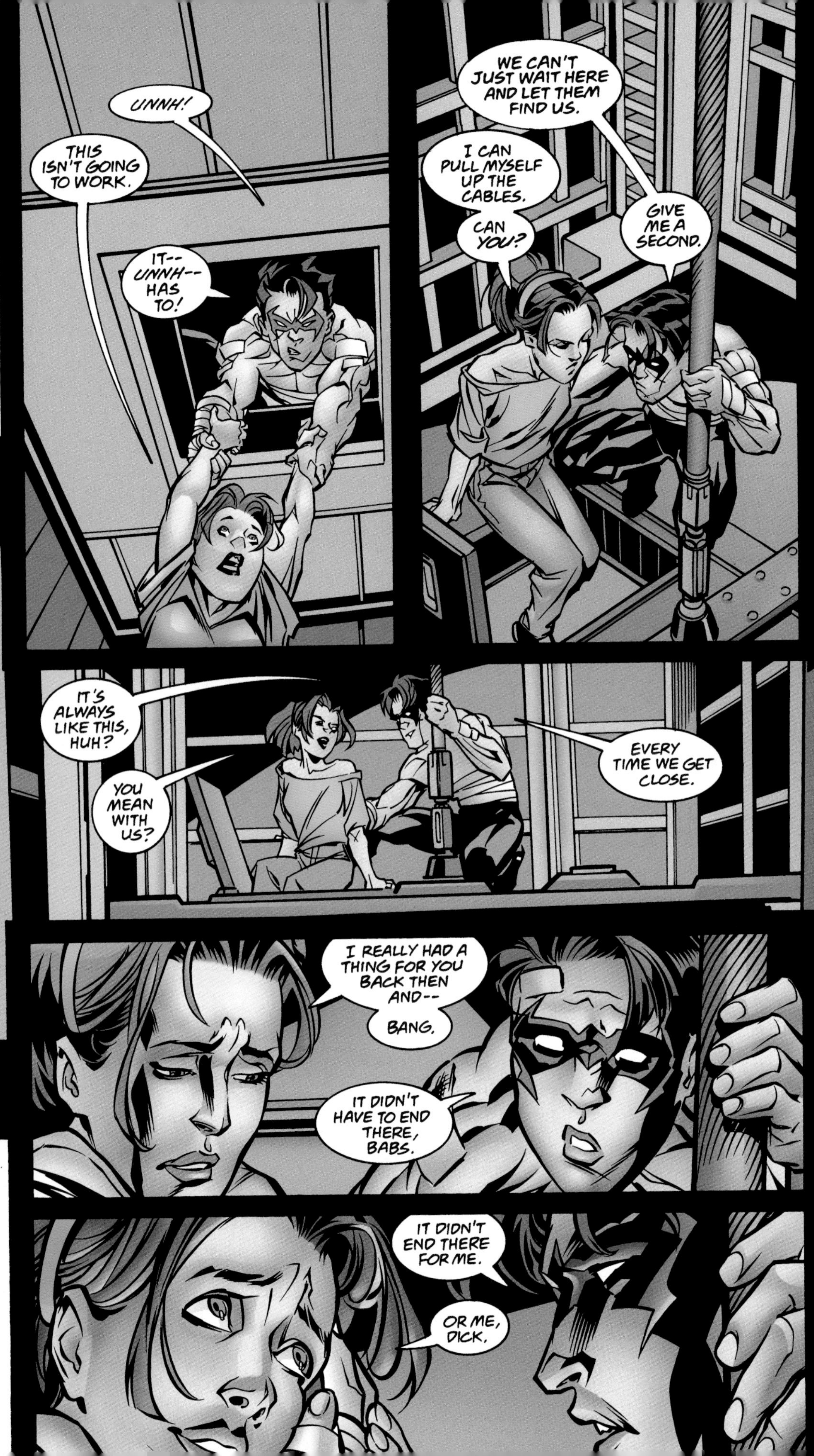
UNNH!
THIS ISN'T GOING TO WORK.
IT-- UNNH-- HAS TO!
WE CAN'T JUST WAIT HERE AND LET THEM FIND US.
I CAN PULL MYSELF UP THE CABLES.
CAN YOU?
GIVE ME A SECOND.
IT'S ALWAYS LIKE THIS, HUH?
YOU MEAN WITH US?
EVERY TIME WE GET CLOSE.
I REALLY HAD A THING FOR YOU BACK THEN AND--
BANG.
IT DIDN'T HAVE TO END THERE, BABS.
IT DIDN'T END THERE FOR ME.
OR ME, DICK.

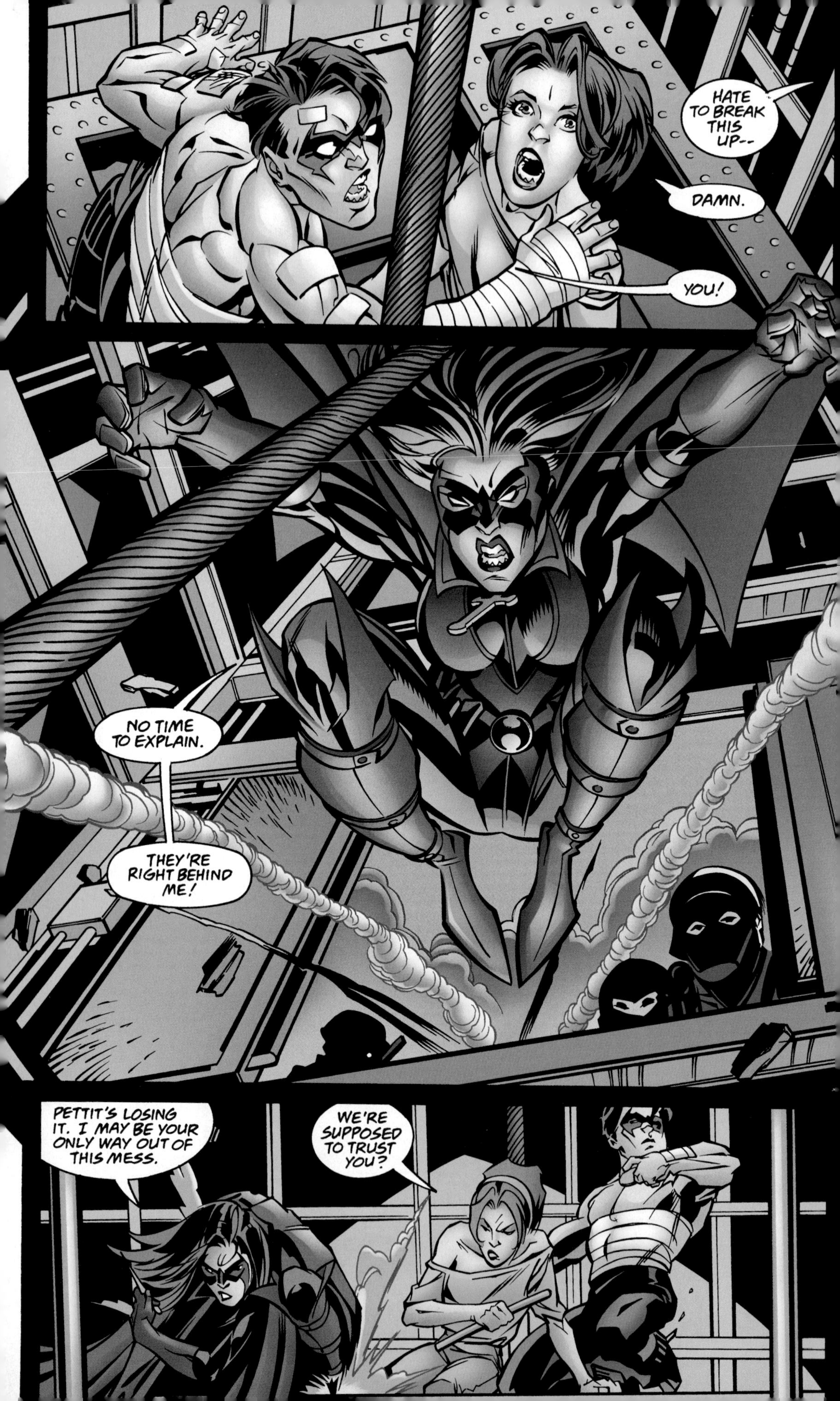
HATE TO BREAK THIS UP--
DAMN.
YOU!
NO TIME TO EXPLAIN.
THEY'RE RIGHT BEHIND ME!
PETTIT'S LOSING IT. I MAY BE YOUR ONLY WAY OUT OF THIS MESS.
WE'RE SUPPOSED TO TRUST YOU?

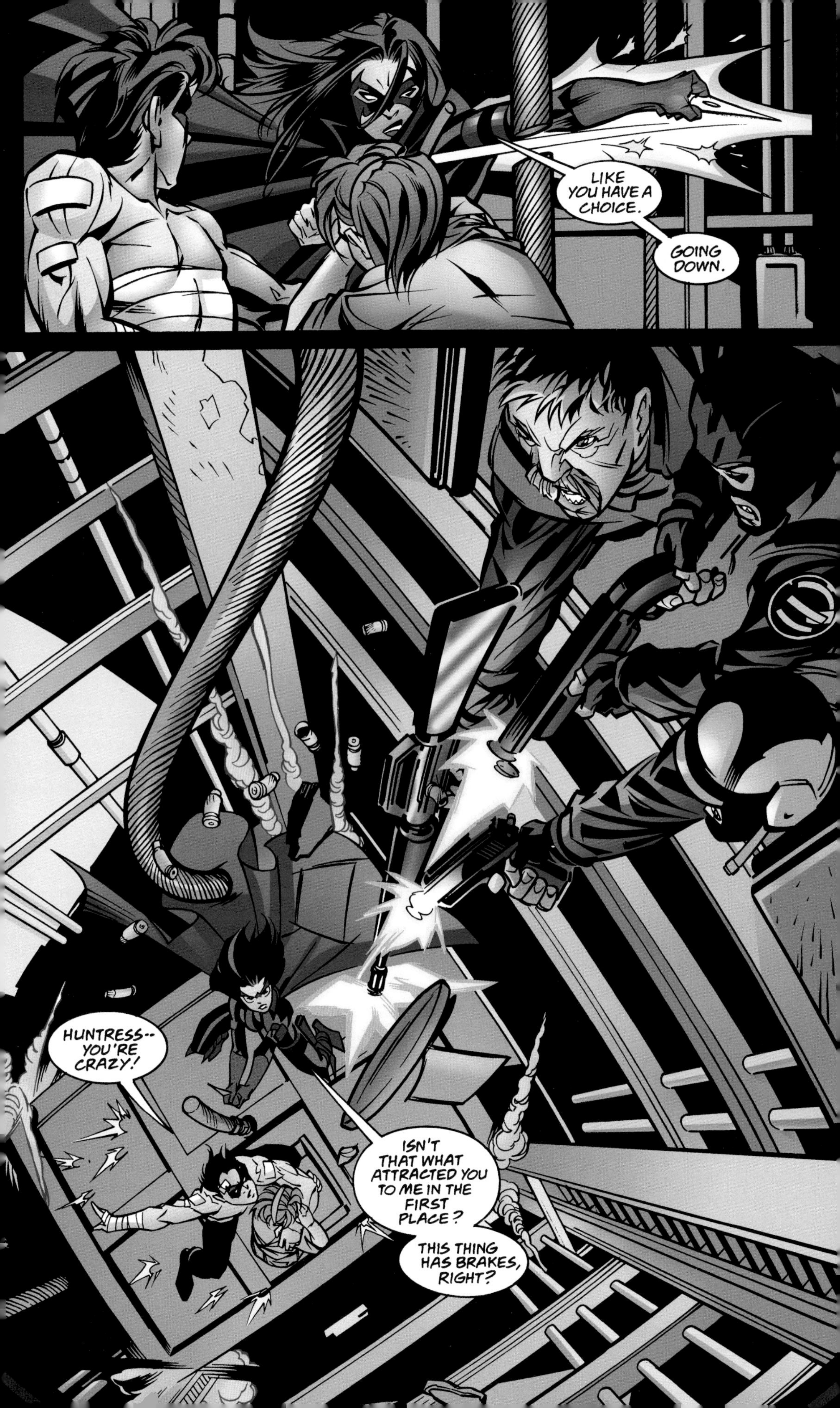
LIKE YOU HAVE A CHOICE.
GOING DOWN.
HUNTRESS-- YOU'RE CRAZY!
ISN'T THAT WHAT ATTRACTED YOU TO ME IN THE FIRST PLACE?
THIS THING HAS BRAKES, RIGHT?

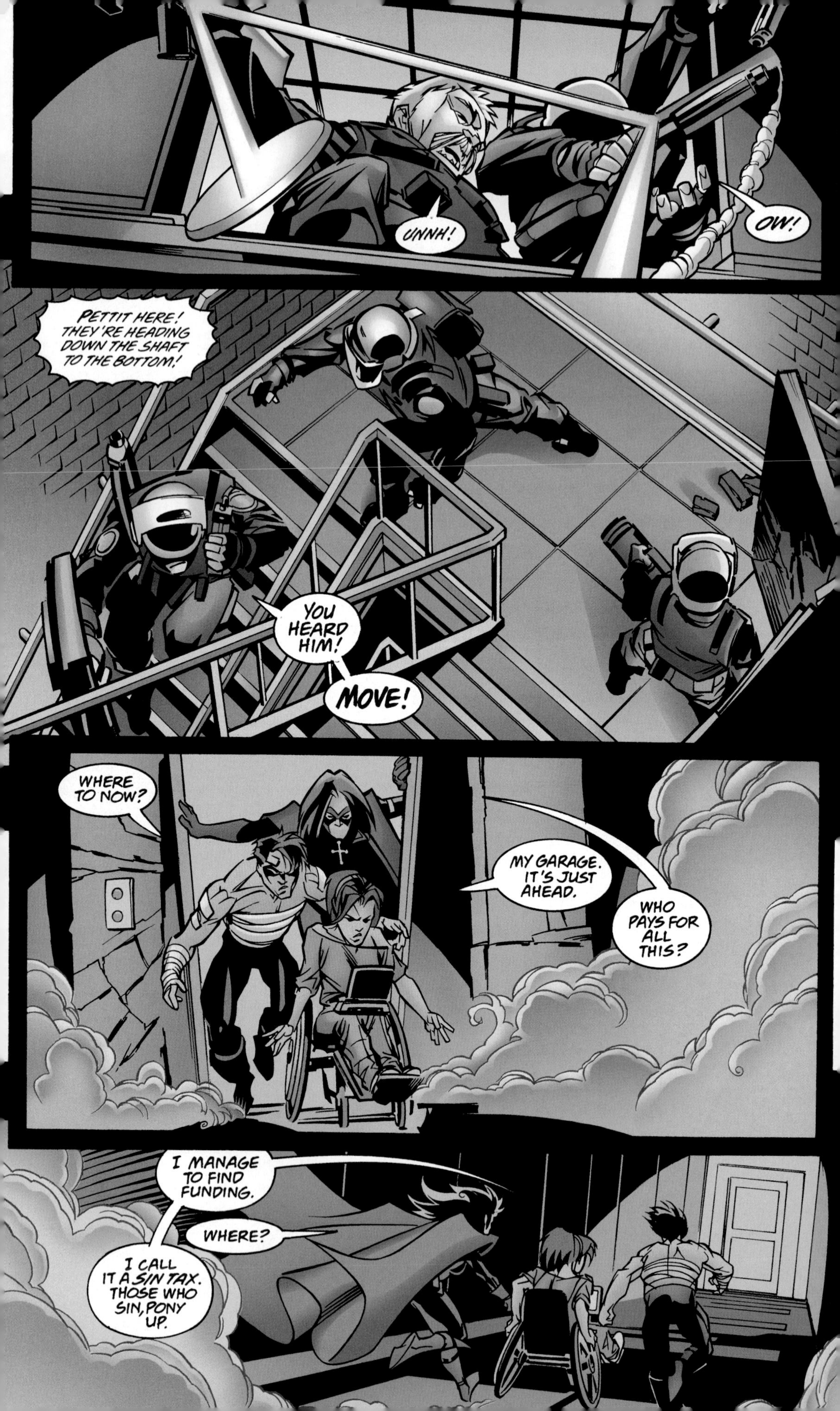
UNNH!
OW!
PETTIT HERE! THEY'RE HEADING DOWN THE SHAFT TO THE BOTTOM!
YOU HEARD HIM!
MOVE!
WHERE TO NOW?
MY GARAGE. IT'S JUST AHEAD.
WHO PAYS FOR ALL THIS?
I MANAGE TO FIND FUNDING.
WHERE?
I CALL IT A SIN TAX. THOSE WHO SIN, PONY UP.

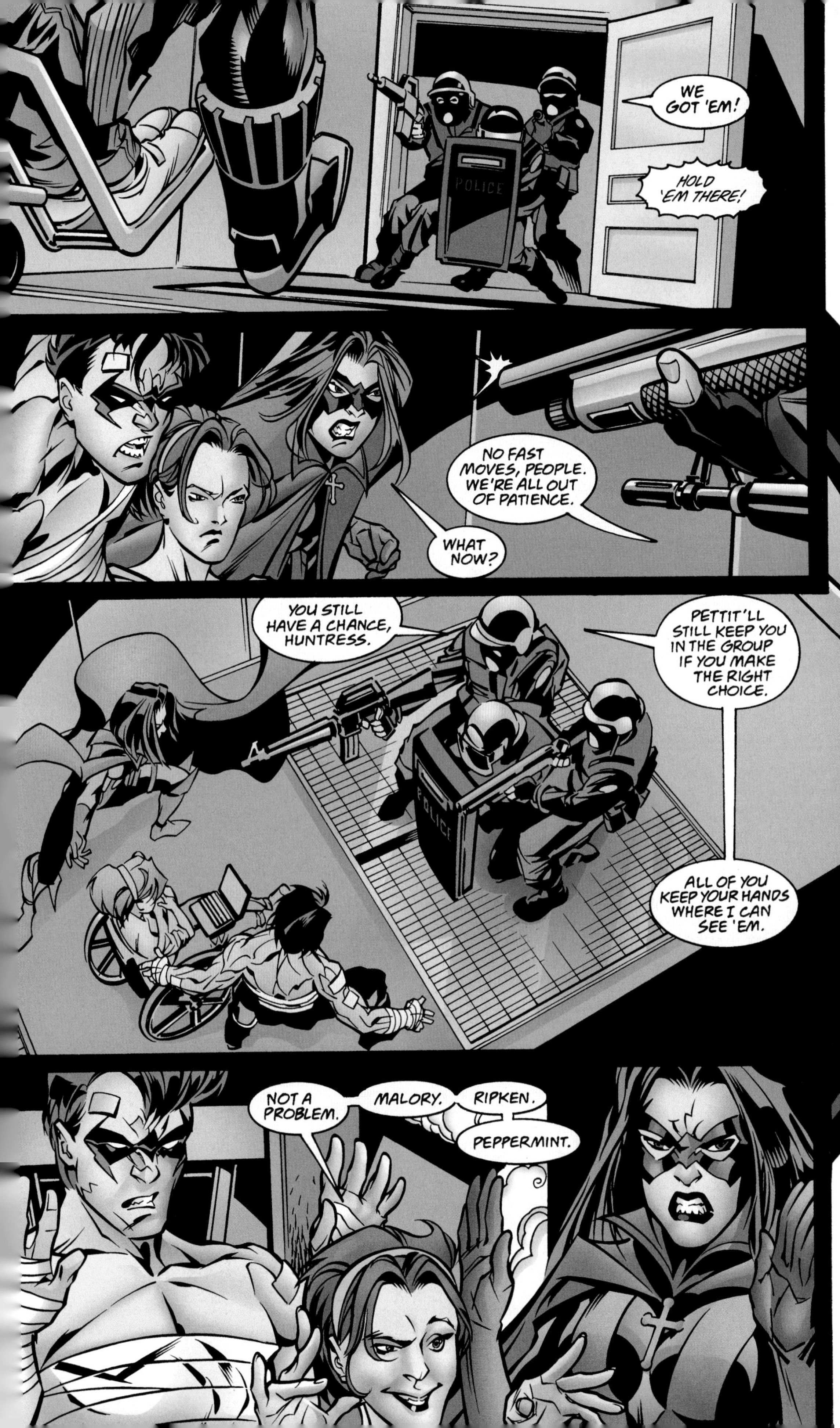
WE GOT 'EM!
HOLD 'EM THERE!
POLICE
NO FAST MOVES, PEOPLE. WE'RE ALL OUT OF PATIENCE.
WHAT NOW?
YOU STILL HAVE A CHANCE, HUNTRESS.
PETTIT'LL STILL KEEP YOU IN THE GROUP IF YOU MAKE THE RIGHT CHOICE.
ALL OF YOU KEEP YOUR HANDS WHERE I CAN SEE 'EM.
POLICE
NOT A PROBLEM.
MALORY.
RIPKEN.
PEPPERMINT.

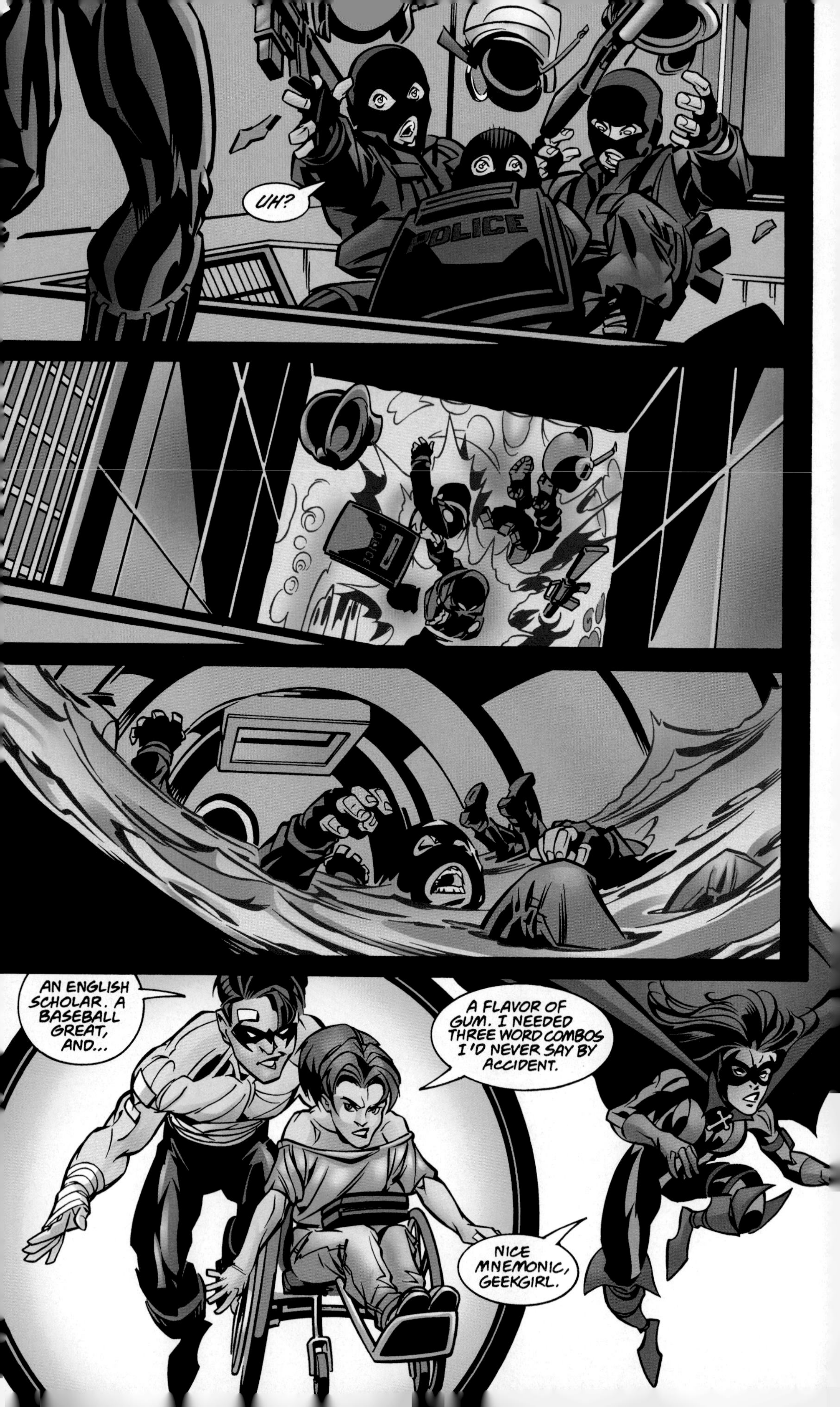
UH?
POLICE
POLICE
AN ENGLISH SCHOLAR. A BASEBALL GREAT, AND...
A FLAVOR OF GUM. I NEEDED THREE WORD COMBOS I'D NEVER SAY BY ACCIDENT.
NICE MNEMONIC, GEEKGIRL.

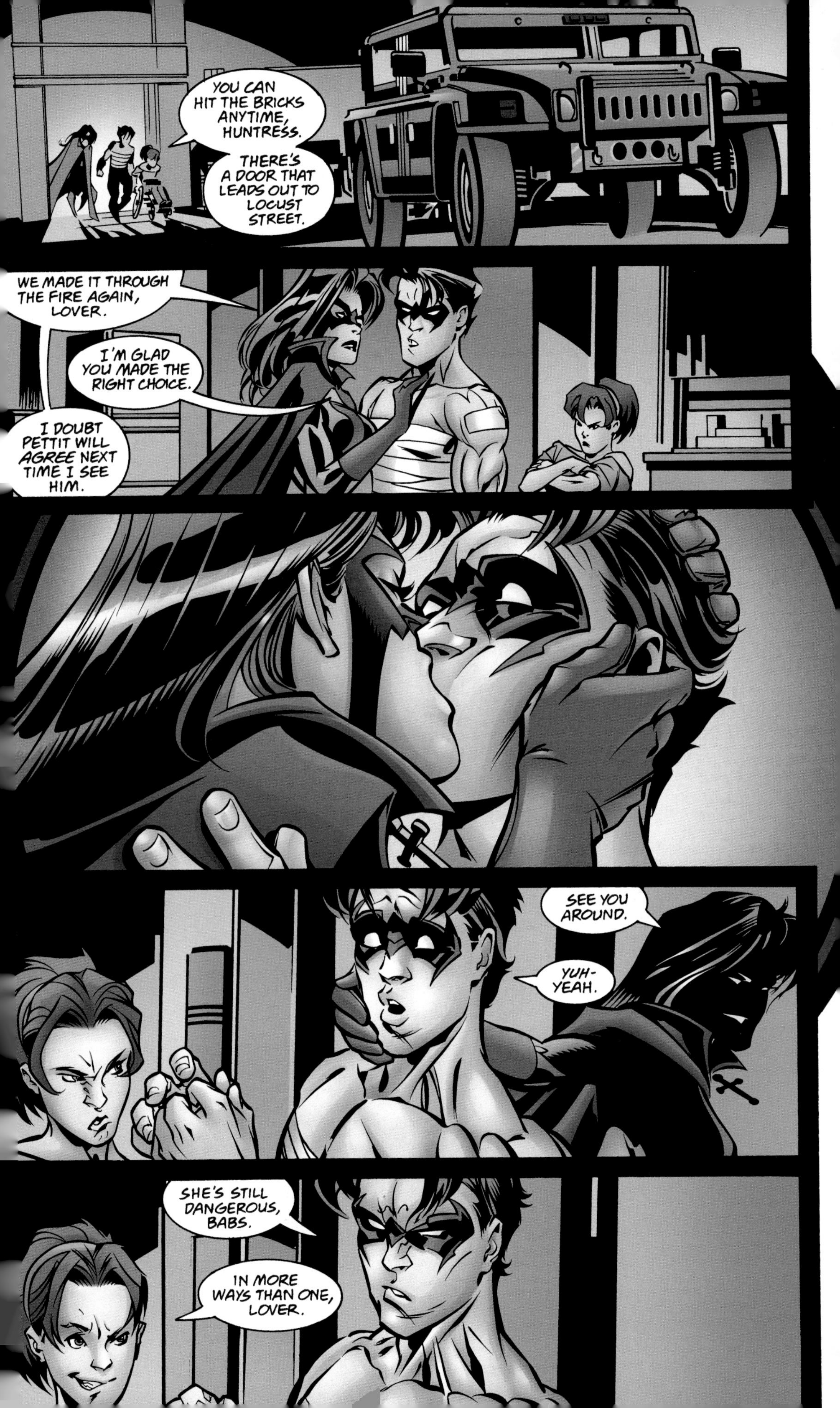

YOU CAN HIT THE BRICKS ANYTIME, HUNTRESS.
THERE'S A DOOR THAT LEADS OUT TO LOCUST STREET.
WE MADE IT THROUGH THE FIRE AGAIN, LOVER.
I'M GLAD YOU MADE THE RIGHT CHOICE.
I DOUBT PETTIT WILL AGREE NEXT TIME I SEE HIM.
SEE YOU AROUND.
YUH-YEAH.
SHE'S STILL DANGEROUS, BABS.
IN MORE WAYS THAN ONE, LOVER.

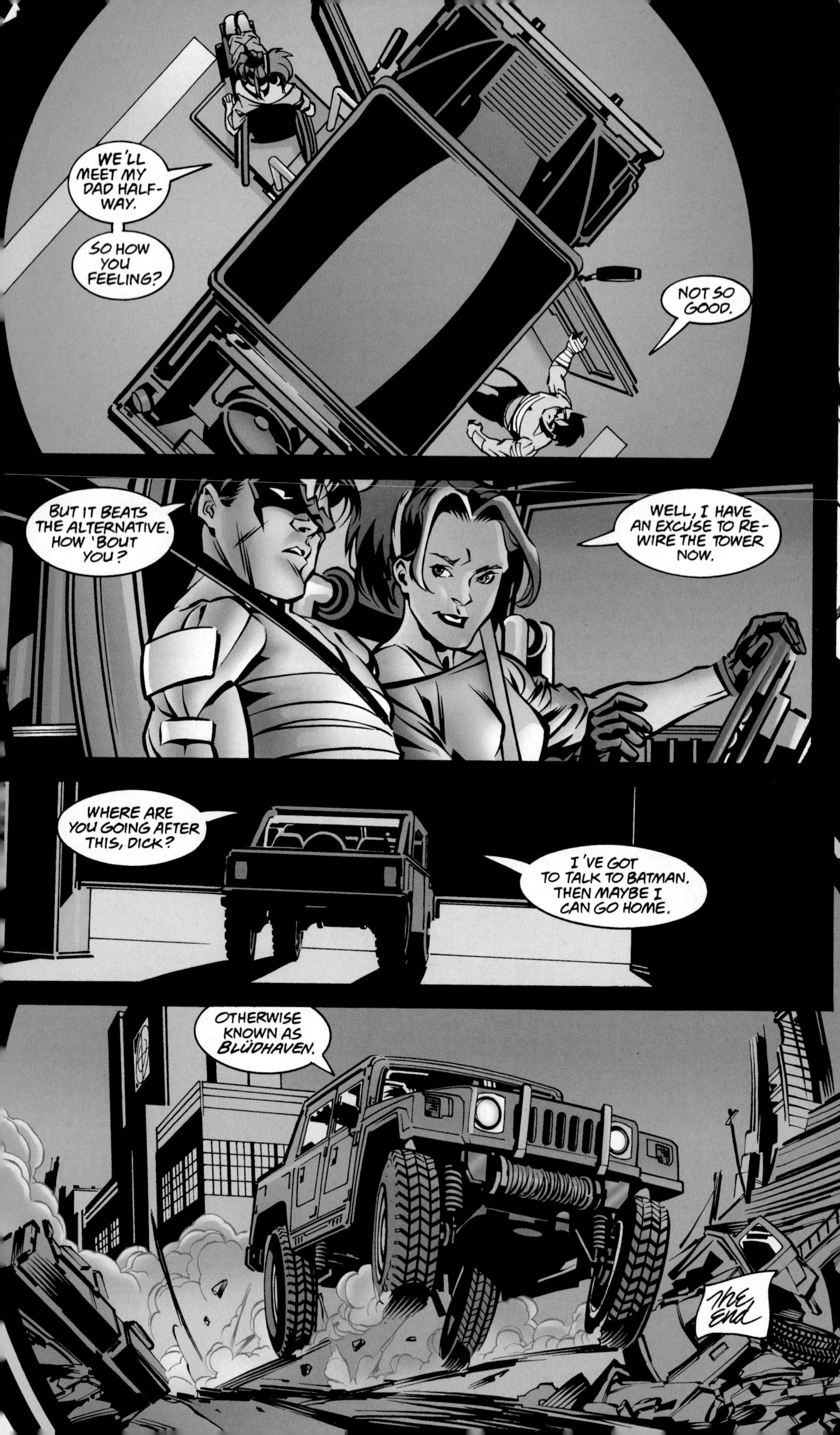

WE'LL MEET MY DAD HALF-WAY.
SO HOW YOU FEELING?
NOT SO GOOD.
BUT IT BEATS THE ALTERNATIVE. HOW 'BOUT YOU?
WELL, I HAVE AN EXCUSE TO RE-WIRE THE TOWER NOW.
WHERE ARE YOU GOING AFTER THIS, DICK?
I'VE GOT TO TALK TO BATMAN. THEN MAYBE I CAN GO HOME.
OTHERWISE KNOWN AS BLÜDHAVEN.
THE END

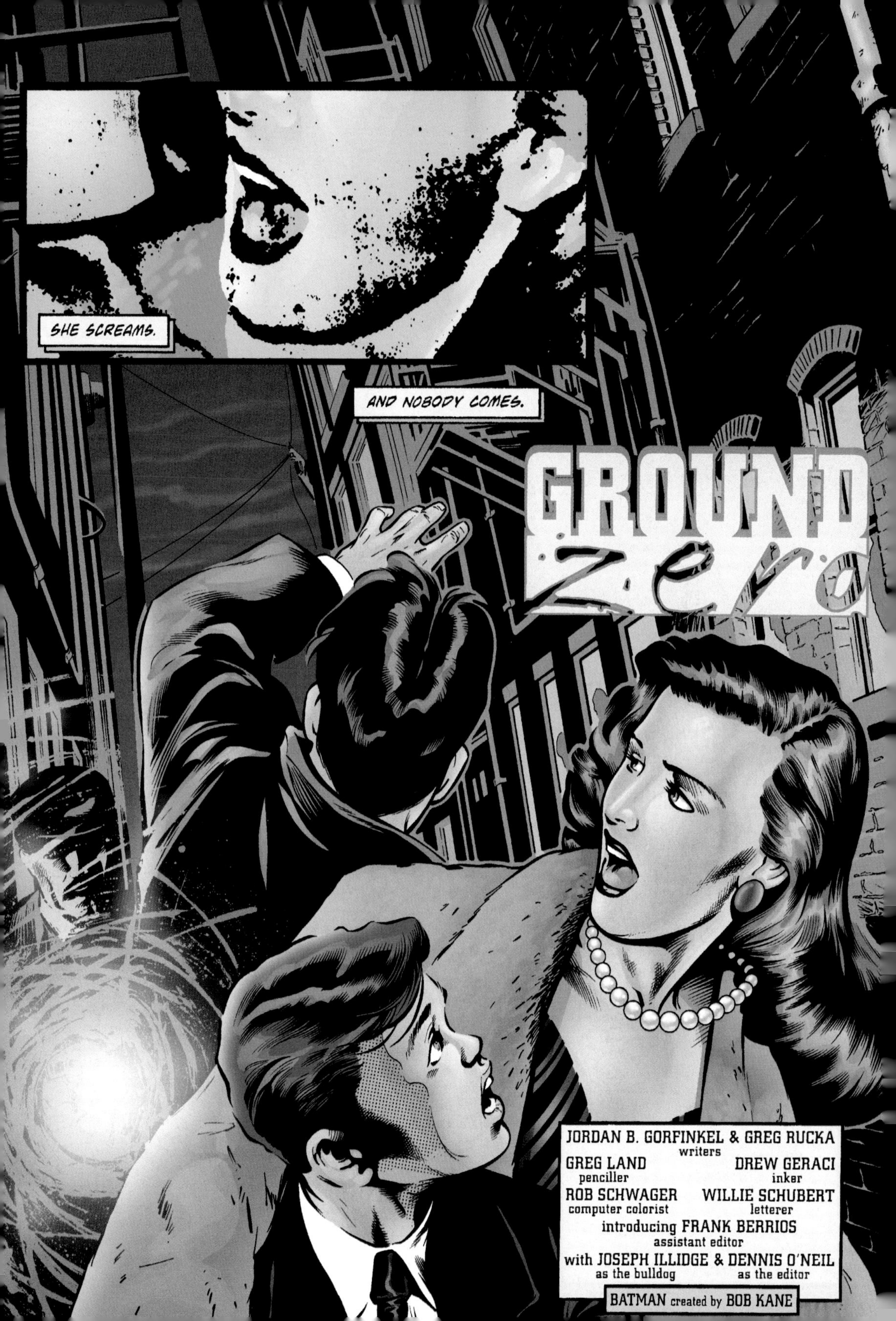

SHE SCREAMS.
AND NOBODY COMES.
GROUND zero
JORDAN B. GORFINKEL & GREG RUCKA writers
GREG LAND penciller
DREW GERACI inker
ROB SCHWAGER computer colorist
WILLIE SCHUBERT letterer
introducing FRANK BERRIOS assistant editor
with JOSEPH ILLIDGE as the bulldog & DENNIS O'NEIL as the editor
BATMAN created by BOB KANE

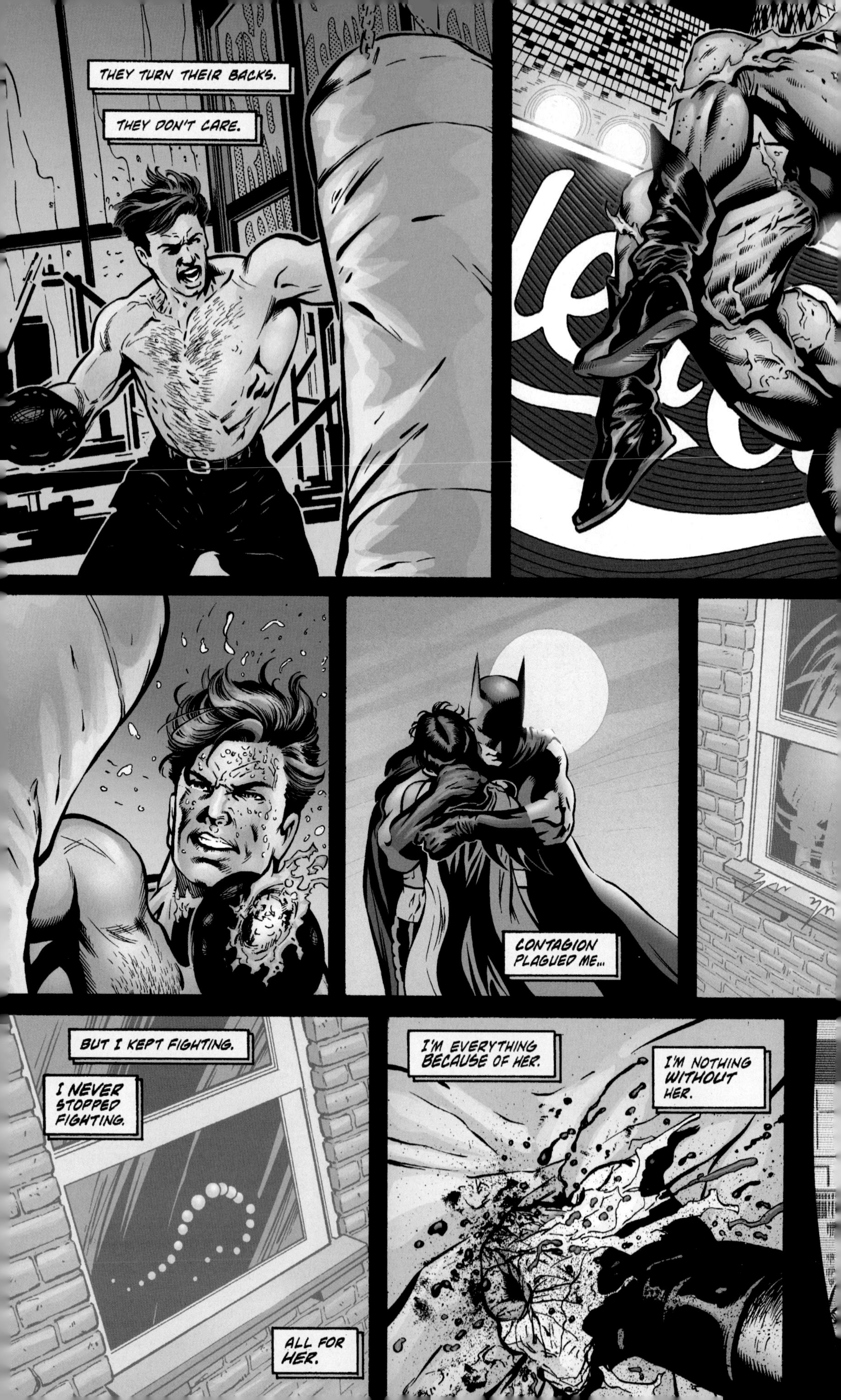
THEY TURN THEIR BACKS.
THEY DON'T CARE.
CONTAGION PLAGUED ME...
BUT I KEPT FIGHTING.
I NEVER STOPPED FIGHTING.
ALL FOR HER.
I'M EVERYTHING BECAUSE OF HER.
I'M NOTHING WITHOUT HER.

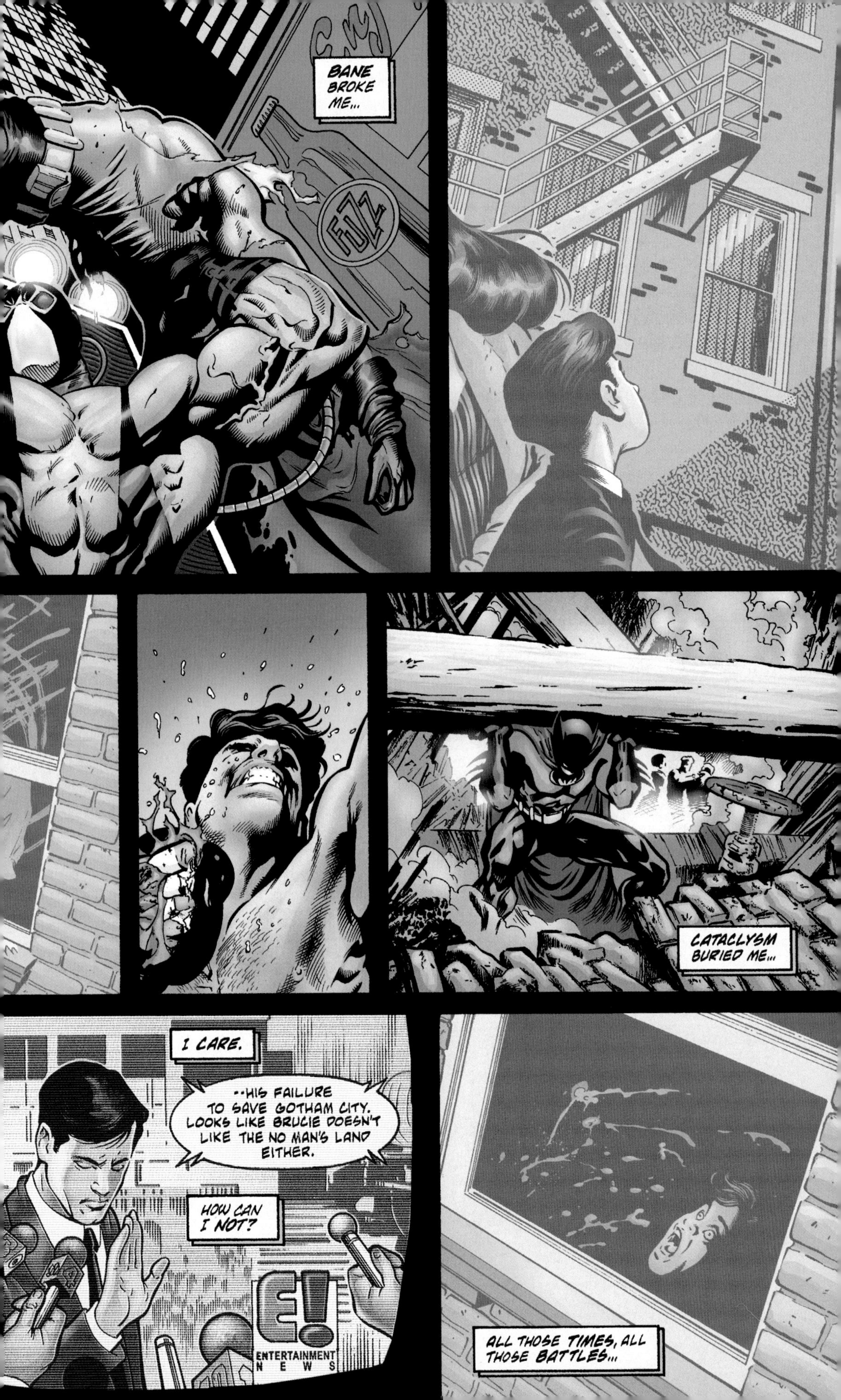

BANE BROKE ME...
CATACLYSM BURIED ME...
I CARE.
--HIS FAILURE TO SAVE GOTHAM CITY. LOOKS LIKE BRUCIE DOESN'T LIKE THE NO MAN'S LAND EITHER.
HOW CAN I NOT?
E! ENTERTAINMENT NEWS
ALL THOSE TIMES, ALL THOSE BATTLES...

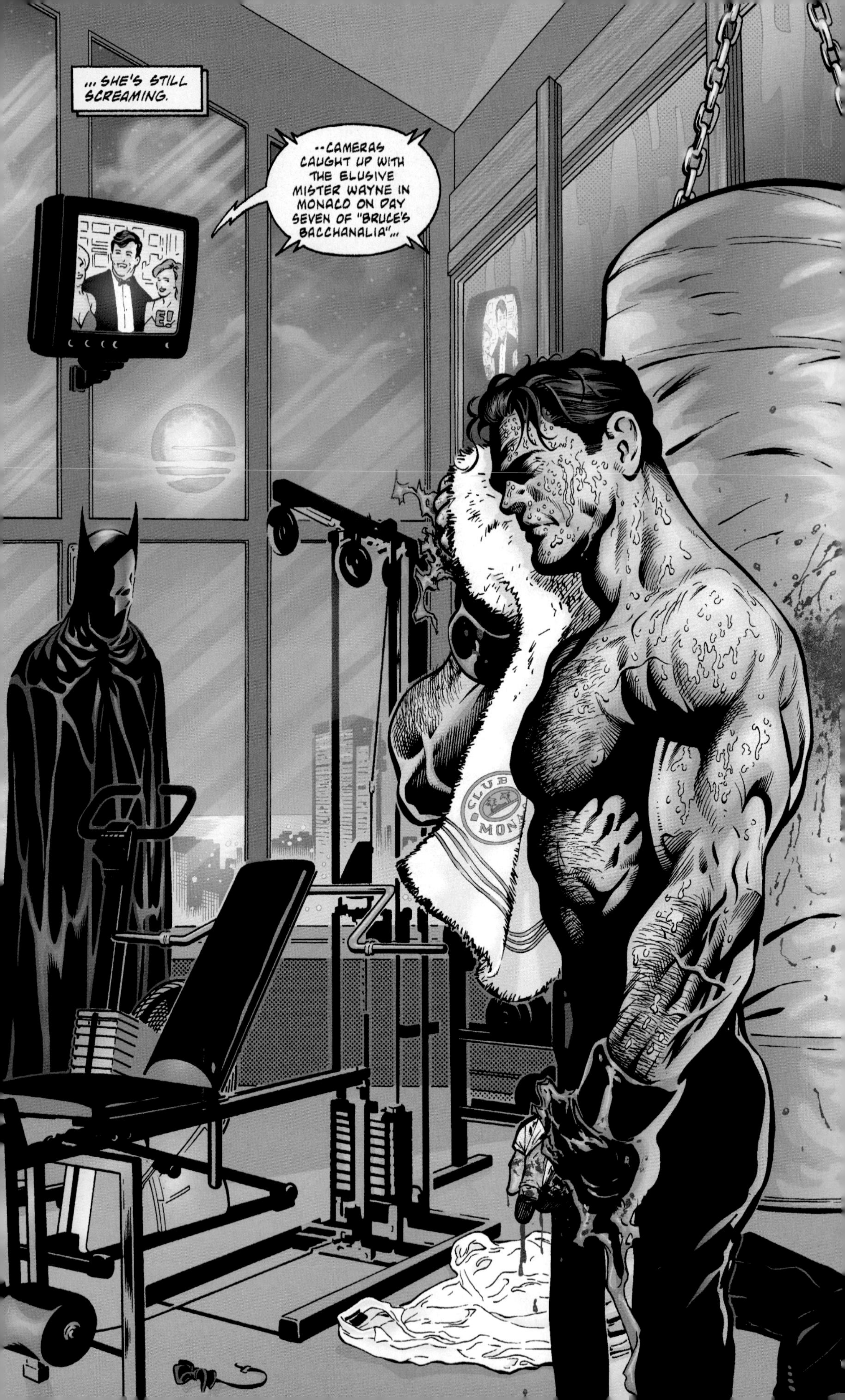
...SHE'S STILL SCREAMING.
--CAMERAS CAUGHT UP WITH THE ELUSIVE MISTER WAYNE IN MONACO ON DAY SEVEN OF "BRUCE'S BACCHANALIA"...
CLUB MONACO

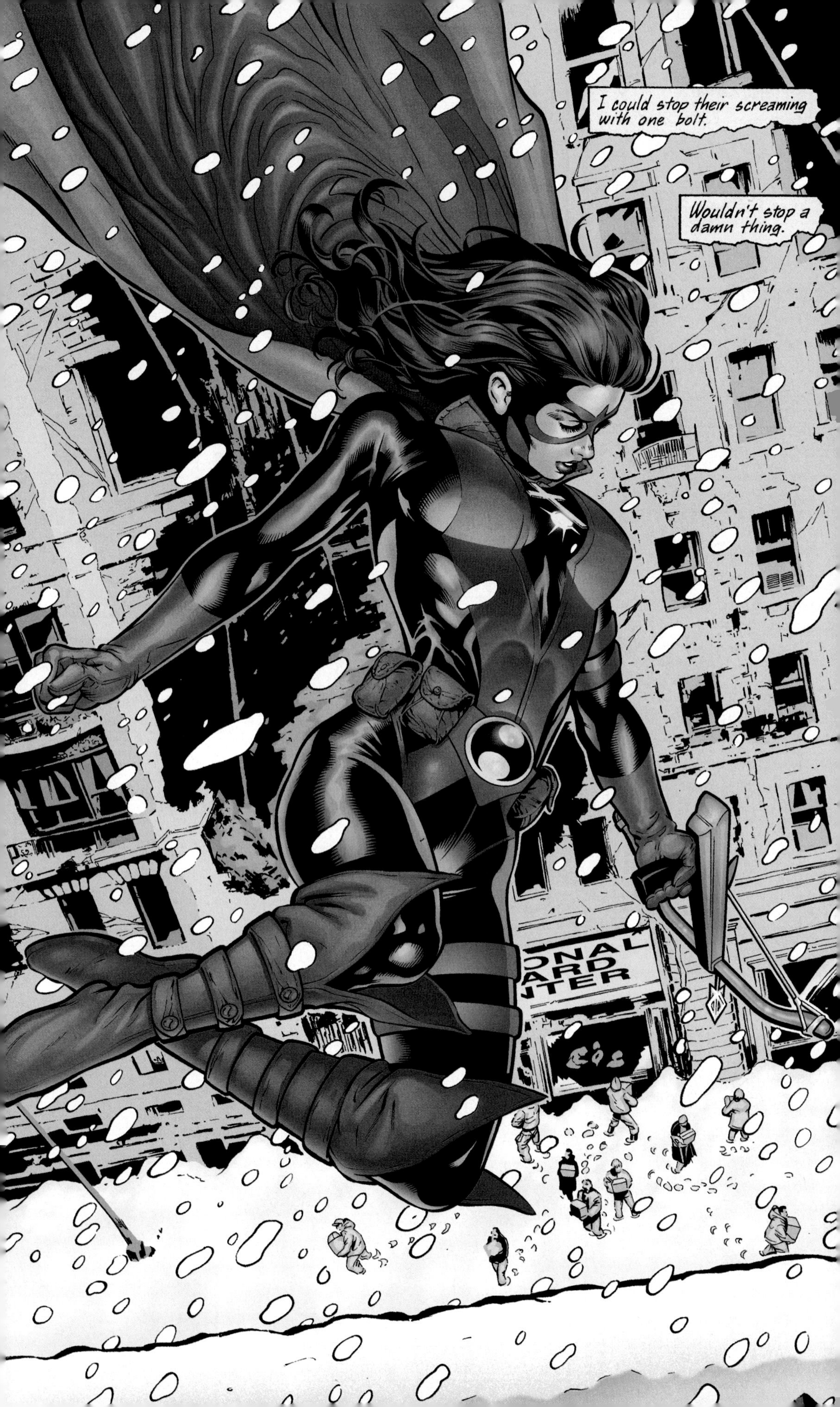
I could stop their screaming with one bolt.
Wouldn't stop a damn thing.

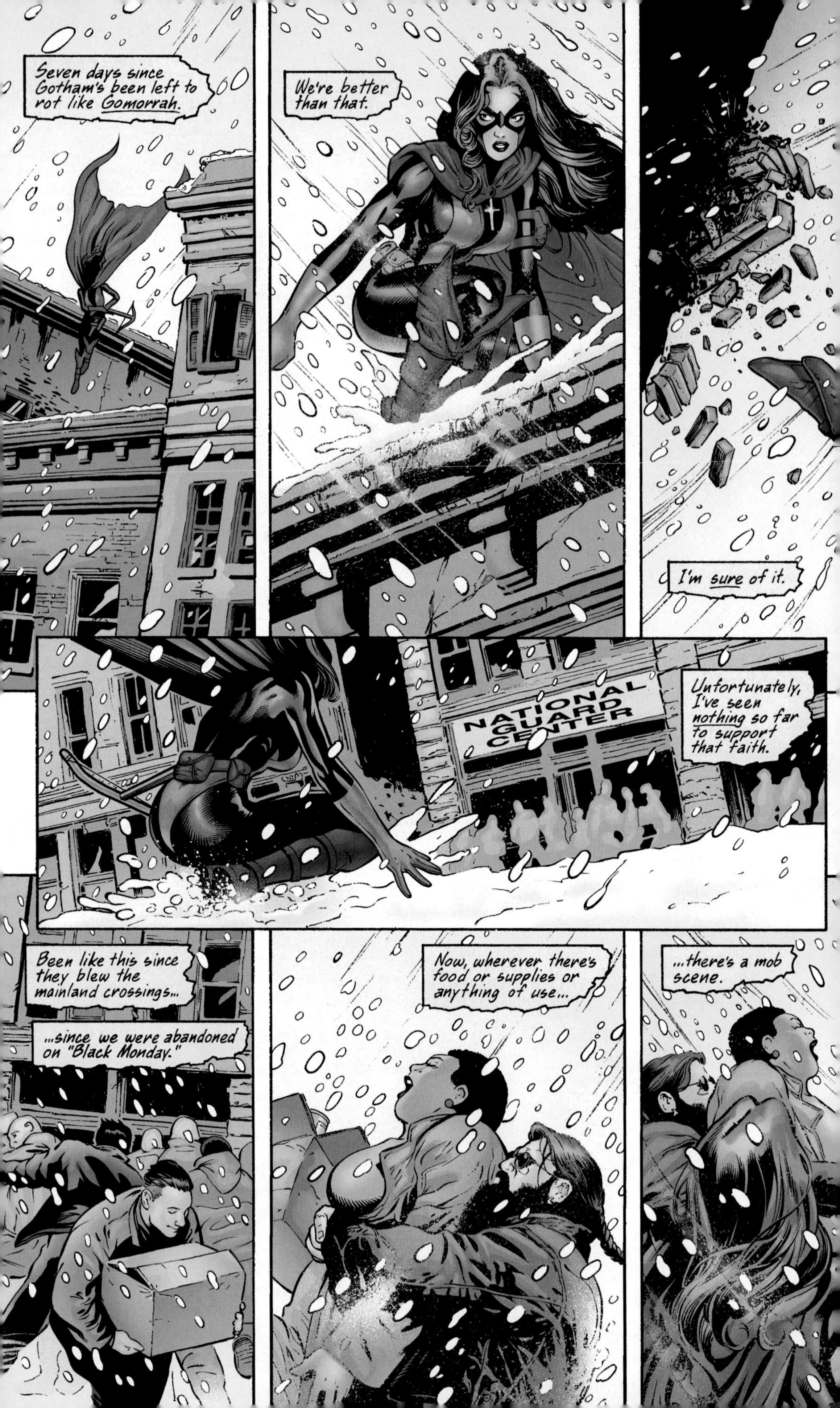
Seven days since Gotham's been left to rot like Gomorrah.
We're better than that.
I'm sure of it.
Unfortunately, I've seen nothing so far to support that faith.
NATIONAL GUARD CENTER
Been like this since they blew the mainland crossings...
...since we were abandoned on "Black Monday."
Now, wherever there's food or supplies or anything of use...
...there's a mob scene.

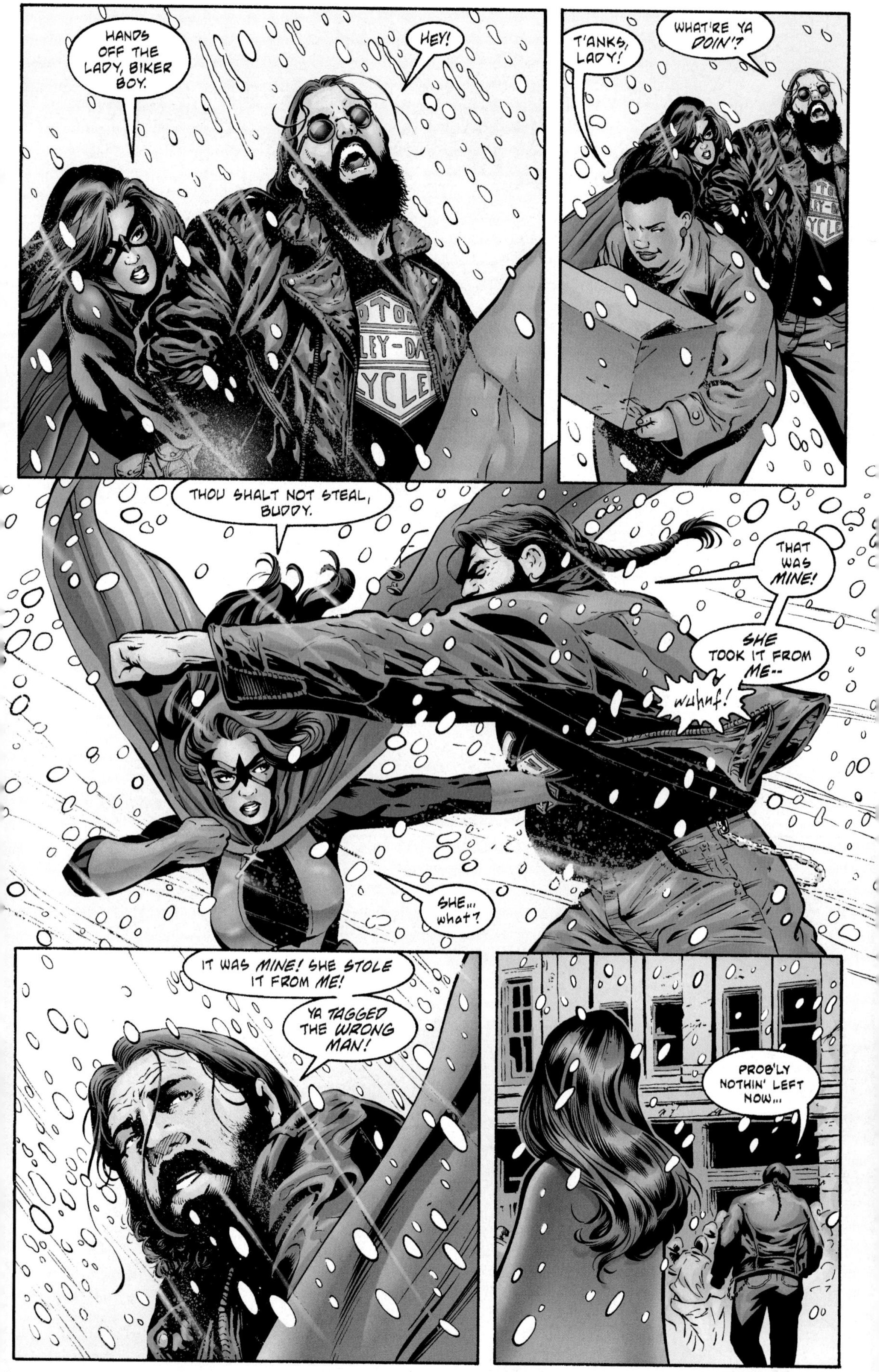
HANDS OFF THE LADY, BIKER BOY.
HEY!
T'ANKS, LADY!
WHAT'RE YA DOIN'?
THOU SHALT NOT STEAL, BUDDY.
THAT WAS MINE!
SHE TOOK IT FROM ME--
wuhnf!
SHE... what?
IT WAS MINE! SHE STOLE IT FROM ME!
YA TAGGED THE WRONG MAN!
PROB'LY NOTHIN' LEFT NOW...

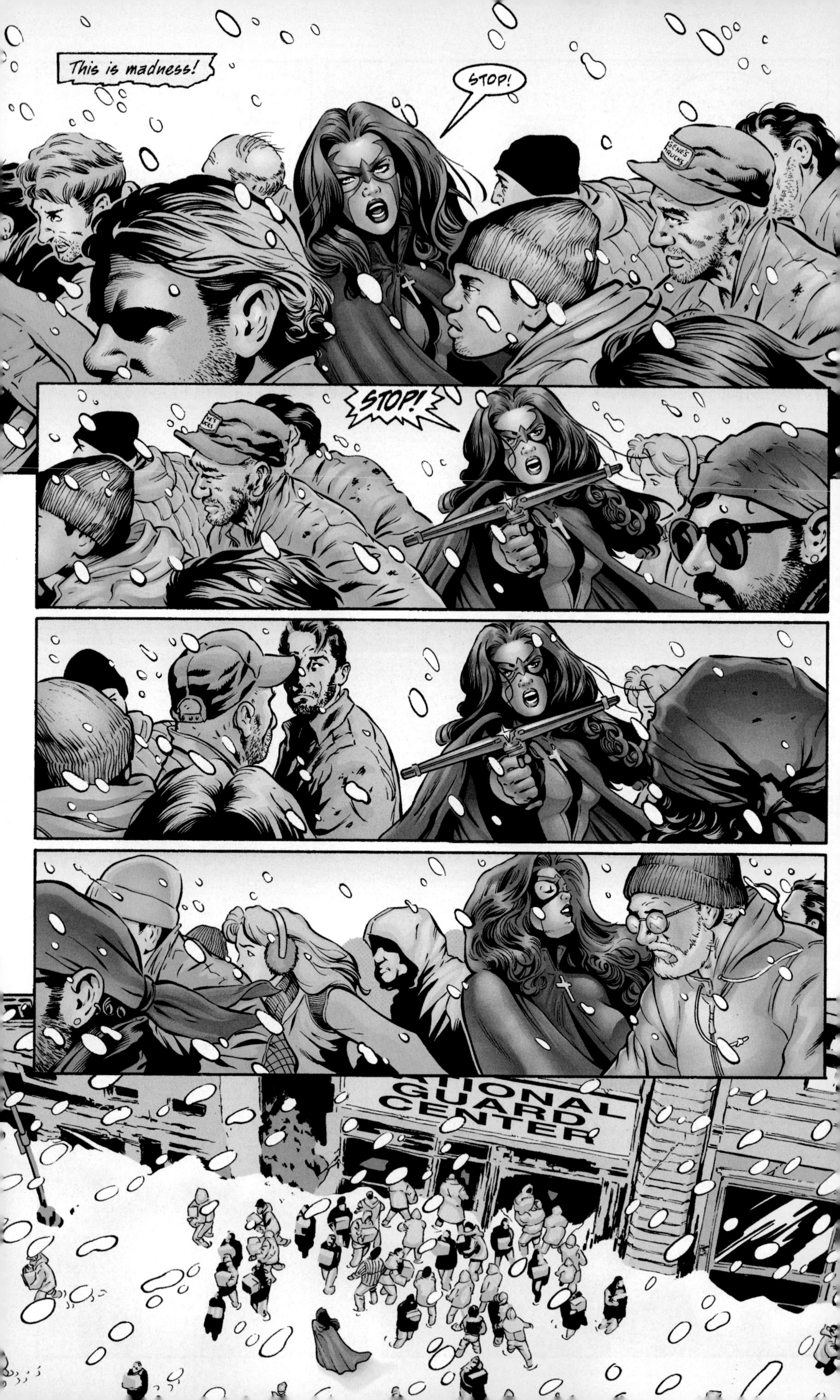

This is madness!
STOP!
GENE'S TRUCKS
STOP!
GUIONAL GUARD CENTER

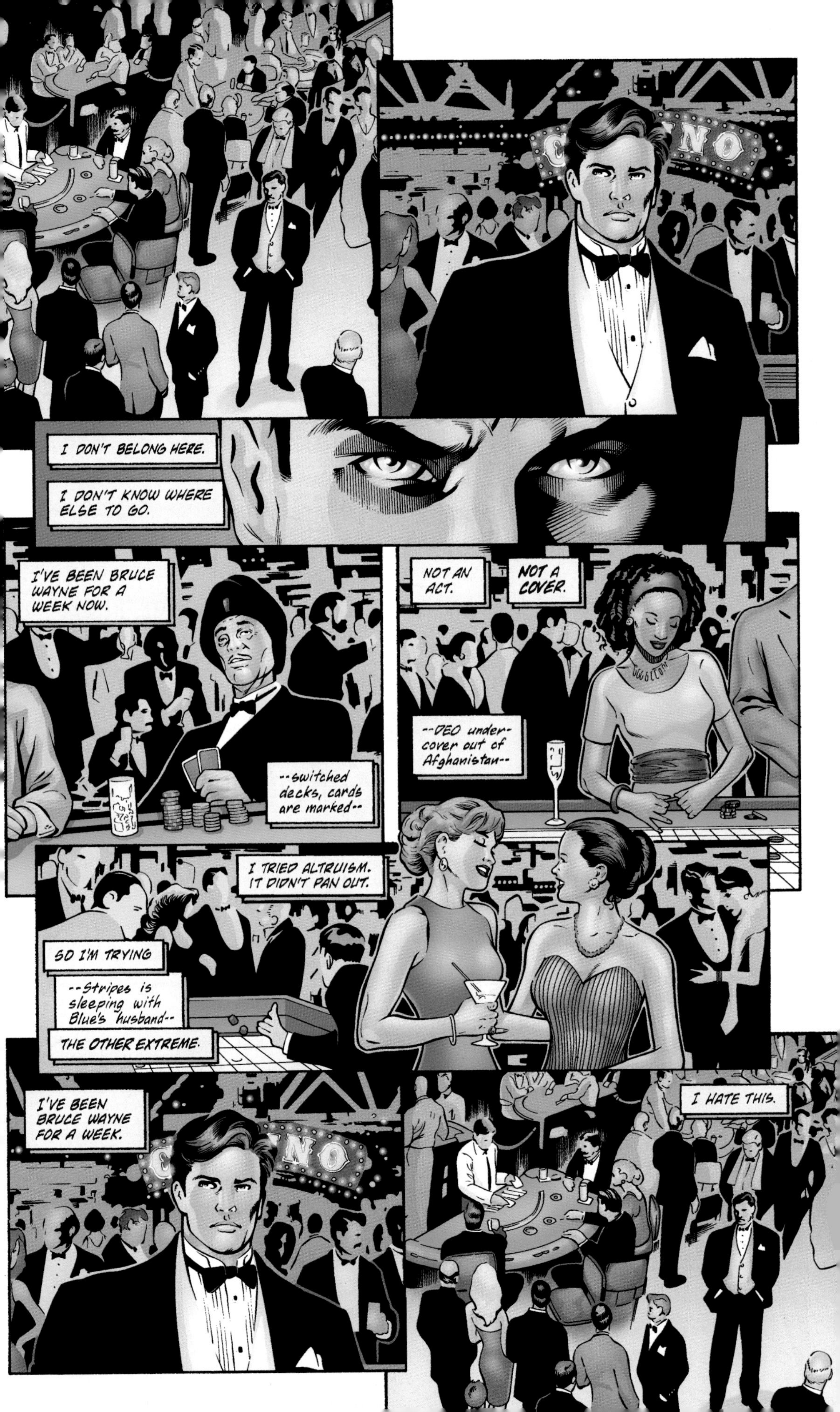

I DON'T BELONG HERE.
I DON'T KNOW WHERE ELSE TO GO.
I'VE BEEN BRUCE WAYNE FOR A WEEK NOW.
--switched decks, cards are marked--
NOT AN ACT.
NOT A COVER.
--DEO under-cover out of Afghanistan--
I TRIED ALTRUISM. IT DIDN'T PAN OUT.
SO I'M TRYING
--Stripes is sleeping with Blue's husband--
THE OTHER EXTREME.
I'VE BEEN BRUCE WAYNE FOR A WEEK.
I HATE THIS.

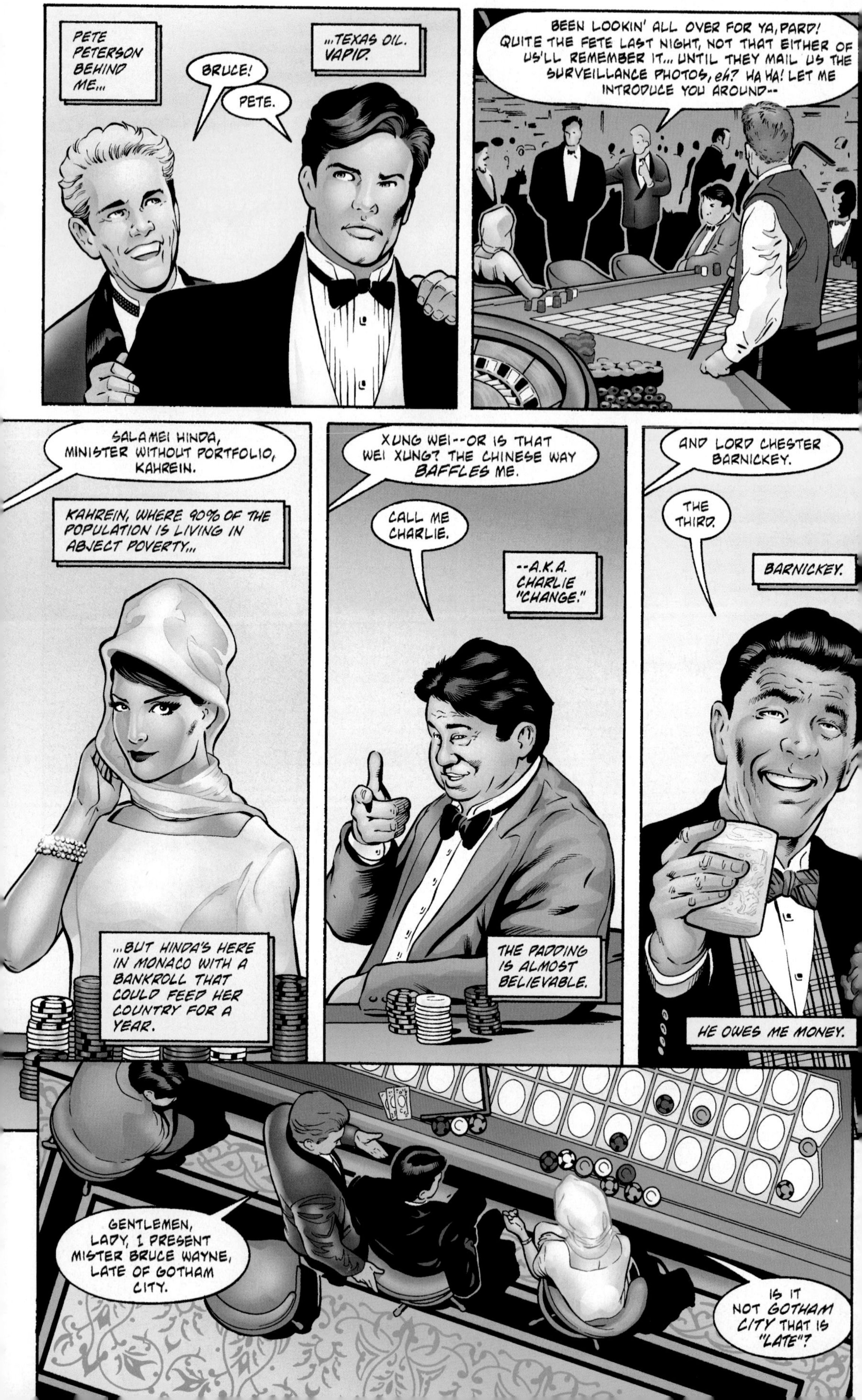
PETE PETERSON BEHIND ME...
BRUCE!
PETE.
...TEXAS OIL. VAPID.
BEEN LOOKIN' ALL OVER FOR YA, PARD! QUITE THE FETE LAST NIGHT, NOT THAT EITHER OF US'LL REMEMBER IT... UNTIL THEY MAIL US THE SURVEILLANCE PHOTOS, eh? HA HA! LET ME INTRODUCE YOU AROUND--
SALAMEI HINDA, MINISTER WITHOUT PORTFOLIO, KAHREIN.
KAHREIN, WHERE 90% OF THE POPULATION IS LIVING IN ABJECT POVERTY...
...BUT HINDA'S HERE IN MONACO WITH A BANKROLL THAT COULD FEED HER COUNTRY FOR A YEAR.
XUNG WEI--OR IS THAT WEI XUNG? THE CHINESE WAY BAFFLES ME.
CALL ME CHARLIE.
--A.K.A. CHARLIE "CHANGE."
THE PADDING IS ALMOST BELIEVABLE.
AND LORD CHESTER BARNICKEY.
THE THIRD.
BARNICKEY.
HE OWES ME MONEY.
GENTLEMEN, LADY, I PRESENT MISTER BRUCE WAYNE, LATE OF GOTHAM CITY.
IS IT NOT GOTHAM CITY THAT IS "LATE"?

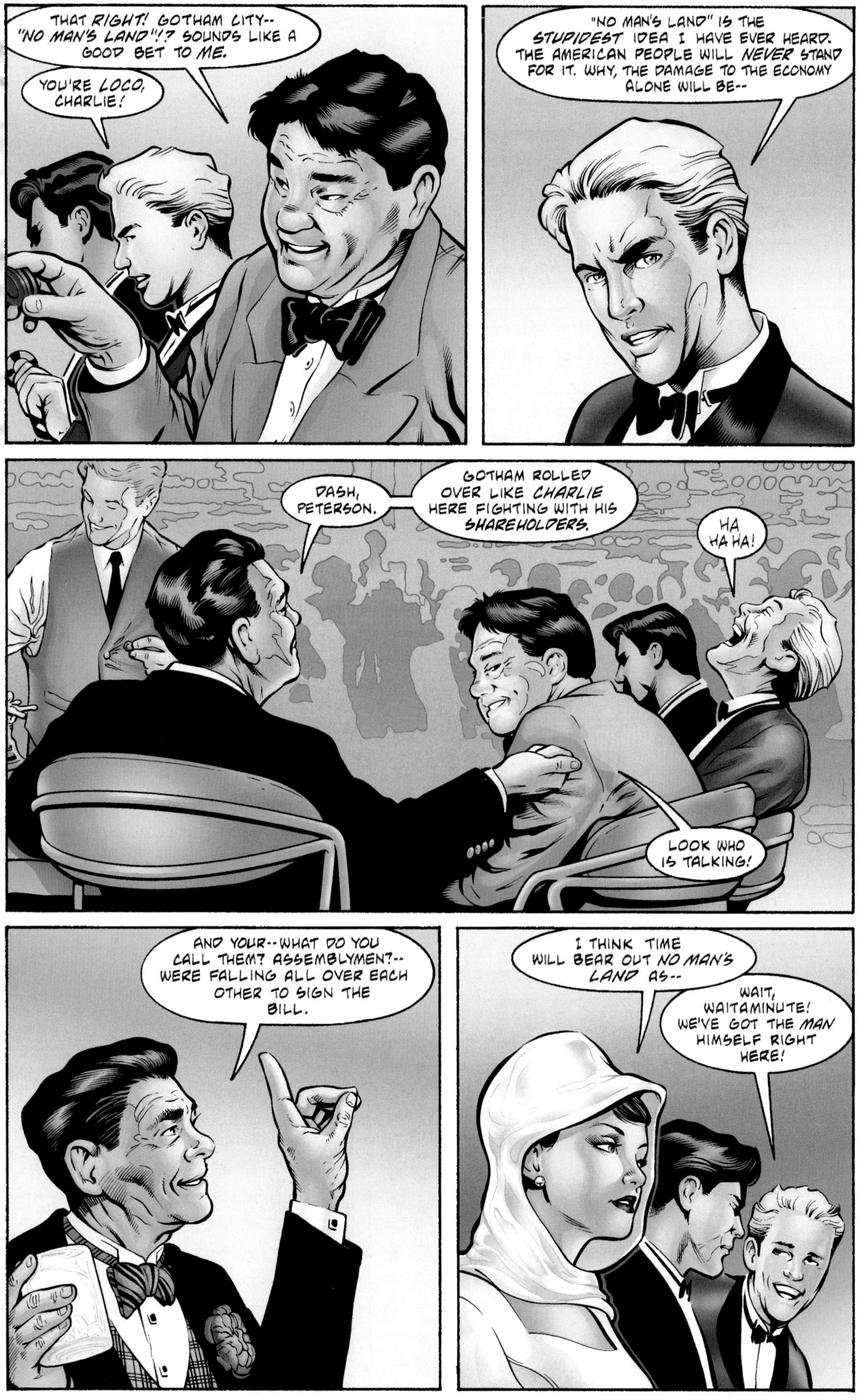

THAT RIGHT! GOTHAM CITY-- "NO MAN'S LAND"!? SOUNDS LIKE A GOOD BET TO ME.
YOU'RE LOCO, CHARLIE!
"NO MAN'S LAND" IS THE STUPIDEST IDEA I HAVE EVER HEARD. THE AMERICAN PEOPLE WILL NEVER STAND FOR IT. WHY, THE DAMAGE TO THE ECONOMY ALONE WILL BE--
DASH, PETERSON.
GOTHAM ROLLED OVER LIKE CHARLIE HERE FIGHTING WITH HIS SHAREHOLDERS.
HA HA HA!
LOOK WHO IS TALKING!
AND YOUR--WHAT DO YOU CALL THEM? ASSEMBLYMEN?--WERE FALLING ALL OVER EACH OTHER TO SIGN THE BILL.
I THINK TIME WILL BEAR OUT NO MAN'S LAND AS--
WAIT, WAITAMINUTE! WE'VE GOT THE MAN HIMSELF RIGHT HERE!

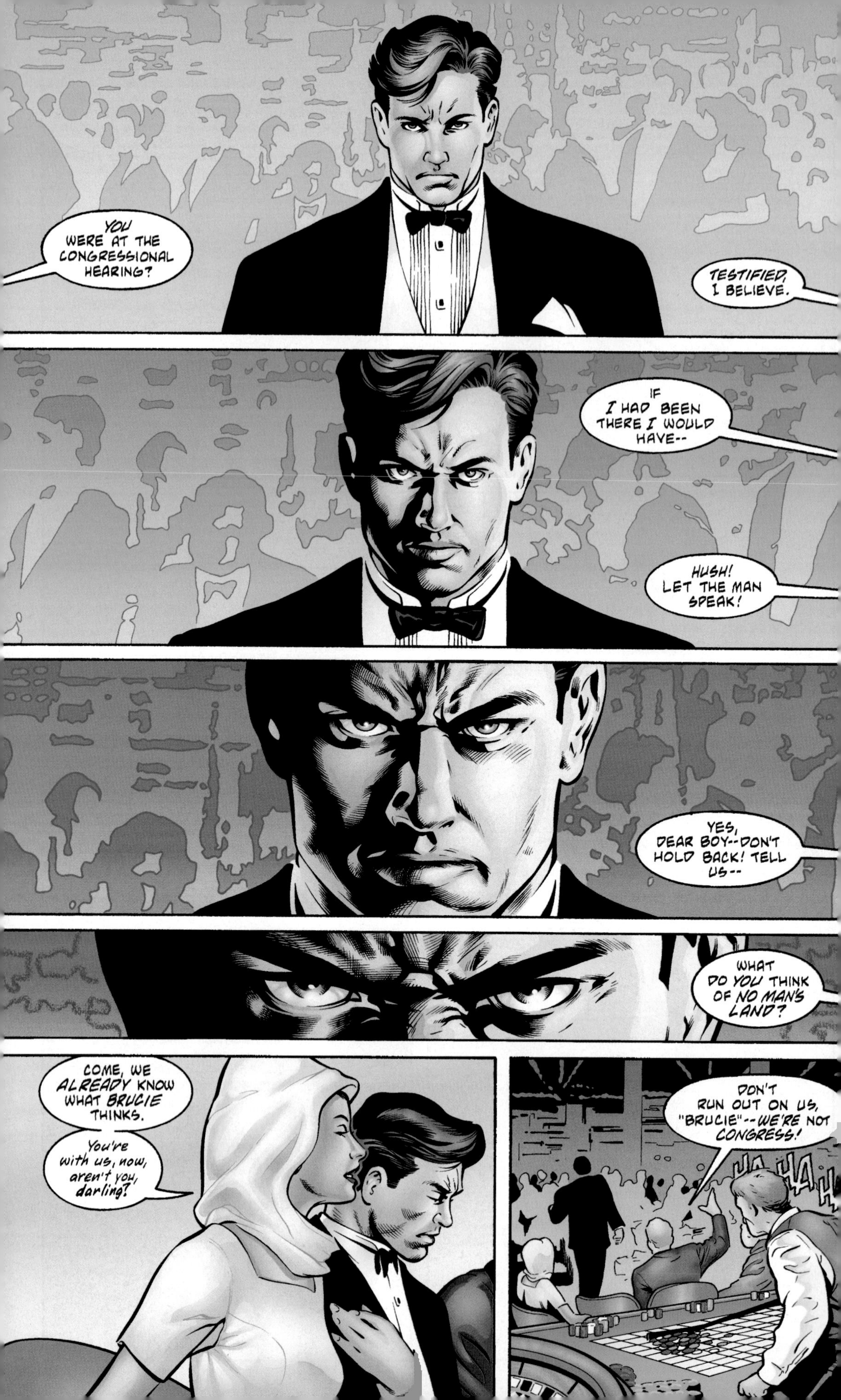

YOU WERE AT THE CONGRESSIONAL HEARING?
TESTIFIED, I BELIEVE.
IF I HAD BEEN THERE I WOULD HAVE--
HUSH! LET THE MAN SPEAK!
YES, DEAR BOY--DON'T HOLD BACK! TELL US--
WHAT DO YOU THINK OF NO MAN'S LAND?
COME, WE ALREADY KNOW WHAT BRUCIE THINKS.
You're with us, now, aren't you, darling?
DON'T RUN OUT ON US, "BRUCIE"--WE'RE NOT CONGRESS!
HA HA H

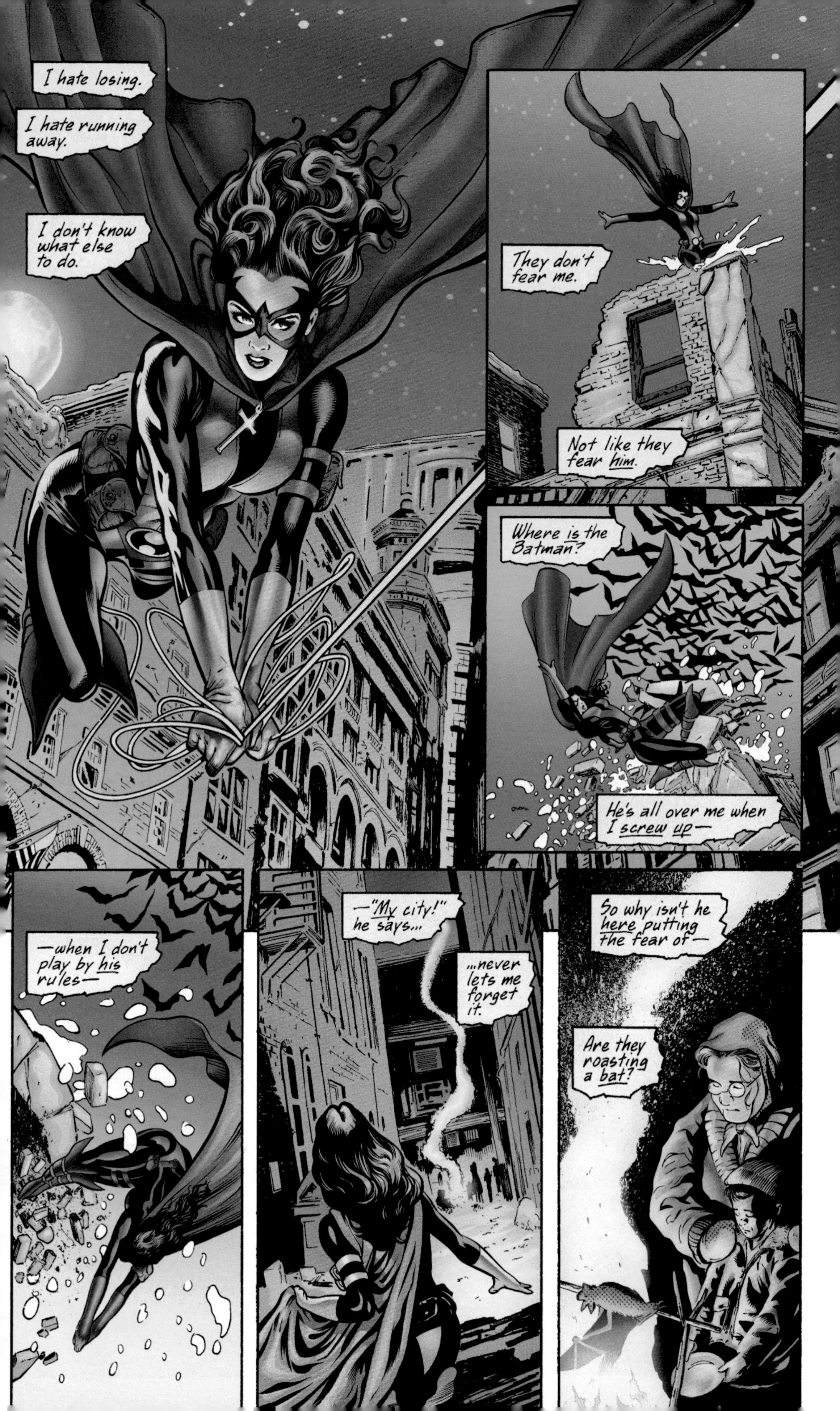
I hate losing.
I hate running away.
I don't know what else to do.
They don't fear me.
Not like they fear him.
Where is the Batman?
He's all over me when I screw up—
—when I don't play by his rules—
—"My city!" he says...
...never lets me forget it.
So why isn't he here putting the fear of—
Are they roasting a bat?

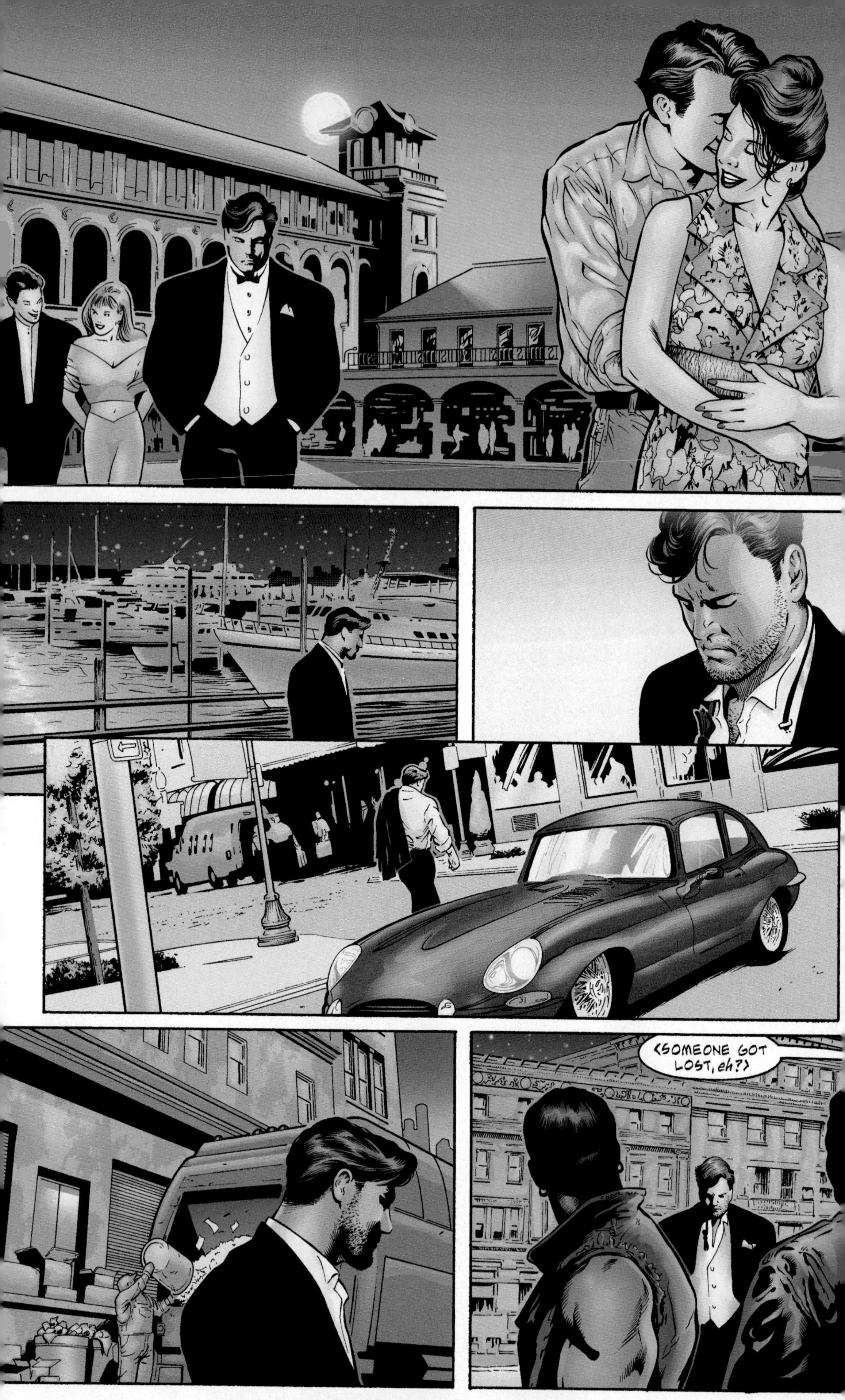
<SOMEONE GOT LOST, eh?>

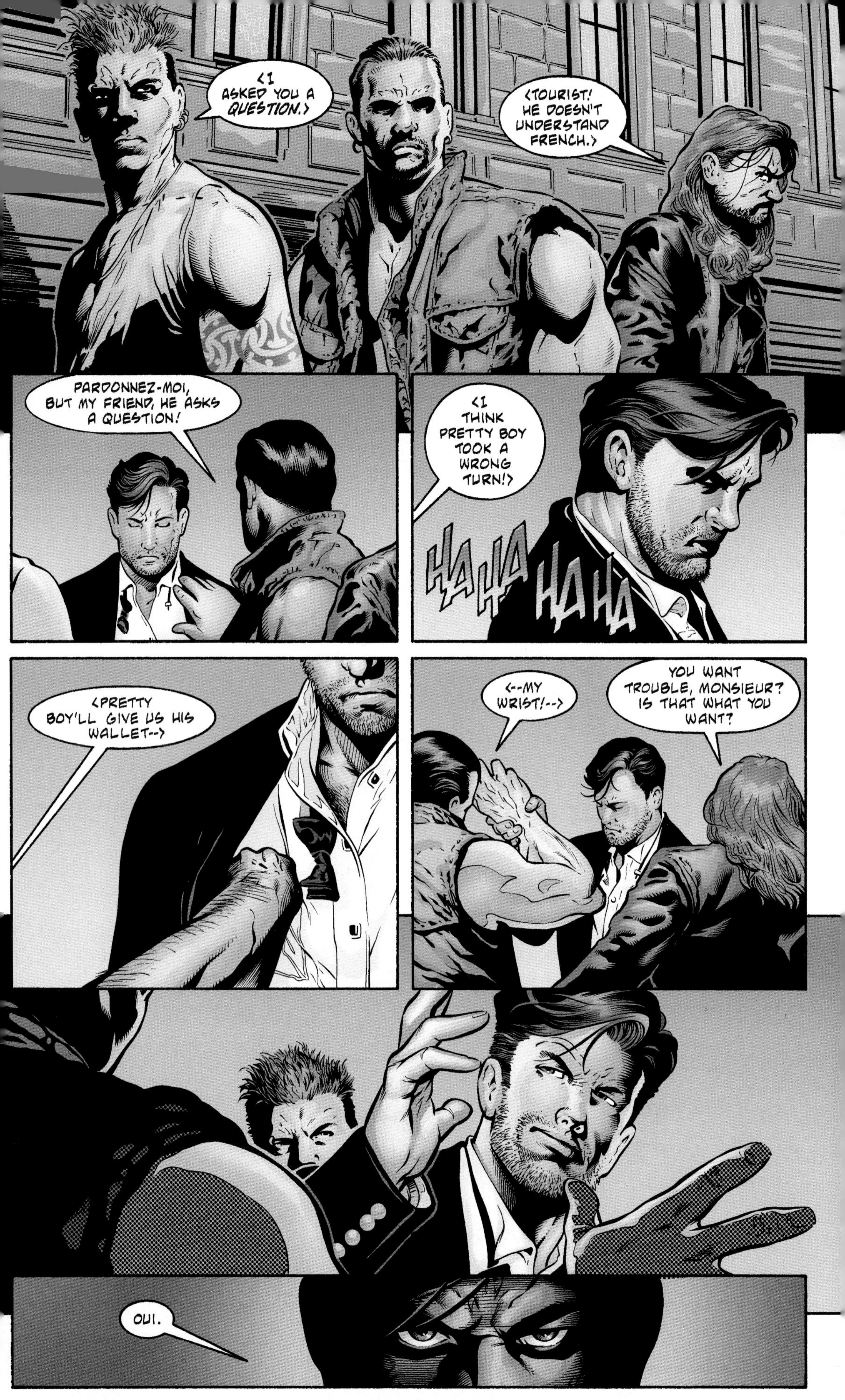

<I ASKED YOU A QUESTION.>
<TOURIST! HE DOESN'T UNDERSTAND FRENCH.>
PARDONNEZ-MOI, BUT MY FRIEND, HE ASKS A QUESTION!
<I THINK PRETTY BOY TOOK A WRONG TURN!>
HAHA HAHA
<PRETTY BOY'LL GIVE US HIS WALLET-->
<--MY WRIST!-->
YOU WANT TROUBLE, MONSIEUR? IS THAT WHAT YOU WANT?
OUI.

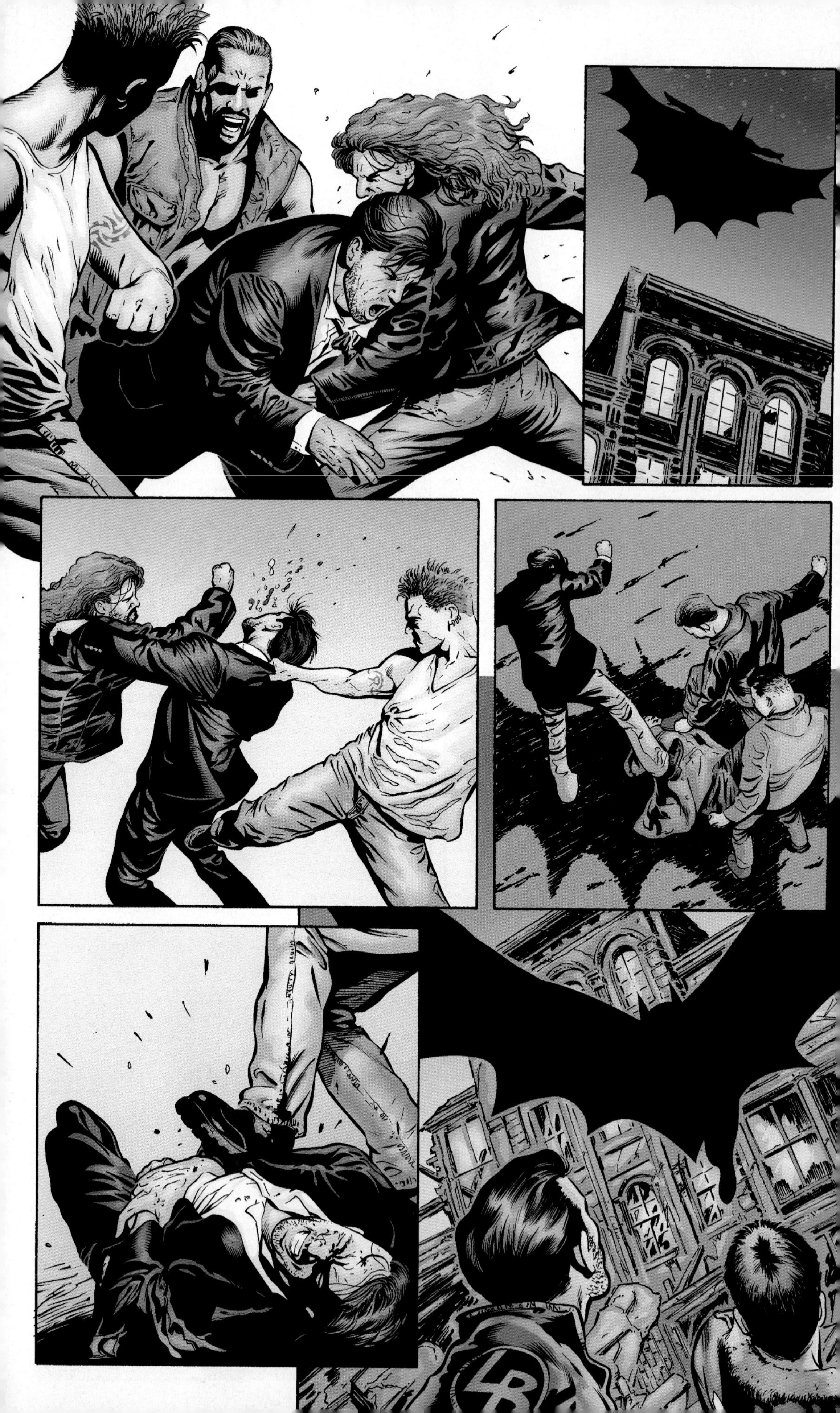

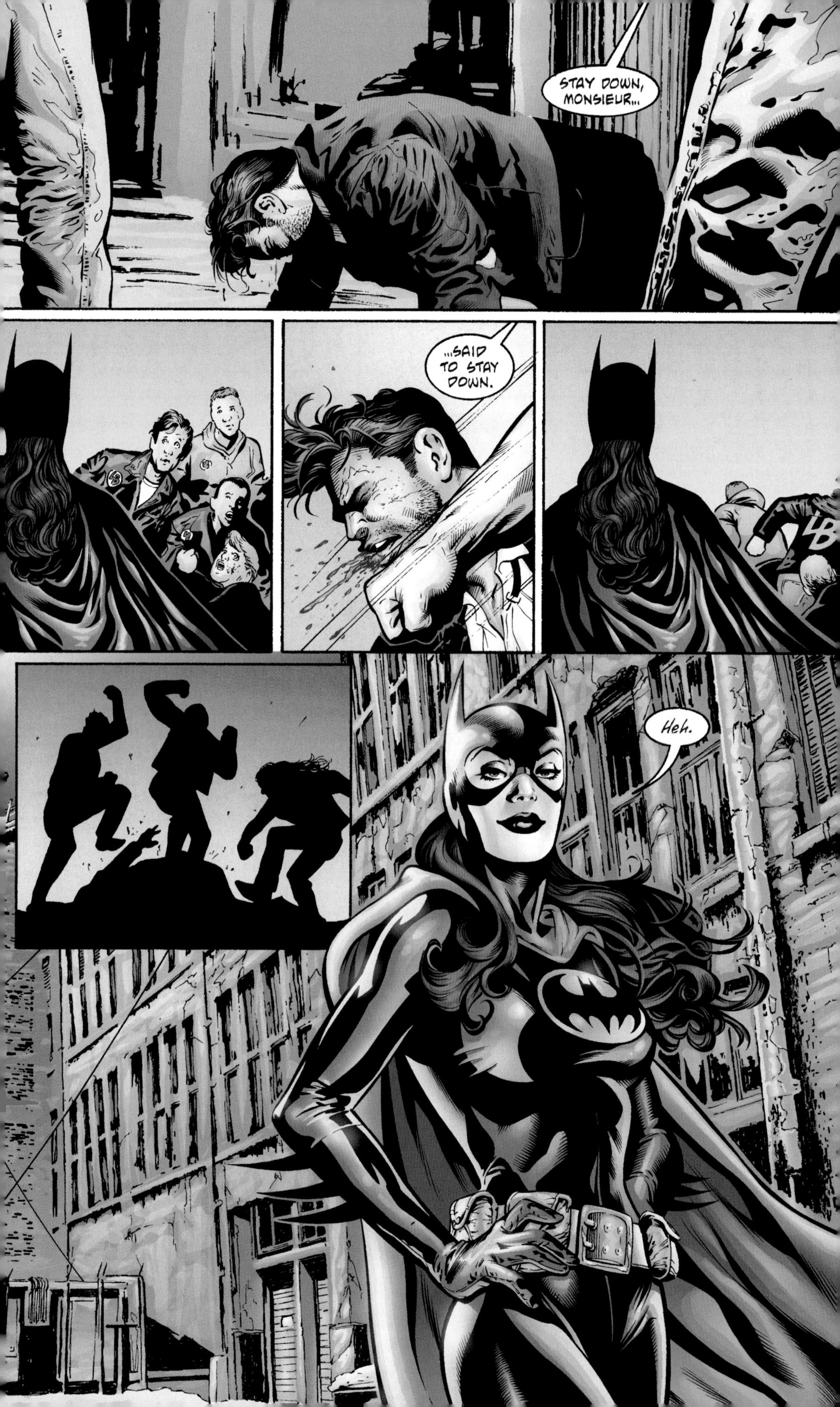
STAY DOWN, MONSIEUR...
...SAID TO STAY DOWN.
Heh.

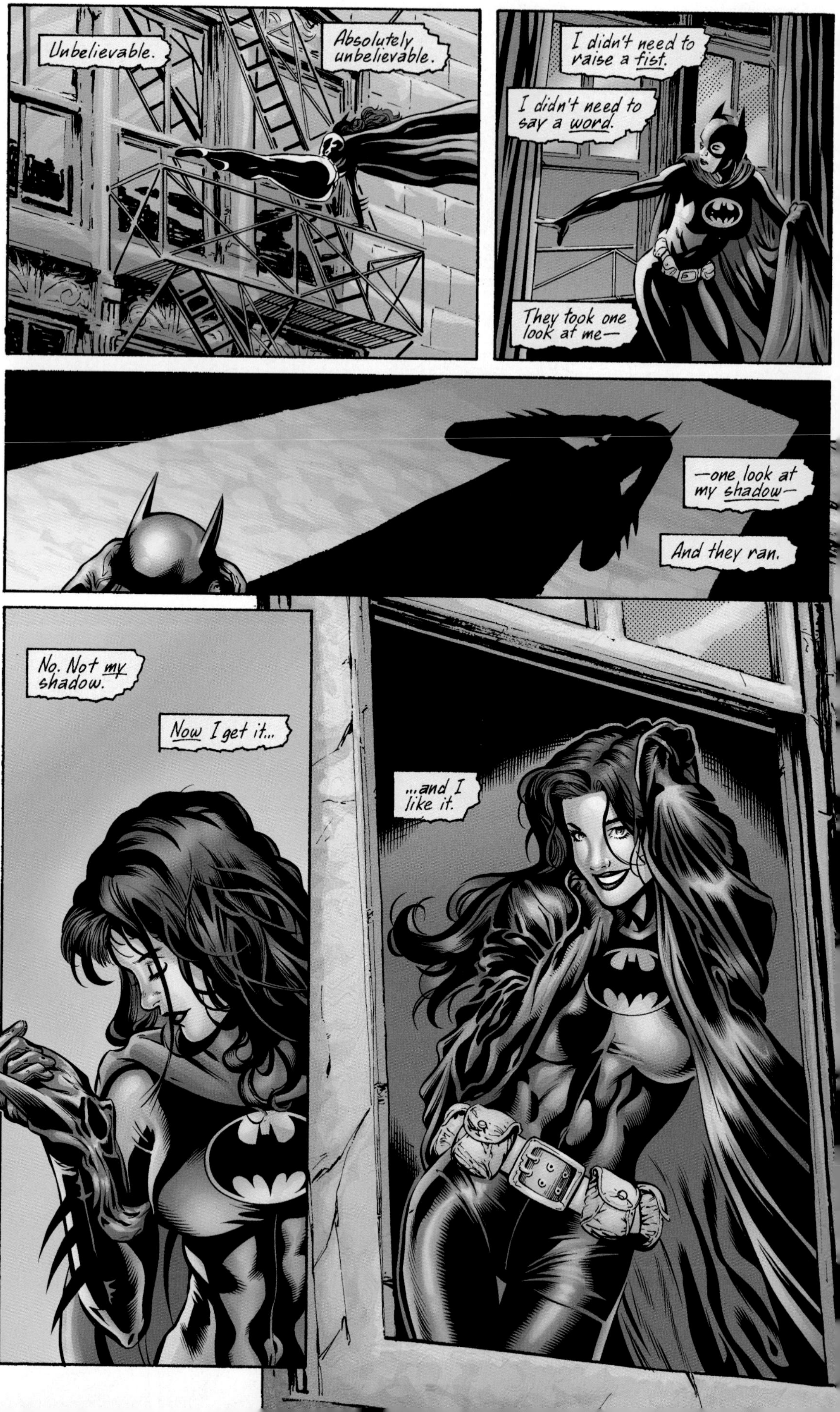
Unbelievable.
Absolutely unbelievable.
I didn't need to raise a fist.
I didn't need to say a word.
They took one look at me—
—one look at my shadow—
And they ran.
No. Not my shadow.
Now I get it...
...and I like it.

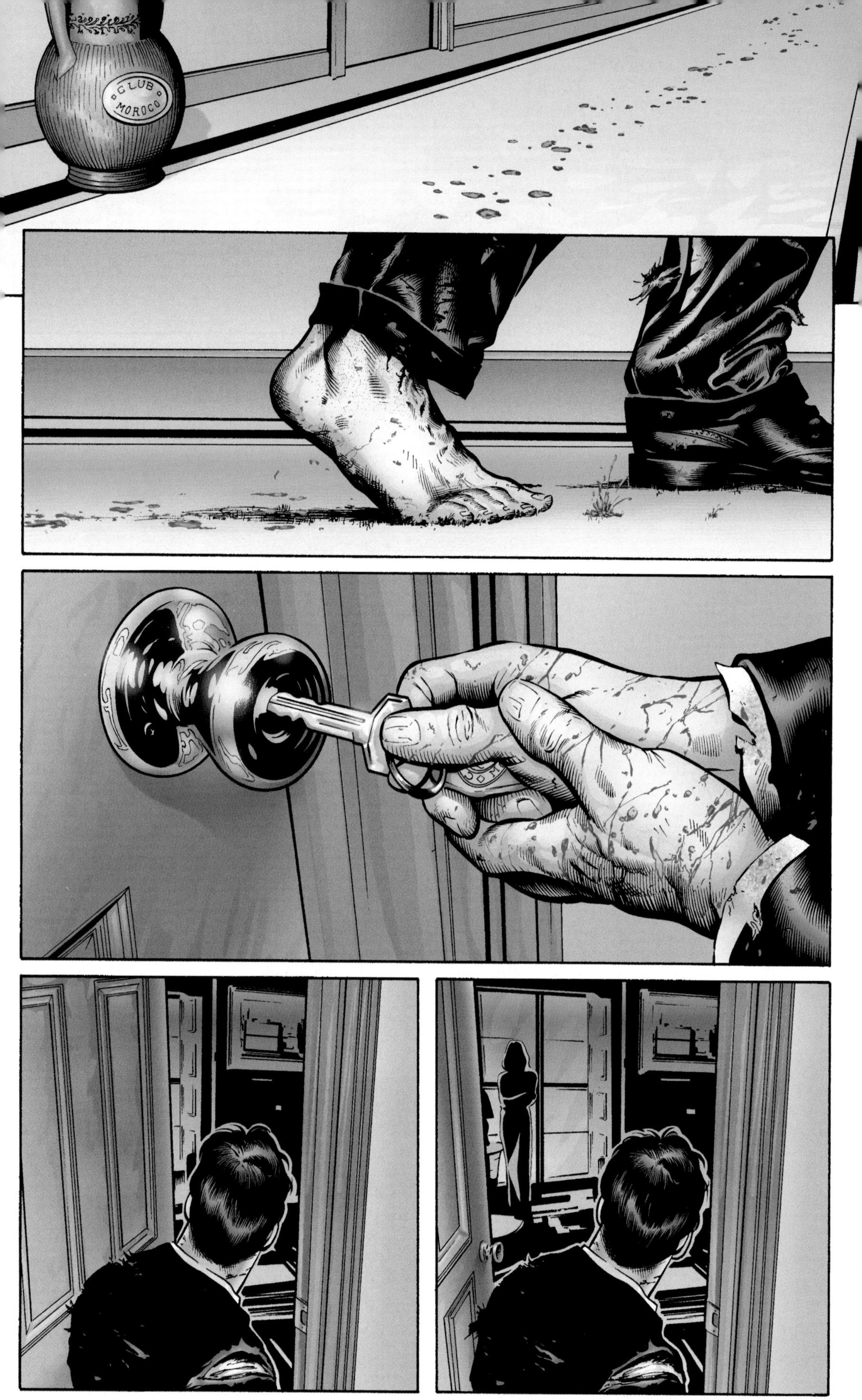

CLUB MOROCO

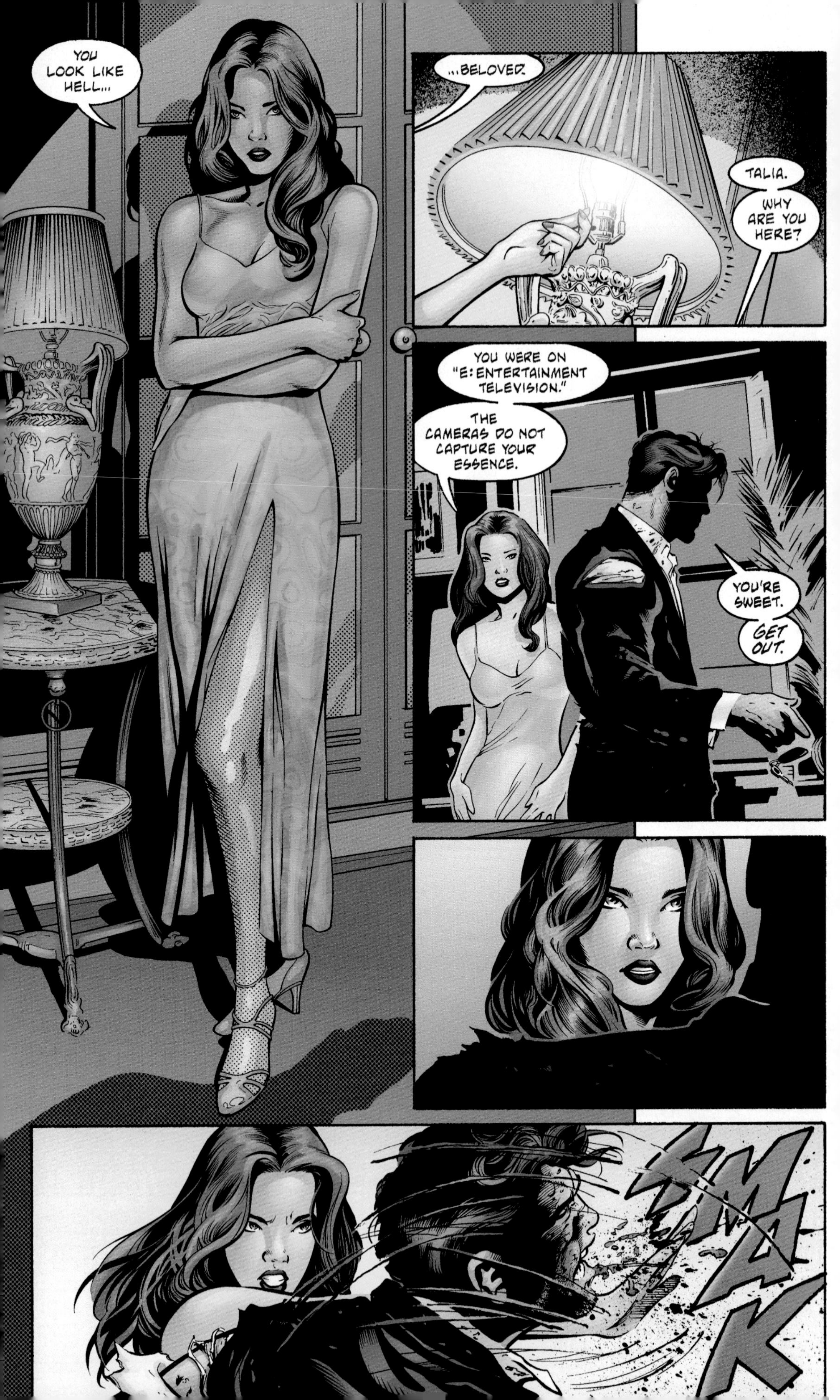

YOU LOOK LIKE HELL...
...BELOVED.
TALIA.
WHY ARE YOU HERE?
YOU WERE ON "E: ENTERTAINMENT TELEVISION."
THE CAMERAS DO NOT CAPTURE YOUR ESSENCE.
YOU'RE SWEET.
GET OUT.
SMAK

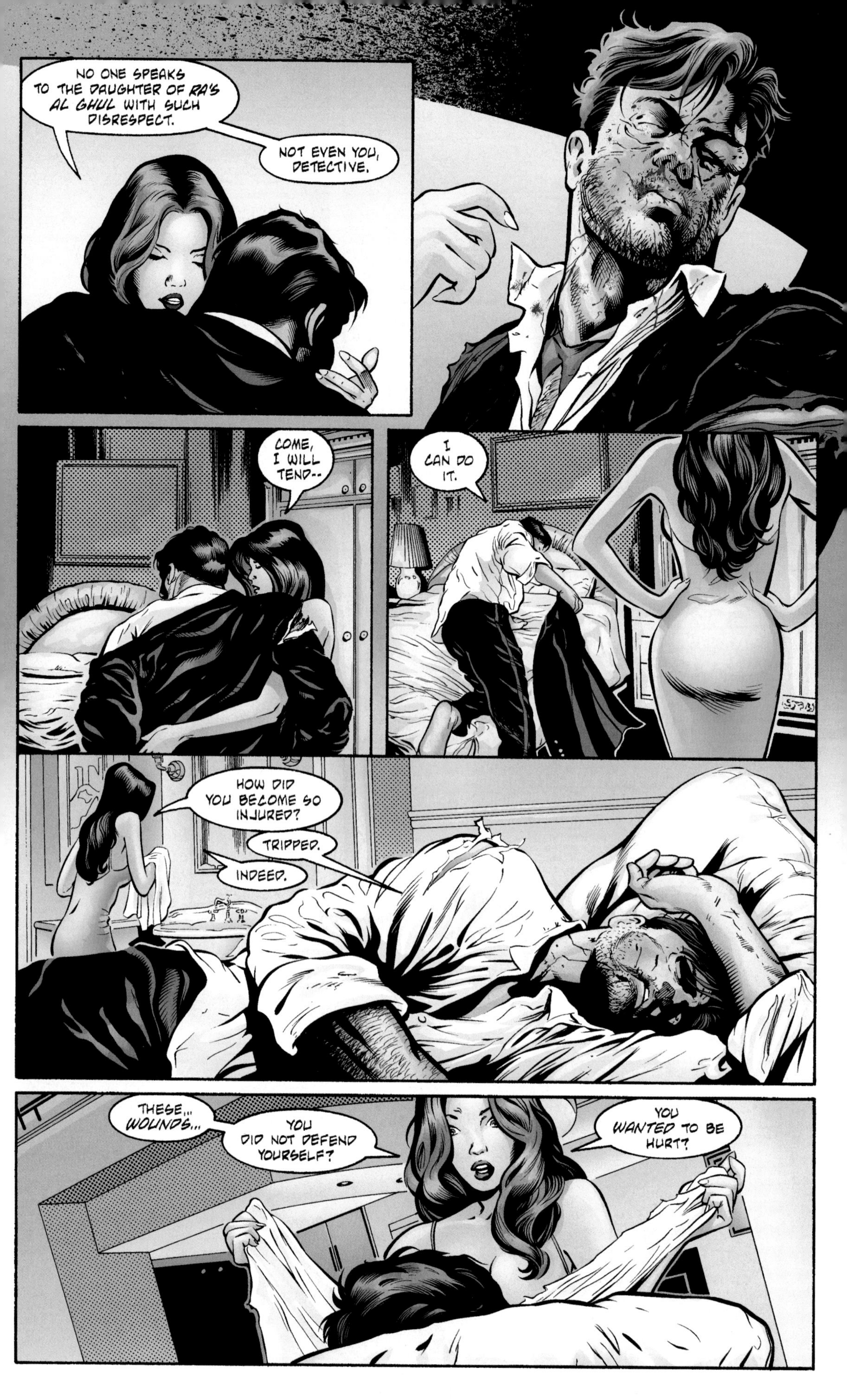
NO ONE SPEAKS TO THE DAUGHTER OF RA'S AL GHUL WITH SUCH DISRESPECT.
NOT EVEN YOU, DETECTIVE.
COME, I WILL TEND--
I CAN DO IT.
HOW DID YOU BECOME SO INJURED?
TRIPPED.
INDEED.
THESE... WOUNDS...
YOU DID NOT DEFEND YOURSELF?
YOU WANTED TO BE HURT?

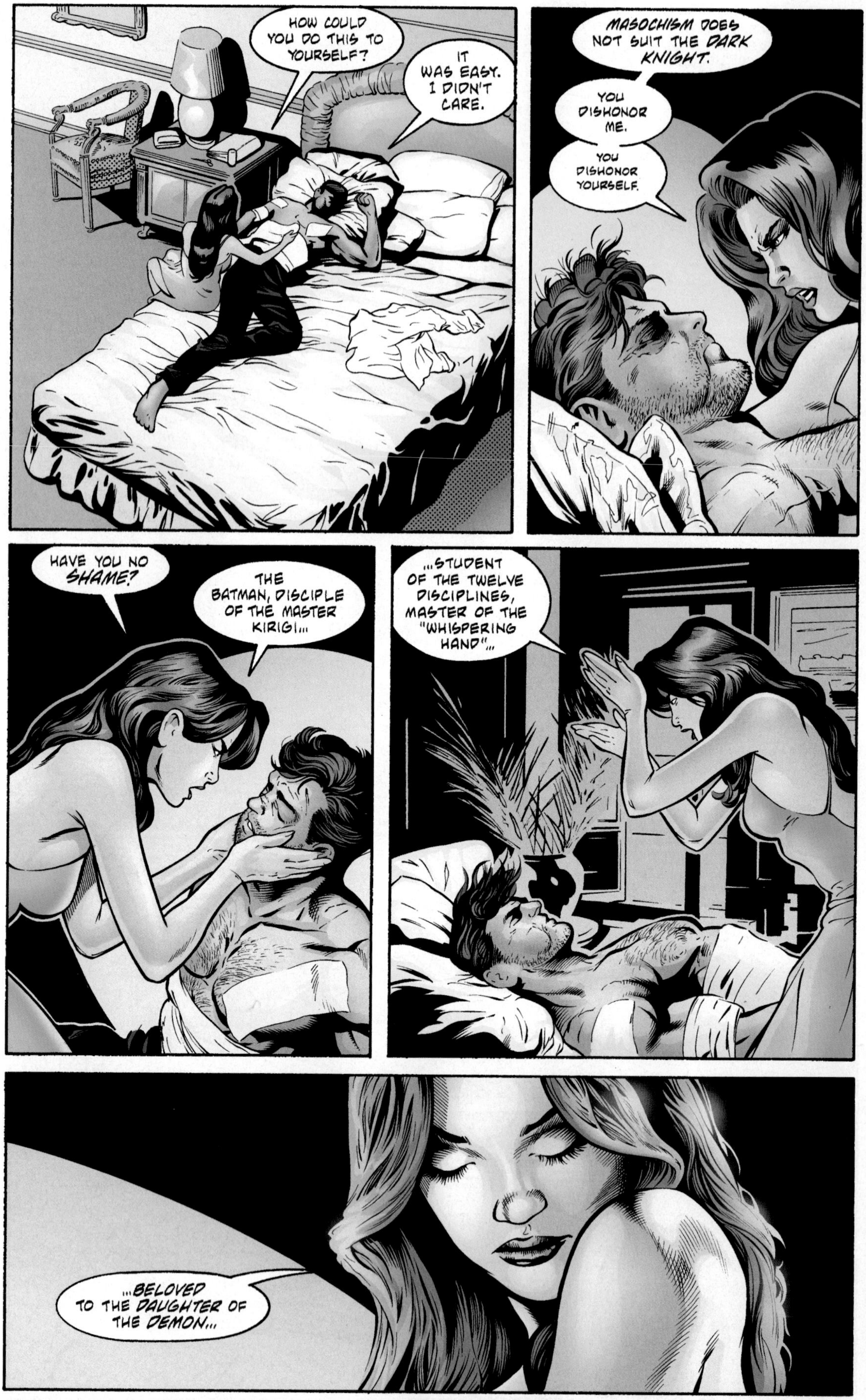
HOW COULD YOU DO THIS TO YOURSELF?
IT WAS EASY. I DIDN'T CARE.
MASOCHISM DOES NOT SUIT THE DARK KNIGHT.
YOU DISHONOR ME.
YOU DISHONOR YOURSELF.
HAVE YOU NO SHAME?
THE BATMAN, DISCIPLE OF THE MASTER KIRIGI...
...STUDENT OF THE TWELVE DISCIPLINES, MASTER OF THE "WHISPERING HAND"...
...BELOVED TO THE DAUGHTER OF THE DEMON...

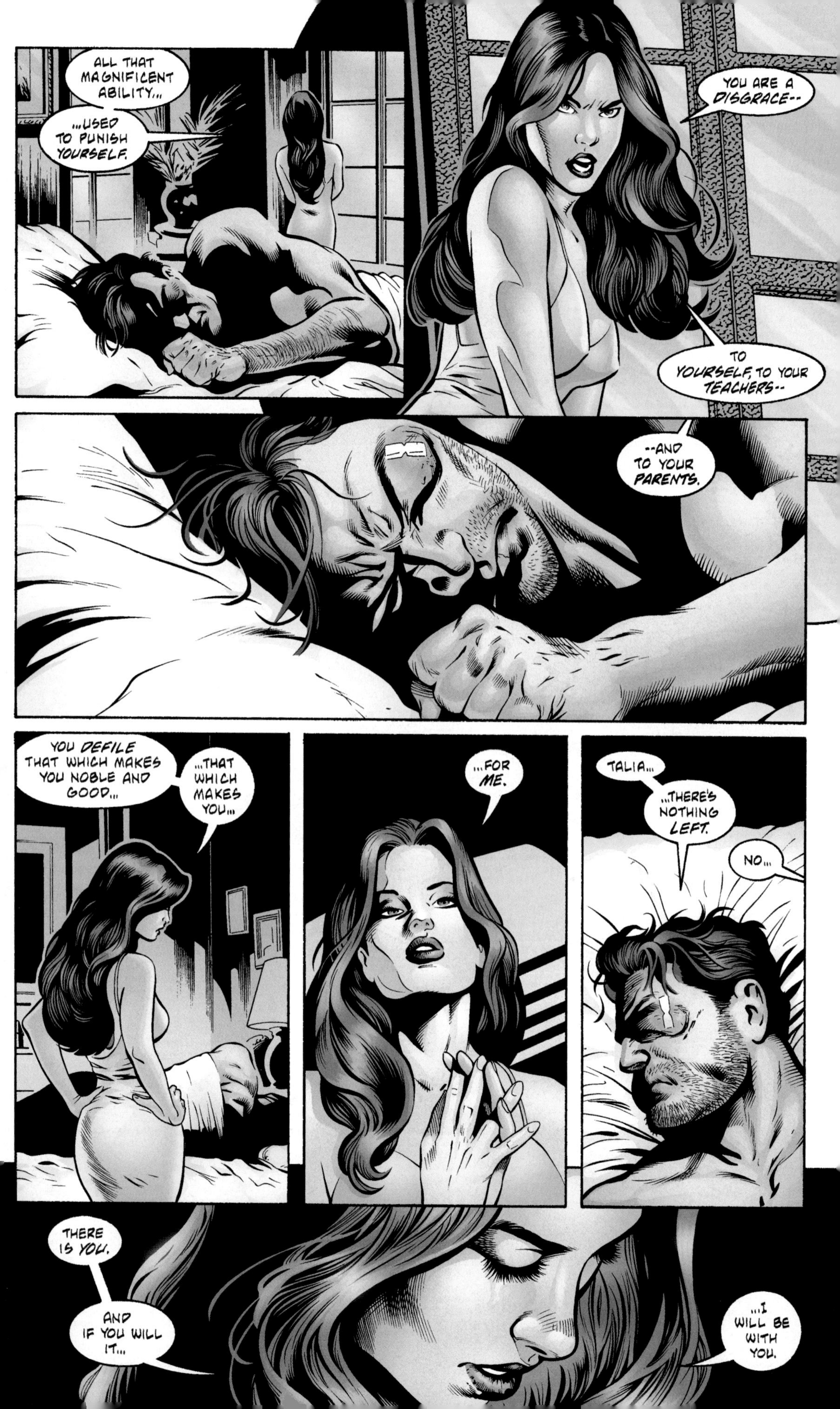
ALL THAT MAGNIFICENT ABILITY...
...USED TO PUNISH YOURSELF.
YOU ARE A DISGRACE--
TO YOURSELF, TO YOUR TEACHERS--
--AND TO YOUR PARENTS.
YOU DEFILE THAT WHICH MAKES YOU NOBLE AND GOOD...
...THAT WHICH MAKES YOU...
...FOR ME.
TALIA...
...THERE'S NOTHING LEFT.
NO...
THERE IS YOU.
AND IF YOU WILL IT...
...I WILL BE WITH YOU.

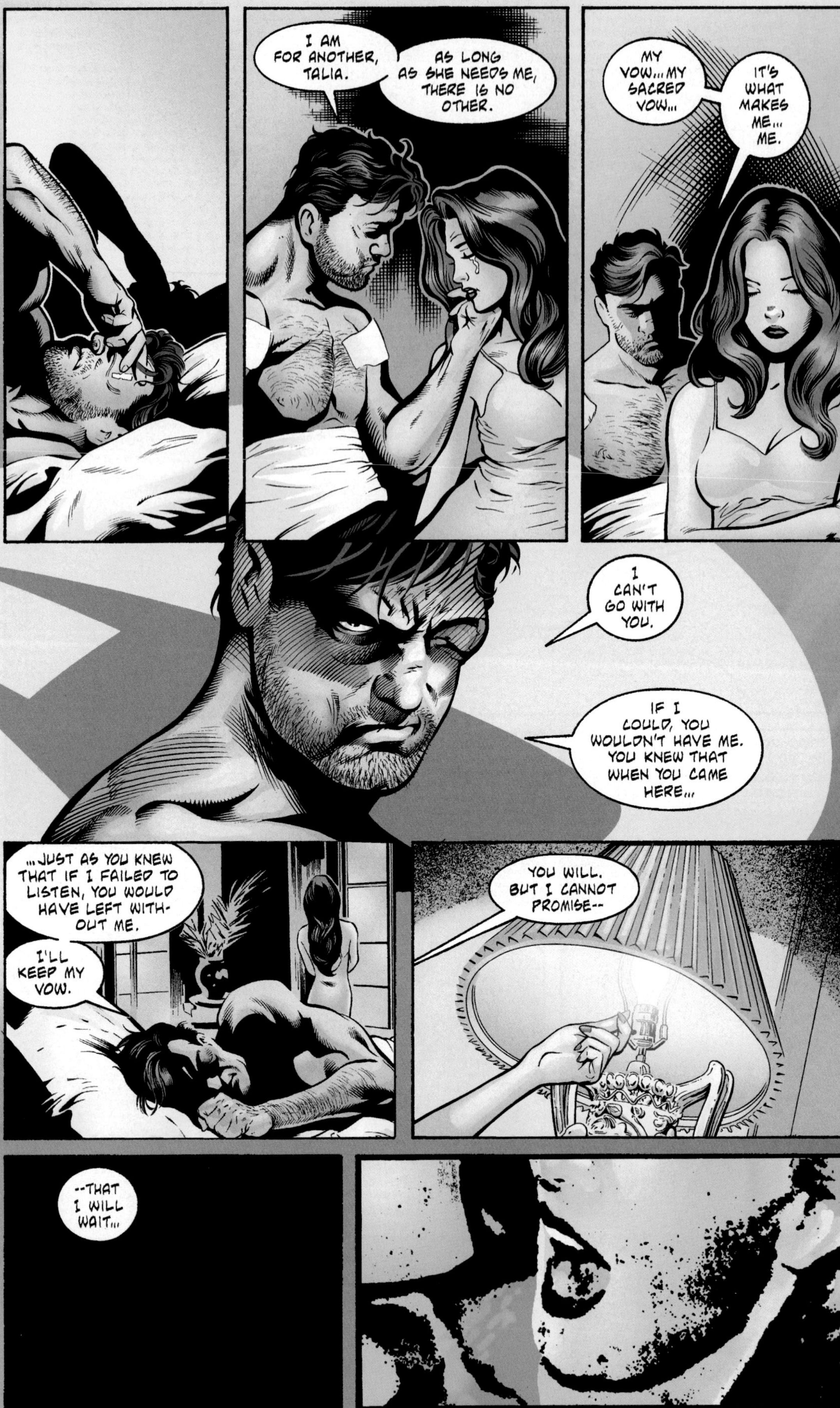
I AM FOR ANOTHER, TALIA.
AS LONG AS SHE NEEDS ME, THERE IS NO OTHER.
MY VOW... MY SACRED VOW...
IT'S WHAT MAKES ME... ME.
I CAN'T GO WITH YOU.
IF I COULD, YOU WOULDN'T HAVE ME. YOU KNEW THAT WHEN YOU CAME HERE...
...JUST AS YOU KNEW THAT IF I FAILED TO LISTEN, YOU WOULD HAVE LEFT WITHOUT ME.
I'LL KEEP MY VOW.
YOU WILL. BUT I CANNOT PROMISE--
--THAT I WILL WAIT...

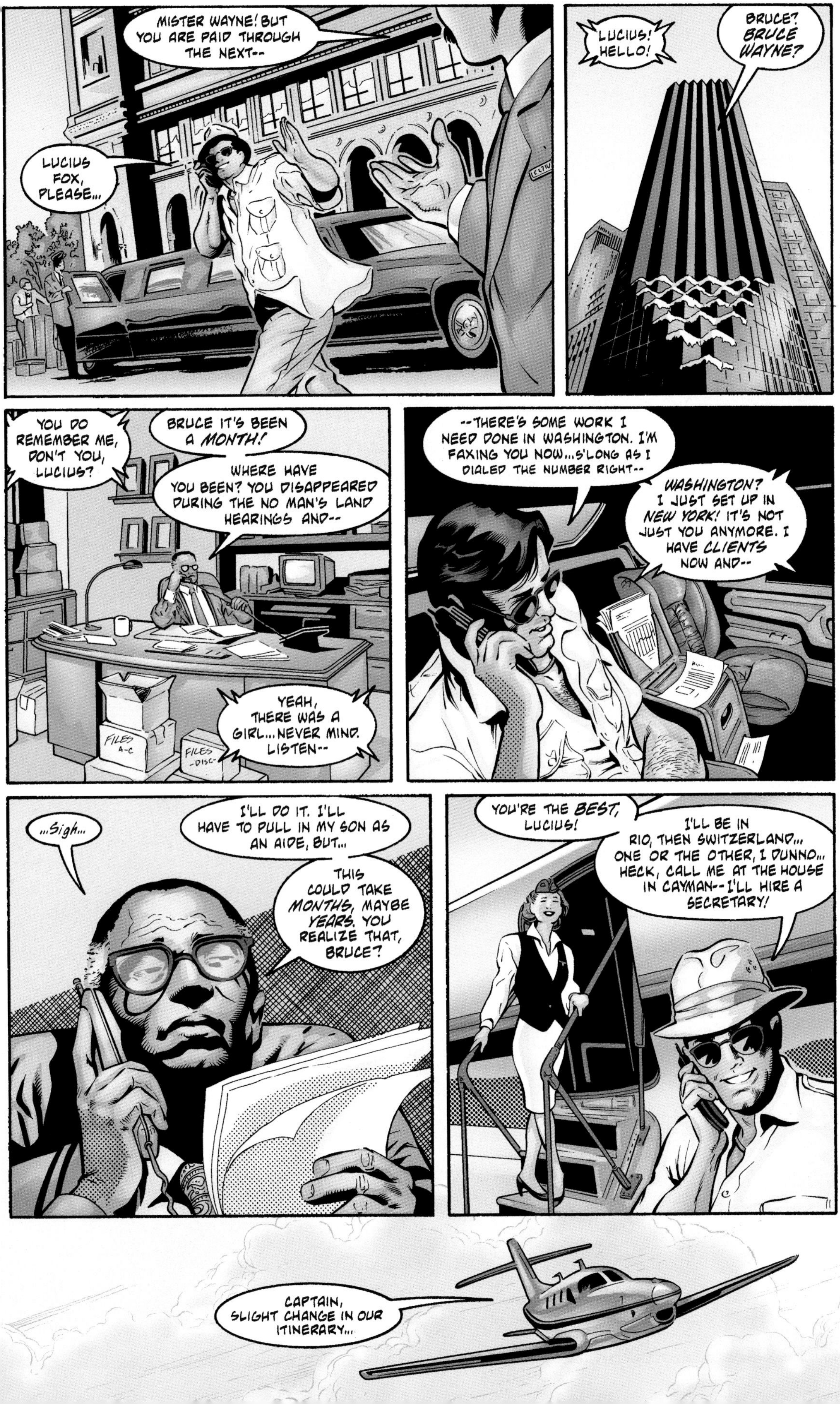

LUCIUS FOX, PLEASE...
MISTER WAYNE! BUT YOU ARE PAID THROUGH THE NEXT--
LUCIUS! HELLO!
BRUCE? BRUCE WAYNE?
YOU DO REMEMBER ME, DON'T YOU, LUCIUS?
BRUCE IT'S BEEN A MONTH!
WHERE HAVE YOU BEEN? YOU DISAPPEARED DURING THE NO MAN'S LAND HEARINGS AND--
YEAH, THERE WAS A GIRL... NEVER MIND. LISTEN--
FILES A-C
FILES -DISC-
--THERE'S SOME WORK I NEED DONE IN WASHINGTON. I'M FAXING YOU NOW... S'LONG AS I DIALED THE NUMBER RIGHT--
WASHINGTON? I JUST SET UP IN NEW YORK! IT'S NOT JUST YOU ANYMORE. I HAVE CLIENTS NOW AND--
...Sigh...
I'LL DO IT. I'LL HAVE TO PULL IN MY SON AS AN AIDE, BUT...
THIS COULD TAKE MONTHS, MAYBE YEARS. YOU REALIZE THAT, BRUCE?
YOU'RE THE BEST, LUCIUS!
I'LL BE IN RIO, THEN SWITZERLAND... ONE OR THE OTHER, I DUNNO... HECK, CALL ME AT THE HOUSE IN CAYMAN--I'LL HIRE A SECRETARY!
CAPTAIN, SLIGHT CHANGE IN OUR ITINERARY...

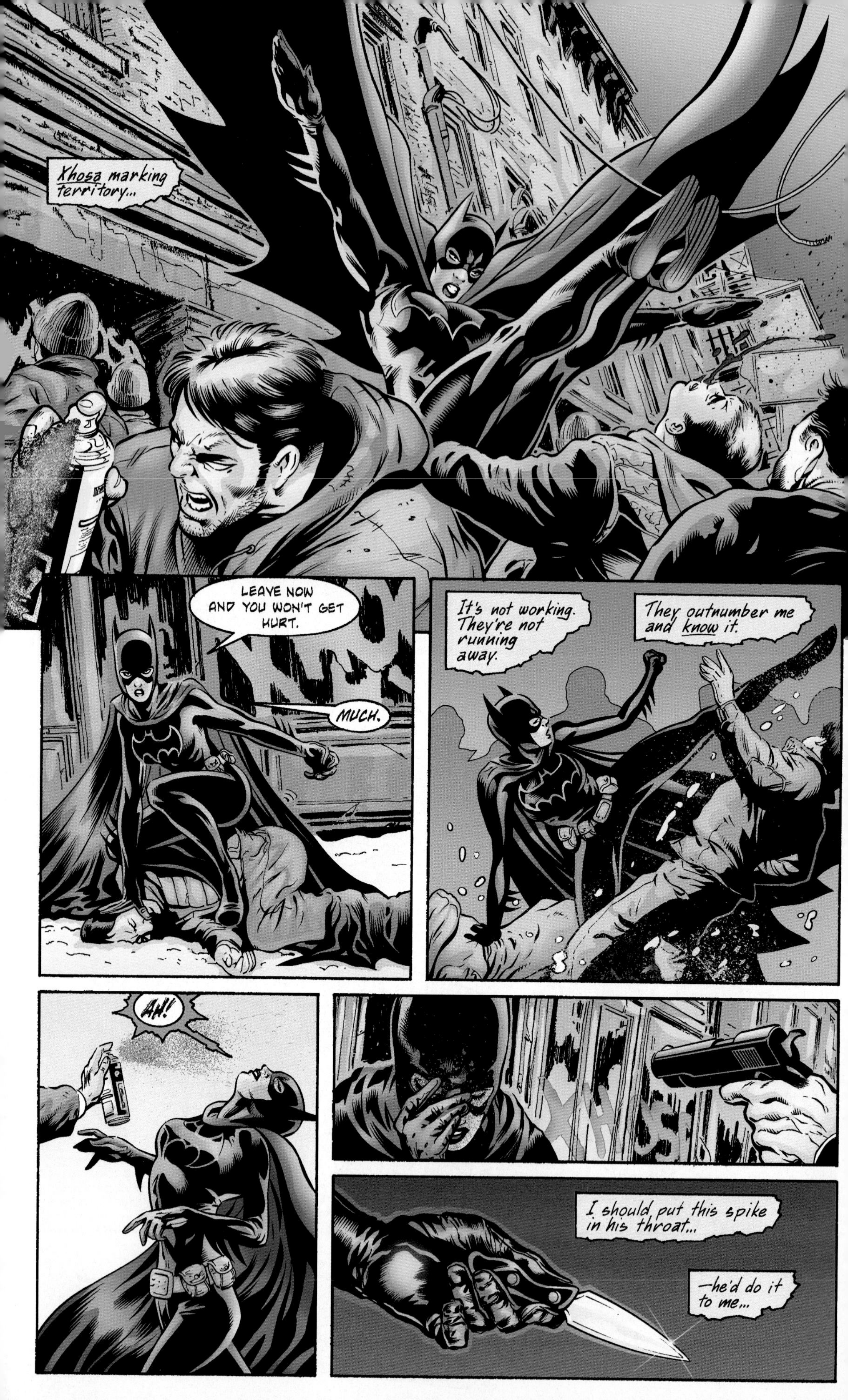

Xhosa marking territory...
LEAVE NOW AND YOU WON'T GET HURT.
MUCH.
It's not working. They're not running away.
They outnumber me and know it.
AH!
I should put this spike in his throat...
—he'd do it to me...

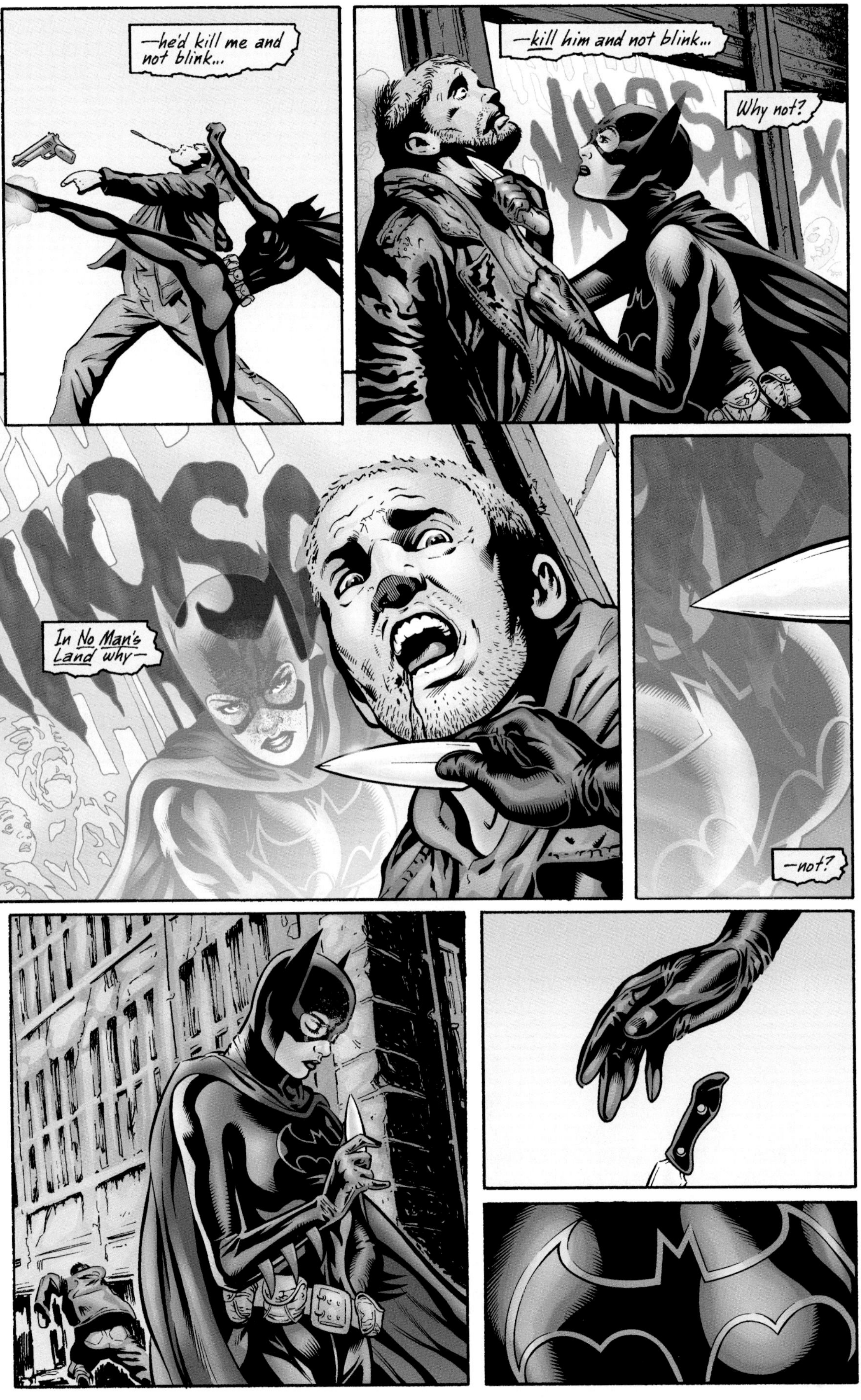
—he'd kill me and not blink...
—kill him and not blink...
Why not?
In No Man's Land why—
—not?

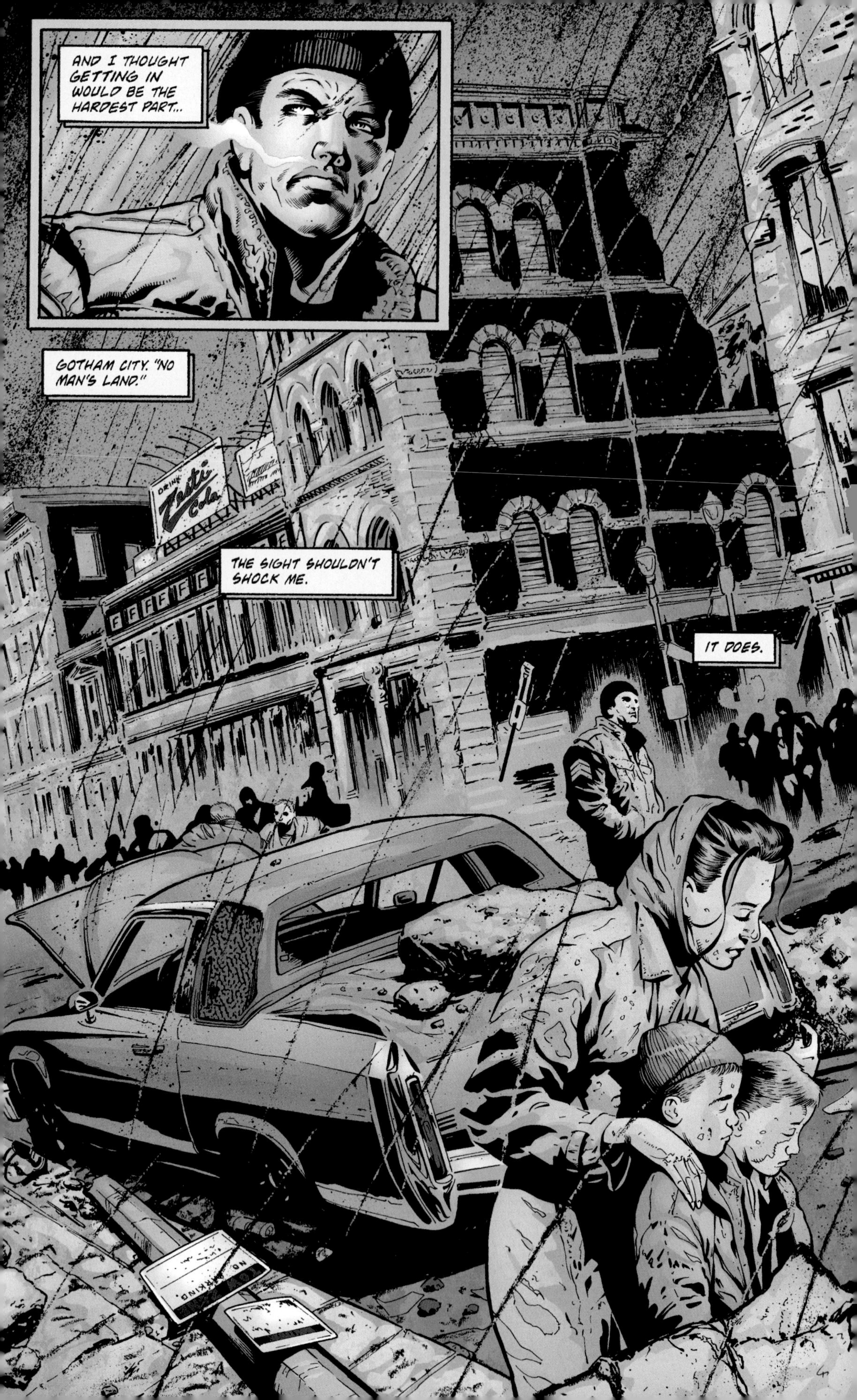
AND I THOUGHT GETTING IN WOULD BE THE HARDEST PART...
GOTHAM CITY. "NO MAN'S LAND."
DRINK Zesti Cola
THE SIGHT SHOULDN'T SHOCK ME.
IT DOES.
NO PARKING

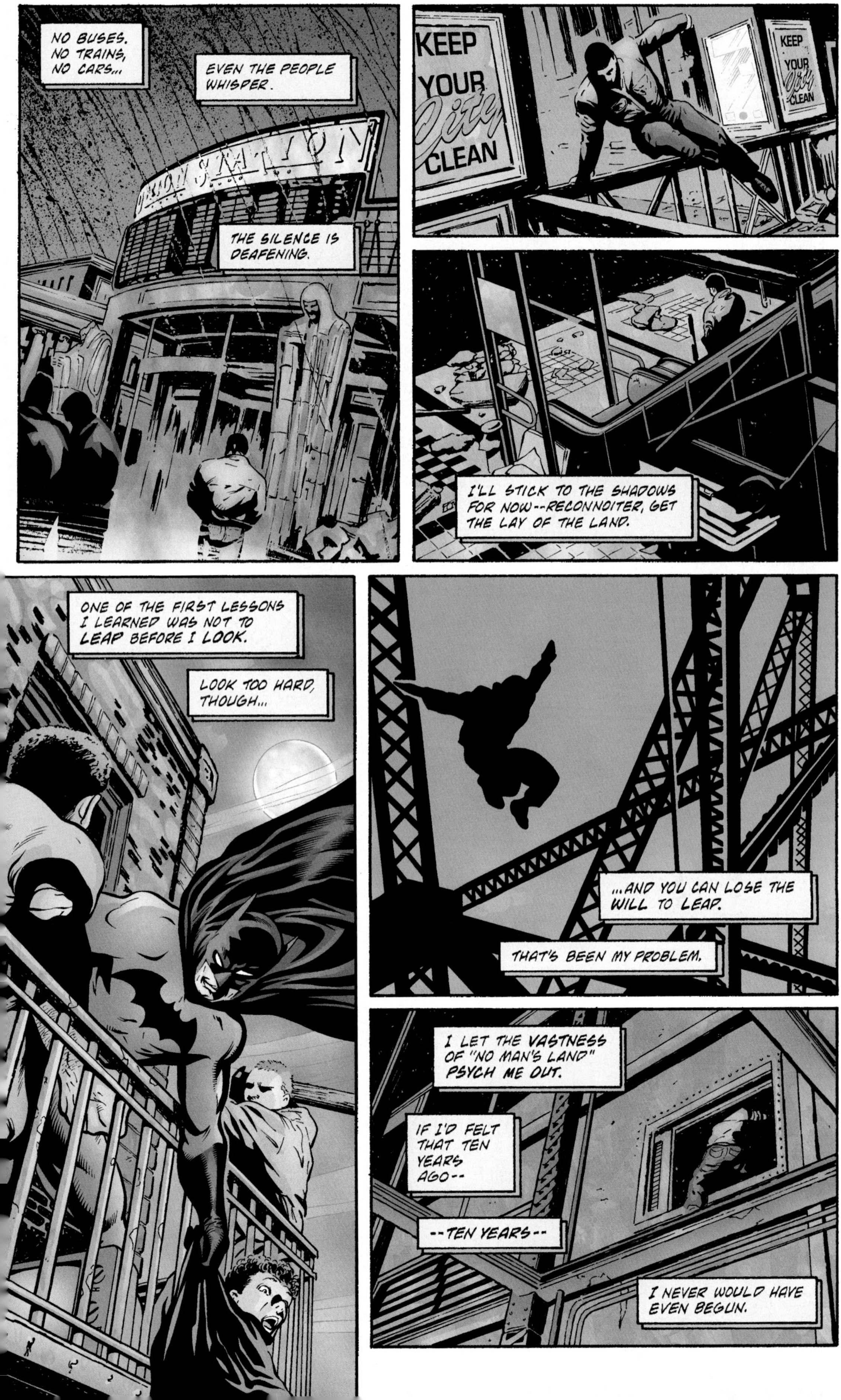
NO BUSES.
NO TRAINS,
NO CARS...
EVEN THE PEOPLE WHISPER.
THE SILENCE IS DEAFENING.
KEEP YOUR City CLEAN
KEEP YOUR City CLEAN
I'LL STICK TO THE SHADOWS FOR NOW--RECONNOITER, GET THE LAY OF THE LAND.
ONE OF THE FIRST LESSONS I LEARNED WAS NOT TO LEAP BEFORE I LOOK.
LOOK TOO HARD, THOUGH...
...AND YOU CAN LOSE THE WILL TO LEAP.
THAT'S BEEN MY PROBLEM.
I LET THE VASTNESS OF "NO MAN'S LAND" PSYCH ME OUT.
IF I'D FELT THAT TEN YEARS AGO--
--TEN YEARS--
I NEVER WOULD HAVE EVEN BEGUN.

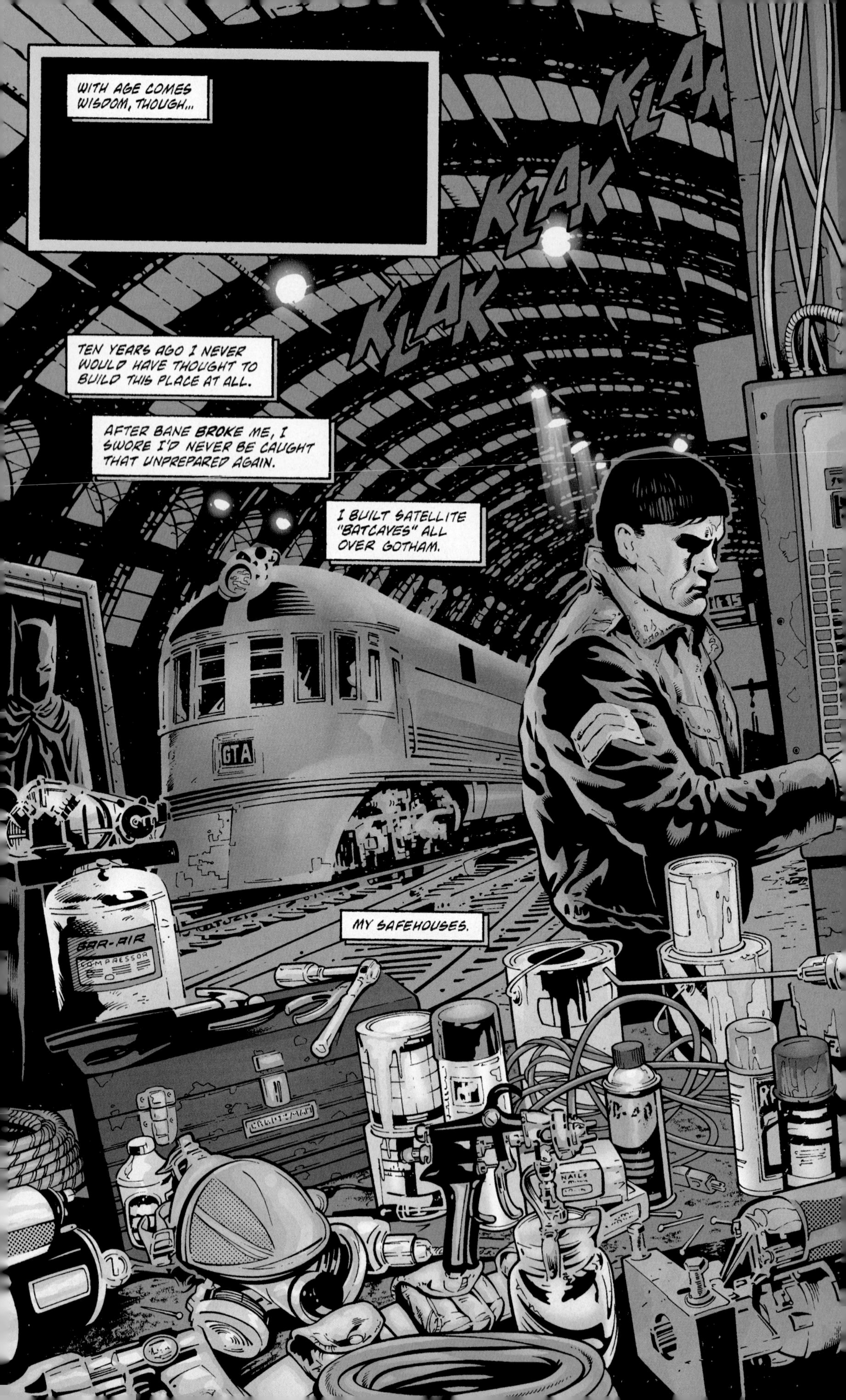
WITH AGE COMES WISDOM, THOUGH...
KLAK KLAK KLAK KLAK
TEN YEARS AGO I NEVER WOULD HAVE THOUGHT TO BUILD THIS PLACE AT ALL.
AFTER BANE BROKE ME, I SWORE I'D NEVER BE CAUGHT THAT UNPREPARED AGAIN.
I BUILT SATELLITE "BATCAVES" ALL OVER GOTHAM.
GTA
MY SAFEHOUSES.
BAR-AIR COMPRESSOR

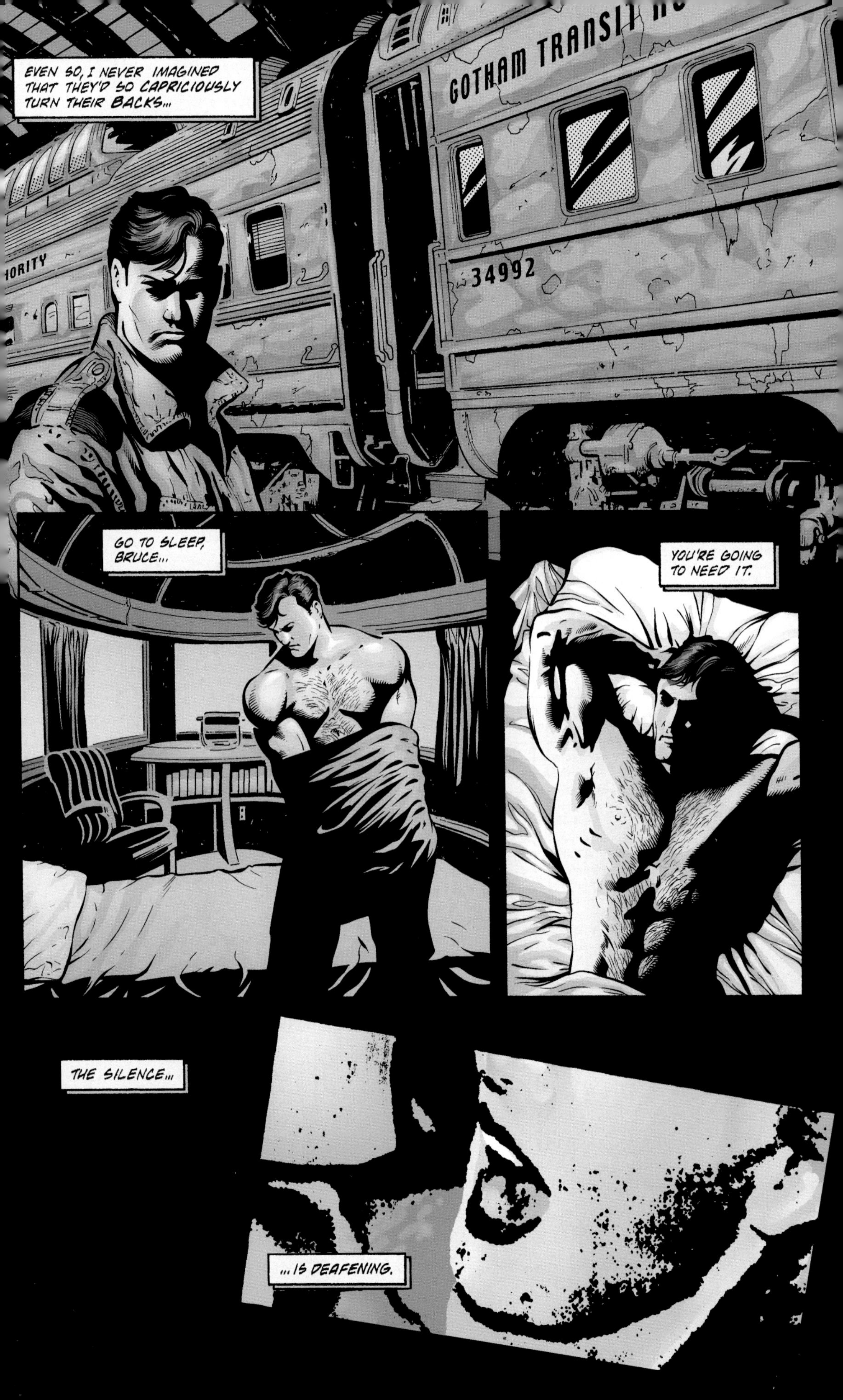
EVEN SO, I NEVER IMAGINED THAT THEY'D SO CAPRICIOUSLY TURN THEIR BACKS...
GOTHAM TRANSIT
34992
GO TO SLEEP, BRUCE...
YOU'RE GOING TO NEED IT.
THE SILENCE...
...IS DEAFENING.

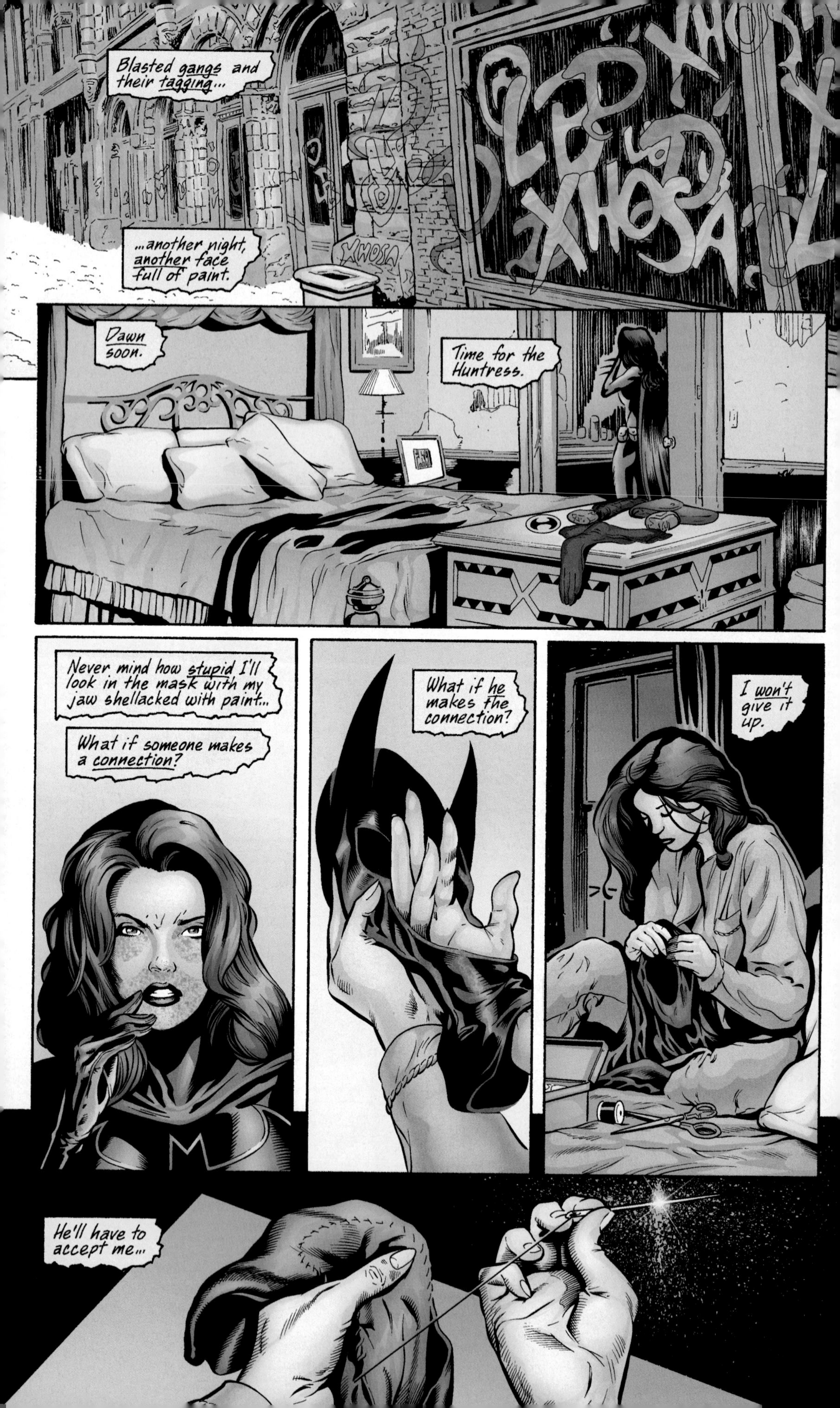
Blasted gangs and their tagging...
...another night, another face full of paint.
XHOSA
Dawn soon.
Time for the Huntress.
Never mind how stupid I'll look in the mask with my jaw shellacked with paint...
What if someone makes a connection?
What if he makes the connection?
I won't give it up.
He'll have to accept me...

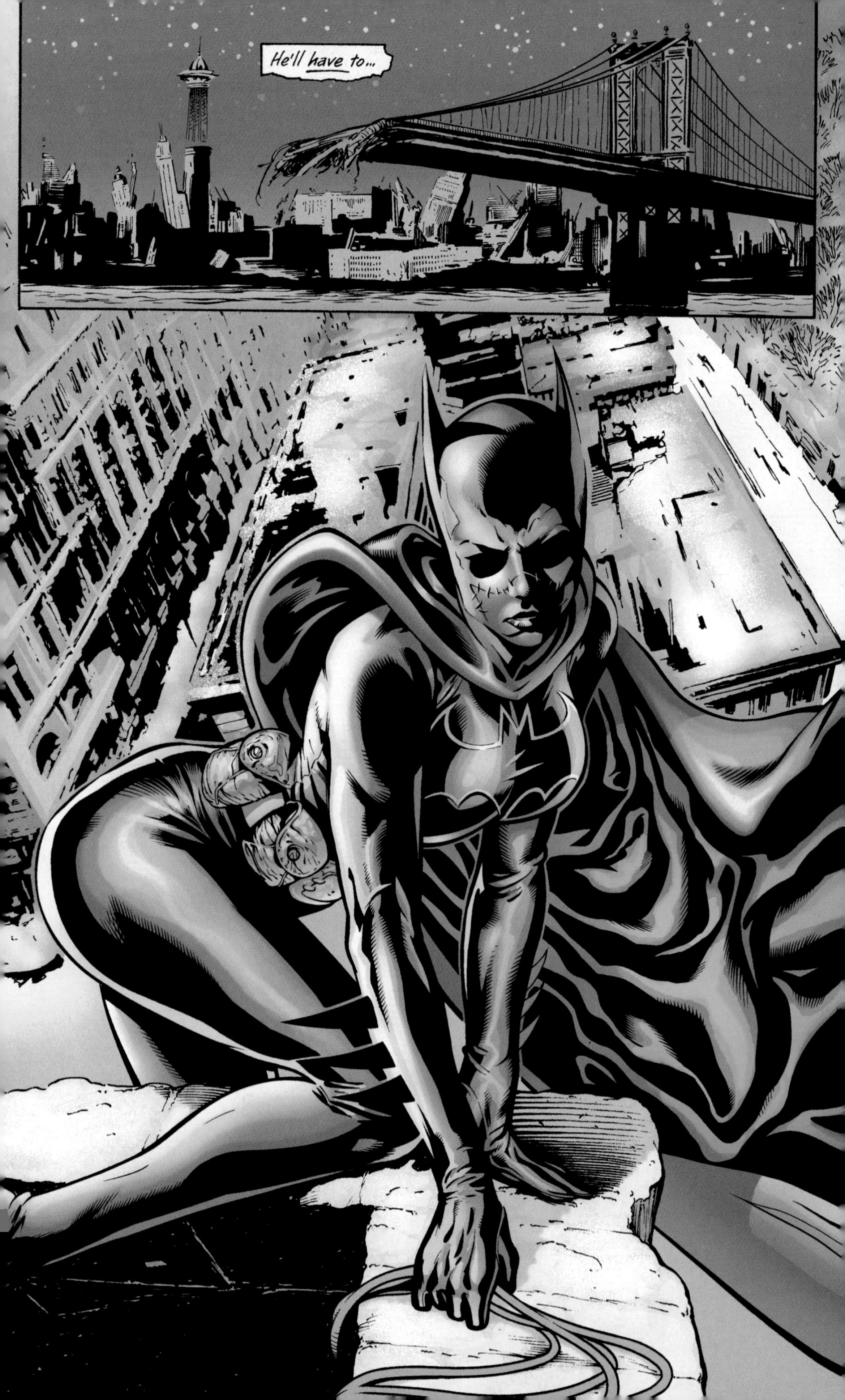
He'll have to...

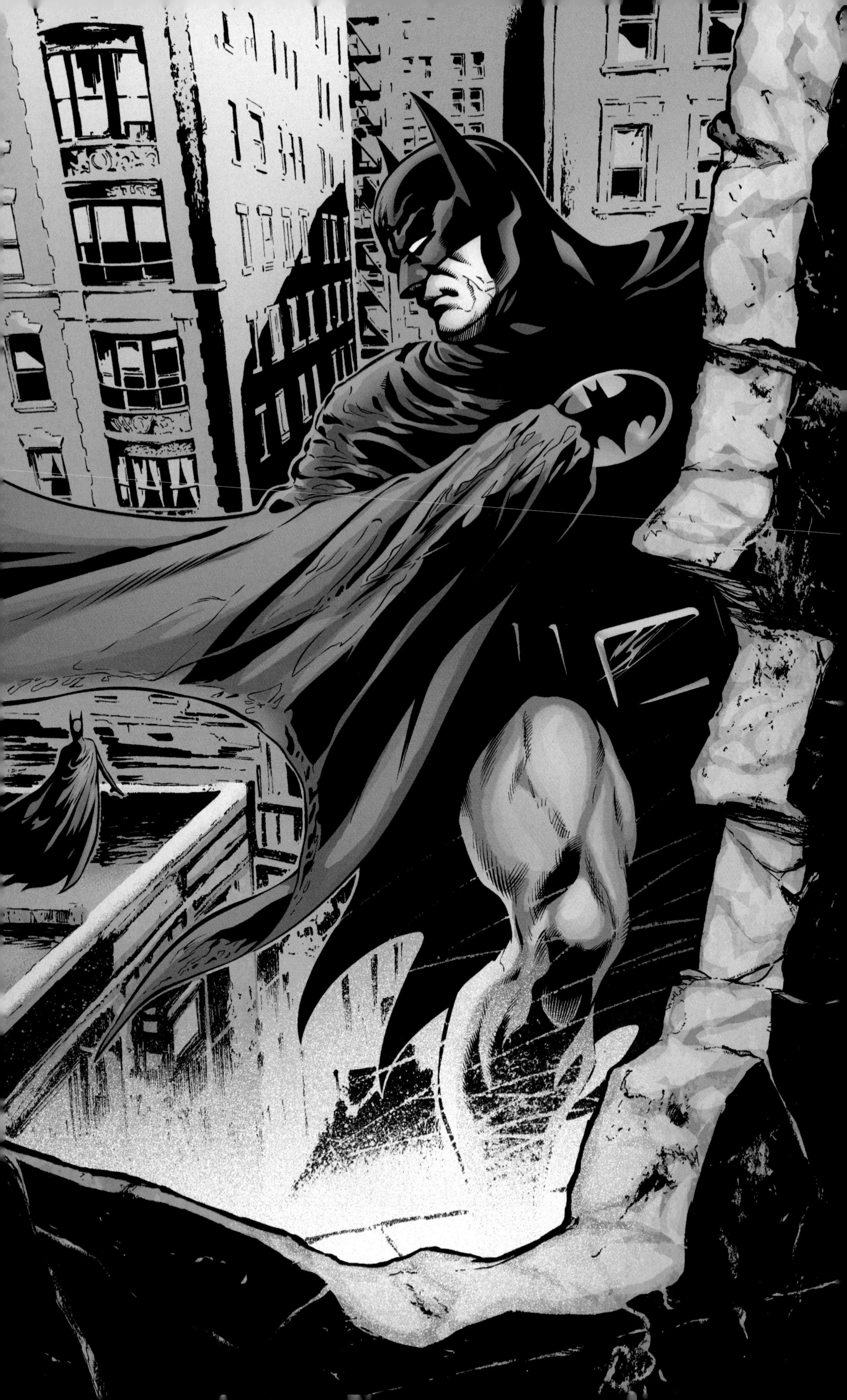

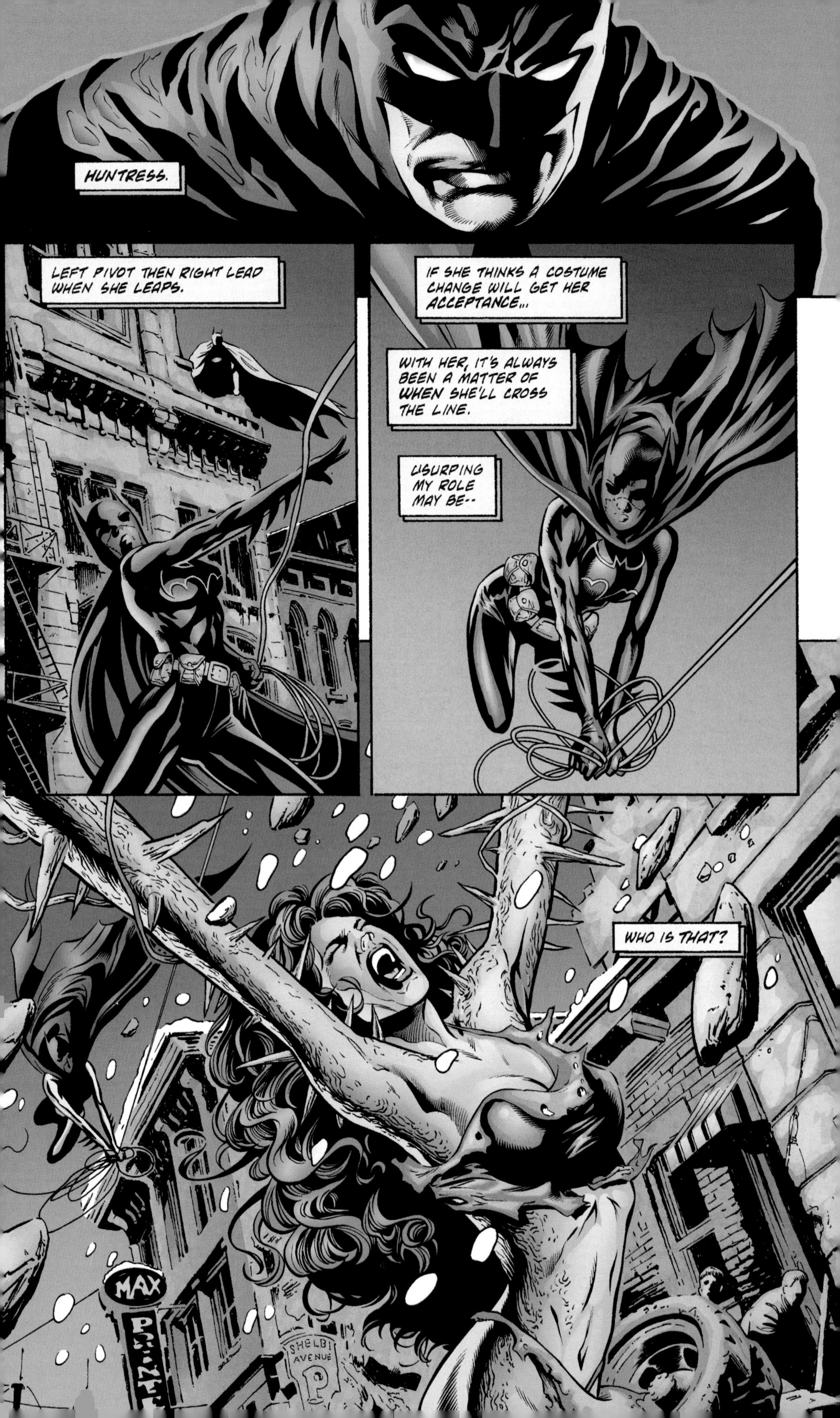
HUNTRESS.
LEFT PIVOT THEN RIGHT LEAD WHEN SHE LEAPS.
IF SHE THINKS A COSTUME CHANGE WILL GET HER ACCEPTANCE...
WITH HER, IT'S ALWAYS BEEN A MATTER OF WHEN SHE'LL CROSS THE LINE.
USURPING MY ROLE MAY BE--
WHO IS THAT?
MAX
SHELBI AVENUE
P

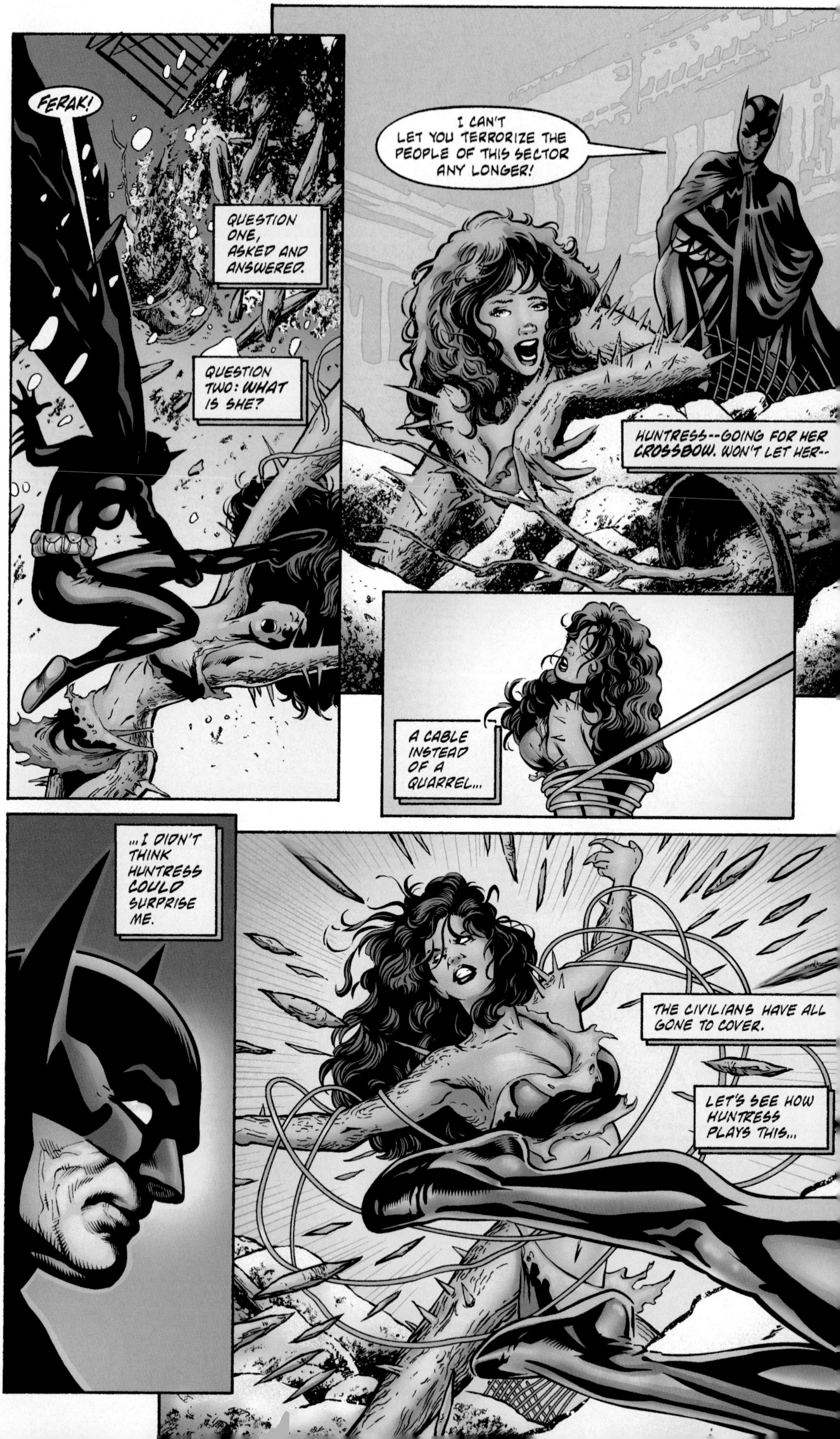

FERAK!
QUESTION ONE, ASKED AND ANSWERED.
QUESTION TWO: WHAT IS SHE?
I CAN'T LET YOU TERRORIZE THE PEOPLE OF THIS SECTOR ANY LONGER!
HUNTRESS--GOING FOR HER CROSSBOW. WON'T LET HER--
A CABLE INSTEAD OF A QUARREL...
...I DIDN'T THINK HUNTRESS COULD SURPRISE ME.
THE CIVILIANS HAVE ALL GONE TO COVER.
LET'S SEE HOW HUNTRESS PLAYS THIS...

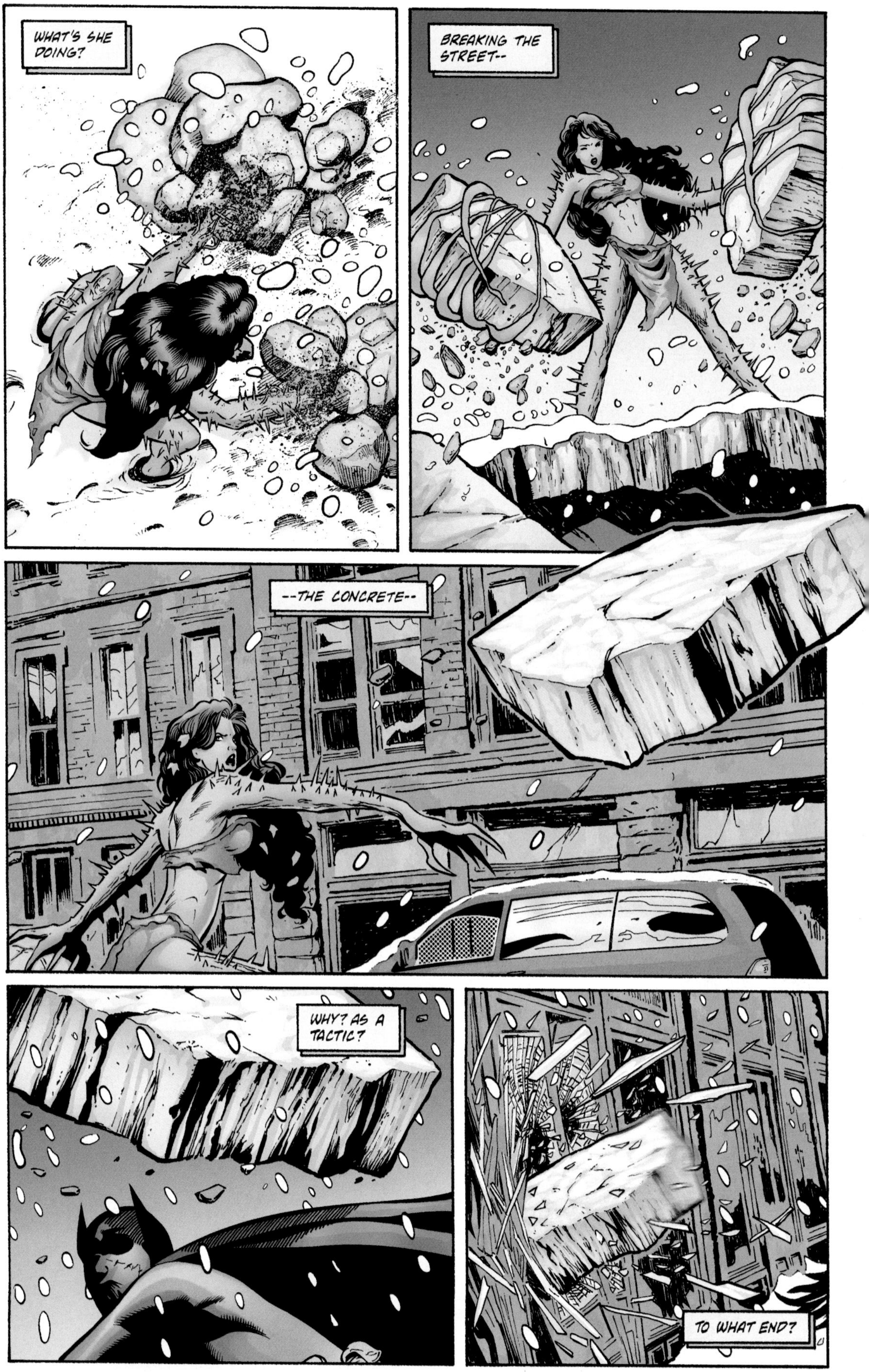
WHAT'S SHE DOING?
BREAKING THE STREET--
--THE CONCRETE--
WHY? AS A TACTIC?
TO WHAT END?

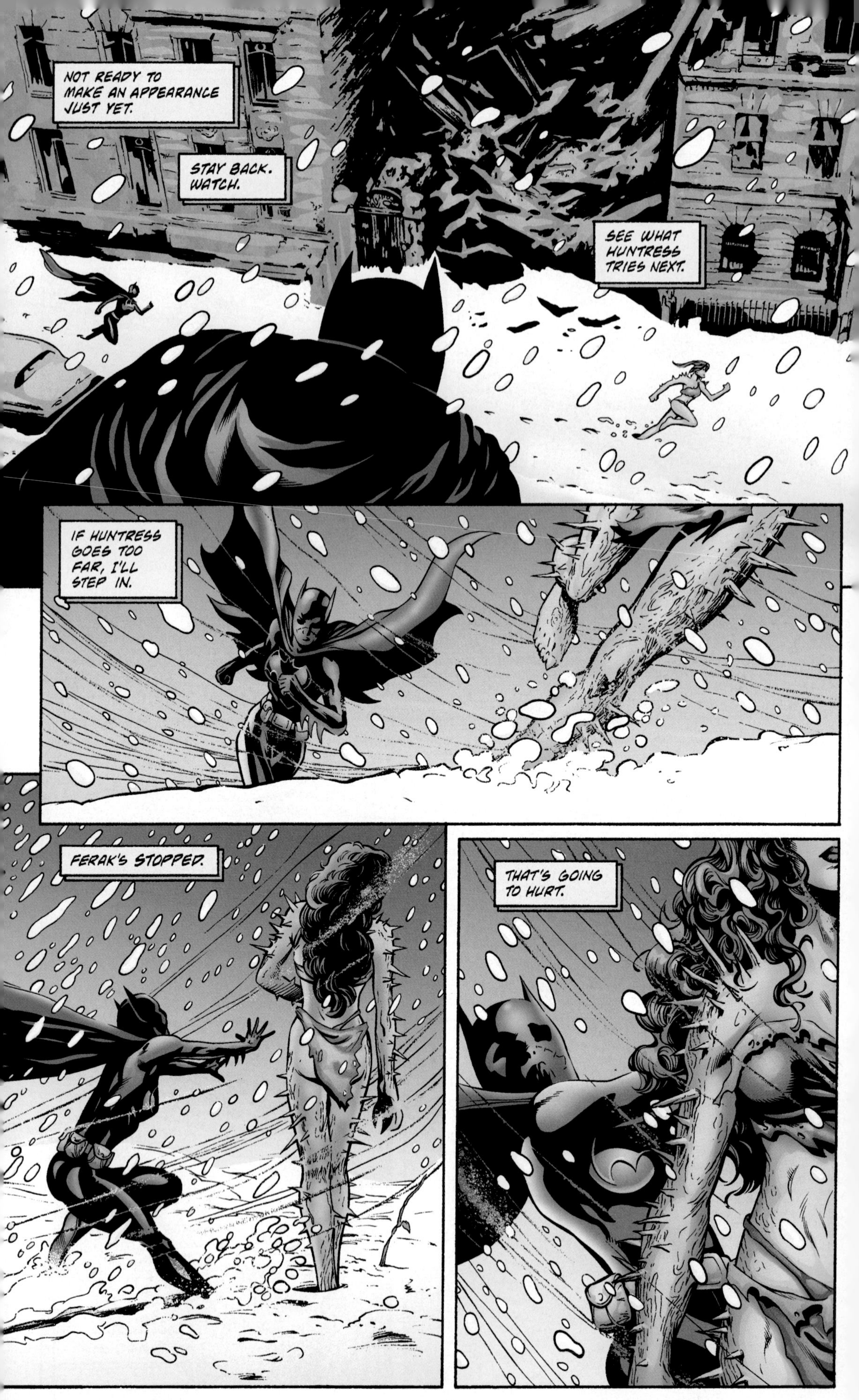

NOT READY TO MAKE AN APPEARANCE JUST YET.
STAY BACK. WATCH.
SEE WHAT HUNTRESS TRIES NEXT.
IF HUNTRESS GOES TOO FAR, I'LL STEP IN.
FERAK'S STOPPED.
THAT'S GOING TO HURT.

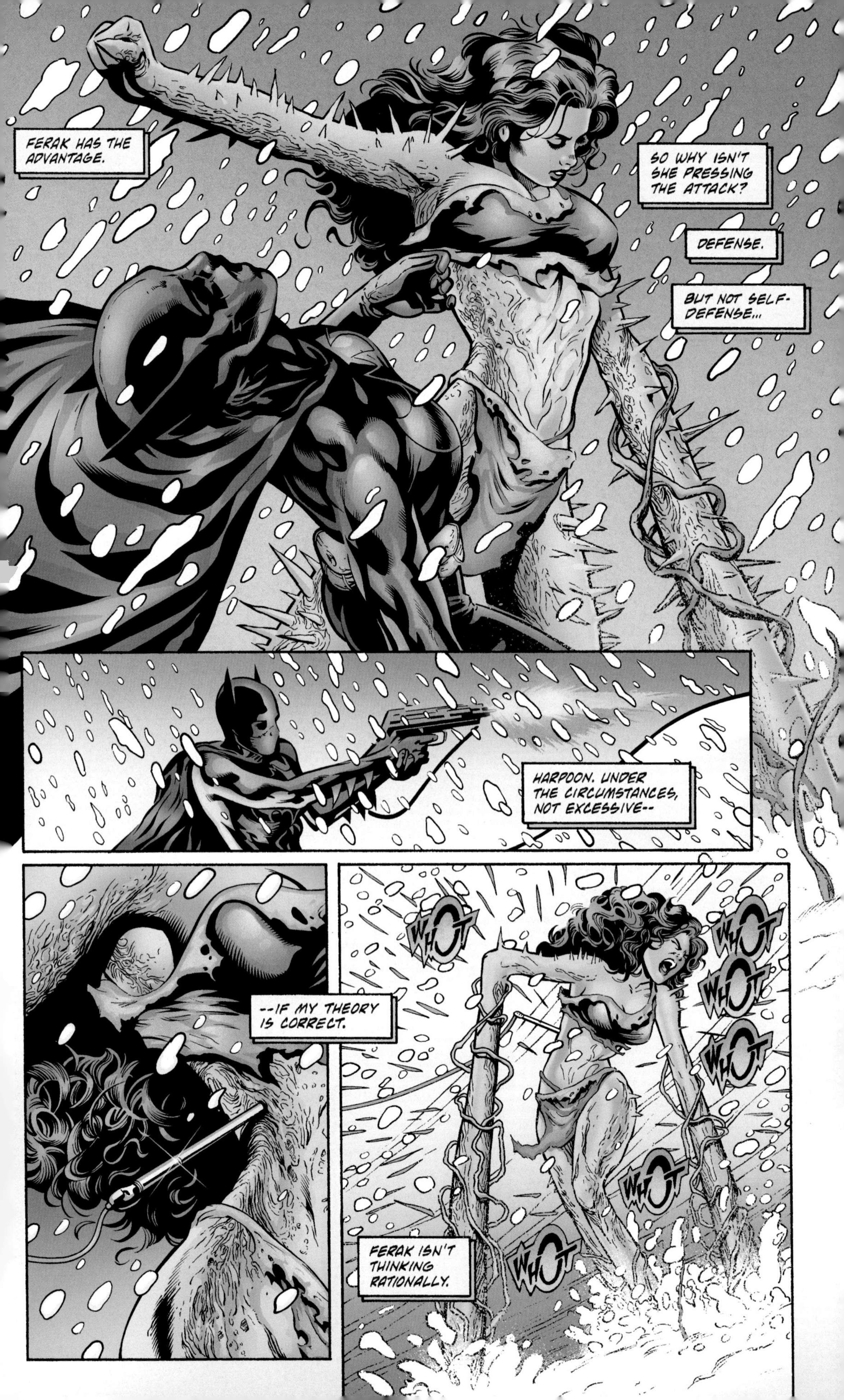
FERAK HAS THE ADVANTAGE.
SO WHY ISN'T SHE PRESSING THE ATTACK?
DEFENSE.
BUT NOT SELF-DEFENSE...
HARPOON. UNDER THE CIRCUMSTANCES, NOT EXCESSIVE--
--IF MY THEORY IS CORRECT.
WHOT
WHOT
WHOT
WHOT
WHOT
WHOT
FERAK ISN'T THINKING RATIONALLY.

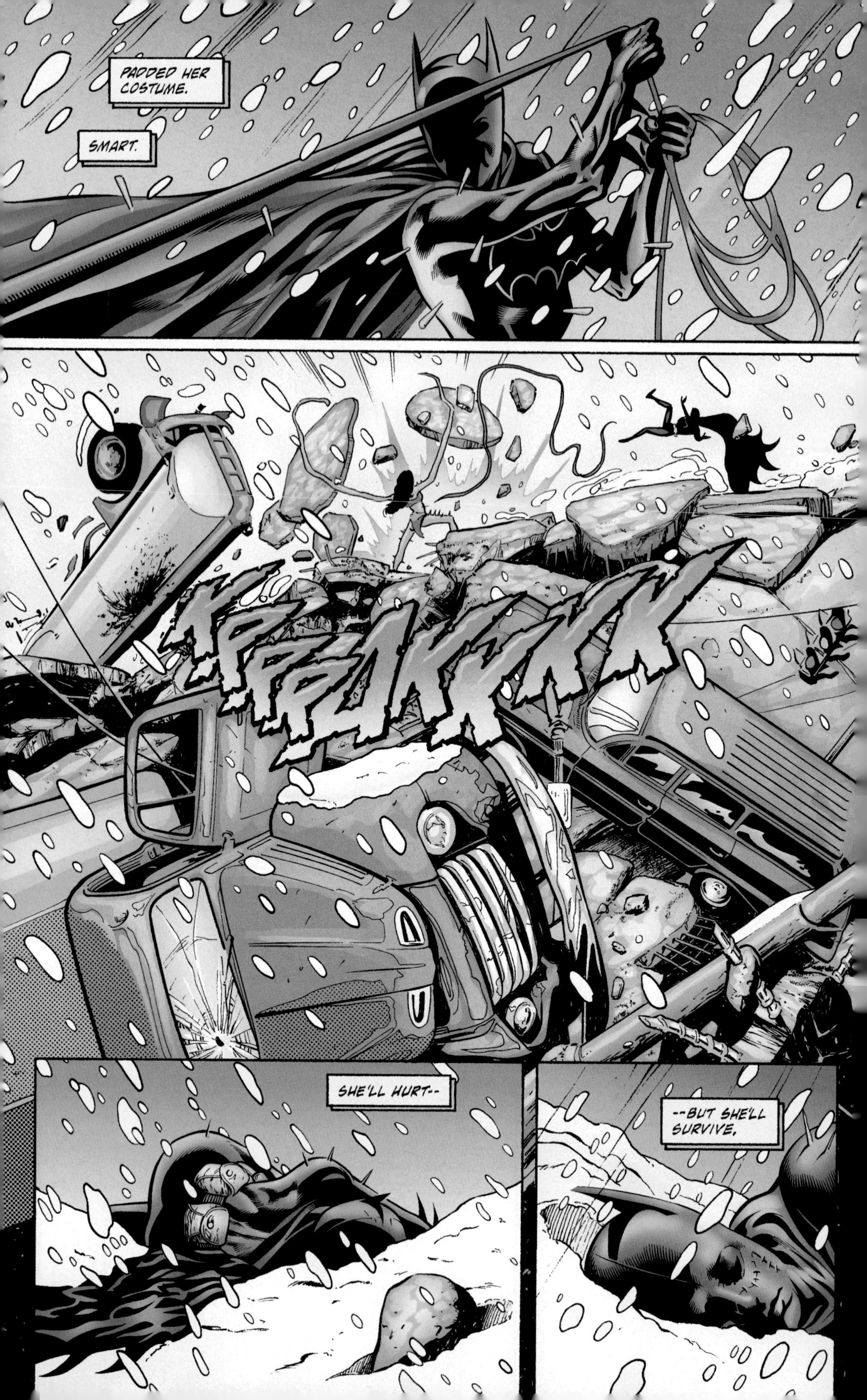
PADDED HER COSTUME.
SMART.
KRAKKK
SHE'LL HURT--
--BUT SHE'LL SURVIVE.

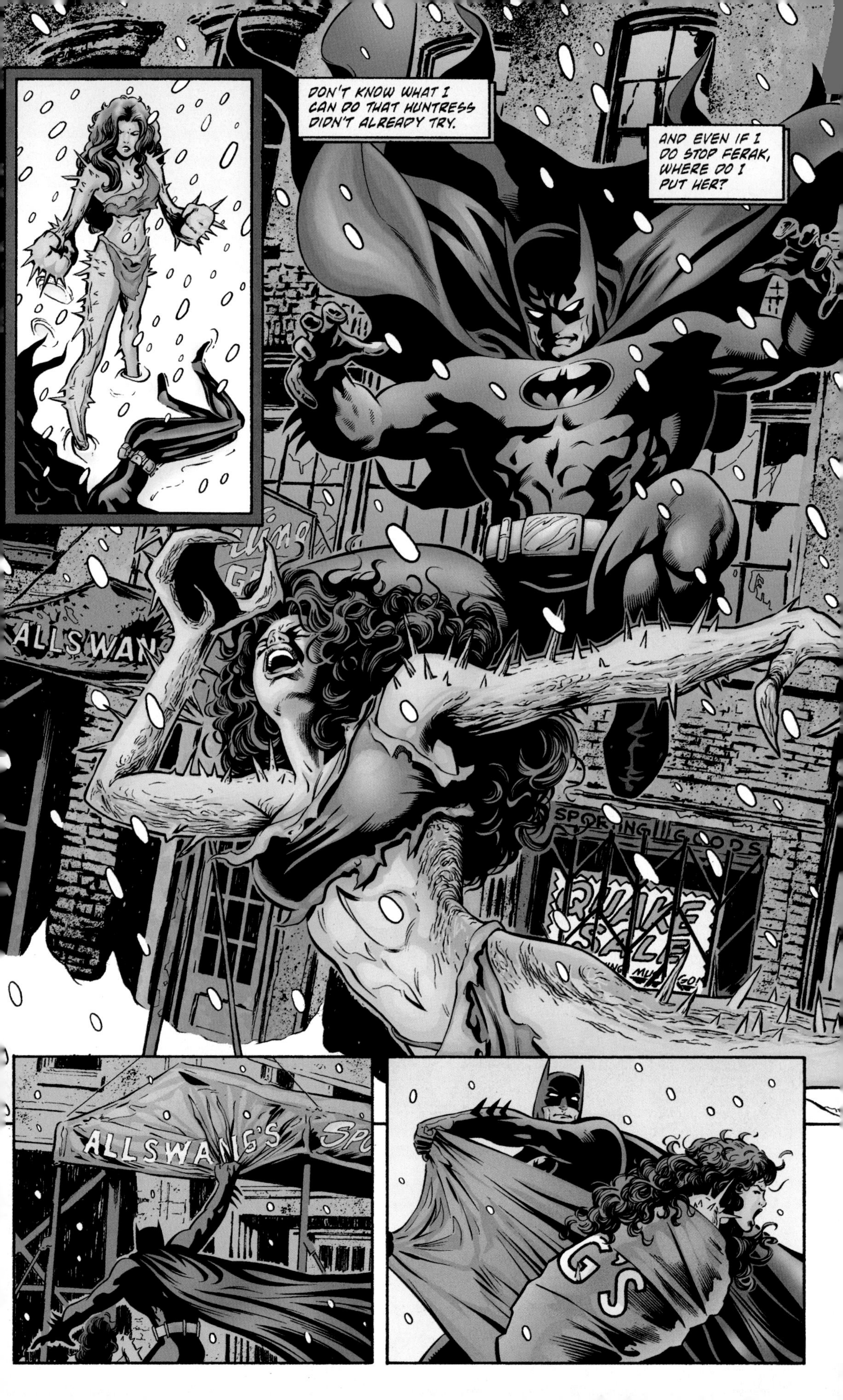
DON'T KNOW WHAT I CAN DO THAT HUNTRESS DIDN'T ALREADY TRY.
AND EVEN IF I DO STOP FERAK, WHERE DO I PUT HER?
ALLSWAN
SPORTING GOODS
QUAKE SALE
ALLSWANG'S
G'S

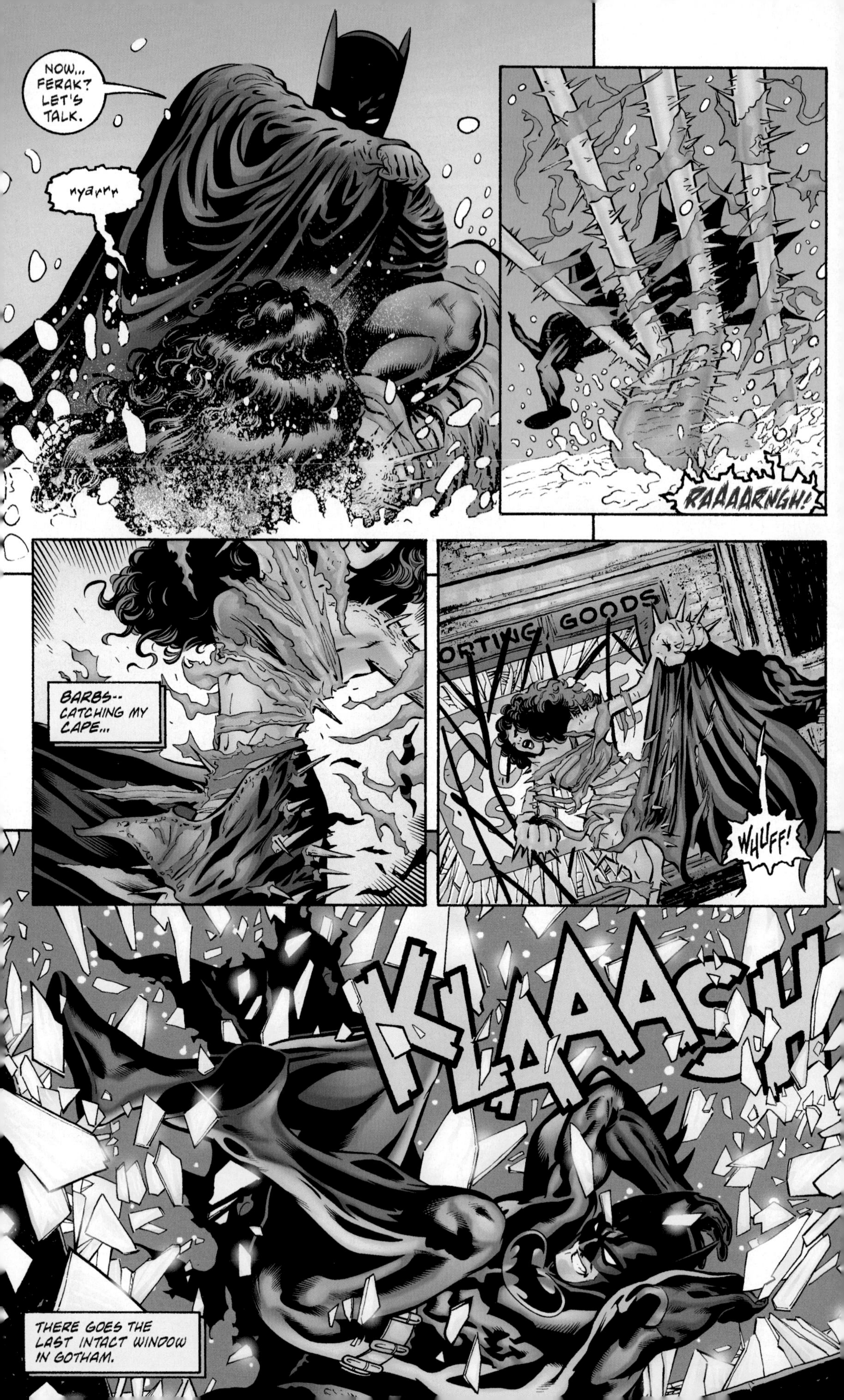
NOW... FERAK? LET'S TALK.
nyarrr
RAAAARNGH!
BARBS-- CATCHING MY CAPE...
ORTING GOODS
WHUFF!
KLAAACH
THERE GOES THE LAST INTACT WINDOW IN GOTHAM.

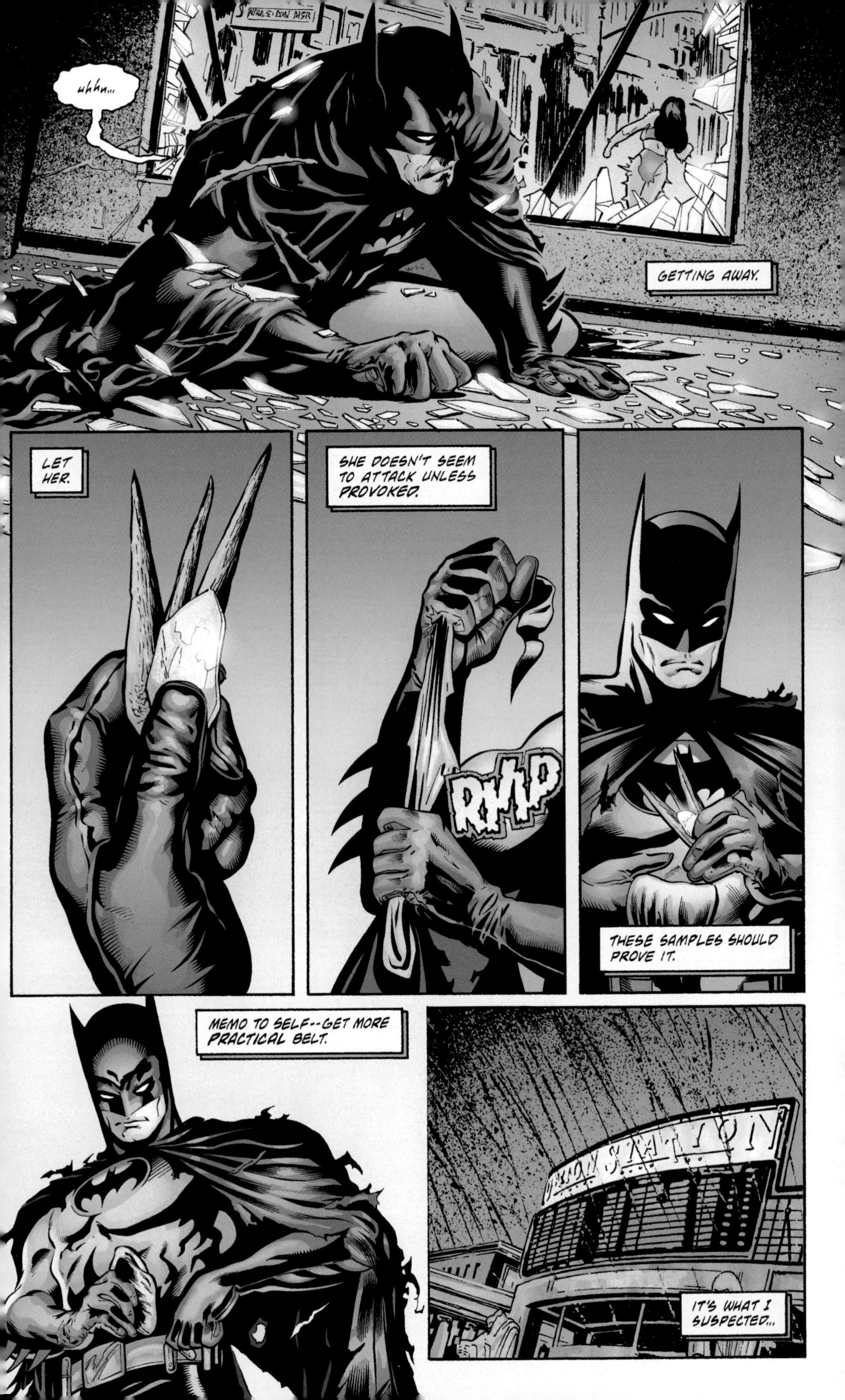

uhhn...
GETTING AWAY.
LET HER.
SHE DOESN'T SEEM TO ATTACK UNLESS PROVOKED.
RIIIP
THESE SAMPLES SHOULD PROVE IT.
MEMO TO SELF--GET MORE PRACTICAL BELT.
IT'S WHAT I SUSPECTED...

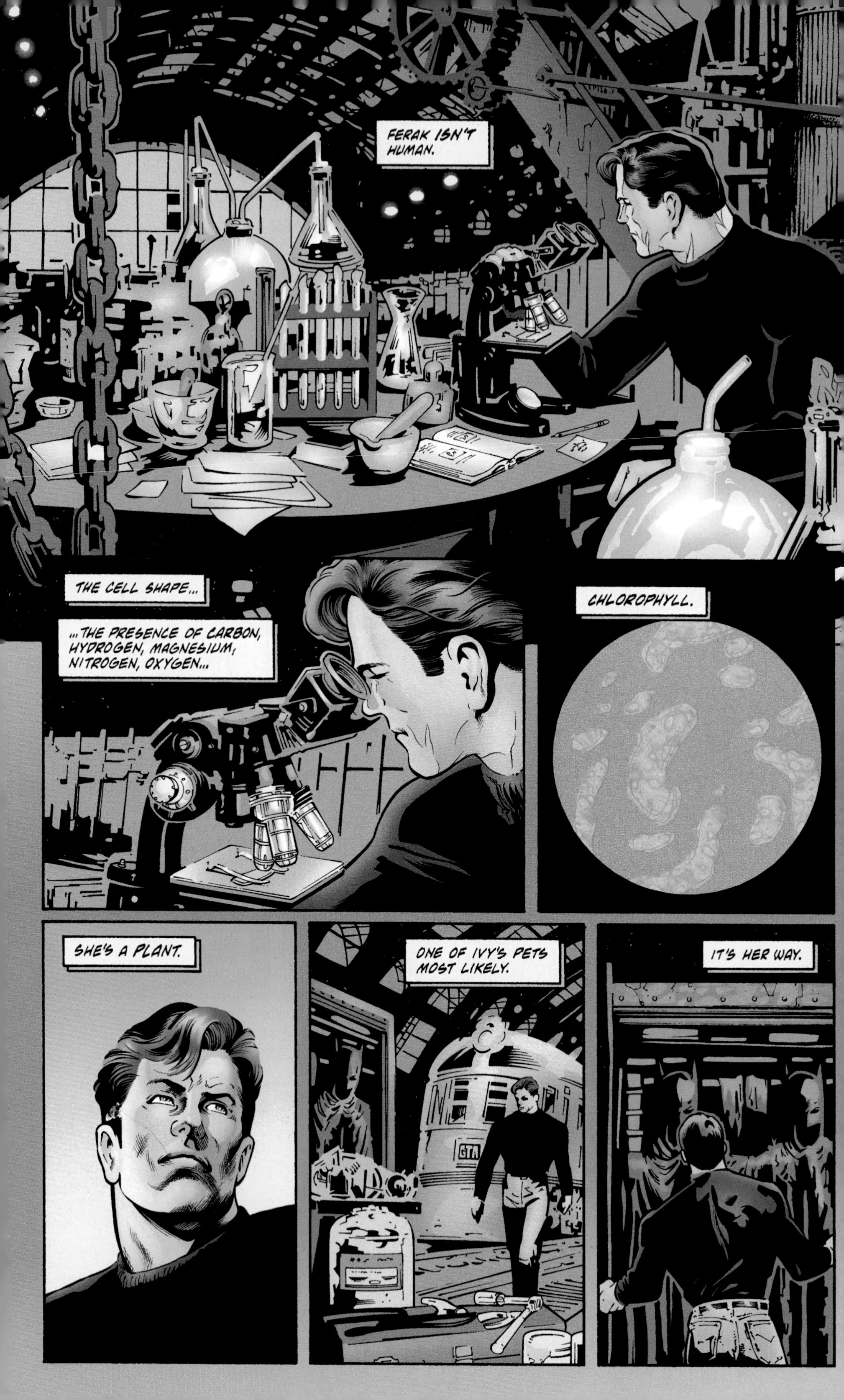
FERAK ISN'T HUMAN.
THE CELL SHAPE...
...THE PRESENCE OF CARBON, HYDROGEN, MAGNESIUM, NITROGEN, OXYGEN...
CHLOROPHYLL.
SHE'S A PLANT.
ONE OF IVY'S PETS MOST LIKELY.
IT'S HER WAY.

FERAK WASN'T ON A RAMPAGE.

SHE WAS ON A HUNT.

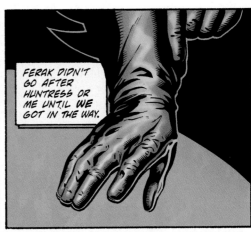

FERAK DIDN'T GO AFTER HUNTRESS OR ME UNTIL WE GOT IN THE WAY.

THAT CREATURE PROBABLY DOESN'T EVEN KNOW WHAT SHE'S LOOKING FOR...

...ONLY THAT SHE'LL KNOW IT WHEN SHE FINDS IT.

HER MEANDERING SEARCH PATTERN, HER PRIMITIVE SPEECH...

...INDICATING AN UNDEVELOPED BRAIN.

HMM...

P.KLATCH

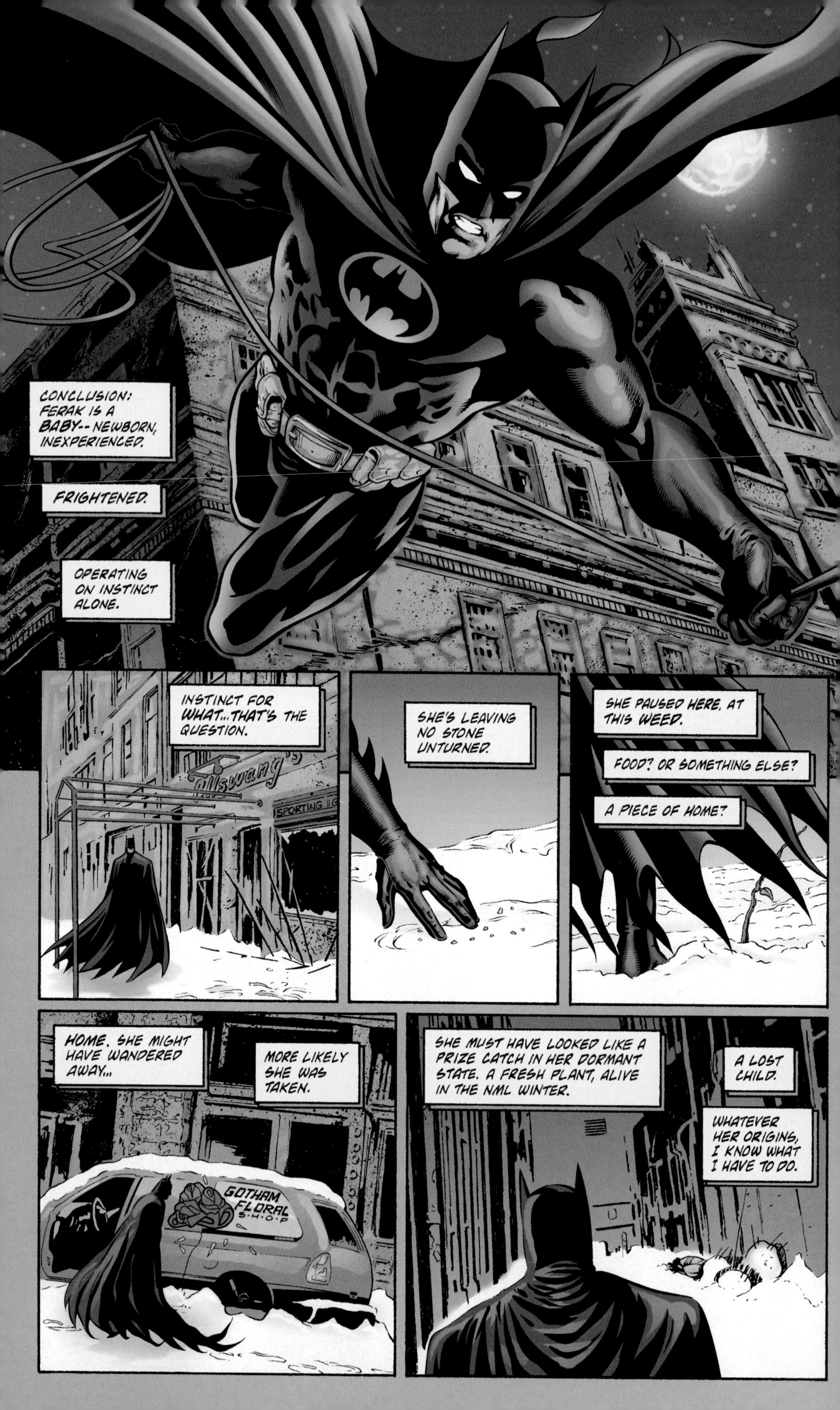
CONCLUSION: FERAK IS A BABY-- NEWBORN, INEXPERIENCED.
FRIGHTENED.
OPERATING ON INSTINCT ALONE.
INSTINCT FOR WHAT...THAT'S THE QUESTION.
SPORTING
SHE'S LEAVING NO STONE UNTURNED.
SHE PAUSED HERE, AT THIS WEED.
FOOD? OR SOMETHING ELSE?
A PIECE OF HOME?
HOME. SHE MIGHT HAVE WANDERED AWAY...
MORE LIKELY SHE WAS TAKEN.
GOTHAM FLORAL S·H·O·P
SHE MUST HAVE LOOKED LIKE A PRIZE CATCH IN HER DORMANT STATE. A FRESH PLANT, ALIVE IN THE NML WINTER.
A LOST CHILD.
WHATEVER HER ORIGINS, I KNOW WHAT I HAVE TO DO.

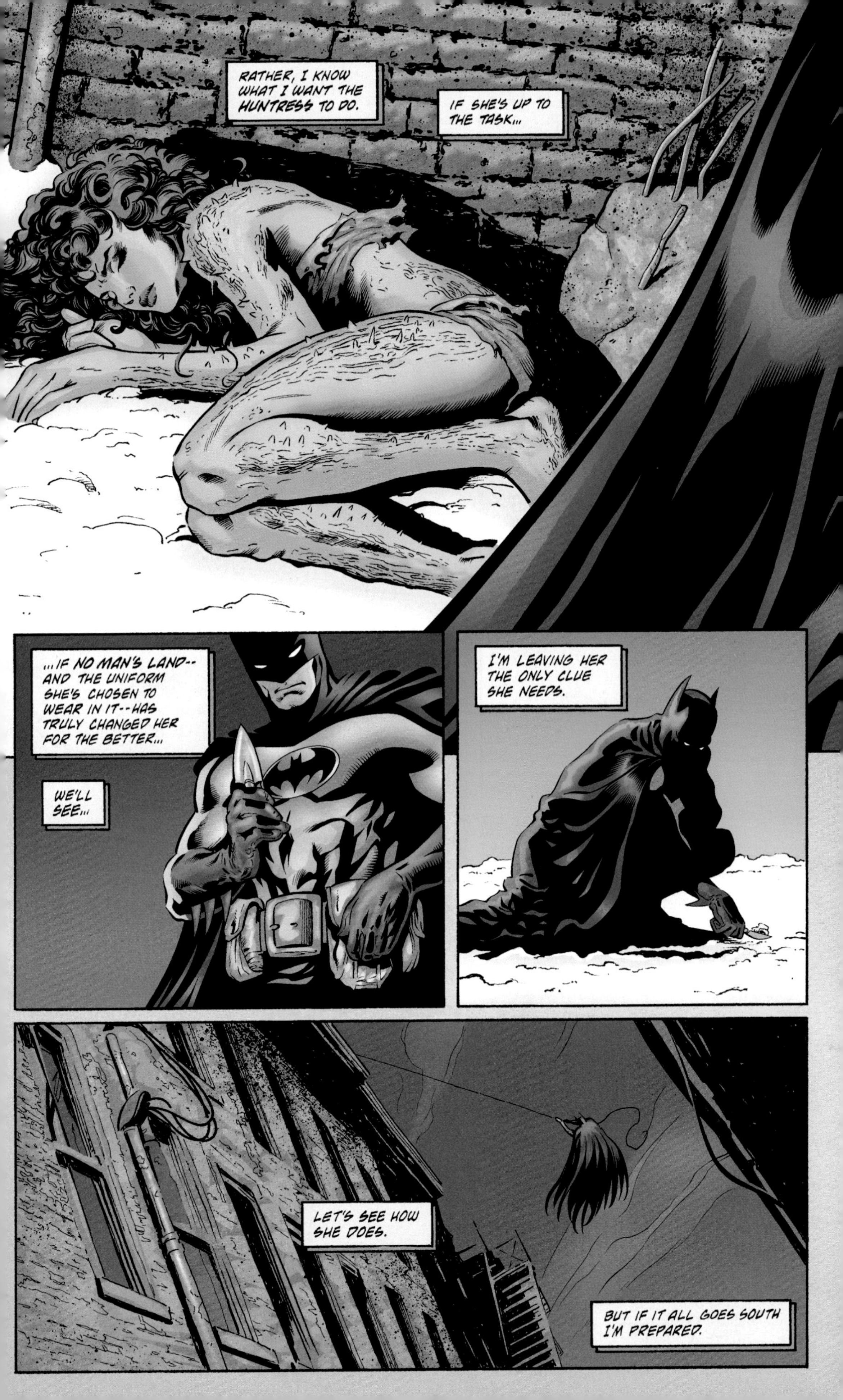
RATHER, I KNOW WHAT I WANT THE HUNTRESS TO DO.
IF SHE'S UP TO THE TASK...
...IF NO MAN'S LAND-- AND THE UNIFORM SHE'S CHOSEN TO WEAR IN IT--HAS TRULY CHANGED HER FOR THE BETTER...
WE'LL SEE...
I'M LEAVING HER THE ONLY CLUE SHE NEEDS.
LET'S SEE HOW SHE DOES.
BUT IF IT ALL GOES SOUTH I'M PREPARED.

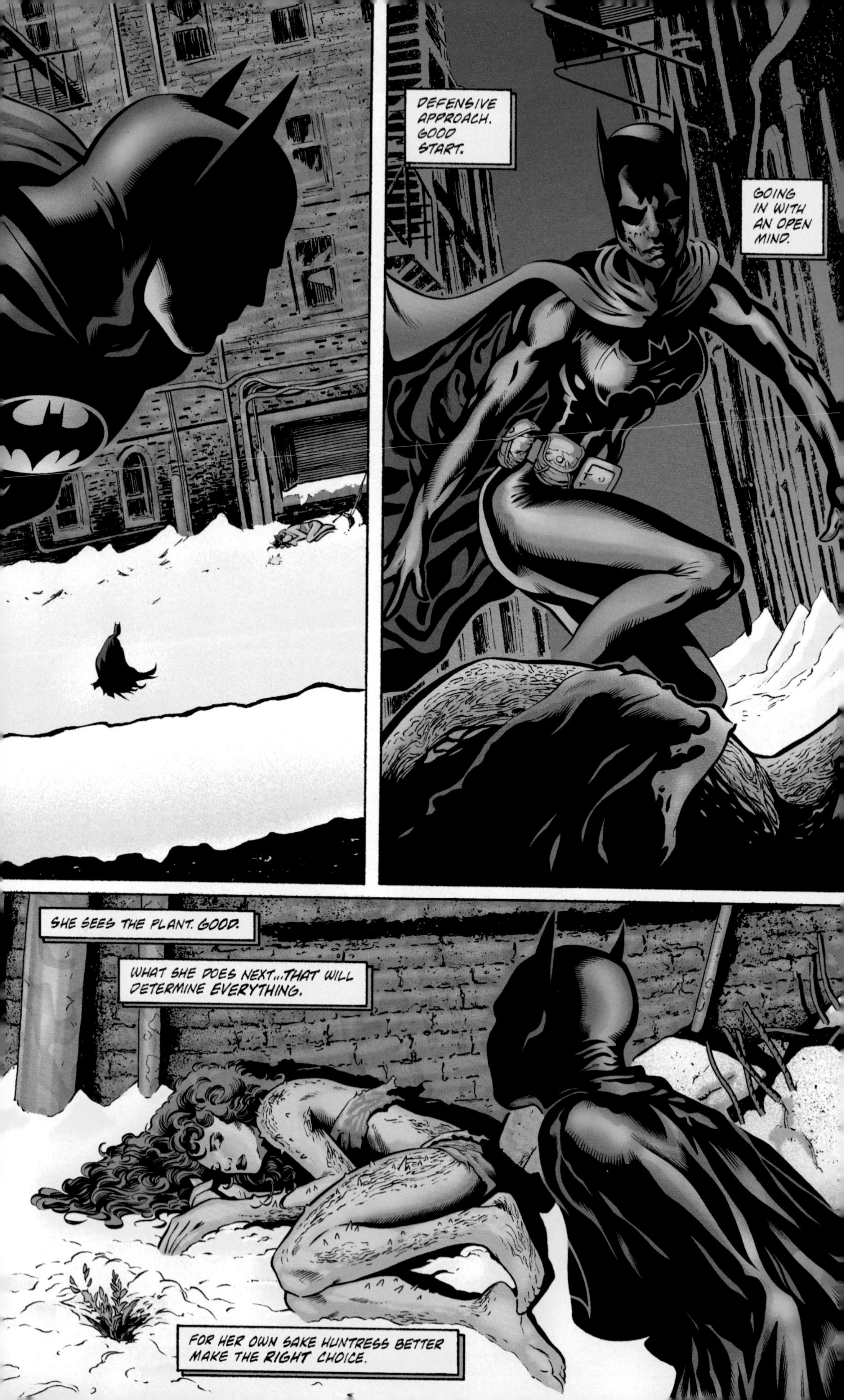
DEFENSIVE APPROACH. GOOD START.
GOING IN WITH AN OPEN MIND.
SHE SEES THE PLANT. GOOD.
WHAT SHE DOES NEXT...THAT WILL DETERMINE EVERYTHING.
FOR HER OWN SAKE HUNTRESS BETTER MAKE THE RIGHT CHOICE.

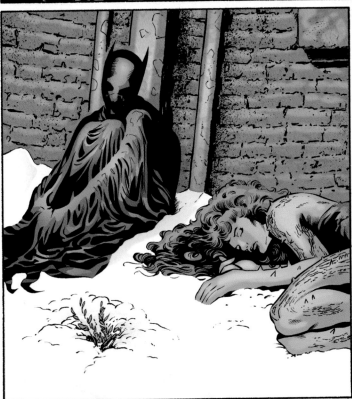

GOOD.

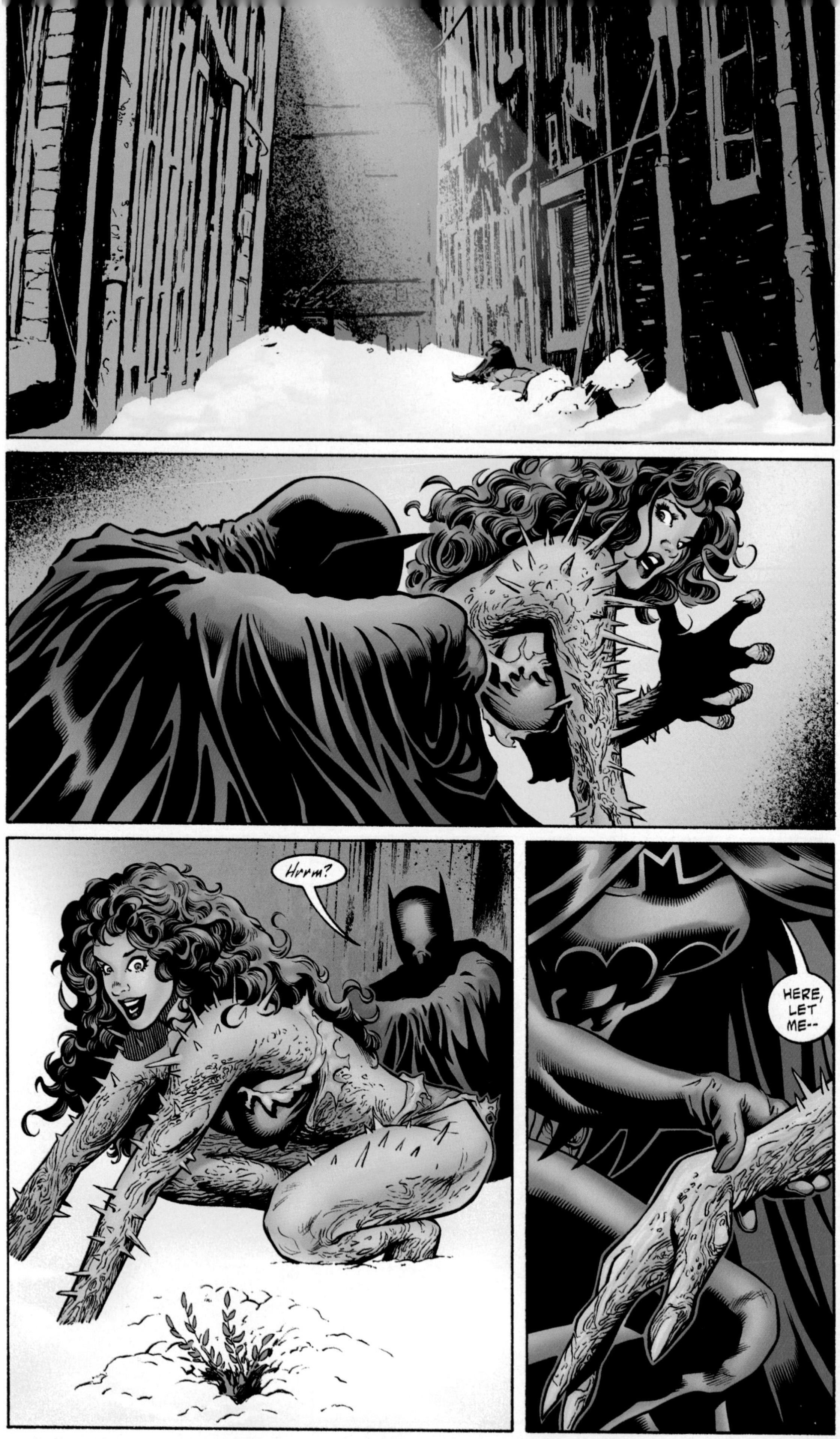
Hrrm?
HERE, LET ME--

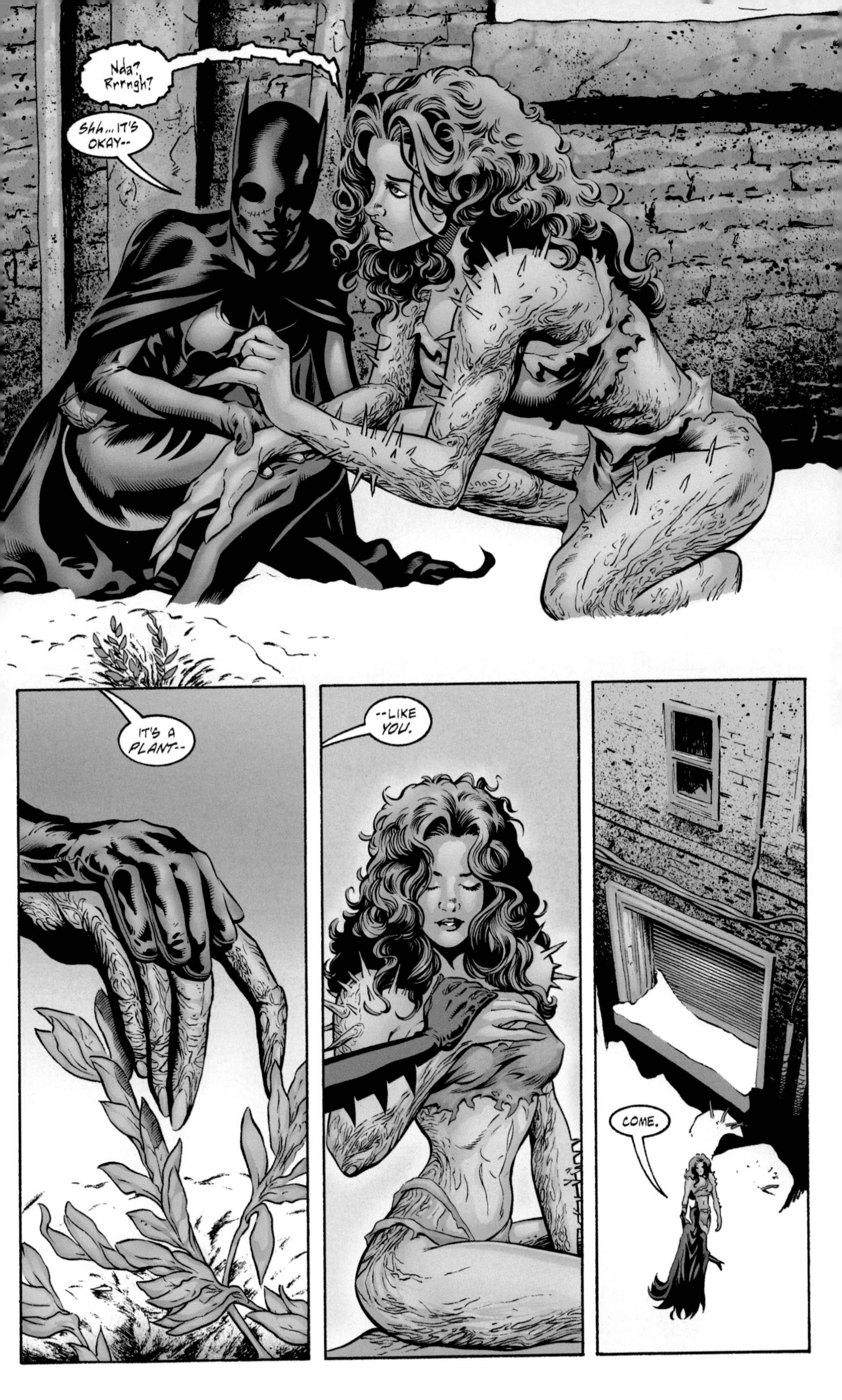
Nda? Rrrngh?
Shh... IT'S OKAY--
IT'S A PLANT--
--LIKE YOU.
COME.

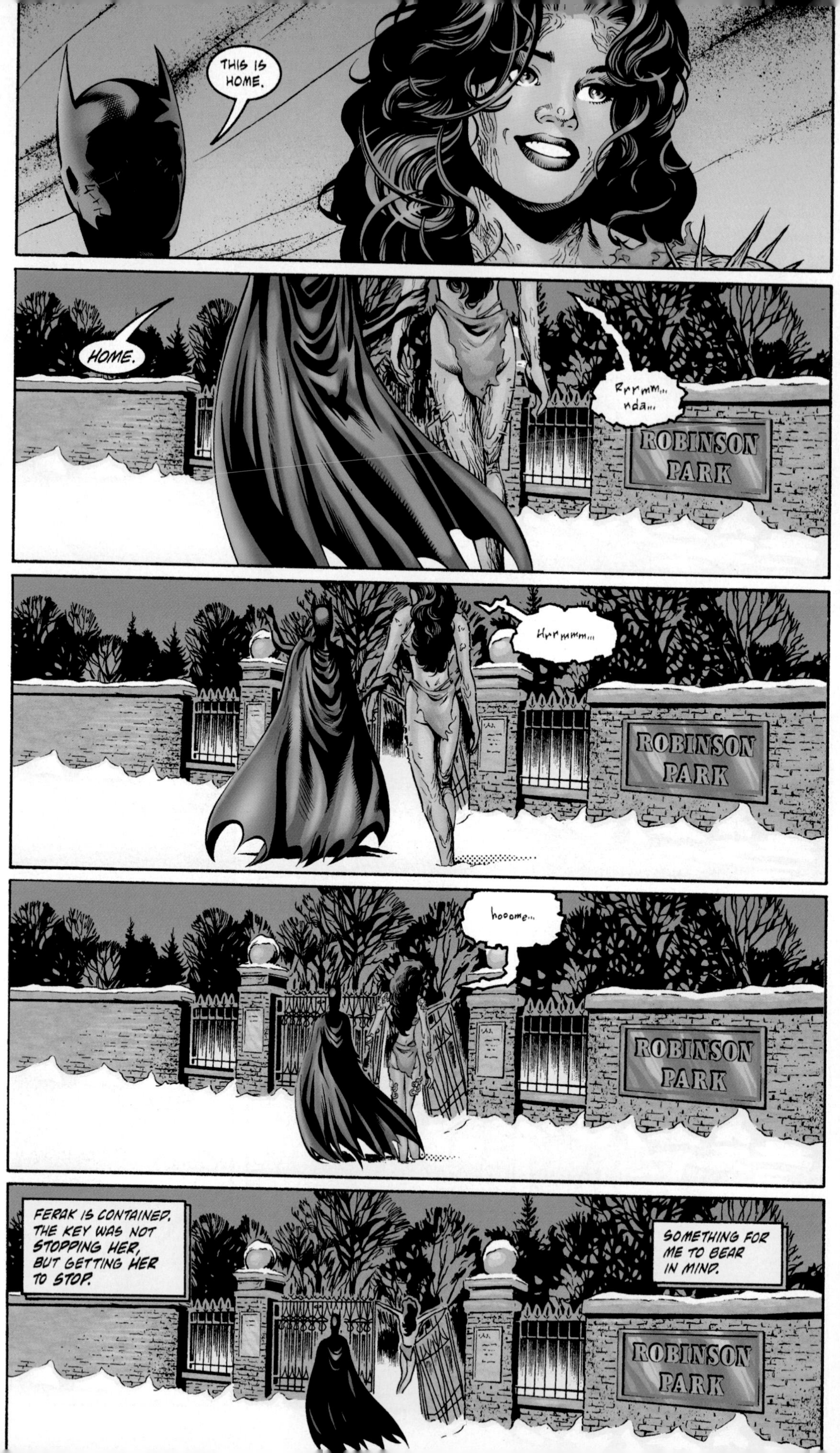
THIS IS HOME.
HOME.
Rrrmm... nda...
ROBINSON PARK
Hrrmmm...
ROBINSON PARK
hooome...
ROBINSON PARK
FERAK IS CONTAINED. THE KEY WAS NOT STOPPING HER, BUT GETTING HER TO STOP.
SOMETHING FOR ME TO BEAR IN MIND.
ROBINSON PARK

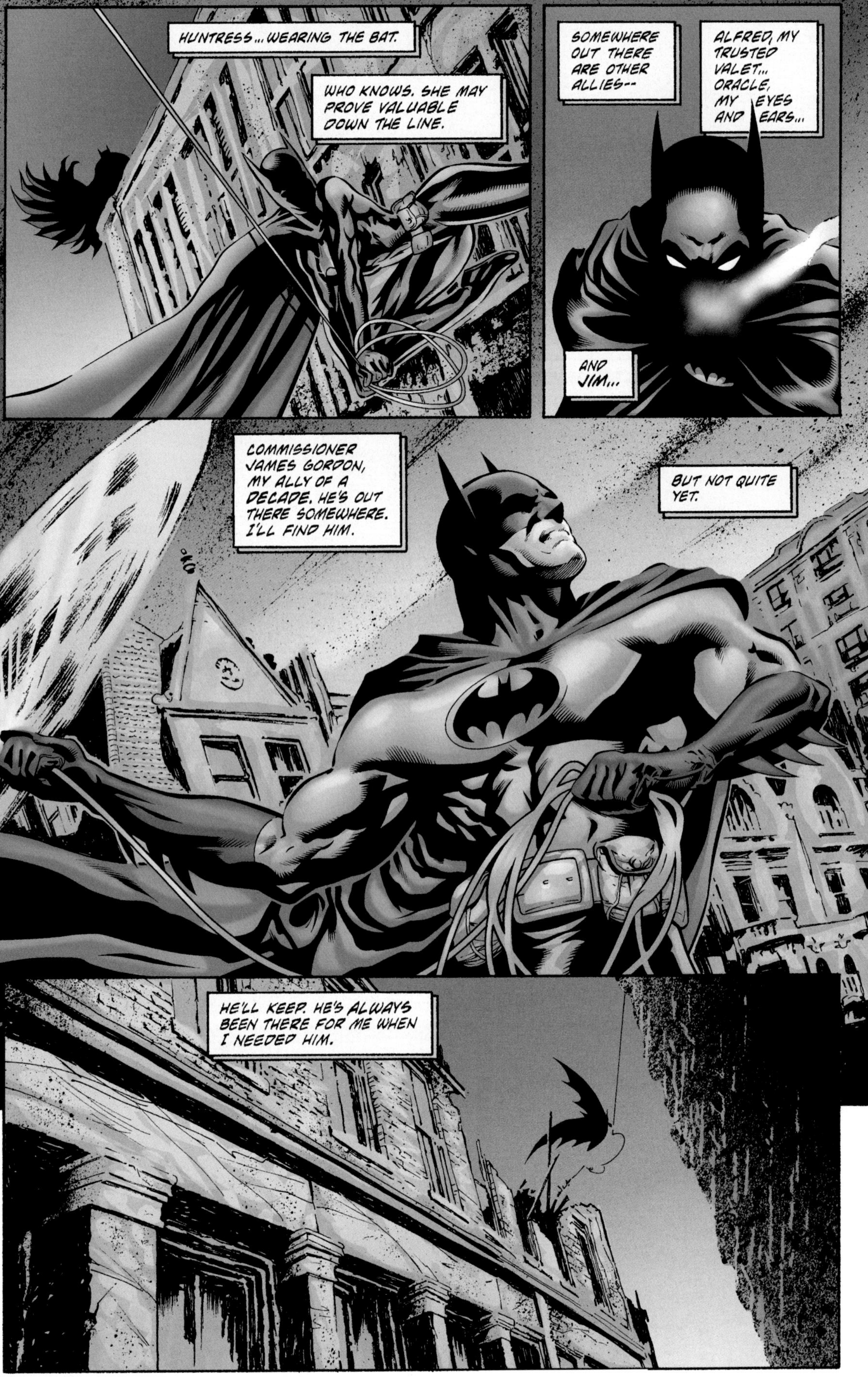
HUNTRESS... WEARING THE BAT.
WHO KNOWS. SHE MAY PROVE VALUABLE DOWN THE LINE.
SOMEWHERE OUT THERE ARE OTHER ALLIES--
ALFRED, MY TRUSTED VALET... ORACLE, MY EYES AND EARS...
AND JIM...
COMMISSIONER JAMES GORDON, MY ALLY OF A DECADE. HE'S OUT THERE SOMEWHERE. I'LL FIND HIM.
BUT NOT QUITE YET.
HE'LL KEEP. HE'S ALWAYS BEEN THERE FOR ME WHEN I NEEDED HIM.

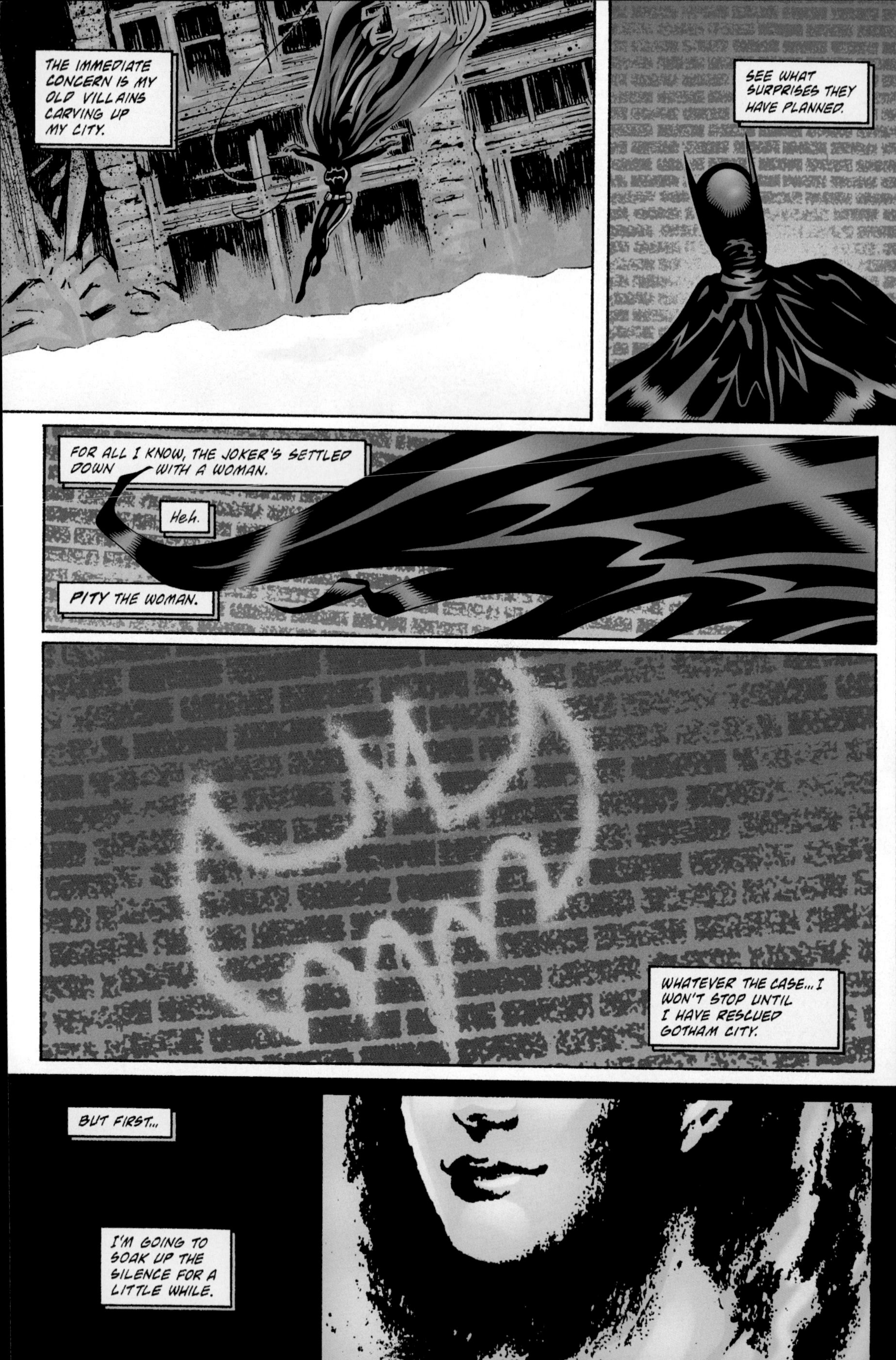
THE IMMEDIATE CONCERN IS MY OLD VILLAINS CARVING UP MY CITY.
SEE WHAT SURPRISES THEY HAVE PLANNED.
FOR ALL I KNOW, THE JOKER'S SETTLED DOWN WITH A WOMAN.
Heh.
PITY THE WOMAN.
WHATEVER THE CASE... I WON'T STOP UNTIL I HAVE RESCUED GOTHAM CITY.
BUT FIRST...
I'M GOING TO SOAK UP THE SILENCE FOR A LITTLE WHILE.

THE BEGINNING...

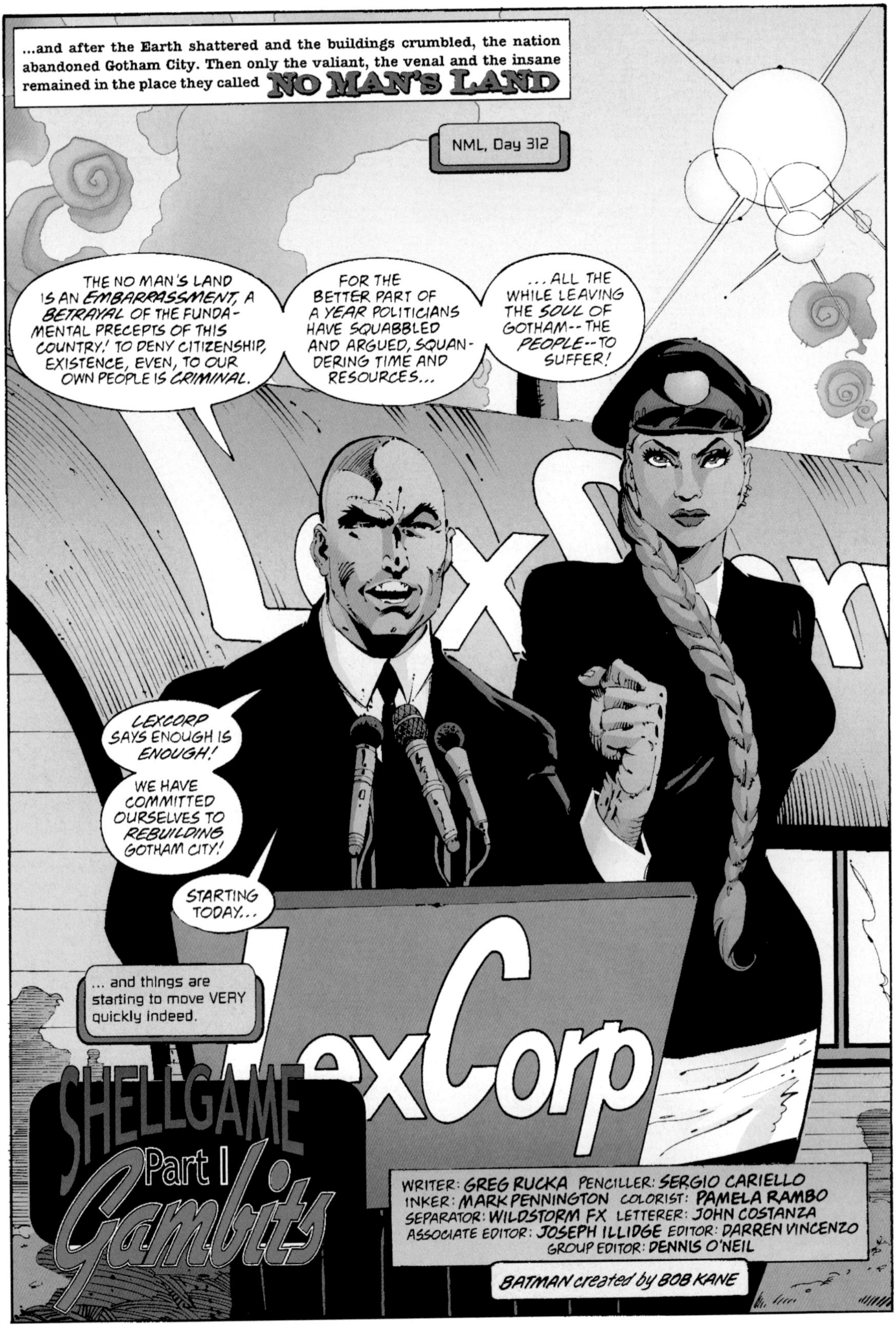
...and after the Earth shattered and the buildings crumbled, the nation abandoned Gotham City. Then only the valiant, the venal and the insane remained in the place they called NO MAN'S LAND
NML, Day 312
THE NO MAN'S LAND IS AN EMBARRASSMENT, A BETRAYAL OF THE FUNDAMENTAL PRECEPTS OF THIS COUNTRY! TO DENY CITIZENSHIP, EXISTENCE, EVEN, TO OUR OWN PEOPLE IS CRIMINAL.
FOR THE BETTER PART OF A YEAR POLITICIANS HAVE SQUABBLED AND ARGUED, SQUANDERING TIME AND RESOURCES...
...ALL THE WHILE LEAVING THE SOUL OF GOTHAM--THE PEOPLE--TO SUFFER!
LEXCORP SAYS ENOUGH IS ENOUGH!
WE HAVE COMMITTED OURSELVES TO REBUILDING GOTHAM CITY!
STARTING TODAY...
... and things are starting to move VERY quickly indeed.
SHELLGAME Part I Gambits
WRITER: GREG RUCKA PENCILLER: SERGIO CARIELLO
INKER: MARK PENNINGTON COLORIST: PAMELA RAMBO
SEPARATOR: WILDSTORM FX LETTERER: JOHN COSTANZA
ASSOCIATE EDITOR: JOSEPH ILLIDGE EDITOR: DARREN VINCENZO
GROUP EDITOR: DENNIS O'NEIL
BATMAN created by BOB KANE

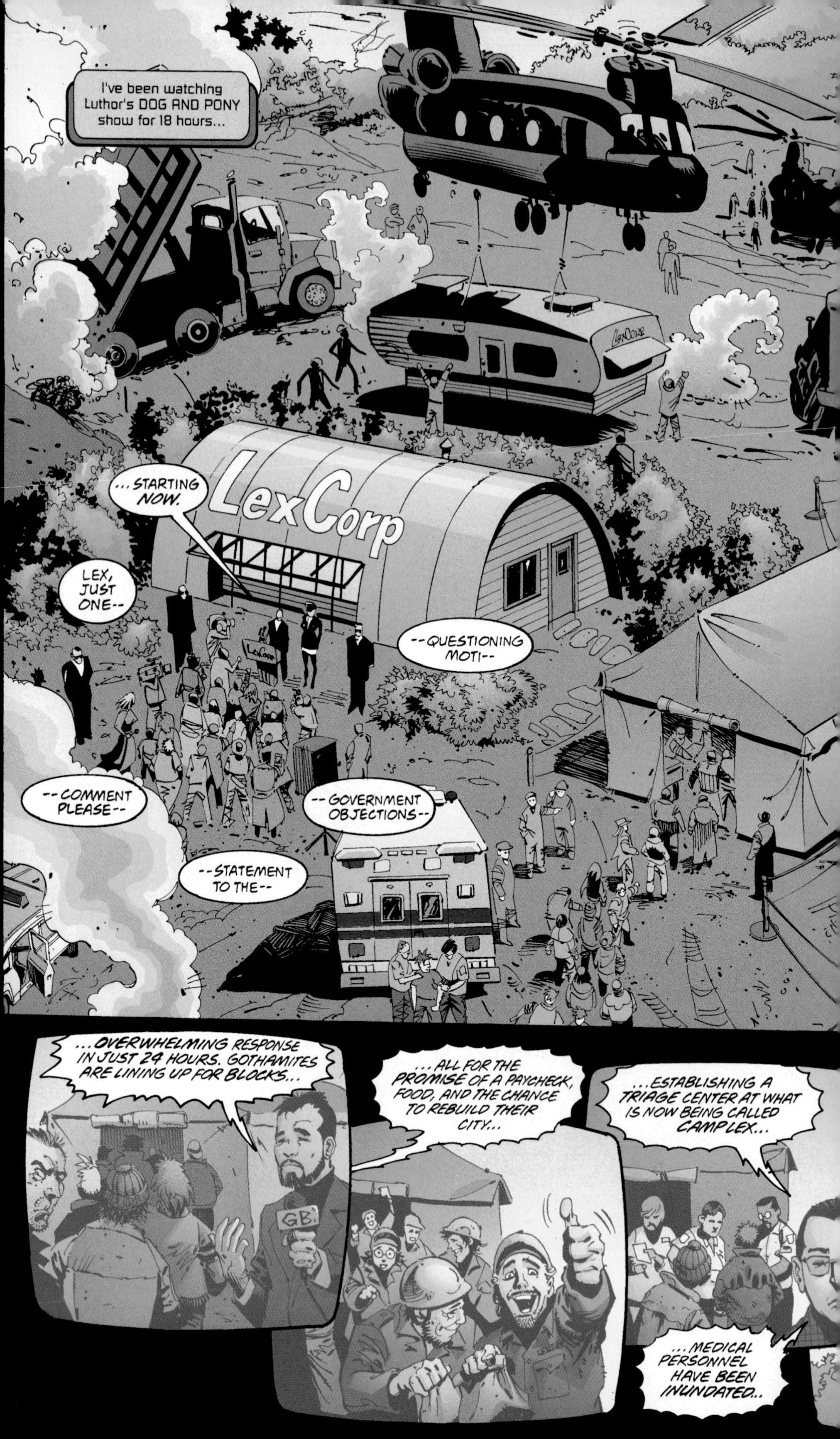
I've been watching Luthor's DOG AND PONY show for 18 hours...
...STARTING NOW.
LexCorp
LEX, JUST ONE--
--QUESTIONING MOTI--
--COMMENT PLEASE--
--GOVERNMENT OBJECTIONS--
--STATEMENT TO THE--
...OVERWHELMING RESPONSE IN JUST 24 HOURS. GOTHAMITES ARE LINING UP FOR BLOCKS...
GB
...ALL FOR THE PROMISE OF A PAYCHECK, FOOD, AND THE CHANCE TO REBUILD THEIR CITY...
...ESTABLISHING A TRIAGE CENTER AT WHAT IS NOW BEING CALLED CAMP LEX...
...MEDICAL PERSONNEL HAVE BEEN INUNDATED...

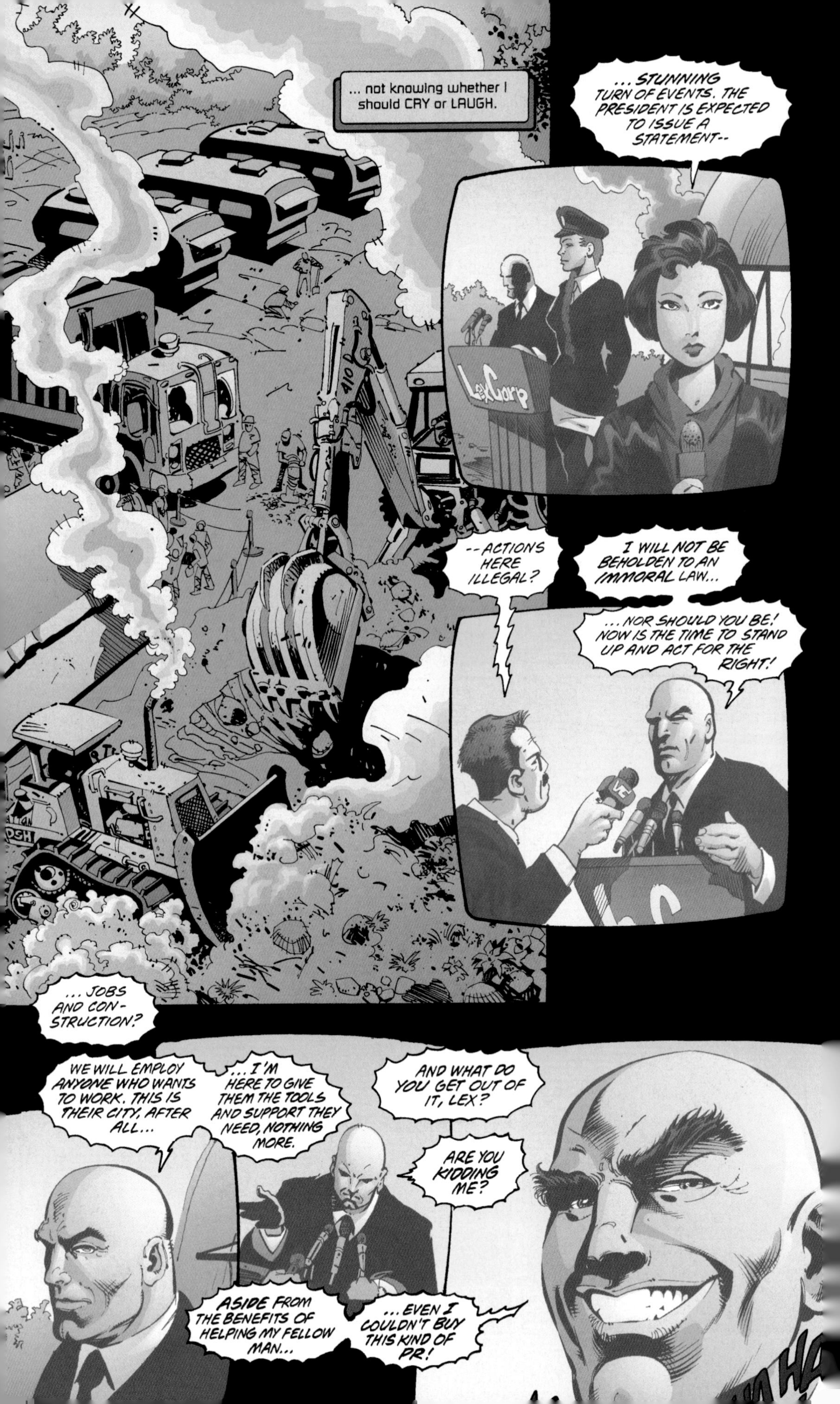

... not knowing whether I should CRY or LAUGH.
... STUNNING TURN OF EVENTS. THE PRESIDENT IS EXPECTED TO ISSUE A STATEMENT--
LexCorp
--ACTIONS HERE ILLEGAL?
I WILL NOT BE BEHOLDEN TO AN IMMORAL LAW...
... NOR SHOULD YOU BE! NOW IS THE TIME TO STAND UP AND ACT FOR THE RIGHT!
410
... JOBS AND CON-STRUCTION?
WE WILL EMPLOY ANYONE WHO WANTS TO WORK. THIS IS THEIR CITY, AFTER ALL...
... I'M HERE TO GIVE THEM THE TOOLS AND SUPPORT THEY NEED, NOTHING MORE.
AND WHAT DO YOU GET OUT OF IT, LEX?
ARE YOU KIDDING ME?
ASIDE FROM THE BENEFITS OF HELPING MY FELLOW MAN...
... EVEN I COULDN'T BUY THIS KIND OF PR!

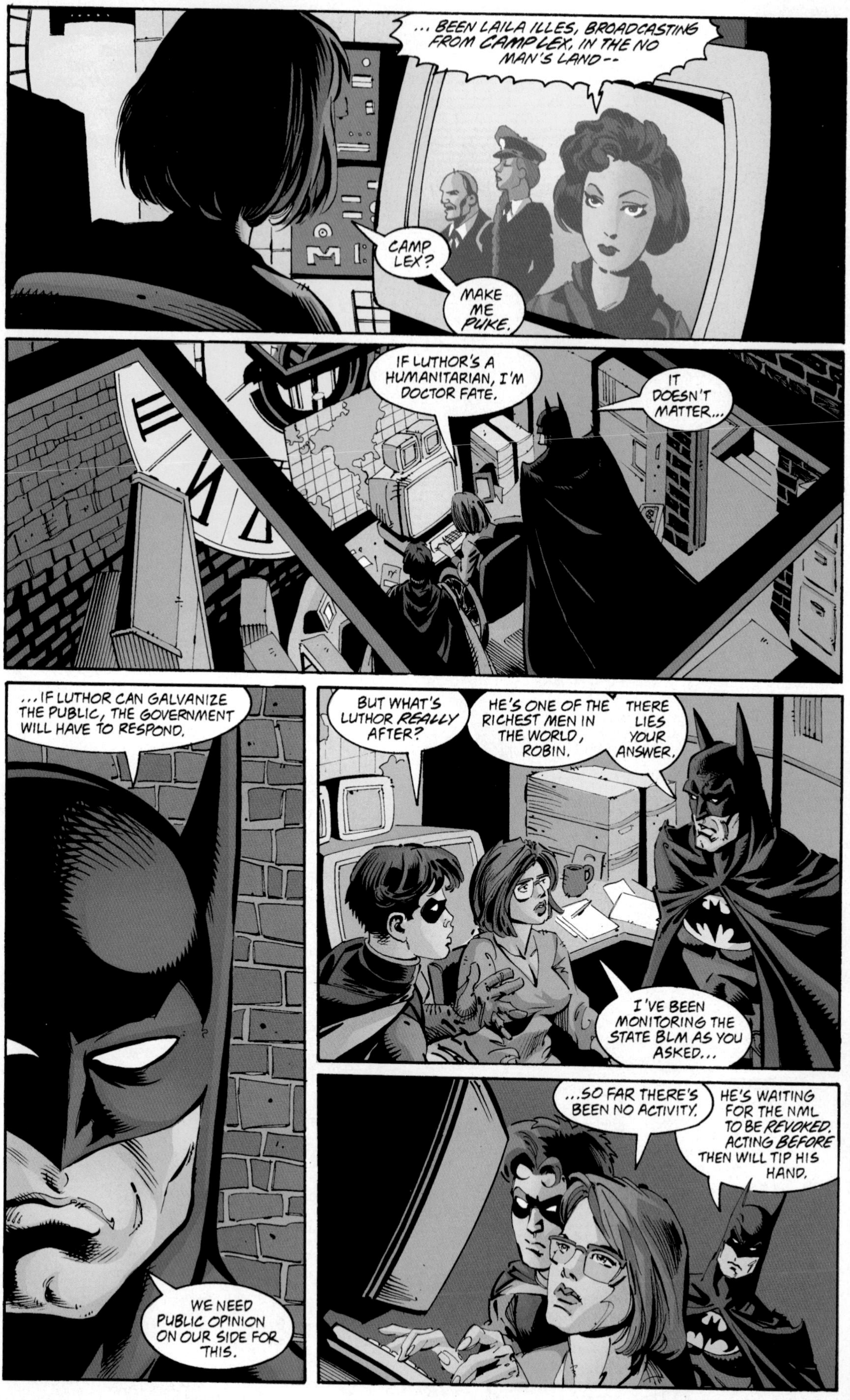

...BEEN LAILA ILLES, BROADCASTING FROM CAMP LEX, IN THE NO MAN'S LAND--
CAMP LEX?
MAKE ME PUKE.
IF LUTHOR'S A HUMANITARIAN, I'M DOCTOR FATE.
IT DOESN'T MATTER...
...IF LUTHOR CAN GALVANIZE THE PUBLIC, THE GOVERNMENT WILL HAVE TO RESPOND.
WE NEED PUBLIC OPINION ON OUR SIDE FOR THIS.
BUT WHAT'S LUTHOR REALLY AFTER?
HE'S ONE OF THE RICHEST MEN IN THE WORLD, ROBIN.
THERE LIES YOUR ANSWER.
I'VE BEEN MONITORING THE STATE BLM AS YOU ASKED...
...SO FAR THERE'S BEEN NO ACTIVITY.
HE'S WAITING FOR THE NML TO BE REVOKED. ACTING BEFORE THEN WILL TIP HIS HAND.

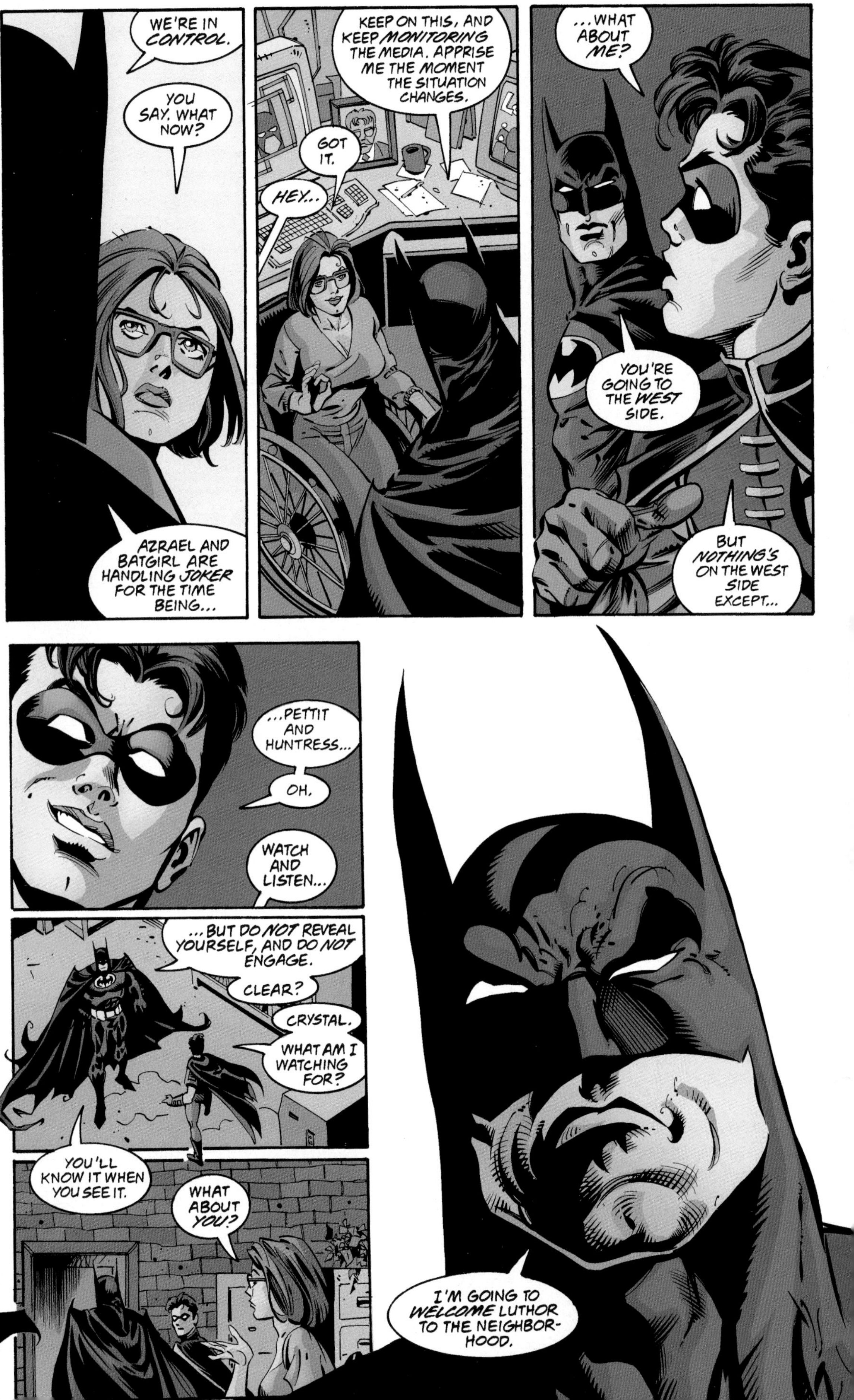

WE'RE IN CONTROL.
YOU SAY. WHAT NOW?
AZRAEL AND BATGIRL ARE HANDLING JOKER FOR THE TIME BEING...
KEEP ON THIS, AND KEEP MONITORING THE MEDIA. APPRISE ME THE MOMENT THE SITUATION CHANGES.
GOT IT.
HEY...
...WHAT ABOUT ME?
YOU'RE GOING TO THE WEST SIDE.
BUT NOTHING'S ON THE WEST SIDE EXCEPT...
...PETTIT AND HUNTRESS...
OH.
WATCH AND LISTEN...
...BUT DO NOT REVEAL YOURSELF, AND DO NOT ENGAGE.
CLEAR?
CRYSTAL.
WHAT AM I WATCHING FOR?
YOU'LL KNOW IT WHEN YOU SEE IT.
WHAT ABOUT YOU?
I'M GOING TO WELCOME LUTHOR TO THE NEIGHBOR-HOOD.

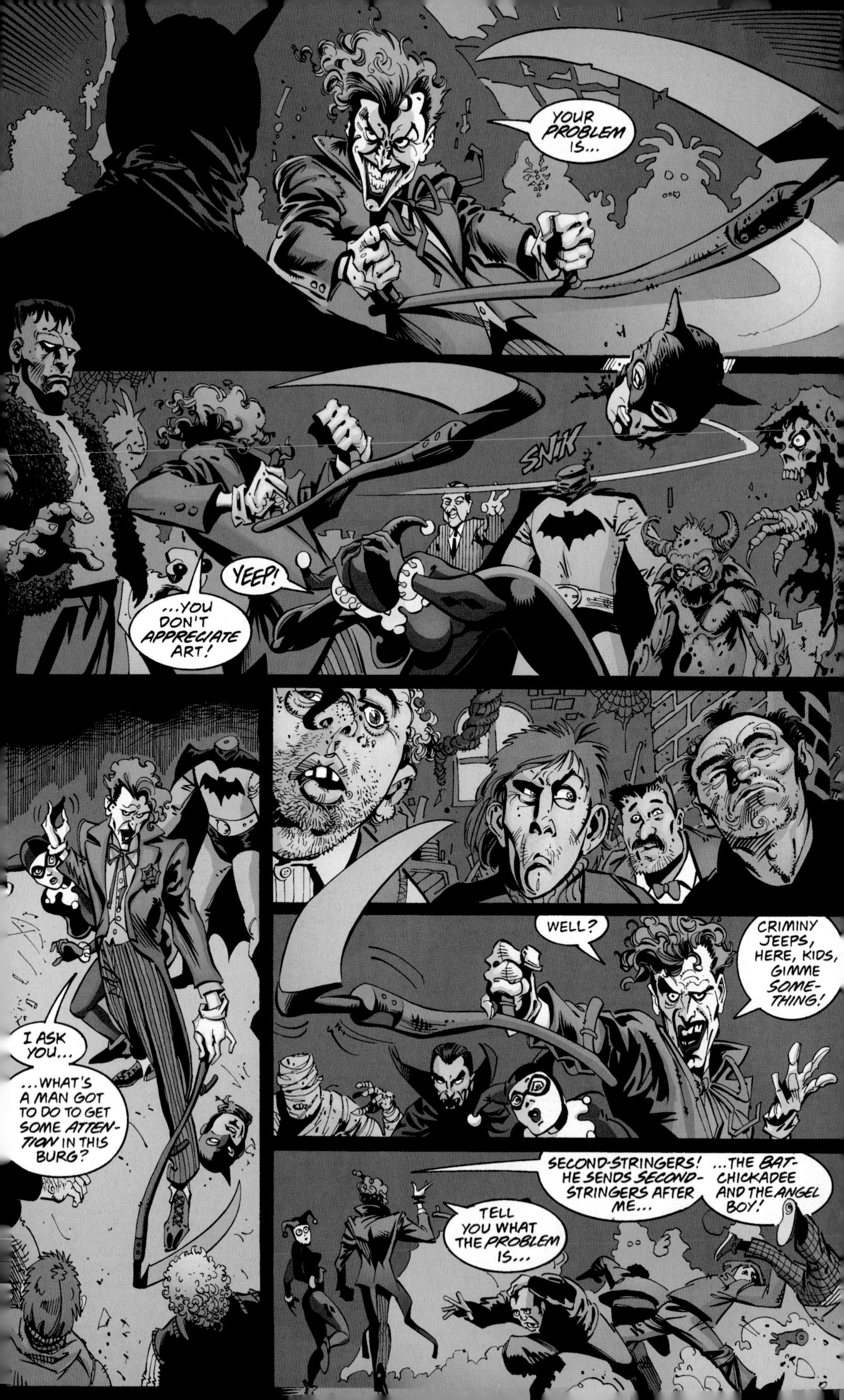
YOUR PROBLEM IS...
SNIK
YEEP!
...YOU DON'T APPRECIATE ART!
I ASK YOU...
...WHAT'S A MAN GOT TO DO TO GET SOME ATTENTION IN THIS BURG?
WELL?
CRIMINY JEEPS, HERE, KIDS, GIMME SOMETHING!
SECOND-STRINGERS! HE SENDS SECOND-STRINGERS AFTER ME...
...THE BAT-CHICKADEE AND THE ANGEL BOY!
TELL YOU WHAT THE PROBLEM IS...

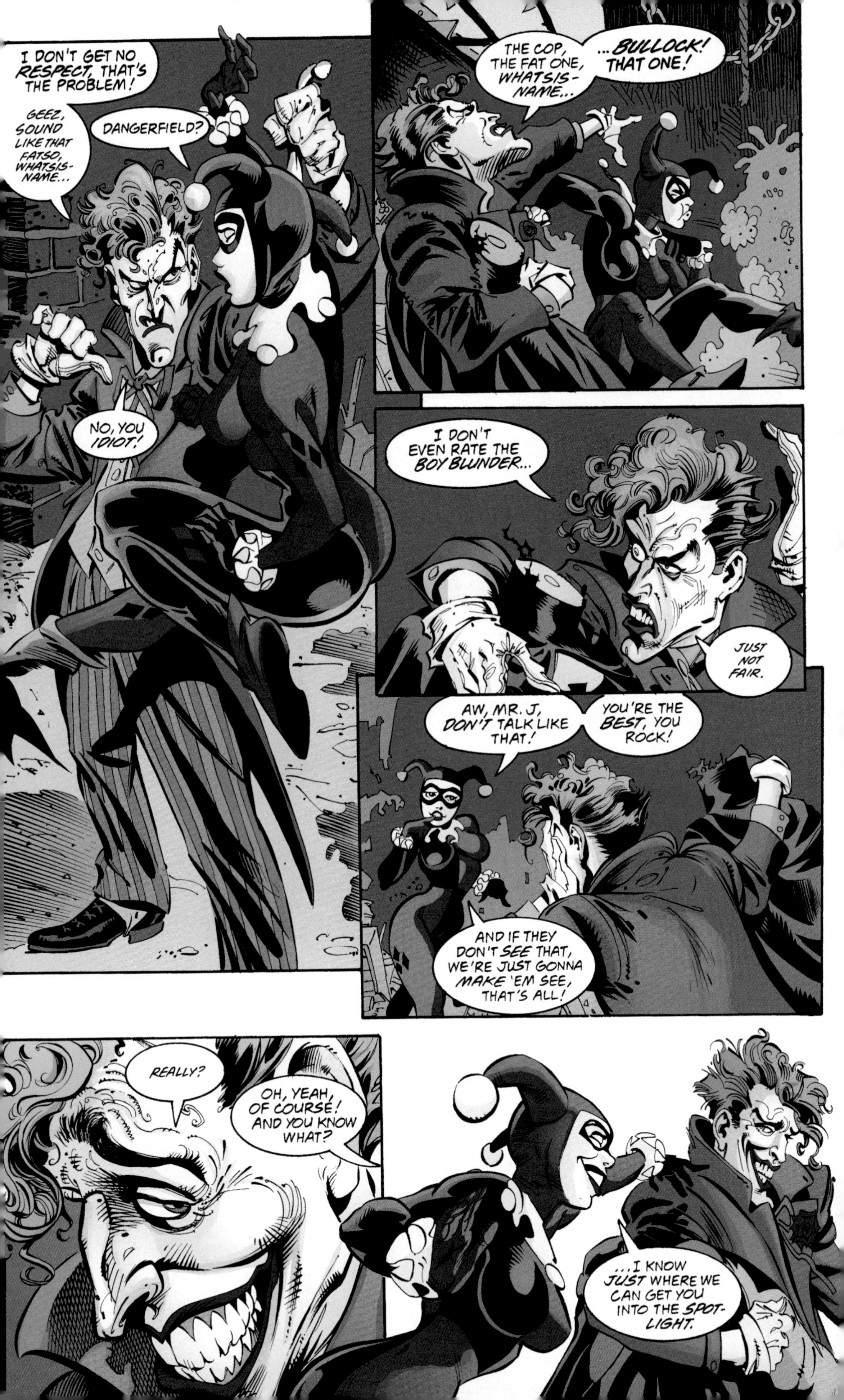
I DON'T GET NO RESPECT, THAT'S THE PROBLEM!
GEEZ, SOUND LIKE THAT FATSO, WHATSIS-NAME...
DANGERFIELD?
NO, YOU IDIOT!
THE COP, THE FAT ONE, WHATSIS-NAME...
...BULLOCK! THAT ONE!
I DON'T EVEN RATE THE BOY BLUNDER...
JUST NOT FAIR.
AW, MR. J, DON'T TALK LIKE THAT!
YOU'RE THE BEST, YOU ROCK!
AND IF THEY DON'T SEE THAT, WE'RE JUST GONNA MAKE 'EM SEE, THAT'S ALL!
REALLY?
OH, YEAH, OF COURSE! AND YOU KNOW WHAT?
...I KNOW JUST WHERE WE CAN GET YOU INTO THE SPOT-LIGHT.

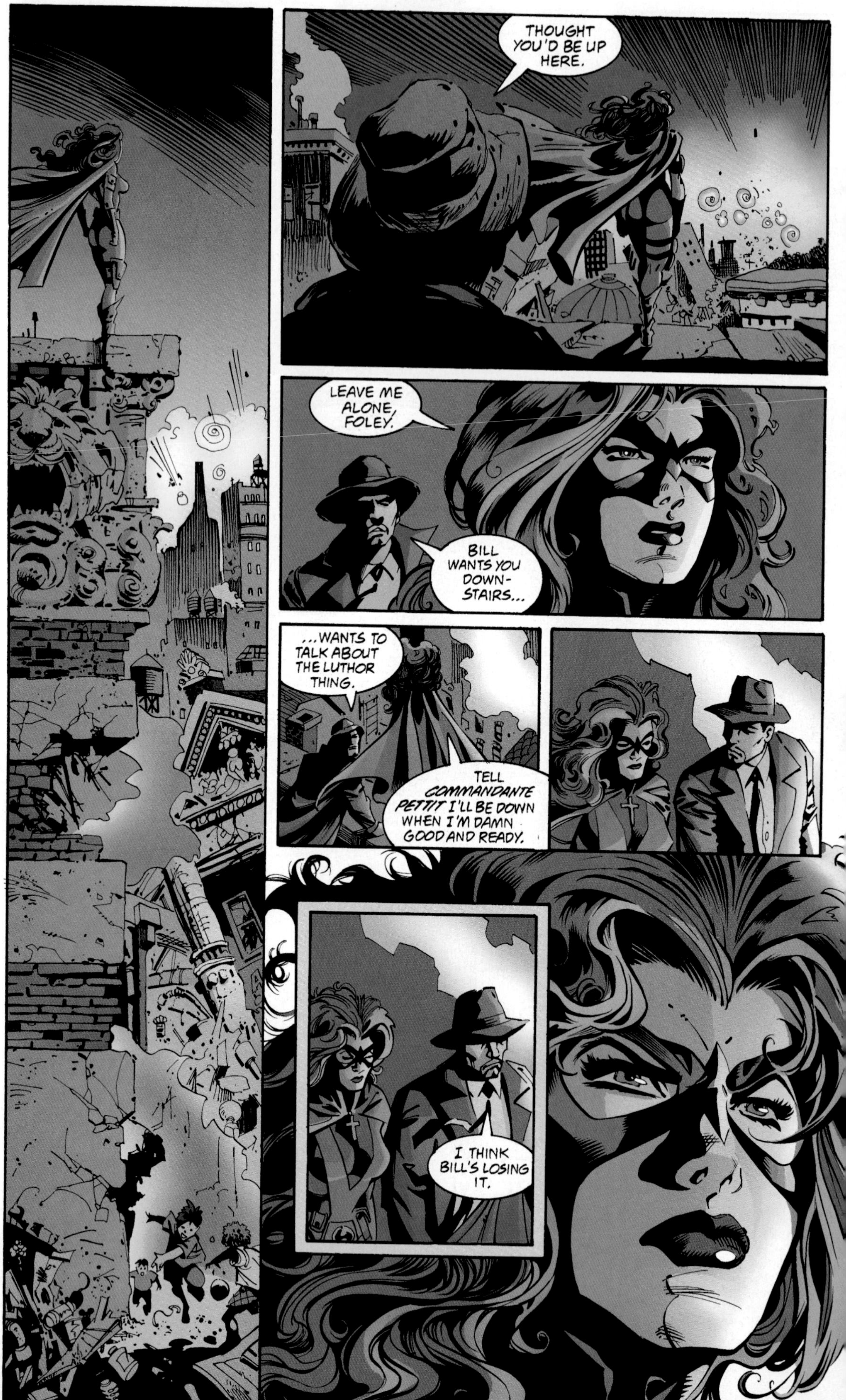
THOUGHT YOU'D BE UP HERE.
LEAVE ME ALONE, FOLEY.
BILL WANTS YOU DOWN-STAIRS...
...WANTS TO TALK ABOUT THE LUTHOR THING.
TELL *COMMANDANTE PETTIT* I'LL BE DOWN WHEN I'M DAMN GOOD AND READY.
I THINK BILL'S LOSING IT.

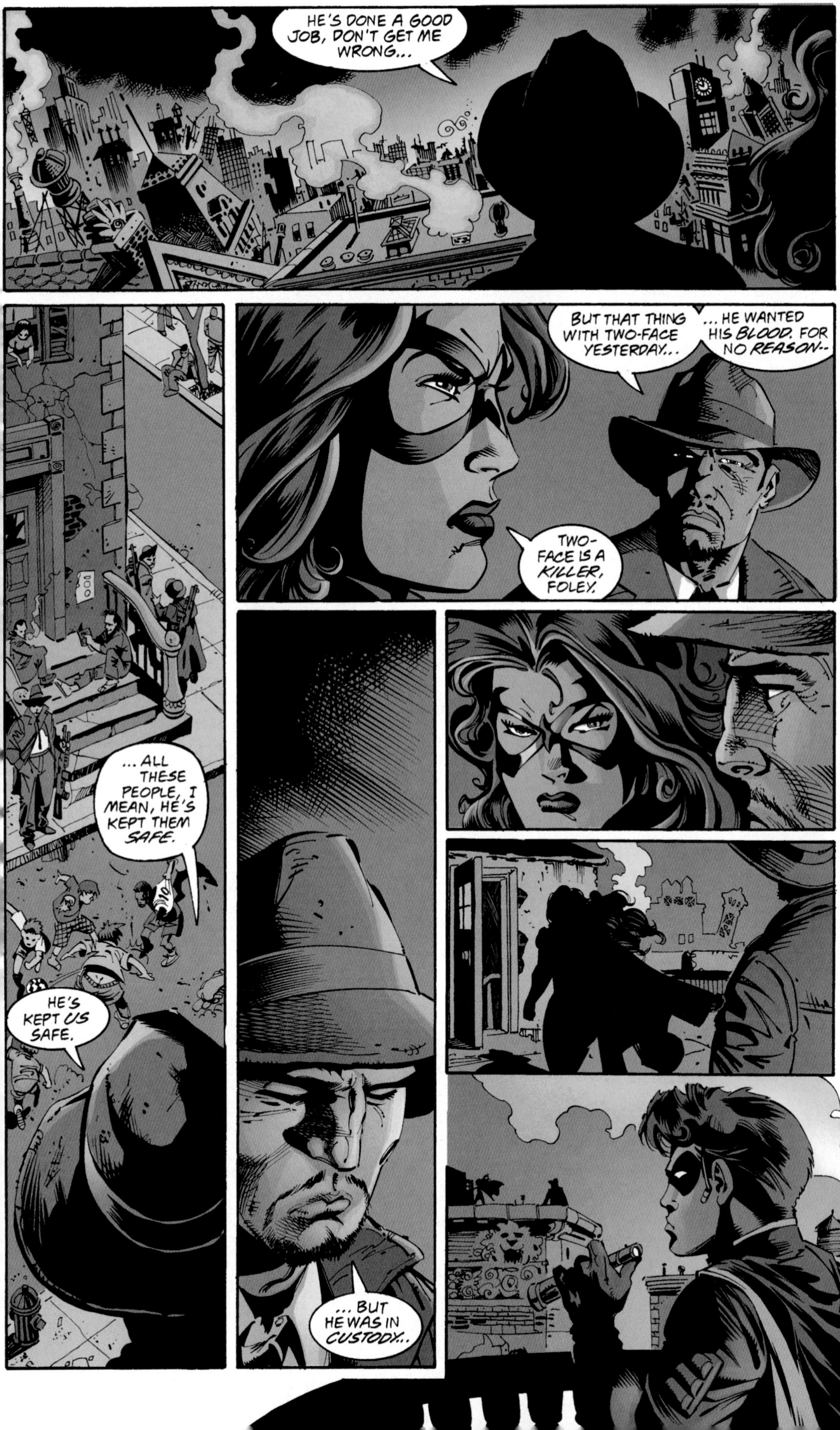

HE'S DONE A GOOD JOB, DON'T GET ME WRONG...
...ALL THESE PEOPLE, I MEAN, HE'S KEPT THEM SAFE.
HE'S KEPT US SAFE.
BUT THAT THING WITH TWO-FACE YESTERDAY...
...HE WANTED HIS BLOOD. FOR NO REASON--
TWO-FACE IS A KILLER, FOLEY.
...BUT HE WAS IN CUSTODY...

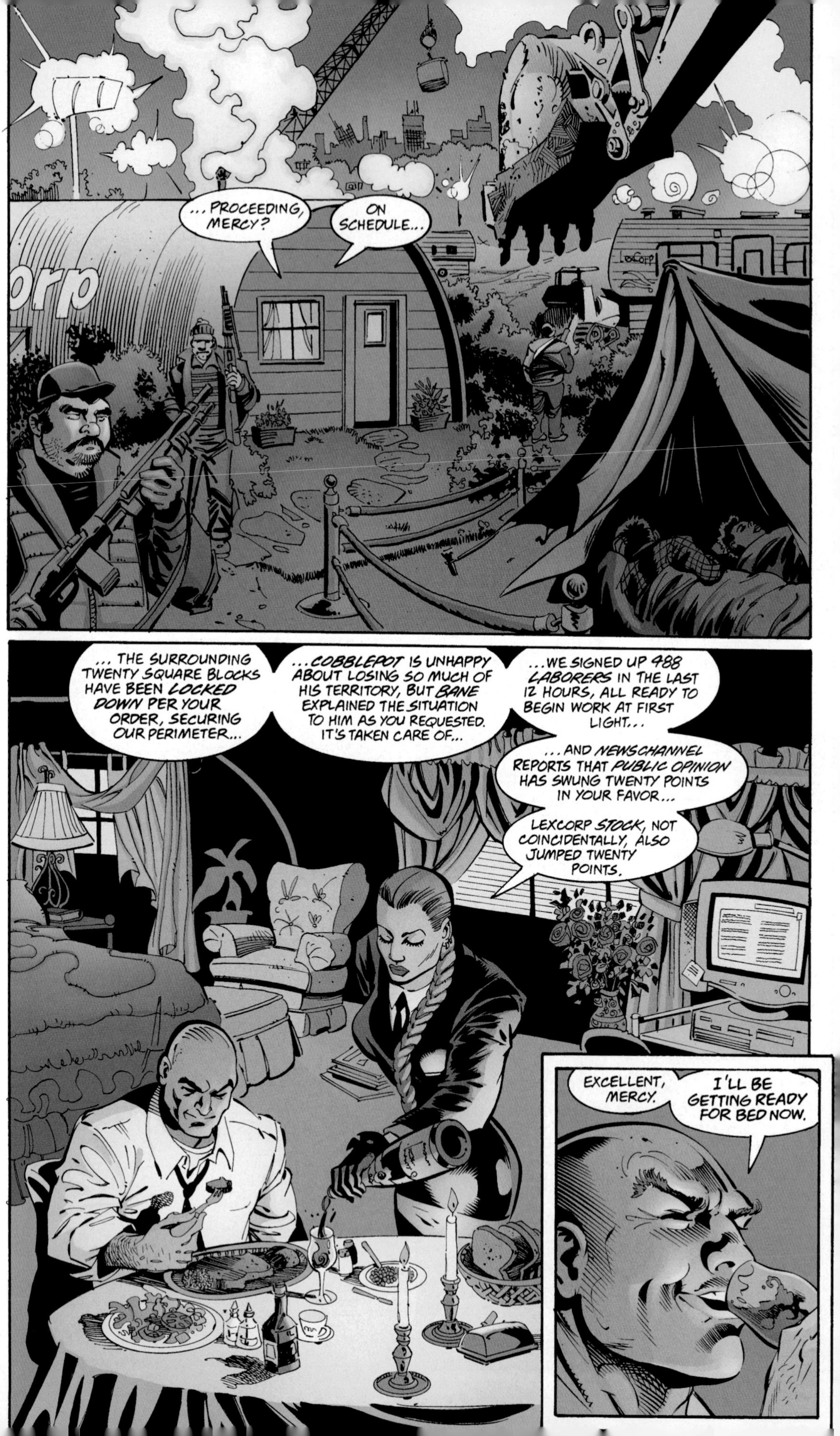
...PROCEEDING, MERCY?
ON SCHEDULE...
...THE SURROUNDING TWENTY SQUARE BLOCKS HAVE BEEN LOCKED DOWN PER YOUR ORDER, SECURING OUR PERIMETER...
...COBBLEPOT IS UNHAPPY ABOUT LOSING SO MUCH OF HIS TERRITORY, BUT BANE EXPLAINED THE SITUATION TO HIM AS YOU REQUESTED. IT'S TAKEN CARE OF...
...WE SIGNED UP 488 LABORERS IN THE LAST 12 HOURS, ALL READY TO BEGIN WORK AT FIRST LIGHT...
...AND NEWSCHANNEL REPORTS THAT PUBLIC OPINION HAS SWUNG TWENTY POINTS IN YOUR FAVOR...
LEXCORP STOCK, NOT COINCIDENTALLY, ALSO JUMPED TWENTY POINTS.
EXCELLENT, MERCY.
I'LL BE GETTING READY FOR BED NOW.

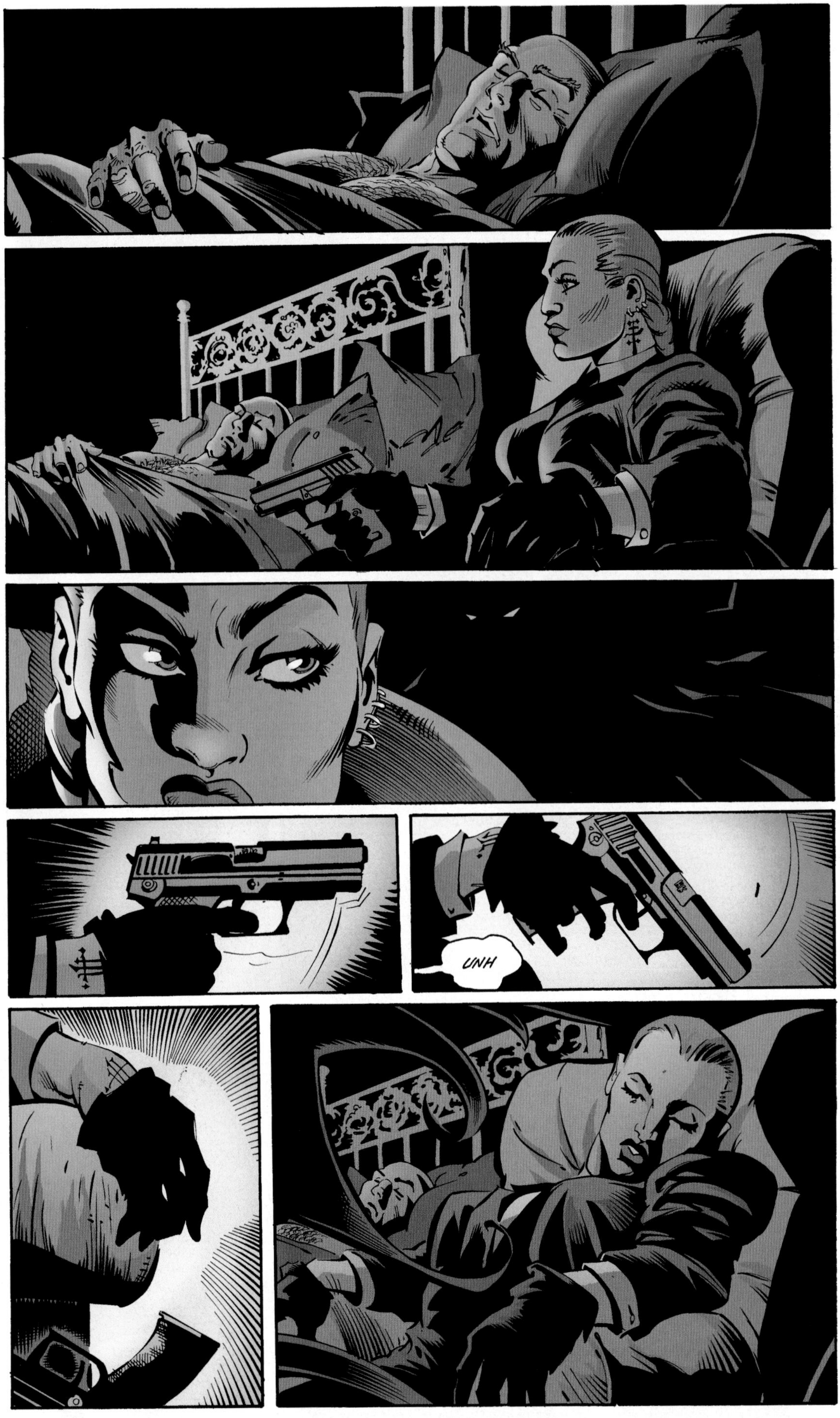
UNH

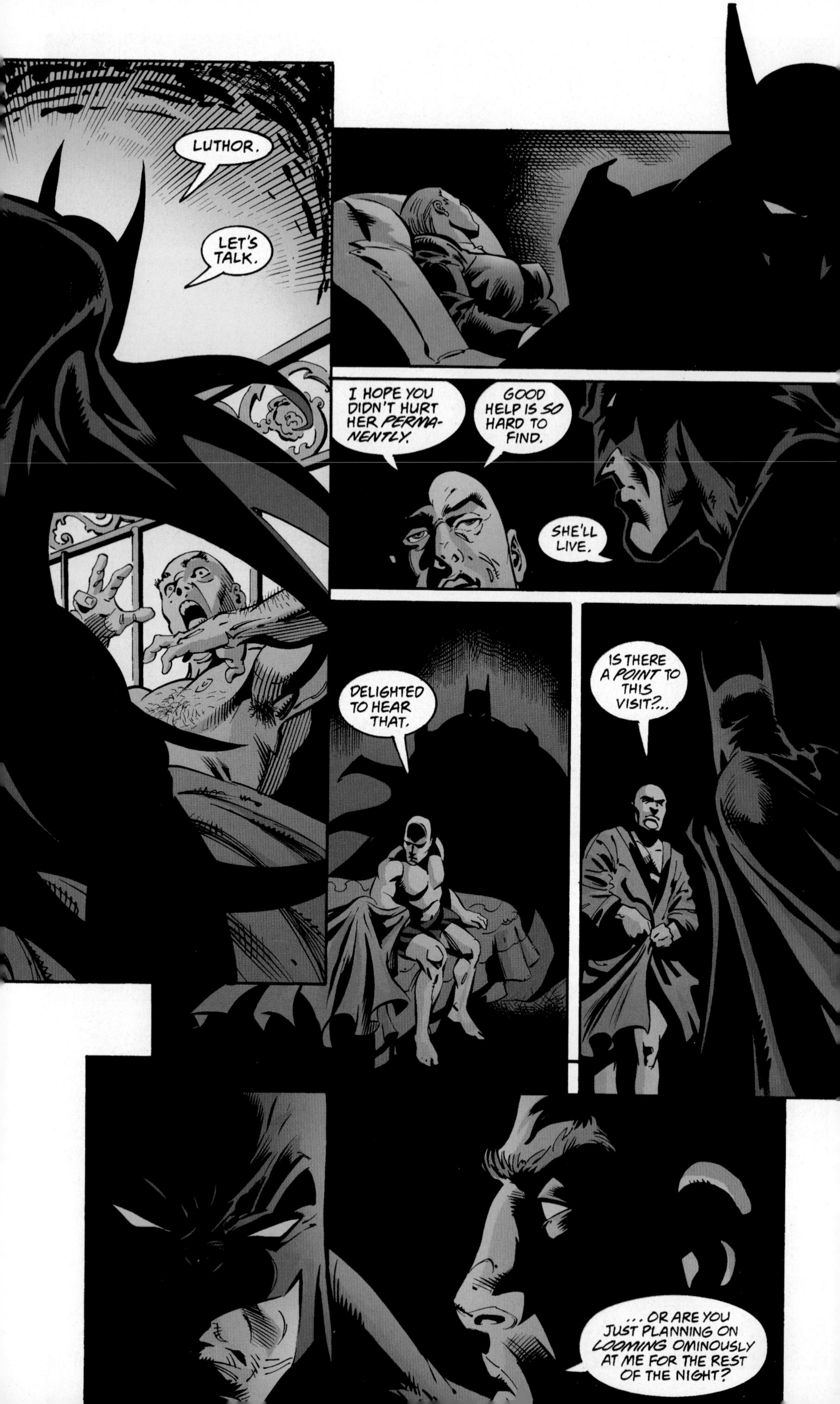
LUTHOR.
LET'S TALK.
I HOPE YOU DIDN'T HURT HER PERMANENTLY.
GOOD HELP IS SO HARD TO FIND.
SHE'LL LIVE.
DELIGHTED TO HEAR THAT.
IS THERE A POINT TO THIS VISIT?...
...OR ARE YOU JUST PLANNING ON LOOMING OMINOUSLY AT ME FOR THE REST OF THE NIGHT?

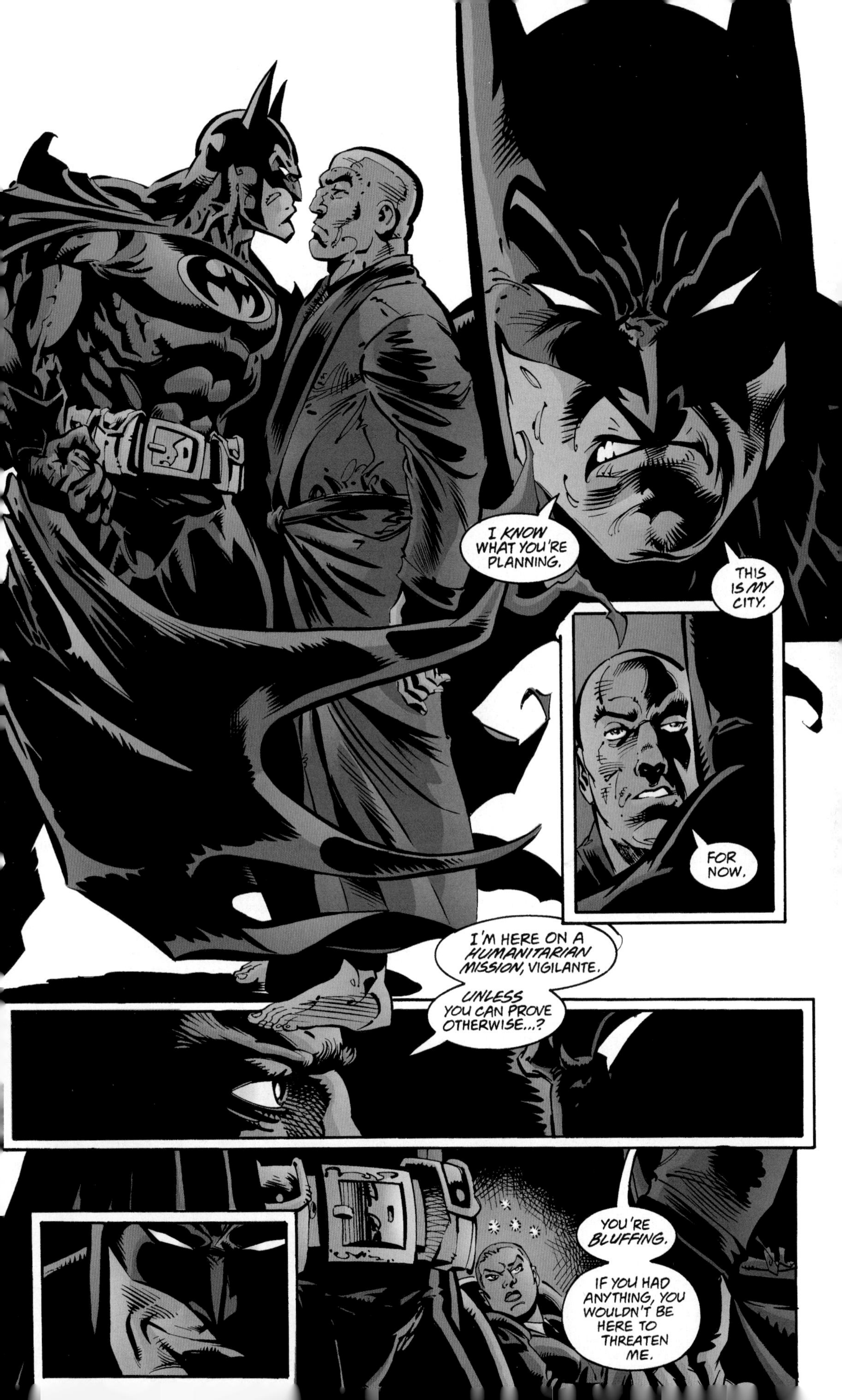
I KNOW WHAT YOU'RE PLANNING.
THIS IS MY CITY.
FOR NOW.
I'M HERE ON A HUMANITARIAN MISSION, VIGILANTE.
UNLESS YOU CAN PROVE OTHERWISE...?
YOU'RE BLUFFING.
IF YOU HAD ANYTHING, YOU WOULDN'T BE HERE TO THREATEN ME.

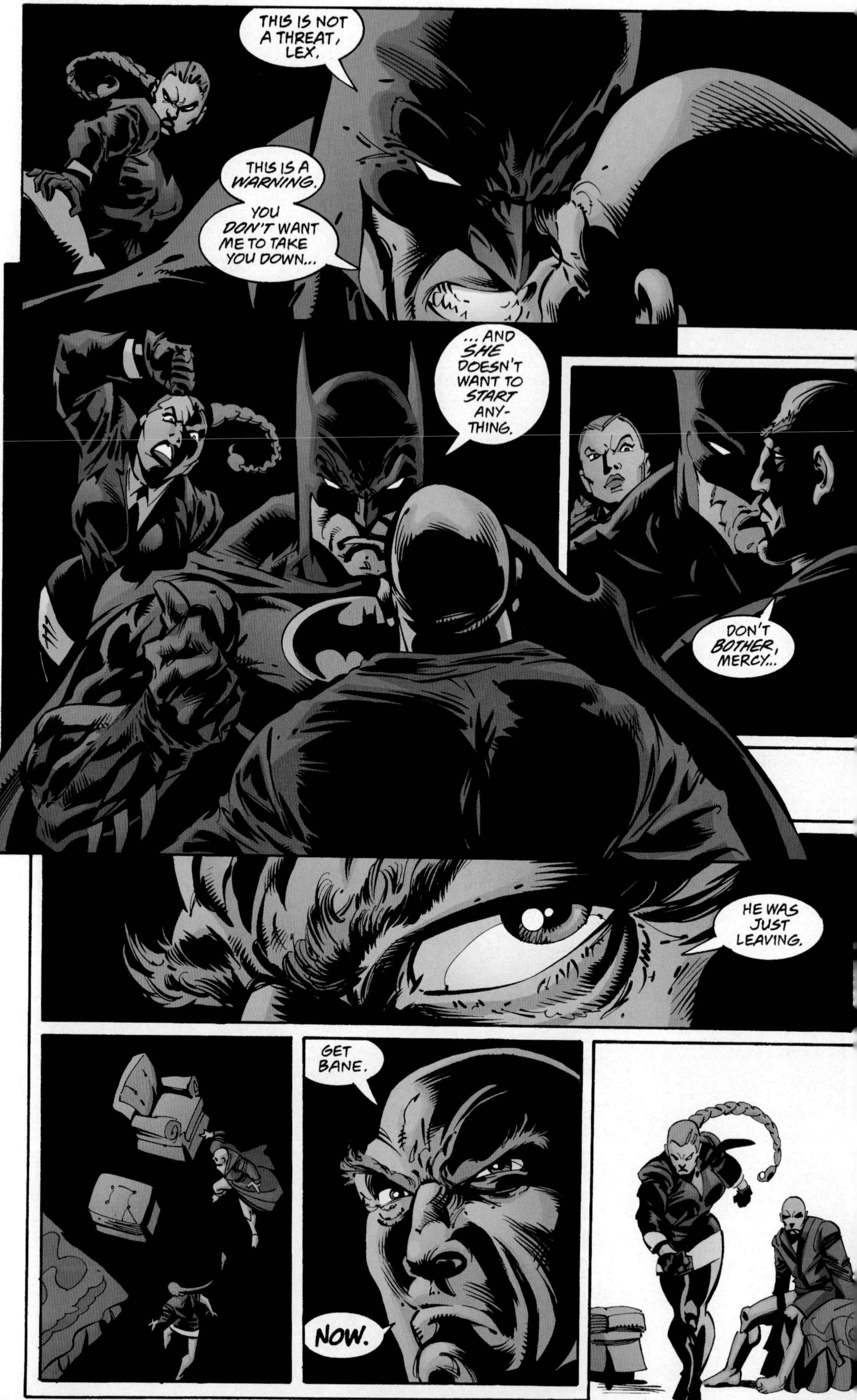
THIS IS NOT A THREAT, LEX.
THIS IS A WARNING.
YOU DON'T WANT ME TO TAKE YOU DOWN...
...AND SHE DOESN'T WANT TO START ANYTHING.
DON'T BOTHER, MERCY...
HE WAS JUST LEAVING.
GET BANE.
NOW.

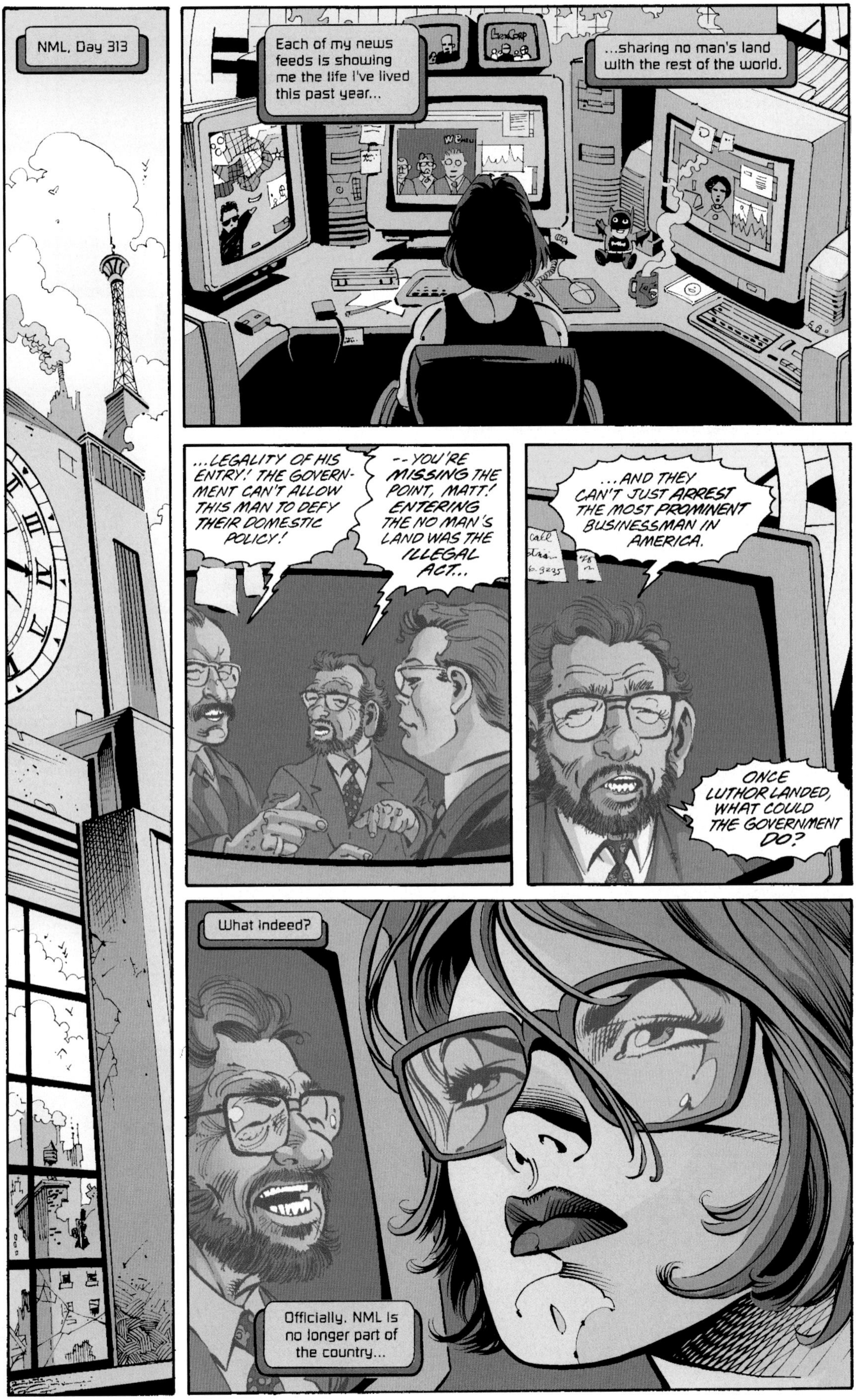

NML, Day 313
Each of my news feeds is showing me the life I've lived this past year...
...sharing no man's land with the rest of the world.
LexCorp
...LEGALITY OF HIS ENTRY! THE GOVERNMENT CAN'T ALLOW THIS MAN TO DEFY THEIR DOMESTIC POLICY!
--YOU'RE MISSING THE POINT, MATT! ENTERING THE NO MAN'S LAND WAS THE ILLEGAL ACT...
...AND THEY CAN'T JUST ARREST THE MOST PROMINENT BUSINESSMAN IN AMERICA.
ONCE LUTHOR LANDED, WHAT COULD THE GOVERNMENT DO?
What indeed?
Officially, NML is no longer part of the country...

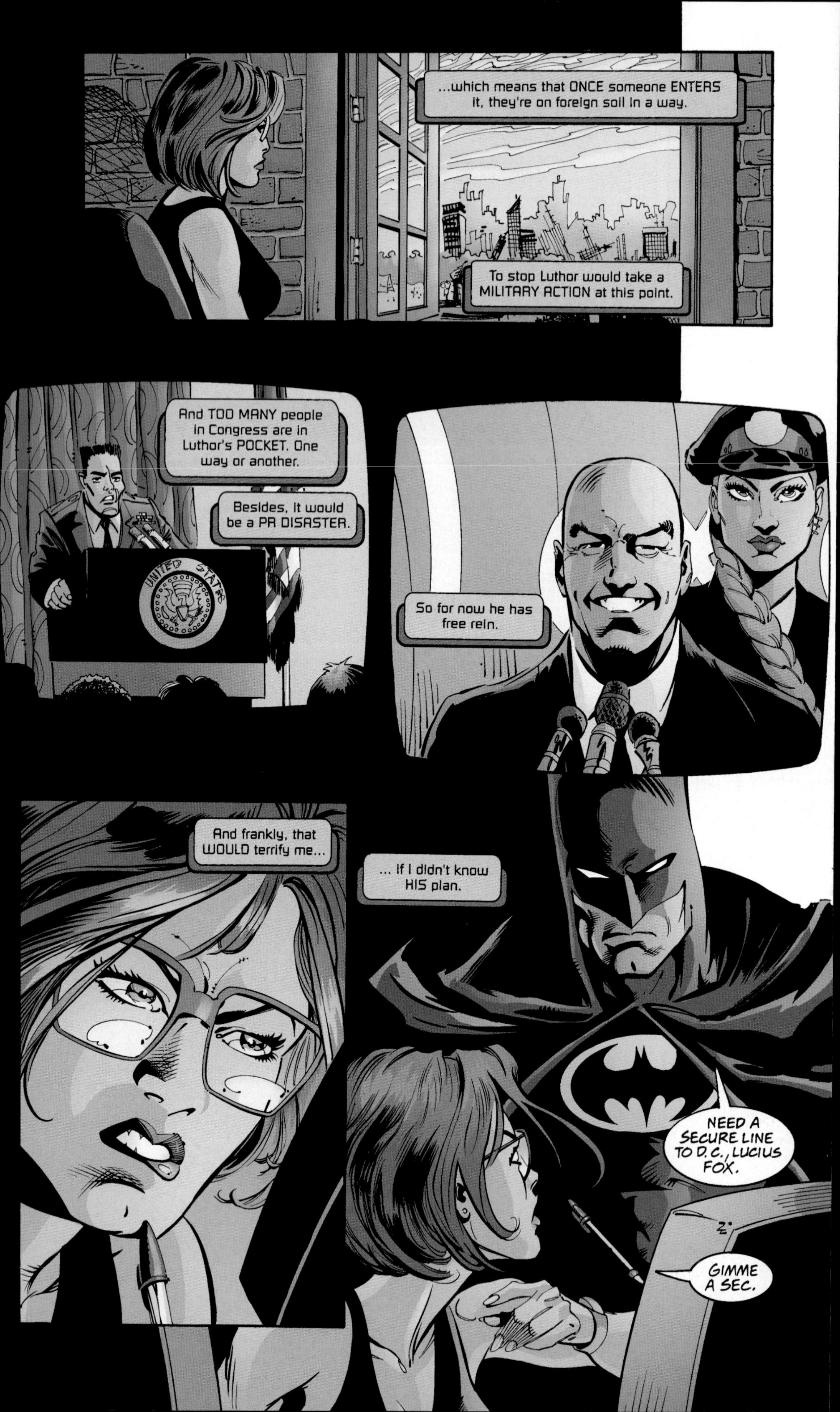
...which means that ONCE someone ENTERS it, they're on foreign soil in a way.
To stop Luthor would take a MILITARY ACTION at this point.
And TOO MANY people in Congress are in Luthor's POCKET. One way or another.
Besides, it would be a PR DISASTER.
So for now he has free rein.
And frankly, that WOULD terrify me...
... if I didn't know HIS plan.
NEED A SECURE LINE TO D.C., LUCIUS FOX.
GIMME A SEC.

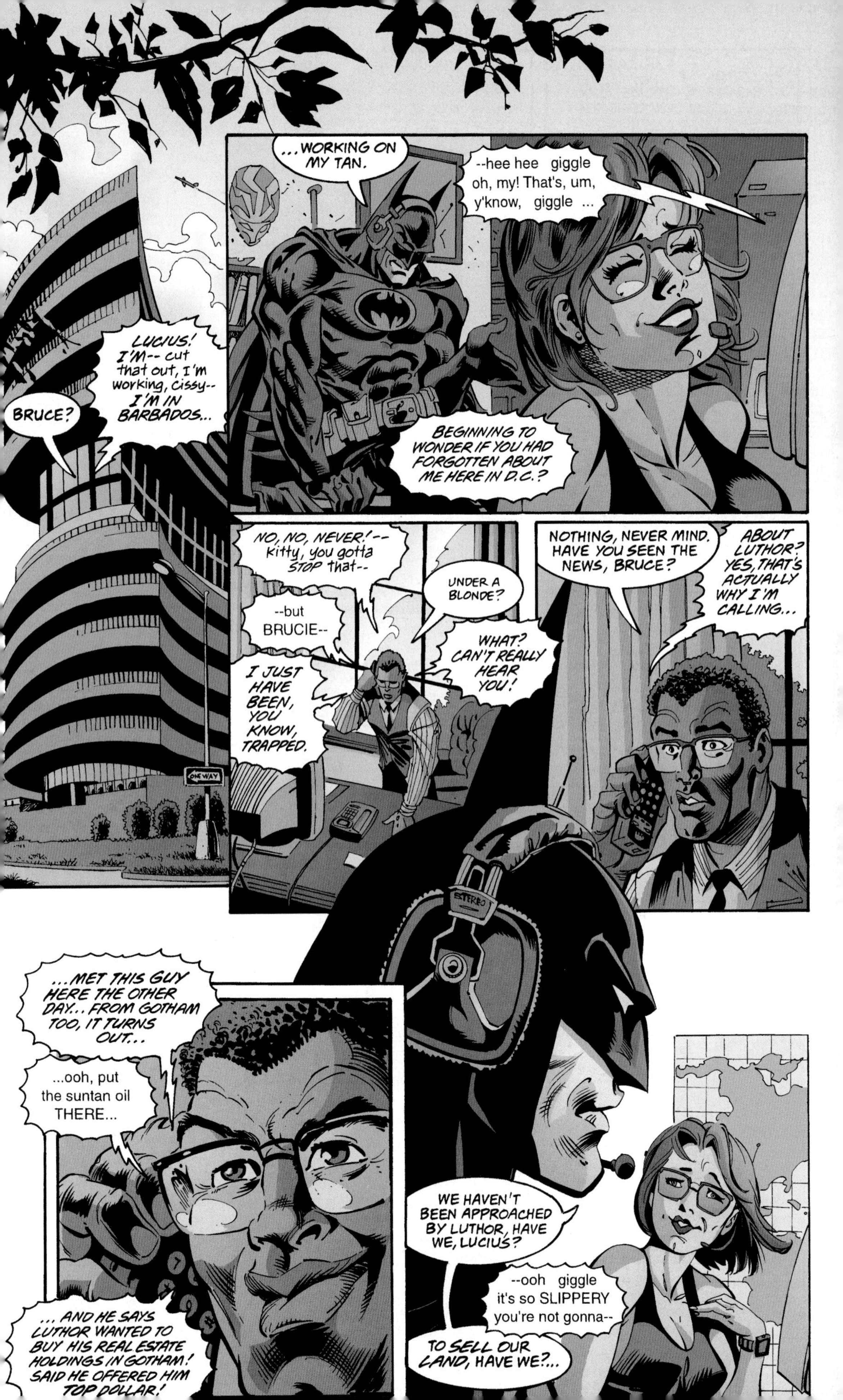
...WORKING ON MY TAN.
--hee hee giggle oh, my! That's, um, y'know, giggle ...
BRUCE?
LUCIUS! I'M-- cut that out, I'm working, cissy-- I'M IN BARBADOS...
BEGINNING TO WONDER IF YOU HAD FORGOTTEN ABOUT ME HERE IN D.C.?
NO, NO, NEVER!-- kitty, you gotta STOP that--
--but BRUCIE--
UNDER A BLONDE?
I JUST HAVE BEEN, YOU KNOW, TRAPPED.
WHAT? CAN'T REALLY HEAR YOU!
NOTHING, NEVER MIND. HAVE YOU SEEN THE NEWS, BRUCE?
ABOUT LUTHOR? YES, THAT'S ACTUALLY WHY I'M CALLING...
ONE WAY
STEREO
...MET THIS GUY HERE THE OTHER DAY... FROM GOTHAM TOO, IT TURNS OUT...
...ooh, put the suntan oil THERE...
...AND HE SAYS LUTHOR WANTED TO BUY HIS REAL ESTATE HOLDINGS IN GOTHAM! SAID HE OFFERED HIM TOP DOLLAR!
WE HAVEN'T BEEN APPROACHED BY LUTHOR, HAVE WE, LUCIUS?
--ooh giggle it's so SLIPPERY you're not gonna--
TO SELL OUR LAND, HAVE WE?...

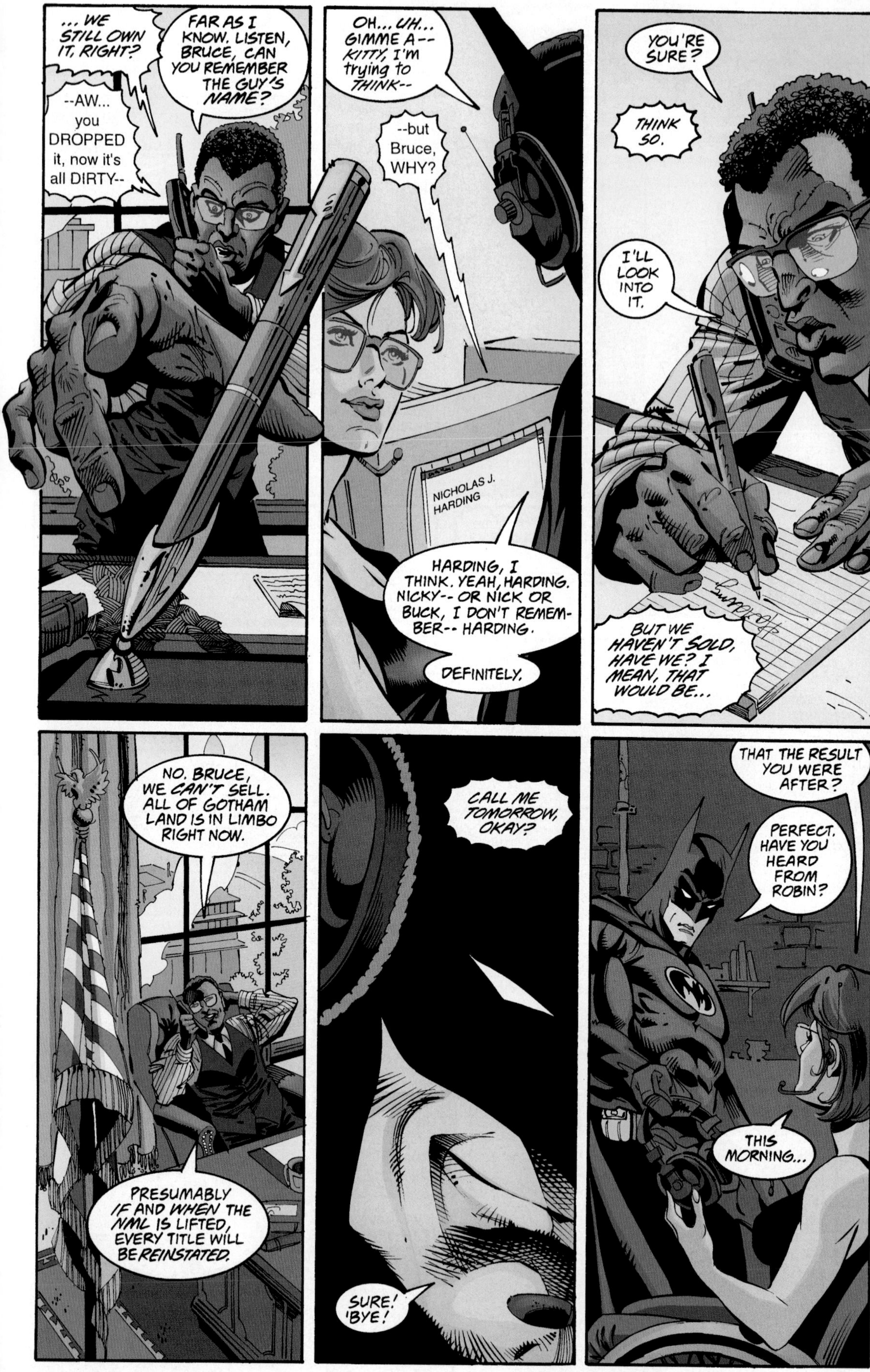
...WE STILL OWN IT, RIGHT?
FAR AS I KNOW. LISTEN, BRUCE, CAN YOU REMEMBER THE GUY'S NAME?
--AW... you DROPPED it, now it's all DIRTY--
OH... UH... GIMME A-- KITTY, I'M trying to THINK--
--but Bruce, WHY?
NICHOLAS J. HARDING
HARDING, I THINK. YEAH, HARDING. NICKY-- OR NICK OR BUCK, I DON'T REMEMBER-- HARDING.
DEFINITELY.
YOU'RE SURE?
THINK SO.
I'LL LOOK INTO IT.
BUT WE HAVEN'T SOLD, HAVE WE? I MEAN, THAT WOULD BE...
NO. BRUCE, WE CAN'T SELL. ALL OF GOTHAM LAND IS IN LIMBO RIGHT NOW.
PRESUMABLY IF AND WHEN THE NML IS LIFTED, EVERY TITLE WILL BE REINSTATED.
CALL ME TOMORROW, OKAY?
SURE! 'BYE!
THAT THE RESULT YOU WERE AFTER?
PERFECT. HAVE YOU HEARD FROM ROBIN?
THIS MORNING...

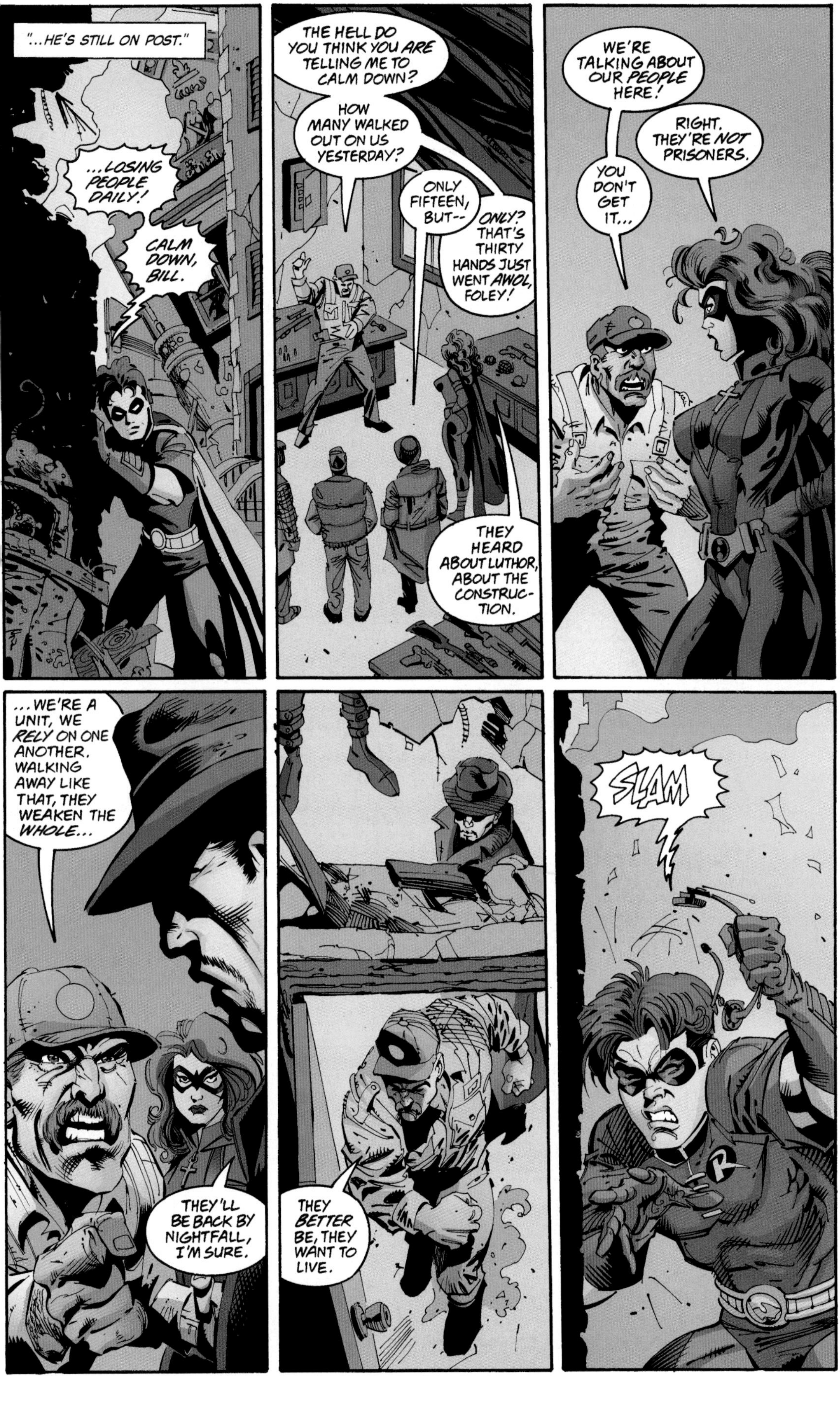
"...HE'S STILL ON POST."
...LOSING PEOPLE DAILY!
CALM DOWN, BILL.
THE HELL DO YOU THINK YOU ARE TELLING ME TO CALM DOWN?
HOW MANY WALKED OUT ON US YESTERDAY?
ONLY FIFTEEN, BUT--
ONLY? THAT'S THIRTY HANDS JUST WENT AWOL, FOLEY!
THEY HEARD ABOUT LUTHOR, ABOUT THE CONSTRUC-TION.
WE'RE TALKING ABOUT OUR PEOPLE HERE!
YOU DON'T GET IT...
RIGHT. THEY'RE NOT PRISONERS.
...WE'RE A UNIT, WE RELY ON ONE ANOTHER. WALKING AWAY LIKE THAT, THEY WEAKEN THE WHOLE...
THEY'LL BE BACK BY NIGHTFALL, I'M SURE.
THEY BETTER BE, THEY WANT TO LIVE.
SLAM

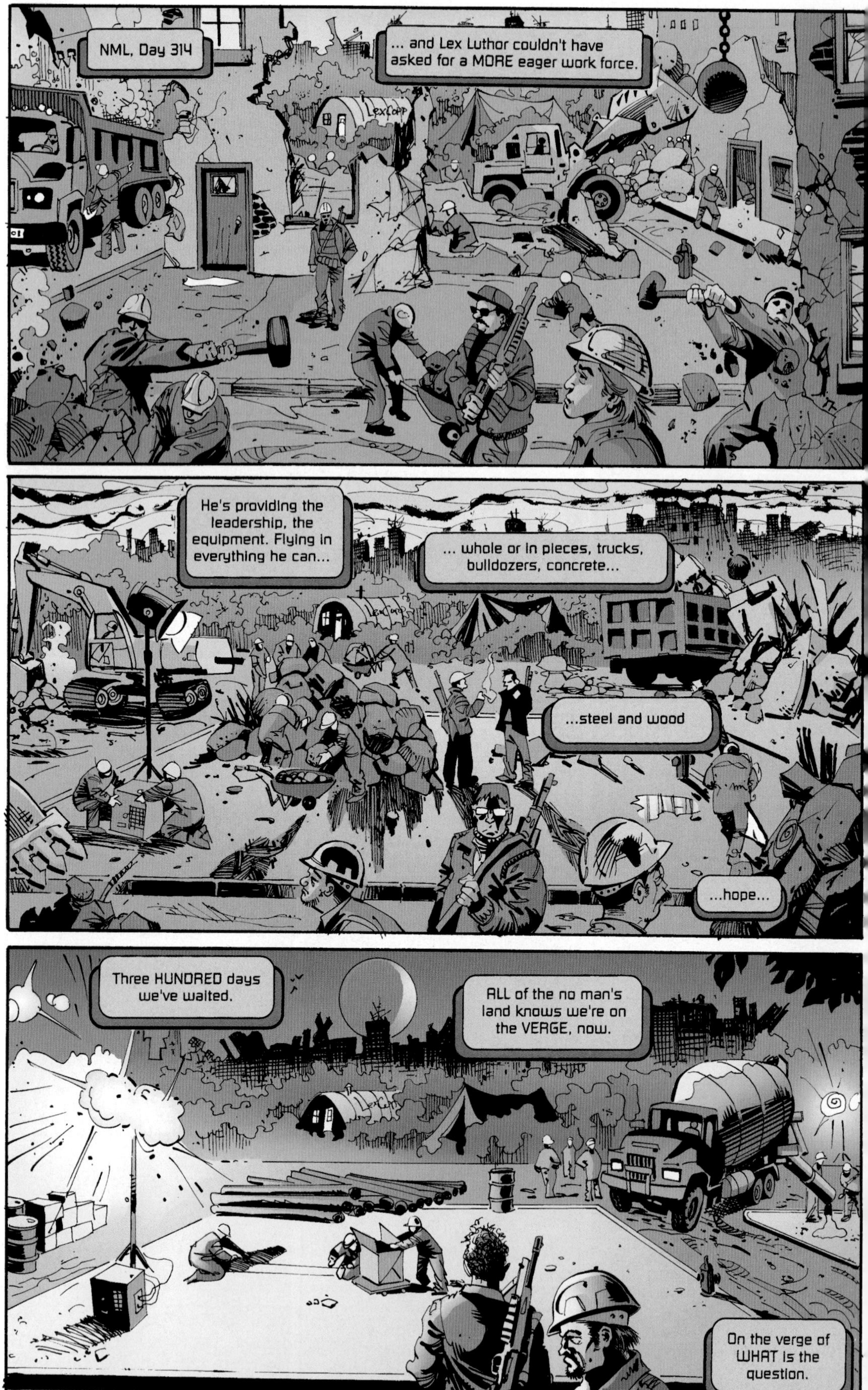
NML, Day 314
... and Lex Luthor couldn't have asked for a MORE eager work force.
He's providing the leadership, the equipment. Flying in everything he can...
... whole or in pieces, trucks, bulldozers, concrete...
...steel and wood
...hope...
Three HUNDRED days we've waited.
ALL of the no man's land knows we're on the VERGE, now.
On the verge of WHAT is the question.

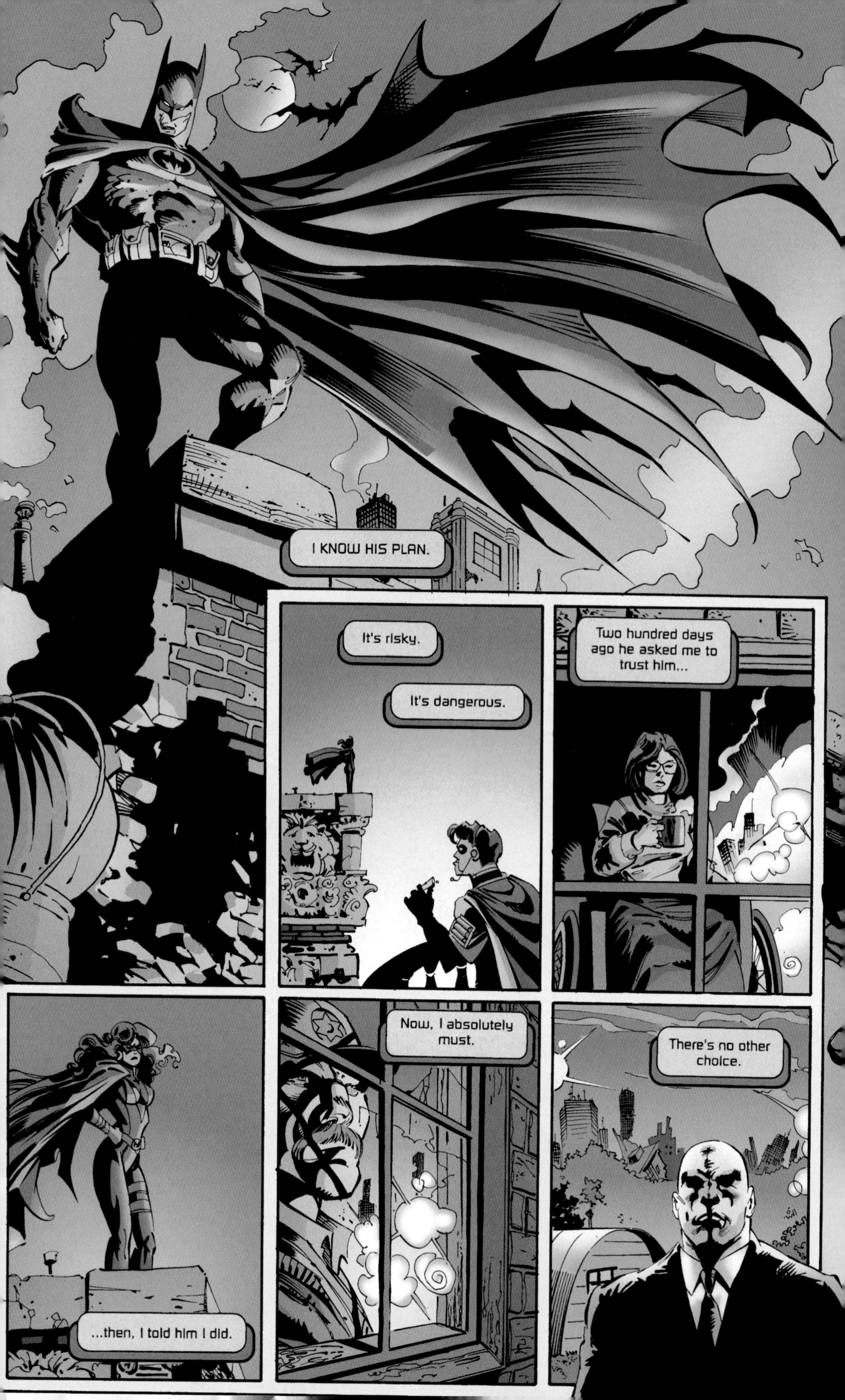
I KNOW HIS PLAN.
It's risky.
It's dangerous.
Two hundred days ago he asked me to trust him...
...then, I told him I did.
Now, I absolutely must.
There's no other choice.

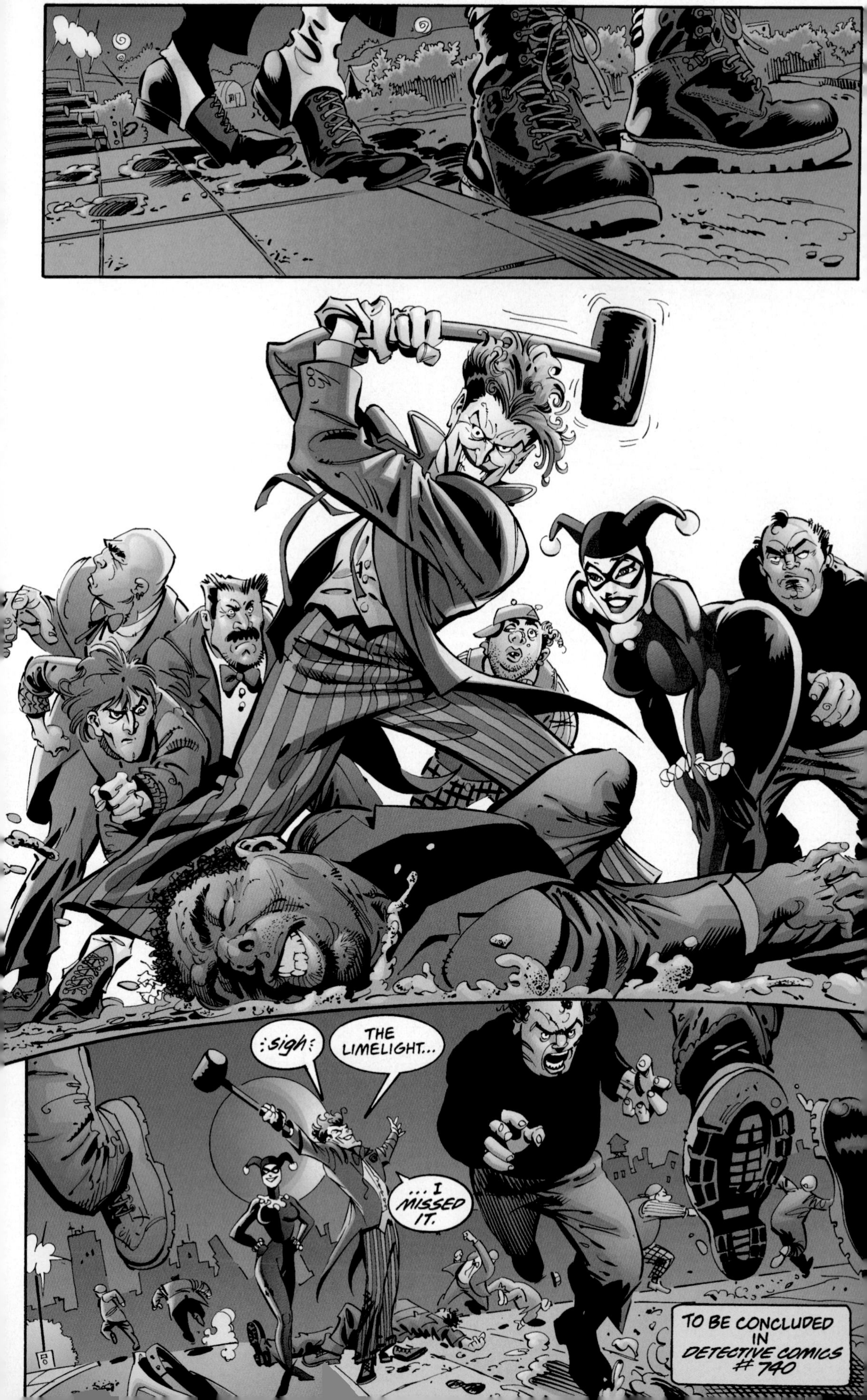

sigh
THE LIMELIGHT...
...I MISSED IT.
TO BE CONCLUDED IN DETECTIVE COMICS #740

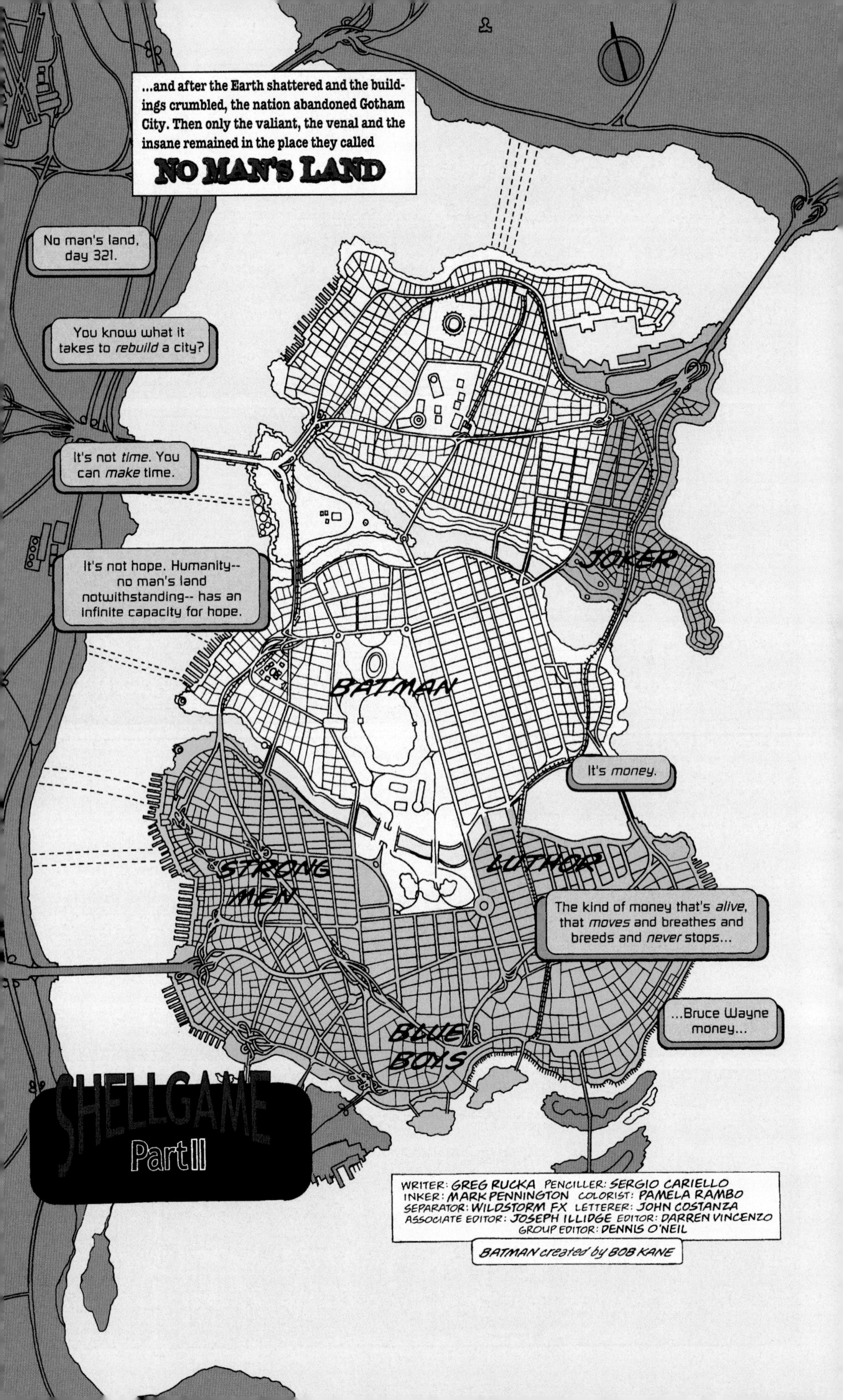

...and after the Earth shattered and the buildings crumbled, the nation abandoned Gotham City. Then only the valiant, the venal and the insane remained in the place they called
NO MAN'S LAND
No man's land, day 321.
You know what it takes to *rebuild* a city?
It's not *time*. You can *make* time.
It's not hope. Humanity-- no man's land notwithstanding-- has an infinite capacity for hope.
JOKER
BATMAN
It's *money*.
STRONG MEN
LUTHOR
The kind of money that's *alive*, that *moves* and breathes and breeds and *never* stops...
...Bruce Wayne money...
BLUE BOYS
SHELLGAME
Part II
WRITER: GREG RUCKA PENCILLER: SERGIO CARIELLO
INKER: MARK PENNINGTON COLORIST: PAMELA RAMBO
SEPARATOR: WILDSTORM FX LETTERER: JOHN COSTANZA
ASSOCIATE EDITOR: JOSEPH ILLIDGE EDITOR: DARREN VINCENZO
GROUP EDITOR: DENNIS O'NEIL
BATMAN created by BOB KANE

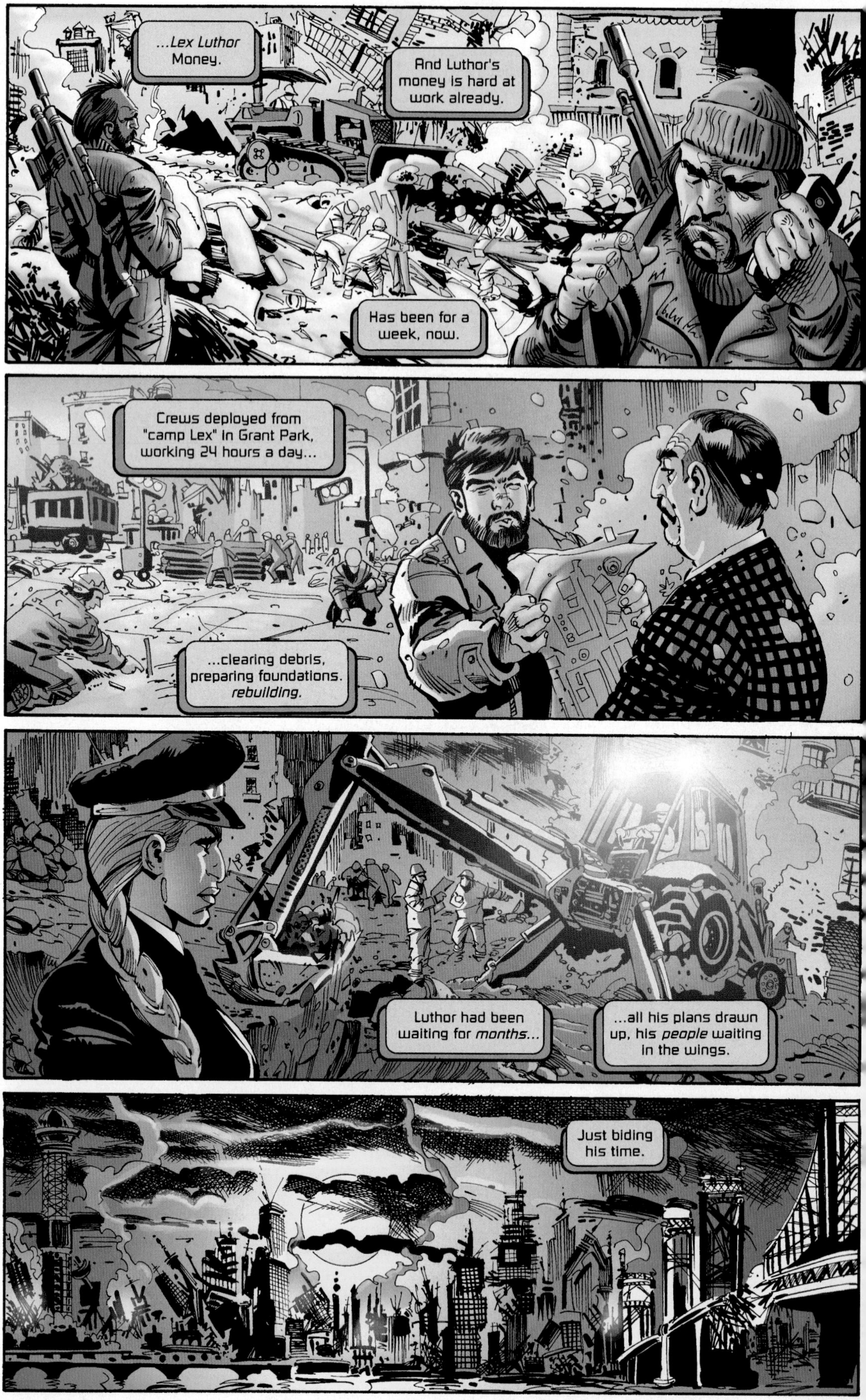
...*Lex Luthor* Money.
And Luthor's money is hard at work already.
Has been for a week, now.
Crews deployed from "camp Lex" in Grant Park, working 24 hours a day...
...clearing debris, preparing foundations. *rebuilding.*
Luthor had been waiting for *months*...
...all his plans drawn up, his *people* waiting in the wings.
Just biding his time.

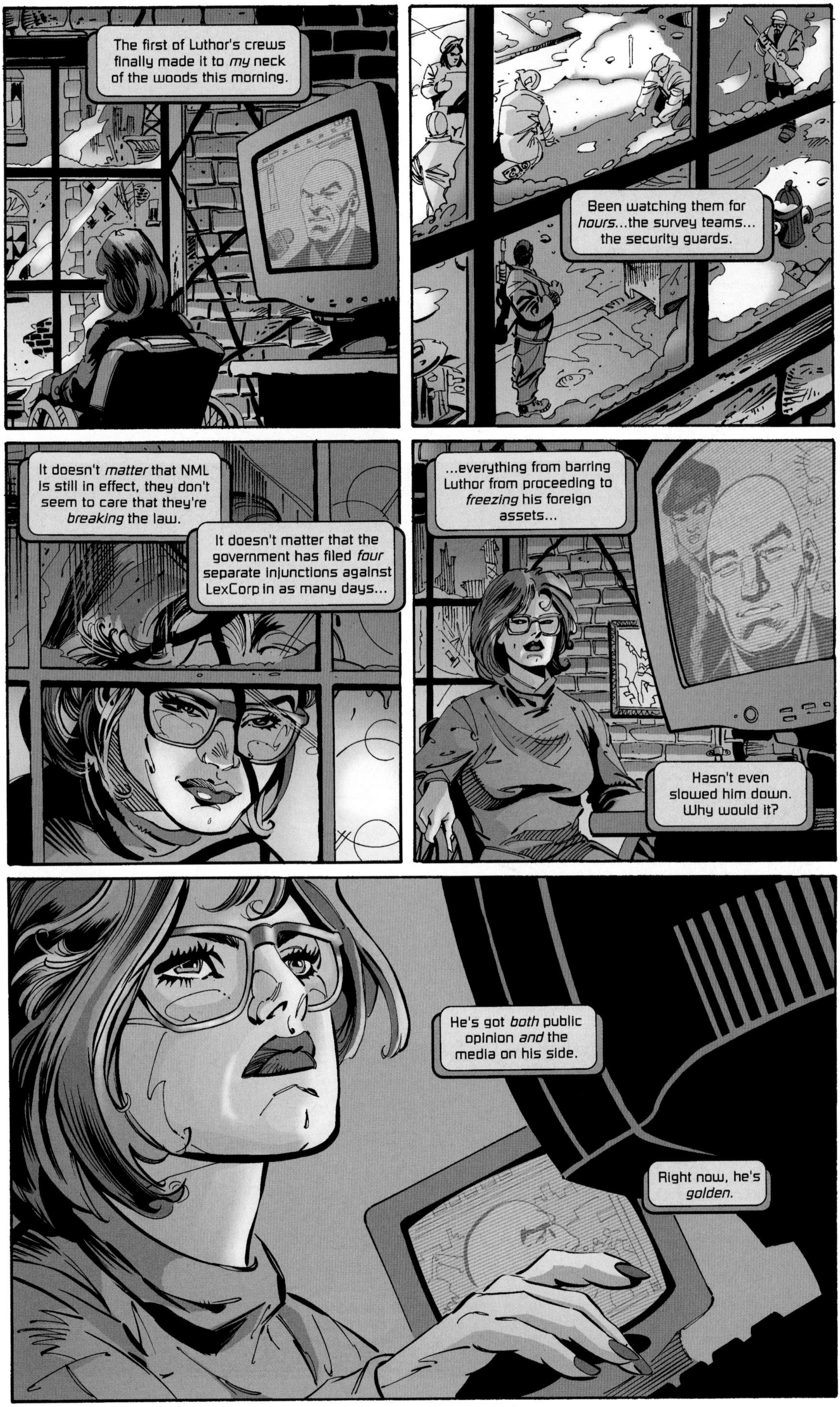
The first of Luthor's crews finally made it to *my* neck of the woods this morning.
Been watching them for *hours*...the survey teams... the security guards.
It doesn't *matter* that NML is still in effect, they don't seem to care that they're *breaking* the law.
It doesn't matter that the government has filed *four* separate injunctions against LexCorp in as many days...
...everything from barring Luthor from proceeding to *freezing* his foreign assets...
Hasn't even slowed him down. Why would it?
He's got *both* public opinion *and* the media on his side.
Right now, he's *golden.*

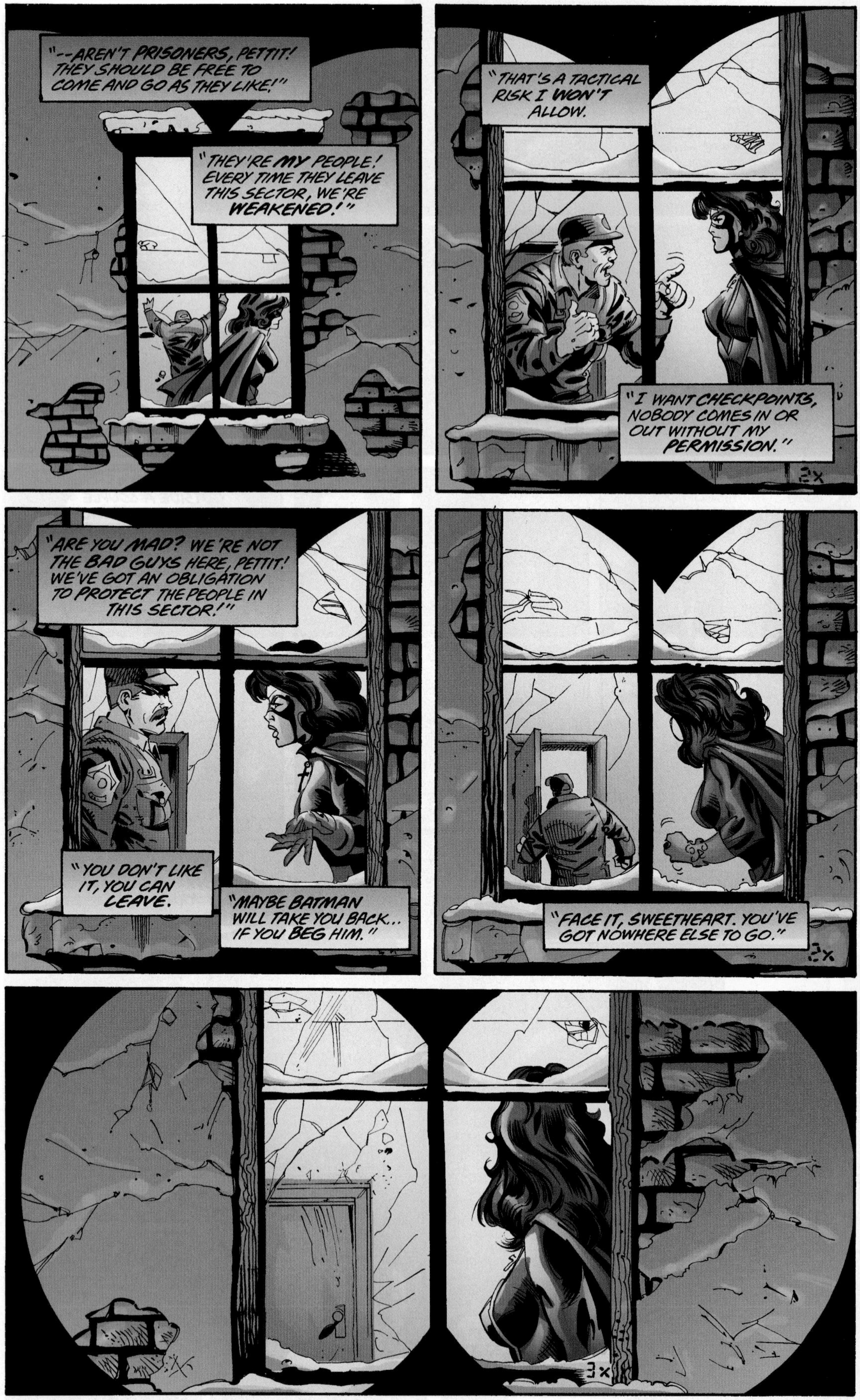
"--AREN'T PRISONERS, PETTIT! THEY SHOULD BE FREE TO COME AND GO AS THEY LIKE!"
"THEY'RE MY PEOPLE! EVERY TIME THEY LEAVE THIS SECTOR, WE'RE WEAKENED!"
"THAT'S A TACTICAL RISK I WON'T ALLOW.
"I WANT CHECKPOINTS, NOBODY COMES IN OR OUT WITHOUT MY PERMISSION."
"ARE YOU MAD? WE'RE NOT THE BAD GUYS HERE, PETTIT! WE'VE GOT AN OBLIGATION TO PROTECT THE PEOPLE IN THIS SECTOR!"
"YOU DON'T LIKE IT, YOU CAN LEAVE.
"MAYBE BATMAN WILL TAKE YOU BACK... IF YOU BEG HIM."
"FACE IT, SWEETHEART. YOU'VE GOT NOWHERE ELSE TO GO."

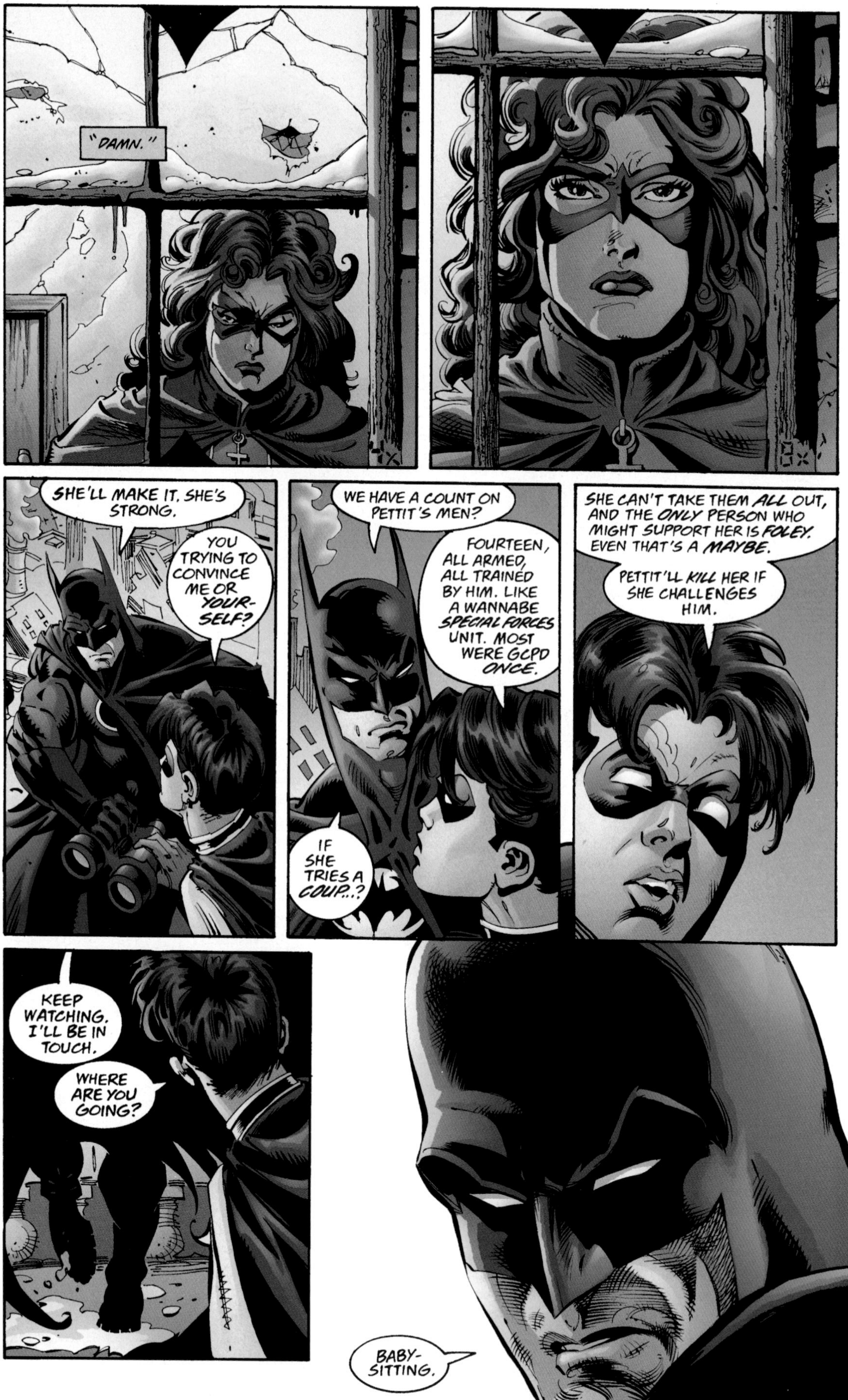
"DAMN."
SHE'LL MAKE IT. SHE'S STRONG.
YOU TRYING TO CONVINCE ME OR YOURSELF?
WE HAVE A COUNT ON PETTIT'S MEN?
FOURTEEN, ALL ARMED, ALL TRAINED BY HIM. LIKE A WANNABE SPECIAL FORCES UNIT. MOST WERE GCPD ONCE.
IF SHE TRIES A COUP...?
SHE CAN'T TAKE THEM ALL OUT, AND THE ONLY PERSON WHO MIGHT SUPPORT HER IS FOLEY. EVEN THAT'S A MAYBE.
PETTIT'LL KILL HER IF SHE CHALLENGES HIM.
KEEP WATCHING. I'LL BE IN TOUCH.
WHERE ARE YOU GOING?
BABY-SITTING.

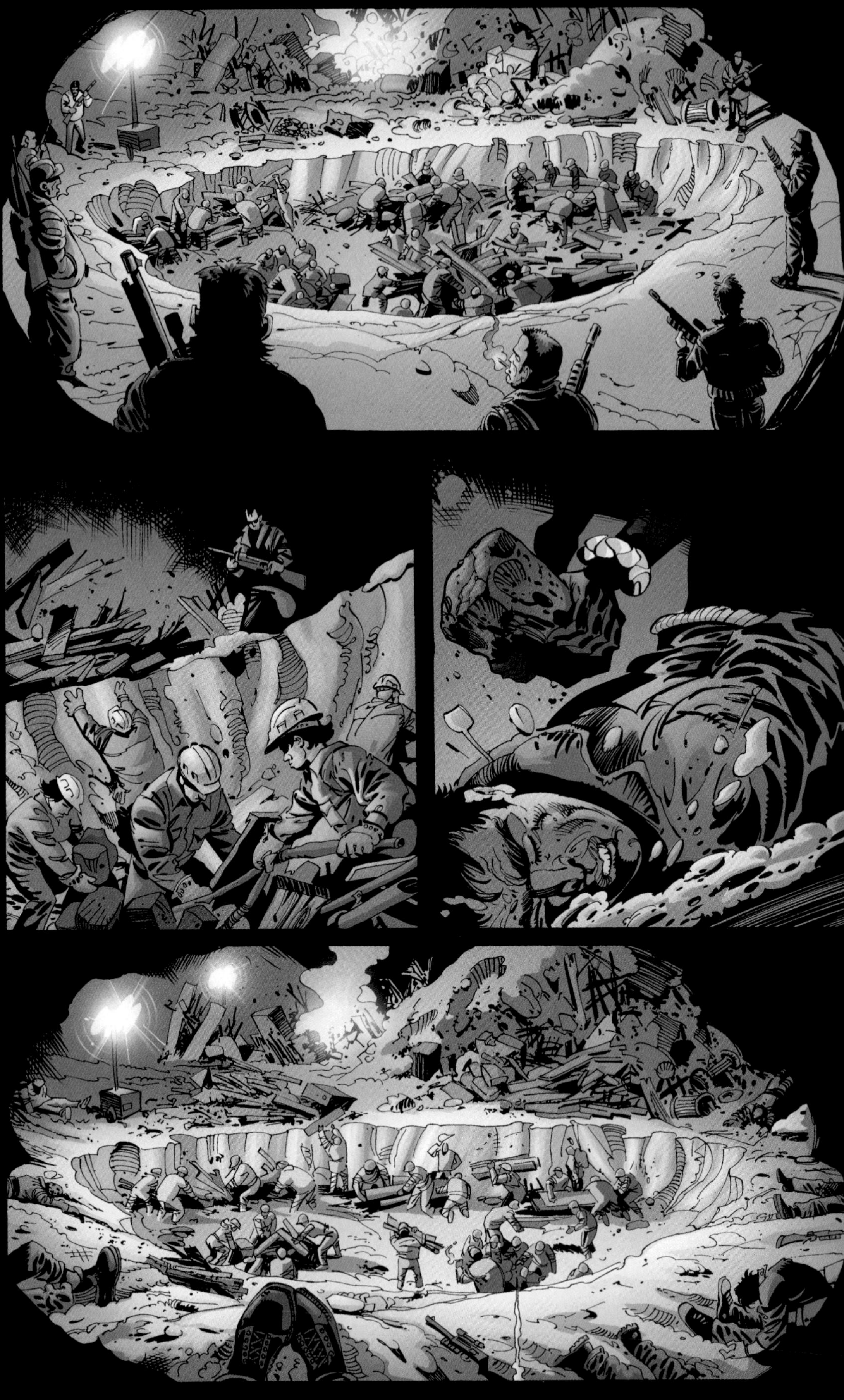

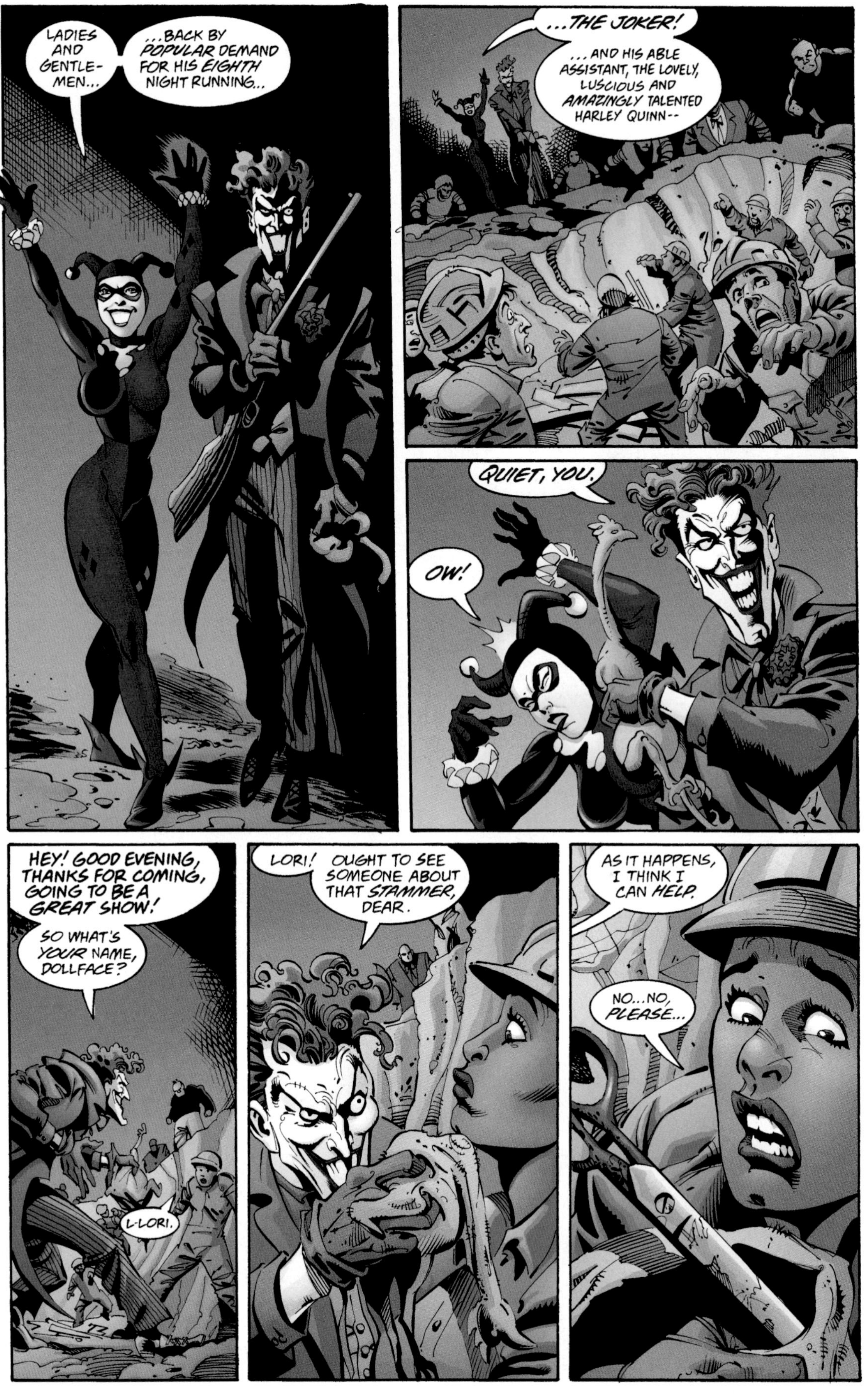
LADIES AND GENTLE-MEN...
...BACK BY POPULAR DEMAND FOR HIS EIGHTH NIGHT RUNNING...
...THE JOKER!
...AND HIS ABLE ASSISTANT, THE LOVELY, LUSCIOUS AND AMAZINGLY TALENTED HARLEY QUINN--
QUIET, YOU.
OW!
HEY! GOOD EVENING, THANKS FOR COMING, GOING TO BE A GREAT SHOW!
SO WHAT'S YOUR NAME, DOLLFACE?
L-LORI.
LORI!
OUGHT TO SEE SOMEONE ABOUT THAT STAMMER, DEAR.
AS IT HAPPENS, I THINK I CAN HELP.
NO...NO, PLEASE...

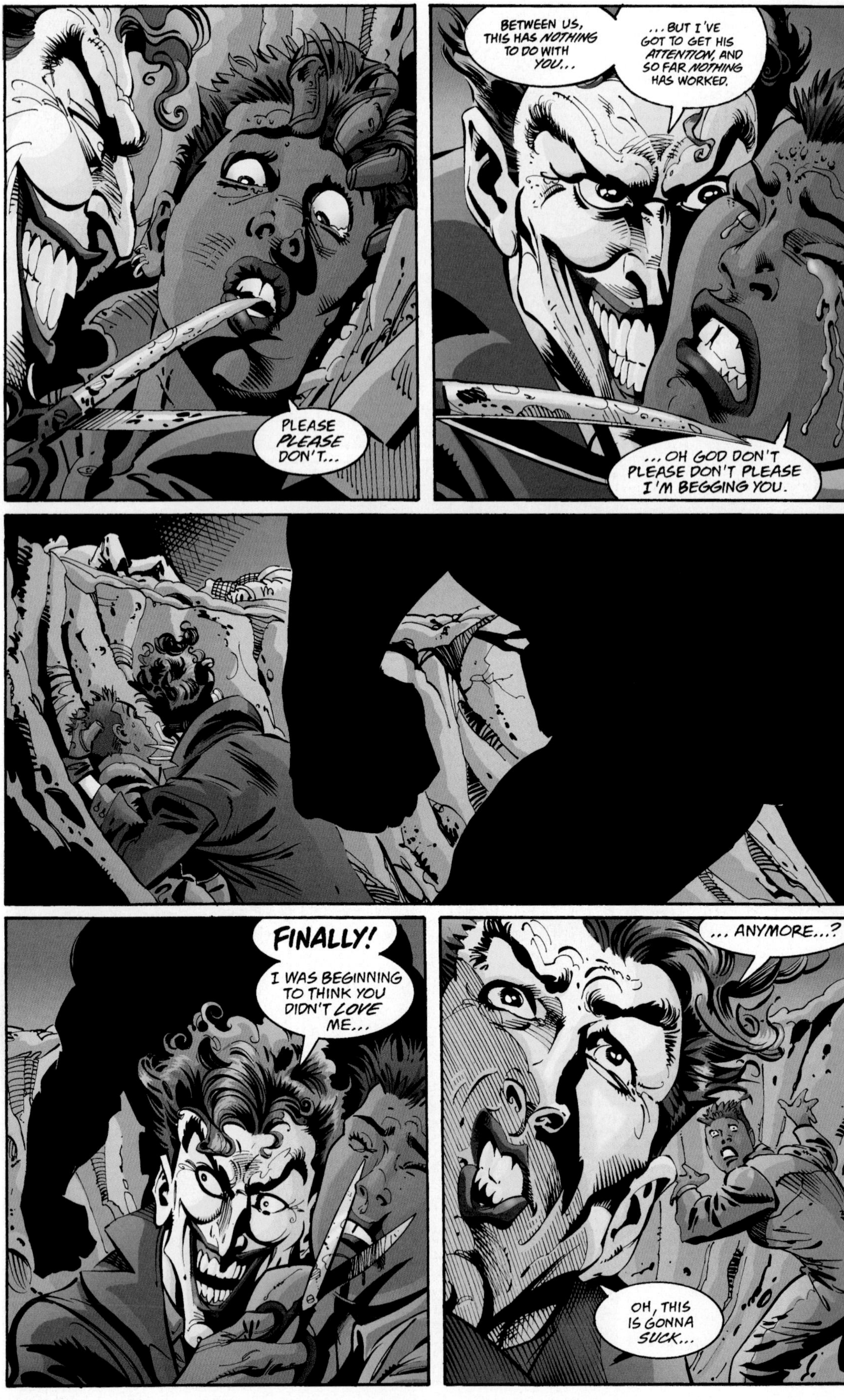
PLEASE PLEASE DON'T...
BETWEEN US, THIS HAS NOTHING TO DO WITH YOU...
...BUT I'VE GOT TO GET HIS ATTENTION, AND SO FAR NOTHING HAS WORKED.
...OH GOD DON'T PLEASE DON'T PLEASE I'M BEGGING YOU.
FINALLY!
I WAS BEGINNING TO THINK YOU DIDN'T LOVE ME...
...ANYMORE...?
OH, THIS IS GONNA SUCK...

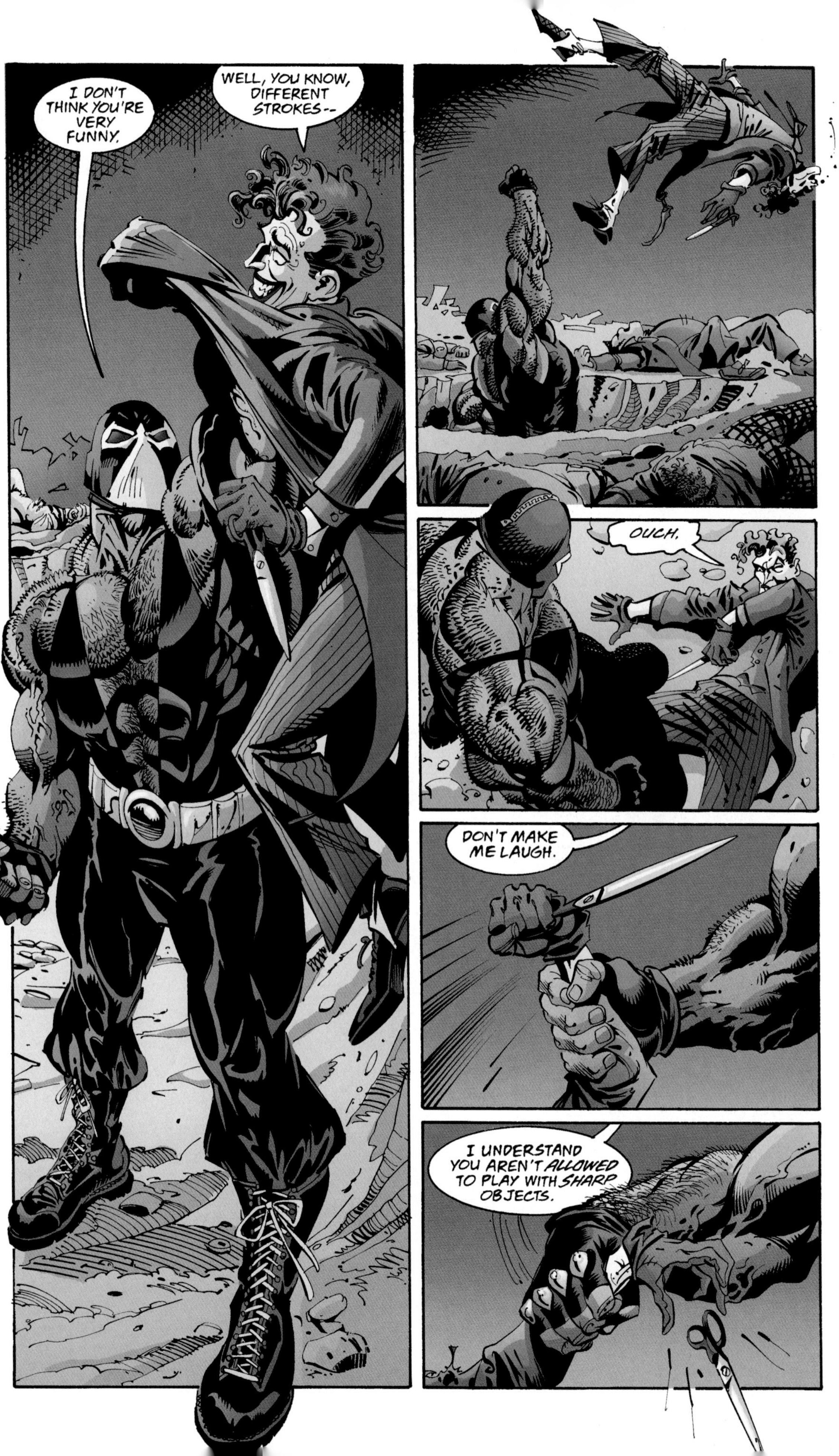
I DON'T THINK YOU'RE VERY FUNNY.
WELL, YOU KNOW, DIFFERENT STROKES--
OUCH.
DON'T MAKE ME LAUGH.
I UNDERSTAND YOU AREN'T ALLOWED TO PLAY WITH SHARP OBJECTS.

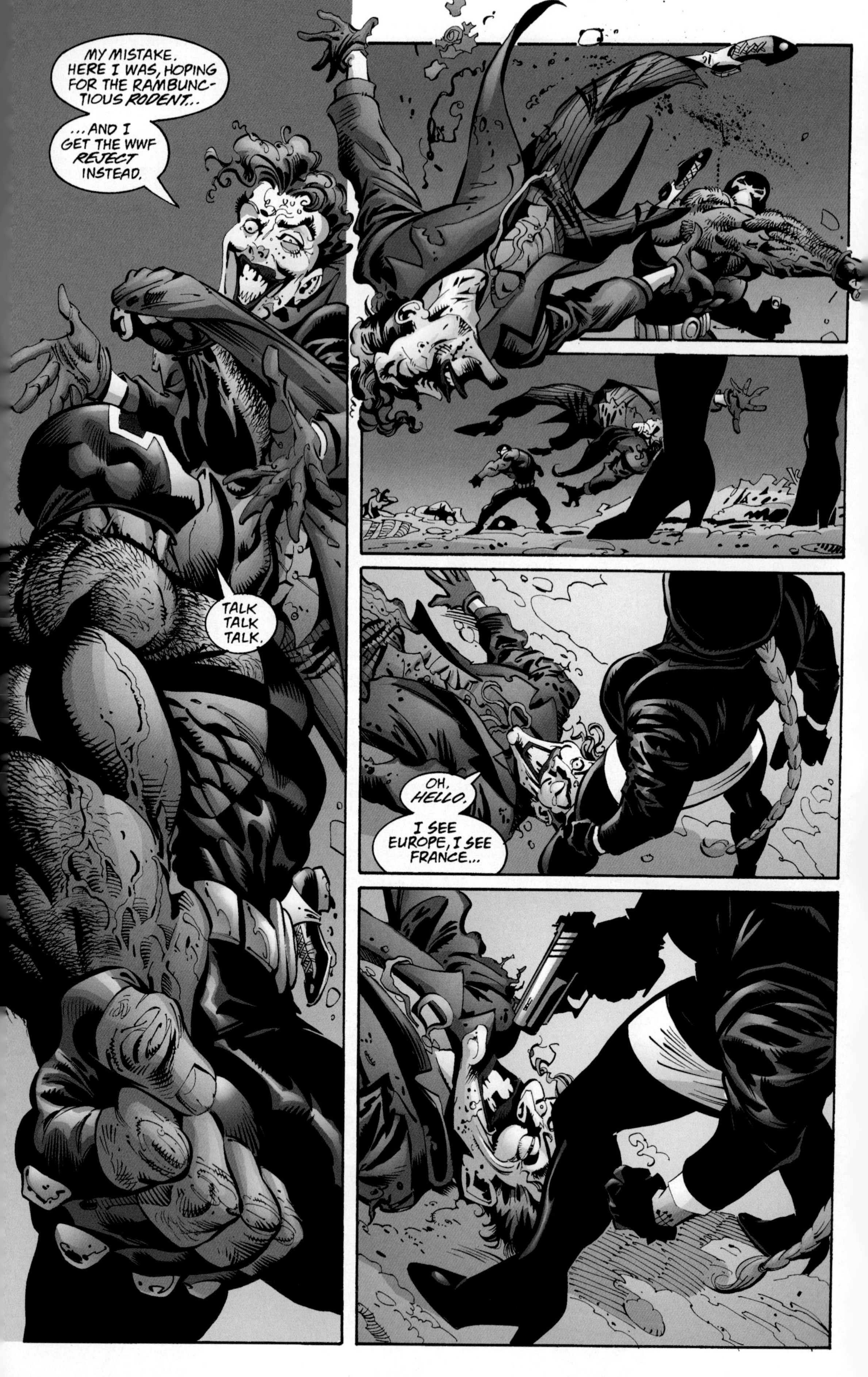
MY MISTAKE. HERE I WAS, HOPING FOR THE RAMBUNCTIOUS RODENT...
...AND I GET THE WWF REJECT INSTEAD.
TALK TALK TALK.
OH, HELLO.
I SEE EUROPE, I SEE FRANCE...

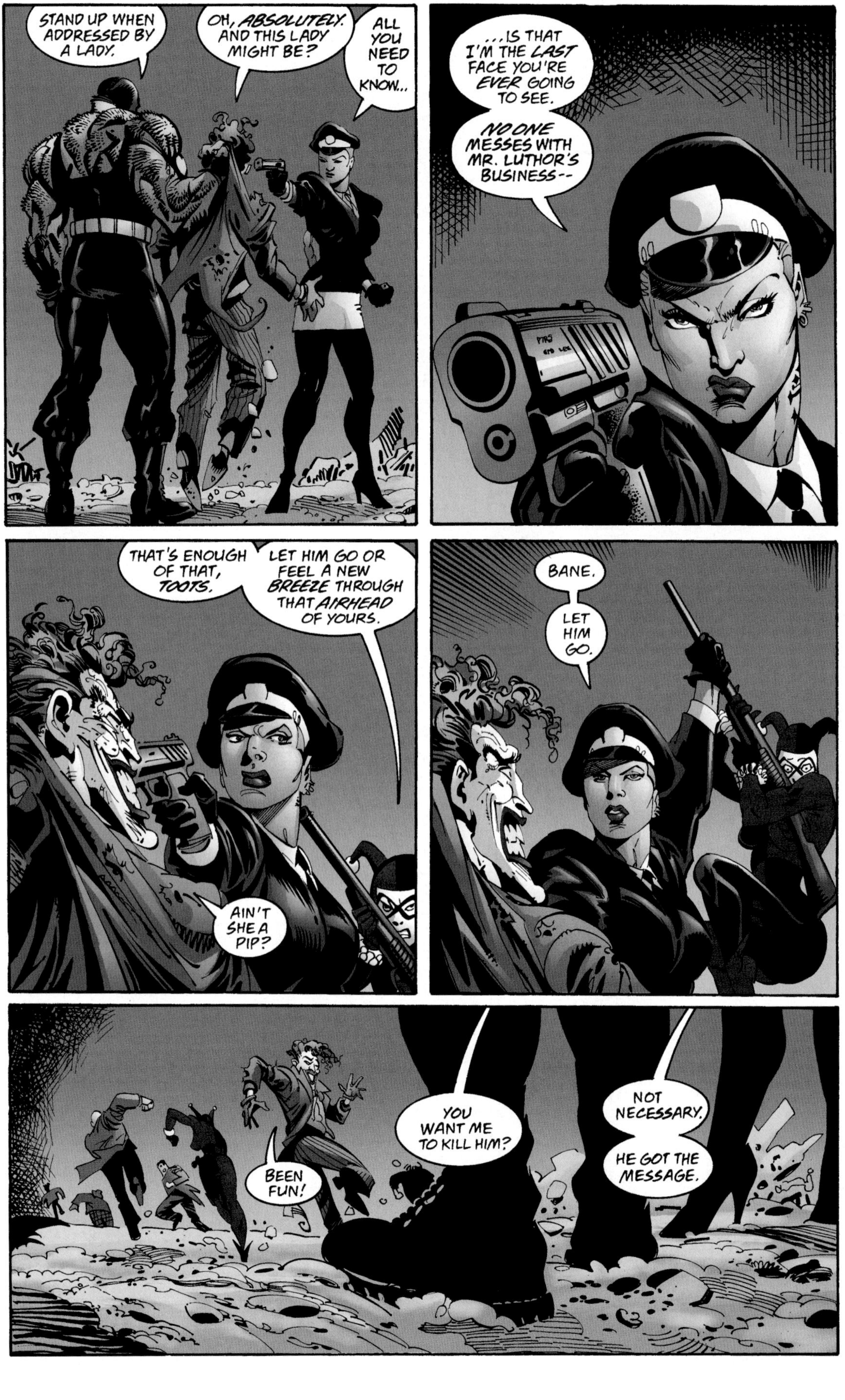
STAND UP WHEN ADDRESSED BY A LADY.
OH, ABSOLUTELY. AND THIS LADY MIGHT BE?
ALL YOU NEED TO KNOW...
...IS THAT I'M THE LAST FACE YOU'RE EVER GOING TO SEE.
NO ONE MESSES WITH MR. LUTHOR'S BUSINESS--
THAT'S ENOUGH OF THAT, TOOTS.
LET HIM GO OR FEEL A NEW BREEZE THROUGH THAT AIRHEAD OF YOURS.
AIN'T SHE A PIP?
BANE.
LET HIM GO.
BEEN FUN!
YOU WANT ME TO KILL HIM?
NOT NECESSARY.
HE GOT THE MESSAGE.

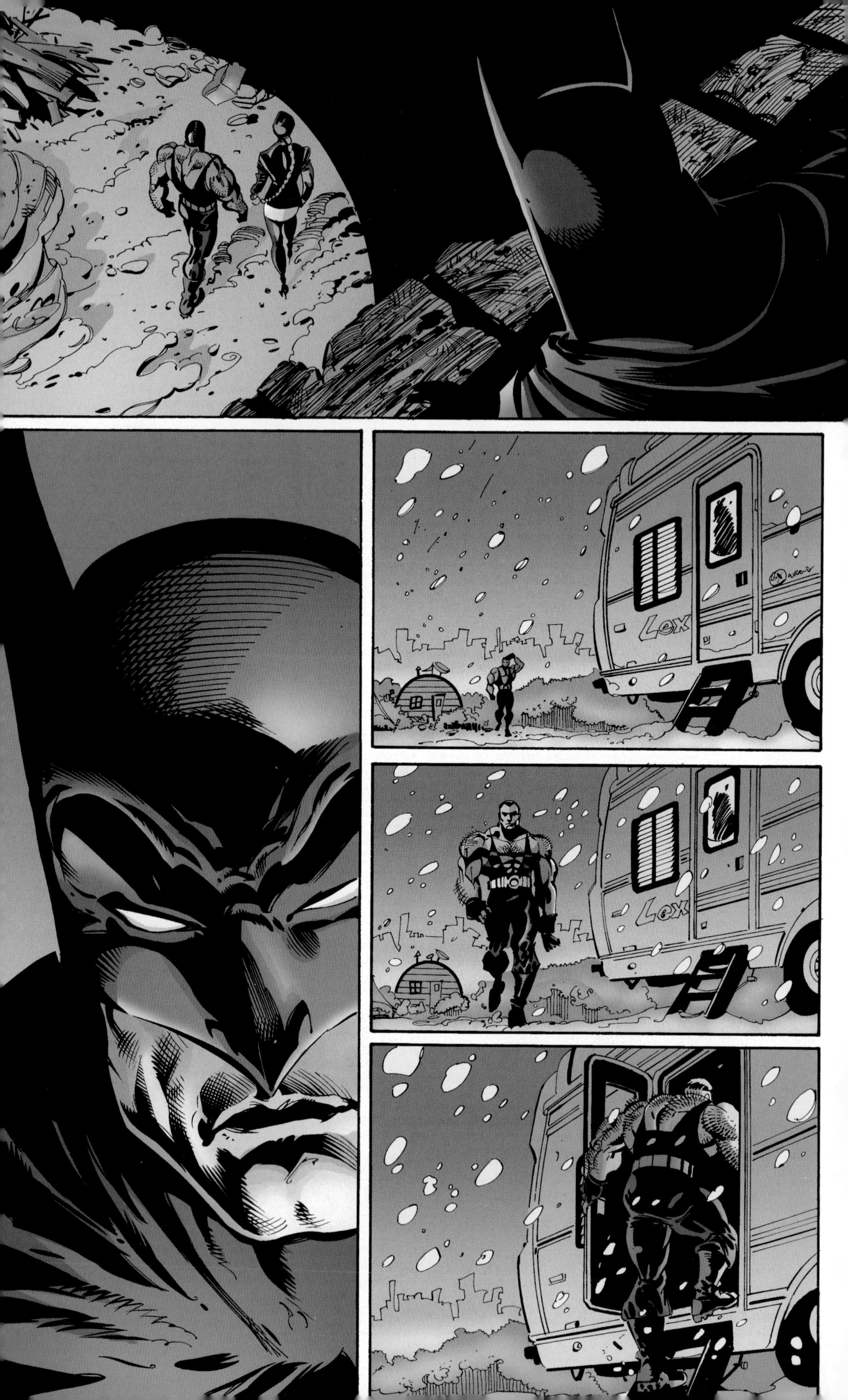
Lex
Lex

BATMAN.

TO WHAT DO I OWE THIS PLEASURE?

IT TOOK ME A WHILE TO FIGURE OUT WHAT YOU WERE DOING...

...WHY YOU *BLEW UP* ALL THOSE *RECORDS* AFTER GOING TO SUCH GREAT LENGTHS TO STOP *ME* FROM DOING THE SAME.

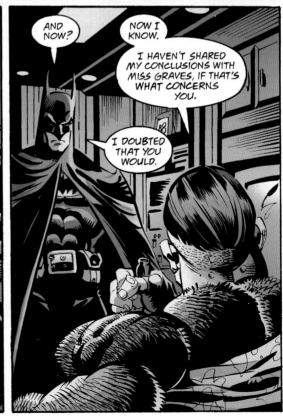

AND NOW?

NOW I KNOW.

I HAVEN'T SHARED MY CONCLUSIONS WITH MISS GRAVES, IF THAT'S WHAT CONCERNS YOU.

I DOUBTED THAT YOU WOULD.

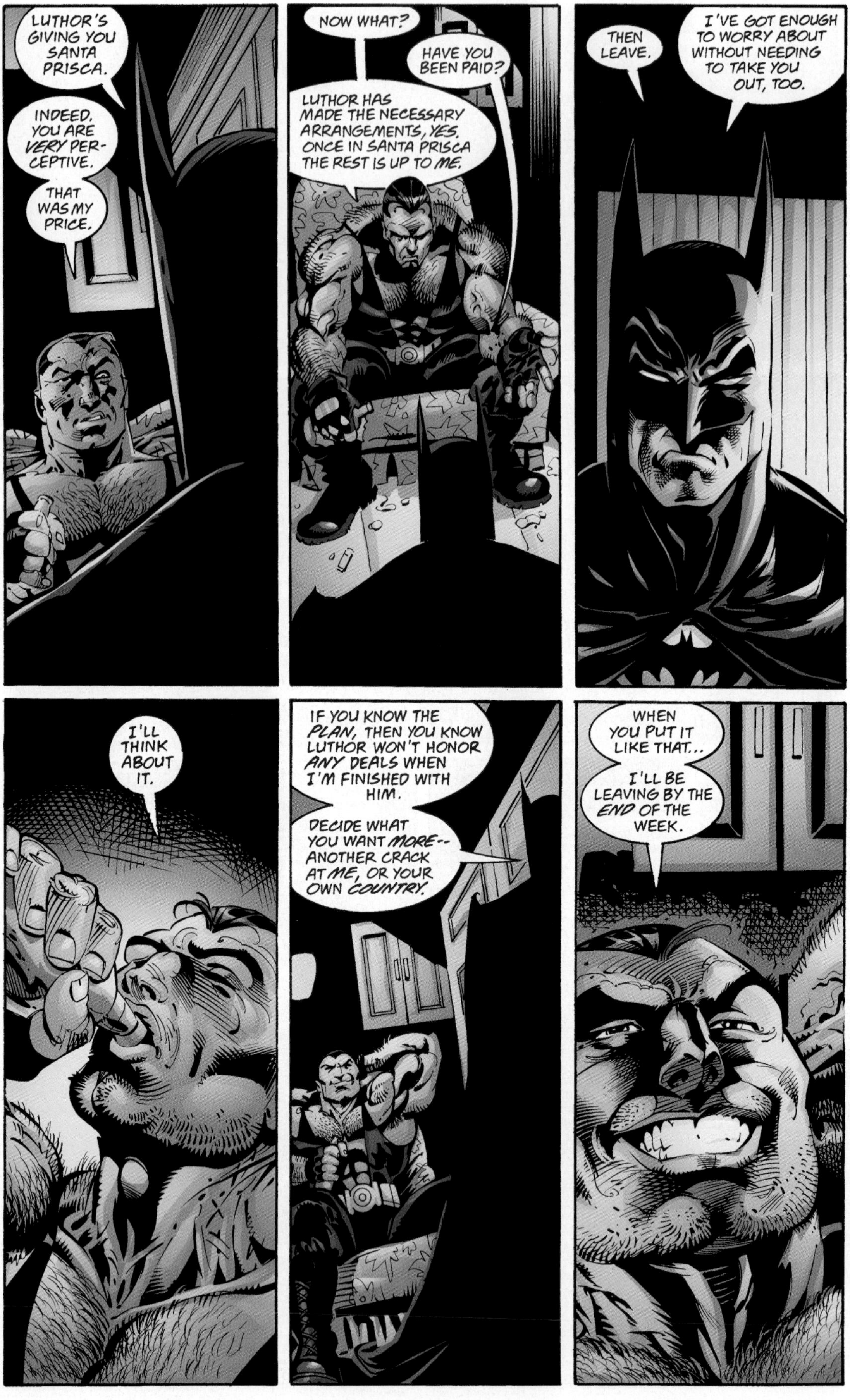
LUTHOR'S GIVING YOU SANTA PRISCA.
INDEED. YOU ARE VERY PERCEPTIVE.
THAT WAS MY PRICE.
NOW WHAT?
HAVE YOU BEEN PAID?
LUTHOR HAS MADE THE NECESSARY ARRANGEMENTS, YES. ONCE IN SANTA PRISCA THE REST IS UP TO ME.
THEN LEAVE.
I'VE GOT ENOUGH TO WORRY ABOUT WITHOUT NEEDING TO TAKE YOU OUT, TOO.
I'LL THINK ABOUT IT.
IF YOU KNOW THE PLAN, THEN YOU KNOW LUTHOR WON'T HONOR ANY DEALS WHEN I'M FINISHED WITH HIM.
DECIDE WHAT YOU WANT MORE-- ANOTHER CRACK AT ME, OR YOUR OWN COUNTRY.
WHEN YOU PUT IT LIKE THAT...
I'LL BE LEAVING BY THE END OF THE WEEK.

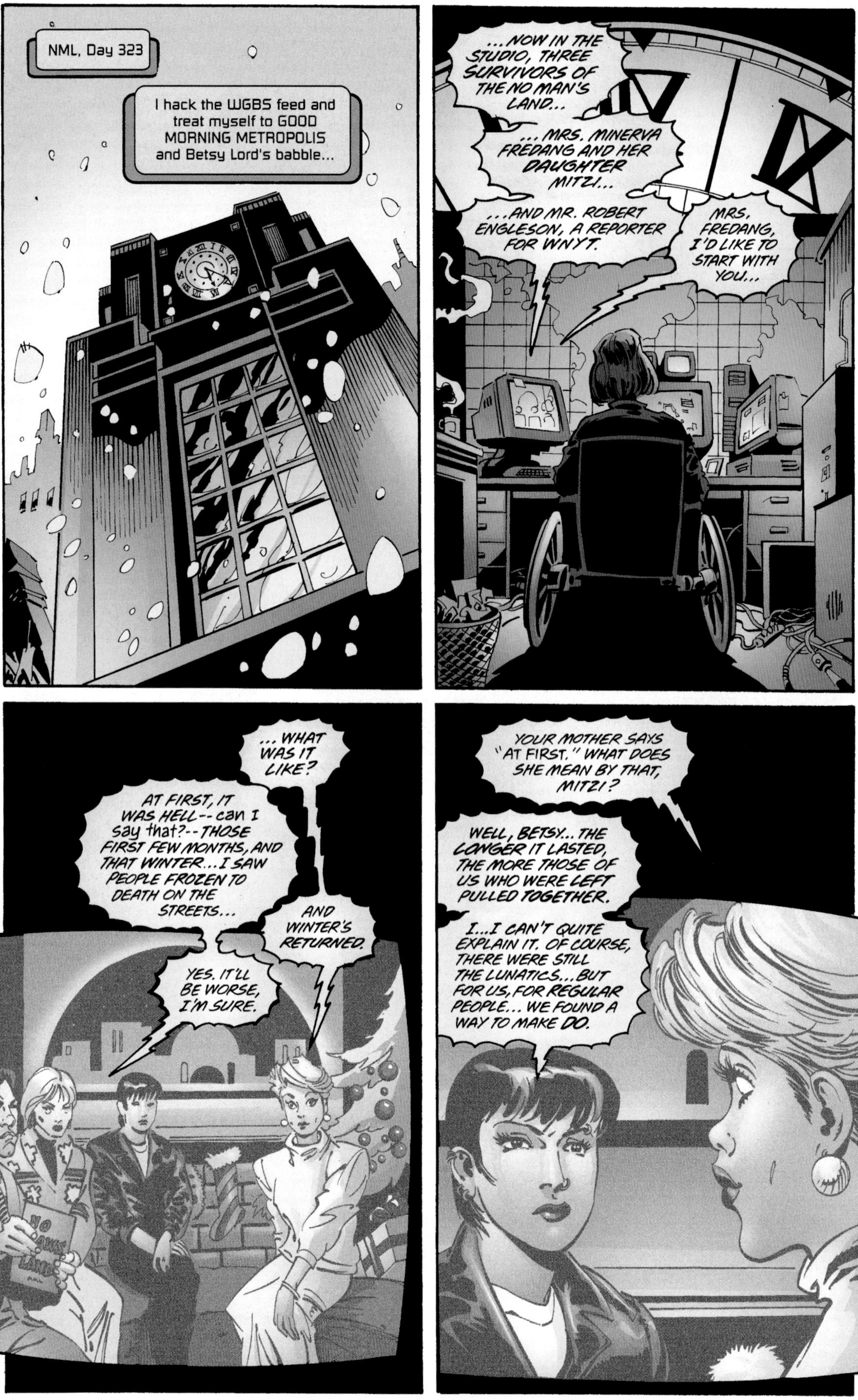
NML, Day 323
I hack the WGBS feed and treat myself to GOOD MORNING METROPOLIS and Betsy Lord's babble...
...NOW IN THE STUDIO, THREE SURVIVORS OF THE NO MAN'S LAND...
...MRS. MINERVA FREDANG AND HER DAUGHTER MITZI...
...AND MR. ROBERT ENGLESON, A REPORTER FOR WNYT.
MRS. FREDANG, I'D LIKE TO START WITH YOU...
...WHAT WAS IT LIKE?
AT FIRST, IT WAS HELL--can I say that?--THOSE FIRST FEW MONTHS, AND THAT WINTER...I SAW PEOPLE FROZEN TO DEATH ON THE STREETS...
AND WINTER'S RETURNED.
YES. IT'LL BE WORSE, I'M SURE.
YOUR MOTHER SAYS "AT FIRST." WHAT DOES SHE MEAN BY THAT, MITZI?
WELL, BETSY...THE LONGER IT LASTED, THE MORE THOSE OF US WHO WERE LEFT PULLED TOGETHER.
I...I CAN'T QUITE EXPLAIN IT. OF COURSE, THERE WERE STILL THE LUNATICS...BUT FOR US, FOR REGULAR PEOPLE...WE FOUND A WAY TO MAKE DO.

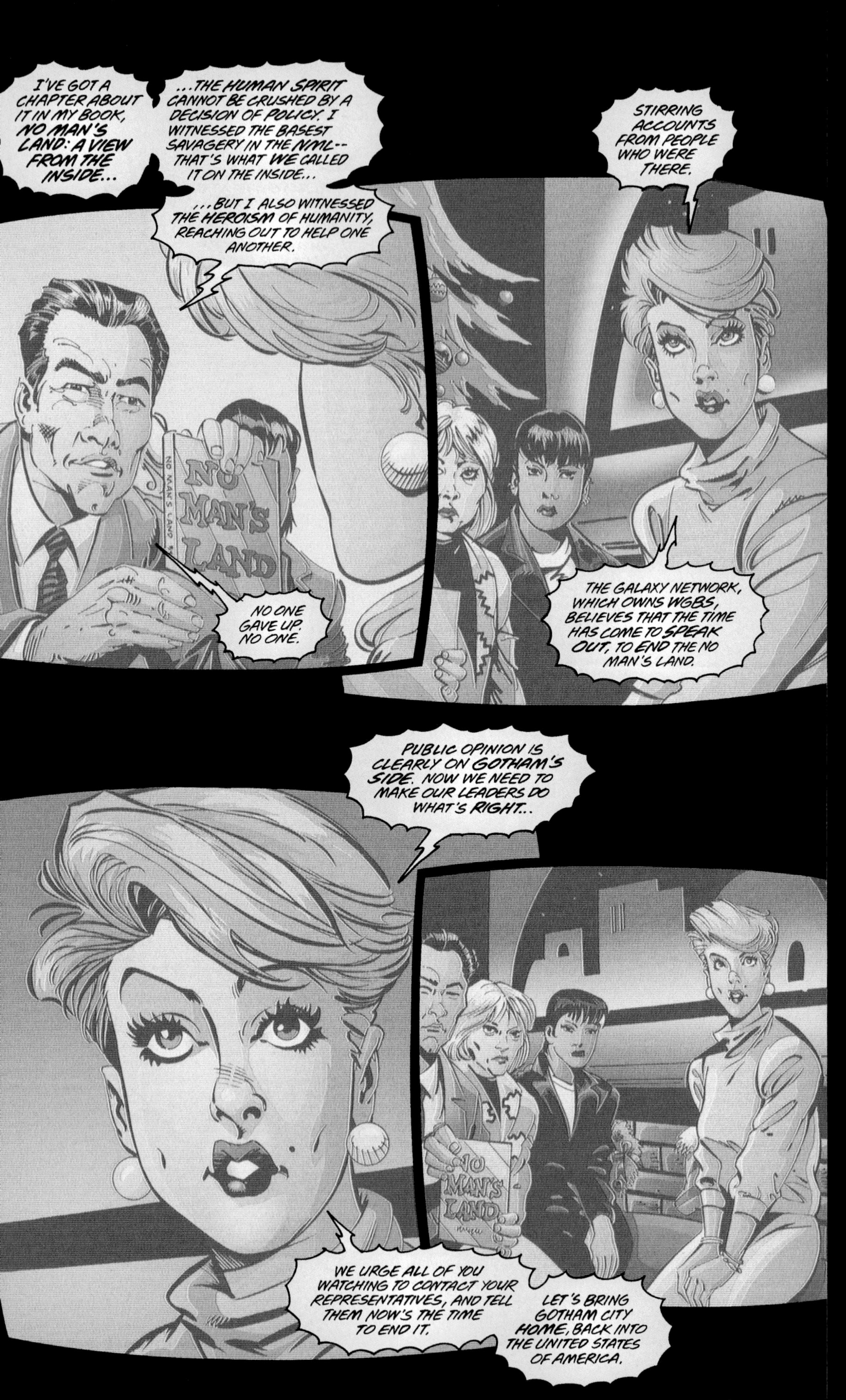
I'VE GOT A CHAPTER ABOUT IT IN MY BOOK, NO MAN'S LAND: A VIEW FROM THE INSIDE...
...THE HUMAN SPIRIT CANNOT BE CRUSHED BY A DECISION OF POLICY. I WITNESSED THE BASEST SAVAGERY IN THE NML-- THAT'S WHAT WE CALLED IT ON THE INSIDE...
...BUT I ALSO WITNESSED THE HEROISM OF HUMANITY, REACHING OUT TO HELP ONE ANOTHER.
NO MAN'S LAND
NO ONE GAVE UP. NO ONE.
STIRRING ACCOUNTS FROM PEOPLE WHO WERE THERE.
THE GALAXY NETWORK, WHICH OWNS WGBS, BELIEVES THAT THE TIME HAS COME TO SPEAK OUT, TO END THE NO MAN'S LAND.
PUBLIC OPINION IS CLEARLY ON GOTHAM'S SIDE. NOW WE NEED TO MAKE OUR LEADERS DO WHAT'S RIGHT...
WE URGE ALL OF YOU WATCHING TO CONTACT YOUR REPRESENTATIVES, AND TELL THEM NOW'S THE TIME TO END IT.
LET'S BRING GOTHAM CITY HOME, BACK INTO THE UNITED STATES OF AMERICA.

SIR, I'M NOT ACCUSTOMED TO BEING KEPT *WAITING*...

...AND YOU'VE KEPT ME WAITING FOR *OVER A WEEK!*

MAKE IT *FAST*, COBBLEPOT. I DON'T WANT TO BE SEEN WITH YOU.

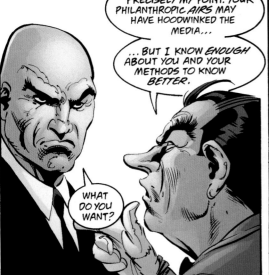

PRECISELY MY POINT. YOUR PHILANTHROPIC *AIRS* MAY HAVE HOODWINKED THE MEDIA...

...BUT I KNOW *ENOUGH* ABOUT YOU AND YOUR METHODS TO KNOW *BETTER.*

WHAT DO YOU WANT?

I WANT A PIECE OF THE *PIE*, MY FRIEND.

OR I GO TO THE *MEDIA* AND TELL THEM ABOUT OUR SHARED DEALINGS VIA YOUR SHAPELY ASSISTANT HERE.

MERCY, IF YOU PLEASE.

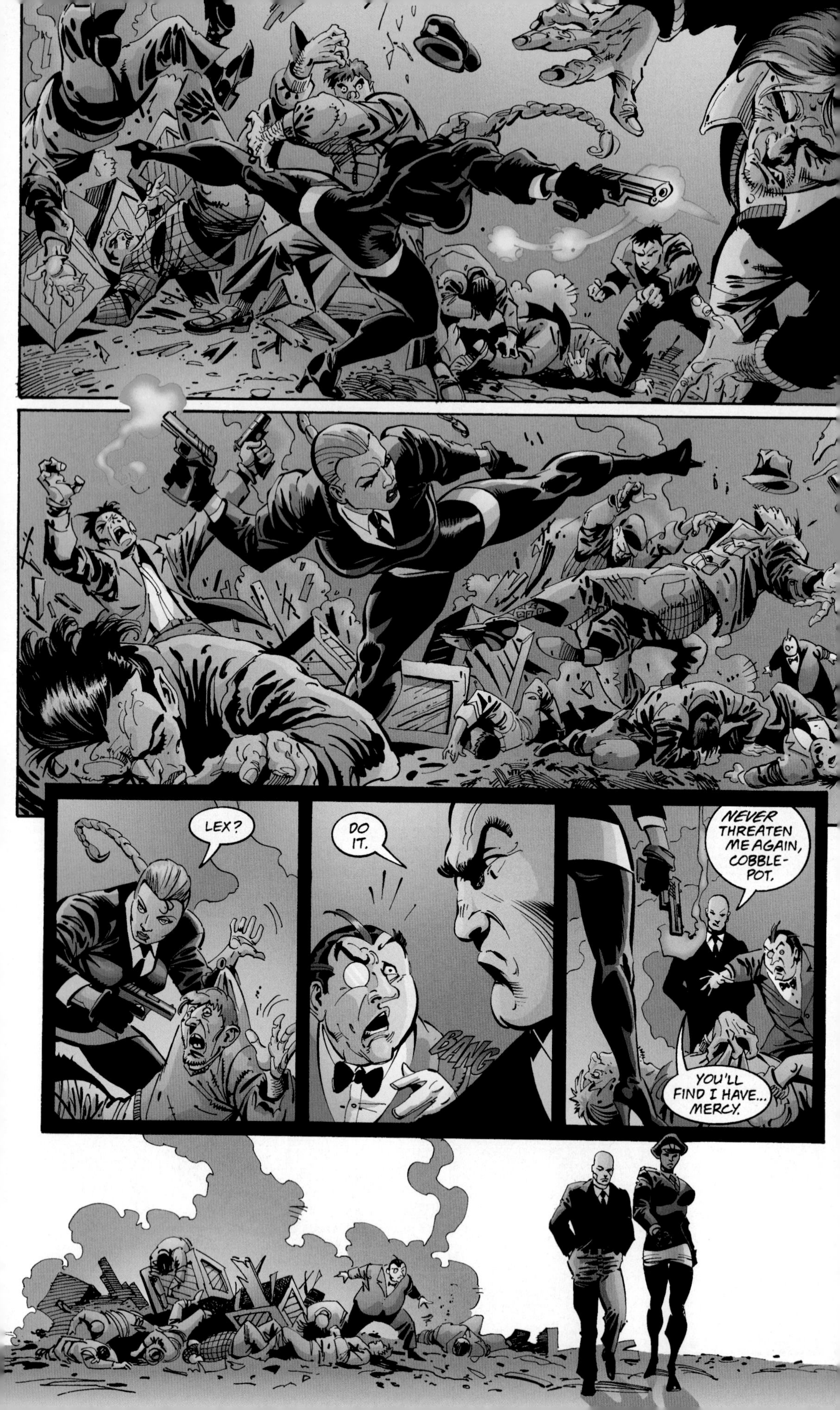
LEX?
DO IT.
BANG
NEVER THREATEN ME AGAIN, COBBLE-POT.
YOU'LL FIND I HAVE... MERCY.

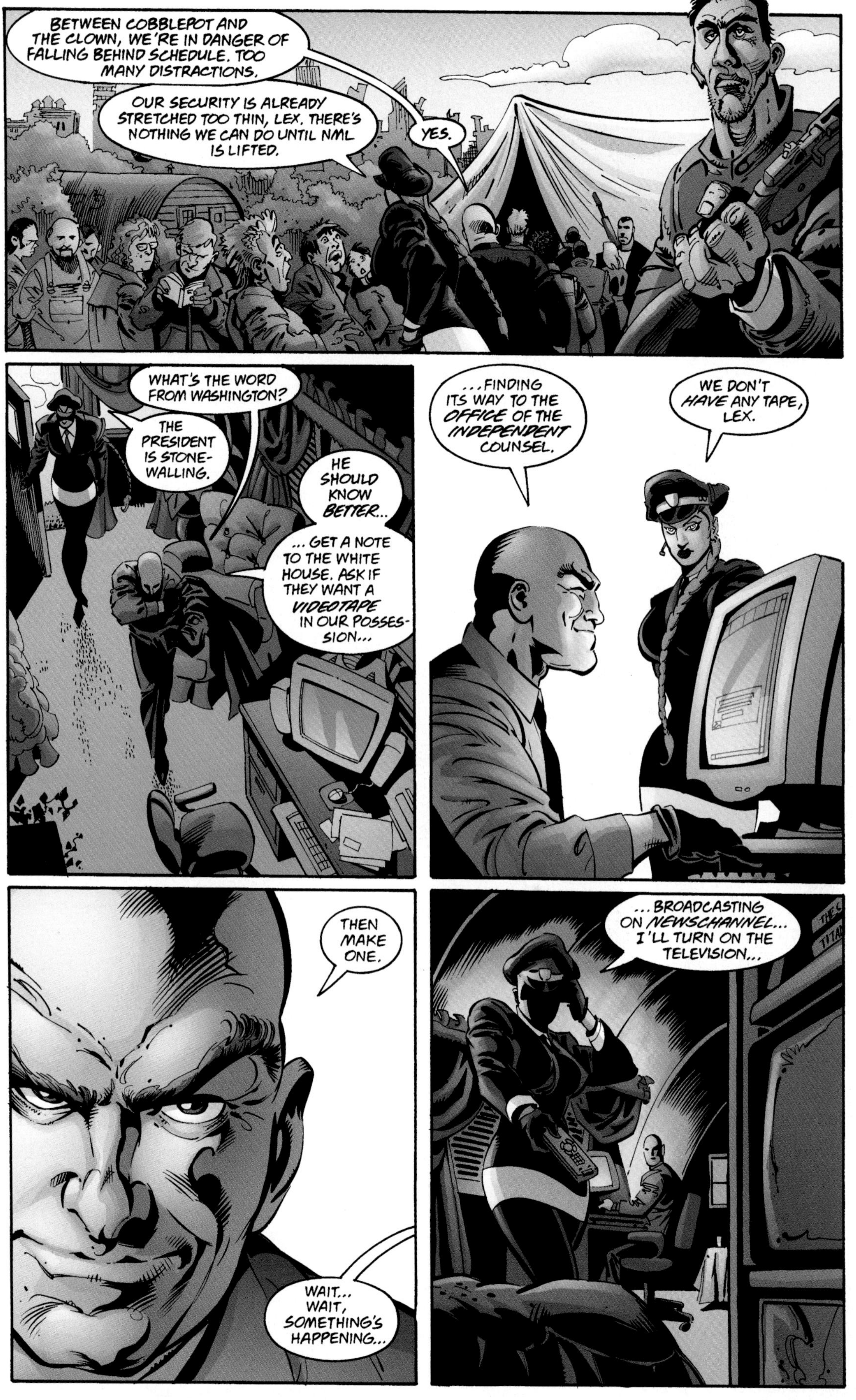
BETWEEN COBBLEPOT AND THE CLOWN, WE'RE IN DANGER OF FALLING BEHIND SCHEDULE. TOO MANY DISTRACTIONS.
OUR SECURITY IS ALREADY STRETCHED TOO THIN, LEX. THERE'S NOTHING WE CAN DO UNTIL NML IS LIFTED.
YES.
WHAT'S THE WORD FROM WASHINGTON?
THE PRESIDENT IS STONE-WALLING.
HE SHOULD KNOW BETTER...
...GET A NOTE TO THE WHITE HOUSE. ASK IF THEY WANT A VIDEOTAPE IN OUR POSSES-SION...
...FINDING ITS WAY TO THE OFFICE OF THE INDEPENDENT COUNSEL.
WE DON'T HAVE ANY TAPE, LEX.
THEN MAKE ONE.
WAIT... WAIT, SOMETHING'S HAPPENING...
...BROADCASTING ON NEWSCHANNEL... I'LL TURN ON THE TELEVISION...

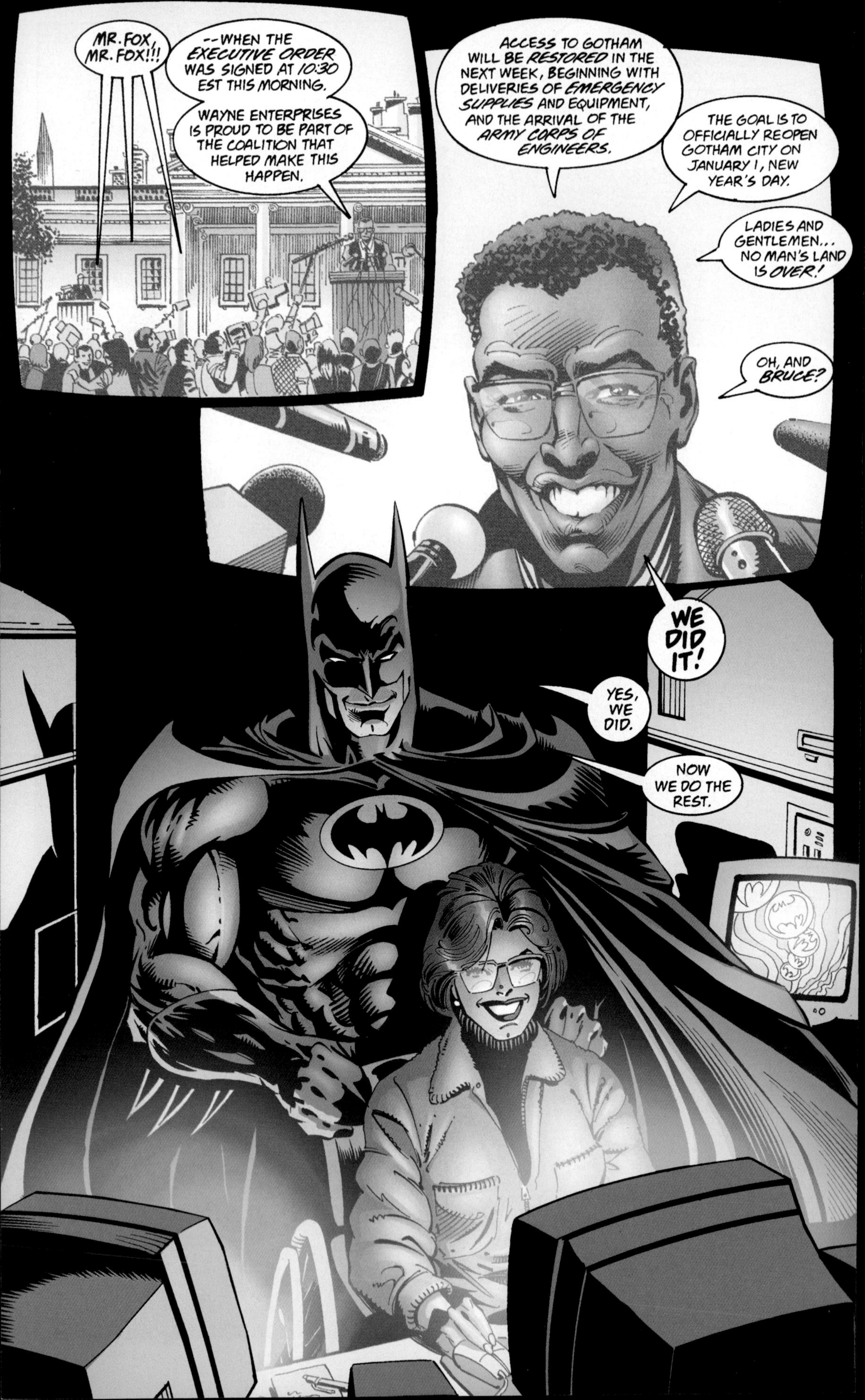
MR. FOX, MR. FOX!!!
--WHEN THE EXECUTIVE ORDER WAS SIGNED AT 10:30 EST THIS MORNING.
WAYNE ENTERPRISES IS PROUD TO BE PART OF THE COALITION THAT HELPED MAKE THIS HAPPEN.
ACCESS TO GOTHAM WILL BE RESTORED IN THE NEXT WEEK, BEGINNING WITH DELIVERIES OF EMERGENCY SUPPLIES AND EQUIPMENT, AND THE ARRIVAL OF THE ARMY CORPS OF ENGINEERS.
THE GOAL IS TO OFFICIALLY REOPEN GOTHAM CITY ON JANUARY 1, NEW YEAR'S DAY.
LADIES AND GENTLEMEN... NO MAN'S LAND IS OVER!
OH, AND BRUCE?
WE DID IT!
YES, WE DID.
NOW WE DO THE REST.

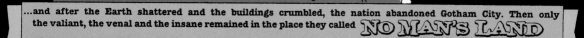

...and after the Earth shattered and the buildings crumbled, the nation abandoned Gotham City. Then only the valiant, the venal and the insane remained in the place they called **NO MAN'S LAND**

EVACUATION

JOKER'LL GO FOR THE INNOCENTS FIRST, TRYING TO DRAW ME OUT.

DON'T LET HIM.

Dennis O'Neil • •writer
Roger Robinson • •penciller
James Pascoe • •inker
Rob Ro & Alex Bleyaert • •
colorists & separators
Ken Bruzenak • •letterer
Mike Carlin • •editor

Azrael created by
Dennis O'Neil
Joe Quesada

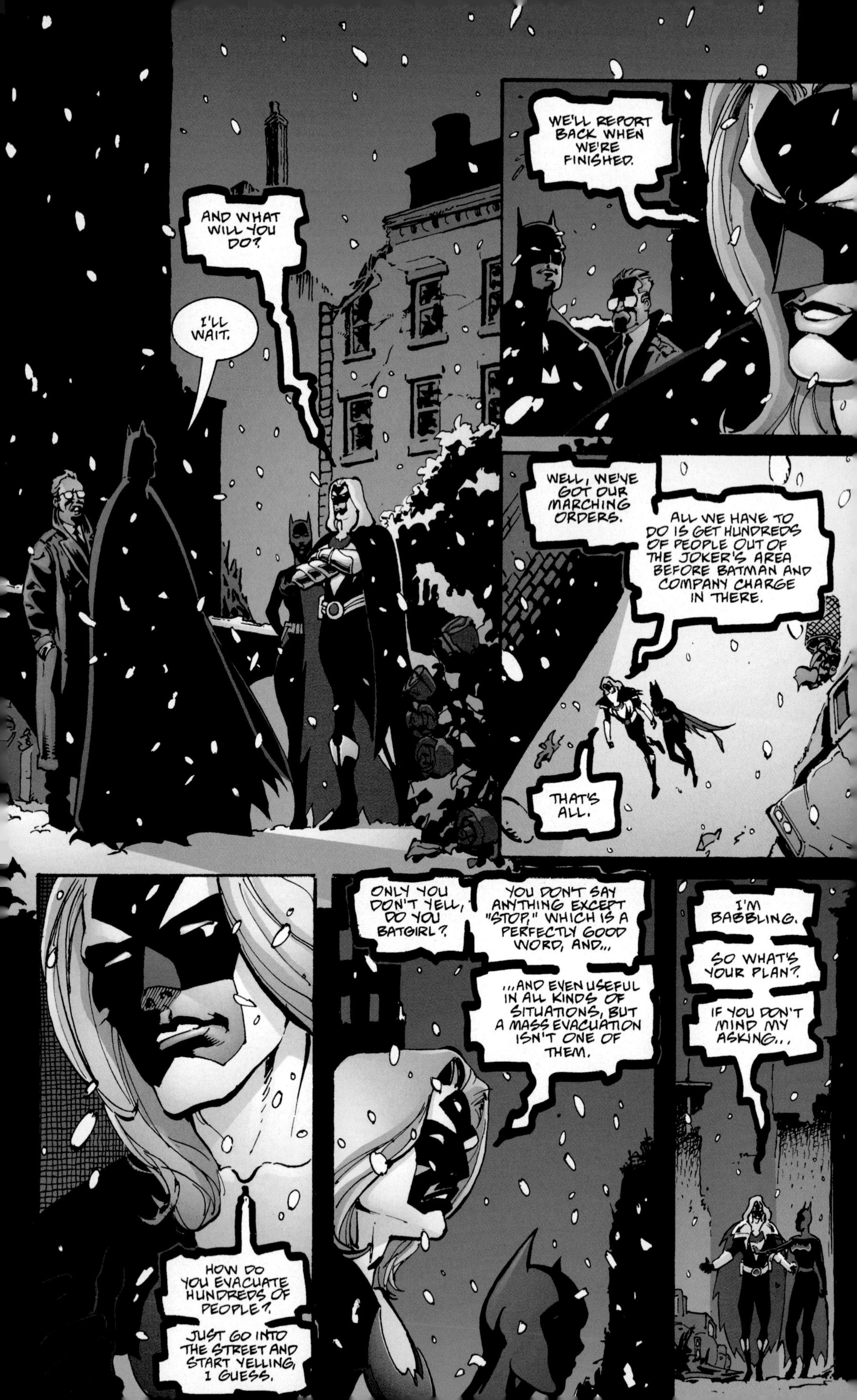
AND WHAT WILL YOU DO?
I'LL WAIT.
WE'LL REPORT BACK WHEN WE'RE FINISHED.
WELL, WE'VE GOT OUR MARCHING ORDERS.
ALL WE HAVE TO DO IS GET HUNDREDS OF PEOPLE OUT OF THE JOKER'S AREA BEFORE BATMAN AND COMPANY CHARGE IN THERE.
THAT'S ALL.
HOW DO YOU EVACUATE HUNDREDS OF PEOPLE?
JUST GO INTO THE STREET AND START YELLING, I GUESS.
ONLY YOU DON'T YELL, DO YOU BATGIRL?
YOU DON'T SAY ANYTHING EXCEPT "STOP," WHICH IS A PERFECTLY GOOD WORD, AND...
...AND EVEN USEFUL IN ALL KINDS OF SITUATIONS, BUT A MASS EVACUATION ISN'T ONE OF THEM.
I'M BABBLING.
SO WHAT'S YOUR PLAN?
IF YOU DON'T MIND MY ASKING...

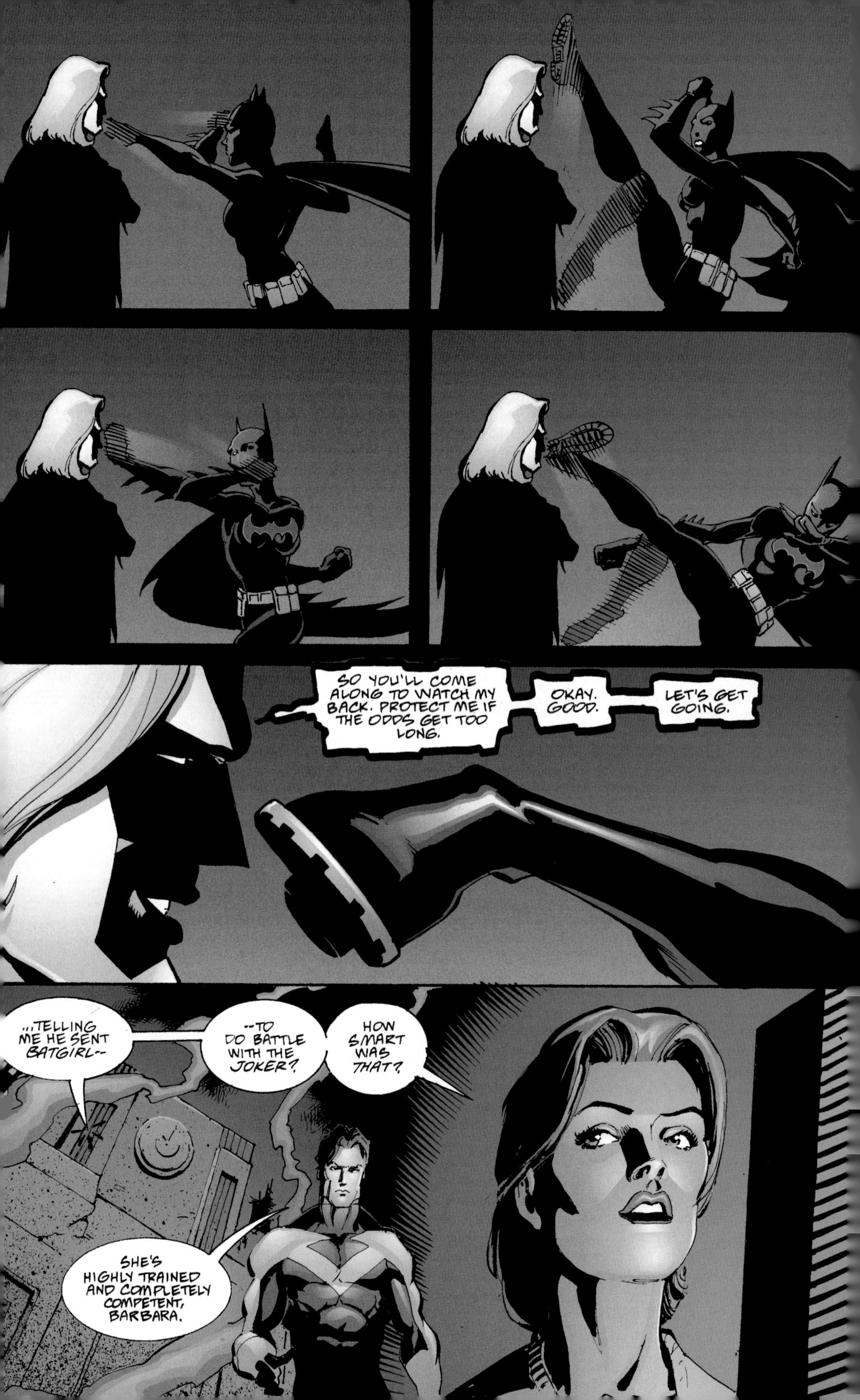
SO YOU'LL COME ALONG TO WATCH MY BACK. PROTECT ME IF THE ODDS GET TOO LONG.
OKAY. GOOD.
LET'S GET GOING.
...TELLING ME HE SENT BATGIRL--
--TO DO BATTLE WITH THE JOKER?
HOW SMART WAS THAT?
SHE'S HIGHLY TRAINED AND COMPLETELY COMPETENT, BARBARA.

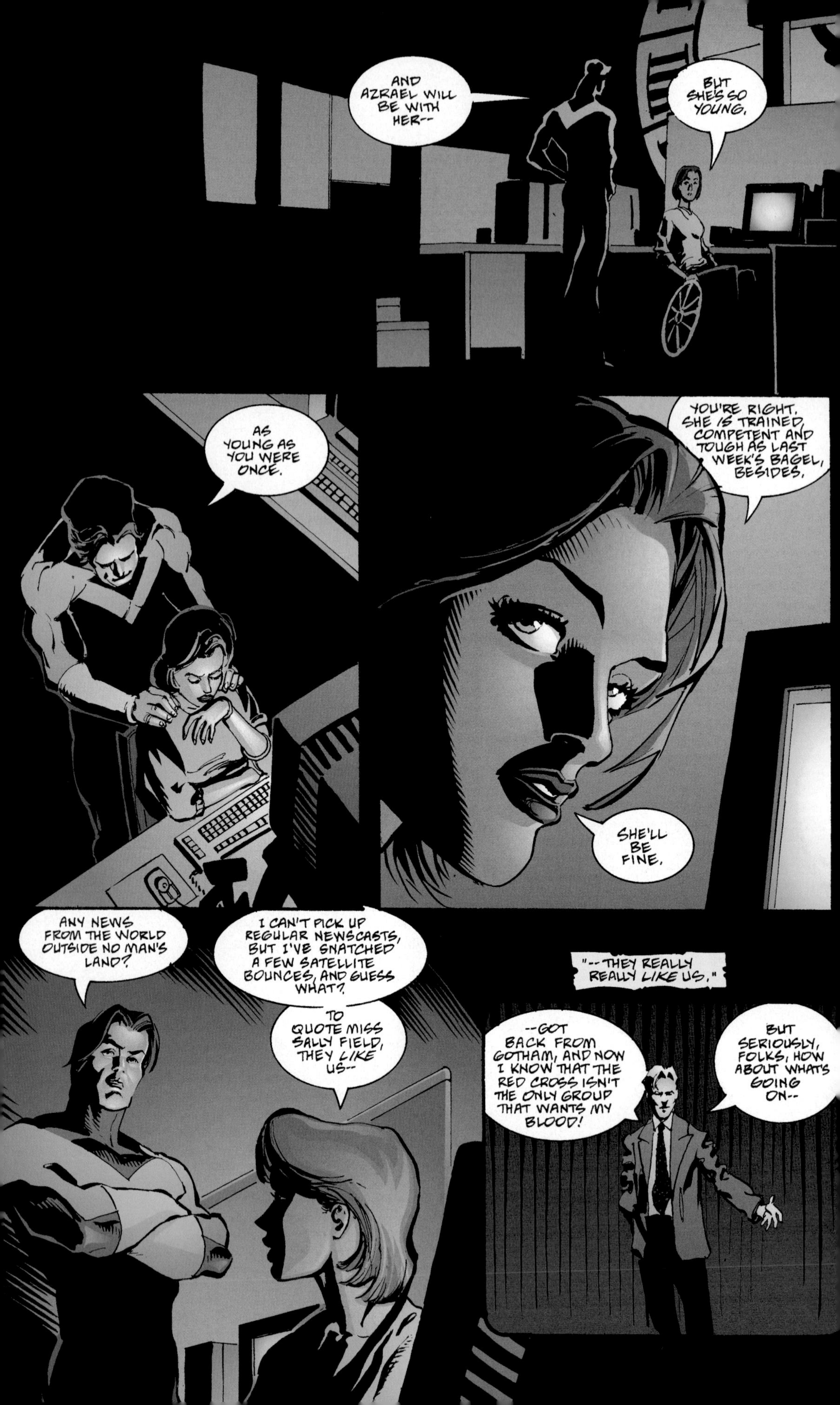

AND AZRAEL WILL BE WITH HER--
BUT SHE'S SO YOUNG.
AS YOUNG AS YOU WERE ONCE.
YOU'RE RIGHT. SHE IS TRAINED, COMPETENT AND TOUGH AS LAST WEEK'S BAGEL. BESIDES,
SHE'LL BE FINE.
ANY NEWS FROM THE WORLD OUTSIDE NO MAN'S LAND?
I CAN'T PICK UP REGULAR NEWSCASTS, BUT I'VE SNATCHED A FEW SATELLITE BOUNCES, AND GUESS WHAT?
TO QUOTE MISS SALLY FIELD, THEY LIKE US--
"--THEY REALLY REALLY LIKE US."
--GOT BACK FROM GOTHAM, AND NOW I KNOW THAT THE RED CROSS ISN'T THE ONLY GROUP THAT WANTS MY BLOOD!
BUT SERIOUSLY, FOLKS, HOW ABOUT WHAT'S GOING ON--

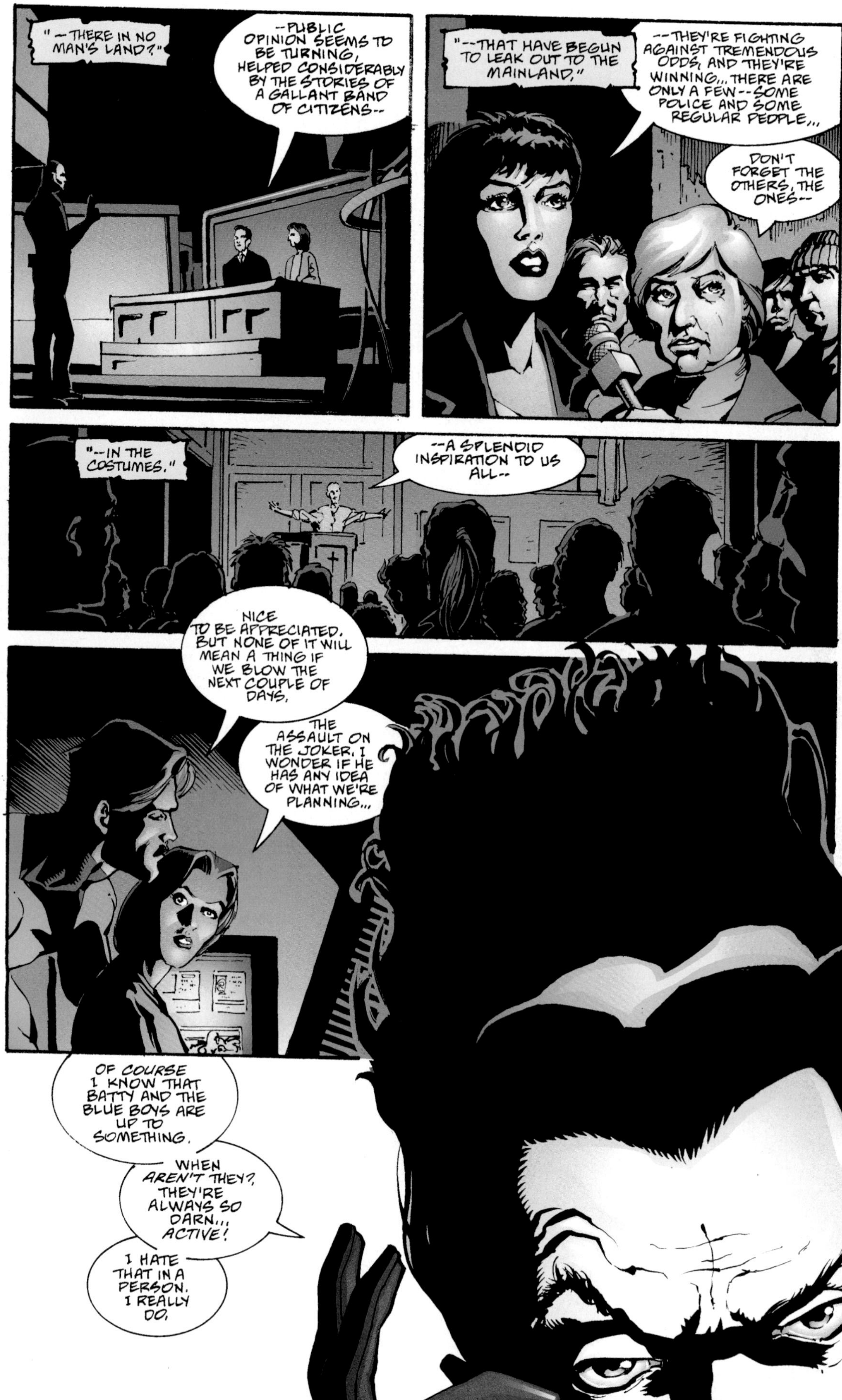
"--THERE IN NO MAN'S LAND?"
--PUBLIC OPINION SEEMS TO BE TURNING, HELPED CONSIDERABLY BY THE STORIES OF A GALLANT BAND OF CITIZENS--
"--THAT HAVE BEGUN TO LEAK OUT TO THE MAINLAND,"
--THEY'RE FIGHTING AGAINST TREMENDOUS ODDS, AND THEY'RE WINNING... THERE ARE ONLY A FEW--SOME POLICE AND SOME REGULAR PEOPLE...
DON'T FORGET THE OTHERS, THE ONES--
"--IN THE COSTUMES."
--A SPLENDID INSPIRATION TO US ALL--
NICE TO BE APPRECIATED. BUT NONE OF IT WILL MEAN A THING IF WE BLOW THE NEXT COUPLE OF DAYS.
THE ASSAULT ON THE JOKER. I WONDER IF HE HAS ANY IDEA OF WHAT WE'RE PLANNING...
OF COURSE I KNOW THAT BATTY AND THE BLUE BOYS ARE UP TO SOMETHING.
WHEN AREN'T THEY? THEY'RE ALWAYS SO DARN... ACTIVE!
I HATE THAT IN A PERSON. I REALLY DO.

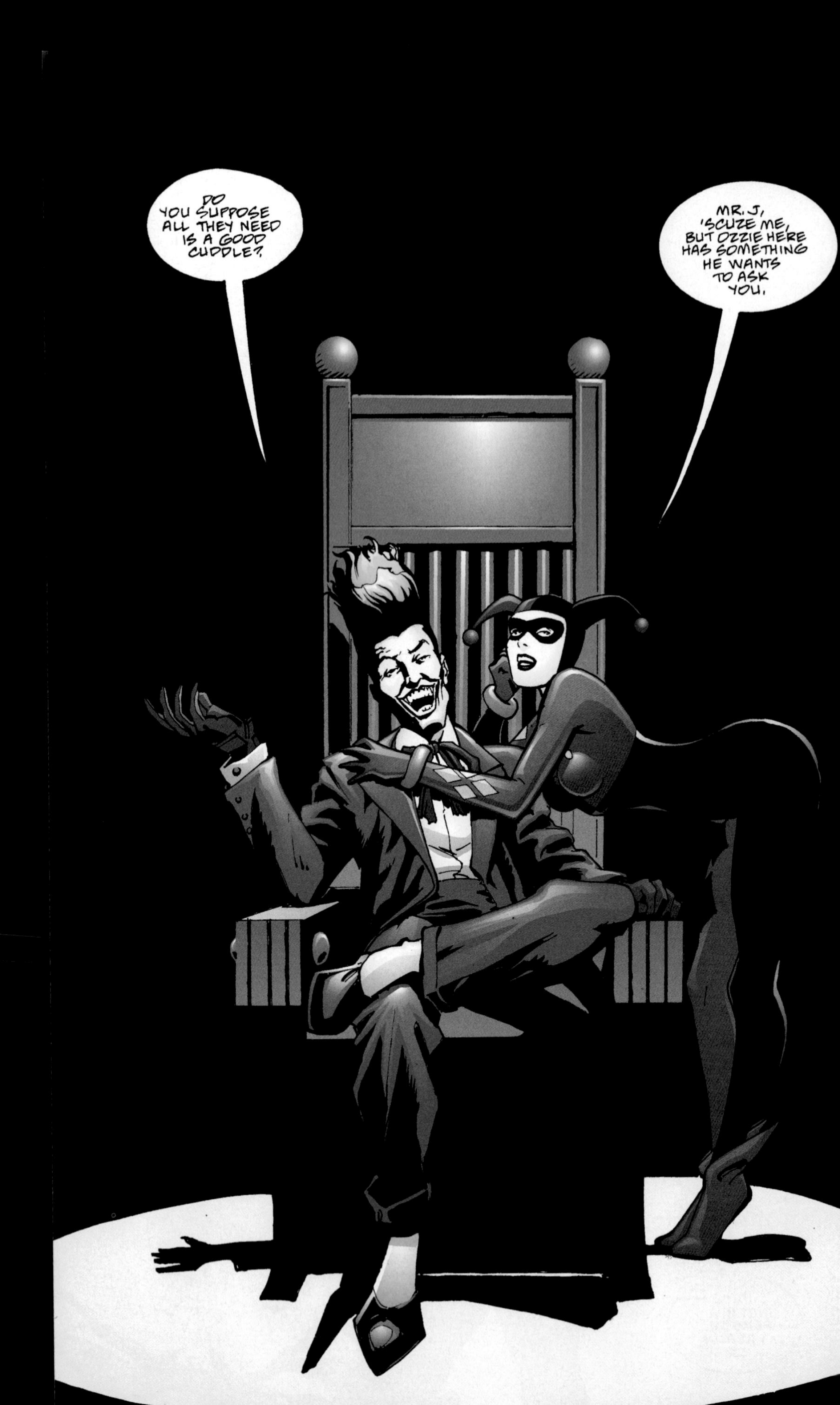
DO YOU SUPPOSE ALL THEY NEED IS A GOOD CUDDLE?
MR. J, 'SCUZE ME, BUT OZZIE HERE HAS SOMETHING HE WANTS TO ASK YOU.

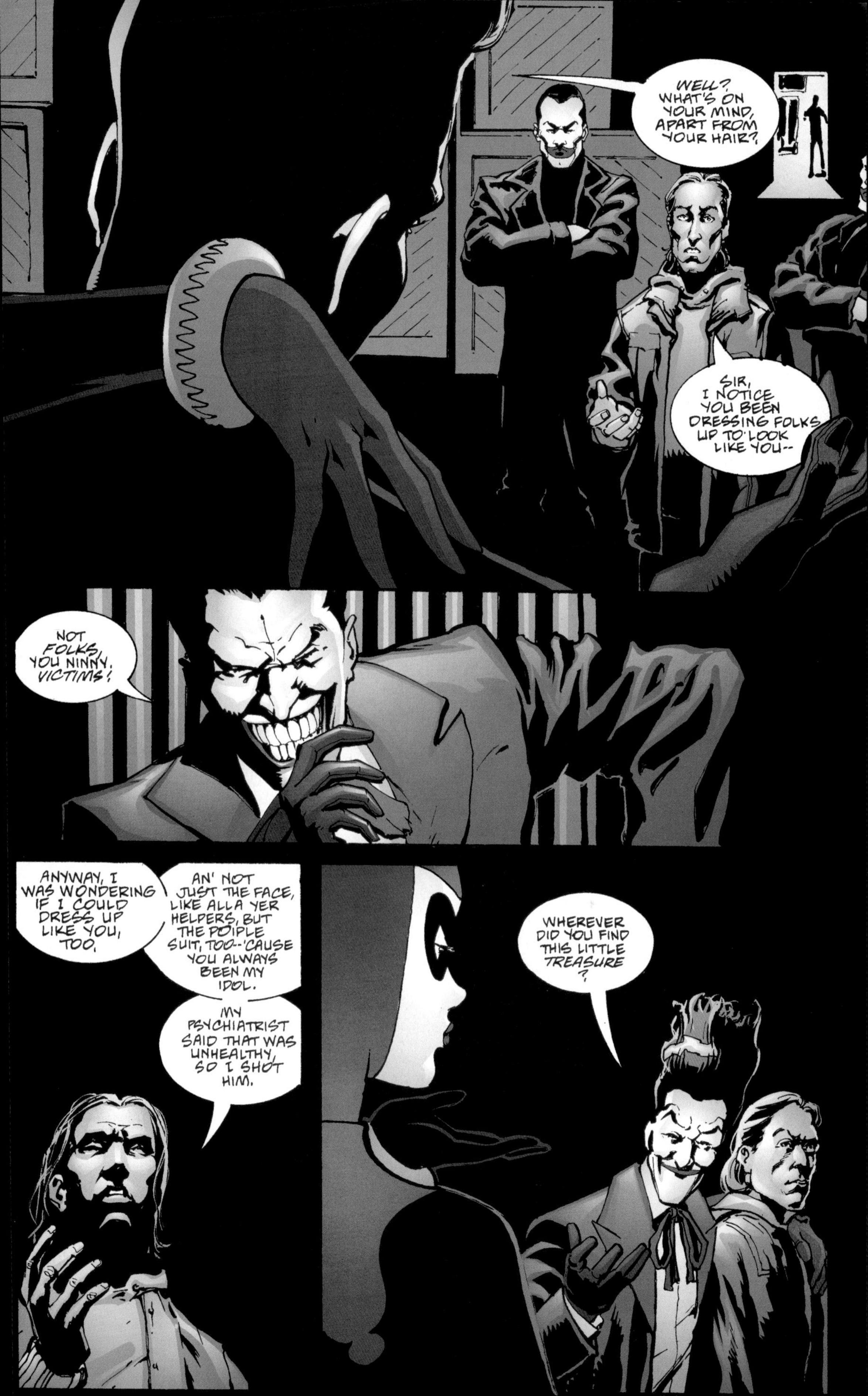
WELL? WHAT'S ON YOUR MIND, APART FROM YOUR HAIR?
SIR, I NOTICE YOU BEEN DRESSING FOLKS UP TO LOOK LIKE YOU--
NOT FOLKS, YOU NINNY. VICTIMS!
ANYWAY, I WAS WONDERING IF I COULD DRESS UP LIKE YOU, TOO.
AN' NOT JUST THE FACE, LIKE ALLA YER HELPERS, BUT THE POIPLE SUIT, TOO--'CAUSE YOU ALWAYS BEEN MY IDOL.
MY PSYCHIATRIST SAID THAT WAS UNHEALTHY, SO I SHOT HIM.
WHEREVER DID YOU FIND THIS LITTLE TREASURE?

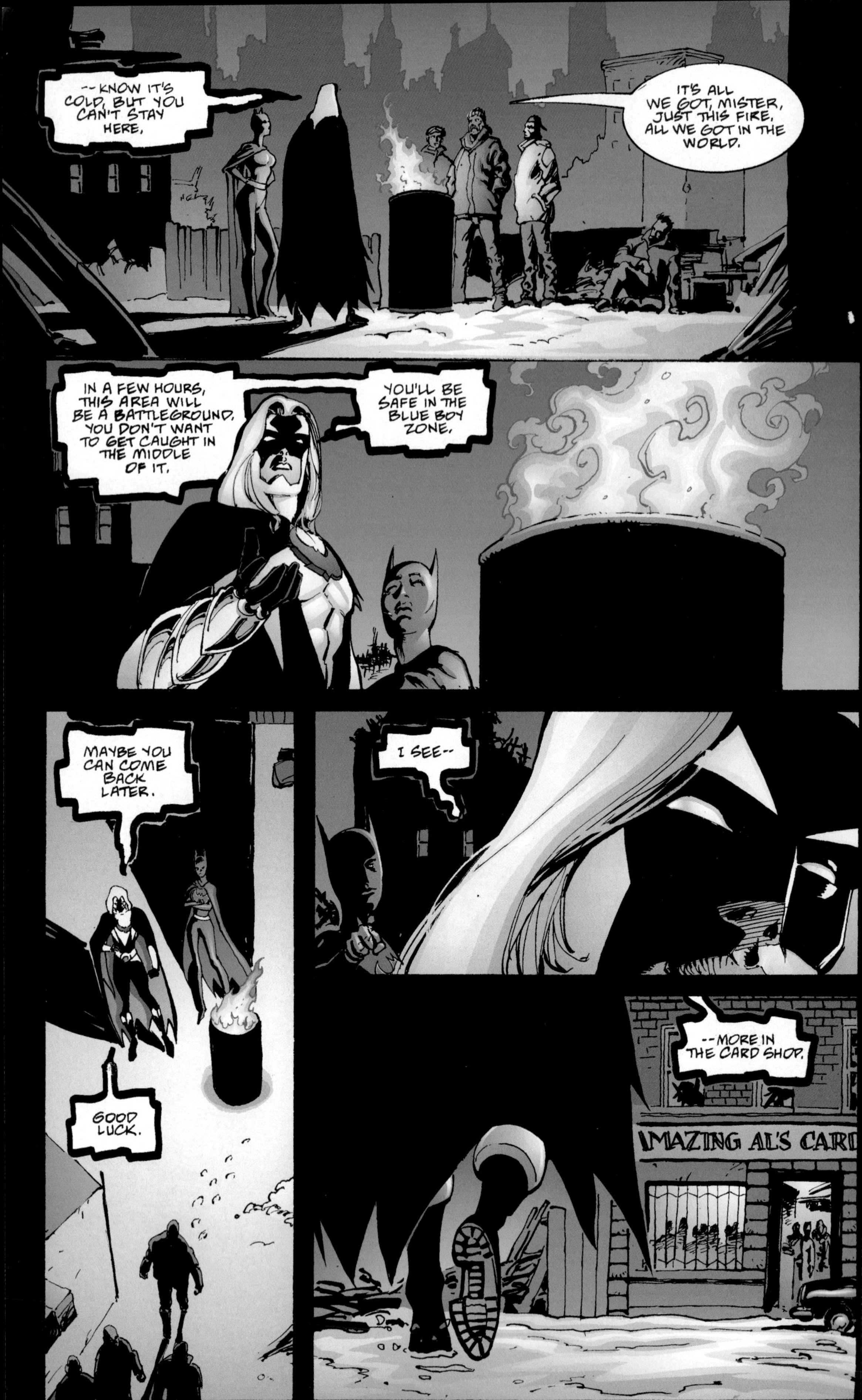
--KNOW IT'S COLD, BUT YOU CAN'T STAY HERE,
IT'S ALL WE GOT, MISTER, JUST THIS FIRE, ALL WE GOT IN THE WORLD.
IN A FEW HOURS, THIS AREA WILL BE A BATTLEGROUND, YOU DON'T WANT TO GET CAUGHT IN THE MIDDLE OF IT,
YOU'LL BE SAFE IN THE BLUE BOY ZONE,
MAYBE YOU CAN COME BACK LATER.
GOOD LUCK.
I SEE--
--MORE IN THE CARD SHOP.
IMAZING AL'S CARD

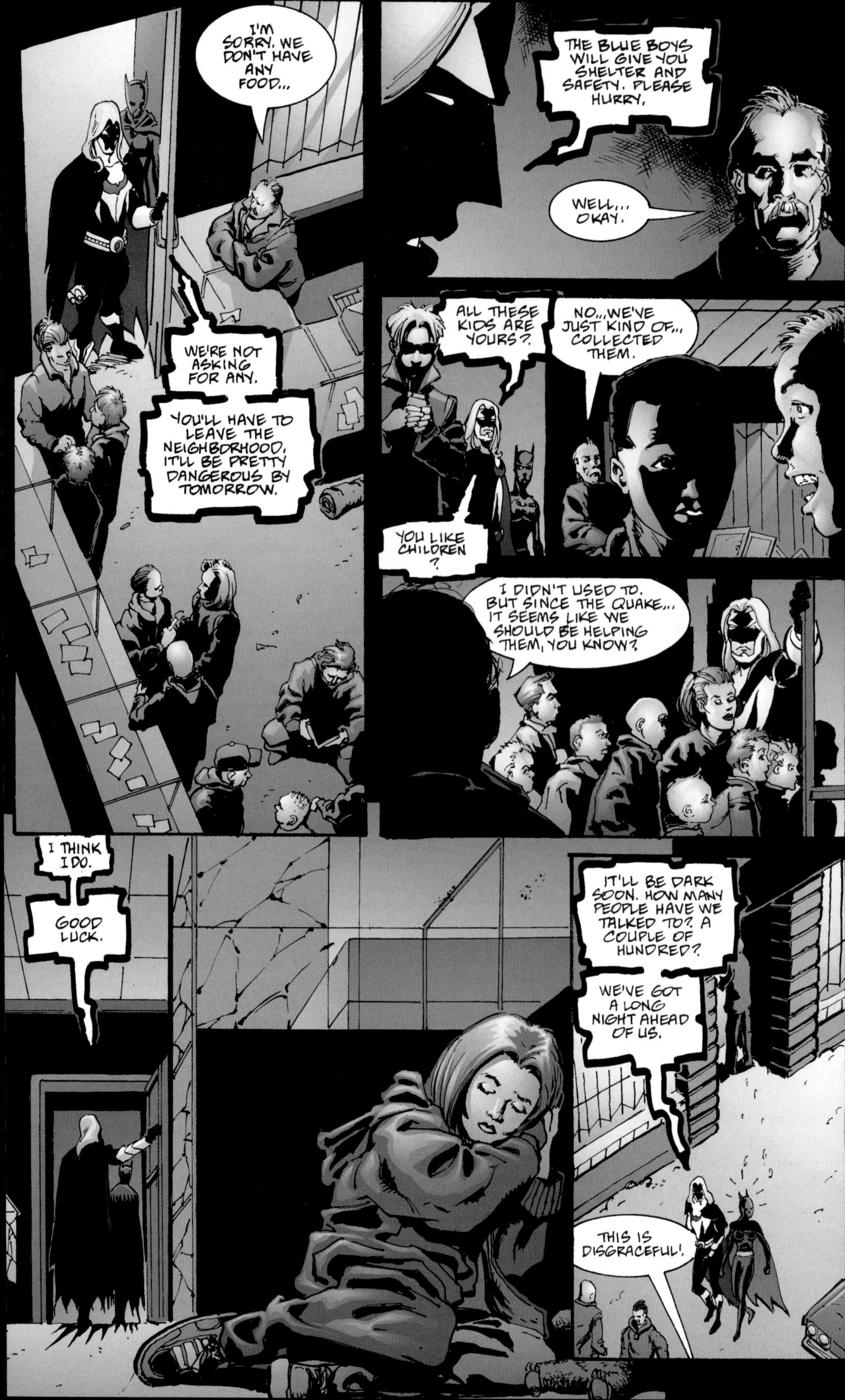
I'M SORRY. WE DON'T HAVE ANY FOOD...
WE'RE NOT ASKING FOR ANY.
YOU'LL HAVE TO LEAVE THE NEIGHBORHOOD. IT'LL BE PRETTY DANGEROUS BY TOMORROW.
THE BLUE BOYS WILL GIVE YOU SHELTER AND SAFETY. PLEASE HURRY.
WELL... OKAY.
ALL THESE KIDS ARE YOURS?
NO... WE'VE JUST KIND OF... COLLECTED THEM.
YOU LIKE CHILDREN?
I DIDN'T USED TO. BUT SINCE THE QUAKE... IT SEEMS LIKE WE SHOULD BE HELPING THEM, YOU KNOW?
I THINK I DO.
GOOD LUCK.
IT'LL BE DARK SOON. HOW MANY PEOPLE HAVE WE TALKED TO? A COUPLE OF HUNDRED?
WE'VE GOT A LONG NIGHT AHEAD OF US.
THIS IS DISGRACEFUL!

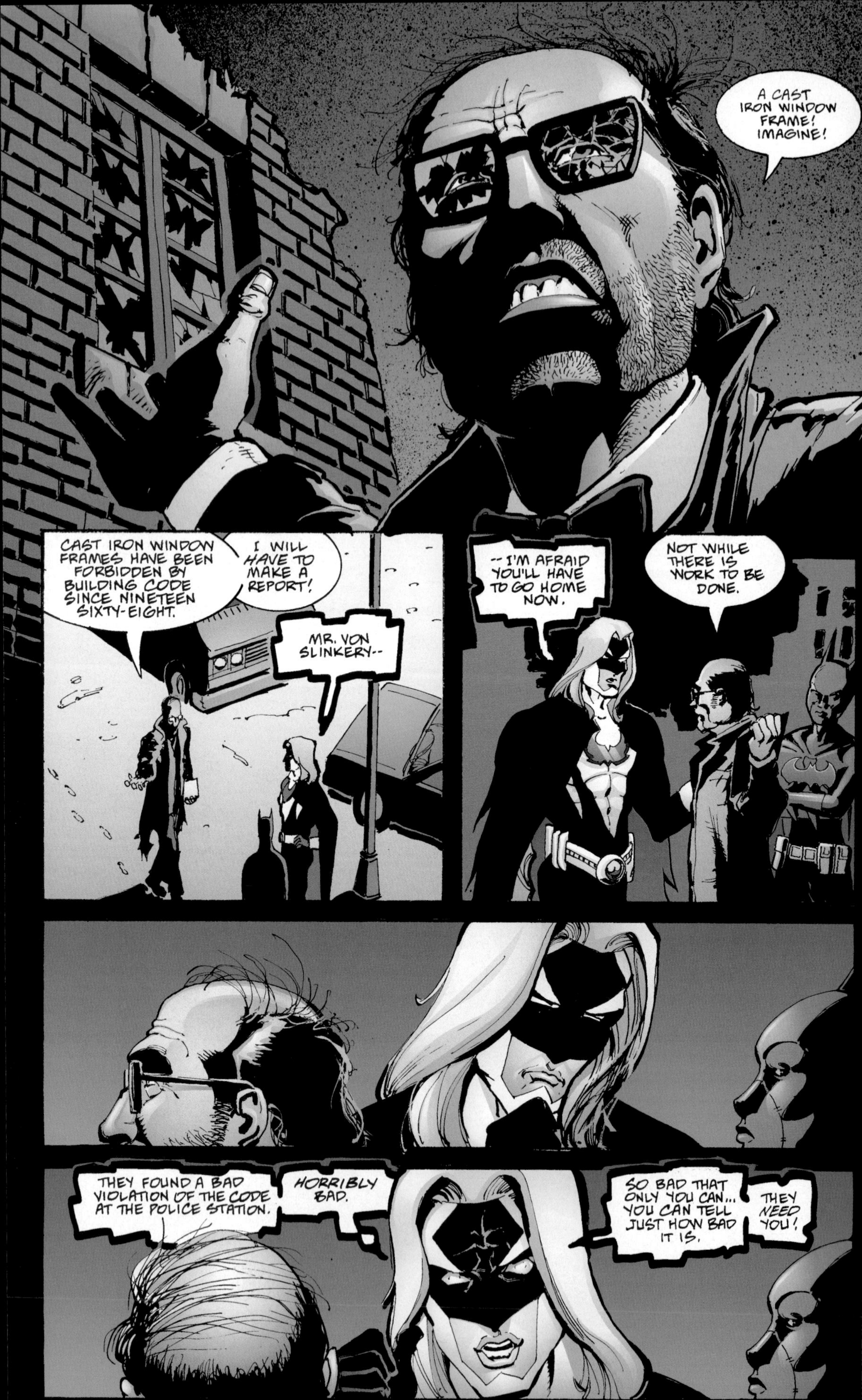
A CAST IRON WINDOW FRAME! IMAGINE!
CAST IRON WINDOW FRAMES HAVE BEEN FORBIDDEN BY BUILDING CODE SINCE NINETEEN SIXTY-EIGHT.
I WILL HAVE TO MAKE A REPORT!
MR. VON SLINKERY--
--I'M AFRAID YOU'LL HAVE TO GO HOME NOW.
NOT WHILE THERE IS WORK TO BE DONE.
THEY FOUND A BAD VIOLATION OF THE CODE AT THE POLICE STATION.
HORRIBLY BAD.
SO BAD THAT ONLY YOU CAN... YOU CAN TELL JUST HOW BAD IT IS.
THEY NEED YOU!

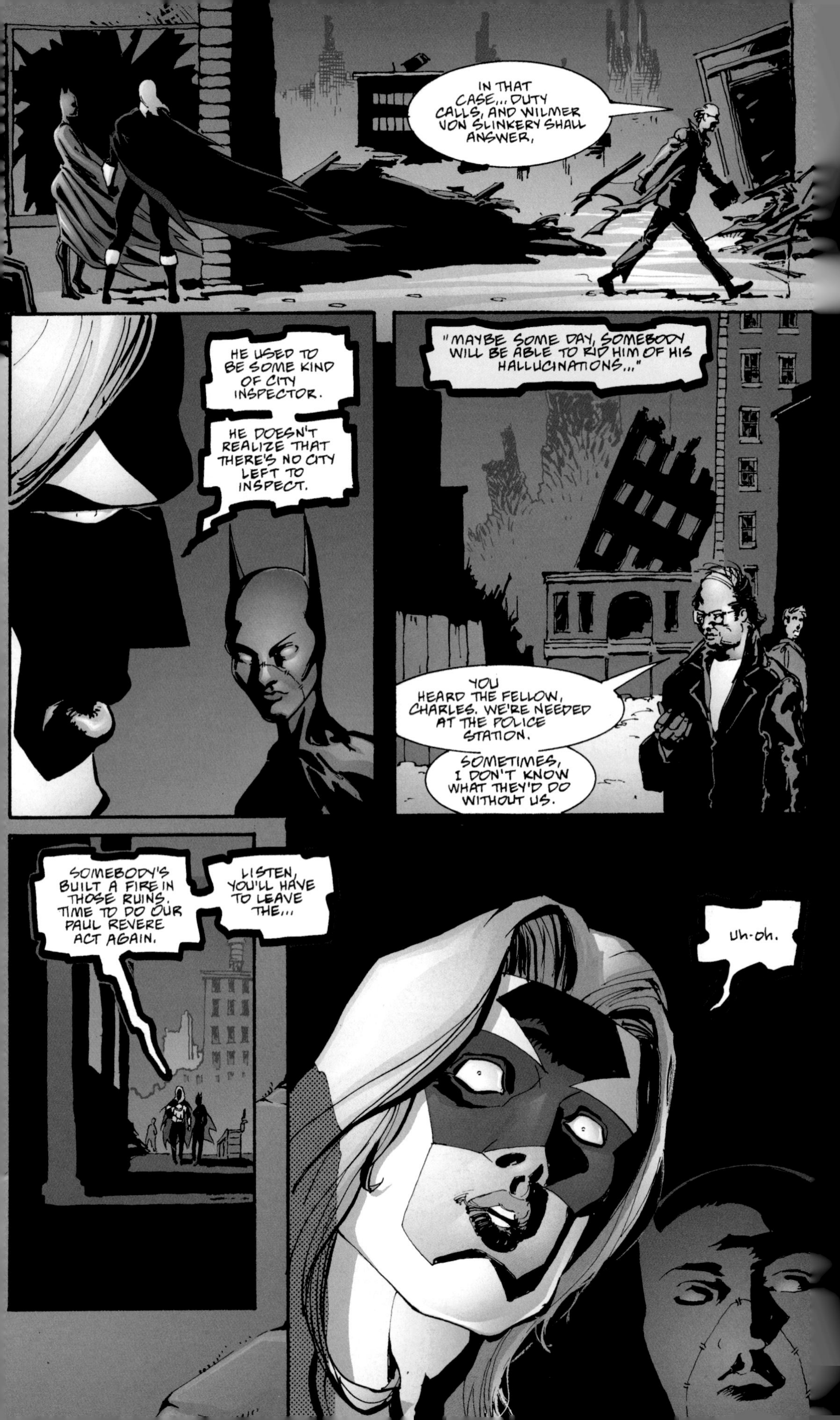
IN THAT CASE... DUTY CALLS, AND WILMER VON SLINKERY SHALL ANSWER.
HE USED TO BE SOME KIND OF CITY INSPECTOR.
HE DOESN'T REALIZE THAT THERE'S NO CITY LEFT TO INSPECT.
"MAYBE SOME DAY, SOMEBODY WILL BE ABLE TO RID HIM OF HIS HALLUCINATIONS..."
YOU HEARD THE FELLOW, CHARLES. WE'RE NEEDED AT THE POLICE STATION.
SOMETIMES, I DON'T KNOW WHAT THEY'D DO WITHOUT US.
SOMEBODY'S BUILT A FIRE IN THOSE RUINS. TIME TO DO OUR PAUL REVERE ACT AGAIN.
LISTEN, YOU'LL HAVE TO LEAVE THE...
Uh-oh.

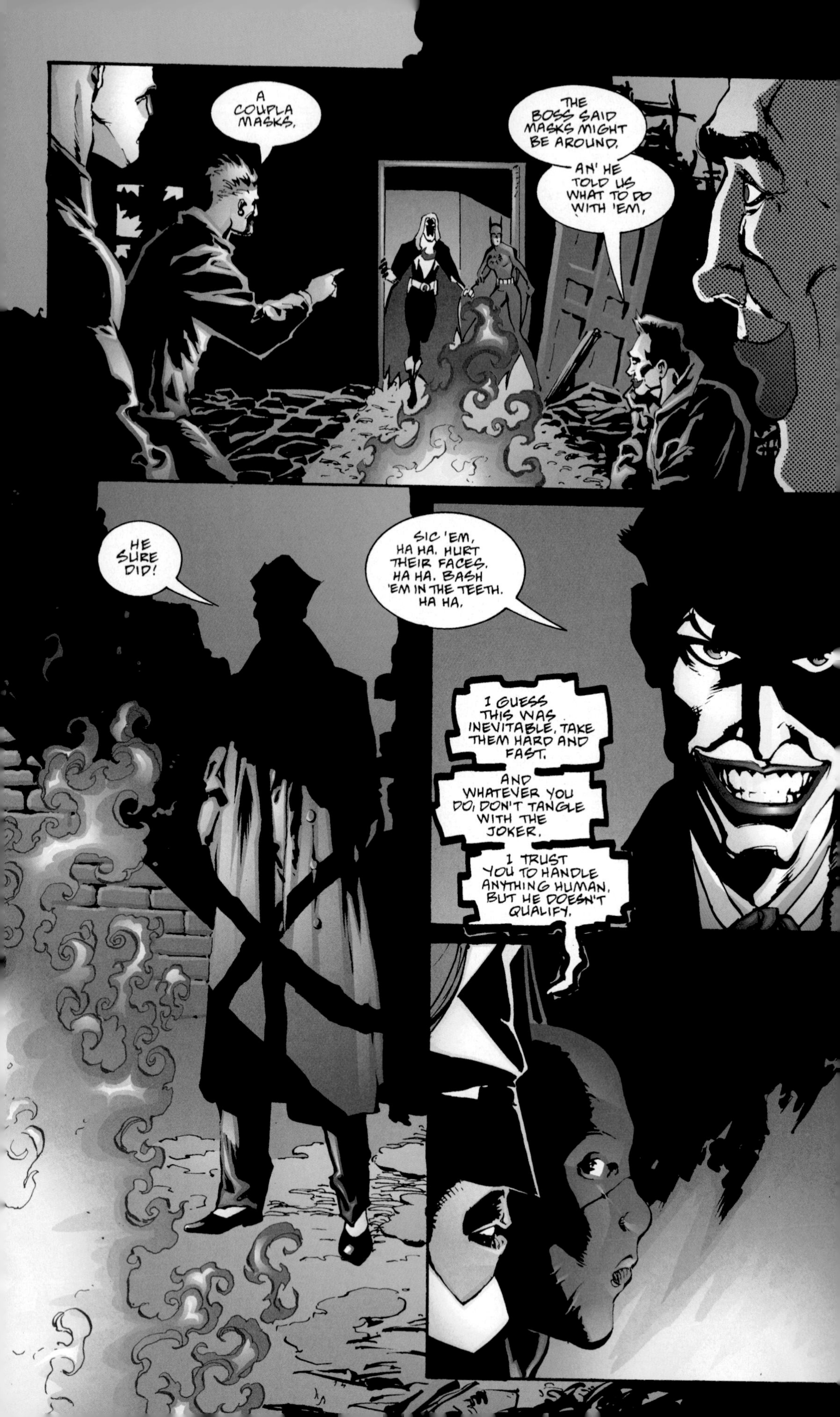
A COUPLA MASKS.
THE BOSS SAID MASKS MIGHT BE AROUND.
AN' HE TOLD US WHAT TO DO WITH 'EM.
HE SURE DID!
SIC 'EM. HA HA. HURT THEIR FACES. HA HA. BASH 'EM IN THE TEETH. HA HA.
I GUESS THIS WAS INEVITABLE. TAKE THEM HARD AND FAST.
AND WHATEVER YOU DO, DON'T TANGLE WITH THE JOKER.
I TRUST YOU TO HANDLE ANYTHING HUMAN. BUT HE DOESN'T QUALIFY.

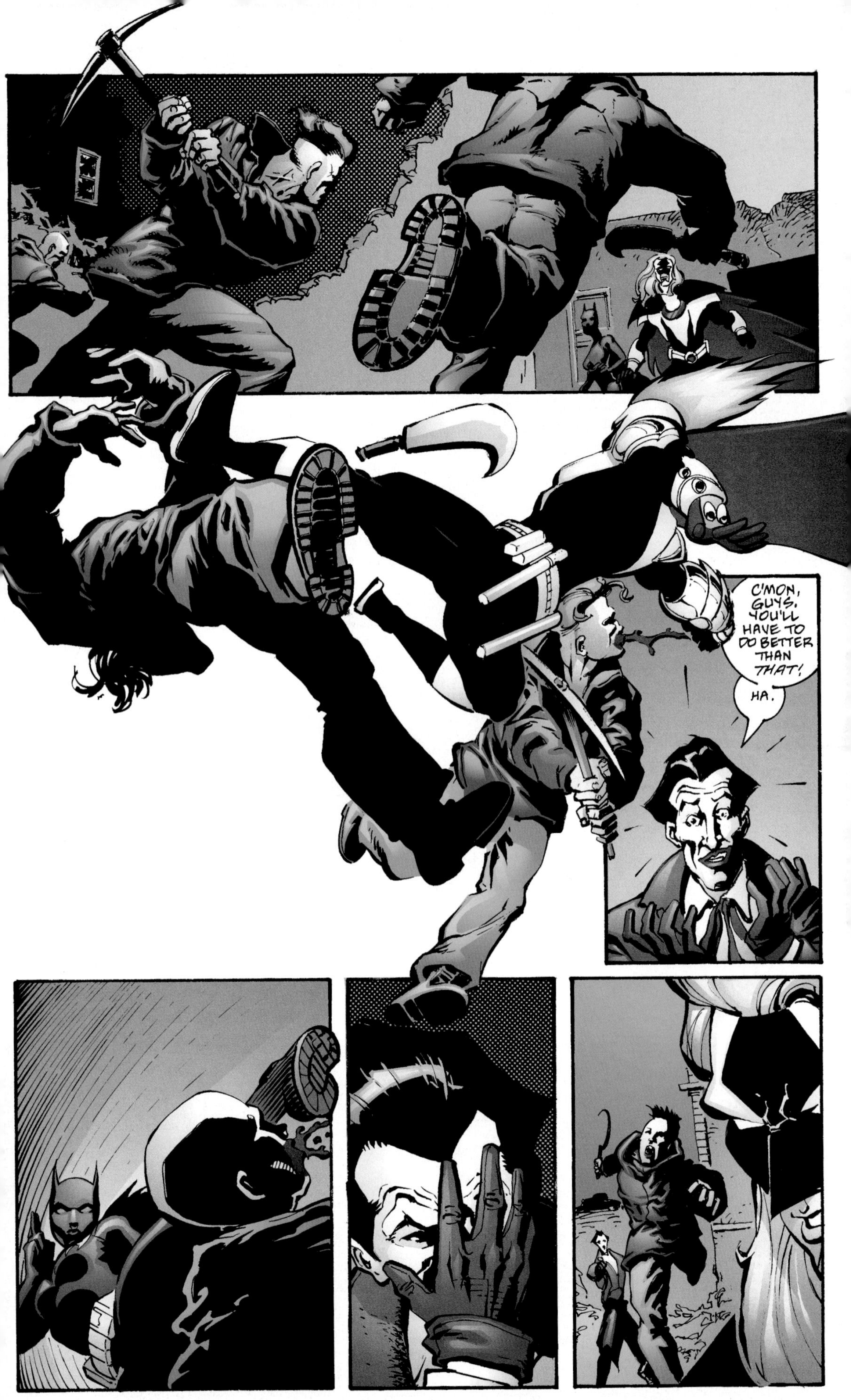
C'MON, GUYS, YOU'LL HAVE TO DO BETTER THAN THAT!
HA.

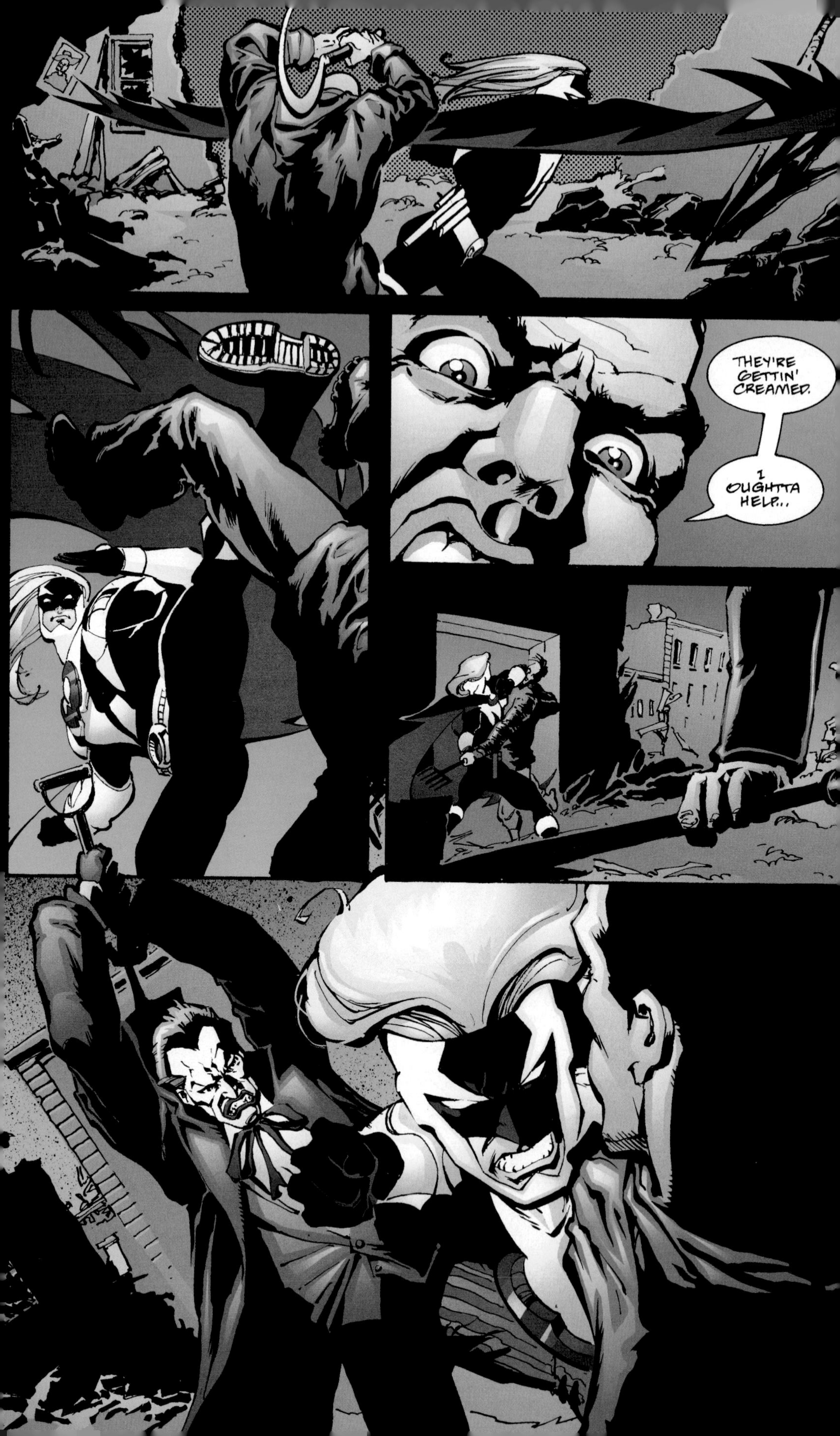
THEY'RE GETTIN' CREAMED.
I OUGHTTA HELP...

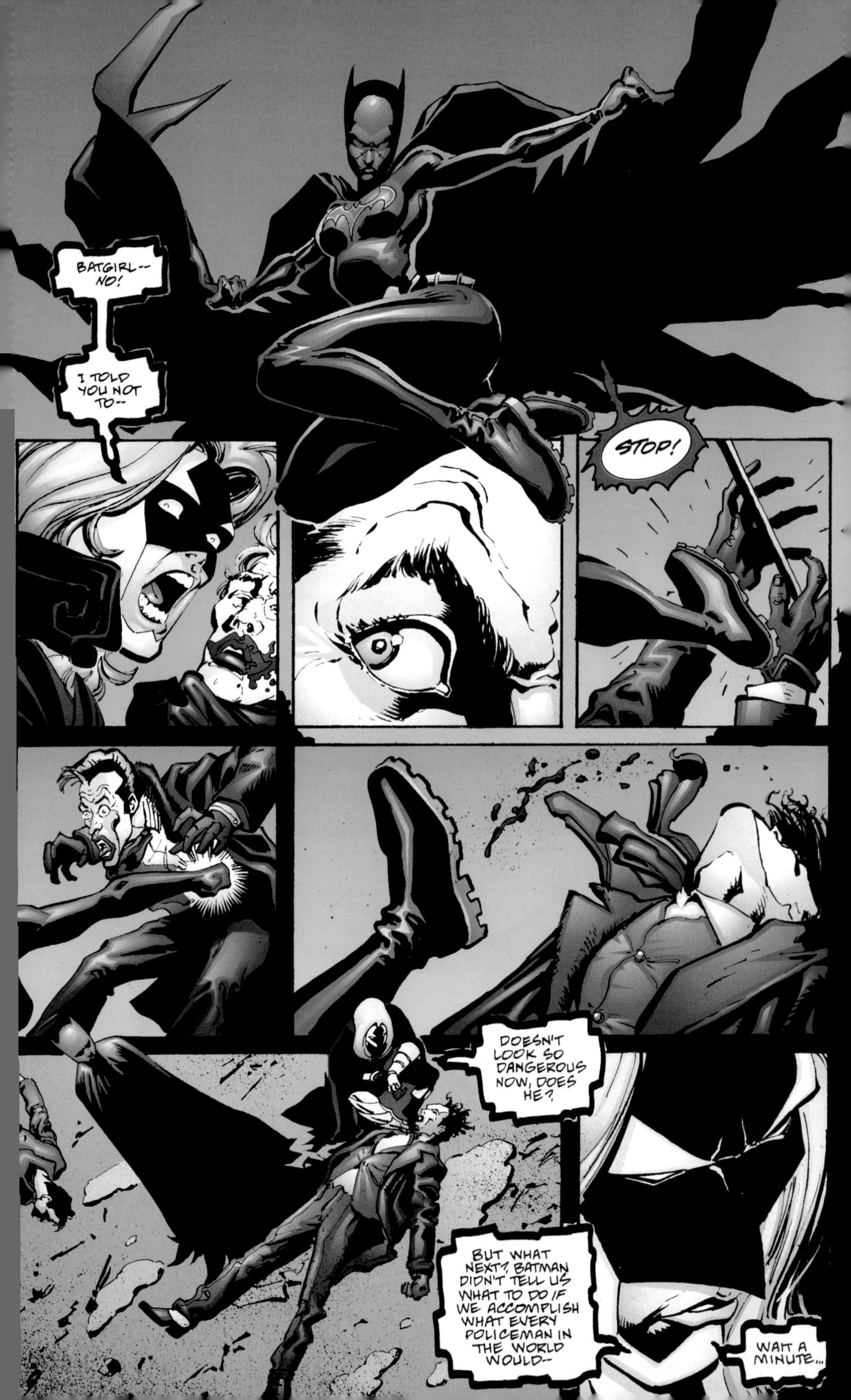
BATGIRL-- NO!
I TOLD YOU NOT TO--
STOP!
DOESN'T LOOK SO DANGEROUS NOW, DOES HE?
BUT WHAT NEXT? BATMAN DIDN'T TELL US WHAT TO DO IF WE ACCOMPLISH WHAT EVERY POLICEMAN IN THE WORLD WOULD--
WAIT A MINUTE...

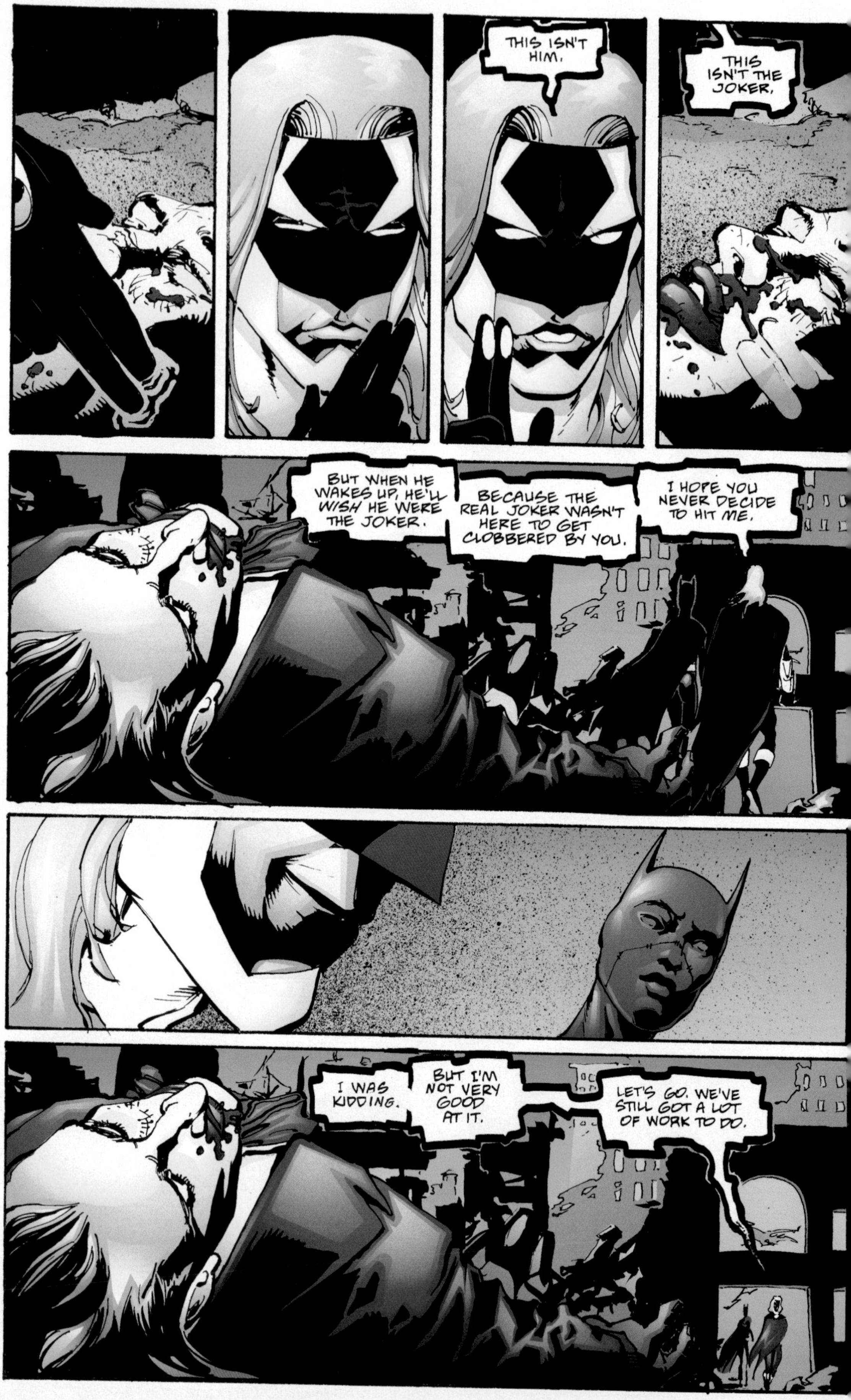
THIS ISN'T HIM.
THIS ISN'T THE JOKER.
BUT WHEN HE WAKES UP, HE'LL *WISH* HE WERE THE JOKER.
BECAUSE THE REAL JOKER WASN'T HERE TO GET CLOBBERED BY YOU.
I HOPE YOU NEVER DECIDE TO HIT *ME*.
I WAS KIDDING.
BUT I'M NOT VERY GOOD AT IT.
LET'S GO. WE'VE STILL GOT A LOT OF WORK TO DO.

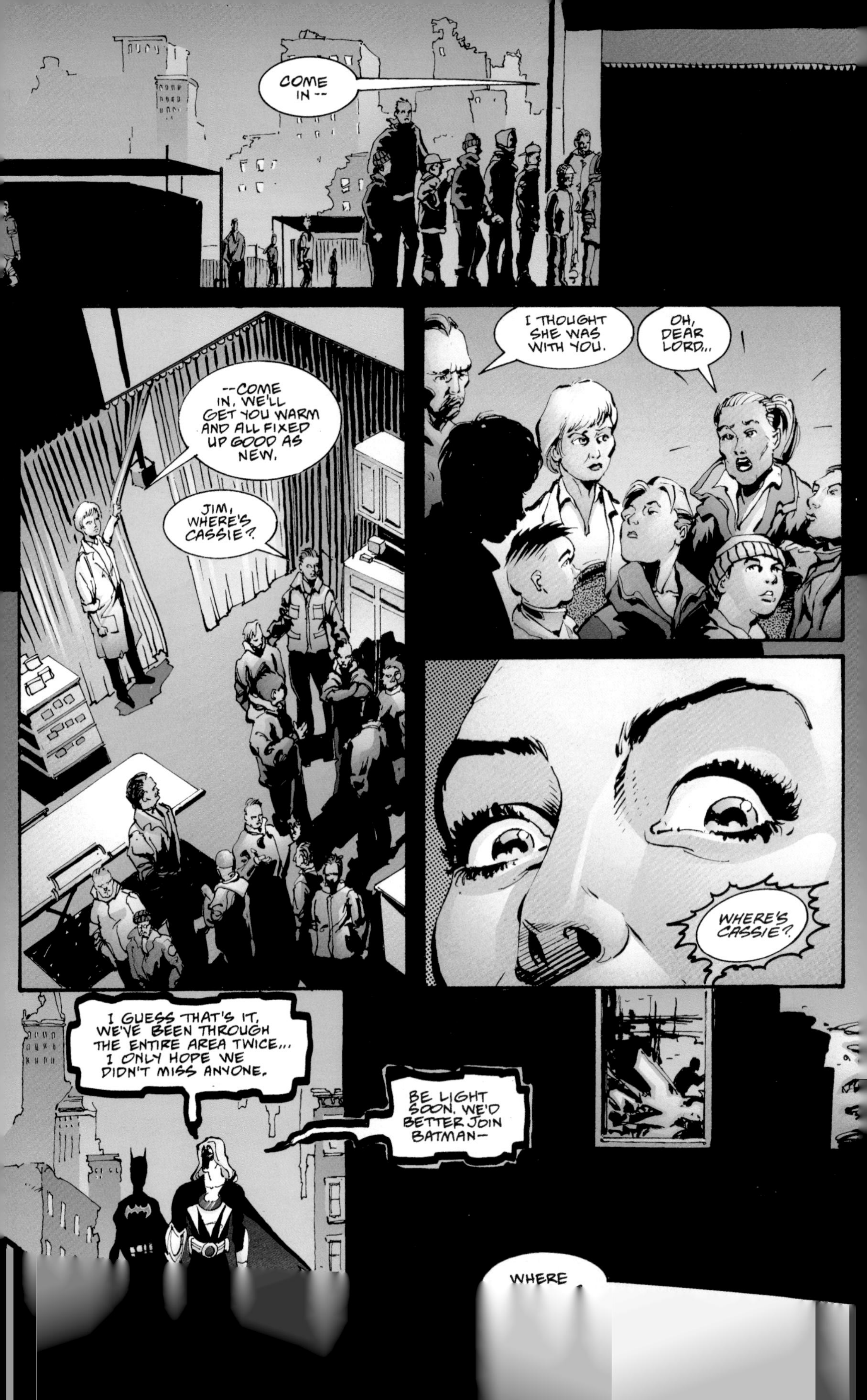
COME IN --
--COME IN. WE'LL GET YOU WARM AND ALL FIXED UP GOOD AS NEW.
JIM, WHERE'S CASSIE?
I THOUGHT SHE WAS WITH YOU.
OH, DEAR LORD...
WHERE'S CASSIE?
I GUESS THAT'S IT. WE'VE BEEN THROUGH THE ENTIRE AREA TWICE... I ONLY HOPE WE DIDN'T MISS ANYONE.
BE LIGHT SOON. WE'D BETTER JOIN BATMAN-
WHERE

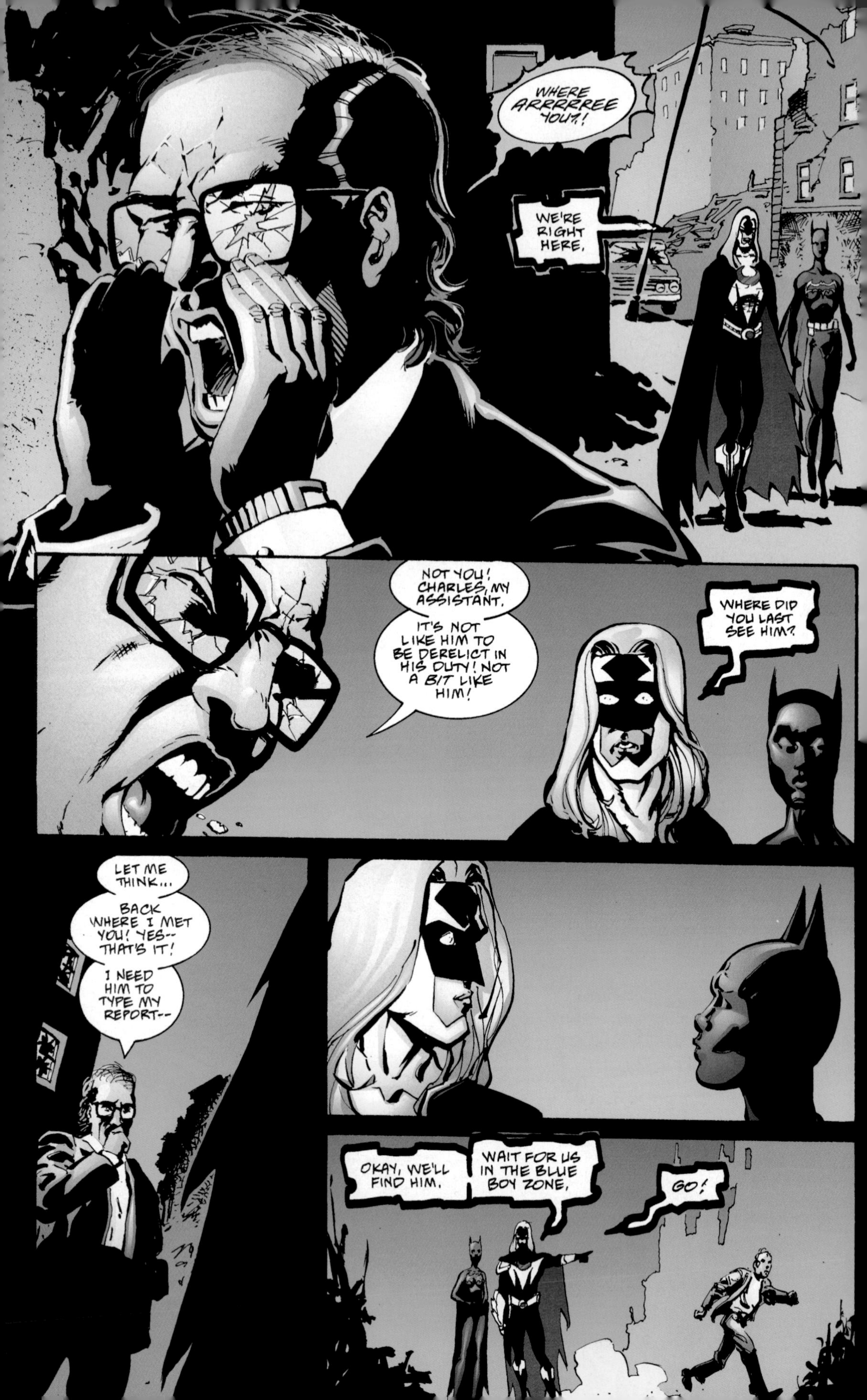
WHERE ARRRRREE YOU?!
WE'RE RIGHT HERE.
NOT YOU! CHARLES, MY ASSISTANT.
IT'S NOT LIKE HIM TO BE DERELICT IN HIS DUTY! NOT A *BIT* LIKE HIM!
WHERE DID YOU LAST SEE HIM?
LET ME THINK...
BACK WHERE I MET YOU! YES-- THAT'S IT!
I NEED HIM TO TYPE MY REPORT--
OKAY, WE'LL FIND HIM.
WAIT FOR US IN THE BLUE BOY ZONE.
GO!

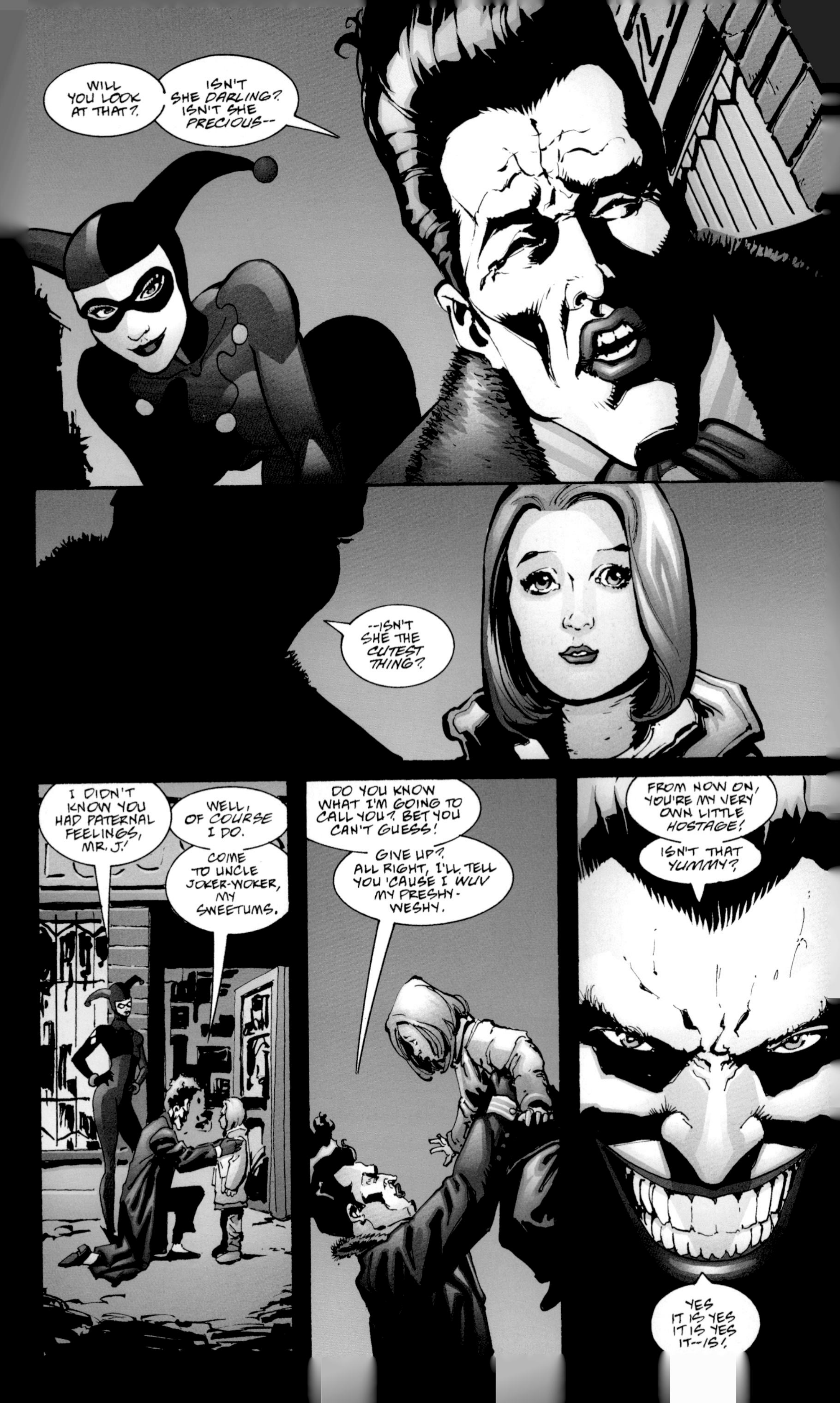
WILL YOU LOOK AT THAT?
ISN'T SHE DARLING? ISN'T SHE PRECIOUS--
--ISN'T SHE THE CUTEST THING?
I DIDN'T KNOW YOU HAD PATERNAL FEELINGS, MR. J.!
WELL, OF COURSE I DO.
COME TO UNCLE JOKER-YOKER, MY SWEETUMS.
DO YOU KNOW WHAT I'M GOING TO CALL YOU? BET YOU CAN'T GUESS!
GIVE UP? ALL RIGHT, I'LL TELL YOU 'CAUSE I WUV MY PRESHY-WESHY.
FROM NOW ON, YOU'RE MY VERY OWN LITTLE HOSTAGE!
ISN'T THAT YUMMY?
YES IT IS YES IT IS YES IT--IS!

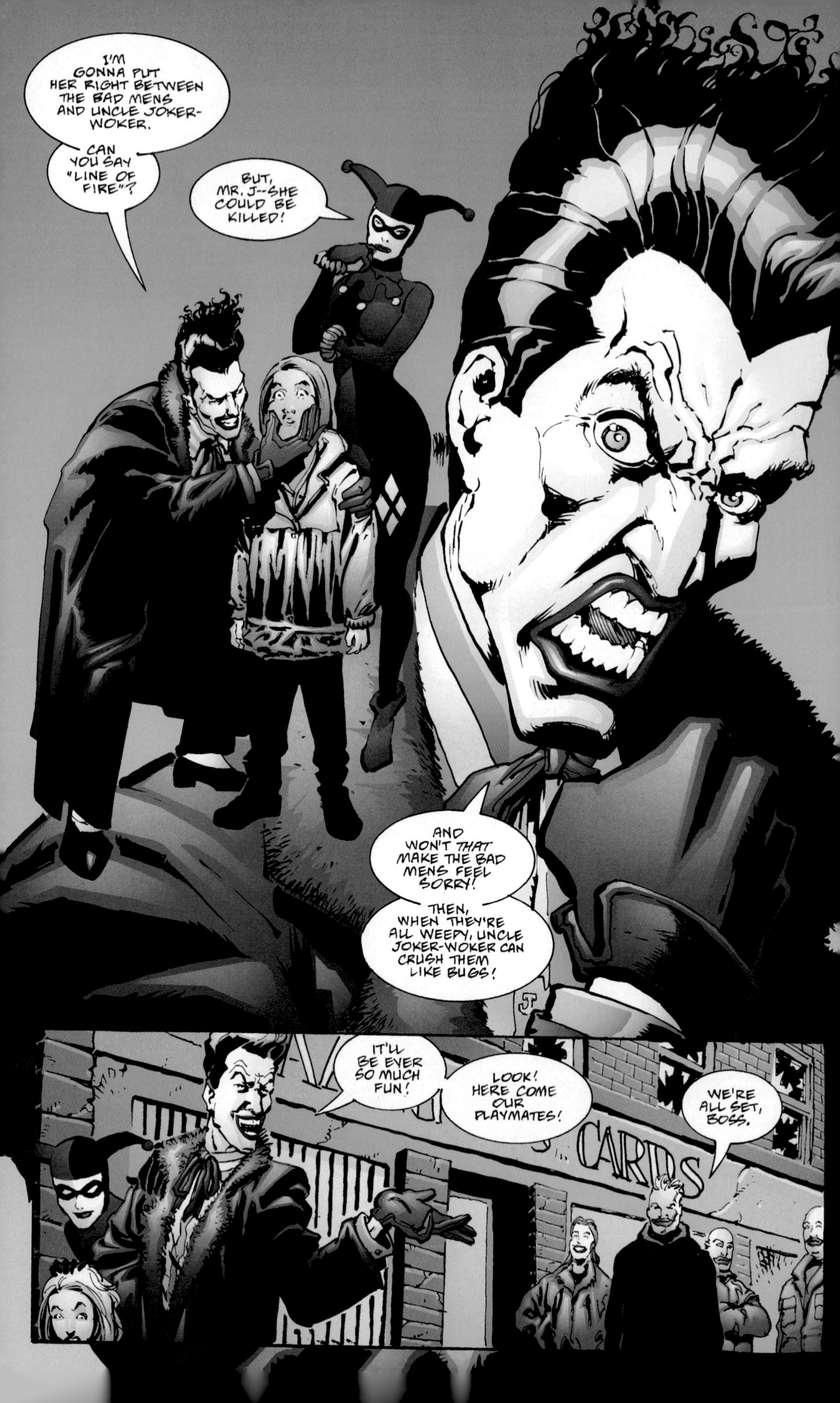

I'M GONNA PUT HER RIGHT BETWEEN THE BAD MENS AND UNCLE JOKER-WOKER.
CAN YOU SAY "LINE OF FIRE"?
BUT, MR. J--SHE COULD BE KILLED!
AND WON'T THAT MAKE THE BAD MENS FEEL SORRY!
THEN, WHEN THEY'RE ALL WEEPY, UNCLE JOKER-WOKER CAN CRUSH THEM LIKE BUGS!
IT'LL BE EVER SO MUCH FUN!
LOOK! HERE COME OUR PLAYMATES!
WE'RE ALL SET, BOSS.
CARDS

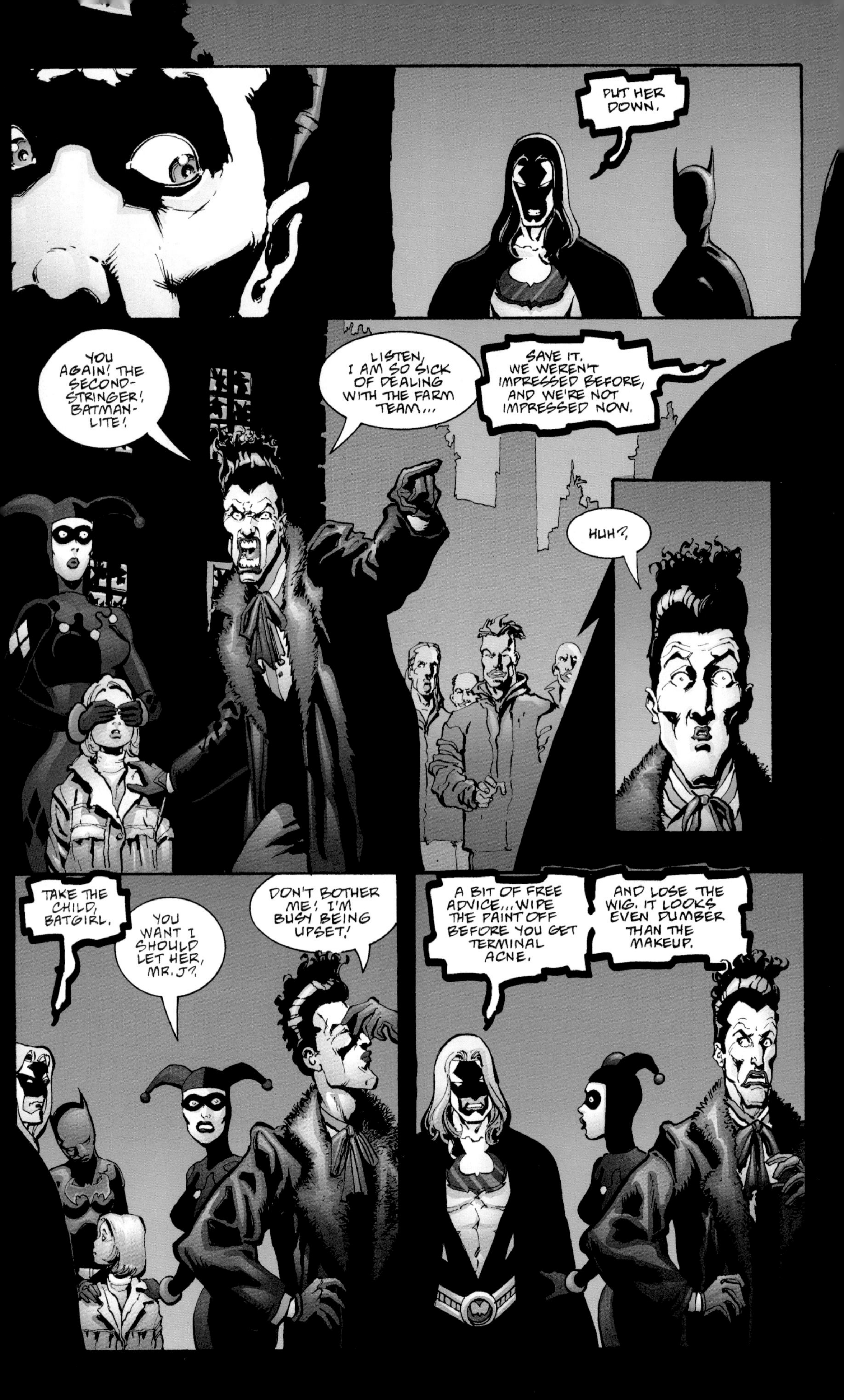
PUT HER DOWN.
YOU AGAIN! THE SECOND-STRINGER! BATMAN-LITE!
LISTEN, I AM SO SICK OF DEALING WITH THE FARM TEAM...
SAVE IT. WE WEREN'T IMPRESSED BEFORE, AND WE'RE NOT IMPRESSED NOW.
HUH?
TAKE THE CHILD, BATGIRL.
YOU WANT I SHOULD LET HER, MR. J?
DON'T BOTHER ME! I'M BUSY BEING UPSET!
A BIT OF FREE ADVICE... WIPE THE PAINT OFF BEFORE YOU GET TERMINAL ACNE.
AND LOSE THE WIG. IT LOOKS EVEN DUMBER THAN THE MAKEUP.

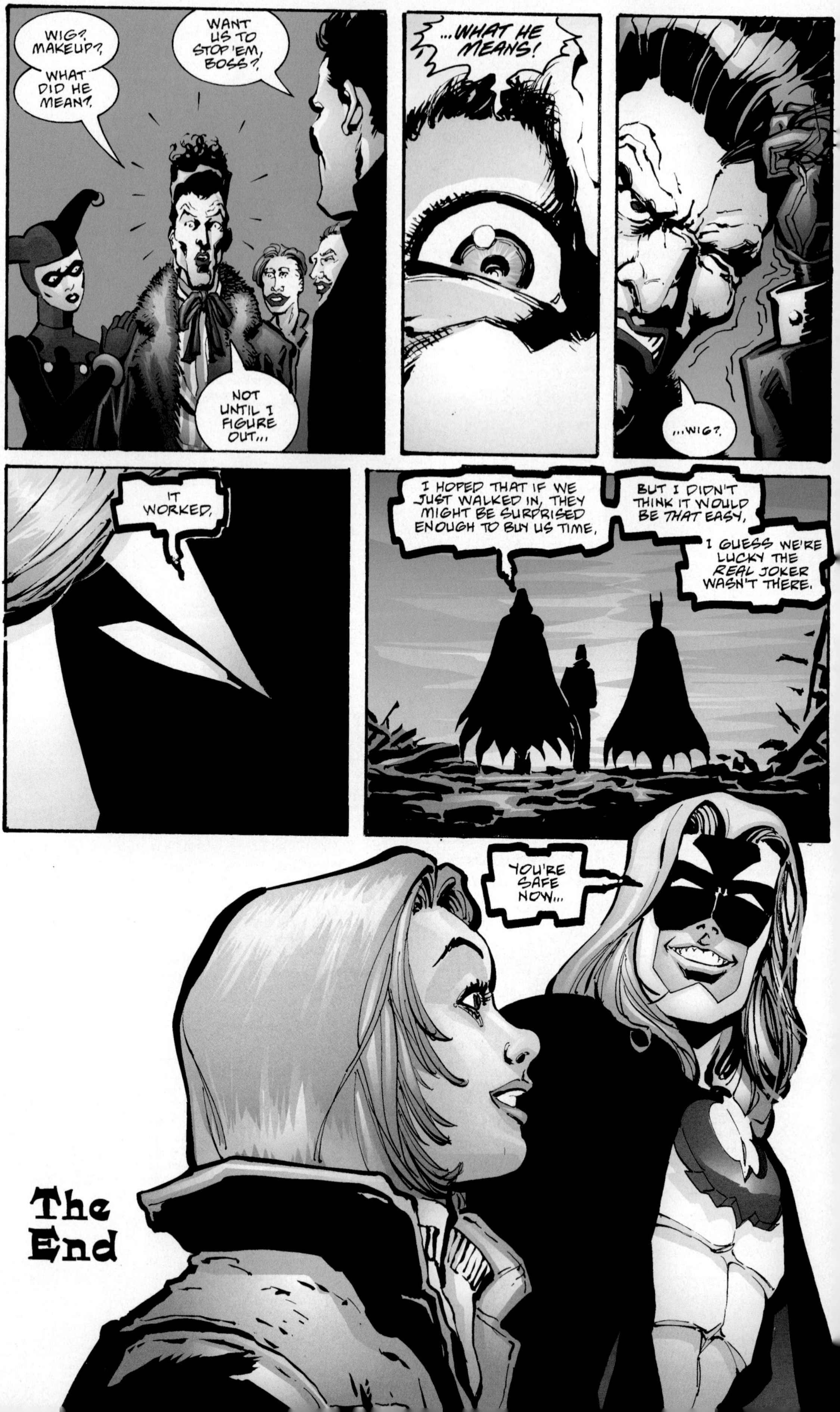
WIG? MAKEUP?
WHAT DID HE MEAN?
WANT US TO STOP 'EM, BOSS?
NOT UNTIL I FIGURE OUT...
...WHAT HE MEANS!
...WIG?
IT WORKED.
I HOPED THAT IF WE JUST WALKED IN, THEY MIGHT BE SURPRISED ENOUGH TO BUY US TIME.
BUT I DIDN'T THINK IT WOULD BE THAT EASY.
I GUESS WE'RE LUCKY THE REAL JOKER WASN'T THERE.
YOU'RE SAFE NOW...
The End

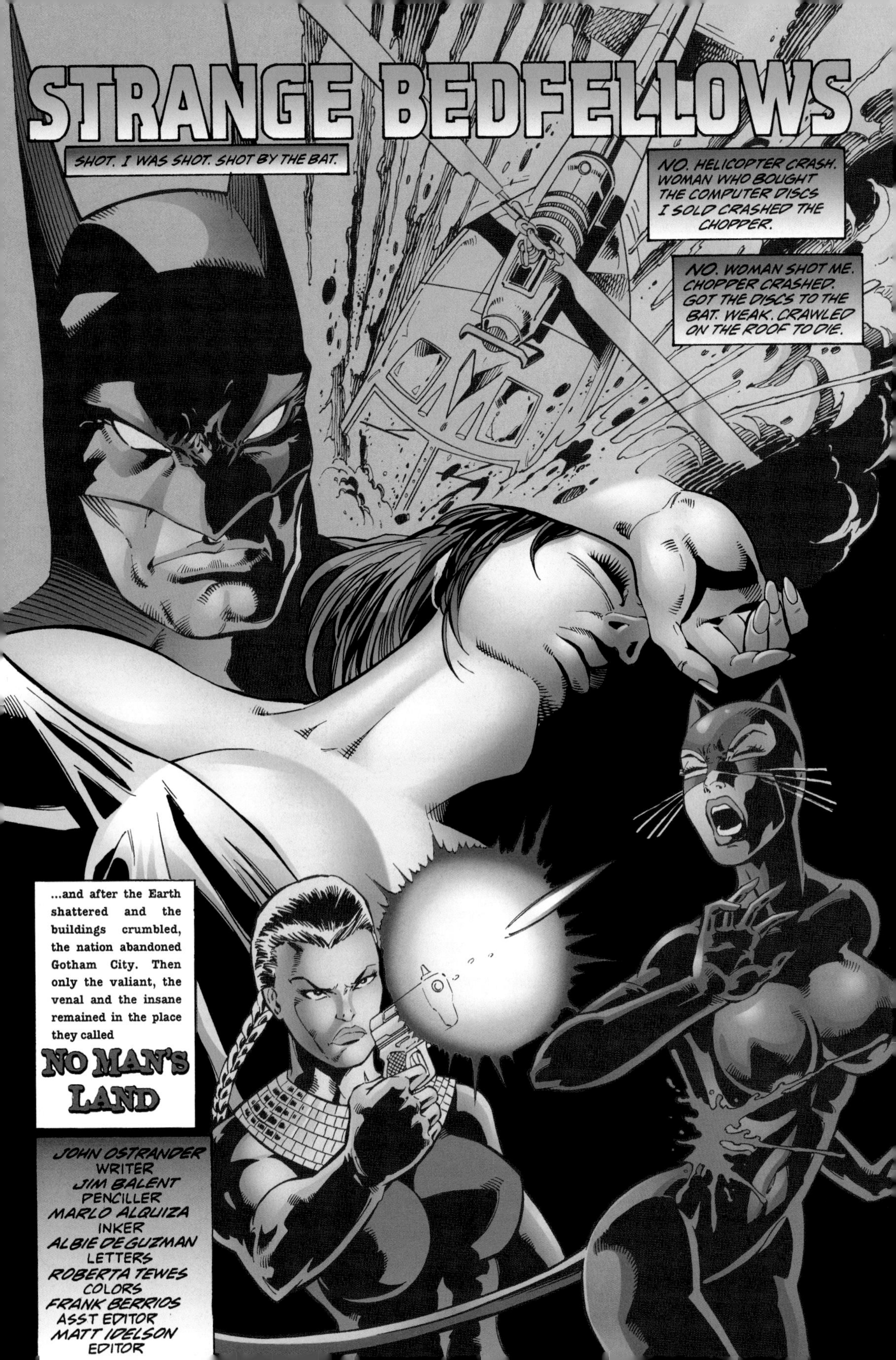

STRANGE BEDFELLOWS
SHOT. I WAS SHOT. SHOT BY THE BAT.
NO. HELICOPTER CRASH. WOMAN WHO BOUGHT THE COMPUTER DISCS I SOLD CRASHED THE CHOPPER.
NO. WOMAN SHOT ME. CHOPPER CRASHED. GOT THE DISCS TO THE BAT. WEAK. CRAWLED ON THE ROOF TO DIE.
...and after the Earth shattered and the buildings crumbled, the nation abandoned Gotham City. Then only the valiant, the venal and the insane remained in the place they called
NO MAN'S LAND
JOHN OSTRANDER WRITER
JIM BALENT PENCILLER
MARLO ALQUIZA INKER
ALBIE DE GUZMAN LETTERS
ROBERTA TEWES COLORS
FRANK BERRIOS ASST EDITOR
MATT IDELSON EDITOR

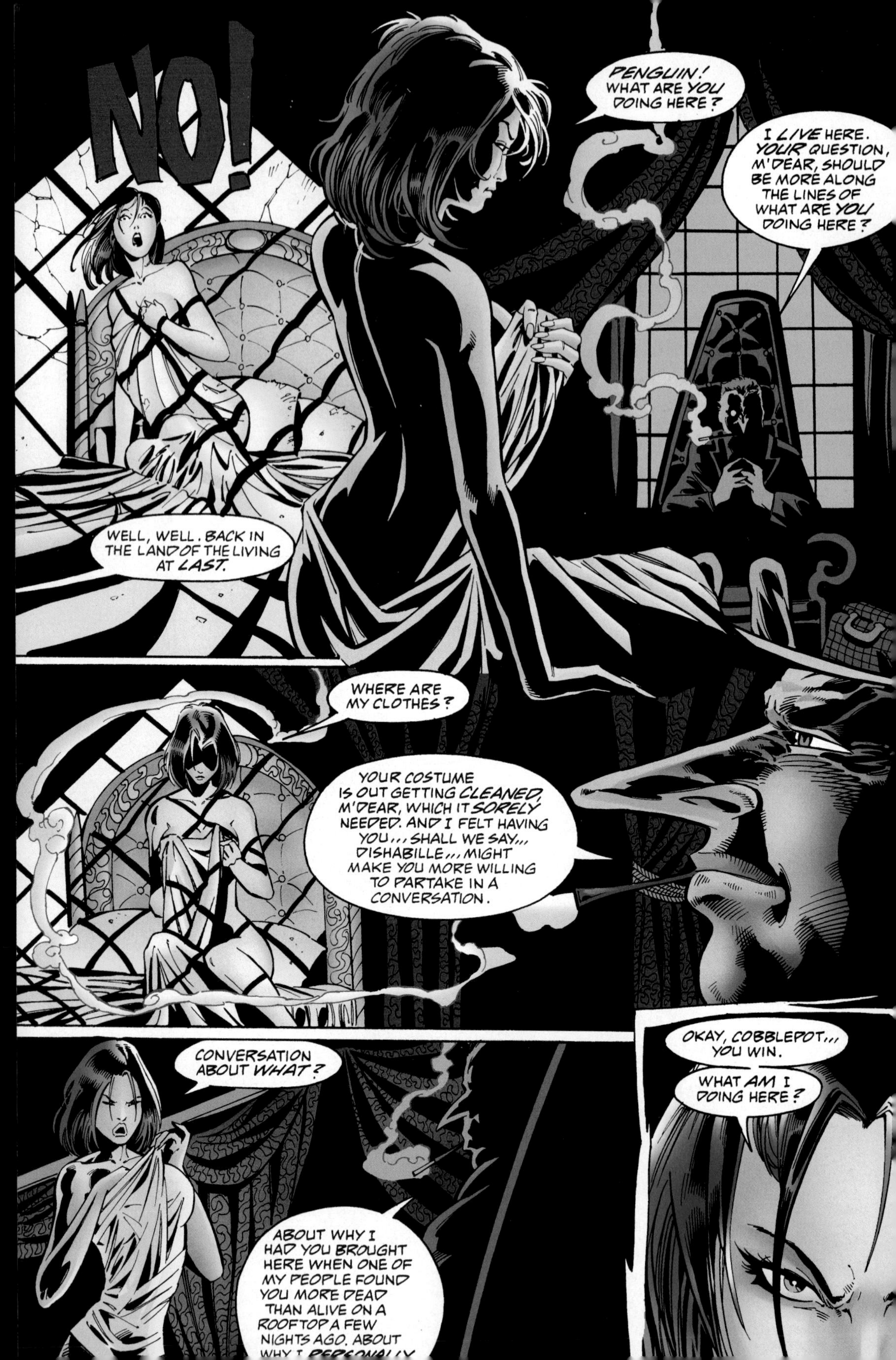
NO!
PENGUIN! WHAT ARE YOU DOING HERE?
I LIVE HERE. YOUR QUESTION, M'DEAR, SHOULD BE MORE ALONG THE LINES OF WHAT ARE YOU DOING HERE?
WELL, WELL. BACK IN THE LAND OF THE LIVING AT LAST.
WHERE ARE MY CLOTHES?
YOUR COSTUME IS OUT GETTING CLEANED, M'DEAR, WHICH IT SORELY NEEDED. AND I FELT HAVING YOU... SHALL WE SAY... DISHABILLE... MIGHT MAKE YOU MORE WILLING TO PARTAKE IN A CONVERSATION.
CONVERSATION ABOUT WHAT?
ABOUT WHY I HAD YOU BROUGHT HERE WHEN ONE OF MY PEOPLE FOUND YOU MORE DEAD THAN ALIVE ON A ROOFTOP A FEW NIGHTS AGO. ABOUT
OKAY, COBBLEPOT... YOU WIN.
WHAT AM I DOING HERE?

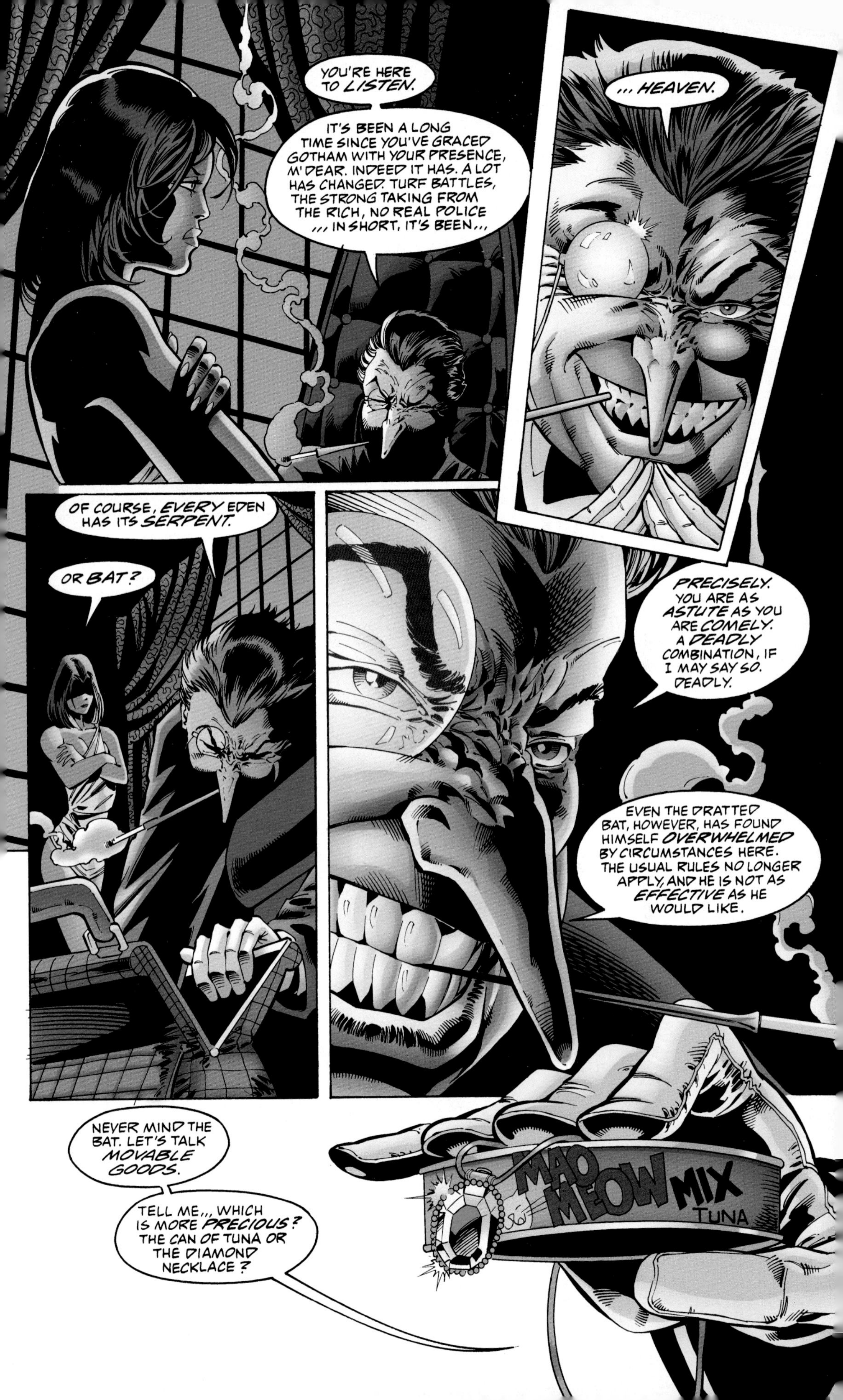

YOU'RE HERE TO LISTEN.
IT'S BEEN A LONG TIME SINCE YOU'VE GRACED GOTHAM WITH YOUR PRESENCE, M'DEAR. INDEED IT HAS. A LOT HAS CHANGED. TURF BATTLES, THE STRONG TAKING FROM THE RICH, NO REAL POLICE ... IN SHORT, IT'S BEEN...
... HEAVEN.
OF COURSE, EVERY EDEN HAS ITS SERPENT.
OR BAT?
PRECISELY. YOU ARE AS ASTUTE AS YOU ARE COMELY. A DEADLY COMBINATION, IF I MAY SAY SO. DEADLY.
EVEN THE DRATTED BAT, HOWEVER, HAS FOUND HIMSELF OVERWHELMED BY CIRCUMSTANCES HERE. THE USUAL RULES NO LONGER APPLY, AND HE IS NOT AS EFFECTIVE AS HE WOULD LIKE.
NEVER MIND THE BAT. LET'S TALK MOVABLE GOODS.
TELL ME... WHICH IS MORE PRECIOUS? THE CAN OF TUNA OR THE DIAMOND NECKLACE?
MAD MEOW MIX TUNA

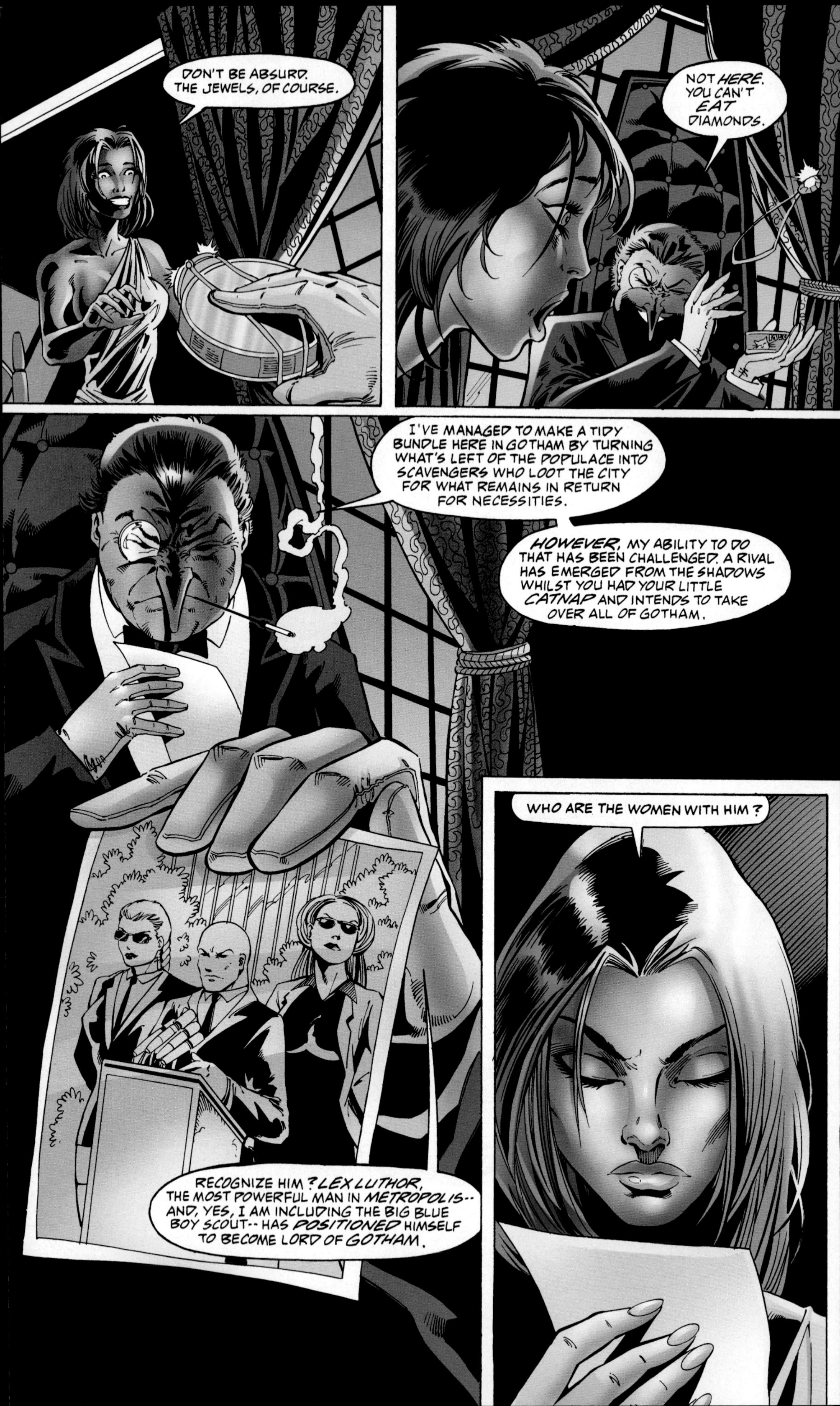
DON'T BE ABSURD. THE JEWELS, OF COURSE.
NOT HERE. YOU CAN'T EAT DIAMONDS.
I'VE MANAGED TO MAKE A TIDY BUNDLE HERE IN GOTHAM BY TURNING WHAT'S LEFT OF THE POPULACE INTO SCAVENGERS WHO LOOT THE CITY FOR WHAT REMAINS IN RETURN FOR NECESSITIES.
HOWEVER, MY ABILITY TO DO THAT HAS BEEN CHALLENGED. A RIVAL HAS EMERGED FROM THE SHADOWS WHILST YOU HAD YOUR LITTLE CATNAP AND INTENDS TO TAKE OVER ALL OF GOTHAM.
RECOGNIZE HIM? LEX LUTHOR, THE MOST POWERFUL MAN IN METROPOLIS-- AND, YES, I AM INCLUDING THE BIG BLUE BOY SCOUT-- HAS POSITIONED HIMSELF TO BECOME LORD OF GOTHAM.
WHO ARE THE WOMEN WITH HIM?

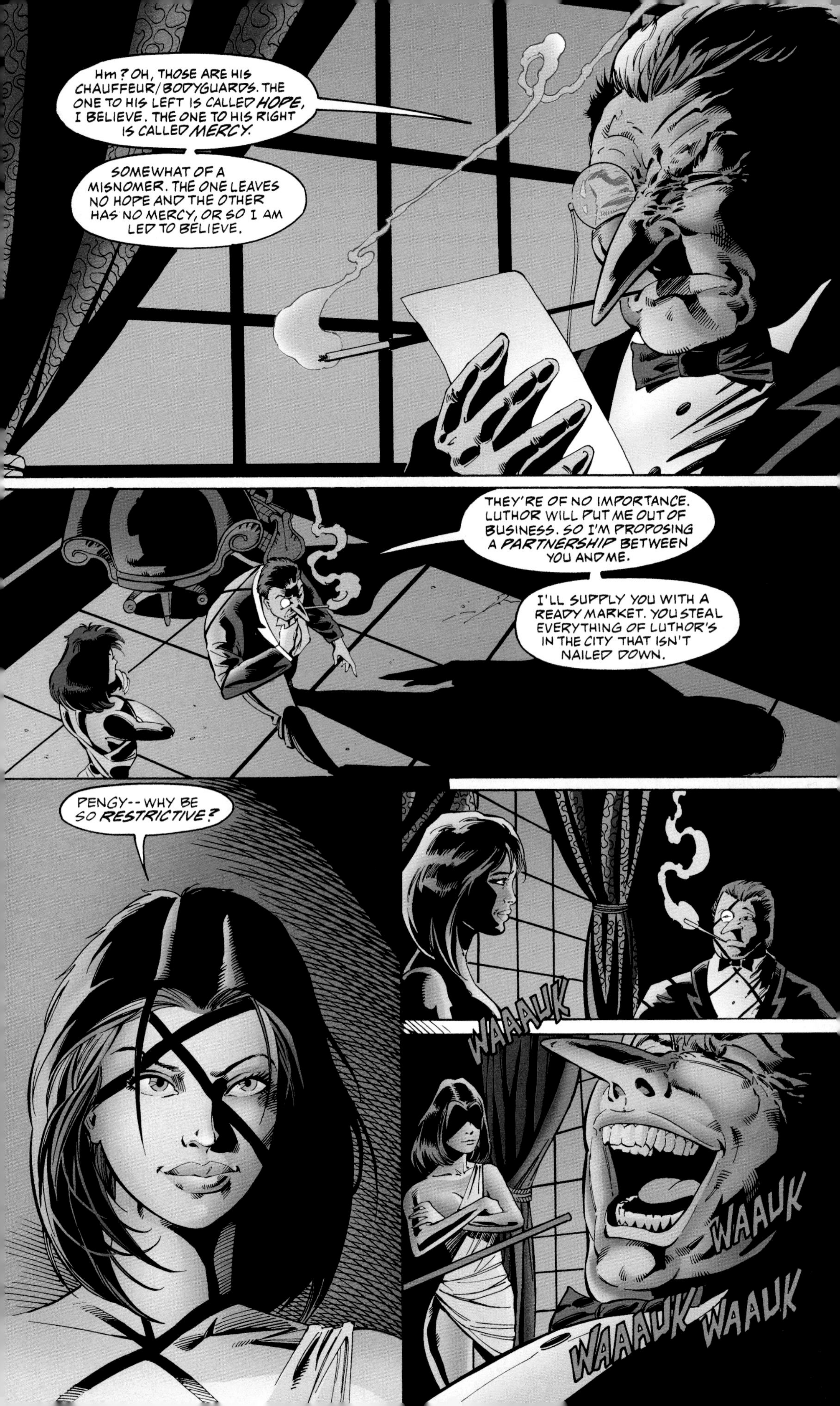
Hm? OH, THOSE ARE HIS CHAUFFEUR/BODYGUARDS. THE ONE TO HIS LEFT IS CALLED *HOPE*, I BELIEVE. THE ONE TO HIS RIGHT IS CALLED *MERCY*.
SOMEWHAT OF A MISNOMER. THE ONE LEAVES NO HOPE AND THE OTHER HAS NO MERCY, OR SO I AM LED TO BELIEVE.
THEY'RE OF NO IMPORTANCE. LUTHOR WILL PUT ME OUT OF BUSINESS. SO I'M PROPOSING A *PARTNERSHIP* BETWEEN YOU AND ME.
I'LL SUPPLY YOU WITH A READY MARKET. YOU STEAL EVERYTHING OF LUTHOR'S IN THE CITY THAT ISN'T NAILED DOWN.
PENGY-- WHY BE SO *RESTRICTIVE*?
WAAAUK
WAAAUK
WAAUK
WAAAUK!
WAAUK

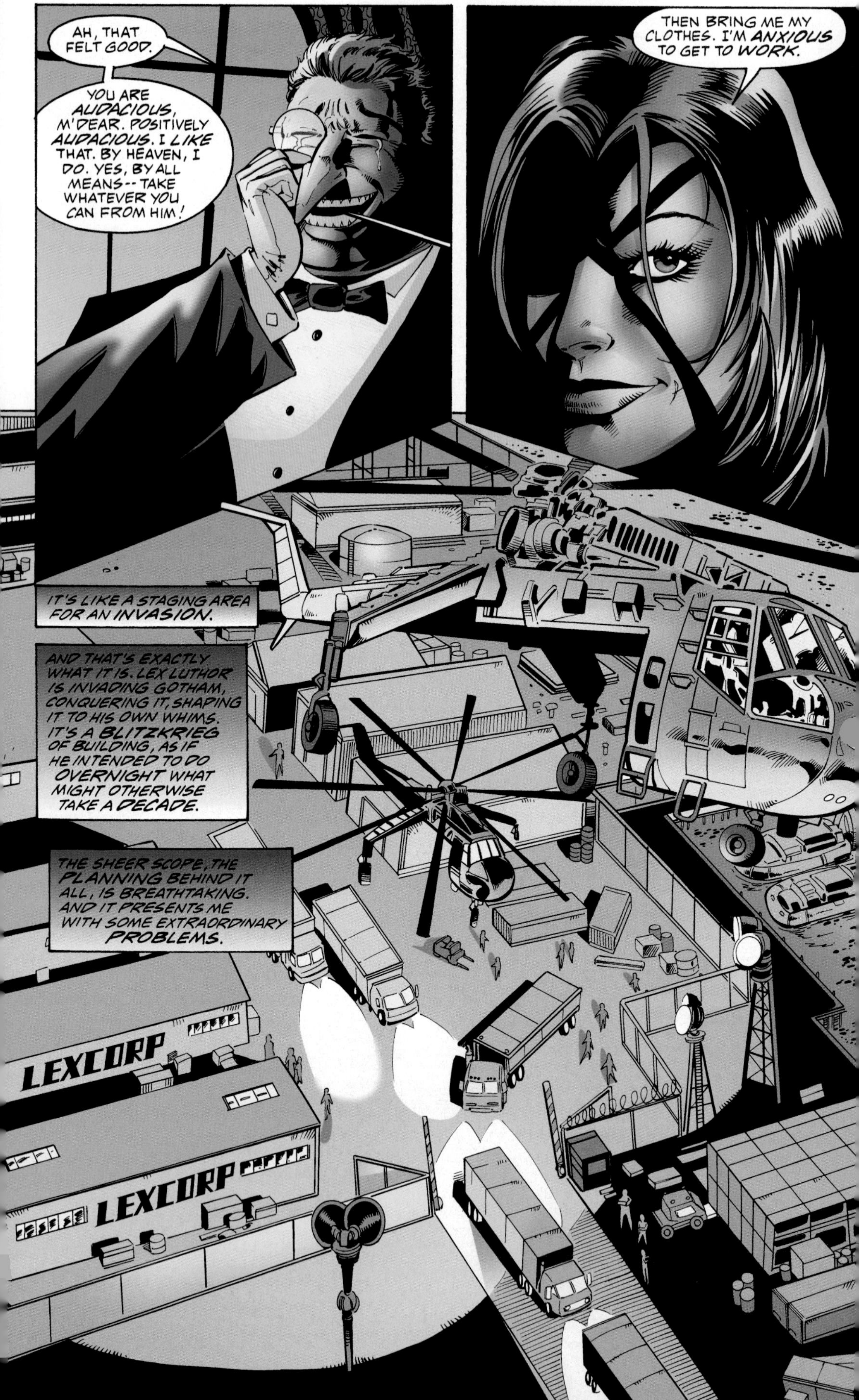

AH, THAT FELT GOOD.
YOU ARE AUDACIOUS, M'DEAR. POSITIVELY AUDACIOUS. I LIKE THAT. BY HEAVEN, I DO. YES, BY ALL MEANS--TAKE WHATEVER YOU CAN FROM HIM!
THEN BRING ME MY CLOTHES. I'M ANXIOUS TO GET TO WORK.
IT'S LIKE A STAGING AREA FOR AN INVASION.
AND THAT'S EXACTLY WHAT IT IS. LEX LUTHOR IS INVADING GOTHAM, CONQUERING IT, SHAPING IT TO HIS OWN WHIMS. IT'S A BLITZKRIEG OF BUILDING, AS IF HE INTENDED TO DO OVERNIGHT WHAT MIGHT OTHERWISE TAKE A DECADE.
THE SHEER SCOPE, THE PLANNING BEHIND IT ALL, IS BREATHTAKING. AND IT PRESENTS ME WITH SOME EXTRAORDINARY PROBLEMS.
LEXCORP
LEXCORP

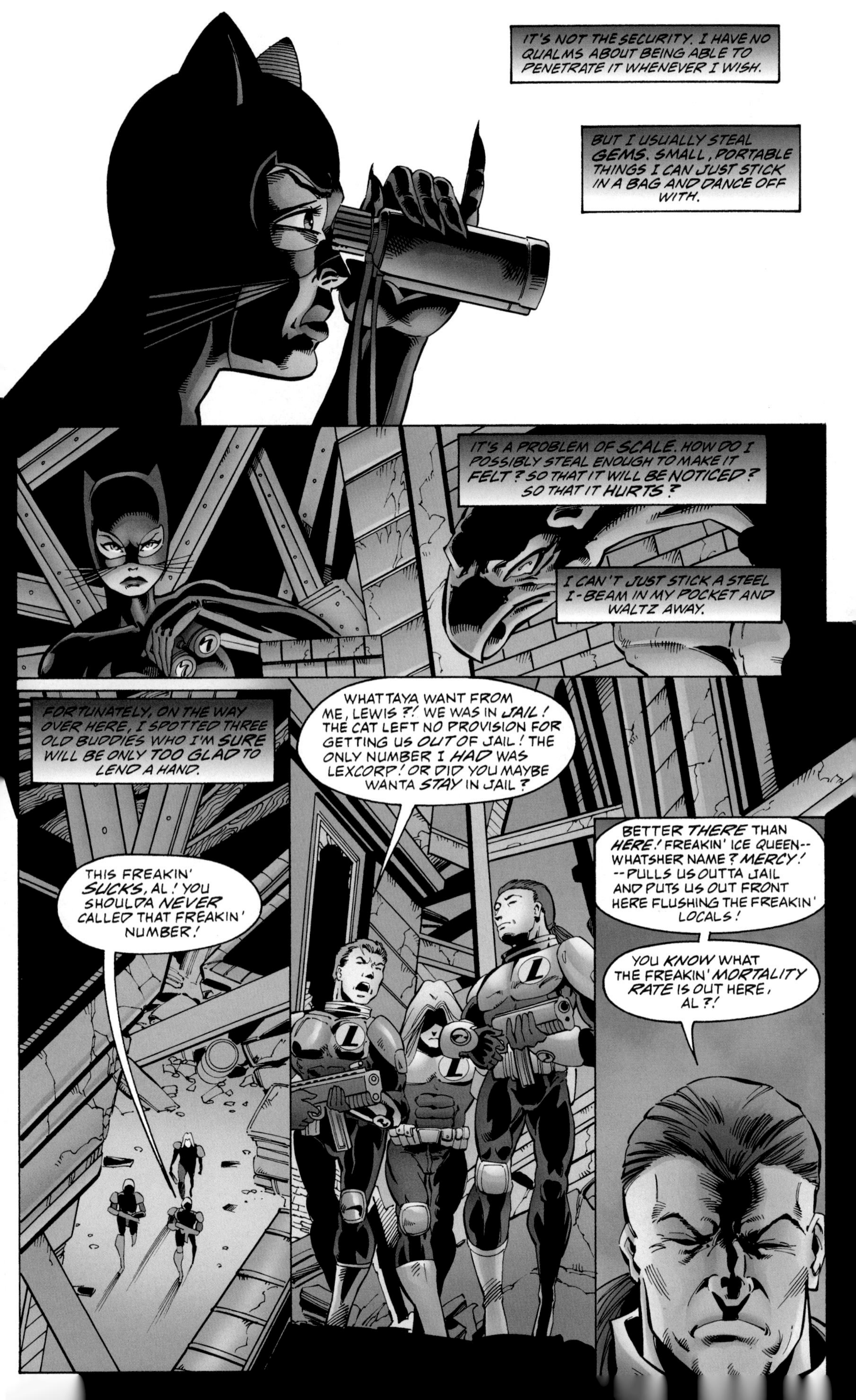

IT'S NOT THE SECURITY. I HAVE NO QUALMS ABOUT BEING ABLE TO PENETRATE IT WHENEVER I WISH.
BUT I USUALLY STEAL GEMS. SMALL, PORTABLE THINGS I CAN JUST STICK IN A BAG AND DANCE OFF WITH.
IT'S A PROBLEM OF SCALE. HOW DO I POSSIBLY STEAL ENOUGH TO MAKE IT FELT? SO THAT IT WILL BE NOTICED? SO THAT IT HURTS?
I CAN'T JUST STICK A STEEL I-BEAM IN MY POCKET AND WALTZ AWAY.
FORTUNATELY, ON THE WAY OVER HERE, I SPOTTED THREE OLD BUDDIES WHO I'M SURE WILL BE ONLY TOO GLAD TO LEND A HAND.
THIS FREAKIN' SUCKS, AL! YOU SHOULDA NEVER CALLED THAT FREAKIN' NUMBER!
WHATTAYA WANT FROM ME, LEWIS?! WE WAS IN JAIL! THE CAT LEFT NO PROVISION FOR GETTING US OUT OF JAIL! THE ONLY NUMBER I HAD WAS LEXCORP! OR DID YOU MAYBE WANTA STAY IN JAIL?
BETTER THERE THAN HERE! FREAKIN' ICE QUEEN-- WHATSHER NAME? MERCY! --PULLS US OUTTA JAIL AND PUTS US OUT FRONT HERE FLUSHING THE FREAKIN' LOCALS!
YOU KNOW WHAT THE FREAKIN' MORTALITY RATE IS OUT HERE, AL?!

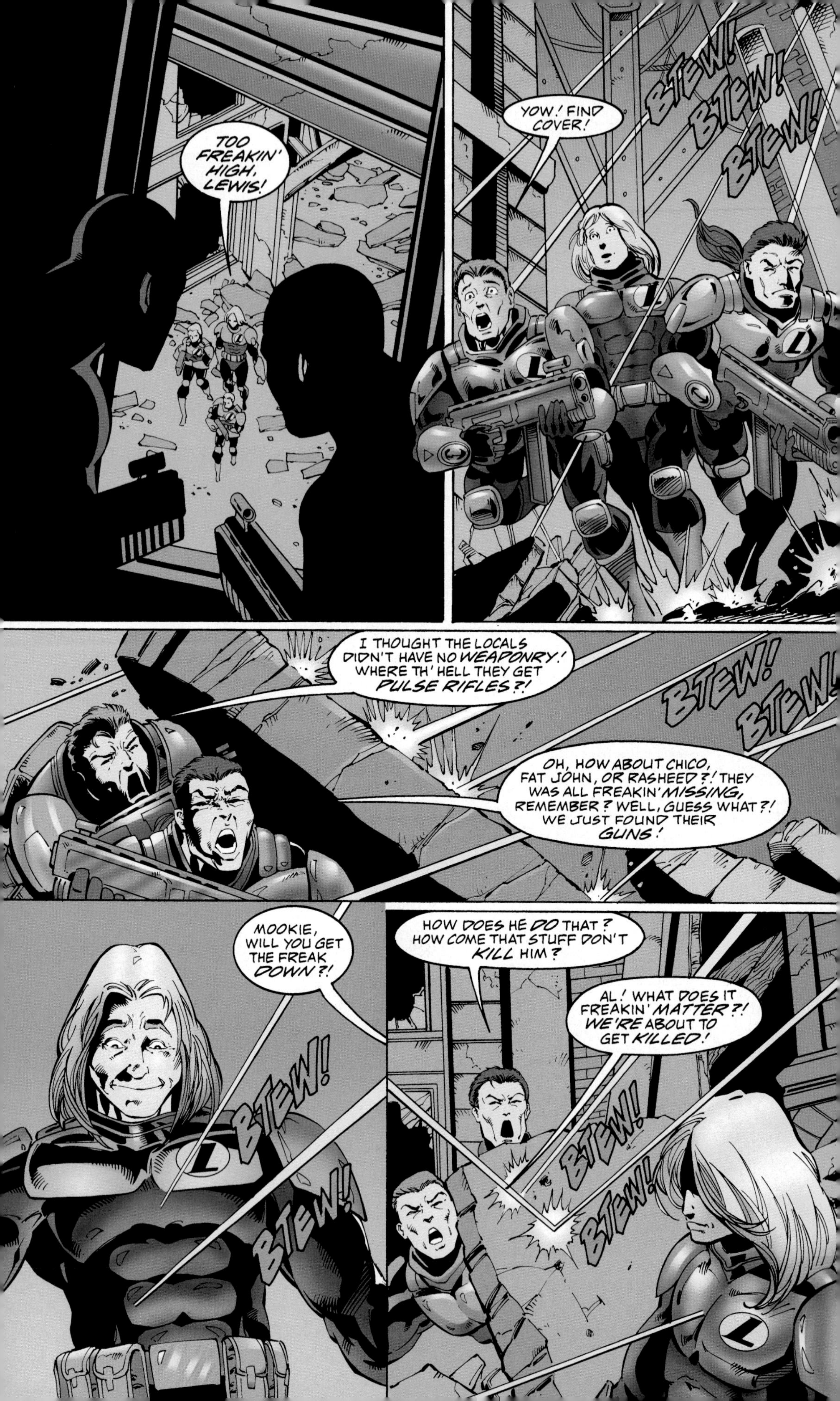

TOO FREAKIN' HIGH, LEWIS!
YOW! FIND COVER!
BTEW! BTEW! BTEW!
I THOUGHT THE LOCALS DIDN'T HAVE NO WEAPONRY! WHERE TH' HELL THEY GET PULSE RIFLES?!
BTEW! BTEW!
OH, HOW ABOUT CHICO, FAT JOHN, OR RASHEED?! THEY WAS ALL FREAKIN' MISSING, REMEMBER? WELL, GUESS WHAT?! WE JUST FOUND THEIR GUNS!
MOOKIE, WILL YOU GET THE FREAK DOWN?!
BTEW!
BTEW!!
HOW DOES HE DO THAT? HOW COME THAT STUFF DON'T KILL HIM?
AL! WHAT DOES IT FREAKIN' MATTER?! WE'RE ABOUT TO GET KILLED!
BTEW!
BTEW!

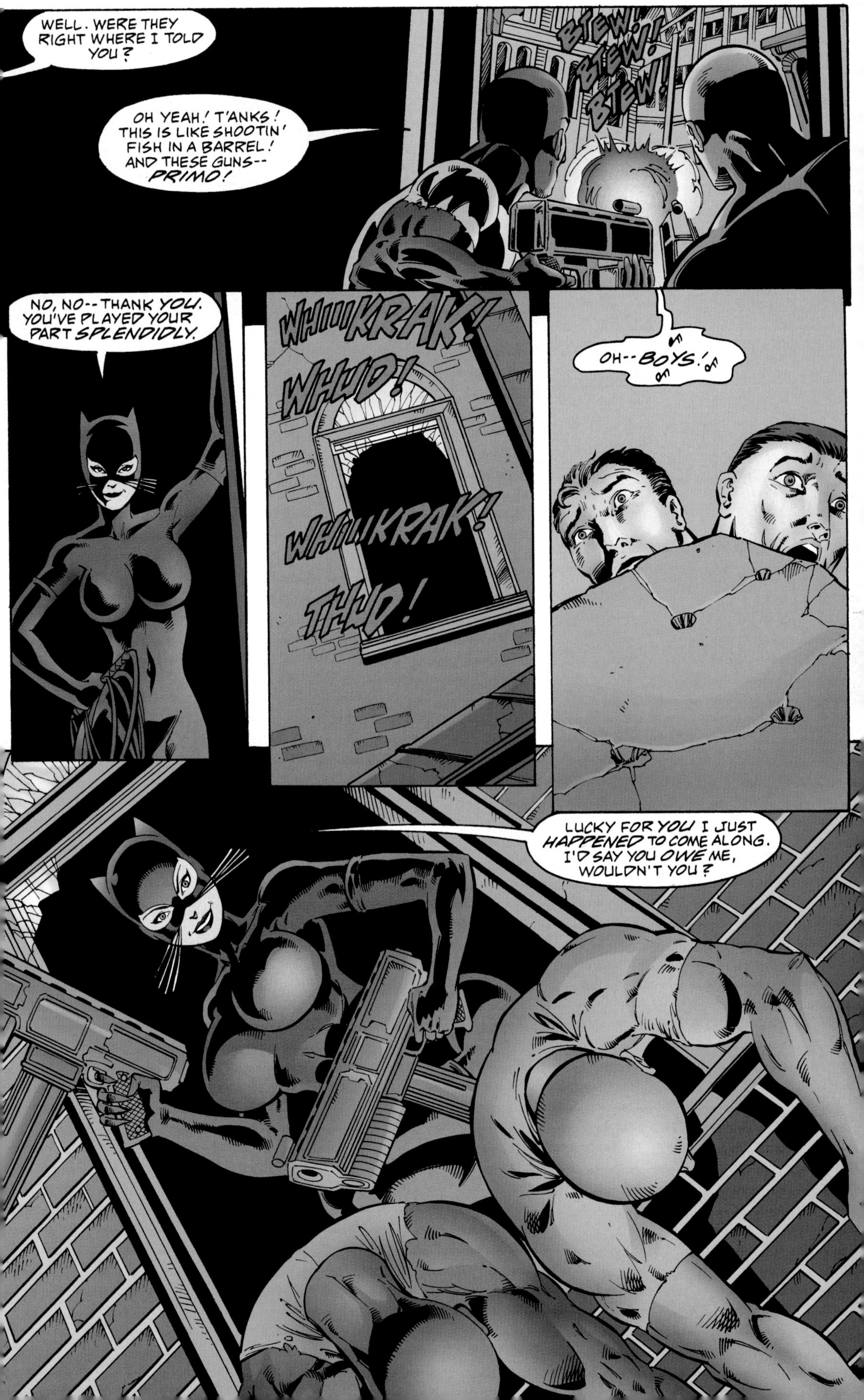
WELL. WERE THEY RIGHT WHERE I TOLD YOU?
BTEW! BTEW! BTEW!
OH YEAH! T'ANKS! THIS IS LIKE SHOOTIN' FISH IN A BARREL! AND THESE GUNS-- PRIMO!
NO, NO-- THANK YOU. YOU'VE PLAYED YOUR PART SPLENDIDLY.
WHIIIKRAK!
WHUD!
WHIIIKRAK!
THUD!
OH-- BOYS!
LUCKY FOR YOU I JUST HAPPENED TO COME ALONG. I'D SAY YOU OWE ME, WOULDN'T YOU?

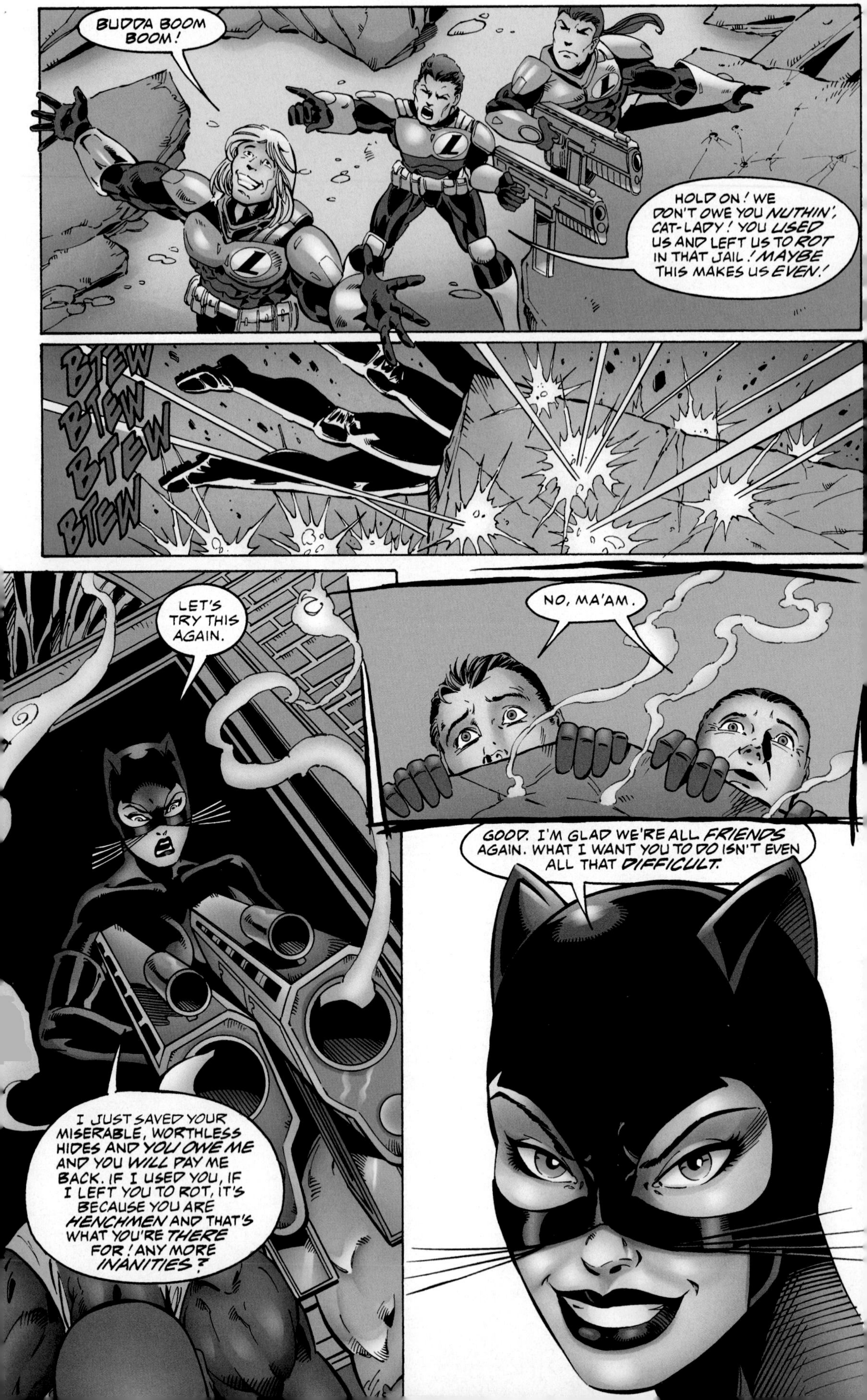
BUDDA BOOM BOOM!
HOLD ON! WE DON'T OWE YOU NUTHIN', CAT-LADY! YOU USED US AND LEFT US TO ROT IN THAT JAIL! MAYBE THIS MAKES US EVEN!
BTEW BTEW BTEW BTEW BTEW
LET'S TRY THIS AGAIN.
I JUST SAVED YOUR MISERABLE, WORTHLESS HIDES AND YOU OWE ME AND YOU WILL PAY ME BACK. IF I USED YOU, IF I LEFT YOU TO ROT, IT'S BECAUSE YOU ARE HENCHMEN AND THAT'S WHAT YOU'RE THERE FOR! ANY MORE INANITIES?
NO, MA'AM.
GOOD. I'M GLAD WE'RE ALL FRIENDS AGAIN. WHAT I WANT YOU TO DO ISN'T EVEN ALL THAT DIFFICULT.

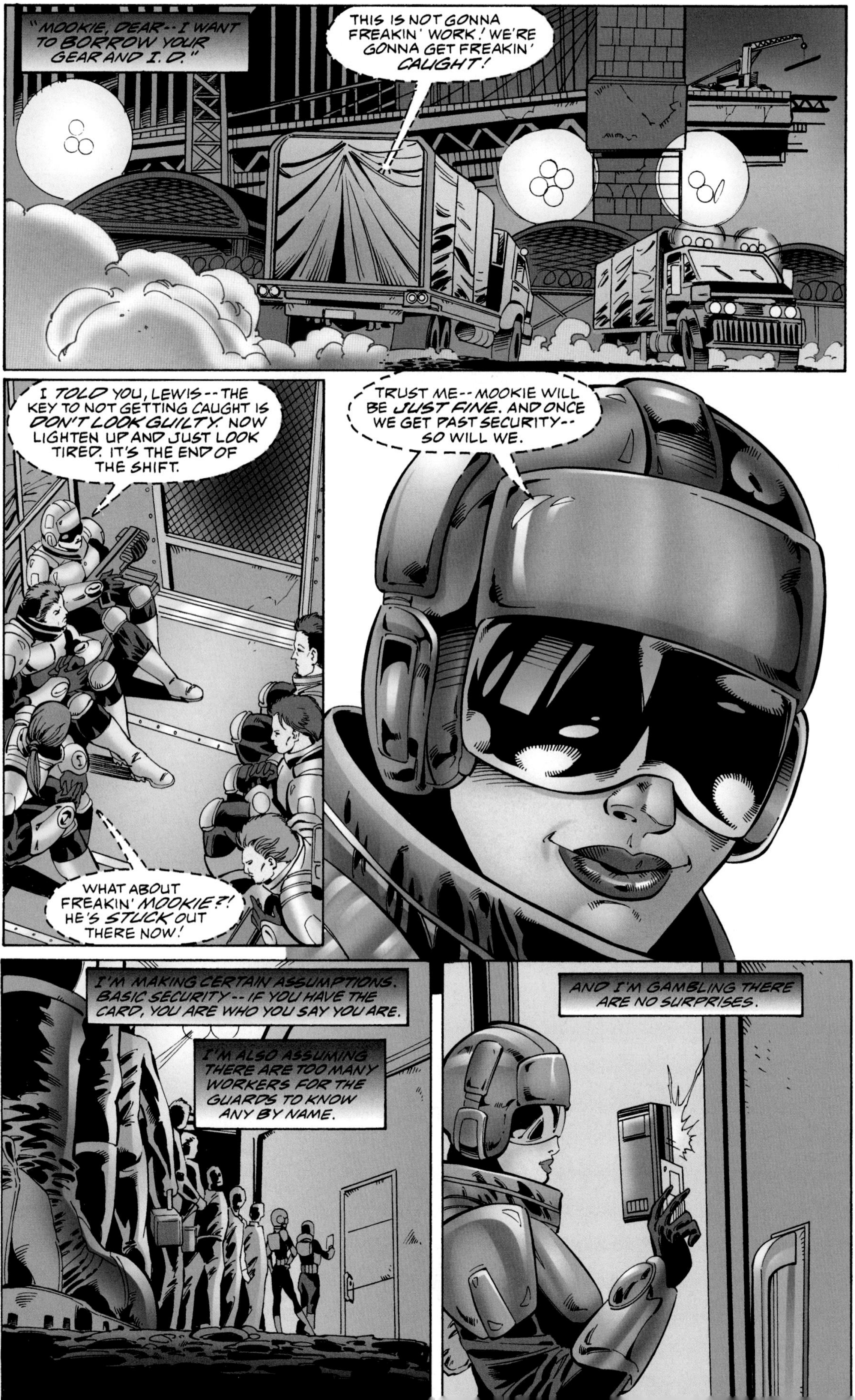
"MOOKIE, DEAR--I WANT TO BORROW YOUR GEAR AND I.D."
THIS IS NOT GONNA FREAKIN' WORK! WE'RE GONNA GET FREAKIN' CAUGHT!
I TOLD YOU, LEWIS--THE KEY TO NOT GETTING CAUGHT IS DON'T LOOK GUILTY. NOW LIGHTEN UP AND JUST LOOK TIRED. IT'S THE END OF THE SHIFT.
WHAT ABOUT FREAKIN' MOOKIE?! HE'S STUCK OUT THERE NOW!
TRUST ME--MOOKIE WILL BE JUST FINE. AND ONCE WE GET PAST SECURITY--SO WILL WE.
I'M MAKING CERTAIN ASSUMPTIONS. BASIC SECURITY--IF YOU HAVE THE CARD, YOU ARE WHO YOU SAY YOU ARE.
I'M ALSO ASSUMING THERE ARE TOO MANY WORKERS FOR THE GUARDS TO KNOW ANY BY NAME.
AND I'M GAMBLING THERE ARE NO SURPRISES.

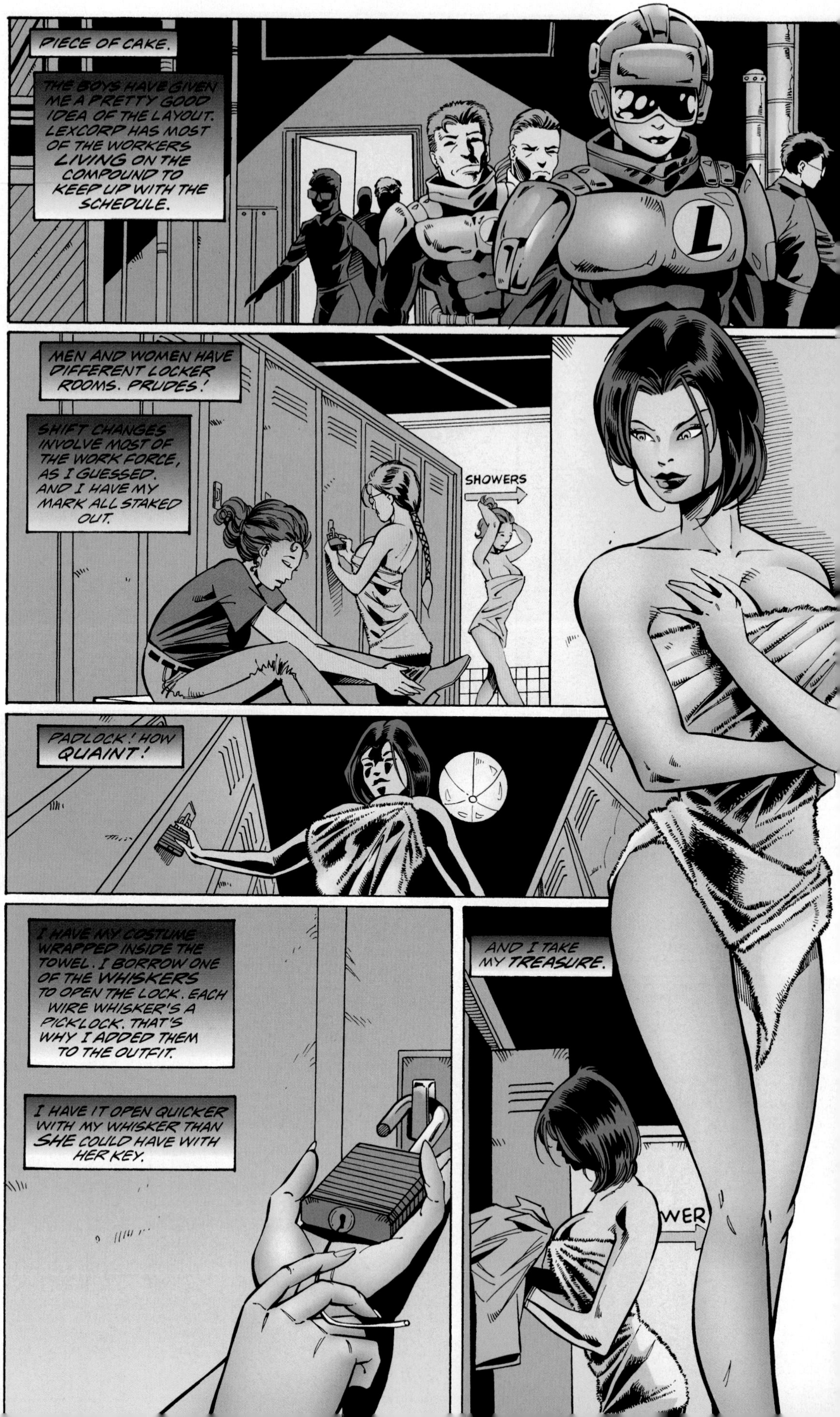
PIECE OF CAKE.
THE BOYS HAVE GIVEN ME A PRETTY GOOD IDEA OF THE LAYOUT. LEXCORP HAS MOST OF THE WORKERS LIVING ON THE COMPOUND TO KEEP UP WITH THE SCHEDULE.
MEN AND WOMEN HAVE DIFFERENT LOCKER ROOMS. PRUDES!
SHIFT CHANGES INVOLVE MOST OF THE WORK FORCE, AS I GUESSED. AND I HAVE MY MARK ALL STAKED OUT.
SHOWERS
PADLOCK! HOW QUAINT!
I HAVE MY COSTUME WRAPPED INSIDE THE TOWEL. I BORROW ONE OF THE WHISKERS TO OPEN THE LOCK. EACH WIRE WHISKER'S A PICKLOCK. THAT'S WHY I ADDED THEM TO THE OUTFIT.
I HAVE IT OPEN QUICKER WITH MY WHISKER THAN SHE COULD HAVE WITH HER KEY.
AND I TAKE MY TREASURE.
WER

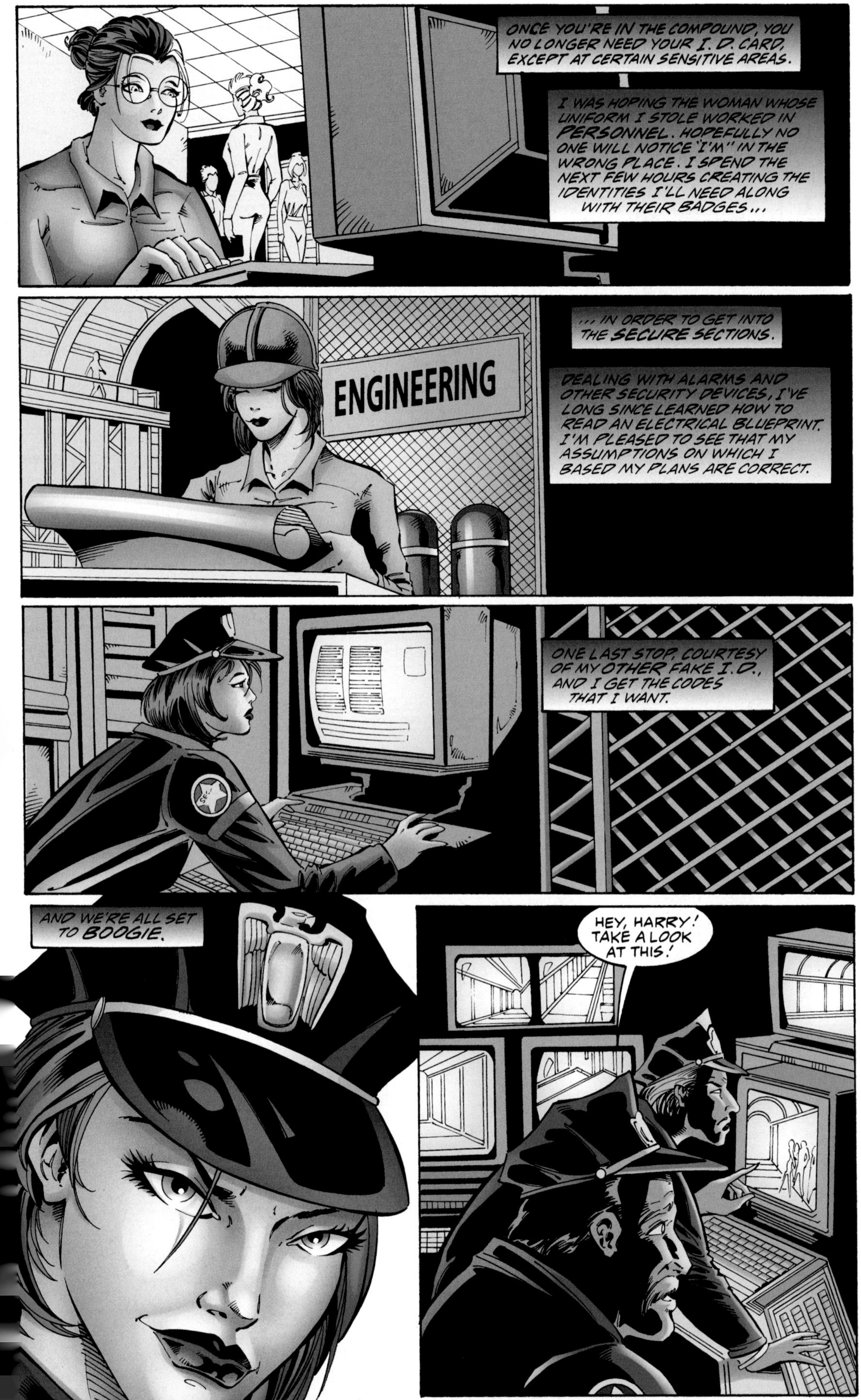
ONCE YOU'RE IN THE COMPOUND, YOU NO LONGER NEED YOUR I. D. CARD, EXCEPT AT CERTAIN SENSITIVE AREAS.
I WAS HOPING THE WOMAN WHOSE UNIFORM I STOLE WORKED IN PERSONNEL. HOPEFULLY NO ONE WILL NOTICE "I'M" IN THE WRONG PLACE. I SPEND THE NEXT FEW HOURS CREATING THE IDENTITIES I'LL NEED ALONG WITH THEIR BADGES...
...IN ORDER TO GET INTO THE SECURE SECTIONS.
ENGINEERING
DEALING WITH ALARMS AND OTHER SECURITY DEVICES, I'VE LONG SINCE LEARNED HOW TO READ AN ELECTRICAL BLUEPRINT. I'M PLEASED TO SEE THAT MY ASSUMPTIONS ON WHICH I BASED MY PLANS ARE CORRECT.
ONE LAST STOP, COURTESY OF MY OTHER FAKE I.D., AND I GET THE CODES THAT I WANT.
AND WE'RE ALL SET TO BOOGIE.
HEY, HARRY! TAKE A LOOK AT THIS!

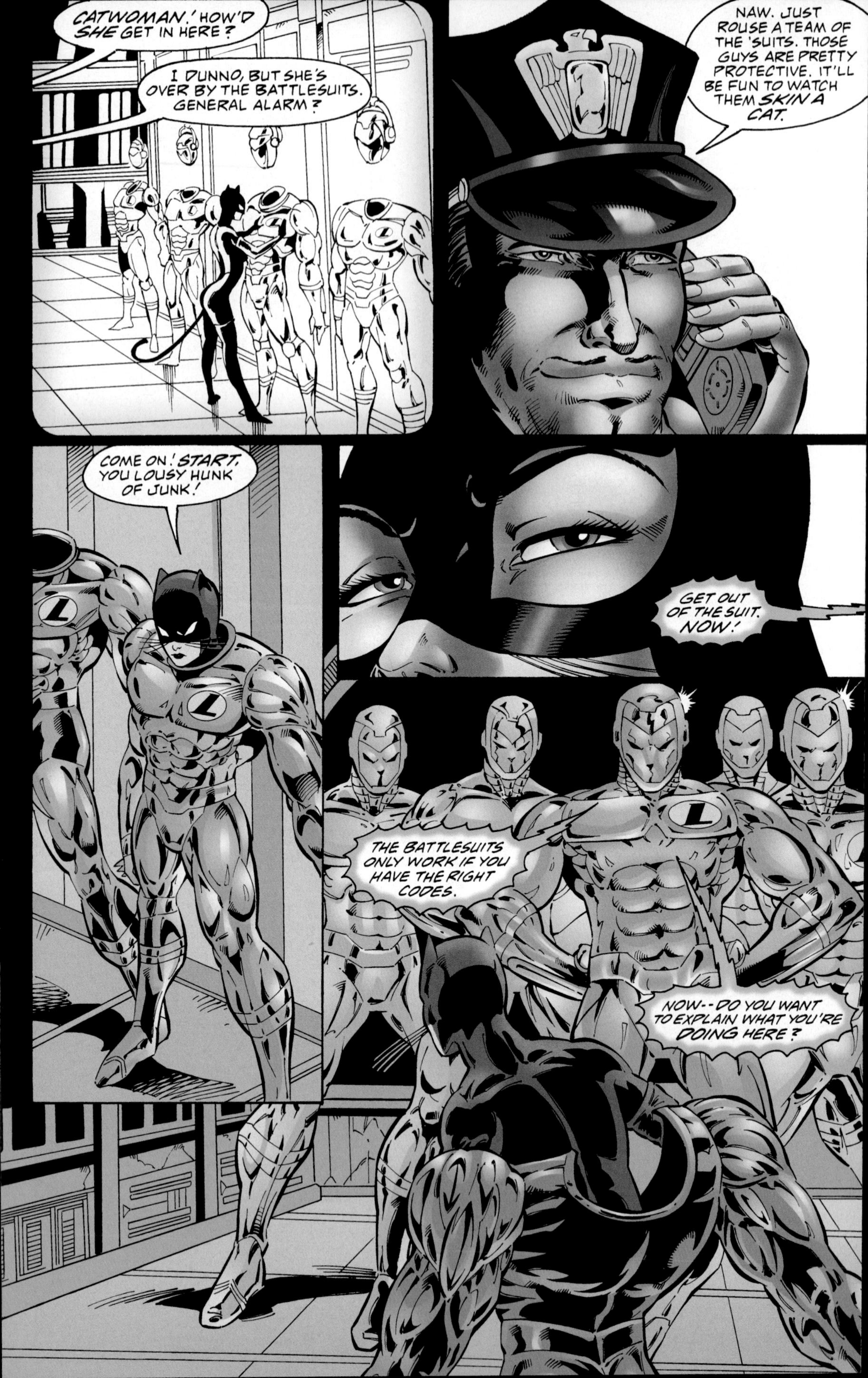

CATWOMAN! HOW'D SHE GET IN HERE?
I DUNNO, BUT SHE'S OVER BY THE BATTLESUITS. GENERAL ALARM?
NAW. JUST ROUSE A TEAM OF THE 'SUITS. THOSE GUYS ARE PRETTY PROTECTIVE. IT'LL BE FUN TO WATCH THEM SKIN A CAT.
COME ON! START, YOU LOUSY HUNK OF JUNK!
GET OUT OF THE SUIT. NOW!
THE BATTLESUITS ONLY WORK IF YOU HAVE THE RIGHT CODES.
NOW--DO YOU WANT TO EXPLAIN WHAT YOU'RE DOING HERE?

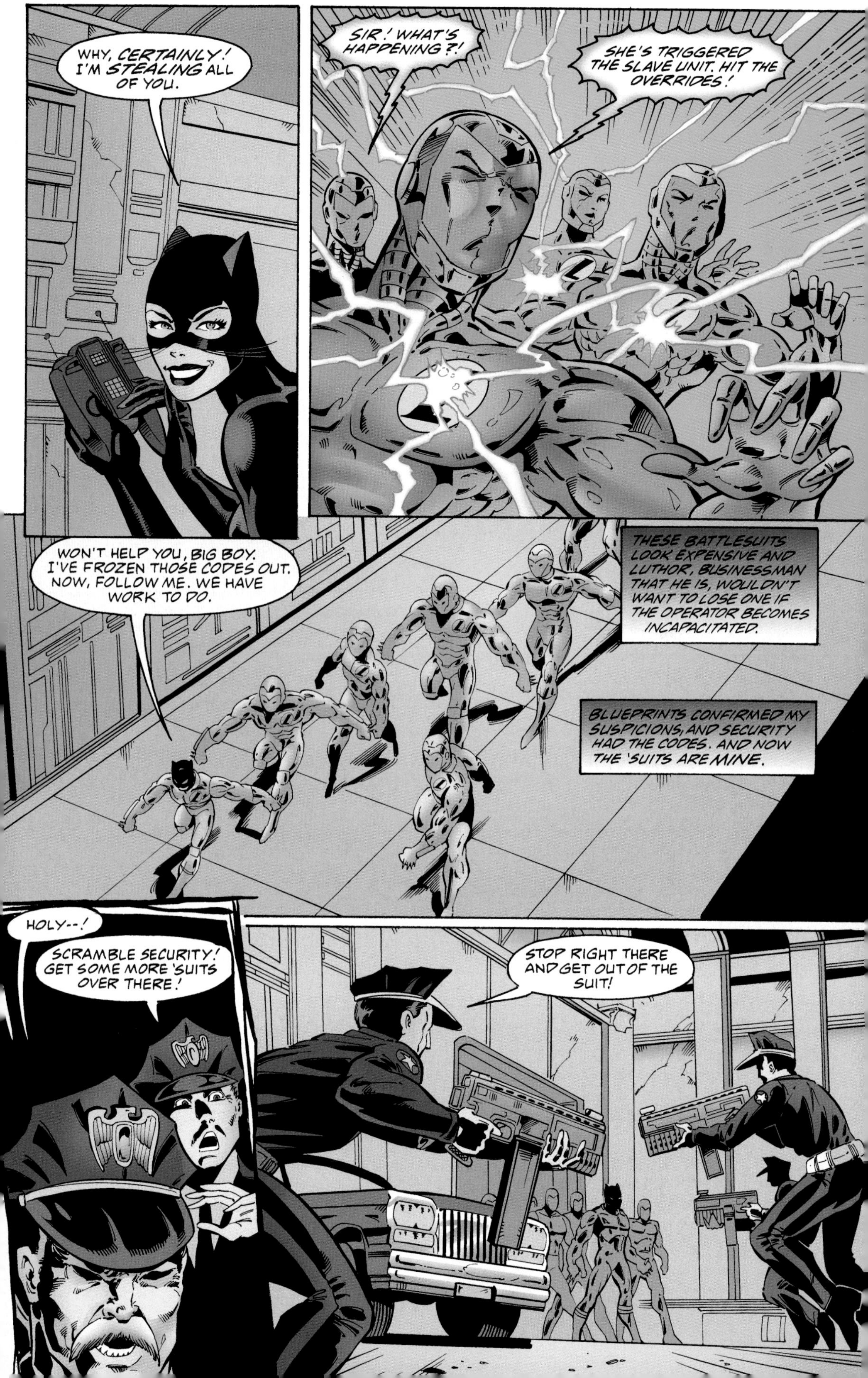
WHY, CERTAINLY! I'M STEALING ALL OF YOU.
SIR! WHAT'S HAPPENING?!
SHE'S TRIGGERED THE SLAVE UNIT. HIT THE OVERRIDES!
WON'T HELP YOU, BIG BOY. I'VE FROZEN THOSE CODES OUT. NOW, FOLLOW ME. WE HAVE WORK TO DO.
THESE BATTLESUITS LOOK EXPENSIVE AND LUTHOR, BUSINESSMAN THAT HE IS, WOULDN'T WANT TO LOSE ONE IF THE OPERATOR BECOMES INCAPACITATED.
BLUEPRINTS CONFIRMED MY SUSPICIONS, AND SECURITY HAD THE CODES. AND NOW THE 'SUITS ARE MINE.
HOLY--!
SCRAMBLE SECURITY! GET SOME MORE 'SUITS OVER THERE!
STOP RIGHT THERE AND GET OUT OF THE SUIT!

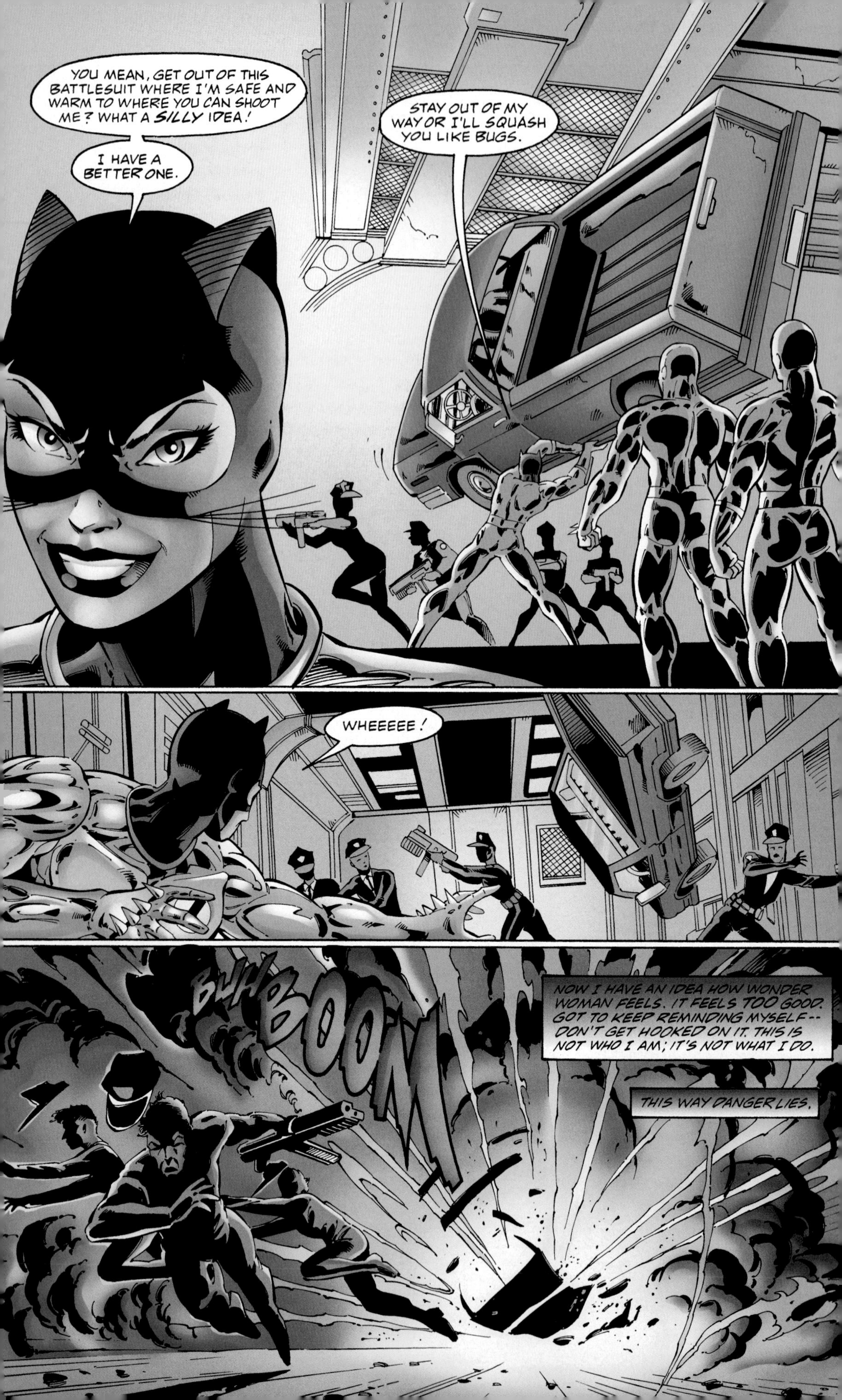
YOU MEAN, GET OUT OF THIS BATTLESUIT WHERE I'M SAFE AND WARM TO WHERE YOU CAN SHOOT ME? WHAT A SILLY IDEA!
I HAVE A BETTER ONE.
STAY OUT OF MY WAY OR I'LL SQUASH YOU LIKE BUGS.
WHEEEEE!
BUHBOOM
NOW I HAVE AN IDEA HOW WONDER WOMAN FEELS. IT FEELS TOO GOOD. GOT TO KEEP REMINDING MYSELF -- DON'T GET HOOKED ON IT. THIS IS NOT WHO I AM; IT'S NOT WHAT I DO.
THIS WAY DANGER LIES.

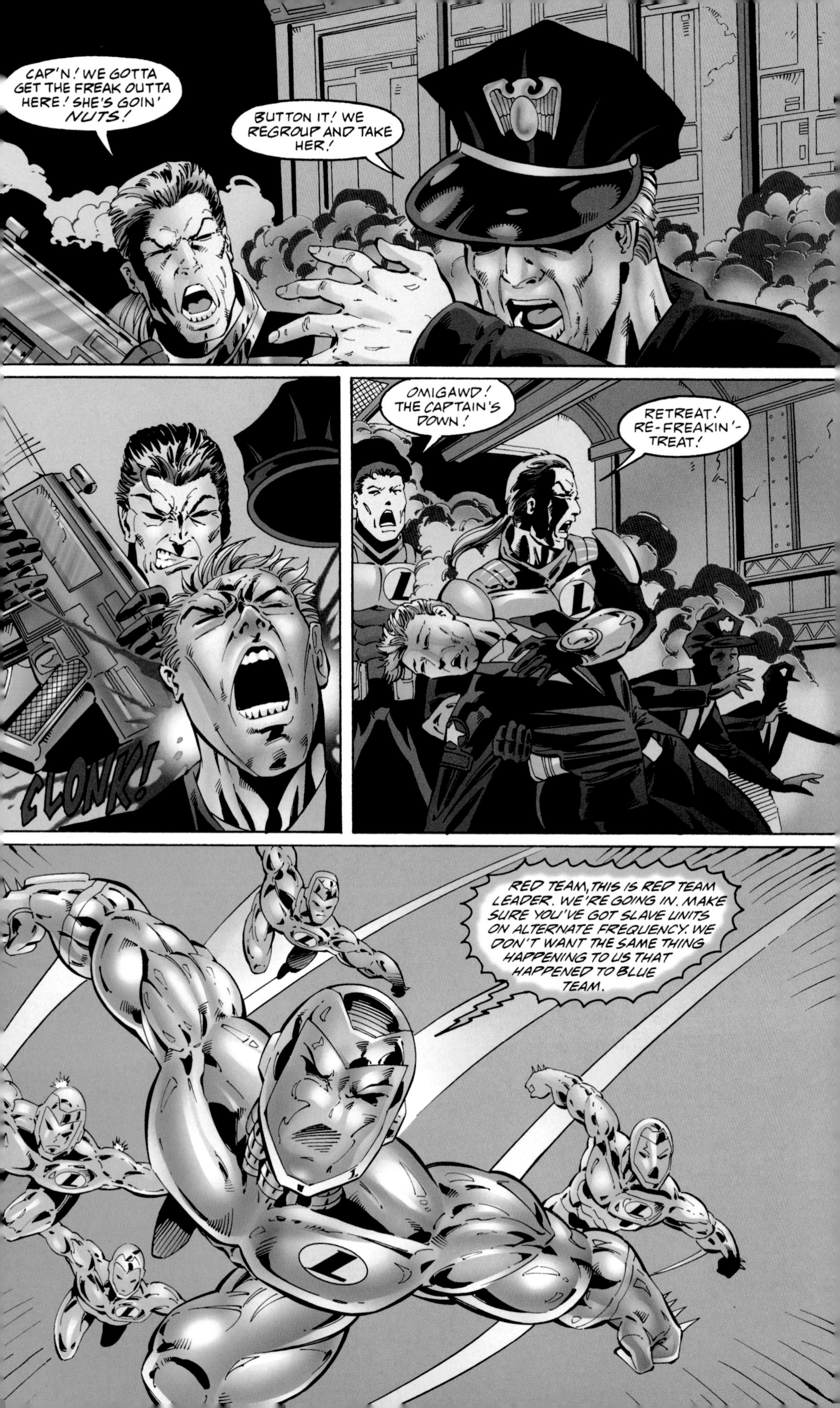
CAP'N! WE GOTTA GET THE FREAK OUTTA HERE! SHE'S GOIN' NUTS!
BUTTON IT! WE REGROUP AND TAKE HER!
CLONK!
OMIGAWD! THE CAPTAIN'S DOWN!
RETREAT! RE-FREAKIN'-TREAT!
RED TEAM, THIS IS RED TEAM LEADER. WE'RE GOING IN. MAKE SURE YOU'VE GOT SLAVE UNITS ON ALTERNATE FREQUENCY. WE DON'T WANT THE SAME THING HAPPENING TO US THAT HAPPENED TO BLUE TEAM.

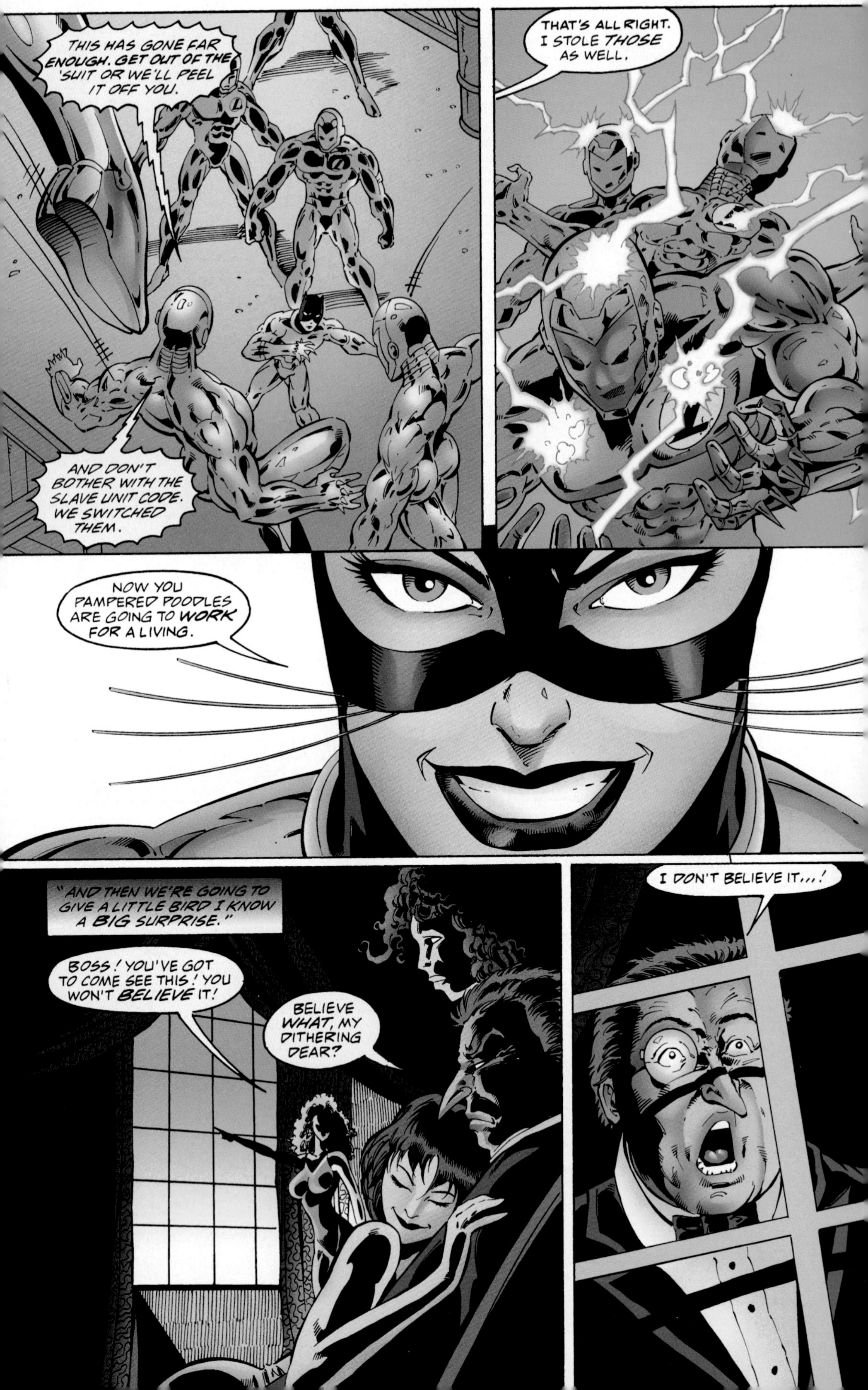
THIS HAS GONE FAR ENOUGH. GET OUT OF THE SUIT OR WE'LL PEEL IT OFF YOU.
AND DON'T BOTHER WITH THE SLAVE UNIT CODE. WE SWITCHED THEM.
THAT'S ALL RIGHT. I STOLE *THOSE* AS WELL.
NOW YOU PAMPERED POODLES ARE GOING TO **WORK** FOR A LIVING.
"AND THEN WE'RE GOING TO GIVE A LITTLE BIRD I KNOW A **BIG** SURPRISE."
BOSS! YOU'VE GOT TO COME SEE THIS! YOU WON'T ***BELIEVE*** IT!
BELIEVE *WHAT*, MY DITHERING DEAR?
I DON'T BELIEVE IT...!

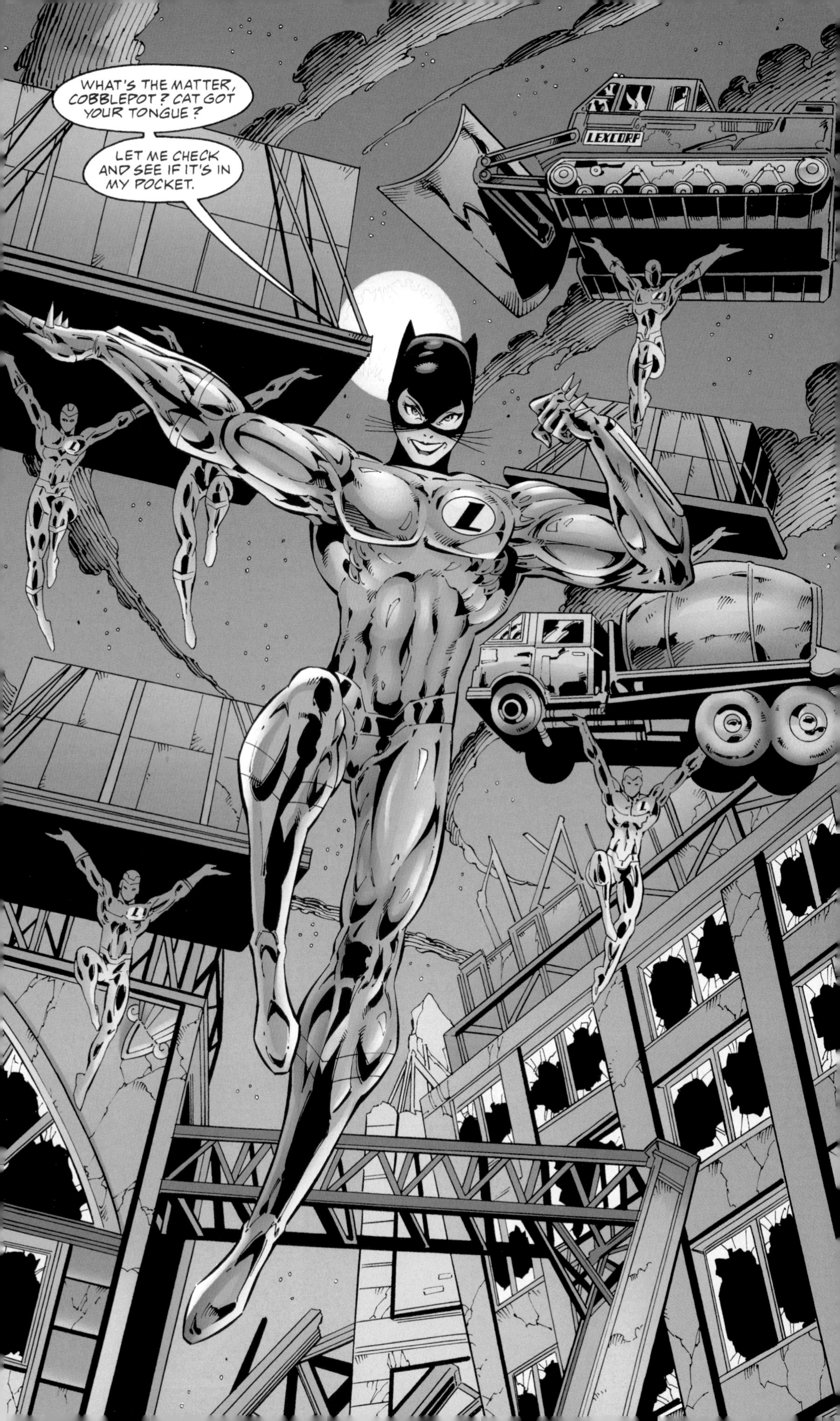
WHAT'S THE MATTER, COBBLEPOT? CAT GOT YOUR TONGUE?
LET ME CHECK AND SEE IF IT'S IN MY POCKET.
LEXCORP

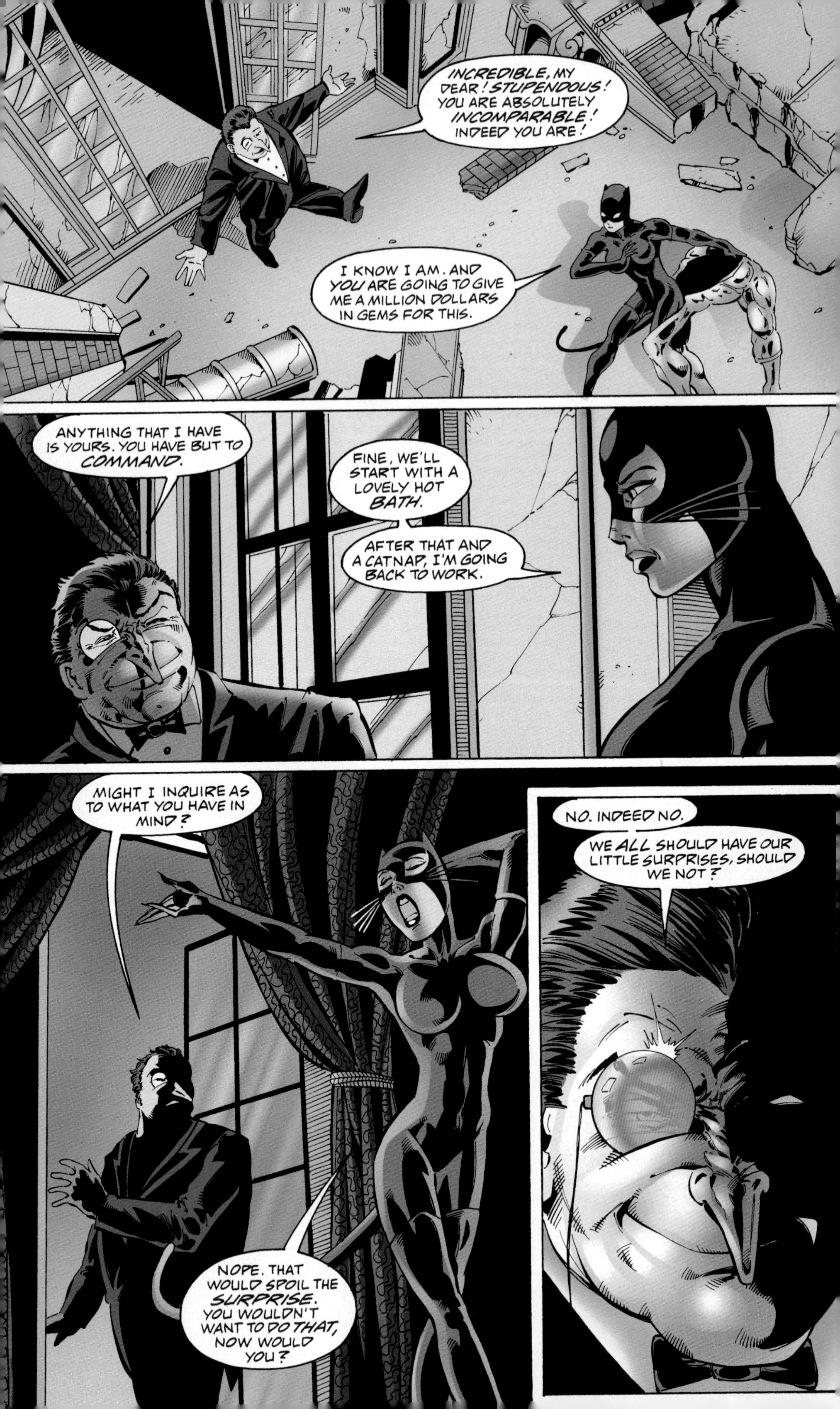
INCREDIBLE, MY DEAR! STUPENDOUS! YOU ARE ABSOLUTELY INCOMPARABLE! INDEED YOU ARE!
I KNOW I AM. AND YOU ARE GOING TO GIVE ME A MILLION DOLLARS IN GEMS FOR THIS.
ANYTHING THAT I HAVE IS YOURS. YOU HAVE BUT TO COMMAND.
FINE, WE'LL START WITH A LOVELY HOT BATH.
AFTER THAT AND A CATNAP, I'M GOING BACK TO WORK.
MIGHT I INQUIRE AS TO WHAT YOU HAVE IN MIND?
NOPE. THAT WOULD SPOIL THE SURPRISE. YOU WOULDN'T WANT TO DO THAT, NOW WOULD YOU?
NO. INDEED NO.
WE ALL SHOULD HAVE OUR LITTLE SURPRISES, SHOULD WE NOT?

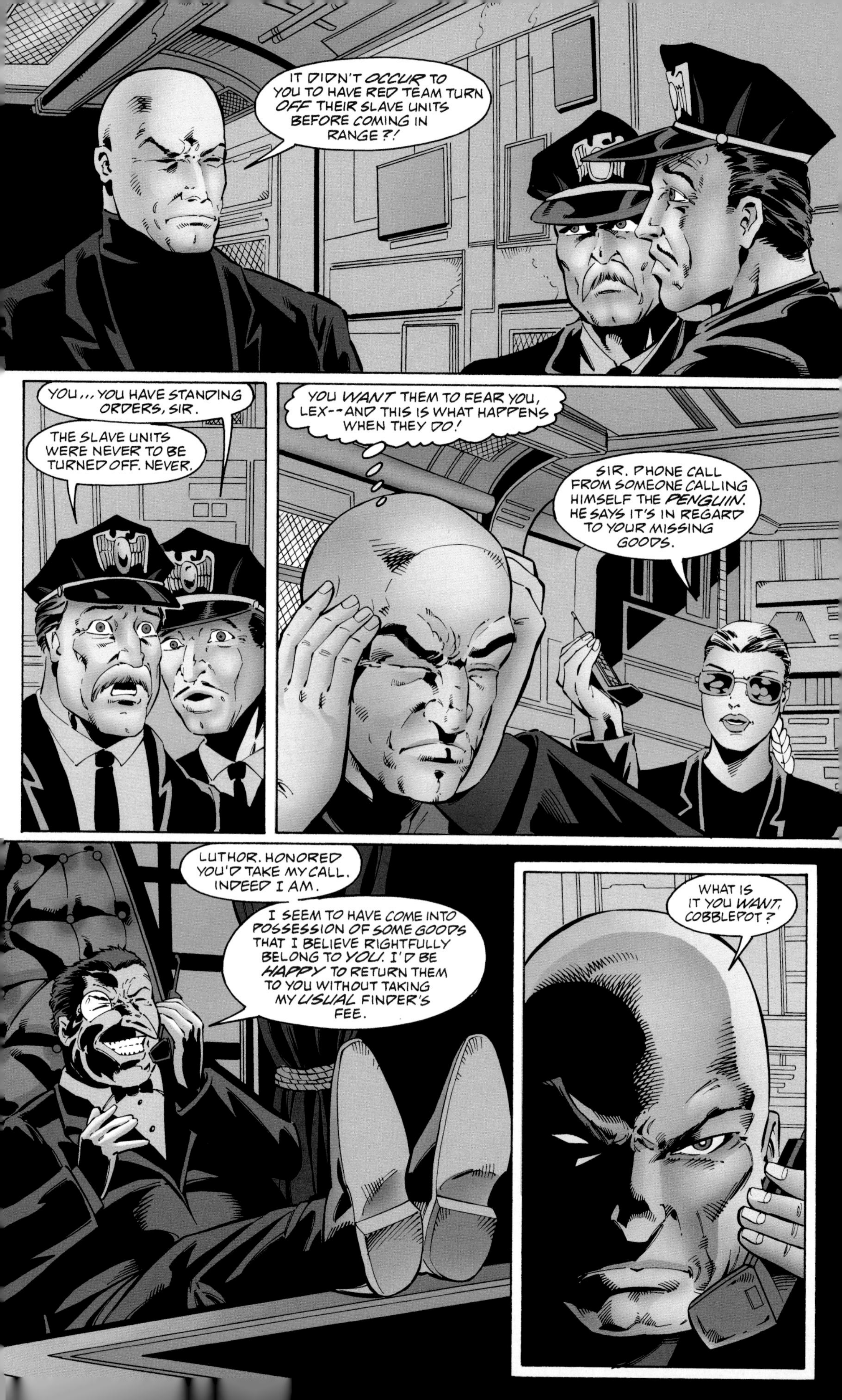

IT DIDN'T OCCUR TO YOU TO HAVE RED TEAM TURN OFF THEIR SLAVE UNITS BEFORE COMING IN RANGE?!
YOU... YOU HAVE STANDING ORDERS, SIR.
THE SLAVE UNITS WERE NEVER TO BE TURNED OFF. NEVER.
YOU WANT THEM TO FEAR YOU, LEX--AND THIS IS WHAT HAPPENS WHEN THEY DO!
SIR. PHONE CALL FROM SOMEONE CALLING HIMSELF THE PENGUIN. HE SAYS IT'S IN REGARD TO YOUR MISSING GOODS.
LUTHOR. HONORED YOU'D TAKE MY CALL. INDEED I AM.
I SEEM TO HAVE COME INTO POSSESSION OF SOME GOODS THAT I BELIEVE RIGHTFULLY BELONG TO YOU. I'D BE HAPPY TO RETURN THEM TO YOU WITHOUT TAKING MY USUAL FINDER'S FEE.
WHAT IS IT YOU WANT, COBBLEPOT?

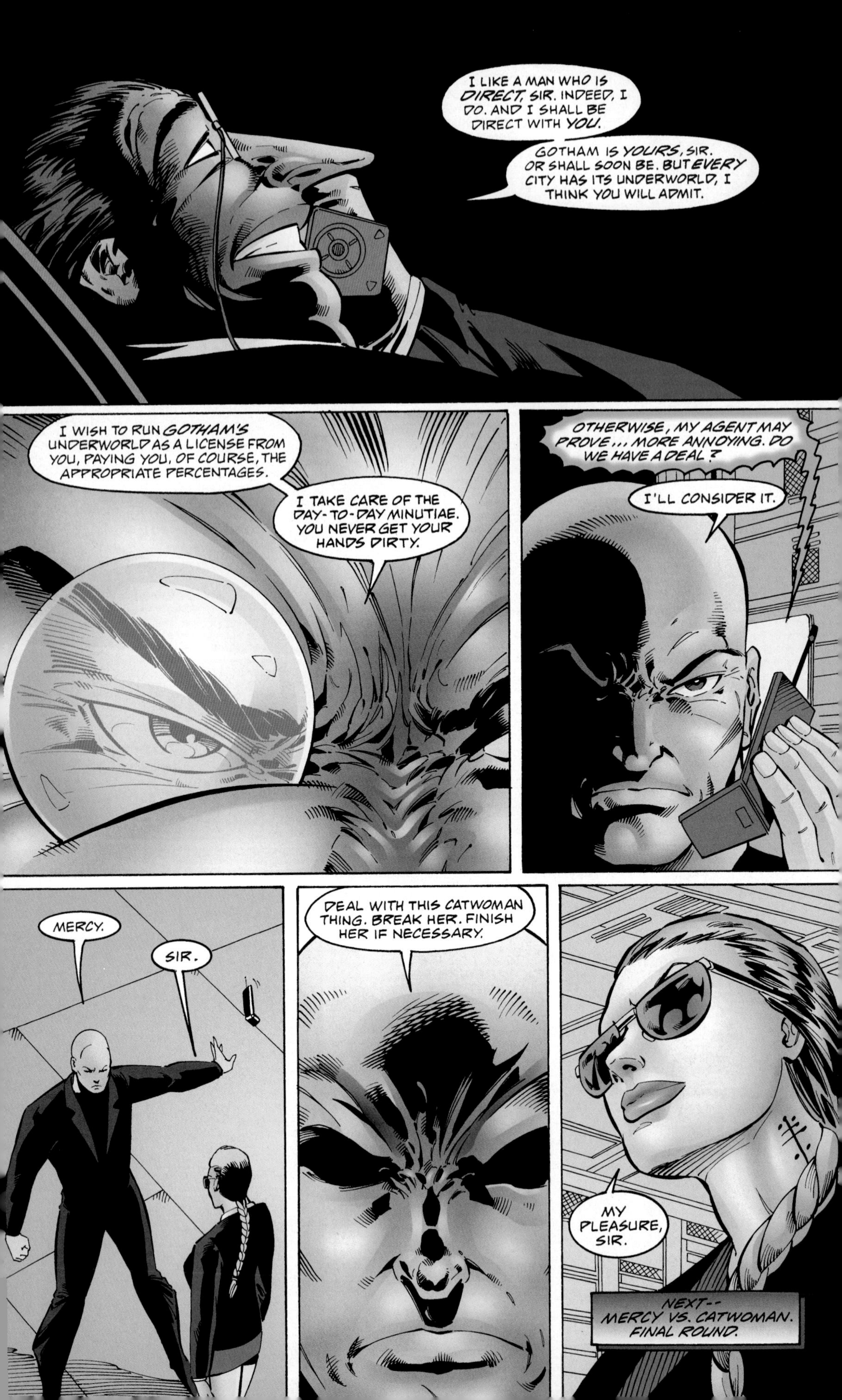
I LIKE A MAN WHO IS DIRECT, SIR. INDEED, I DO. AND I SHALL BE DIRECT WITH YOU.
GOTHAM IS YOURS, SIR. OR SHALL SOON BE. BUT EVERY CITY HAS ITS UNDERWORLD, I THINK YOU WILL ADMIT.
I WISH TO RUN GOTHAM'S UNDERWORLD AS A LICENSE FROM YOU, PAYING YOU, OF COURSE, THE APPROPRIATE PERCENTAGES.
I TAKE CARE OF THE DAY-TO-DAY MINUTIAE. YOU NEVER GET YOUR HANDS DIRTY.
OTHERWISE, MY AGENT MAY PROVE... MORE ANNOYING. DO WE HAVE A DEAL?
I'LL CONSIDER IT.
MERCY.
SIR.
DEAL WITH THIS CATWOMAN THING. BREAK HER. FINISH HER IF NECESSARY.
MY PLEASURE, SIR.
NEXT-- MERCY VS. CATWOMAN. FINAL ROUND.

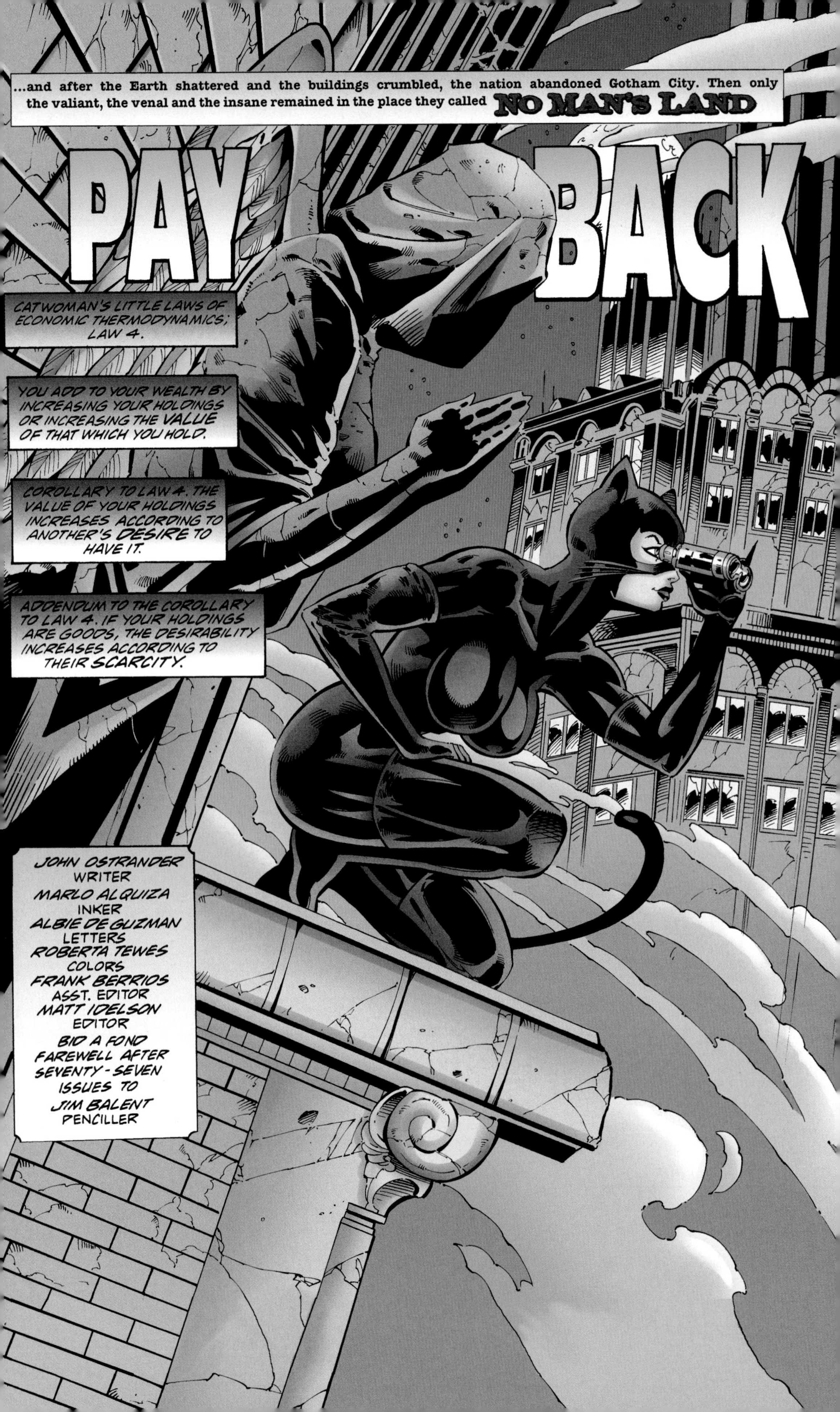
...and after the Earth shattered and the buildings crumbled, the nation abandoned Gotham City. Then only the valiant, the venal and the insane remained in the place they called NO MAN'S LAND
PAY BACK
CATWOMAN'S LITTLE LAWS OF ECONOMIC THERMODYNAMICS; LAW 4.
YOU ADD TO YOUR WEALTH BY INCREASING YOUR HOLDINGS OR INCREASING THE VALUE OF THAT WHICH YOU HOLD.
COROLLARY TO LAW 4. THE VALUE OF YOUR HOLDINGS INCREASES ACCORDING TO ANOTHER'S DESIRE TO HAVE IT.
ADDENDUM TO THE COROLLARY TO LAW 4. IF YOUR HOLDINGS ARE GOODS, THE DESIRABILITY INCREASES ACCORDING TO THEIR SCARCITY.
JOHN OSTRANDER WRITER
MARLO ALQUIZA INKER
ALBIE DE GUZMAN LETTERS
ROBERTA TEWES COLORS
FRANK BERRIOS ASST. EDITOR
MATT IDELSON EDITOR
BID A FOND FAREWELL AFTER SEVENTY-SEVEN ISSUES TO JIM BALENT PENCILLER

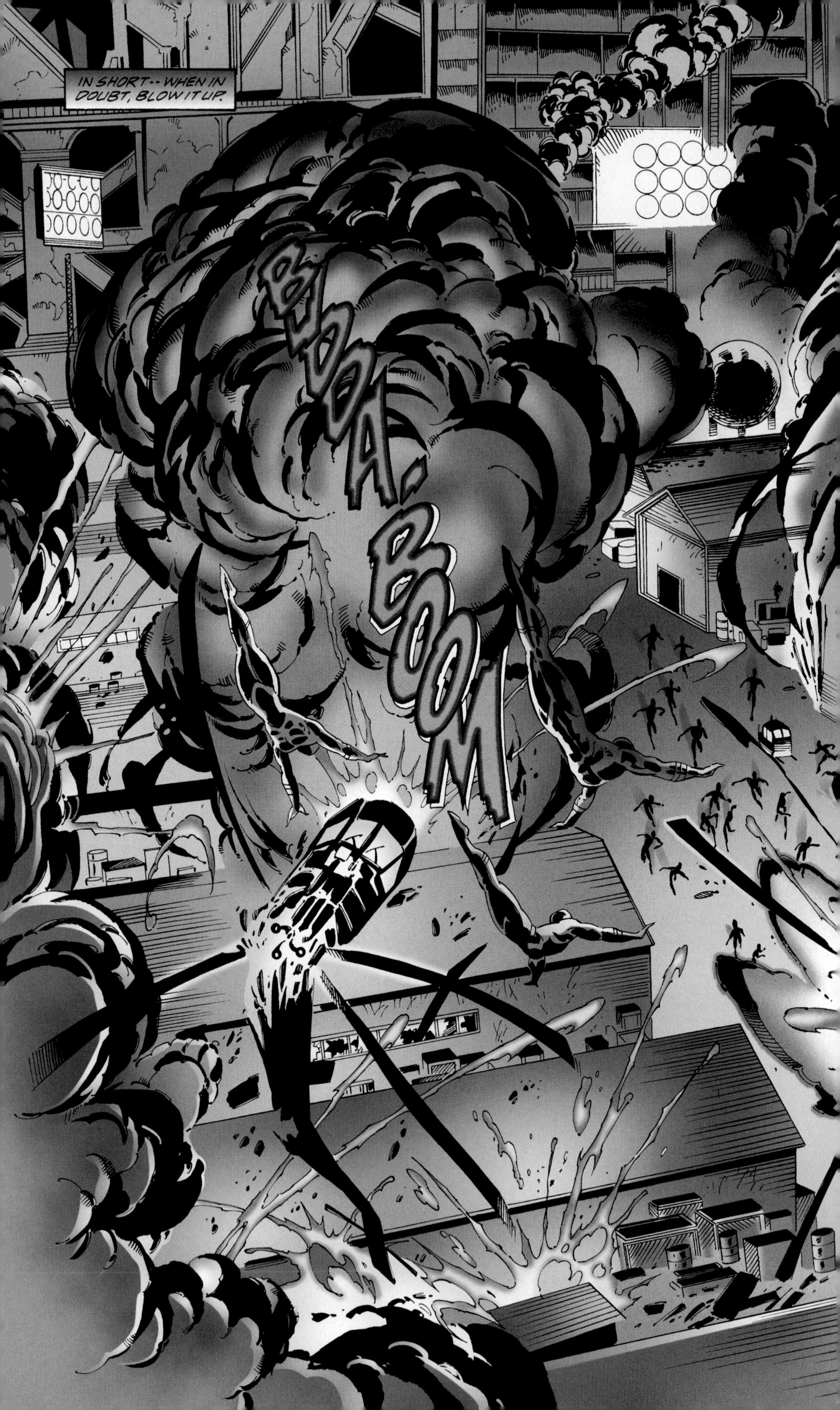
IN SHORT-- WHEN IN DOUBT, BLOW IT UP.
BUDDA-BOOM

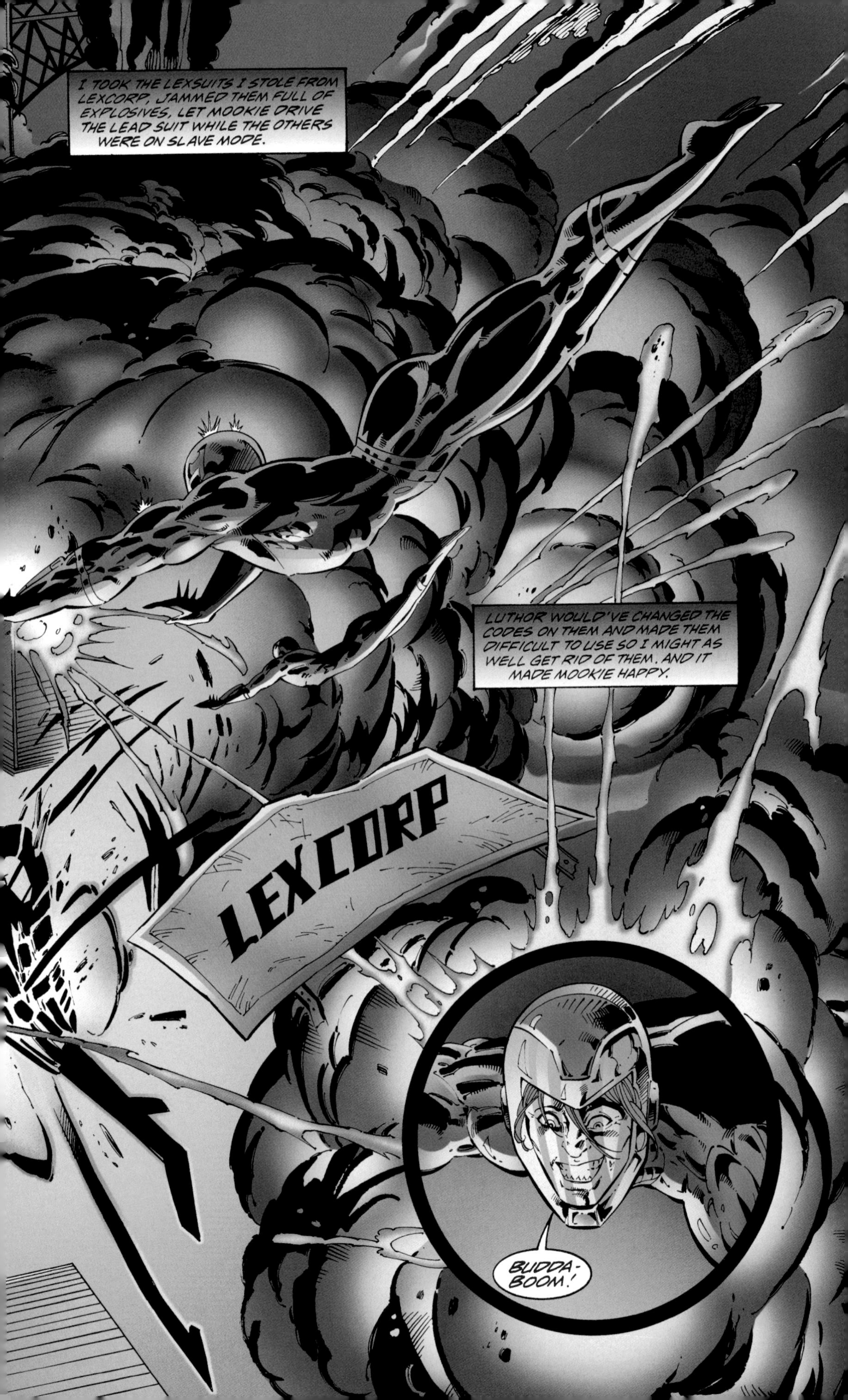
I TOOK THE LEXSUITS I STOLE FROM LEXCORP, JAMMED THEM FULL OF EXPLOSIVES, LET MOOKIE DRIVE THE LEAD SUIT WHILE THE OTHERS WERE ON SLAVE MODE.
LUTHOR WOULD'VE CHANGED THE CODES ON THEM AND MADE THEM DIFFICULT TO USE SO I MIGHT AS WELL GET RID OF THEM. AND IT MADE MOOKIE HAPPY.
LEXCORP
BUDDA-BOOM!

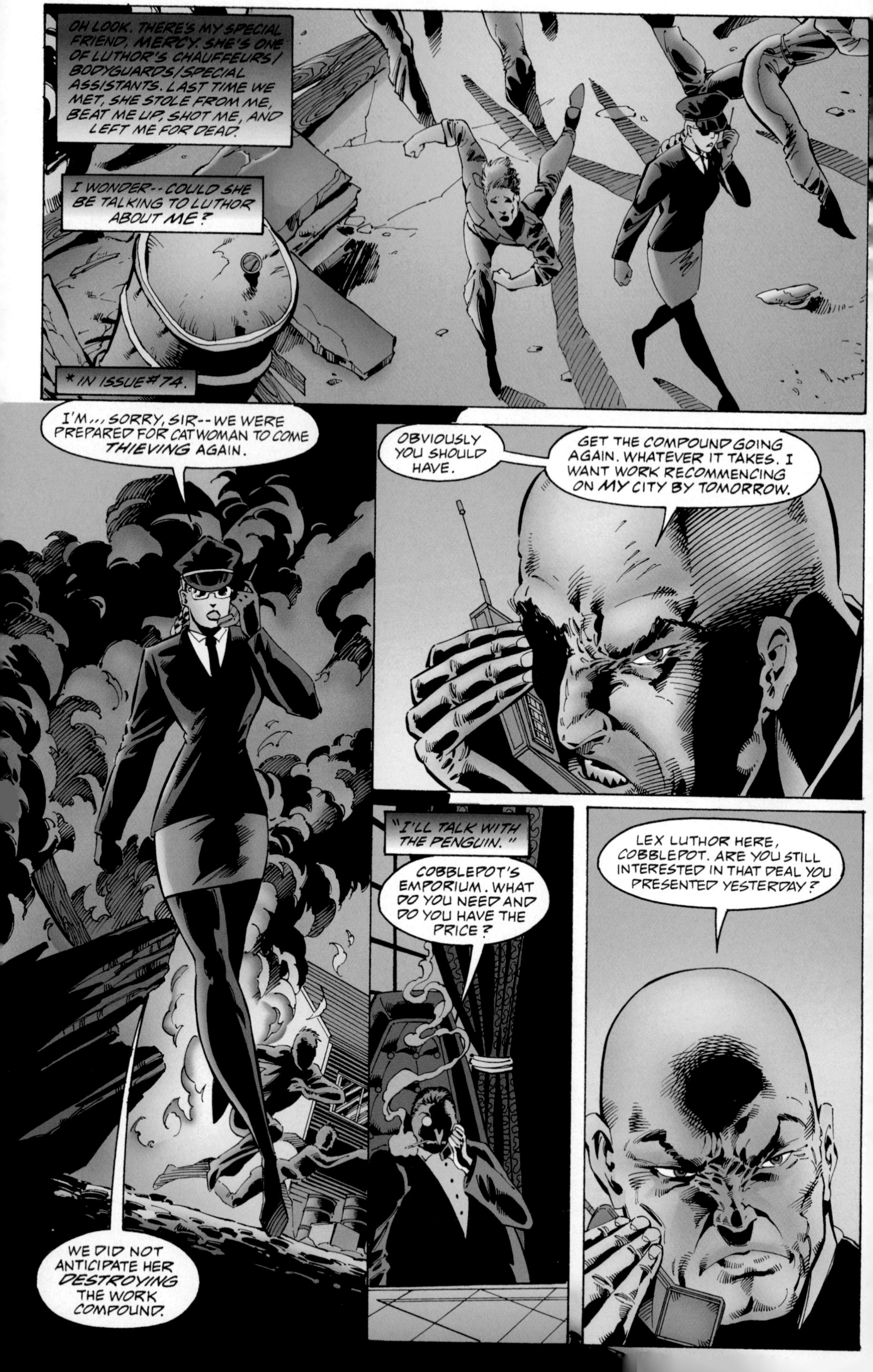
OH LOOK. THERE'S MY SPECIAL FRIEND, MERCY. SHE'S ONE OF LUTHOR'S CHAUFFEURS/ BODYGUARDS/SPECIAL ASSISTANTS. LAST TIME WE MET, SHE STOLE FROM ME, BEAT ME UP, SHOT ME, AND LEFT ME FOR DEAD.*
I WONDER--COULD SHE BE TALKING TO LUTHOR ABOUT ME?
* IN ISSUE #74.
I'M... SORRY, SIR--WE WERE PREPARED FOR CATWOMAN TO COME THIEVING AGAIN.
WE DID NOT ANTICIPATE HER DESTROYING THE WORK COMPOUND.
OBVIOUSLY YOU SHOULD HAVE.
GET THE COMPOUND GOING AGAIN. WHATEVER IT TAKES. I WANT WORK RECOMMENCING ON MY CITY BY TOMORROW.
"I'LL TALK WITH THE PENGUIN."
COBBLEPOT'S EMPORIUM. WHAT DO YOU NEED AND DO YOU HAVE THE PRICE?
LEX LUTHOR HERE, COBBLEPOT. ARE YOU STILL INTERESTED IN THAT DEAL YOU PRESENTED YESTERDAY?

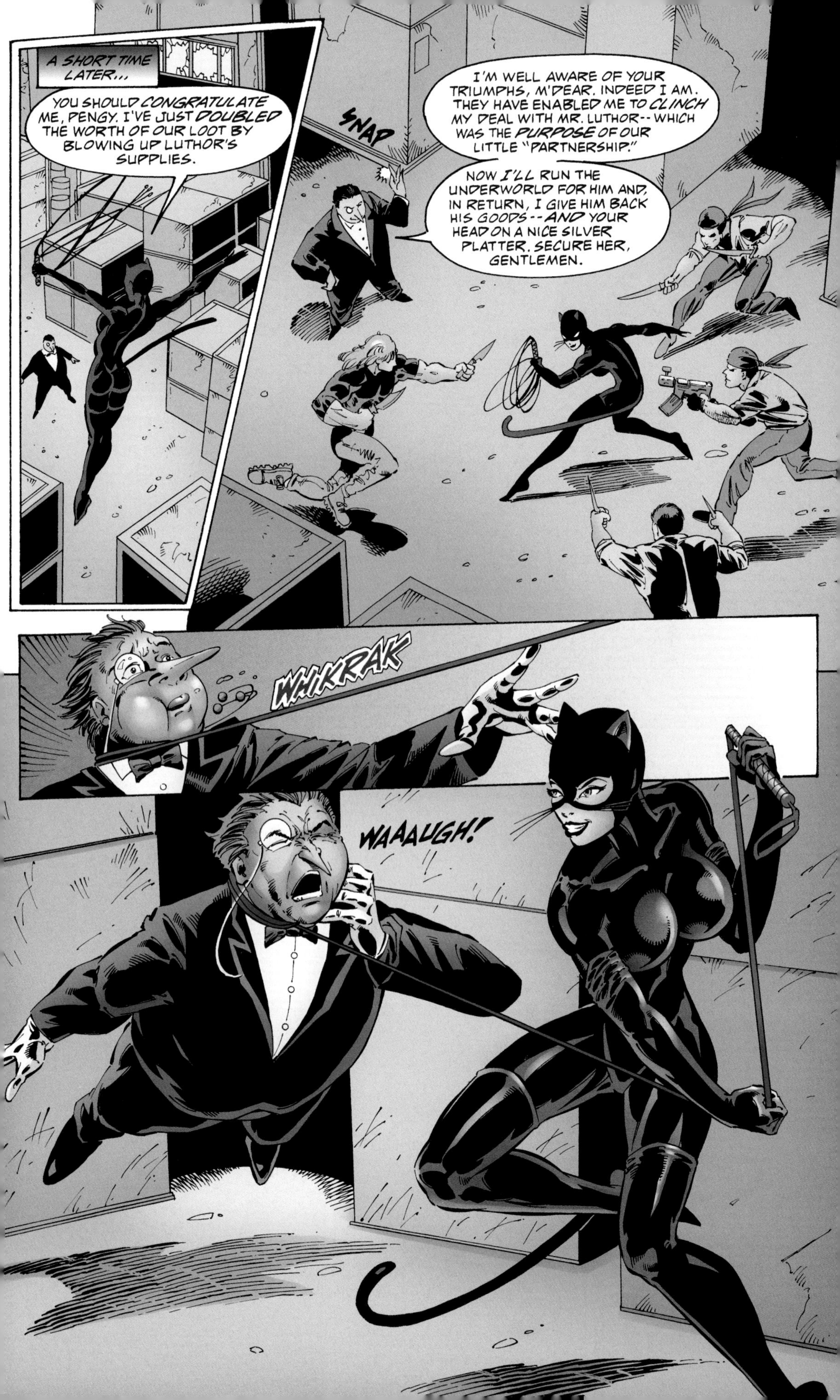

A SHORT TIME LATER...
YOU SHOULD CONGRATULATE ME, PENGY. I'VE JUST DOUBLED THE WORTH OF OUR LOOT BY BLOWING UP LUTHOR'S SUPPLIES.
SNAP
I'M WELL AWARE OF YOUR TRIUMPHS, M'DEAR. INDEED I AM. THEY HAVE ENABLED ME TO CLINCH MY DEAL WITH MR. LUTHOR-- WHICH WAS THE PURPOSE OF OUR LITTLE "PARTNERSHIP."
NOW I'LL RUN THE UNDERWORLD FOR HIM AND, IN RETURN, I GIVE HIM BACK HIS GOODS--AND YOUR HEAD ON A NICE SILVER PLATTER. SECURE HER, GENTLEMEN.
WHIKRAK
WAAAUGH!

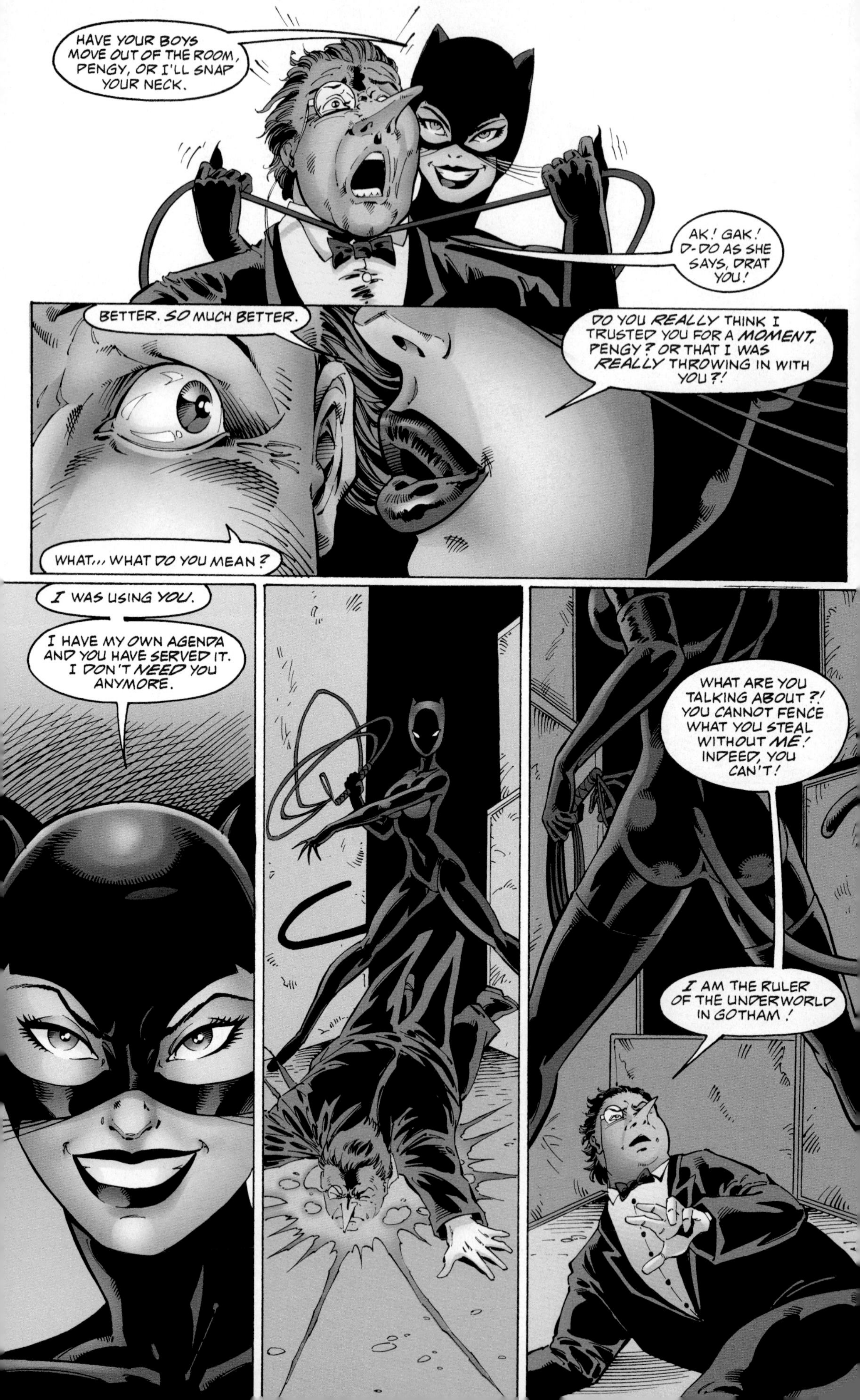
HAVE YOUR BOYS MOVE OUT OF THE ROOM, PENGY, OR I'LL SNAP YOUR NECK.
AK! GAK! D-DO AS SHE SAYS, DRAT YOU!
BETTER. SO MUCH BETTER.
DO YOU REALLY THINK I TRUSTED YOU FOR A MOMENT, PENGY? OR THAT I WAS REALLY THROWING IN WITH YOU?!
WHAT... WHAT DO YOU MEAN?
I WAS USING YOU.
I HAVE MY OWN AGENDA AND YOU HAVE SERVED IT. I DON'T NEED YOU ANYMORE.
WHAT ARE YOU TALKING ABOUT?! YOU CANNOT FENCE WHAT YOU STEAL WITHOUT ME! INDEED, YOU CAN'T!
I AM THE RULER OF THE UNDERWORLD IN GOTHAM!

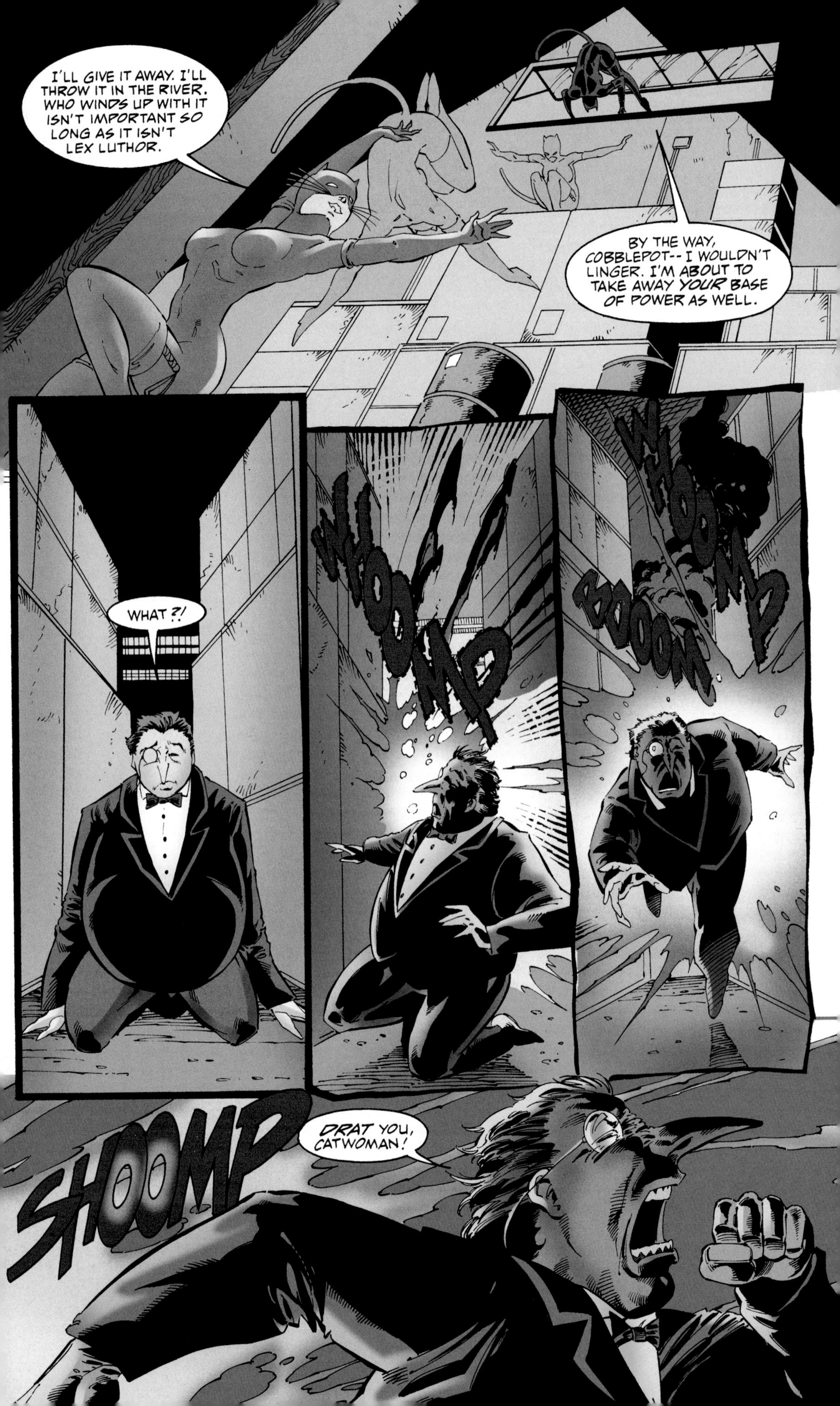
I'LL GIVE IT AWAY. I'LL THROW IT IN THE RIVER. WHO WINDS UP WITH IT ISN'T IMPORTANT SO LONG AS IT ISN'T LEX LUTHOR.
BY THE WAY, COBBLEPOT-- I WOULDN'T LINGER. I'M ABOUT TO TAKE AWAY YOUR BASE OF POWER AS WELL.
WHAT?!
WHOOOMD
WHOOOMD
BOOOOM
SHOOMP
DRAT YOU, CATWOMAN!

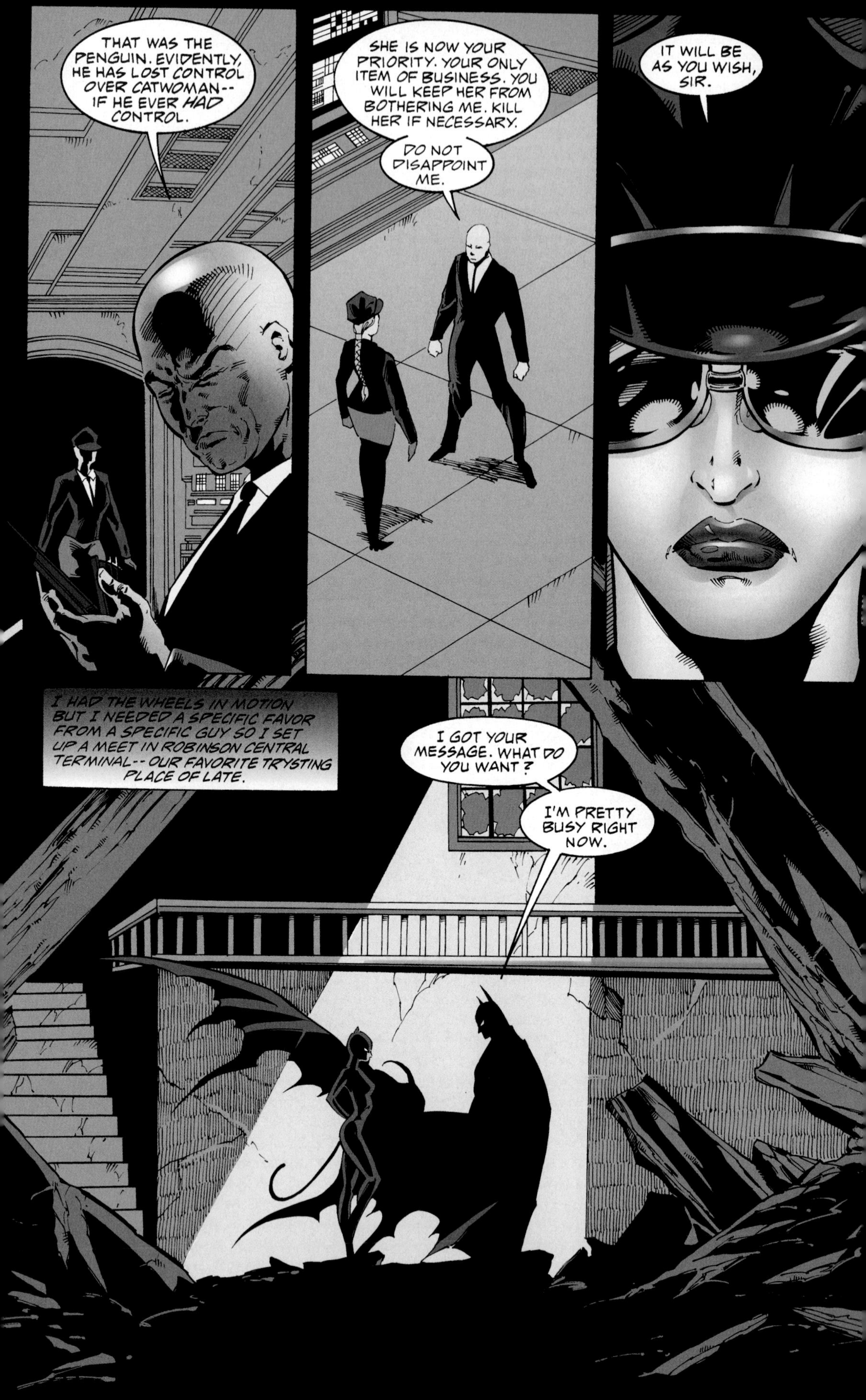
THAT WAS THE PENGUIN. EVIDENTLY, HE HAS LOST CONTROL OVER CATWOMAN-- IF HE EVER HAD CONTROL.
SHE IS NOW YOUR PRIORITY. YOUR ONLY ITEM OF BUSINESS. YOU WILL KEEP HER FROM BOTHERING ME. KILL HER IF NECESSARY.
DO NOT DISAPPOINT ME.
IT WILL BE AS YOU WISH, SIR.
I HAD THE WHEELS IN MOTION BUT I NEEDED A SPECIFIC FAVOR FROM A SPECIFIC GUY SO I SET UP A MEET IN ROBINSON CENTRAL TERMINAL-- OUR FAVORITE TRYSTING PLACE OF LATE.
I GOT YOUR MESSAGE. WHAT DO YOU WANT?
I'M PRETTY BUSY RIGHT NOW.

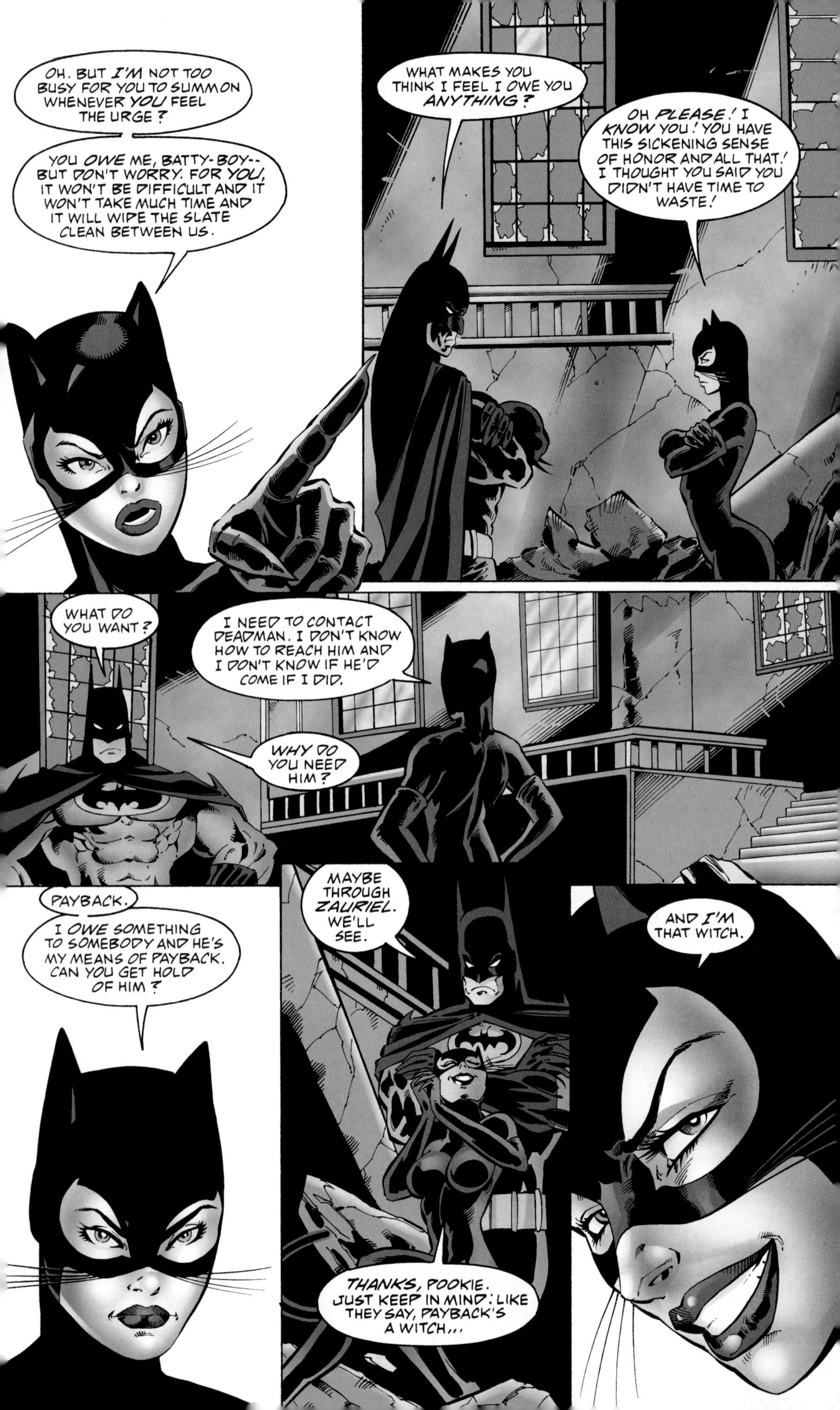

OH. BUT I'M NOT TOO BUSY FOR YOU TO SUMMON WHENEVER YOU FEEL THE URGE?
YOU OWE ME, BATTY-BOY-- BUT DON'T WORRY. FOR YOU, IT WON'T BE DIFFICULT AND IT WON'T TAKE MUCH TIME AND IT WILL WIPE THE SLATE CLEAN BETWEEN US.
WHAT MAKES YOU THINK I FEEL I OWE YOU ANYTHING?
OH PLEASE! I KNOW YOU! YOU HAVE THIS SICKENING SENSE OF HONOR AND ALL THAT! I THOUGHT YOU SAID YOU DIDN'T HAVE TIME TO WASTE!
WHAT DO YOU WANT?
I NEED TO CONTACT DEADMAN. I DON'T KNOW HOW TO REACH HIM AND I DON'T KNOW IF HE'D COME IF I DID.
WHY DO YOU NEED HIM?
PAYBACK.
I OWE SOMETHING TO SOMEBODY AND HE'S MY MEANS OF PAYBACK. CAN YOU GET HOLD OF HIM?
MAYBE THROUGH ZAURIEL. WE'LL SEE.
THANKS, POOKIE. JUST KEEP IN MIND: LIKE THEY SAY, PAYBACK'S A WITCH...
AND I'M THAT WITCH.

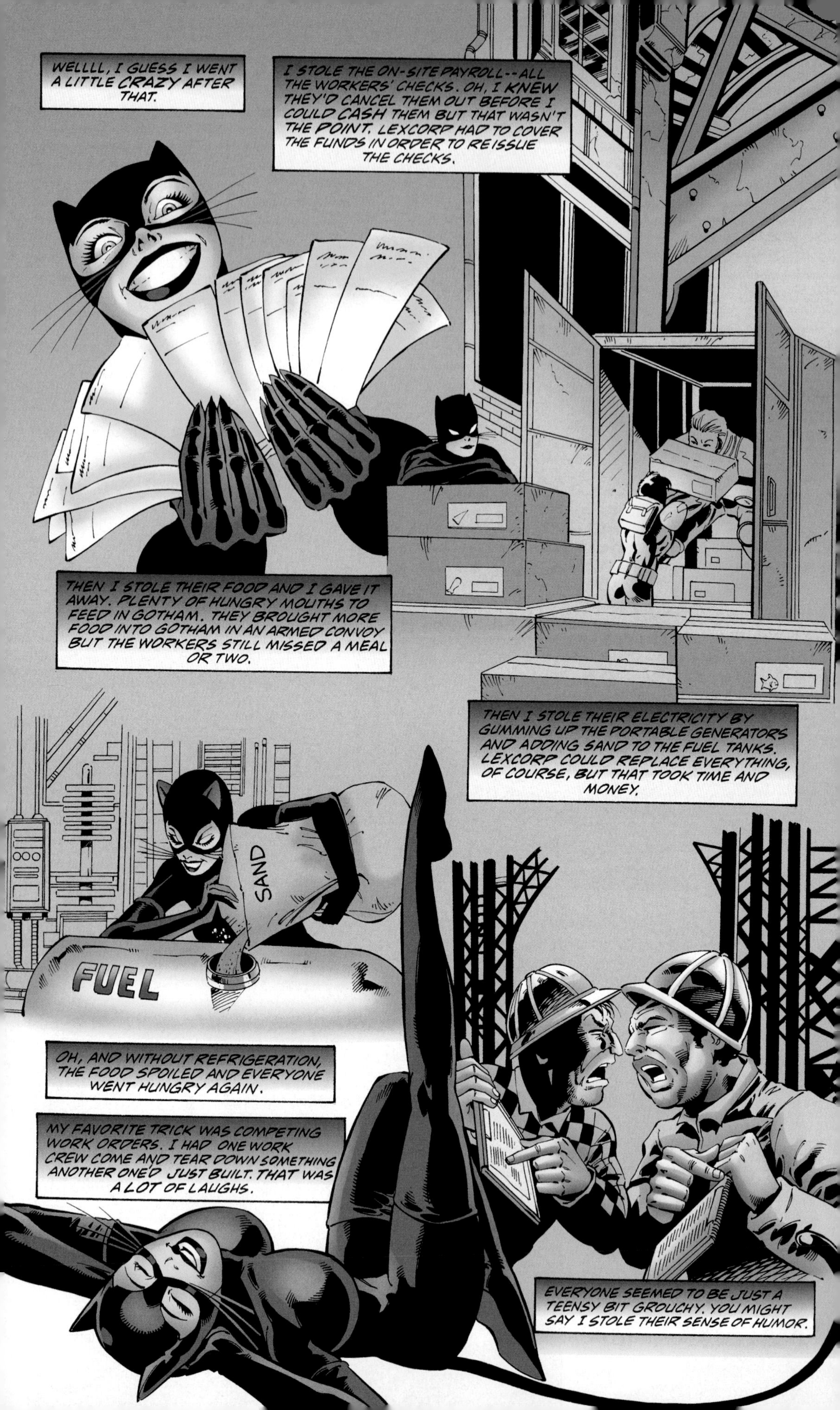
WELLLL, I GUESS I WENT A LITTLE CRAZY AFTER THAT.
I STOLE THE ON-SITE PAYROLL--ALL THE WORKERS' CHECKS. OH, I KNEW THEY'D CANCEL THEM OUT BEFORE I COULD CASH THEM BUT THAT WASN'T THE POINT. LEXCORP HAD TO COVER THE FUNDS IN ORDER TO REISSUE THE CHECKS.
THEN I STOLE THEIR FOOD AND I GAVE IT AWAY. PLENTY OF HUNGRY MOUTHS TO FEED IN GOTHAM. THEY BROUGHT MORE FOOD INTO GOTHAM IN AN ARMED CONVOY BUT THE WORKERS STILL MISSED A MEAL OR TWO.
THEN I STOLE THEIR ELECTRICITY BY GUMMING UP THE PORTABLE GENERATORS AND ADDING SAND TO THE FUEL TANKS. LEXCORP COULD REPLACE EVERYTHING, OF COURSE, BUT THAT TOOK TIME AND MONEY.
SAND
FUEL
OH, AND WITHOUT REFRIGERATION, THE FOOD SPOILED AND EVERYONE WENT HUNGRY AGAIN.
MY FAVORITE TRICK WAS COMPETING WORK ORDERS. I HAD ONE WORK CREW COME AND TEAR DOWN SOMETHING ANOTHER ONE'D JUST BUILT. THAT WAS A LOT OF LAUGHS.
EVERYONE SEEMED TO BE JUST A TEENSY BIT GROUCHY. YOU MIGHT SAY I STOLE THEIR SENSE OF HUMOR.

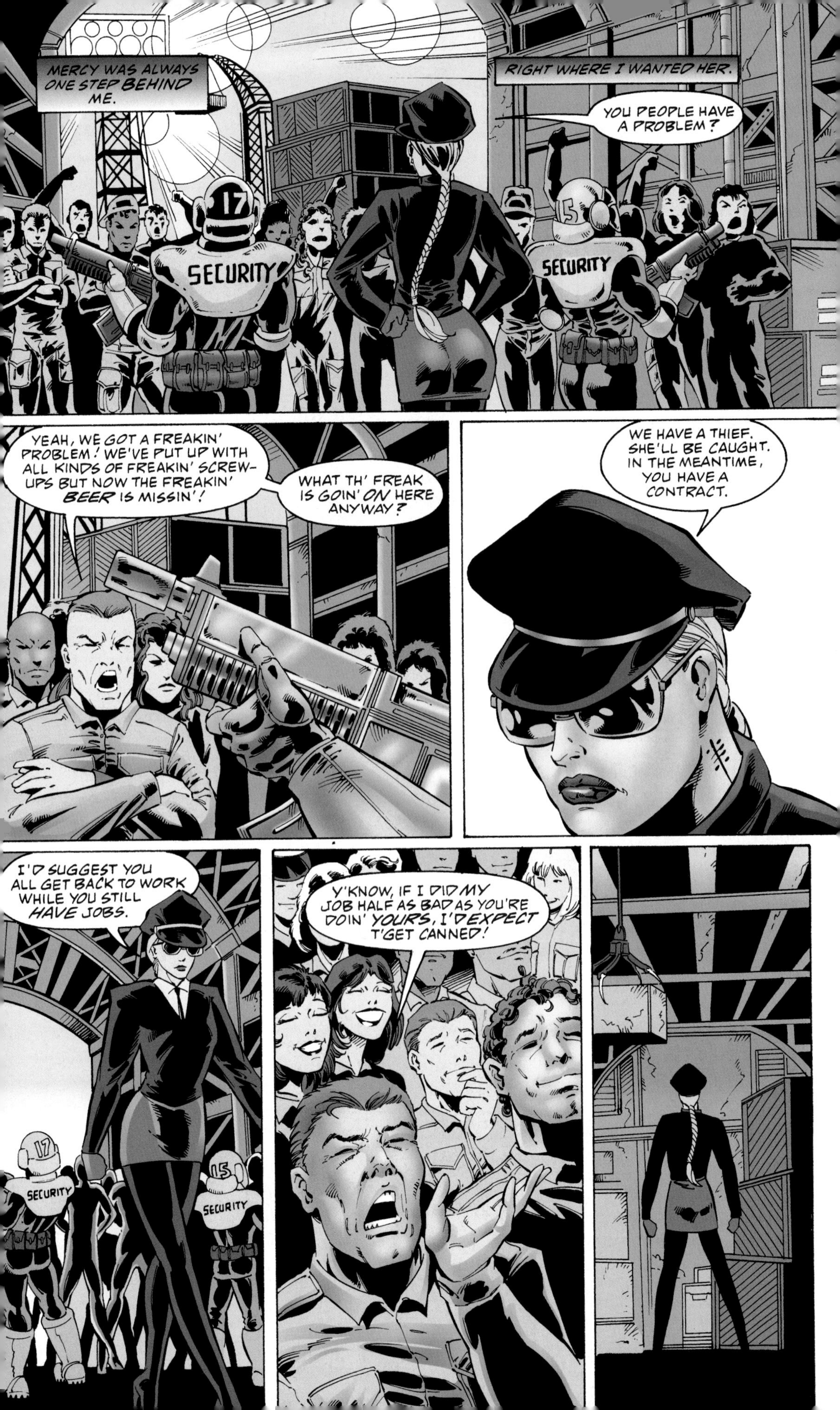
MERCY WAS ALWAYS ONE STEP BEHIND ME.
RIGHT WHERE I WANTED HER.
YOU PEOPLE HAVE A PROBLEM?
SECURITY
SECURITY
YEAH, WE GOT A FREAKIN' PROBLEM! WE'VE PUT UP WITH ALL KINDS OF FREAKIN' SCREW-UPS BUT NOW THE FREAKIN' BEER IS MISSIN'!
WHAT TH' FREAK IS GOIN' ON HERE ANYWAY?
WE HAVE A THIEF. SHE'LL BE CAUGHT. IN THE MEANTIME, YOU HAVE A CONTRACT.
I'D SUGGEST YOU ALL GET BACK TO WORK WHILE YOU STILL HAVE JOBS.
SECURITY
SECURITY
Y'KNOW, IF I DID MY JOB HALF AS BAD AS YOU'RE DOIN' YOURS, I'D EXPECT T'GET CANNED!

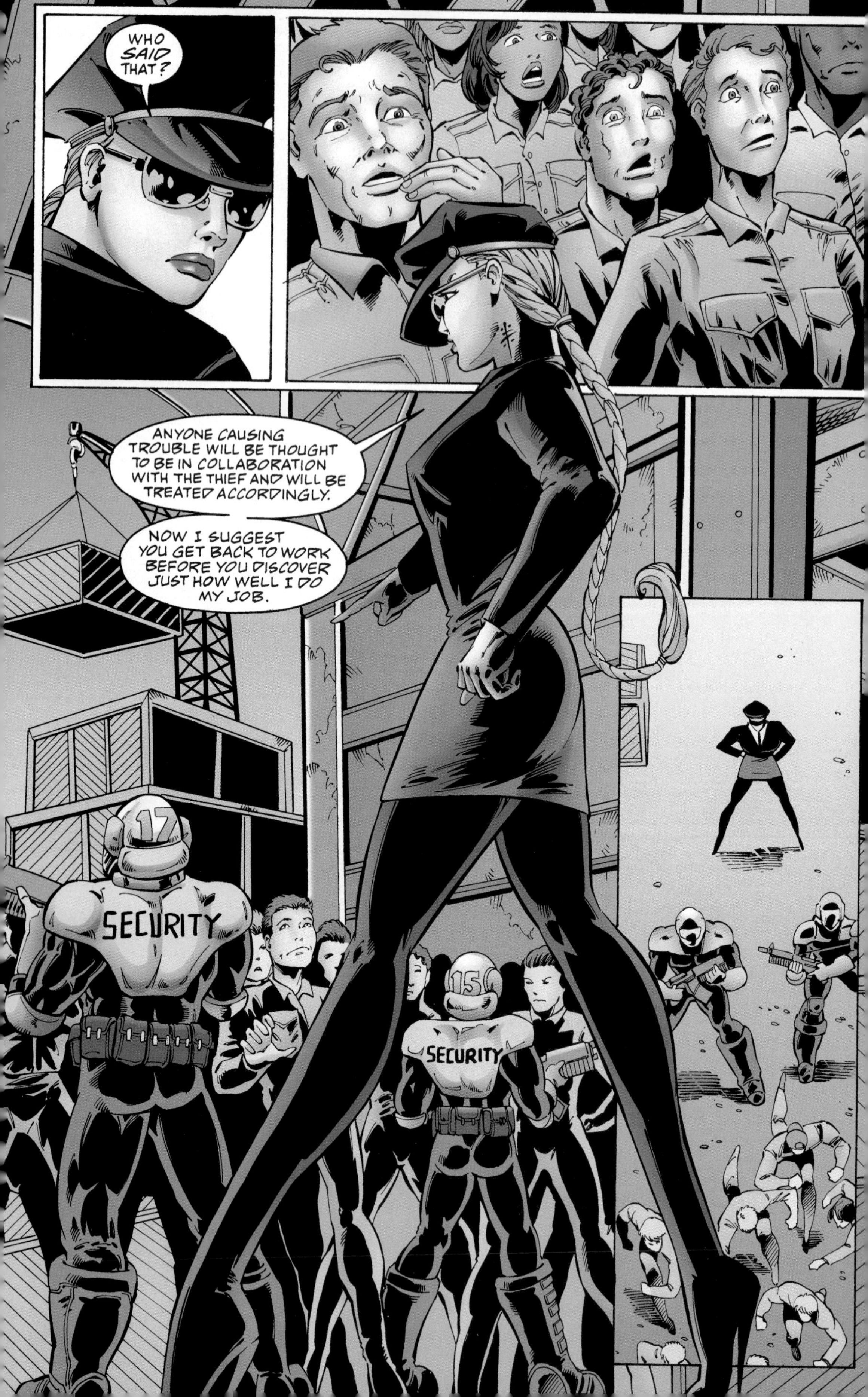
WHO SAID THAT?
ANYONE CAUSING TROUBLE WILL BE THOUGHT TO BE IN COLLABORATION WITH THE THIEF AND WILL BE TREATED ACCORDINGLY.
NOW I SUGGEST YOU GET BACK TO WORK BEFORE YOU DISCOVER JUST HOW WELL I DO MY JOB.
17
SECURITY
15
SECURITY

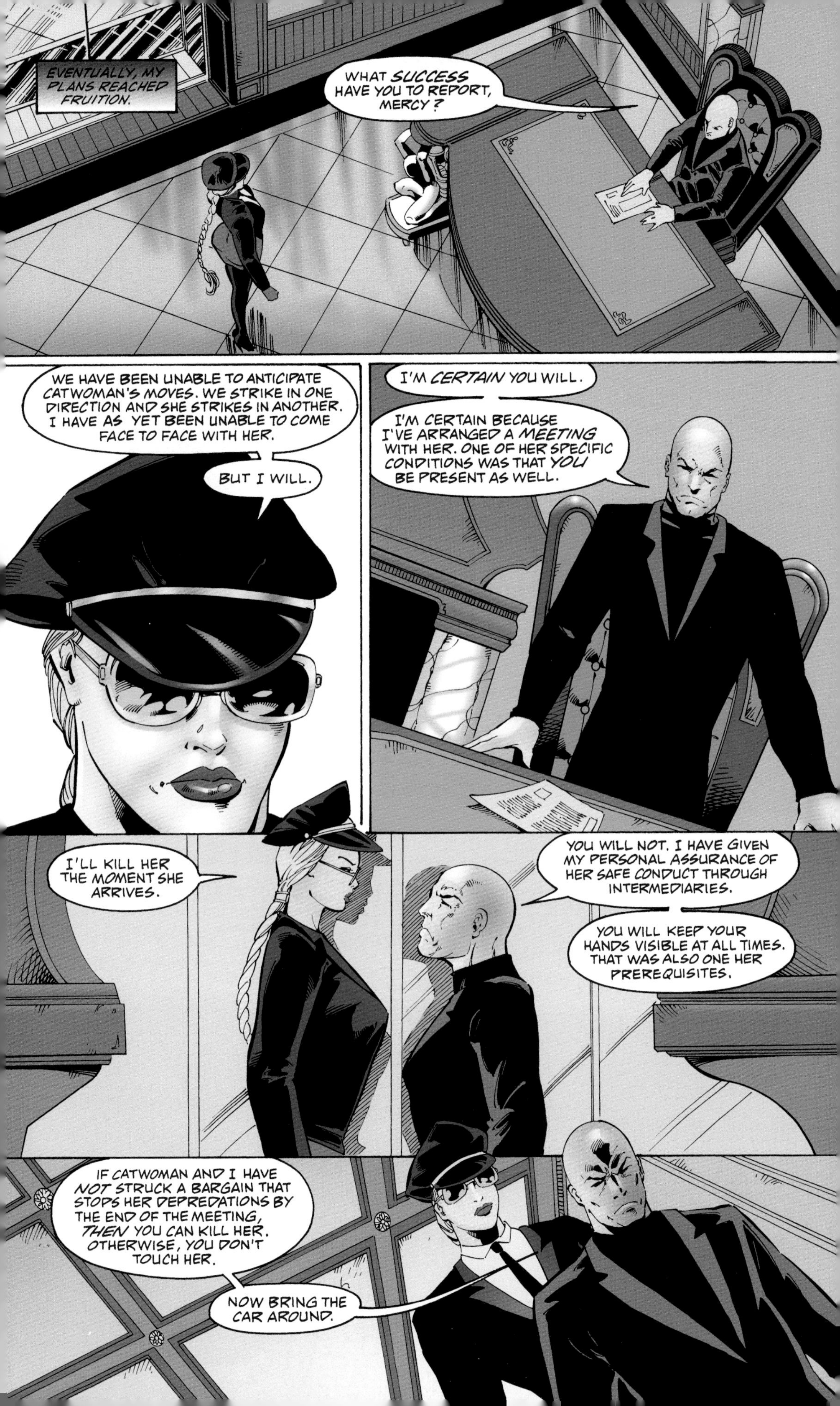
EVENTUALLY, MY PLANS REACHED FRUITION.
WHAT SUCCESS HAVE YOU TO REPORT, MERCY?
WE HAVE BEEN UNABLE TO ANTICIPATE CATWOMAN'S MOVES. WE STRIKE IN ONE DIRECTION AND SHE STRIKES IN ANOTHER. I HAVE AS YET BEEN UNABLE TO COME FACE TO FACE WITH HER.
BUT I WILL.
I'M CERTAIN YOU WILL.
I'M CERTAIN BECAUSE I'VE ARRANGED A MEETING WITH HER. ONE OF HER SPECIFIC CONDITIONS WAS THAT YOU BE PRESENT AS WELL.
I'LL KILL HER THE MOMENT SHE ARRIVES.
YOU WILL NOT. I HAVE GIVEN MY PERSONAL ASSURANCE OF HER SAFE CONDUCT THROUGH INTERMEDIARIES.
YOU WILL KEEP YOUR HANDS VISIBLE AT ALL TIMES. THAT WAS ALSO ONE HER PREREQUISITES.
IF CATWOMAN AND I HAVE NOT STRUCK A BARGAIN THAT STOPS HER DEPREDATIONS BY THE END OF THE MEETING, THEN YOU CAN KILL HER. OTHERWISE, YOU DON'T TOUCH HER.
NOW BRING THE CAR AROUND.

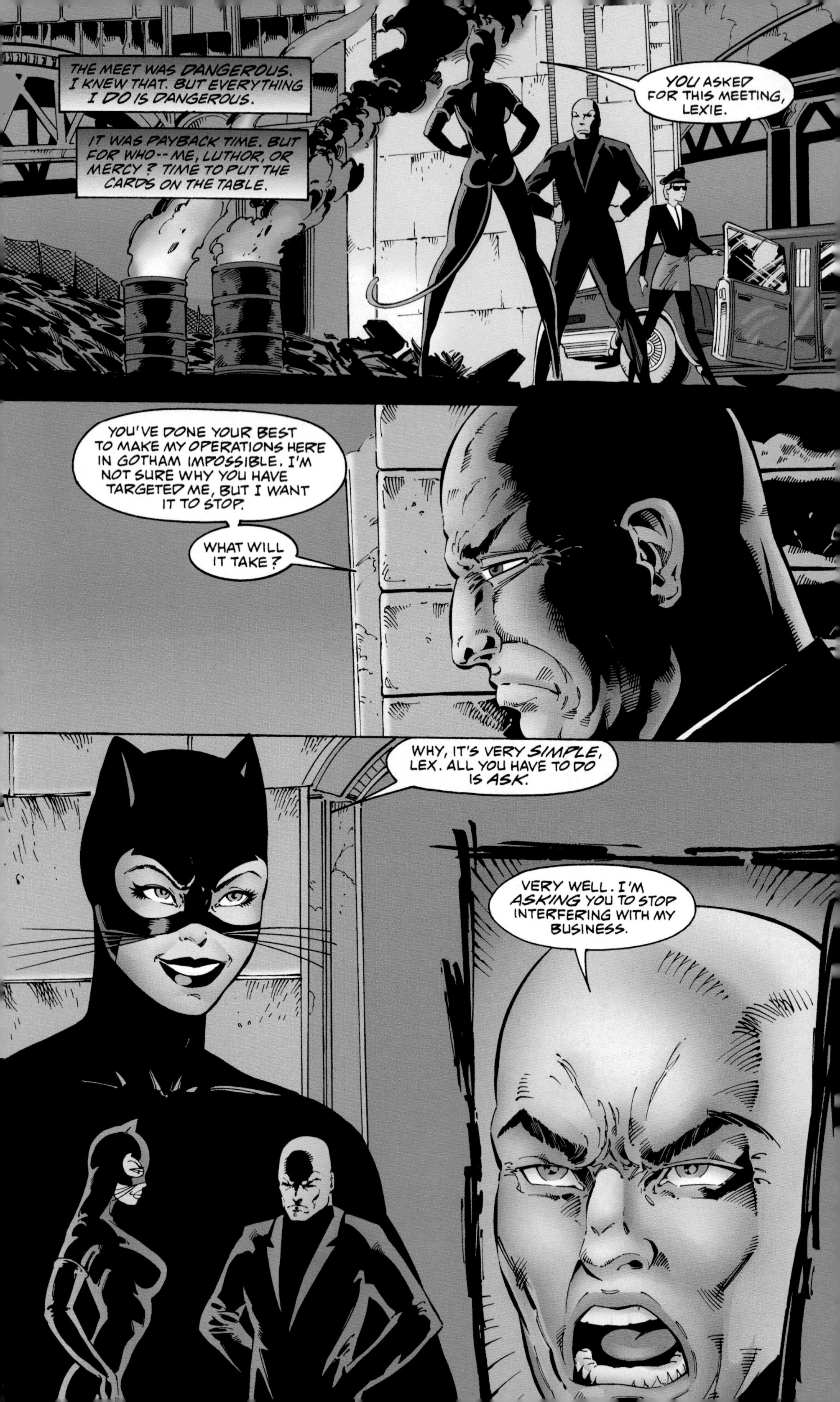
THE MEET WAS DANGEROUS. I KNEW THAT. BUT EVERYTHING I DO IS DANGEROUS.
IT WAS PAYBACK TIME. BUT FOR WHO-- ME, LUTHOR, OR MERCY? TIME TO PUT THE CARDS ON THE TABLE.
YOU ASKED FOR THIS MEETING, LEXIE.
YOU'VE DONE YOUR BEST TO MAKE MY OPERATIONS HERE IN GOTHAM IMPOSSIBLE. I'M NOT SURE WHY YOU HAVE TARGETED ME, BUT I WANT IT TO STOP.
WHAT WILL IT TAKE?
WHY, IT'S VERY SIMPLE, LEX. ALL YOU HAVE TO DO IS ASK.
VERY WELL. I'M ASKING YOU TO STOP INTERFERING WITH MY BUSINESS.

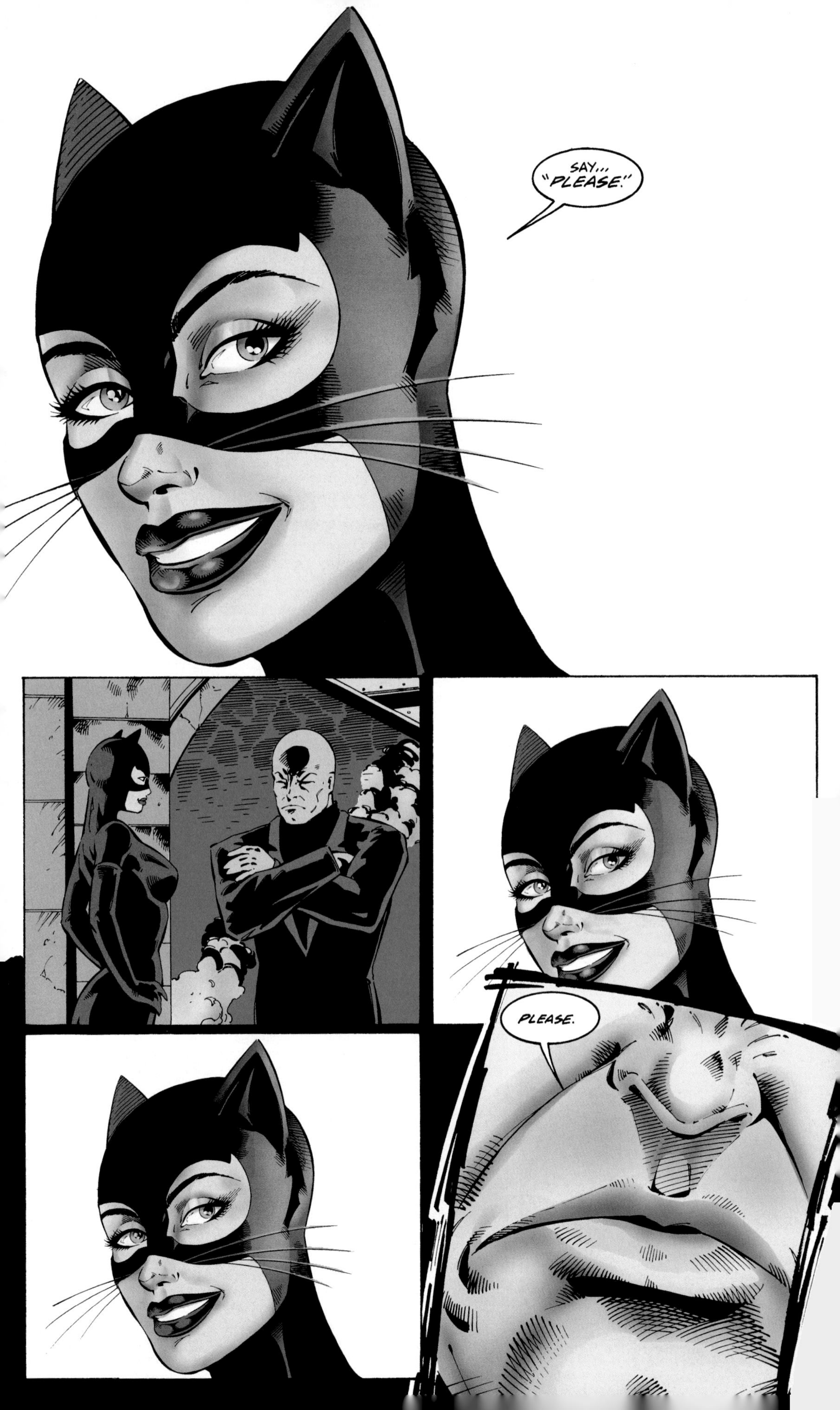
SAY... "PLEASE."
PLEASE.

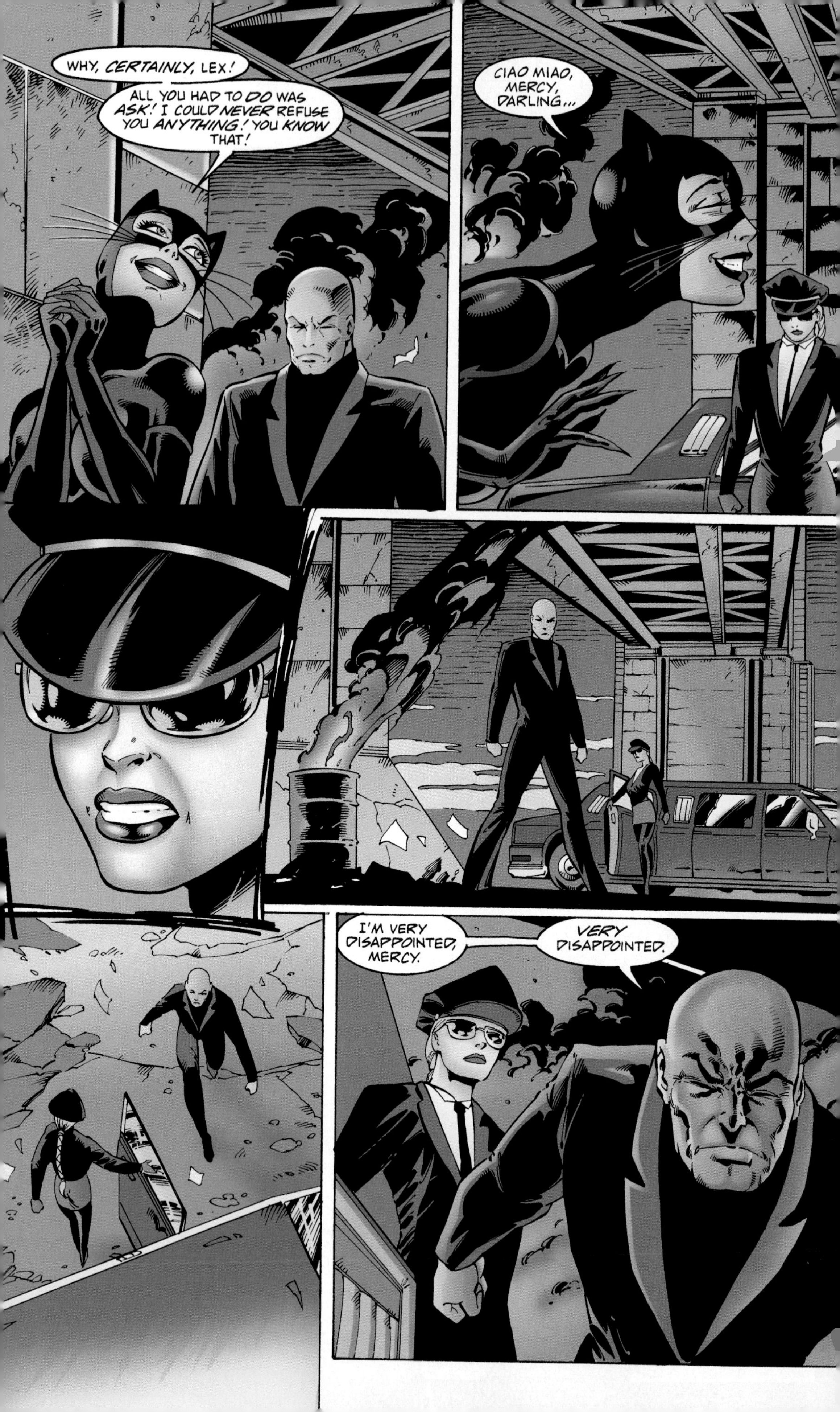
WHY, CERTAINLY, LEX!
ALL YOU HAD TO DO WAS ASK! I COULD NEVER REFUSE YOU ANYTHING! YOU KNOW THAT!
CIAO MIAO, MERCY, DARLING...
I'M VERY DISAPPOINTED, MERCY.
VERY DISAPPOINTED.

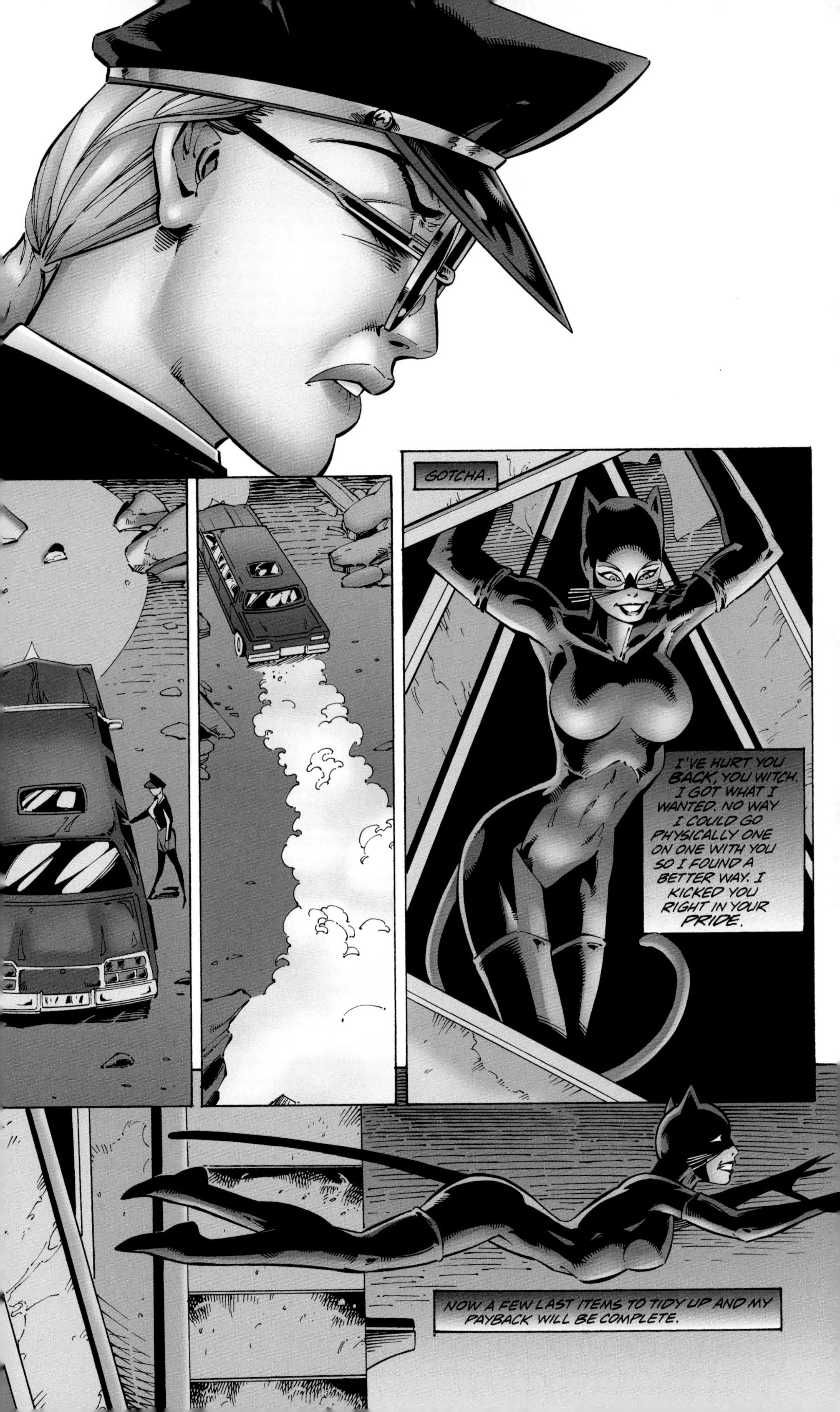
GOTCHA.
I'VE HURT YOU BACK, YOU WITCH. I GOT WHAT I WANTED. NO WAY I COULD GO PHYSICALLY ONE ON ONE WITH YOU SO I FOUND A BETTER WAY. I KICKED YOU RIGHT IN YOUR PRIDE.
NOW A FEW LAST ITEMS TO TIDY UP AND MY PAYBACK WILL BE COMPLETE.

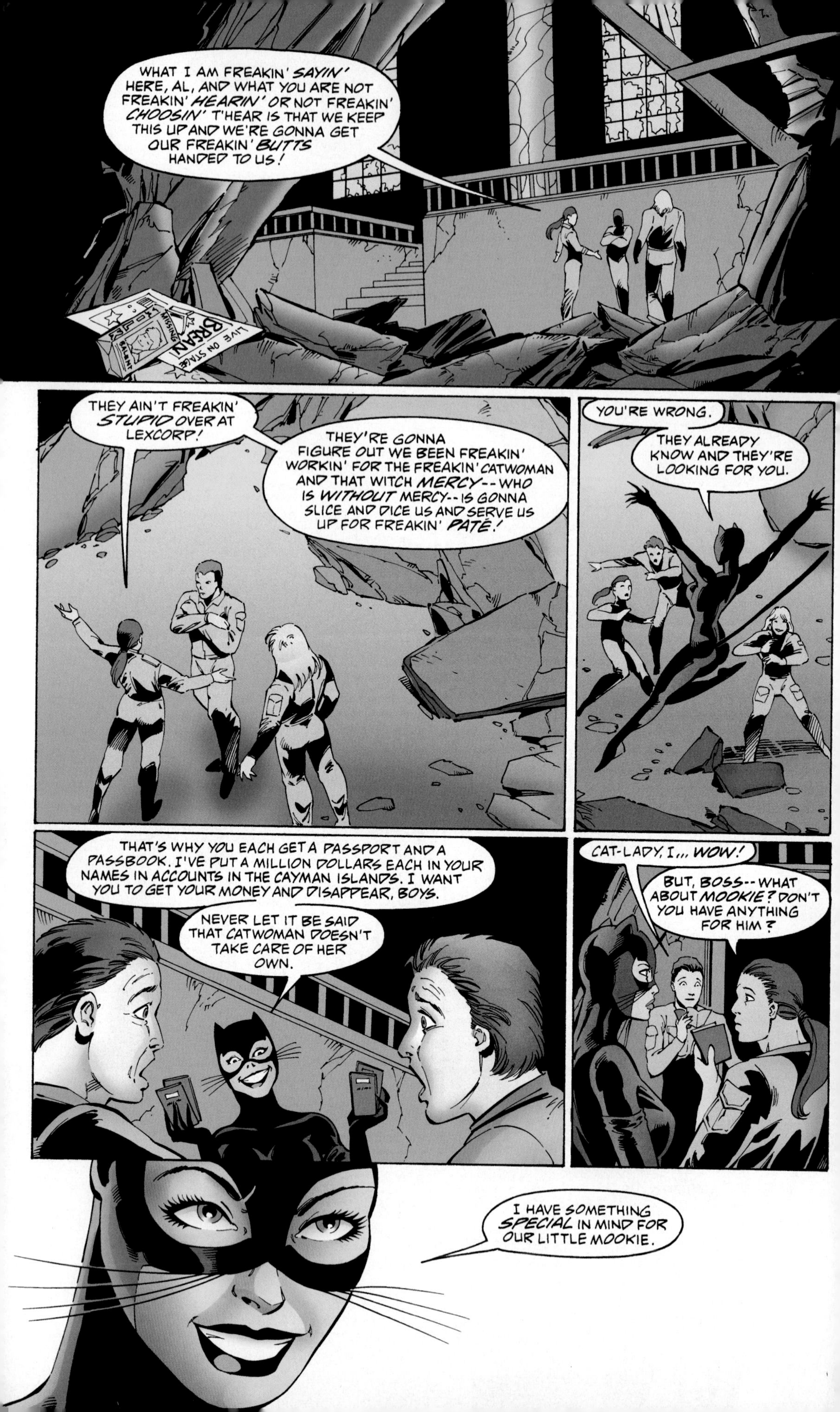

WHAT I AM FREAKIN' SAYIN' HERE, AL, AND WHAT YOU ARE NOT FREAKIN' HEARIN' OR NOT FREAKIN' CHOOSIN' T'HEAR IS THAT WE KEEP THIS UP AND WE'RE GONNA GET OUR FREAKIN' BUTTS HANDED TO US!
MISSING
BREAN
LIVE ON STAGE
THEY AIN'T FREAKIN' STUPID OVER AT LEXCORP!
THEY'RE GONNA FIGURE OUT WE BEEN FREAKIN' WORKIN' FOR THE FREAKIN' CATWOMAN AND THAT WITCH MERCY-- WHO IS WITHOUT MERCY-- IS GONNA SLICE AND DICE US AND SERVE US UP FOR FREAKIN' PATÉ!
YOU'RE WRONG.
THEY ALREADY KNOW AND THEY'RE LOOKING FOR YOU.
THAT'S WHY YOU EACH GET A PASSPORT AND A PASSBOOK. I'VE PUT A MILLION DOLLARS EACH IN YOUR NAMES IN ACCOUNTS IN THE CAYMAN ISLANDS. I WANT YOU TO GET YOUR MONEY AND DISAPPEAR, BOYS.
NEVER LET IT BE SAID THAT CATWOMAN DOESN'T TAKE CARE OF HER OWN.
CAT-LADY, I... WOW!
BUT, BOSS-- WHAT ABOUT MOOKIE? DON'T YOU HAVE ANYTHING FOR HIM?
I HAVE SOMETHING SPECIAL IN MIND FOR OUR LITTLE MOOKIE.

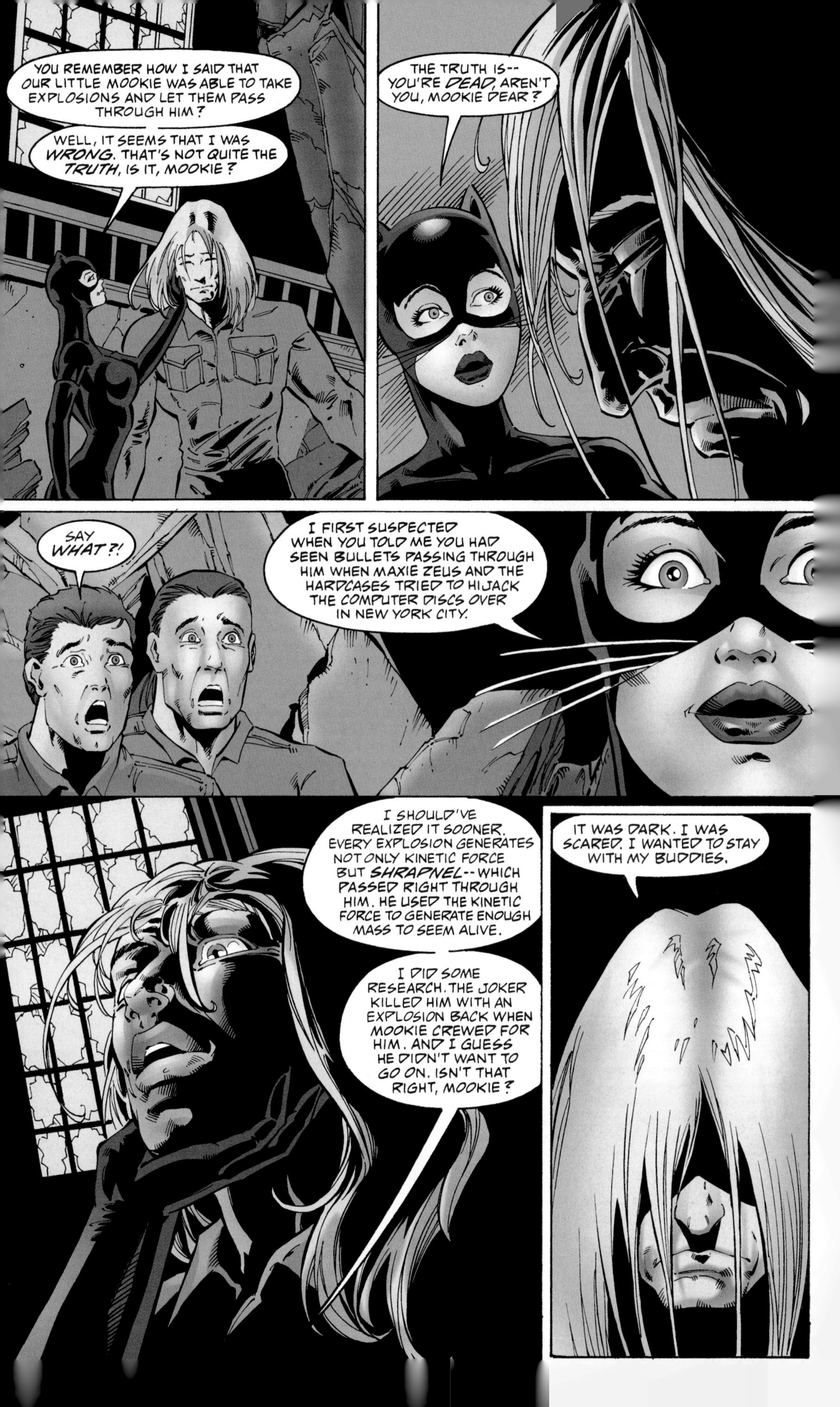

YOU REMEMBER HOW I SAID THAT OUR LITTLE MOOKIE WAS ABLE TO TAKE EXPLOSIONS AND LET THEM PASS THROUGH HIM?
WELL, IT SEEMS THAT I WAS *WRONG*. THAT'S NOT QUITE THE *TRUTH*, IS IT, MOOKIE?
THE TRUTH IS-- YOU'RE *DEAD*, AREN'T YOU, MOOKIE DEAR?
SAY *WHAT?!*
I FIRST SUSPECTED WHEN YOU TOLD ME YOU HAD SEEN BULLETS PASSING THROUGH HIM WHEN MAXIE ZEUS AND THE HARDCASES TRIED TO HIJACK THE COMPUTER DISCS OVER IN NEW YORK CITY.
I SHOULD'VE REALIZED IT SOONER. EVERY EXPLOSION GENERATES NOT ONLY KINETIC FORCE BUT *SHRAPNEL*-- WHICH PASSED RIGHT THROUGH HIM. HE USED THE KINETIC FORCE TO GENERATE ENOUGH MASS TO SEEM ALIVE.
I DID SOME RESEARCH. THE JOKER KILLED HIM WITH AN EXPLOSION BACK WHEN MOOKIE CREWED FOR HIM. AND I GUESS HE DIDN'T WANT TO GO ON. ISN'T THAT RIGHT, MOOKIE?
IT WAS DARK. I WAS SCARED. I WANTED TO STAY WITH MY BUDDIES.

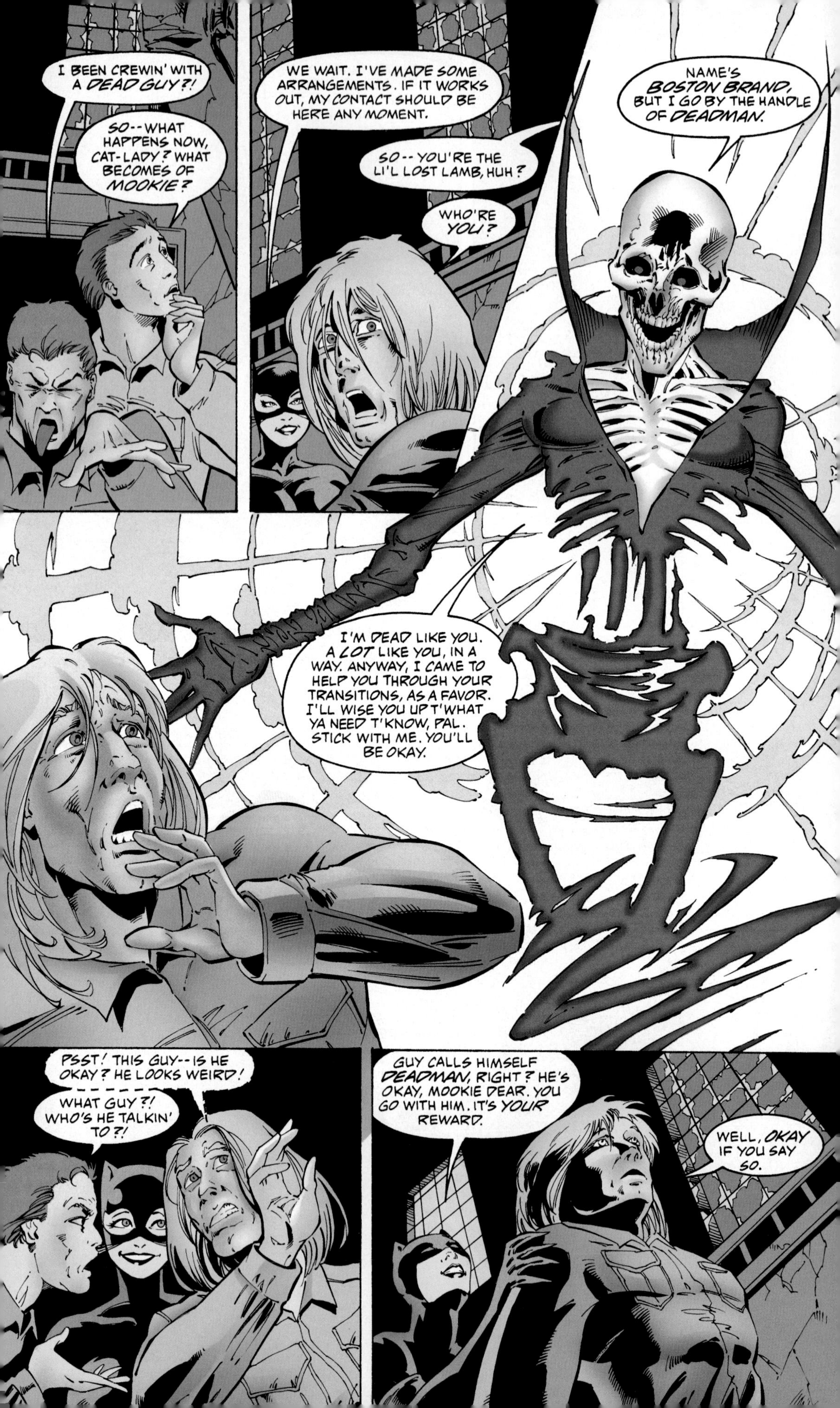
I BEEN CREWIN' WITH A DEAD GUY?!
SO--WHAT HAPPENS NOW, CAT-LADY? WHAT BECOMES OF MOOKIE?
WE WAIT. I'VE MADE SOME ARRANGEMENTS. IF IT WORKS OUT, MY CONTACT SHOULD BE HERE ANY MOMENT.
SO--YOU'RE THE LI'L LOST LAMB, HUH?
WHO'RE YOU?
NAME'S BOSTON BRAND, BUT I GO BY THE HANDLE OF DEADMAN.
I'M DEAD LIKE YOU. A LOT LIKE YOU, IN A WAY. ANYWAY, I CAME TO HELP YOU THROUGH YOUR TRANSITIONS, AS A FAVOR. I'LL WISE YOU UP T'WHAT YA NEED T'KNOW, PAL. STICK WITH ME. YOU'LL BE OKAY.
PSST! THIS GUY--IS HE OKAY? HE LOOKS WEIRD!
WHAT GUY?! WHO'S HE TALKIN' TO?!
GUY CALLS HIMSELF DEADMAN, RIGHT? HE'S OKAY, MOOKIE DEAR. YOU GO WITH HIM. IT'S YOUR REWARD.
WELL, OKAY IF YOU SAY SO.

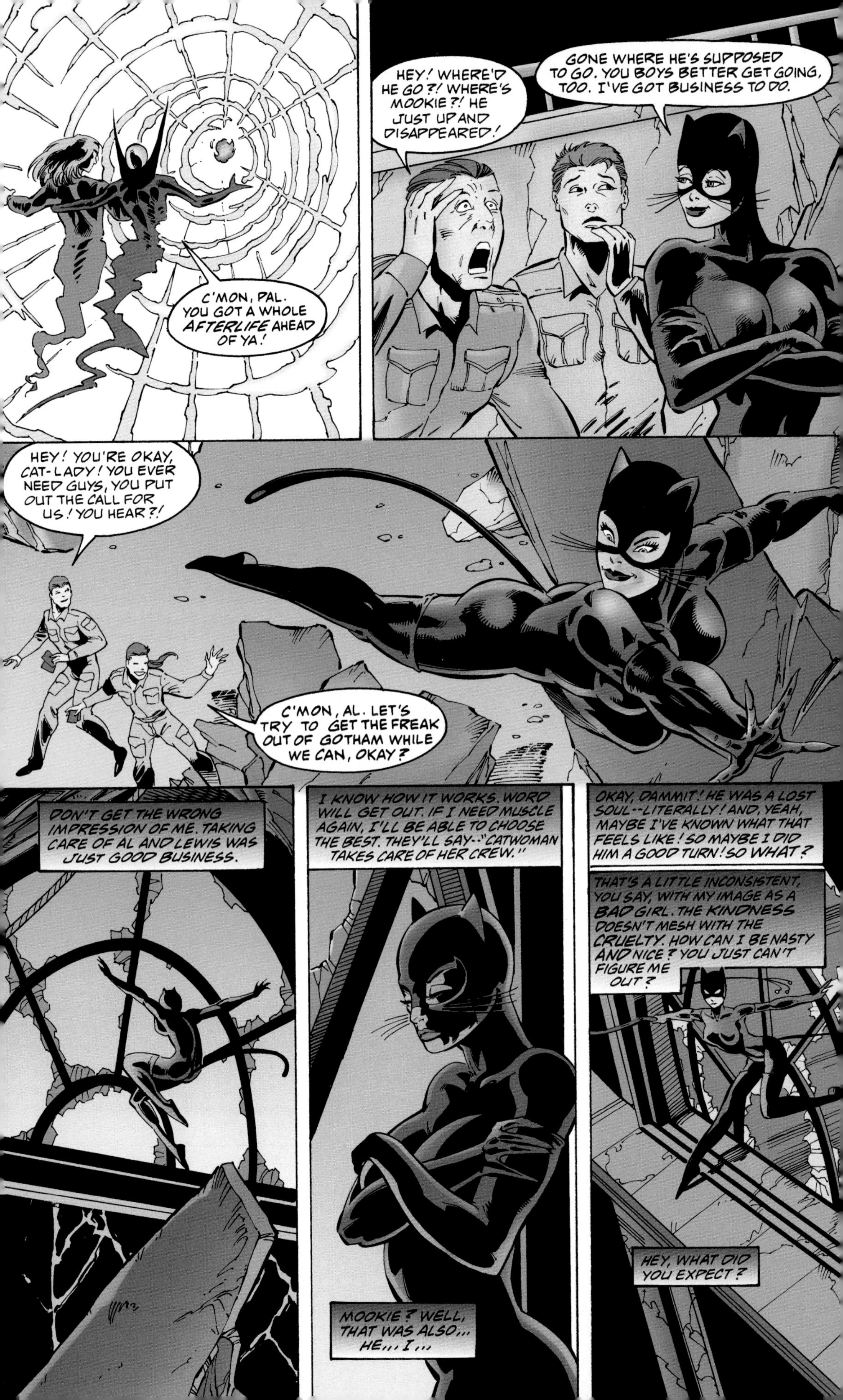
C'MON, PAL. YOU GOT A WHOLE AFTERLIFE AHEAD OF YA!
HEY! WHERE'D HE GO?! WHERE'S MOOKIE?! HE JUST UP AND DISAPPEARED!
GONE WHERE HE'S SUPPOSED TO GO. YOU BOYS BETTER GET GOING, TOO. I'VE GOT BUSINESS TO DO.
HEY! YOU'RE OKAY, CAT-LADY! YOU EVER NEED GUYS, YOU PUT OUT THE CALL FOR US! YOU HEAR?!
C'MON, AL. LET'S TRY TO GET THE FREAK OUT OF GOTHAM WHILE WE CAN, OKAY?
DON'T GET THE WRONG IMPRESSION OF ME. TAKING CARE OF AL AND LEWIS WAS JUST GOOD BUSINESS.
I KNOW HOW IT WORKS. WORD WILL GET OUT. IF I NEED MUSCLE AGAIN, I'LL BE ABLE TO CHOOSE THE BEST. THEY'LL SAY--"CATWOMAN TAKES CARE OF HER CREW."
MOOKIE? WELL, THAT WAS ALSO... HE... I...
OKAY, DAMMIT! HE WAS A LOST SOUL--LITERALLY! AND, YEAH, MAYBE I'VE KNOWN WHAT THAT FEELS LIKE! SO MAYBE I DID HIM A GOOD TURN! SO WHAT?
THAT'S A LITTLE INCONSISTENT, YOU SAY, WITH MY IMAGE AS A BAD GIRL. THE KINDNESS DOESN'T MESH WITH THE CRUELTY. HOW CAN I BE NASTY AND NICE? YOU JUST CAN'T FIGURE ME OUT?
HEY, WHAT DID YOU EXPECT?

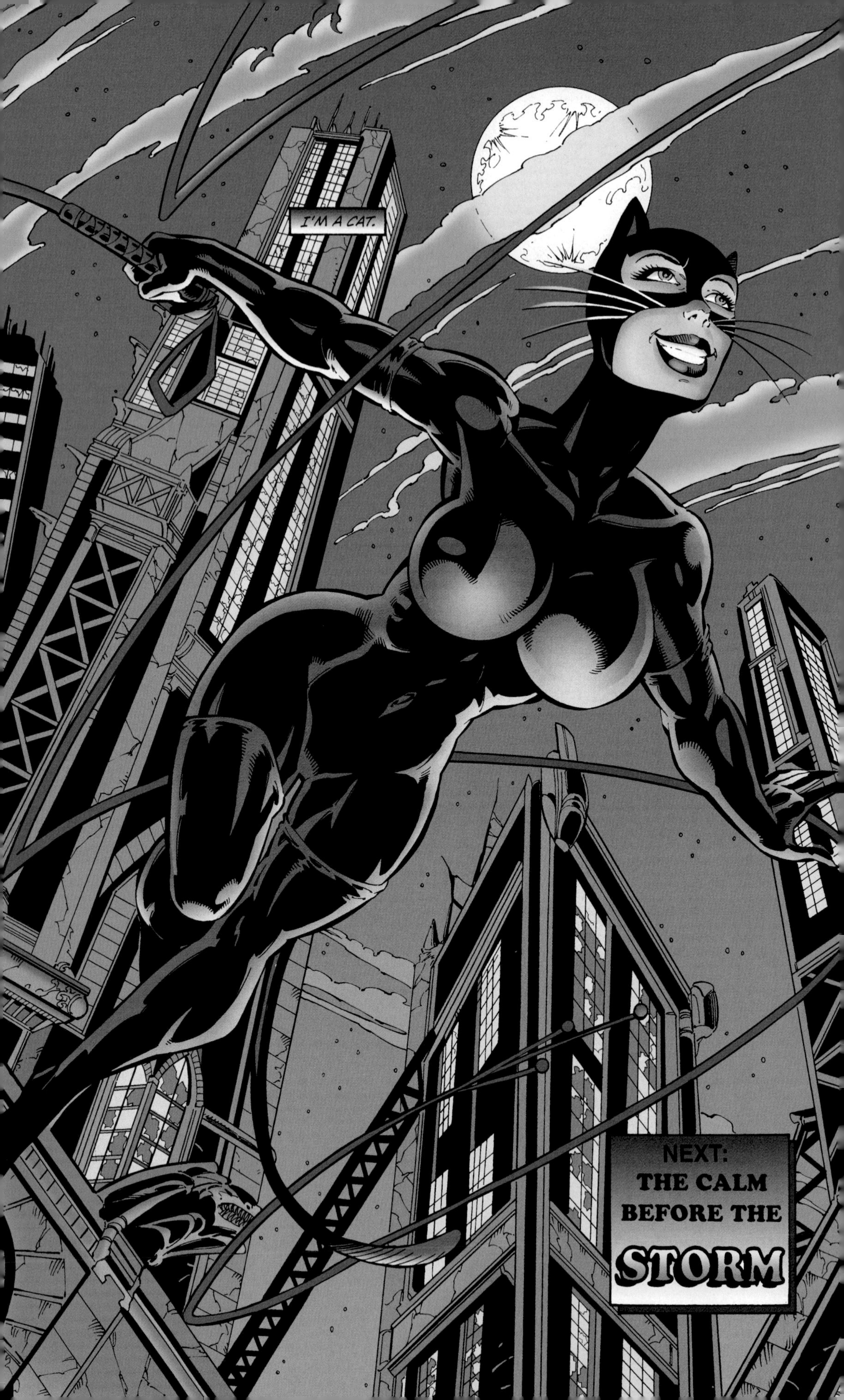
I'M A CAT.
NEXT:
THE CALM BEFORE THE
STORM

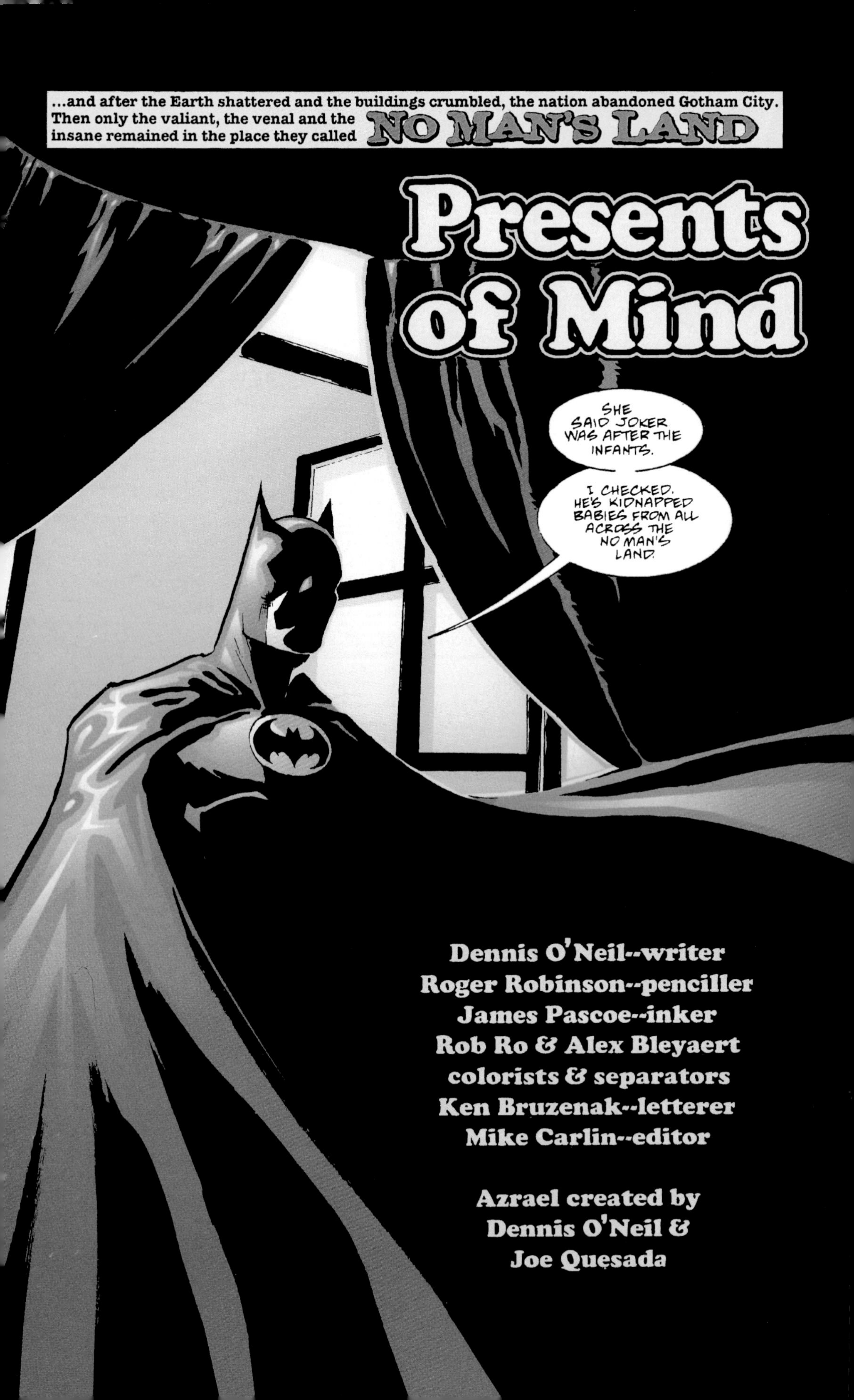
...and after the Earth shattered and the buildings crumbled, the nation abandoned Gotham City. Then only the valiant, the venal and the insane remained in the place they called NO MAN'S LAND
Presents of Mind
SHE SAID JOKER WAS AFTER THE INFANTS.
I CHECKED. HE'S KIDNAPPED BABIES FROM ALL ACROSS THE NO MAN'S LAND.
Dennis O'Neil--writer
Roger Robinson--penciller
James Pascoe--inker
Rob Ro & Alex Bleyaert
colorists & separators
Ken Bruzenak--letterer
Mike Carlin--editor
Azrael created by
Dennis O'Neil &
Joe Quesada

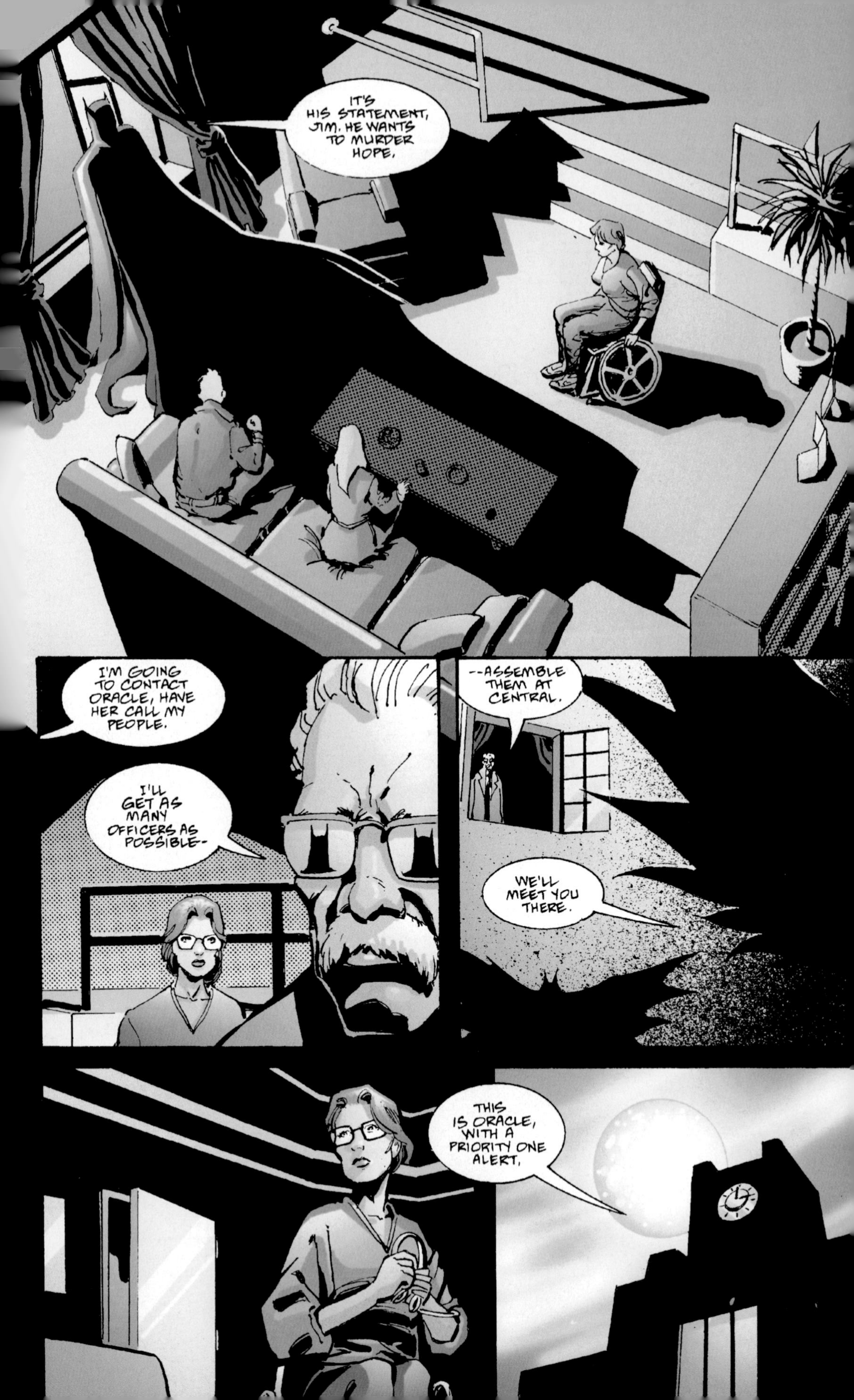
IT'S HIS STATEMENT, JIM. HE WANTS TO MURDER HOPE.
I'M GOING TO CONTACT ORACLE, HAVE HER CALL MY PEOPLE.
I'LL GET AS MANY OFFICERS AS POSSIBLE--
--ASSEMBLE THEM AT CENTRAL.
WE'LL MEET YOU THERE.
THIS IS ORACLE, WITH A PRIORITY ONE ALERT.

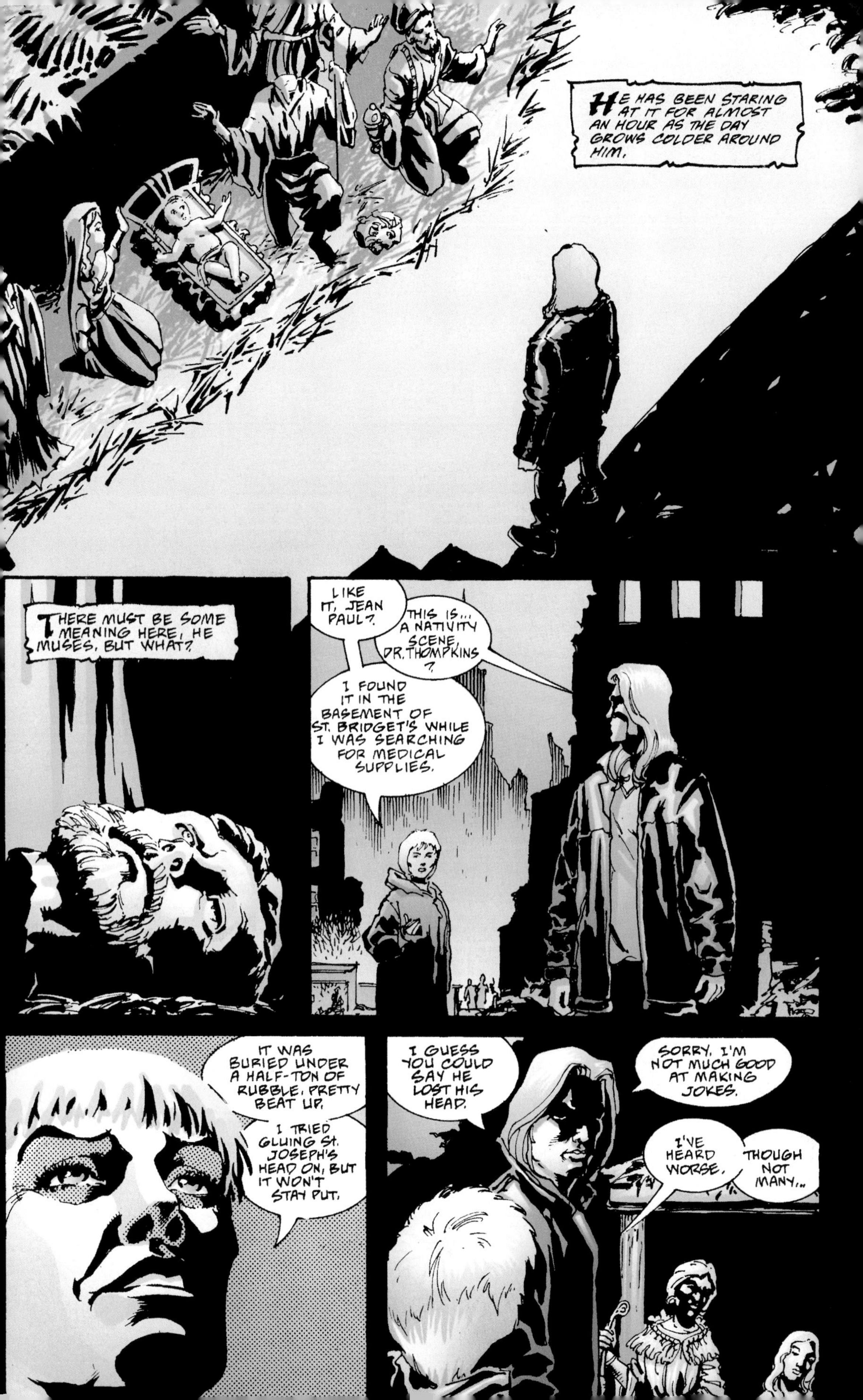
HE HAS BEEN STARING AT IT FOR ALMOST AN HOUR AS THE DAY GROWS COLDER AROUND HIM.
THERE MUST BE SOME MEANING HERE, HE MUSES, BUT WHAT?
LIKE IT, JEAN PAUL?
THIS IS... A NATIVITY SCENE, DR. THOMPKINS?
I FOUND IT IN THE BASEMENT OF ST. BRIDGET'S WHILE I WAS SEARCHING FOR MEDICAL SUPPLIES.
IT WAS BURIED UNDER A HALF-TON OF RUBBLE, PRETTY BEAT UP.
I TRIED GLUING ST. JOSEPH'S HEAD ON, BUT IT WON'T STAY PUT.
I GUESS YOU COULD SAY HE LOST HIS HEAD.
SORRY. I'M NOT MUCH GOOD AT MAKING JOKES.
I'VE HEARD WORSE.
THOUGH NOT MANY...

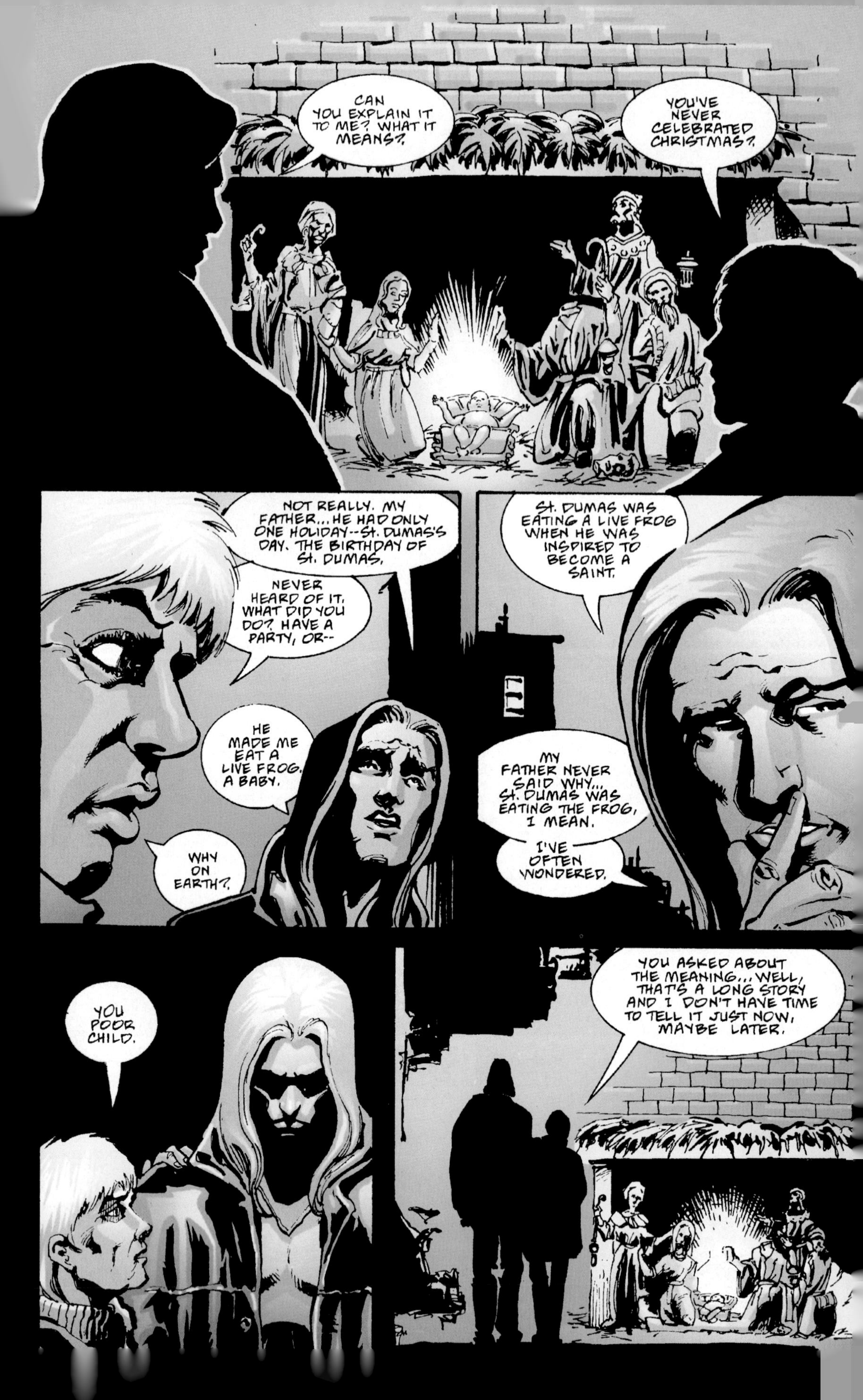
CAN YOU EXPLAIN IT TO ME? WHAT IT MEANS?.
YOU'VE NEVER CELEBRATED CHRISTMAS?.
NOT REALLY. MY FATHER... HE HAD ONLY ONE HOLIDAY--ST. DUMAS'S DAY. THE BIRTHDAY OF ST. DUMAS.
NEVER HEARD OF IT. WHAT DID YOU DO? HAVE A PARTY, OR--
HE MADE ME EAT A LIVE FROG. A BABY.
WHY ON EARTH?.
ST. DUMAS WAS EATING A LIVE FROG WHEN HE WAS INSPIRED TO BECOME A SAINT.
MY FATHER NEVER SAID WHY... ST. DUMAS WAS EATING THE FROG, I MEAN.
I'VE OFTEN WONDERED.
YOU POOR CHILD.
YOU ASKED ABOUT THE MEANING... WELL, THAT'S A LONG STORY AND I DON'T HAVE TIME TO TELL IT JUST NOW. MAYBE LATER.

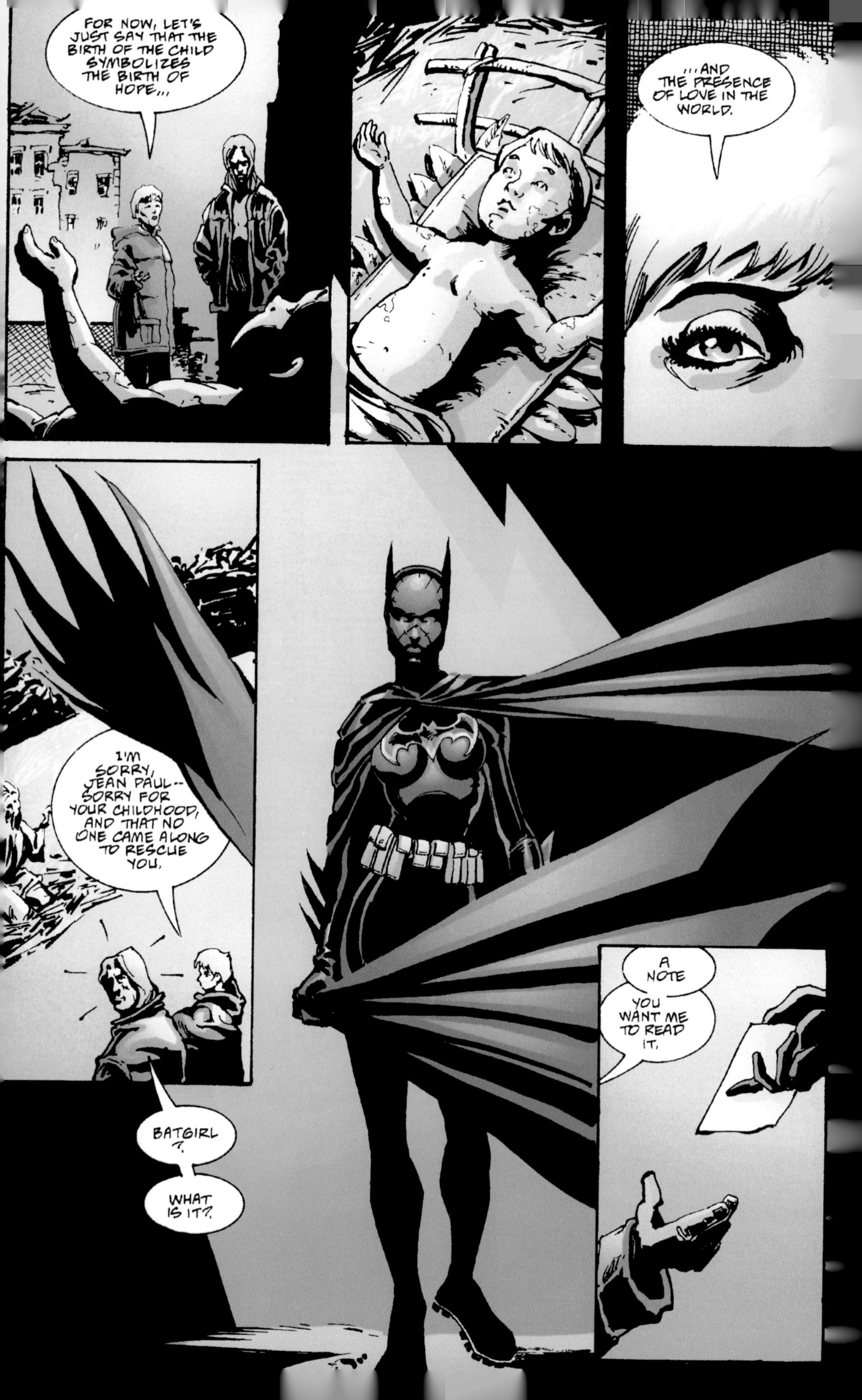
FOR NOW, LET'S JUST SAY THAT THE BIRTH OF THE CHILD SYMBOLIZES THE BIRTH OF HOPE...
...AND THE PRESENCE OF LOVE IN THE WORLD.
I'M SORRY, JEAN PAUL-- SORRY FOR YOUR CHILDHOOD, AND THAT NO ONE CAME ALONG TO RESCUE YOU.
BATGIRL?
WHAT IS IT?
A NOTE
YOU WANT ME TO READ IT.

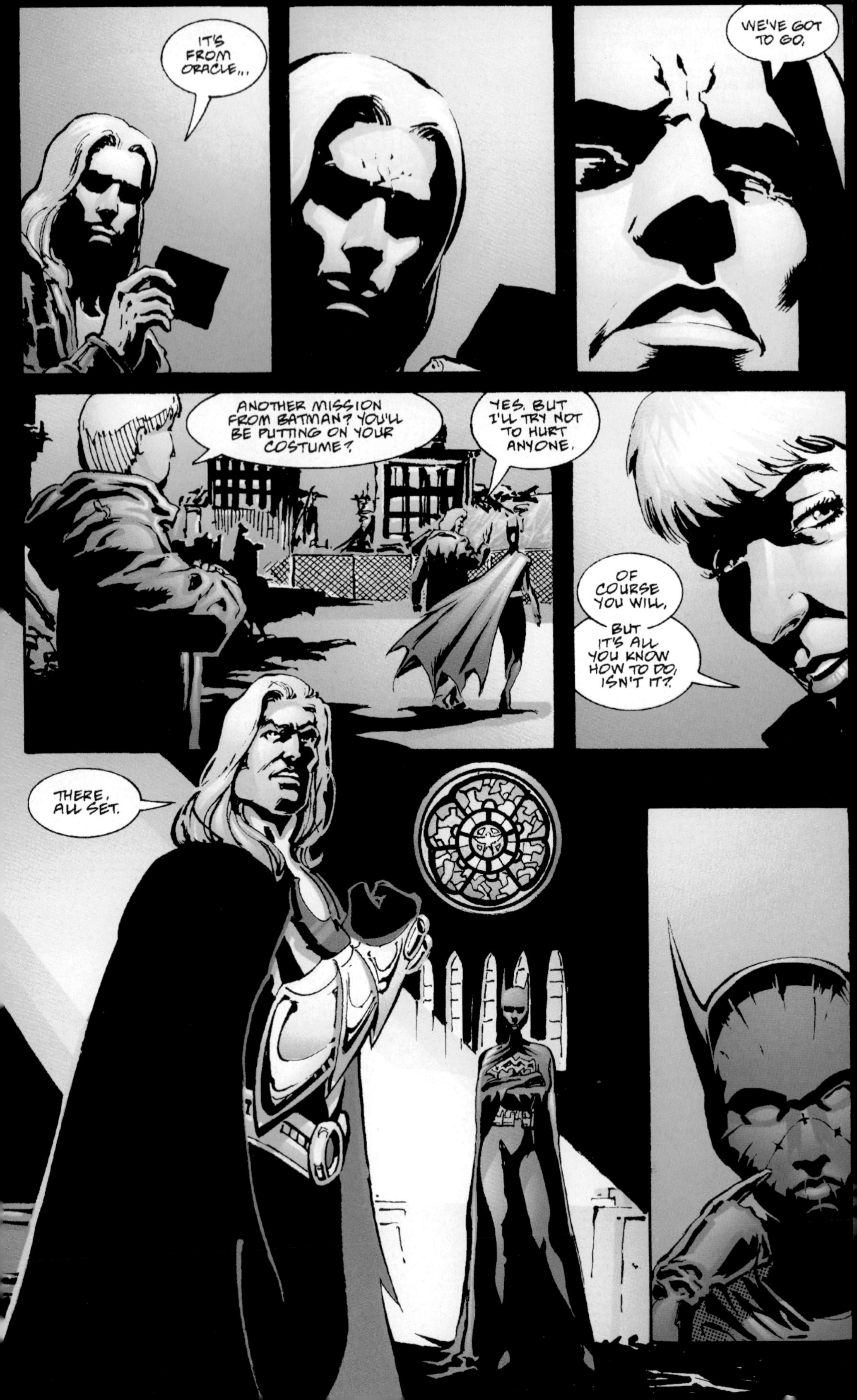
IT'S FROM ORACLE...
WE'VE GOT TO GO.
ANOTHER MISSION FROM BATMAN? YOU'LL BE PUTTING ON YOUR COSTUME?
YES. BUT I'LL TRY NOT TO HURT ANYONE.
OF COURSE YOU WILL.
BUT IT'S ALL YOU KNOW HOW TO DO, ISN'T IT?
THERE. ALL SET.

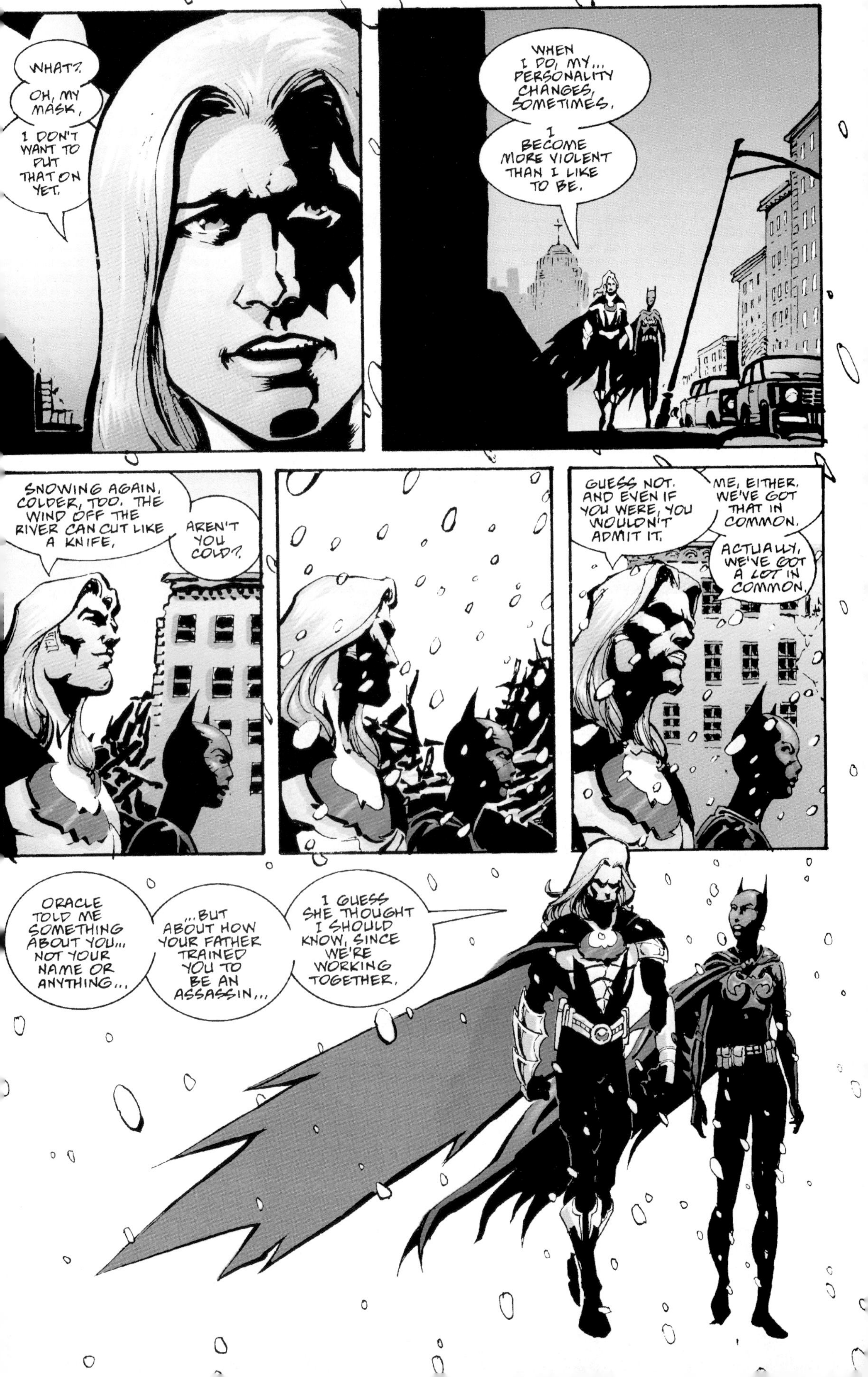

WHAT?
OH, MY MASK,
I DON'T WANT TO PUT THAT ON YET.
WHEN I DO, MY... PERSONALITY CHANGES, SOMETIMES.
I BECOME MORE VIOLENT THAN I LIKE TO BE.
SNOWING AGAIN. COLDER, TOO. THE WIND OFF THE RIVER CAN CUT LIKE A KNIFE.
AREN'T YOU COLD?
GUESS NOT. AND EVEN IF YOU WERE, YOU WOULDN'T ADMIT IT.
ME, EITHER. WE'VE GOT THAT IN COMMON.
ACTUALLY, WE'VE GOT A LOT IN COMMON.
ORACLE TOLD ME SOMETHING ABOUT YOU... NOT YOUR NAME OR ANYTHING...
...BUT ABOUT HOW YOUR FATHER TRAINED YOU TO BE AN ASSASSIN...
I GUESS SHE THOUGHT I SHOULD KNOW, SINCE WE'RE WORKING TOGETHER.

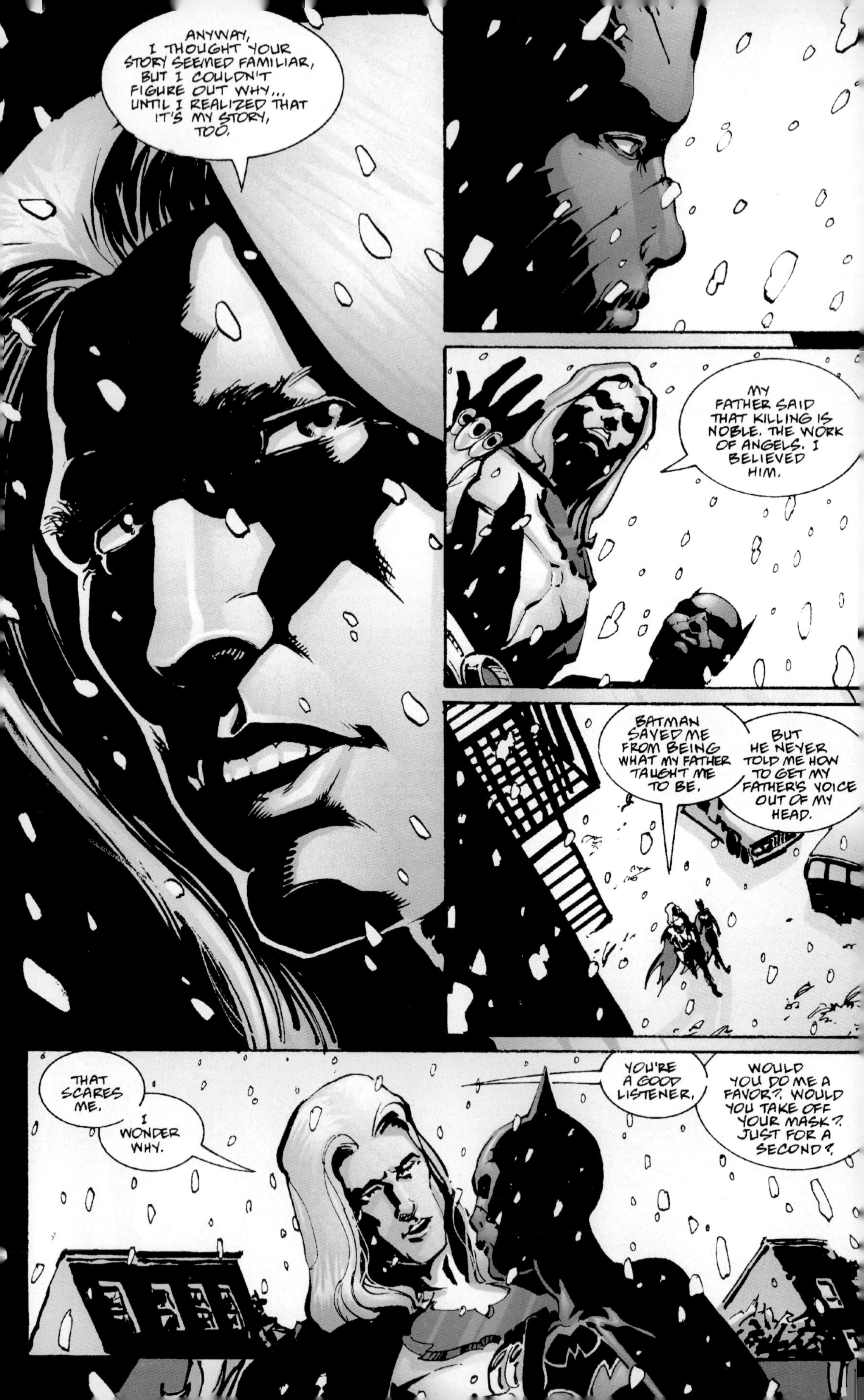
ANYWAY, I THOUGHT YOUR STORY SEEMED FAMILIAR, BUT I COULDN'T FIGURE OUT WHY... UNTIL I REALIZED THAT IT'S MY STORY, TOO.
MY FATHER SAID THAT KILLING IS NOBLE. THE WORK OF ANGELS. I BELIEVED HIM.
BATMAN SAVED ME FROM BEING WHAT MY FATHER TAUGHT ME TO BE.
BUT HE NEVER TOLD ME HOW TO GET MY FATHER'S VOICE OUT OF MY HEAD.
THAT SCARES ME.
I WONDER WHY.
YOU'RE A GOOD LISTENER.
WOULD YOU DO ME A FAVOR? WOULD YOU TAKE OFF YOUR MASK? JUST FOR A SECOND?

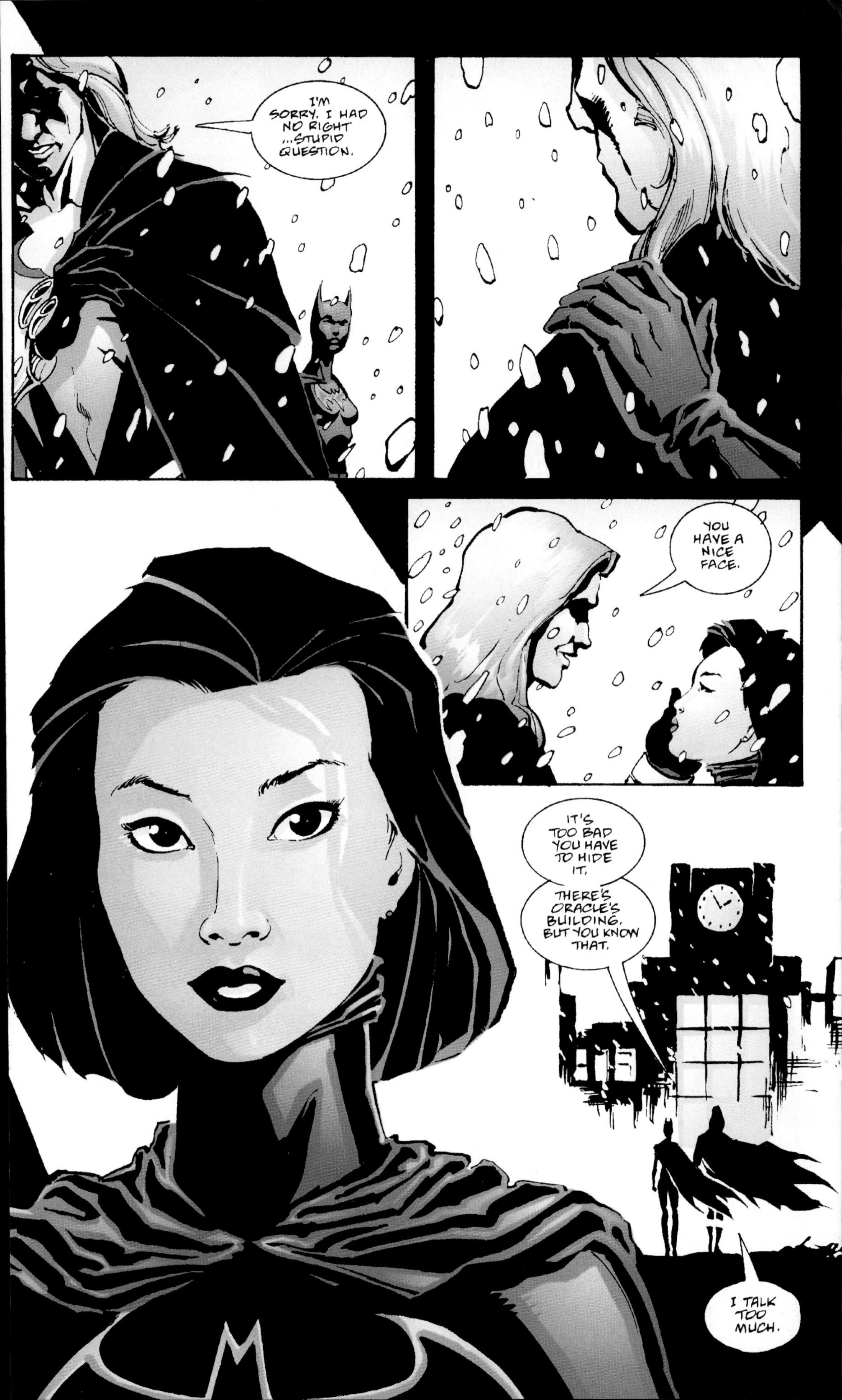
I'M SORRY. I HAD NO RIGHT ...STUPID QUESTION.
YOU HAVE A NICE FACE.
IT'S TOO BAD YOU HAVE TO HIDE IT.
THERE'S ORACLE'S BUILDING. BUT YOU KNOW THAT.
I TALK TOO MUCH.

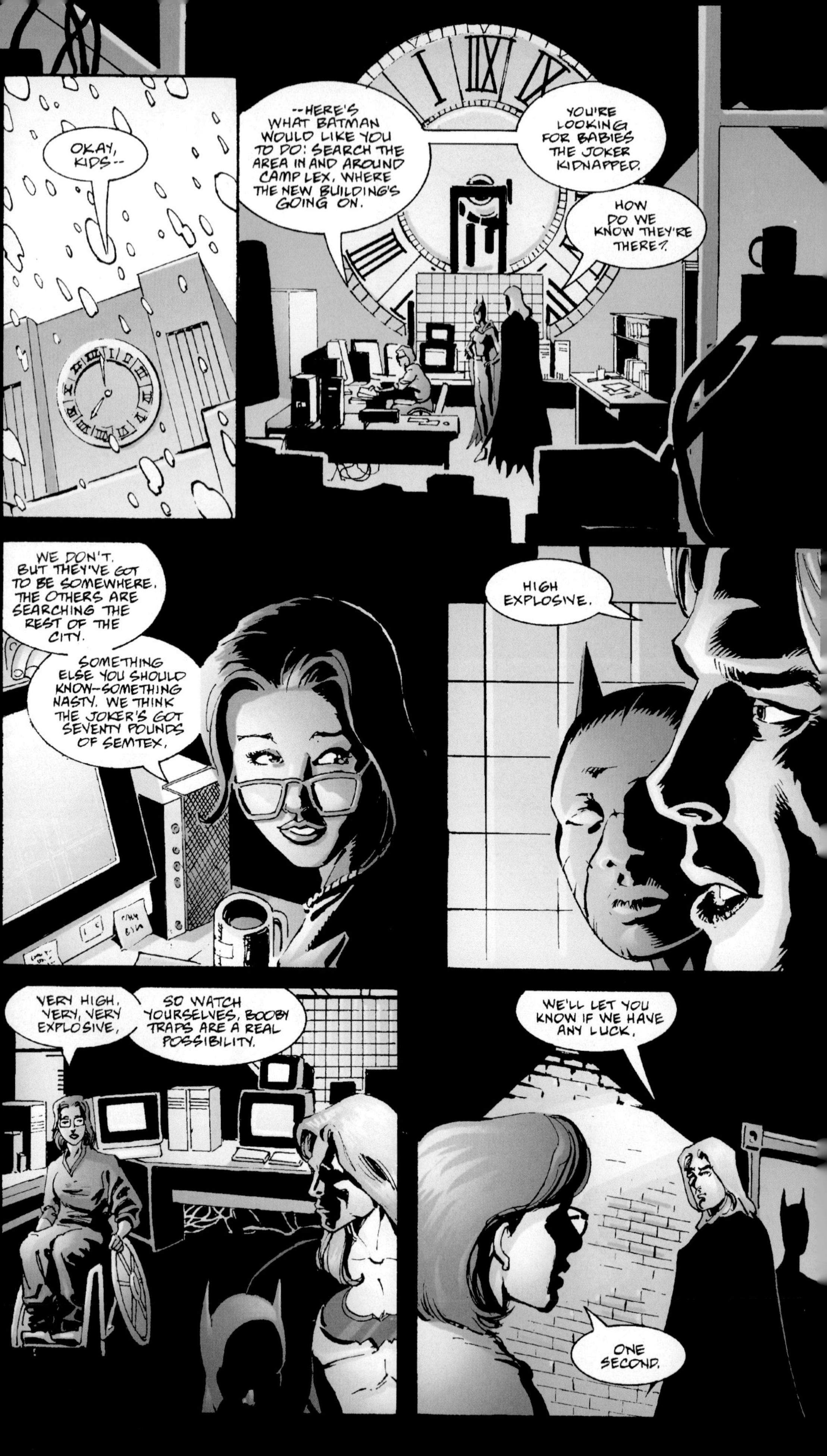
OKAY, KIDS--
--HERE'S WHAT BATMAN WOULD LIKE YOU TO DO: SEARCH THE AREA IN AND AROUND CAMP LEX, WHERE THE NEW BUILDING'S GOING ON.
YOU'RE LOOKING FOR BABIES THE JOKER KIDNAPPED.
HOW DO WE KNOW THEY'RE THERE?
WE DON'T. BUT THEY'VE GOT TO BE SOMEWHERE. THE OTHERS ARE SEARCHING THE REST OF THE CITY.
SOMETHING ELSE YOU SHOULD KNOW--SOMETHING NASTY. WE THINK THE JOKER'S GOT SEVENTY POUNDS OF SEMTEX,
HIGH EXPLOSIVE.
VERY HIGH, VERY, VERY EXPLOSIVE,
SO WATCH YOURSELVES, BOOBY TRAPS ARE A REAL POSSIBILITY.
WE'LL LET YOU KNOW IF WE HAVE ANY LUCK.
ONE SECOND.

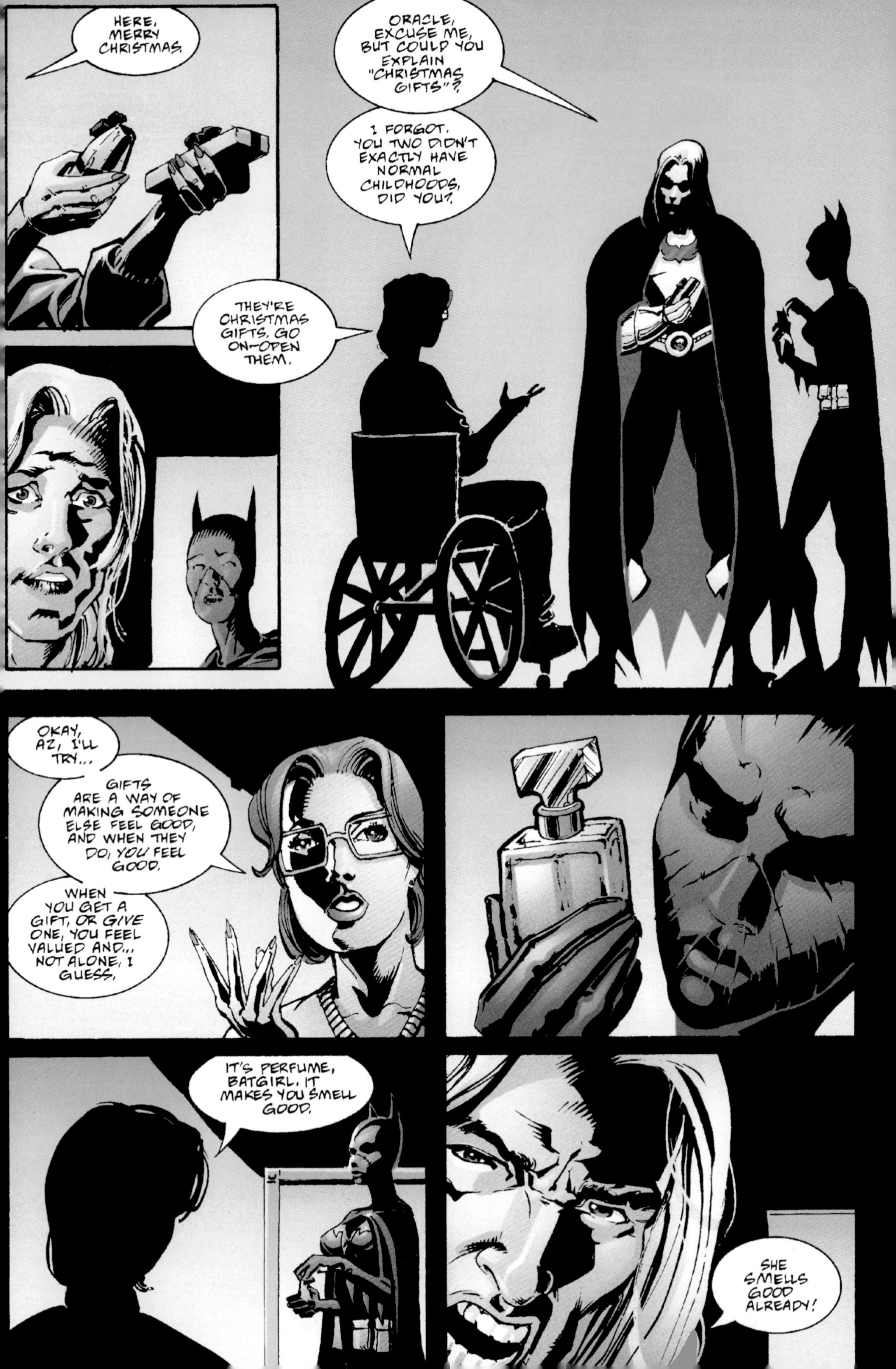
HERE, MERRY CHRISTMAS.
ORACLE, EXCUSE ME, BUT COULD YOU EXPLAIN "CHRISTMAS GIFTS"?
I FORGOT. YOU TWO DIDN'T EXACTLY HAVE NORMAL CHILDHOODS, DID YOU?
THEY'RE CHRISTMAS GIFTS. GO ON--OPEN THEM.
OKAY, AZ, I'LL TRY...
GIFTS ARE A WAY OF MAKING SOMEONE ELSE FEEL GOOD, AND WHEN THEY DO, YOU FEEL GOOD.
WHEN YOU GET A GIFT, OR GIVE ONE, YOU FEEL VALUED AND... NOT ALONE, I GUESS.
IT'S PERFUME, BATGIRL. IT MAKES YOU SMELL GOOD.
SHE SMELLS GOOD ALREADY!

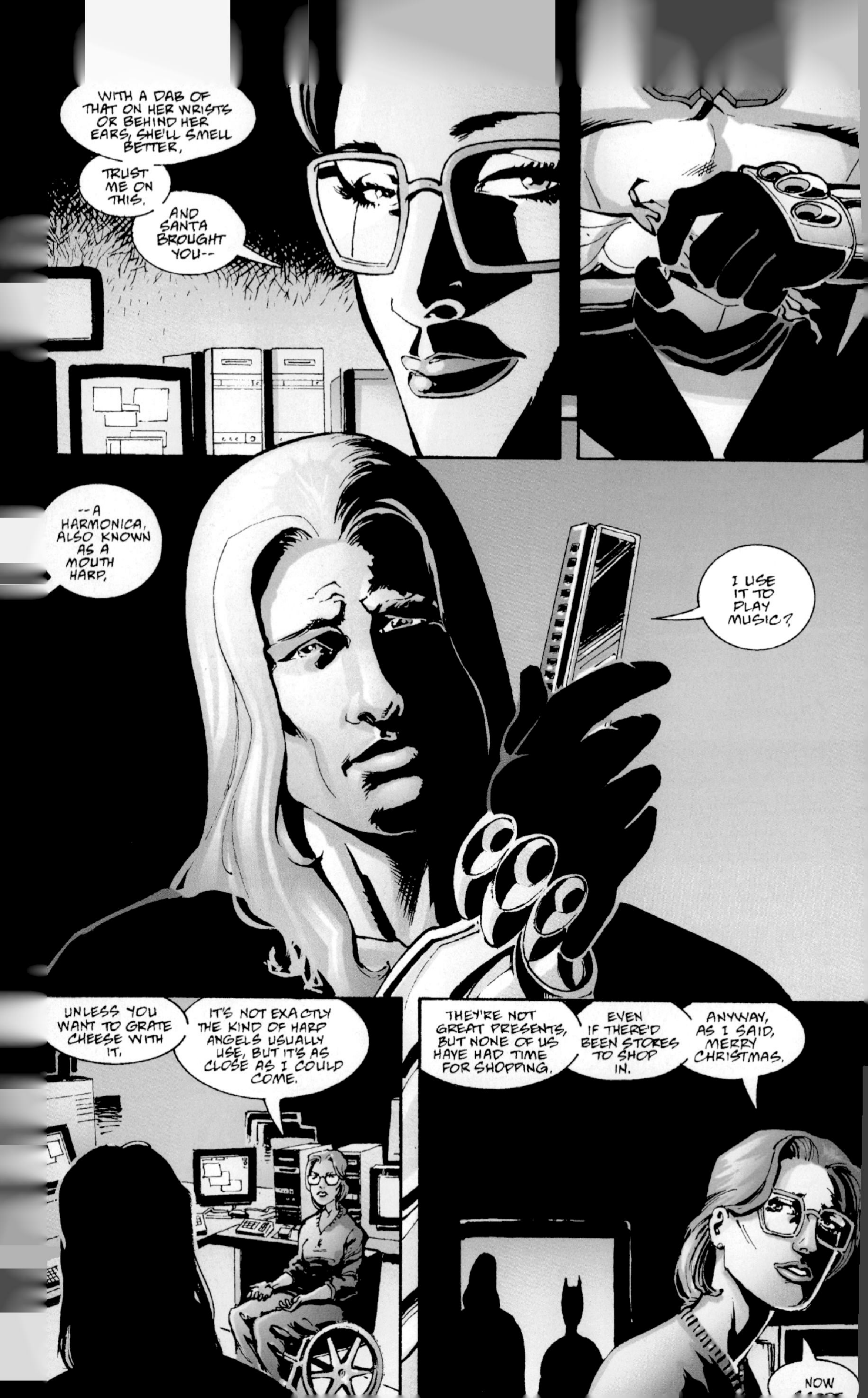
WITH A DAB OF THAT ON HER WRISTS OR BEHIND HER EARS, SHE'LL SMELL BETTER.
TRUST ME ON THIS.
AND SANTA BROUGHT YOU--
--A HARMONICA, ALSO KNOWN AS A MOUTH HARP.
I USE IT TO PLAY MUSIC?
UNLESS YOU WANT TO GRATE CHEESE WITH IT.
IT'S NOT EXACTLY THE KIND OF HARP ANGELS USUALLY USE, BUT IT'S AS CLOSE AS I COULD COME.
THEY'RE NOT GREAT PRESENTS, BUT NONE OF US HAVE HAD TIME FOR SHOPPING.
EVEN IF THERE'D BEEN STORES TO SHOP IN.
ANYWAY, AS I SAID, MERRY CHRISTMAS.
NOW

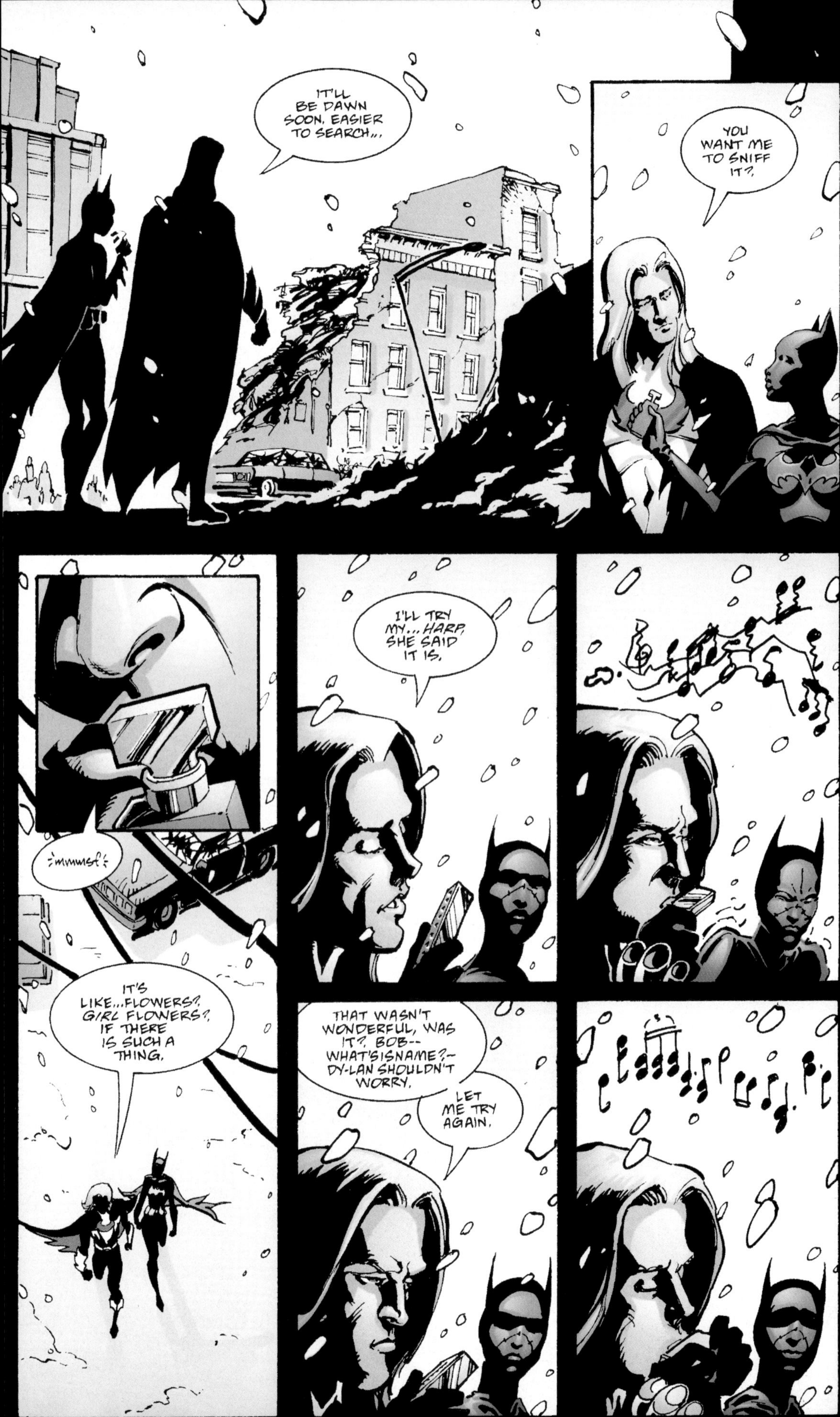
IT'LL BE DAWN SOON. EASIER TO SEARCH...
YOU WANT ME TO SNIFF IT?
I'LL TRY MY... HARP, SHE SAID IT IS.
mmmsf
IT'S LIKE...FLOWERS? GIRL FLOWERS? IF THERE IS SUCH A THING.
THAT WASN'T WONDERFUL, WAS IT? BOB--WHAT'SISNAME?--DY-LAN SHOULDN'T WORRY.
LET ME TRY AGAIN.

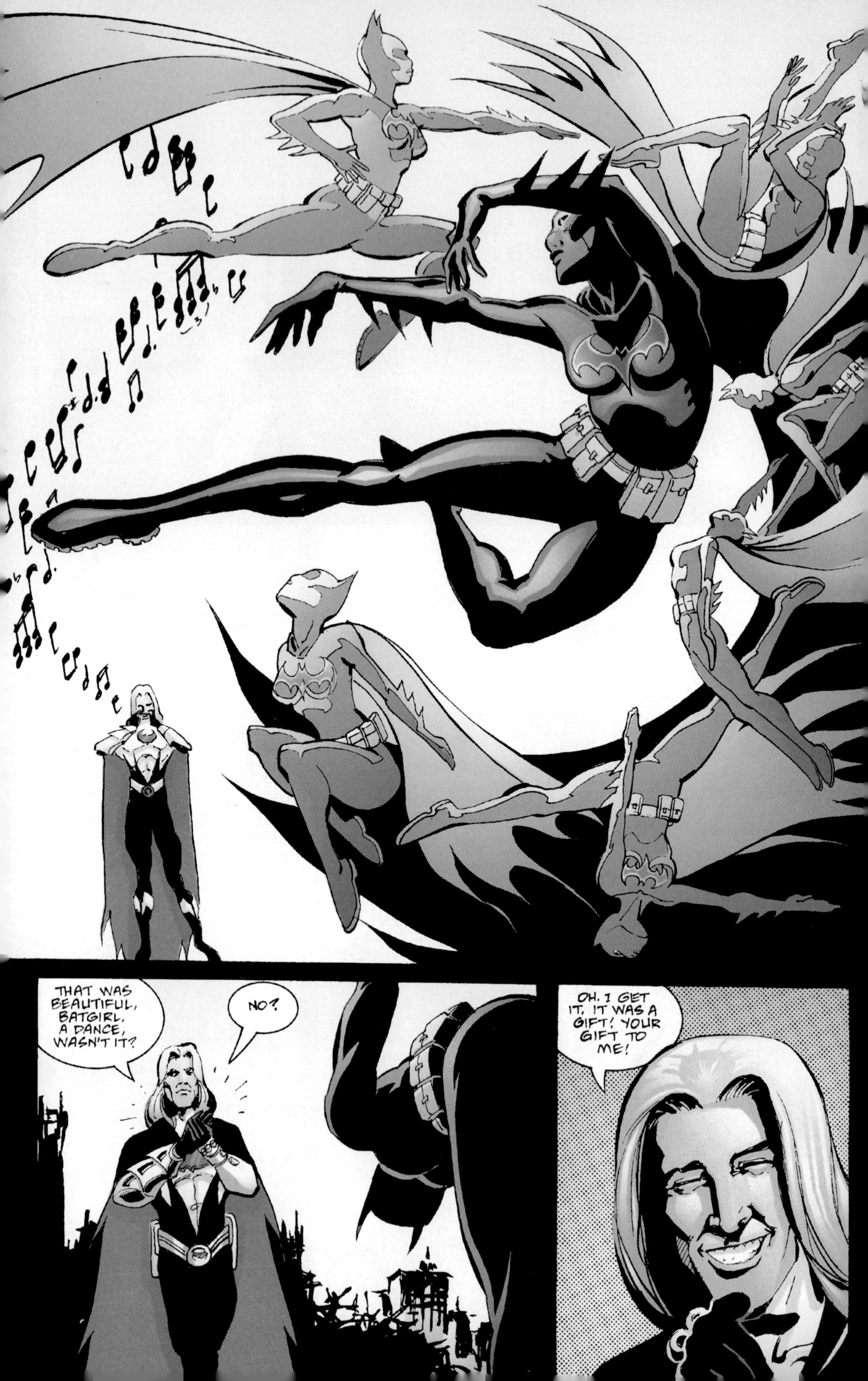
THAT WAS BEAUTIFUL, BATGIRL. A DANCE, WASN'T IT?
NO?
OH. I GET IT. IT WAS A GIFT! YOUR GIFT TO ME!

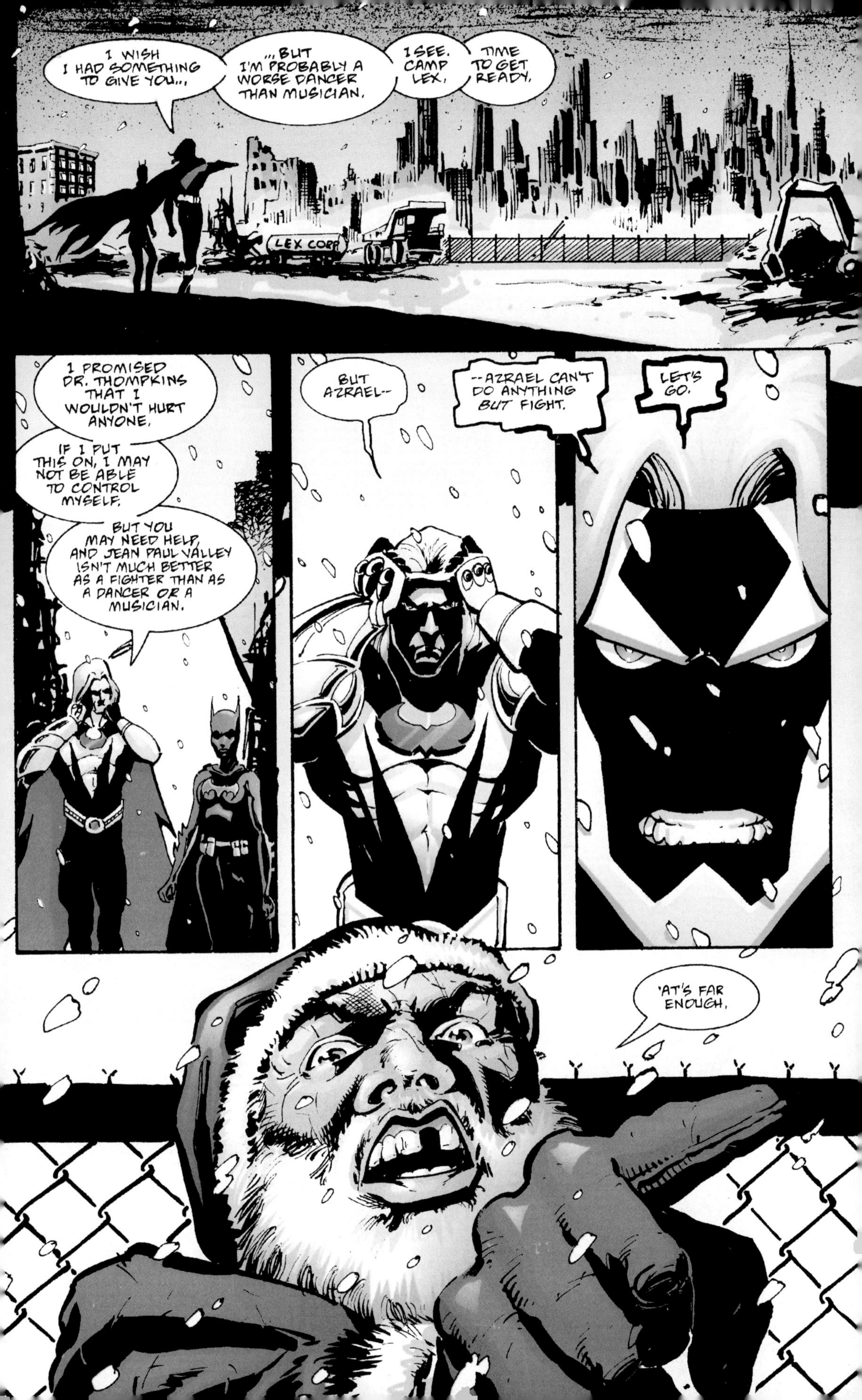
I WISH I HAD SOMETHING TO GIVE YOU...
...BUT I'M PROBABLY A WORSE DANCER THAN MUSICIAN.
I SEE. CAMP LEX.
TIME TO GET READY.
LEX CORP
I PROMISED DR. THOMPKINS THAT I WOULDN'T HURT ANYONE.
IF I PUT THIS ON, I MAY NOT BE ABLE TO CONTROL MYSELF.
BUT YOU MAY NEED HELP, AND JEAN PAUL VALLEY ISN'T MUCH BETTER AS A FIGHTER THAN AS A DANCER OR A MUSICIAN.
BUT AZRAEL--
--AZRAEL CAN'T DO ANYTHING BUT FIGHT.
LET'S GO.
'AT'S FAR ENOUGH.

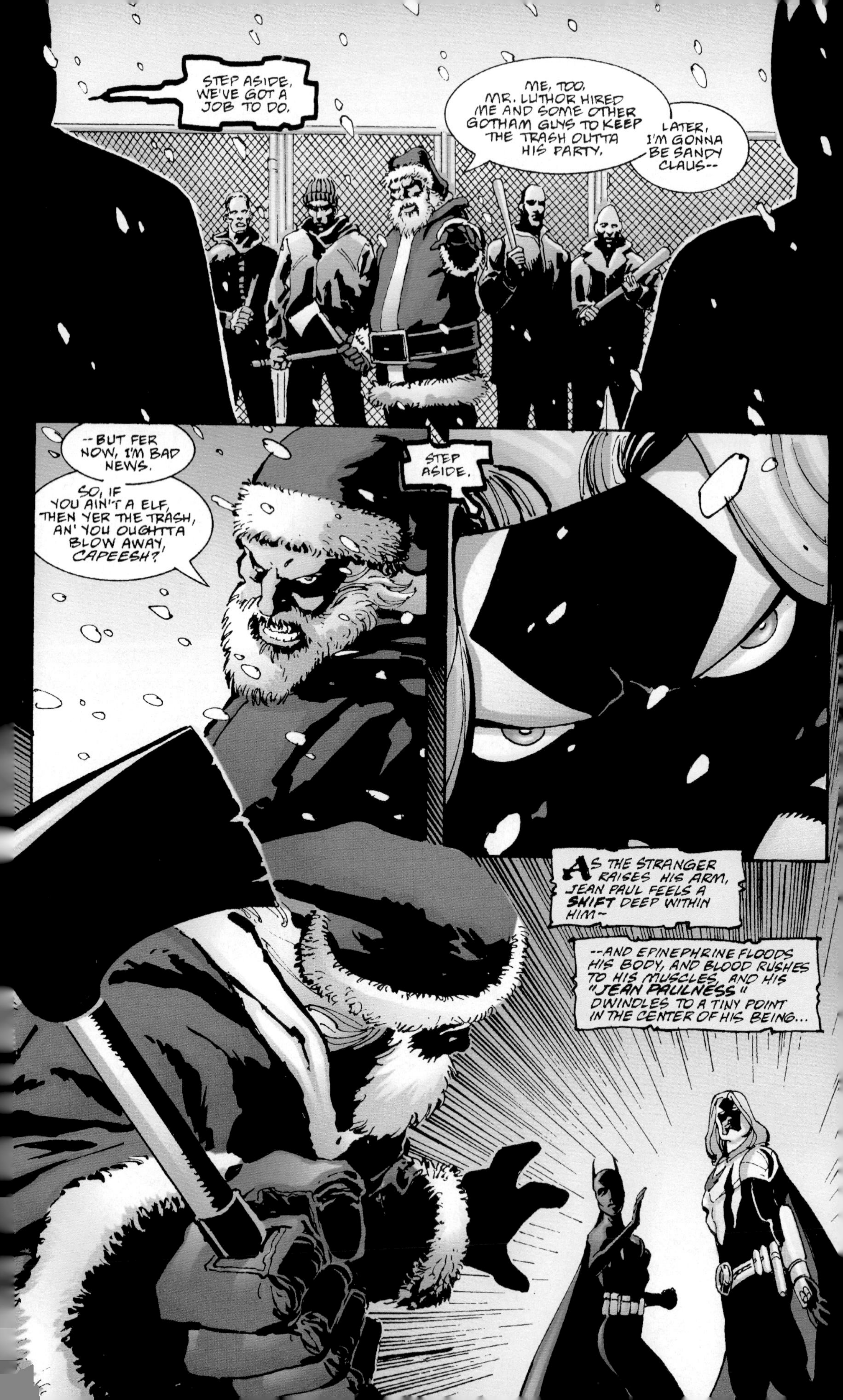
STEP ASIDE, WE'VE GOT A JOB TO DO.
ME, TOO, MR. LUTHOR HIRED ME AND SOME OTHER GOTHAM GUYS TO KEEP THE TRASH OUTTA HIS PARTY.
LATER, I'M GONNA BE SANDY CLAUS--
--BUT FER NOW, I'M BAD NEWS.
SO, IF YOU AIN'T A ELF, THEN YER THE TRASH, AN' YOU OUGHTTA BLOW AWAY, CAPEESH?
STEP ASIDE.
AS THE STRANGER RAISES HIS ARM, JEAN PAUL FEELS A SHIFT DEEP WITHIN HIM--
--AND EPINEPHRINE FLOODS HIS BODY, AND BLOOD RUSHES TO HIS MUSCLES, AND HIS "JEAN PAULNESS" DWINDLES TO A TINY POINT IN THE CENTER OF HIS BEING...

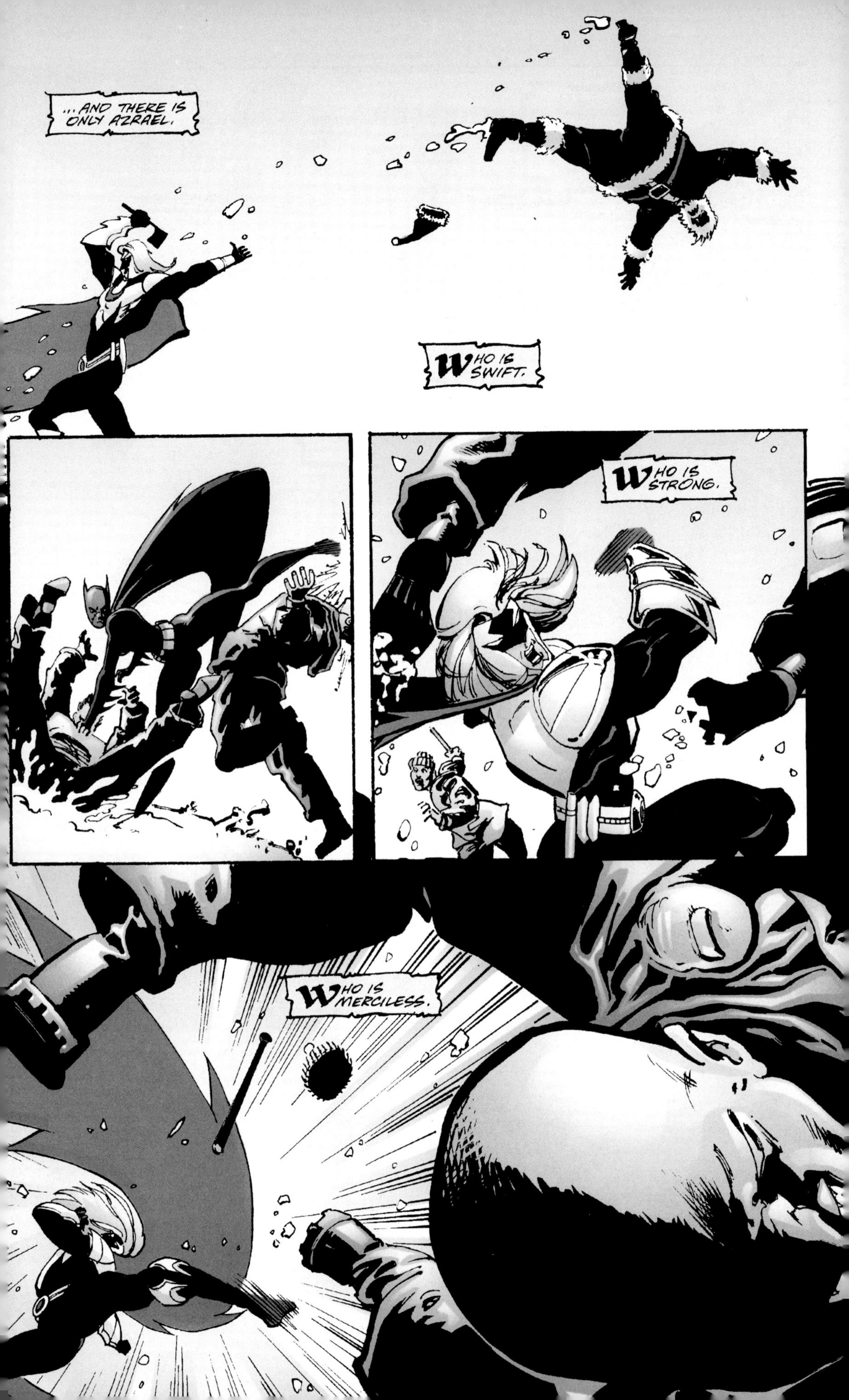
...AND THERE IS ONLY AZRAEL.
WHO IS SWIFT.
WHO IS STRONG.
WHO IS MERCILESS.

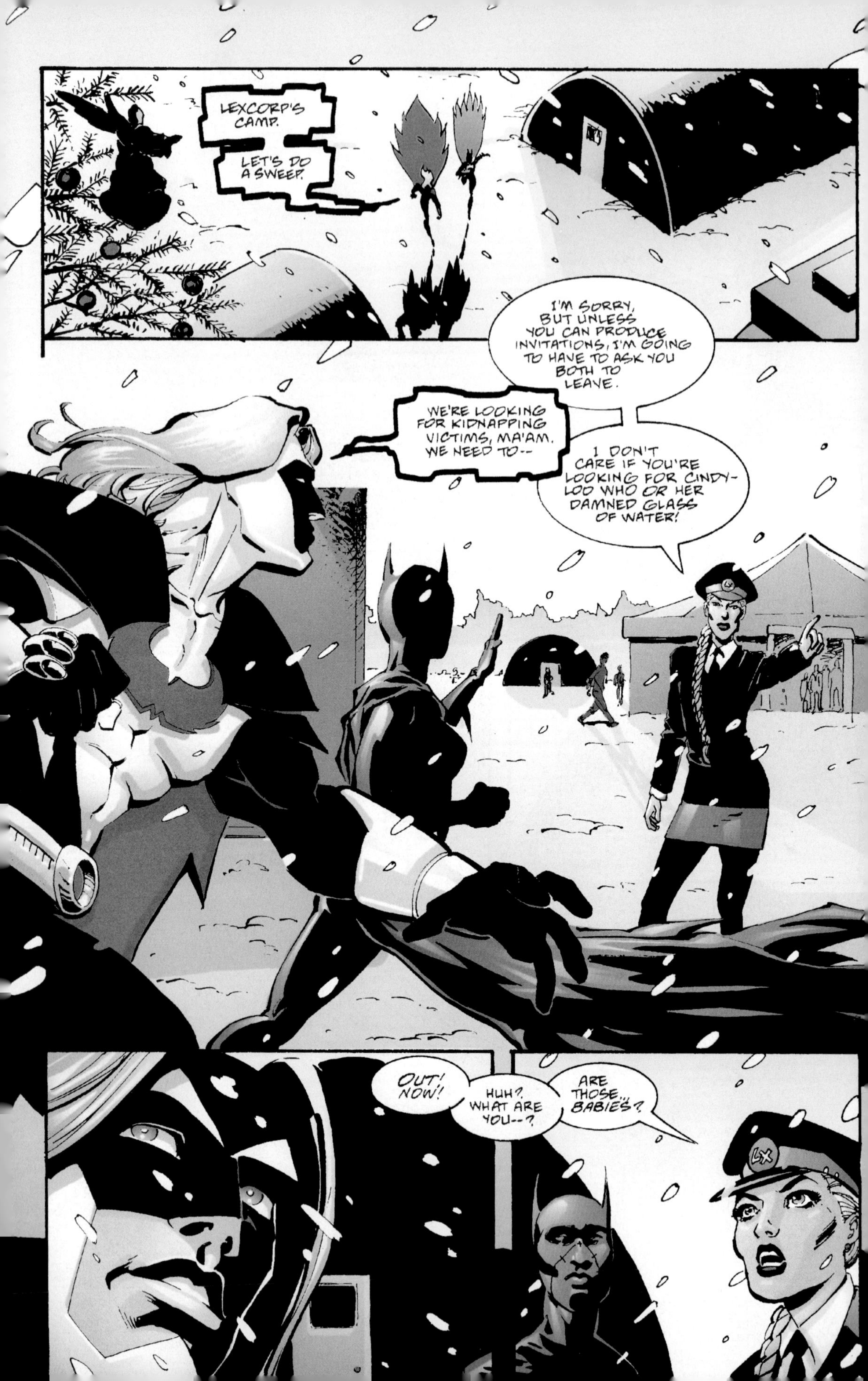

LEXCORP'S CAMP.
LET'S DO A SWEEP.
I'M SORRY, BUT UNLESS YOU CAN PRODUCE INVITATIONS, I'M GOING TO HAVE TO ASK YOU BOTH TO LEAVE.
WE'RE LOOKING FOR KIDNAPPING VICTIMS, MA'AM. WE NEED TO--
I DON'T CARE IF YOU'RE LOOKING FOR CINDY-LOO WHO OR HER DAMNED GLASS OF WATER!
OUT! NOW!
HUH?. WHAT ARE YOU--?
ARE THOSE... BABIES?

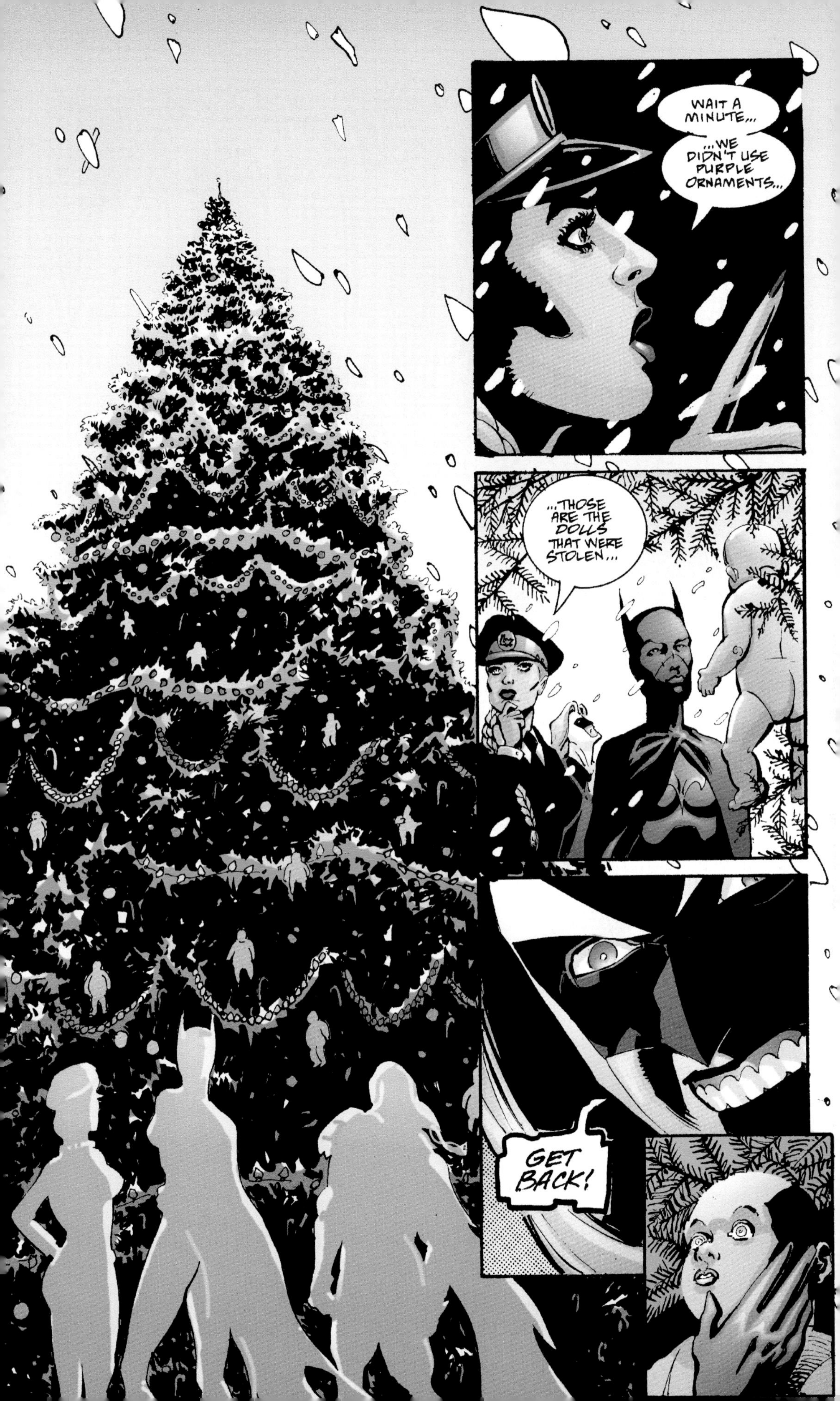
WAIT A MINUTE...
...WE DIDN'T USE PURPLE ORNAMENTS...
...THOSE ARE THE DOLLS THAT WERE STOLEN...
GET BACK!

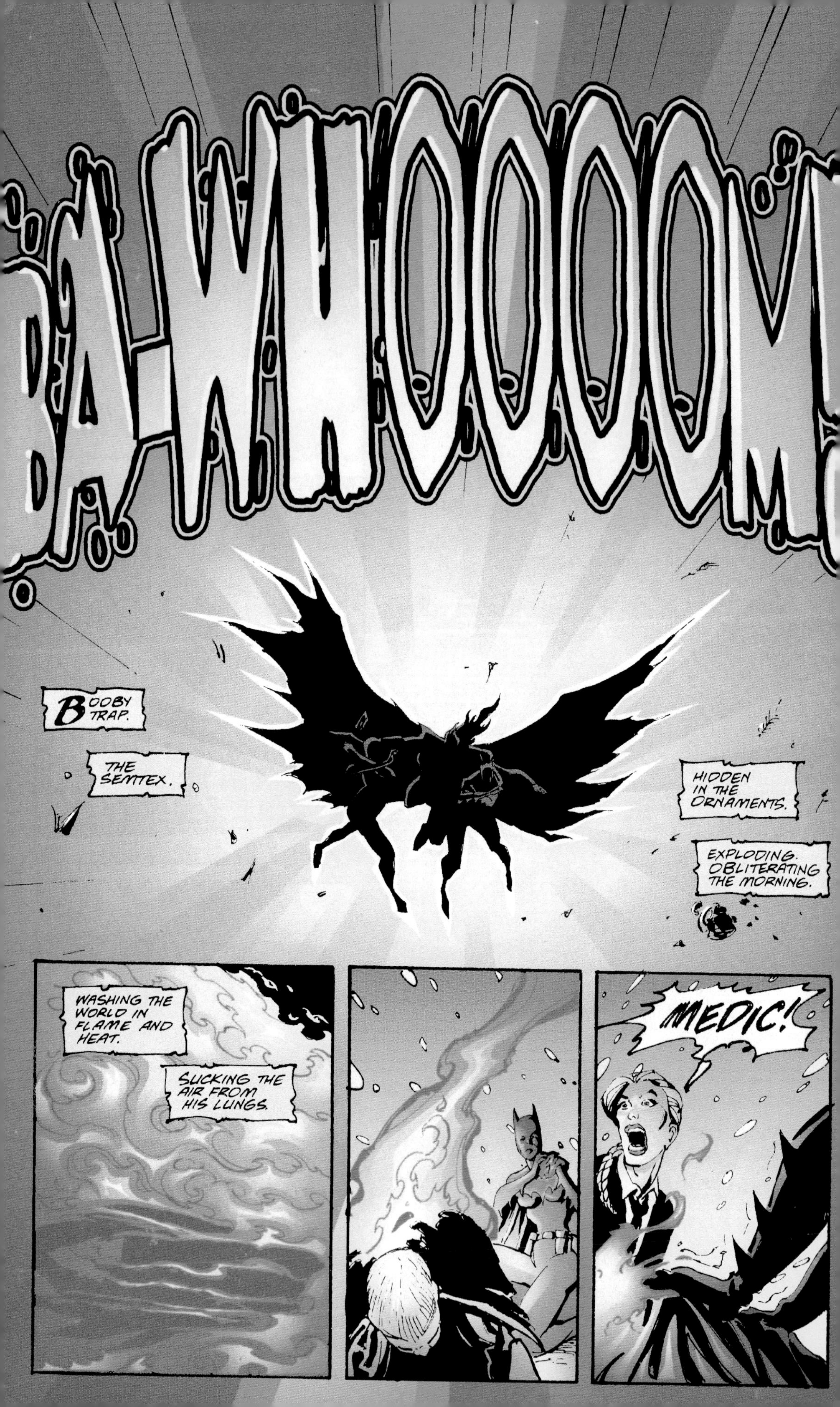
BA-WHOOOOM
BOOBY TRAP.
THE SEMTEX.
HIDDEN IN THE ORNAMENTS.
EXPLODING. OBLITERATING THE MORNING.
WASHING THE WORLD IN FLAME AND HEAT.
SUCKING THE AIR FROM HIS LUNGS.
MEDIC!

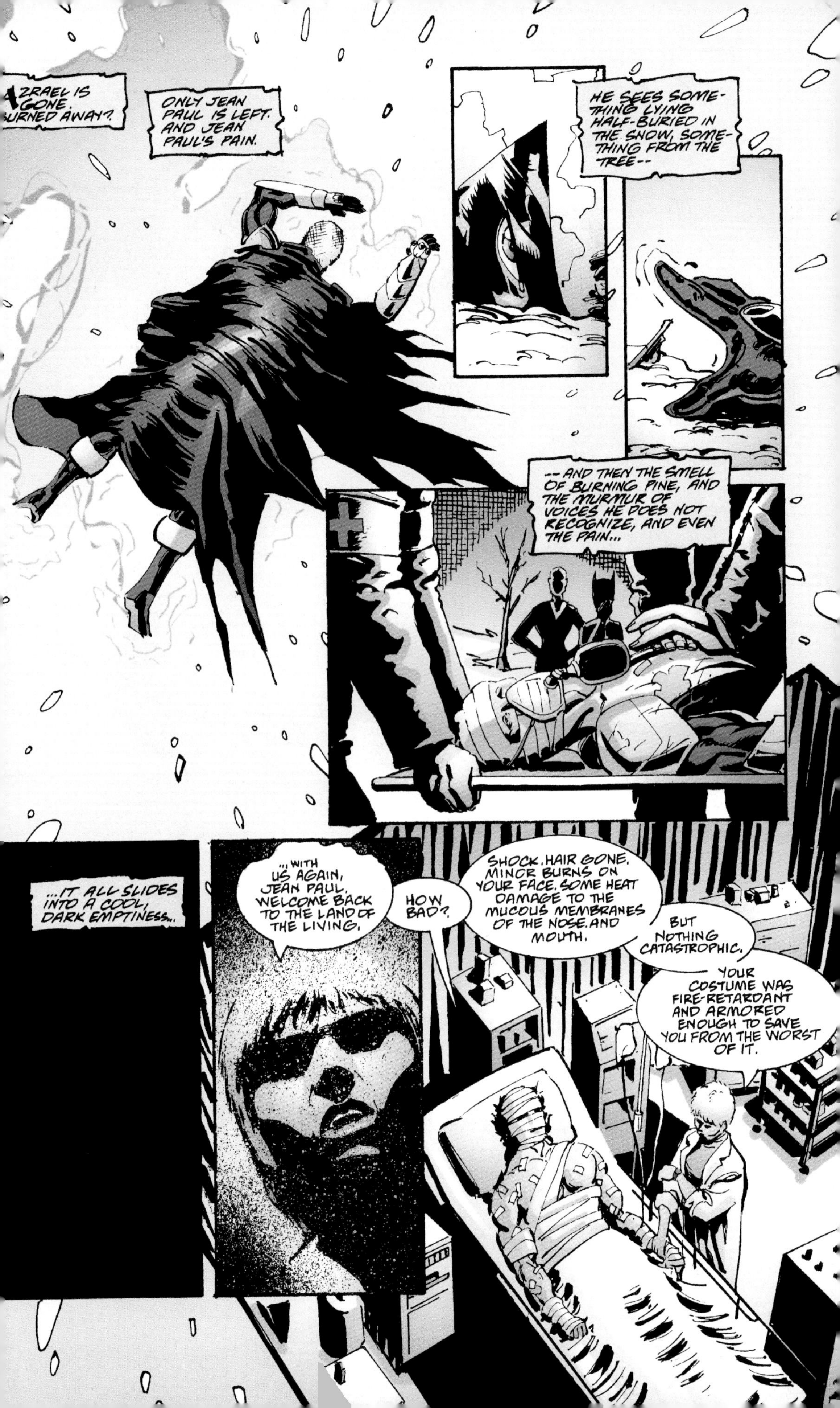
AZRAEL IS GONE. BURNED AWAY?
ONLY JEAN PAUL IS LEFT. AND JEAN PAUL'S PAIN.
HE SEES SOMETHING LYING HALF-BURIED IN THE SNOW, SOMETHING FROM THE TREE--
--AND THEN THE SMELL OF BURNING PINE, AND THE MURMUR OF VOICES HE DOES NOT RECOGNIZE, AND EVEN THE PAIN...
...IT ALL SLIDES INTO A COOL, DARK EMPTINESS...
...WITH US AGAIN, JEAN PAUL. WELCOME BACK TO THE LAND OF THE LIVING.
HOW BAD?
SHOCK. HAIR GONE. MINOR BURNS ON YOUR FACE. SOME HEAT DAMAGE TO THE MUCOUS MEMBRANES OF THE NOSE AND MOUTH.
BUT NOTHING CATASTROPHIC.
YOUR COSTUME WAS FIRE-RETARDANT AND ARMORED ENOUGH TO SAVE YOU FROM THE WORST OF IT.

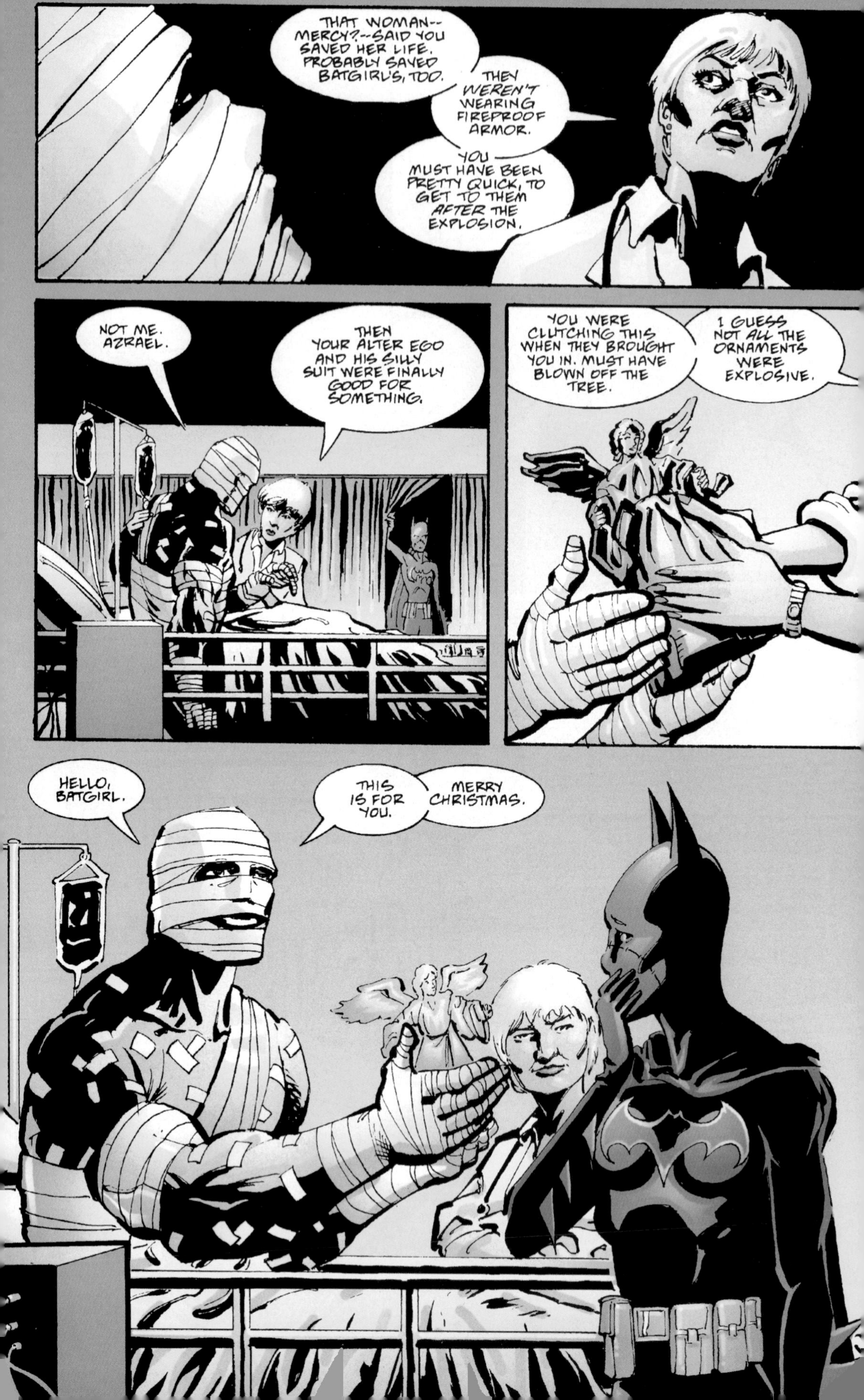
THAT WOMAN--MERCY?--SAID YOU SAVED HER LIFE. PROBABLY SAVED BATGIRL'S, TOO.
THEY WEREN'T WEARING FIREPROOF ARMOR.
YOU MUST HAVE BEEN PRETTY QUICK, TO GET TO THEM AFTER THE EXPLOSION.
NOT ME. AZRAEL.
THEN YOUR ALTER EGO AND HIS SILLY SUIT WERE FINALLY GOOD FOR SOMETHING.
YOU WERE CLUTCHING THIS WHEN THEY BROUGHT YOU IN. MUST HAVE BLOWN OFF THE TREE.
I GUESS NOT ALL THE ORNAMENTS WERE EXPLOSIVE.
HELLO, BATGIRL.
THIS IS FOR YOU.
MERRY CHRISTMAS.

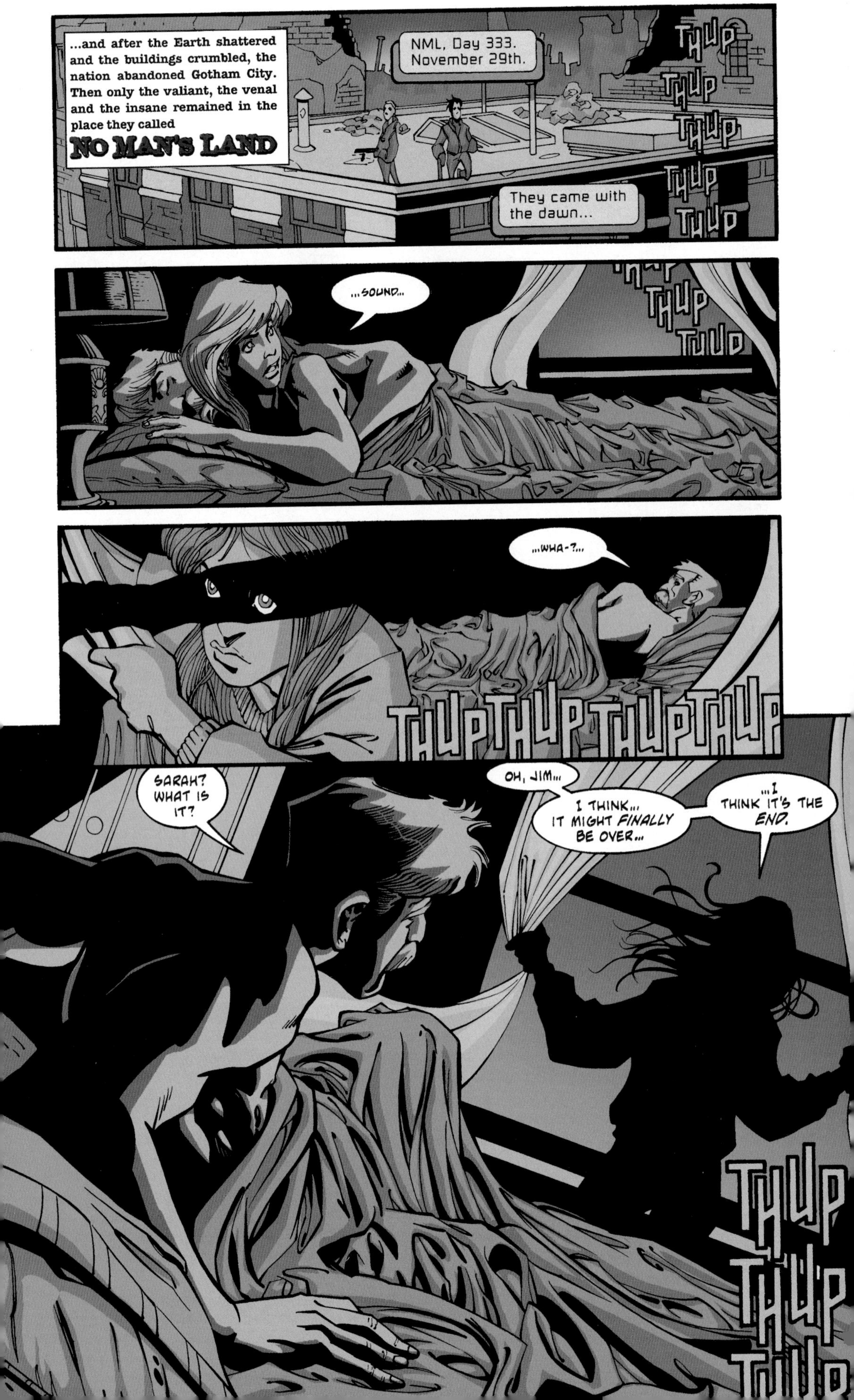

...and after the Earth shattered and the buildings crumbled, the nation abandoned Gotham City. Then only the valiant, the venal and the insane remained in the place they called
NO MAN'S LAND
NML, Day 333. November 29th.
They came with the dawn...
THUP THUP THUP THUP THUP
THUP THUP THUP
...SOUND...
...WHA-?...
THUPTHUPTHUPTHUP
SARAH? WHAT IS IT?
OH, JIM...
I THINK... IT MIGHT FINALLY BE OVER...
...I THINK IT'S THE END.
THUP THUP THUP

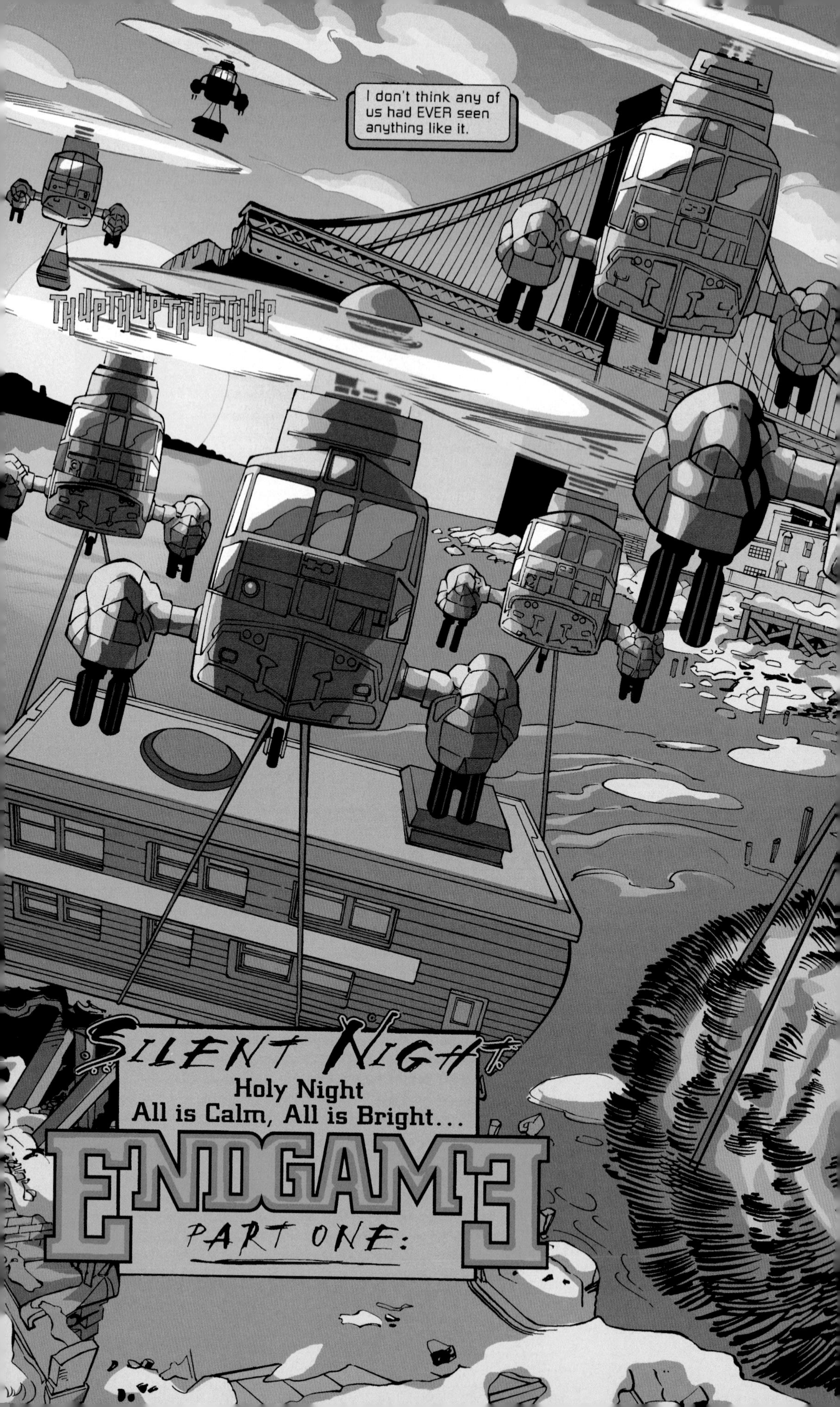

I don't think any of us had EVER seen anything like it.
THUPTHUPTHUPTHUP
SILENT NIGHT
Holy Night
All is Calm, All is Bright...
ENDGAME
PART ONE:

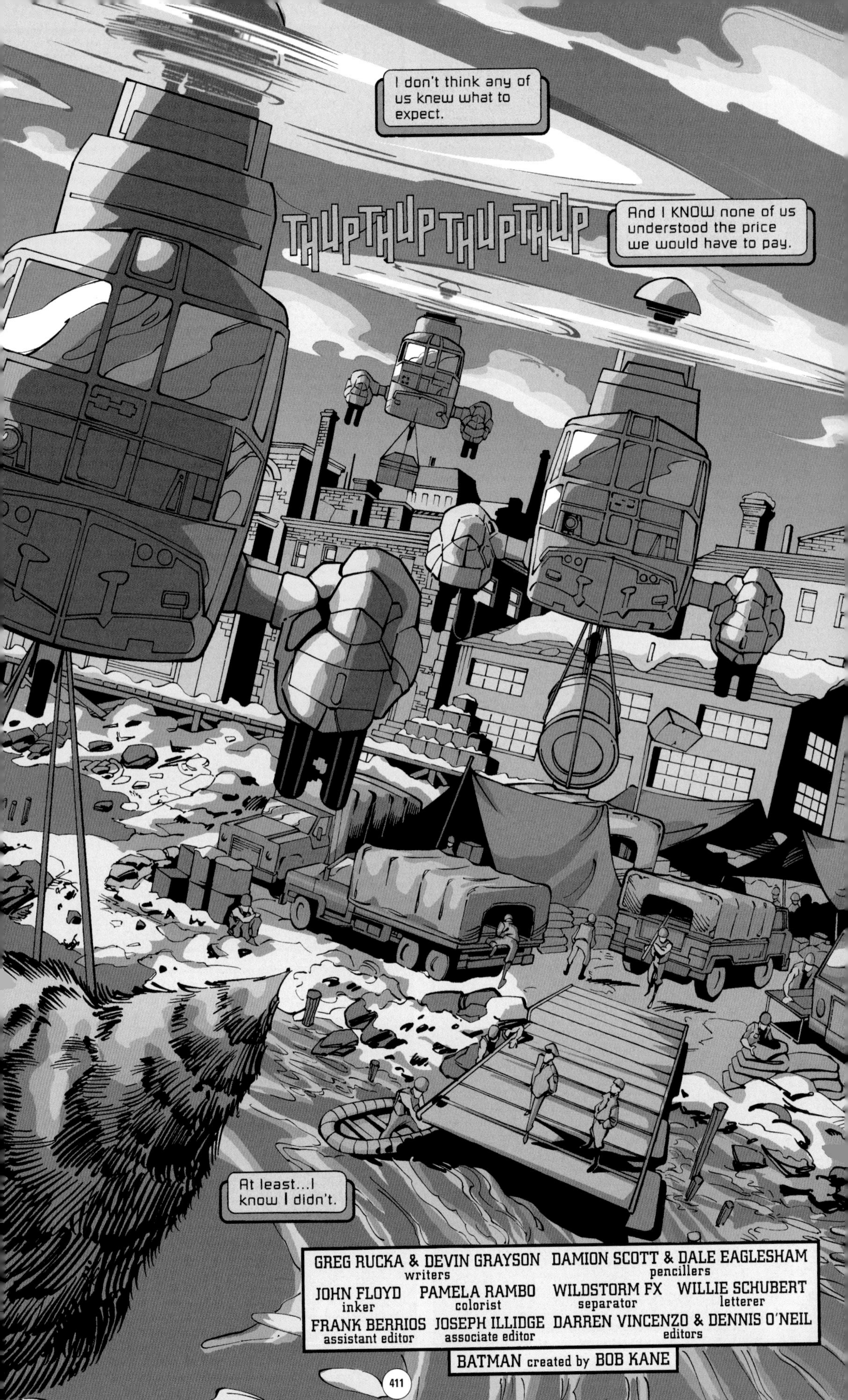
I don't think any of us knew what to expect.
THUPTHUPTHUPTHUP
And I KNOW none of us understood the price we would have to pay.
At least...I know I didn't.
GREG RUCKA & DEVIN GRAYSON writers
DAMION SCOTT & DALE EAGLESHAM pencillers
JOHN FLOYD inker
PAMELA RAMBO colorist
WILDSTORM FX separator
WILLIE SCHUBERT letterer
FRANK BERRIOS assistant editor
JOSEPH ILLIDGE associate editor
DARREN VINCENZO & DENNIS O'NEIL editors
BATMAN created by BOB KANE

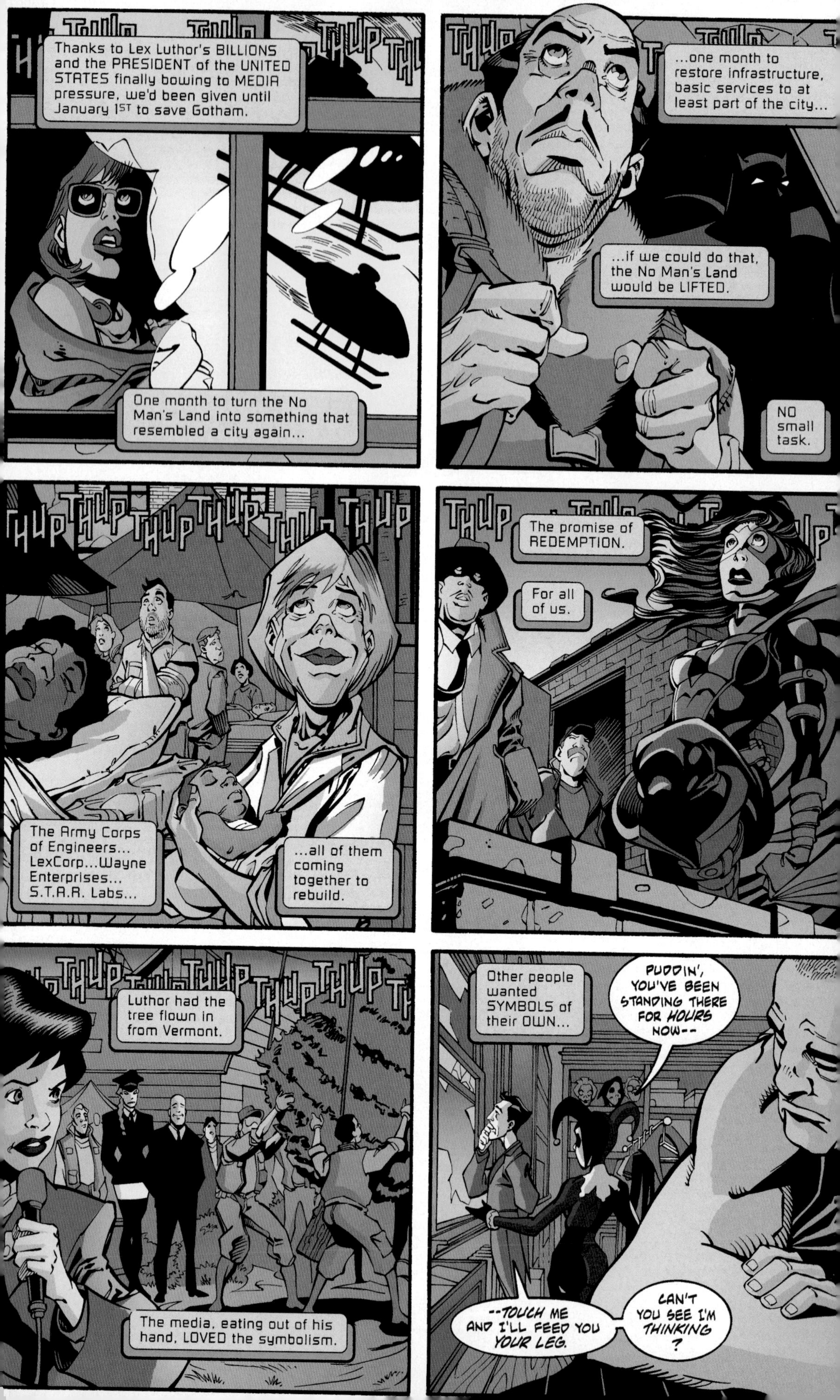

Thanks to Lex Luthor's BILLIONS and the PRESIDENT of the UNITED STATES finally bowing to MEDIA pressure, we'd been given until January 1ST to save Gotham.
One month to turn the No Man's Land into something that resembled a city again...
...one month to restore infrastructure, basic services to at least part of the city...
...if we could do that, the No Man's Land would be LIFTED.
NO small task.
THUP THUP THUP THUP THUP THUP
The Army Corps of Engineers... LexCorp...Wayne Enterprises... S.T.A.R. Labs...
...all of them coming together to rebuild.
THUP
The promise of REDEMPTION.
For all of us.
THUP THUP THUP THUP THUP
Luthor had the tree flown in from Vermont.
The media, eating out of his hand, LOVED the symbolism.
Other people wanted SYMBOLS of their OWN...
PUDDIN', YOU'VE BEEN STANDING THERE FOR HOURS NOW--
--TOUCH ME AND I'LL FEED YOU YOUR LEG.
CAN'T YOU SEE I'M THINKING?

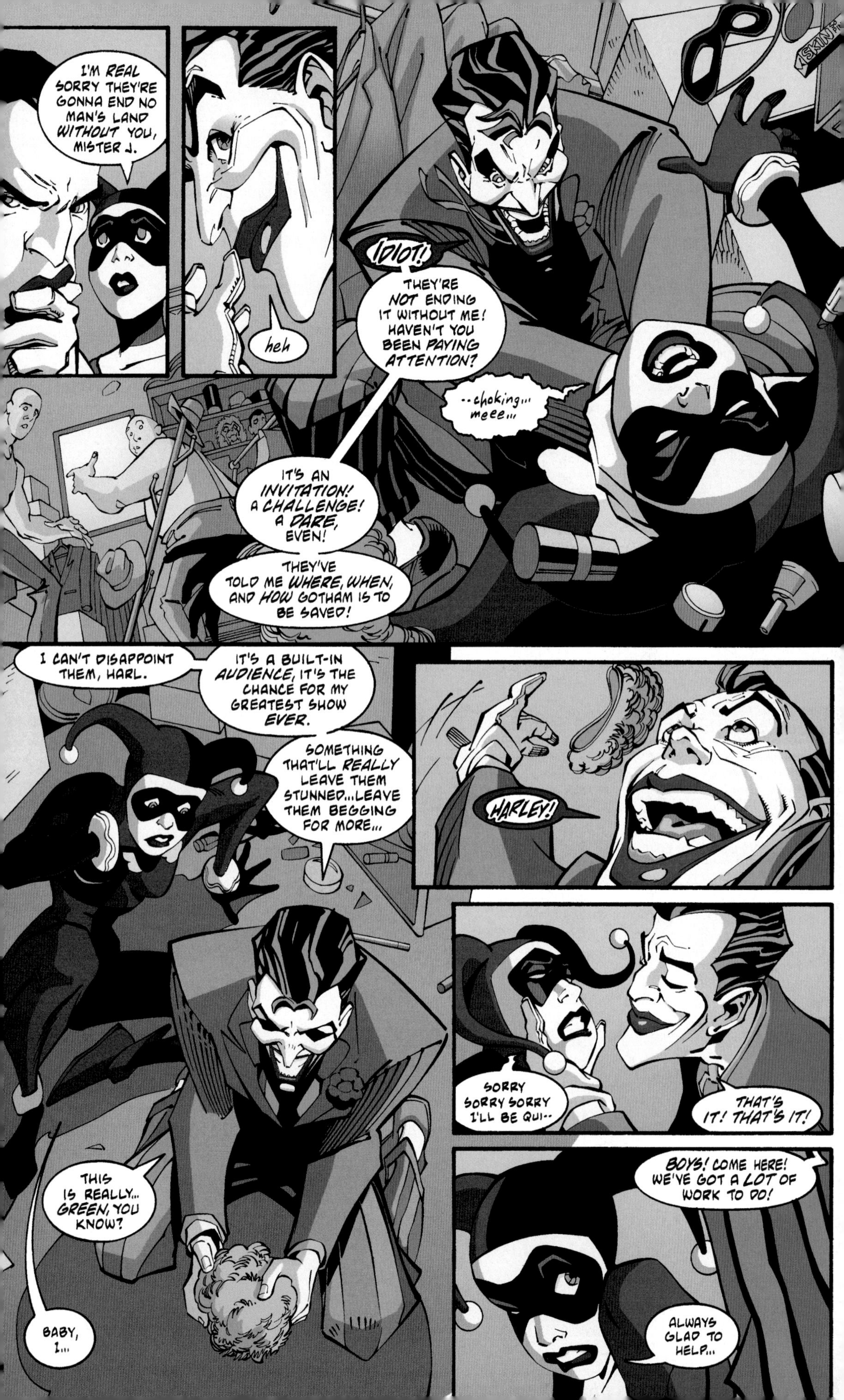
I'M REAL SORRY THEY'RE GONNA END NO MAN'S LAND WITHOUT YOU, MISTER J.
heh
IDIOT!
THEY'RE NOT ENDING IT WITHOUT ME! HAVEN'T YOU BEEN PAYING ATTENTION?
..choking... meee...
IT'S AN INVITATION! A CHALLENGE! A DARE, EVEN!
THEY'VE TOLD ME WHERE, WHEN, AND HOW GOTHAM IS TO BE SAVED!
I CAN'T DISAPPOINT THEM, HARL.
IT'S A BUILT-IN AUDIENCE, IT'S THE CHANCE FOR MY GREATEST SHOW EVER.
SOMETHING THAT'LL REALLY LEAVE THEM STUNNED...LEAVE THEM BEGGING FOR MORE...
HARLEY!
THIS IS REALLY... GREEN, YOU KNOW?
BABY, I...
SORRY SORRY SORRY I'LL BE QUI--
THAT'S IT! THAT'S IT!
BOYS! COME HERE! WE'VE GOT A LOT OF WORK TO DO!
ALWAYS GLAD TO HELP...

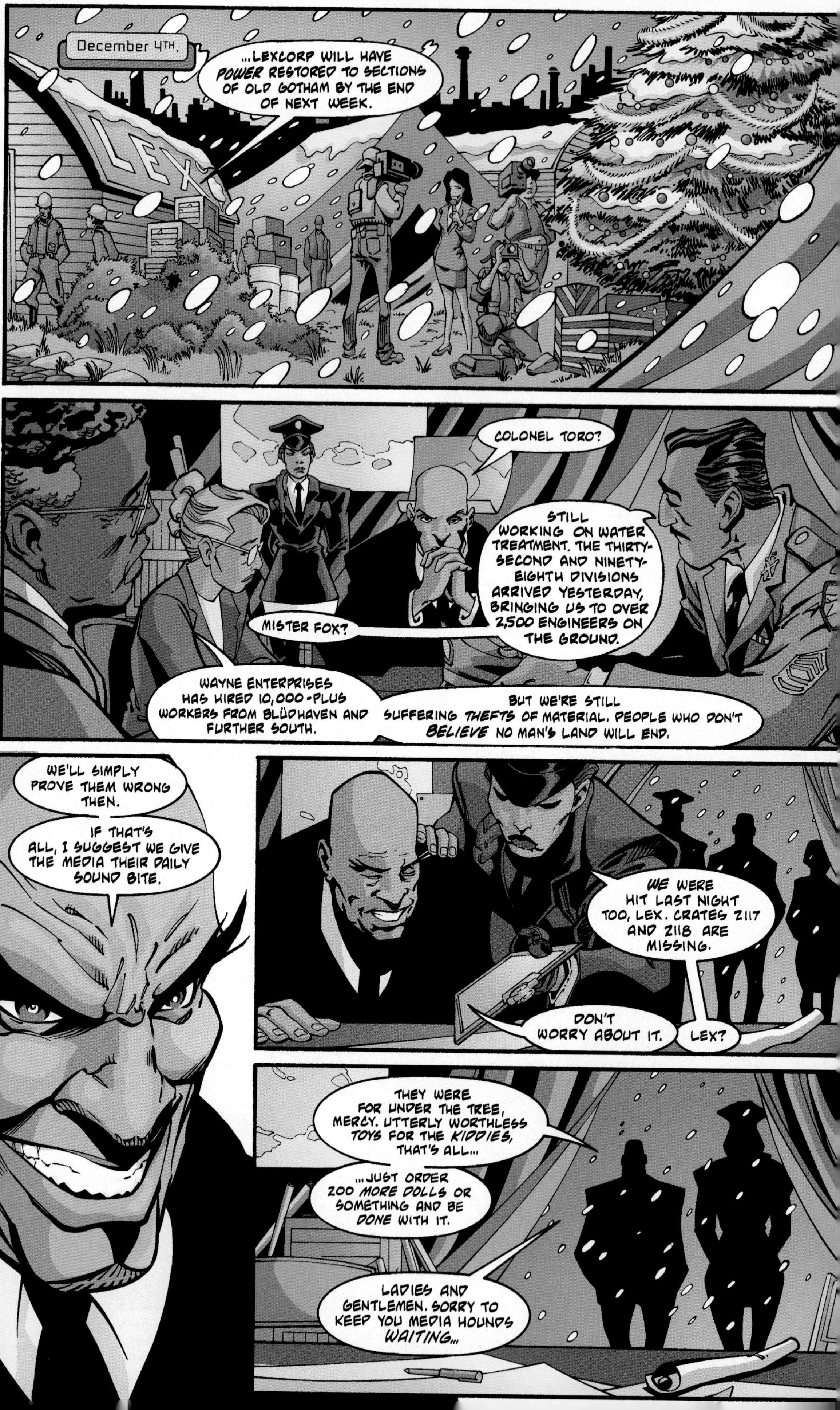
December 4TH.
...LEXCORP WILL HAVE POWER RESTORED TO SECTIONS OF OLD GOTHAM BY THE END OF NEXT WEEK.
COLONEL TORO?
STILL WORKING ON WATER TREATMENT. THE THIRTY-SECOND AND NINETY-EIGHTH DIVISIONS ARRIVED YESTERDAY, BRINGING US TO OVER 2,500 ENGINEERS ON THE GROUND.
MISTER FOX?
WAYNE ENTERPRISES HAS HIRED 10,000-PLUS WORKERS FROM BLÜDHAVEN AND FURTHER SOUTH.
BUT WE'RE STILL SUFFERING THEFTS OF MATERIAL. PEOPLE WHO DON'T BELIEVE NO MAN'S LAND WILL END.
WE'LL SIMPLY PROVE THEM WRONG THEN.
IF THAT'S ALL, I SUGGEST WE GIVE THE MEDIA THEIR DAILY SOUND BITE.
WE WERE HIT LAST NIGHT TOO, LEX. CRATES 2117 AND 2118 ARE MISSING.
DON'T WORRY ABOUT IT.
LEX?
THEY WERE FOR UNDER THE TREE, MERCY. UTTERLY WORTHLESS TOYS FOR THE KIDDIES, THAT'S ALL...
...JUST ORDER 200 MORE DOLLS OR SOMETHING AND BE DONE WITH IT.
LADIES AND GENTLEMEN. SORRY TO KEEP YOU MEDIA HOUNDS WAITING...

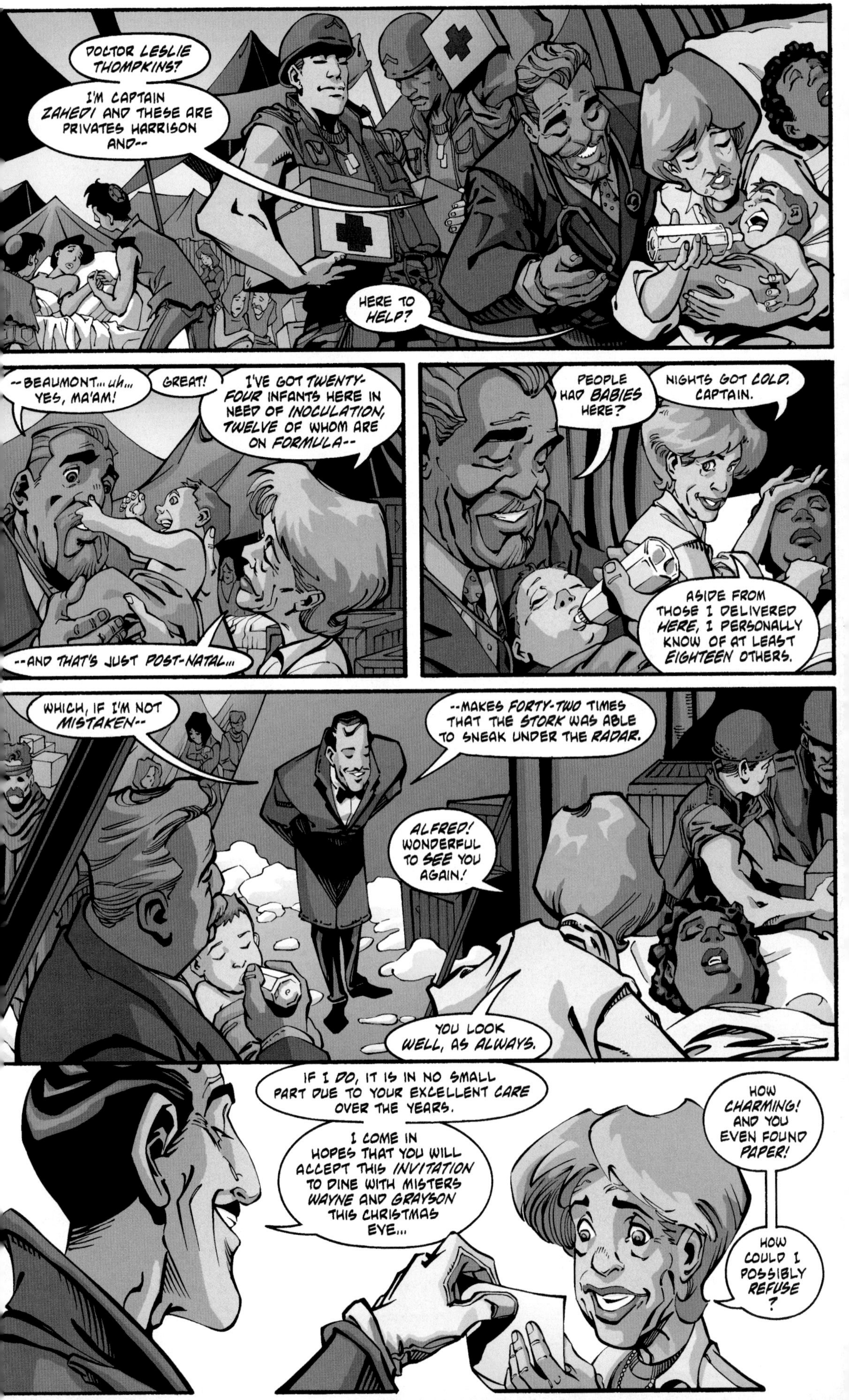
DOCTOR LESLIE THOMPKINS?
I'M CAPTAIN ZAHEDI AND THESE ARE PRIVATES HARRISON AND--
HERE TO HELP?
--BEAUMONT... uh... YES, MA'AM!
GREAT!
I'VE GOT TWENTY-FOUR INFANTS HERE IN NEED OF INOCULATION, TWELVE OF WHOM ARE ON FORMULA--
--AND THAT'S JUST POST-NATAL...
PEOPLE HAD BABIES HERE?
NIGHTS GOT COLD, CAPTAIN.
ASIDE FROM THOSE I DELIVERED HERE, I PERSONALLY KNOW OF AT LEAST EIGHTEEN OTHERS.
WHICH, IF I'M NOT MISTAKEN--
--MAKES FORTY-TWO TIMES THAT THE STORK WAS ABLE TO SNEAK UNDER THE RADAR.
ALFRED! WONDERFUL TO SEE YOU AGAIN!
YOU LOOK WELL, AS ALWAYS.
IF I DO, IT IS IN NO SMALL PART DUE TO YOUR EXCELLENT CARE OVER THE YEARS.
I COME IN HOPES THAT YOU WILL ACCEPT THIS INVITATION TO DINE WITH MISTERS WAYNE AND GRAYSON THIS CHRISTMAS EVE...
HOW CHARMING! AND YOU EVEN FOUND PAPER!
HOW COULD I POSSIBLY REFUSE?

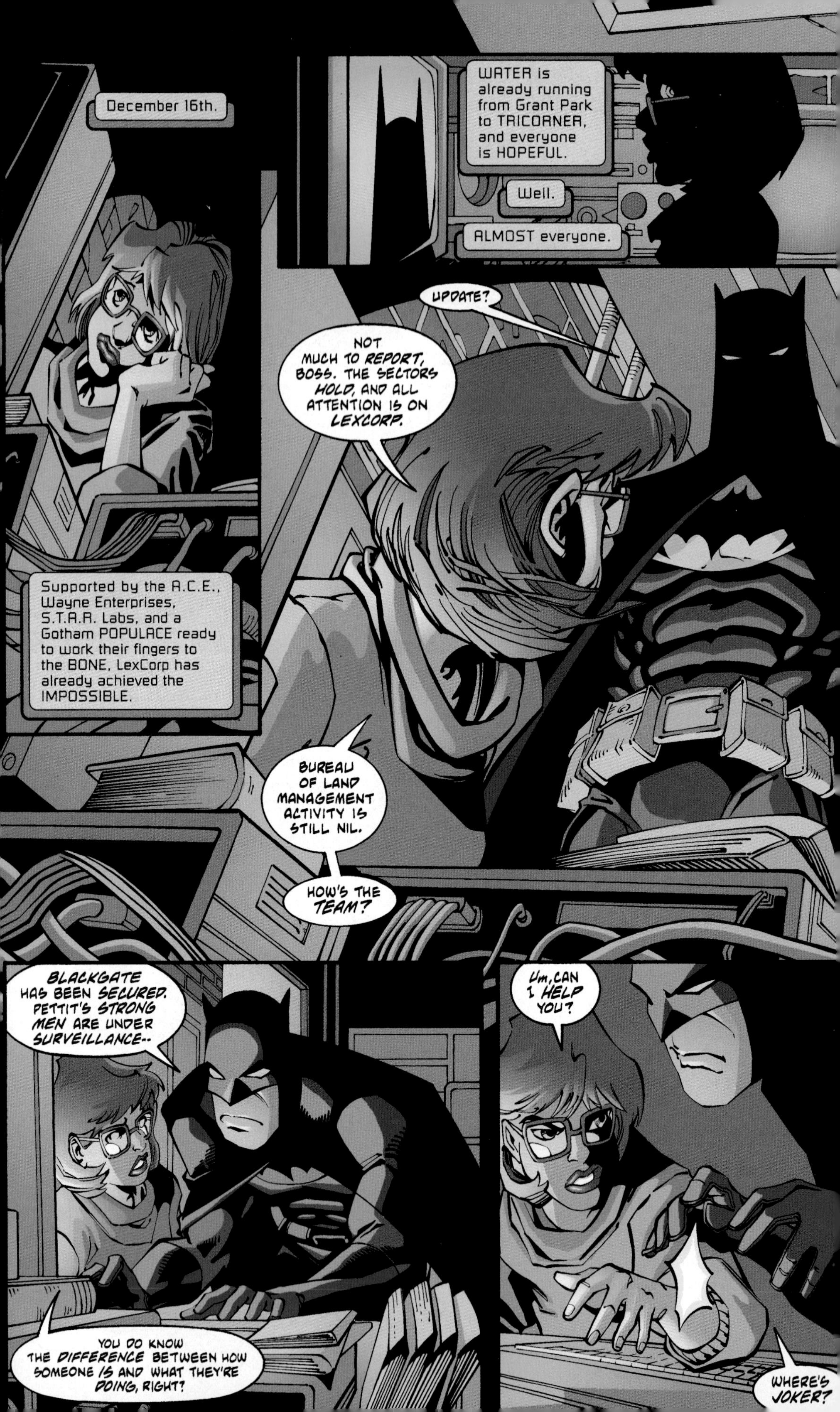

December 16th.
WATER is already running from Grant Park to TRICORNER, and everyone is HOPEFUL.
Well.
ALMOST everyone.
Supported by the A.C.E., Wayne Enterprises, S.T.A.R. Labs, and a Gotham POPULACE ready to work their fingers to the BONE, LexCorp has already achieved the IMPOSSIBLE.
UPDATE?
NOT MUCH TO REPORT, BOSS. THE SECTORS HOLD, AND ALL ATTENTION IS ON LEXCORP.
BUREAU OF LAND MANAGEMENT ACTIVITY IS STILL NIL.
HOW'S THE TEAM?
BLACKGATE HAS BEEN SECURED. PETTIT'S STRONG MEN ARE UNDER SURVEILLANCE--
YOU DO KNOW THE DIFFERENCE BETWEEN HOW SOMEONE IS AND WHAT THEY'RE DOING, RIGHT?
UM, CAN I HELP YOU?
WHERE'S JOKER?

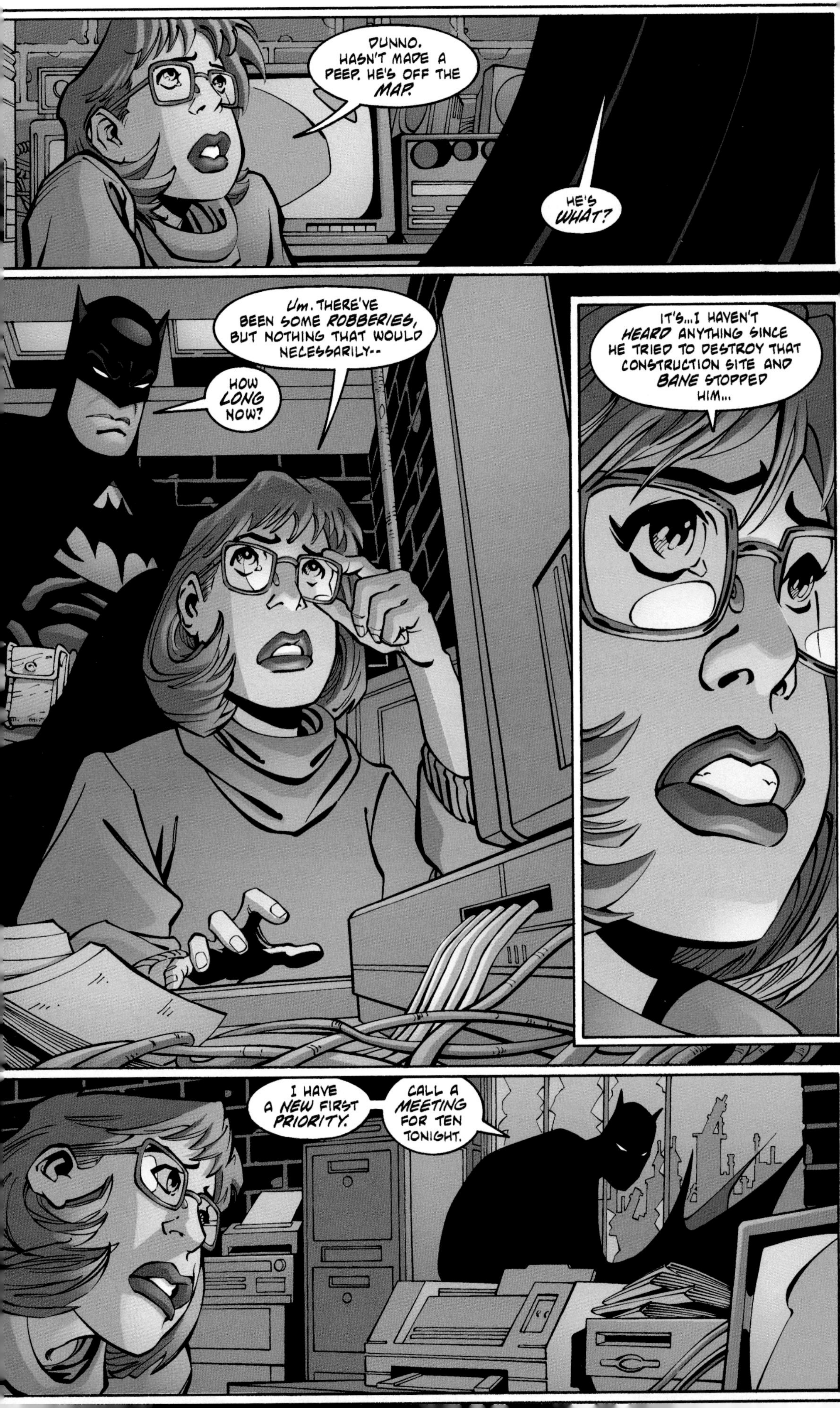
DUNNO. HASN'T MADE A PEEP. HE'S OFF THE *MAP.*
HE'S *WHAT?*
Um. THERE'VE BEEN SOME *ROBBERIES,* BUT NOTHING THAT WOULD NECESSARILY--
HOW *LONG* NOW?
IT'S...I HAVEN'T *HEARD* ANYTHING SINCE HE TRIED TO DESTROY THAT CONSTRUCTION SITE AND *BANE* STOPPED HIM...
I HAVE A *NEW FIRST PRIORITY.*
CALL A *MEETING* FOR TEN TONIGHT.

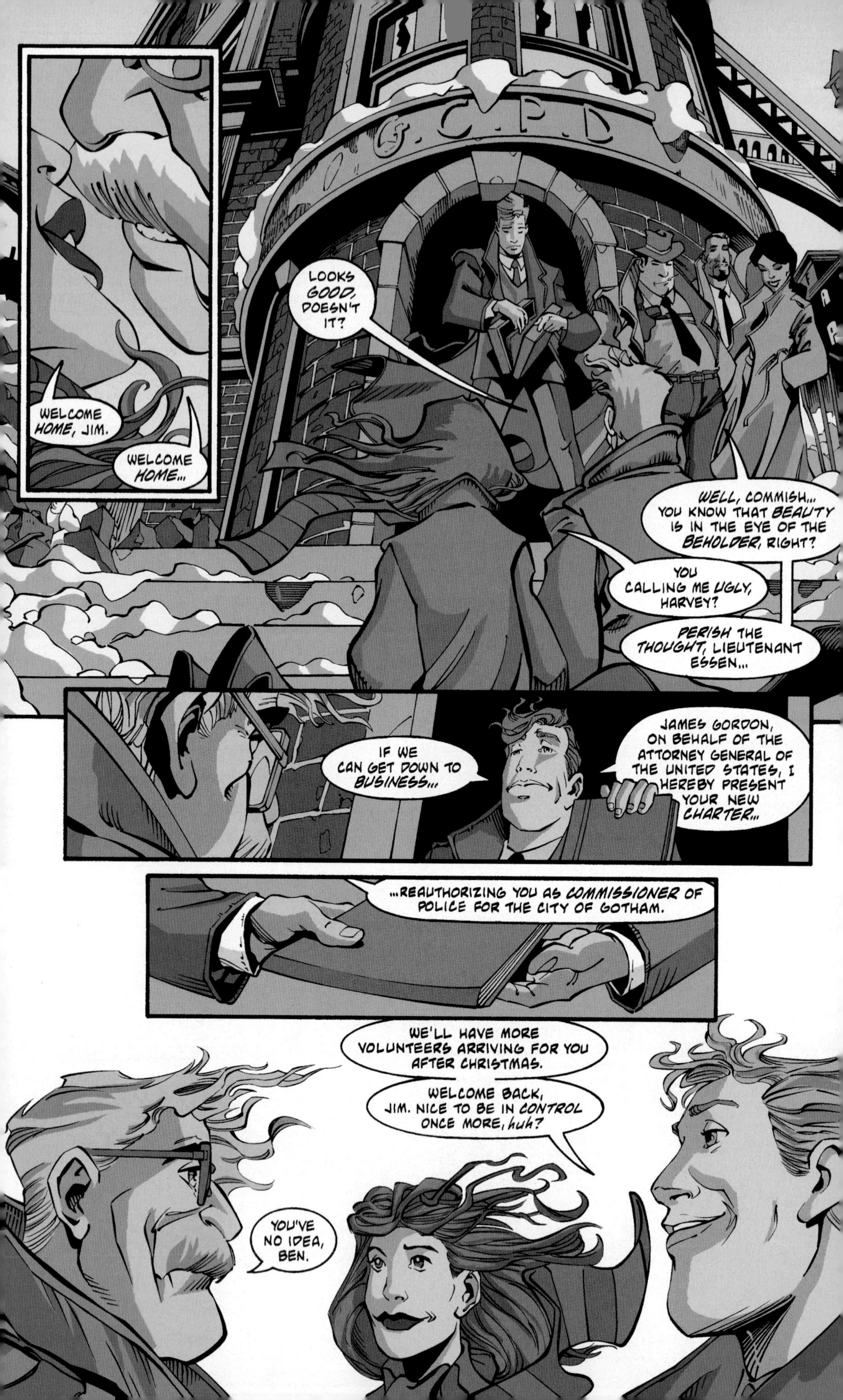
WELCOME HOME, JIM.
WELCOME HOME...
LOOKS GOOD, DOESN'T IT?
WELL, COMMISH... YOU KNOW THAT BEAUTY IS IN THE EYE OF THE BEHOLDER, RIGHT?
YOU CALLING ME UGLY, HARVEY?
PERISH THE THOUGHT, LIEUTENANT ESSEN...
G.C.P.D
IF WE CAN GET DOWN TO BUSINESS...
JAMES GORDON, ON BEHALF OF THE ATTORNEY GENERAL OF THE UNITED STATES, I HEREBY PRESENT YOUR NEW CHARTER...
...REAUTHORIZING YOU AS COMMISSIONER OF POLICE FOR THE CITY OF GOTHAM.
WE'LL HAVE MORE VOLUNTEERS ARRIVING FOR YOU AFTER CHRISTMAS.
WELCOME BACK, JIM. NICE TO BE IN CONTROL ONCE MORE, huh?
YOU'VE NO IDEA, BEN.

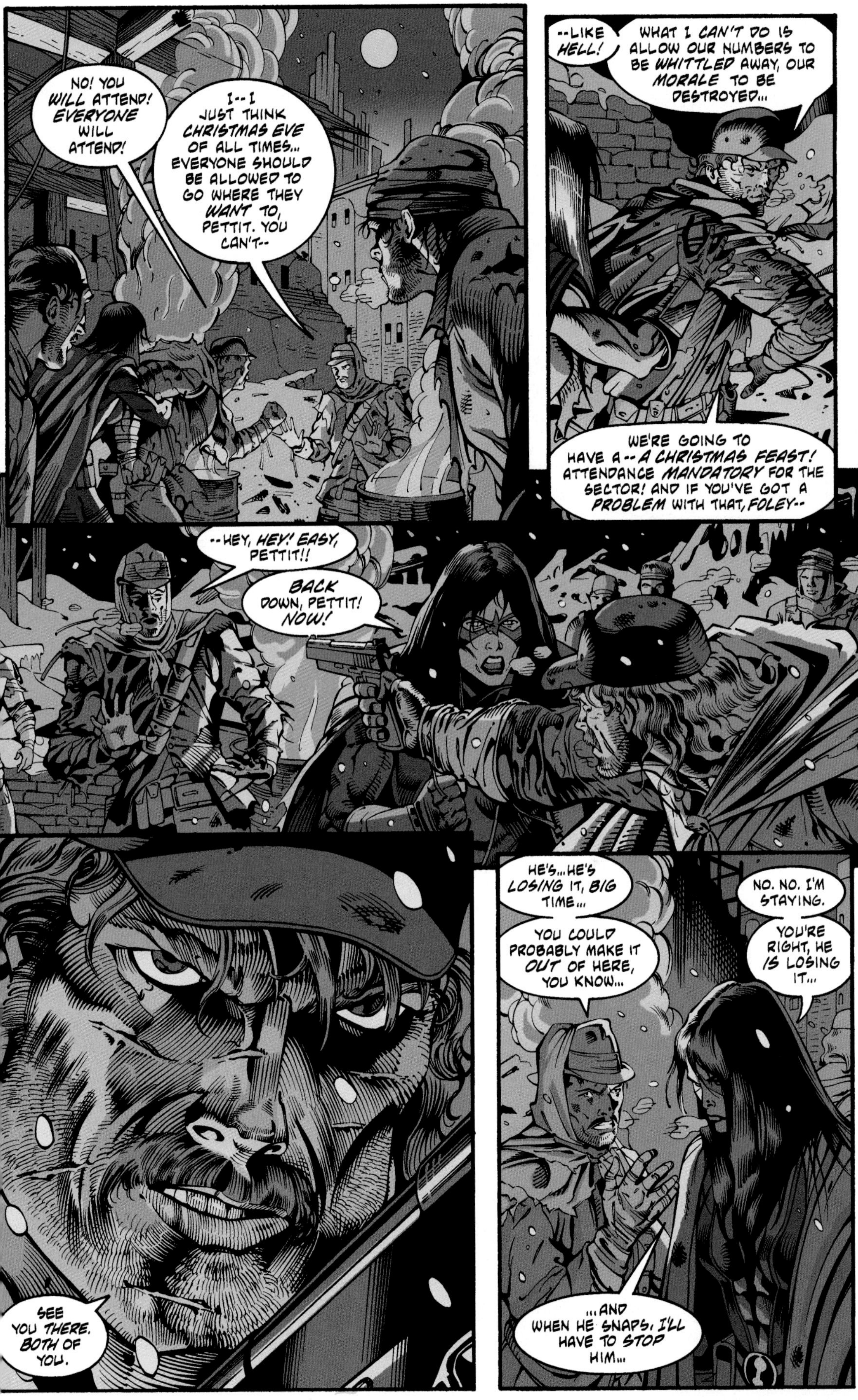
NO! YOU WILL ATTEND! EVERYONE WILL ATTEND!
I--I JUST THINK CHRISTMAS EVE OF ALL TIMES... EVERYONE SHOULD BE ALLOWED TO GO WHERE THEY WANT TO, PETTIT. YOU CAN'T--
--LIKE HELL!
WHAT I CAN'T DO IS ALLOW OUR NUMBERS TO BE WHITTLED AWAY, OUR MORALE TO BE DESTROYED...
WE'RE GOING TO HAVE A--A CHRISTMAS FEAST! ATTENDANCE MANDATORY FOR THE SECTOR! AND IF YOU'VE GOT A PROBLEM WITH THAT, FOLEY--
--HEY, HEY! EASY, PETTIT!!
BACK DOWN, PETTIT! NOW!
SEE YOU THERE. BOTH OF YOU.
HE'S...HE'S LOSING IT, BIG TIME...
YOU COULD PROBABLY MAKE IT OUT OF HERE, YOU KNOW...
NO. NO. I'M STAYING.
YOU'RE RIGHT, HE IS LOSING IT...
...AND WHEN HE SNAPS, I'LL HAVE TO STOP HIM...

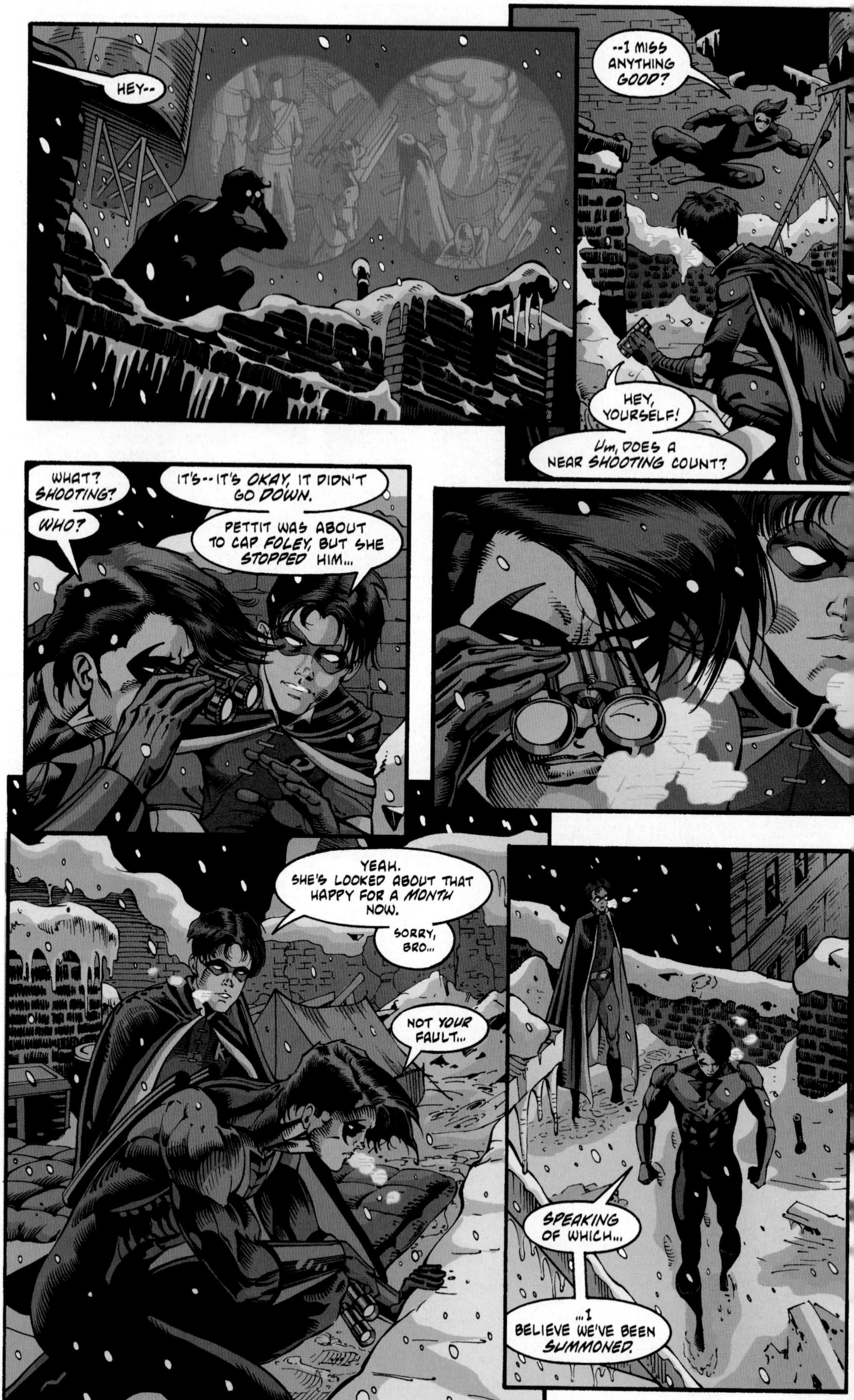
HEY--
--I MISS ANYTHING GOOD?
HEY, YOURSELF!
Um, DOES A NEAR SHOOTING COUNT?
WHAT? SHOOTING?
WHO?
IT'S--IT'S OKAY, IT DIDN'T GO DOWN.
PETTIT WAS ABOUT TO CAP FOLEY, BUT SHE STOPPED HIM...
YEAH. SHE'S LOOKED ABOUT THAT HAPPY FOR A MONTH NOW.
SORRY, BRO...
NOT YOUR FAULT...
SPEAKING OF WHICH...
...I BELIEVE WE'VE BEEN SUMMONED.

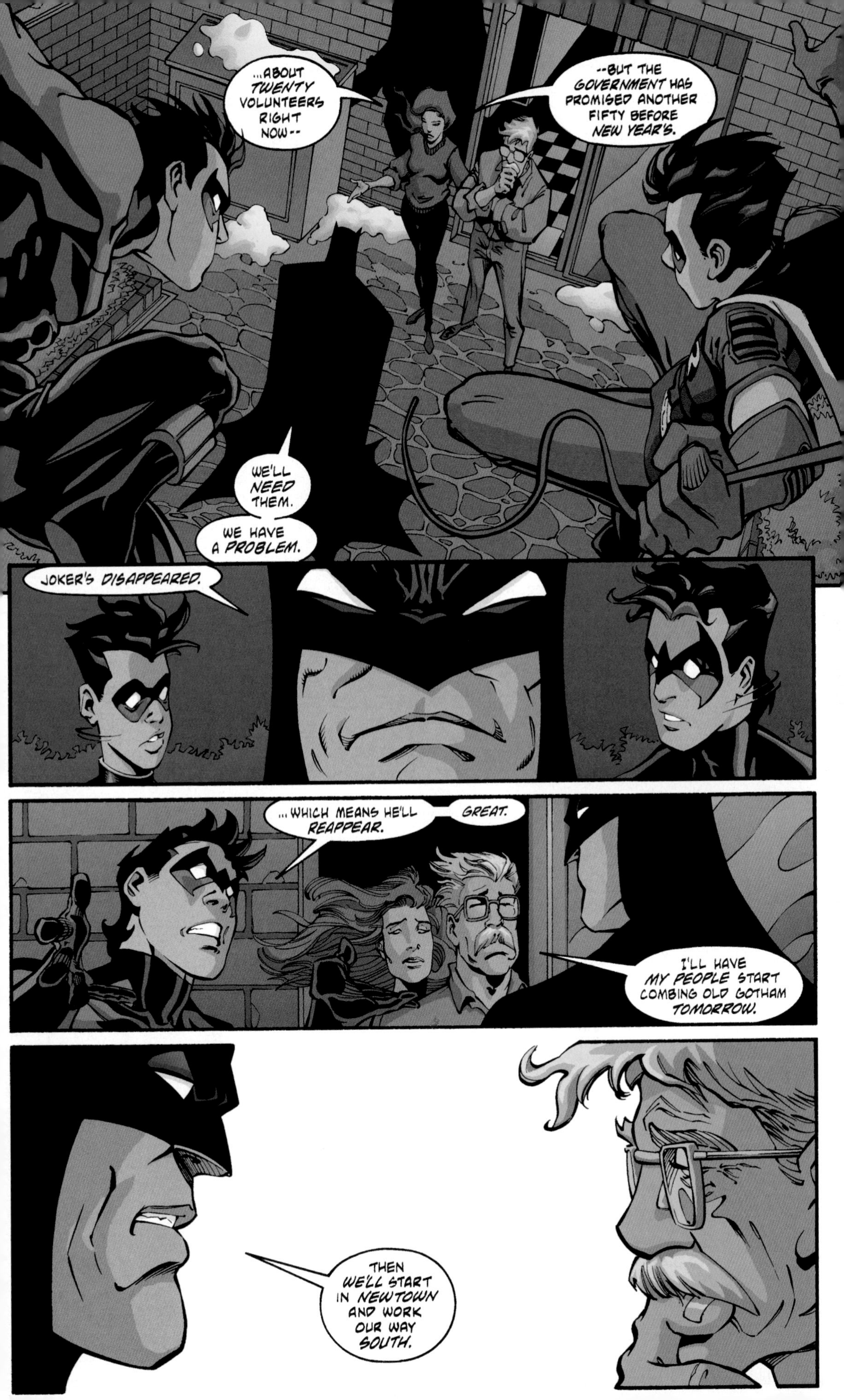
...ABOUT TWENTY VOLUNTEERS RIGHT NOW--
--BUT THE GOVERNMENT HAS PROMISED ANOTHER FIFTY BEFORE NEW YEAR'S.
WE'LL NEED THEM.
WE HAVE A PROBLEM.
JOKER'S DISAPPEARED.
...WHICH MEANS HE'LL REAPPEAR.
GREAT.
I'LL HAVE MY PEOPLE START COMBING OLD GOTHAM TOMORROW.
THEN WE'LL START IN NEWTOWN AND WORK OUR WAY SOUTH.

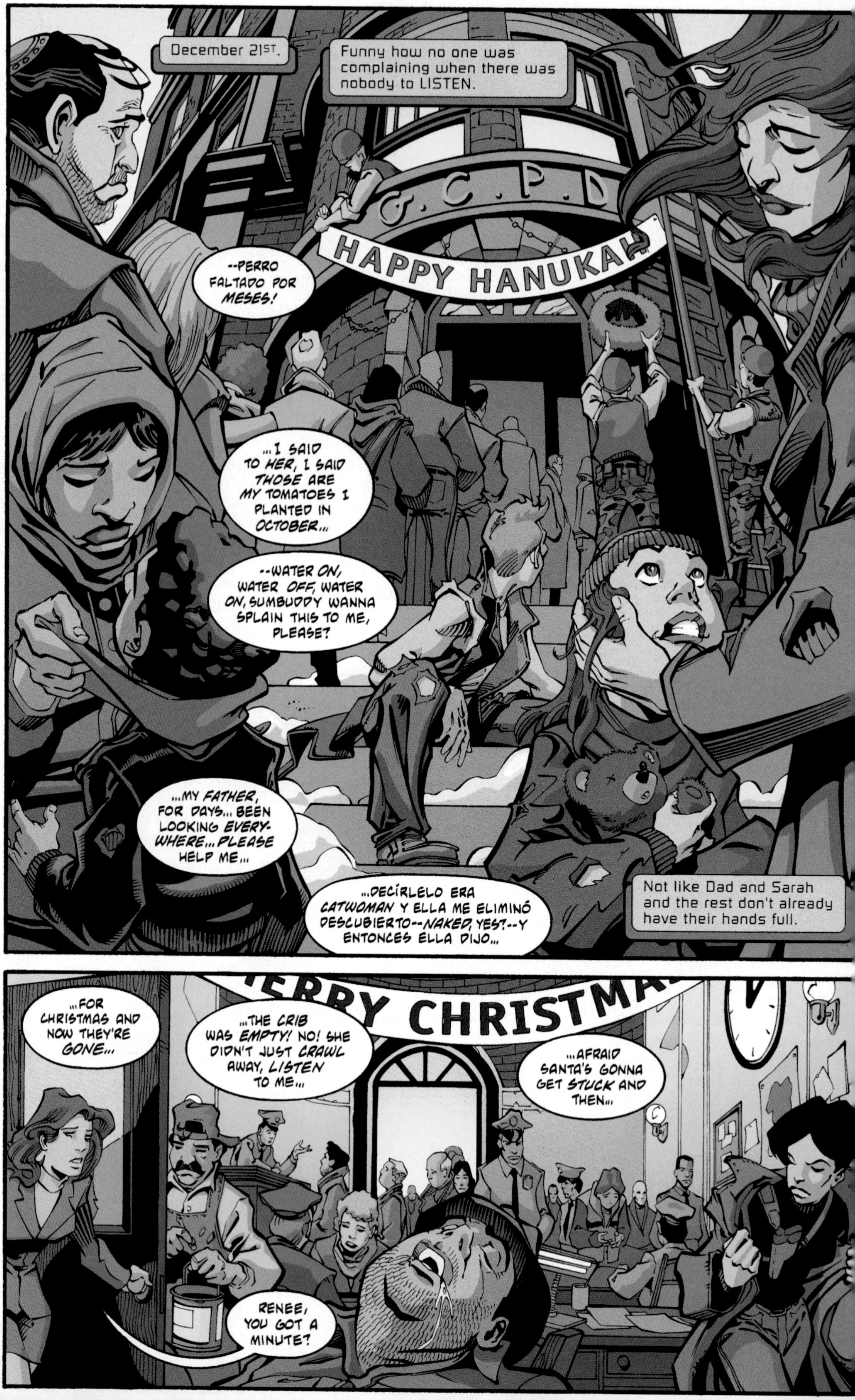

December 21ST.
Funny how no one was complaining when there was nobody to LISTEN.
G.C.P.D
HAPPY HANUKAH
--PERRO FALTADO POR MESES!
...I SAID TO HER, I SAID THOSE ARE MY TOMATOES I PLANTED IN OCTOBER...
--WATER ON, WATER OFF, WATER ON, SUMBUDDY WANNA SPLAIN THIS TO ME, PLEASE?
...MY FATHER, FOR DAYS... BEEN LOOKING EVERY-WHERE... PLEASE HELP ME...
...DECÍRLELO ERA CATWOMAN Y ELLA ME ELIMINÓ DESCUBIERTO--NAKED, YES?--Y ENTONCES ELLA DIJO...
Not like Dad and Sarah and the rest don't already have their hands full.
ERRY CHRISTMA
...FOR CHRISTMAS AND NOW THEY'RE GONE...
...THE CRIB WAS EMPTY! NO! SHE DIDN'T JUST CRAWL AWAY, LISTEN TO ME...
...AFRAID SANTA'S GONNA GET STUCK AND THEN...
RENEE, YOU GOT A MINUTE?

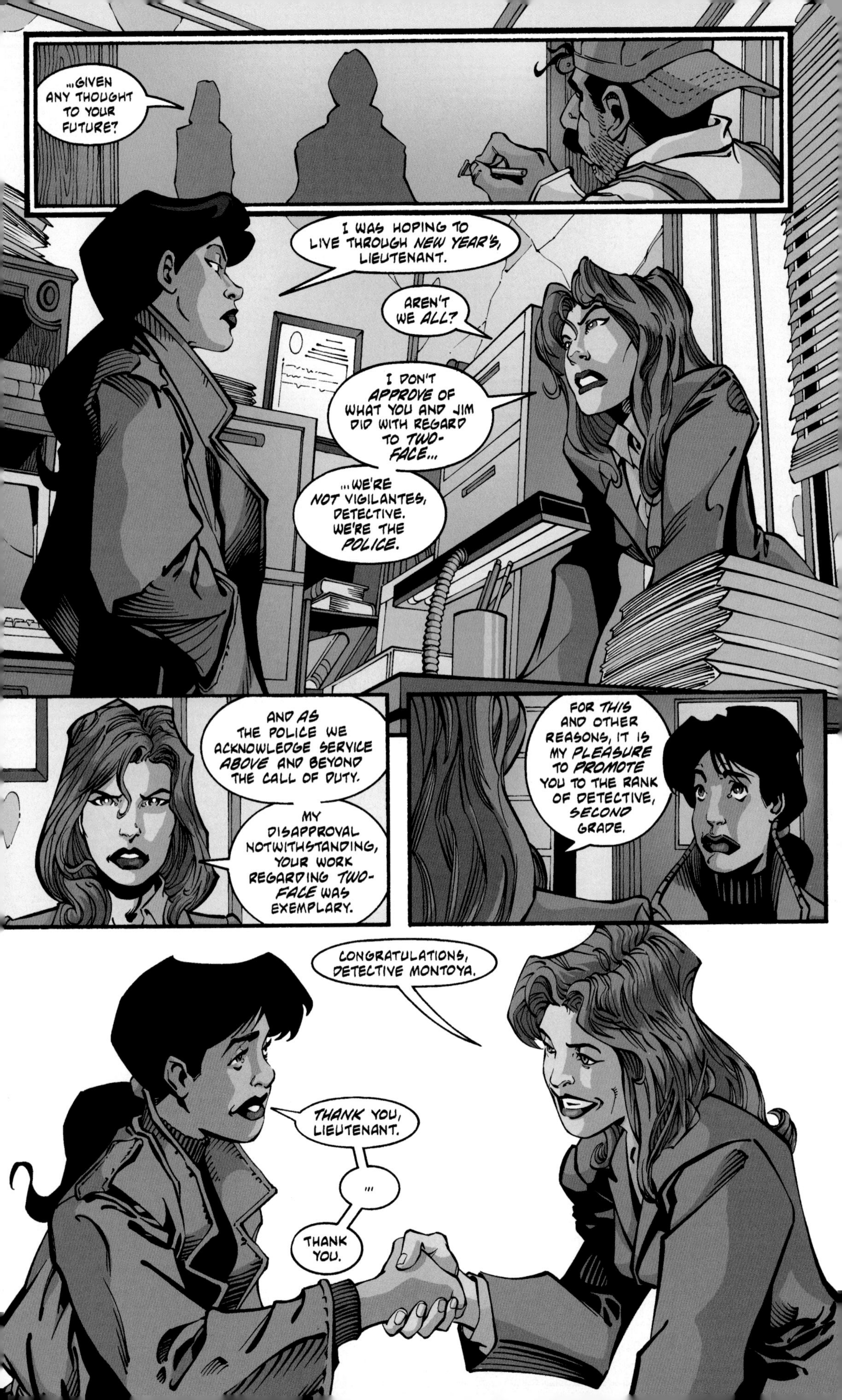
...GIVEN ANY THOUGHT TO YOUR FUTURE?
I WAS HOPING TO LIVE THROUGH NEW YEAR'S, LIEUTENANT.
AREN'T WE ALL?
I DON'T APPROVE OF WHAT YOU AND JIM DID WITH REGARD TO TWO-FACE...
...WE'RE NOT VIGILANTES, DETECTIVE. WE'RE THE POLICE.
AND AS THE POLICE WE ACKNOWLEDGE SERVICE ABOVE AND BEYOND THE CALL OF DUTY.
MY DISAPPROVAL NOTWITHSTANDING, YOUR WORK REGARDING TWO-FACE WAS EXEMPLARY.
FOR THIS AND OTHER REASONS, IT IS MY PLEASURE TO PROMOTE YOU TO THE RANK OF DETECTIVE, SECOND GRADE.
CONGRATULATIONS, DETECTIVE MONTOYA.
THANK YOU, LIEUTENANT.
...
THANK YOU.

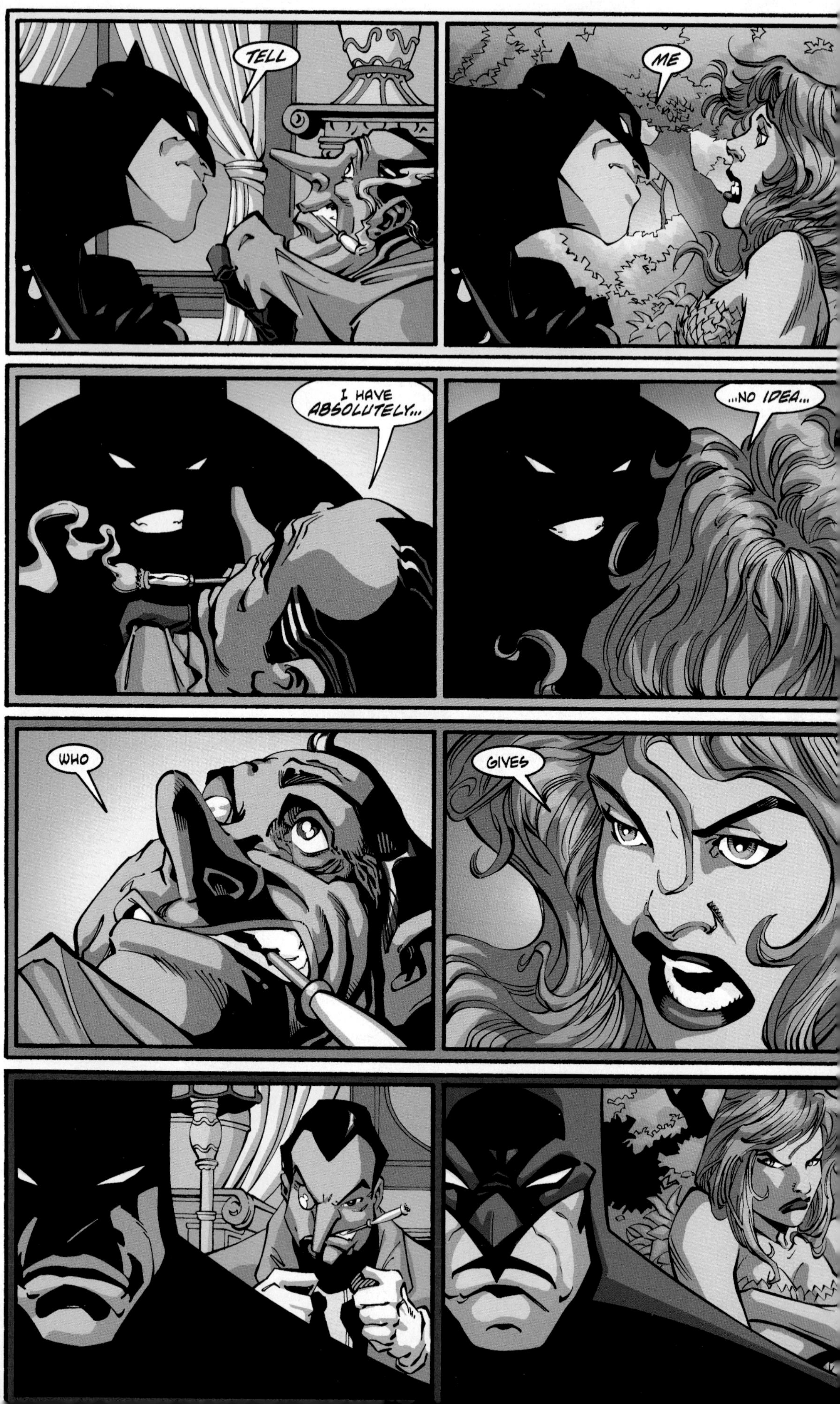
TELL
ME
I HAVE ABSOLUTELY...
...NO IDEA...
WHO
GIVES

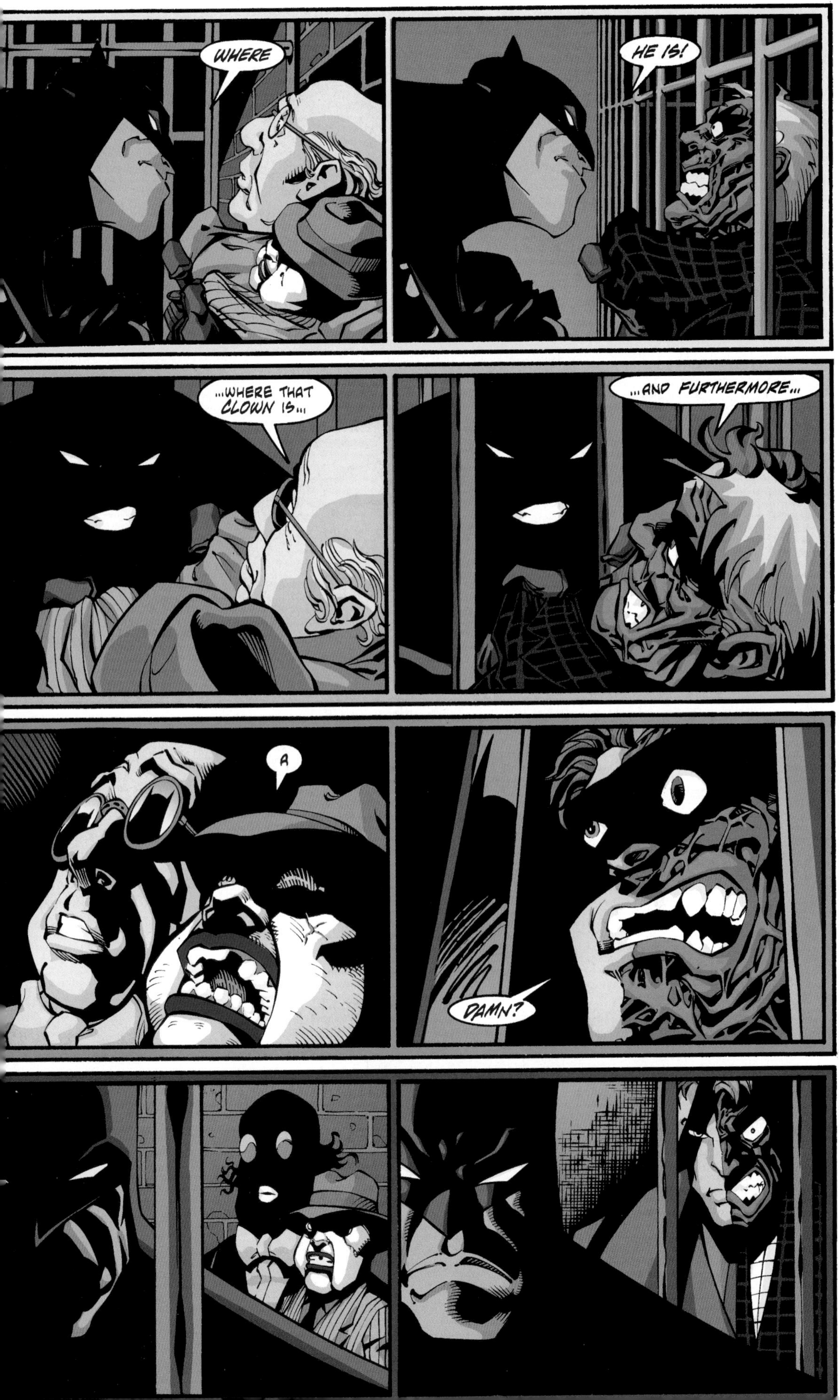
WHERE
HE IS!
...WHERE THAT CLOWN IS...
...AND FURTHERMORE...
A
DAMN?

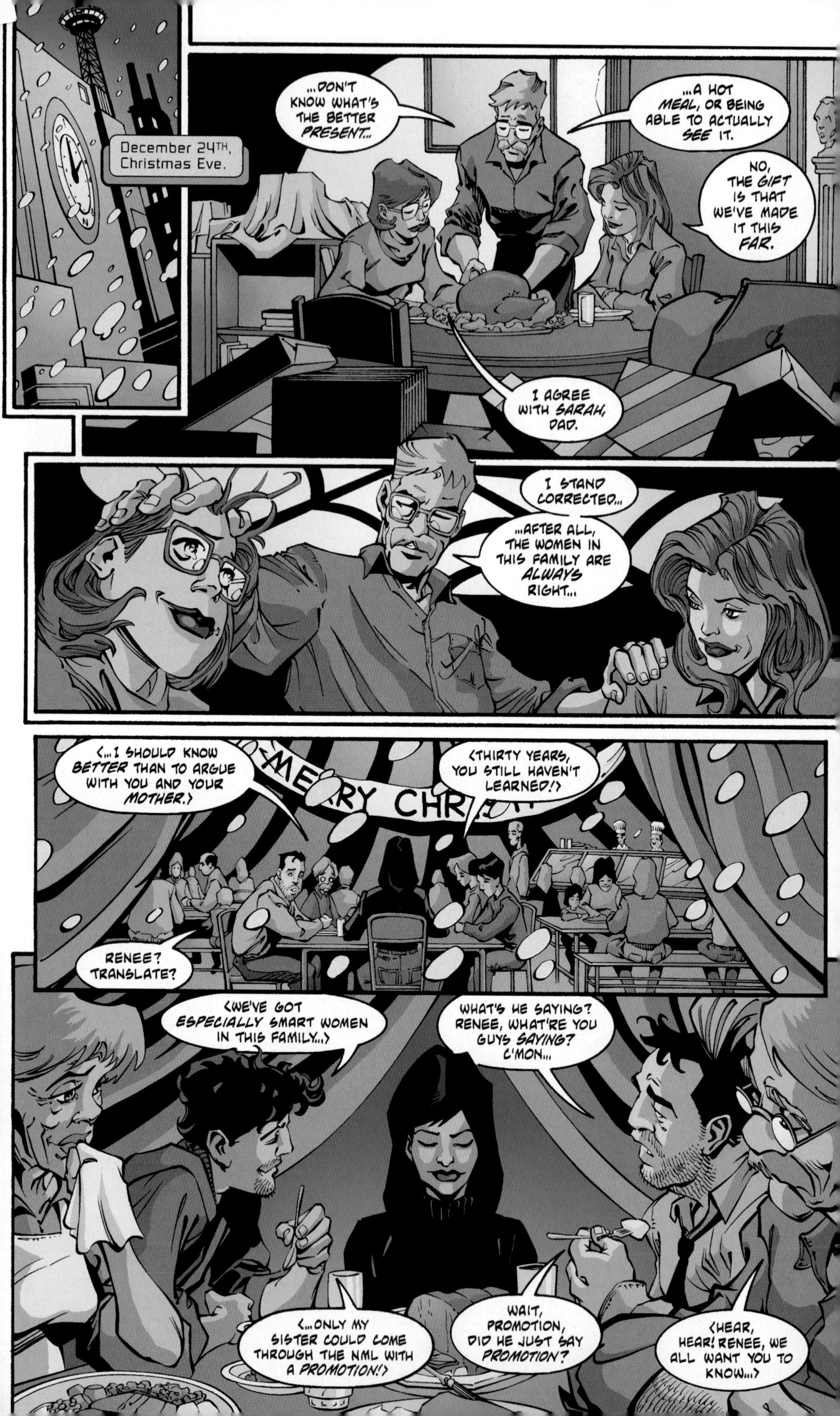
December 24TH, Christmas Eve.
...DON'T KNOW WHAT'S THE BETTER PRESENT...
...A HOT MEAL, OR BEING ABLE TO ACTUALLY SEE IT.
NO, THE GIFT IS THAT WE'VE MADE IT THIS FAR.
I AGREE WITH SARAH, DAD.
I STAND CORRECTED...
...AFTER ALL, THE WOMEN IN THIS FAMILY ARE ALWAYS RIGHT...
MERRY CHR
<...I SHOULD KNOW BETTER THAN TO ARGUE WITH YOU AND YOUR MOTHER.>
<THIRTY YEARS, YOU STILL HAVEN'T LEARNED!>
RENEE? TRANSLATE?
<WE'VE GOT ESPECIALLY SMART WOMEN IN THIS FAMILY...>
WHAT'S HE SAYING? RENEE, WHAT'RE YOU GUYS SAYING? C'MON...
<...ONLY MY SISTER COULD COME THROUGH THE NML WITH A PROMOTION!>
WAIT, PROMOTION, DID HE JUST SAY PROMOTION?
<HEAR, HEAR! RENEE, WE ALL WANT YOU TO KNOW...>

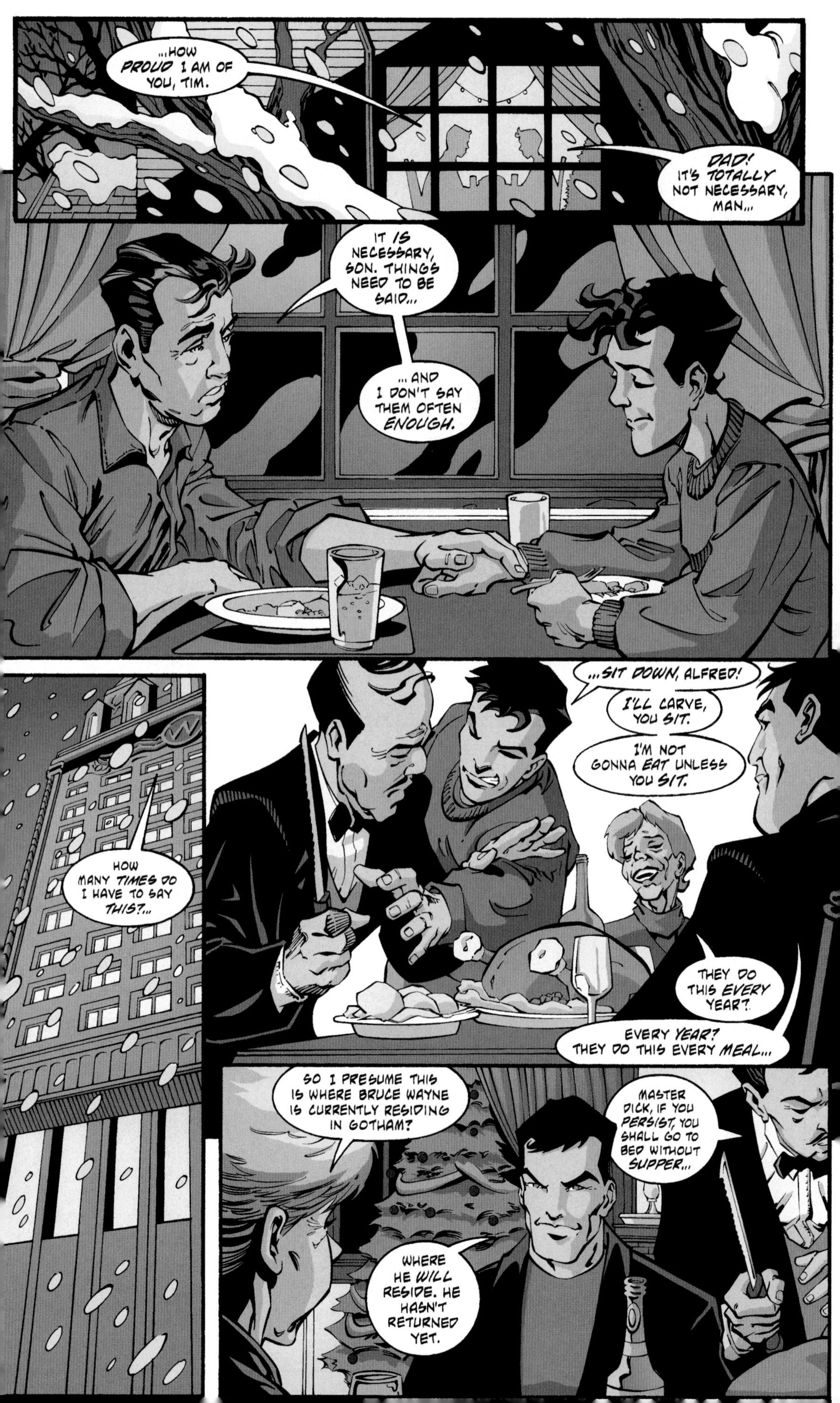
...HOW PROUD I AM OF YOU, TIM.
DAD! IT'S TOTALLY NOT NECESSARY, MAN...
IT IS NECESSARY, SON. THINGS NEED TO BE SAID...
... AND I DON'T SAY THEM OFTEN ENOUGH.
HOW MANY TIMES DO I HAVE TO SAY THIS?...
...SIT DOWN, ALFRED!
I'LL CARVE, YOU SIT.
I'M NOT GONNA EAT UNLESS YOU SIT.
THEY DO THIS EVERY YEAR?
EVERY YEAR? THEY DO THIS EVERY MEAL...
SO I PRESUME THIS IS WHERE BRUCE WAYNE IS CURRENTLY RESIDING IN GOTHAM?
MASTER DICK, IF YOU PERSIST, YOU SHALL GO TO BED WITHOUT SUPPER...
WHERE HE WILL RESIDE. HE HASN'T RETURNED YET.

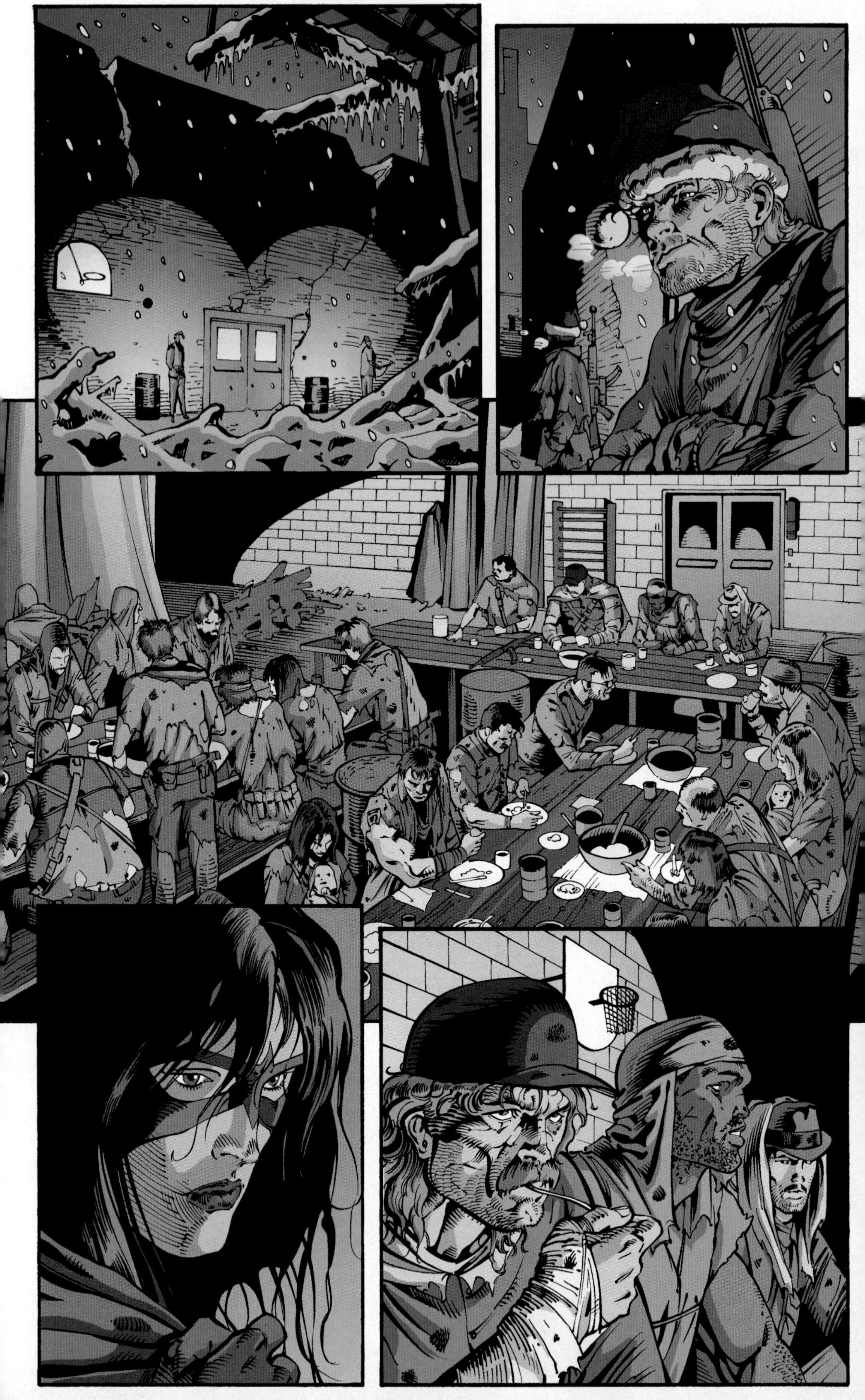

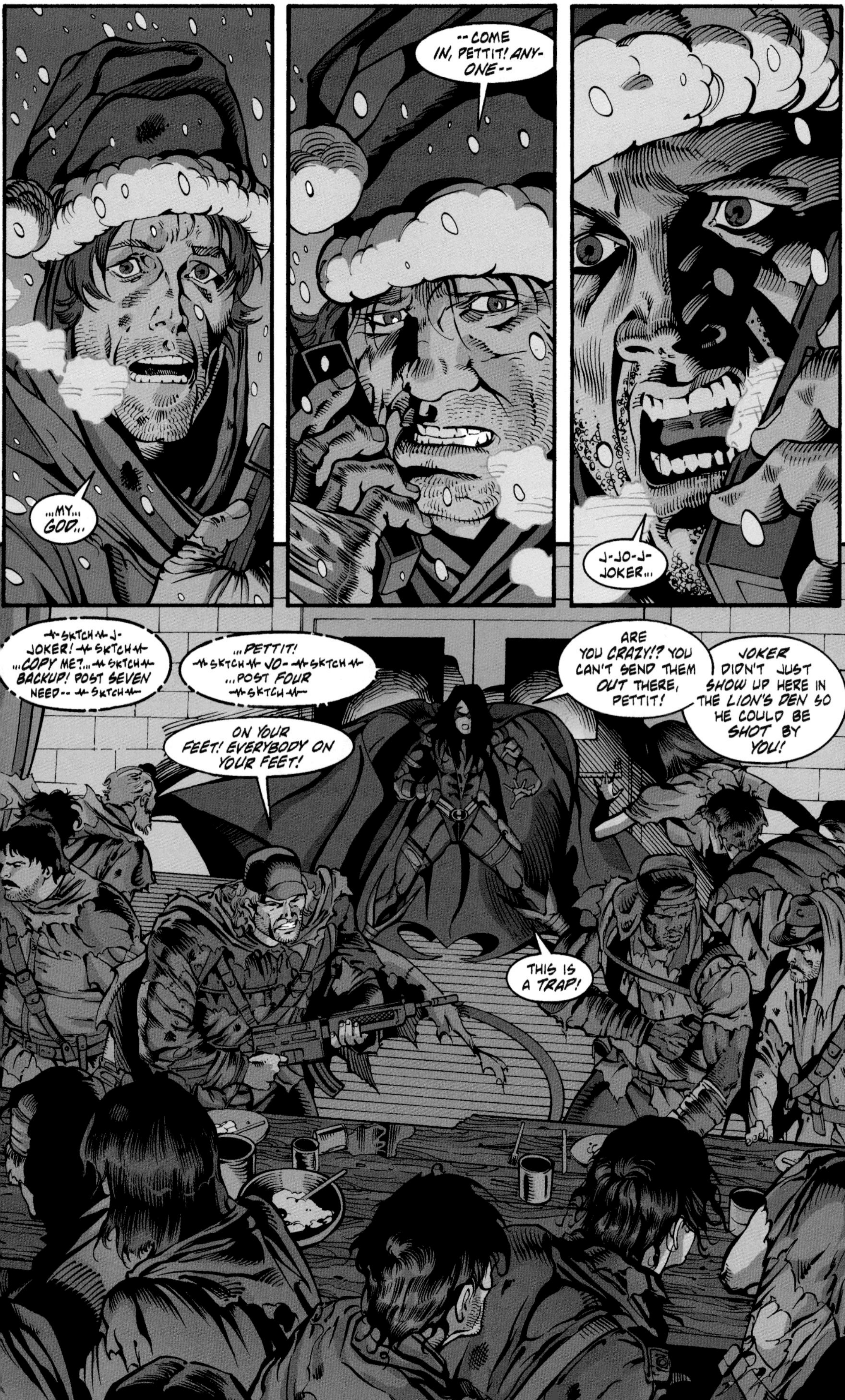
...MY... GOD...
--COME IN, PETTIT! ANY-ONE--
J-JO-J-JOKER...
SKTCH J-JOKER! SKTCH ...COPY ME?... SKTCH BACKUP! POST SEVEN NEED-- SKTCH
...PETTIT! SKTCH JO- SKTCH ...POST FOUR SKTCH
ON YOUR FEET! EVERYBODY ON YOUR FEET!
ARE YOU CRAZY!? YOU CAN'T SEND THEM OUT THERE, PETTIT!
JOKER DIDN'T JUST SHOW UP HERE IN THE LION'S DEN SO HE COULD BE SHOT BY YOU!
THIS IS A TRAP!

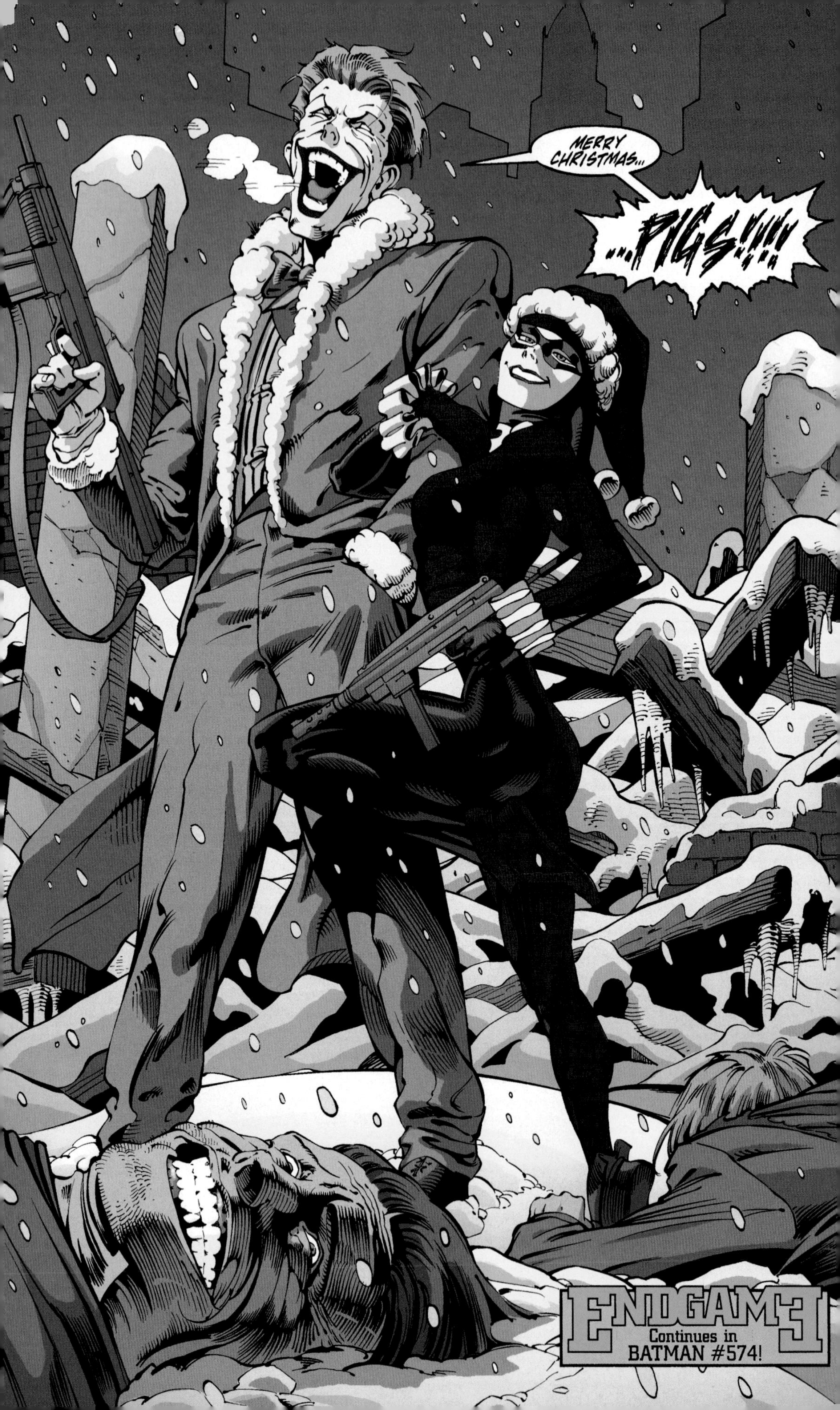
MERRY CHRISTMAS...
...PIGS!!!!
ENDGAME
Continues in BATMAN #574!

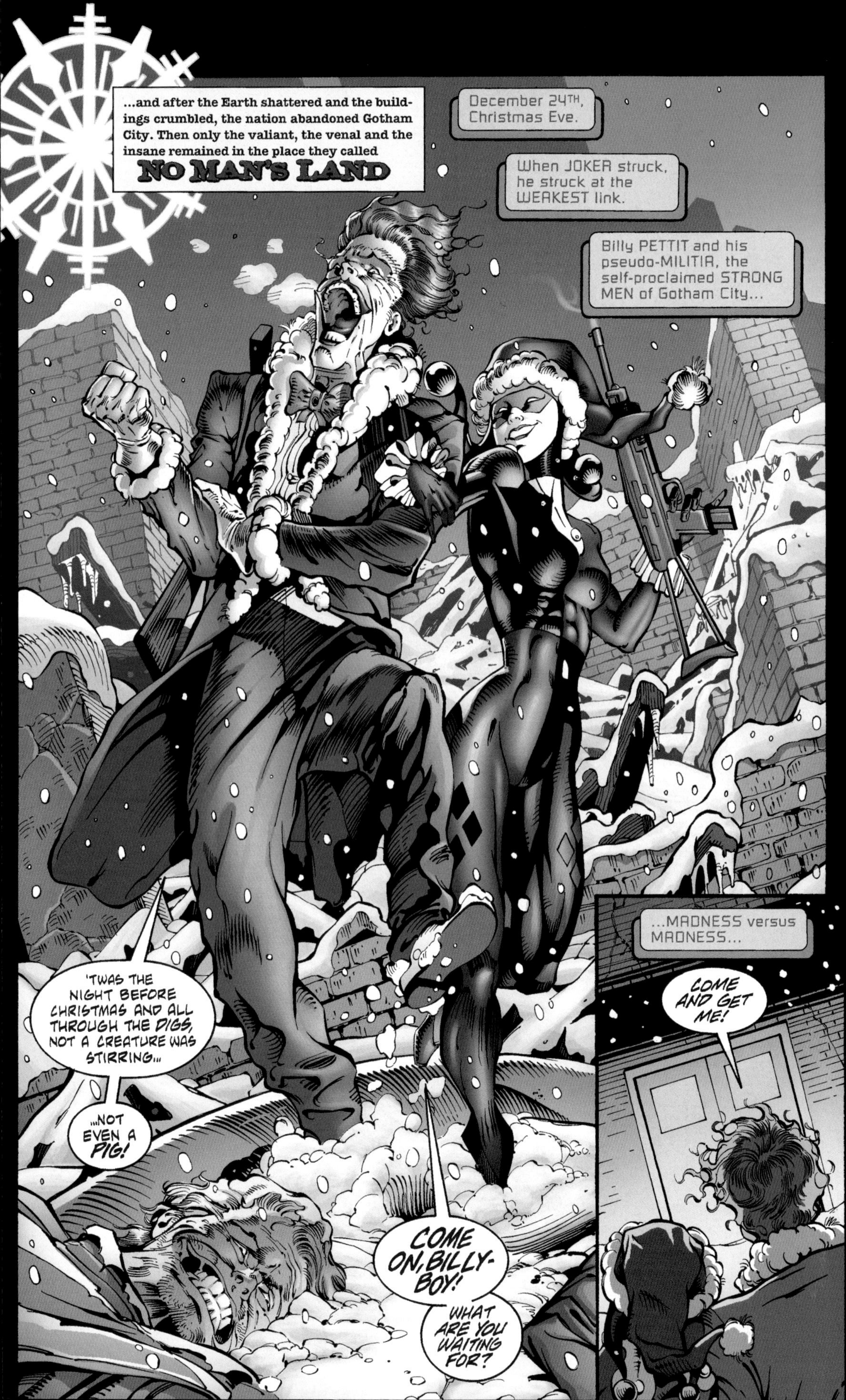
...and after the Earth shattered and the buildings crumbled, the nation abandoned Gotham City. Then only the valiant, the venal and the insane remained in the place they called
NO MAN'S LAND
December 24TH, Christmas Eve.
When JOKER struck, he struck at the WEAKEST link.
Billy PETTIT and his pseudo-MILITIA, the self-proclaimed STRONG MEN of Gotham City...
...MADNESS versus MADNESS...
'TWAS THE NIGHT BEFORE CHRISTMAS AND ALL THROUGH THE DIGS, NOT A CREATURE WAS STIRRING...
...NOT EVEN A PIG!
COME ON, BILLY-BOY!
WHAT ARE YOU WAITING FOR?
COME AND GET ME!

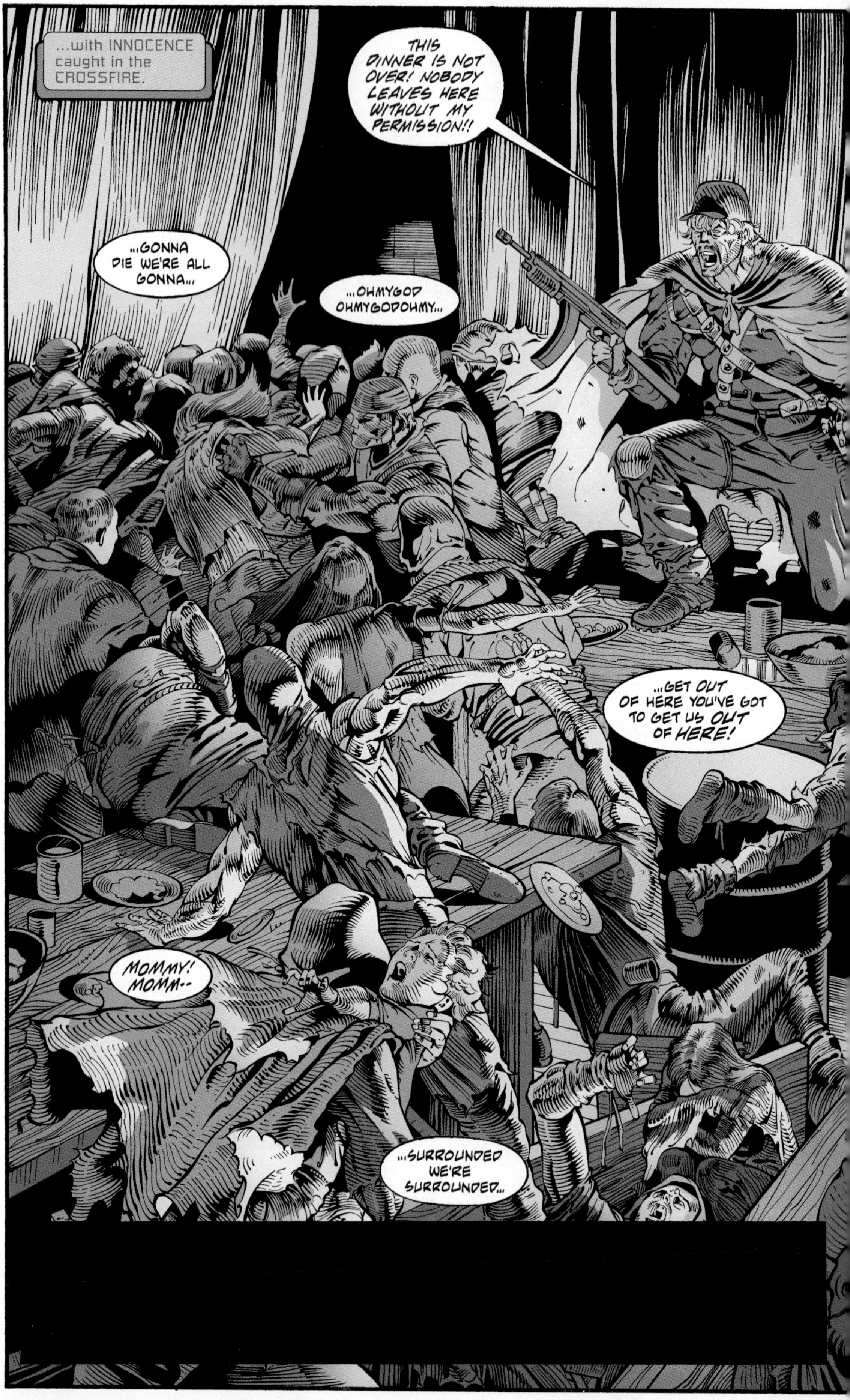
...with INNOCENCE caught in the CROSSFIRE.
THIS DINNER IS NOT OVER! NOBODY LEAVES HERE WITHOUT MY PERMISSION!!
...GONNA DIE WE'RE ALL GONNA...
...OHMYGOD OHMYGODOHMY...
...GET OUT OF HERE YOU'VE GOT TO GET US OUT OF HERE!
MOMMY! MOMM--
...SURROUNDED WE'RE SURROUNDED...
[redacted]

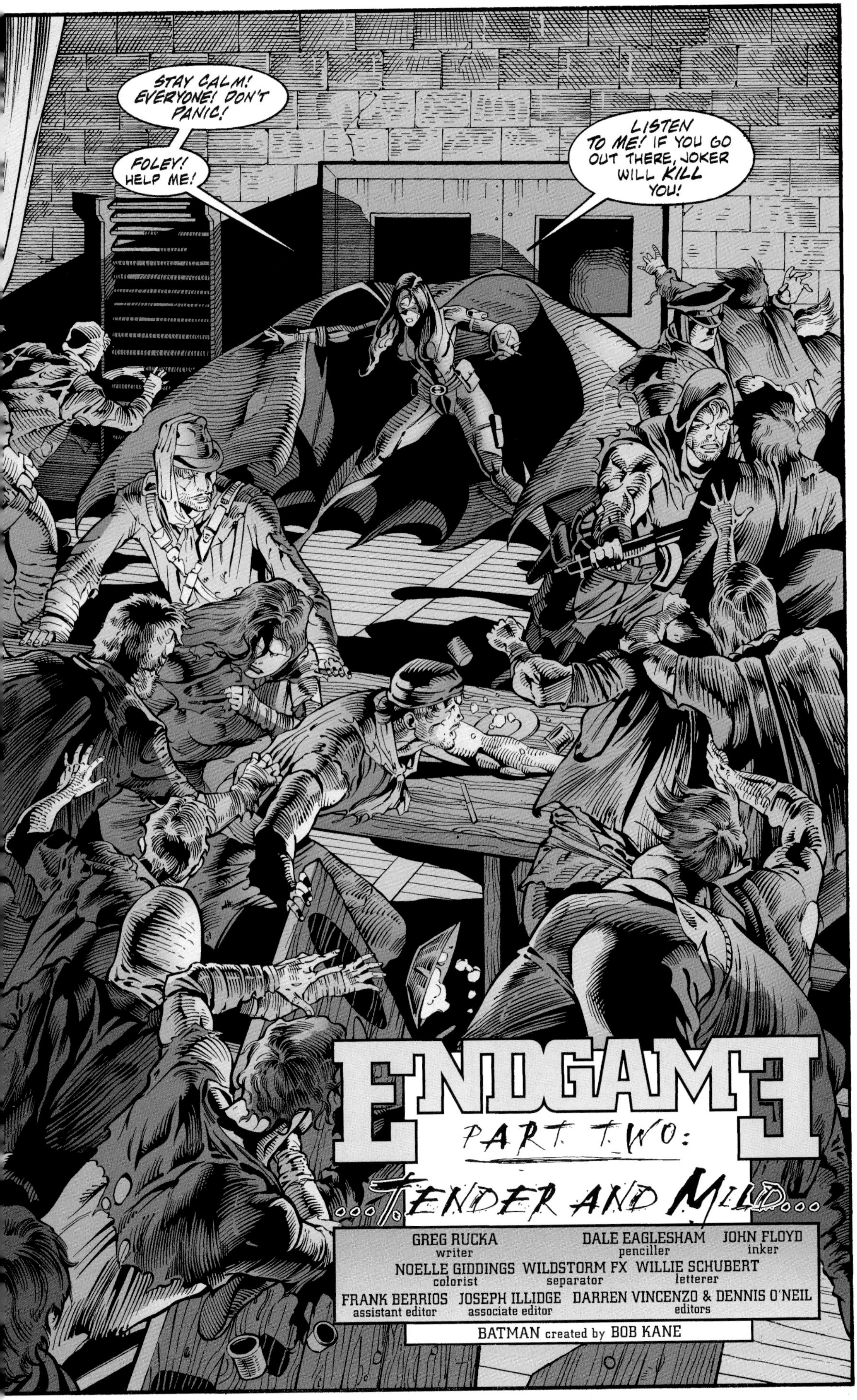
STAY CALM! EVERYONE! DON'T PANIC!
FOLEY! HELP ME!
LISTEN TO ME! IF YOU GO OUT THERE, JOKER WILL KILL YOU!
ENDGAME
PART TWO:
...TENDER AND MILD...
GREG RUCKA writer
DALE EAGLESHAM penciller
JOHN FLOYD inker
NOELLE GIDDINGS colorist
WILDSTORM FX separator
WILLIE SCHUBERT letterer
FRANK BERRIOS assistant editor
JOSEPH ILLIDGE associate editor
DARREN VINCENZO & DENNIS O'NEIL editors
BATMAN created by BOB KANE

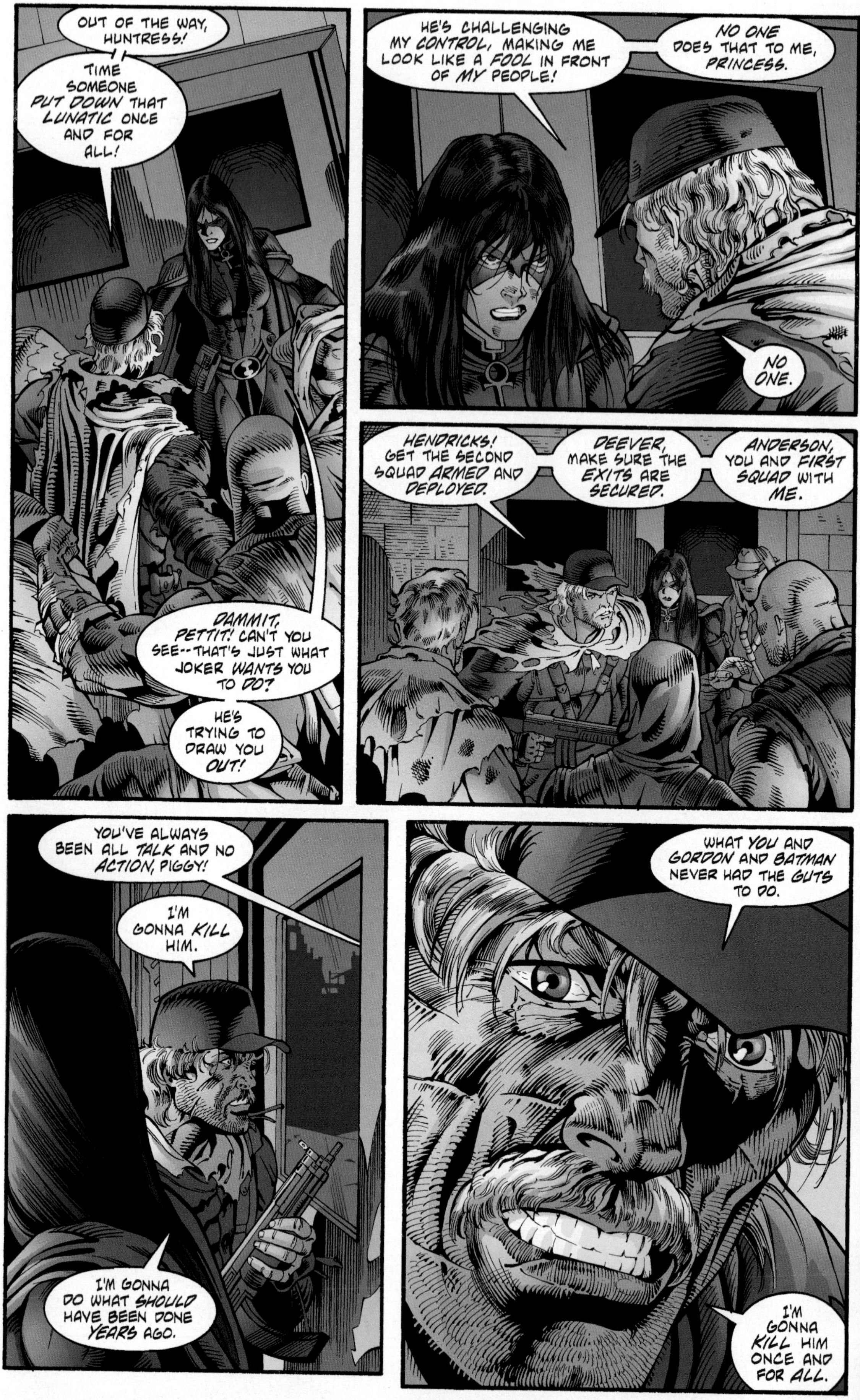

OUT OF THE WAY, HUNTRESS!
TIME SOMEONE PUT DOWN THAT LUNATIC ONCE AND FOR ALL!
DAMMIT, PETTIT! CAN'T YOU SEE--THAT'S JUST WHAT JOKER WANTS YOU TO DO?
HE'S TRYING TO DRAW YOU OUT!
HE'S CHALLENGING MY CONTROL, MAKING ME LOOK LIKE A FOOL IN FRONT OF MY PEOPLE!
NO ONE DOES THAT TO ME, PRINCESS.
NO ONE.
HENDRICKS! GET THE SECOND SQUAD ARMED AND DEPLOYED.
DEEVER, MAKE SURE THE EXITS ARE SECURED.
ANDERSON, YOU AND FIRST SQUAD WITH ME.
YOU'VE ALWAYS BEEN ALL TALK AND NO ACTION, PIGGY!
I'M GONNA KILL HIM.
I'M GONNA DO WHAT SHOULD HAVE BEEN DONE YEARS AGO.
WHAT YOU AND GORDON AND BATMAN NEVER HAD THE GUTS TO DO.
I'M GONNA KILL HIM ONCE AND FOR ALL.

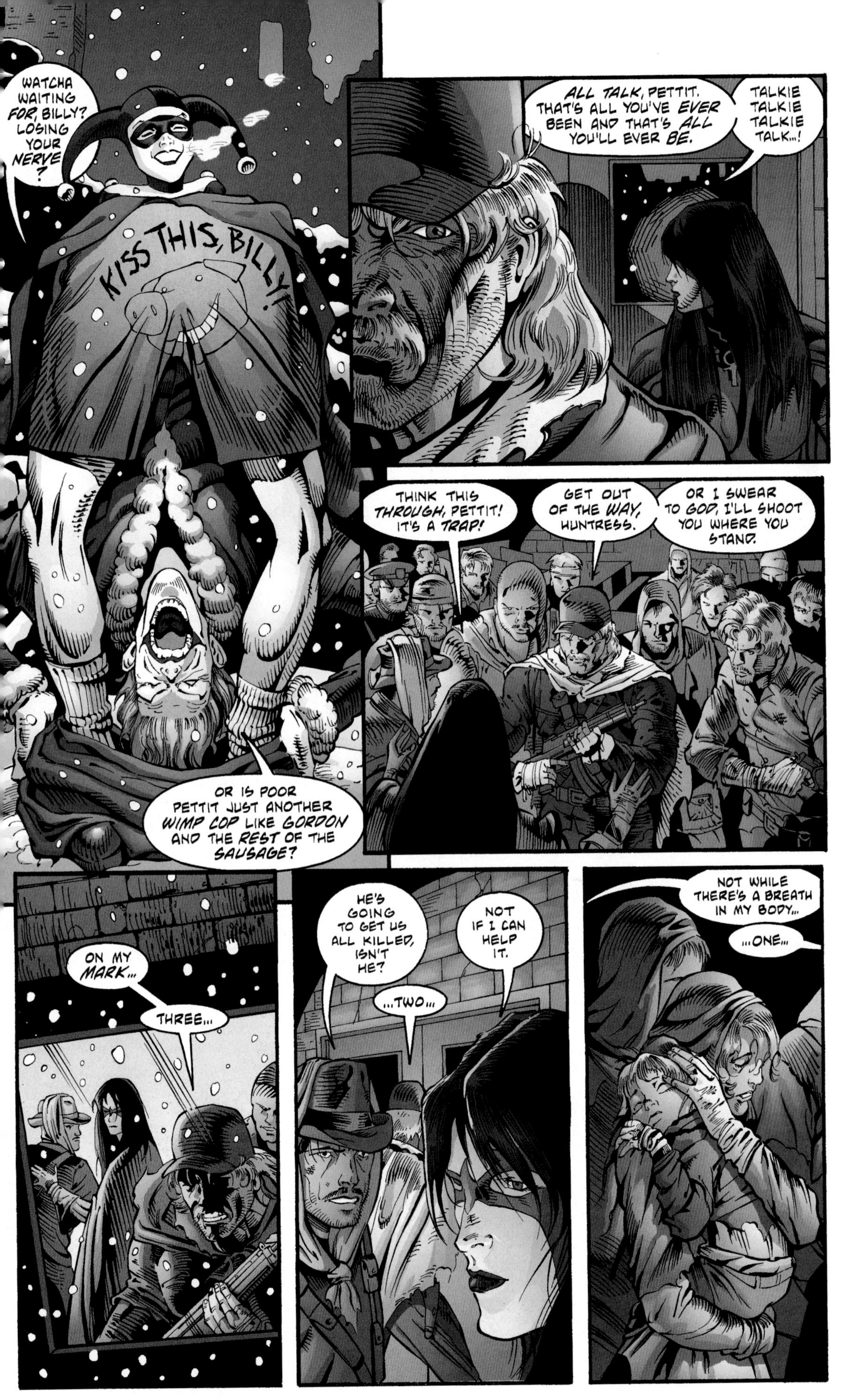
WATCHA WAITING FOR, BILLY? LOSING YOUR NERVE?
KISS THIS, BILLY!
ALL TALK, PETTIT. THAT'S ALL YOU'VE EVER BEEN AND THAT'S ALL YOU'LL EVER BE.
TALKIE TALKIE TALKIE TALK...!
OR IS POOR PETTIT JUST ANOTHER WIMP COP LIKE GORDON AND THE REST OF THE SAUSAGE?
THINK THIS THROUGH, PETTIT! IT'S A TRAP!
GET OUT OF THE WAY, HUNTRESS.
OR I SWEAR TO GOD, I'LL SHOOT YOU WHERE YOU STAND.
ON MY MARK...
THREE...
HE'S GOING TO GET US ALL KILLED, ISN'T HE?
NOT IF I CAN HELP IT.
...TWO...
NOT WHILE THERE'S A BREATH IN MY BODY...
...ONE...

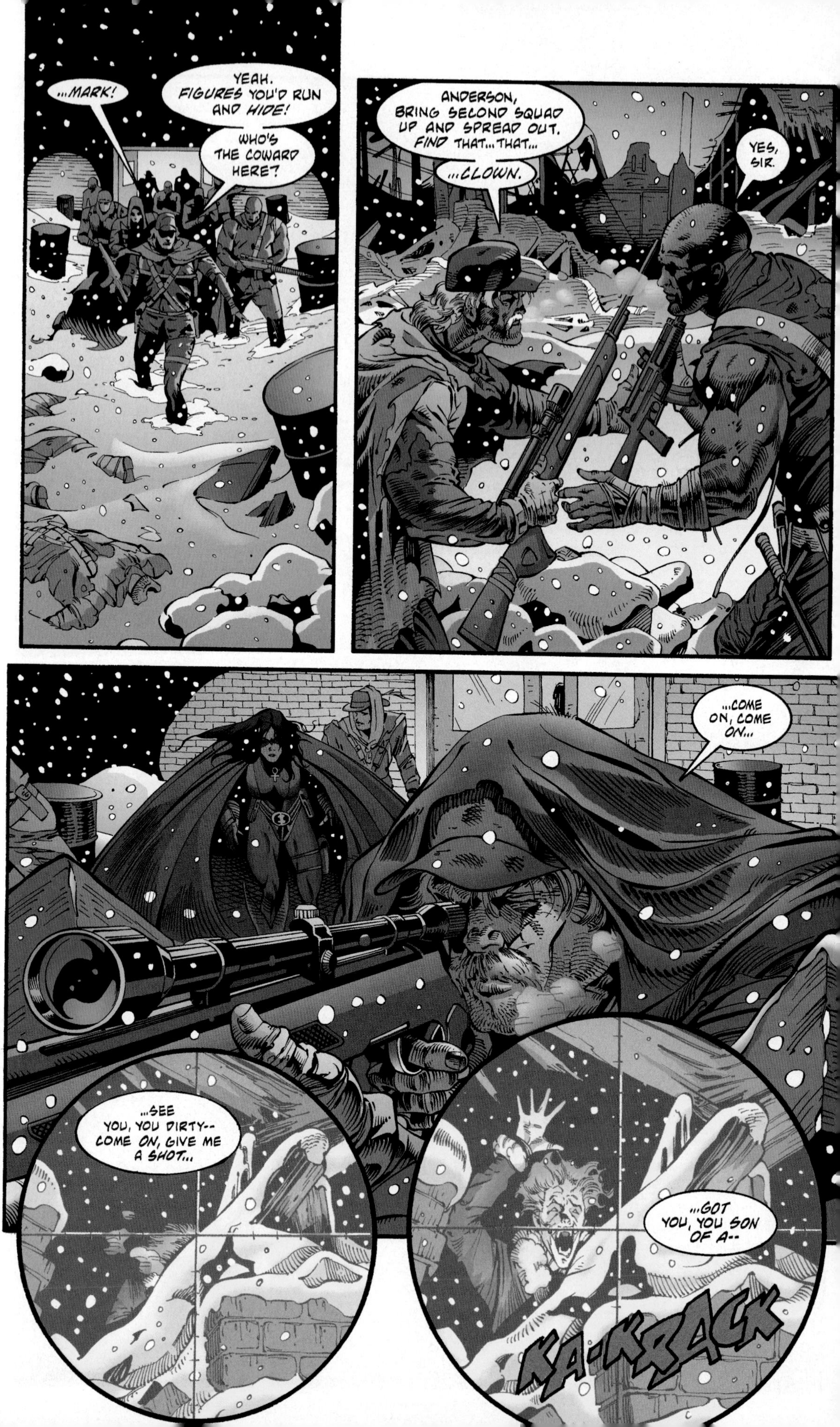
...MARK!
YEAH. FIGURES YOU'D RUN AND HIDE!
WHO'S THE COWARD HERE?
ANDERSON, BRING SECOND SQUAD UP AND SPREAD OUT. FIND THAT...THAT...
...CLOWN.
YES, SIR.
...COME ON, COME ON...
...SEE YOU, YOU DIRTY-- COME ON, GIVE ME A SHOT...
...GOT YOU, YOU SON OF A--
KA-KRACK

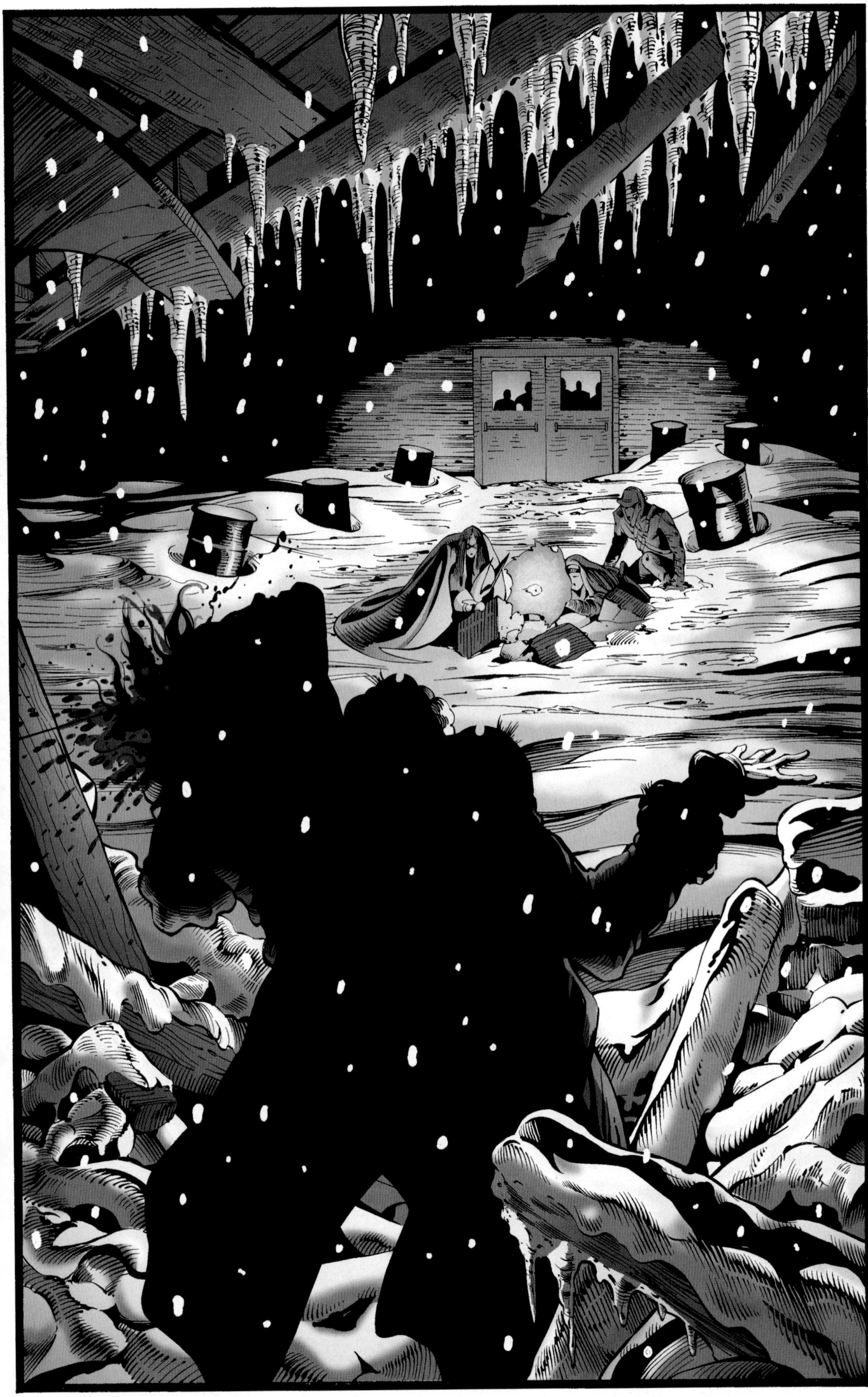

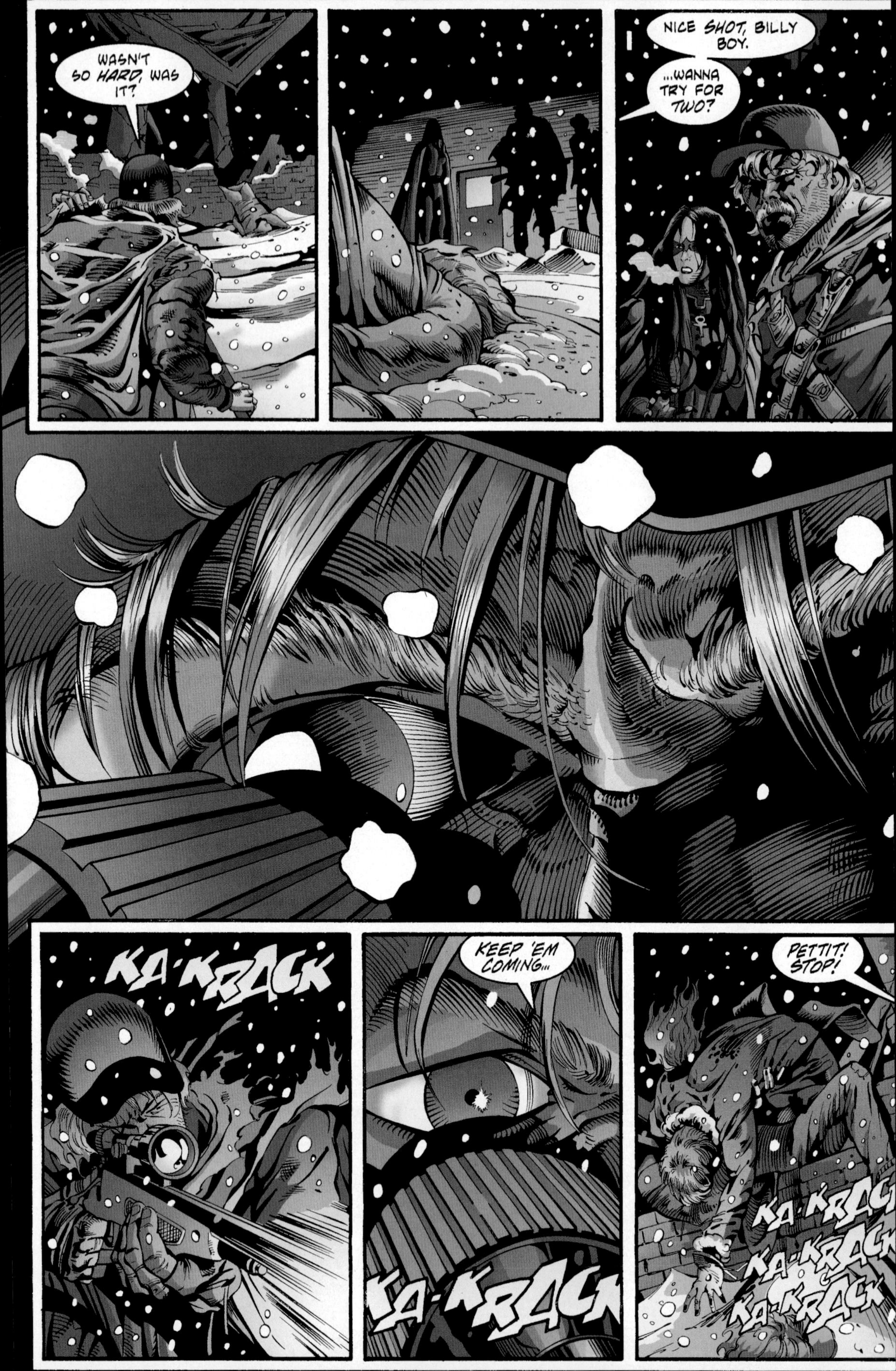
WASN'T SO HARD, WAS IT?
NICE SHOT, BILLY BOY.
...WANNA TRY FOR TWO?
KA-KRACK
KEEP 'EM COMING...
KA-KRACK
PETTIT! STOP!
KA-KRACK
KA-KRACK
KA-KRACK

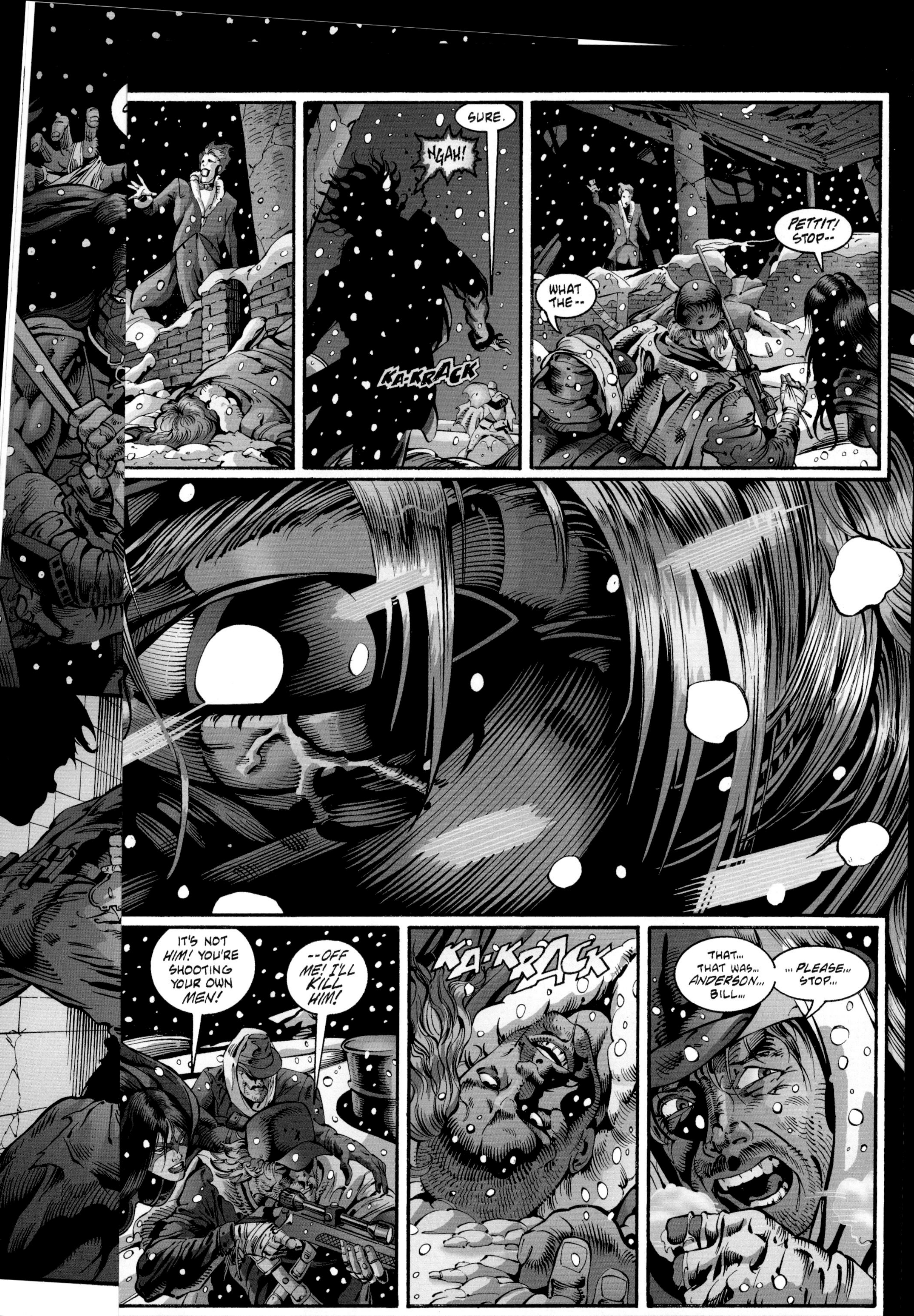
SURE.
NGAH!
KA-KRACK
PETTIT! STOP--
WHAT THE--
IT'S NOT HIM! YOU'RE SHOOTING YOUR OWN MEN!
--OFF ME! I'LL KILL HIM!
KA-KRACK
THAT... THAT WAS... ANDERSON... BILL...
...PLEASE... STOP...

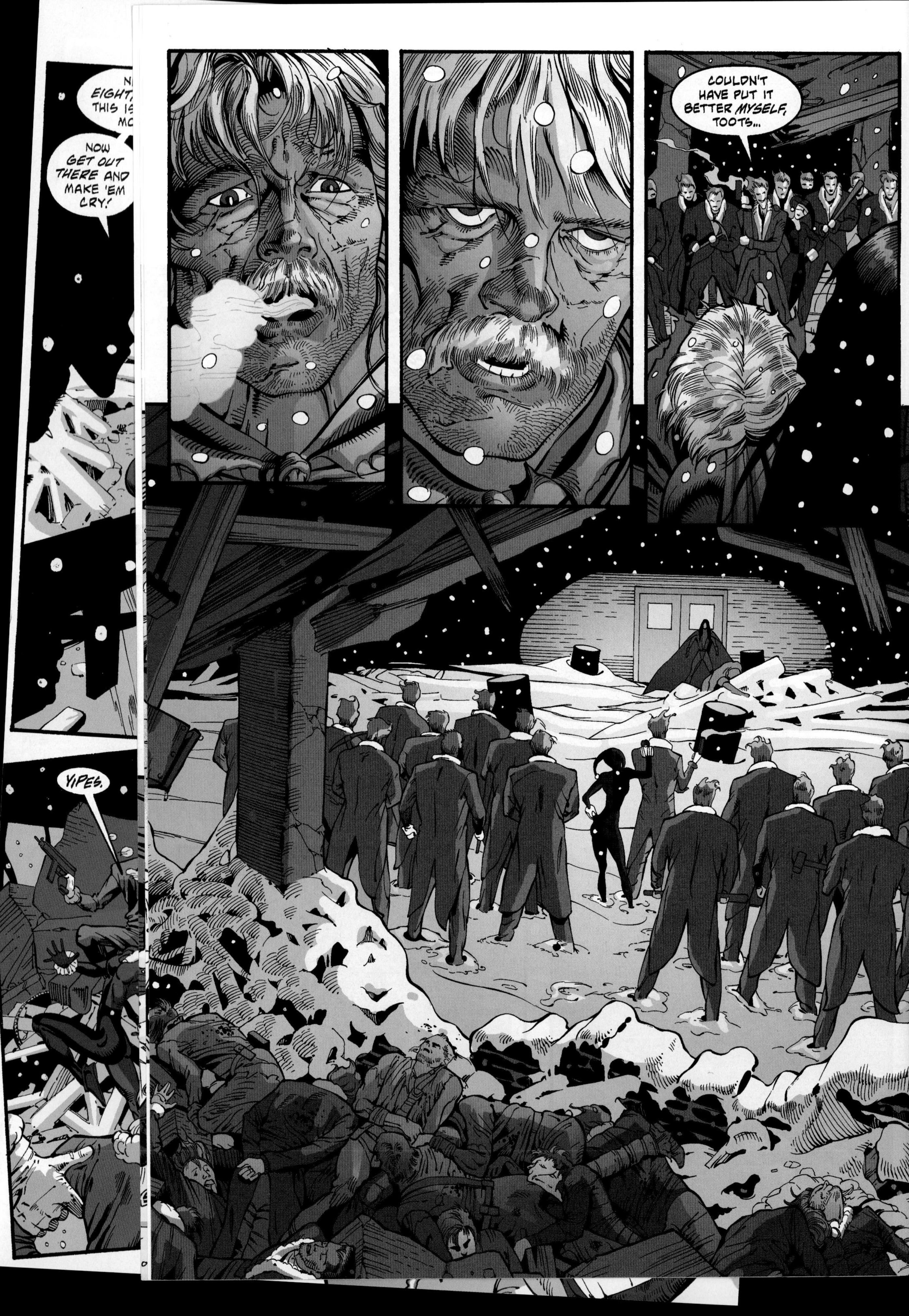
NOW GET OUT THERE AND MAKE 'EM CRY!
YIPES.
COULDN'T HAVE PUT IT BETTER MYSELF, TOOTS...

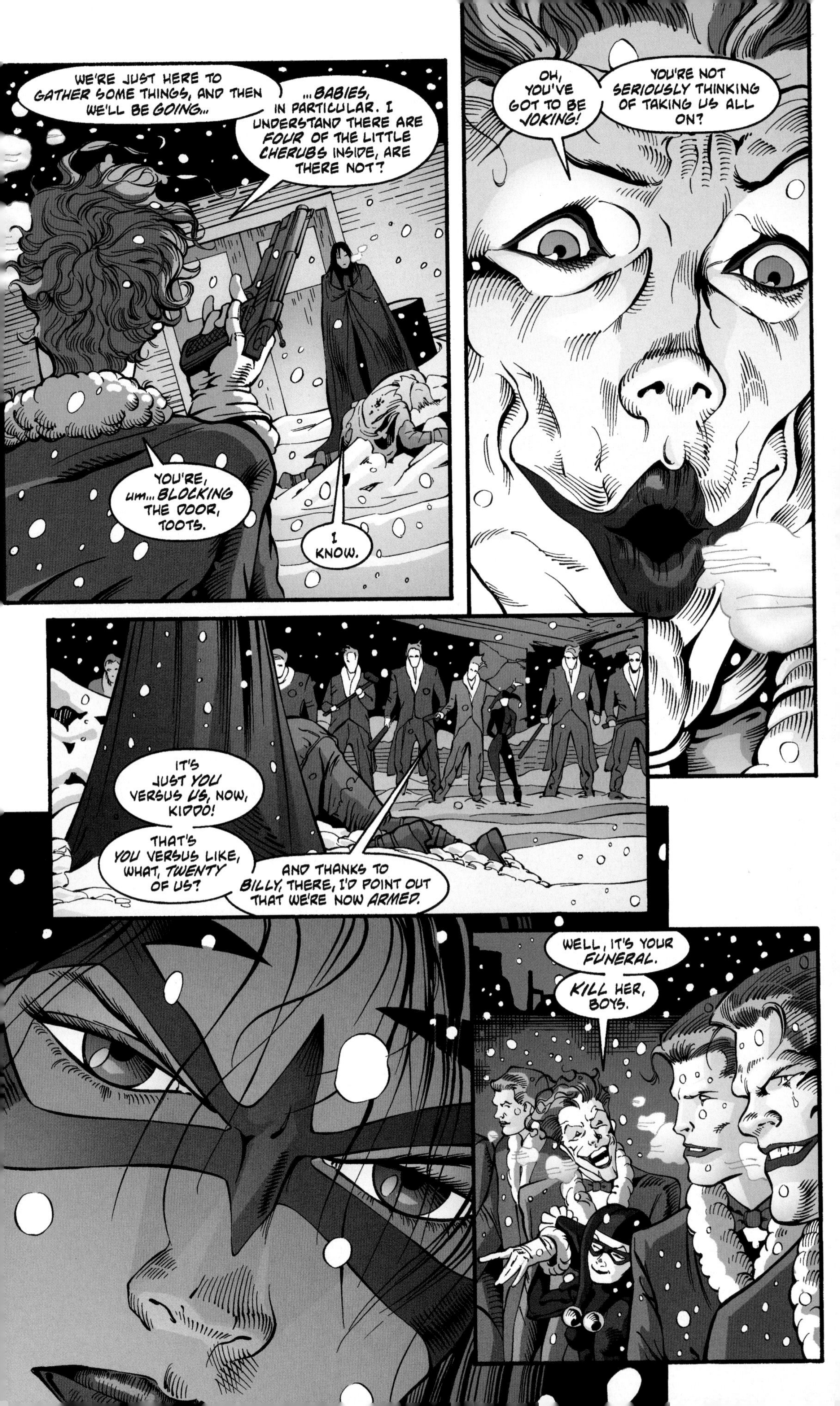

WE'RE JUST HERE TO GATHER SOME THINGS, AND THEN WE'LL BE GOING...
...BABIES, IN PARTICULAR. I UNDERSTAND THERE ARE FOUR OF THE LITTLE CHERUBS INSIDE, ARE THERE NOT?
YOU'RE, um... BLOCKING THE DOOR, TOOTS.
I KNOW.
OH, YOU'VE GOT TO BE JOKING!
YOU'RE NOT SERIOUSLY THINKING OF TAKING US ALL ON?
IT'S JUST YOU VERSUS US, NOW, KIDDO!
THAT'S YOU VERSUS LIKE, WHAT, TWENTY OF US?
AND THANKS TO BILLY, THERE, I'D POINT OUT THAT WE'RE NOW ARMED.
WELL, IT'S YOUR FUNERAL.
KILL HER, BOYS.

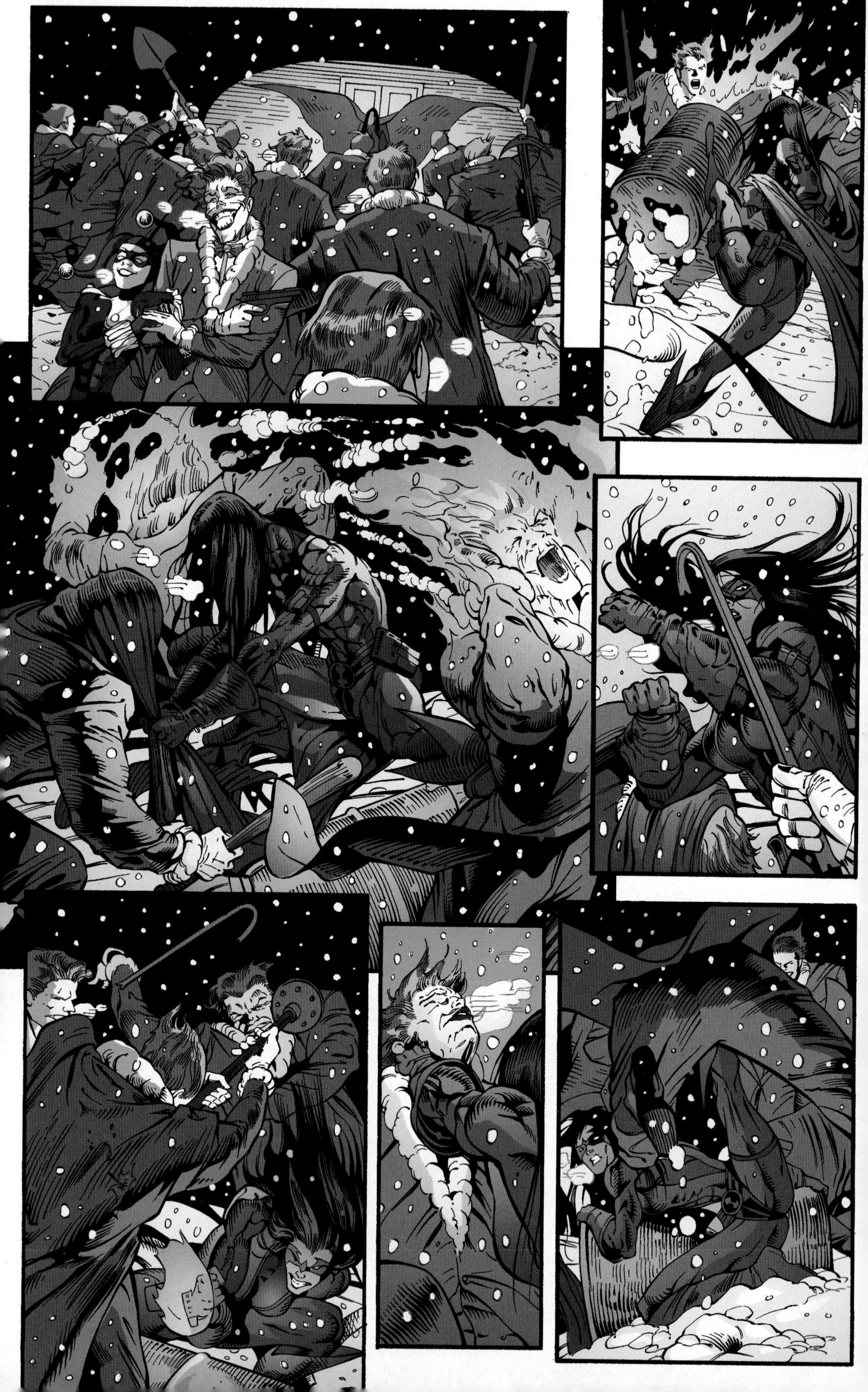

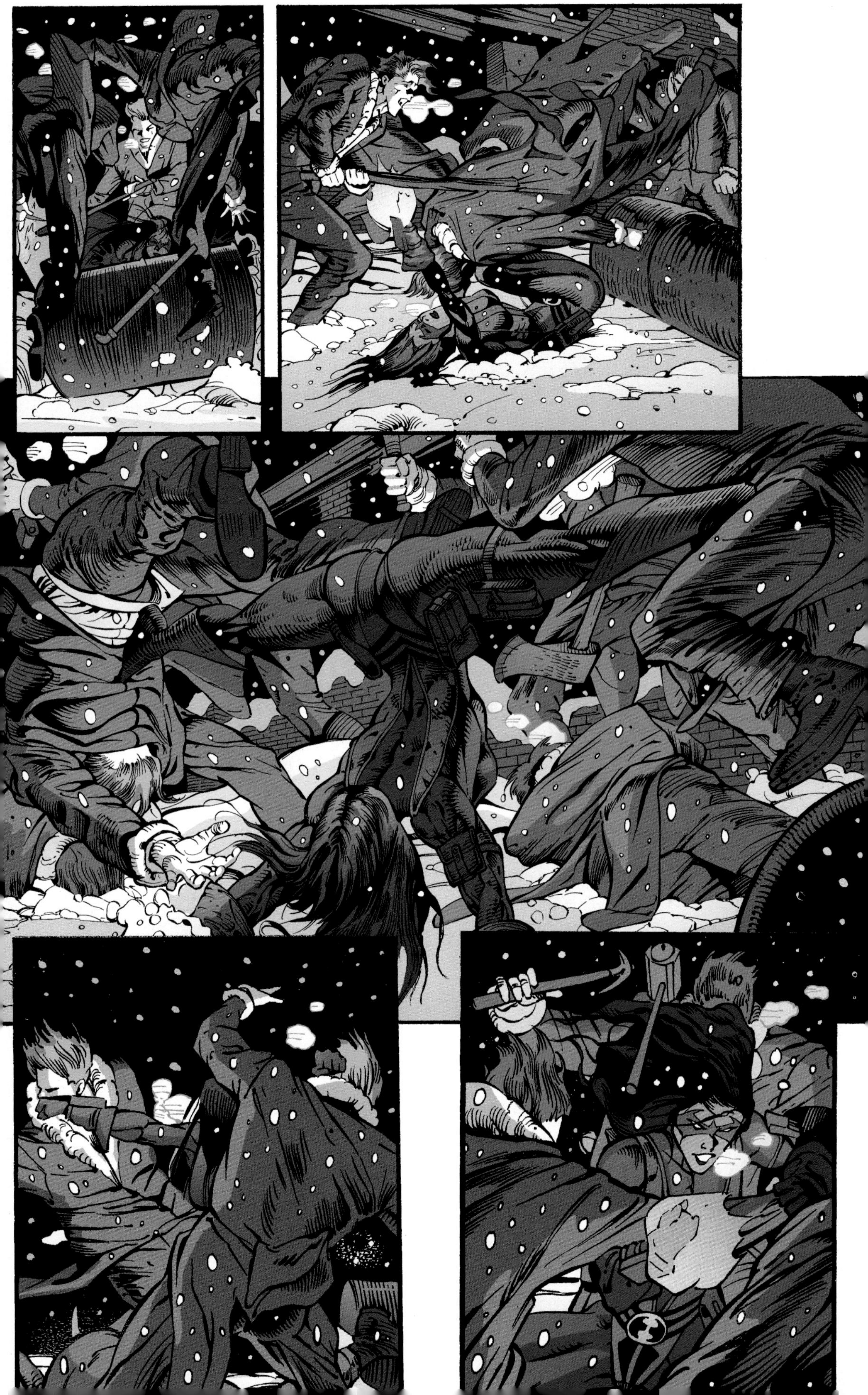

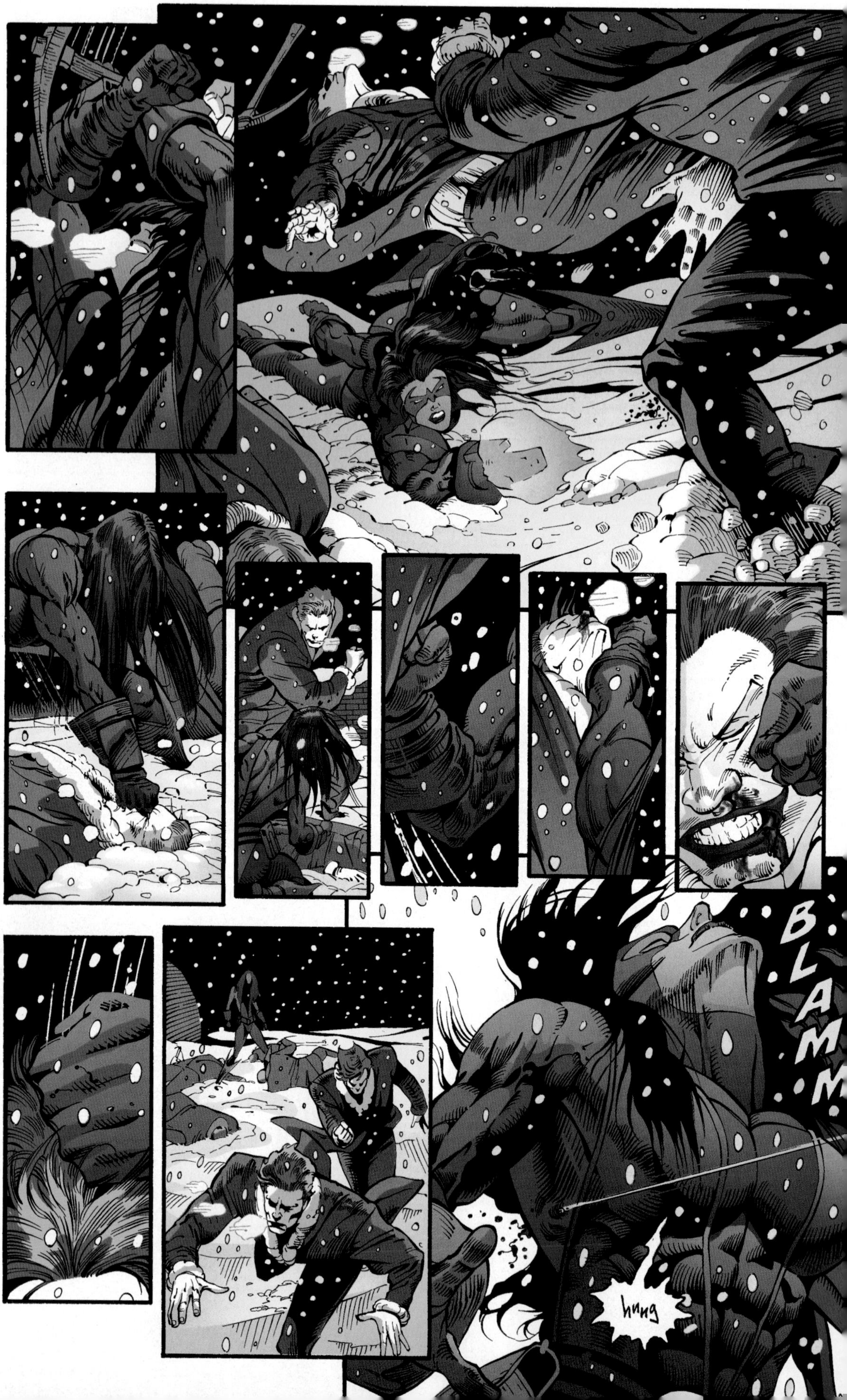
BLAMM
hnng

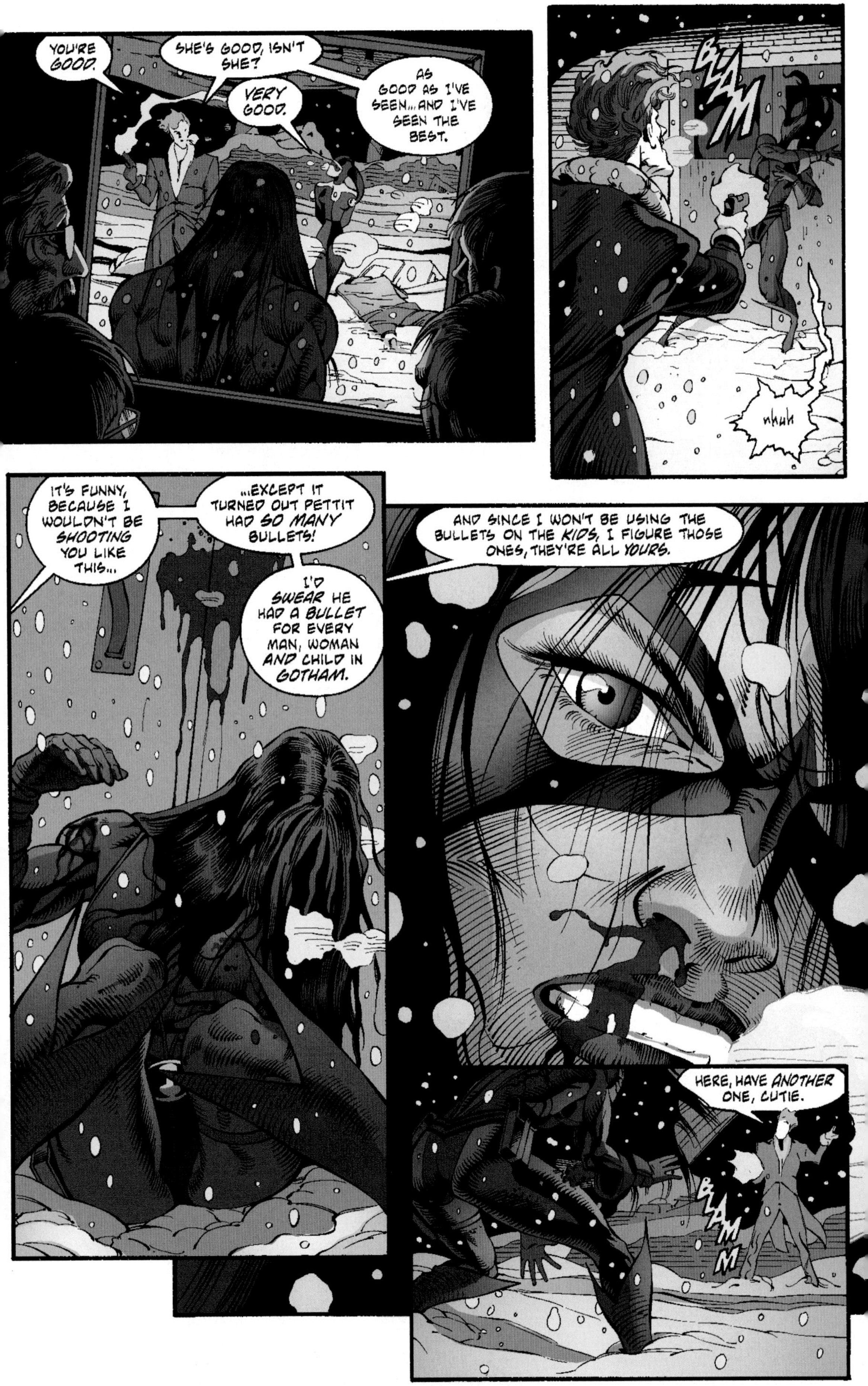
YOU'RE GOOD.
SHE'S GOOD, ISN'T SHE?
VERY GOOD.
AS GOOD AS I'VE SEEN... AND I'VE SEEN THE BEST.
BLAM
nhuh
IT'S FUNNY, BECAUSE I WOULDN'T BE SHOOTING YOU LIKE THIS...
...EXCEPT IT TURNED OUT PETTIT HAD SO MANY BULLETS!
I'D SWEAR HE HAD A BULLET FOR EVERY MAN, WOMAN AND CHILD IN GOTHAM.
AND SINCE I WON'T BE USING THE BULLETS ON THE KIDS, I FIGURE THOSE ONES, THEY'RE ALL YOURS.
HERE, HAVE ANOTHER ONE, CUTIE.
BLAMM

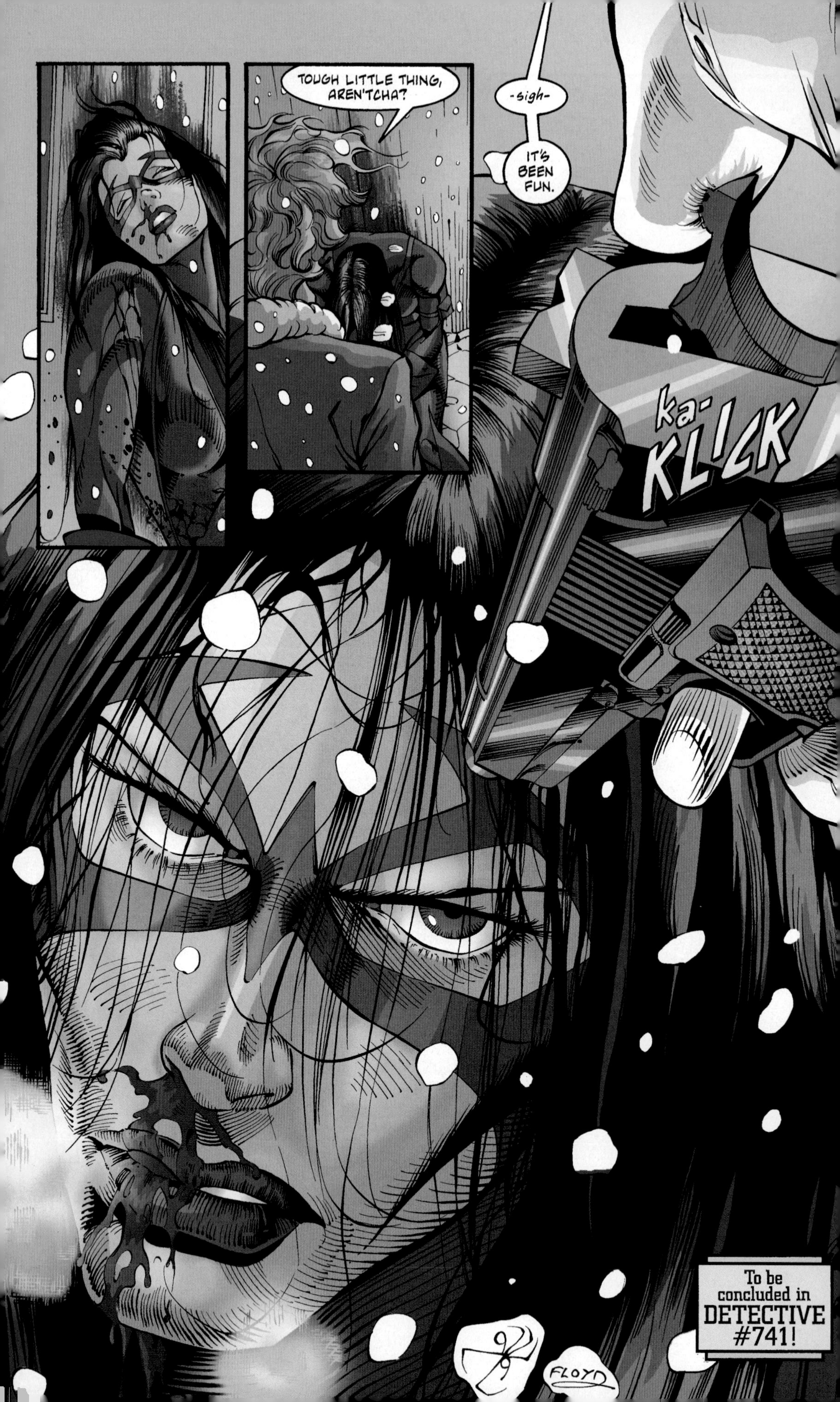

TOUGH LITTLE THING, AREN'TCHA?
-sigh-
IT'S BEEN FUN.
ka-KLICK
To be concluded in DETECTIVE #741!
FLOYD

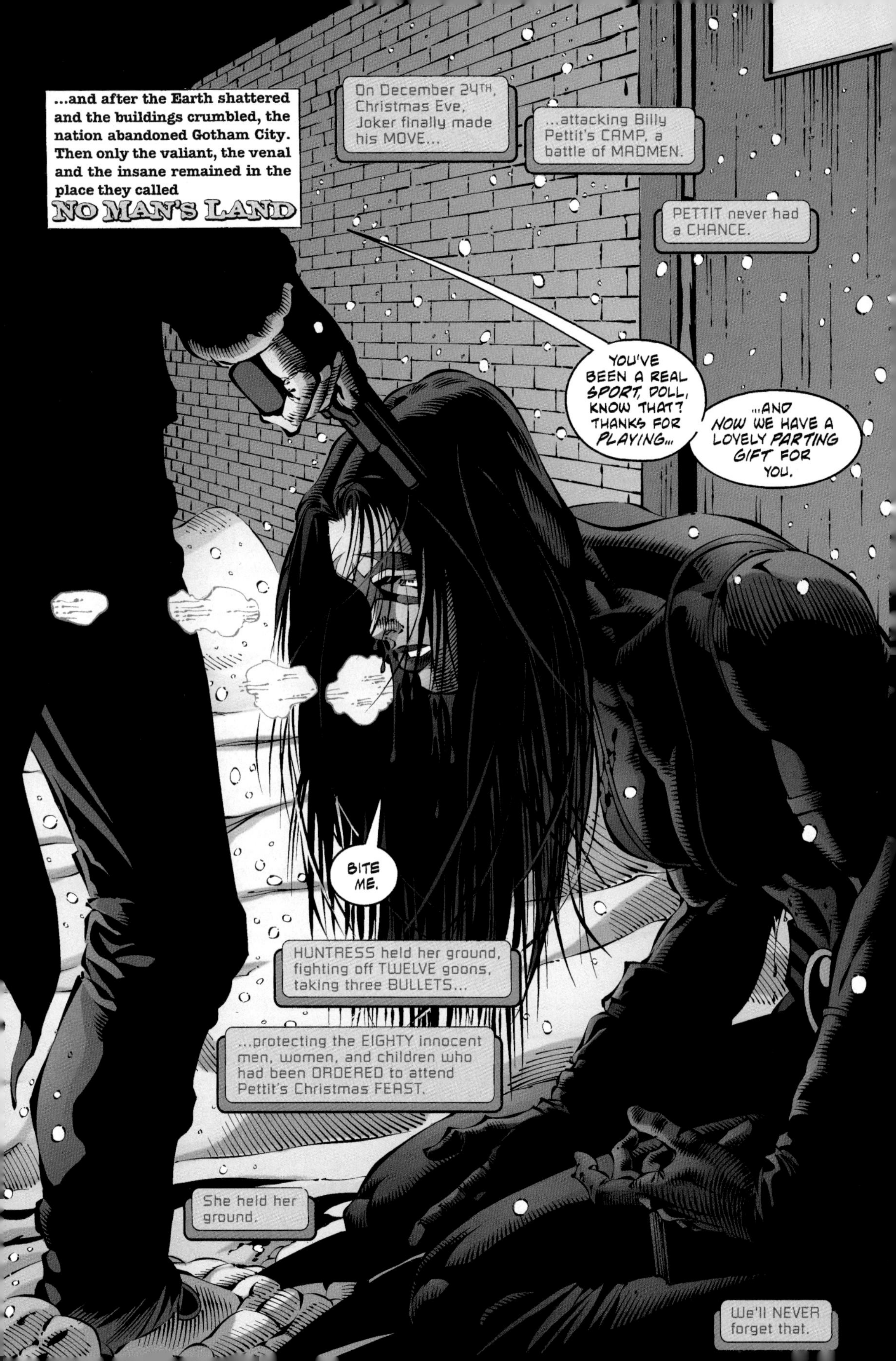
...and after the Earth shattered and the buildings crumbled, the nation abandoned Gotham City. Then only the valiant, the venal and the insane remained in the place they called
NO MAN'S LAND
On December 24TH, Christmas Eve, Joker finally made his MOVE...
...attacking Billy Pettit's CAMP, a battle of MADMEN.
PETTIT never had a CHANCE.
YOU'VE BEEN A REAL SPORT, DOLL, KNOW THAT? THANKS FOR PLAYING...
...AND NOW WE HAVE A LOVELY PARTING GIFT FOR YOU.
BITE ME.
HUNTRESS held her ground, fighting off TWELVE goons, taking three BULLETS...
...protecting the EIGHTY innocent men, women, and children who had been ORDERED to attend Pettit's Christmas FEAST.
She held her ground.
We'll NEVER forget that.

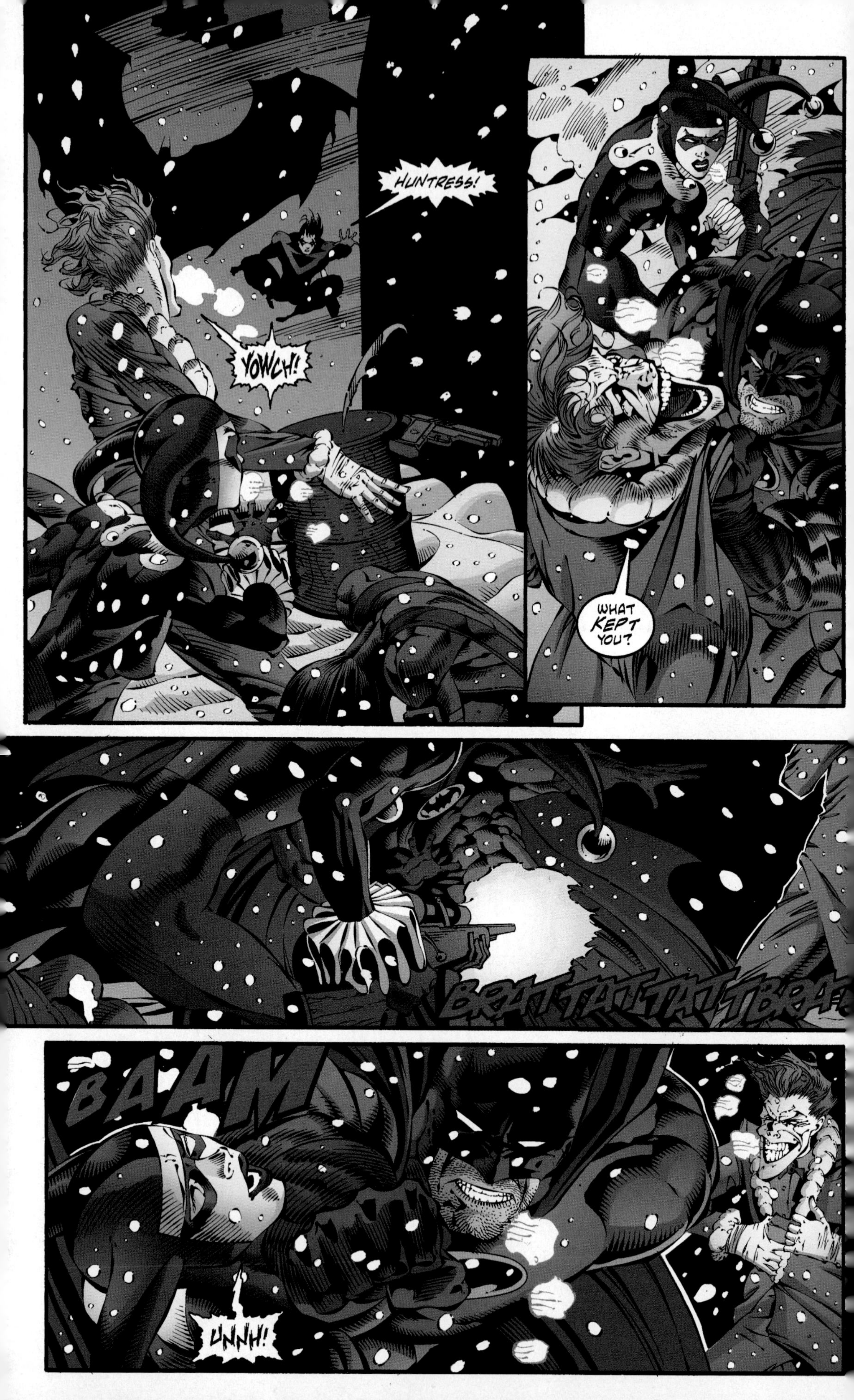
HUNTRESS!
YOWCH!
WHAT KEPT YOU?
BRATTATTATTBRA
BAAM
UNNH!

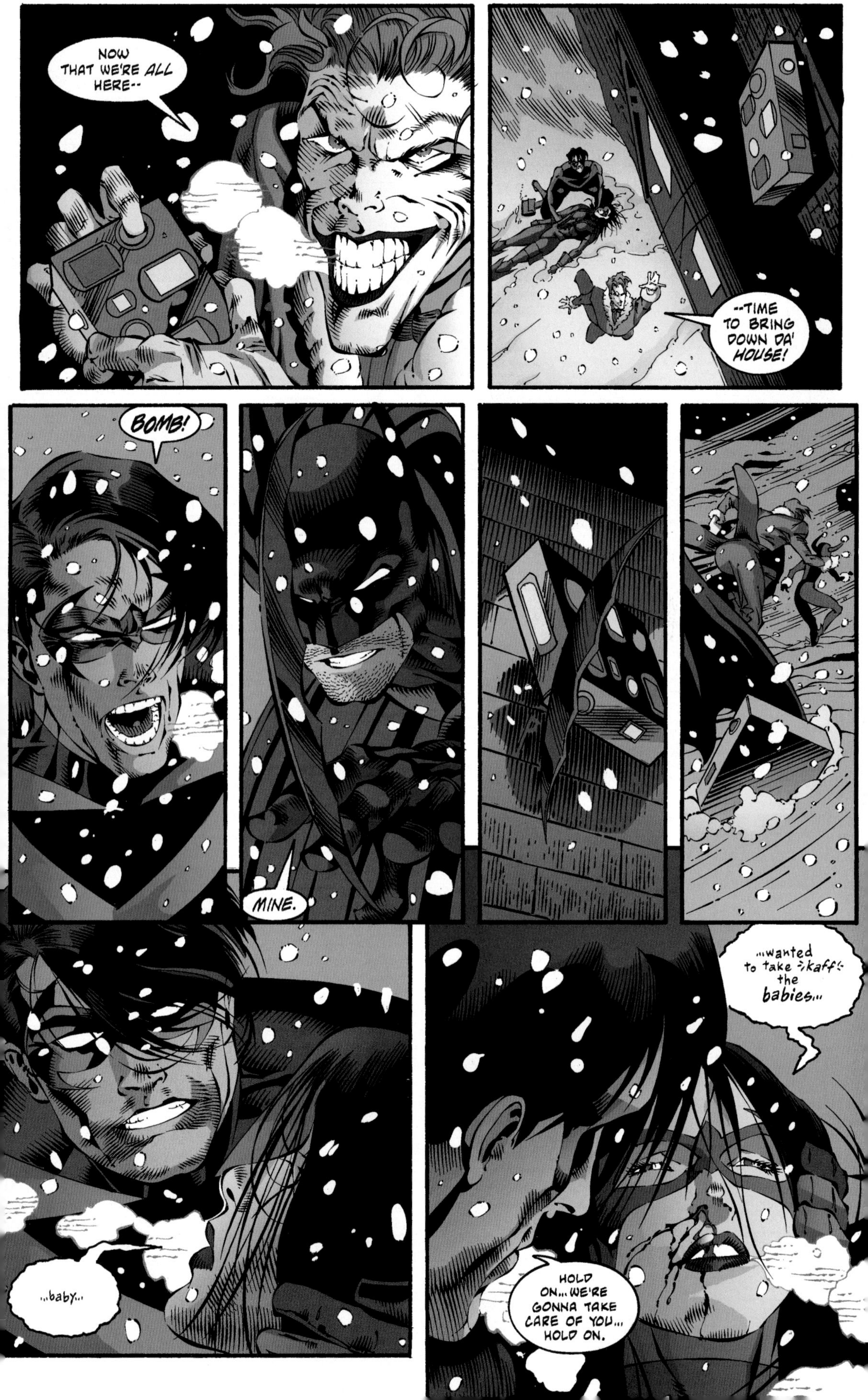
NOW THAT WE'RE ALL HERE--
--TIME TO BRING DOWN DA' HOUSE!
BOMB!
MINE.
...wanted to take -kaff- the babies...
...baby...
HOLD ON... WE'RE GONNA TAKE CARE OF YOU... HOLD ON.

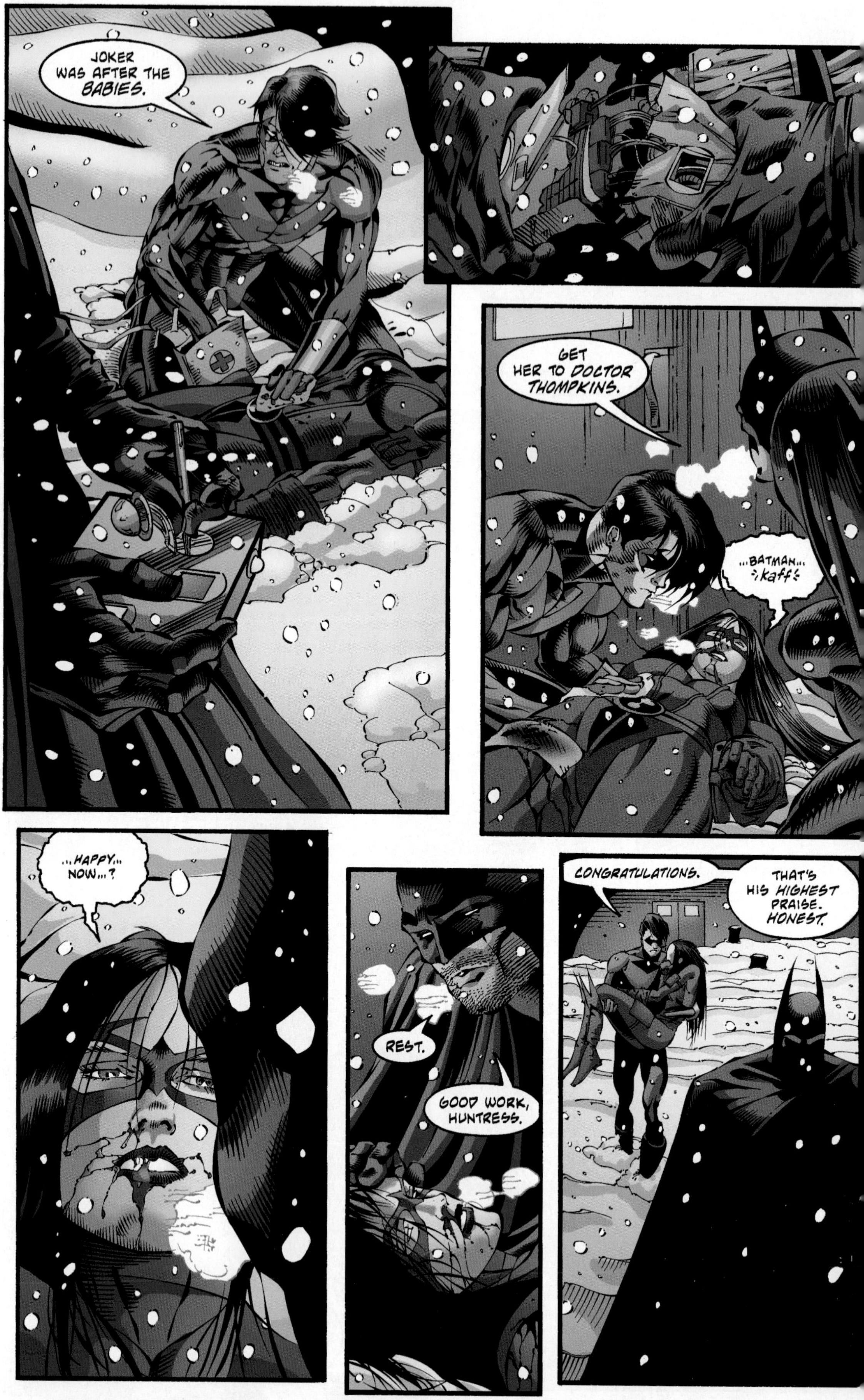
JOKER WAS AFTER THE BABIES.
GET HER TO DOCTOR THOMPKINS.
...BATMAN... kaff
...HAPPY... NOW...?
REST.
GOOD WORK, HUNTRESS.
CONGRATULATIONS.
THAT'S HIS HIGHEST PRAISE. HONEST.

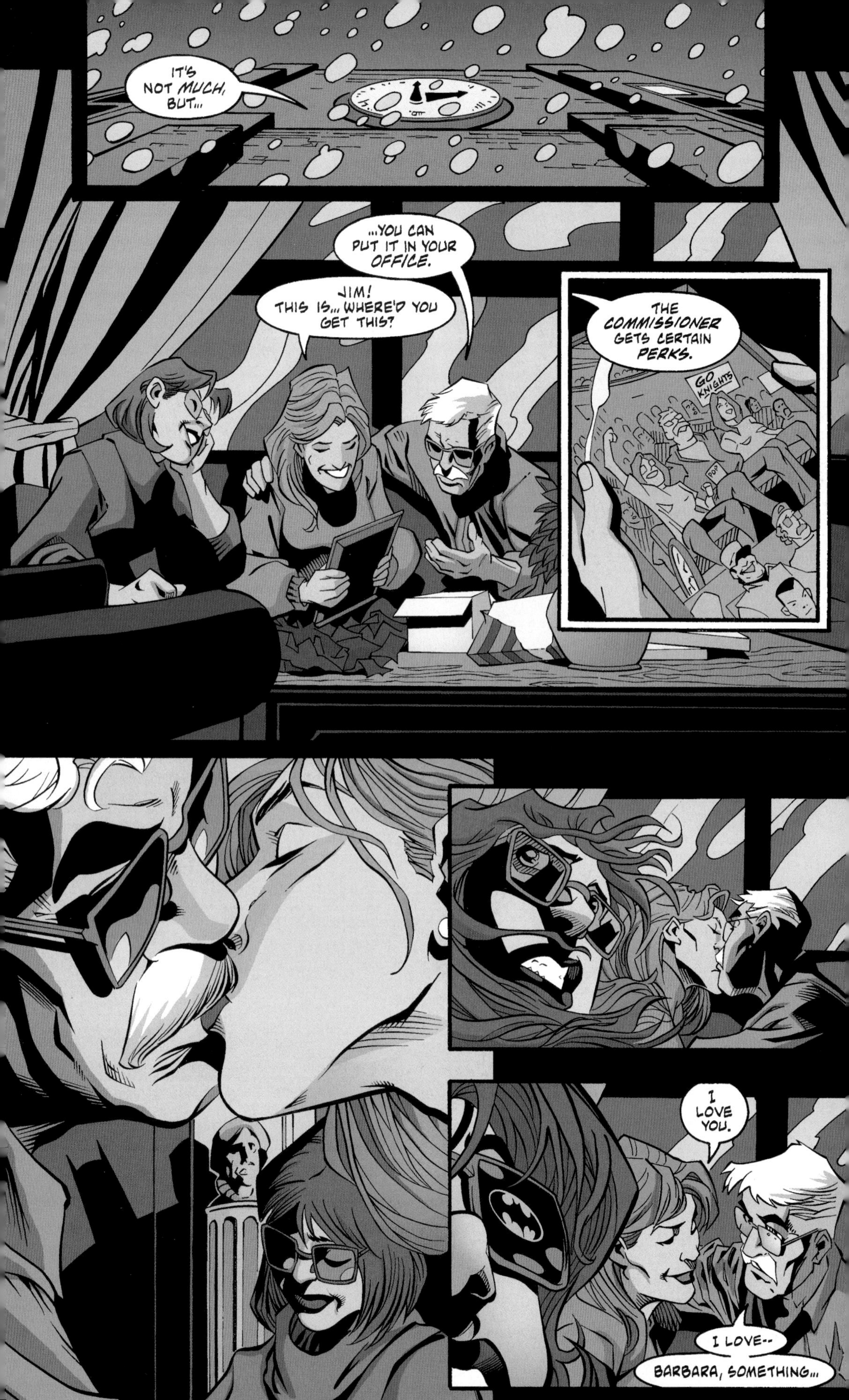
IT'S NOT MUCH, BUT...
...YOU CAN PUT IT IN YOUR OFFICE.
JIM! THIS IS... WHERE'D YOU GET THIS?
THE COMMISSIONER GETS CERTAIN PERKS.
GO KNIGHTS
I LOVE YOU.
I LOVE--
BARBARA, SOMETHING...

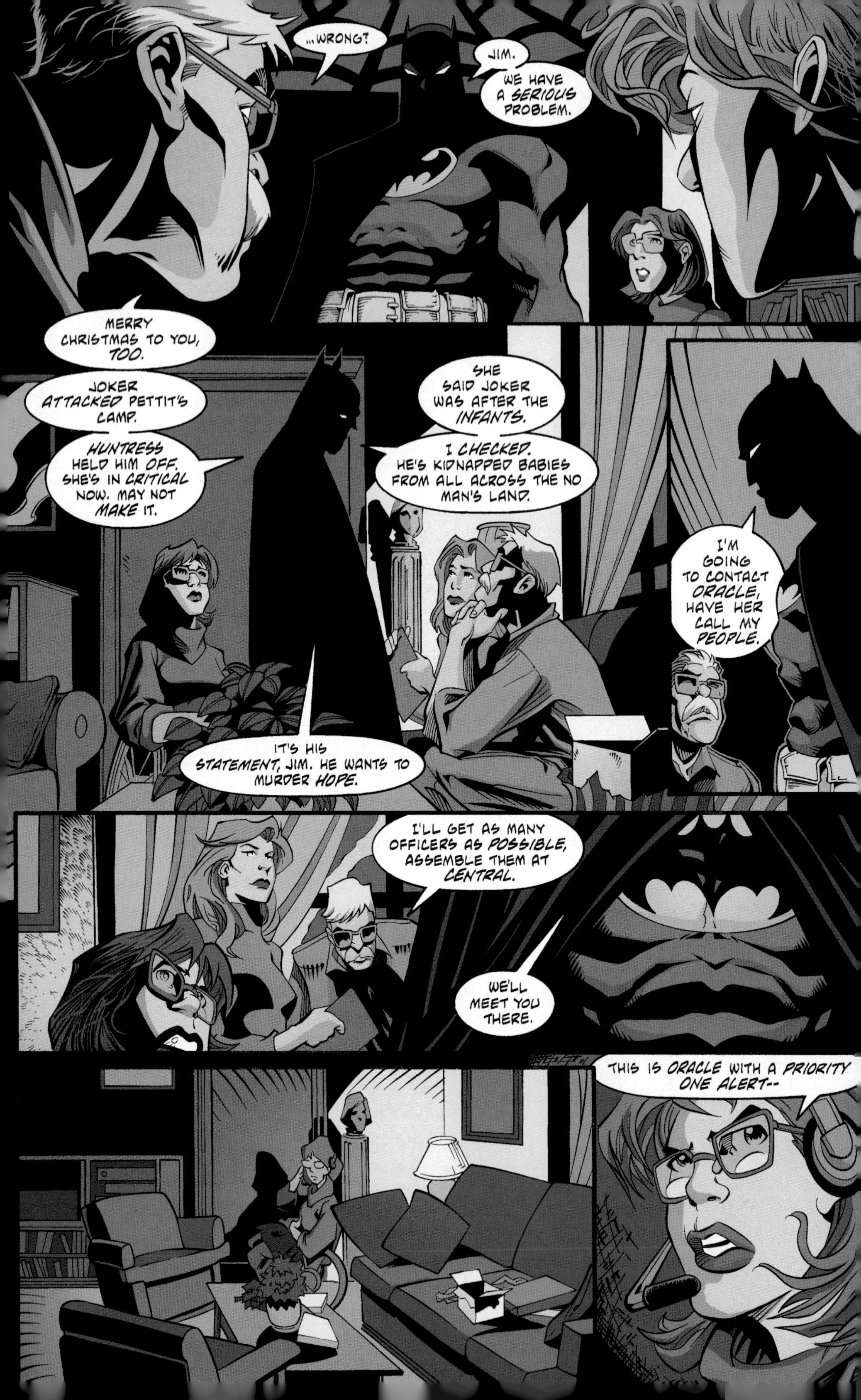
...WRONG?
JIM.
WE HAVE A SERIOUS PROBLEM.
MERRY CHRISTMAS TO YOU, TOO.
JOKER ATTACKED PETTIT'S CAMP.
HUNTRESS HELD HIM OFF. SHE'S IN CRITICAL NOW. MAY NOT MAKE IT.
SHE SAID JOKER WAS AFTER THE INFANTS.
I CHECKED. HE'S KIDNAPPED BABIES FROM ALL ACROSS THE NO MAN'S LAND.
IT'S HIS STATEMENT, JIM. HE WANTS TO MURDER HOPE.
I'M GOING TO CONTACT ORACLE, HAVE HER CALL MY PEOPLE.
I'LL GET AS MANY OFFICERS AS POSSIBLE, ASSEMBLE THEM AT CENTRAL.
WE'LL MEET YOU THERE.
THIS IS ORACLE WITH A PRIORITY ONE ALERT--

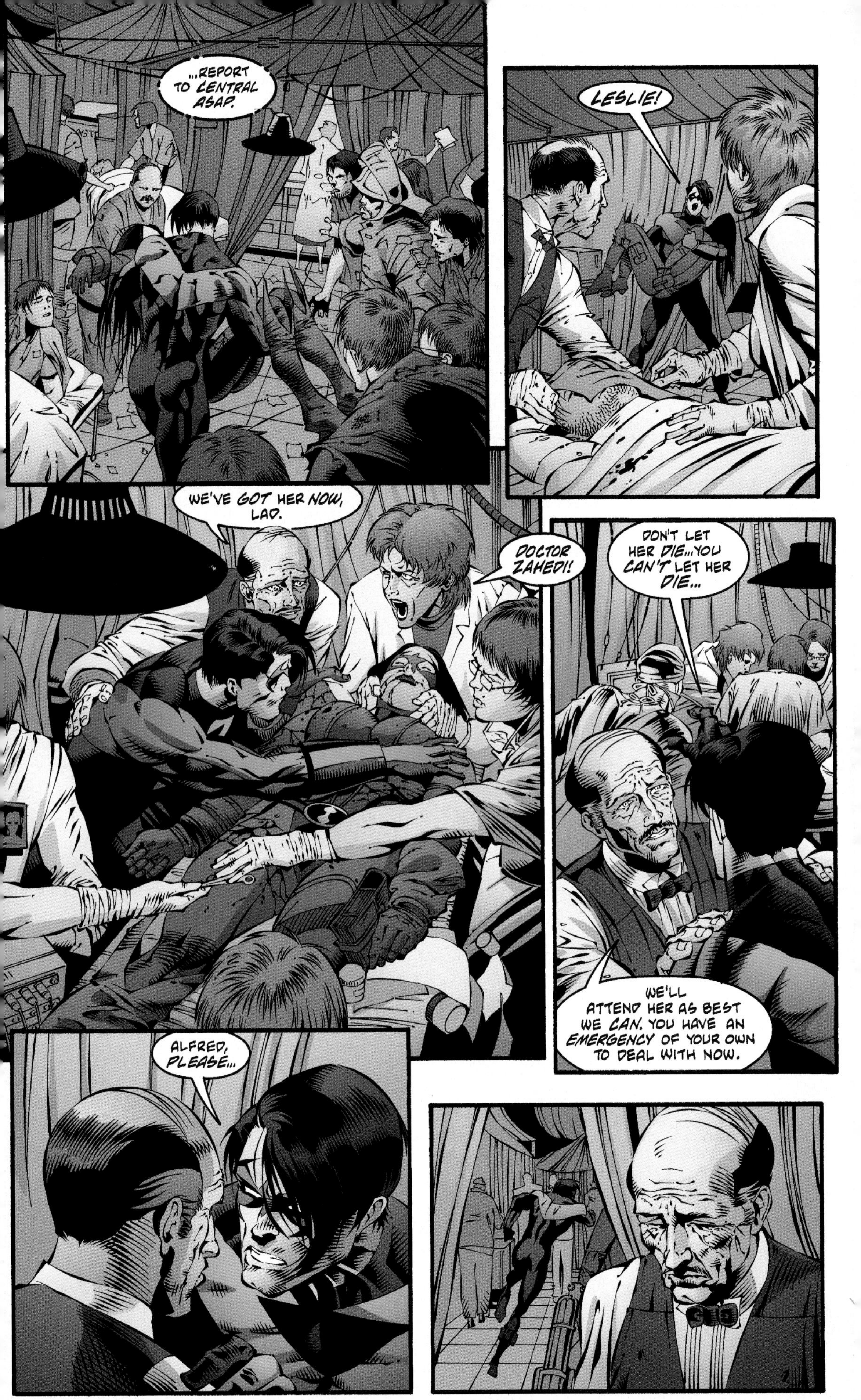
...REPORT TO CENTRAL ASAP.
LESLIE!
WE'VE GOT HER NOW, LAD.
DOCTOR ZAHEDI!
DON'T LET HER DIE...YOU CAN'T LET HER DIE...
WE'LL ATTEND HER AS BEST WE CAN. YOU HAVE AN EMERGENCY OF YOUR OWN TO DEAL WITH NOW.
ALFRED, PLEASE...

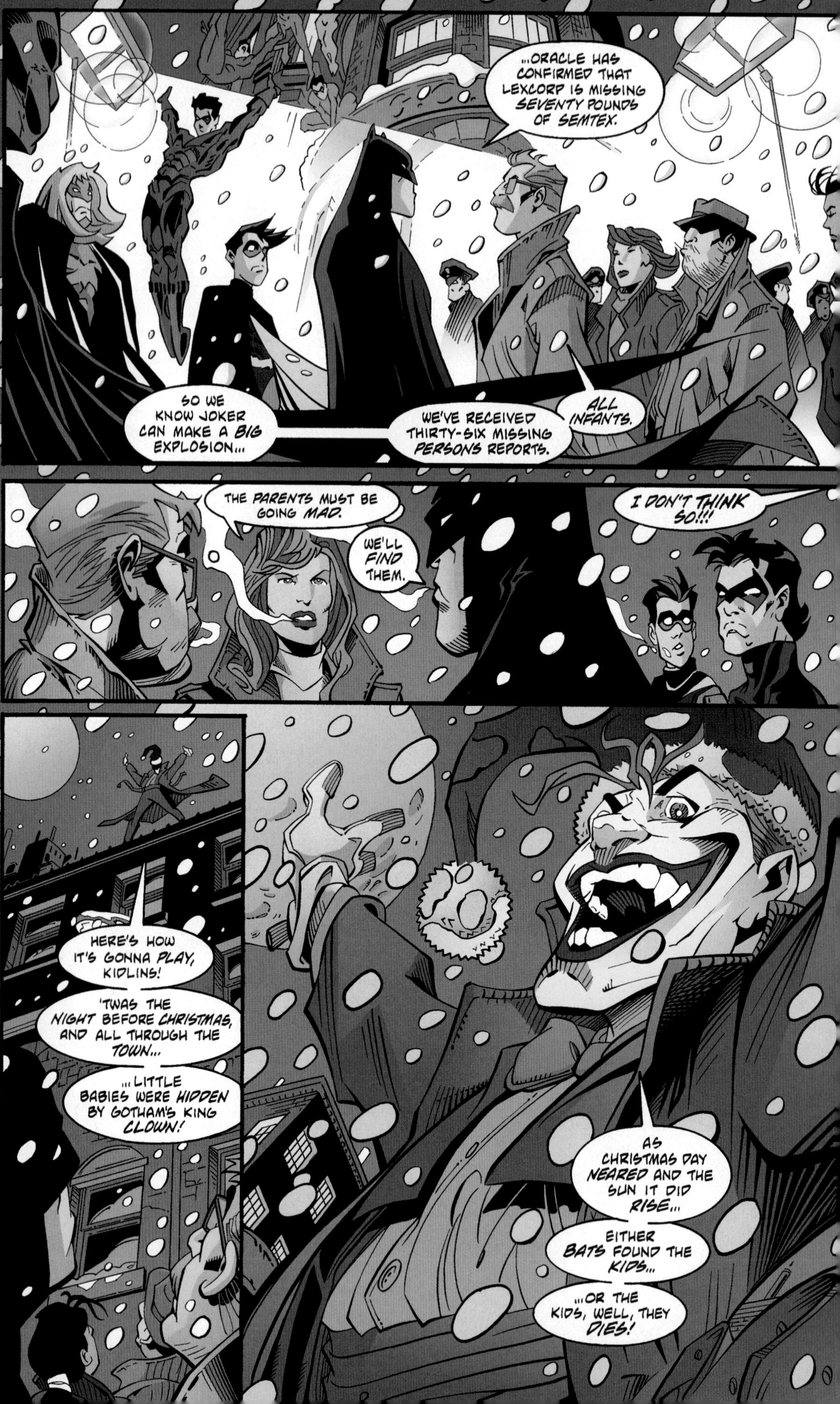
...ORACLE HAS CONFIRMED THAT LEXCORP IS MISSING SEVENTY POUNDS OF SEMTEX.
SO WE KNOW JOKER CAN MAKE A BIG EXPLOSION...
WE'VE RECEIVED THIRTY-SIX MISSING PERSONS REPORTS.
ALL INFANTS.
THE PARENTS MUST BE GOING MAD.
WE'LL FIND THEM.
I DON'T THINK SO!!!
HERE'S HOW IT'S GONNA PLAY, KIDLINS!
'TWAS THE NIGHT BEFORE CHRISTMAS, AND ALL THROUGH THE TOWN...
...LITTLE BABIES WERE HIDDEN BY GOTHAM'S KING CLOWN!
AS CHRISTMAS DAY NEARED AND THE SUN IT DID RISE...
EITHER BATS FOUND THE KIDS...
...OR THE KIDS, WELL, THEY DIES!

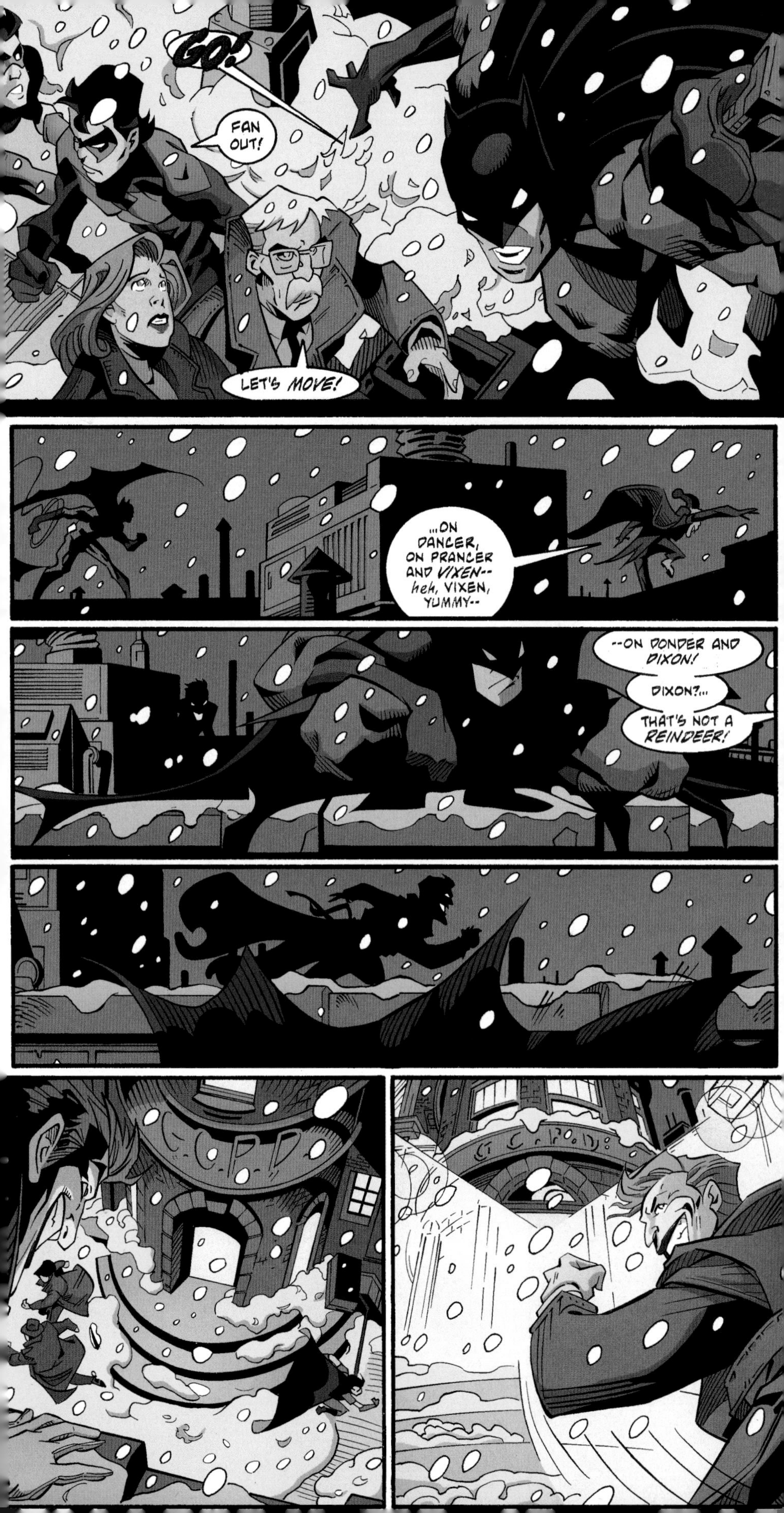
GO!
FAN OUT!
LET'S MOVE!
...ON DANCER, ON PRANCER AND VIXEN--heh, VIXEN, YUMMY--
--ON DONDER AND DIXON!
DIXON?...
THAT'S NOT A REINDEER!

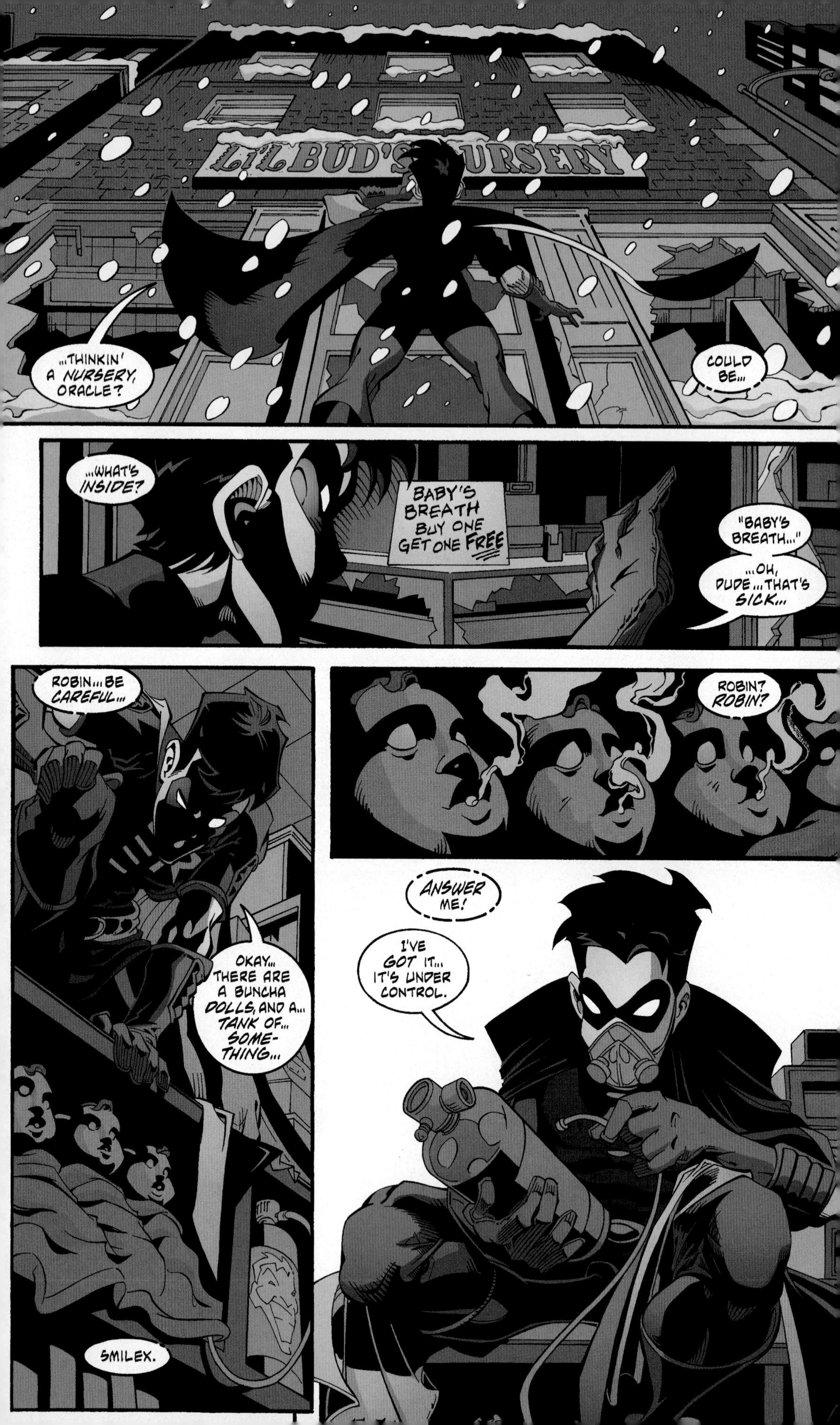
L'iL BUD'S NURSERY
...THINKIN' A NURSERY, ORACLE?
COULD BE...
...WHAT'S INSIDE?
BABY'S BREATH BUY ONE GET ONE FREE
"BABY'S BREATH..."
...OH, DUDE...THAT'S SICK...
ROBIN...BE CAREFUL...
OKAY... THERE ARE A BUNCHA DOLLS, AND A... TANK OF... SOME-THING...
SMILEX.
ROBIN? ROBIN?
ANSWER ME!
I'VE GOT IT... IT'S UNDER CONTROL.

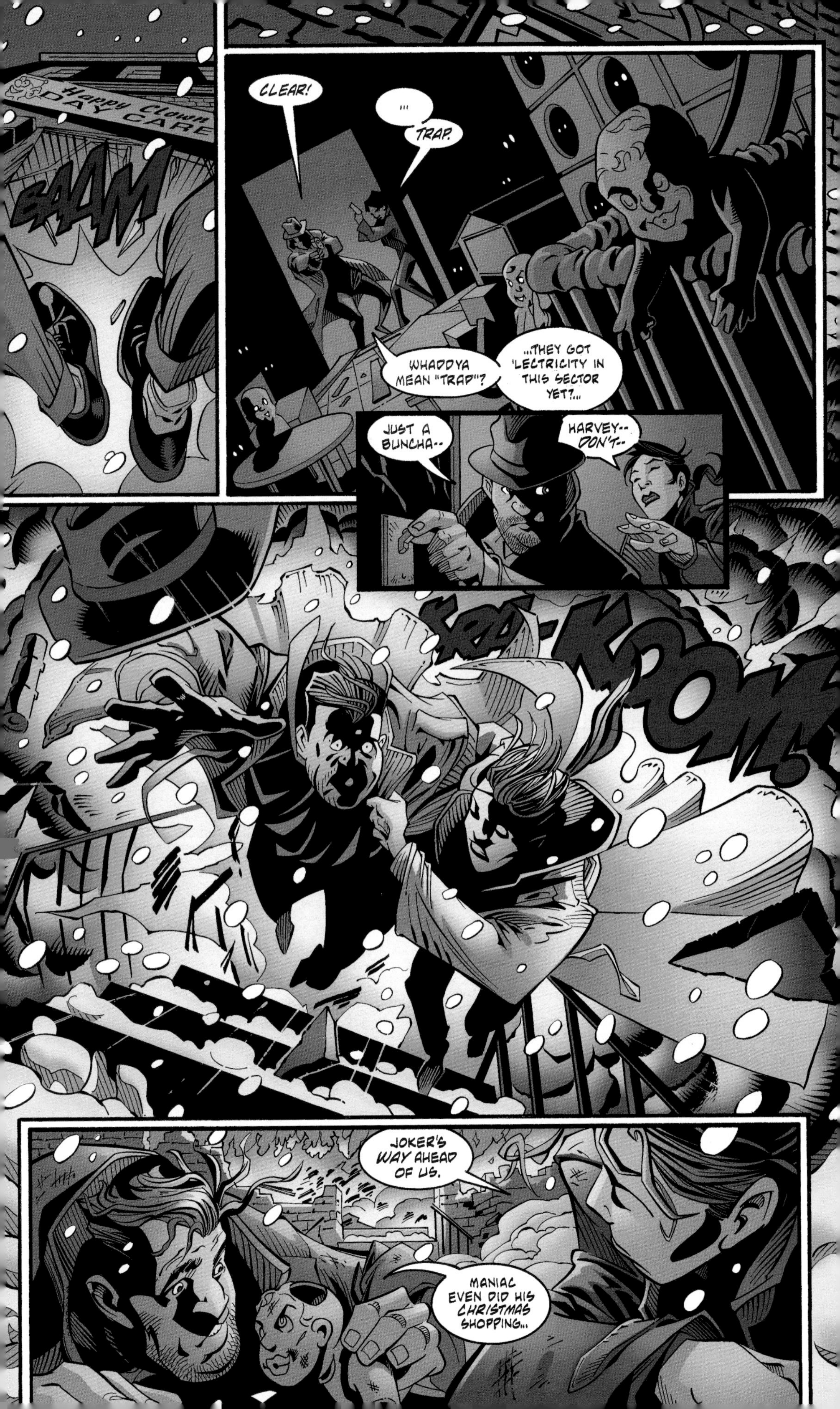
Happy Clown DAY CARE
BLAM
CLEAR!
... TRAP.
WHADDYA MEAN "TRAP"?
...THEY GOT 'LECTRICITY IN THIS SECTOR YET?...
JUST A BUNCHA--
HARVEY-- DON'T--
JOKER'S WAY AHEAD OF US.
MANIAC EVEN DID HIS CHRISTMAS SHOPPING...

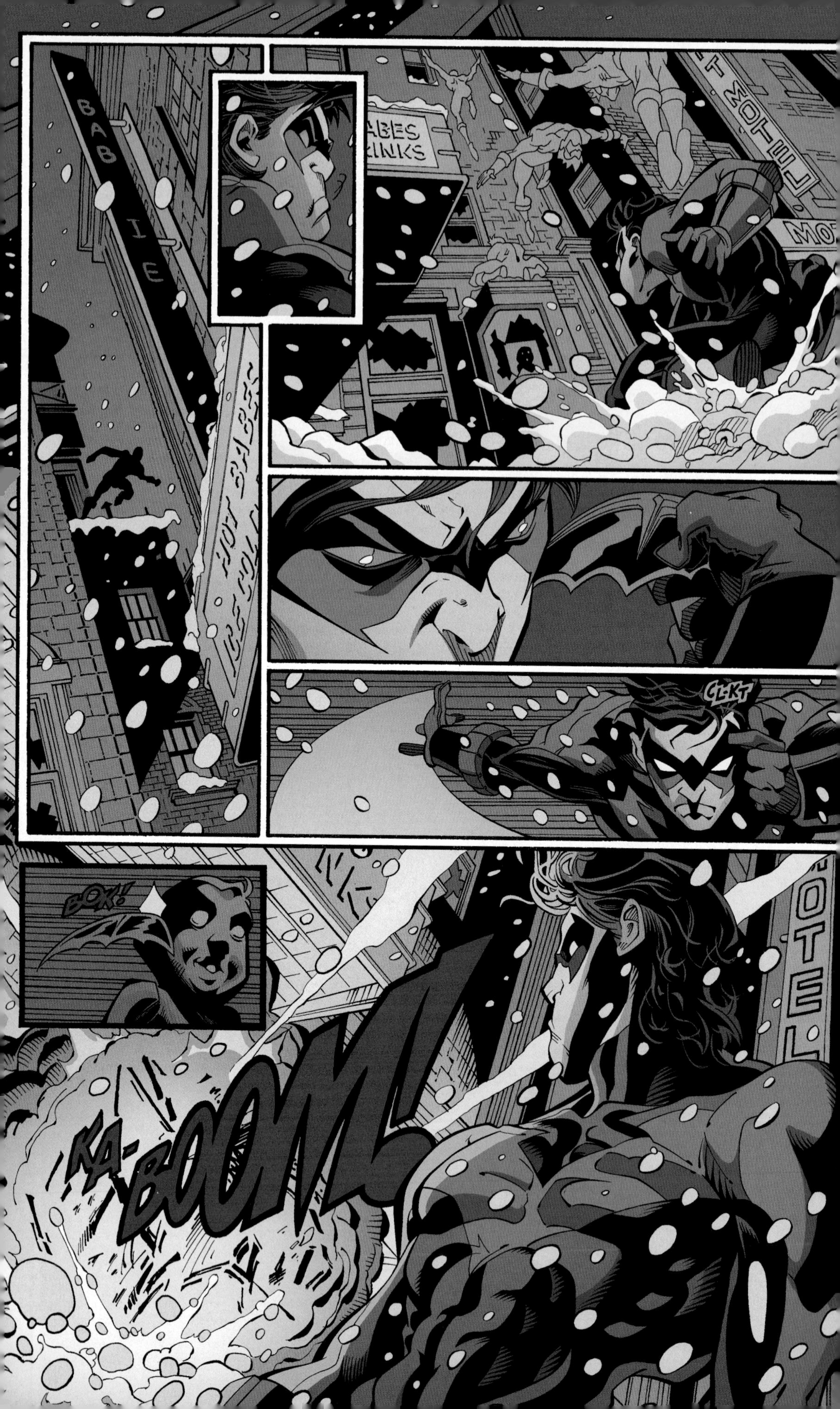

ABES
KINKS
CL-KT
BOK!
KA-BOOM!
OTEL

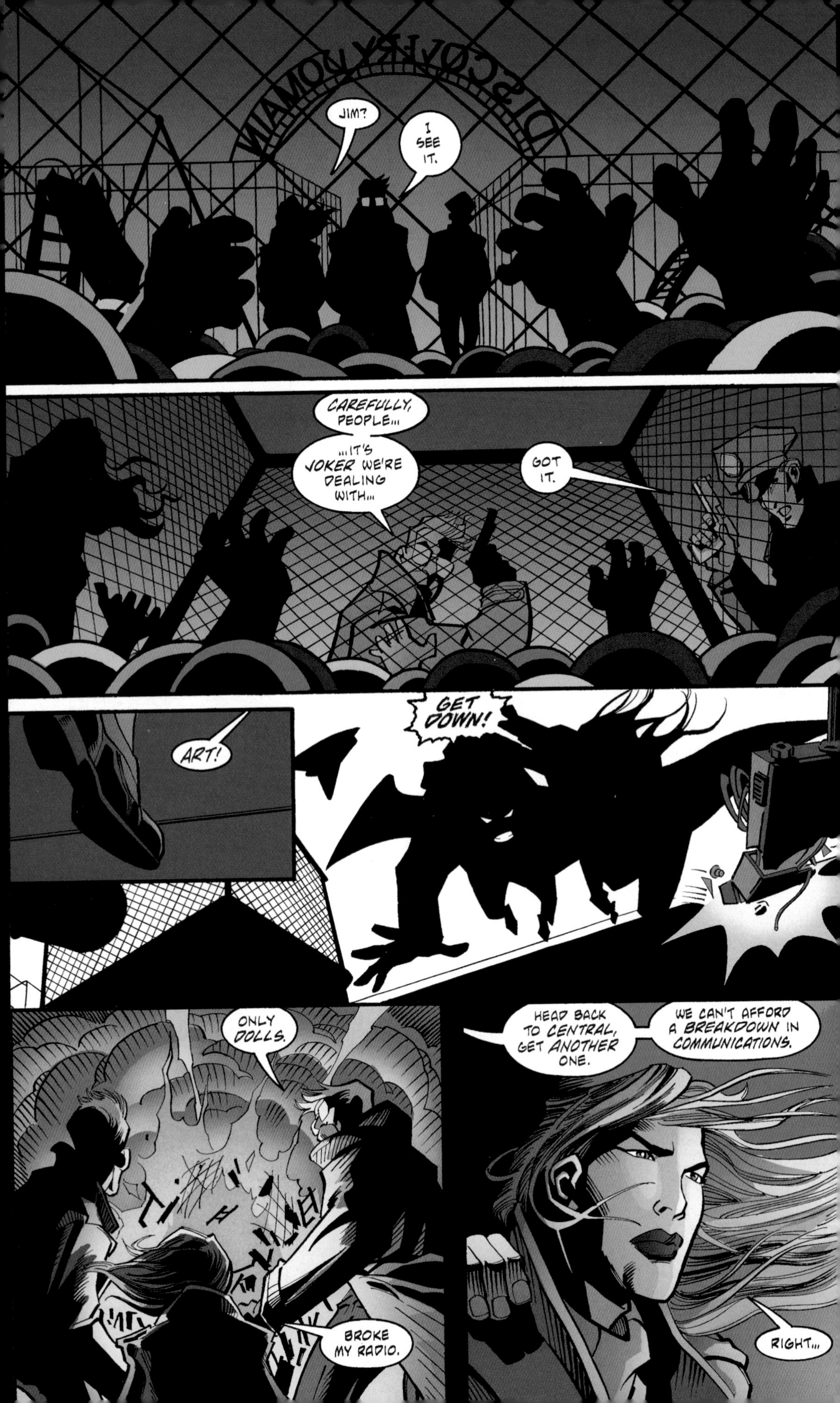
JIM?
I SEE IT.
CAREFULLY, PEOPLE...
...IT'S JOKER WE'RE DEALING WITH...
GOT IT.
ART!
GET DOWN!
ONLY DOLLS.
BROKE MY RADIO.
HEAD BACK TO CENTRAL, GET ANOTHER ONE.
WE CAN'T AFFORD A BREAKDOWN IN COMMUNICATIONS.
RIGHT...

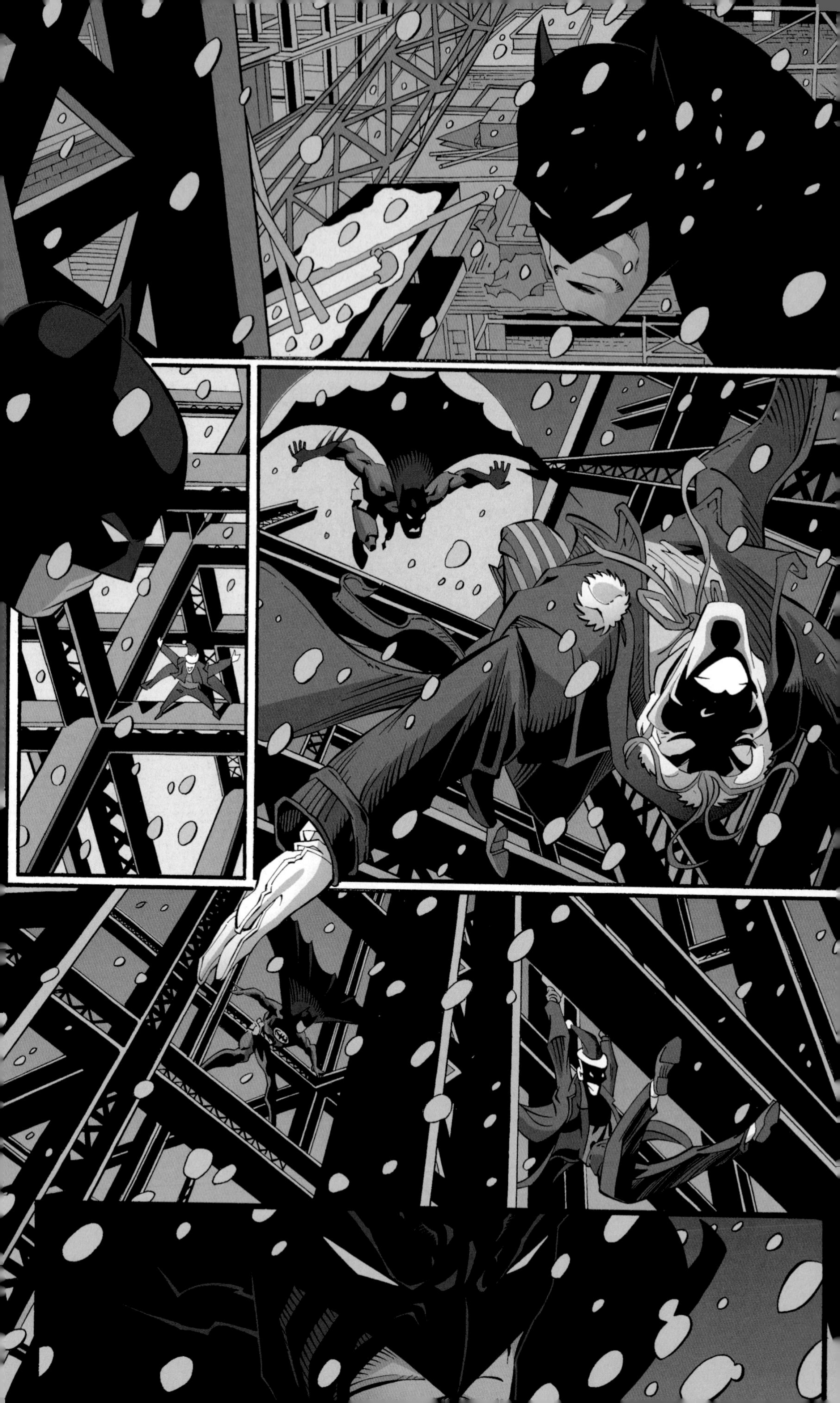

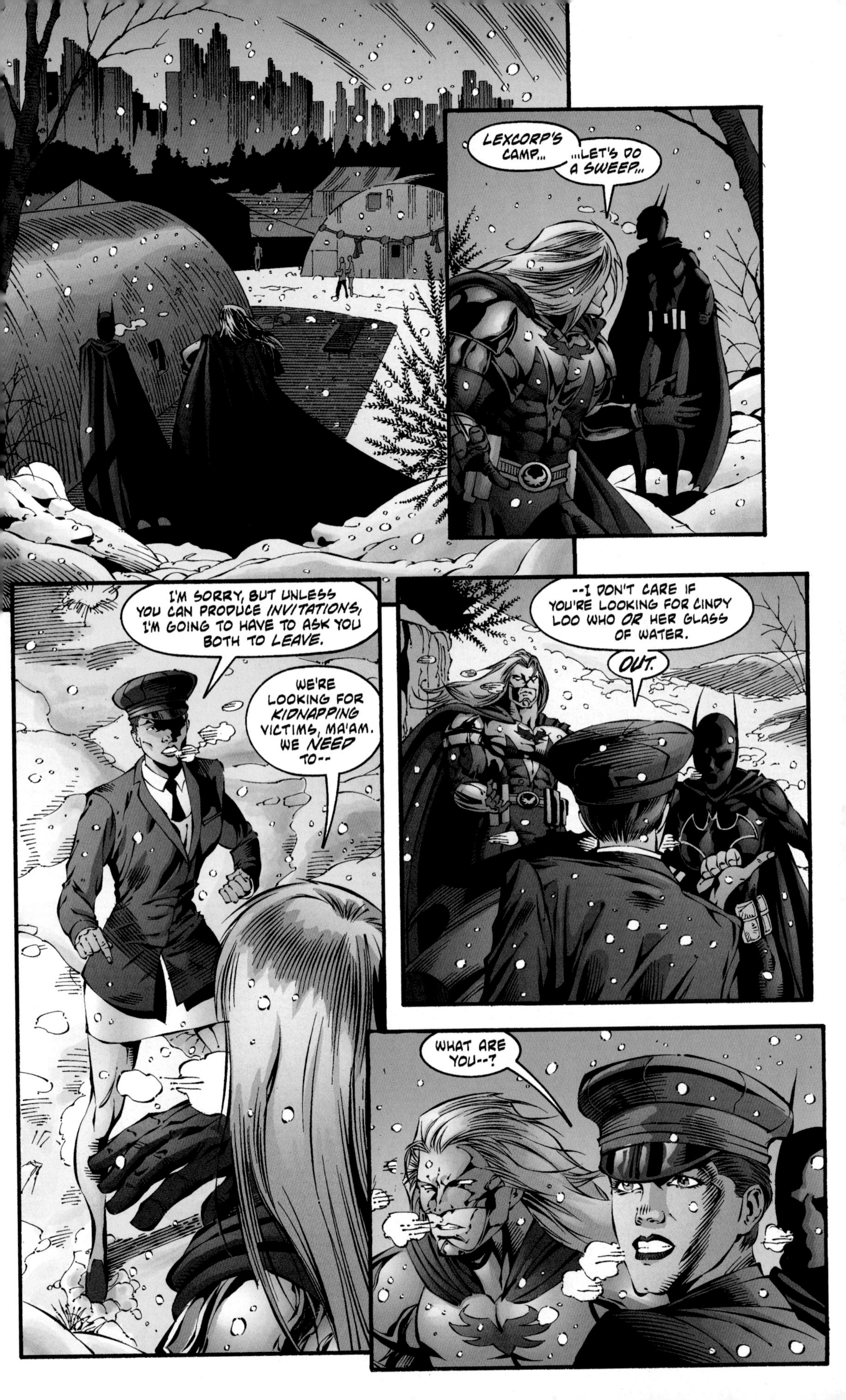
LEXCORP'S CAMP...
...LET'S DO A SWEEP...
I'M SORRY, BUT UNLESS YOU CAN PRODUCE INVITATIONS, I'M GOING TO HAVE TO ASK YOU BOTH TO LEAVE.
WE'RE LOOKING FOR KIDNAPPING VICTIMS, MA'AM. WE NEED TO--
--I DON'T CARE IF YOU'RE LOOKING FOR CINDY LOO WHO OR HER GLASS OF WATER.
OUT.
WHAT ARE YOU--?

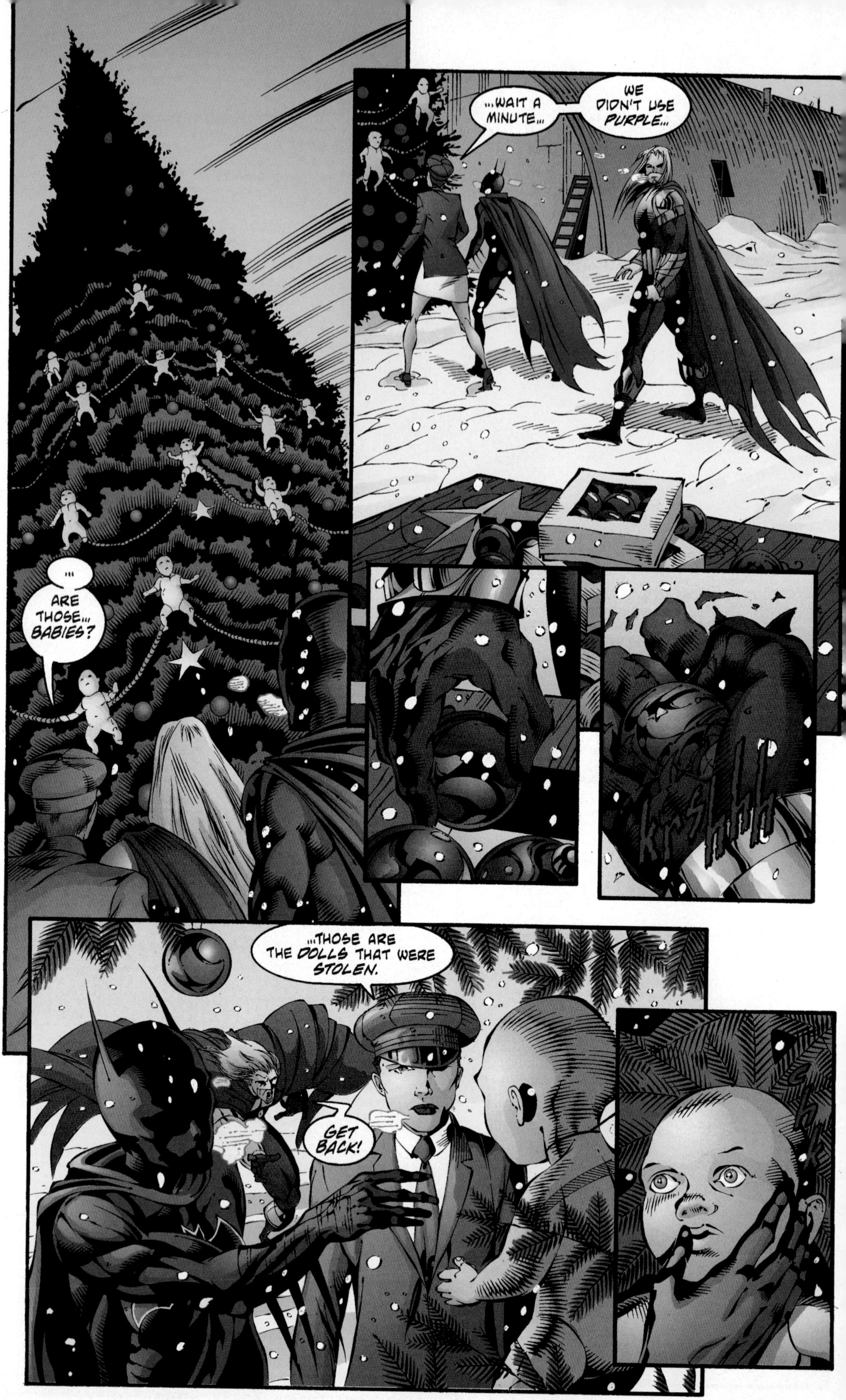

... ARE THOSE... BABIES?
...WAIT A MINUTE...
WE DIDN'T USE PURPLE...
krshhh
...THOSE ARE THE DOLLS THAT WERE STOLEN.
GET BACK!

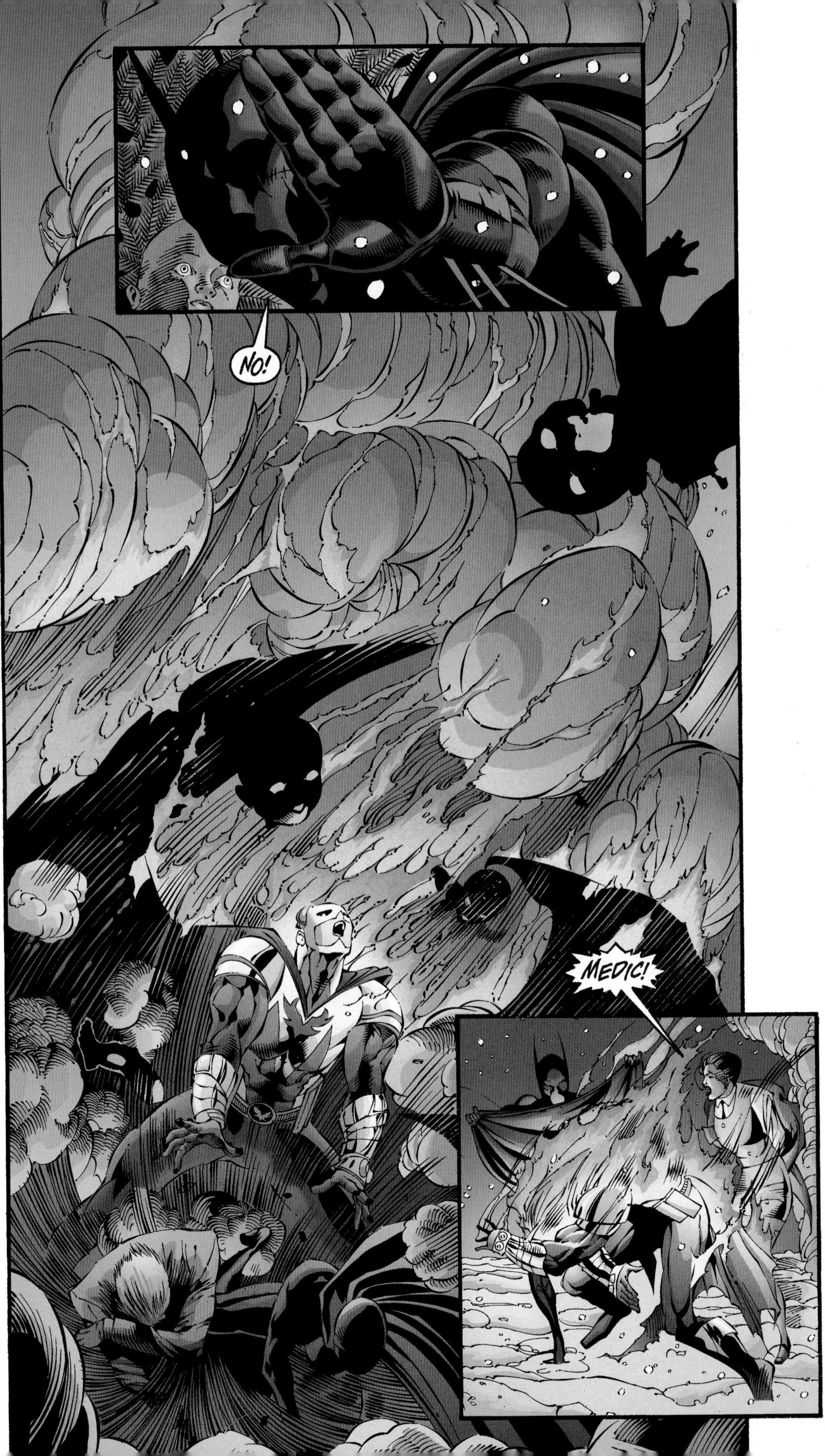
NO!
MEDIC!

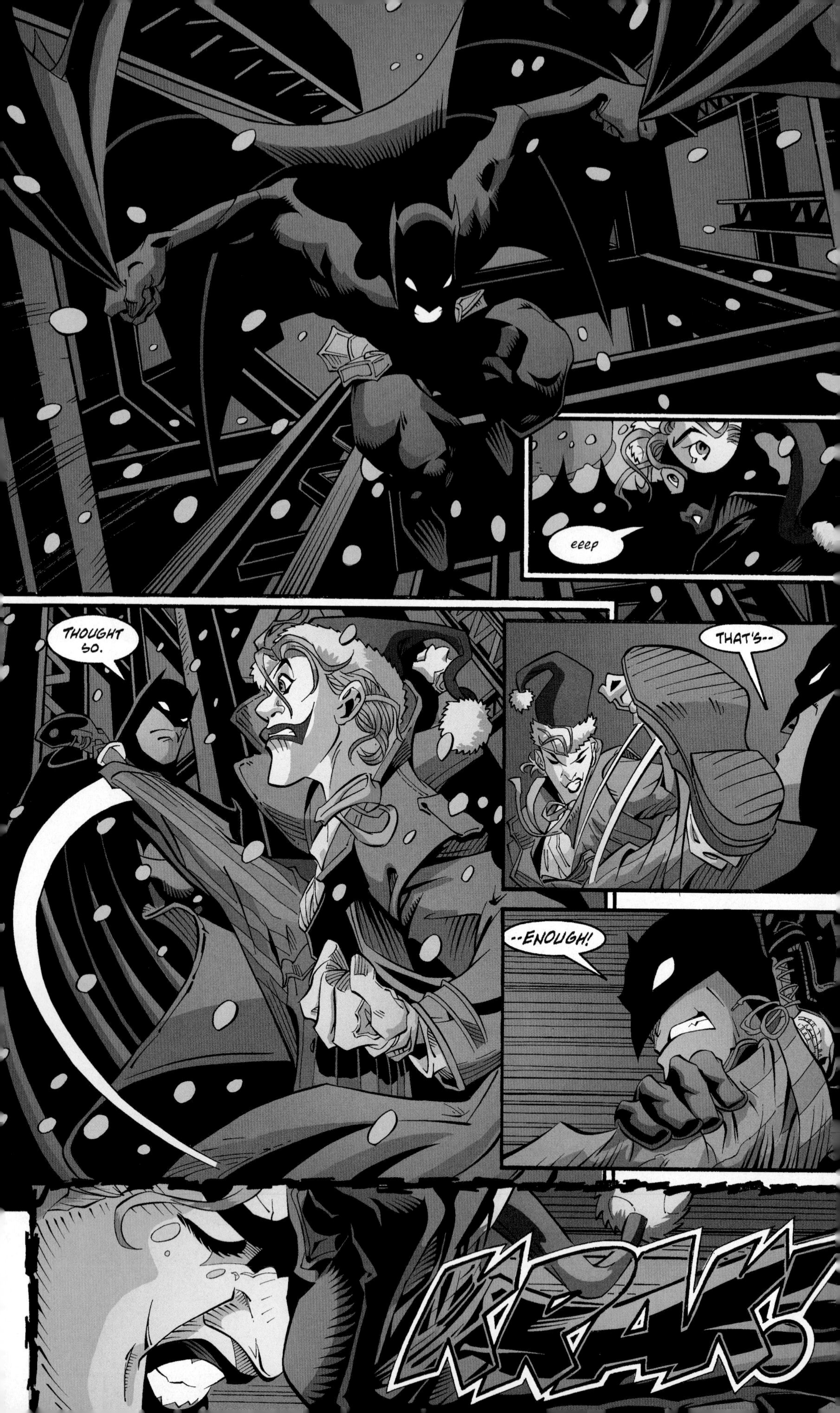
eeep
THOUGHT SO.
THAT'S--
--ENOUGH!

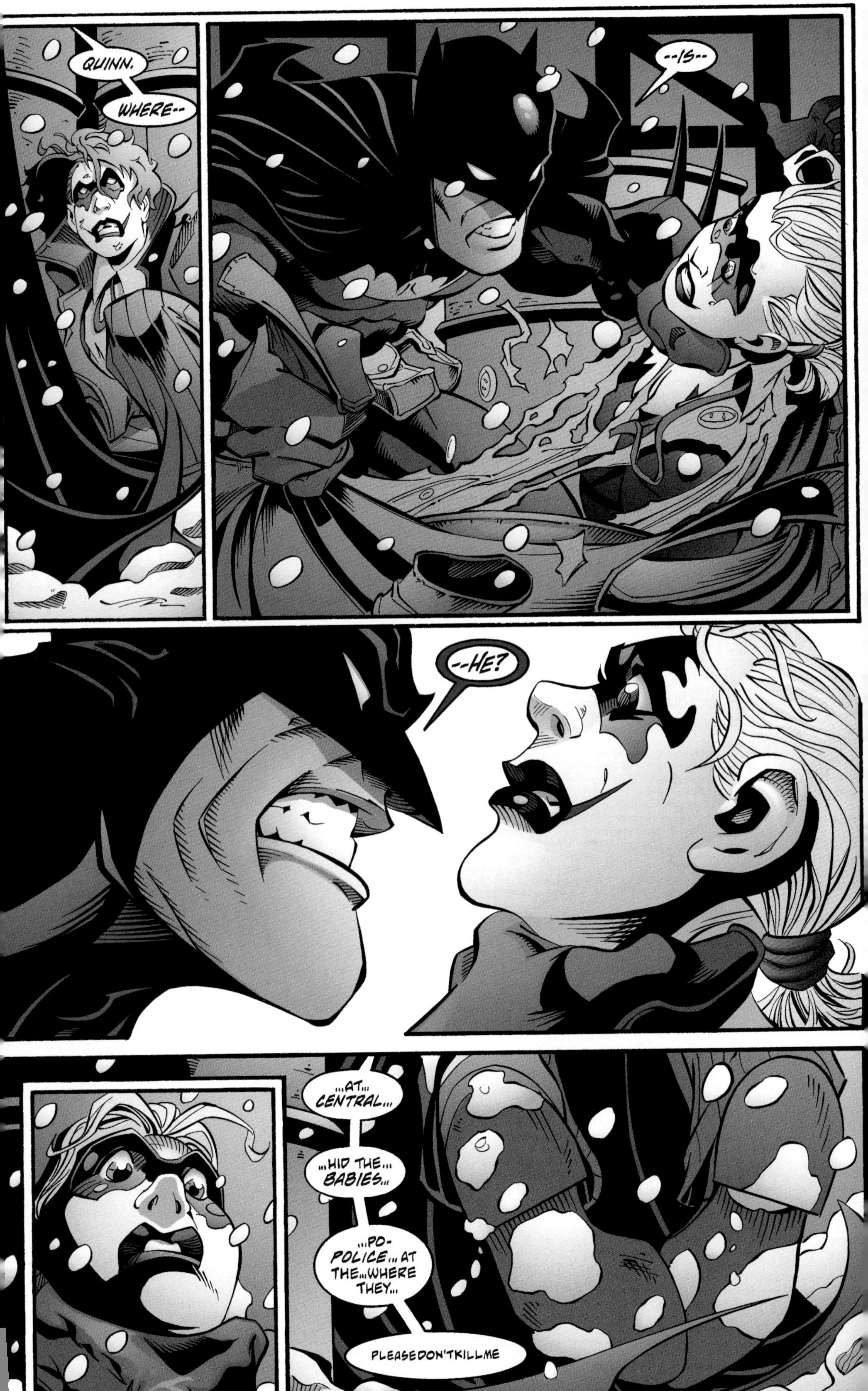
QUINN.
WHERE--
--IS--
--HE?
...AT CENTRAL...
...HID THE... BABIES...
...PO-POLICE... AT THE...WHERE THEY...
PLEASEDON'TKILLME

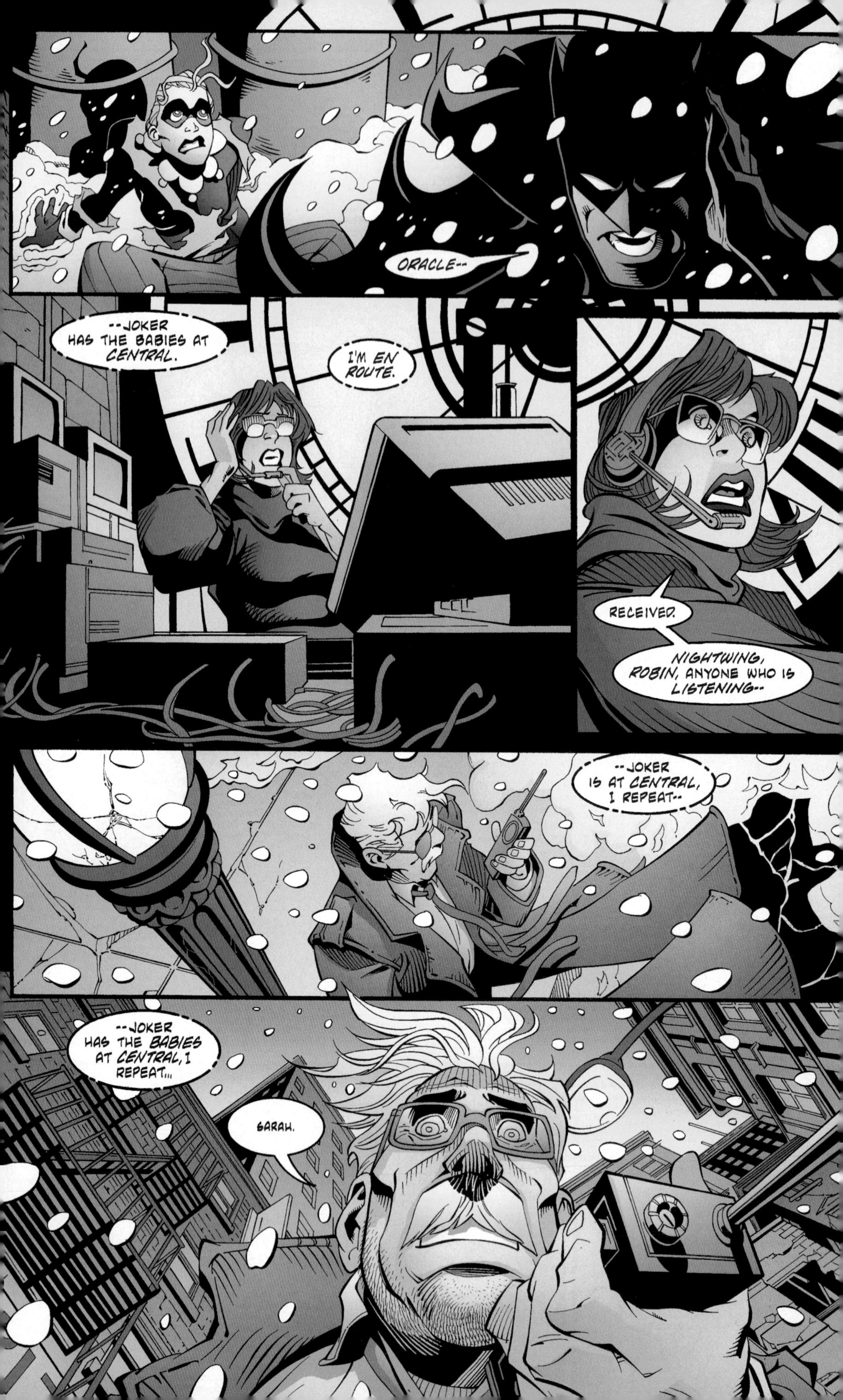
ORACLE--
--JOKER HAS THE BABIES AT CENTRAL.
I'M EN ROUTE.
RECEIVED.
NIGHTWING, ROBIN, ANYONE WHO IS LISTENING--
--JOKER IS AT CENTRAL, I REPEAT--
--JOKER HAS THE BABIES AT CENTRAL, I REPEAT...
SARAH.

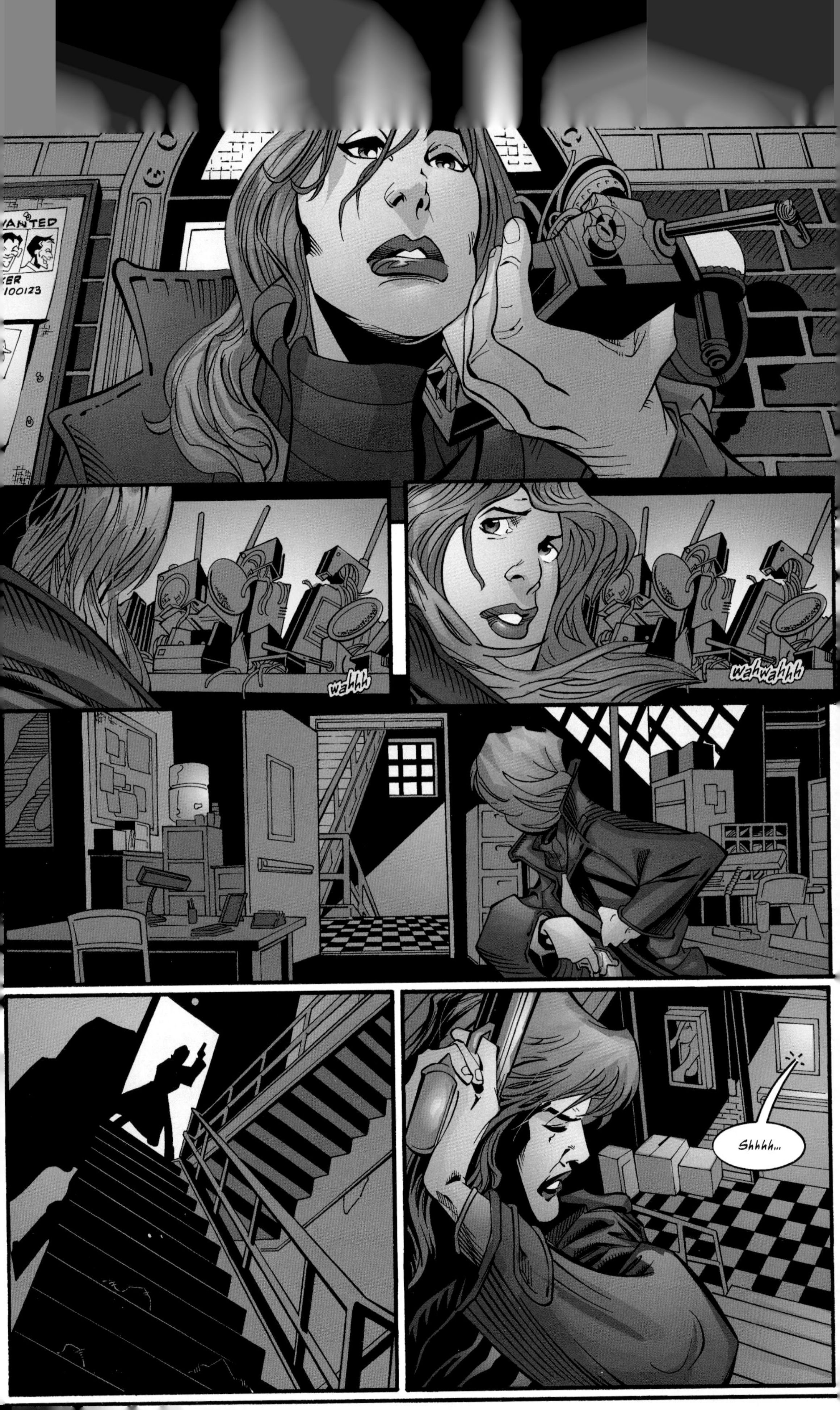

WANTED
KER
100123
wahhh
wahwahhh
Shhhh...

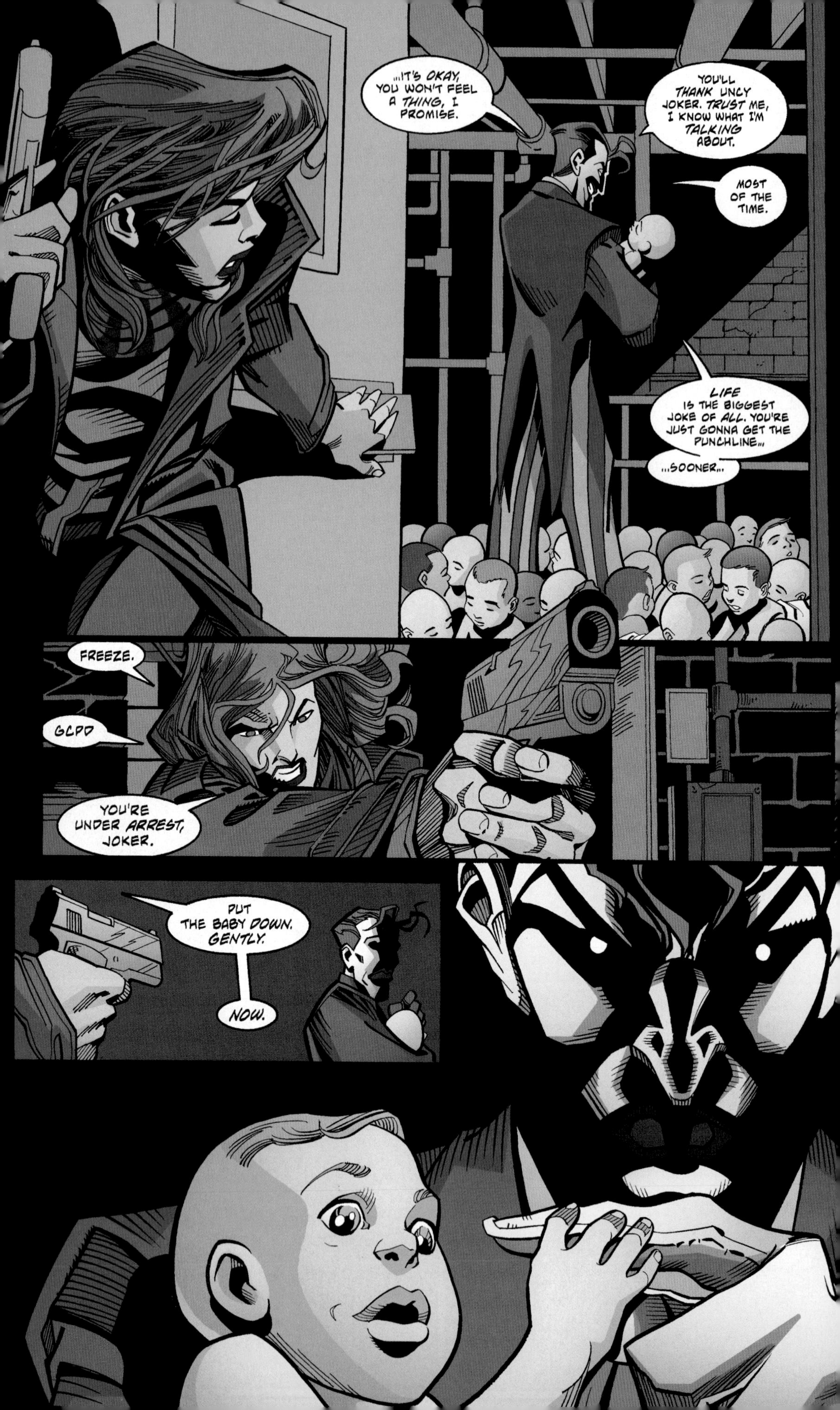
...IT'S OKAY, YOU WON'T FEEL A THING, I PROMISE.
YOU'LL THANK UNCY JOKER. TRUST ME, I KNOW WHAT I'M TALKING ABOUT.
MOST OF THE TIME.
LIFE IS THE BIGGEST JOKE OF ALL. YOU'RE JUST GONNA GET THE PUNCHLINE...
...SOONER...
FREEZE.
GCPD
YOU'RE UNDER ARREST, JOKER.
PUT THE BABY DOWN. GENTLY.
NOW.

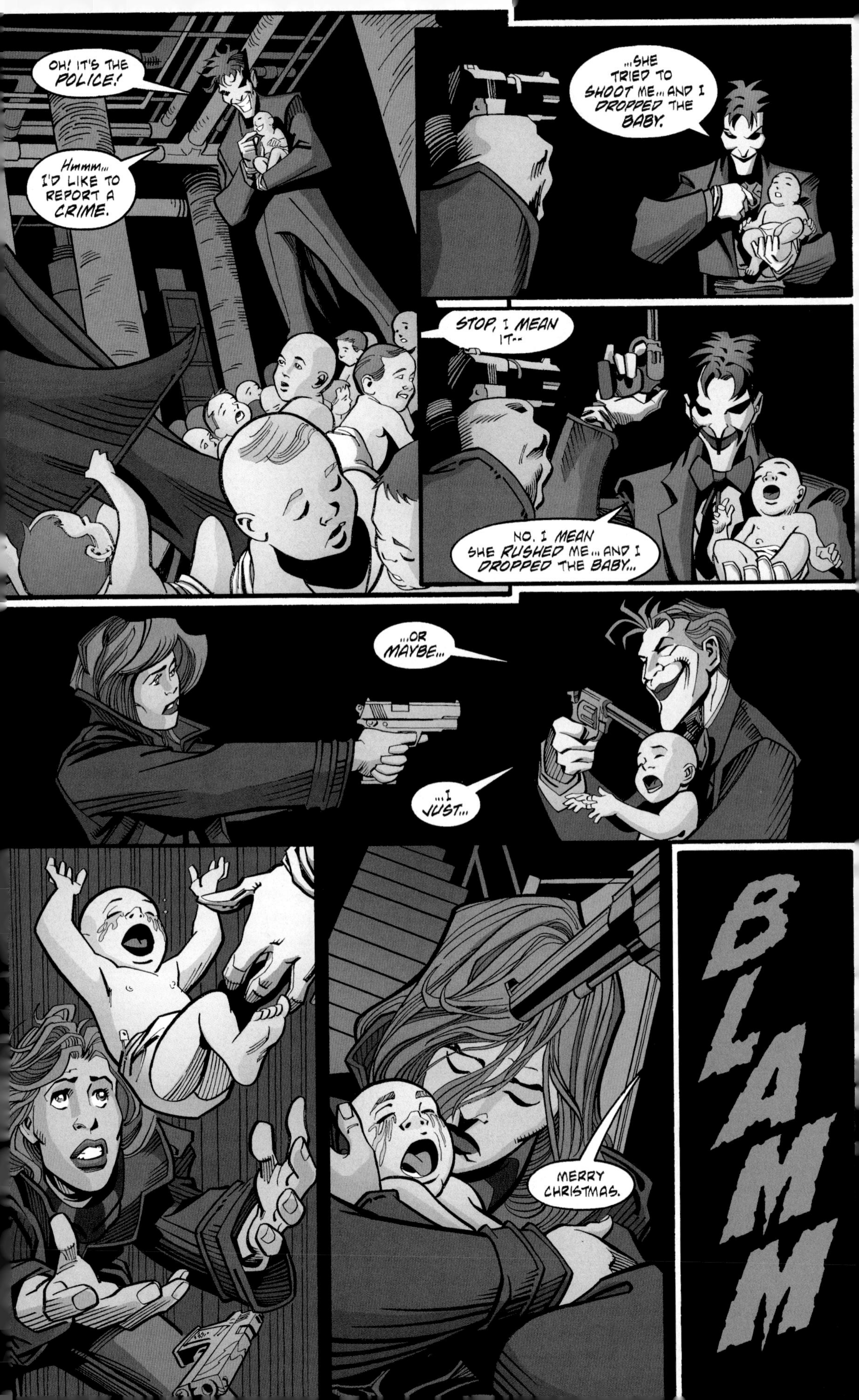
OH! IT'S THE POLICE!
Hmmm... I'D LIKE TO REPORT A CRIME.
...SHE TRIED TO SHOOT ME... AND I DROPPED THE BABY.
STOP, I MEAN IT--
NO. I MEAN SHE RUSHED ME... AND I DROPPED THE BABY...
...OR MAYBE...
...I JUST...
MERRY CHRISTMAS.
BLAMM

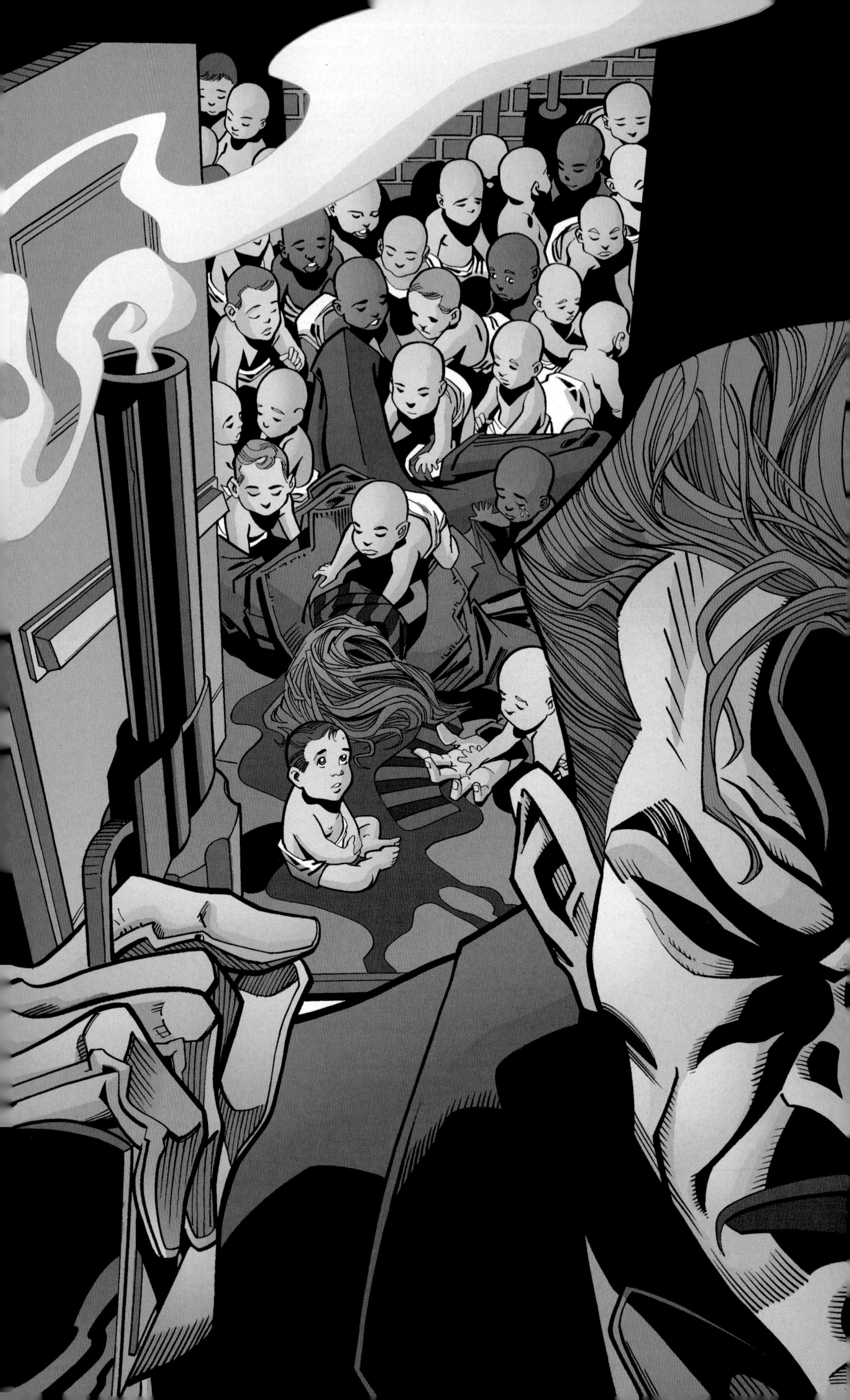

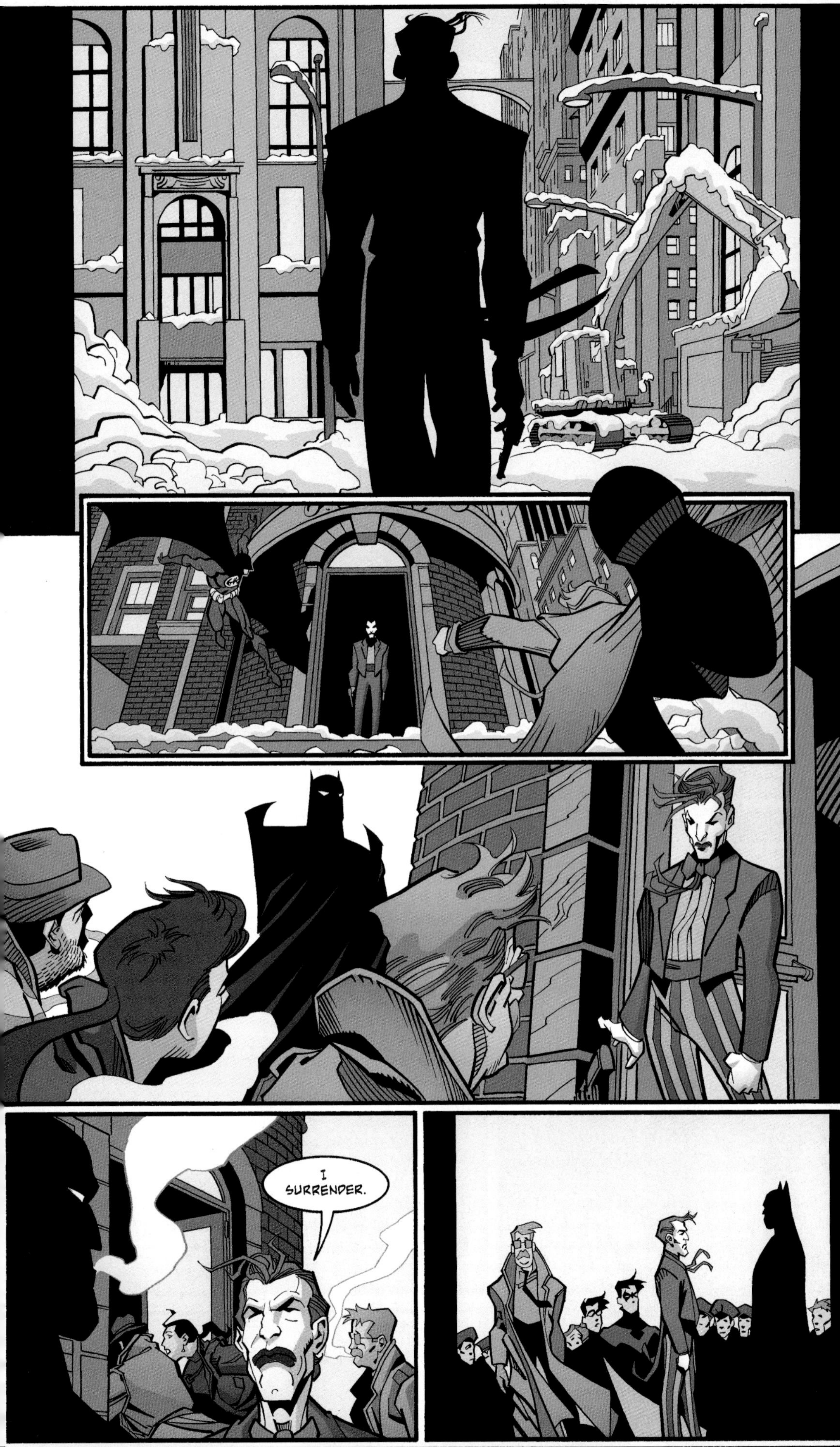
I SURRENDER.

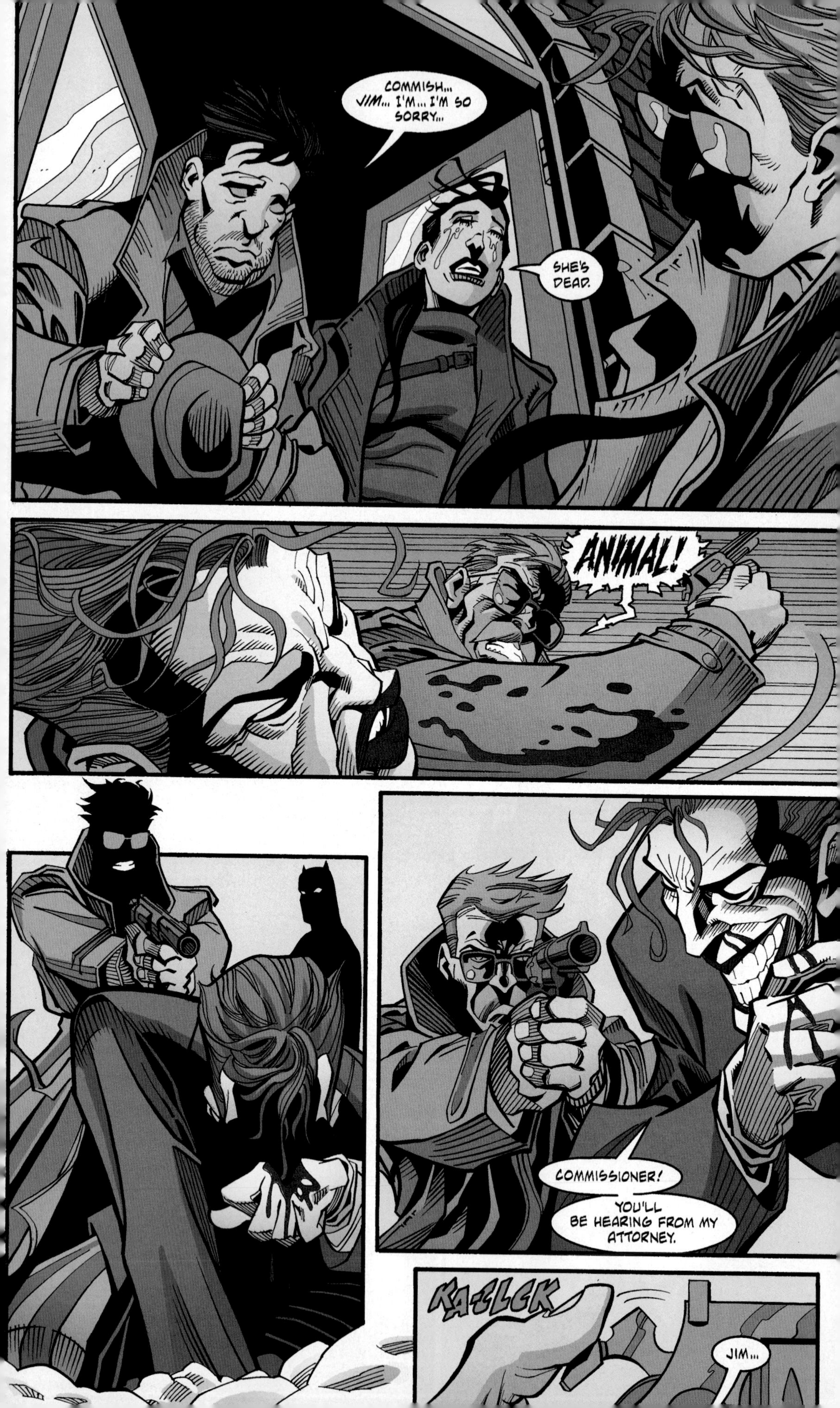
COMMISH... JIM... I'M... I'M SO SORRY...
SHE'S DEAD.
ANIMAL!
COMMISSIONER!
YOU'LL BE HEARING FROM MY ATTORNEY.
KA-CLCK
JIM...

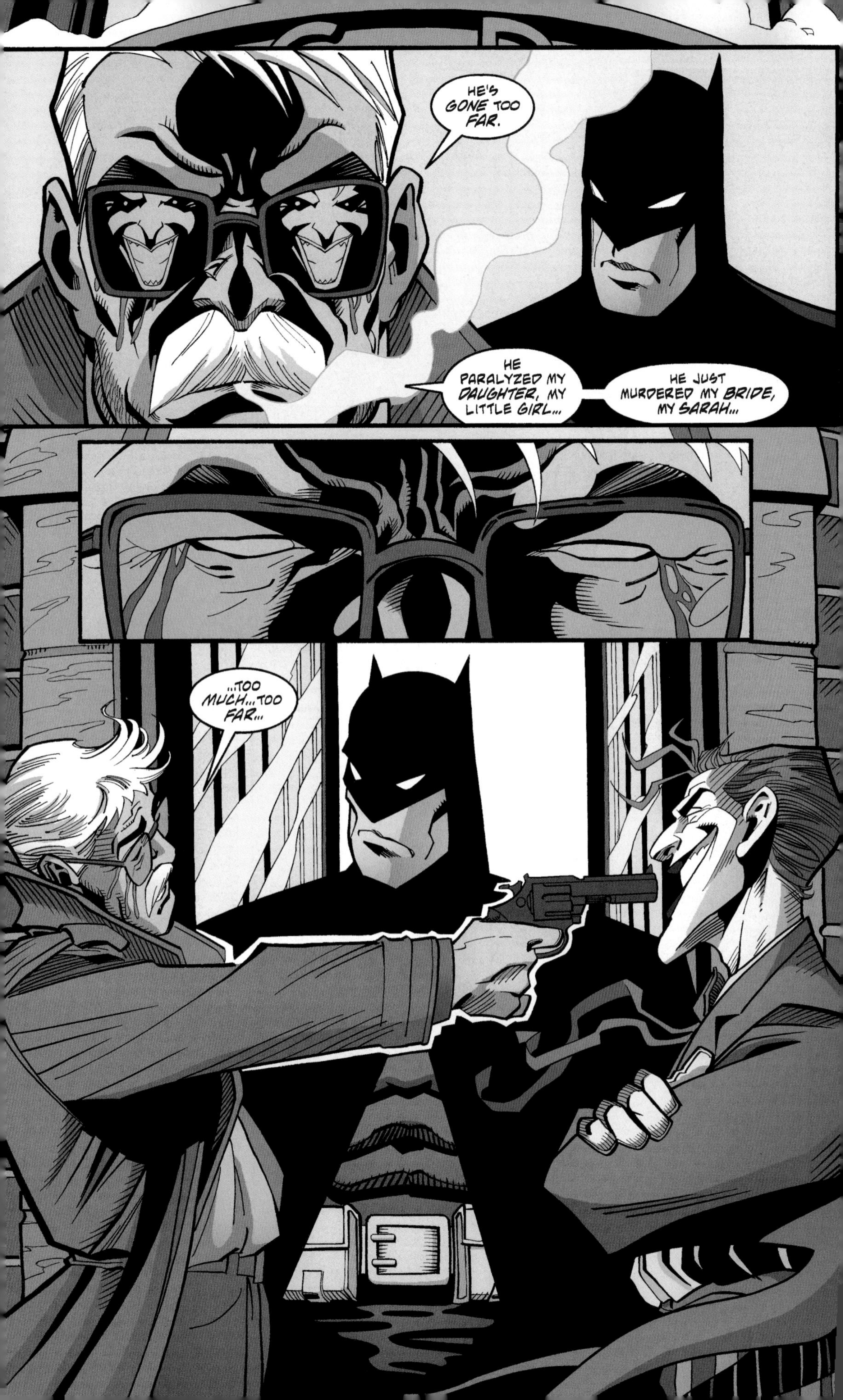
HE'S GONE TOO FAR.
HE PARALYZED MY DAUGHTER, MY LITTLE GIRL...
HE JUST MURDERED MY BRIDE, MY SARAH...
...TOO MUCH...TOO FAR...

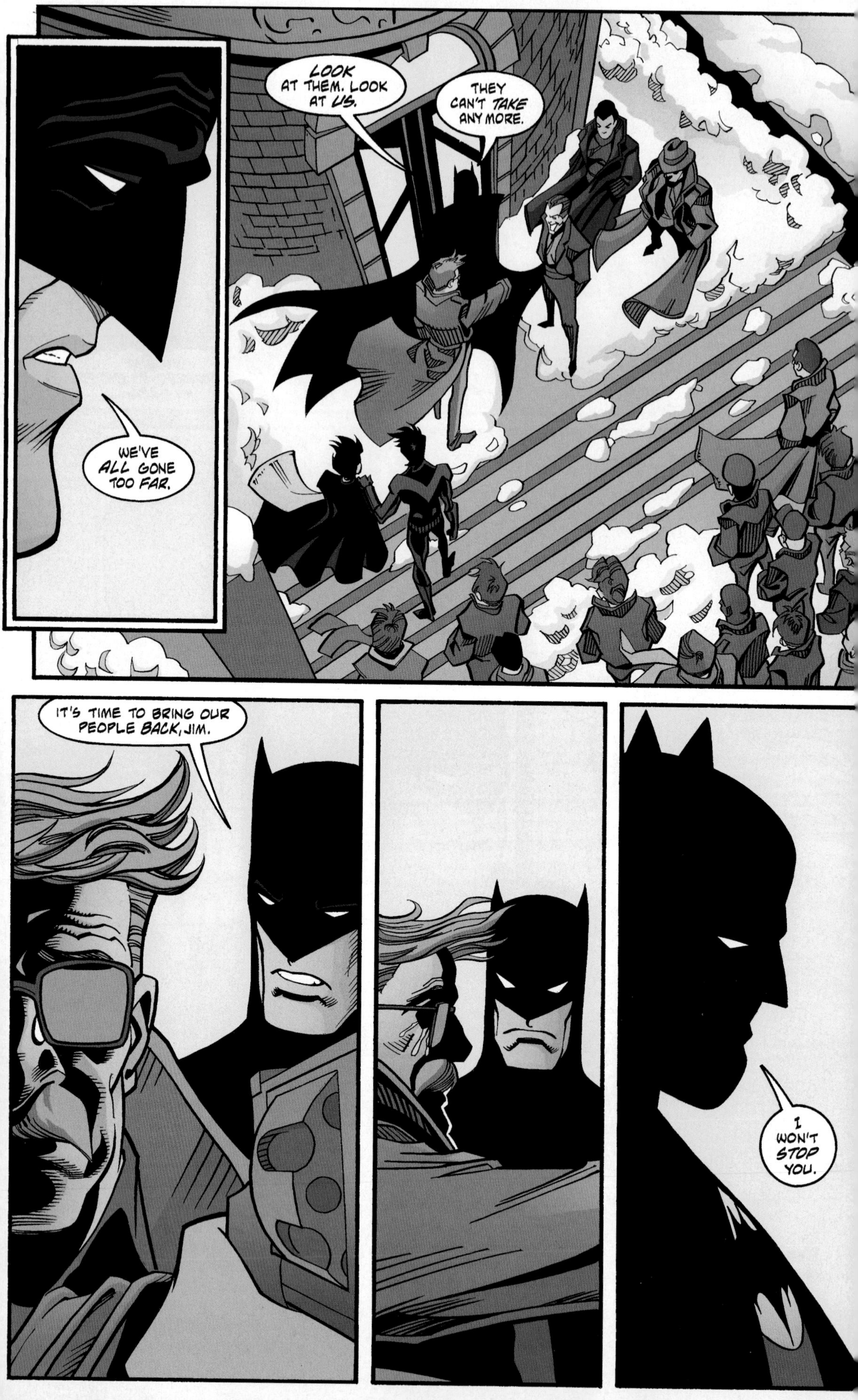
LOOK AT THEM. LOOK AT US.
THEY CAN'T TAKE ANY MORE.
WE'VE ALL GONE TOO FAR.
IT'S TIME TO BRING OUR PEOPLE BACK, JIM.
I WON'T STOP YOU.

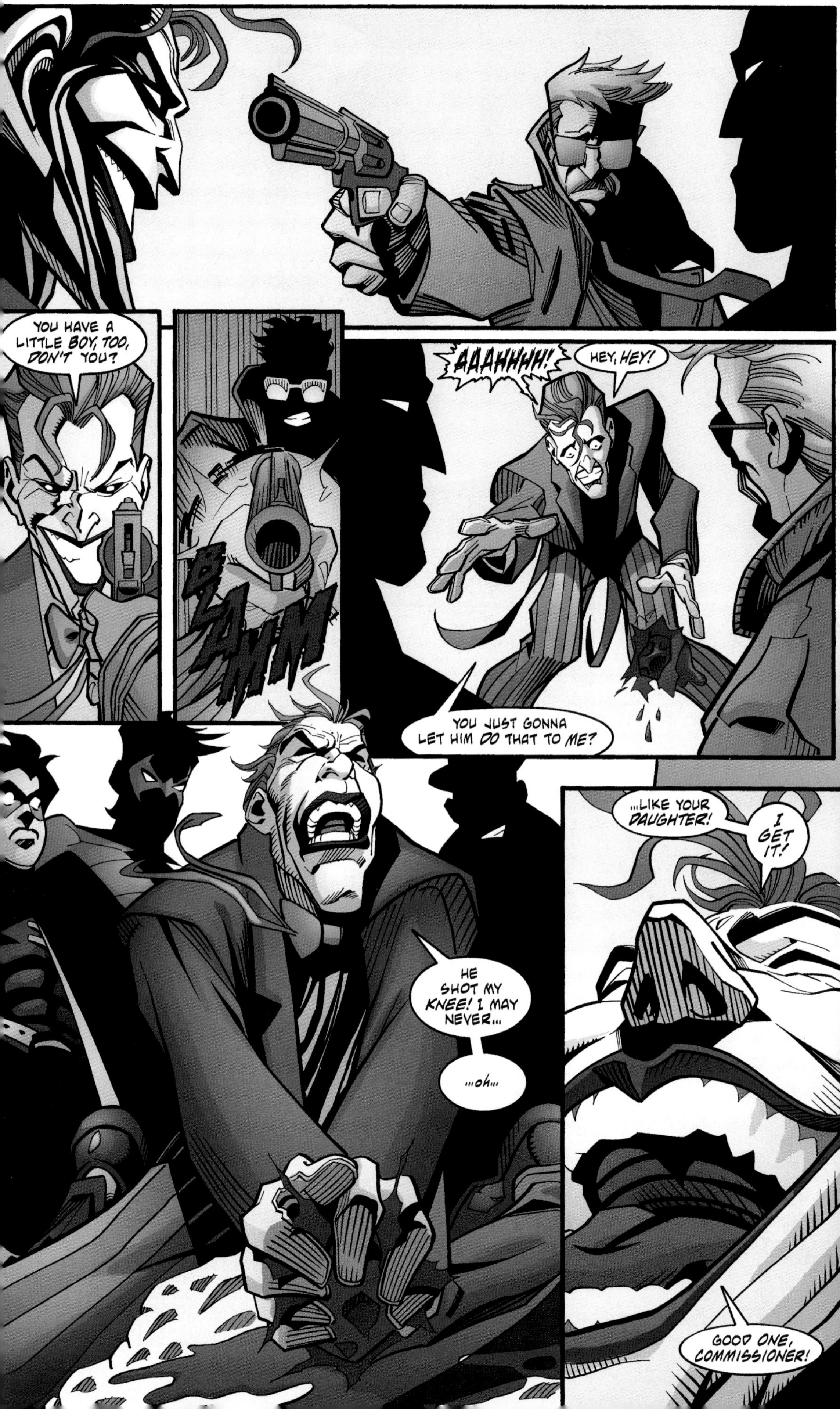
YOU HAVE A LITTLE BOY, TOO, DON'T YOU?
BLAMM
AAAHHHH!
HEY, HEY!
YOU JUST GONNA LET HIM DO THAT TO ME?
HE SHOT MY KNEE! I MAY NEVER...
...oh...
...LIKE YOUR DAUGHTER!
I GET IT!
GOOD ONE, COMMISSIONER!

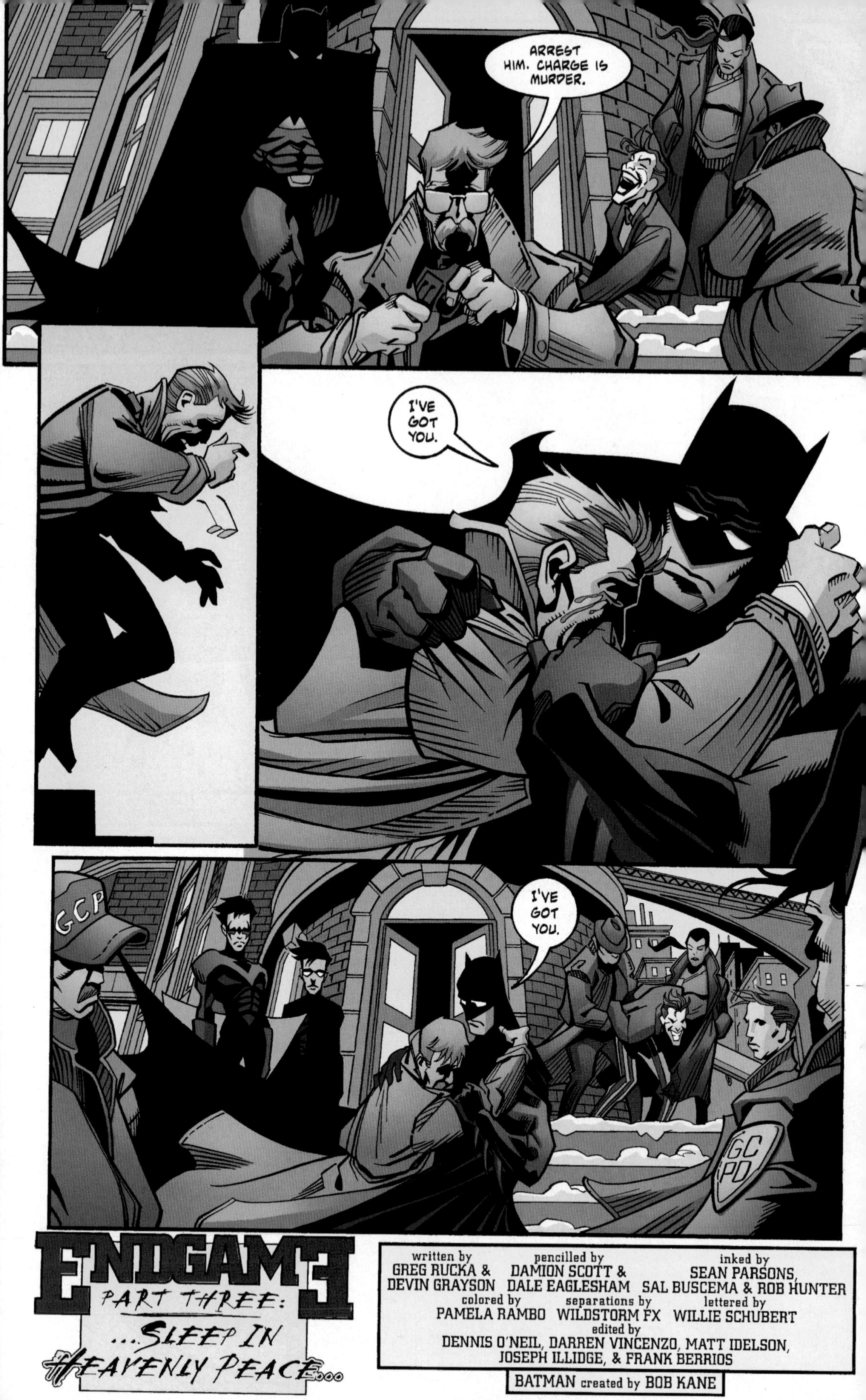
ARREST HIM. CHARGE IS MURDER.
I'VE GOT YOU.
I'VE GOT YOU.
GCP
GC PD

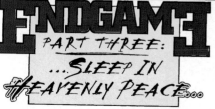

ENDGAME

PART THREE: ...SLEEP IN HEAVENLY PEACE...

written by GREG RUCKA & DEVIN GRAYSON
pencilled by DAMION SCOTT & DALE EAGLESHAM
inked by SEAN PARSONS, SAL BUSCEMA & ROB HUNTER
colored by PAMELA RAMBO
separations by WILDSTORM FX
lettered by WILLIE SCHUBERT
edited by DENNIS O'NEIL, DARREN VINCENZO, MATT IDELSON, JOSEPH ILLIDGE, & FRANK BERRIOS

BATMAN created by BOB KANE

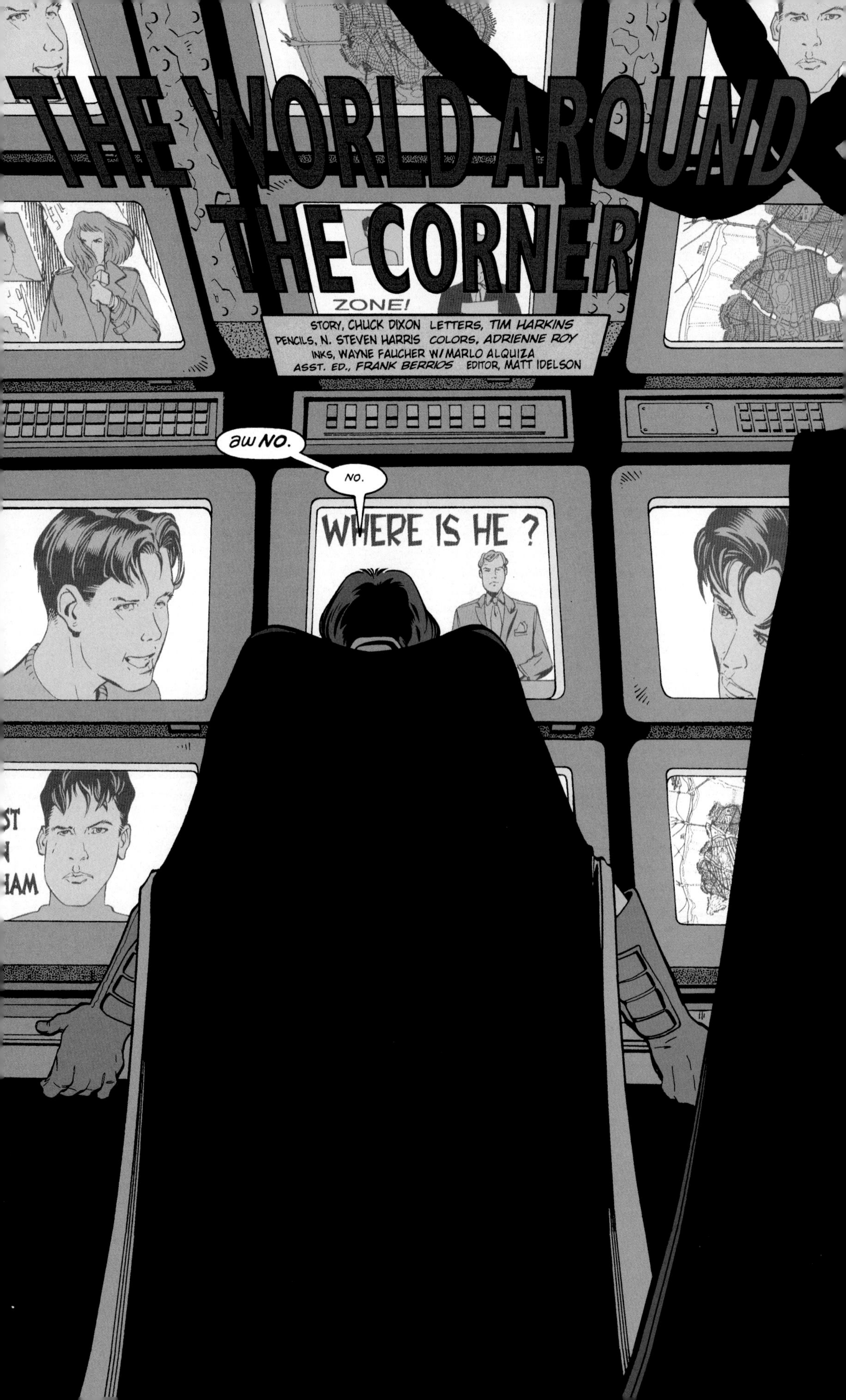
THE WORLD AROUND THE CORNER
ZONE!
STORY, CHUCK DIXON LETTERS, TIM HARKINS
PENCILS, N. STEVEN HARRIS COLORS, ADRIENNE ROY
INKS, WAYNE FAUCHER W/MARLO ALQUIZA
ASST. ED., FRANK BERRIOS EDITOR, MATT IDELSON
aw NO.
NO.
WHERE IS HE ?

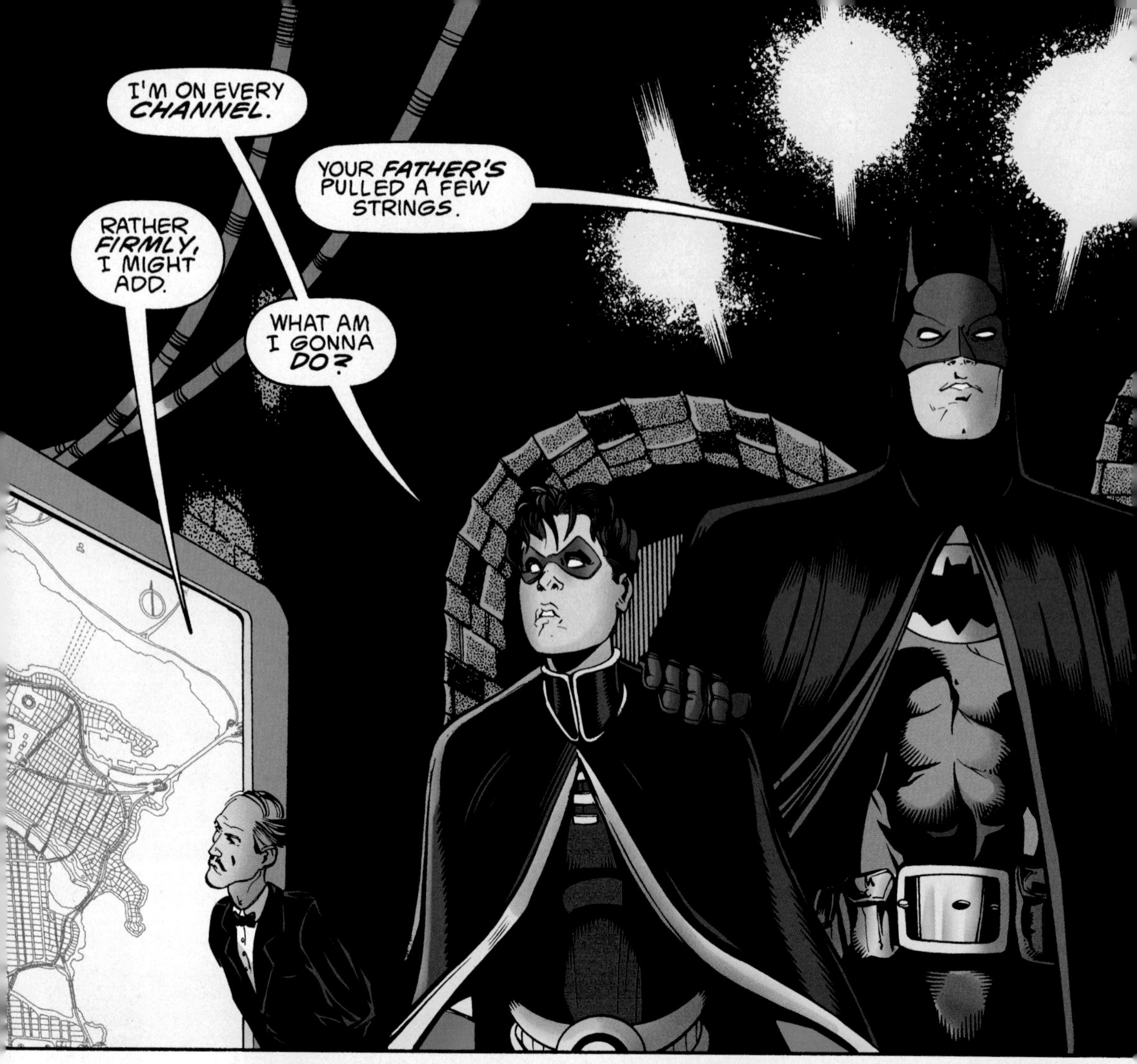
I'M ON EVERY CHANNEL.
YOUR FATHER'S PULLED A FEW STRINGS.
RATHER FIRMLY, I MIGHT ADD.
WHAT AM I GONNA DO?

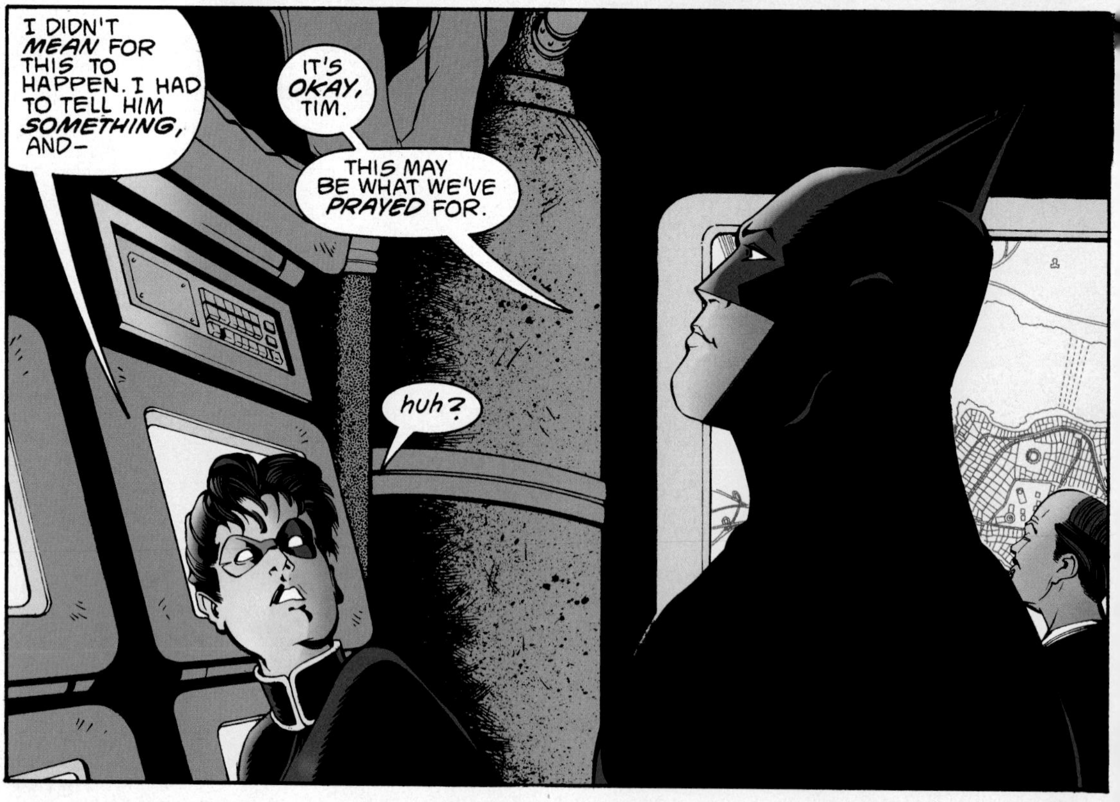
I DIDN'T MEAN FOR THIS TO HAPPEN. I HAD TO TELL HIM SOMETHING, AND–
IT'S OKAY, TIM.
THIS MAY BE WHAT WE'VE PRAYED FOR.
huh?

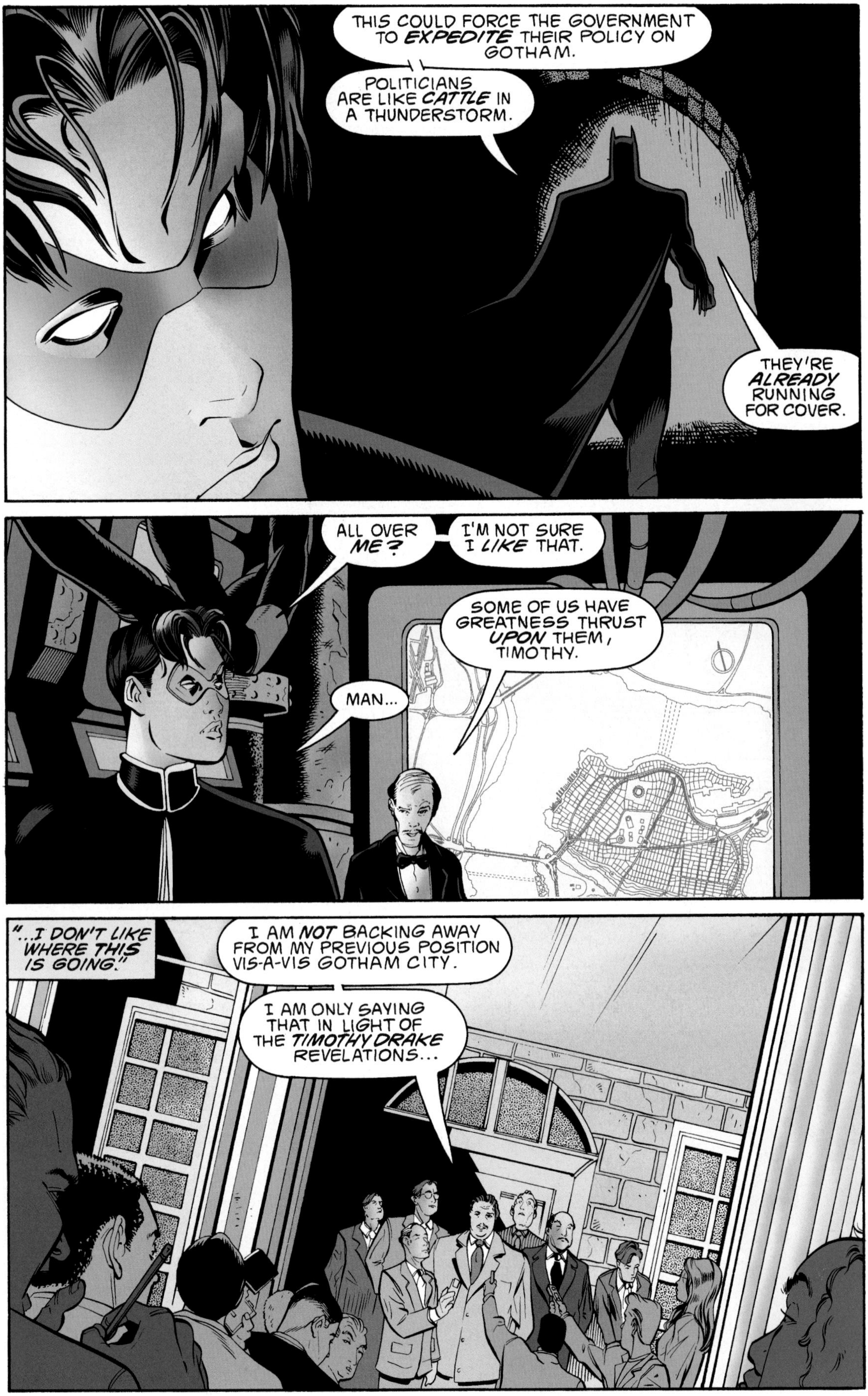
THIS COULD FORCE THE GOVERNMENT TO EXPEDITE THEIR POLICY ON GOTHAM.
POLITICIANS ARE LIKE CATTLE IN A THUNDERSTORM.
THEY'RE ALREADY RUNNING FOR COVER.
ALL OVER ME?
I'M NOT SURE I LIKE THAT.
SOME OF US HAVE GREATNESS THRUST UPON THEM, TIMOTHY.
MAN...
"...I DON'T LIKE WHERE THIS IS GOING."
I AM NOT BACKING AWAY FROM MY PREVIOUS POSITION VIS-A-VIS GOTHAM CITY.
I AM ONLY SAYING THAT IN LIGHT OF THE TIMOTHY DRAKE REVELATIONS...

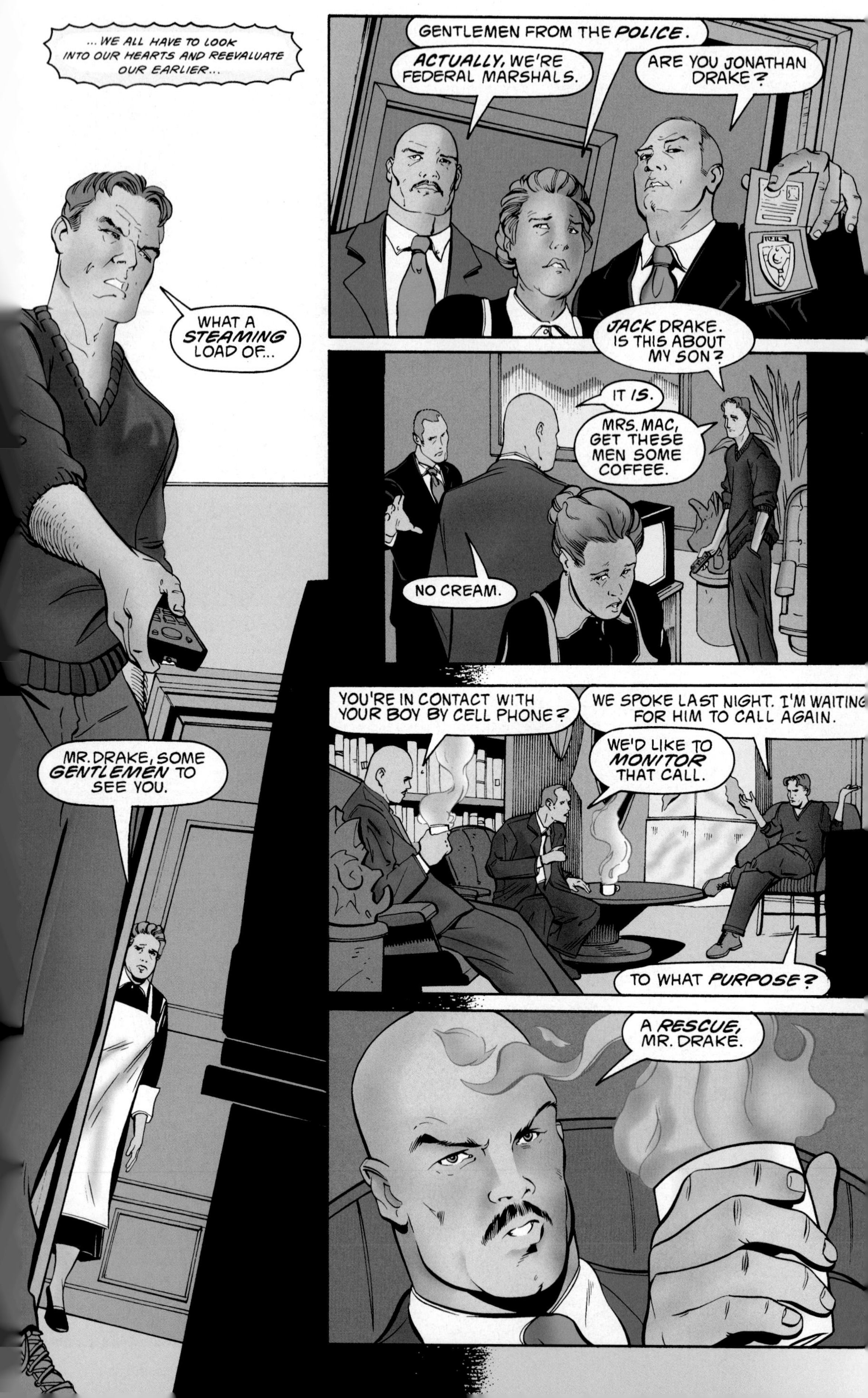
...WE ALL HAVE TO LOOK INTO OUR HEARTS AND REEVALUATE OUR EARLIER...
WHAT A STEAMING LOAD OF...
MR. DRAKE, SOME GENTLEMEN TO SEE YOU.
GENTLEMEN FROM THE POLICE.
ACTUALLY, WE'RE FEDERAL MARSHALS.
ARE YOU JONATHAN DRAKE?
JACK DRAKE. IS THIS ABOUT MY SON?
IT IS.
MRS. MAC, GET THESE MEN SOME COFFEE.
NO CREAM.
YOU'RE IN CONTACT WITH YOUR BOY BY CELL PHONE?
WE SPOKE LAST NIGHT. I'M WAITING FOR HIM TO CALL AGAIN.
WE'D LIKE TO MONITOR THAT CALL.
TO WHAT PURPOSE?
A RESCUE, MR. DRAKE.

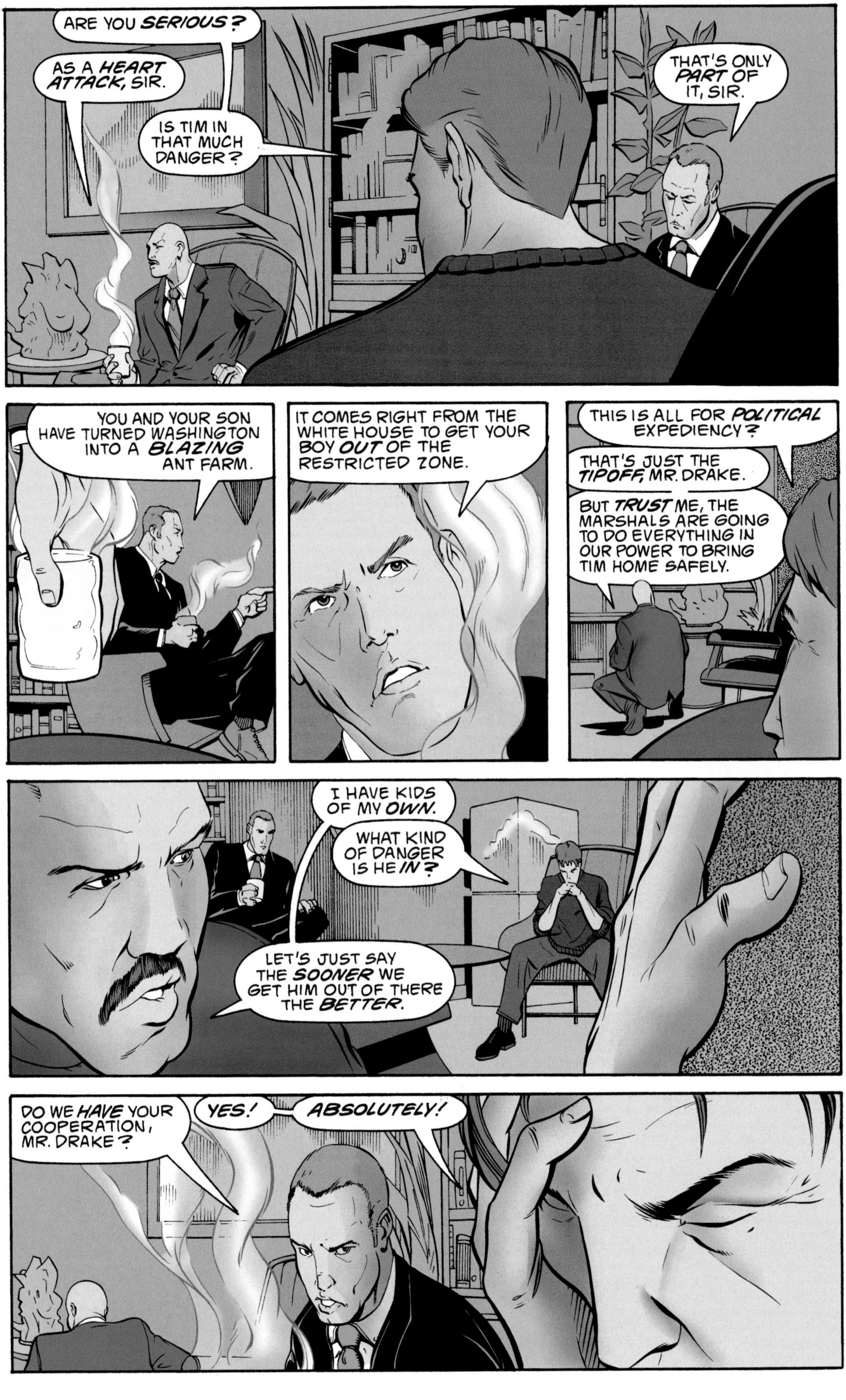
ARE YOU SERIOUS?
AS A HEART ATTACK, SIR.
IS TIM IN THAT MUCH DANGER?
THAT'S ONLY PART OF IT, SIR.
YOU AND YOUR SON HAVE TURNED WASHINGTON INTO A BLAZING ANT FARM.
IT COMES RIGHT FROM THE WHITE HOUSE TO GET YOUR BOY OUT OF THE RESTRICTED ZONE.
THIS IS ALL FOR POLITICAL EXPEDIENCY?
THAT'S JUST THE TIPOFF, MR. DRAKE.
BUT TRUST ME, THE MARSHALS ARE GOING TO DO EVERYTHING IN OUR POWER TO BRING TIM HOME SAFELY.
I HAVE KIDS OF MY OWN.
WHAT KIND OF DANGER IS HE IN?
LET'S JUST SAY THE SOONER WE GET HIM OUT OF THERE THE BETTER.
DO WE HAVE YOUR COOPERATION, MR. DRAKE?
YES!
ABSOLUTELY!

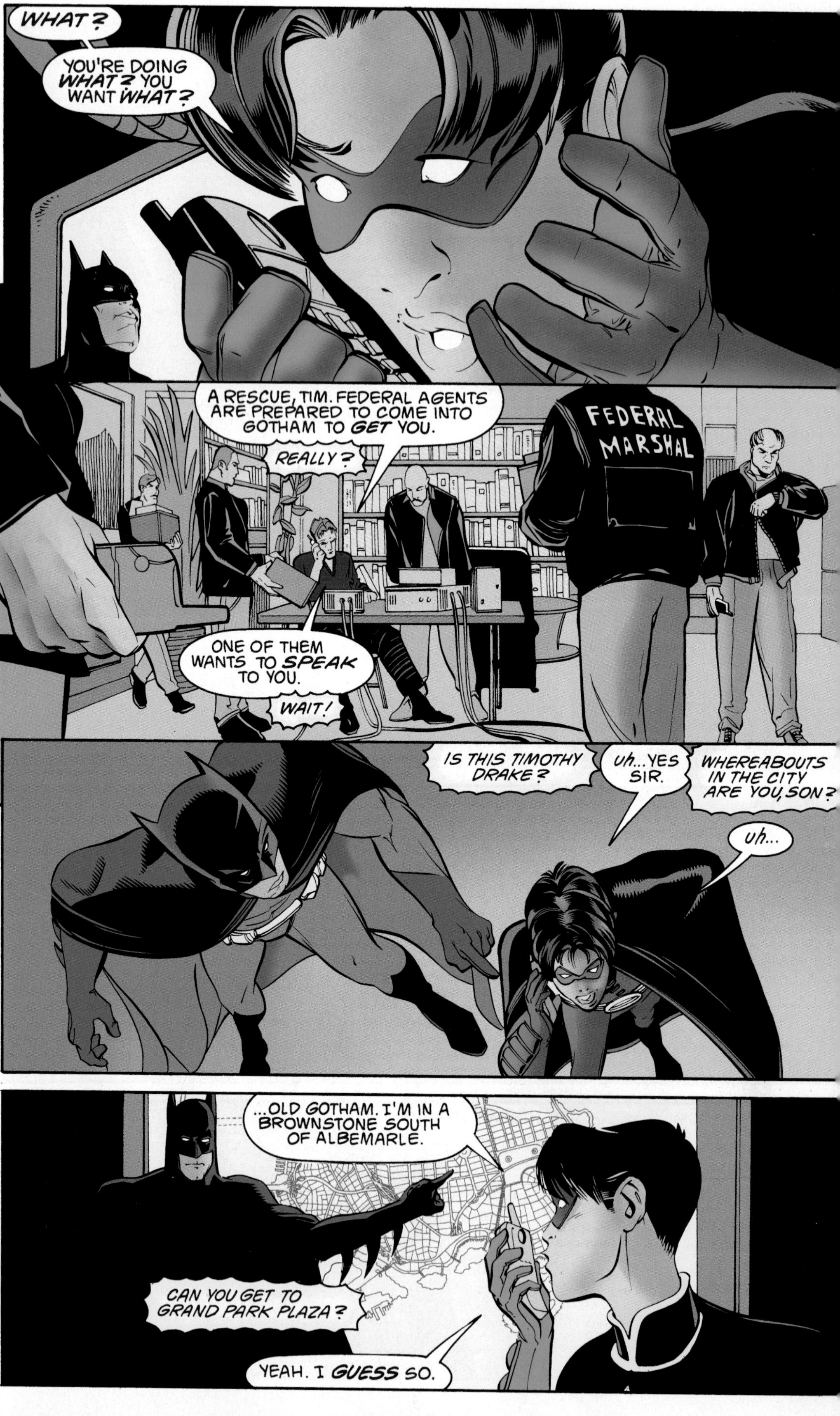
WHAT?
YOU'RE DOING WHAT? YOU WANT WHAT?
A RESCUE, TIM. FEDERAL AGENTS ARE PREPARED TO COME INTO GOTHAM TO GET YOU.
REALLY?
FEDERAL MARSHAL
ONE OF THEM WANTS TO SPEAK TO YOU.
WAIT!
IS THIS TIMOTHY DRAKE?
Uh... YES SIR.
WHEREABOUTS IN THE CITY ARE YOU, SON?
Uh...
...OLD GOTHAM. I'M IN A BROWNSTONE SOUTH OF ALBEMARLE.
CAN YOU GET TO GRAND PARK PLAZA?
YEAH. I GUESS SO.

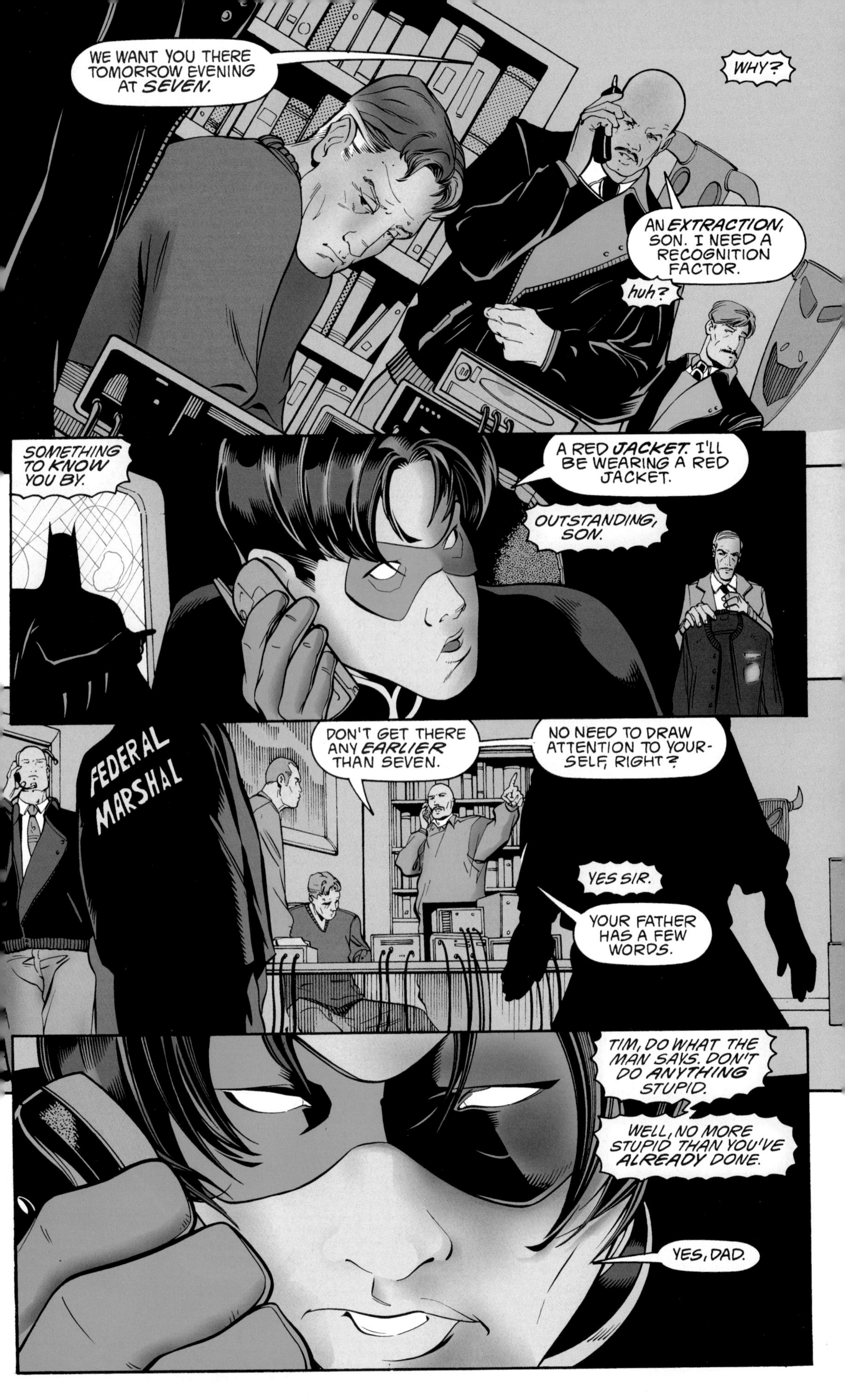
WE WANT YOU THERE TOMORROW EVENING AT SEVEN.
WHY?
AN EXTRACTION, SON. I NEED A RECOGNITION FACTOR.
huh?
SOMETHING TO KNOW YOU BY.
A RED JACKET. I'LL BE WEARING A RED JACKET.
OUTSTANDING, SON.
FEDERAL MARSHAL
DON'T GET THERE ANY EARLIER THAN SEVEN.
NO NEED TO DRAW ATTENTION TO YOURSELF, RIGHT?
YES SIR.
YOUR FATHER HAS A FEW WORDS.
TIM, DO WHAT THE MAN SAYS. DON'T DO ANYTHING STUPID.
WELL, NO MORE STUPID THAN YOU'VE ALREADY DONE.
YES, DAD.

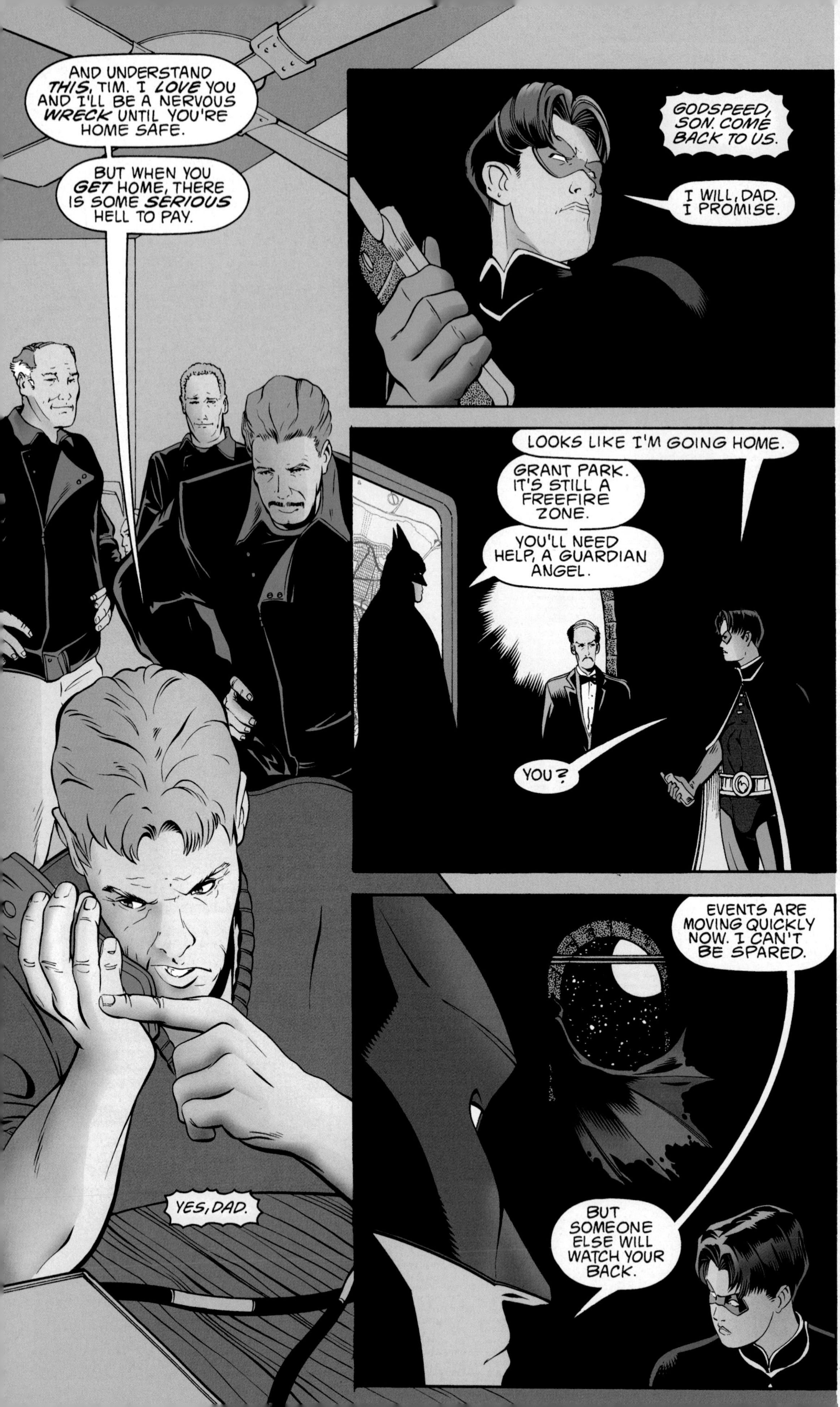

AND UNDERSTAND THIS, TIM. I LOVE YOU AND I'LL BE A NERVOUS WRECK UNTIL YOU'RE HOME SAFE.
BUT WHEN YOU GET HOME, THERE IS SOME SERIOUS HELL TO PAY.
YES, DAD.
GODSPEED, SON. COME BACK TO US.
I WILL, DAD. I PROMISE.
LOOKS LIKE I'M GOING HOME.
GRANT PARK. IT'S STILL A FREEFIRE ZONE.
YOU'LL NEED HELP, A GUARDIAN ANGEL.
YOU?
EVENTS ARE MOVING QUICKLY NOW. I CAN'T BE SPARED.
BUT SOMEONE ELSE WILL WATCH YOUR BACK.

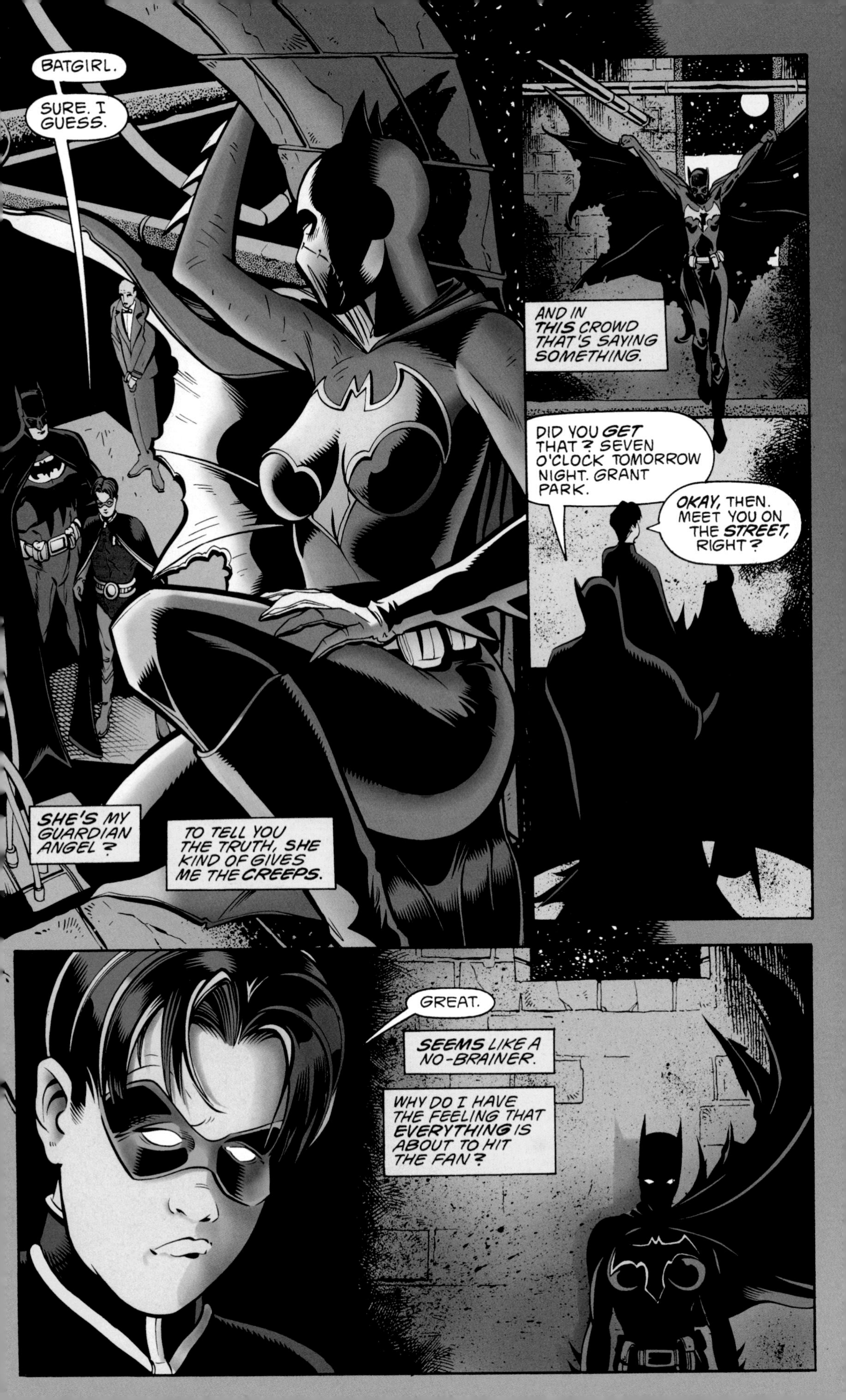
BATGIRL.
SURE. I GUESS.
SHE'S MY GUARDIAN ANGEL?
TO TELL YOU THE TRUTH, SHE KIND OF GIVES ME THE CREEPS.
AND IN THIS CROWD THAT'S SAYING SOMETHING.
DID YOU GET THAT? SEVEN O'CLOCK TOMORROW NIGHT. GRANT PARK.
OKAY, THEN. MEET YOU ON THE STREET, RIGHT?
GREAT.
SEEMS LIKE A NO-BRAINER.
WHY DO I HAVE THE FEELING THAT EVERYTHING IS ABOUT TO HIT THE FAN?

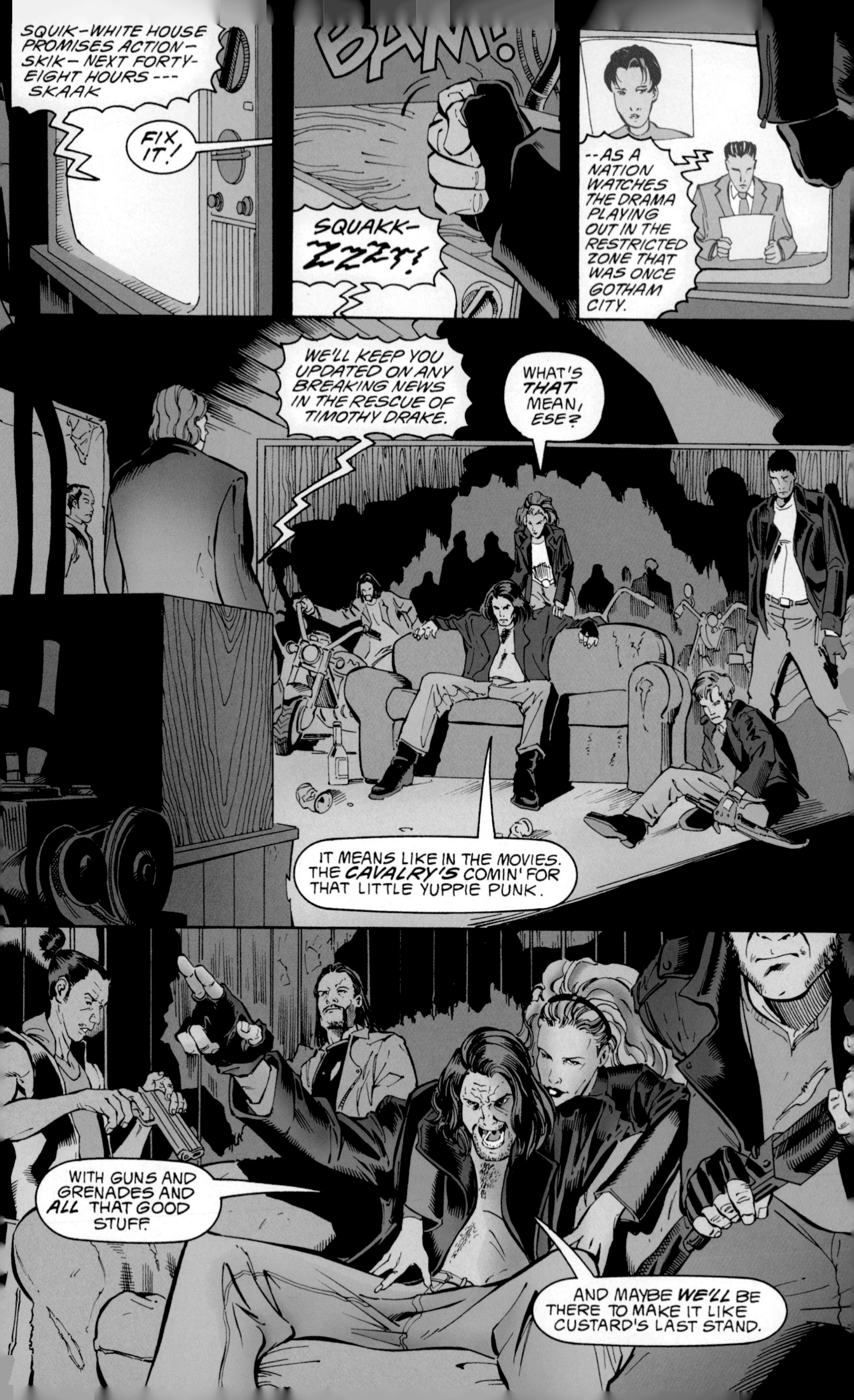
SQUIK–WHITE HOUSE PROMISES ACTION– SKIK– NEXT FORTY-EIGHT HOURS--- SKAAK
FIX IT!
BAM!
SQUAKK-ZZZZT!
--AS A NATION WATCHES THE DRAMA PLAYING OUT IN THE RESTRICTED ZONE THAT WAS ONCE GOTHAM CITY.
WE'LL KEEP YOU UPDATED ON ANY BREAKING NEWS IN THE RESCUE OF TIMOTHY DRAKE.
WHAT'S THAT MEAN, ESE?
IT MEANS LIKE IN THE MOVIES. THE CAVALRY'S COMIN' FOR THAT LITTLE YUPPIE PUNK.
WITH GUNS AND GRENADES AND ALL THAT GOOD STUFF.
AND MAYBE WE'LL BE THERE TO MAKE IT LIKE CUSTARD'S LAST STAND.

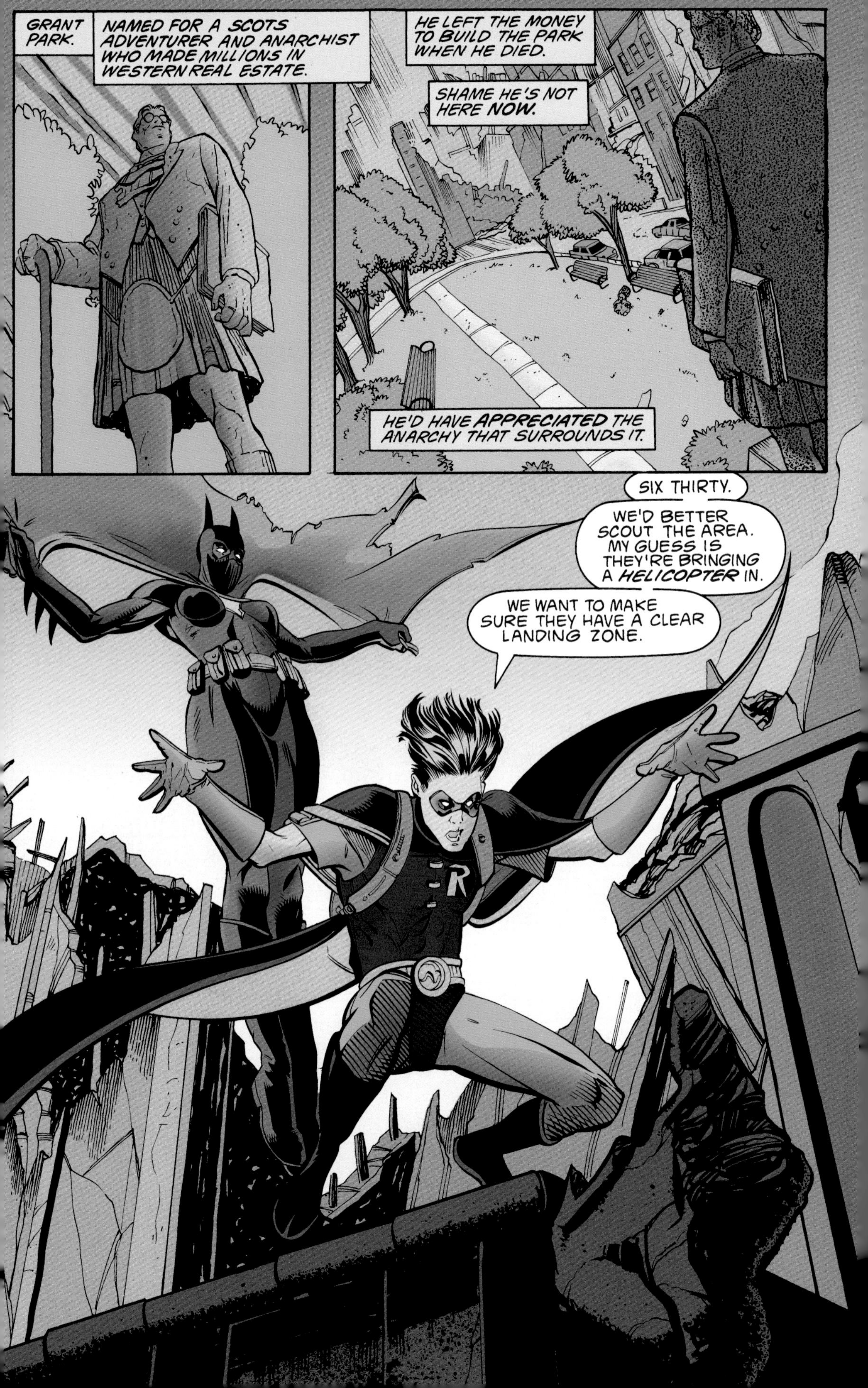
GRANT PARK.
NAMED FOR A SCOTS ADVENTURER AND ANARCHIST WHO MADE MILLIONS IN WESTERN REAL ESTATE.
HE LEFT THE MONEY TO BUILD THE PARK WHEN HE DIED.
SHAME HE'S NOT HERE NOW.
HE'D HAVE APPRECIATED THE ANARCHY THAT SURROUNDS IT.
SIX THIRTY.
WE'D BETTER SCOUT THE AREA. MY GUESS IS THEY'RE BRINGING A HELICOPTER IN.
WE WANT TO MAKE SURE THEY HAVE A CLEAR LANDING ZONE.

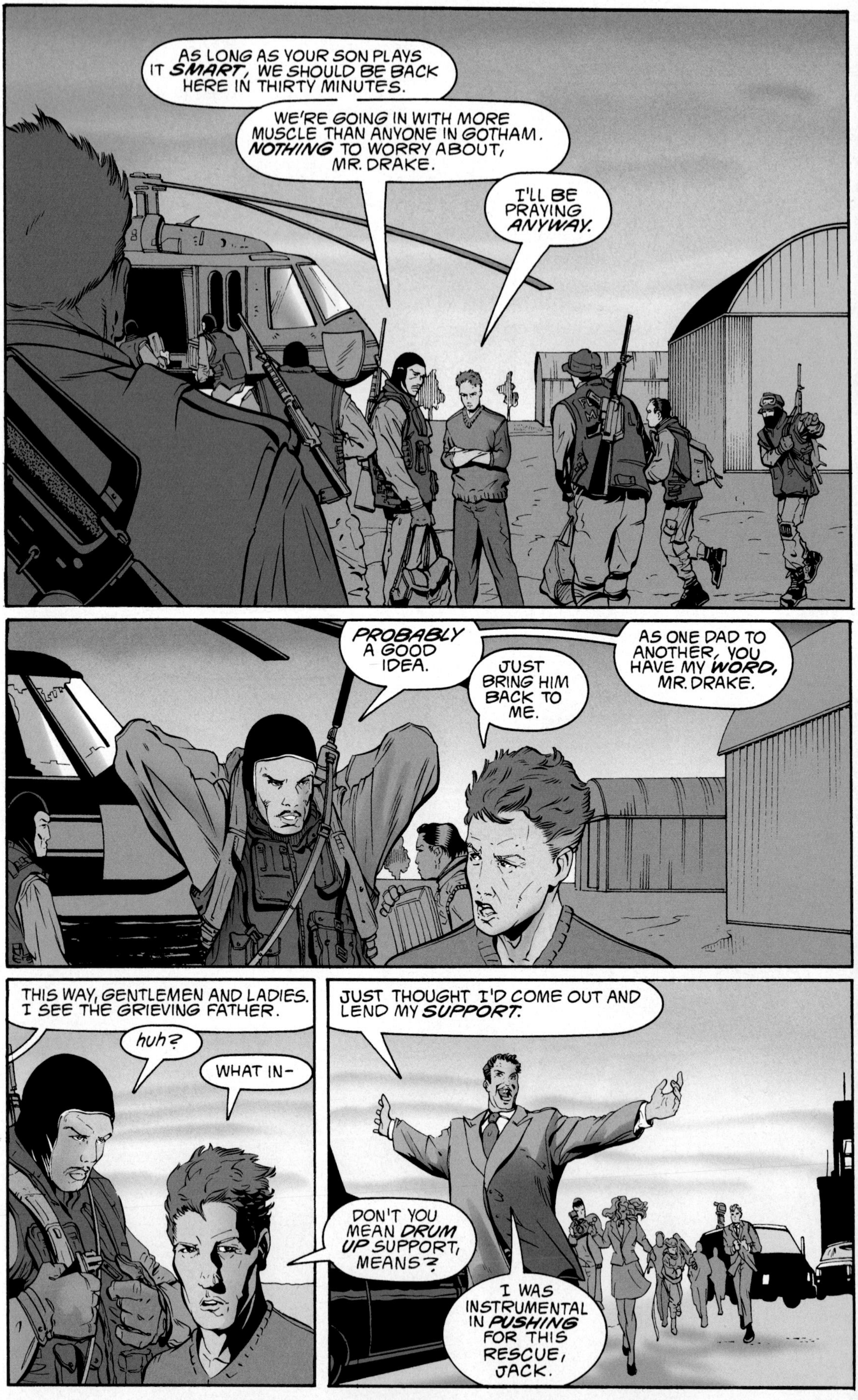
AS LONG AS YOUR SON PLAYS IT SMART, WE SHOULD BE BACK HERE IN THIRTY MINUTES.
WE'RE GOING IN WITH MORE MUSCLE THAN ANYONE IN GOTHAM. NOTHING TO WORRY ABOUT, MR. DRAKE.
I'LL BE PRAYING ANYWAY.
PROBABLY A GOOD IDEA.
JUST BRING HIM BACK TO ME.
AS ONE DAD TO ANOTHER, YOU HAVE MY WORD, MR. DRAKE.
THIS WAY, GENTLEMEN AND LADIES. I SEE THE GRIEVING FATHER.
huh?
WHAT IN-
JUST THOUGHT I'D COME OUT AND LEND MY SUPPORT.
DON'T YOU MEAN DRUM UP SUPPORT, MEANS?
I WAS INSTRUMENTAL IN PUSHING FOR THIS RESCUE, JACK.

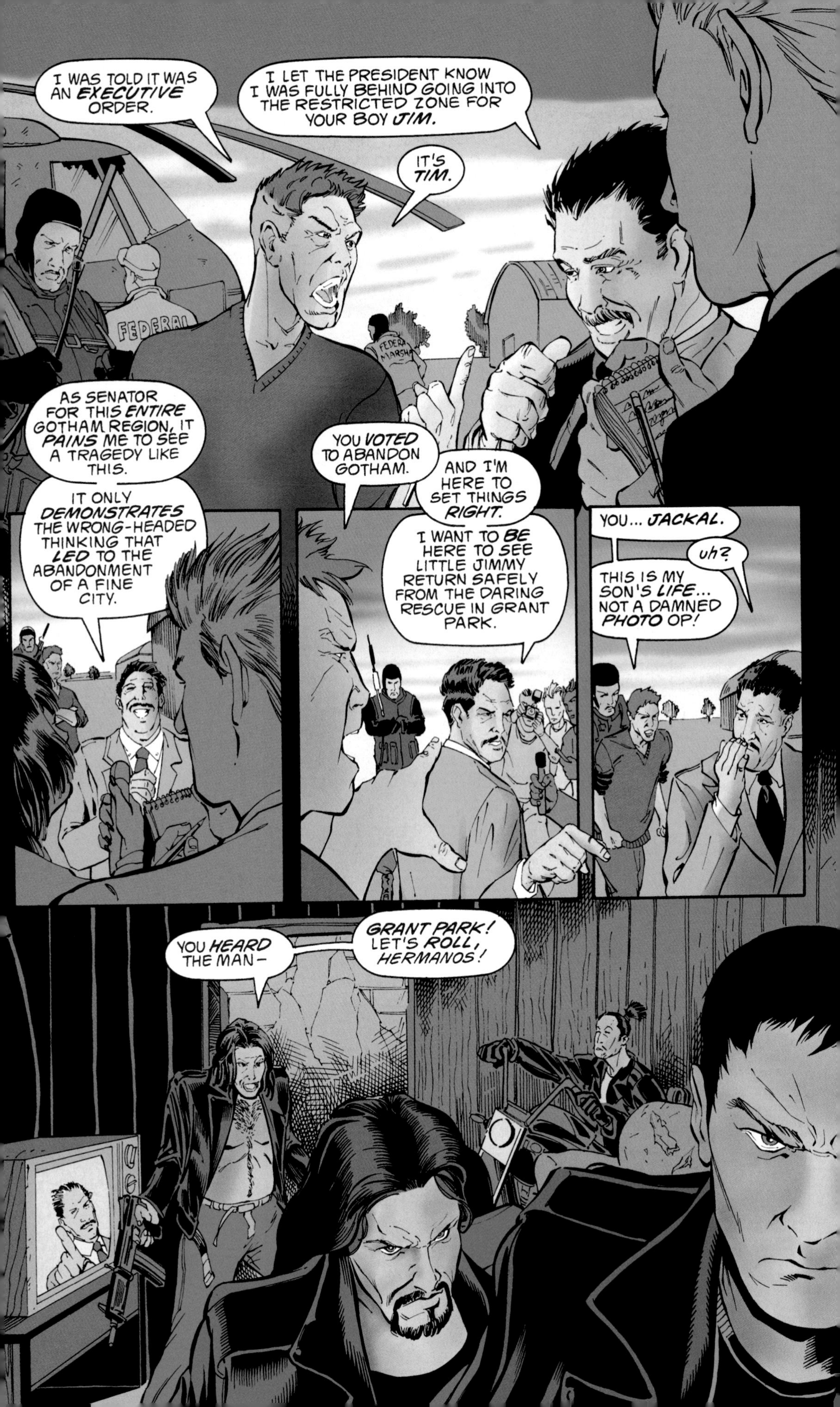

I WAS TOLD IT WAS AN EXECUTIVE ORDER.
I LET THE PRESIDENT KNOW I WAS FULLY BEHIND GOING INTO THE RESTRICTED ZONE FOR YOUR BOY JIM.
IT'S TIM.
FEDERAL
AS SENATOR FOR THIS ENTIRE GOTHAM REGION, IT PAINS ME TO SEE A TRAGEDY LIKE THIS.
IT ONLY DEMONSTRATES THE WRONG-HEADED THINKING THAT LED TO THE ABANDONMENT OF A FINE CITY.
YOU VOTED TO ABANDON GOTHAM.
AND I'M HERE TO SET THINGS RIGHT.
I WANT TO BE HERE TO SEE LITTLE JIMMY RETURN SAFELY FROM THE DARING RESCUE IN GRANT PARK.
YOU... JACKAL.
uh?
THIS IS MY SON'S LIFE... NOT A DAMNED PHOTO OP!
YOU HEARD THE MAN—
GRANT PARK! LET'S ROLL, HERMANOS!

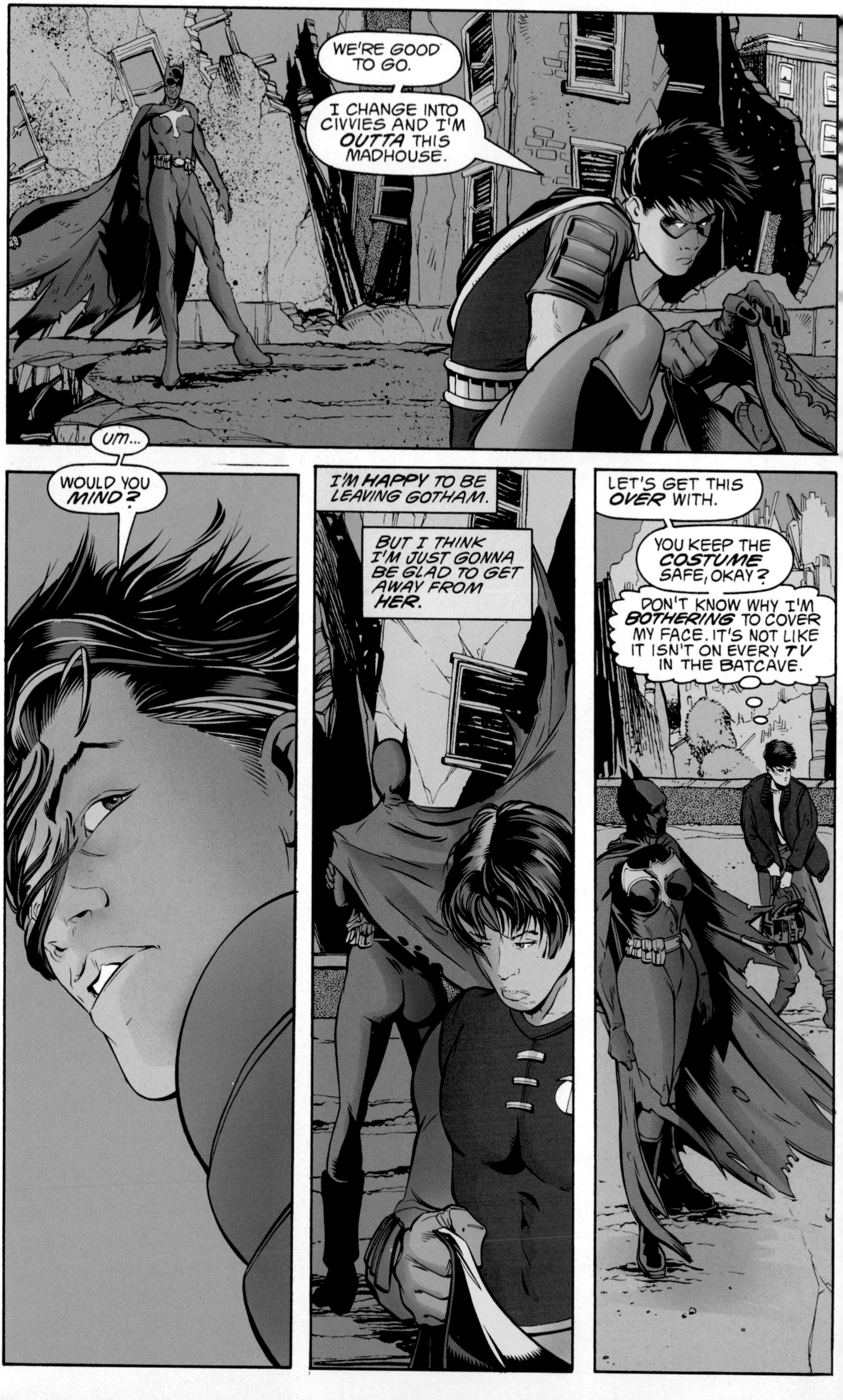

WE'RE GOOD TO GO.
I CHANGE INTO CIVVIES AND I'M OUTTA THIS MADHOUSE.
UM...
WOULD YOU MIND?
I'M HAPPY TO BE LEAVING GOTHAM.
BUT I THINK I'M JUST GONNA BE GLAD TO GET AWAY FROM HER.
LET'S GET THIS OVER WITH.
YOU KEEP THE COSTUME SAFE, OKAY?
DON'T KNOW WHY I'M BOTHERING TO COVER MY FACE. IT'S NOT LIKE IT ISN'T ON EVERY TV IN THE BATCAVE.

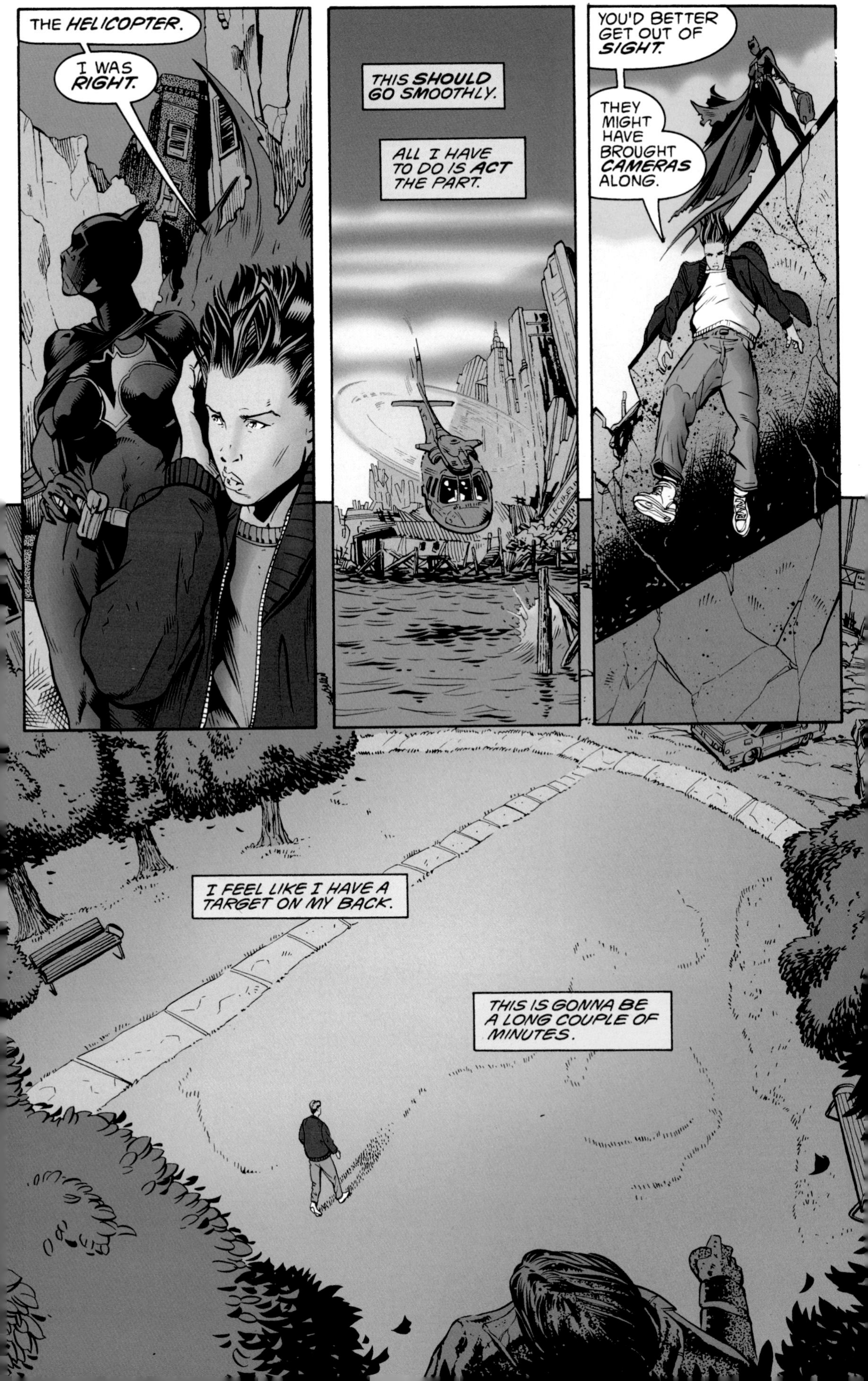

THE HELICOPTER.
I WAS RIGHT.
THIS SHOULD GO SMOOTHLY.
ALL I HAVE TO DO IS ACT THE PART.
YOU'D BETTER GET OUT OF SIGHT.
THEY MIGHT HAVE BROUGHT CAMERAS ALONG.
I FEEL LIKE I HAVE A TARGET ON MY BACK.
THIS IS GONNA BE A LONG COUPLE OF MINUTES.

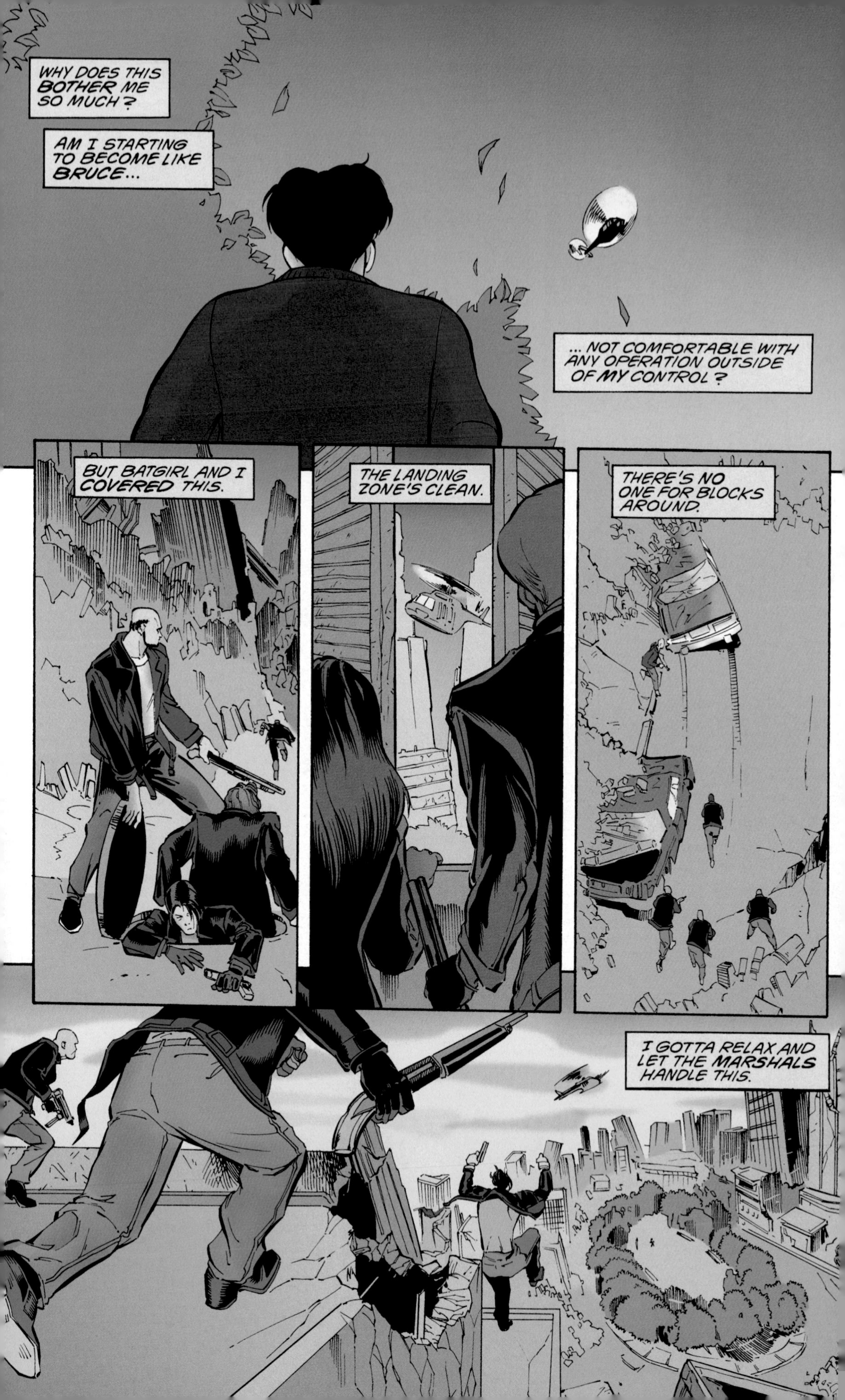
WHY DOES THIS BOTHER ME SO MUCH?
AM I STARTING TO BECOME LIKE BRUCE...
...NOT COMFORTABLE WITH ANY OPERATION OUTSIDE OF MY CONTROL?
BUT BATGIRL AND I COVERED THIS.
THE LANDING ZONE'S CLEAN.
THERE'S NO ONE FOR BLOCKS AROUND.
I GOTTA RELAX AND LET THE MARSHALS HANDLE THIS.

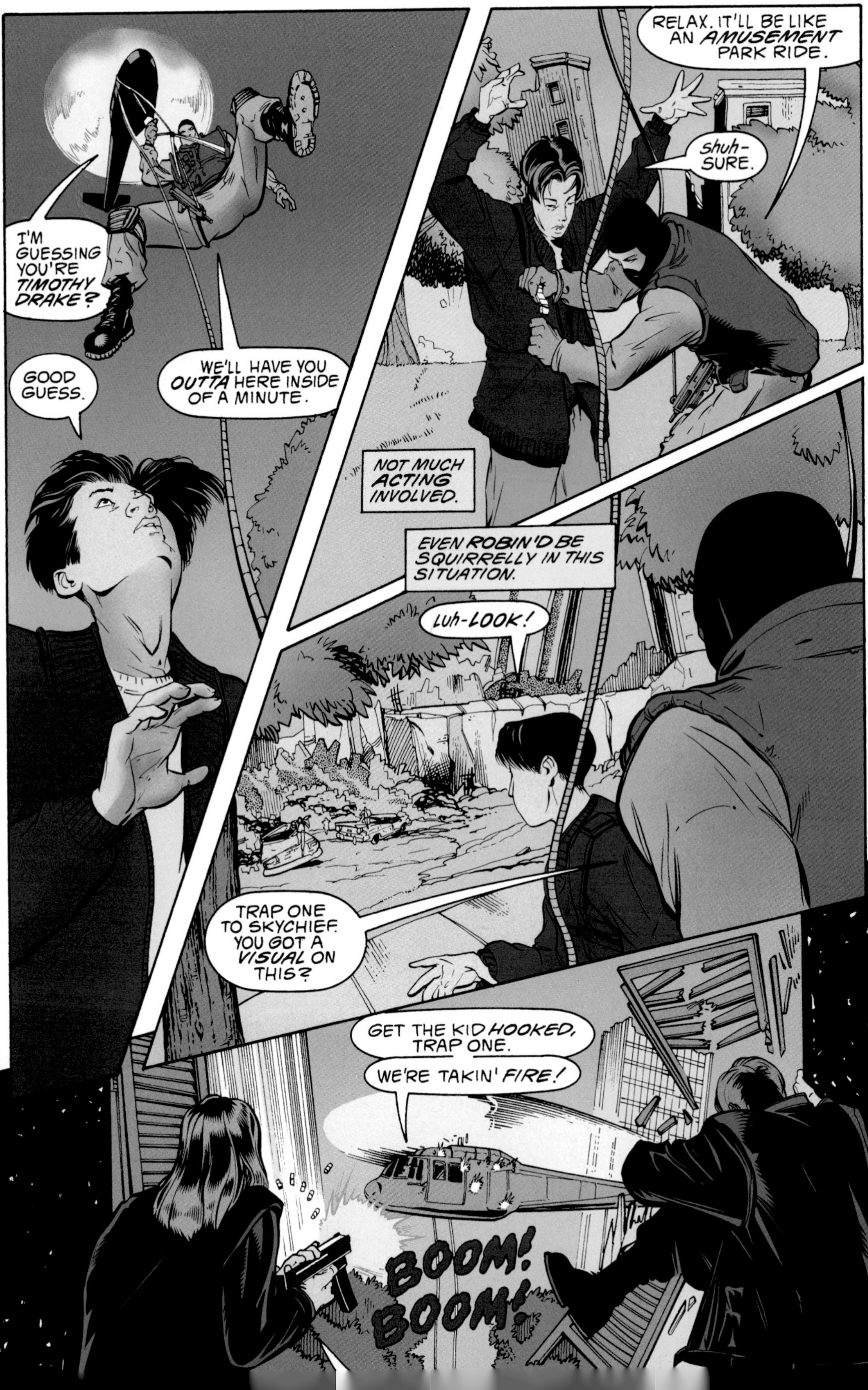
I'M GUESSING YOU'RE TIMOTHY DRAKE?
GOOD GUESS.
WE'LL HAVE YOU OUTTA HERE INSIDE OF A MINUTE.
RELAX. IT'LL BE LIKE AN AMUSEMENT PARK RIDE.
SHUH-SURE.
NOT MUCH ACTING INVOLVED.
EVEN ROBIN'D BE SQUIRRELLY IN THIS SITUATION.
LUH-LOOK!
TRAP ONE TO SKYCHIEF. YOU GOT A VISUAL ON THIS?
GET THE KID HOOKED, TRAP ONE.
WE'RE TAKIN' FIRE!
BOOM! BOOM!

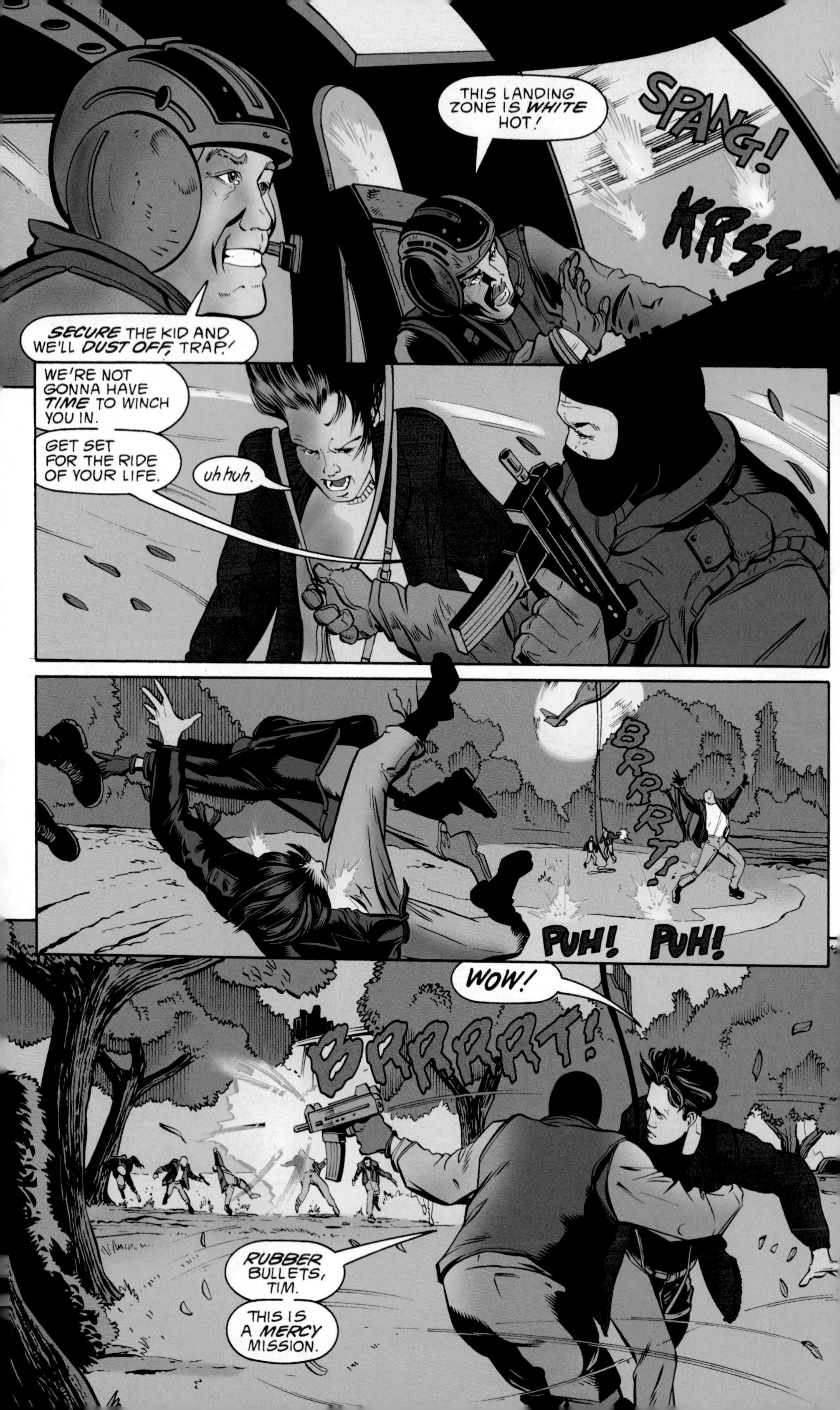
THIS LANDING ZONE IS *WHITE* HOT!
SPANG!
KRSSS
SECURE THE KID AND WE'LL *DUST OFF*, TRAP!
WE'RE NOT GONNA HAVE *TIME* TO WINCH YOU IN.
GET SET FOR THE RIDE OF YOUR LIFE.
uh huh.
BRRRT!
PUH! PUH!
WOW!
BRRRRT!
RUBBER BULLETS, TIM.
THIS IS A *MERCY* MISSION.

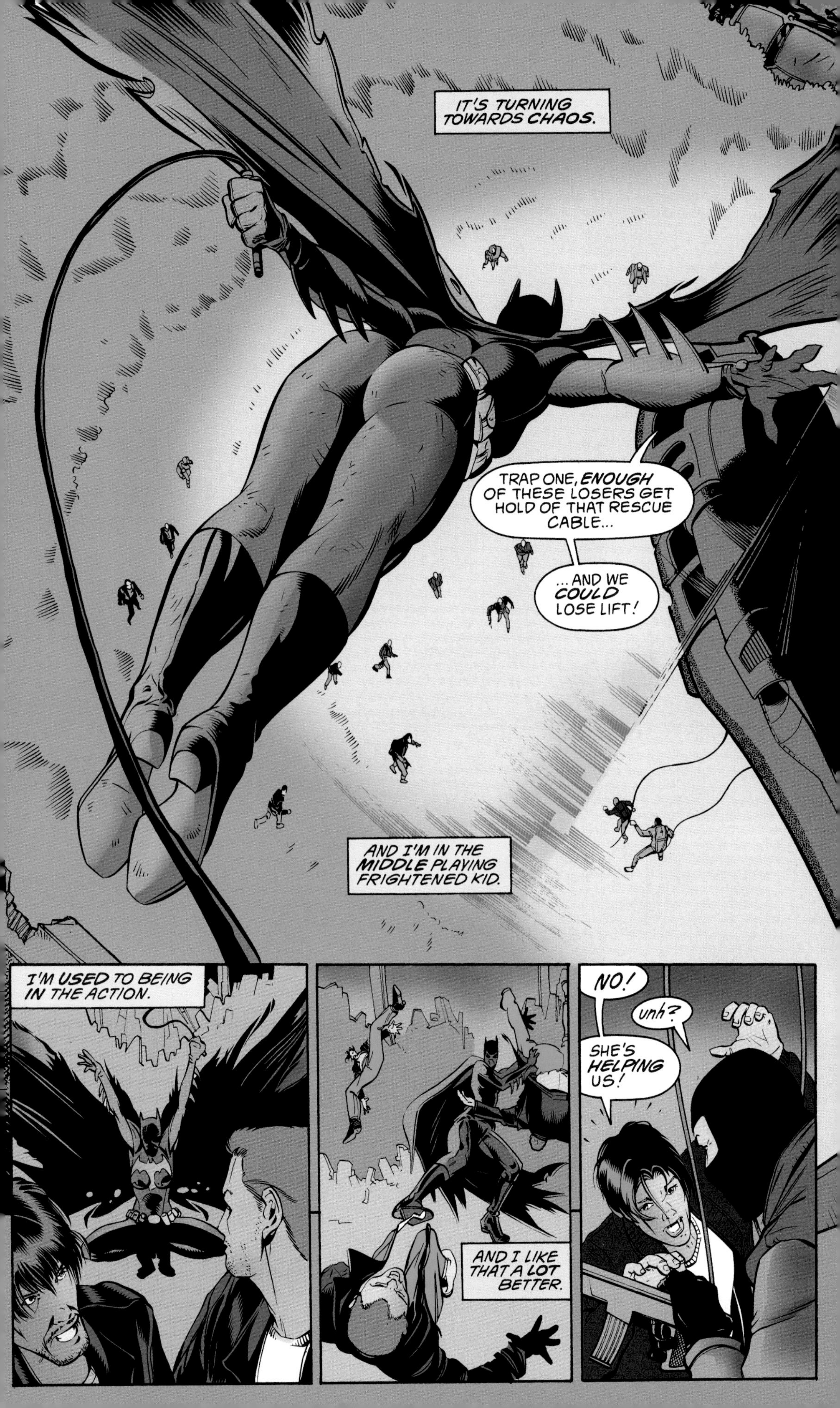

IT'S TURNING TOWARDS CHAOS.
TRAP ONE, ENOUGH OF THESE LOSERS GET HOLD OF THAT RESCUE CABLE...
...AND WE COULD LOSE LIFT!
AND I'M IN THE MIDDLE PLAYING FRIGHTENED KID.
I'M USED TO BEING IN THE ACTION.
AND I LIKE THAT A LOT BETTER.
NO!
unh?
SHE'S HELPING US!

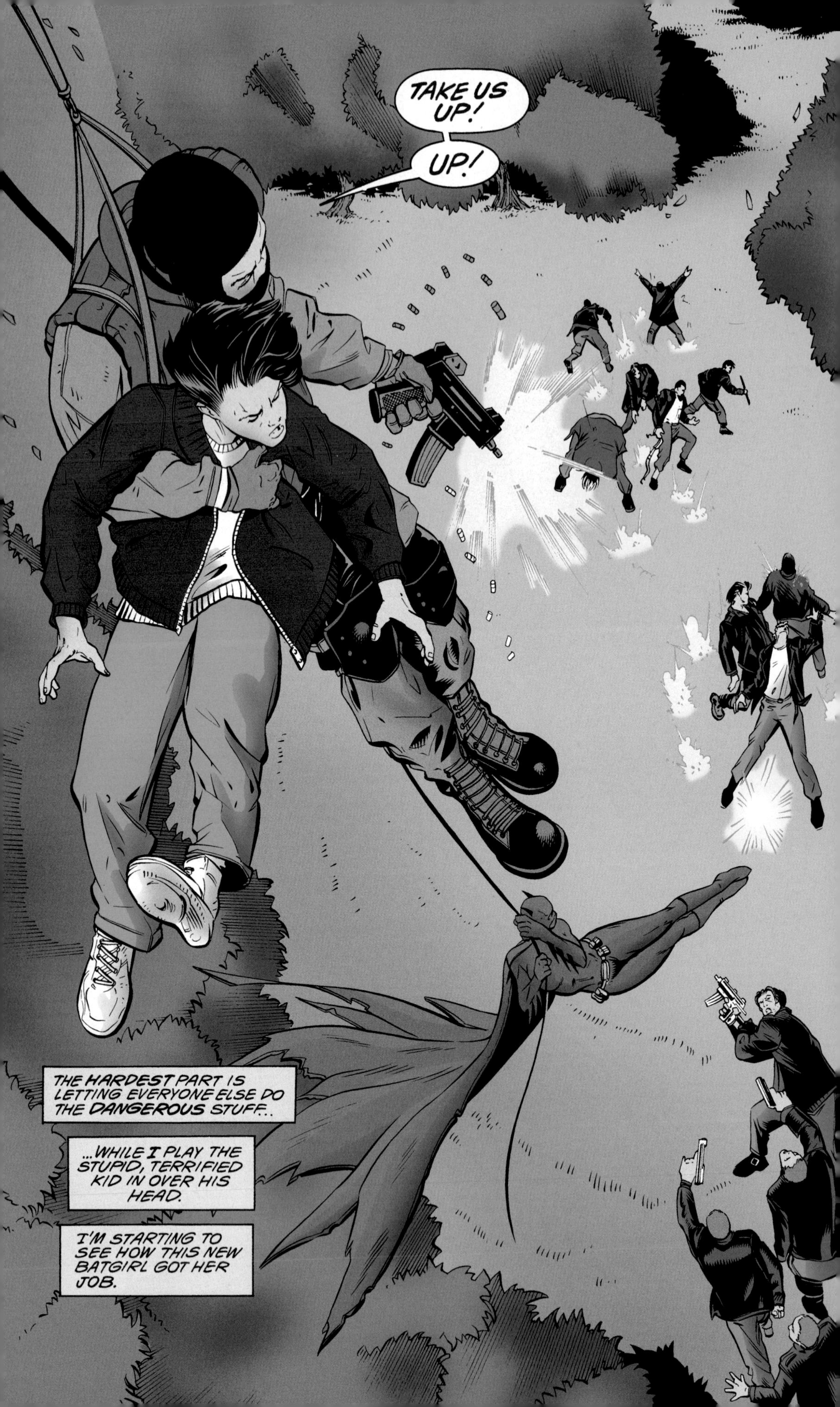
TAKE US UP!
UP!
THE HARDEST PART IS LETTING EVERYONE ELSE DO THE DANGEROUS STUFF...
...WHILE I PLAY THE STUPID, TERRIFIED KID IN OVER HIS HEAD.
I'M STARTING TO SEE HOW THIS NEW BATGIRL GOT HER JOB.

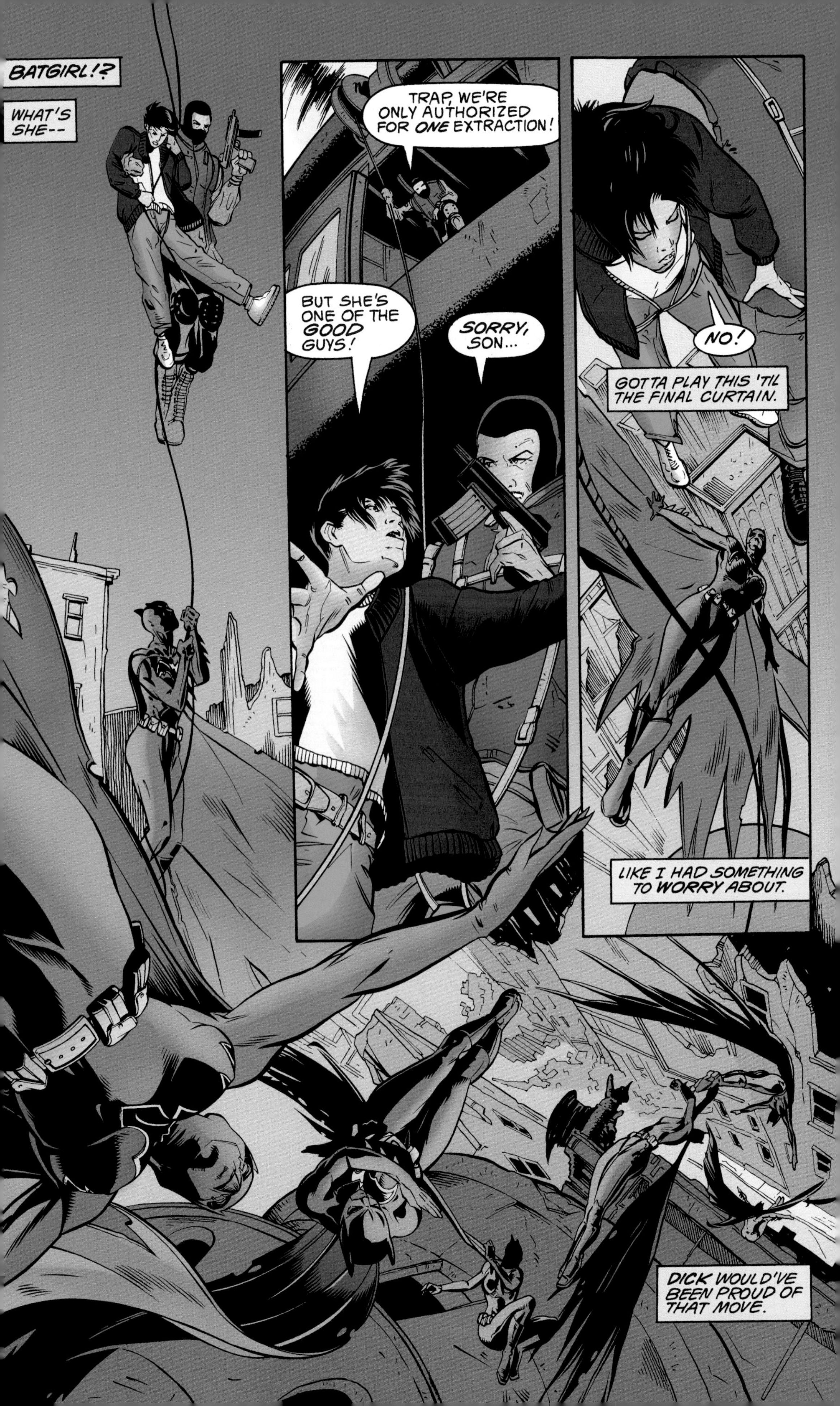

BATGIRL!?
WHAT'S SHE--
TRAP, WE'RE ONLY AUTHORIZED FOR ONE EXTRACTION!
BUT SHE'S ONE OF THE GOOD GUYS!
SORRY, SON...
NO!
GOTTA PLAY THIS 'TIL THE FINAL CURTAIN.
LIKE I HAD SOMETHING TO WORRY ABOUT.
DICK WOULD'VE BEEN PROUD OF THAT MOVE.

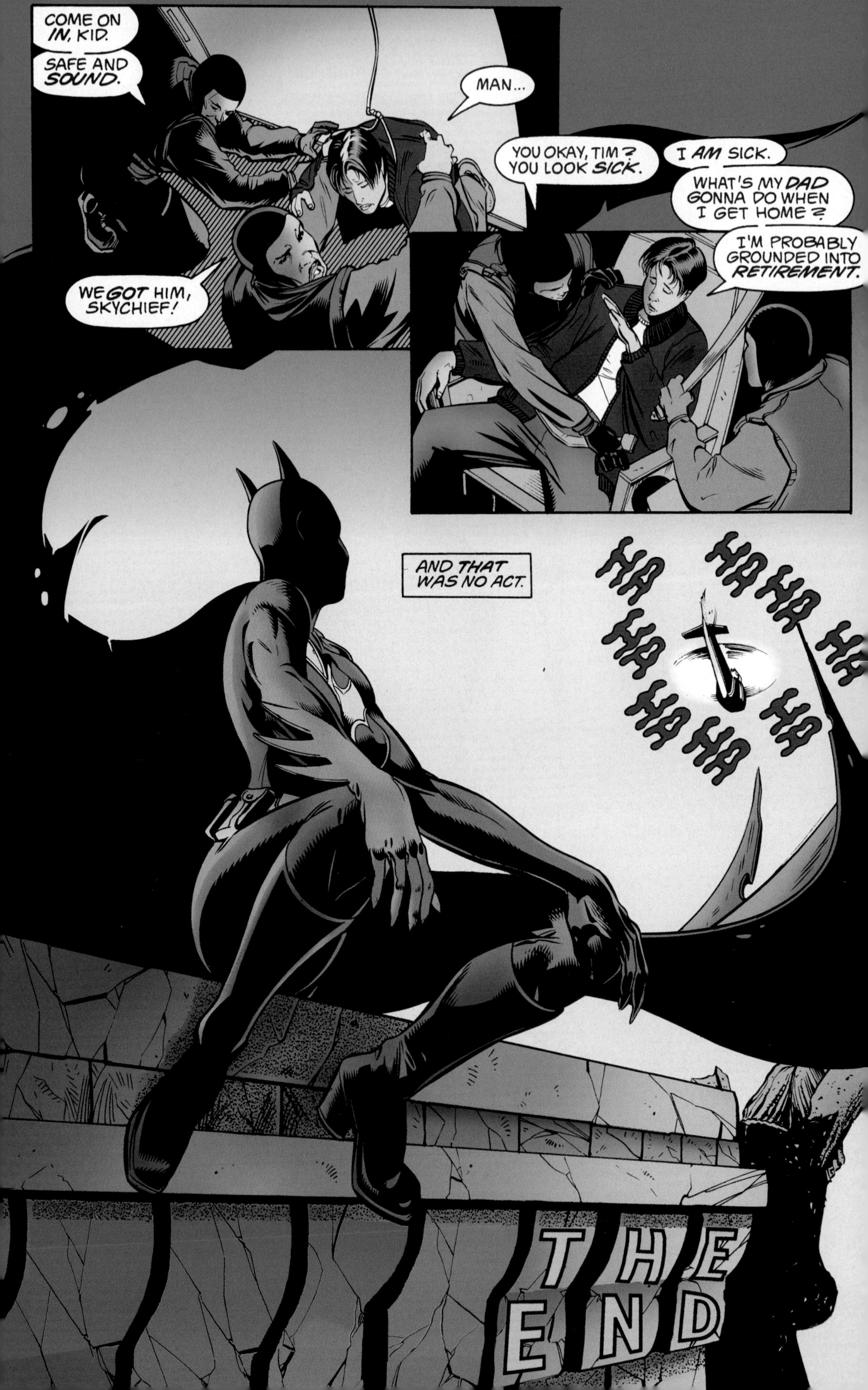
COME ON IN, KID.
SAFE AND SOUND.
MAN...
WE GOT HIM, SKYCHIEF!
YOU OKAY, TIM? YOU LOOK SICK.
I AM SICK.
WHAT'S MY DAD GONNA DO WHEN I GET HOME?
I'M PROBABLY GROUNDED INTO RETIREMENT.
AND THAT WAS NO ACT.
HA HA HA HA HA HA HA HA HA HA HA
THE END

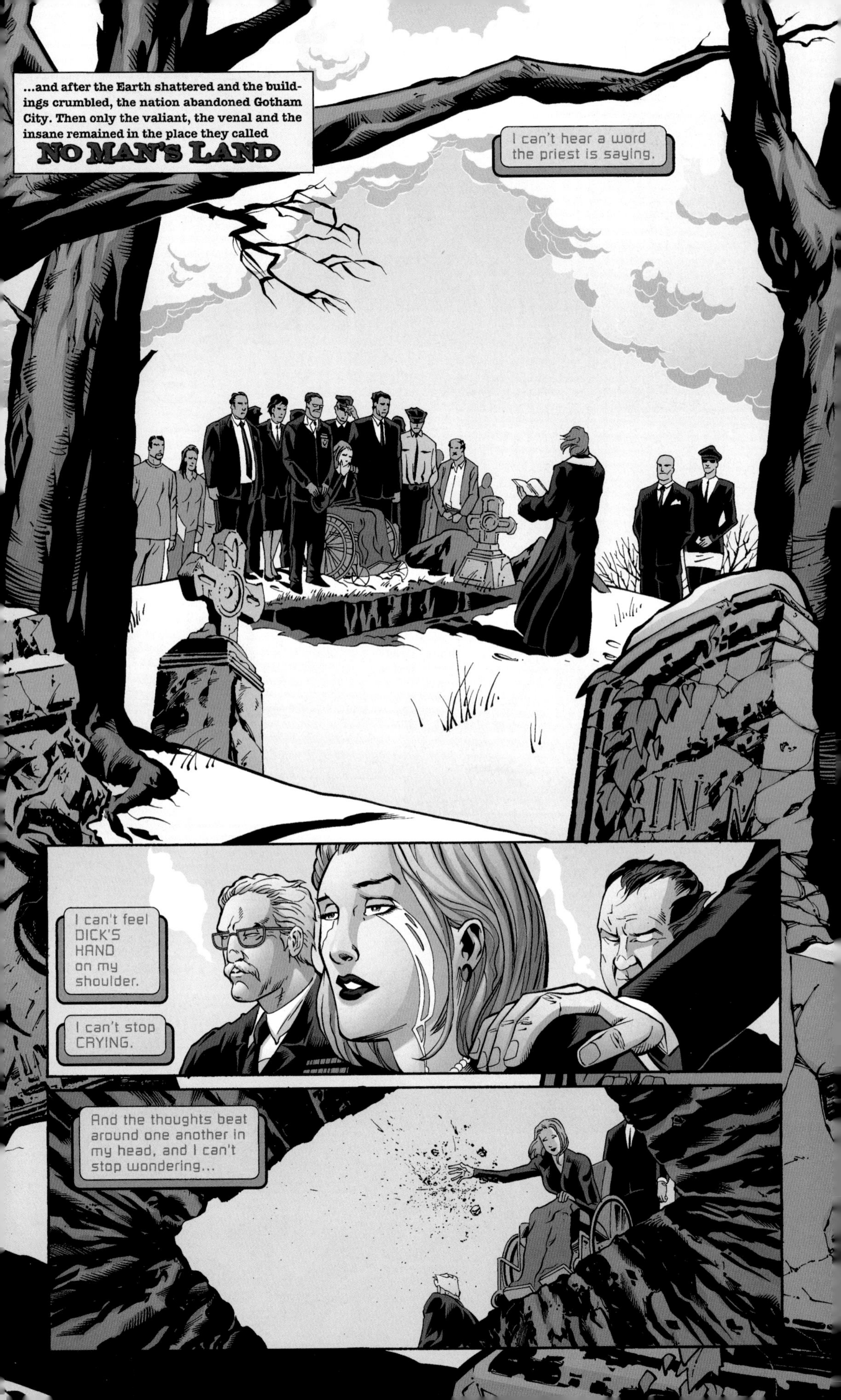
...and after the Earth shattered and the buildings crumbled, the nation abandoned Gotham City. Then only the valiant, the venal and the insane remained in the place they called
NO MAN'S LAND
I can't hear a word the priest is saying.
IN M
I can't feel DICK'S HAND on my shoulder.
I can't stop CRYING.
And the thoughts beat around one another in my head, and I can't stop wondering...

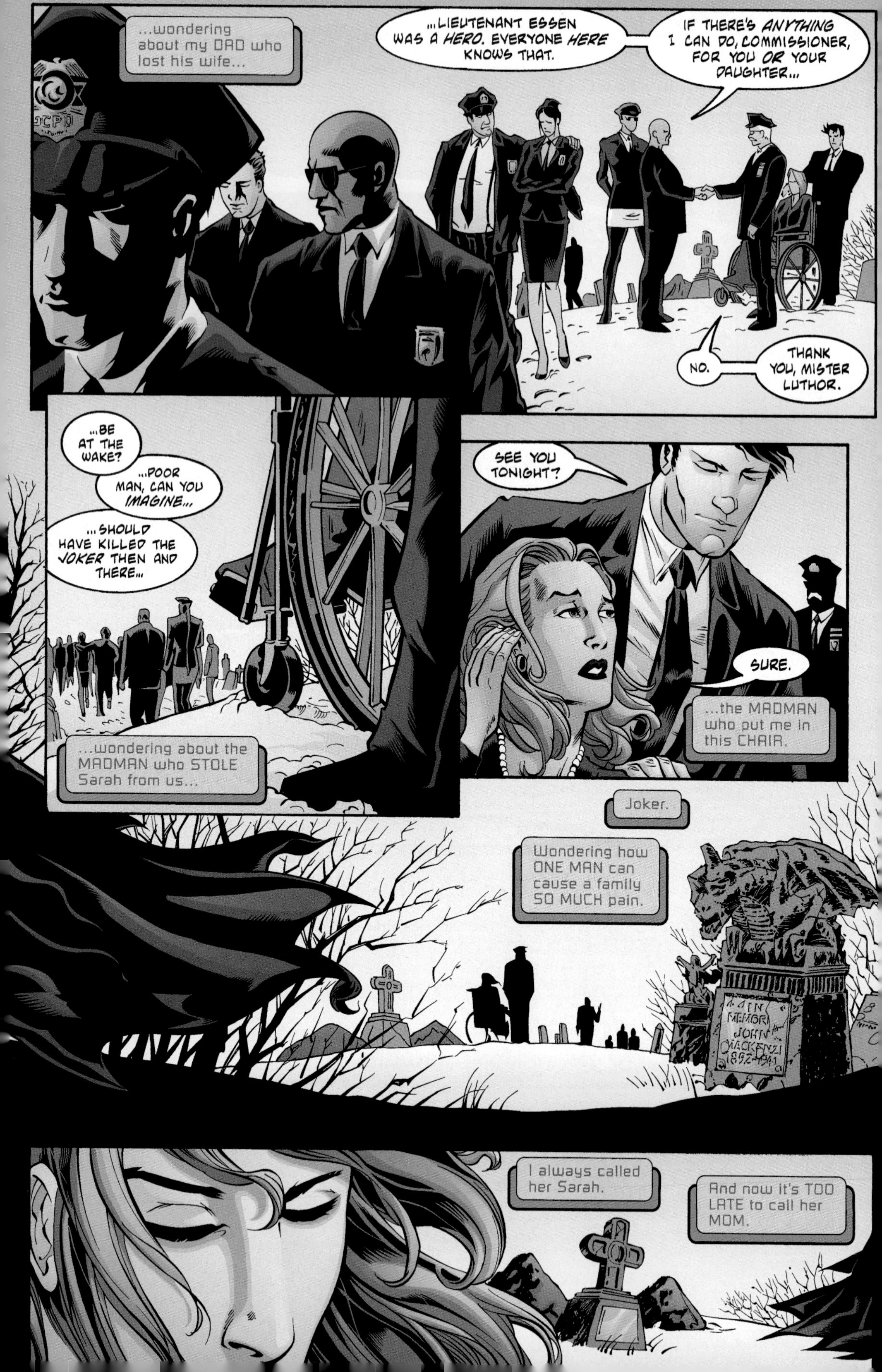

...wondering about my DAD who lost his wife...
...LIEUTENANT ESSEN WAS A HERO. EVERYONE HERE KNOWS THAT.
IF THERE'S ANYTHING I CAN DO, COMMISSIONER, FOR YOU OR YOUR DAUGHTER...
NO.
THANK YOU, MISTER LUTHOR.
...BE AT THE WAKE?
...POOR MAN, CAN YOU IMAGINE...
...SHOULD HAVE KILLED THE JOKER THEN AND THERE...
...wondering about the MADMAN who STOLE Sarah from us...
SEE YOU TONIGHT?
SURE.
...the MADMAN who put me in this CHAIR.
Joker.
Wondering how ONE MAN can cause a family SO MUCH pain.
I always called her Sarah.
And now it's TOO LATE to call her MOM.

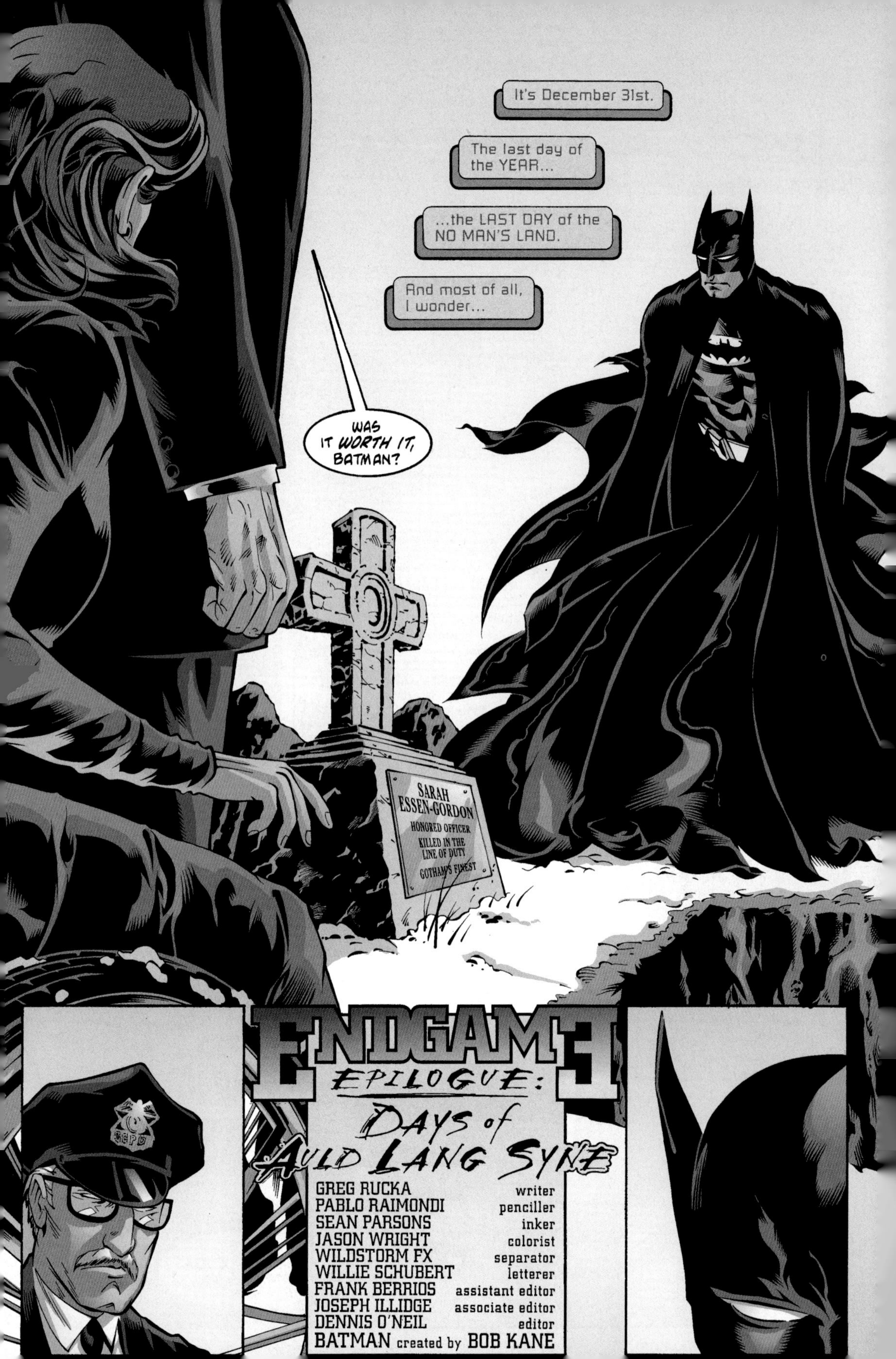

It's December 31st.
The last day of the YEAR...
...the LAST DAY of the NO MAN'S LAND.
And most of all, I wonder...
WAS IT WORTH IT, BATMAN?
SARAH ESSEN-GORDON
HONORED OFFICER
KILLED IN THE LINE OF DUTY
GOTHAM'S FINEST
GCPD
ENDGAME
EPILOGUE:
DAYS of AULD LANG SYNE
GREG RUCKA writer
PABLO RAIMONDI penciller
SEAN PARSONS inker
JASON WRIGHT colorist
WILDSTORM FX separator
WILLIE SCHUBERT letterer
FRANK BERRIOS assistant editor
JOSEPH ILLIDGE associate editor
DENNIS O'NEIL editor
BATMAN created by BOB KANE

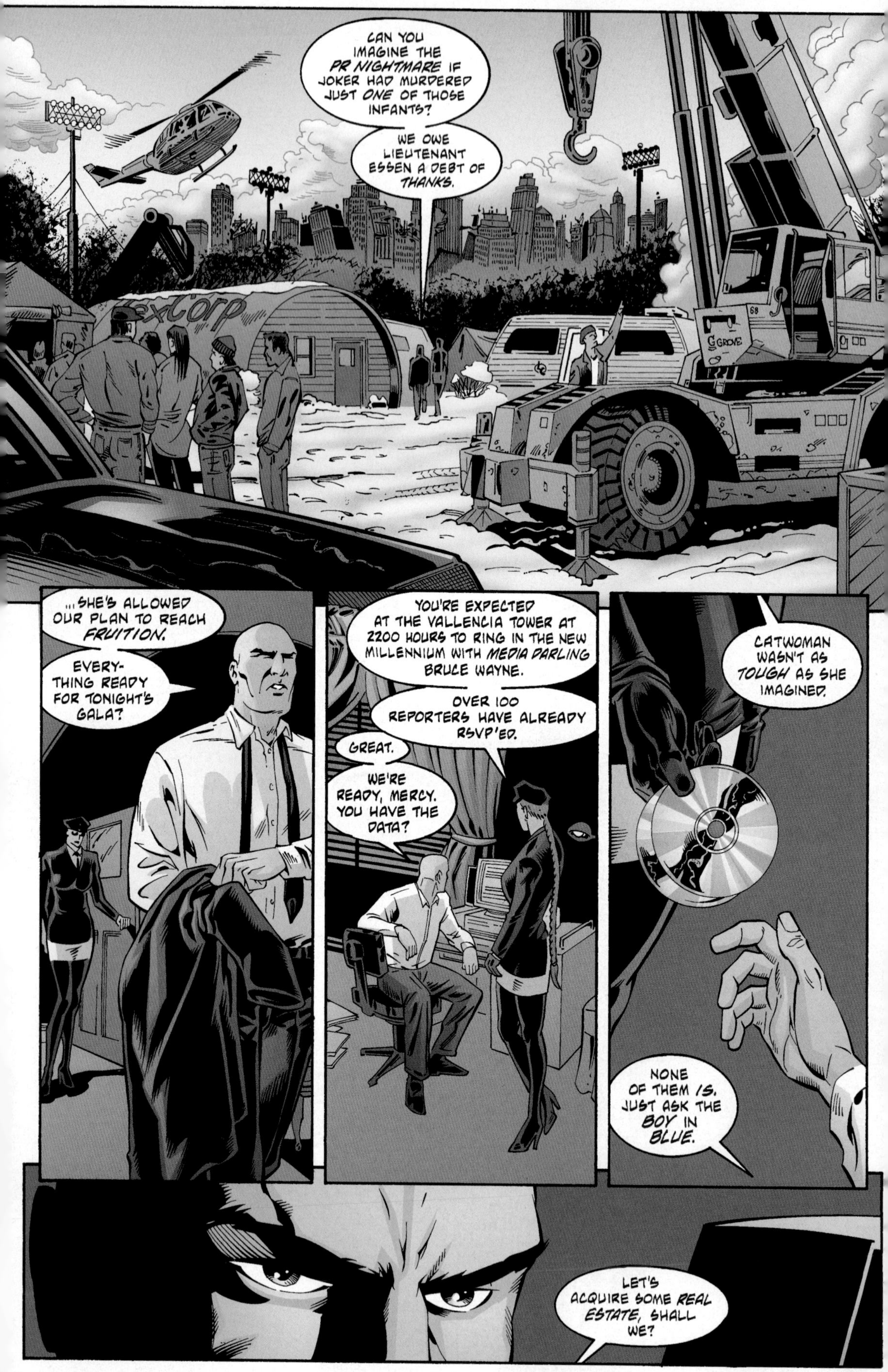
CAN YOU IMAGINE THE PR NIGHTMARE IF JOKER HAD MURDERED JUST ONE OF THOSE INFANTS?
WE OWE LIEUTENANT ESSEN A DEBT OF THANKS.
LEXCORP
GROVE
...SHE'S ALLOWED OUR PLAN TO REACH FRUITION.
EVERY-THING READY FOR TONIGHT'S GALA?
YOU'RE EXPECTED AT THE VALLENCIA TOWER AT 2200 HOURS TO RING IN THE NEW MILLENNIUM WITH MEDIA DARLING BRUCE WAYNE.
OVER 100 REPORTERS HAVE ALREADY RSVP'ED.
GREAT.
WE'RE READY, MERCY. YOU HAVE THE DATA?
CATWOMAN WASN'T AS TOUGH AS SHE IMAGINED.
NONE OF THEM IS. JUST ASK THE BOY IN BLUE.
LET'S ACQUIRE SOME REAL ESTATE, SHALL WE?

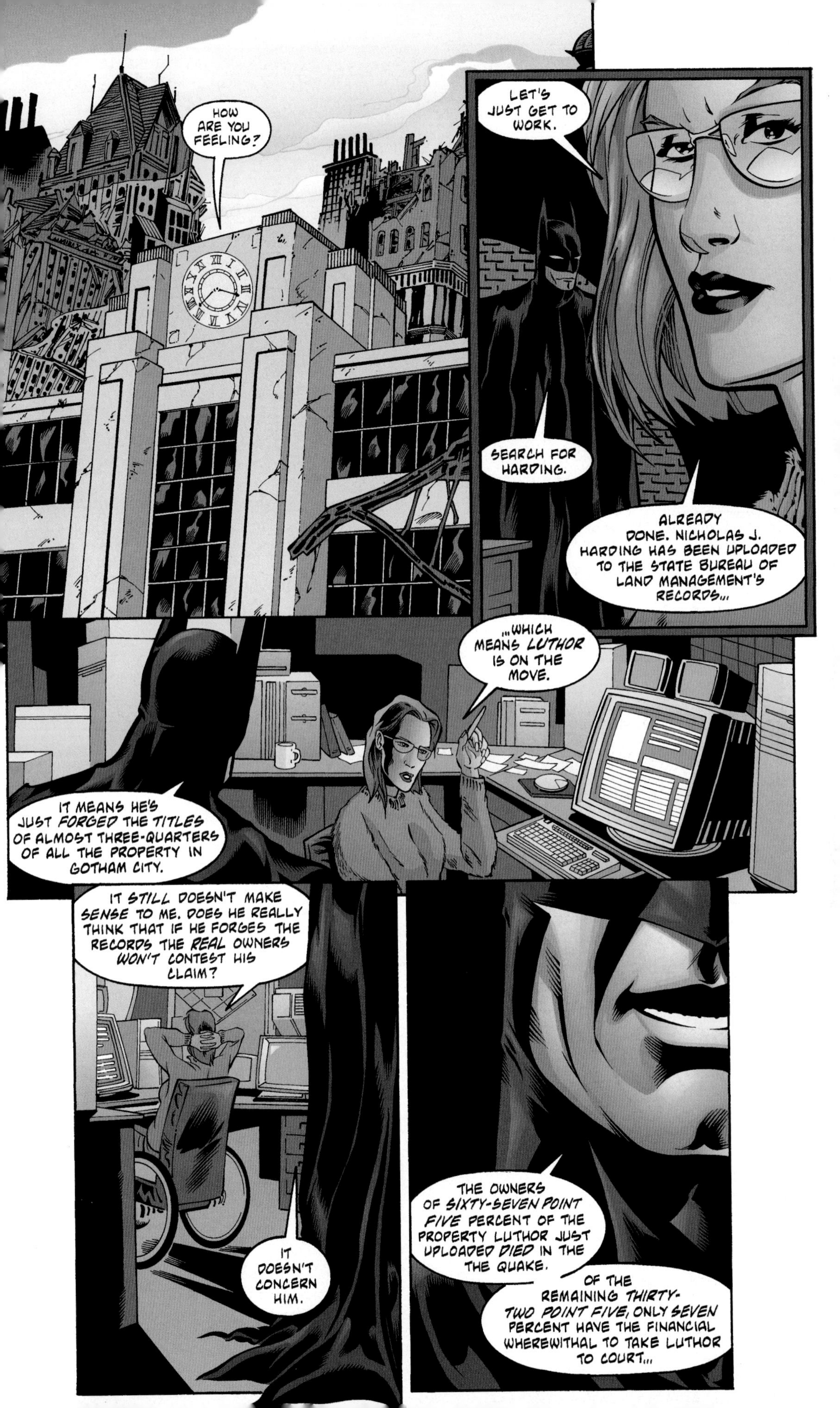
HOW ARE YOU FEELING?
LET'S JUST GET TO WORK.
SEARCH FOR HARDING.
ALREADY DONE. NICHOLAS J. HARDING HAS BEEN UPLOADED TO THE STATE BUREAU OF LAND MANAGEMENT'S RECORDS...
...WHICH MEANS LUTHOR IS ON THE MOVE.
IT MEANS HE'S JUST FORGED THE TITLES OF ALMOST THREE-QUARTERS OF ALL THE PROPERTY IN GOTHAM CITY.
IT STILL DOESN'T MAKE SENSE TO ME. DOES HE REALLY THINK THAT IF HE FORGES THE RECORDS THE REAL OWNERS WON'T CONTEST HIS CLAIM?
IT DOESN'T CONCERN HIM.
THE OWNERS OF SIXTY-SEVEN POINT FIVE PERCENT OF THE PROPERTY LUTHOR JUST UPLOADED DIED IN THE THE QUAKE.
OF THE REMAINING THIRTY-TWO POINT FIVE, ONLY SEVEN PERCENT HAVE THE FINANCIAL WHEREWITHAL TO TAKE LUTHOR TO COURT...

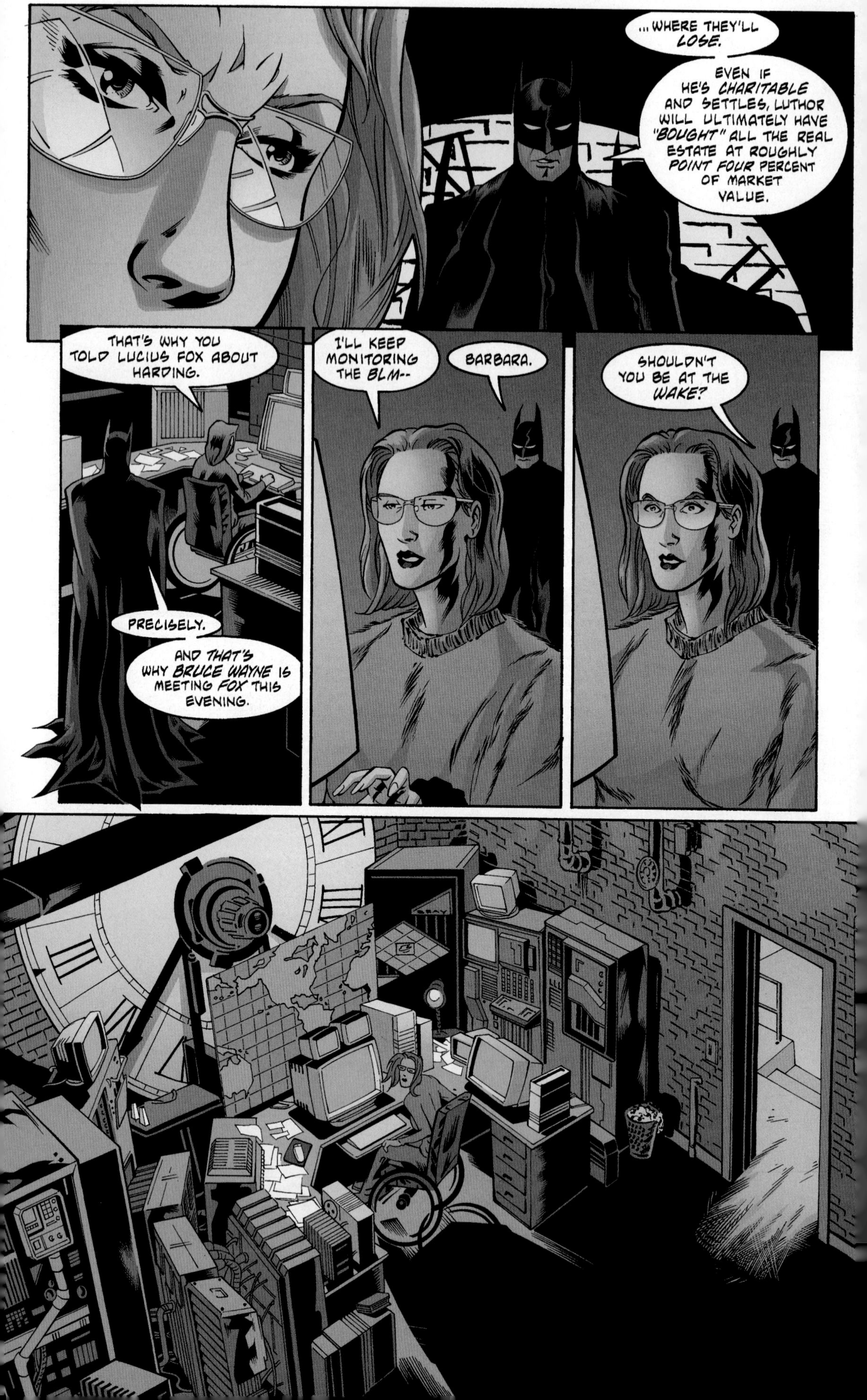
...WHERE THEY'LL LOSE.
EVEN IF HE'S CHARITABLE AND SETTLES, LUTHOR WILL ULTIMATELY HAVE "BOUGHT" ALL THE REAL ESTATE AT ROUGHLY POINT FOUR PERCENT OF MARKET VALUE.
THAT'S WHY YOU TOLD LUCIUS FOX ABOUT HARDING.
PRECISELY.
AND THAT'S WHY BRUCE WAYNE IS MEETING FOX THIS EVENING.
I'LL KEEP MONITORING THE BLM--
BARBARA.
SHOULDN'T YOU BE AT THE WAKE?

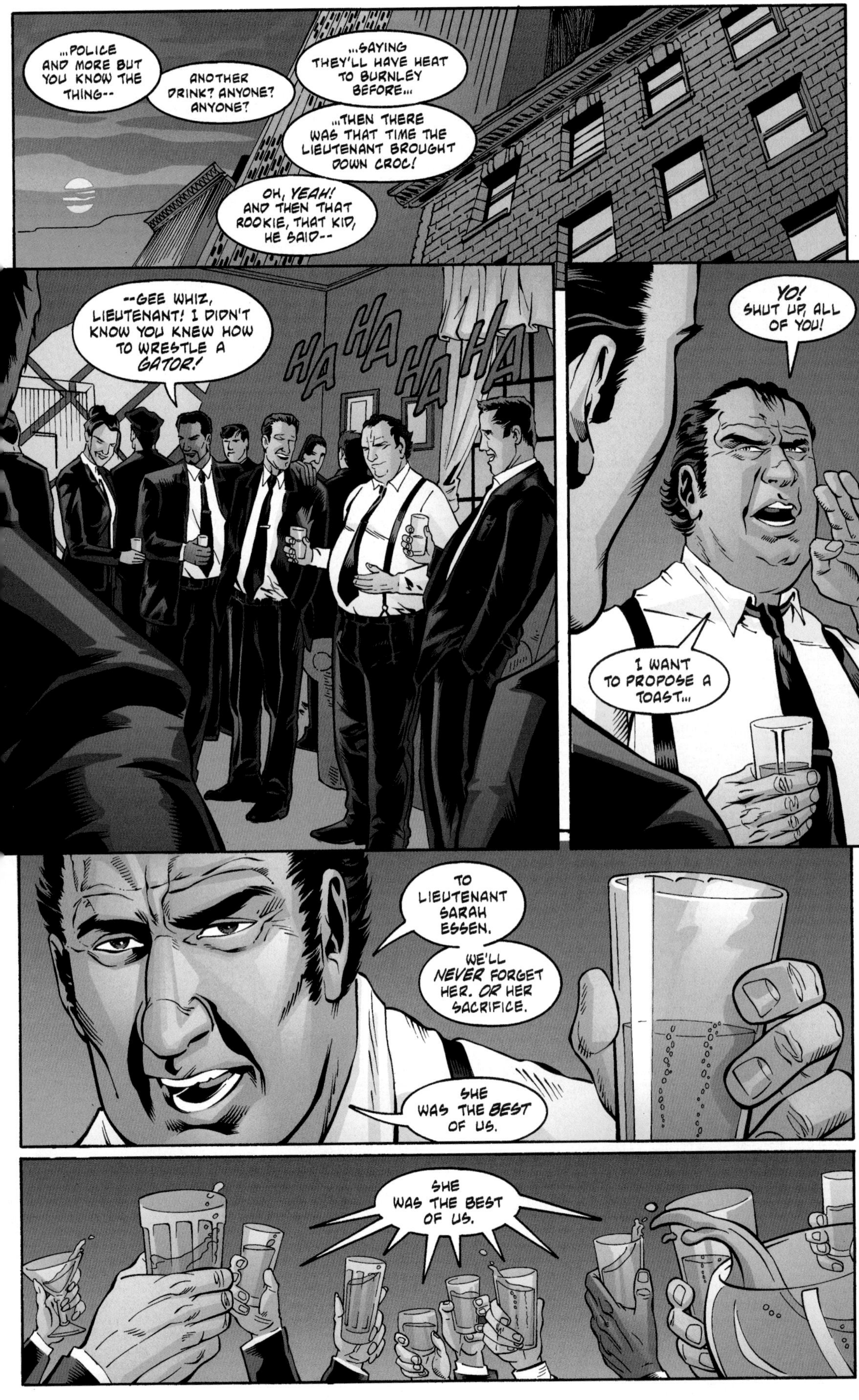
...POLICE AND MORE BUT YOU KNOW THE THING--
ANOTHER DRINK? ANYONE? ANYONE?
...SAYING THEY'LL HAVE HEAT TO BURNLEY BEFORE...
...THEN THERE WAS THAT TIME THE LIEUTENANT BROUGHT DOWN CROC!
OH, YEAH! AND THEN THAT ROOKIE, THAT KID, HE SAID--
--GEE WHIZ, LIEUTENANT! I DIDN'T KNOW YOU KNEW HOW TO WRESTLE A GATOR!
HA HA HA HA HA HA
YO! SHUT UP, ALL OF YOU!
I WANT TO PROPOSE A TOAST...
TO LIEUTENANT SARAH ESSEN.
WE'LL NEVER FORGET HER. OR HER SACRIFICE.
SHE WAS THE BEST OF US.
SHE WAS THE BEST OF US.

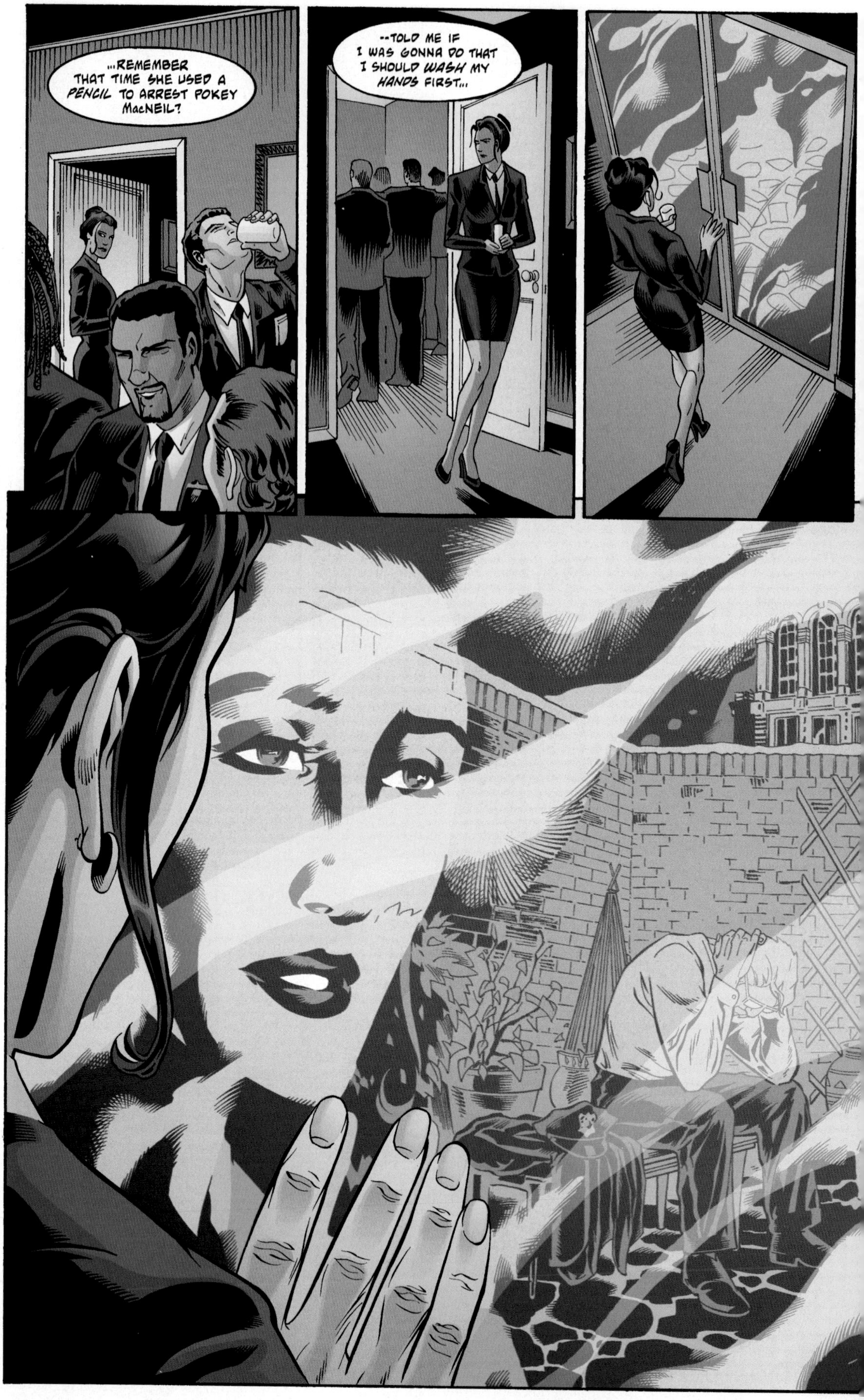
...REMEMBER THAT TIME SHE USED A PENCIL TO ARREST POKEY MacNEIL?
--TOLD ME IF I WAS GONNA DO THAT I SHOULD WASH MY HANDS FIRST...

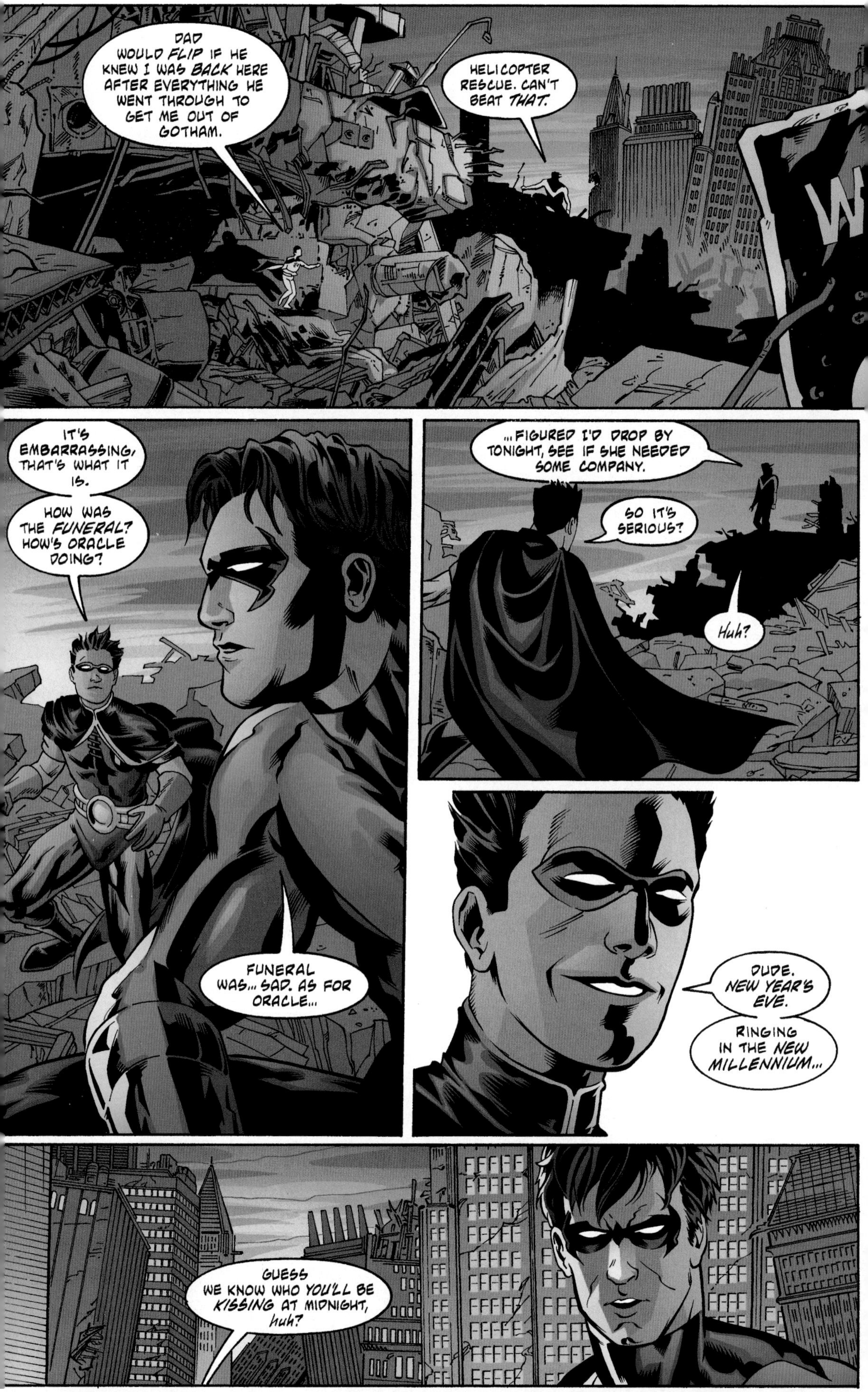
DAD WOULD *FLIP* IF HE KNEW I WAS *BACK* HERE AFTER EVERYTHING HE WENT THROUGH TO GET ME OUT OF GOTHAM.
HELICOPTER RESCUE. CAN'T BEAT *THAT.*
IT'S EMBARRASSING, THAT'S WHAT IT IS.
HOW WAS THE *FUNERAL?* HOW'S ORACLE DOING?
FUNERAL WAS... SAD. AS FOR ORACLE...
...FIGURED I'D DROP BY TONIGHT, SEE IF SHE NEEDED SOME COMPANY.
SO IT'S SERIOUS?
Huh?
DUDE. *NEW YEAR'S EVE.*
RINGING IN THE *NEW MILLENNIUM...*
GUESS WE KNOW WHO *YOU'LL* BE *KISSING* AT MIDNIGHT, *huh?*

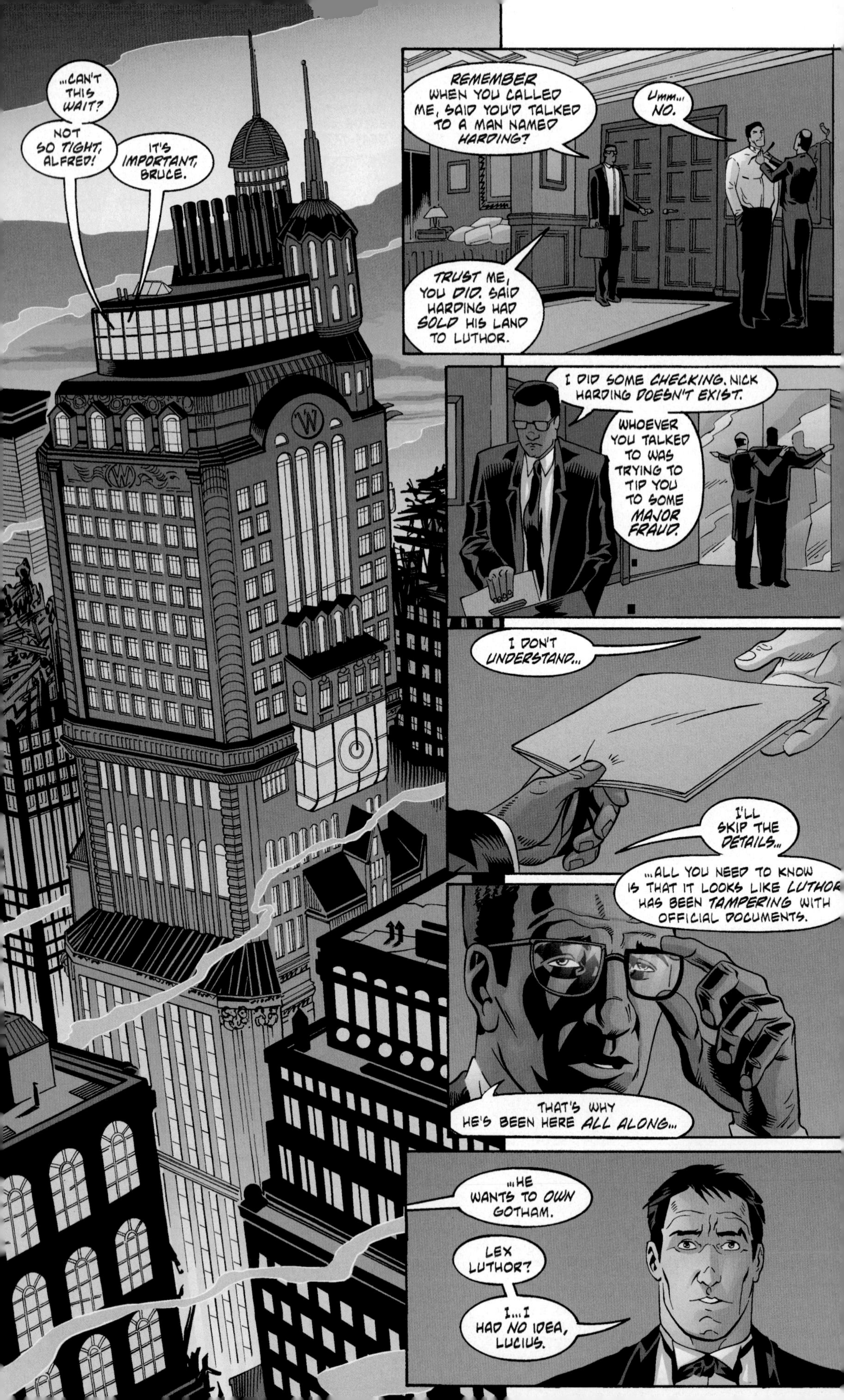
...CAN'T THIS WAIT?
NOT SO TIGHT, ALFRED!
IT'S IMPORTANT, BRUCE.
REMEMBER WHEN YOU CALLED ME, SAID YOU'D TALKED TO A MAN NAMED HARDING?
Umm... NO.
TRUST ME, YOU DID. SAID HARDING HAD SOLD HIS LAND TO LUTHOR.
I DID SOME CHECKING. NICK HARDING DOESN'T EXIST.
WHOEVER YOU TALKED TO WAS TRYING TO TIP YOU TO SOME MAJOR FRAUD.
I DON'T UNDERSTAND...
I'LL SKIP THE DETAILS...
...ALL YOU NEED TO KNOW IS THAT IT LOOKS LIKE LUTHOR HAS BEEN TAMPERING WITH OFFICIAL DOCUMENTS.
THAT'S WHY HE'S BEEN HERE ALL ALONG...
...HE WANTS TO OWN GOTHAM.
LEX LUTHOR?
I...I HAD NO IDEA, LUCIUS.

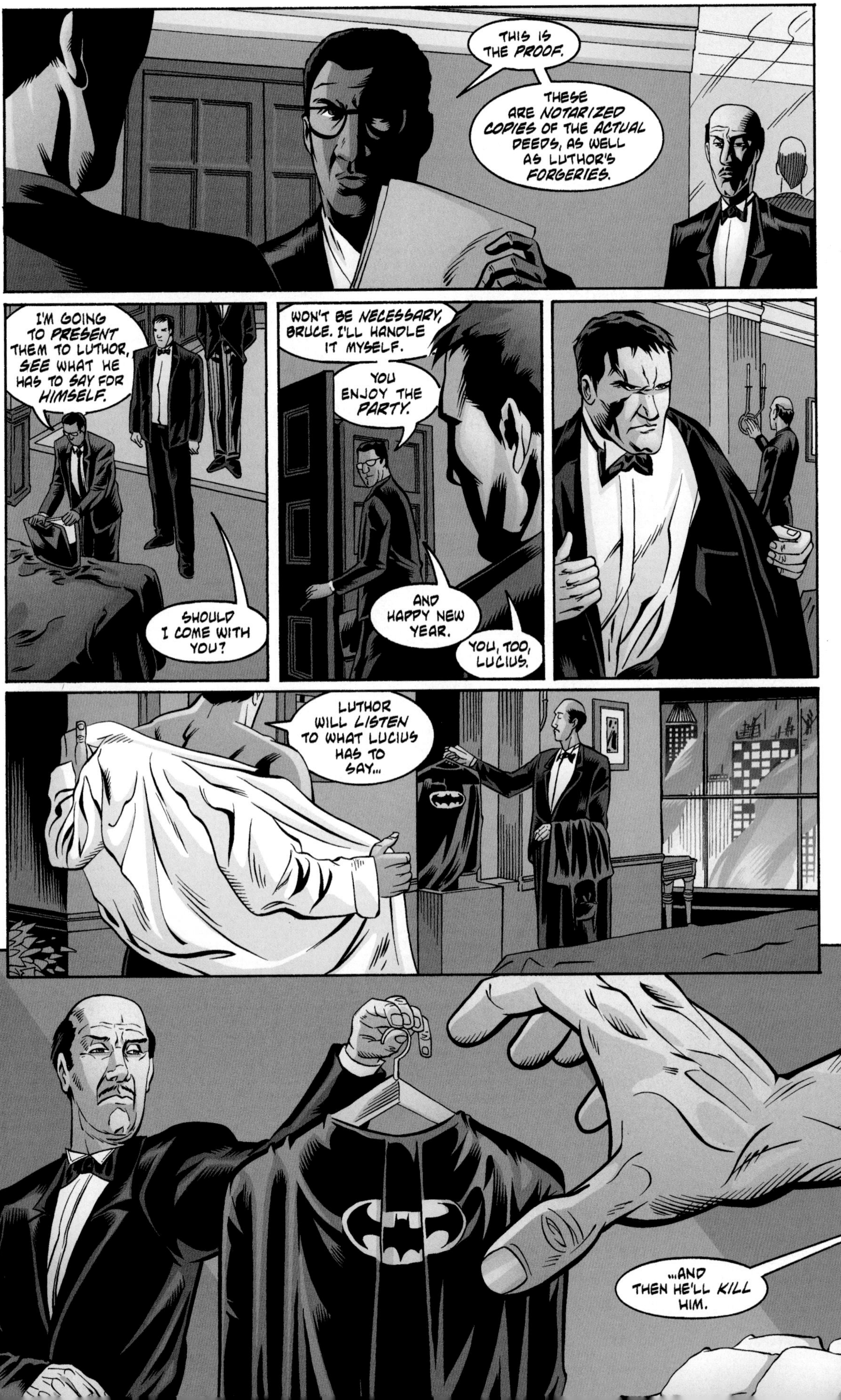
THIS IS THE PROOF.
THESE ARE NOTARIZED COPIES OF THE ACTUAL DEEDS, AS WELL AS LUTHOR'S FORGERIES.
I'M GOING TO PRESENT THEM TO LUTHOR, SEE WHAT HE HAS TO SAY FOR HIMSELF.
SHOULD I COME WITH YOU?
WON'T BE NECESSARY, BRUCE. I'LL HANDLE IT MYSELF.
YOU ENJOY THE PARTY.
AND HAPPY NEW YEAR.
YOU, TOO, LUCIUS.
LUTHOR WILL LISTEN TO WHAT LUCIUS HAS TO SAY...
...AND THEN HE'LL KILL HIM.

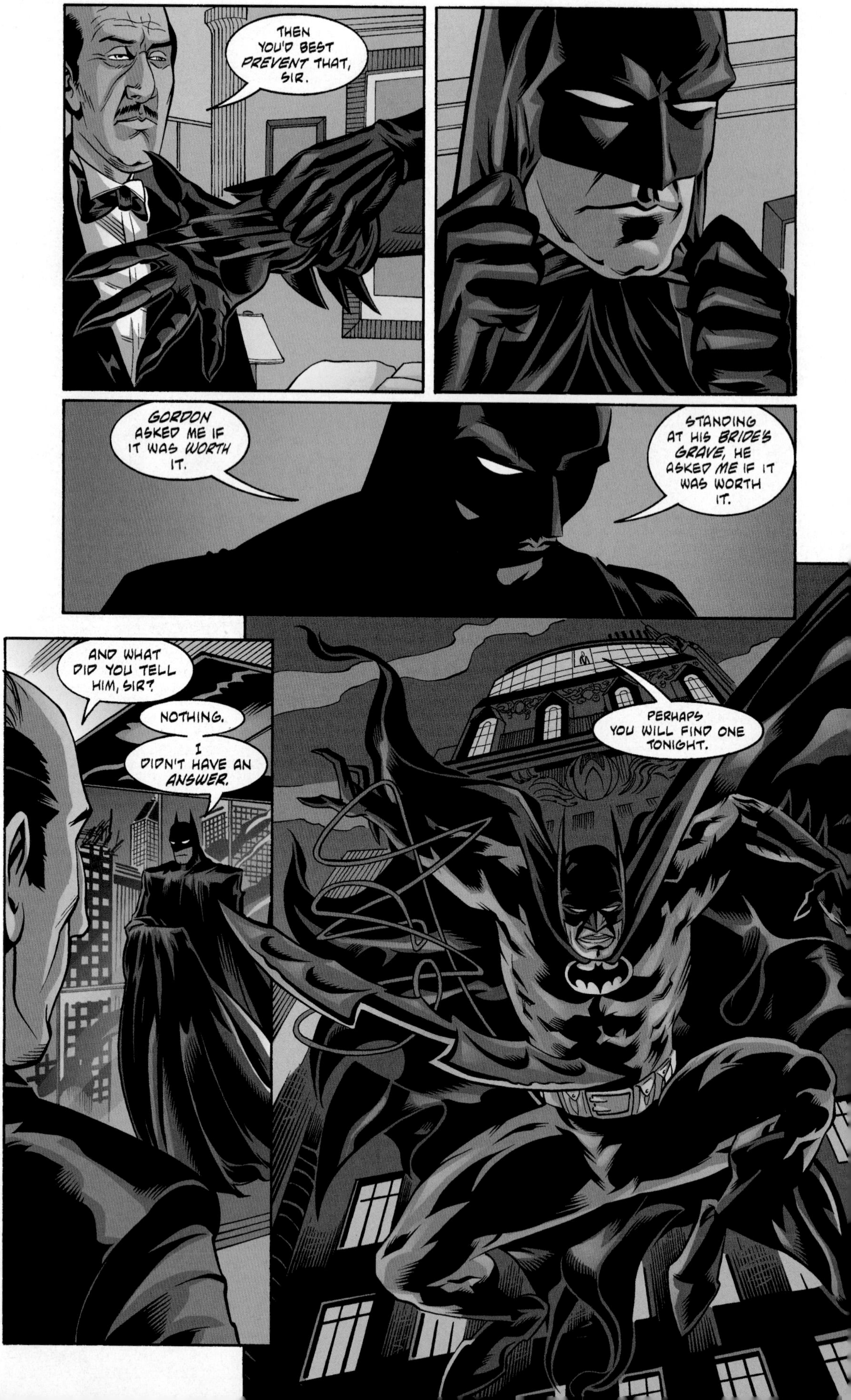

THEN YOU'D BEST PREVENT THAT, SIR.
GORDON ASKED ME IF IT WAS WORTH IT.
STANDING AT HIS BRIDE'S GRAVE, HE ASKED ME IF IT WAS WORTH IT.
AND WHAT DID YOU TELL HIM, SIR?
NOTHING.
I DIDN'T HAVE AN ANSWER.
PERHAPS YOU WILL FIND ONE TONIGHT.

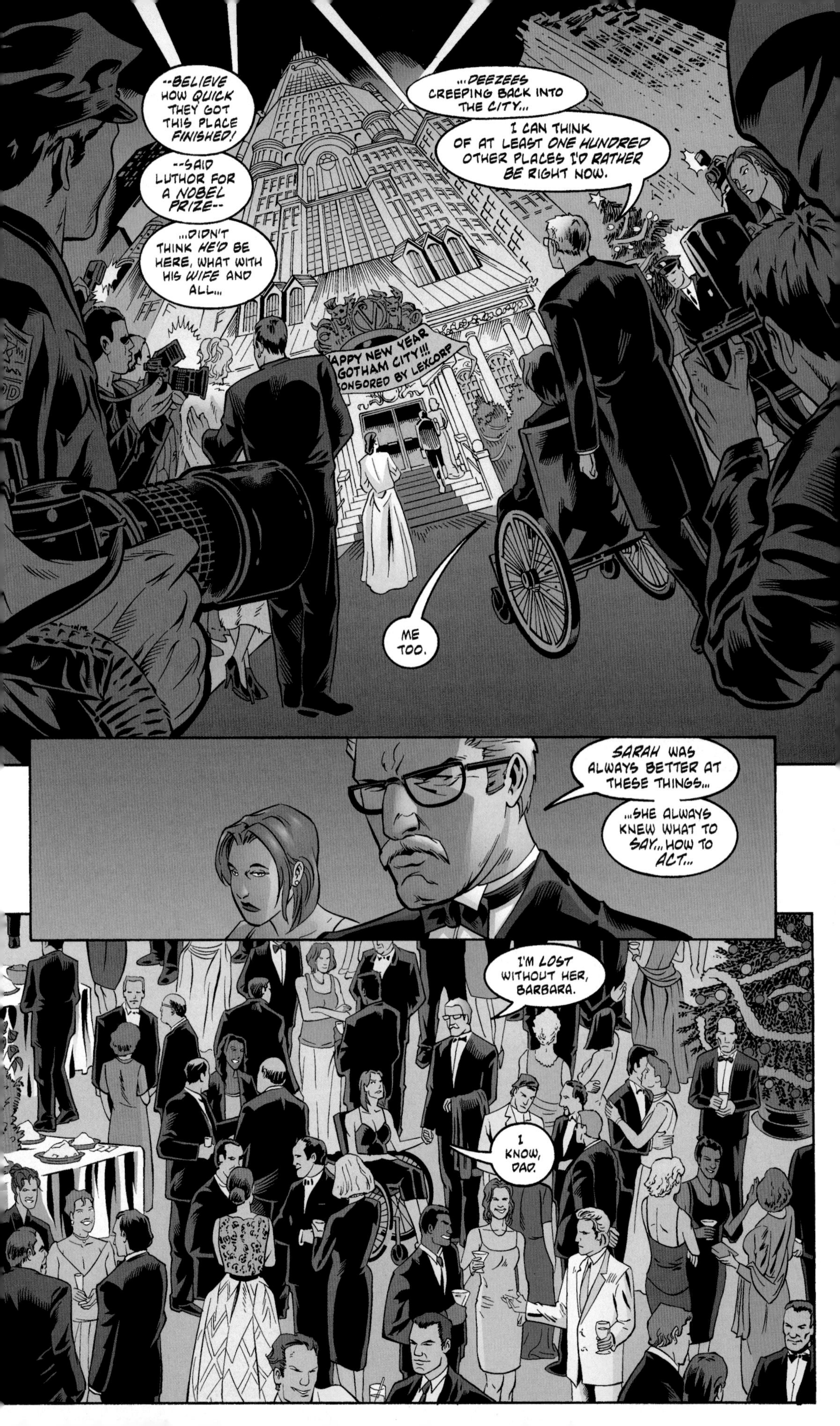
--BELIEVE HOW QUICK THEY GOT THIS PLACE FINISHED!
--SAID LUTHOR FOR A NOBEL PRIZE--
...DIDN'T THINK HE'D BE HERE, WHAT WITH HIS WIFE AND ALL...
...DEEZEES CREEPING BACK INTO THE CITY...
I CAN THINK OF AT LEAST ONE HUNDRED OTHER PLACES I'D RATHER BE RIGHT NOW.
APPY NEW YEAR GOTHAM CITY!!! ONSORED BY LEXCORP
ME TOO.
SARAH WAS ALWAYS BETTER AT THESE THINGS...
...SHE ALWAYS KNEW WHAT TO SAY... HOW TO ACT...
I'M LOST WITHOUT HER, BARBARA.
I KNOW, DAD.

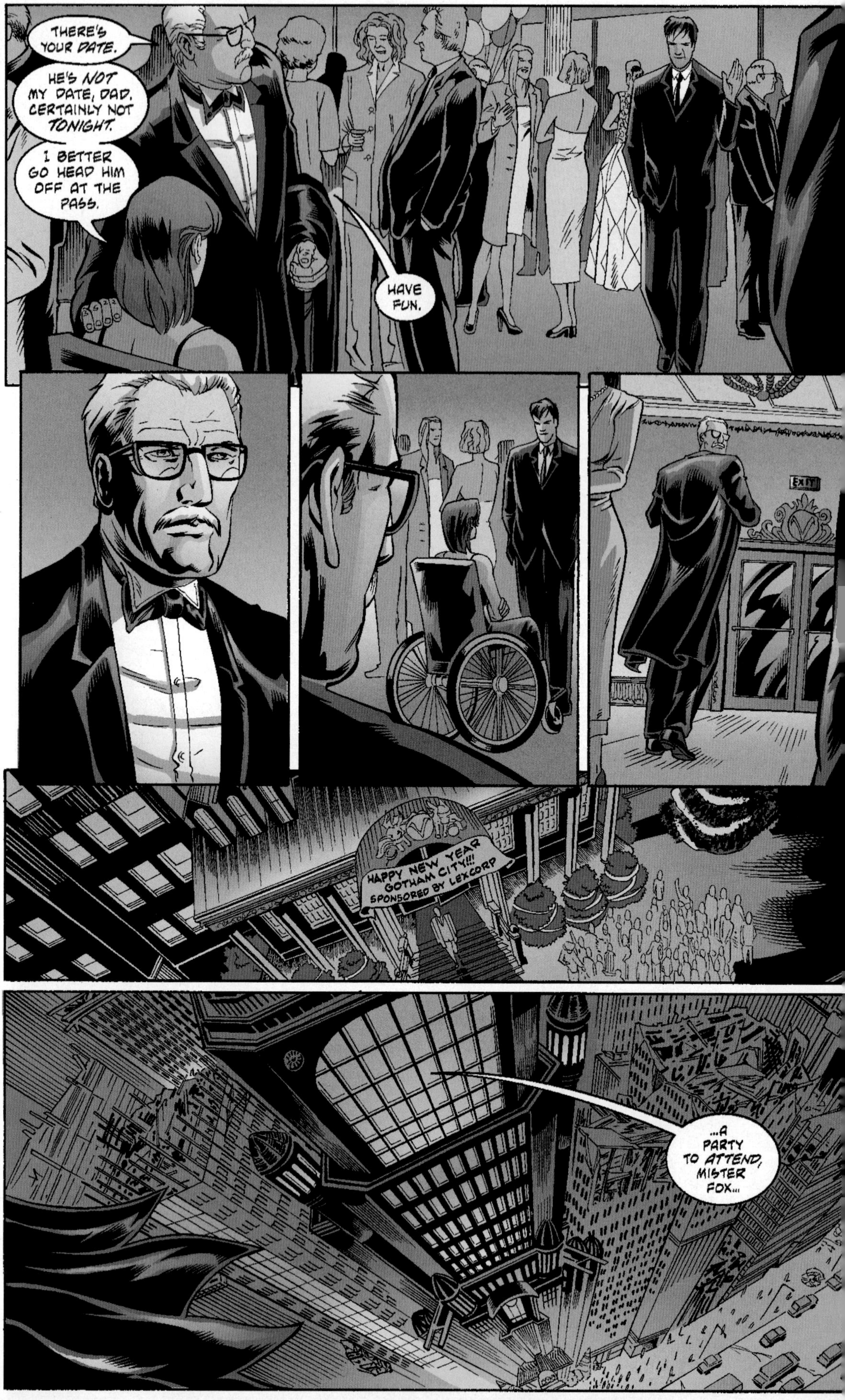
THERE'S YOUR DATE.
HE'S NOT MY DATE, DAD. CERTAINLY NOT TONIGHT.
I BETTER GO HEAD HIM OFF AT THE PASS.
HAVE FUN.
EXIT
HAPPY NEW YEAR GOTHAM CITY!!! SPONSORED BY LEXCORP
...A PARTY TO ATTEND, MISTER FOX...

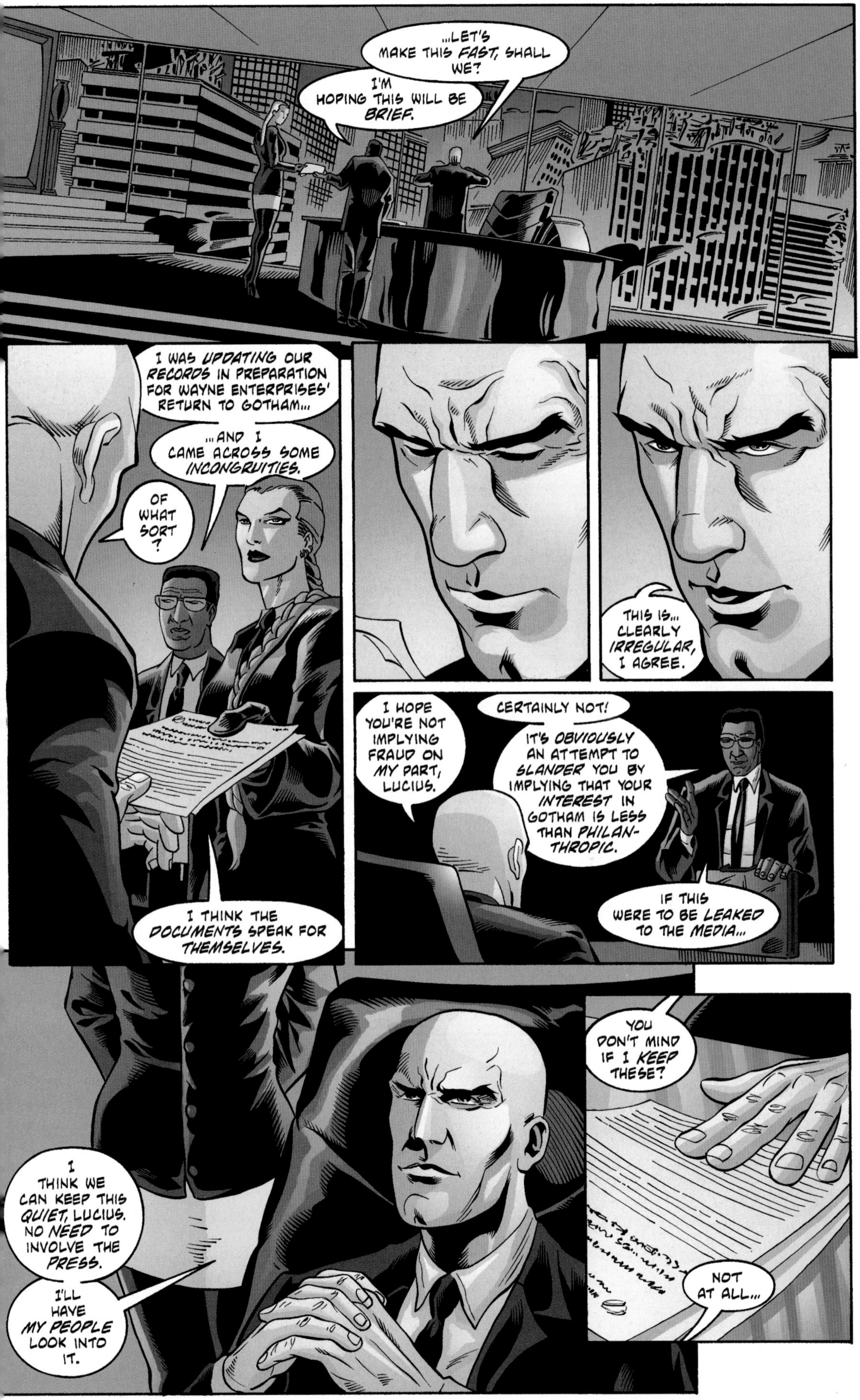
...LET'S MAKE THIS FAST, SHALL WE?
I'M HOPING THIS WILL BE BRIEF.
I WAS UPDATING OUR RECORDS IN PREPARATION FOR WAYNE ENTERPRISES' RETURN TO GOTHAM...
...AND I CAME ACROSS SOME INCONGRUITIES.
OF WHAT SORT?
I THINK THE DOCUMENTS SPEAK FOR THEMSELVES.
THIS IS... CLEARLY IRREGULAR, I AGREE.
I HOPE YOU'RE NOT IMPLYING FRAUD ON MY PART, LUCIUS.
CERTAINLY NOT!
IT'S OBVIOUSLY AN ATTEMPT TO SLANDER YOU BY IMPLYING THAT YOUR INTEREST IN GOTHAM IS LESS THAN PHILAN-THROPIC.
IF THIS WERE TO BE LEAKED TO THE MEDIA...
I THINK WE CAN KEEP THIS QUIET, LUCIUS. NO NEED TO INVOLVE THE PRESS.
I'LL HAVE MY PEOPLE LOOK INTO IT.
YOU DON'T MIND IF I KEEP THESE?
NOT AT ALL...

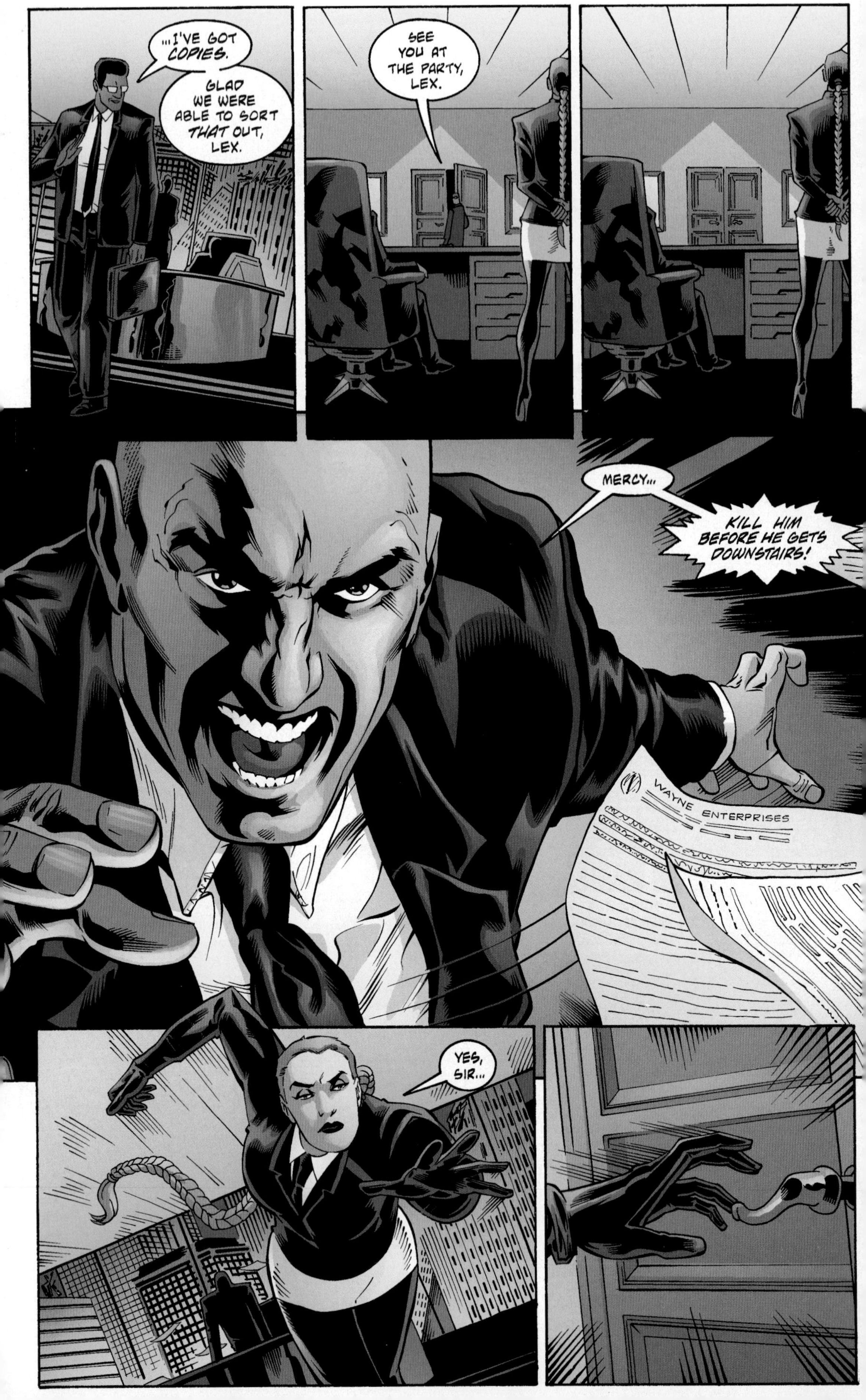
...I'VE GOT COPIES.
GLAD WE WERE ABLE TO SORT THAT OUT, LEX.
SEE YOU AT THE PARTY, LEX.
MERCY...
KILL HIM BEFORE HE GETS DOWNSTAIRS!
WAYNE ENTERPRISES
YES, SIR...

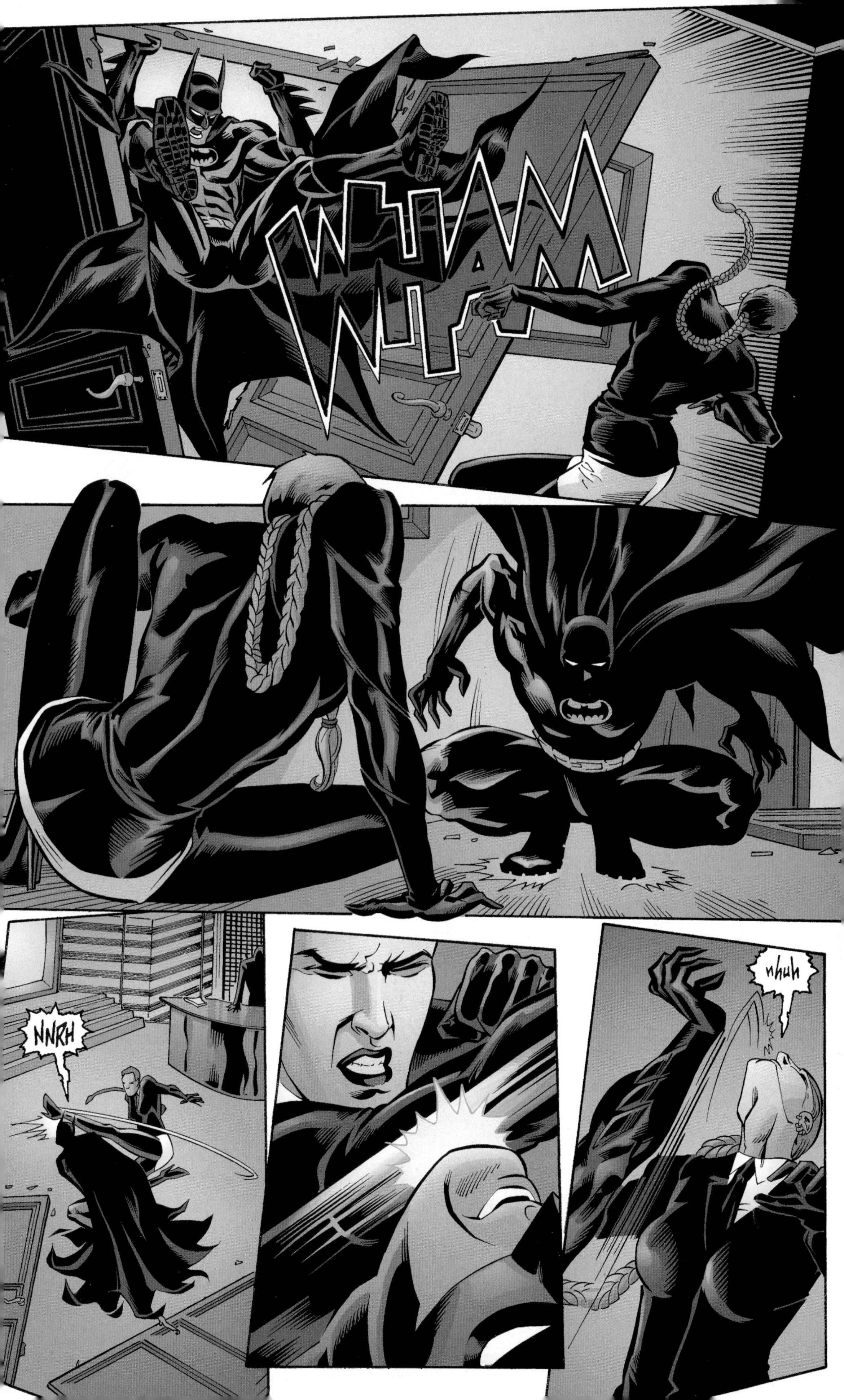
WHAM
WHAM
NNRH
nhuh

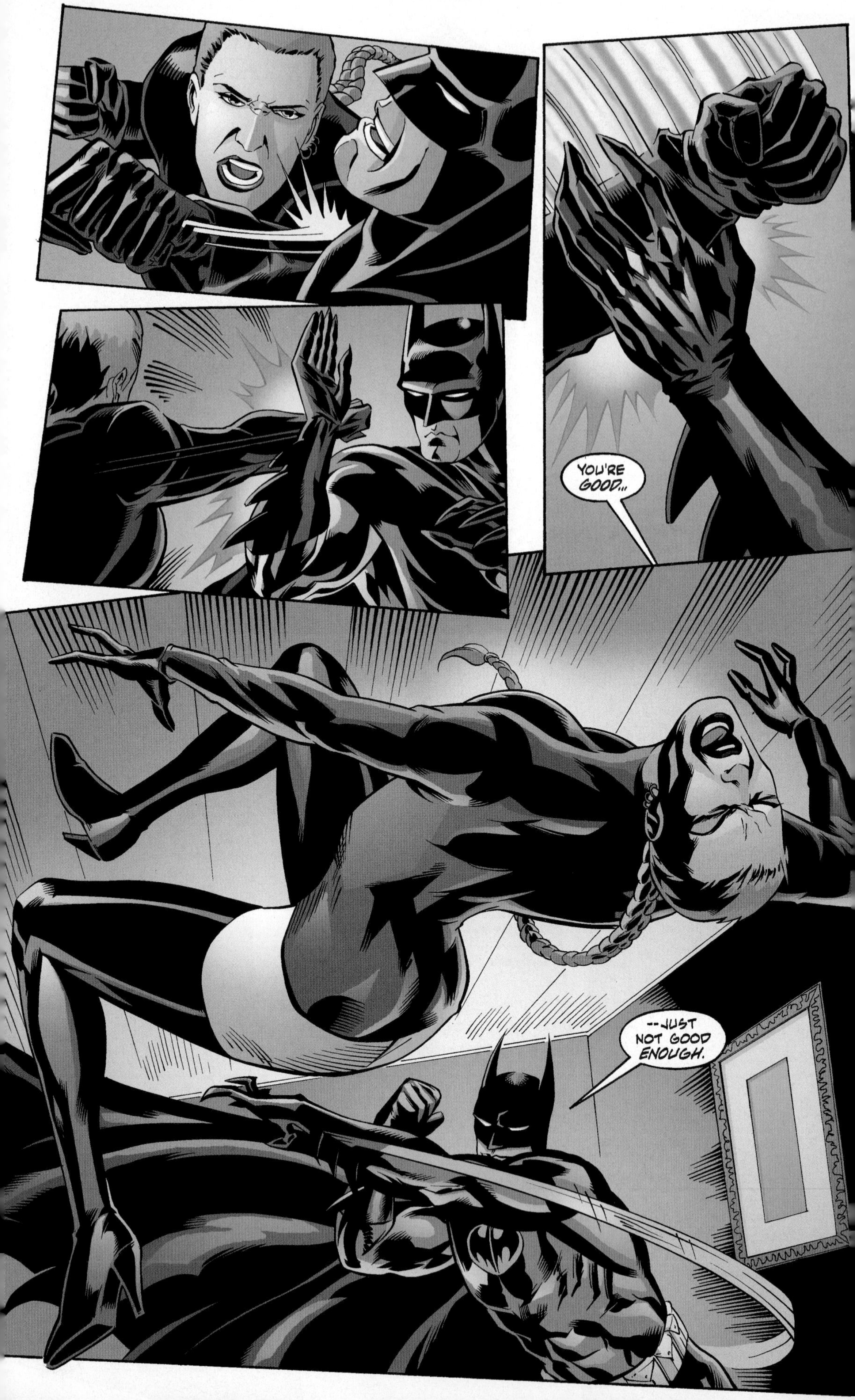
YOU'RE GOOD...
--JUST NOT GOOD ENOUGH.

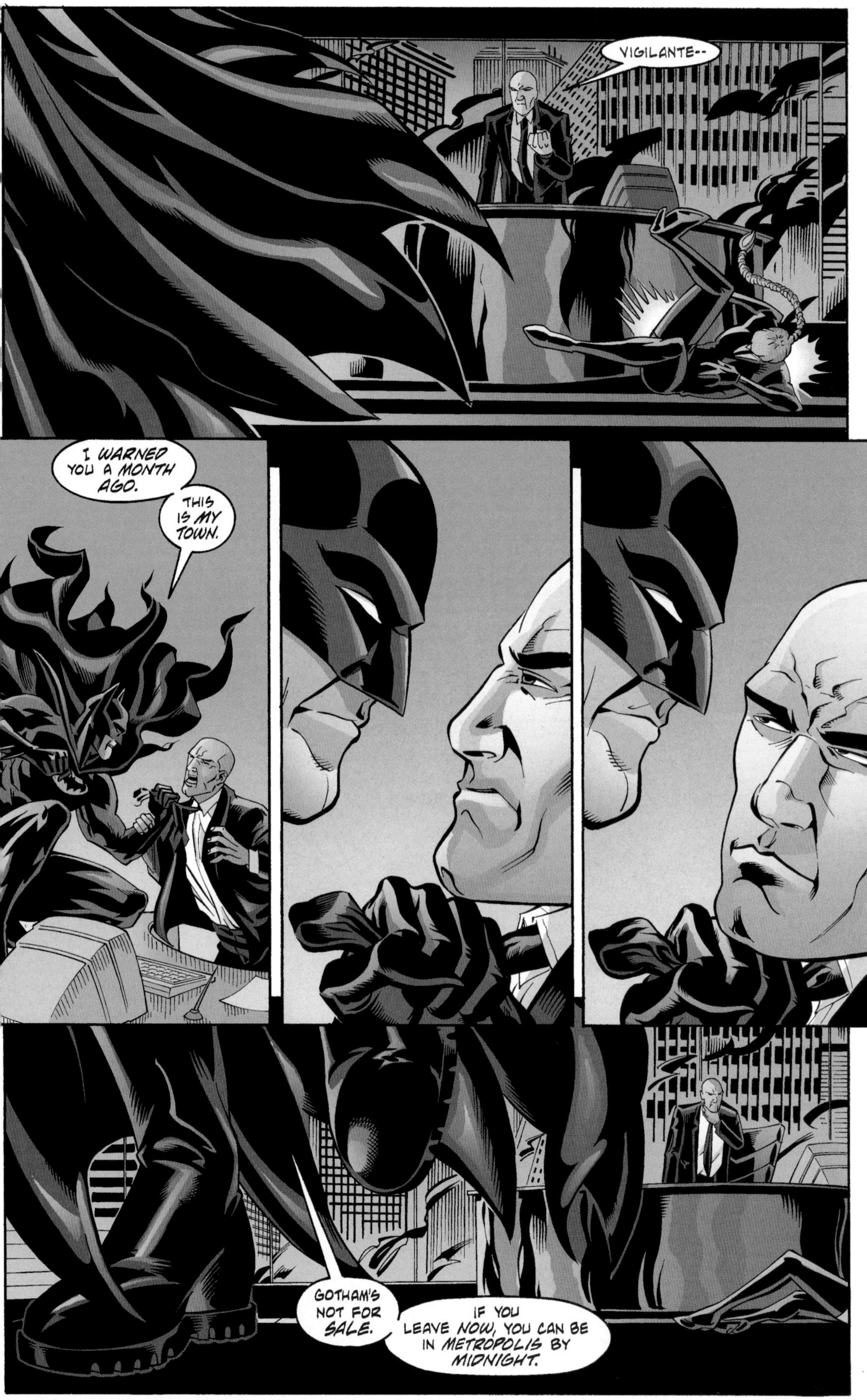
VIGILANTE--
I WARNED YOU A MONTH AGO.
THIS IS MY TOWN.
GOTHAM'S NOT FOR SALE.
IF YOU LEAVE NOW, YOU CAN BE IN METROPOLIS BY MIDNIGHT.

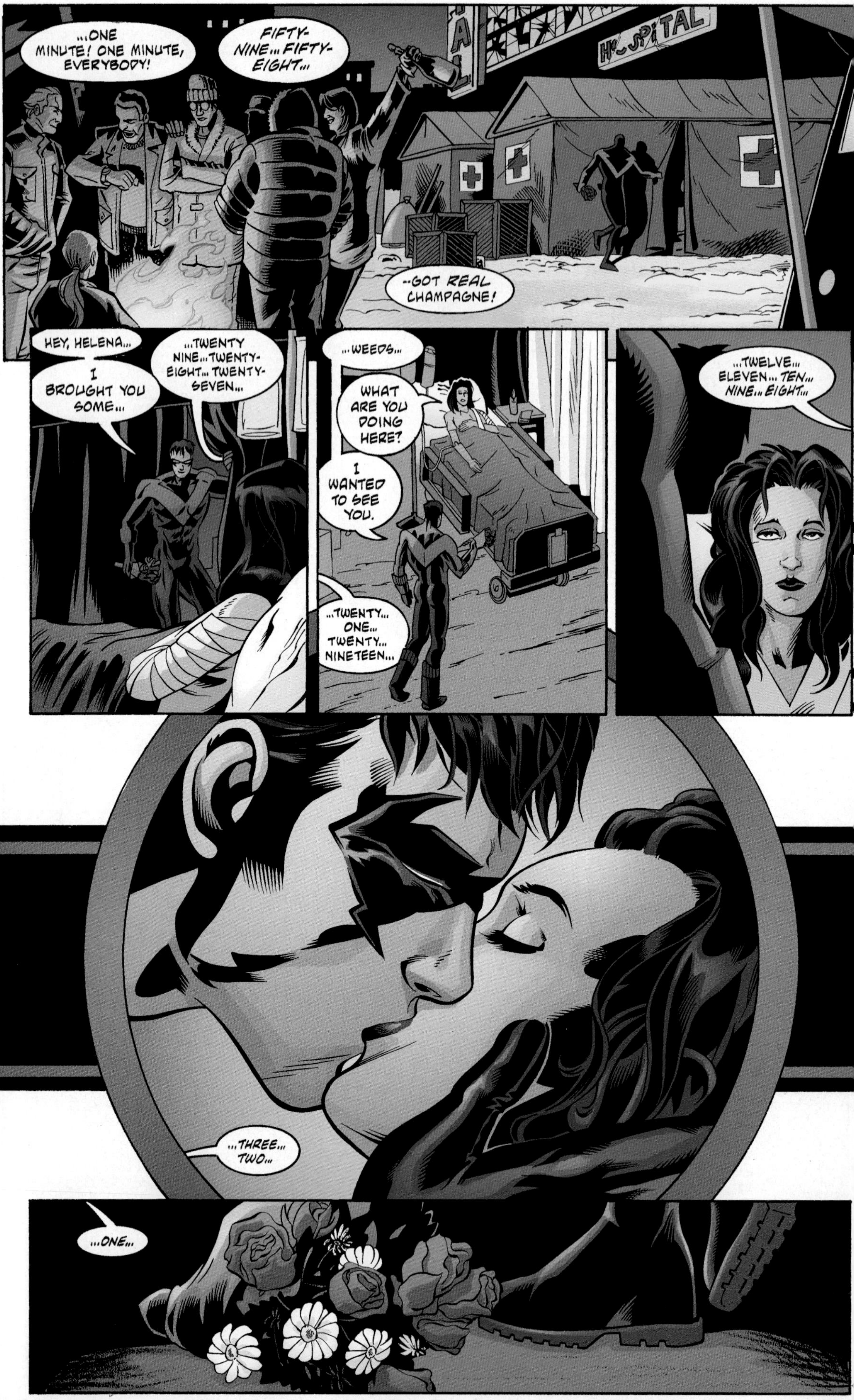
...ONE MINUTE! ONE MINUTE, EVERYBODY!
FIFTY-NINE... FIFTY-EIGHT...
HOSPITAL
--GOT REAL CHAMPAGNE!
HEY, HELENA...
I BROUGHT YOU SOME...
...TWENTY NINE... TWENTY-EIGHT... TWENTY-SEVEN...
...WEEDS...
WHAT ARE YOU DOING HERE?
I WANTED TO SEE YOU.
...TWENTY... ONE... TWENTY... NINETEEN...
...TWELVE... ELEVEN... TEN... NINE... EIGHT...
...THREE... TWO...
...ONE...

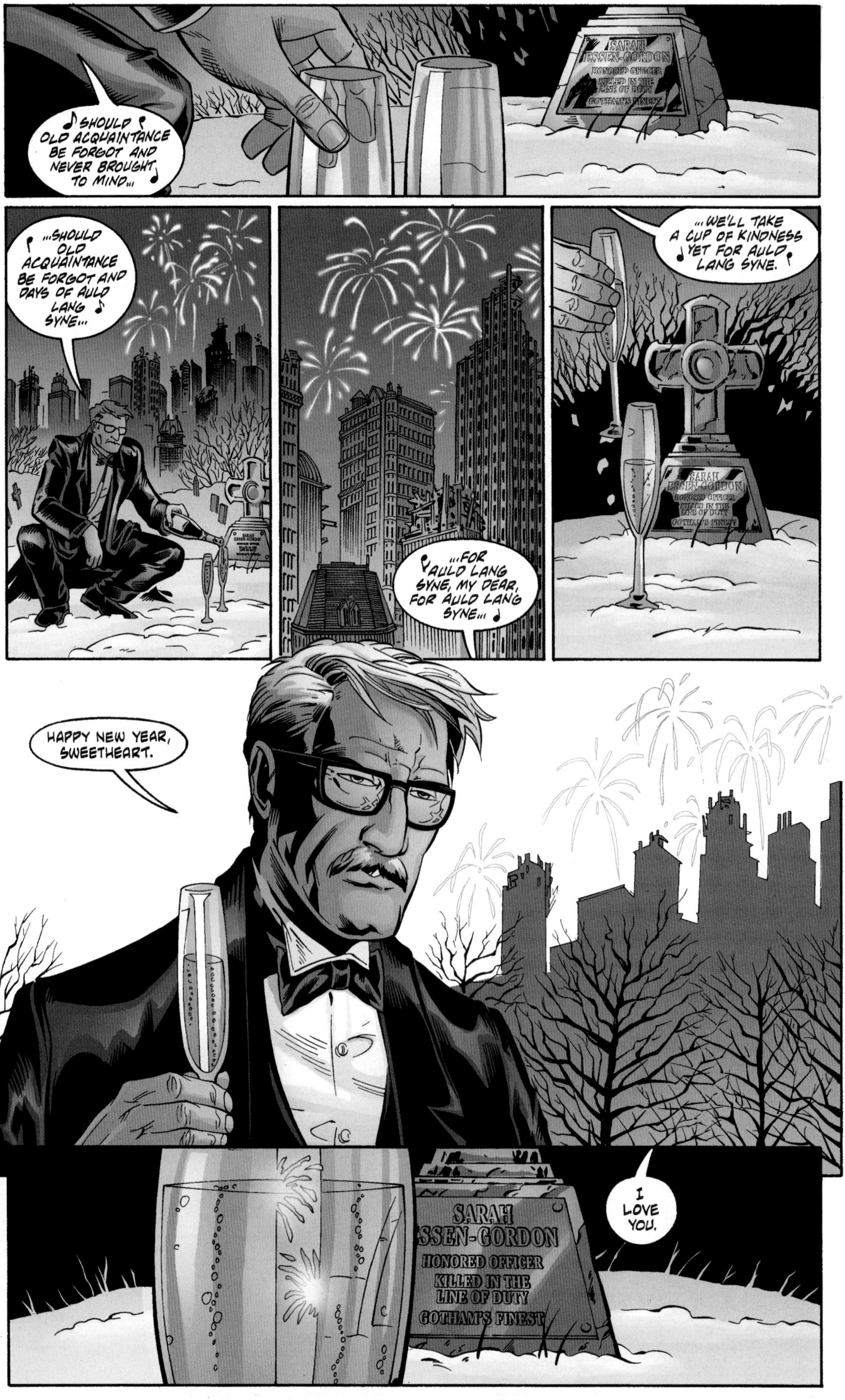
SARAH ESSEN-GORDON
HONORED OFFICER
KILLED IN THE LINE OF DUTY
GOTHAM'S FINEST
♪ SHOULD OLD ACQUAINTANCE BE FORGOT AND NEVER BROUGHT TO MIND... ♪
♪ ...SHOULD OLD ACQUAINTANCE BE FORGOT AND DAYS OF AULD LANG ♪ SYNE...
♪ ...FOR AULD LANG SYNE, MY DEAR, FOR AULD LANG SYNE... ♪
...WE'LL TAKE A CUP OF KINDNESS ♪ YET FOR AULD LANG SYNE. ♪
SARAH ESSEN-GORDON
HONORED OFFICER
KILLED IN THE LINE OF DUTY
GOTHAM'S FINEST
HAPPY NEW YEAR, SWEETHEART.
SARAH
ESSEN-GORDON
HONORED OFFICER
KILLED IN THE
LINE OF DUTY
GOTHAM'S FINEST
I LOVE YOU.

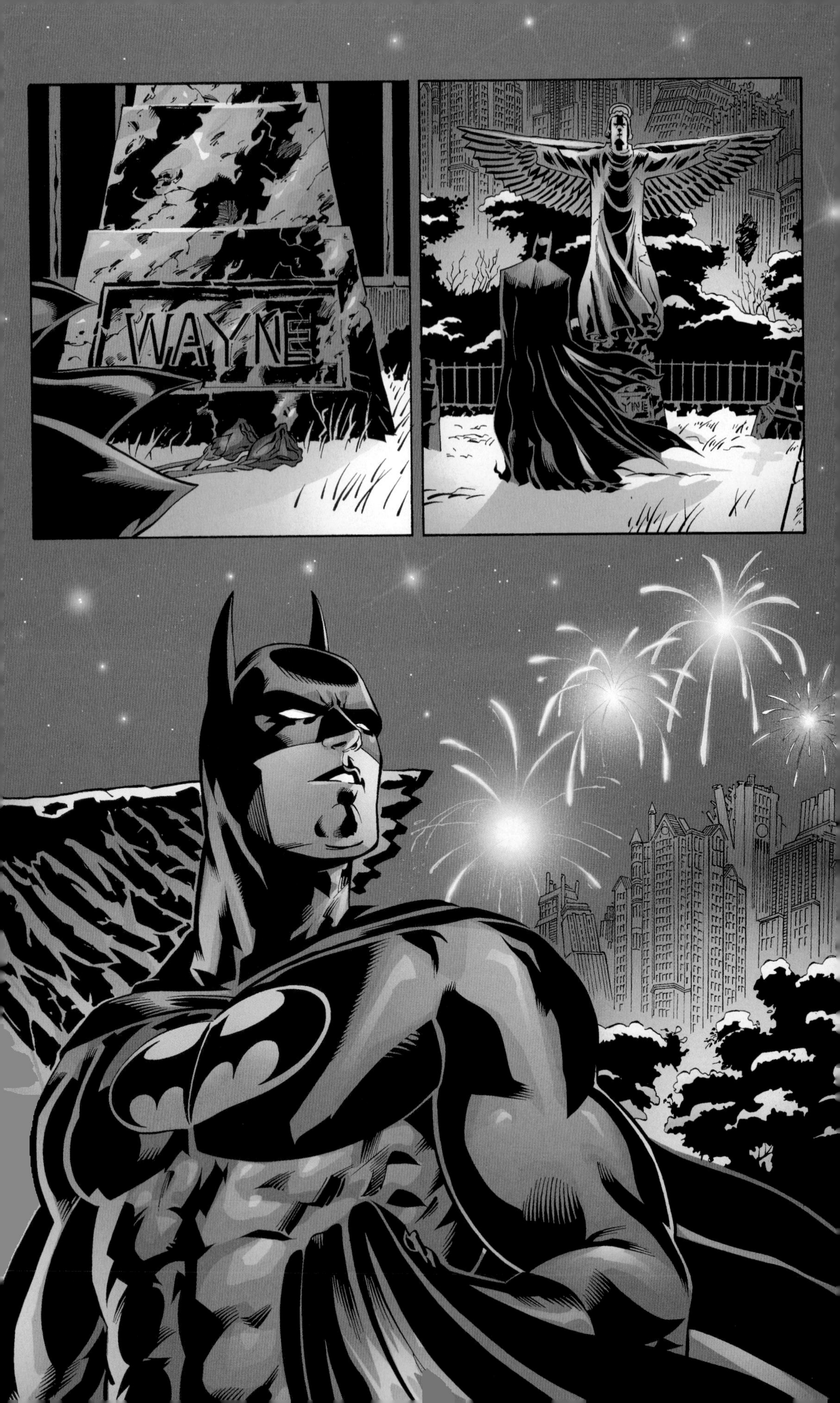
WAYNE

COVER GALLERY

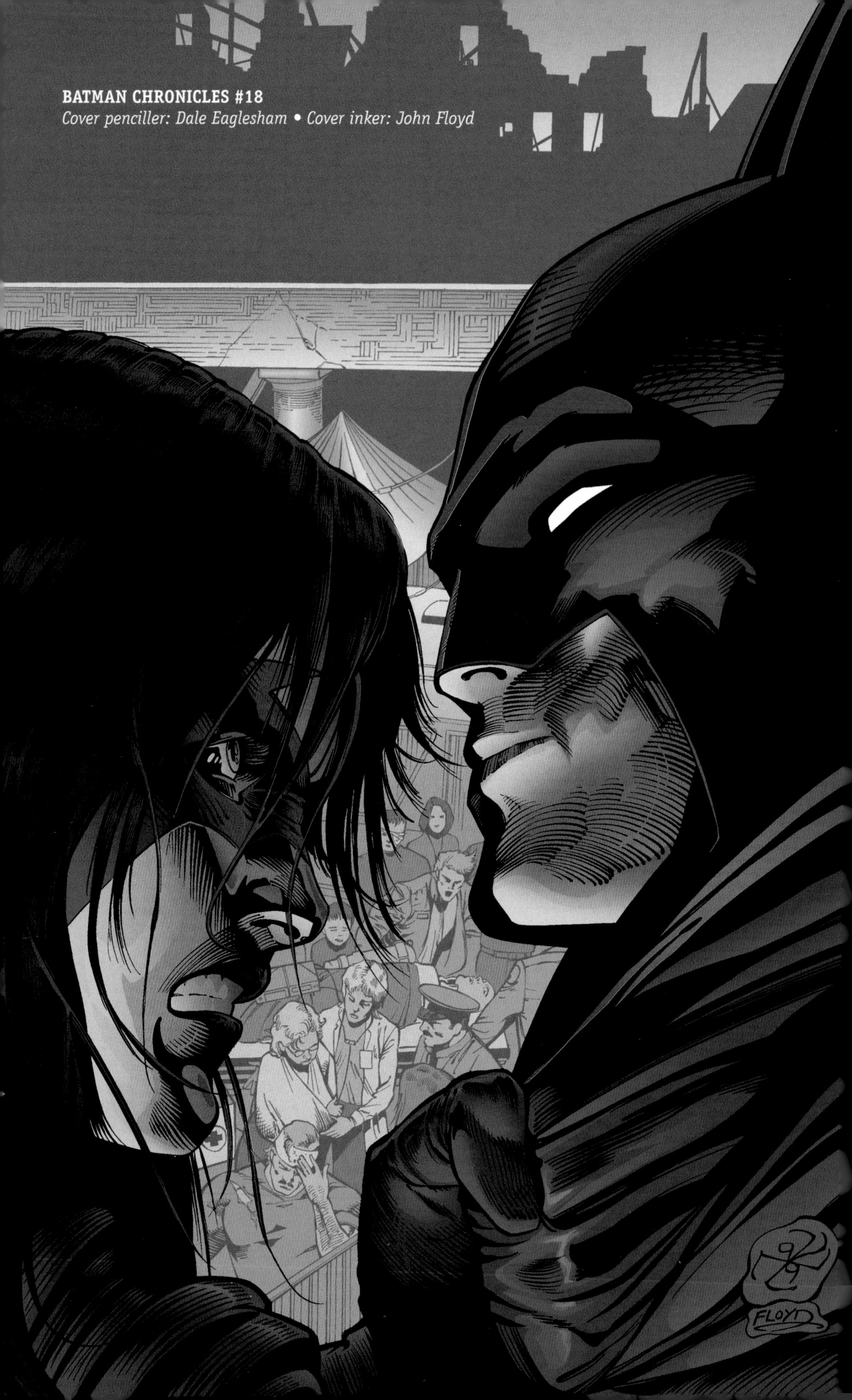
FLOYD

BATMAN CHRONICLES #18
Cover penciller: Dale Eaglesham • Cover inker: John Floyd

BATMAN #572
Cover artist: John Cassaday

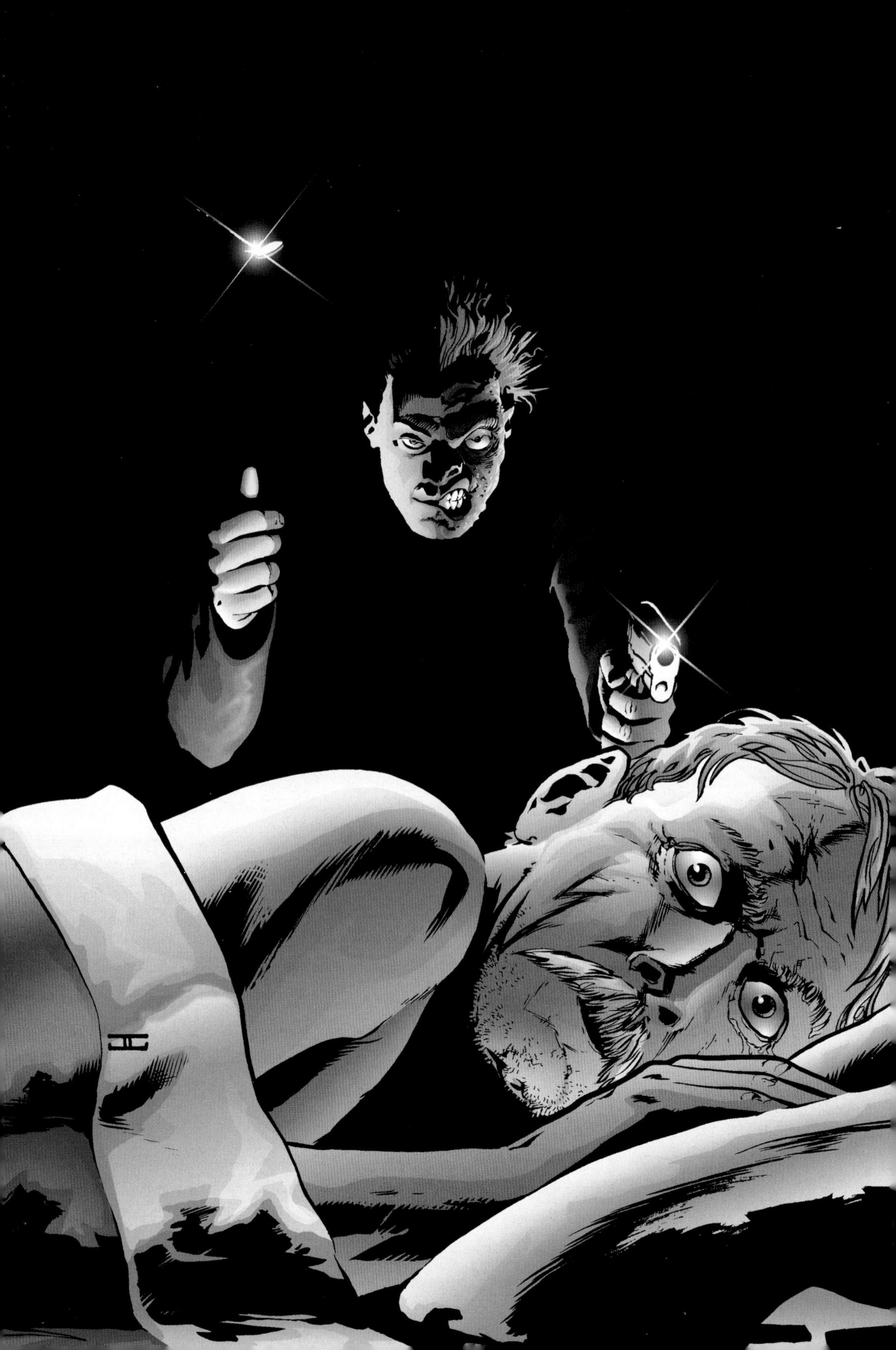
JC

DETECTIVE COMICS #739
Cover artist: John Cassaday

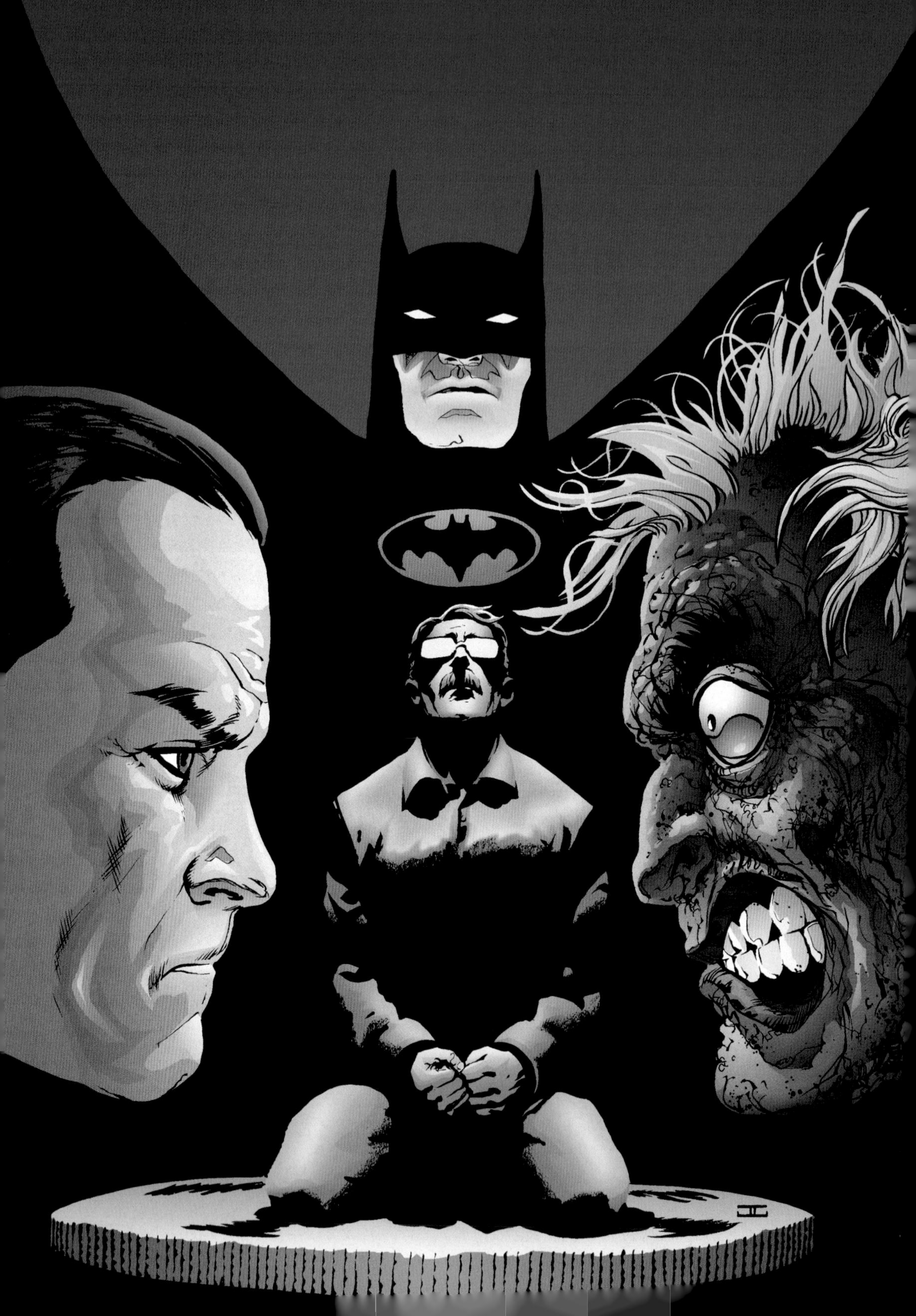

BATMAN: LEGENDS OF THE DARK KNIGHT #125
Cover artist: Jim Aparo • Cover inker: Jesse Delperdang

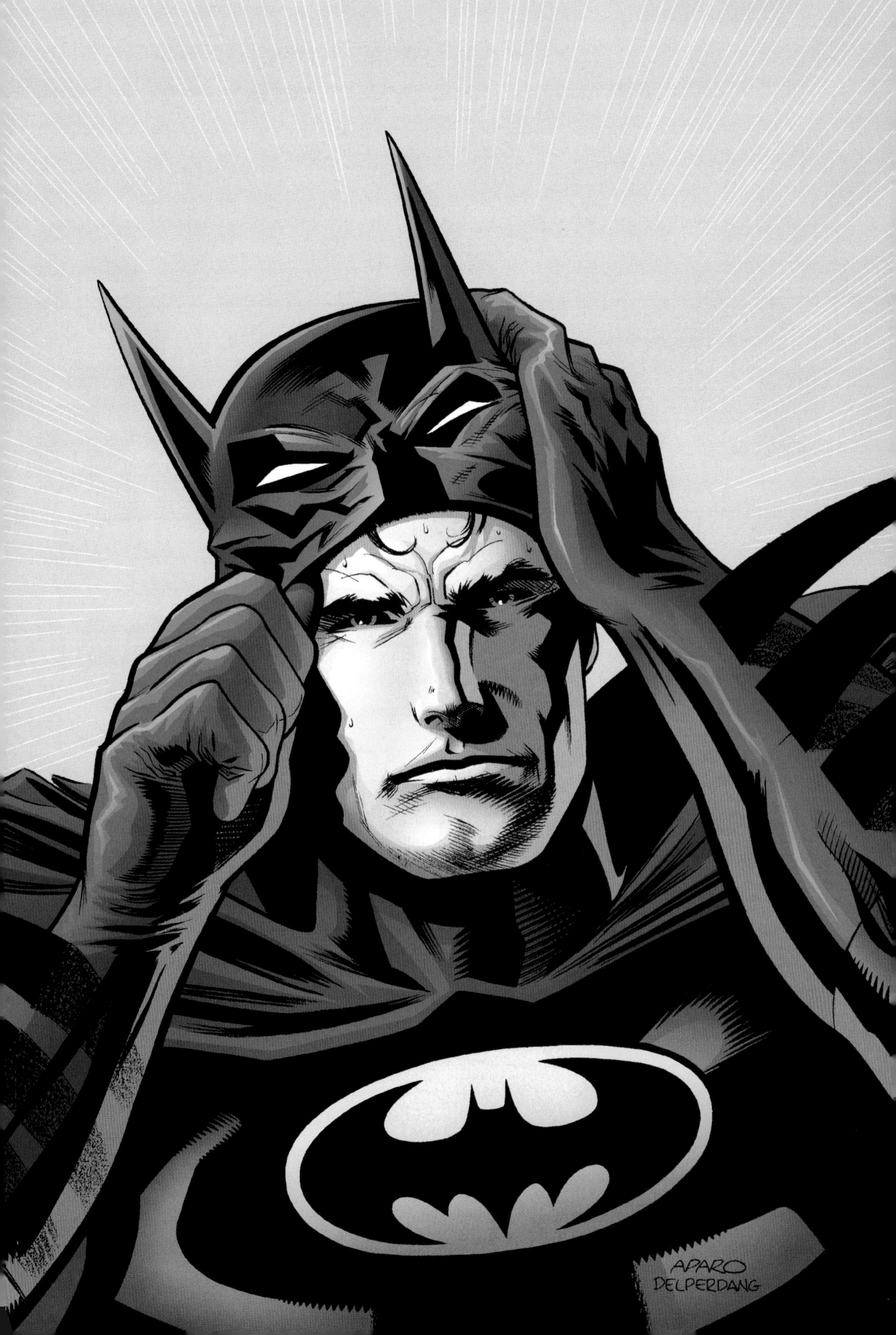
APARO
DELPERDANG

Cover penciller: Roger Robinson • Cover inker: James Pascoe

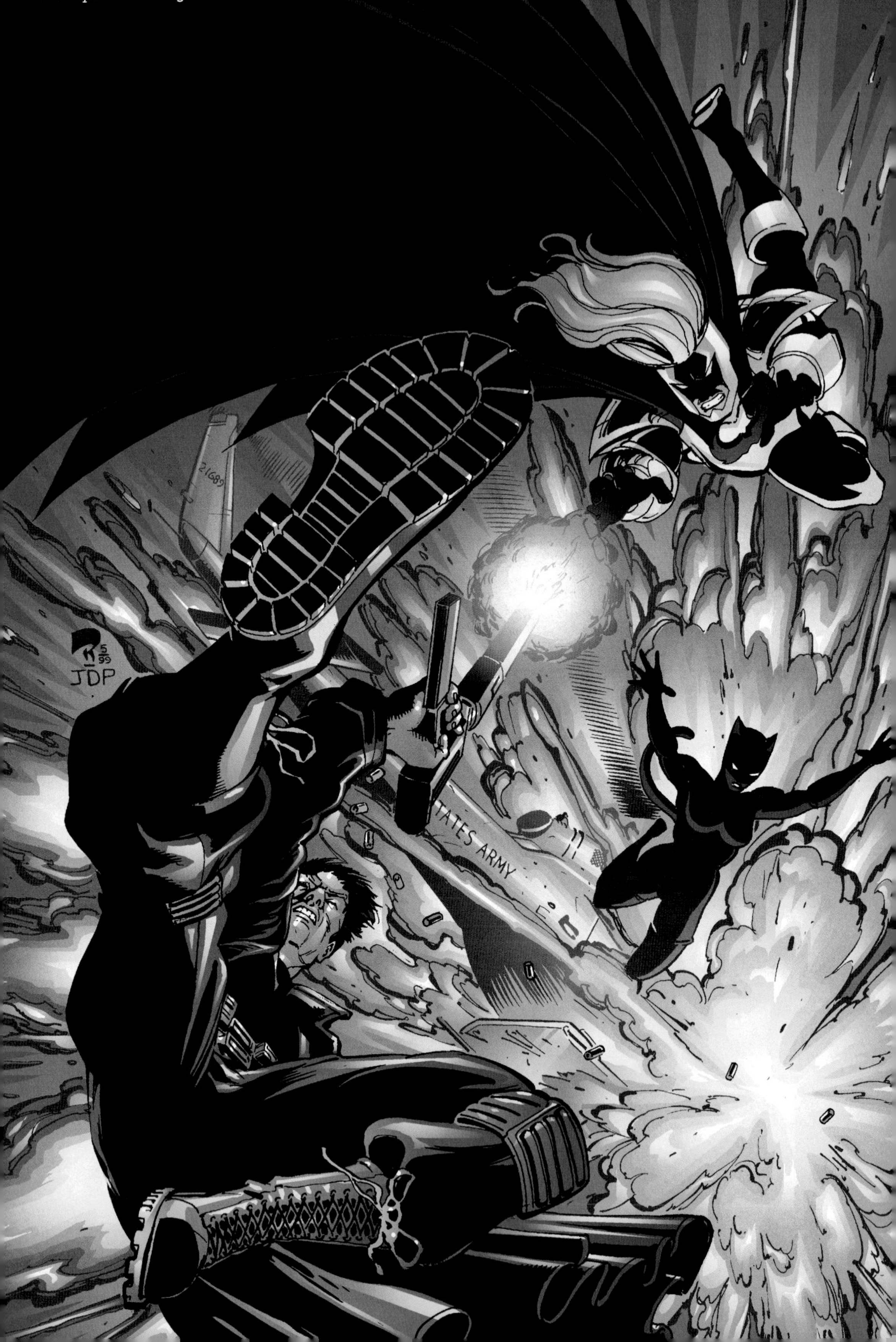
21689
JDP
TATES ARMY

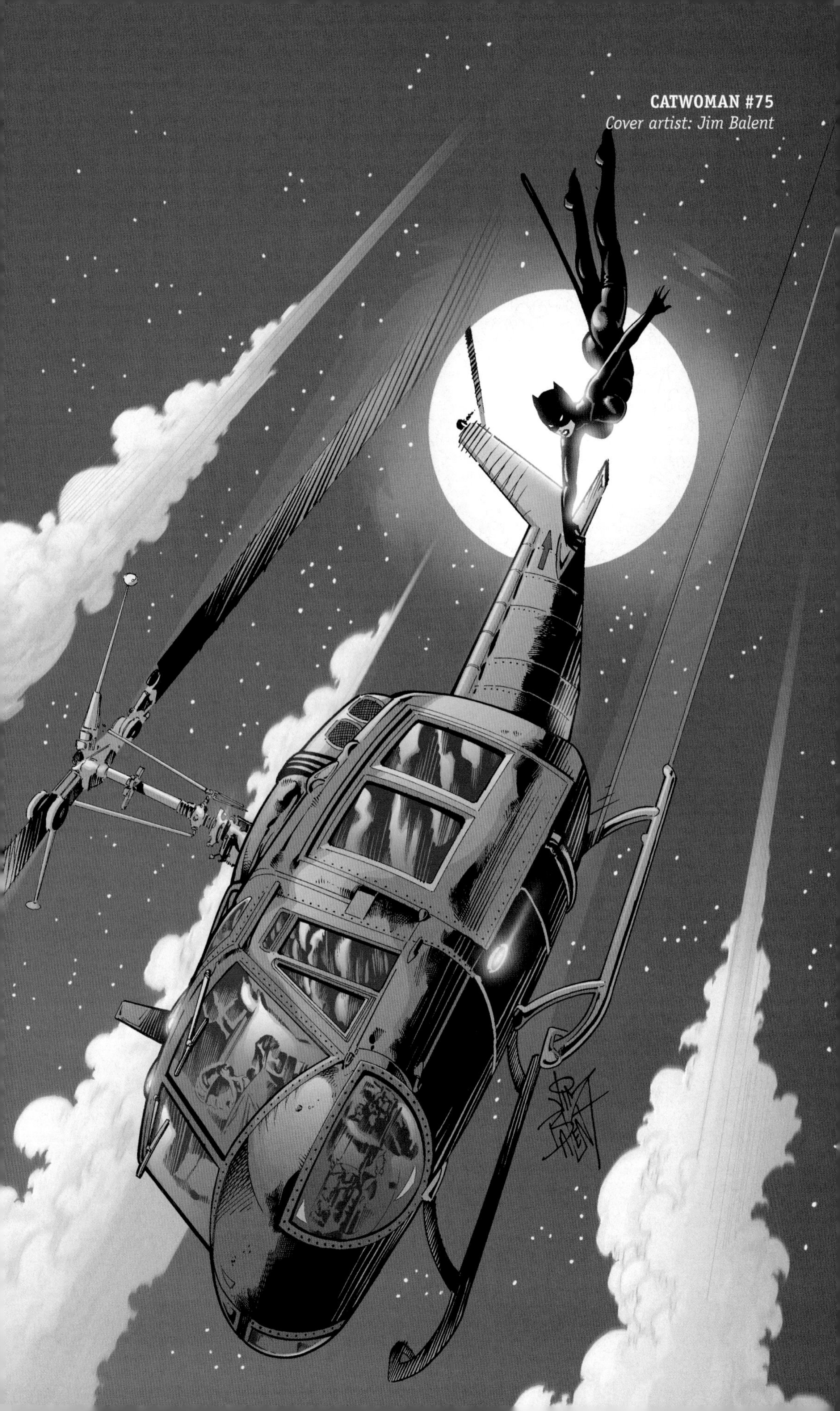

CATWOMAN #75
Cover artist: Jim Balent

BATMAN: SHADOW OF THE BAT #93
Cover penciller: Dale Eaglesham • Cover inker: Danny Miki

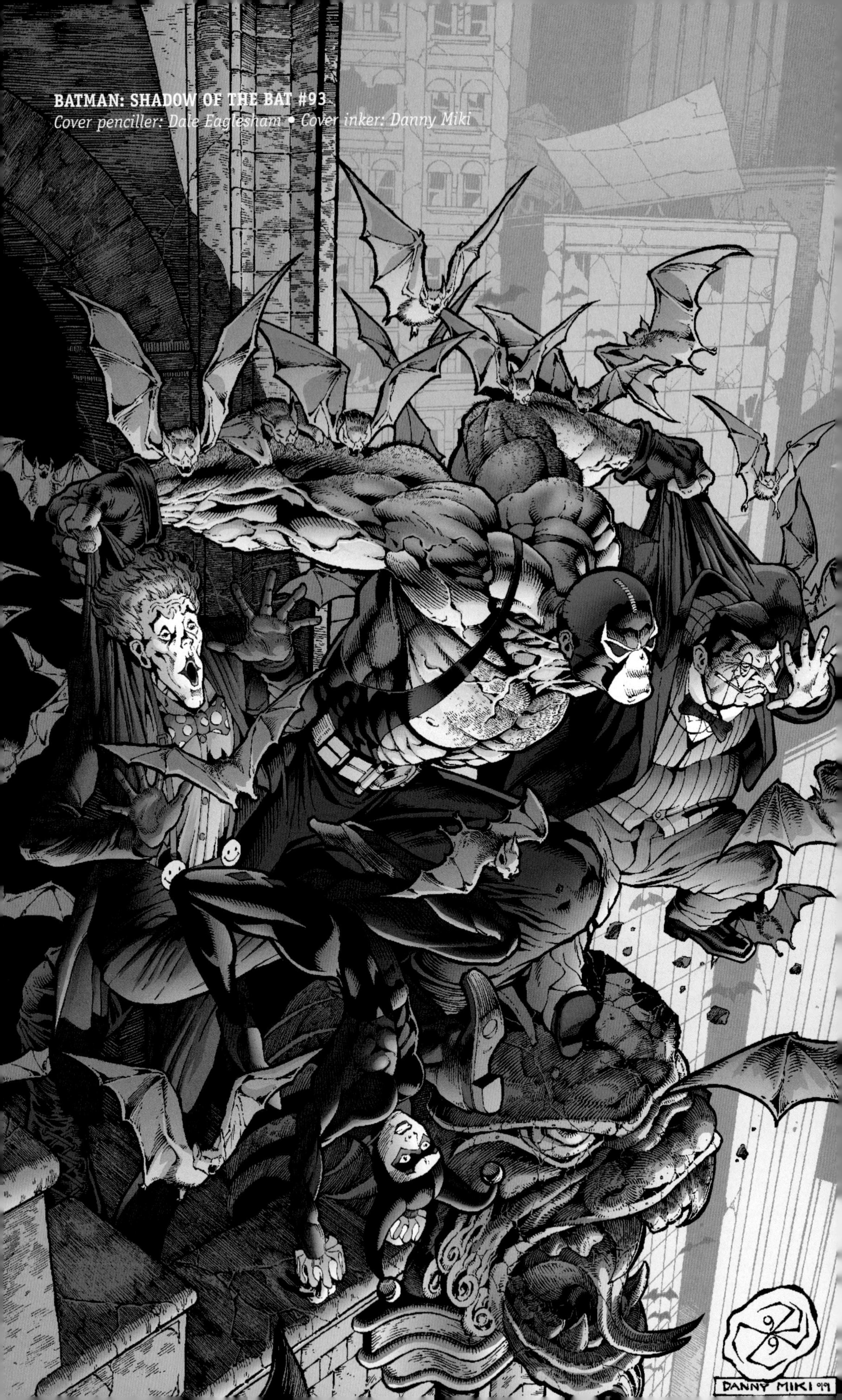
DANNY MIKI '99

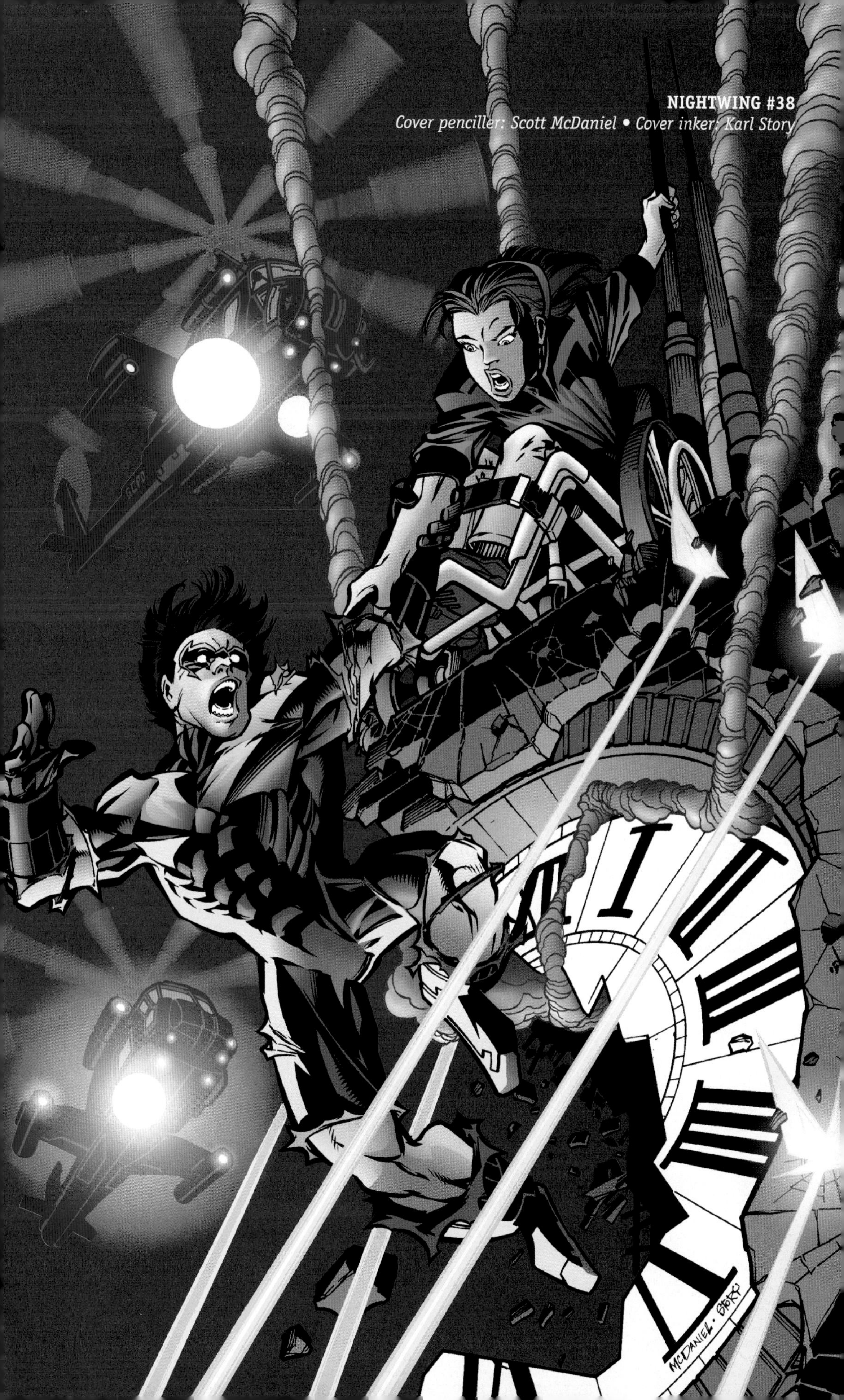
McDANIEL · STORY

NIGHTWING #38
Cover penciller: Scott McDaniel • Cover inker: Karl Story

NIGHTWING #39
Cover penciller: Scott McDaniel • Cover inker: Karl Story

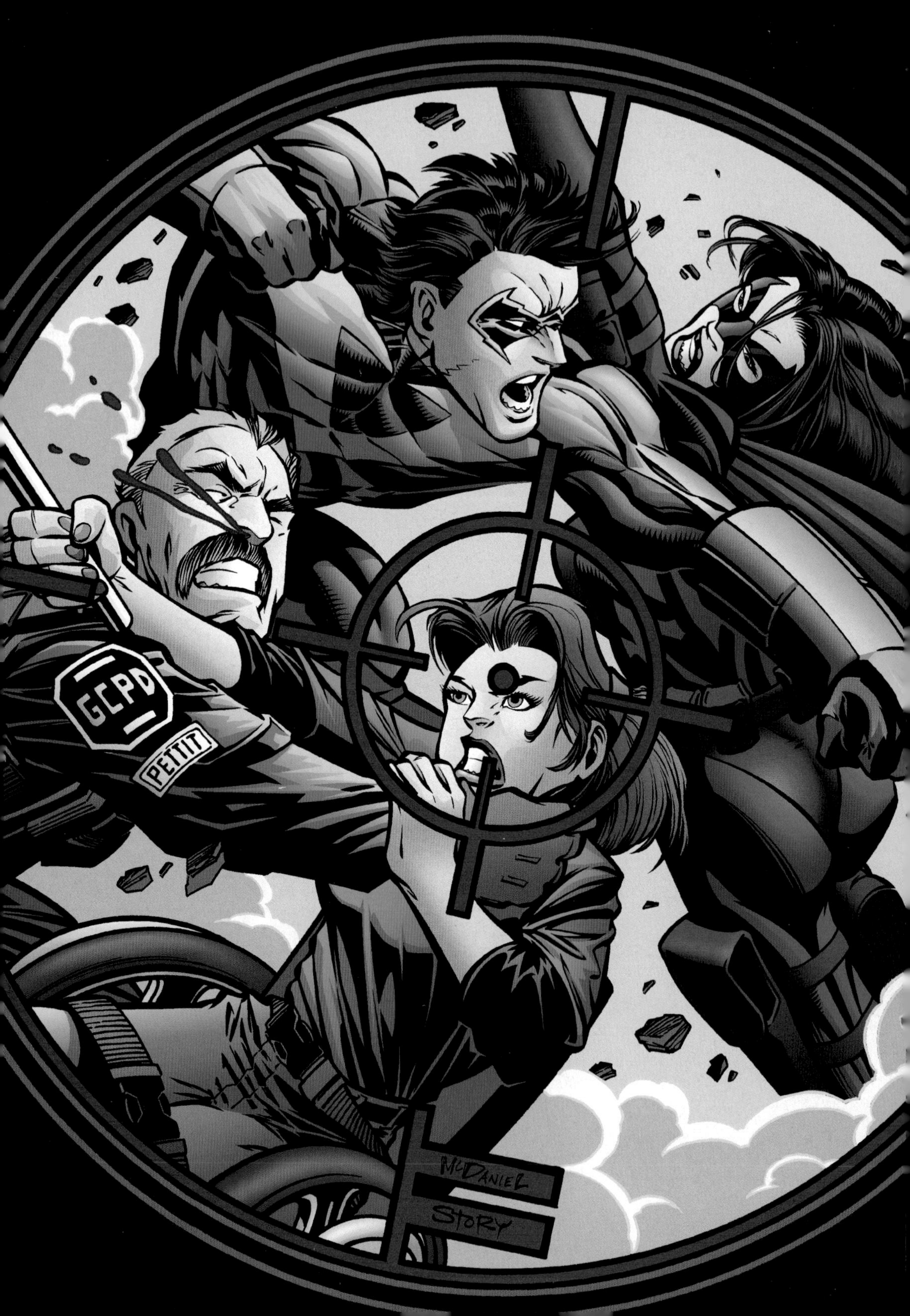
GCPD
PETTIT
McDANIEL
STORY

BATMAN: NO MAN'S LAND #0
Cover artist: Glenn Orbik

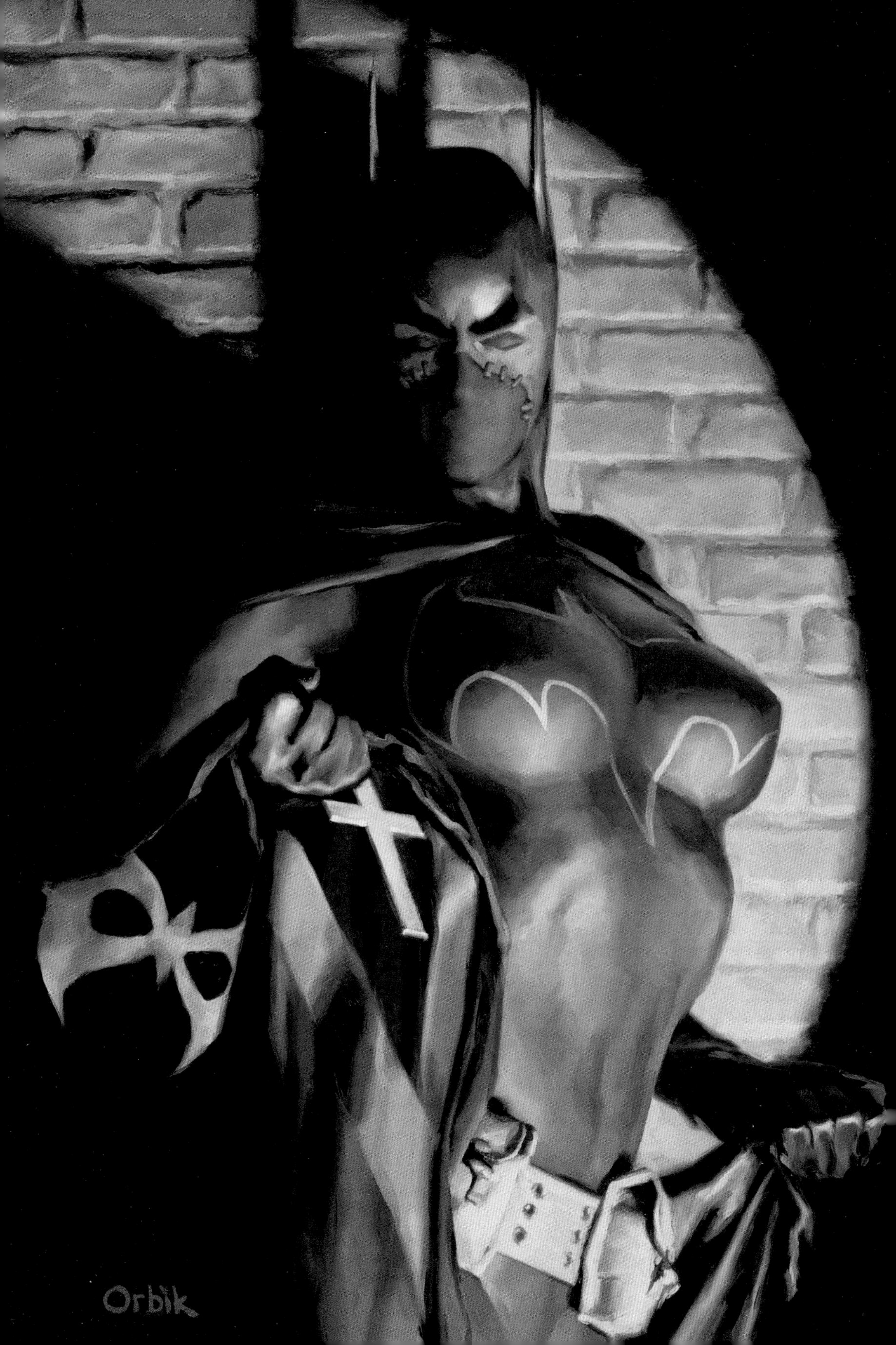
Orbik

BATMAN #573

Cover penciller: Doug Mahnke • Cover inker: Tom Nguyen

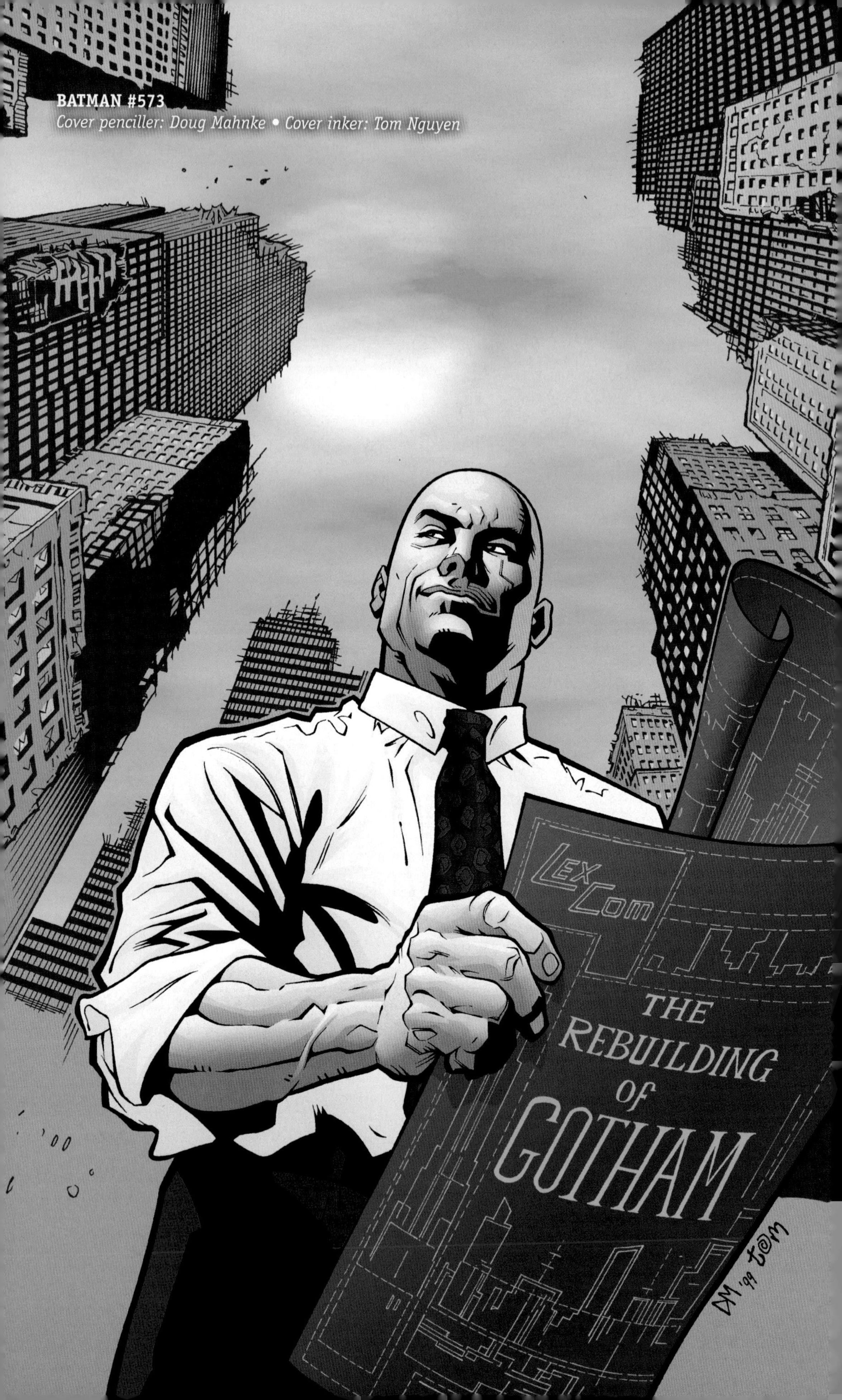

LEX COM
THE REBUILDING OF GOTHAM
DM '99 t@m

DETECTIVE COMICS #740
Cover artist: John Cassaday

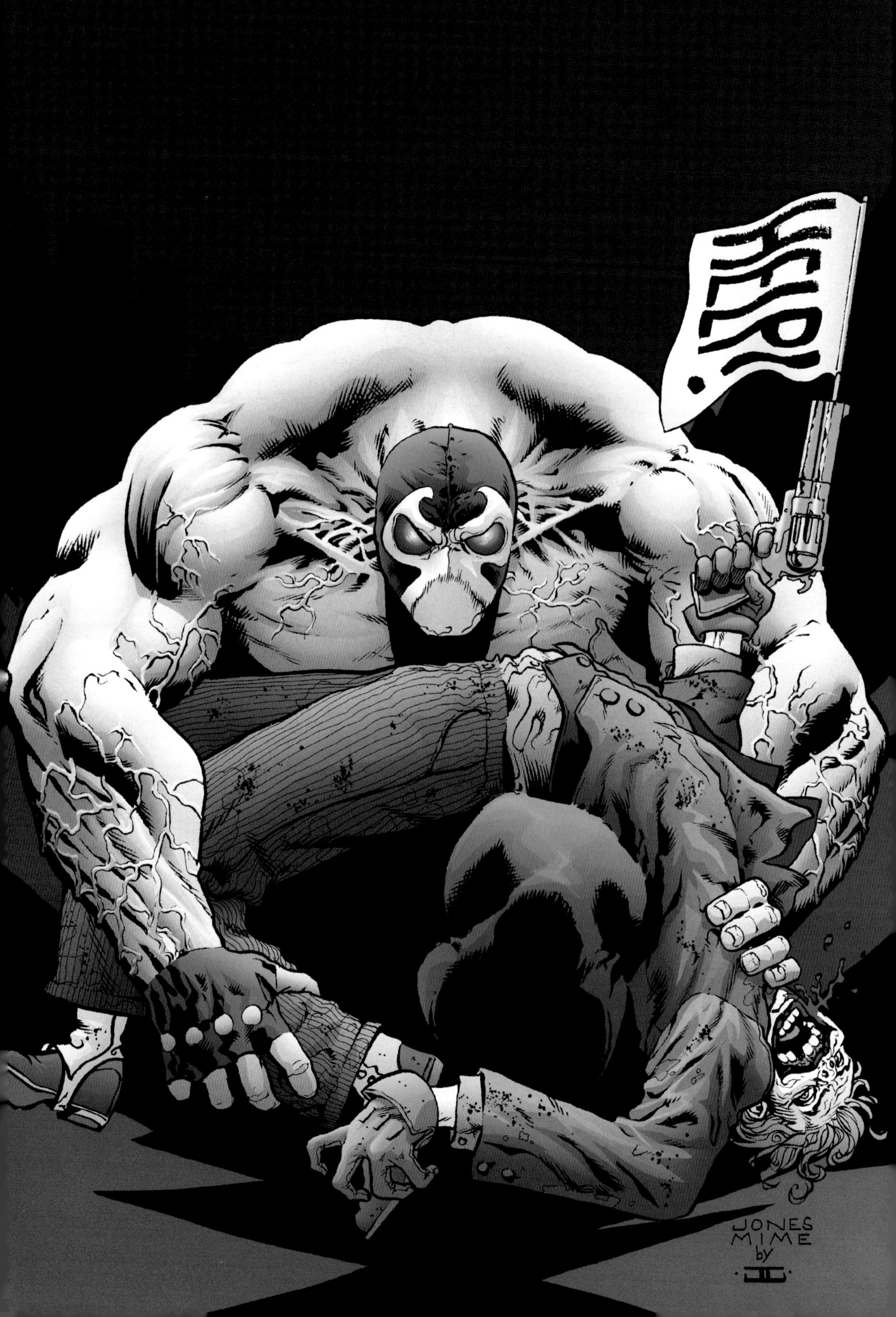
HELP!
JONES
MIME
by

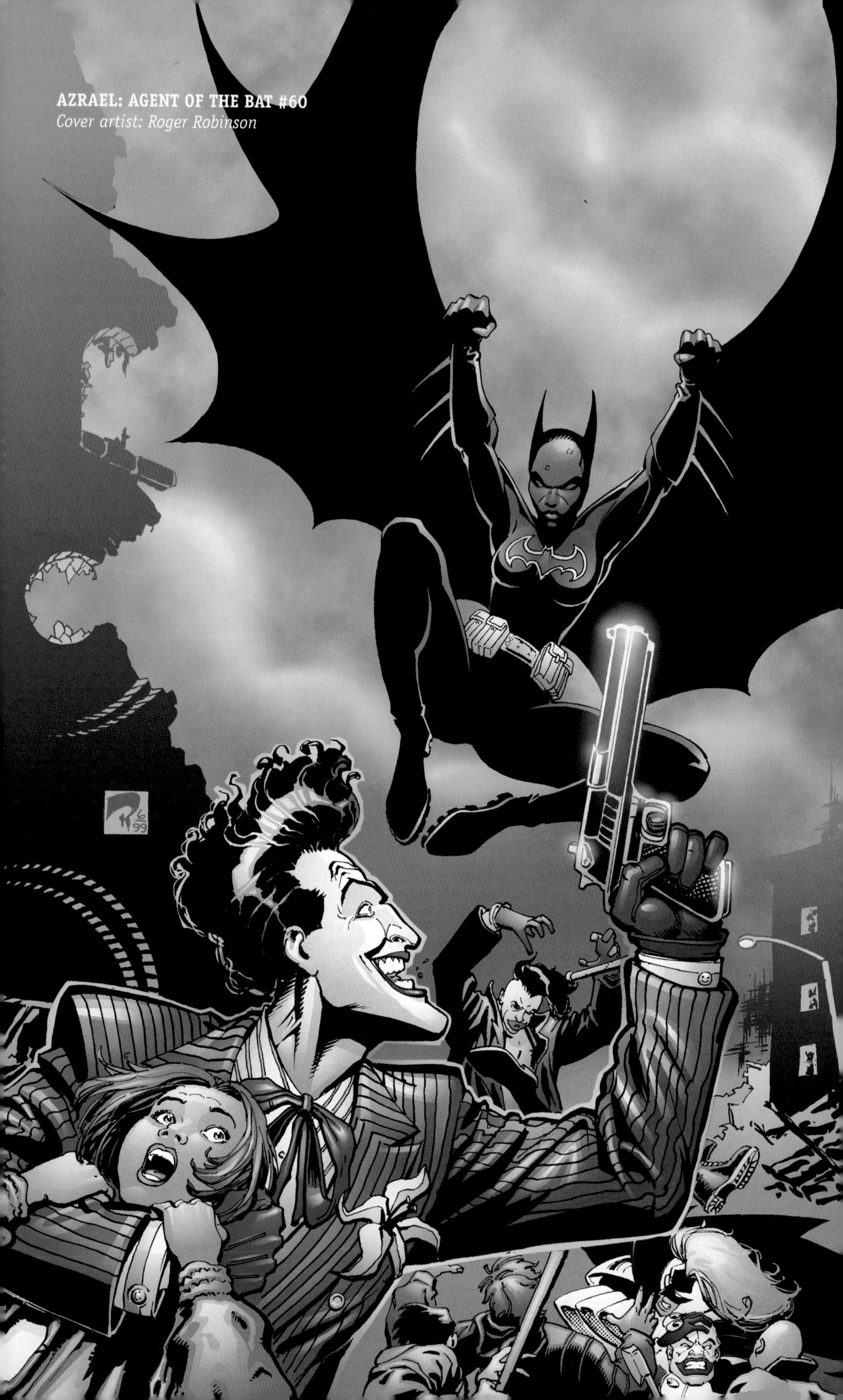

AZRAEL: AGENT OF THE BAT #60
Cover artist: Roger Robinson

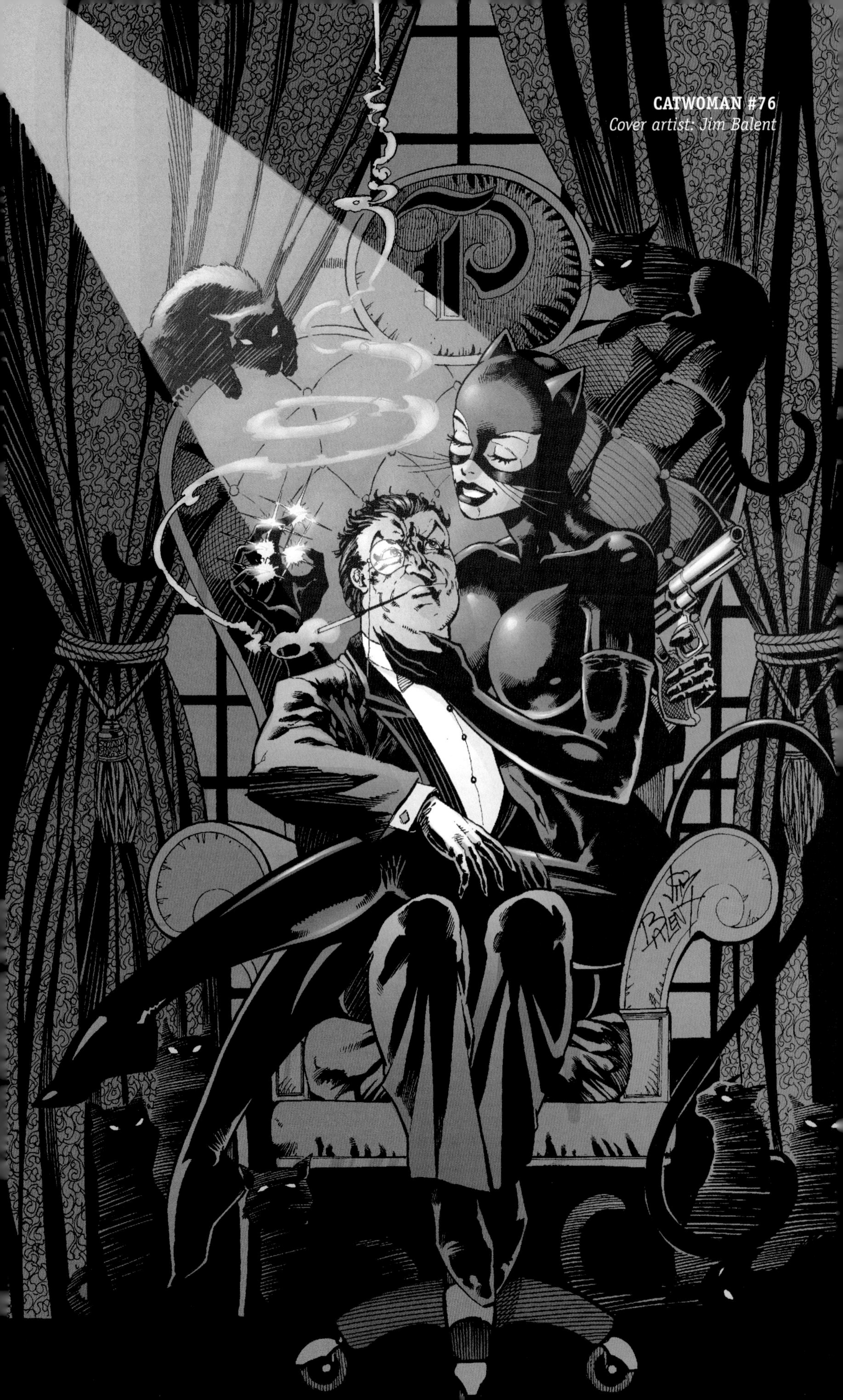

CATWOMAN #76
Cover artist: Jim Balent

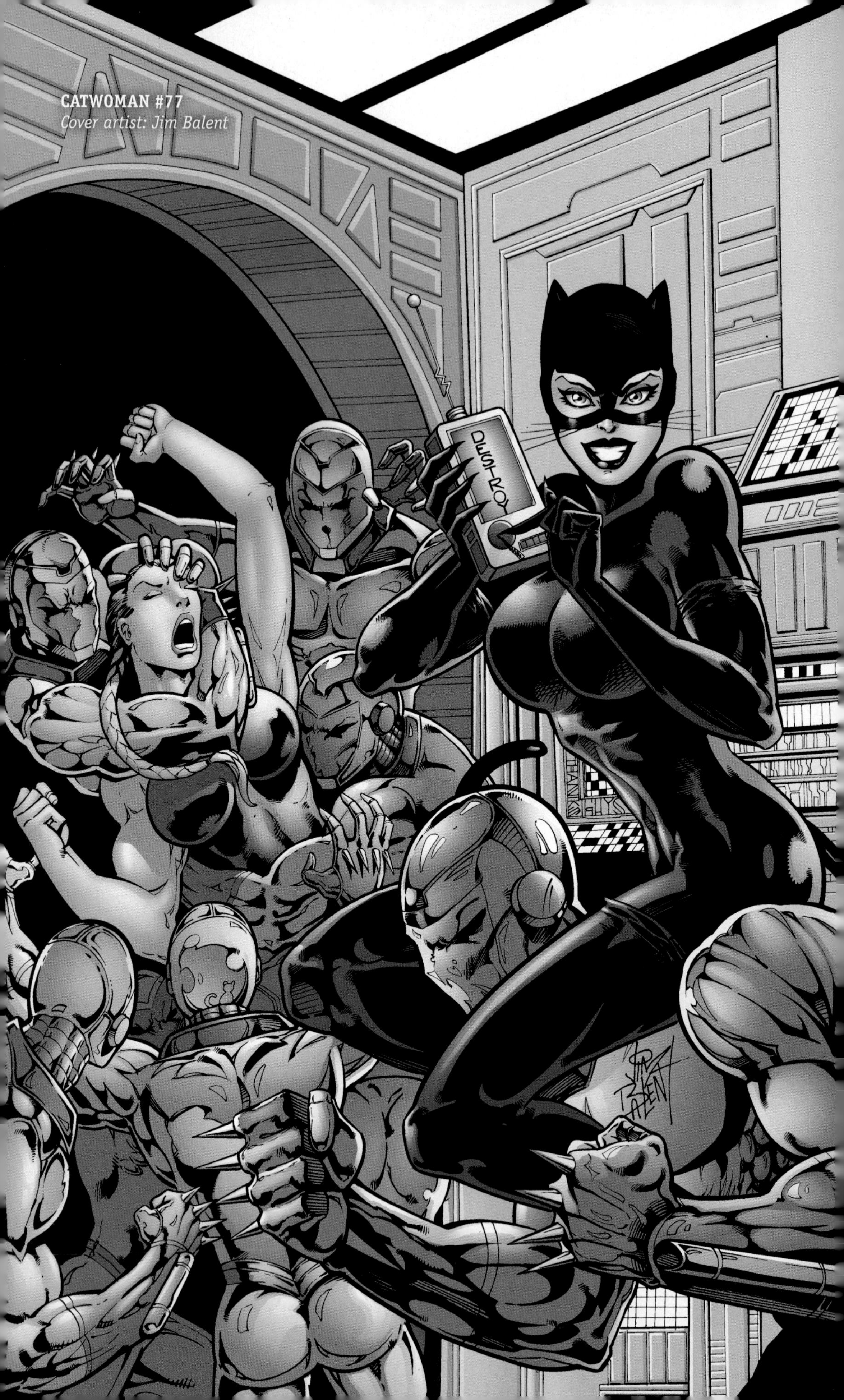
DESTROY

CATWOMAN #77
Cover artist: Jim Balent

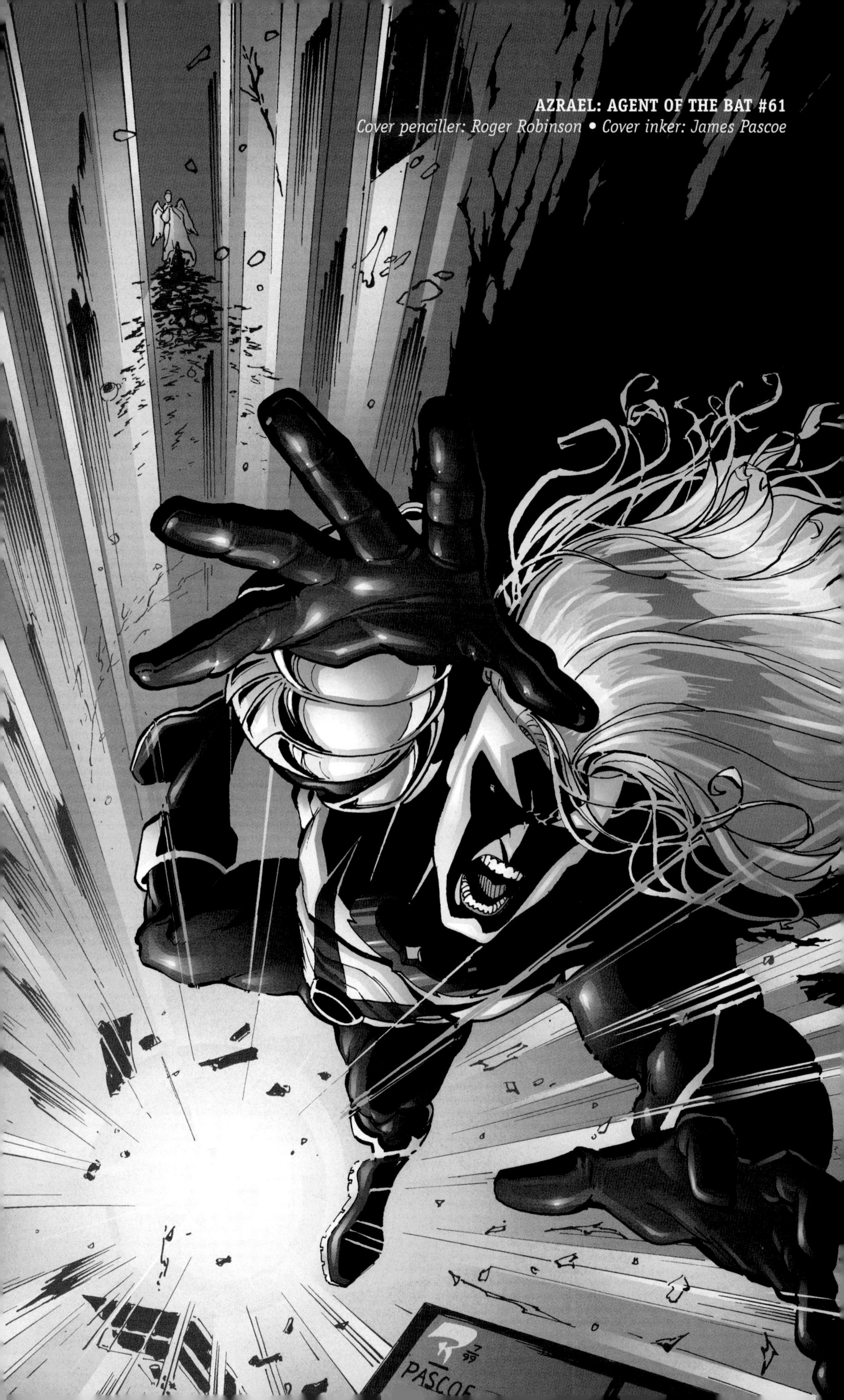

AZRAEL: AGENT OF THE BAT #61
Cover penciller: Roger Robinson • Cover inker: James Pascoe

BATMAN: LEGENDS OF THE DARK KNIGHT #126
Cover penciller: Alex Maleev • Cover inker: Wayne Faucher

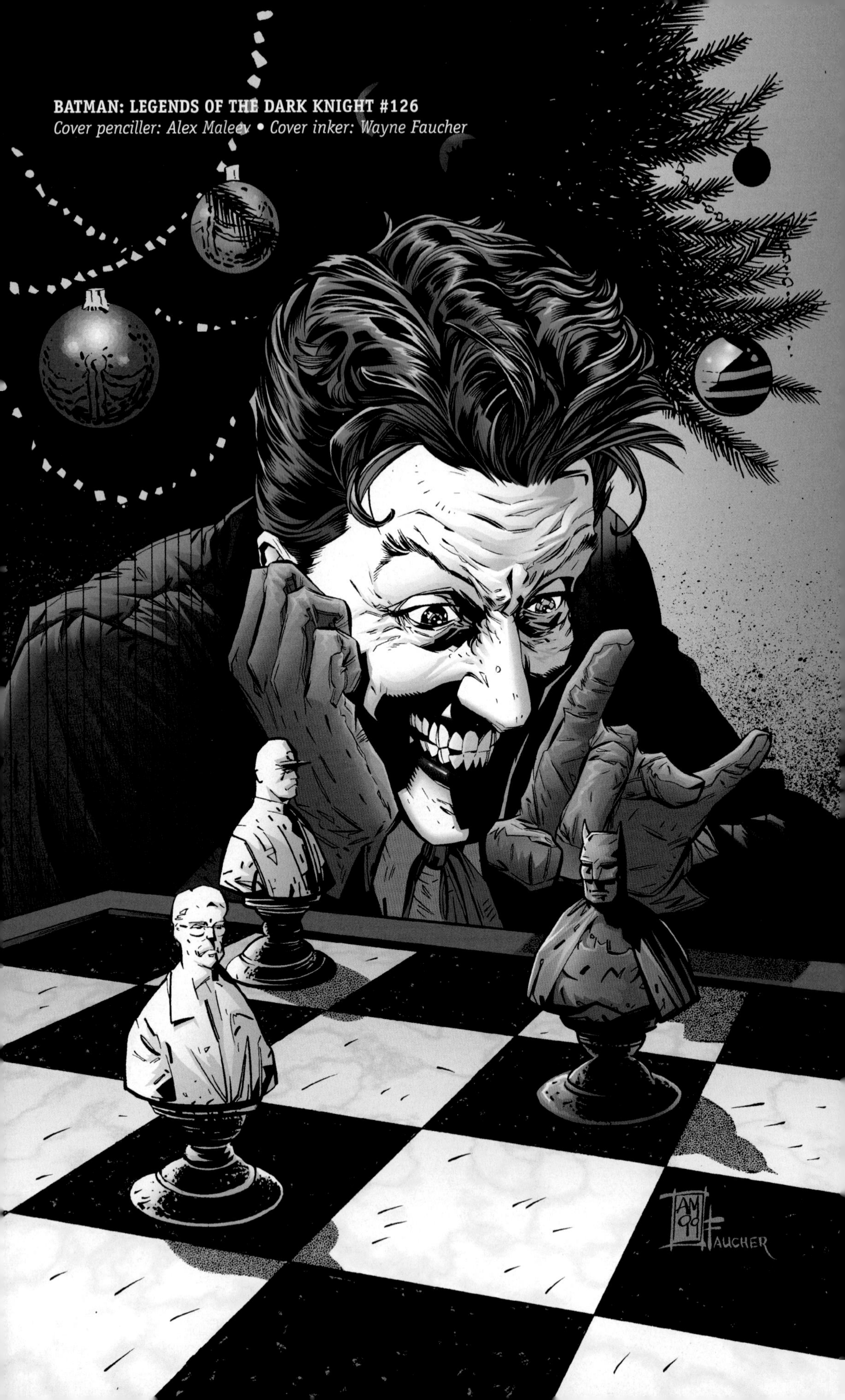
FAUCHER

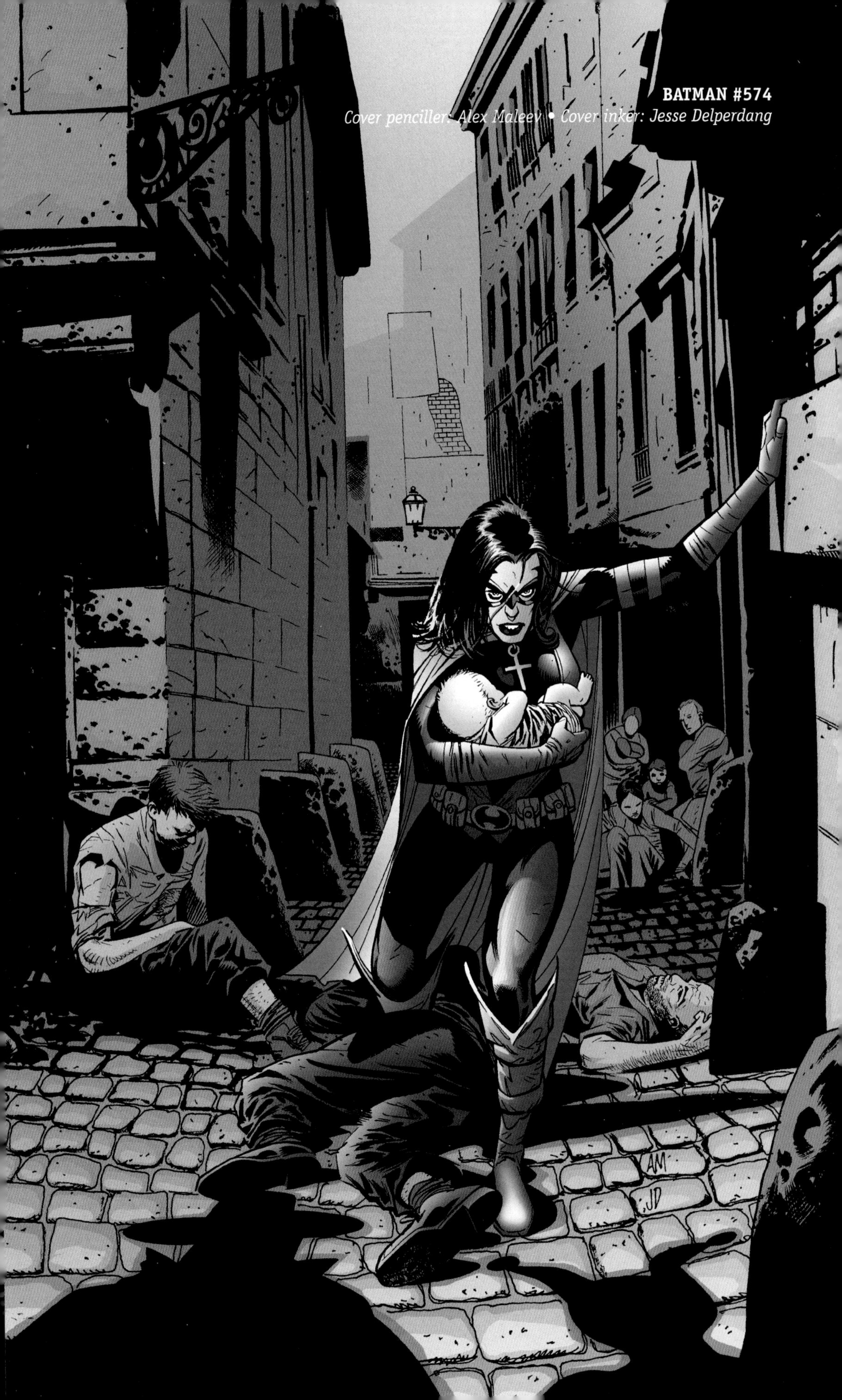
AM
JD

BATMAN #574

Cover penciller: Alex Maleev • Cover inker: Jesse Delperdang

DETECTIVE COMICS #741
Cover penciller: Alex Maleev • Cover inker: Bill Sienkiewicz

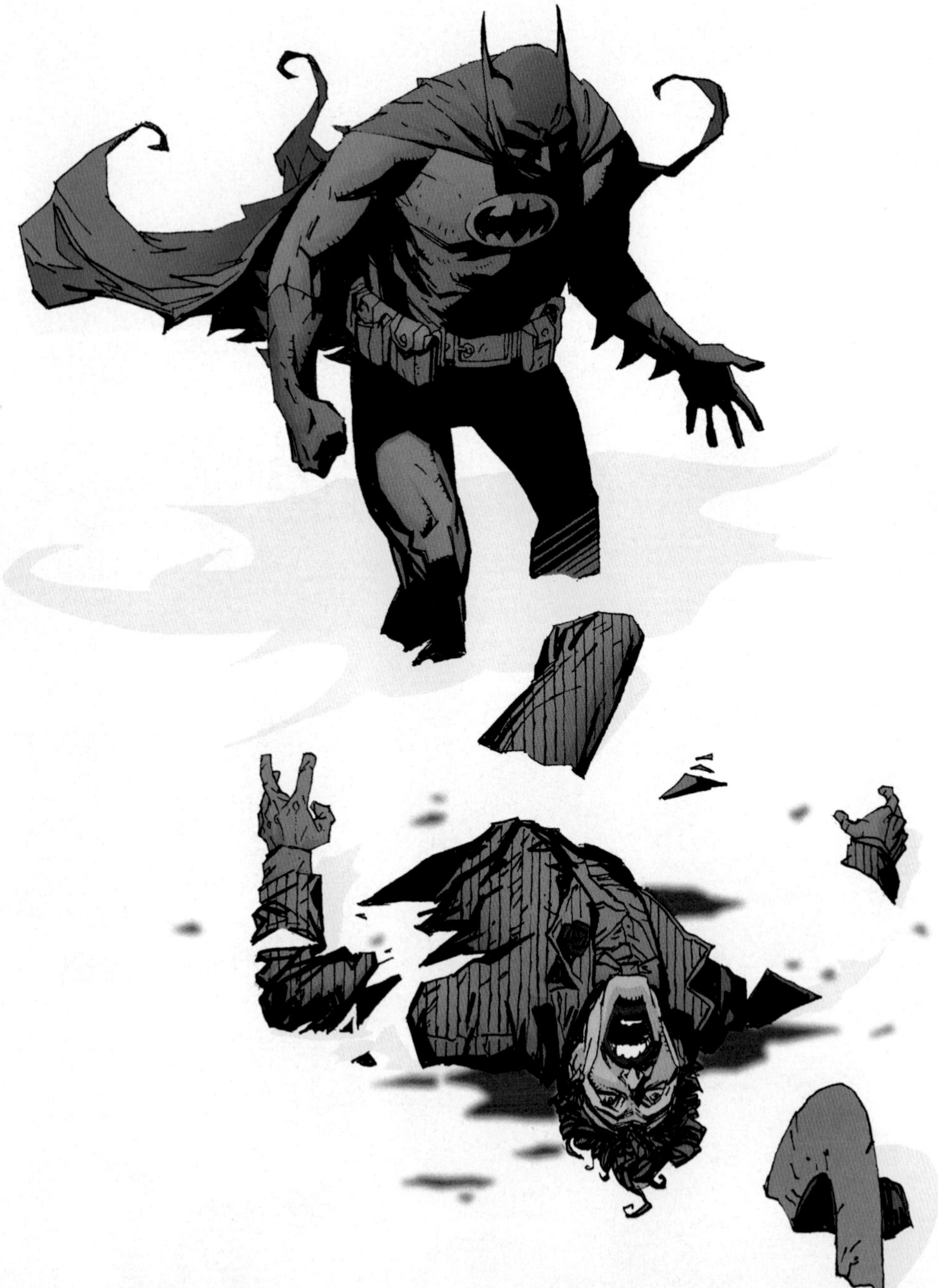
AM
BS
99

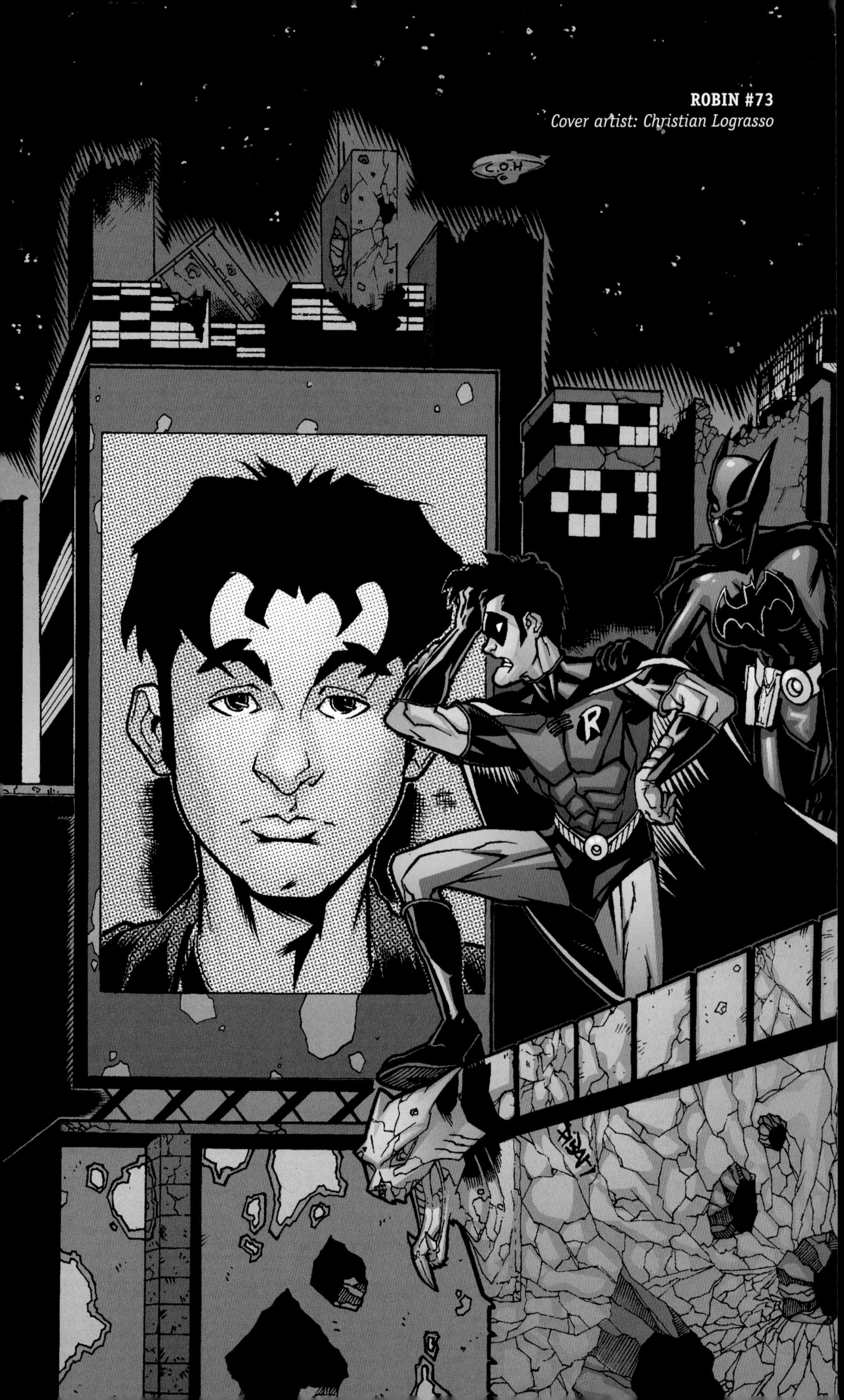
C.O.H

ROBIN #73
Cover artist: Christian Lograsso

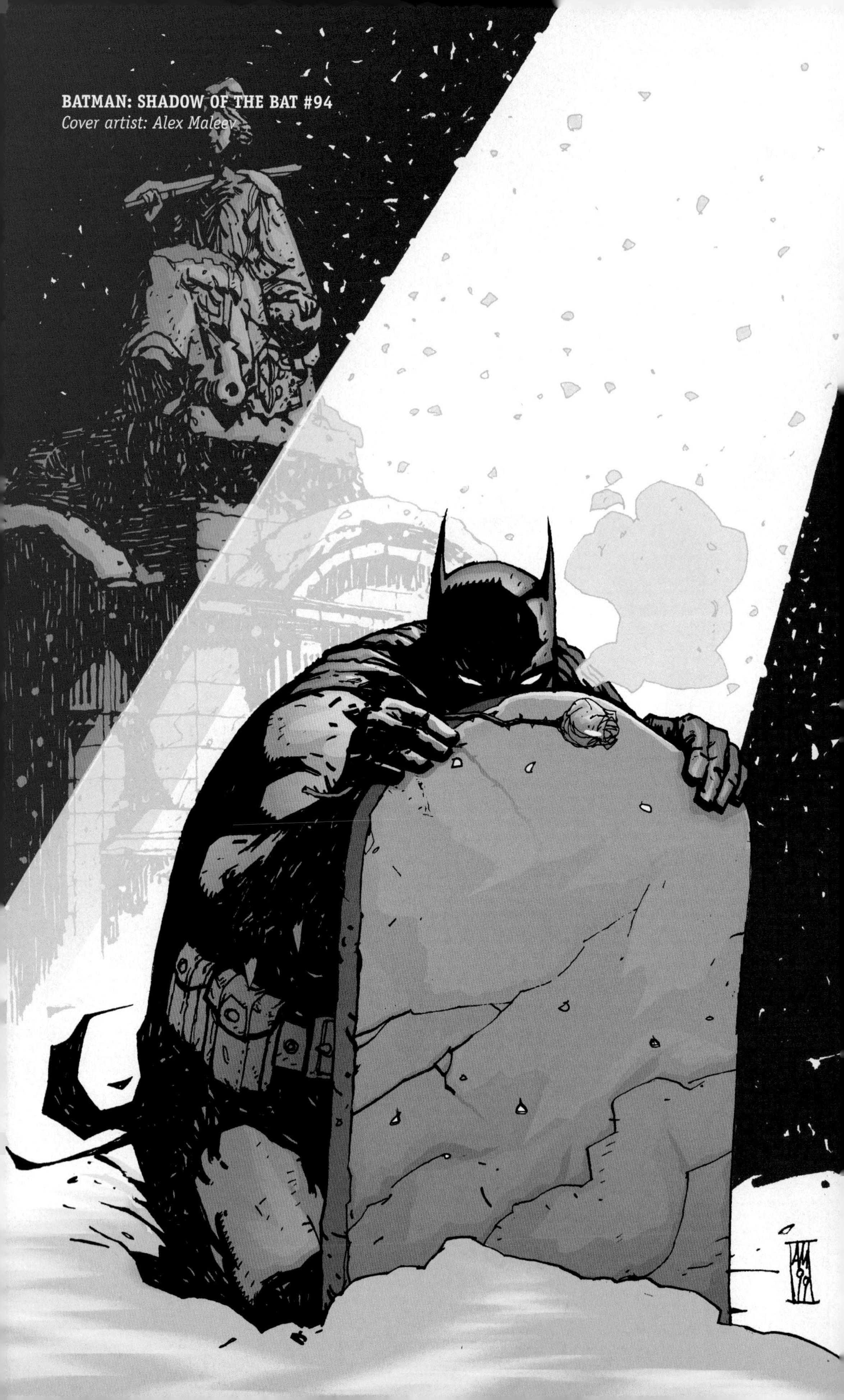

BATMAN: SHADOW OF THE BAT #94
Cover artist: Alex Maleev

NO MAN'S LAND GALLERY
Art by Jason Minor

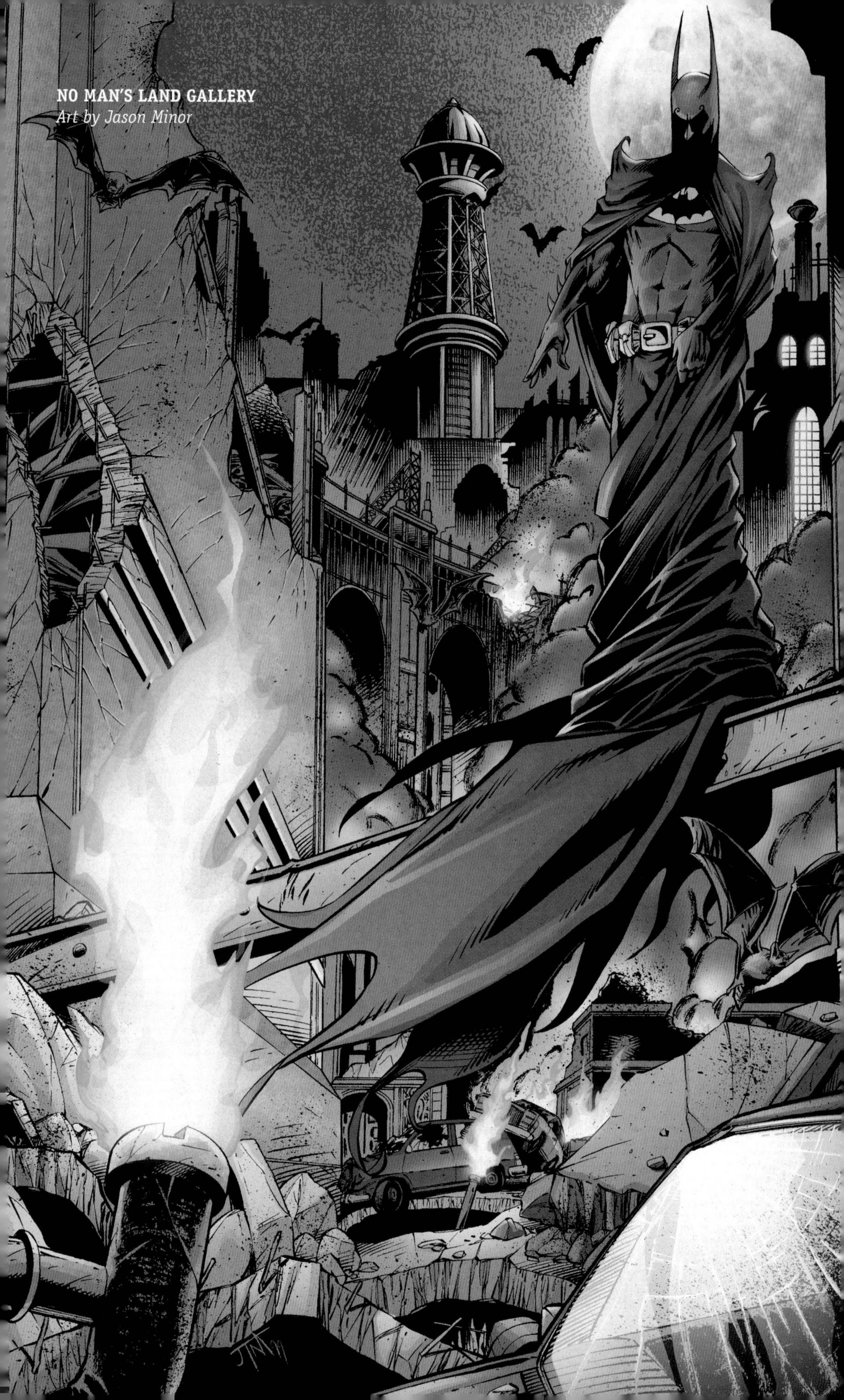

NO MAN'S LAND GALLERY

Art by Chriscross & Rob Stull

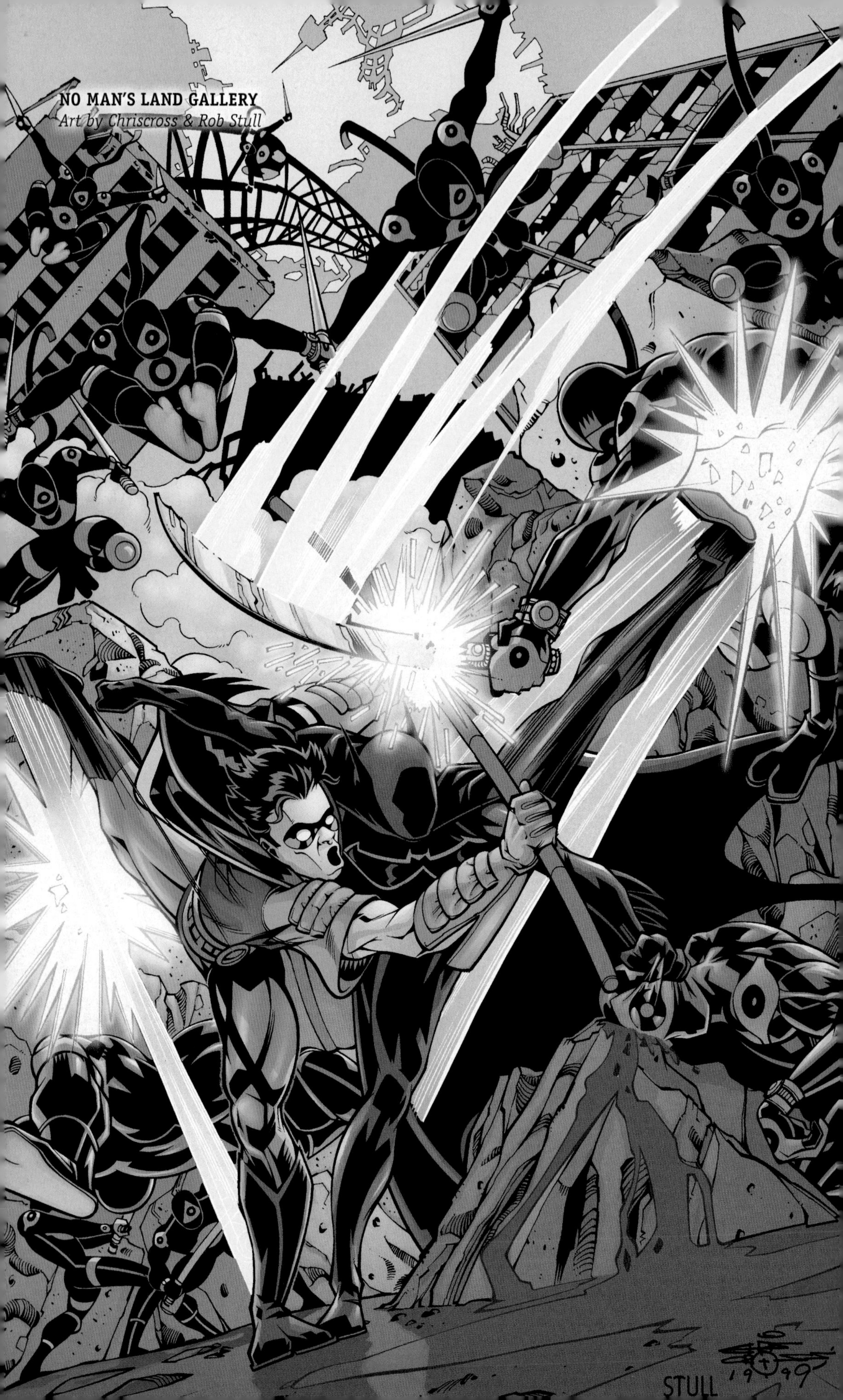
STULL

NO MAN'S LAND GALLERY
Art by Rodolfo Damaggio

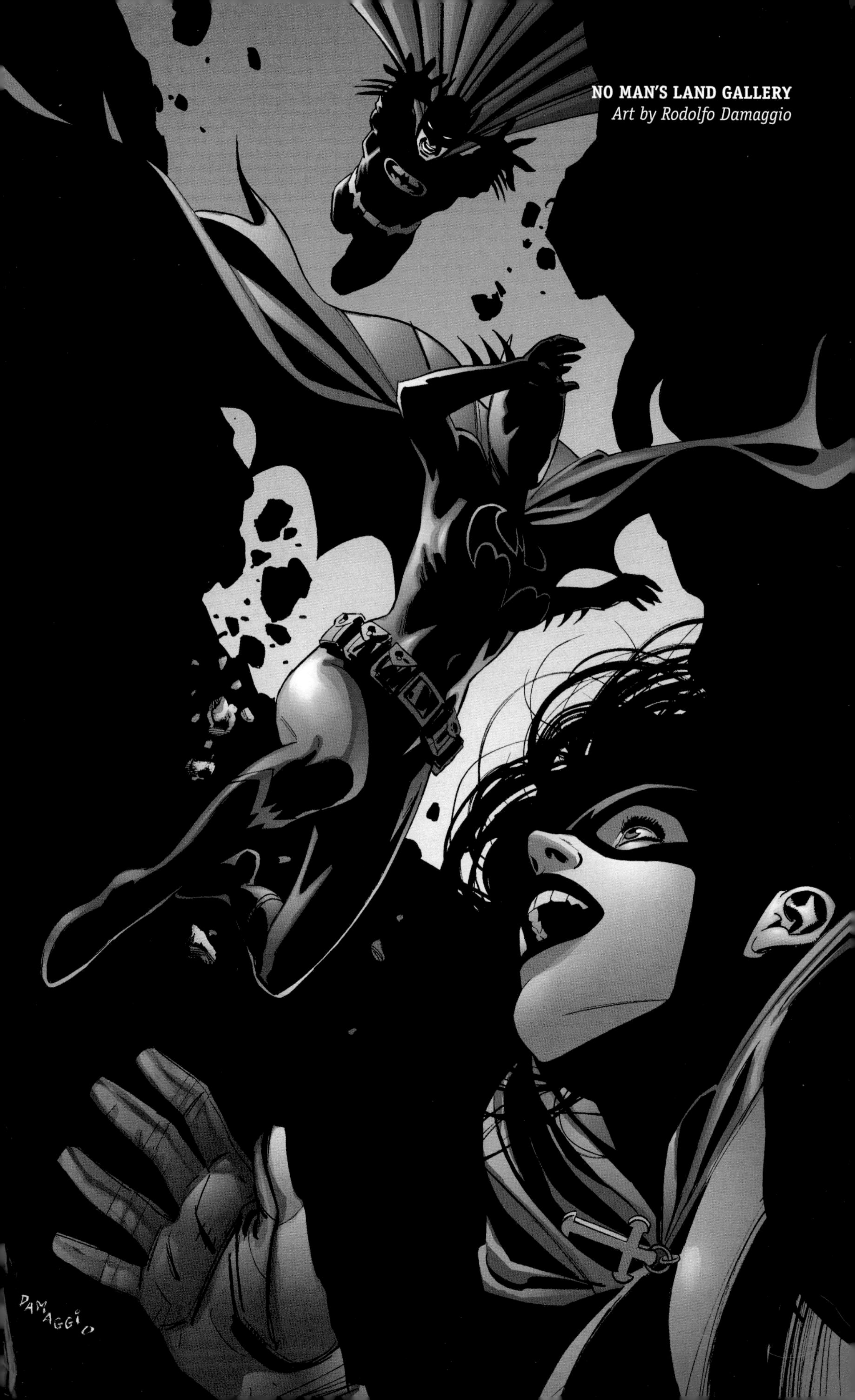
DAMAGGIO

NO MAN'S LAND GALLERY
Art by Craig Rousseau & Terry Beatty

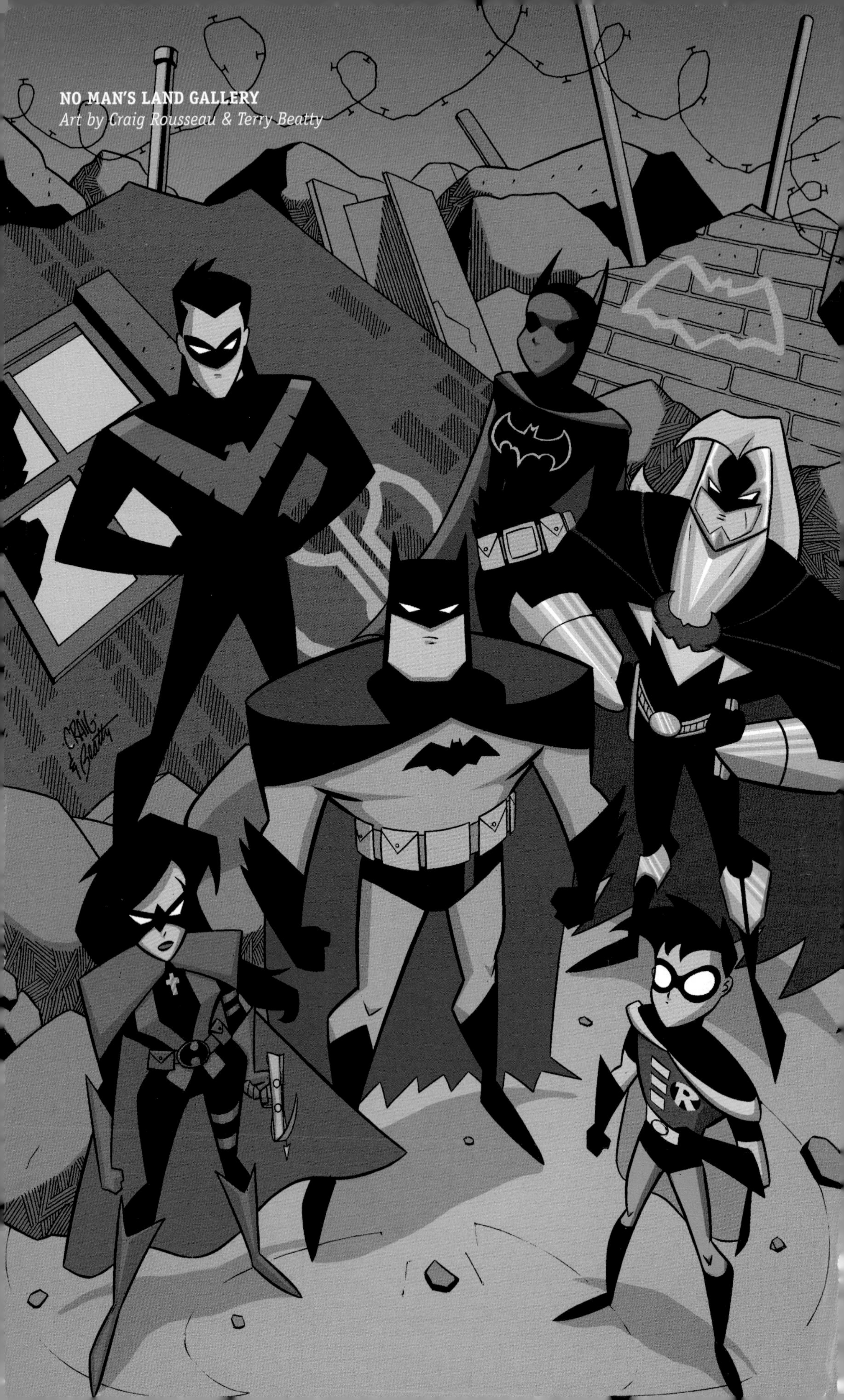

CRAIG & Beatty